CW01560559

An Anthology of Informal 1

Fifty Texts with Translations and Linguistic Commentary

This book contains over fifty passages of Latin from 200 BC to AD 900, each with translation and linguistic commentary. It is not intended as an elementary reader (though suitable for university courses), but as an illustrative history of Latin covering more than a millennium, with almost every century represented. Conventional histories cite constructions out of context, whereas this work gives a sense of the period, genre, stylistic aims and idiosyncrasies of specific passages. 'Informal' texts, particularly if they portray talk, reflect linguistic variety and change better than texts adhering to classicising norms. Some of the texts are of recent discovery or little known. Writing tablets are well represented, as are literary and technical texts down to the early medieval period, when striking changes appear. The Commentaries identify innovations, discontinuities and phenomena of long duration. Readers will learn much about the diversity and development of Latin.

J. N. ADAMS CBE FBA is an Emeritus Fellow of All Souls College, Oxford, an Honorary Fellow of Brasenose College, Oxford, and an Honorary Research Fellow, University of Manchester. He is the author of many books and articles on the Latin language, including the trilogy *Bilingualism and the Latin Language* (Cambridge 2003), *The Regional Diversification of Latin 200 BC – AD 600* (Cambridge 2007) and *Social Variation and the Latin Language* (Cambridge 2013). He was awarded the Kenyon Medal for Classical Studies of the British Academy in 2009.

AN ANTHOLOGY OF INFORMAL LATIN, 200 BC – AD 900

Fifty Texts with Translations and Linguistic Commentary

J. N. ADAMS

CAMBRIDGE
UNIVERSITY PRESS

CAMBRIDGE
UNIVERSITY PRESS

University Printing House, Cambridge CB2 8BS, United Kingdom

One Liberty Plaza, 20th Floor, New York, NY 10006, USA

477 Williamstown Road, Port Melbourne, VIC 3207, Australia

314-321, 3rd Floor, Plot 3, Splendor Forum, Jasola District Centre, New Delhi - 110025, India

79 Anson Road, #06-04/06, Singapore 079906

Cambridge University Press is part of the University of Cambridge.

It furthers the University's mission by disseminating knowledge in the pursuit of education, learning and research at the highest international levels of excellence.

www.cambridge.org
Information on this title: www.cambridge.org/9781108729970

First published 2016
First paperback edition 2018

A catalogue record for this publication is available from the British Library

ISBN 978-1-107-03977-3 Hardback
ISBN 978-1-108-72997-0 Paperback

CONTENTS

PREFACE

I originally intended to put a selection of texts at the end of my last book (Adams 2013), but there was not space, certainly for translations and commentaries or for the range of texts in this volume.

I have as ever consulted and learned from many people, to all of whom I am extremely grateful: Iveta Adams, Philip Alexander, Jose Miguel Baños, John Briscoe, Philip Burton, Brian Campbell, Anna Chahoud, James Clackson, Kathleen Coleman, Wolfgang de Melo, Eleanor Dickey, Katherine Dunbabin, Trevor Evans, Panagiotis Filos, Patrick Finglass, Michèle Fruyt, Jan Felix Gaertner, Giovanbattista Galdi, Jane Gardner, Roy Gibson, Christa Gray, Hilla Halla-aho, Gerd Haverling, Simon Hornblower, Bob Kaster, David Langslow, Michael Lapidge, Adam Ledgeway, John Lee, Alex Mullen, Marijke Ottink, Costas Panayotakis, Stelios Panayotakis, Tim Parkin, Mair Parry, Giuseppe Pezzini, Harm Pinkster (who generously let me see in advance some parts of his work *The Oxford Latin Syntax*, which was published after the present book was sent to the press), Philomen Probert, Joseph Reisdoerfer, Danuta Shanzer, Richard Sharpe, William Slater, Olga Spevak, John Trumper, Nigel Vincent, Tony Woodman and George Woudhuysen. It is not unlikely that I have forgotten some names, in which case I offer apologies (and thanks) to those persons omitted.

Again I have to acknowledge a great debt to All Souls College, which bestows its generous academic support even on Emeritus Fellows. I have continued to use the incomparable resources of the Oxford libraries. I have also had a (renewed) attachment to the University of Manchester, and profited from the University Library and also the John Rylands Library.

Finally, I would like to give warm thanks to Michael Sharp, Emma Collison and their colleagues at Cambridge University Press for ongoing support and efficiency, to Iveta Adams for saving the book from many inconsistencies and inadequacies by her exacting copy-editing, and to the very efficient proof reader Anthony Hippisley.

ABBREVIATIONS

CC	*Corpus Christianorum, series Latina* (Turnholt, 1954–).
CEL	*See* Cugusi (1992), (2002).
CHG	E. Oder and C. Hoppe, *Corpus hippiatricorum Graecorum*, 2 vols. (Leipzig, 1924–7).
ChLA	A. Bruckner, R. Marichal *et al., Chartae Latinae antiquiores* (Olten, Lausanne etc., 1954).
CIL	*Corpus inscriptionum Latinarum* (Berlin, 1862–).
CLE	F. Bücheler, A. Riese and E. Lommatzsch, *Carmina Latina epigraphica*, 3 vols. (Leipzig, 1897–1926).
CSEL	*Corpus scriptorum ecclesiasticorum Latinorum* (Vienna, 1866).
DMLBS	*Dictionary of Medieval Latin from British Sources* (Oxford, 1975–2013).
FEW	W. von Wartburg, *Französisches etymologisches Wörterbuch* (Bonn, 1928–).
FRH	T. J. Cornell *et al., The Fragments of the Roman Historians*, 3 vols. (Oxford, 2013).
GL	H. Keil, *Grammatici Latini*, 8 vols. (Leipzig, 1855–80).
ILCV	E. Diehl, *Inscriptiones Latinae Christianae ueteres*, 3 vols. (Berlin, 1925–31).
ILLRP	A. Degrassi, *Inscriptiones Latinae liberae rei publicae*, 2 vols. (I 2nd edn 1965, II 1963).
LEI	M. Pfister and W. Schweickard, *LEI: Lessico etimologico italiano* (Wiesbaden, 1979–).
LSJ	H. G. Liddell and R. Scott, *A Greek–English Lexicon* (revised and augmented by H. S. Jones, with a revised supplement) (Oxford, 1996).
O. Bu Njem	R. Marichal, *Les ostraca de Bu Njem* (Libya antiqua Supplement 7) (Assraya al Hamra, 1992).
O. Claud.	*See* Bingen *et al.* (1992), (1997).
O. Faw.	O. Guéraud, 'Ostraca grecs et latins de l'Wâdi Fawâkhir', *BIFAO* 41 (1942), 141–96.
OCD	*Oxford Classical Dictionary*, 2nd edn (Oxford, 1970), 3rd edn (Oxford, 1996).

OLD	*Oxford Latin Dictionary* (Oxford, 1968–82).
ORF	H. Malcovati, *Oratorum Romanorum fragmenta liberae rei publicae*, 4th edn (Turin, 1976).
P. Rainer Cent.	*Festschrift zum 100-jährigen Bestehen der Papyrussammlung der Österreichischen Nationalbibliothek, Papyrus Erzherzog Rainer* (Vienna, 1983).
REW	W. Meyer-Lübke, *Romanisches etymologisches Wörterbuch*, 3rd edn (Heidelberg, 1935).
Tab. Sulis	*See* Tomlin (1988).
Tab. Vindol.	*See* Bowman and Thomas (1983), (1994), (2003).
Tab. Vindon.	M. A. Speidel, *Die römischen Schreibtafeln von Vindonissa* (Baden-Dättwil).
Tablettes Albertini	*See* Courtois *et al.* (1952).
TLL	*Thesaurus linguae Latinae* (Leipzig, 1900–).
TPSulp.	*See* Camodeca (1999).

Abbreviations of editions of papyri and ostraca not given in this list may be found in J. F. Oates *et al., Checklist of Editions of Greek, Latin, Demotic and Coptic Papyri, Ostraca and Tablets*, available online at: http://library.duke.edu /rubenstein/scriptorium/papyrus/texts/clist.html. Abbreviations of biblical texts used in this book are those found in R. Weber and R. Gryson eds., *Biblia sacra iuxta vulgatam versionem*, 5th edn (Stuttgart, 2007).

INTRODUCTION

More than fifty texts or extracts are collected in this volume, covering over 1,000 years of the history of Latin. I have tried to select passages that do not simply reflect the classical language associated particularly with Cicero and codified in modern grammars of Latin. The word 'informal' in the title is appropriate only up to a point, and has been used for want of a better term. Some of the texts would have been looked on by their writers not as informal, but as their best effort at expressing themselves in formal writing. All, however, have departures from the norms prescribed by some ancient and modern grammarians, and all have something to offer in illustrating changes in the language over time.

The texts fall into various categories.

The first five (or six) texts are early republican, and antedate any standardisation movement that might have occurred (therein lies a question in itself: see the concluding chapter). Most are conversational or informal.

Eight passages belong to the Ciceronian or Augustan periods. Cicero has been excluded, except in the collection numbered 10, which are jokes mainly from the late Republic quoted by Cicero himself and also by others. Jokes tend to be made off-the-cuff, and are often spoken. They may be risqué, and admit language not used in formal writing.

There are eighteen writing tablets from the first century BC to about the eighth century AD (6, 13–15, 19–24, 32–7, 41, 46). These comprise private letters and curse tablets (some of which have been published for the first time in recent decades), and also two legal documents (15, 41) that are linguistically noteworthy; one (15) has two versions, by an educated scribe and by an uneducated freedman. Parts of two imperial literary letters have also been included, one by Seneca (17), the other extant in Augustine's correspondence, from a certain Publicola to Augustine (31). Augustine's reply survives, and some comparisons are made between Publicola's language and that of the reply. These are two texts of the same date and same genre dealing with the same subject.

The Latin Bible translations were influential in the late period, but their Latin is not straightforward. Bible translations were influenced by popular varieties of the language, but are also full of constructions from Greek and even Hebrew. Much surviving late Latin was written by Christians, and Christian writers drew on the Bible as a stylistic model. Some of these constructions found their way into Christian writings. Could translationese have had an influence on the language in general? I have included two versions of a passage from the Gospel of John (38), eight overtly Christian texts (27, 31, 39, 40, 44, 45, 47, 49), and another with a pagan theme but subject to biblical influence (43). The Latin written in the Christian period on biblical themes cannot without reservation be assumed to represent a stage in the language's development, as it may to some extent be biblical pastiche, remote from the way people spoke. The difficulty of interpreting such material comes up particularly in an assessment of the Latin of the Irish/British writer Patrick (see 39, 40). Does his Latin reflect the Latin spoken in Britain or Ireland (or indeed on the Continent), or is it bookish, i.e. based on Bible translations?

Many technical texts (e.g. medical, veterinary) are extant from different centuries. From the earlier period there are here two passages of Cato's *De agricultura* (4, 5), and a long passage from Vitruvius (11). Vitruvius was almost contemporary with Cicero, and his Latin alongside that of Cicero shows up a lack of standardisation in the classical period. A long Algerian inscription set up by a surveyor (25) has also been included as a specimen of a practical man's way of expressing himself. The one medical text in the collection (42), and one of the two veterinary (30), have different 'versions' (on this phenomenon see further below).

As well as the surveyor's inscription I have quoted a short Pompeian verse inscription (16), and also a text found on a mosaic from North Africa depicting a beast hunt (28). This purports to record acclamations uttered by the crowd attending the show.

There are five texts from very late antiquity or the early medieval period, from Spain, Francia and northern Italy (46–50). All display regional or proto-Romance features that had either been kept at bay in earlier writing, or had not been established at all in the language until very late. Two of these texts have an obligatory definite article (49, 50). One, a text on falcon medicine from northern Italy (50), has been quoted at length because it is so advanced in many respects towards a Romance vernacular.

One of the private letters (21), from Vindolanda, is by a woman, Claudia Severa, who was married to a military officer. A passage (27) from the *Passio sanctarum Perpetuae et Felicitatis* claims to be a woman's own account of her dream, and it has attracted attention recently as a possible specimen of female writing. The authorship of this narrative will be discussed: is it really in the words of Perpetua herself, or has the redactor attributed words to her?

Many of the passages present 'talk' in one form or another: of characters in a play (2, 3), of mundane persons as depicted condescendingly by a rhetorician

(7, 8), of the sort heard in jokes (10), of slaves in a letter of Seneca in dialogue with their master (17), of an uneducated freedman of Greek origin in a novel by a writer of high education (18), of the crowd at a beast hunt (28), of a character in a late novelistic work (43), of humble characters in Gregory the Great's *Dialogues* (45), and of occupants of an early medieval monastery (47). Private letters too, though they have stereotyped formulae, are conversational.

The only narrative texts (44, 48) are very late. The *Itinerarium Antonini Placentini* is heavily Christian and exists in more than one recension. The other, the *Annales regni Francorum*, also has two versions, one of which has regional features.

These are not the only texts in this volume that have more than one version, such as a classicising one and one less correct (see 15, 30, 42, 43; note too the Bible translation, 38). It may be hard to determine whether a scribe or redactor of one version has corrected non-standard Latin, or barbarised correct Latin. This question will be considered in the Commentaries on some of the texts just listed. Sometimes however two versions cannot be reduced to the classification correct versus non-correct: there are many reasons why a scribe or redactor might change the text he had before him. The existence of two versions of a work raises problems for an editor. I stress that I do not have in mind mere spelling variations between manuscripts. A manuscript with phonetic spellings should not be classified as a specimen of 'vulgar Latin', because the spellings in most cases will represent the sounds of educated, or general, as distinct from exclusively uneducated, speech: e.g. *e* for *ae*, omission of initial *h*, omission of final *m* and various vocalic misspellings reflected spoken features widespread in the language across all classes. A scribe might have been a bad speller, but his speech need not have differed from that of a good speller. It is usually impossible to know what the spelling of the original author was like. Even if we knew, we would be the wiser about his level of literacy, but not about any distinctive character of his speech.

The passages are in rough chronological order (as far as that can be determined), though I have not attempted to establish a definitive order of the writing tablets numbered 20–4 and 26, which belong loosely to the second century. I have also put six British curse tablets into a 'late' group (32–7), again without seeking to impose a strict relative chronology. In each case there is usually an introduction giving a few facts about the text. There follow the text, a literal translation, a linguistic commentary, and finally a conclusion. The aim of the conclusions is to highlight general linguistic themes arising from each passage, and to summarise features of the Latin relevant to genre, date of composition, diachronic change and social variation. The volume might serve as a sort of practical or illustrative history of the Latin language over about 1,000 years. For that reason there is a concluding chapter summarising some of the themes that arise from the selections. Many of the notes in the volume inevitably deal with isolated or miscellaneous usages, but an effort has been made throughout to keep important topics and continuities to the fore. The book might be used by students, but is not intended as an elementary reader. It is wide-ranging in its treatment of many topics, and offers some revisions of standard accounts of the history of the language, and a good deal that is new or little known.

Numbering in the Commentaries

In the Commentaries on verse passages, line numbers from the original text are used. In a few non-literary documents printed here with their original format, the original line numbers are again given. In (literary) prose passages traditional section numbers (if these have been used in standard editions) within chapters are printed in bold in the text and translation. These same numbers are used in the Commentary to mark lemmata. If however a text does not have section numbers in standard editions, I have numbered the lemmata consecutively (NOT in bold), and inserted these numbers in the text in brackets (again not in bold) at the relevant points. Finally, in standard editions of some works traditional section numbers are so widely spaced that they have proved inadequate here for the numbering of lemmata. In passages taken from such editions the section numbers are given (as above) in bold, but in addition the lemmata are numbered consecutively (not in bold), and these numbers are inserted in the text in brackets (not in bold).

A note on cross-referencing

Many of the phenomena discussed in the Commentaries come up more than once. Cross-references are not by page number, but by the number of the text, accompanied by the number of the lemma. Alternatively I have sometimes inserted in the Commentaries at appropriate points references of the type 'see index, "temporal adverbs, repetitious"'.

TEXTS

1

ENNIUS, *EVHEMERVS* III (VΛHLEN)

Introduction

Ennius (239–169 BC) is known now mainly from his poetic works, the *Annals* and tragedies, but we also have fragments of his prose *Euhemerus*, a work based on the Sacred Scripture of Euhemerus of Messene (late fourth, early third century BC). The fragments come from Lactantius, and that presented here from *Div. Inst.* 1.14.1–7. It is of course possible that Lactantius altered the wording of the original, but a good case has been made that I, III, IV, V, VI, VII, XI are authentic (see Laughton 1951, Fraenkel 1951: 55 = 1964: II.58). In the passage discussed here I have found only one possible anachronism, alongside a lot of features that look right for the period. Some comparisons are made below with Ennius' other writings, and with Cato and various other early writers, particularly annalists, since these too wrote narratives about the past. For the text see Vahlen (1928: 223–4), Warmington (1961: 418–20), Winiarczyk (1991: 34–5), Courtney (1999: 27–8).

Text

Haec Ennii uerba sunt. Exim (1) Saturnus uxorem duxit Opem. Titan qui maior natu erat postulat ut ipse regnaret (2). ibi Vesta (3) mater eorum et sorores Ceres atque Ops suadent Saturno, uti de regno ne concedat fratri (4). ibi Titan, qui facie deterior esset quam Saturnus, idcirco et quod (5) uidebat matrem atque sorores suas (6) operam dare uti Saturnus regnaret (7), concessit ei ut is regnaret (8). itaque pactus est cum Saturno, uti si quid liberum uirile secus ei natum esset, ne quid educaret (9). id eius rei causa fecit, uti ad suos gnatos regnum rediret (10). tum Saturno filius qui primus natus est, eum necauerunt (11). deinde posterius (12) nati sunt gemini, Iuppiter atque Iuno. tum Iunonem Saturno in conspectum dedere (13) atque (14) Iouem clam abscondunt dantque eum Vestae educandum celantes Saturnum (15). item Neptunum clam Saturno (16) Ops parit eumque clanculum abscondit (17). ad eundem modum tertio partu Ops parit geminos, Plutonem et Glaucam. Pluto Latine est Dis pater, alii Orcum uocant. ibi filiam Glaucam Saturno ostendunt, at filium Plutonem celant atque abscondunt. deinde Glauca parua emoritur (18). haec ut scripta sunt

Iouis fratrumque eius stirps atque cognatio (19): in hunc modum nobis ex sacra scriptione traditum est.

Translation

These are the words of Ennius. Then Saturn took Ops as wife. Titan, who was the elder, demanded that he should be the one to be king. Then Vesta their mother and their sisters Ceres and Ops urged Saturn not to give in to his brother over the kingship. Then Titan, since he was more unpleasant in appearance than Saturn, and also because he could see that his mother and sisters were applying themselves so that Saturn should be king, conceded to him that he should be king. And so he agreed with Saturn that if any child, of male sex, should have been born to him, he would not raise it. This he did for this reason, that the kingship might come instead to his own sons. Then the son who was born first to Saturn, him they killed. Then afterwards there were born twins, Jupiter and Juno. Then they allowed Saturn a sight of Juno, yet they concealed Jupiter secretly and gave him to Vesta to be brought up, hiding this from Saturn. In addition Ops bore Neptune without the knowledge of Saturn and concealed him secretly. Likewise in a third birth Ops bore twins, Pluto and Glauca. Pluto in Latin is Dis pater, but others call him Orcus. Then they showed the daughter Glauca to Saturn, but the son Pluto they hid and concealed. Then Glauca died as a child. These as they have been recorded in writing are the stock and kinsfolk of Jupiter and his brothers: in this form has it been handed down to us from the Sacred Scripture.

Commentary

1 exim: the indexes of Vahlen (1928: 270) and Skutsch (1985: 816) list two instances of *exim* from the *Annals* and three of *exin*; *exinde* does not occur. This is the only instance of any of the forms in *Euhemerus*. None of these forms is attested in Ennius' tragic fragments, but note Accius *praet.* 25 *exim prostratum terra*. Skutsch (1985: 199) states: 'both *exim* and *exin* occur only before consonants, and *exim* therefore is not a formation like *olim* or *interim* but a variant of *exin(de)* which has developed the final *m* under the influence of those adverbs.' This last clause may be right, but it is just as likely that *exim* arose as a phonetic variant of *exin* determined originally by a following bilabial consonant (note the example from Accius above). *Exinde* is a secondary form showing the particle *-de*. *Exim* (along with *exin*) turns up mainly in early Latin or in high-style texts later. Similarly *deinde* far outnumbers *dein* throughout recorded Latin (see the table at *TLL* V.1.407). Plautus has *exin* and *exim* once or twice each (with some textual uncertainty), and *exinde* three times. Information about the distribution of *exim* (*exin*) may be found at *TLL* V.2.1506.54ff. (also Woodman and Martin 1996: 152–3). The one prose writer who uses *exim/-n* frequently (to the exclusion of *exinde*) is Tacitus (*TLL* 1506.73, Woodman and Martin loc. cit.). Cicero has four examples of the base form in verse, but only three in prose works, all in special contexts (*TLL* 1506.69f. for references), one in a comment on the word (*Orat.* 154), one in a fragment of the *Leg.* (in the words of a law), and a third in a quotation from Coelius Antipater (*Div.* 1.55). This last example (*exin*) is almost certainly Coelius' own wording, given that the word is not one of Cicero's own prose terms (for the fragment see *FRH* II.15.F48; it is not printed as a verbatim quotation). The one example (*exim*) in Livy (27.5.6) might equally have been taken from Coelius, one of the sources of the third decade (information from John Briscoe: see Briscoe at *FRH* I.261 n. 37). We thus have a few examples in (stylised) early prose that might be seen as precursors of the Tacitean examples.

On Vahlen's punctuation there are fourteen sentences in this fragment, of which eight begin with a temporal adverb (or with a pair of such): *exim, ibi, ibi, tum, deinde posterius, tum, ibi, deinde*. Another four begin with adverbials of different types (*itaque, item, ad eundem modum, in hunc modum*). This monotonous presentation was a feature of a contrived style of popular narrative, found for example in folk tales (see Norden 1956: 377 n. 1; Fraenkel 1951: 50–7 = 1964: I.53–7 for the Greco-Roman background and parallels from both languages; also below, Appendix 3, for parallel passages from Terence; and *TLL* VII.1.151.40f. '*ibi* temporale repetitur in narrationibus'). In Latin it is not exclusively a feature of the early period but persists for centuries (see index, 'temporal adverbs, repetitious').

2 postulat ut ipse regnaret: in the fragments considered to have Ennius' wording there are five instances of *ut* and four of *uti*. Four of the five of *ut* are before a vowel (here, and at III *ut is*, V *ut eum*, VII *ut insulis*; the exception is at V, *ut caueret*), whereas three of the four of *uti* are before consonants (III *uti de, uti Saturnus, uti si*; the exception is at III, *uti ad*). Vahlen's index (1928: 297) shows that *ut* is the preferred form throughout Ennius, and that it is used indifferently before vowels and consonants. *Vti* on the other hand occurs just three times in works other than the *Euhemerus,* always before consonants. Similarly Lodge (1924–33: II.919) remarks of *uti* in Plautus: 'Plerumque ante consonantes locum obtinet, raro ante vocales.' The use of *uti* in the *Euhemerus* fragments looks authentic for Ennius.

Manuscripts, particularly of a prose work, are not, however, a reliable guide to the distribution of *uti* versus *ut*. For what it is worth there does seem to be variability from writer to writer in the early period. Cato's practice contrasts with that of Ennius. He has *uti* 129 times in the *De agricultura*, 27 times before vowels (21 per cent of cases), and *ut* 34 times, 24 times before vowels (69 per cent of cases). In the fragments of the *Origines* there are only four instances of the word, two in the form *uti* (one before a consonant, *FRH* II.5. F9, the other before *haec*, F87).

See further below, 11.6 on Vitruvius.

3 ibi Vesta: there are three temporal examples of *ibi* in this passage, two indeed at the start of successive sentences at this point (so *ibi Titan*; cf. *ibi filiam*). On the distribution of this temporal (as distinct from the more common local) use see *TLL* VII.1.141.9ff. '*ibi* temporale ... frequentant scaenici veteres, recipiunt poetae ... rarius scriptores'. Cicero for example has *ibi tum* three times, always in early speeches, *Quinct., Caec., Verr.* (an old pleonastic combination, where the temporal meaning is established by *tum*; for a collection of examples, from Ennius through to Cicero, see Thomsen 1930: 82–3; also *TLL* VII.1.150.52ff. 'per pleonasmum de tempore'), but *ibi* on its own just once, again in an early speech (*Cat.* 3.12: *TLL* 141.11f., 145.72). For temporal examples (including cases from Ennius' *Annals* and *scenica*) see *TLL* VII.1.145.62ff. Usage in the fragments is in accord with that of the early period and of Ennius himself (see also Fraenkel 1951: 50 = 1964: I.53).

4 uti de regno ne concedat fratri: *ut(i) ne* for the usual final negative of classical Latin, *ne*, is old. It occurs twice in our passage (cf. below, *uti si quid . . . ne quid*). *Ne* on its own occurs once (V *caueret ne*). By this period the full form of expression was probably recessive. In Plautus' *Miles gloriosus*, for example, I have noted about forty examples of *ne* but only five of *ut ne*. The first of these latter is in a quasi-legal context (164 *ut ne legi fraudem faciant aleariae,* | *adcuratote*) (cf. 185a, 199, 227, 1050). In Cato's *De agricultura uti ne* appears four times (*ut ne* never) but *ne* on its own well over a hundred times. *Vt ne* is however not infrequent in Terence, though outnumbered (see McGlynn 1963–7: I.388). *Vt ne* persisted in legal Latin, and there are occasional examples even in Cicero. For details of its later distribution see Hofmann and Szantyr (1965: 643).

5 idcirco et quod: for the attachment of a *quod*-clause to a causal expression of a different type Laughton (1951: 37–8) compares Cato, *FRH* II.5.F76 *defetigatum uulneribus atque quod sanguen eius defluxerat*, finding it crude. By contrast such lack of rhetorical balance in Tacitus would be deemed artistic. *Idcirco* is in fact ambiguous here. On the one hand it might be resumptive, after causal *qui* ('since he was ..., for that reason, and because ...'), or it might anticipate the following *quod*, with anastrophe of the connective ('and (also) for this reason, because . . .').

6 matrem atque sorores suas: the fragments of this work (i.e. I, III, IV, V, VI, VII, XI) are exceptional in that the mundane connective *et* is outnumbered by its higher-style alternatives. *Et* itself occurs just eight times, compared with nineteen cases of *-que*. *Atque* is a striking presence: it is found seven times before consonants, and eight times before vowels (see the end of this note for the examples). Thus *atque* as well as *-que* outnumbers *et*. There are also two instances of *ac*, both before consonants (both in V). By contrast in Cato's *De agricultura* there are about 500 instances of *et*, 215 instances of *-que* (many of them in special contexts: see below, 4.2, 4.6) but just five instances of *atque* (as a connective; there is also a comparative use), three of them before consonants. On the other hand the fragments of Cato's *Origines* present a very different picture. There (in the verbatim fragments as set out in *FRH* II.5) there are twenty-one instances of *atque*, sixteen of them before consonants, compared with twelve of *et*. There are also twelve of *-que* (all these examples are quoted below in Appendix 1). Again the high-style alternatives outnumber *et*. The difference between Cato's two works shows clearly that *atque* was a formal connective, at home in higher-level prose. The pre-consonantal examples are conspicuous in both Ennius' prose and the *Origines*, but in Ennius' verse it is a different matter (see below).

In the *Annals* Skutsch's index (1985: 816, 823) shows that *-que* outnumbers *et*, by 67:36. Skutsch (1985: 63) gives full information about *atque* in the *Annals* and tragic fragments. In the *Annals* Ennius elides *atque* twelve times (i.e. has it before vowels) and places it before consonants only twice in textually certain contexts (both times in association with alliteration: 74 *sedet atque secundam | solus auem seruat, atque manu magna*). In the scenic fragments there are twenty-seven or twenty-eight cases of elision, and just two of the full form. Skutsch makes a comparison between Ennius' verse and the *Euhemerus* fragments, where (as we have seen) there is a substantial body of instances before consonants.

The Latin of the *Euhemerus* fragments looks mundane and very simple, but the artifice in the use of connectives suggests that that simplicity is contrived.

Here are the examples of *atque* in the *Euhemerus*, first (a) those cases before consonants and then (b) those before vowels: (a) I *instituit atque parauit*, III *matrem atque sorores, Iuppiter atque Iuno, Saturno in conspectum dedere atque Iouem clam abscondunt, stirps atque cognatio*, V *patrem atque matrem*, XI *amicis atque cognatis*; (b) III *Ceres atque Ops, celant atque abscondunt*, IV *procreatos atque educatos, Saturnum atque Opem,* V *circumsaeptos atque in uincula coniectos, atque ita* (on which see Norden 1956: 376 with n. 2, citing parallels from annalists; also Courtney 1999: 33), *eleuandae sortis atque effugiendi periculi gratia, consedisse . . . atque ei regnum portendisse.* In many cases the terms linked, particularly when a consonant follows, are near-synonyms or associated in some way (father and mother, mother and sisters, Jupiter and Juno). In Cato (see below, Appendix 1) pre-consonantal *atque* has an even more conspicuous tendency to link alliterative or synonymous terms.

I offer some statistics from two contrasting narrative passages of Plautus. The first is the prologue of the *Miles gloriosus* (99–144), which is in a straightforward style with repetitions of demonstratives and an abundance of temporal adverbs (for an analysis of the passage see Courtney 1999: 154–5). Here there are not many connectives at all, as the sentences are short and coordination is not a feature of the narrative. There are just four examples of *et* and three of *-que*; *atque* does not occur. The other passage is far more elaborate, a battle narrative in a grandiose epic style at *Amph.* 188–261 (omitting the intrusions at 197–202 and 248–9) (for discussion see Oniga 1985, Christenson 2000: 172–3; for a brief specimen from this narrative see Appendix 4 below). Here again we see the higher-style connectives *-que* and *atque* jointly outnumbering *et*, by 16:10 (*-que* ten times, *atque* six).

For *atque* before vowels in Plautus see below, 2.10. On Lucilius see Chahoud (forthcoming) II.1.

7–8 operam dare uti Saturnus regnaret, concessit ei ut is regnaret: *regnaret* is twice within a few words in *ut*-clauses, and it is used identically in the second sentence of the passage. The passage has verbal repetitions quite apart from those of temporal adverbs and the pronoun *is* (for the former see above and for the latter the next note). Cf. *concedat . . . concessit, natum esset . . . natus est . . . nati sunt, clam . . . clam . . . clanculum, abscondunt . . . abscondit, parit . . . parit, celantes . . . celant,* and see too Norden (1956: 376 n. 2) (for Norden on repetitions see also the next note). The indifference to repetition is no doubt deliberate and a marker of a contrived 'simple' narrative style. A notable specimen of this style in an annalist is at Cato, *FRH* II.5.F76, where alongside obvious stylistic artificiality manifested for example in the choice of connectives (*atque* occurs four times, *-que* four times but *et* not at all), in the use of the perfect ending *-ere* (five times, against no examples of *-erunt*) (see below, 1.11 on *necauerunt*) and in lexical features (note *claritudinis inclitissimae*), we find constant use of the pronoun *is* (seven times in what is a short passage), and other repetitions (*euenit . . . euenit, illoque facto . . . id eius*

factum ... pro factis, simile apud Thermopylas fecit ... qui idem fecerat). With
the last compare in our passage of Ennius *id eius rei causa fecit.*

8 concessit ei ut is regnaret: there is a constant, and sometimes redundant,
use of *is* in the fragments, which has been identified as a feature of deliberately simple narrative (see e.g. Fraenkel 1951: 57 = 1964: I.54–5; cf. the
fragment of a speech by C. Gracchus quoted by Gellius 10.3.5 and cited with
some bibliography by Hofmann and Ricottilli 2003: 390; also Calpurnius
Piso, *FRH* II.9.F29.2, cited in this connection along with Cato, *FRH* II.5.F76,
by Laughton 1951: 37–8, and containing *isque, eumque, isque*; see too
Appendix 3 below). Here the second *is* could be deleted. The repetitive use
of demonstratives is by no means confined to early Latin (see index, 'pronouns, redundantly used'; also s.v. *is*, 'repetitively used'). The clearest cases
of redundancy in our fragments are in XI. Note *eumque Curetes filii sui
curauerunt decoraueruntque eum.* Here the linking of the two transitive
verbs by *-que* creates a presumption that the second verb too will govern
eumque, yet *eum* is repeated. There follows immediately *et sepulchrum eius
est in Creta in oppido Gnosso*, after which comes *inque sepulchro eius est
inscriptum*, where there is no possibility that a second *sepulchrum* has been
introduced, and *eius* is needless. On this passage Norden (1956: 376 n. 2)
notes that the noun is repeated (in a different form) at the start of the
next sentence, and compares Cassius Hemina, *FRH* II.6.F35 *lapidem fuisse
quadratum circiter in media arca ... in eo lapide* and Quadrigarius, *FRH*
II.24.F57 *erat consul. ei consuli* (see Wills 1996: 272).

9 uti si quid liberum uirile secus ei natum esset, ne quid educaret: if
(liberum) uirile secus here were the primary subject, preceded by an adjectival
indefinite, *quod* would have been used, not *quid. Quid* must be pronominal, and the primary subject, which means that *uirile secus* is appositional,
literally 'if any child had been born to him, of male sex'. *Virile (muliebre)
secus* is neuter, and is regularly appositional. It is a type of apposition
whereby a specifying noun is attached to another, as in the Plautine
lapidem silicem 'stone that is flint' (see below, 5.35), and might also be
described as partitive (see also index, 'apposition, partitive/specifying/
defining'). A close parallel is provided by the use of *femina*, as in *lupus
femina* 'wolf that is female' (cf. *leo femina*, but with reversed order at
Plaut. *Vid.* frg. 18: on such reversals see below, this paragraph); so here
'anything that was male'.

Where *uirile/muliebre secus* differs from *femina* is that it is indeclinable, and
does not change its case to match that of the head noun. Here are two instances
from annalists where the case of the term (noun, pronoun) specified by the

phrase varies: Sempronius Asellio, *FRH* II.20.F8 *eum, quem uirile secus tum in eo tempore habebat, produci iussit* ('that one, the male one [with *uirile secus* taken into the relative clause], whom he had at that time, he ordered to be brought forth', i.e. 'his male child of that time he …'; he might have had a female child as well; here the head term is accusative), Sisenna, *FRH* II.26.F90 *tum in muro uirile ac muliebre secus populi multitudine omni conlocata* (translated 'then, when the whole mass of the people, men and women, had been placed on the wall'; here the phrase specifies *populi* in the genitive, and the adjectival role of the original appositive is so much to the fore that the expected order is reversed; one might compare in this respect appositional phrases containing *id genus* or the like, which not only occur in the expected order, with the specifier following, as at Suet. *Aug.* 75 *alia id genus*, but are also sometimes reversed, as at Petron. 71.7 *omne genus … poma*) (see Adams 2003b: 20 with n. 18 for bibliography).

On the phrase *uirile/muliebre secus* see Hofmann and Szantyr (1965: 47). It was old and stylised, and found mainly in historians, including annalists (see *OLD* s.v. *secus*). Wackernagel (1926–8: I.298) = Langslow (2009: 374) says that it functions 'as a genitive of quality', which in practical terms is correct but obscures the syntactic origin of the phrase.

The use of a neuter pronoun of a newborn or unborn child seen in *quid* (*natum esset*) occurs sometimes. Note Cic. *Att.* 10.18.1 *quod quidem est natum perimbecillimum* ('as for the baby, it is very weakly', Shackleton Bailey 1965–70: IV.291) (of a premature boy, born at seven months; *puerum* precedes). See further *TLL* IX.1.89.44ff. For *quod* of the foetus see Ovid *Her.* 6.61–2 *quod tamen e nobis grauida celatur in aluo,* | *uiuat et eiusdem simus uterque parens.* The idea seems to be that the foetus or newborn is not yet fully human, and in addition the sex of the foetus (or infant) may be unknown (as in the second passage above), though in the Ennian example and that from Cicero just quoted that is not the case; see however Christenson (2000: 230) on Plaut. *Amph.* 501 *quod erit natum tollito*; cf. *Truc.* 399 *si quod peperissem id <non> necarem ac tollerem.* Compare *TLL* X.1.954.22 f. on the use of *pecus* n. 'animal' of the foetus: 'technice de fetu humano, qui nondum homo sed animal habetur'. Also worth noting is the Greek neuter τέκνον meaning 'child'. Wackernagel (1926–8: II.16) = Langslow (2009: 420) remarks (in the context of gender) of such a coinage: 'No thought is given here to the personhood of the being, merely to its coming into being.' Cf. Eng. 'it', not infrequently used to refer to a newborn baby.

Liberum is mistranslated by Warmington (1961: 419) as 'free-born'. It is the usual genitive plural in -*um* of *liberi* 'child/children' (see *OLD* s.v.), here used, as it can be, of a single child. See Courtney (1999: 31), citing Hofmann and Szantyr (1965: 56) for the construction (*quid* + genitive).

ne quid: this second *quid* is redundant. It resembles the resumptive pronouns that are particularly common in Cato (see below, 5.7–8; also index, 'pronouns, resumptive'), and has something in common too with the redundant second indefinites that are found in some clauses in early Latin (see 3.431–2). On the latter see Hofmann and Szantyr (1965: 801), with bibliography.

10 uti ad suos gnatos regnum rediret: this is the first (nominal) use of *(g)natus = filius* in prose (see *TLL* IX.1.112.50). In the early annalists by contrast there are four examples of *filius* but none of *natus*. There is a treatment of *natus* versus *filius* in early Latin by Köhm (1905: 122–36), with comparative statistics at 126. Both are common (Plautus for example has *natus* and *nata* 108 times, and *filius* and *filia* 373 times) and used without semantic distinction (Köhm 1905: 125), but there is a difference in their distribution. *Filius* and *filia* are far preferred in comedy (Plautus, Terence and comic fragments) (by 401:185), whereas *natus* and *nata are* preferred in tragic fragments (by 23:4/5), a distribution which leads Köhm (1905: 126) to conclude that *filius* and *filia* were the everyday terms, whereas *natus* and *nata* belonged to high style. In prose of the Republic *filius* and *filia* are much preferred, with just a scattering of examples of the latter, in e.g. Cicero and Varro (see *TLL* IX.1.111.34f., 112.50ff.). This is the only example of *natus/ nata* in the fragments considered here, whereas *filius* and *filia* occur eight times, in the singular and plural. Ennius seems to have allowed himself the high-style term just occasionally in prose.

Rediret does not mean 'return to', since his sons, not yet born, have not had the kingship in the first place. The prefix *re-* often lacks specificity (see Svennung 1929: 55–6; also 1935: 602–3, citing e.g. the preface of Cato *Agr.* § 4, *ut ad rem redeam*).

11 tum Saturno filius qui primus natus est, eum necauerunt: most relative constructions in the fragments are of the 'normal' type, with the antecedent preceding the relative clause (which follows either immediately or after intervening words), and taking its case from the main clause, not the relative clause (for this type in general see e.g. Probert 2015: 126–8, a work with detailed classifications of relative clauses). Cf. III *Titan, qui maior natu erat, postulat; Titan, qui facie . . . esset . . ., concessit ei;* V *fugasse Saturnum, qui cum iactatus esset . . . uix in Italia locum . . . inuenit; persequentibus armatis, quos . . . Iuppiter miserat;* VI *in montem, qui uocatur; in caelum, quod nunc nos nominamus; quod supra mundum erat, quod aethera uocabatur; idque Iuppiter quod* *aether uocatur ... caelum nominauit; eamque hostiam quam ibi sacrificauit totam adoleuit.*

In our passage, however, the nominative *filius* has the case of the relative pronoun, not the case it would have had in the main clause (accusative). In this type of construction (usually called 'attractio inversa': see recently e.g. Pompei 2011: 468–72, Probert 2015: 162–7) the relative clause, preceded by the antecedent (here *filius*), comes before the main clause, and there tends to be a resumptive pronoun (or noun) in the main clause. For early examples see e.g. Plaut. *Mil.* 140–2 *unum conclaue, concubinae quod dedit | miles ... | in eo conclaui ego perfodi parietem, Lex Cornelia de XX quaestoribus* (*CIL* I².587.31; Crawford 1996 col. II.31–2) *uiatores praecones quei ex hac lege lectei sublectei erunt, eis uiatoribus praeconibus ... dato.* It is sometimes said that the construction is basically of the relative-correlative type (= *qui filius primus natus est, eum necauerunt*; cf. e.g. Cic. *De orat.* 2.248 *quoscunque locos attingam, ... ex eisdem locis fere etiam grauis sententias posse duci*, and see further below, this note), but with 'fronting' of the noun out of the relative clause (see Watkins 1995: 541 with n. 2, Probert 2015: 163–4, with refinements). That seems to be so in the Plautine example above, where *concubinae* is fronted from the same clause.

Similar in the present text is VI (*idque quod supra mundum erat, quod aether uocabatur, de sui aui nomine caelo nomen indidit*), where *idque* does not take its case from the main clause, in which, like *caelo* there, it would have been dative, but it has the same case as the relative pronoun immediately following.

Attractio inversa is not uncommon, particularly but not exclusively in early Latin (see also below, 4.11; for late examples see e.g. Adams 2007: 444, and now Halla-aho, forthcoming). There is scope for an extensive search for examples in later works.

In VII on the other hand (*quae secundum mare loca essent, omnibus regnaret*) *loca* is within the relative clause and is resumed by *omnibus* in the main clause. This is the relative-correlative type (on which see in general Probert 2015: 142–4).

As in the *Euhemerus* fragments, so in another early narrative text, Cato's *Origines*, most relative constructions are of the normal type (with an antecedent preceding the relative) rather than relative-correlative (for which, and variants, in Ennius himself, mainly in poetic works, see Vonlaufen 1974: 31–3). In Cato's *De agricultura* on the other hand relative-correlatives are particularly common (see below, 4.11, Vonlaufen 1974: 15–31, and Probert and Dickey, forthcoming, on their passage (22)). In the earlier period a high incidence of the construction was probably determined at least partly by genre, with instructional texts more likely to have it (see Laughton 1960: 6–7 on its frequency in Varro; also Probert and Dickey, forthcoming on (22)). The nature of an utterance was a factor, with gnomic generalisations, e.g. in late sermons, often showing the pattern (see below, 39.10; note e.g., earlier, Lucr. 4.954–5). There was possibly a decline in the frequency of the relative-correlative pattern over time (see Probert and Dickey, forthcoming, §§6–7), though that requires further investigation.

I have listed in Appendix 2 all relative constructions in the fragments of Cato's *Origines*, with those that are not of the normal type marked with an asterisk. See further Vonlaufen (1974: 15–45), Pompei (2011: 494–9), and for descriptive issues, Pinkster (2012); see also index, 'relative clauses, relative-correlative type'.

tum: *tum* occurs twice in the fragments as presented by Lactantius, *tunc* not at all. Manuscripts are not a trustworthy guide to the distribution of the pair, but the preference apparently displayed here is in accord with what can be deduced about their history from the evidence such as it is. *Tum* is strongly preferred in texts of the early period, even the only form in some texts, whereas *tunc* becomes more frequent in later Latin (Hofmann and Szantyr 1965: 519–20; also below, 11.9 on Vitruvius; also index s.v. *tum/tunc*). Skutsch's index (1985: 826) to the *Annals* lists eleven examples of *tum*, four of *tunc*. Vahlen's index (1928: 296) lists six examples of *tum* from the *scenica*, none of *tunc*. The index to *FRH* at III.720 lists thirteen examples of *tum* from the fragmentary (mainly early) historians, two of *tunc*.

necauerunt: *neco* is regularly used of the putting to death of an infant, as here (see Adams 1990d: 235–8), one of the early categories of killing that might sometimes be described as executing (given that it might be effected by some-one in virtue of his possession of *patria potestas*); *neco* is frequently employed of execution (Adams 1990d: 232–51). Here however it is someone else's offspring that is killed. There are two other instances of *neco* in the fragments, both, like that above, referring to the dynastic killing of rivals: V *insidiatum Ioui, ut eum necaret*, V *quos ad eum comprehendendum uel necandum Iuppiter miserat*. Such examples are difficult to classify semantically. They do not refer to random acts of killing, but to killing for a higher purpose, with the sense 'execute' discernible but shading into 'murder' (for this sort of ambiguity see Adams 1990d: 253). The meaning 'murder' in a legal or quasi-legal sense was well established for the verb (Adams 1990d: 251–4).

In the *Annals* of Ennius there is just one example of *neco* (573 Skutsch *hos pestis necuit*), of a type of death not involving a weapon or human agent, which foreshadows later uses of the verb (for which see the whole of Adams 1991a, and for this passage, 1991a: 116–17). For the tragedies see 178 Jocelyn *quis parentem aut hospitem* | *necasset* (of specific categories of murder: see Adams 1990d: 252, comparing Plaut. *Most.* 479 *hospes necauit hospitem* and Cic. *S. Rosc.* 70 *qui parentem necasset*), 206 *mea necetur filia* (so in our passage of the *Euhemerus* it is *filium* that is implied object; in both cases it is someone else's offspring that is put to death), 362 *extemplo acceptum me necato et filium*. The association of the verb in various of these passages with *filius/filia* may be significant, reflecting in origin phraseology applied to the putting to death of an infant.

The classical form of the third person plural perfect ending in *necauerunt* is the main one attested in the fragments: cf. XI *curauerunt decoraueruntque* (also X *fuerunt*). On the other hand a few lines later in our passage there is *in conspectum dedere* (a phrase which Courtney 1999: 32 notes is in the *Annals* at 47 Skutsch, though there with the verb form *dedit*). In the *Annals* and the *scenica* on the other hand '-*erunt* is only half as frequent as -*ere*': Skutsch 1985: 62). Skutsch concludes that '[a]pparently Ennius felt -*erunt* to be the normal form'.

There is a contrast between Ennius' prose and that of Cato's *Origines*, where the archaic/archaising form -*ere* outnumbers the other (in the *De agricultura* -*ere* does not occur: see Bauer 1933: 67): *FRH* II.5.F18 *fuere*, F34b *meminere*, F76 *dedere . . . cognouere . . . sustulere . . . decorauere . . . habuere*, F77 *decessere*, F79 *resciuere*, F88 *noluere . . . metuere . . . adiuuere*, F117 *accessitauere* (thirteen examples). The -*erunt* form occurs just twice, once in a speech: F24 *habuerunt* (narrative), F92 *fecerunt* (speech).

Later annalists prefer -*erunt*. Here are all cases of the third person plural perfect in three writers:

Cassius Hemina (*FRH* II.6)

F10 manserunt
F14 praefecerunt . . . fecerunt
F30 demessuerunt.

Quadrigarius (*FRH* II.24)

F14 rescierunt . . . prouolarunt
F29 exegerunt
F38 habuerunt
F48 reuerterunt
F52 urserunt
F77 decreuerunt
F84 quiuerunt
F97 coeperunt.

Sisenna (*FRH* II.26)
F57 supersederunt
F61 exhauserunt
F97 uiderunt
F135 suffragauerunt.

On -*ere* in Plautus see Bauer (1933: 33–7) (almost all examples are connected with formal or archaic language: see 37), and in Terence, Bauer (1933: 40) (just four examples). On other early writers and on later periods see Bauer (1933: 64–75).

12 deinde posterius: this is the only example of the combination cited at *TLL* X.2.212.6f., where it is labelled a 'iunctura pleonastica', an accurate description of the only two-word temporal phrase occurring in a vague chronology of sequential events of which the others are introduced by a single temporal adverb (*exim, ibi, ibi, tum, (deinde posterius), tum, ibi, deinde*). For pairs of adverbials (adverbs, prepositional phrases or a combination of both) in the fragments cf. V *post haec deinde*, VI *ibique in eo monte*, VIII *eo ad eum in ius ueniebant*, XI *in Creta in oppido Gnosso*. Of these the most noteworthy is *post haec deinde*, which is similar to *deinde posterius*. See further Thomsen (1930: 21), citing various comparable phrases, including *post tum* in the *Censoriae tabulae* quoted by Varro *Ling.* 6.87. *Deinde* is often combined pleonastically with other temporal adverbs, such as *post* or *postea* (see *TLL* V.1.408.58ff. for an extensive collection of examples; see also Hofmann and Szantyr 1965: 525, 799). Particularly striking is the threefold pleonasm *postid [agam] igitur deinde* found at Plaut. *Stich.* 86 (for further such examples see Petersmann 1973: 107 ad loc.; for temporal *igitur* in early Latin = *tum*, see e.g. Lindsay 1900: 316–17 on Plaut. *Capt.* 870). *Postid* with *deinde* is very similar to *post haec deinde* above (a combination not illustrated by the *TLL* loc. cit.). From Ennius himself elsewhere note *Ann.* 9 Skutsch *post inde uenit* (with Skutsch's note, 1985: 163). This expression is also at Lucr. 3.531, on which Munro (1886: II.202) cites both the Ennian example above and Cic. *Pis.* 89; he also lists parallel phrases from Lucretius himself, *post deinde, post hinc, tum deinde*.

There are many other such pleonasms illustrated by Thomsen (1930), of which I mention just *deinde postea* (20 n. 2), which is at Cic. *Tusc.* 4.2 (see also below, this paragraph), *tum postea* (64–5) and *tum in eo tempore* (Sempronius Asellio, *FRH* II.20.F8 *quem uirile secus tum in eo tempore habebat*; cf. Lucr. 3.862 *in eo tum tempore*: see Thomsen 1930: 103 n. 2;

also Hofmann and Szantyr 1965: 525, 799). See further, for a variety of expressions, Kühner and Stegmann (1955: II.573–4). Figures are not available for the distribution of this form of adverbial pleonasm, but it does seem to be more common in early Latin and later archaisers than in classical prose; examples can be found in Cicero (see above, 1.3 on *ibi tum*), but they are not numerous. In the Latin translation of Irenaeus *post deinde* occurs more than fifty times, usually translating a single Greek word (see Lundström 1943: 108), and that suggests that this is a pleonasm that persisted into late Latin (cf. E. Löfstedt 1911: 59–64, but dealing with various different phenomena). On *post deinde* (and variants, with reversal of the order and also *postea* for *post*) in republican and imperial Latin see the collection of material by Lindholm (1931: 30–1). Anna Chahoud points out to me that *poi dopo* is very common in Italian in informal speech.

The examples quoted above from Ennius' *Euhemerus* fall into two categories. *Deinde posterius* and *post haec deinde* are indeed 'iuncturae pleonasticae'. In the other cases, however, the second, appositional, term adds a specification (e.g. *in Creta in oppido Gnosso*). This latter type is discussed and illustrated at length by Müller (1895), and it is common in all varieties of the language (see below, 3.421, and index, 'locative/temporal expressions, double'). The specifying type is well illustrated by Aug. *Serm.* 12.4, *CC* 41, p. 168.109–10 *non extrinsecus per aures eius aut oculos, sed intus in animo*. Here both elements have a point: there is an 'outside/inside' contrast, and the contrasting locations are then specified.

13 in conspectum dedere: see above, 1.11.

14 atque Iouem: this is the 'slightly adversative' use of *atque* (*OLD* s.v. 9). Compare in a similar context later in the passage <u>at</u> *filium . . . celant*.

15 celantes Saturnum: this is the use of *celo* + acc. meaning 'conceal from (someone)' (see *OLD* s.v. 5). There are only two present participles in the (genuine) fragments considered here, both of them with an accusative object: cf. VI *idque Iuppiter quod aether uocatur placans primus caelum nominauit* 'Jupiter, appeasing that called ether, was the first to name it *caelum*'. The standard opinion is that the classical uses of the present participle were not fully current in early Latin (see e.g. Clackson and Horrocks 2007: 191–2). In particular the present participle with an accusative object is said to be rare, though becoming common by Cicero's later period (for this development see e.g. Laughton 1964: 21–3; for Varro, in whom it is quite common, see Marouzeau 1910: 15). According to Hofmann and Szantyr (1965: 384), the present participle with an accusative object in early Latin is found mainly in passages of high style. They say that it is found only twice in Plautus but more frequently in Terence (and later classical Latin) (for Plautus see also Marouzeau 1910: 13–14, and for Terence Marouzeau 1910: 14–15; also Laughton 1964: 21). In Cato it occurs only once, in the Rhodian speech: *FRH* II.5.93 *id obiectantes quod mihi et liberis meis minime dici uelim*. In Ennius' other works note *Ann.* 184 Skutsch *non cauponantes bellum*, 251 *miscent inter sese inimicitias agitantes* (but ambiguous), 282 *multa tenens antiqua*, 283 (textually uncertain), 294 *tonsamque tenentes*, 398 *tela manu iacientes, scen.* 55 Jocelyn *pacem petens*, 63 *exspectantes nuntium*, 105 *bellum gerentes*, 169 *flammam halitantes*, 297 *saxa spargens*. It seems that in Ennius' *Annals* and tragedies the present participle + object was not uncommon, in contrast to its rarity in Plautine comedy. There is indeed a suggestion here of an early generic distinction, with higher genres (under Greek influence?) admitting the construction, it would seem, freely. Only in a qualified sense then can one speak of a later development of the language: the construction was established early but was not generally used. One should not however exaggerate the role of Cicero as an innovator in prose. Early literary prose is very fragmentary, and we have seen three instances in these fragmentary prose narrative texts. It is worth noting above the similarity between the second case in the *Euhemerus* and that in the speech of Cato (*id* + pres. part. + *quod*).

16 clam Saturno: *clam* with the ablative looks like an anachronism. The early Latin construction is *clam* + accusative (*TLL* III.1247.33ff.: Plautus, Terence, Caecilius; also at *B. Hisp.* 3.2; for the archaising tendencies of this work see the next note). *Clam* + ablative is quoted only from the late Republic onwards (*TLL* III.1247.51ff.). It seems that Lactantius has modernised here, or the text could have been altered in transmission.

17 clanculum abscondit: *clanculum* (originally an adjective, *clanculus*, converted to an adverb in the neuter) is very much a term of early Latin (see *TLL* s.v.), found for example twenty-nine times in Plautus, sometimes in Terence, in Afranius and Lucilius. There is also an example at *B. Hisp.* 32.8, an illustration of the archaising element in the ps.-Caesarian military texts (see Adams 2005a: 79–83). The author of the *B. Hisp.* twice cites Ennius (Adams 2005a: 84).

18 Glauca parua emoritur: for the attributive (and often pathetic or emotive) use of *paruus* of a child see *TLL* X.1.558.12ff. This usage is found mainly in poetry, but that merely reflects the subject matter of poetic genres (there are a few instances in Cicero).

19 haec ut scripta sunt ... **stirps atque cognatio:** it might be tempting to take *haec* as feminine singular with *stirps atque cognatio*, but that would leave *scripta sunt* without a subject. The alternative is to take it as neuter plural (as in the translation, 'these, as they are recorded, are ...'). *Sunt* would be understood in the main clause, and the neuter pronoun would be that summarising use of neuter pronominals that can embrace referents of any gender (see index, 'gender, neuter pronouns/adjectives, resuming noun of another gender (or number)').

Appendix 1: connectives in Cato's *Origines* (*FRH* II.5)

atque

F28   in maximum decus atque in excelsissimam claritudinem

F29   in nauis putidas atque sentinosas

F30   securim atque lorum ferunt

F48   terna atque quaterna milia (cf. *Agr.* 65.2 *triduum atque quatriduum*).

F76   atque quod

F76   fortem atque strenuam

F76   gloriam atque gratiam

F76   fecerat atque rem seruauerat

F87   secundis atque prolixis atque prosperis

F87   animum excellere atque superbiam atque ferociam augescere atque crescere

F87   consulendo atque intellegendo

F88   atque ego

F88   multos populos atque multas nationes

F91   atque nos

F95   equitibus atque alis

F97   eduxit foras atque instruxit

F111   magnus atque pulcher

F138   inter se natinari atque factiones esse.

Fronto mocks Cato's taste for *atque* at *Epist.* p. 34.20–1 van den Hout *nam uni M. Porcio me dedicaui atque despondi atque delegaui. hoc etiam ipsum 'atque' unde putas? ex ipso furore.*

et

F33   rem militarem et argute loqui

F41   populi et boni et strenui

F66b   tauro et uacca

F66b   sustollat et portet

F66b   et portam uocet

F77   quattuor et uiginti
F86   publicati et execrati
F87   edomant et docent
F93   mihi et liberis meis
F142 et in Italia
F143 primo pedatu et secundo.

-que
F76   eumque
F76   isque
F76   saepeque
F76   illoque
F76   aliisque
F83   proelium factum depugnatumque
F87   dico suadeoque
F89   ultro citroque
F94   urbes insulasque omnis
F109 opertae auro purpuraque
F112 iurum legumque
F143 stipendio agrique parte multati.

Appendix 2: relative constructions in Cato's *Origines*

An asterisk marks those in which the relative clause is preposed or there is some noteworthy feature.

*F24   agrum quem Volsci habuerunt, campestris plerus, Aboriginum fuit (attractio inversa).
F30   Libui, qui aquatum ut lignatum uidentur ire, securim atque lorum ferunt.
F38   ex sale qui apud Carthaginienses fit.
F40   idem in montibus serit, ubi hordeum idem iterum metit.
F46   ager Gallicus Romanus uocatur qui uiritim ... datus est.
F47   caprae ferae sunt, quae saliunt.
*F66b qui urbem nouam condet, tauro et uacca aret (preposed relative clause, but without resumptive pronoun in main clause).
F76   illoque facto, quod illos milites subduxit, exercitum ceterum seruauit.
*F76   Leonides Laco, qui simile apud Thermopylas fecit, propter eius uirtutes (hanging nominative rather than attractio inversa).
F76   at tribuno militum parua laus pro factis relicta, qui idem fecerat.
F77   post dimissum bellum, quod quattuor et uiginti annos fuit.

F80   non lubet scribere quod in tabula apud pontificem maximum est.

F87   ne quid . . . eueniat quod nostras secundas res confutet.

*F89   quod illos dicimus uoluisse facere, id nos priores facere occupabimus? (relative-correlative).

*F90   qui acerrime aduersus eos dicit, ita dicit (preposed relative clause without resumptive pronoun in main clause).

F90   ecquis est tandem qui uestrorum . . . aequum censeat.

F91   ecqua tandem lex est tam acerba quae dicat.

F93   id obiectantes quod mihi et liberis meis minime dici uelim.

?F108   qui magistratum curulem cepisset, calceos malleos . . . ceteri peronei.

F140   praeda quae capta est uiritim diuisa.

*F147   qua mollissimum est, adoriantur (preposed 'relative' clause, but with adverbial relative, without resumption in main clause).

Appendix 3: two passages from Terence (*Andr.* 220–4, 922–37 with omissions) exemplifying the popular narrative style (on which see above 1.1, 7, 8)

220–4

Et fingunt quondam inter se nunc fallaciam
ciuem Atticam esse hanc: 'fuit olim quidam senex
mercator; nauim is fregit apud Andrum insulam;
is obiit mortem.' ibi tum hanc eiectam Chrysidis
patrem recepisse orbam paruam. fabulae!

922–5

nam ego quae dico uera an falsa audierim iam sciri potest.
Atticus quidam olim naui fracta ad Andrum eiectus est
et istaec una parua uirgo. tum ille egens forte adplicat
primum ad Chrysidis patrem se.

926–8

tum is mihi cognatus fuit
qui eum recepit. ibi ego auidui ex illo sese esse Atticum.
is ibi mortuost.

935–7

is bellum hinc fugiens meque in Asiam persequens proficiscitur:
tum illam relinquere hic est ueritus. postilla hoc primum audio
quid illo sit factum.

Exemplified here are the frequent use of temporal adverbs (*olim, ibi tum* (note the pleonasm, and the temporal use of *ibi*), *olim, tum, tum, ibi, tum, postilla*), and the repetitive use of demonstrative pronouns (most notably *is . . . is* in the first passage). Also of note are the short and uncomplicated sentences.

Appendix 4: a brief passage from Plautus illustrating a completely different narrative style (*Amph.* 188–94)

uictores uictis hostibus legiones reueniunt domum,
duello exstincto maxumo atque internecatis hostibus.
quod multa Thebano poplo acerba obiecit funera,   190
id ui et uirtute militum uictum atque expugnatum oppidum est.
imperio atque auspicio mei eri Amphitruonis maxume.
praedaque agroque adoriaque adfecit popularis suos
regique Thebano Creoni regnum stabiliuit suom.

I have cited this passage (from a much longer military narrative: see above, 1.6, where some bibliography can also be found) to provide a contrast with the passage that precedes (in Appendix 3) and also with our passage of the *Euhemerus*. This narrative is far from 'simple' stylistically, and it offers a corrective to any assumption that the simplicity of style adopted sometimes in the early period by some writers was a reflection of the 'primitiveness' of the period or of the undeveloped state of the Latin language. If a writer such as Plautus or Ennius ever adopts a simple style, he does so deliberately.

Et occurs just once, whereas there are three instances of *atque* and four of *-que*, with a notable polysyndeton in the second last line. The ablative absolute is found three times, a construction that hardly occurs in Plautus but was associated with military narrative (see Adams 2005a: 74–5). There is at least one archaic form (*duello*). *Vi et uirtute* is an alliterative combination of near-synonyms of ascending length, and *agroque adoriaque adfecit* shows an alliterative pair of nouns with the alliteration further extended.

Conclusions

This passage of Ennius is written in what looks like an informal and simple style, marked by short sentences, an indifference to verbal repetition, redundant use of the pronoun *is* and constant use of temporal adverbs at the start of sentences. These last two features in particular are a mark of a popular narrative style that first turns up in Latin in the early period (see Appendix 3) and does not disappear entirely later.

It is however a contrived simplicity, which on close inspection turns out to have artificialities. As Courtney (1999: 38) puts it, 'Ennius' translation is written in a very simple narrative style, but it has touches which run counter to any suggestion that this was the only way Ennius knew how to write prose.' The use of connectives in the *Euhemerus* fragments is comparable to that in Cato's *Origines* but quite different from that in the *De agricultura*, and is a mark of an early high style. *Gnatus* too seems to have been a stylistically marked alternative to *filius*. Also significant is the construction present participle + object, which is all but absent from the comedies of Plautus but common (it seems from what is extant) in the *Annals* and tragedies of Ennius. Here is another generic distinction of early Latin: the *Euhemerus* fragments are to be associated with the usage of epic and tragedy rather than comedy. On the other hand Ennius' apparent preference for *-erunt* over *-ere* sets him apart from Cato in the *Origines*: he seems to have preferred the more mundane form, though the examples are not numerous enough to justify any confidence. Relative constructions by contrast are comparable to those in the *Origines* but differ from those in the didactic text *De agricultura*. In the early period prose was already stylistically diverse, with genre an influence, and one should avoid any temptation to use the term 'primitive' as a blanket description. Clearly the style of the *Euhemerus* was complex, and is not to be dismissed as naive.

For the most part the Latin of our passage looks authentic for the period and for Ennius himself, for example in the use of *uti, ut(i) ne, ibi,* the pleonasm *deinde posterius, tum* versus *tunc, exim* and *clanculum.* Quite a few parallels of different types were cited from early annalists. We noted just one apparent anachronism, *clam* + ablative.

2
PLAUTUS, *MILES GLORIOSVS* 5–27

Introduction

This is the opening scene of the play, preceding the delayed prologue, which begins at 79. The metre is iambic senarii. The soldier Pyrgopolinices, 'capturer of towers and cities', enters, followed by the parasite Artotrogus, the 'bread eater' (see on line 9). The pair proceed to act in character, engaging in boasting and flattery. Some typical Plautine elements are in evidence, such as the personification of a weapon, and the passage brings out some of the diversity of Plautine Latin. The text printed here is that of de Melo (2011b), with just one change, in line 11, where de Melo does not print *se*.

Text

PY. Nam ego hanc machaeram mihi consolari uolo,	5
ne lamentetur neue animum despondeat,	
quia se iam pridem feriatam gestitem,	
quae misera gestit fartem facere ex hostibus.	
sed ubi Artotrogus hic est? AR. stat propter uirum	
fortem atque fortunatum et forma regia.	10
tam bellatorem Mars se haud ausit dicere	
neque aequiperare suas uirtutes ad tuas.	
PY. quemne ego seruaui in campis Curculioniis,	
ubi Bumbomachides Clytomestoridysarchides	
erat imperator summus, Neptuni nepos?	15
AR. memini. nempe illum dicis cum armis aureis,	
quoius tu legiones difflauisti spiritu,	
quasi uentus folia aut peniculus tectorium.	
PY. istuc quidem edepol nihil est. AR. nihil hercle hoc quidem est	
praeut alia dicam – quae tu numquam feceris.	20
periuriorem hoc hominem si quis uiderit	
aut gloriarum pleniorem quam illic est,	
me sibi habeto, ego me mancupio dabo;	
nisi unum, epityra estur insanum bene.	

PY. ubi tu es? AR. eccum. edepol uel elephanto in India,   25
quo pacto ei pugno praefregisti brachium.
PY. quid 'bracchium'? AR. illud dicere uolui, 'femur'.

Translation

PY. I want to console this sword so that it does not lament or lose heart because
I have been carrying it around for a long time now on holidays, when the poor
thing is itching to make stuffing of the enemy. But where here is Artotrogus?
AR. He is standing near a real man, brave and fortunate and of royal beauty.
Mars would not dare to call himself so much of a warrior nor to compare
his deeds of valour to yours. PY. Do you mean the one whom I saved in the
Curculonian Fields, where Bumbomachides Clytomestoridysarchides, grand-
son of Neptune, was supreme commander? AR. I remember. No doubt you
mean him with the golden arms, whose legions you scattered with your breath,
as the wind scatters leaves or the plasterer's brush the plaster. PY. That for sure
is nothing. AR. Nothing indeed is it, compared with other things I might say –
which you never did. If anyone sees a greater liar than him, or one more full of
boasts than this one is, he can have me as his own, I will hand over ownership
of myself; except for one thing, his olive spread is amazingly good to eat. PY.
Where are you? AR. Here I am. Or for example the elephant in India – how
you broke its arm with your fist! PY. What? Its 'arm'? AR. I meant to say this –
'thigh'.

Commentary

5 machaeram: Plautus does not use the Latin word for 'sword', *gladius*, except
in passages with a Roman feel (see Shipp 1955: 149–50). *Merc.* 613 (*demisisti
gladium in iugulum: iam cadam*) is proverbial and metaphorical, and is not
a reference to a literal case of stabbing. *Truc.* 492 (*illi quorum lingua gladiorum
aciem praestringit domi*) contrasts oratory with the sword, and is typically
Roman. At *Cas.* 909 *gladius* is in a sexual pun (see MacCary and Willcock 1976
on 907). *Machaera* is Plautus' regular word for the weapon of Greek mercenaries, and its choice over the Latin *gladius* is clearly a piece of linguistic
characterisation. Shipp showed that *machaera* was not taken over by Plautus
from Greek New Comedy. There the sword of mercenaries was regularly
σπάθη (see Men. *Sam.* 659, 660, 687, 720). Μάχαιρα does occur in New
Comedy, but it was a piece of cook's equipment (*Sam.* 283; found occasionally
in this sense from Pindar onwards).

Machaera was not confined to comedy in early Latin. It also occurs in other genres of Greek origin (tragedy and epic), in which again it could not have come from Greek originals or models. Jocelyn (1967: 291–2) on Ennius *scen.* 149 notes that *machaera* is found once in early Latin tragedy, and that, though the word occurs once in Attic tragedy (in Euripides) and in comedy, it never there indicates a military weapon. In Attic tragedy 'soldiers wield the ξίφος or the φάσγανον', whereas in comedy they wield the σπάθη (examples are cited, and see above). Note also Skutsch (1985: 671) on Enn. *Ann.* 519: 'The Greek word μάχαιρα is firmly established in the language of the Roman people at the end of the third century BC. It . . . practically disappears from literature after Accius.' The word occurs just a few times in Homer, where it means 'knife' (see Ebeling 1885: 1021: 'pugio, culter, quem heroes iuxta gladium suspensum gerunt, . . . quo imprimis, ut videtur, utuntur ad mactandas victimas'), and it cannot be a literary borrowing in Ennius' *Annales* in the sense that it has there.

Μάχαιρα had almost certainly entered Latin in the early period not from literature but from contemporary (koine) Greek. It is common in the sense 'sword' in Polybius (twenty times: see Mauersberger 1975: 1514; ξίφος is used only six times: Mauersberger 1975: 1678), who was born *c.* 200 and was thus almost contemporary with Plautus (on the influence on Polybius of the koine see Horrocks 2010: 97–8). Polybius has it, for example (6.23.6), of the Roman *gladius Hispaniensis* (for which see Livy 7.10.5, with Oakley 1998: 134–5 ad loc., and also 38.21.13), so called because it was thought to have been adopted from Spanish mercenaries fighting for the Carthaginians in the First Punic War. Polybius also uses μάχαιρα of the Gallic sword (2.33.3), for which Livy at 7.10.9 adopts *ensis* (see Oakley 1998: 135); Mauersberger loc. cit. classifies the examples according to the origin of the users. Μάχαιρα is also common in the Septuagint and in papyri of the last three centuries BC (information from John Lee, and <papyri.info> on 12.10.14): in papyri of s. III–I BC there are about thirty-five examples, and in those of s. III alone about fourteen. In addition there are about forty-nine examples of μαχαιροφόρος in s. III–I. A proper survey of the papyrological evidence would have to sift all examples to rule out cases meaning 'knife', but the meaning 'sword' is definitely attested (see e.g. *PRyl* 2.256.3, s. I BC), and the currency of the term clear. In the imperial period μάχαιρα was definitely alive in the koine: it, not ξίφος, is the standard word for 'sword' in the Greek New Testament (see Bauer, Arndt and Gingrich 1957, s.vv.); ῥομφαία also occurs, but it was an exotic implement used particularly by barbarian peoples (Bauer, Arndt and Gingrich 1957: 744).

Plautine Latin is full of popular, as distinct from literary, borrowings from Greek, as will be shown below, and these throw light on cultural contacts between Greeks and Italians in the early republic.

mihi consolari uolo: it is possible to take *mihi* either as possessive with *machaeram* (so de Melo 2011b), or as a 'pleonastic' reflexive dative of advantage with *uolo* (literally 'I want for myself, for my purposes'). Such reflexive datives may have a variety of nuances at different periods (see on 2.23 below), but they sometimes verge on the pleonastic (see Dahlén 1964, Adams 2013, chapter XVI). Plautus uses for example *quid tibi uis* and *quid uis* interchangeably (Adams 2013: 349). For this reflexive construction complemented, as possibly here, by an infinitive see Lucr. 3.772 *quidue foras sibi uult membris exire senectis?* (see Adams 2013: 350). In his note on this last passage Bailey (1947: II.1122) translates 'why does it wish to?', and adds 'not in the frequent idiomatic sense of "what does it mean?"' He was clearly taking the pronoun as pleonastic. See further below on 2.23, and index, 'dative, reflexive, pleonastic'.

6 animum despondeat: the *machaera* is personified. For 'animating the inanimate' in Plautus see Fraenkel ([1922] 2007: 72–7) (with instruments of punishment at 75). In this play cf. 1398 (*culter* is subject) *quin iamdudum gestit moecho hoc abdomen adimere.*

7–8 gestitem… gestit: a word play with verbs of the same root but different suffixal forms (cf. Accius *praet.* 30 *quaeque agunt uigilantes agitantque*). Word plays of different types are constant in Plautus (see e.g. Lorenz 1869: 63, quoting diverse examples from this play, e.g. at 33–4, 325, 938, 1424).

Gestio is a derivative of *gestus* (cf. *singultus > singultire*), which is a derivative of *gero*. *Gestito* is a derivative of *gesto, -are*, which also is a derivative of *gero*. *Gestio* here is accompanied in the frequent classical manner by an infinitive and can be translated 'desire', but there are places in Plautus where it is unaccompanied and refers to agitated bodily movement, like the base noun *gestus* (for which, of '[m]ovement of the limbs, etc., bodily action', see *OLD* s.v. 1): *Amph.* 323 *gestiunt pugni mihi*, *Bacch.* 596 *ita dentifrangibula haec meis manibus gestiunt.* The infinitive complement can be interpreted in origin as an infinitive of purpose with a verb of motion, 'to be in a state of agitation/to move agitatedly to do something' (for this use of the infinitive see index, 'infinitive, final'). The two examples just quoted both refer to weapons exhibiting agitated movement, and the same is so in our passage, but with the infinitive added; cf. also *Mil.* 1398, quoted in the previous note.

9 sed ubi Artotrogus hic est?: the speaking name (of a parasite) combines ἄρτος 'bread' and τρώγω, possibly in the sense 'eat'. This verb, 'gnaw' in classical Greek, in the sense 'eat' 'comes into prominence in *NT*, though no doubt older' (Shipp 1979: 540) (for the semantic change cf. *manduco*). Τρώγω rather than ἐσθίω is the word for 'eat' in John's Gospel, and it was to survive in modern Greek (for further details see Shipp 1967: 129, 1979: 540–1). It will come up later in connection with the *Vetus Latina* (38.53). Here we may see the new meaning in a Latin text several centuries before the New Testament, and taken no doubt from the popular language if this interpretation is right. There is however an ambiguity: does the name mean rather 'bread chewer/nibbler'?

ubi … hic: this expression ('where here') is of common type in Plautus. The pairing of locativals came up earlier (1.12) in passing (in Ennius' *in Creta in oppido Gnosso*), where it was noted that the second term was not a pleonastic apposition but adds a specification. In the present passage *hic* could certainly be left out without the audience noticing anything untoward, but it does add something: it shows that the speaker knows that Artotrogus is in the vicinity. Cf. Ter. *Heaut.* 829 *ubi Clitipho hic est?* Many such expressions in Plautus can plausibly be related to staging, with *hic* signalling a gesture by the speaker. See further below, on 3.421, and also index, 'locative/temporal expressions, double'.

10 fortem atque fortunatum et forma regia: note the triple alliteration of *f*, a letter that starts Latin words relatively rarely and was therefore probably more noticeable in an alliterative sequence than, say, *p* (see Goodyear 1972: 338–9). The tricolon is also of ascending length, with its elements having two, four and five syllables ('Behaghel's law': see Behaghel 1909, Collinge 1985: 241–2, West 2007: 117–19). It fills the line (on which see Lindholm 1931: 113). *Fortis* and its adverb *fortiter* are attested in numerous alliterative combinations (see Wölfflin 1933: 260 for examples). Wölfflin cites only this case of *fortis fortunatus*, but the nouns *fors* (not connected etymologically with *fortis*) and *fortuna* not infrequently occur in asyndeton together ('Chance Luck'), as do *forte* and *fortuna*. Our passage alongside these combinations raises the possibility that a popular etymological connection was felt between *fortis* and *fors*; note too the proverb *fortes fortuna adiuuat* (Ter. *Ph.* 203 with Otto 1890: 144).

The use of two alliterative (and almost synonymous) terms linked by *atque*, placed before a consonant rather than the usual vowel, is also stylistically marked. Note the following three groups of passages from Plautus:

(a) *Cas.* 418 pietate . . . mea atque maiorum meum, *Curc.* 77 multibiba atque merobiba, *Men.* 459 contioni ... atque comitieis, 572 molesto atque multo, *Mil.* 887 male atque malitiose, *Trin.* 829 damnare atque domare.

(b) *Bacch.* 763 truculento mi atque saeuo, *Cas.* 382, 402 quod bonum atque fortunatum sit mihi, 477 sodalem meum atque uicinum, *Curc.* 649 timidam atque pauidam, *Epid.* 523 legum atque iurum, *Merc.* 21 magno atque solido, *Poen.* 1223 lepide hercle atque commode, *Truc.* 345 magna atque luculenta.

(c) *Capt.* 135 ossa atque pellis sum, *Men.* 88 esca atque potione, *Capt.* 744, *Cist.* 116, *Curc.* 522, 588 uale atque salue.

In group (a) *atque* before a consonant links alliterative terms (which in several cases are closely related in meaning, or have other features of assonance). In (b) there are pairs of near-synonyms or complementary terms (*legum atque iurum*), and again there is some assonance, most notably in *timidam atque pauidam*. The terms in (c) form set phrases, skin and bone, food and drink.

The stylised character of this use of *atque* can be seen particularly from the well-known fragment of a speech by Cato: *ap.* Gell. 6.3.14 = 13.25.14 (*FRH* II.5. F87): *scio solere plerisque hominibus rebus secundis* <u>atque</u> *prolixis* <u>atque</u> *prosperis animum excellere* <u>atque</u> *superbiam* <u>atque</u> *ferociam augescere* <u>atque</u> *crescere*. Here one sees an alliterative pair, pairs of synonyms, and a homoeoteleuton in *augescere atque crescere* (cf. *multibiba atque merobiba, damnare atque domare, timidam atque pauidam*).

See further on Cato's *Origines*, 1 Appendix 1; and on Ennius' prose, 1.6.

11 tam bellatorem Mars se haud ausit dicere: the text here is that of Bothe (1811). *Tam* is an emendation for *tum*, and *se* is an insertion. If *tum* is retained it means 'moreover', and *bellatorem* is an additional epithet of *uirum*. The problem with this reading is that *Mars haud ausit dicere* (which is introduced with a dash by both Leo and Lindsay, who retain *tum*) is left hanging without a dependent construction. Moreover *tam* is often confused with *tum* in manuscripts. The addition of *se* (with the change of *tum* to *tam*) gives good sense but is not strictly necessary (as long as *dicere* is not translated 'call (himself)', an interpretation surely requiring *se*), as subject accusatives in the acc. + inf. construction are often left out in Plautus (see de Melo 2006). However, for this position of the reflexive in relation to *dicere*, see *Amph.* 373 *tun <u>te</u> audes Sosiam esse* <u>dicere</u>. *Audeo* + *dicere*, with an acc. + inf. dependent on *dicere*, is a common construction in Plautus: see Lodge (1924–33: I.187 col. 1) for examples.

tam: *tantum* might have been used here, but *tam* is explicable from the fact that *bellator* is a verbal noun.

bellatorem: a term ('warrior') of laudatory tone appropriate in high-style, even epic, contexts. Cf. *Bacch.* 927 *Atridae duo fratres cluent fecisse facinus maxumum,* | *quom Priami patriam Pergamum diuina moenitum manu* | *armis equis exercitu atque eximiis bellatoribus* | *milli cum numero nauium decumo anno post subegerunt, Capt.* 68 *ualete, iudices iustissimi* | *domi, duellique duellatores optumi* (note the archaic form here).

ausit: on this old sigmatic subjunctive form, which was probably still current in this word, see de Melo (2007: 194–5).

12 suas uirtutes: *uirtutes* = *facta bellica, res gestae* (Lodge 1924–33: II.879 col. 1), 'deeds of prowess, valour'. This use of the plural is common in Plautus (see Lodge) and recurs throughout Latin (see *OLD* s.v. 1b), particularly in poetry but not only there: note e.g. *B. Afr.* 81.1 *circum milites concursans uirtutesque ueteranorum proeliaque superiora commemorans blandeque appellans animos eorum excitabat.* See also Fordyce (1961: 285) on Catull. 64.51, citing three other examples from Catullus and also Virg. *Aen.* 1.566. This is a usage that closely resembles the plural use of ἀρετή found e.g. at Hdt. 1.176 ('brave deeds', LSJ s.v. 1a), and it may have come into educated Latin under the influence of the Greek use.

16 illum dicis cum armis aureis: 'you mean him with the golden arms'. *Cum armis aureis* is adnominal, and attached here to a pronoun. For this type of adnominal see *Curc.* 191 *tun etiam cum noctuinis oculis 'odium' me uocas, Pseud.* 158 *te cum securi caudicali praeficio prouinciae,* Enn. *Ann.* 26 Skutsch *teque pater Tiberine tuo cum flumine sancto,* 50 *uix aegro cum corde meo me somnus reliquit,* Caecilius 114 *ut te di omnes infelicitent cum male monita memoria,* Cic. *Mur.* 64 *te . . ., Cato, cum ista natura,* Virg. *Aen.* 8.72 *tuque o Thybri tuo genitor cum flumine sancto.* On adnominal prepositional expressions see Jocelyn (1967: 232) on Enn. *trag.* 70, Fraenkel (1968: 67), Wharton (2009), Adams (2013: 288–9, 296–7, 373–4), below, 2.25, 11.3 and 11.30 (on Vitruvius), and index, 'adnominal prepositional expressions'. They have had something of a reputation of being non-standard (so Fraenkel above), but are widespread, with variations of frequency in different authors and genres, as will be shown here in later Commentaries.

18 quasi uentus folia aut peniculus tectorium: on the text here see Hall (1923). *Tectorium* as a noun (neuter, here accusative) means 'plaster' (*OLD* s.v.). *Peniculus* (an emendation for *peniculum*) means 'little brush', here of a plasterer's brush, and there is a double (nom./acc.) comparison with the scattering of legions: 'just as the wind scatters leaves or the plasterer's brush scatters the plaster'. Here is probably a Plautine reference to a scene from everyday life.

21–2 periuriorem hoc hominem si quis uiderit | aut gloriarum pleniorem quam illic est: there are two striking features of this clause. First, the ablative of comparison *hoc* is followed by a comparative *quam*-construction which has the same referent. *Quam illic est* is redundant. Second, *hoc* and *illic* are in the same sentence yet express no contrast of deixis. Both refer to the same person. Normally if *hic* and *ille* occur together a contrast of the 'this/that' type is expected.

It is just possible that there is implicit in the variation a stage direction, with the soldier moving further away as the parasite speaks, but such a view seems over-subtle (though implicit stage directions are identifiable in Plautus: see below on 3.418 and 3.421). The variation would not be so striking if the order of the two pronouns were reversed: the soldier would be somewhat distant (*illic*), but having been brought to the attention of the audience would achieve a metaphorical proximity, or familiarity, to them, expressed by *hic*. So in the prologue later the *miles*, who is no longer present, is first referred to by *ille* (88), but then several times by *hic* (104, 109, 120). Note too the alternation between *istuc* and *hoc* with the same referent at line 19, with *istuc* coming first. In the present case one might have expected after *hoc* the deictically neutral *is* instead of *illic*.

Demonstratives do not always conform to the rules of modern grammar books. We will see later in the *Passio Perpetuae* an almost identical, unmotivated switch from *hic* to *ille* in the same sentence with the same referent (27.9), and in the same text switches from *is* to *ille* with the same referent in a short space, and parallels will be quoted from other late texts (27.11). *Ille* was to intrude into the territory of *is* and eventually to replace it by the time of the Romance languages, and in at least some of these cases we see an anticipation of that development (i.e. a loss of deixis by *ille*). See below, 18.6, and also index, 'demonstrative/anaphoric pronouns/adjectives/adverbs', with cross-references.

On the reinforced form *illic* see 6.5.

23 me sibi habeto: *habeo* construed with a reflexive dative (of advantage) often implies indifference on the part of the speaker, here 'let him have me, I don't care' (see Fordyce 1961: 86 commenting on Catull. 1.8, Powell 1988: 222 with bibliography, and Adams 2013: 351). Note *Men.* 690 *eandem nunc reposcis: patiar. tibi habe, aufer, utere | uel tu uel tua uxor*. In this usage the reflexive is not pleonastic (indeed in 23 there is hiatus after *sibi*, which may be for emphasis), though there are other expressions (notably *quid tibi uis*) in which the dative reflexive seems not to add anything (see above on 2.5). Often however the pronoun is not to be regarded as merely empty (see Adams 2013: 361–2 and the whole of chapter XVI).

24 nisi unum, epityra estur insanum bene: the *nisi*-construction here is elliptical, = 'except (that there is) one thing'), *nisi quod unum est*. For the full *nisi quod*-construction see Cic. *Sest.* 133 *mihi nullo meo merito, nisi quod bonis placere cupiebam, omnis est insidias ... machinatus*. There are a few examples of the elliptical construction in Cicero: see *S. Rosc.* 99 *nescio, nisi hoc uideo, Capitonem in his bonis esse socium* (with Landgraf 1914: 196), *Fam.* 13.73.2 *de re nihil possum iudicare, nisi illud mihi persuadeo, te ... nihil temere fecisse*. See further *OLD* s.v. *nisi* 5, Kühner and Stegmann (1955: II. 415–16), Shackleton Bailey (1977: 416) on Cic. *Fam.* 4.5.3 ('a colloquial use, belonging mainly to Comedy and familiar letters'), and below, 11.6. Here then is a case of continuity between comic language and familiar language in the late Republic.

epityra estur: ἐπίτυρον is not an Attic word and (like *machaera*) cannot have been taken by Plautus from the Greek original. Varro associates both the word and the food to which it refers with Sicily, and the term must have entered Latin from Magna Graecia as a popular borrowing: *Ling.* 7.86 *epityrum uocabulum est cibi, quo frequentius Sicilia quam Italia usa*. According to the *OLD* it denoted a preserve made with olives (eaten with cheese?). For another word from Sicilian Greek that had found its way into Latin by the time of Plautus cf. *colaphus* (with Adams 2003a: 351 n. 100; see also below, 10.5.1). Similarly *glaucumam* in this play (148) not only shows a switch of gender from (Greek) neuter to feminine (see below), but betrays by the *ū* for ω in the second syllable the influence of a southern Italic language, and it too probably came into popular Latin from Greek in the south of Italy (see Adams 2013: 408 for details).

Epityra looks like a neuter plural, but if so it would have to be construed as object of an impersonal passive *estur* (given that Plautus does not admit gross syntactic Grecisms, such as the construing of a neuter plural subject with a singular verb). But the impersonal passive with accusative object is a dubious construction, in that the examples adduced by some (see e.g. Lindsay 1907: 53, Jocelyn 1967: 338 on Enn. *scen.* 202) are invariably open to alternative explanations or to easy emendation. For the disputed credentials of such a construction see e.g. Calboli (1962: 6–56), Hofmann and Szantyr (1965: 39), Wistrand (1972: 158–60), Adams (2013: 240–2) (but contrast Adams (2013) 242 on Petron. 71.10 with Wistrand (1972) 160 on the same alleged example).

There is no need to emend the text here. *Epityra* can be taken as one of those Latin feminine singulars derivable from a neuter plural, like *ostrea*, which is in Plautus himself and elsewhere (Adams 2013: 408, 416–17); for the type see André (1968). Others are *carota* (late Latin, < καρωτόν), *cala* 'fire-wood' (< κᾶλον) (see André 1968: 3) and *gerra* 'screen, hurdle made of wicker-work' (< γέρρον). There are Romance feminine nouns derived from Greek neuter plurals (see Väänänen 1981a: 103).

insanum bene: *insanum* is adverbial and forms an intensive superlative with *bene* ('insanely well'), a substitute for the usual inflected type of superlative (*optime*). Such an intensifier would have had a slangy feel: cf. in a freedman's speech Petron. 68.7 *desperatum ualde ingeniosus est* (with Hofmann and Ricottilli 2003: 206).

On a more general level this example illustrates the trend for analytic superlatives to encroach on the inflected, synthetic, type, an encroachment that was to triumph by the time of the Romance languages. I am referring here to what I called above the 'intensive' superlative, e.g. to the use of *celerrimus* in a sentence such as 'this boat is very fast', as distinct from an explicit comparative use ('this boat is the fastest of the three').

Such analytic superlatives were early and common in informal style. *Valde* for example as an intensifier is particularly frequent in Cicero's letters. Pinkster (2010: 192) notes that *ualde* occurs about twenty-five times in the speeches of Cicero, but 250 times in the letters, including those of his correspondents (Caelius has eight examples in a small corpus). Pinkster does not give separate figures for examples with gradable adjectives and adverbs, but there would be the same high proportion of these too in letters (see Hofmann and Ricottilli 2003: 202–3, with bibliography, and also Maltby, forthcoming).

The extent of this encroachment already by the time of Plautus may be seen from a comparison of synthetic versus analytic (intensive) superlatives in this play. There are two lists below, first of the synthetic type and then of the analytic:

(a) 75 opere ... maxumo, 99 adulescens optumus, 246 immo optume!, 246 sed simillumas, 279 maxumum in malum, 388 suspicionem maxumam, 547 maxumum ... malum (but possibly a real superlative), 602 saepissume, 703 in diuitiis maxumis, 941 lepidissume et comissume, 1098 clementissume, 1210 ero ... optumo, 1312 pulcherrume, 1382 uir ledipissume.

There are fifteen examples here, eight of which are in the commonplace forms *maxumus* and *optumus*.

(b) 24 insanum bene, 68 nimis pulchrum ... hominem (but the meaning of *nimis/nimium* is often difficult to determine, = *ualde* or 'too, excessively'; all examples of the two adverbs listed here, this one apart, are classified by Lodge 1924–33: II.168, 169 as being 'vi attentuata', = *multum, ualde*), 248 nimis doctum dolum!, 258 docte tibi illam perdoctam (but *docte* can be given its full semantic force), 370 ego stulta et mora multum, 377 nimis mirum est facinus, 443 stulta multum, 591 nimium festiuam ... operam, 716 nimis bona ratione, 794 est prime cata, 852 nimis loculi lubrici, 871 mulierem | nimis lepida forma, 918 haec carina satis probe fundata, 926 nimis lepide, 998 hominem nimium lepidum et nimia pulchritudine (= *pulcherrimum*), 1003 illa ipsa est nimium lepida nimisque nitida femina, 1142 nimis facete nimisque facunde.

There are nineteen examples here (disregarding the ablatival phrase at 998). What is most striking is the number of intensifiers, *insanum, nimis, nimium, docte, multum, prime, satis* (seven). Only one of these (*multum*) could be described as possibly a Romance anticipation. This variety shows that, while such analytic expressions were commonplace in informal speech, no one term had been grammaticalised. It was to be centuries before the diversity was dropped and the language settled on a few banal intensifiers (notably *bene* and *multum*). It is however of interest that, if the two banal suffixal superlatives *maxumus* and *optumus* are left aside, the analytic type is much preferred. There is only one replacement for *maxumus/optumus* above (*nimis bona*).

25 PY. ubi tu es? AR. eccum: 'Where are you?' 'Here I am.' *Eccum* etymologically has third person reference (*ecce* + **hom* 'there he is'), but though it is still used in that way in comedy its etymology was no longer felt and it was not tied to the third person. Cf. Ter. *Haut.* 829 *ubi Clitipho hic est?*:: '*eccum me inque.*:: *eccum hic tibi*, and see Adams (2013: 469).

elephanto in India: the prepositional expression is adnominal (see above, 2.16 with references). The phrase is dislocated leftwards to the start of the sentence as a focal element (see index, 'hanging (focal?) expressions'), and is picked up with a resumptive pronoun later (*ei*). *Elephanto* is in the case (dative) required by the syntax of the sentence (and therefore the resumptive pronoun is redundant), but sometimes a hanging initial noun resumed by a pronoun in an oblique case is in the nominative, unconstrued (see further below on 3.416, and index, 'pronouns, resumptive').

That *elephantus* was a popular (acoustic) borrowing, made in the spoken not written language, is clear from the fact that it is based on the genitive form of the Greek word (< ἐλέφας, ἐλέφαντος). For other such deformed borrowings see ἄβαξ, ἄβακος > *abacus* (Cato onwards), δελφίς, δελφῖνος > *delphinus* (Accius onwards), τρυγών, τρυγόνος > *trygonus* (Plaut. *Capt.* 851) (in contrast to imperial *trygon*) (see in general Kahle 1918: 16, André 1956). *Elephas* (like *trygon*) was a learned re-borrowing in the classical period, but *elephantus* continued in the oblique cases in (e.g.) Cicero (details at *TLL* V.2.354.18ff.). *Elephantus* occurs six times in Plautus, but contrast *Cas.* 846 *institit plantam quasi Luca bos*, where the old expression 'Lucanian ox' is used instead (on which see Varro *Ling.* 7.39 *nostri, cum ... in Lucanis Pyrrhi bello primum uidissent apud hostis elephantos, ... Lucam bouem appellasse<nt>*). It occurs in the *Cas.* above in an expression of proverbial type ('she stood on my foot like an elephant'), and must have lingered on in such comparisons after the borrowing of *elephantus*.

On popular borrowings see also below, 16.2.

27 illud dicere uolui, 'femur': punctuated thus *illud* is not that use of a neuter demonstrative equivalent to a definite article in Greek ('the word *femur*') (for this article-type see Adams 2013: 485), but is the primary object of *dicere*, with *femur* in apposition. When a word is commented on it may be uninflected (i.e. not adapted to the context in which it occurs) and in apposition to a supporting term, perhaps most notably *nomen* (Adams 2013: 220–3), though here there is no inconcinnity of case. The type of joke whereby a speaker uses the wrong word and then corrects himself is quite common, and found not only in Plautus. Cf. in this play 819 *sorbet dormiens.* | *quid, 'sorbet'? illud 'stertit' uolui dicere*; also Cic. *Cael.* 32 *nisi intercederent mihi inimicitiae cum istius mulieris uiro – fratrem uolui dicere.* The juxtaposition of *illud* with *stertit* at 819 makes *illud* look articloid but the appositional interpretation is still possible.

Conclusions

The conclusions to the next Commentary (text 3) will cover the above passage as well.

3
PLAUTUS, *MILES GLORIOSVS* 416–35

Introduction

Philocomasium, the concubine of the soldier, comes forth from the house of the old man Periplectomenus, friend and host of the youth Pleusicles, with whom Philocomasium is really in love. She is accosted by Sceledrus, her guard, but in keeping with a plan denies that she is really Philocomasium. Also present is Palaestrio, a former slave of Pleusicles but now in the possession of the soldier. The metre is trochaic septenarii. The text is that of de Melo (2011b).

Text

SC. Haec mulier, quae hinc exit modo, estne erilis concubina
Philocomasium an non est ea? PA. hercle opinor, ea uidetur.
sed facinus mirum est quo modo haec hinc huc transire potuit,
si quidem ea est. SC. an dubium tibi est eam esse hanc? PA. ea uidetur.
SC. adeamus, appellemus. heus, quid istuc est, Philocomasium?   420
quid tibi istic in istisce aedibus debetur, quid negoti est?
quid nunc taces? tecum loquor. PA. immo edepol tute tecum;
nam haec nihil respondet. SC. te adloquor, uiti probrique plena,
quae circum uicinos uagas. PH. quicum tu fabulare?
SC. quicum nisi tecum? PH. quis tu homo es aut mecum quid est negoti?   425
SC. me rogas, hem, qui sim? PH. quin ego hoc rogem quod nesciam?
PA. quis ego sum igitur, si hunc ignoras? PH. mihi odiosus, quisquis es,
et tu et hic. SC. non nos nouisti? PH. neutrum. SC. metuo maxume.
PA. quid metuis? SC. enim ne <nos> nosmet perdiderimus uspiam;
nam nec te neque me nouisse ait haec. PA. persectari hic uolo,   430
Sceledre, nos nostri an alieni simus, ne dum quispiam
nos uicinorum inprudentis aliquis immutauerit.
SC. certe equidem noster sum. PA. et pol ego. quaeris tu, mulier, malum.
tibi ego dico, heus, Philocomasium! PH. quae te intemperiae tenent
qui me perperam perplexo nomine appelles?   435

Translation

SC. This woman who just now came out of here, is she master's concubine Philocomasium or is she not her? PA. Indeed I think it seems to be her. But it's a wondrous thing how she could have passed from here to here, if indeed it is her. SC. Are you then doubting that this one is her? PA. It seems to be her. SC. Let's go and address her. Hey, what's going on, Philocomasium? What is owed to you there in this house, what's your business? Why are you now saying nothing? I am speaking to you. PA. On the contrary you are speaking to yourself, for she is not replying at all. SC. I am addressing you, you creature full of vice and disgrace, you who are wandering around the neighbours' houses. PH. Who are you speaking with? SC. Who except you? PH. Who are you, and what's your business with me? SC. You ask me, for heaven's sake, who I am? PH. Why shouldn't I ask what I don't know? PA. Who am *I* therefore, if you don't know him? PH. You are a nuisance to me, whoever you are, you and him too. SC. Don't you know us? PH. Neither of you. SC. I am very afraid. PA. Afraid of what? SC. That we have lost our identity somewhere, for she says that she knows neither you nor me. PA. I want to investigate now, Sceledrus, whether we belong to our household or to someone else's, in case someone or other of the neighbours in the meantime has switched us without our knowledge. SC. Certainly I belong to our household. PA. And so do I. You are looking for trouble, woman. Hey, Philocomasium, I'm talking to you. PH. What madness has got hold of you, since you're addressing me wrongly by a false name?

Commentary

416 Haec mulier, quae hinc exit modo, estne . . .: the noun *mulier* and its qualifying word and clause are fronted before the question marker *estne*. *-ne* is usually attached to the first word of the clause, but in Plautus postponement is not uncommon: see Lodge (1924–33: 123, s.v. II Collocatio) 'apud Pl. saepius tertio loco (14 ex.), etiam quarto, quinto, sexto loco aliquando legitur (*As* 579, *Ba* 75, *Tri* 350; *Poen* 731, *Tri* 1162; *As* 444, *Ba* 882)' (a quotation of an earlier dissertation). Cf. e.g. *Asin.* 444 *scyphos quos utendos dedi Philodamo, rettulitne?* In our passage *-ne* is attached to the seventh word in the sentence. Fronting (and not only before *-ne*) of a noun or phrase, which may be picked up by a resumptive pronoun, is a common means of focusing the noun or phrase, for example to mark a change of subject. Here attention is drawn to the new arrival. For some different types, cf. *Mil.* 25–6, commented on above (2.25), 1434–5 *scelus uiri Palaestrio,* | *is me in hanc inlexit fraudem* (in both of these the phrase dislocated to the left has the same case as the resumptive pronoun, and the pronoun is redundant), Men. 57–9 *Epidamniensis ille, quem dudum dixeram,* | . . . | *ei liberorum nisi diuitiae nihil erat* (here, however, the dislocated nominative is left hanging, in that it is resumed by a dative; for this type see Cato, *FRH* II.5.F76, quoted above at 1 Appendix 2), Catull. 10.29–30 *meus sodalis, . . . is sibi parauit* (noun and pronoun in same case again), Sall. *Cat.* 37.4, Virg. *Georg.* 2.434–5 with Mynors (1990: 158) (see further below, 4.10, 5.7–8 on Cato, and also Adams, Lapidge and Reinhardt 2005: 17, Adams 2005a: 92 with n. 94, id. 2013: 215–16).

In Plautus *puella* is usually used of a female child, and only occasionally of a young woman, whose youth is particularly stressed (see Adams 1983b: 345–8 for details). *Mulier* could be used of a woman of mature years, but it is also the regular word for a young woman, and not least one who is a prostitute: a *leno* possesses *mulieres* not *puellae* in Plautus. Philocomasium in this play is a young woman and *meretrix*. In the late Republic and early Empire usage changed slightly. *Puella* widened its range. It still might denote a young girl, but could also be applied to a young woman past puberty, and often one by implication of easy virtue. *Mulier* was thus partially rivalled by *puella*.

erilis: an old possessive adjective for genitive (for the type, e.g. *Virgo Vestalis, Campus Martius*, see Wackernagel 1926–8: II.70–2 = Langslow 2009: 487–90, E. Löfstedt 1956: I.107–24), found mainly in the early period and no doubt obsolescent already. In Plautus it alternates with the genitive *eri* (for which see Lodge 1924–33: I.516–17). E. Löfstedt (1956: I.116) points out that *erilis* in Plautus occurs mainly with *filius, filia, amica* and *concubina*, and has an institutional feel to it. *Eri* is used more variably, whereas *erilis* was becoming restricted; outside these set phrases it was probably high-style ('pathetic'?: see Haffter 1934: 121 n. 6).

A feature of the phrases such as *erilis filius* is the placement of the adjective. It regularly comes before the noun (e.g. twenty times with *filius/filia*, and never postponed: see Adams 1976b: 89–90), whereas e.g. in *Virgo Vestalis* and *Campus Martius* adjectives of this type regularly are placed after the noun. The four phrases with *erilis* listed above almost by definition belonged to slave language, and the fronting of 'master's' might reflect slave idiom, with the placement marked and respectful. For a slave idiom see below, 3.433, and index, 'slave idioms/address'.

concubina: in this play Philocomasium is regularly referred to as *amica* in her relationship to the *adulescens* (105, 114, 122, 263, 507), but as *concubina* in her relationship to the *miles* (140, 146, 337, 362, 416, 458, 470, 508, 549, 814, 937, 1095, 1145). *Amica* had a favourable meaning at this time and was associated with a romantic attachment (it was however later to deteriorate into a term for a prostitute), whereas *concubina* implied an element of coercion and is used of a sexual liaison (see Adams 1983b: 348–50 for details; also Watson 1967: 1–2, Treggiari 1981: 60). For legal and other aspects of *concubinatus* see McGinn (1998: 410 s.vv. *concubinae, concubinatus*).

417 hercle opinor, ea uidetur: *opinor* is here paratactic or parenthetical rather than construed with a dependent acc. + inf. For *opinor* used thus see *TLL* IX.2.723.63ff., Hofmann and Ricottilli (2003: 250). It is common in comedy and scattered about in classical Latin, including Cicero (not least in letters and early speeches). For this type of parataxis (with a variety of verbs) see below, 15.19–20, and also index, 'parataxis, parenthetical use of verbs of saying and the like'. Such usages are always in the first person.

418 facinus mirum est: *facinus* in early Latin was not yet specialised in its later, unfavourable, sense 'crime', but it does indicate an act which is out of the ordinary, as here something which causes surprise. Cf. *Rud.* 162 *quod facinus uideo!* Note the three examples at *Mil.* 616–21, all of *facinora puerilia* 'childish deeds' that a *senex* is requested to carry out (and hence not conforming to the norm for such a person). Instances of the neutral/favourable use in classical Latin are mainly in archaisers such as Sallust (see *Cat.* 53.2). See further Manessy-Guitton (1964, especially 53, citing also l. 377).

   quo modo haec hinc huc transire potuit: this looks like an indirect question with an indicative verb, but many such indicative clauses in early Latin can alternatively be read as free-standing questions or exclamations (see Adams 2013: 747–51, with bibliography). Here: 'It is a strange thing – how could she have...?'. In late Latin the indicative again became acceptable (Adams 2013: 766–70), whereas in classical and early imperial Latin its status is not easy to grasp (see Adams 2013: 752–66 for discussion of both periods, and below, 31.6, 47.17).

   hinc huc: 'from here to here', a curious phrase but explicable from staging: the speaker is equidistant from both places and points to each in turn; so also at 143 and 377. Outside the *Miles* the phrase is only at *Cist.* 702 *hinc huc iit, hinc nusquam abiit.* There are other aspects of demonstrative use in Plautus that might be explained from staging (see below, 3.421 and above, 2.21–2).

   The comparable correlations of *huc* with *huc* (rather than *eo* or *illuc*) and *hic* with *hic* (rather than *ille*) turn up as stylised and vivid idioms in poetic texts. For the former see Catull. 61.34 *huc et huc ... errans*, Virg. *Aen.* 12.743 *et nunc huc, inde huc incertos implicat orbis*, Hor. *Epod.* 4.9 *ut ora uertat huc et huc euntium* (see Watson 2003: 159). For *hic ... hic* see Meader and Wölfflin (1902: 250–1), quoting poetic examples (e.g. Virg. *Aen.* 7.506–7, on which see

Horsfall 2000: 338 for further cases), Woytek (1970: 72), Horsfall (2000: 318–19), Hofmann and Ricottilli (2003: 340 n. 1).

420 adeamus, appellemus: asyndeton bimembre will come up often in this book. In Latin it was more stylised than longer asyndetic groups, and tends to occur in old formulae and certain genres (e.g. religious and legal texts, curse tablets), or to be of old (inherited) types. For the type here (a pair of compounds with repeated fore-element) see West (1988: 156): 'the device of pairing (often with asyndeton) adjectives which share the same fore-element' (usually ἀ-privative, εὐ- (e.g. *Od.* 15.406) or πολυ-) is 'closely paralleled in the Veda and Avesta, and evidently an inherited Graeco-Aryan feature'; also West (2007: 109–10), citing examples from a variety of I.-E. languages (but not Latin). Cf. e.g. Enn. *scen.* 117 Jocelyn *alia fluctus differt dissupat | uisceratim membra,* Plaut. *Epid.* 118 *differor difflagitor, Men.* 342 *adplicant adglutinant, Merc.* 192 *complicandis componendis, Trin.* 689 *sed ut inops infamis ne sim,* Ter. *Ad.* 795 *repressi redii, Haut.* 473 *consusurrant conferunt | consilia,* Pomponius 139 Frassinetti *adportas nuntium | nobis disparem, diuisum,* Sall. *Cat.* 11.3 *infinita insatiabilis est,* and in Umbrian *Tab. Ig.* VI b.60 *preplotatu preuilatu* (part of a long sequence of asyndetic pairs) (see also below, 19.10). In our passage the two (subjunctive) verbs express sequential acts, as is often the case when two verbs are in asyndeton or apparent asyndeton (cf. Cic. *S. Rosc.* 101 *ueniat modo, explicet,* with Landgraf 1914: 199 on such pairings at the start of a sentence; see however below, 4.3–4, on the difficulty of classifying verb pairs). See further 6.41 (on synonymous pairs), 45.14 (on pairs of imperatives), and index, 'asyndeton bimembre'.

istuc: on this reinforced form (with -*c(e)*) see Lindsay (1900: 338–40), who concludes (340) that the usual classical neuter *istud* and the plural *ista* were not admitted by Plautus and Terence, who used instead *istuc* and *istaec. Istuc* continued to be used into the classical period, but from the Augustan period receded before *istud* (see Adams 2013: 456–8). The plural *istaec* for its part had only a limited survival into the classical period, but in informal registers and conversational style (Adams 2013: 457–8). Two other case forms of this pronoun, *istic* and *istunc,* will come up in later texts (see 8.1, 17.3); see also 6.5 on *illunc.* The history of the (reinforced) adverb *istic* is also relevant (see the third note below). Modern grammar books do not always offer a true picture of pronominal diversity (cf. 2.21–2).

421 quid tibi istic in istisce aedibus debetur, quid negoti est?: *quid tibi debetur* is a formula that occurs at least eight times with variations in Plautus (but never in Terence). It means 'what is owed to you?', i.e. 'are you a creditor?', but was subject to semantic weakening, 'what is your business?', 'why are you acting aggressively?'. Note here the following *quid negoti est?* The formula had its origins in Roman popular methods of achieving justice, and is worthy of a special discussion: see below, Appendix.

istic in istisce aedibus: a locatival (appositional) pairing, with the local prepositional phrase specifying the preceding local adverb ('there – in that house') (see also on 2.9 above). Such phrases, as was remarked earlier, can sometimes be related in Plautus, where they are common, to staging: the speaker points (*istic*), and then explains (see above, 3.418 on *hinc huc*): cf. *Cist.* 546 *hinc ex hisce aedibus ... | ... uidi exeuntem mulierem, Mil.* 1136 *exeuntis uideo hinc ex proxumo, Most.* 405 *aedis occludam hinc foris.* But they are not confined to comedy: note e.g. Cic. *Leg. agr.* 2.94 *hinc Roma qui ueneramus,* Virg. *Aen.* 7.209 *hinc illum Corythi Tyrrhena ab sede profectum.* In these double locatives there is usually a progression from the general to the specific, or from the whole to the part, as for example at Livy 32.4.7 *in Macedoniam in hiberna copias reduxit,* but the reverse order sometimes occurs (e.g. Caes. *Gall.* 1.54.2 *in hiberna in Sequanos exercitum deduxit;* see also below, 26.16), in which the second (usually prepositional) element is not so much appositional as adnominal. There is an extensive collection of such double locatives in Müller (1895); see also e.g. *TLL* VI.2.2807.50ff. (with *hinc*), 3071.14ff. (with *huc*). An example from Ennius, *Euhemerus* XI (*in Creta in oppido Gnosso*) was quoted at 1.12, and the phenomenon will come up again (see index, 'locative/temporal expressions, double').

istic: it was mentioned above (3.420) that various forms of the pronouns *iste* and *ille* reinforced by *-c(e)* have a distinctive distribution. The same is true of some comparable adverbial forms (see also below, 9.10 on *istoc*). The adverb *istic* is frequent in Plautus and Terence and found in other comic genres such as farce. By the late republican and Augustan periods it seems to be restricted to special contexts suggestive of a colloquial character. Cicero has it four times, always in early speeches, as at *S. Rosc.* 84 *quoniam istic sedes ac te palam aduersarium esse profiteris;* the same collocation is also at 104 in a markedly colloquial passage, again of direct address, also containing Cicero's only instance of *ausculto: quid? tu, uir optime, ecquid habes quod dicas? mihi ausculta ... nihil opus fuit te istic sedere;* Plautus too combines *isti(c)* with *sedeo* at *Stich.* 93. Landgraf (1914: 172) notes on *S. Rosc.* 84 that the adverb is equivalent to *in accusatorum subselliis.* The second person reference is strong, and there is probably a note of contempt. Another example in an early speech is at *Verr.* 2.104 (*quid fuit istic antea scriptum*) in direct address and in a verb phrase in which it occurs in Plautus (*Bacch.* 788, 1023). The context suggests that the phrase might have been current in court when written evidence was presented (the imperative *cedo* occurs in the same passage of the *Verrines* –

cedo, quaeso, codicem: another colloquial survival in a special context). The fourth instance in a speech, at *Tull.* 20, is again in direct (peremptory) address, this time of a slave: '*quid uobis' inquit 'istic negoti in meo est?*' The same expression is also addressed to a slave at Ter. *Andr.* 849 *quid istic tibi negotist?* It is a striking fact that in our present passage of Plautus *istic* occurs in the same line as *quid negoti est*, with which it is juxtaposed also in the passages of Cicero and Terence just quoted.

In the rhetorical works, at *Brut.* 217 the word is put into the mouth of a *homo impurus, sed admodum ridiculus* (216) in a remark of slangy appearance: *qui nisi se suo more iactauisset, hodie te istic muscae comedissent* (a colloquial use of *hodie* too: see Hofmann and Ricottilli 2003: 154, 209). Another instance in a piece of dialogue is at Cic. *Fin.* 5.78.

By contrast *istic* is common in the letters (thirty times in *Fam.* and fifteen times in *Att.*). In the *Ad familiares* ten of the thirty examples (4.5.1, 5.10a.3, 8.7.1, 8.10.2, 8.10.3, 8.17.2, 10.23.6, 11.11.2, 11.20.2, 12.13.4) are in letters to Cicero by various correspondents. Caelius, whose style has been characterised as 'slangy' (see on 13.10), has *istic* four times (*Fam.* 8.7.1, 8.10.2, 8.10.3, 8.17.2; both *istinc* and *istic* occur in the first few sentences of *Fam.* 8.7.1). There are two instances in letters from D. Brutus to Cicero (11.11.2, 11.20.2). Cicero himself seems to have used the term especially in letters to certain correspondents. There are six examples in letters to Trebatius, some of which are marked by jokes (7.10.2, 7.11.3, 7.13.2 twice, 7.15.1 twice), three in letters to Cornificius (12.18.2, 12.25a.2, 12.28.1), and three in letters to members of his family (14.3.5, 14.7.2, 14.14.2).

Certain phrases recur, some with parallels in Plautus. For *quid istic agitur* (et sim.) see *Att.* 3.8.2, *Fam.* 11.20.2, 12.25a.2, 14.14.2. With this cf. Plaut. *Most.* 939 *quid istic agitis?* In a letter to Tiro there is the juxtaposition *tu istic* (*Fam.* 16.22.1), which occurs a number of times in Plautus (see Lodge 1924–33: I.859 col. 1). Note too *uos istic* at *Fam.* 10.23.6 (Plancus), and *te istic* at *Att.* 3.12.2, 3.19.3, 5.19.1, 7.20.2, 11.7.5, 14.4.1, *Fam.* 7.13.2, 7.15.1, 14.3.5. *Recte istic esse* is at *Att.* 16.15.6, *Fam.* 10.20.3. Note too the examples linked to the idiomatic use of *calere* at *Att.* 7.20.2 *etsi te ipsum istic iam calere puto* and *Fam.* 7.10.2 *uos nunc istic satis calere audio.*

The *TLL* also quotes examples from (e.g) a short poem of Catullus (37.14, where it is juxtaposed with *consedit*; see above on *sedeo* + *istic*), Hor. *Epist.* 1.14.37, a speech in Virgil (*Aen.* 10.557) (with *iaceo*), an address of a *mentula* at Ovid *Am.* 3.7.69 (again with *iaceo*), and speeches in Livy (1.47.3, 7.40.13) (the only examples in Livy). In the second passage of Livy the adverb is associated with both *inuitus*, as it is at Cic. *Fam.* 7.13.2, and *uolens*, just as Cicero has it with *libenter* at *Fam.* 7.15.1.

What this case demonstrates is a continuity of usage between early comic dialogue and informal/conversational varieties in the classical and Augustan periods. After Plautus and Terence the adverb has a marked tendency to occur in conversations.

422 tecum loquor. PA. immo edepol tute tecum: note the implication of reciprocity (*cum*) appropriate to a 'middle' verb. *Loquor* is often used with *cum* (see Lodge 1924–33: I.907–8), usually of a two-way conversation. The verb may also take the dative (Lodge 1924–33: I.909), but then of peremptory address rather than a conversation. Most of the examples listed by Lodge with the complement *mihi* are much the same as the following: *Capt.* 564 *at etiam, furcifer,* | *male loqui mi audes?* (of an abusive remark directed at someone).

A parallel distinction of constructions is provided by another deponent verb, *osculor*. In the *Miles osculor* is constantly accompanied by *cum* in reference to Philocomasium kissing the *adulescens* or vice versa (243, 245, 264, 288, 320, 338, 366–7, 390, 461, 555), i.e. applied to an act that is reciprocated. To these examples should be added 1433, where the verb is accompanied by *inter se*. But when the kissing is not reciprocal, that is when one of the participants wishes it to take place but the other is reluctant, then the plain accusative is used: e.g. *Asin.* 669 *ten osculetur, uerbero?*, 895 *nauteam* | *bibere malim … quam illam oscularier, Merc.* 575 *senex hircosus tu osculere mulierem?*

423 uiti probrique plena: *plenus* is often used with abstract nouns in the genitive in expressions of praise or contempt (see *TLL* X.1.2410.26ff., 2411.68ff.). What is unusual about this phrase is that it is vocative. Dickey's list (2002: 173–6) of vocative insults contains many adjectives in the vocative, but in almost every case they seem to be used as single words. She does cite (147) some longer phrases with a respectful implication.

424 circum uicinos uagas: 'around the neighbours' houses', a common type of brevity in Plautus: cf. e.g. 154 *sed foris concrepuit hinc a uicino sene* 'but the door just creaked – here, from our old neighbour's house' (see Brix and Niemeyer 1901b ad loc. for further parallels).

Vago is active here but at *Per.* 319 deponent. In classical Latin it is a deponent verb. The *OLD* s.v. lists five instances of the active from early Latin (as well as Varro *Men.* 438), and these are not only in comedy but also in tragic fragments. A substantial list of such actives for deponents in the tragedies of Pacuvius may be found in Schierl (2006: 673 s.v. 'Diathesenwechsel'), and this includes *uagat* at 204 (302 Ribbeck). For examples in the tragedies of Ennius see Jocelyn (1967: 286, 288, 317, 388). Skutsch (1985: 326) on Enn. *Ann.* 162 *misererent* observes that the 'active form, found also at *scen.* 197; Lucr. 3.881, seems to be earlier than the deponent'. For a considerable number of such forms listed from Plautus himself see Brix and Niemeyer (1901b: 44) on *Mil.* 172 (*tumultuas*). Note also Lindsay (1907: 53–4) (on *opino, uago, mereo, ludifico, apiscor*, passive at *Trin.* 367). See also below, 6.7, 26.5.

The widespread distribution of such forms in different genres, some of them elevated, in early Latin shows that it would be mistaken to say that the phenomenon at the time was substandard (see in general Flobert 1975). In some cases, as Skutsch says, the active may be earlier (with the deponent use a later analogical development), and in other cases there may have been oscillation in educated usage between deponent and active, with the language starting to move away from the category deponent. The regular use as deponents later in classical Latin of virtually all the verbs listed in the above sources might have been due to an effort by the educated (and grammarians) in the late Republic to preserve the category, though that would be hard to establish. From that point on actives for deponents might have been stigmatised in some circles. On this view there is not any continuity of attitude to 'actives for deponents' between the early Latin period and later Latin. From a very late (early medieval) period we will discuss a text in which deponents have been mainly activised (see on 47.15), but even there the writer was making some effort to retain the type.

quicum tu fabulare: *fabulor* is in alternation here with *loquor* (422), and has the same construction (with *cum*). The verb could, however, be used absolutely, or with a direct object or acc. + inf., or introducing direct speech. *Fabulor* is very common in Plautus (fifty-six times) but in Terence it occurs only twice. Thereafter the decline continues. The word is absent from Cicero and the whole of classical Latin. There is a scattering of imperial examples, some of them in significant contexts, and the word survives particularly in the Romance of the Iberian peninsula (*REW* 3125: Sp. *hablar*, Pg. *falar*; also Old Italian and Occitan) (see *TLL* VI.1.35.4ff. for the Latin distribution; also Adams 2007: 383–5, with details about its use). The history of *fabulor* is not unlike that of *ausculto* (see 16.2): it must have had a life in varieties of Latin largely submerged after Plautus. There is just one instance in Augustan literature, in a speech in Livy (45.39.15), where in the words of *TLL* VI.1.36.13f. it is used 'per contemptum de oratione futtili'. In Tacitus there are just two examples, both in the *Dialogus*, that at 23.3 implying contempt (*quos more prisco apud iudicem fabulantes non auditores* *sequuntur, non populus audit, uix denique litigator perpetitur*), and that at 39.1 with much the same implication.

425 quis tu homo es: interrogative *quis* is here adjectival (unless *homo* is to be taken as appositional: see below). The school rule, that the distinction between *quis* and *qui* in interrogative clauses is that the former is substantival and the latter adjectival, has little foundation (see E. Löfstedt 1956: II.79, Hofmann and Szantyr 1965: 541; cf. also Powell 1988: 185, 263 on *si qui(s) deus* in Cicero), except in the neuter singular, where usually *quid* is substantival and *quod* adjectival (see E. Löfstedt 1956: II.81 n. 2). The overlap between the two masculine forms used adjectivally can be seen e.g. from Cic. *Mur.* 82 on the one hand (*qui locus est, iudices, quod tempus, qui dies, quae nox . . . ?*) and Cic. *Verr.* 3.42 on the other (*quis arator te praetore decumam dedit?*; note however the vowel following, and see the next note). Plautus uses both *qui* and *quis* with *homo* adjectivally, with what at first sight looks like a functional distinction. *Quis homo* (nominative) occurs seventeen times (Lodge 1924–33: I.718 col. 1), invariably in direct questions. Interrogative *qui homo* (nominative) occurs three or four times (*Men.* 301 (changed to *quis* by editors), *Trin.* 849, 960), always in indirect questions. However, in the latter two of these examples *homo* is separated from *qui*, which stands before *sit*, and it may be the first letter of the verb that determines the form *qui* (see below, next note) rather than the fact that the question is indirect. *Qui homo* (nominative) also occurs nine times in relative clauses (see Lodge 1924–33: I.718 col. 2). These figures are for the nominative singular alone. In other cases and in the plural there is usually no formal distinction between *quis* and *qui*.

What particularly stands out is the redundancy of *homo*. Nor is *homo* only used thus with *quis*. It also accompanies indefinites, including *(ali)quis* (*TLL* VI.2.2883.45ff.), *alius* (*TLL* 2883.51ff.), *quisquam* (2883.65ff.), *quisque* and *quiuis* (2883.76ff.) and *ullus* (2883.84ff.). It is also used with the interrogative *ecquis* (2884.4ff.) and with *nemo* (2884.42ff.). The distribution of these expressions as it emerges from the *TLL* article (Brink) is of some interest. They are particularly common in early Latin (Plautus, Terence, Ennius, Cato, Lucilius). From Cicero they are quoted mainly from early works, such as the *Inv.*, *S. Rosc., Quinct., Verr.* (also the anonymous *Rhet. Her.*, of early first-century date), and letters (note *Att.* 10.18.3 *ecquem tu hominem infeliciorem?*; cf. for the phraseology Plaut. *Capt.* 540 *quis homost me hominum miserior?*), and only occasionally later from significant contexts, such as speeches in Livy (e.g. 23.12.16 *ecquis homo . . . transfugerit?*). They appear to have been recessive, though holding on to some extent in informal varieties.

The distribution specifically of *quis homo* is much the same (*TLL* VI.2884.8ff.). A word search turns up only one instance of the nominative singular *quis homo* in the whole of Cicero (*Tusc.* 4.77), but there in a quotation of Ennius. There are two instances only of interrogative/exclamatory *qui homo* (*S. Rosc.* 39, *Planc.* 27), where the form *qui* for *quis* (but equivalent in meaning to *qualis*: see Landgraf 1914: 95) is in line with the school rule alluded to above. A few examples in other cases are cited by Brink, again mainly from early works. Also of note is Hor. *Sat.* 1.6.29 *quis homo hic est?* Was Horace drawing on colloquial language, or using comic phraseology? The same question might be asked of the accusative example at Cic. *Att.* 10.18.3 cited in the previous paragraph.

Sometimes in interrogative/indefinite phrases in Plautus *homo* is separated from the modifier, as at *Mil.* 160 *quemque a milite hoc uideritis hominem in nostris tegulis* and *Pseud.* 971 *ecquem in angiporto hoc hominem tu nouisti?* Do these phrases show a conventional hyperbaton? *Homo* here has a similarity to postponed redundant indefinites in early Latin standing in apposition to an initial indefinite (see below, 3.431–2), and one wonders whether in *quis homo* the noun was originally an appositional indefinite rather than part of a syntactic unit.

426 me rogas, hem, qui sim?: the school rule is that pronominal *qui* is relative and *quis* interrogative (with *qui* confined to adjectival use when interrogative: see the preceding note). Accordingly *quis* might have been expected here introducing an indirect question. The reality is more complicated. At Catull. 66. 42, for example, it is (pronominal) *qui* that introduces a question (*qui se ferro postulet esse parem?*). It is the start of the following word that seems here to determine the form of the interrogative (on *qui/quis* see particularly E. Löfstedt 1956: II.82–96), with *qui* preferred before a word beginning with *s* (cf. Fordyce 1961: 145 on Catull. 17.22, and 243 on 61.46; also 334 on 66.42, where Kroll 1929: 205 merely states that this use of *qui* is 'altertümlich'). *Qui sim/sis/sit* is commonplace, and not least in Cicero (see E. Löfstedt 1956: II.84 n. 1), though there are different manuscript readings (see also Dyck 2008: 183).

A cursory look at the use by Plautus of *qui* and *quis* introducing indirect questions is worthwhile, but it is all but impossible to compile precise figures, because scribes will have regularised in line with the school rule above and there is a lot of variation in manuscripts. There follows a very small selection of classified examples that I have managed to extract from Lodge's lexicon (1924–33).

qui introducing indirect questions

followed immediately by *sim/sis/sit*
Amph. 130 qui siem
Amph. 844 qui sim
Asin. 348 qui siet
Aul. 1 qui sim
Aul. 714 qui sim
Bacch. 555 qui sit
Capt. 560 qui siet
Cist. 164 qui siet
Epid. 458 qui sit
Mil. 426 qui sim
Most. 627 qui sit
Poen. 649 qui siet
Poen. 993 qui sit
Poen. 1121 qui siet
Trin. 994 qui sis.

followed by but separated from *sim/sis/sit*
Capt. 248 qui nunc sis
Mil. 1365 qui bonus sit, qui malus
Rud. 385 qui fur sit
Trin. 994 qui non sis (following *qui sis*: see above).

followed by other parts of the verb 'to be'
Amph. 127 qui essem
Capt. 248 qui fueris et qui nunc sis
Mil. 261 qui fuerit
Trin. 1141 qui esset.

followed by other verbs or terms
Aul. 773 qui apstulerit
Aul. 774 qui apstulerit
Rud. 1312 qui inuenerit
Truc. 708 qui foras ueniat.

Incomplete collections of material are not meaningful statistically, but there are some trends apparent, which would probably be upheld if it were possible to collect every relevant example in the corpus. There are twenty-seven instances cited. In fifteen places *qui* is immediately followed by a part of the verb 'to be' starting with *s* (see above for Löfstedt on *qui sim*). In twenty-three cases *qui* introduces a clause containing the verb 'to be'. In only five of the twenty-seven cases does *qui* precede a word beginning with a vowel.

quis introducing indirect questions

followed by but separated from *sim/sis/sit*
Amph. 1029 quis ego sim
Men. 279 <quis> ego sim
Men. 302 quis ego sim
Mil. 925 quis ego sim.

followed immediately by other parts of the verb 'to be'
Amph. 1016 quis fuerit
Merc. 634 quis esset
Truc. 816 quis esset.

followed by other terms
Aul. 716 quis eam apstulerit
Cist. 679 quis eam abstulerit
Epid. 506 quis eam liberau<er>it
Merc. 941 quis eam uexerit
Rud. 16 quis hic quaerat
Truc. 708 quis eat
Truc. 821 quis integram stuprauerit.

Fourteen instances of *quis* are collected above, none of which is followed by a word beginning with *s*. In almost every case (thirteen) *quis* is followed by a word beginning with a vowel (or, in one case, *h*) (cf. *quis arator* cited in the preceding note).

On this evidence the main differences between *qui* and *quis* introducing indirect questions are that *qui* frequently precedes a word beginning with *s*, whereas *quis* frequently precedes a vowel. Notable is *quis ego sim* alongside *qui sim*.

427 quis ego sum: see immediately above.

428 metuo maxume: there is a magisterial article on *metuo/metus* and synonyms, particularly *timeo/timor*, by Ernout (1957b: 7–56); see also *TLL* VIII. 901–2 for a table of distributions. In Plautus *metuo/metus* far outnumber the other pair (by 176:40) (Ernout 1957b: 12), and *timeo/timor* appear 'comme des mots nouveaux, encore rares, soumis à certaines restrictions' (Ernout 1957b: 14). *Metuo/metus* are also preferred by Terence. In Cicero the beginnings of a change can be seen. *Metuo/metus* are the preferred terms in the speeches, philosophica and rhetorical works, whereas in the letters *timeo/timor* out-number the other two. In Caesar *timeo/timor* markedly predominate. Thereafter this pair grows in favour, though typically the archaiser Tacitus prefers *metuo/metus* by 441:60 (further details in Ernout 1957: 14).

429 enim: in first position as here *enim* is restricted to early Latin and later to archaisers (Hofmann and Szantyr 1965: 507–8). On the function of *enim (ne)* here (= 'lest, of course') see Kroon (1995: 176–7).

431 ne dum: *dum* here is possibly a freestanding adverb = *interim* (see *TLL* V.1.2200.75ff., Hofmann and Szantyr 1965: 610, 617–18), though there are doubts hanging over the two or three examples, all from Plautus, listed by the *TLL* (see both the *TLL* and Hofmann and Szantyr; also Ernout and Meillet 1959: 187).

431–2 quispiam | . . . uicinorum . . . aliquis: there is a special type of pleonasm here, that in which an indefinite (*quispiam*) is followed later by another, redundant, appositional indefinite (*aliquis*). It is a type that is common in early Latin (notably Plautus), and then recurs in late Latin: see in general, with bibliography, Hofmann and Szantyr (1965: 195, 801–2), and the discussion of E. Löfstedt (1956: II.191–4). For *aliquis* used thus see some of the examples cited at *TLL* I.1612.15ff. and E. Löfstedt (1956) II.192. Cf. e.g. *Asin.* 785–6 *ne quid sui | membri commoueat quicquam in tenebris*, and, in a direct question, *Most.* 256 *quid illa pote peius quicquam muliere memorarier?*; also Ter. *Andr.* 90–1 *comperibam nil ad Pamphilum | quicquam attinere*. The occasional occurrence of such usages after early Latin and then their appearances in late substandard texts suggest that they never died out at a submerged level. Note *Mul. Chir.* 522 *in hoc sexto libro omnia demonstro, ne quid minus aliquid in ceteris libris subiectum sit.*

Another possible manifestation of this phenomenon in early Latin may be the phrase *quis homo* (see above, 3.425).

432 immutauerit: *TLL* VII.1.515.18ff. Cf. *Amph.* 845–6 *Amphitruo es profectus, caue sis ne tu te usu perduis: | ita nunc homines immutantur, postquam peregre aduenimus* ('you set out as Amphitruo, but take care lest you lose your identity through someone else's taking possession of you. To such an extent do people now get transformed since we arrived from abroad'). Compare *perduis* here with *perdiderimus* at 429 (of losing one's identity and being transformed into someone else). See further *Amph.* 456, where *perdo* and *immuto* again occur together: *ubi ego perii? ubi immutatus sum? ubi ego formam perdidi?*

How could neighbours transform the slaves? Presumably by *usucapio* 'acquisition of ownership', as in *Amph.* 845 above (*usu* = *usucapione*: see

OLD s.v. *usus* 5). Cf. Plin. *Nat.* 16.233 for the reflexive use of *perdo: placuit deinde materiem et in mari quaeri. testudo in hoc secta, nuperque portentosis ingeniis principatu Neronis inuentum, ut pigmentis <u>perderet se</u> plurisque ueniret imitata lignum* ('[n]ext came the fancy of ransacking even the sea for material: tortoiseshell was cut up to provide it, and recently, in the principate of Nero, it was discovered by miraculous devices how to cause it to lose its natural appearance by means of paints and fetch a higher price by imitating wood', Loeb).

433 noster sum: *noster (sum/est)* is a slave idiom, = 'belonging to our household': see *OLD* s.v. 3, Brix and Niemeyer 1901b on *Mil.* 350 *nam illic noster est fortasse circiter triennium | nec quoiquam quam illic in nostra meliust famulo familia,* '[h]e's been one of us for perhaps something like three years, and yet no servant in our household has it better than him' (de Melo 2011b). Brix and Niemeyer cite half a dozen further examples. Cf. 458 *est … nostra erilis concubina,* 'she is the master's concubine, (a slave) from our household/our fellow slave' (not 'our master's concubine'). The point in our passage is that Sceledrus still belongs to his original household and has not changed ownership. For slave idioms in Latin see Adams (2013: 16–17), and index, 'slave idioms/address'.

   et pol ego: the oath *pol* is here put into the mouth of a man. In Terence it is mainly a female word (forty-five times; only ten times in the mouths of males, who speak the majority of lines: see Adams 1984b: 48, 50). Women on average in Terence use the term once every 14.9 lines, whereas men use it once every 540.5 lines (Adams 1984b: 50). In Plautus the majority of examples are in male speech (159:84), but *pol* nevertheless had something of a female character, as it occurs once every 31.2 lines in female speech but only once every 116.9 lines in male (Adams 1984b: 51). In Terence female speech is more distinctive than it is in Plautus. See further on *pol* below, 10.3.6.

Appendix: *quid tibi debetur*

There is a formula (with some minor variants) that occurs at least eight times in Plautus, *quid tibi debetur?* (see above, 3.421). There is nothing like it in Terence. Literally it means 'what is owed to you?', and its use is generated by a particular context, when a stranger is found hammering on someone's door or is lurking outside with possible aggressive intent. It is a phrase that has to be placed and interpreted in the context of methods of 'Italian popular justice' (in the sense in which that expression has been used by Fraenkel 1961 and others) in the early period. The question must have originated as a response to the behaviour typical of those attempting to recover a debt, but an examination of the passages in which it occurs would suggest that it was tending to be generalised towards some such weaker meaning as 'what is your business?' In some contexts, however, the original meaning of the question is still felt, and there is one passage in which it is associated quite clearly with the activity that has been called *flagitatio* (3). We will come to this below.

(1)   *Mil.* 420–1

adeamus, appellemus. heus, quid istuc est, Philocomasium?
quid tibi istic in istisce aedibus debetur, quid negoti est?

Philocomasium, who is pretending to be her fictitious twin sister to deceive the slave Sceledrus (the speaker of the above lines), has just come out of the house of Periplectomenus and called back inside to the slaves within instructing them to light a fire on an altar to express thanks to Diana of Ephesus for her safe arrival from abroad. Sceledrus is wondering what her business is in the house. He asks first what is owed to her in the house, and then more vaguely what her business is. There is no suggestion that she has acted aggressively, and no reason in the context why she should have been owed money, and *quid tibi ... debetur* hardly differs in meaning from *quid negoti est.*

(2)   *Bacch.* 884–5

quid nunc, impure? numquid debetur tibi?
quid illi molestu's? quid illum morte territas?

What is this now, you filthy creature? Are you owed anything? Why are you bothering this man? Why are you threatening him with death?

The soldier Cleomachus has come to demand back some money (see 868–9). He makes the demand of Nicobulus (882), who, prompted by Chrysalus (aside), promises it (883). Then Chrysalus rounds on the soldier (having set up the exchange), and demands to know if they owe him any money. The expression here refers to a specific demand for money, and is without the generality of the formula in the previous passage.

(3)   *Most.* 615–18

quis illic est? quid illic petit?
quid Philolachetem gnatum compellat <meum>
sic et praesenti tibi facit conuicium?
quid illi debetur?

Who is that? What is he after? Why does he accost my son Philolaches by this means and abuse you in his stead? What is owed to him?

The money-lender Misargyrides has come to demand interest on a loan made to the *adulescens* Philolaches. He makes his demands to the slave Tranio. The *senex* Theopropides, the father of Philolaches, comes on the scene and asks what is being demanded of his son and by whom. What is owed to the stranger?

Earlier in the scene (603), in calling for his interest, the money-lender had used a refrain (*cedo faenus, redde faenus, faenus reddite*) which Fraenkel (1961: 50 = 1964: II.122) associated with the practice of *flagitatio* (chanting outside the house of a wrongdoer to bring disgrace – *flagitium* – on him).

It is of interest that the old man describes the conduct of the money-lender as abusive (*facit conuicium*). This is a significant phrase. Festus p. 190.32–6 Lindsay in a discussion of the practice of *occentatio* defines the ancient verb *occentassint*, which occurs at Cic. *Rep.* 4.20 c [12] in a citation of the Twelve Tables (*nostrae contra XII Tabulae, cum perpaucas res capite sanxissent, in eis hanc quoque sanciendam putauerunt, si quis occentauisset siue carmen condidisset quod infamiam faceret flagitiumue alteri*), as equivalent now to *conuicium fecerint*, giving in the process a definition of *occentatio: occentassint antiqui dicebant quod nunc conuicium fecerint dicimus, quod id clare et cum quodam canore fit, ut procul exaudiri possit. quod turpe habetur, quia non sine causa fieri putatur* ('The ancients used to say *occentassint* of what we now call "making abuse", because that is done clearly and with a sort of chant, so that it can be heard far off. This is considered a disgrace, because it is thought to be done with good reason') (see Lintott 1968: 8).

Whatever the wording of the law might have been, it is clear from allusions to it that chants to the detriment of another person were expressly forbidden. Note Cic. *Tusc.* 4.4 *quamquam id quidem etiam XII Tabulae declarant, condi iam tum solitum esse carmen, quod ne liceret fieri ad alterius iniuriam, lege sanxerunt* ('And yet as much as this is formally shown also by the Twelve Tables, namely, that by that time the composition of songs was regularly practised: because it is expressly enacted that this may not be done to a neighbour's detriment', King, Loeb). Note too Hor. *Epist.* 2.1.152–4 *quin etiam lex | poenaque lata, malo quae nollet carmine quemquam | describi* ('There was even a law with a penalty passed, which forbade the portrayal of anyone in an abusive song'). There is much the same at Hor. *Sat.* 2.1.80–3 *sed tamen ut monitus caueas, ne forte negoti | incutiat tibi quid sanctarum inscitia legum: | si mala condiderit in quem quis carmina, ius est | iudiciumque* ('but nevertheless be warned and beware, in case by chance ignorance of sacred laws should inflict upon you some trouble: if anyone shall compose abusive verses against another, there is legal redress'). In Plautus in those passages in which the *quid tibi debetur* formula occurs, aggressive behaviour in the street and hammering at someone's door regularly elicit an angry response from the victim or an observer, and that must reflect an attitude deriving from the old law.

(4) *Pseud.* 1137, 1339

1337 HA. heus ubi estis uos? BA. heus adulescens, quid istic debetur tibi?

HA. Hey, where are you all? BA. Hey, young man! What is owed to you there?

1139 HA. ecquis hoc aperit? BA. heus chlamydate, quid istic debetur tibi?

HA. Is anyone going to open this door? BA. Hey, you with the cloak, what is owed to you there?

The soldier's slave Harpax arrives on behalf of his master to pay off a debt so that the girl Phoenicium can be taken back to the soldier. Here there is no suggestion that Harpax is owed money, but it is assumed that anyone who knocks on a door and summons loudly those within must be a creditor calling to make a commotion to get his money back.

(5) *Truc.* 256–61

TR. quis illic est qui tam proterue nostras aedis arietat?
AS. ego sum, respice ad me. TR. quid 'ego'? <AS.> nonne 'ego' uideor tibi?
TR. quid tibi ad hasce accessio aedis est prope aut pultatio?
AS. salue. TR. sat mihi est tuae salutis. nil moror. non salueo.
aegrotare malim quam esse tua salute sanior.
sed uolo scire, quid debetur hic tibi nostrae domi?

TR. Who is it who is so aggressively ramming our house?
AS. It is me, do have a look at me. TR. Me? AS. Don't I seem to you to be me?
TR. Why this approach by you to this house of ours, or why this hammering?
AS. Good health. TR. That's enough of your good healths, I don't care for such things. I am not in good health. I would prefer to be ill than to be healthier because of your good healths. But I want to know: what is owed to you here at our house?

Astaphium, the slave of Phronesium, arrives at the house of Strabax on an errand from her mistress, and strikes on the door (253 *feriam*), well aware that this will have consequences, because the door is presided over by the rough slave Truculentus, who tries to keep women away (250–2). There is no question of debt collecting here, as she has supposedly come to see the women of the house (283). Any hammering on a house door that might be interpreted as aggressive is enough to put the householders (and audience) in mind of debt collectors, and to inspire the *quid tibi debetur* formula. Heavy knocking could generate the formula as a default response, even though there might be no reason in the context for the householder to expect a debt collector. Such a response offers an insight into the behaviour expected of creditors, and the formula would hardly have recurred throughout Plautus had not such scenes of aggression once been common in the city. We are taken into the world of ancient Italian popular justice. Self-help, in the form of noisy aggression at the house of a debtor, may be a substitute for formalised legal action. That is not to say that the householder would readily give in, as the knocking tends to inspire an angry response (see above on (3)).

(6)   *Poen.* 1232–7

HA. moramini. in ius uos uoco, nisi honestiust prehendi.
ADE. quid in ius uocas nos? quid tibi debemus? . . .
. . . quid nos fecimus tibi? HA. fures estis ambae.

HA. You are wasting my time. I am summoning you to court, unless it is more honourable to be seized. ADE. Why are you summoning us to court? What do we owe you? . . . What have we done to you? HA. You are both thieves.

Hanno, addressing his two long-lost daughters, summons them to court (1232 *in ius uos uoco*), using the verb-phrase from the start of the XII Tables. The girls' response is to ask *quid tibi debemus?* (1233). The question is repeated in a more general form at 1237 *quid nos fecimus tibi?*, which again suggests that phrases of the type *quid tibi debetur* were tending to be generalised.

(7)   *Trin.* 893–5

CH. eloquere, isti tibi quid homines debent quos tu quaeritis?
SY. pater istius adulescentis dedit has duas mi epistulas,
     Lesbonici.

CH. Tell me, what do those men whom you are looking for owe you?
SY. The father of this youth, Lesbonicus, gave me these two letters.

The old man Charmides arrives home from abroad to find a stranger in the street making for his house. The stranger, the sycophant, hammers on the door and calls out for anyone inside (870–1). The old man's reaction to such conduct (above) is to ask the familiar question *tibi quid homines debent?*, which in the Loeb of Nixon is translated generally ('What's your business with those men you're looking for?'; de Melo 2011b translates literally). The sycophant replies that he has letters to deliver to the youth Lesbonicus, the son of Charmides. In this context no debt is due.

(8) *Rud.* 115–17

et impudicum et impudentem hominem addecet
molestum ultro aduenire ad alienam domum,
quoi debeatur nil.

And a man must be indecent and shameless if he comes as a nuisance to a stranger's house of his own accord, even though nothing is owed to him. (de Melo 2012a)

The slave Sceparnio and the old man Daemones come out of the farmhouse to find Plesidippus and three others lurking in the street. Plesidippus (110) asks them whether they live there, and it is this question that prompts the above observation from Sceparnio. A person has no justification in approaching a stranger's house if he is owed nothing.

  The phrase must be old and have originated from the activities of debt collectors harassing householders in the street, sometimes by means of chants intended to bring disgrace on the debtor. The manifest disapproval conveyed by those using the phrase must be seen in the light of the law of the Twelve Tables banning such chants. Athough the question could still be used with its literal sense to the fore, it was tending to be weakened such that it might be little different from *quid istuc est?* or *quid negoti est?*. This weakening must have been followed by the demise of the phrase, given that it disappears from view after Plautus.

Conclusions

The Latin of Plautus is immensely varied in register, and historically interesting. It represents a stage of the language that in many ways had passed by the classical period. On the other hand it is by definition conversational, and some informal features persisted in informal varieties in classical Latin and even later. Given the theme of this book it is this continuity that is most important here, and particularly anticipations of the Romance languages. In this section a comprehensive summary is attempted of the features of these passages (texts 2, 3).

Greek loan-words

The Greek words in these lines and others adduced in the Commentary bring out the character of contacts with Greek speakers in this early period. Plautus did not take Greek words from the Greek originals he was adapting. Borrowings are not literary but a consequence of contact with Greek spoken in Italy itself, or with koine Greek in general. *Machaera, epityra, colaphus* and *glaucoma* all fall into this category, and *elephantus* is a typical popular borrowing marked by a deformation. It had probably entered Latin during the battles with Pyrrhus in about 280 BC, when Latin speakers first encountered elephants. The plural use of *uirtutes* may also reflect Greek influence, of a more sophisticated type.

Old Latin features

This is not the place to dwell on early usages that were to be dropped from the language, but see on *ausit* (2.11), *erilis* (3.416), *facinus* (3.418), *uagas* and the active use of deponents (3.424), *quis homo* (3.425), *metuo* (3.428), *enim* (3.428), *dum* (3.431), pleonastic indefinites (3.431–2).

Continuities with later/conversational Latin

We saw two verbs used with reflexive datives of advantage (2.5 *uolo* (?), 2.23 *habeo*). Loosely there is an anticipation here of reflexive verbs in Romance, but usually in Latin the dative is clearly motivated (though that is not the case with *uolo*). Double locativals (2.9, 3.421) persisted for centuries. Adnominal prepositional expressions (2.16, 2.25) are variable in frequency in different writers, but they have a notably high incidence in Vitruvius (11.30) and a very late text that has marked proto-Romance features (46.5–6). Statistics are not available for their frequency in Plautus. The pronoun *illic* seems to be used at 2.22 without its usual deixis, possibly as an anticipation of the later deictically neutral use of *ille* = *is*. Of particular interest (2.24) is the high incidence of intensive superlatives of the Romance, analytic, type, though the intensifiers are far more varied than was to be the case later. Paratactic uses of verbs of saying, thinking et sim. (3.417) continued for centuries in informal texts. One continuity between Plautus and conversational style in the late Republic that was demonstrated in detail lies in the use of the reinforced adverb *istic* (3.421). On the other hand it was suggested that the apparent continuity in the active use of deponents (3.424) is misleading. *Fabulor* (3.424) is one of those lexical items that is common in Plautus but went underground by the classical period, to emerge again in Romance.

The familiar parallelism between Plautine Latin and that of the letters of Cicero has been noted from time to time (2.24 *nisi, ualde*, 3.417 *opinor*, 3.420 *istaec*, 3.421 *istic* (adv.)), but it is also of interest that in three places we have commented on usages of Plautine type in speeches in Livy (3.421 *istic*, 3.424 *fabulor*, 3.425 *homo*). Informal elements in Livy's speeches ought to be investigated systematically, and might have something to do with the charge of *Patauinitas*.

Register variation

Most of the usages listed in the previous section were probably informal, but, as was remarked at the start, the Latin of Plautus varies in register. Plautus was capable of adopting a native rhetoric (see on 2.10), and makes liberal use of plays on words (2.7–8). He has high-style terms where appropriate (2.11, 2.12), and also sometimes adapts his language to character types. There is no female speech in this selection (but see on 3.433), but we did note several slave idioms (3.416, 3.433).

4
CATO, *DE AGRICVLTVRA* 33.5–35

Introduction

Cato was born in 234 BC and died in 149. The *De agricultura* cannot be dated precisely because its composition was probably spread over a long period, with bits added from time to time. We also have fragments of his speeches and historical works, the *Origines*. The style of the Latin surviving under Cato's name is notably diverse, reflecting in part differences of genre, with the speeches and *Origines* more contrived in language than the agricultural treatise. The *Agr.* itself is variable in style. Alongside mundane directives to do with agricultural procedures, containing technical terms, rustic words and careless syntax, there are old prayers in traditional language, a formal preface and medical instructions. I have selected, first (text 4), a purely agricultural passage, and second (text 5), a medical. The text is that of Mazzarino (1982).

Text

33.5 Salictum (1) suo tempore caedito, glubito arteque alligato (2). librum conseruato, cum opus erit in uinea, ex eo in aquam coicito (3), alligato (4). uimina, unde corbulae fiant, conseruato (5).

34.1 redeo ad sementim. ubi quisque locus frigidissimus aquosissimusque (6) erit (7), ibi primum serito. in calidissimis locis sementim postremum fieri (8) oportet. terram caue cariosam tractes (9). **2** ager rubricosus et terra pulla, materina, rudecta, harenosa, item quae aquosa non erit, ibi lupinum bonum fiet (10). in creta et uligine et rubrica et ager qui aquosus erit (11), semen adoreum (12) potissimum serito. quae loca sicca et non herbosa erunt, aperta ab umbra, ibi triticum serito.

35.1 fabam in locis ualidis non calamitosis (13) serito. uiciam et fenum graecum (14) quam minime herbosis locis serito. siliginem triticum (15) in loco aperto celso, ubi sol quam diutissime siet, seri oportet. lentim in rudecto et rubricoso loco, qui herbosus non siet, serito. **2** hordeum, qui locus nouus erit, aut qui restibilis fieri poterit, serito. trimestre, quo in loco sementim maturam facere non potueris et qui locus restibilis crassitudine fieri poterit, seri oportet.

rapinam et coles rapicii unde fiant (16) et raphanum in loco stercorato bene aut in loco crasso serito.

Translation

33.5 Cut willows at the proper time, strip the bark and tie tightly together. Keep the bark, and when it is needed among the vines, throw some of it in water and tie together. Save the withies so that baskets can be made from them.

34.1 I return to sowing. In places that are the coldest and the most watery, sow there first. In the warmest places sowing should be done last. Avoid working decaying earth. **2** Land rich in red clay, and earth that is friable, woody (?), full of stones and sandy and likewise that which is not watery – there lupins will do well. In chalk and marsh and red earth and land that is watery, sow for preference the seed of emmer wheat. Places that are dry and not grassy, free of shade, there sow wheat.

35.1 Sow beans in thriving places not subject to disasters. Sow vetch and fenugreek in the least grassy places. Soft wheat and wheat ought to be sown in an open place that is high, where there is sun as long as possible. Sow lentils in a place full of stones and rich in clay, which is not grassy. **2** Sow barley (in a place) which is new or which will be capable of being planted without lying fallow. Three-month wheat should be sown in a place where you will not have been able to produce a ripe crop and which because of its thickness will be capable of being planted without lying fallow. Sow turnips and that from which turnip stalks may grow and radishes in well-manured ground or in ground that is thick.

Commentary

1 salictum: may denote a place where willows grow, an osier-bed, but here and elsewhere it is a collective, 'willows'.

2 caedito glubito arteque alligato: the old connective *-que* (see e.g. Penney 2005, and above, 1.6, 1 Appendix 1), which always had a formal or stylised ring in Latin and does not survive in Romance, is ubiquitous in the *Agr*. We see it in its most extreme form in the prayer at 141.2–3, where it occurs sixteen times in the complete absence of the other connectives *et* and *atque*. The pattern here, AB*Cque*, occurs in the following cases.

First, there are seven examples in prayers: 141.1 *fundum agrum terramque meam*, 141.2 *mihi domo familiaeque nostrae*, 141.2 *agrum terram fundumque meum*, 141.2 *prohibessis defendas auerruncesque*, 141.3 *mihi domo familiaeque nostrae*, 141.3 *fundi terrae agrique mei*, 141.4 *porcum immolabis, agnum uitulumque.* These passages are in an old formal language.

Second, three instances comprise imperatives in *-to*, with the last linked by *-que*: 41.4 *oblinito alligato integitoque*, 49.2 *statuito alligato flexatoque*, 161.2 *aperito sarito runcatoque.* We may include our passage in this group, though strictly it is to an adverb that *-que* is attached. Of similar type is 33.4 *uites subligato, pampinato, uuasque expellito.*

Third, there are two adjectival groups that look formulaic: 119 *epityrum album nigrum uariumque*, 119 *oleis albis nigris uariisque.*

Fourth, also with a formulaic or at least formal appearance are two groups of present passive infinitives, with the first pairs (*legi teri, legi seri*) echoing each other: 70 *haec . . . legi teri darique oportet*, 151.1 *semen . . . legi seri propagarique oporteat.*

Finally, there remain just two places where names of plants, crops or the like have this pattern: 2.1 *quid factum uini, frumenti aliarumque rerum omnium*, 5.8 *rapinam, pabulum lupinumque serito.* Lists of plants and the like of this length usually have asyndeton, and the second of these two examples is unusual; the first ends with a summarising phrase, a pattern.

There are thus sixteen to eighteen examples of the pattern ABC*que* (depending on one's view of the marginal cases in the second group), about 40 per cent of which are in prayers. Thirteen or fourteen have a stylised appearance. The imperative in *-to* was associated with generalising instructions as found for example in the languages of the law and religion. *-que* is constantly used with this type of imperative.

There are 215 instances of *-que* in the *Agr.*, of which fifty-nine are attached to imperatives in *-to*. The *Agr.* is an informal text, but it also consists largely of directives intended particularly for the *uilicus*, a subordinate of the *dominus*, and that may be one factor motivating a quasi-legal style. *-que* is not uncommon in laws and *senatus consulta.* It also long retained a place in didactic style: it is frequent, for example, in Pelagonius. It is of some interest that *-que* linking imperatives in *-to* in Cato outnumbers *et* linking such imperatives, and that despite the greater frequency of *et* overall in the text. I have noted just twenty-two instances of *-to et -to* (with the imperatives juxtaposed), out of a total of about 500 instances of *et* in the text. There seems to have been an affinity between this verb form and *-que*.

For further remarks about the use of *-que* in this text see below, 4.6, 4.14–15.

It is hard to get detailed information about this pattern ABC*que* elsewhere. Kühner and Stegmann (1955: II.31–2) cite a few examples from Cicero and Sallust, but not in such a way as to allow any generalisation about its frequency or determinants. Sjögren (1900: 138) lists quite a few cases from Plautus. Note the following: Plaut. *Asin.* 554 *eae nunc legiones copiae exercitusque eorum | ui pugnando, peiiuriis nostris fugae potiti, Capt.* 517 *nunc spes opes auxiliaque a me segregant* (with accumulation of synonyms in both passages), *Merc.* 19 *cura aegritudo nimiaque elegantia, Mil.* 107 *uino ornamentis opiparisque opsoniis* (extended alliteration), 656 *Venerem amorem amoenitatemque accubans exerceo* (alliteration), *Most.* 1160 *faenus sortem sumptumque omnem, Poen.* 1240 *atque equidem ingenuas leiberas summoque genere gnatas* (ascending length), *Pseud.* 173 *in munditiis mollitiis deliciisque* (alliteration and assonance), Pac. *trag.* 262.3 Schierl *atrox incerta instabilisque* (alliteration showing privative adjectives), Lucr. 1.56 *creet res auctet alatque* (with alliteration), 2.457 *fumum nebulas flammasque.* Such examples seem to be a mark of high style in early Latin, but here is a subject that might repay detailed investigation.

Finally, since Varro's *Res rusticae* deals with the same subject as the *Agr.* but is about a century later, it may be worthwhile to make some comparisons between his practice and that of Cato. Throughout the Commentary on the present passage observations will be made about Varro, and particularly about his use of connectives or lack thereof (see also the Appendix on asyndeton bimembre in Varro).

-que is less numerous in the *Rust.* than in Cato. There are just seventy-seven examples in the work, compared with about 1,150 of *et* (see the concordance of Briggs 1983), whereas in Cato, as we saw above, *-que* is outnumbered by *et* by little more than 2:1. On the other hand in Varro's *De lingua Latina* and fragments as indexed by Salvatore (1995) there are approximately 383 examples of *-que*. It would seem that Varro did not associate this connective with the subject matter of the *Rust.*, whereas it has a presence in the scholarly treatise. The attachment of *-que* to imperatives in *-to*, which was seen above to occur fifty-nine times in Cato, is not found at all in the *Rust.* So the pattern ABC*que* does not appear.

3 ex eo in aquam coicito: here the partitive prepositional phrase *ex eo* ('(some) of it') stands in an object relation to the verb *coicito.* Cf. e.g. Plaut. *Trin.* 742 *ex ea largiri te illi,* Gell. 4.11.1 *opinio uetus falsa … conualuit Pythagoram philosophum non esitauisse ex animalibus* (see *TLL* V.2.1115.27ff., Hofmann and Szantyr 1965: 58). At Varro *Ling.* 5.86 the partitive phrase is subject of the verb: *ex his mittebantur, ante quam conciperetur, qui res repeterent* ('Some of them were sent before war should be declared, to demand restitution of the stolen property', Kent, Loeb). For such examples in the Vulgate under Greek influence see Hofmann and Szantyr (1965: 59), and below, 38.51. A few late examples may be found in E. Löfstedt (1956: I.147), and see below, index s.v.

ex, 'expressing partitive object'. Examples from later Latin may be found below at 40.5, 42.16.

This is the only example of partitive *ex* standing as object of a verb in the *Agr.*, but compare 70.2 *ter triduum de ea potione unicuique boui dato*. Such uses of *de*, which are found from an early period, are forerunners of the Romance partitive article (see Adams 2013: 273–5 for examples and discussion, and the index to the present work, s.v. *de*, 'expressing partitive object'), particularly when combined with an articloid use of a demonstrative (see below, 49.14, 50.29–30). *De* eventually displaced *ex* and the latter does not survive in the Romance languages, and that is why it is *de* that produces the Romance partitive uses. Nevertheless before its disappearance *ex* is found in some Romance-like constructions that were later to be restricted to *de* (see e.g. Adams 2013: 265–6 on *ex* as similar to an objective and subjective genitive).

In late Latin *exinde* is sometimes used like *ex eo* above in an object (partitive) relation to a verb (*TLL* V.2.1512.23ff., but add Pelagonius 456 *exinde animali . . . linito*, 'smear from there on the animal', i.e. 'smear some of that').

3–4 coicito, alligato: punctuated thus this looks like an asyndeton bimembre. Certainly a connective such as *et* might be inserted. However, an example such as this highlights the difficulty of classifying asyndeta bimembria, particularly when the two members are verbs (see above, 3.420). The two processes here are not closely related temporally. The bark is to be thrown in water to soak, presumably for some time. Then it is to be removed and the pieces tied together. It would be possible to put a full stop after *coicito* without affecting the sense, and arguably if there is a marked pause between the two actions one should not use the term asyndeton. On the other hand (e.g.) in the curse tablet Audollent (1904), no. 250A a second verb intensifies the first, and this may be treated as a genuine asyndeton: *obliges perobliges Maurussum* (line 2; cf. 22) (see below, 6.7 on *l]uct[ent, deluctent* for this type). So too pairs of synonymous verbs may be classified as asyndeta (see 6.41). Asyndeton bimembre in this text as a whole is discussed below, 4.14–15.

5 uimina, unde corbulae fiant: *unde* is the standard relative in this text indicating that 'from which' something is made (ten examples). Here are the other nine:

14.3 terram unde lutum fiat ('earth from/with which mortar may be made').
31.1 uti sit unde corbulae fiant et ueteres sarciantur ('so that there is something from/with which baskets may be made and old ones repaired').

31.1 fibulae unde fiant, scidae iligneae (things 'from which pins may be made').

37.2 stercus unde facias: stramenta, lupinum . . . ('things with which you can make manure . . .').

38.4 neque lapidem habebis unde calcem coquas ('. . . from which you may burn lime').

58 oleas tempestiuas, unde minimum olei fieri poterit ('mature olives, from which little oil will be able to be made').

59 prius ueterem accipito, unde centones fiant ('. . . from/with which quilts may be made').

76.1 farinae siligineae l. II, unde solum facias ('. . . from/with which to make the crust').

112.2 unde uinum Coum facere uoles, uuas relinquito in uinea ('leave the grapes from which you intend to make Coan wine on the vine').

There is no comparable example of *quibus*, a form which occurs only nine times. Six of those examples are dative and the other three are either temporal or locatival (= 'in'). *Quo* and *qua* if ablatival are local in meaning rather than instrumental. The only other relative form in the text used with instrumental force or the like is the fossilised instrumental *qui*: see 6.4 *uti siet qui uineam alliges* ('so that there are (withies) with which to tie the vines'), 10.5 *qui nucleos succernat* ('(pestle) with which to crack kernels'), 11.2 *cola qui florem demant III* ('three strainers with which they may remove the flower'), 12 *fibulas XL constibilis ligneas qui arbores conprimat* ('forty stout wooden pins with which to brace the posts'), 26 *priuasque scopulas in dolia facito habeas illi rei, qui labra doliorum circumfrices* ('and see that you provide each jar with its own broom with which to wipe off the edges', Hooper and Ash, Loeb), 39.2 *qui colorem eundem facias, cretae crudae partes duas, calcis tertiam commisceto* ('mix two parts of crude chalk and one of lime with/from which to make the colour uniform'). These examples are indifferently plural or singular. One is in a context (with *facio*) in which *unde* might have been used.

Vnde in the type of idiom in our passage corresponds to the prepositions *ex* and *de* complementing *facio* in expressions denoting that from which a thing is made. For *facio ex* in Cato see 31.2 *prelum ex carpino atra potissimum facito*; cf. 3.4, 18.9, 20.2. For *facio de* see 92 *lutum de amurca facito*; cf. 18.7, 111.

The plain ablative is also found in such contexts: see 21.5 *cupam materia ulmea aut faginea facito*. For the ablative of a conventional relative pronoun see Varro *Rust.* 1.24.3 *exinde ut uasa olearia quot et quanta habeant, quibus conficiunt illut*, 2.2.9 *crates aut retia quibus cohortes in solitudine faciant* ('. . . with which to make enclosures . . .'). Varro also has *unde* in the context of making at *Rust.* 1.23.6 *ubi cannabim linum iuncum spartum, unde nectas bubus soleas lineas restis funes.* It follows that *unde* might in theory have been replaced in Cato by *e quibus, de quibus* or *quibus* without a preposition.

What is interesting in Cato is the complete absence of the ablatives *quibus, quo* or *qua*, either dependent on *ex/de* (in which context *unde* is used), or as unambiguous instrumentals (for which the fossilised *qui* is used). Instrumental *qui* was recessive in the later history of Latin (for the contexts in which it occurs still in Cicero see Powell 1988: 106–7; see also below, 12 Conclusions), though it lived on in *quicum*. This usage in Cato to the exclusion of *quibus* etc. represents an early state of the language. On the other hand *unde* looks forward to the Romance languages. In current Italian the present example would be rendered by *vimini dai/con i quali si fanno i canestri*, but in literary and high-register varieties of Italian one could also say *onde si fanno i canestri* (or *donde*, < *de unde*)[1] (this and the following information I owe to Giuseppe Pezzini). *Onde* and *donde* are standard in early Italian, but today have become artificial. Their main meaning is 'from where', but the meaning 'with which, of which, from which' is well attested (see *Dizionario dell'Accademia della Crusca* s.v. *onde*).[2]

For the same use of *unde* in Plautus see *Mil.* 687 *eme, mi uir, lanam, unde tibi pallium* | ... *conficiatur.* An example was quoted above from Varro of *quibus* introducing a clause containing this same verb *conficio.*

6 frigidissimus aquosissimusque: *-que* linking adjectives is rare in the *Agr.* Here are the other examples that I have noted (two of them in the preface), leaving aside those in the pattern ABC*que* discussed above: praef. 3 *strenuum studiosumque* (alliterative), 1.3 *uia bona celebrisque*, 34.1 *locus frigidissimus aquosissimusque* (superlatives with inevitable assonance), 131 *rudecta harenosaque*, 141.2 *uisos inuisosque* (opposites with assonance, in a prayer; this is a type of expression in which asyndeton bimembre is also found: cf. Plaut. *Asin.* 247 *dignos indignos*, *Bacch.* 401 *iustus iniustus*, and note particularly the Umbrian expression *Tab. Ig.* VIa.28 *tuer perscler <u>uirseto auirseto</u> uas est* (= *tui sacrificii uisum inuisum uitium est*)). We might add to the list above the pair of

---

[1] A striking parallel in early Latin for the later hypercharacterised compound *de unde/donde* is found in a fragment of C. Gracchus *ap.* Terentianus Maurus, *De syllabis* lines 988–9 (Cignolo 2002: I.71) *dixerit si forte quidam 'scrobs abunde fossa est* | *stirps', uelut dixit disertus Gracchus alter Gaius* ('a hole from which was dug a stump'). *Abunde* must be a compound *ab-unde*: see Cignolo (2002: II.394–5), citing for a late parallel Löfstedt (1911: 227).

[2] Giuseppe Pezzini draws my attention to A. Pellegrini, *Il dialetto greco-calabro di Bova* (Rome and Turin, 1880), s.v. *splóno* (p. 227): 'splóno [to?]. Pianta onde si fanno i canestri.' Here *onde* is in exactly the same context as *unde* in our passage.

superlative adverbs derived from adjectives at 66.1, *mundissime purissimeque.*
Most of these combinations are clearly stylised.

In Varro *Rust.* there is just a single instance of *-que* joining adjectives, and
these, as in our present passage, are superlatives: 2.8.3 *amplissimum
formosissimumque.*

Cato's usual way of linking adjectives (and adverbs) was by *et* (e.g. 3.3, 3.4, 6.1
twice, 6.2, 8.1, 17.1, 50.2, 54.2, 54.4, 76.2, 133.2 etc.). There are two examples in
our passage (34.2 *loca sicca et non herbosa,* 35.1 *in rudecto et rubricoso loco*).
On asyndeton bimembre, which is equally stylised and alternates with *-que* in
some phrases (see above on *uisos inuisosque*), see below, 4.14–15.

aquosissimus: adjectives in *-osus* abound in this passage and in the whole
Agr. There are two other instances of *aquosus* in the passage, and also *cariosus,
rubricosus* (twice), *harenosus, herbosus* (three times), *calamitosus.* Further
examples are listed by Cooper (1895: 127). It is a semantic property of the
suffix that causes its frequency in a treatise to do with the land and its use. It
expresses the idea of 'abounding in', especially in reference to concrete
features, and hence is suited to the description of the landscape (see Adams
2013: 571–8). It is not intrinsically 'vulgar' or 'rustic', but clearly had
a significant place in agricultural discourse.

6–7 ubi quisque … erit: here, in a preposed relative clause (i.e. a relative
clause that does not follow an antecedent but is picked up later by a correlative,
here *ibi*: see further below, 4.11 on such relatives), the future is used. The same
future is in the previous section, in a *cum*-clause (*cum opus erit*). In the rest of
the extract we have *quae aquosa non erit, ager qui aquosus erit, quae loca …
non herbosa erunt, qui locus nouus erit, qui restibilis fieri poterit, qui locus
restibilis crassitudine fieri poterit.* There is no example of the present (e.g. *est,
sunt*) in such a context in the passage. On the other hand there are two
conventional (classical-type) relative clauses where the relative follows an
antecedent, in which we have not the future but the (generic) subjunctive: *in
loco aperto celso, ubi sol quam diutissime siet, in … rubricoso loco, qui herbosus
non siet.* This distinction between the clause types is not however the absolute
determinant in the text of the one construction against the other, as there is
some alternation between future and subjunctive in the same types of context:
note e.g. 151.2 *serito in loco, ubi terra tenerrima erit …, ubi aqua propter siet.*
Dalby (1998: 215) translates here: 'Sow … in ground where the earth is very
tender, … where there is water nearby', clearly finding no distinction between
the future and the subjunctive.

This use of the future is ubiquitous in the text. I have counted 157 cases
of *erit*, many of them in relative (including *ubi-*) clauses, compared with 82

cases of *est*, only some of which are in relative clauses (see 6.1, 13.1, 18.3, 67.2, 108.2, 136, 139, 156.7). This generalising future is not easy to characterise. It does not seem to be quite the same as the so-called gnomic use of the future (see Kühner and Stegmann 1955: I.143, Hofmann and Szantyr 1965: 310). In the present sentence it is possible to see a future reference of sorts, if we put ourselves into the place of the addressee. The reader is instructed (in future) to sow where he shall at some future time find the coldest and wettest place.

8 sementim . . . fieri: Cato has this phrase three times in this sense. *Sementis* is a derivative of *semen*, and may denote the sowing (of seed). As such with *facio* it may approach *sero* in meaning. A notable example is at 27: *sementim facito, ocinum, uiciam, fenum graecum, fabam, eruum, pabulum bubus* ('Sow clover, vetch, fenugreek, beans, bitter-vetch as forage for cattle', Loeb; so Dalby 1998). Here *ocinum* and the following nouns are loosely in apposition to *sementim* ('do a sowing: clover etc.'), but the translation catches the force of the phrase, which could simply be replaced by *serito*, an imperative that is common in the text. *Sementim facito* here is on the way to displaying a type of 'incorporation', such that a verb–object combination comes to govern an accusative (see Rosén 1981: 142 on this example; on other types of incorporation in Latin see Marini 2015). A classic case is the frequent Plautine expression *ludos facere* + object, as e.g. at *Amph.* 571 *rogasne, inprobe, etiam qui ludos facis me*, which is equivalent to *ludificor* at 565: *tun me, uerbero, audes erum ludificari*. See Rosén (1981: 141), Baños (2012), and for the Plautine examples Lodge (1924–33: I.912 s.v. *ludus* 3). Cf. 37.2–3, 47.3 for incorporation of this type.

In the present passage *sementim . . . fieri oportet* follows *serito* in the previous sentence. *Seri oportet* is a phrase that occurs ten times in the work, but with an expressed subject accusative, whereas if it had been used here it would have been impersonal, and therein lies Cato's motive in this context: the nominal phrase stands in for impersonal *seri* in a generalisation.

The third example of *sementis* is at 30: *ubi sementim facturus eris, ibi oues delectato*. Here the use of the phrase corresponds to the absolute use of *seres* at e.g. 45.3 *si in scrobibus aut in sulcis seres* (for *sero* used absolutely see also Varro *Rust.* 1.34.1, 3.1.7). The phrase occurs in a proverb at Cic. *De orat.* 2.261 *ut sementim feceris, ita metes*; note too Col. 2.15.1 *si autumno sementem facturus est*, alongside (same section) *antea . . . quam erit saturus* (the absolute use of the verb again).

Other such periphrastic expressions in Cato are 27 *alteram et tertiam sationem facito* (following *sementim facito*, above; here the periphrasis allows the use of adjectives specifying aspects of the sowing; the same is so at

60 *pabulum cum seres, multas sationes facito*), 134.1 *prius quam messim facies* (cf. Varro *Rust.* 1.32.1 *inter solstitium et caniculam plerique messem faciunt*), 141.3 *lustrandi lustrique faciendi* (from a prayer, with *lustrum facere* repeating *lustrare*). *Sanum facere* is common, but *sanare* does not occur; in a phrase such as *sanum facies* (157.13) it is equivalent to the later *sanabis* (e.g. Pel. 457).

The verb phrase at 57 (*ubi uindemia facta erit*; cf. Varro *Rust.* 1.34.2) had a later correspondent in *uindemiare*. *Munditias facere* 'to do the tidying up' (2.4, 39.2) was a set phrase (cf. Plaut. *Stich.* 347), and not quite the same as *mundare*.

Later in our passage (35.2) *sementim maturam facere* has a different meaning (see the translation).

Facio in such combinations is usually referred to as a 'support' verb or the like, which causes the verbal idea to be expressed in nominal form, thereby allowing the addition of adjectives (see above): see in general Hofmann and Szantyr (1965: 755), Rosén (1981: 130–44), Moreda (1987), Flobert (1996), Fruyt (2011a: 150), Baños (2012), and for equivalent expressions in Greek, Horrocks (2010: 75). Another case of this type is *tempestiuam stercorationem facere* at Col. 2.15.2, in a passage in which *stercoretur* occurs twice. Often, however, such phrases are mere periphrases (note 27 above) with no adjective present (see below, 8.4). A feature of these support-verb constructions is that they often overlap or are even interchangeable with a precise verb, as *sementim facere* with *serere*, though the nominalisation does offer possibilities not provided by the simple verb. Nominalisation incidentally is a far more extensive stylistic variant on verbal style than in the form in which we see it here (see e.g. Langslow 2000: 515, index s.v. 'nominalization').

The periphrases with *facio* were probably sometimes down-to-earth in style, but in other cases one suspects a technical character (see e.g. on nominalisations in medical literature Langslow 2000, chapter 6). We will see some evidence that they prompted disapproval among 'purists' (see 8.4, 48.2.5), but they were nevertheless well established in literary language: purists often unknowingly adopt usages of which they think there is reason to disapprove. Other support verbs are *do/dono* and *habeo* (see 47.3, 48.4.5, and note e.g. in French *avoir peur*). The expression *lustrum facere* alongside *lustrare* in the prayer in Cato above shows the antiquity of the usage and of its equivalence to the precise verb.

9 terram caue cariosam tractes: the prohibitive *caue(to)* usually in Cato has *ne* + subjunctive rather than the pure subjunctive, as in the similar context 5.6 *terram cariosam caue ne ares*. *Ne* occurs fifteen times, the subjunctive alone four times. On the use of the two constructions in Cato and comedy see in particular de Melo (2007: 119–29, especially 120). In Cicero the plain subjunctive is the norm (see Kühner and Stegmann 1955: I.205–6).

On *cariosam* as a technical term used by rustics see Col. 2.4.5 *obseruabimus ne lutosus ager tractetur neue exiguis nimbis semimadidus, quam terram rustici uariam cariosamque appellant.* The word occurs three times in Cato (see the preceding paragraph and 37.1). It is a derivative of *caries*, 'A decaying or shrivelling-up: esp. . . . (of wood) rot' (*OLD* s.v. 1), a noun that is used of soil at Col. 3.11.2. The meaning seems to be in doubt. The *OLD* 1c offers no translation, and the Loeb of Cato leaves the word untranslated. So Dalby (1998) renders 'carious land'. Ernout (1949: 15) says plausibly enough 'qui se décompose, pourri, qui tombe en poussière' (cf. *TLL* III.458.83 'putredine affectus'). Goujard (1975: 136) on *Agr.* 5.6 paraphrases Columella above: 'terre mouillée en surface par une petite pluie après la sécheresse'. It is not certain that Columella knew what the word meant, as his reference to rain and dampness is hard to relate to the idea of rot. Moreover Pliny's speculations about Cato's meaning (*Nat.* 17.34 *quid putamus hac appellatione ab eo tantopere reformidari, ut paene uestigiis quoque interdicat?*, 'What do we infer from this designation to have been the thing that so much alarmed him that he almost prohibits even setting foot on it?', Rackham, Loeb) are not consistent with Columella's remark. Pliny finds a reference to *uitia aridae, fistulosae* etc., where *aridae* is at variance with Columella's *semimadidus*. It is possible that the word was no longer in use by the first century AD, or that it had never been in use outside rural communities.

10 ager rubricosus et terra pulla, materina, rudecta, harenosa, item quae aquosa non erit, ibi lupinum bonum fiet: the construction from *ager rubricosus* through to *erit* is left hanging (see above, 2.25, 3.416; also index, 'hanging (focal?) expressions'). Cato not infrequently leaves a nominative (or accusative) hanging in this work (see below, 5.7–8), though the examples vary in type. The present example seems derivable from a relative-correlative construction which has been truncated, = *qui ager rubricosus et quae terra pulla . . . erit* etc., *ibi/in eo*. Here is a selection of imperfect constructions with some comments:

(a) 9 prata inrigiua, si aquam habebis, id potissimum facito (here *id facito* must refer to the planting of osier-beds, *salicta*, mentioned at the start of the chapter; there we have the logical construction *salicta locis aquosis . . . seri oportet*, whereas here *prata* is not in the ablative but is apparently a hanging nominative (or accusative? see the next passage); this example does however have similarities to that above in our passage (10), in that

Cato starts by stating the type of land in which something is to be done but fails to adapt the case to the ensuing directive).

(b) 128 terram quam maxime cretosam uel rubricosam, eo amurcam infundito (this time the term stating the terrain required is unambiguously in the accusative).

(c) 18.7 ceterum pauimentum totum fundamenta p. II facito ('the whole of the rest of the pavement, make the foundation 2 ft deep'; *ceterum pauimentum totum* is without the expected (genitive) case marker; this example differs from those cited above; *fundamenta* stands in a partitive relation to *pauimentum*).

Here are two unusual examples that are different again:

(d) 15 (maceriam) altam p. V et columen p. I, crassam p. IS, longam p. XIV (the measurements of an enclosure wall are given, with a series of adjectives agreeing with *maceriam*, which is understood; *columen*, referring to the coping of the wall, is not an adjective but a noun, and it is given no case, = *cum columine*, or *habentem columen*).

(e) 22.4 si orbes in ueteres trapetos parabis, medios crassos p. I digitos III, altos p. I, foramen semipedem quoquouorsum (here *foramen* is syntactically unattached in the same way as *columen* above).

Varro *Rust.* 1.2.25 has one of his speakers quote a passage from the books on agriculture by the Sasernas (father and son), of about 100 BC: *fel bubulum cum aceto mixtum, unguito lectum. Fel bubulum* might have been in the (instrumental) ablative, but instead it is a hanging (accusative?). It is easy to understand a directive such as *cape, sume*, or there might have been a verb understood from the wider context. For a similar construction in Cato see 135.1, where there is a string of accusatives without a verb: *Romae: tunicas, togas, saga, centones, sculponeas*. Here we might understand an imperative = 'buy'. A particularly striking accusatival list without a verb is in a passage of Metellius Pius (cos. 52 BC) describing the foods at a pontiff's dinner (Macr. 3.13.12). It begins with *cena haec fuit*, and then proceeds entirely in the accusative: *ante cenam echinos, ostreas crudas quantum uellent, peloridas* etc. Here the introductory phrase contains the verb 'to be' (*haec fuit*), and the accusatival list is independent of any transitive verb.

In the same context of Cato a little later (135.2) there is a string of nominatives instead: *hamae, urnae oleariae, urcei aquarii, urnae uinariae, alia uasa ahenea Capuae, Nolae*. Lists are sometimes in the nominative as well as accusative without any attempt at verbal syntax (see Adams 2013: 226–31).

terra pulla: *pullus,* a colour term in origin, was used in Campania of a type of friable soil, also marked by its dark colour (note the first passage that follows): Col. 1.praef.24 *atque in aliis regionibus nigra terra, quam pullam uocant, ut in Campania, est laudibilis,* 2.10.18 *putre solum, quod Campani pullum uocant, plerumque desiderant.* The association of the word (and soil) with Campania is also implicit at Cato *Agr.* 135.2: *aratra in terram ualidam Romanica bona erunt, in terram pullam Campanica* ('Roman ploughs will be good for *terra ualida,* Campanian for *terra pulla'*). Cato's comment at 151.2 (*ubi terra tenerrima erit (quam pullam uocant)*) is also suggestive of a special or local term. The word survives with this sense in the south of Italy (Calabria) (*REW* 6829, along with references in Adams 2007: 207 n. 38 and *TLL* X.2.2591.44ff.). See further *TLL* X.2.2592.31ff., Adams (2007: 206–7).

materina: described by the *OLD* s.v. as doubtful, adding that some have derived it from *materia.* The *TLL* (VIII.467.21) also puts a question mark against the form, but then adds: 'a materia; ad formationem cf. *sterquilinus'.* Goujard (1975: 207) mentions a conjecture *macerina = macra.* At first sight this would seem to have point, as *macer* 'thin' is used of soil (*TLL* VIII.5.71ff.), as indeed by Cato himself at 6.2 *qui ager frigidior et macrior erit.* Morphologically however there are problems. Such a formation would presumably have to have the diminutive suffix *-īnus* found both in nouns and adjectives (*miserinus, calidinus*), given that the suffix in its other functions has noun bases (see the classification of Leumann 1977: 326–7). One difficulty lies in the fact that such diminutives belong to late Latin (see Adams 2013: 566–9 for a collection of examples, including the adjectives just cited, and also further bibliography). It does not seem convincing to find an example of the suffix used with diminutive function as early as this. More conclusively, *macer +* *-inus* would give *macrinus* not *macerinus* (cf. *macritudo, macritas*). There remains a doubt about what Cato wrote and the meaning (see also the next note).

rudecta: this adjective means 'full of small stones' (*OLD*), and is based on *rudus -eris* 'rubble, stones'. For the formation see Leumann (1977: 335). *Rudectus* is found only in Cato (three times) in the period covered by the *OLD,* but it must have been a familiar term in the countryside. The presence in the passage of *terra* that is full of stones might encourage one to think that *terra* that is *materina* might be full of twigs and wood fallen from trees, but *-īnus* did not normally form adjectives of material.

ibi lupinum bonum fiet: *lupinum* is neuter here, and at 37.2. It is masculine (*lupinus*) at 96.1 (and indeterminate in several other places). For masculine examples see *TLL* VII.2.1849.57ff., and for both neuter and masculine examples, Neue and Wagener (1892–1905: I.799–800). In early Latin there is a huge amount of gender variation, particularly in Plautus (see Adams 2013: 392–419, with examples too from Cato at 394, 401, 404, 411–12). But standard-isation of gender was never fully achieved except in the idealised world of grammar books. This word is for example neuter at Col. 2.15.5–6, but mascu-line (plural) at Col. 6.25. For a few instances of the plural *lupini* see *TLL* VII.2.1849.60ff.

Lupinum is often in the singular, a collective or generic use that is common in plant names (such as *faba*: see in general E. Löfstedt 1956: I.14). Other examples in this extract (cited by Löfstedt loc. cit.) are *uicia* 'vetch' (35.1) and *raphanus* 'radish' (35.2) (the latter of which is plural at 6.1).

Bonus is ubiquitous (sixty times) in the *Agr.*, of plants, soil, equipment, water, soil, regions, wine, personnel, climate etc. It has the look of a multi-purpose farmer's term of approval, a mark of a naive style indifferent to variation and subtle semantic distinctions. See the remarks of Marouzeau (1962: 189) and De Meo (1983: 35).

11 in creta et uligine et rubrica et ager qui aquosus erit: an obvious change of the superficially ungrammatical *ager* would be to *agro*, as in the dependent passage of Pliny *Nat.* 18.163 *in creta et rubrica et aquosiore agro adoreum (serendum)*, but the text has been defended (see E. Löfstedt 1911: 226, Svennung 1934: 17–18, Norberg 1943: 83; see also Hofmann and Szantyr 1965: 567). The construction here can be derived from a relative-clause type showing *attractio inversa* (on which in general see above, 1.11, with biblio-graphy), but here with omission of the resumptive element in the main clause, i.e. = *ager qui aquosus erit, (in eo agro) serito*, though it is a complication that *ager* is coordinated with nouns dependent on *in*. For straightforward cases of *attractio inversa* in Cato, see 51 *pulli qui nascentur, eos in terram deprimito*, 64.2 *olea quae diu fuerit in terra. . ., inde olei minus fiet*. I am suggesting that Cato initially had in mind a sentence such as *in creta et uligine et rubrica et, ager qui aquosus erit, in eo semen serito.*

Later in our extract, at 35.2, there is something very similar: *hordeum, qui locus nouus erit, aut qui restibilis fieri poterit, serito*, translated at the start as 'sow barley (in a place) which is new or which will be capable of being planted without lying fallow'. Here *in eo loco* has to be understood with *serito*. The next sentence has another example: *trimestre, . . . qui locus restibilis crassitudine fieri poterit, seri oportet*. The only difference between these two cases and the one we are commenting on here is that in these the noun *locus* is within the relative clause (i.e. it resembles the initial part of a relative-correlative rather than an *attractio inversa*), whereas *ager* is outside it, fronted.

For other deletions of oblique case elements expected in a main clause see 6.4 *qui locus uino optimus dicetur esse et ostentus soli, amminium minusculum et geminum . . . conserito*, 41.2 *quos (surculos) inseres, medullam cum melle componito* (*eorum* omitted), 144.3 *qui oleam legerit, qui deportarit, in singulas deportationes SS.n. II deducentur* ('he who has gathered olives and who has carried them off, a deduction of 2 sesterces per load will be made (from him)'), 156.5 *quibus tormina molesta erunt, brassicam in aquam macerare oportet* (it is necessary to understand *eos* or *eis*), 157.10 *quibus oculi parum clari sunt, eo lotio inunguito* (*eos* needed).

Usually in Cato where there is a preposed relative clause the resumptive element is expressed in the main clause, either as a pronoun or adverb. Alternatively the resumptive element may be omitted if it would have been in the same case as the relative pronoun. These preposed relatives are a very common type of construction in the text. Here is a selection of examples of the types just defined (with adverbial resumptions underlined):

40.2 quem ramum insiturus eris, praecidito.

42 quod genus aut ficum aut oleam esse uoles, <u>inde</u> librum scalpro eximito.

44 quae arida erunt . . . ea omnia eximito.

50.2 ea loca primum arato, quae siccissima erunt, et quae crassissima et aquosissima erunt, ea postremo arato (here *ea loca . . . quae* is the normal type of relative construction, with the antecedent preceding the relative, but then Cato switches to the other type).

52.1 quae diligentius propagari uoles, in aullas . . . propagari oportet.

54.2 quae herbosissima erunt in tecto condito . . . deinde <u>ea</u> pro feno dato (in the first main clause, which is omitted here, there is no resumptive pronoun, but Cato inserts one in the second clause).

54.3 quod falcula secaueris, non renascetur.

105.1 qui ager longe a mari aberit, <u>ibi</u> uinum graecum sic facito.

133.2 quae diligentius seri uoles, in calicibus seri oportet.

135.7 trapetum . . . ubi statues, <u>ibi</u><d>e<m> commodato concinnatoque (here *trapetum* is fronted out of the *ubi*-clause).

144.1 quod ipse ole<a>e delegerit, pro eo nemo soluet.

144.2 quod is legerit omne, pro eo argentum nemo dabit.

For discussion of some of the constructions seen here see Kühner and Stegmann (1955: II.283), Hofmann and Szantyr (1965: 564), Vonlaufen (1974: 15–19), Adams, Lapidge and Reinhardt (2005: 18–19 with n. 24), Pompei (2011), Probert (2015: 142–4, 162–7), Halla-aho (forthcoming), Probert and Dickey (forthcoming).

12 adoreum: *ador* and the adjective *adoreum* almost certainly refer to *triticum dicoccum*, or emmer (see Moritz 1958: xxii).

13 in locis ualidis non calamitosis: there was an old rustic use of *calamitas* specifically denoting disaster befalling crops, whether from disease or the weather (Serv. on Virg. *Georg.* 1.151 *robigo autem genus uitii quo culmi pereunt, quod a rusticanis calamitas dicitur*). Both the noun and derivative adjective are represented in Cato, as in the prayer at 141.2 *calamitates intemperiasque prohibessis defendas auerruncesque* (cf. Plaut. *Cas.* 913). For the adjective see 1.2 *uti bonum caelum habeat; ne calamitosum siet; solo bono, sua uirtute ualeat.*

The use of *ualidus* is of some interest. There is a good deal of overlap later between *ualidus* and *firmus* (both often translatable as 'strong'), with the latter more widespread and *ualidus* favoured in some higher genres, including poetry (see Adams 1974a: 59–60). But in Cato there are still signs of a semantic difference between the two terms. In the *Agr.* the only instance of *firmus* is applied to an inanimate (100 *ipsa metrata firmior erit*, 'the jar itself will be stronger'). *Validus* occurs five times. At 157.1 (*ualidam habet naturam*) the subject is the first of several types of cabbage that are listed, which has a strong (hardy?) nature. The example in our passage is applied to soil that is the opposite of disaster-prone in the sense of inflicting disaster on crops, i.e. strong perhaps in the sense of healthy or health-giving. At 135.2 *ualidus* also refers to soil: *aratra in terram ualidam Romanica bona erunt* ('Roman ploughs will be good for heavy (?) soil'). An example at 157.2 refers to the second type of cabbage, which is *ualidior ad curationem*, more effective in treatment. The final example, at 1.3, is in the clause *oppidum ualidum prope siet* ('near it there should be a flourishing town', Loeb). The passage is about choosing farmland, with the emphasis on the salubrious aspects of the site: it should have a good climate and good, healthy soil, be at the foot of a mountain, look to the south, be in a location not prone to *calamitas*, and so on. In this context a town that was merely strong because, say, well defended would not seem appropriate. Cato must be referring to a town that is strong in the sense of doing well, and 'flourishing' seems appropriate.

Thus all examples can be interpreted as referring in different ways to strength as displayed by health or health-giving properties, and the connection of the word with *ualeo* is manifest. Indeed at 1.2 *ualeat* is used of soil, as *ualidus* is above: *solo bono, sua uirtute ualeat.* *Valeo* is regularly used by Cato in the sense 'be healthy', for example of oxen (73 twice, 83, 103.1), vines (33.2, 33.3) or humans (5.5).

14 uiciam et fenum graecum: the usual way of linking pairs of nouns in this text is by means of *et* (approximately eighty-five examples). There is nothing unusual about that, but the alternatives are of some interest. Asyndeton bimembre (where the two members are nouns) is dealt with immediately below, next note. For pairs of nouns linked by *-que*, see 2.2 *operum opera-rumque*, 5.6 *aratra uomeresque*, 5.7 *ouibus bubusque*, 18.5 *arbores stipitesque*, 19.1 *stipites arboresque*, 28.2 *festucis uectibusque*, 32.1 *uineas arboresque*, 33.1 *uinarios custodesque*, 37.2 *ouibus bubusque*, 50.2 *lignorum uirgarumque*, 66.2 *fraces amurcamque*, 74 *manus mortariumque*, 141.2 *Ianum Iouemque*, 141.2 *uiduertatem uastitudinemque*, 141.2 *calamitates intemperiasque*, 141.2 *uineta uirgultaque*, 141.3 *pastores pecuaque*, 141.3 *salutem ualetudinemque*, 141.4 *neque agnum uitulumque*, 146.1 *ponderibus modiisque*,151.2 *ab herba grami-nibusque*, 155.1 *ferreis sarculisque*, 156.4 *tantum bilis pituitaeque*, 157.3 *uul-nera putida canceresque*, 161.1 *dextra sinistraque* (twenty-five examples).

This list comprises six alliterative combinations, two pairs of synonyms (*calamitates intemperiasque, salutem ualetudinemque*), one pair of opposites (*dextra sinistraque*), one pair of divine names, and numerous terms that are closely associated semantically, embracing for example two related types of tool, material, plant, condition or animal, in other words collective phrases (e.g. *aratra uomeresque, arbores stipitesque, festucis uectibusque, lignorum uirgarumque, herba graminibusque, uulnera . . . canceresque*). Many members of the list fall into this category. It is also worth noting that seven examples are in religious contexts.

Such pairs are obviously far from mundane. They are semantically unified, are found particularly in high-style religious language, and tend to have features of assonance. They are also far less common than the ubiquitous combinations showing *et*.

Varro's use of *-que* to connect nouns in the *Rust.* is even more restrictive than that of Cato. I have counted just twelve instances, and most of these fall into the familiar categories: pairs of opposites or complementary terms (1.9.3 *tempore locoque*, 2.1.8 *mari terraque*, 2.6.2 *mares feminasque*, 3.8.2 *dies noct-esque*), collectives (1.35.2 *uineas arbustumque*, 1.36 *uineas arbustaque*, 2.10.5 *furtis noxisque*), an alliterative pair (1.59.2 *parietes pauimentaque*), and finally 3.2.18 *uim formamque*.

14–15 siliginem triticum in loco aperto celso: *siligo*, according to the *OLD*, is a 'soft variety of wheat, *Triticum vulgare*'. *Triticum* is possibly *triticum durum* (see *OLD* s.v. 1), but there is a lack of clarity about the precise meanings of this term (as emerges from Moritz: 1958: xxii, xxix). Dalby (1998: 119 n. 128) asserts a distinction between the three words for types of wheat in this section, but without explanations. In the translation I have not given *triticum* a precise meaning.

The first two words form an asyndeton bimembre. On the other hand I would take *aperto* and *celso* as differing in rank ('an open place that is high', rather than a 'place high and open'), though that is a subjective judgment; Dalby (1998) by contrast translates 'in open, high fields', a rendering which gives the adjectives the same status and treats them as asyndetic.

Asyndeton bimembre, which came up at 3.420, is quite common in Cato. I list below, first, pairs of nouns, unaccompanied by epithets (except where a single epithet goes with both nouns), second, adjectives, third, adjectives that appear formulaic or special in some way, and finally verbs. The list is tolerably complete, though some examples might have been missed. It would be extended if phrases were included, or noun + noun with adjective. I have not punctuated with commas. Some general comments on the phenomenon, and a comparison with Varro, will be offered below.

Nouns

2.2 rationem inire oportet operarum dierum.

2.3 centones cuculiones familiam oportuisse sibi sarcire.

2.7 uinum frumentum quod supersit uendat.

7.4 oleas, orcites posias ('of olives, the orcite and posea', Loeb).

14.5 uilla ex calce caementis (cf. 14.1 *calce et caementis*).

18.6 trabes, quae insuper arbores stipites stant.

18.8 arbores stipites robustas facito aut pineas (cf. 18.5 *insuper arbores stipitesque trabem planam imponito*, 19.1 *stipites arboresque*).

35.1 siliginem triticum (the present example).

37.2 ex segeti uellito ebulum cicutam.

39.1 bubile ouile, cohortem uillam bene purgato (two pairs).

40.1 seminariis uitiariis locum uerti.

48.3 semen pirorum malorum serito.

132.1 in domo familia mea (prayer).

134.1 <u>thure uino</u> Iano Ioui Iunoni praefato (religious context).

142 cibaria uestimenta familiae dari oportet.

157.3 ad omnia uulnera tumores.

157.5 sale aceto sparsam.

This type of combination is quite well represented (eighteen examples), but like that with -*que* is far less numerous than the type with *et*. There are some similarities to the pairs above with -*que*. *Arbores stipites* occurs twice, whereas twice elsewhere these unitary terms are linked by -*que*. *Bubile ouile* may be compared with *ouibus bubusque*. There are several cases of alliteration (*centones cuculiones, calce caementis*) and of sound effects across more than one syllable (*centones cuculiones, bubile ouile, seminariis uitiariis, pirorum malorum*). Two examples are in religious contexts, and again there are some collective pairs. It would seem that asyndeton bimembre was one option available in listing the types of concrete objects with which a landowner might concern himself, but that it was stylised.

Incidentally, *lapides silices* at 18.3 and *aceto oxymeli* at 157.7 I do not take as asyndeta but as appositions, with the second member adding specification to the first (see below, 5.35).

Adjectives connected by -*que* are divided below into two groups, the first group comprising semantically run-of-the-mill pairs (though in most cases with a shared feature of another kind), and the second group comprising 'special' pairs.

Ordinary adjectives (or participles used adjectivally)

2.5 rationes putare argentariam frumentariam.

2.5 rationem uinariam oleariam.

3.2 cellam oleariam uinariam.

37.2 frondem iligneam querneam.

90 fabam coctam tostam.

103 quarto quinto quoque die.

143.2 focum purum circumuersum cotidie . . . habeat (cf. in the same passage *conuersam mundeque*).

156.6 uini atri duri (but possibly with a difference of rank, 'black wine that is hard').

157.7 coriandrum concisam siccam.

157.13 uinum lene dilutum (but possibly with a difference of rank, 'mild wine watered down').

These nine (or ten) examples are marked in a number of cases by assonance, showing up usually in more syllables than one. In four cases the pairs share a suffix of more than one syllable. At 90 both the root vowel and the ending are the same, and at 103 there is alliteration.

Special pairs of adjectives

13.1 fiscinas nouas ueteres (cf. 157.14 *uetera et noua*).

18.2 dextra sinistra (also 21.2 twice, 21.3, 160; but at 161.1 *dextra sinistraque*).

21.3 lamminas sub lamminas pollulas minutas supponito (the only example of the phrase *pollulus minutus* quoted at *TLL* X.1.829.54).

134.2 (twice) uolens propitius (prayer: also 139, 141.2).

157.6 lautam siccam (but textual problems).

There are twelve examples here. Seven show pairs of opposites (if we include *lautam siccam* 'washed and dried'). Five have pairs of synonyms or near-synonyms, i.e. the instances of the prayer formula *uolens propitius* and the apparently unique *pollulas minutas* (cf. Eng. 'tiny little'). Synonyms and

opposites often occur in asyndeton bimembre. Asyndeton bimembre comprising adjectives has an artificial look in this text. It is confined to formulae,
formulaic types and pairs with assonance.

Verbs

23.1 corbulae sarciantur picentur.
23.1 quala parentur sarciantur.
33.5 coicito alligato.
42 eximito apponito in eum locum unde . . . (surely a pause here, with a full
stop possible).
133.1 eos in terram deprimito extollito (possibly adversative: 'press back . . .
but raise', Loeb).
156.3 conicito contundito.
157.13 spargito opponito.
158.2 bibe interquiesce.

Pairs of verbs, as noted above (4.3–4; cf. 3.420), are difficult to interpret, as
they may refer to temporally distinct actions and not be conceived as unitary.[3]
We saw above, however (4.2), that there are about eighty instances overall of
imperatives in -to linked either by -que (the preferred connective in this
context) or et, and the small handful here (five examples) of asyndetic pairs
of such verb forms is a drop in the ocean.

In linking pairs of concrete nouns in contexts that are list-like Cato was not
averse to asyndeton bimembre, though even such nominal examples tend to
have a stylised look. Adjectives stand together mainly when there is something
special about them.

Pairs of directives (verbs) are only rarely without connectives.

In the Appendix below I have collected all examples of asyndeton bimembre
in Varro's *Res rusticae*, a work dealing with the same subject. Asyndeton
bimembre continues to turn up throughout Latin, particularly in some genres
and styles, but it was recessive (see the concluding chapter), and it is interesting
therefore to compare the incidence and nature of the phenomenon in the two
works.

16 rapinam et coles rapicii unde fiant: '(sow) turnips and that from which
turnip stalks may grow'. The expression *coles rapicii* is obscure to me. André
(1985) does not mention it, and translators throw no light on it. The Loeb has

---

[3] A clear example is at 58: *eas condito, parcito, uti quam diutissime durent*. This is the
punctuation of the Loeb, but Mazzarino places a colon after *condito*, and Goujard
a semi-colon. Olives are to be stored, and then issued only sparingly. There are two distinct
activities here.

'Plant turnips, kohlrabi seed', and Dalby (1998) renders 'Sow turnip, field rape' (both without a note). The *OLD* s.v. *rapicius* cites *rapicii* (plural) from Plin. *Nat.* 18.127 with the comment '(as sb. ?sc. *caules*) turnip-tops'. I have merely given a literal translation.

Here *unde* has no antecedent: = '(that) from which'. This usage is elsewhere in Cato: 31.1 *uti sit unde corbulae fiant*, 151.4 *si non habebis unde inriges* ('if you do not have (something) from which you can irrigate'). The instrumental *qui* is used in the same way: 6.4 *uti siet qui uineam alliges* ('so that there is (something) with which to tie the vines'). Cf. Plaut. *Per.* 302 *paratum iam esse dicito unde argentum sit futurum*, Ter. *Ad.* 122 *est unde haec fiant*. The *OLD* s.v. 10b quotes further examples from classical Latin, including Cic. *Har.* 29 *si habuerit unde tibi soluat*. These indefinite uses are variants of the classical *est qui* ('there is someone who') construction.

This is the only instance of the 'rustic' spelling *colis* attested by the manuscripts of Cato, whereas *caulis* occurs four times. The diminutive form *coliculus*, however, occurs twice but *cauliculus* not all (see Adams 2013: 84–5, and below, 26.11). It is possible that the non-standard *o*-form was better established in the diminutive, but no reliance can be placed on manuscript spellings.

Appendix: asyndeton bimembre in Varro's *Res rusticae*

Nouns

3.9.14 e capite, e collo eorum crebro eligendi pedes (lice must be picked from the head and neck often; a distinctive type showing two prepositional expressions: cf. e.g. Plaut. *Cas.* 664 *sub arcis sub tectis latentes*, *Curc.* 289 *suffarcinati cum libris cum sportulis*; it is possible that the second *e* in the passage of Varro is a corruption of *et*).

This is the only pair of nouns in asyndeton bimembre that I have found in the *Rust.*, which is a rather longer text than Cato's *Agr.* By contrast at 3.5.11 (*in limine, in lateribus dextra et sinistra*) I take it that there is not an asyndeton, which would be replaceable by a connective, but that *in lateribus* is an apposition introducing a specification ('at the entrance, on the right-hand side and on the left') (on such appositions see below, 5.35).

On the other hand Varro freely juxtaposes sets of three or more nouns without a connective. For example, from 3.3 onwards there is a discussion of animals that might be reared around the villa, and there are many combinations of nouns. When there are three or more members asyndeton is common. When there are two, a connective is always used. Note the following contrasting groups of examples:

Groups of three

3.3.1 ornithones leporaria piscinae

3.3.3 pauones turtures turdi

3.3.3 anseres querquedulae anates

3.3.3 aper caprea lepus

3.3.3 apes cochleae glires

3.3.4 aucupes uenatores piscatores

3.3.4 aucupis uenatoris piscatoris

3.3.4 glires cochlias gallinas.

Groups of two

3.3.6 oua et pulli

3.3.7 turdi ac pauones (contrast 3.3.3 above, where the same two nouns are in asyndeton when a third noun is present).

3.3.8 multos apros ac capreas

3.5.1 turdorum ac merularum

3.5.2 miliariae ac coturnices

3.5.7 hirundines et grues

3.5.7 gallinae et columbae

3.5.7 turtures ac coturnices

3.5.14 lusciniolae ac merulae.

Adjectives

1.4.2 quam si est fructuosus turpis ('than if it is profitable but unsightly', an adversative type).

1.48.1 acus tenuis longa (but there could be a difference of rank, of a thin needle that is long rather than short).

1.60 orcites nigras aridas (this comes from Cato *Agr.* 7.4, which has *orcites ubi nigrae erunt et siccae*; Varro might however have taken the adjectives as differing in rank).

1.68 sorbum <u>maturum mite</u> conditum citius promi oportet ('sorbs that are stored ripe and soft ought to be brought out immediately'; this is a definite (alliterative) case).

2.3.2 uidendum ut sint firmae magnae.

2.5.8 cruribus ... minoribus rectis.

2.5.8 genibus eminulis distantibus inter se (this is included though the second member has a complement).

2.11.7 tonsas recentes (oues) ... perungunt (this seems to mean 'recently shorn', as if *recens* had been used adverbially, as it is in the previous sentence, *recens lana tonsa* 'recently shorn wool'; in our passage the second adjective is a specifier, 'shorn, fresh').

3.5.12 qui est ultra rutundus columnatus.

3.7.2 hoc genus ... sine albo, uario (the first member is a prepositional phrase, but is the equivalent of a colour adjective; the second member may be adversative, 'not white but variegated').

Varro also has sets of three adjectives in asyndeton: e.g. 2.2.6 *luscam surdam minam* (old formula of sale), 2.7.5 *iuba crebra fusca subcrispa*, 3.9.5 *rostro breui pleno acuto*, 3.9.18 *gallina ... grandes uariae gibberae*, 3.16.18 *niger ruber uarius*, 3.16.19 *parua uaria rutunda*.

There are lots of other pairs of adjectives without connectives in the text, but the members of the pairs differ in rank (as indeed may be the case with some of the pairs above). For example, at 3.6.6 (*augurali aditiali cena*) *cena auguralis* denotes the dinner given by an augur on taking up office (so Cic. *Fam.* 7.26.2). *Aditialis* means 'on taking up office'. The meaning therefore is 'admissions dinner for an augur', with *auguralis* qualifying the phrase *aditialis cena*. Here is a small selection of cases where I find differences of rank between the adjectives: 2.9.16 *per calles siluestres longinquos*, 2.10.10 *rationes dominicas pecuarias*, 3.1.10 *pauimentis nobilibus lithostrotis*, 3.6.6 *seueri boni uiri* (*boni uiri* is probably a unit), 3.9.6 *duae caueae coniunctae magnae* ('two connected henhouses that are large').

Verbs

3.2.2 itaque imus, uenimus in uillam ('and so we go, and come to the villa'; this should probably not be called an asyndeton, as there could be a marked pause: see on 4.3–4 above).

There are only about nine or ten asyndeta bimembria in the whole work, most of them adjectival. Asyndeton itself is common, but only when a group has three or more components. In just one place Varro appears to have introduced an adjectival asyndeton bimembre that is not in the source Cato (1.60: see above), but in other cases his usage may be contrasted with that of Cato. For example, whereas Cato has *dext(e)ra sinistra* five times (with *dextra sinistraque* only once), Varro regularly writes *dextra et sinistra* (1.47, 2.9.3, 3.5.10, 3.5.11, 3.5.12, 3.16.16 (with *ac*)). Note too *Rust.* 1.13.6 *cellam uinariam et oleariam* alongside *Agr.* 3.2 *cellam oleariam uinariam*.

Conclusions

In this short passage the imperative form *serito* occurs at the end of sentence after sentence (eight times), and there are two instances of *seri oportet* in the same position. Cato was conveying instructions in the most succinct and direct form, and there was no place for stylistic variation. The mundane repetitive style was no doubt adapted to the expected readership. The lexical items too would have been heard in farmers' talk. Notable are the technical terms *cariosus* and *pullus*, the former of which was later ascribed by the educated to 'rustics', and the latter of which survived for centuries in southern parts of Italy, and also *rudectus*, *ualidus* (in the meanings it has in this text), *calamitosus* (of a base that was generalised in meaning in literary Latin), *restibilis*, possibly *materinus*, and various other adjectives and nouns. The multi-purpose adjective *bonus* is suggestive of communication with no frills. Twelve times in the passage terms for plants, crops and the like are in the collective singular, and such singulars must have been widespread in rural areas. The only plural is *coles rapicii*.

The hanging nominatives and seemingly ungrammatical relative constructions are a conspicuous feature of the passage. Should we speak of 'incoherence' or bad Latin? I have suggested that the relative constructions can be derived either from the type with attractio inversa, or the relative-correlative type. A writer attuned to adopting these patterns, as Cato was in his agricultural treatise, might sometimes have fallen into shorthand variations on them. How these variations might have been judged by an educated reader of the time it is impossible to say, but it is likely that they reflect the writer's indifference in a practical text to strict grammatical norms. On syntactic incoherence in informal writing see Halla-aho (2009: 90–120).

The Latin of Cato in the *Agr.* in some ways betrays its date. A noteworthy usage discussed above is that of instrumental *qui* (with *unde*: see below) to the exclusion of *quibus*, *quo* and *qua*. *Qui* later fell out of use. Asyndeton bimembre is also more common in this text than in the longer agricultural work of Varro, though its use by Cato looks stylistically marked rather than mundane. Such asyndeton receded in the history of Latin, but it was always available for exploitation by an artificial stylist.

-*que* also seems to be used more freely by Cato than by Varro (*Rust.*), but again mere statistics tell us little, because it has a restricted and artificial look even as used by Cato. The pattern ABC*que*, which we noted as quite well represented in Cato but absent from Varro's *Rust.*, also seems stylised.

There remains the question of continuity with later Latin. *Pullus* in its sense here lived on into Romance but was never a literary word. It had its life at a spoken level in certain regions. The full history of *unde* in its quasi-instrumental senses is still to be written, but it did continue into Romance with these functions, and is already Cato's relative of choice in one type of context.

5
CATO, *DE AGRICVLTVRA* 157.3–7

Introduction

This passage is about the medicinal qualities of a type of cabbage, described as the 'mild' (157.2 *lenis*), which is the third in a threefold classification that is made at the start of the chapter (1–2). The preceding chapter (156) is also more generally about the salubrious effects of cabbage.

Dalby (1998: 27) has suggested that 157 is not genuine, and he prints it as a supplement to the text at the end (227–33). I quote his words in full (cf. also his remarks at 227 n. 283):

> I cannot accept that it was composed by Cato. Its repetitiousness is of a different kind from his. In any one passage, Cato writes concisely, even if he may afterwards revert to a topic and determinedly or absent-mindedly repeat himself. The composer of this chapter wrote laxly, repeating thoughts and words haphazardly from sentence to sentence. I suggest its origin is in notes made from some medical lecture. Because the subject matter fitted, these notes were incorporated alongside Cato's own chapter on cabbage (chapter **156**) by one of the earliest scribes who made a copy of his book. Whether the addition had his authority I see no way to determine.

This is rather vague, apart from the speculative reference to notes possibly taken at a medical lecture. Cato's book is definitely in a highly varied style, not least because he included ready-made material from sources (most notably prayers and religious passages), but also probably because he put it together over a long period. It is certainly possible that material of a medical kind might have been added by someone at a later date (some late medical texts were added to in this way), but proving that that has happened in the present case would be a difficult matter, requiring more than assertions of repetitiousness and lax writing. Even the preface, which has marks of careful writing, has striking repetitions, such as four instances of *existimo* within a short space, and four of *laudo* (see von Albrecht 1989: 5–7 on 'verbal repetition'). We saw above (4 Conclusions) that seven sentences in a short passage end with *serito*. The disorder and doublets in the work have indeed in the past been put down not to later accretions but to Cato himself (see Reeve in Reynolds

1983: 42 with n. 22). It is not my aim here to adjudicate on the authenticity of
157, but one obvious question that will be kept in mind throughout is whether
features of the Latinity can be paralleled in other parts of the work (see the
Conclusions).

Text

157.3 Ad omnia uulnera tumores eam contritam imponito (1): haec omnia
ulcera purgabit sanaque faciet sine dolore; eadem tumida concoquit (2), eadem
erumpit (3), eadem (4) uulnera putida canceresque purgabit sanosque faciet,
quod medicamentum facere non potest. uerum prius quam id imponas, aqua
calida multa lauato (5): postea bis in die contritam imponito: ea omnem
putorem adimet (6). cancer ater (7), is olet et saniem spurcam mittit, albus
purulentus est, sed fistulosus et subtus suppurat sub carne (8). **4** in ea uulnera
(9) huiusce modi teras brassicam: sanum (10) faciet; optima est ad huiusce
modi uulnus. et luxatum si quod est (11), bis die aqua calida foueto (12),
brassicam tritam opponito: cito sanum faciet; bis die id opponito: dolores
auferet. et si quid contusum est, erumpet: brassicam tritam opponito: sanum
faciet. et si quid in mammis ulceris natum et (13) carcinoma, brassicam tritam
opponito: sanum faciet. **5** et si ulcus acrimoniam eius ferre non poterit,
farinam hordeaceam (14) misceto, ita opponito: huiusce modi ulcera omnia
haec sanum faciet (15), quod aliud medicamentum facere non potest neque
purgare (16). et puero et puellae (17) si ulcus erit huiusce modi, farinam
hordeaceam addito. et si uoles eam consectam, lautam, siccam, sale aceto
sparsam esse (18), salubrius nihil est. **6** quo libentius edis (19), aceto mulso
spargito; lautam siccam et rutam, coriandrum sectam sale sparsam paulo
libentius edes (20). id bene faciet (21) et mali nihil sinet in corpore consistere (22) et aluum bonam faciet (23). si quid antea mali intus erit (24),
omnia sana faciet, et de capite et de oculis omnia deducet et sanum faciet
(25). hanc mane esse oportet ieiunum (26). **7** et si bilis atra est et si lienes
turgent (27) et si cor dolet et si iecur aut pulmones aut praecordia: uno
uerbo, omnia sana faciet, et intro quae dolitabunt (28). eodem (29) silpium
inradito: bonum est. nam (30) uenae omnes, ubi sufflatae sunt ex cibo, non
possunt perspirare in toto corpore: inde aliqui morbus nascitur. ubi ex
multo cibo aluus non it (31), pro portione brassica si uteris (id ut te
moneo) (32), nihil istorum usu ueniet morbis (33). uerum morbum articu-
larium nulla res (34) tam purgat, quam brassica cruda (si edes concisam et
rutam et coriandrum concisam siccam et sirpicium inrasum) et brassica ex
aceto oxymeli (35) et sale sparsa.

Translation

157.3 For all sores and swellings put that (cabbage) on, crushed: this will clear all sores and make them healthy without pain. The same (substance) brings swellings to a head, and also bursts them, and also will clear infected wounds and ulcers and make them healthy, which medicine cannot do. But before you put it on, wash with a lot of hot water. Afterwards twice a day put it on, crushed; it will remove all putridity. A black ulcer – that smells and emits a foul discharge. A white ulcer is purulent but fistulous, and it suppurates under the flesh. **4** For these sores of this kind crush cabbage: it will make them healthy. It is excellent for a sore of this kind. And if there is any dislocation, twice a day wash with hot water, and put on crushed cabbage: it will quickly make it healthy. Twice a day put it on: it will remove pains. And if anything has been bruised, it will cause (it) to burst. Put on crushed cabbage: it will make it healthy. And if any ulcer has developed on the breasts – and a carcinoma – put on crushed cabbage: it will make it healthy. **5** And if the sore cannot bear the sharpness of it, mix barley-flour and in this way put on: it will make all sores of this kind healthy, which another medicine cannot do, nor clear. And if there shall be a sore of this kind on a boy or girl, add barley-flour. And if you want to eat it (cabbage) chopped, washed, dried, sprinkled with salt and vinegar, nothing is more health-giving. **6** So that you may eat it more willingly, sprinkle with honeyed vinegar: you will eat it a little more willingly washed and dried – and rue and coriander chopped and sprinkled with salt.[1] It will be of benefit and will allow no disease to stay in the body and will make the bowels good. If any disease is beforehand within, it will make everything healthy. And it will draw everything out of the head and eyes and make it healthy. It is necessary to eat it in the morning, fasting. **7** And if there is black bile and if the spleen is swollen and if the heart is in pain, and if the liver or lungs or diaphragm (are in pain): in one word, it will make everything healthy – and whatever pains there shall be within. Grate silphium into the aforementioned: it is good. Again, all the veins, when they are puffed up from food, cannot breathe in the whole body: from that some disease develops. When the bowel contents from a lot of food do not go, if you employ cabbage in the proper degree (doing that as I am instructing you), none of these things will occur as the result of diseases. But nothing so clears joint disease as raw cabbage (if you eat it chopped, and rue and chopped coriander that is dry and grated *sirpicium*) and cabbage with vinegar of the honeyed type and sprinkled with salt.

---

[1] See however the Commentary on the text here.

Commentary

1 ad omnia uulnera tumores eam contritam imponito: there is a (final) use of *ad* here that was to become commonplace in medical Latin (see Langslow 2000: 367–8, Adams 2013: 292), namely *ad* + disease name meaning 'for the treatment of'. While *ad* is used + disease name, the dative is used of the patient, with some interchange between the two constructions (thus Cato at 159 has the dative rather than *ad* of the disease (*intertrigini remedium*: contrast e.g. Pelagonius 139 *remedium ad dysuriam*) and at 123 *ad* of the patient (*uinum ad isciacos sic facito*)). For the construction in the present passage see 125 *id est ad aluum crudam et ad lateris dolorem et ad coeliacum*, 126 *ad tormina et si aluus non consistet*, 127.1 *ad dyspepsiam et stranguriam mederi* (an interesting case, = 'to treat (someone) for dyspepsia and strangury'; the verb usually takes the dative, and one can understand a dative of the patient here), 156.1 *lotiumque ad omnes res salubre est*, 157.14 *ad omnia ulcera uetera et noua contritam cum melle opponito*. See also below, 42.14.

    uulnera tumores: asyndeton bimembre (see above, 4.14–15).

    eam contritam: here Cato uses the compound participle with the verb of placing. He uses it again a couple of sentences later (*contritam imponito*). Then in the next section (4) he switches (three times) to the simplex with the same referent and in the same context (*brassicam tritam opponito*). This is a case of iteration of a compound by its simplex, a very old pattern found in the Twelve Tables, which continues to turn up from time to time in technical texts even of a late date (see Adams 1995a: 635–6, with bibliography and examples from such texts; cf. also below, 6.8). Note 161.4 *euellito, sic circumfodito, ut facile uellere possis*; also 157.14–15 *contritam cum melle opponito: sanum faciet. et si polypus in naso intro erit, brassicam erraticam aridam tritam in malam conicito*.

    Another element here that was to be long-lived in medical language is the use of the participle (*contritam*) in association with the imperative verb (*imponito*). Cf. Pel. 180 *contritum ulceri superpone* (Adams 1995a: 636; on such continuities see Adams 1995a: 635–9).

2 tumida concoquit: the substantival neuter adjective *tumida* here is indistinguishable from *tumores*. In medical Latin this type of substantivisation is perhaps more familiar in perfect participles (see further below, 5.11). *Malum* however is used twice in the present passage of disease (see below, 5.22). For *luxum* (from the adjective *luxus*) in the sense 'dislocation' see 160 (for the passage see below, 5.11 on *luxatum si quod est*), and also Scrib. Larg. 208. Önnerfors (1956: 22) cites *aegrum*, for which at *TLL* I.940.57ff. the meanings 'pars aegra corporis' (Sen. *Dial.* 5.9.5 *numquam sine querella aegra tanguntur*) and 'morbus' (Plin. *Nat.* 30.64) are given. Langslow (2000: 341–2) lists instances of *biliosa, glutinosa* and *spumosa* used substantivally. See also below, 11.13 for a substantival neuter adjective in another technical writer (Vitruvius).

Concoquit means 'brings to maturity', i.e. brings to a head' (the rendering of Courtney 1999: 71).

2–4 eadem . . . eadem . . . eadem: the repetition may look like the sort of rhetorical artifice that one is accustomed to in literary language, but I would see it as the technical 'specifying' style marked by redundant use of anaphorics (see e.g. Adams 2013: 496, and below, 24.6–7). It is usually *is* that is repeated in this way. Note e.g. 157.10–11 *id* (*lotium*) . . . *eo* . . . *eo lotio* . . . *eo lotio* . . . *eo lotio*; also 41.4 *eos* . . . *eos*, 48.2 *eam* . . . *eo* . . . *eo*, 81 *id* . . . *id* . . . *eam*, 93 *eae* . . . *ad eas*, 143.1 *eam* . . . *ea* . . . *ea*. See further below, 11.31, and index, 'repetitions, verbal', 'technical writing'.

3 erumpit: a transitive use, of causing swellings to burst (*OLD* s.v. 7).

5 uerum prius quam id imponas, aqua calida multa lauato: the reference in *id* is to *brassica* f., which has just been referred to several times by the feminine *eadem*; in the next clause with the same verb (*imponito*) there is a switch back to the feminine (*contritam* and then *ea*). One might be tempted to think that *id* is a constructio ad sensum, influenced by *medicamentum* in the preceding clause. However, in the next section (4) there is the same variation between feminine and neuter: *brassicam tritam opponito: cito sanum faciet; bis die id opponito*. Both *brassicam tritam* and *id* are object of the same verb. *Brassica* is the topic throughout.

The neuter pronoun *id* as used by Cato often shows lack of concord (of number or gender) with its antecedent (see further below, 5.21). Cf. 6.1 *rapa, raphanos, milium, panicum, id maxime seri oportet* (with inconcinnity of number), 39.2 *cretae crudae partes duas, calcis tertiam conmisceto; inde laterculos facito, coquito in fornacem, eum conterito idque inducito* (here a plausible emendation is of *eum* to *tum*; *tum* is several times elsewhere followed by an imperative in -*to*; *id* however refers to pieces of crushed brick), 44 *qua locus ferax non erit, id plus concidito aratoque* (referring back to *locus*), 81 *eadem omnia indito, quae in placentam. id permisceto in alueo, id indito in irneam fictilem* (here *id* picks up *eadem omnia*), 83 *farris l. III et lardi p. IIIIS et pulpae p. IIIIS, uini s. III, id in u<nu>m uas liceto coicere* (*id* refers to a plurality), 85 *libram alicae in aquam indito, facito uti bene madeat. id infundito in alueum purum* (*id* refers back to a feminine, or to two feminines if *aqua* is embraced as well; but it is fundamentally the wheat, *alica*, that is to be cooked), 87 *siliginem purgato bene, postea in alueum indat, eo addat aquam bis in die. die decimo aquam exsiccato, exurgeto bene, in alueo puro misceto bene: facito tamquam faex fiat. id in linteum nouum indito* (the substance here prepared is *siligo* f.; the water is drained off and it is the *siligo*, or the *faex* (f.) therefrom, that is placed in the linen bag).

Neuter pronouns have a generalising quality, and there is not infrequently a lack of concord (of either number or gender) between the pronoun and its antecedent (see e.g. E. Löfstedt 1911: 307–10, 1956: I.8–9, Svennung 1935: 263, Hofmann and Szantyr 1965: 431–2). Cf. e.g. Plaut. *Aul.* 108–9 *diuidere argenti dixit <u>nummos</u> in uiros; | <u>id</u> si relinquo . . .* (see further Stockert 1983: 209).

For the pattern seen in *uerum prius . . . lauato* (i.e. 'put something on, but before you put it on do X') as lasting into late Latin see Adams (1995a: 637–8); it also occurs at 98.2 (*sed prius*), leading as here to an imperative in *-to*.

6 postea bis in die contritam imponito: ea omnem putorem adimet: paratactic syntax containing what might be interpreted as an imperative replaceable by a conditional (see Kühner and Stegmann 1955: II.165, Hofmann and Szantyr 1965: 481, 657, Hofmann and Ricottilli 2003: 256, and especially L. Löfstedt 1966: 100–3): 'do X; you will achieve Y', = 'if you do X you will achieve Y'. The same usage is the norm in this passage: 157.4 *in ea uulnera huiusce modi teras brassicam: sanum faciet* (with jussive subjunctive rather than imperative), *brassicam tritam opponito: cito sanum faciet; bis die id opponito: dolores auferet* (two examples), 5 *farinam hordeaceam misceto, ita opponito: huiusce modi ulcera omnia haec sanum faciet, 7 eodem silpium inradito: bonum est.* For explicit *si*-clauses in the same contexts in the chapter see 5 *et si uoles eam consectam, lautam, siccam, sale aceto sparsam esse, salubrius nihil est, 7 pro portione brassica si uteris . . ., nihil istorum usu ueniet morbis,* and see below, 5.15. The construction is found in the parody of doctors' language (discussed below, 5.15) at Plaut. *Merc.* 139 *resinam ex melle Aegyptiam uorato: saluom feceris.* L. Löfstedt (1966: 100–1) notes that it persists not only in popular language but in more elevated genres, citing an example from Cicero (*S. Rosc.* 48). A few other Ciceronian instances are quoted by Kühner and Stegmann, but the usage does seem to be a mark of conversational style (cf. Virg. *Aen.* 9.291, in a speech). L. Löfstedt (1966: 102) cites examples from Old and modern French.

bis in die: Cato prefers the prepositional expression to the plain ablative in this type of phrase, though twice below in 157.4 *bis die* occurs. The latter two instances are the only ones of the kind in the work. *Bis in die* occurs six times, *ter in die* once and *aliquotiens in die* once (eight examples in all). Varro reverses Cato's preference. In the *Rust.* he has *bis/ter die* five times, but *bis/ter in die* not at all. He also has *bis/ter* with the plain ablative of the names of seasons (*aestate, hieme*) four times, but such phrases with *in* not at all. On the other hand with just two nouns, *annus* and *mensis*, he prefers the prepositional expressions (three times, no examples of *bis anno/mense*).

Cato's preference for *bis/ter in die* seems to be an anticipation of much later practice. Pelagonius has *bis/ter in die* four times, the ablative not at all (see Adams 1995a: 166).

The frequent use of prepositions in temporal expressions is a general feature of Cato's prose in the *Agr.* It is to be seen in references to the seasons. *Per hiemem* occurs eight times, *hieme* not at all. So *per aestatem* is used three times, *aestate* once. *Per autumnum* occurs once, *autumno* not at all. There is also one case of *ad autumnum*: 161.3 *semen maturum fit ad autumnum* ('The seed ripens in autumn', Loeb; so Dalby 1998, but see below). Finally, *per uer* occurs eight times and *ad uer* once: 105.2 *ad uer diffundito in amphoras* ('rack off into amphorae in the spring', Loeb; so Dalby 1998). It is however likely that these *ad*-phrases have a different implication, 'towards autumn/spring', i.e. 'in late summer/winter'. *Vere* appears in the ablative four times, but always with *primo*, a set phrase used for example nine times by Livy and requiring the ablative to mark the precise point of time. The substantival adjective *uernum* is found three times in the ablative in the meaning 'in spring'.

Such *per*-phrases occur with nouns denoting seasons twenty-times, and as well there are the two *ad*-phrases, which are best left aside here. On the other hand plain ablatives occur just four times (leaving aside *primo uere*). *Primo uere* itself is a phrase of some interest, as it produced with a change of gender Romance words for 'spring' (It., Sp. *primauera*; cf. OPr. *primuer*; see e.g. Bloch and von Wartburg 1968: 511, s.v. *primavera*).

Is there a genuine semantic distinction between e.g. *aestate* and *per aestatem*? *Per aestatem* certainly refers to something that may go on for an extended period during the summer, but then that is usually the implication of the ablative too. Note Cato's one instance of *aestate*: 14.5 *loco pestilenti, ubi aestate fieri non potest*, translated by the Loeb as '[i]n an unwholesome situation, where summer work is impossible'; cf. Dalby 1998 'where work cannot go on in summer'. Here *per aestatem* would also have been possible. Not infrequently of course there is a semantic point to one construction or the other. The *per*-phase for example may stress the continuing of an activity through a specific (dateable) season, as at Sall. *Hist.* 4.59 *quamquam naues caudicariae occulte per hiemem fabricatae aderant* (of ships built secretly during a particular winter). On the other hand if a point of time is to be highlighted, *per* would not be possible (*media aestate* would rarely be replaced by *per mediam aestatem*). In generalisations on the other hand in didactic works about activities to be carried out in certain seasons, there may be no discernible difference between *per* and the ablative, and a writer would have had a choice open to him. We may compare a few passages of Cato containing *per*-expressions with similar passages in Varro containing the plain ablative of an activity repeated throughout the season: *Agr.* 104.1 *uinum familiae per hiemem qui utatur* alongside *Rust.* 1.54.3 *pro uino operariis datur hieme; Agr.* 73 *per aetatem boues aquam bonam et liquidam bibant* alongside *Rust.* 1.13.3 *boues enim ex aruo aestate reducti hic bibunt; Agr.* 151.2 *per uer serito in loco, ubi* alongside *Rust.* 1.27.2 *uere sationes quae fiunt.* There does however seem to be a difference in Cato between *per uer* and *uerno.* All three examples of *uerno* (e.g. 131 *postea uerno arare incipito*) refer to the <u>beginning</u> of something (at a point) in spring (cf. 50.2, 54.3), whereas *per uer* indicates something done during winter.

The distinctiveness of Cato's usage becomes clear from figures for Varro. Varro uses the ablative often but phrases with *per* (with names of seasons) never. *Hieme* occurs twenty-one times in the *Rust.*, *aestate* eighteen, *uere* five and *autumno* five (a total of forty-nine, to which may be added nine instances of *uerno tempore*: for this type of temporal circumlocution see below, 11.10–11). Varro, as in the passages quoted in the last paragraph, was capable of using the ablative in references to events recurring throughout the season (note e.g. 1.12.1 *quod aestate habet umbram, hieme solem*).

Cato manifests a taste for prepositions in temporal expressions in contexts in which the ablative would often have been possible.

7 cancer ater: there are two words for 'black' in Latin, *ater* and *niger*. The difference between them in classical Latin is explained by Marouzeau (1949a: 67–8, 1962: 166). *Niger* means 'black' in a neutral sense, as opposed to 'white'. *Ater* is an emotive term, designating blackness in its sinister, threatening or lugubrious aspects (note *TLL* II.1018.40f. 'subest multis locis nota terroris, abominationis, damni, perniciei').

The question arises whether this distinction already obtains in early Latin. *Ater* occurs twice in our passage, both times of entities that threaten the body (cf. 157.7 *si bilis atra est*). Three other examples in the work are applied to *ueratrum* (114.1 (but an editorial addition), 115.1, 115.2), some sort of 'black hellebore'. Many varieties of hellebore are poisonous. However, it was probably not that feature which inspired the use of this adjective with the noun, but a popular etymology connecting *ueratrum* with *atrum*. Marouzeau's characterisation is not entirely accurate for Cato, as there are two further examples in reference to plants or trees (8.1, of figs, 31.2, of hornbeam), and another of wine (156.6 *uini atri duri*). *Niger* occurs nine times, and is always a neutral term used mainly of plants or the like, and in one case wine (126 *uini nigri austeri*). Four times *niger* is opposed to *albus* (8.2, 119 twice, 133.2). Thus there are signs of the emotive force for *ater* proposed by Marouzeau, but still a good deal of overlap between *ater* and *niger*. Incidentally, throughout Latin *atra* was the usual epithet of *bilis* (*TLL* II.1987.59ff.), though there are occasional instances of *nigra*.

The same variability is to be seen in Plautus' use of *ater*. It is his usual term for 'black'. *Niger* is found only once (*Capt.* 647), in a physical description of a man, *corpore albo, oculis nigris*, in a contrast with the colour white. It appears as usual to be neutral. There are eleven examples of *ater*. At *Men.* 915 it is used neutrally, of 'black' versus 'white' wine.[2] At *Pseud.* 814 it is also neutral, in a plant name (*holus atrum*, which is sometimes written as a single word and persists throughout Latin: see *OLD* s.v. *holus* 2). Another neutral use is in reference to the colour of the hair (*Merc.* 306), in a contrast with other colour terms. At *Vid.* 36 *ater* refers to the effect of the sun on the skin, and must again be neutral. There are four examples of *ater* in this paragraph.

In seven other places the colour designated by *ater* can be interpreted as threatening or unpleasant. There are two instances of the phrase *atra bilis* (*Amph.* 727, *Capt.* 596*)*. Another two examples are in threats to turn someone 'black and blue' (*Poen.* 1290 *ita <eam> repplebo atritate, atrior multo ut siet | quam Aegyptini, Rud.* 1000 *fiet tibi puniceum corium, postea atrum denuo*). Similarly an example applied to the skin (supposedly) of fish (*Rud.* 998 *sunt alii puniceo corio, magni item; atque atri*) has the function merely of leading up to one of these threats (that at *Rud.* 1000 quoted above), and it is not really neutral. There is one example of a threatening dark cloud (in the context of sea travel) (*Merc.* 879), and finally one of black pitch as a threatening substance (*Capt.* 597).

---

[2] It is clear from two of the passages from Cato cited in the previous paragraph that 'black' (both *ater* and *niger*) was used of dark wine, versus 'white'. Gratwick (1993: 224) on Plaut. *Men.* 915 (*album an atrum uinum potas*) states that 'this has to strike Men. and the audience as a "loony" question', and he goes on to call it 'quite meaningless', citing an article which supposedly shows that the ancients did not draw our sharp distinction between red and white wine. It is untrue to imply that a distinction was not made between 'black' and 'white' wine. 'Black' we have seen; for *albus* of wine see Cato, *Agr.* 106.2, Hor. *Sat.* 2.4.29 and *TLL* I.1505.79ff. At Varro, *Men.* 575 there is mention of three types of wine, black, white and medium: *non uides apud Mnesitheum scribi tria genera esse uini, nigrum, album, medium.* Our own white wine is not white at all, and our red wine can look black in the bottle, with a reddish tinge seen only in the glass.

7–8 cancer ater, is olet: the type of pronominal resumption seen in *is* is very common in the *Agr*. There are various motivations and types discernible (see also above, 2.25, 3.416). First, here (and e.g. at 5.3, quoted below) it places the emphasis on the preposed noun, which is new to the context. *Cancer* has occurred earlier, but it is the contrasting black and white types that are now introduced. Second, when there is a string of nouns at the head of a sentence the resumptive pronoun may be used for clarity, stressing that the verbal process applies to every member of the list. Third, when there is an interruption between an initial noun and the verb, resumption may again be used for clarity. Of similar type to this last is the resumption that tends to follow attractio inversa (for the type see above, 1.11, and also 4.11 on Cato).

Here is a list of examples of the varying types: 5.3 *amicos domini, eos habeat sibi amicos*, 5.8 *faenum cordum, sicilimenta de prato, ea omnia condito* (see further below, on *haec omnia*), 6.1 *rapa, raphanos, milium, panicum, id maxime seri oportet* (without agreement of number), 8.1 *Africanas et Herculaneas, Sacontinas, hibernas, Tellanas atras pediculo longo, eas in loco crassiore ... serito*, 8.2 *Abellanas, Praenestinas, Graecas, haec facito uti serantur*, 20.1 *columellam ferream, quae in miliario stat, eam rectam stare oportet*, 28.2 *arbores crassiores digitis quinque quae erunt, eas praecisas serito*, 46.1 *locum quam optimum et apertissimum et stercorosissimum poteris et quam simillimum genus terrae eae, ubi semina positurus eris, et uti ne nimis longe semina ex seminario ferantur, <u>eum locum</u> bipalio uertito*, 51 *ficum, oleam, malum opunicum, ... laurum, myrtum, nuces praenestinas, platinum, <u>haec omnia</u> a capite propagari ... oportet* (so 73, 143.3; *omnia* on its own is at 54.2, 68; for the persistence of *haec omnia* used thus in recipes until late antiquity see Adams 1995a: 637; see also below, 42.8–9), 58 *postea oleas tempestiuas, unde minimum olei fieri poterit, eas condito, parcito, uti quam diutissime durent*.

8 subtus suppurat sub carne: there is multiple pleonasm here, with *subtus* anticipating *sup-* and *sub*. For this type of structure (showing an adverb associated with a preposition of the same semantic field) see 157.15 *et si polypus in naso intro erit*, and also below, 44.37.5. For adverbs duplicating semantically the prefix of a verb see particularly Lucr. 2.130 *retroque repulsa reuerti*, 2.200 *foras emergant exsiliantque*, 2.283 *retroque residit*, 4.310 *inde retro rursum redit*, Virg. *Aen.* 2.378 *retroque pedem cum uoce repressit*, and also index, 'pleonasm, of adverb and verbal prefix'). Müller (1895) deals with double local expressions (usually of the type where the second element adds a specification), but the distribution of the type here might be further investigated. In the first of the passages of Cato in this paragraph (8) the adverb is completely redundant, but at 157.15 *intro* makes it clear that the polyp is in and not on the nose.

The classical adverb with the meaning of *subtus* ('in a lower position, underneath, below') was *subter*. *Subtus* must originally have meant 'from underneath' (cf. e.g. *intus*, which sometimes in Plautus retains the meaning 'from within'; also *funditus, penitus* etc.: see Adams 2013: 589), but it had lost that separative sense by the historical period (on this fate of separative adverbs see Adams 2013: 590 and the whole of chapter XXIII) and come into rivalry with *subter*, but only in lower genres. It has a very restricted distribution in the period covered by the *OLD*. It is used three times by Cato *Agr.* (cf. e.g. 121), who does not have *subter* in that work, twice by Varro (*Rust.* 1.57.3, 2.9.3), who has *subter* twice in the *Rust.*, in a fragment of the fourth digest of Metellus Pius (cos. 52 BC) describing a pontiff's dinner (*Macr.* 3.13.12 *turdum asparagos subtus*: an asyndeton bimembre, 'thrush, asparagus under; the passage has other asyndeta bimembria in the list of courses, *patinam ostrearum peloridum*, and *lumbos capruginos apruginos*), in an inscription (*CIL* VI.36537), and finally in a passage of Festus (p. 474.29 Lindsay). The word also occurs as a preposition in Vitruvius (4.2.5), a writer who has *subter* only once (as a preposition). For details of the distribution of *subtus* in late Latin see Hofmann and Szantyr (1965: 280), describing it as 'vulgärer' than *subter*, and citing places where it occurs in an Old Latin version of the Bible but not in the corresponding passage of the Vulgate (which has *subter*).

This word has a considerable interest, as it survives widely in the Romance languages (e.g. It. *sotto*, Fr. *sous*: *REW* 8402), whereas *subter* lives on nowhere. It is the absence of *subter* from the *Agr.* that is striking. *Subtus* looks like one of those republican low-register words that continued into the Romance languages.

9 in ea uulnera: *uulnera* here, picking up the two types of *cancer*, can hardly refer to a 'wound' in the sense of an injury inflicted by external agency. It means in a general sense 'sores' of whatever cause (a meaning not given by the *OLD*). So in the first sentence of our passage *uulnera tumores* is picked up by *omnia ulcera*.

9–10 uulnera . . . sanum: for the discord (of number) and its significance see below, 5.15.

11 et luxatum si quod est: the use of *quod* here is of interest. Note first the following clauses in this same passage: §4 *et si quid contusum est . . . si quid in* *mammis ulceris natum. Si quid* is found seventeen times in the text, *si quod* twice. In theory there is a distinction between *si quid* and *si quod* in classical Latin. If the indefinite after *si* is pronominal, *quid* is used. If it is adjectival, it is *quod*. In the masculine *si qui* (originally adjectival) encroaches on *si quis* as a pronominal fairly early, but it is far harder to find definite cases of such encroachment in the neuter (i.e. of *si quod* pronominal for the expected *si quid*). This question is discussed further below, 14.8. The similarity between the first two passages quoted at the start of this note, both with a neuter past participle accompanied by *est* but one with *si quod* and the other with *si quid*, might suggest that in *luxatum si quod est* we have the first attested instance of *si quod* used pronominally, and it is presumably for that reason that some editors have changed to *quid*.

Luxatum can however alternatively be taken as substantival, = 'dislocation', with *quod* therefore adjectival as usual. In technical prose neuter past participles are often substantivised, particularly as pathological terms. For the nominal use of *luxatum* see *TLL* VII.2.1918.43ff., Önnerfors (1956: 24), and for the general phenomenon, Önnerfors (1956: 23–7), Adams (1995a: 320), Langslow (2000: 286–7). Possible early cases of *si quod* for *si quid* are usually open to another explanation. What is interesting here is that in *luxatum si quod est* almost alongside *si quid contusum est* we see the substantivisation of a neuter past participle taking place before our eyes. Such participles were of ambiguous status: they could be treated as either verbal or nominal.

The other instance of *si quod* is similar: 160 *luxum si quod est. Luxum* is the adjective *luxus -a -um* substantivised in the neuter. Cf. later in 160 *ad luxum aut ad fracturam alliga.*

The point should finally be made that *quid* and *quod* are easily confused in manuscripts, where they are abbreviated, and the classical distinction observed in modern editions may in some cases at least have been artificially imposed by editors.

12 aqua calida foueto: this expression occurs in identical form at Pel. 44.2 (Adams 1995a: 637), and is another of the traditional elements maintained for centuries in medical language.

13 et si quid in mammis ulceris natum et: the ellipse of *esse* in subordinate clauses is said to be unusual, but for some examples in *si*-clauses (and some other types of clauses) from e.g. Plautus and Celsus see Hofmann and Szantyr (1965: 421). Goodyear (1972: 350), after a trenchant discussion of the phenomenon in Tacitus (and of literature on the subject), remarked that the 'whole subject of the use of ellipse in Latin literature needs fuller and more intelligent discussion than it has yet received'. This is the only instance in Cato after *si quid*, and it is not impossible that *est* has fallen out before *et*.

14 farinam hordeaceam: *hordeaceus* is the early adjective of material based on *hordeum*. Later there is *hordearius*. There is a good deal of semantic overlap and interchange between different adjectival suffixes in the history of Latin (see e.g. Adams 2013, chapter XXII).

15 ulcera omnia haec sanum faciet: *haec* here is nominative singular. The accusative expression is interesting in several ways. First, the phrase *sanum facere* occurs ten times in this short passage, in every case with the verb in the future, = 'it will make (something) better'. There is reason to suppose that this is the way doctors were thought to express themselves at the time. A character (Charinus) at Plaut. *Merc.* 139 says *resinam ex melle Aegyptiam uorato: saluom feceris* 'swallow Egyptian resin dipped in honey; you will make yourself well'. Here the use of *ex*, the imperative in *-to*, the construction comprising imperative followed by future prediction ('do X – you will achieve Y') of a type that might have been replaced by a conditional sentence (see above, 5.6), and finally the future perfect with *saluom*, a synonym of *sanum*, can all be paralleled in medical texts and suggest that Charinus is parodying doctors' talk (see Langslow 2000: 31). Also relevant is *Men.* 893–4, where a doctor and *senex* are conversing. The old man says that he is hiring the doctor 'to make someone well' (*quin ea te causa duco . . . | . . . illum ut <u>sanum facias</u>*). The doctor predicts, using the future, that he 'will be well' (*sanum futurum*). In our present passage six of the futures of the type *sanum faciet* follow imperatives, as in the first passage of Plautus. Another three follow explicit conditional clauses rather than imperatives, a fact which brings out the equivalence of the imperative type to a conditional clause.

There are in all eighteen instances of *sanum* et sim. *facies/faciet* in the *Agr.*, all of them in 157. There are two further instances of the future passive *sanus fiet* in 157 (8, 9), and two of *sanum fiet* at 161. For *sanus fiet* centuries later see Pel. 15.

Second, there is an absence of agreement between the primary (plural) object of *faciet* (*ulcera omnia*), and the secondary (singular) complement (*sanum*). Elsewhere in the passage there are cases of agreement, as in *sanaque faciet* and *sanosque faciet* earlier. On the other hand at §4 there is an example transitional between the two types: *in ea uulnera huiusce modi teras brassicam: sanum faciet*. Here it is *uulnera* that are to be treated and *sanum* is singular, but there is a strong break between the clause with *uulnera* and that with *sanum*, such that *sanum faciet* has a certain independence. *Sanum faciet* was tending to be treated as an invariant formula, used sometimes as a fixed phrase unadapted to the number of the primary object. There is a good republican parallel in a letter by Pompey: Cic. *Att.* 8.12B.2 *impetrare ut cohortis quae ex Piceno et Camerino uenerunt, quae fortunas suas reliquerunt, ad me missum facias.* Here it is *missum* (with *cohortes*) that is fossilised in the commonplace phrase *missum facere* (for which see below, 28.25-6), in which the participle usually agrees in gender and number with the object (see further Thielmann 1885: 547, Hofmann and Szantyr 1965: 392, Svennung 1935: 264, with a few other parallels). In much later Latin there are cases of a lack of agreement between a past participle associated with *habeo* and the primary object of the verb, as at *Comp. Luc.* S 21 *nos omnia probatum habemus.* This is a vague anticipation of the construction in some Romance varieties, where the noun is treated as direct object of the invariant unit 'have' + participle (see e.g. Adams 2013: 645-6).

16 quod ... neque purgare: a crude and not strictly logical addition. What the substance cannot 'clear' are *ulcera omnia*, but *quod* does not refer to the sores but to the act of making them healthy: strictly the present phrase means that the substance cannot clear the making of the sores healthy. *Neque purgare* is an unconstrued afterthought, a mark of a genre in which literary frills are not usually aspired to. Earlier in the passage (§3) Cato had coordinated *sanum facere* and *purgare* logically (*canceresque purgabit sanosque faciet*), and it is that type of coordinated phrase that lies behind the present careless combination.

17-18 et puero et puellae si ulcus erit: the meaning cannot be 'if there is a sore on both a boy and a girl'. The first *et* is a sentence connective, a usage that recurs throughout the passage (as at the start of the next sentence). The second *et* is used loosely, and is interchangeable with *aut*. There are occasional examples of this use in earlier Latin (see *TLL* V.2.894.30ff., Hofmann and Szantyr 1965: 484, both works with further bibliography).

18 si uoles eam consectam ... esse: literally 'if you shall be willing to eat it' (see below, 5.19 on *esse*), but *uoles esse* resembles a future periphrasis: later in the passage (§7) Cato writes instead *si edes concisam.* See however Pinkster (1985, 1987b) for reservations about such periphrases, the extent of which has been exaggerated. The first clause of the next section throws light on the semantic force of *uoles* (see below, 5.19).

  sale aceto: another asyndeton bimembre (see above, 4.14-15); contrast Eng. 'salt and vinegar'.

19 quo libentius edis: 'so that you may eat it the more willingly'. The substance untreated is unpleasant to eat, a fact which puts *si uoles* above into perspective:

the patient might not <u>be willing</u> to eat it. The idea continues in the last clause of the sentence (*paulo libentius edes*).

Cato's *Agr.* is one of those republican texts in which the normal verb for 'eat' is *edo* rather than the compound *comedo* (for a table showing the relative frequencies see *TLL* V.2.100, though omitting Cato; in Plautus *edo* is preferred by 81:23, in Varro *Rust.* by 11:1; Cicero however has *comedo* thirteen times, *edo* ten, and Terence *comedo* twice, *edo* once; for *edo* much later in Bible translations see 38.53, and see also below, 12 Conclusions). In Cato *edo* outnumbers *comedo* by 23:3 (*comesto* is at 156.1, following *esto* in the same sentence and also earlier in the section, with no obvious semantic difference between simplex and compound; the participle *comestus* is at 50.2, and the alternative and original form *comesus* at 58.1). Cato uses only early forms of the simplex. The subjunctive here and elsewhere (e.g. 53 *quod edint boues, edit* jussive twice at 156.6) is of the *edim, edis* type, whereas the remodelled *edam, edas* is perhaps already at Plaut. *Poen.* 534 (but see the *app. crit.* of the editions of Leo and Lindsay) and in classical Latin (*TLL* V.2.98.72ff.). The infinitive in Cato is *esse* (eight times, including two examples in this passage) rather than *edere*, which does not turn up until much later (*TLL* V.2.99.26ff.).

20 lautam siccam et rutam, coriandrum sectam sale sparsam paulo libentius edes: a problematic passage. *Lautam siccam* agrees with *brassicam*, and the phrase picks up the wording of an earlier sentence (§5), which runs *si uoles eam consectam lautam siccam sale aceto sparsam esse, salubrius nihil est* ('if you are willing to eat it chopped, washed, dried and sprinkled with salt and vinegar, nothing is more health-giving'). The lemma above is translated by the Loeb as: 'and you will like it a little better when washed, dried, and seasoned with rue, chopped coriander and salt'. This rendering bears little resemblance to the Latin, in that the apparent accusatives *rutam* and *coriandrum sectam* seem to be taken as ablatives, complementing *sparsam* ('sprinkled with ...') and coordinated with the real ablative *sale*. Goujard (1975) is closer to the Latin: 'lavé, séché, avec de la rue et de la coriandre, haché, saupoudré de sel, vous le mangerez avec un peu plus d'appétit'. Dalby (1998) seems to have followed Goujard. Literally we might translate: 'you will eat it a little more willingly washed and dried – and rue and chopped coriander sprinkled with salt'.

The curious use of *et* (*rutam* ...) tacking on additional ingredients as if by an expression with *cum* ('you will eat cabbage washed and dried more willingly <u>along with</u> ...') has a parallel later in §7: *si edes concisam et rutam et coriandrum concisam siccam et sirpicium inrasum* ('if you eat it chopped – and rue, chopped dry coriander and grated *sirpicium*'). See also below, 5.28 on the use of *et* in *et intro quae dolitabunt*.

On the face of it in both §§6 and 7 the accusative *coriandrum* is feminine (i.e. from nominative *coriandrus*), since it is followed in the first case by *sectam* and in the second by *concisam siccam*. *Coriandrum* is usually neuter, and the *OLD* does not acknowledge the feminine variant. The *TLL* however (IV.950.70f.) cites these two examples as feminine and adds two examples from later Latin. We have already seen gender variation in Cato, including variation in a plant name (see above, 4.10 on *lupinum*). However, although the feminine might be defensible, there are lingering doubts about the text here (see also Flobert 2011: 245). At the end of 5, quoted near the start of this note, the words *consectam lautam siccam sale ... sparsam* form a long epithet applied to *brassica*, and it would make sense if immediately afterwards Cato had written (again of *brassica*) *lautam siccam sectam sale sparsam, et rutam, coriandrum*. Could it be that the phrase *et rutam, coriandrum* has been misplaced? If we rewrite on this assumption, the feminine instance of *coriandrum* would disappear. At 7 too (see the last paragraph) Cato might have written *si edes concisam siccam et rutam et coriandrum et sirpicium inrasum*. If *concisam siccam* had been misplaced after *coriandrum*, an (adjectival) object of *edes* might have been added (*concisam*). There is thus an element of doubt about these early feminine uses of *coriandrum*.

21 id bene faciet: another generalising use of *id*, referring to a plurality of substances, or possibly to the act of eating.

22 mali nihil sinet in corpore consistere: *malum* here and in the next sentence is substantivised in the neuter, of disease, illness, a widespread usage (see *OLD* s.v. 7b).

23 aluum bonam faciet: a clear instance of the multi-purpose use of the adjective commented on above (4.10); *saluam* might have been expected. In the next section Cato writes *bonum est* of an effective remedy.

24 si quid antea mali intus erit: here Cato uses *intus* in its usual classical static sense, whereas a few sentences later in §7 he uses *intro* in the same way (*intro quae dolitabunt*), though the latter is usually directional ('to within'), as at 157.14. At 157.15 *intro* is again static: *si polypus in naso intro erit*. The confusion of the pair is mentioned as a solecism by Quintilian (1.5.50), but a failure to keep the two apart is sometimes to be seen in literary works, most notably in the use of *intus* in a directional sense. For further details see below, 26.13–14.

25 omnia deducet et sanum faciet: in *omnia* followed by *sanum* we again see the indifference to concord of number in the use of generalising neuters.

26 hanc mane esse oportet ieiunum: Cato has just, it seems, used *id* of the combination of substances he is recommending. His thoughts now turn to cabbage again, and he switches to the feminine *hanc*, even though it must still be the whole mixture that he is referring to. The feminine had last been used at the start of section §6 (*lautam* etc.), and just before that in the previous section. There is little sign of planning or consistency.

27 si lienes turgent: *lien* is the old word in Latin for 'spleen'. *Splen*, a borrowing from Greek, turns up for the first time in Vitruvius (1.4.10), and in most late medical texts becomes the normal term; only *splen* survives in Romance languages (*REW* 8164) (see on the two words André 1991: 155–6). Both Cato and Plautus use *lien* only. The plural here is of note. André (1991: 155) rejects the remark of Ernout and Meillet (1959 s.v.) that *lien* was used also in the plural, asserting that 'ce pluriel s'applique toujours à un ensemble de personnes ou d'animaux'. But our passage shows that Ernout and Meillet were right. The plural here is in a generalising context in which the singular is otherwise used of body parts that do not come in pairs: thus *cor* and *iecur* in the same sentence, alongside *pulmones* of the (two) lungs, and *praecordia*, which is normal in the plural. We must look for another motivation of the plural here, and it is undoubtedly the fact that internal organs that were little understood were sometimes expressed in the plural even if strictly there was only one of them: see below, 6.29, and also index, 'plural for singular, of anatomical terms'.

28 et intro quae dolitabunt: if it will cure, 'in a word', everything (*omnia*), *omnia* would embrace internal pains as well, and there is no need for this clause. *Et* rather crudely introduces an afterthought. If the transmitted text is kept at the start of §6 above (*et rutam, coriandrum*), there we would have much the same use of *et*.

On the meaning of *intro* see above, 5.24.

This is the only instance of the frequentative *dolito* cited by the *TLL* from its entire corpus. Frequentatives are very common in Plautus but recessive in Terence (see Hofmann and Szantyr 1965: 297). Some others listed by Wölfflin (1887b: 205) from Cato are *accessito, dato, disserto* and *esito* (see *OLD* s.vv.; most are from the fragmentary works, but *esito* is at *Agr.* 157.10, where it seems to have full frequentative force). Most of these words are shared with Plautus. Another is *uecto* (10.1, also of habitual action). Here the frequentative presumably refers to chronic pain.

29 eodem: adverbial, 'to/in the same place', several times used by Cato in recipes.

30 nam: I take this to be transitional to a new subject (*OLD* s.v. 4).

31 ubi ex multo cibo aluus non it: *TLL* V.2.644.5ff. (s.v. *eo*) cites this passage under the vague heading 'de cibis in corpus ingestis'. The *OLD* s.v. *aluus* 2b gives as one meaning of the noun 'the bowels or their excremental contents', citing as an example Hor. *Sat.* 2.4.27 *si dura morabitur aluus* ('if hard bowel contents shall delay'). Bowel contents that do not 'delay', 'go'. Thus at *Agr.* 156.4 there is a euphemistic use of *ibit* without an expressed subject: *postea ubi deorsum uersus ibit* ('afterwards, when it (the bowel contents) shall go down', i.e. 'be evacuated). In the next sentence Cato writes *si amplius ibit* ('if it (the bowel contents) shall go too freely'). In our context the bowel contents arising from abundance of food 'do not go' (for the general meaning 'depart' see *OLD* s.v. *eo* 4). In this idiom it is not only faeces that 'go', but also urine: *Agr.* 156.7 *quibus aegre lotium it*. There is obviously an idiomatic use of *ire* here, of excretion of one sort or the other, with the subject of the verb either expressed or unexpressed. The other examples quoted by the *TLL* cited above from a few other writers are not really of the same type: they do not denote excreta exiting the body. Do we have here an ephemeral idiom, or one that belonged mainly to speech?

32 id ut te moneo: another vague use of *id*, 'as I instruct you in that matter', i.e. in the use of cabbage.

33 nihil istorum usu ueniet morbis: a puzzling clause, mainly because of the presence of *morbis*. How is it to be construed? According to Kühner and Stegmann (1955: I.345) *usu uenit* means the same as *accidit*, 'happens', i.e. 'turns out through experiencing'. Cf. *OLD* s.v. *usus* 8a, 'To occur in one's experience'. A crucial phrase here is *nihil istorum* 'none of these' (for the phrase, in direct speech, see Cic. *De orat.* 2.287). What does it refer to? The whole preceding section, which begins with the transitional *nam*, is about overeating. The veins get puffed up and cannot breathe, and the bowels do not move. This may lead to disease (*inde aliqui morbus nascitur*). Not, however, if you use Cato's cabbage recipes. *Nihil istorum* must surely refer to these various manifestations of overeating, and the desired meaning would be something like 'none of these things, such as inflated veins and motionless bowels, will lead to disease'. That is how Goujard (1975) translates: 'ces excès n'entraineront aucune maladie' (note 'ces excès', these excesses). The excesses can be stopped in their tracks and not cause disease, if you follow Cato's instructions. Dalby (1998) is similar: 'you will develop no illness from overeating'. Such renderings pay no attention to the syntax of the Latin, and the problem of *morbis*. The Loeb version is even vaguer ('you will have no ill effects from these').

How can *usu ueniet morbis* be made to mean something like 'will (not) lead to diseases'? One possibility that I have considered is that the idiom *usu ueniet* 'will turn out, happen' has had its elements relexicalised: thus 'will turn out in the experiencing of diseases' (i.e. 'will result in diseases'), with *morbis* an ablative dependent on *usus*, a noun of a verbal root that governs the ablative. So it is that in the similar phrase *usus uenit*, which means 'the need arises', *usus* may be construed with an ablative of the thing required (see *OLD* s.v. *usus* 13b). But *usu uenire* is very definitely a fixed phrase with a clear meaning, and it seems far-fetched to break it up like this, and it is by no means clear that it could really convey the meaning just proposed. The only other possibility (apart from emendation of the text) is to take *morbis* as a causal ablative or ablative of source: 'none of these things will happen as a result of diseases' (i.e. you may suffer inflated veins and bowel troubles from overeating, but not from diseases if you eat cabbage). I am grateful to Wolfgang de Melo for help with this note.

Another oddity of this passage is *istorum*. It is not clear what exactly it refers to, and it is not in the manner of Cato to use the pronoun in this way.

34–5 nulla res tam purgat: the same phrase is at 157.12: *nulla res tam bene purgabit*. *Nulla res* is quite widespread for *nihil*, having the advantage that it offered the full range of oblique case endings (note particularly the alternations at Cic. *Mur.* 61 below). See e.g. Plaut. *Amph.* 728 *nulla res tam delirantis homines concinnat cito*, Mil. 802 *nisi adulterio studiosus rei nullae aliae* ('except for adultery (he is) interested in no other thing'; for dative of *nihil aliud*), Most. 1094 *nullam rem sapis* (cf. *Bacch.* 820 *iam nil sapit*), Stich. 720 *nulli rei erimus postea* ('we will be fit for nothing afterwards'), Pac. 272 Schierl *nulla res | nec cicurare neque mederi potis est*, Cato, *FRH* II.5.F153 *qui tantisper nulli rei sies, dum nihil agas*, Coelius Antipater, *FRH* II.15.F35 *nullius alius rei nisi amicitiae eorum causa*, Publil. *Sent.* 570 *rei nulli prodest mora nisi iracundiae*, Lucr. 1.304 *tangere . . . nulla potest res*, Cic. *Mur.* 61 *sapientem nihil opinari, nullius rei paenitere, nulla in re falli, sententiam mutare numquam*, *Tusc.* 1.43 *in quo nulla re egens aletur*, 1.47 *cum autem nihil erit praeter animum, nulla res obiecta inpediet*, Sen. *Epist.* 12.2 *in nulla re cessare curam tuam*. Also worth mention is Tert. *Anim.* 25.2 *nulla interest*, where *re* may be understood. It is not clear what motivates the occasional uses of the phrase in the nominative and accusative. In Lucretius *nulla potest res* (for which see above, 1.304) is a quasi-formulaic line ending (cf. 1.443, 1.485, and compare the metrically identical *nulla daret* *res* at 1.339), but he also has more complex examples, as at 1.773 *nulla tibi ex illis poterit res esse creata*. I am grateful to Marijke Ottink of the *TLL* and Costas Panayotakis for information used here.

35 ex aceto oxymeli: the cabbage is to be eaten 'out of', i.e. 'with' vinegar mixed with honey. For this use of *ex*, which is well attested in technical texts, see Adams (1995a: 438–9). Cf. Plaut. *Merc.* 139 *resinam ex melle Aegyptiam uorato* (on which passage see above, 5.6, 5.15).

Oxymeli is a noun not an adjective (*TLL* IX.2.1209.73ff.), indicating a mixture of vinegar and honey. *TLL* 1210.56f. notes that it has been deleted here as a gloss, 'vix recte': 'tamquam glossema delevit Boscherini, Atene e Roma 4, 1959, 152 and. 4'. If the text is sound we might have a disjunctive asyndeton bimembre ('vinegar, or vinegar mixed with honey'; cf. 103 *quarto quinto quoque die* 'every fourth or fifth day: usually later a disjunctive particle is added in phrases of this type: Wölfflin and Miodoński 1889: 78; for examples of disjunctive asyndeton see e.g. Kühner and Stegmann 1955: II.151, 152). That however is unlikely. If the substance is to be made more palatable pure vinegar would not serve the purpose as one of two possible additives. Earlier, at 6, so that the patient may take something 'more willingly', Cato instructs *aceto mulso spargito*. In this phrase *mulsus* is an adjective meaning 'mixed with honey' (*OLD* s.v.), and similarly in our passage Cato must mean that the cabbage is to be treated with the type of vinegar that is mixed with honey, with *oxymeli* specifying *aceto*.

But what type of specification would this be? *Oxymeli* must be in apposition to *aceto*, a type of apposition in which the second noun has an adjectival role (see Hofmann and Szantyr 1965: 157–8 on 'adjectivising' of nouns). Examples include *lupus femina* 'wolf that is a female' and *lapis silex* 'stone that is flint, flintstone'. The latter is in Cato himself (18.3 *inibi lapides silices*) and also at Plaut. *Poen.* 290 *lapidem silicem*. The meaning here would be 'vinegar that is the honeyed type', and the phrase a variant of the earlier *aceto mulso*. Another possible instance is in the legal phrase *damnum iniuria*, which can be interpreted as meaning 'loss that is a wrongdoing' (as distinct e.g. from a chance loss) (for a full discussion of this phrase with the evidence, though offering a different interpretation of the syntax from that here, see Rodger 2006). See further index, 'apposition, partitive/specifying/defining'.

Conclusions

The whole of chapter 157 and a few other parts of the *Agr.* are our first specimen of 'medical Latin'. Four of the usages seen here (the conditional imperative, the use of the imperative in *-to*, the formula 'it will make it well' and the use of *ex* commented on at 5.35) are all in the short piece of Plautus (*Merc.* 139) that seems to parody doctors' talk. Many of the features here became entrenched in medical prose and persisted for centuries (on such continuity see in general Adams 1995a: 635–9), and it is to be assumed that they were already current in discussion of illness. This list will bring out their sheer extent: *ad* + disease names, iteration of compound by simplex, substantivisation in the neuter of adjectives and perfect participles, the formula *sanum faciet* (or the like), the pattern *uerum prius . . . lauato*, the conditional imperative, the use of *ater* with *bilis*, the expression *aqua calida foueto*.

On the other hand there is an informality to the language, marked by afterthoughts, careless or illogical forms of expression, violations of concord and the odd low-register usage that was to continue (in speech, mainly) and survive into Romance. Throughout the passage and also elsewhere in the work the neuter anaphoric pronoun *id* is used in a generalising sense with indifference to the number and gender of its antecedent(s). Such lack of concord is particularly striking in the case of the expression *sanum facere* (where *sanum* is neuter) used when the primary object of *facere* is plural. Much later a very similar type of discord turns up in the Romance perfect construction in which the participle associated with the reflex of *habeo* is not in agreement with the object of *habeo*. Marked carelessness of expression is to be seen in the afterthought *quod . . . neque purgare*. Other afterthoughts are tacked on by *et*. Of low-register usages, notable are the employment of *subtus* for *subter* (rare in republican Latin but surviving into Romance), of *subtus* preceding redundantly the preposition *sub*, of *intro* with the same sense as *intus* nearby, and probably of *it* as an excretory euphemism. The conditional imperative also continued into Romance. We noted too that in certain types of temporal expressions Cato has a predilection for prepositions over plain cases. This is loosely anticipatory of things to come, but is only the beginning (in the historical period) of the competition between prepositions and bare inflections.

This is also a specimen of early Latin, and some features are suggestive of its date (the varied use of *ater, lien* for *splen* and *edo* for *comedo*, with retention of the early inflections).

It was noted at the start that Dalby (1998) has suggested that 157 was not written by Cato himself. That view is not entirely borne out by the Commentary above. Numerous usages commented on here also occur elsewhere in the work: compound–simplex iteration (see 5.1), the neuter pronoun *id* showing lack of concord with its antecedent (5.5), pronominal resumption (5.7–8), *subtus* instead of CL *subter* (5.8), forms of *edo* (5.19), *bonus* as a multi-purpose term (5.23), and specifying apposition (5.35). On the other hand *sanum facere* occurs only (and repeatedly) in this chapter (5.15), but then the chapter has a special subject (medical treatment), and is much the longest section of its kind in the work. Another oddity is the clause *nihil istorum usu ueniet morbis*, which is hard to understand in the context and is not in the style of Cato. It is possible that the material of the chapter comes from some outside source (like for example the religious chapters), but if so it had in the source, or has been given, for the most part early Latin and Catonian features.

6

ONE OF THE JOHNS HOPKINS *DEFIXIONES* ('PLOTIUS'), OF REPUBLICAN DATE (*c.* 100 BC?)

Introduction

The Johns Hopkins *defixiones* consist of five lead tablets, each cursing an individual (Plotius, Avonia, Maxima Vesonia, Aquila and an unknown man). The texts are fragmentary but clearly contained the same phraseology, and can be supplemented from one another to establish a composite text. The *defixiones* were acquired by the Department of Classical Archaeology, Johns Hopkins University in 1908. At the time their provenance was uncertain, but they were thought to be Roman. As Sherwood Fox (1912: 11) put it, '[t]he person through whom the acquisition was made possible was unable to give a definite assurance as to their provenience, but stated his belief that they had been found at Rome'. Later in the same piece (55–7) Sherwood Fox advanced arguments in favour of a Roman origin for the texts. Confirmation of this view was forthcoming more than ten years later. Vetter (1923: 65) revealed that two years before the acquisition of the tablets by Johns Hopkins University they had been seen and (partly) read by his friend R. Egger while they were in the possession of a dealer in antiquities in Rome. The dealer revealed that they had been discovered just outside the porta Salaria.

The date of the tablets is thought to be first century BC (for collections of opinions see Petersmann 1973: 79 with footnotes). Evidence for their comparatively early date will be collected in the Conclusions.

For texts of 'Plotius' and others see Sherwood Fox (1912), Warmington (1940: 280–4), Ernout (1957a) 140A ('Avonia'), Kropp (2008a) 1.4.4/8–4/12 (the full corpus). See too *CIL* I².2520 (a composite text derived from the whole corpus), with *CIL* I² fasc. 4, p. 967 (with bibliography). The text printed here is taken from Warmington (1940: 280–4) and Kropp (2008) 1.4.4/8. The gaps have been filled from other texts in the corpus, for which see Kropp (2008a) 1.4.4/8–4/12. See further Vendryes (1912), Kroll (1915), Lazzeroni (1962), Petersmann (1973), Adams (2007: 444–51). The text is punctuated with very regular interpuncta, which are not presented here because editors usually omit them.

Text

bona pulchra Proserpina, [P]lut[o]nis uxsor,
seiue me Saluiam deicere oportet,
eripias salutem, c[orpus, co]lorem, uires, uirtutes
Ploti. tradas [Plutoni] uiro tuo. ni possit cogitationibus
sueis hoc uita[re. tradas] illunc   5
febri quartan[a]e, t[ertian]ae, cottidia[n]ae,
quas [cum illo l]uct[ent, deluctent; illunc]
eu[in]cant, [uincant], usq[ue dum animam
eiu]s eripia[nt. quare ha]nc uictimam
tibi trad[o, Prose]rpi[na, seiu]e me,   10
Proserpin[a, sei]ue m[e Ach]eruosiam dicere
oportet. m[e mittas a]rcessitum canem
tricepitem, qui [Ploti] cor eripiat. polliciarus
illi te daturum t[r]es uictimas –
palma[s, ca]rica[s], por[c]um nigrum –   15
hoc sei pe[rfe]cerit [ante mensem]
M[artium. haec, P]r[oserpina Saluia, tibi dabo]
cum compote fe[cer]is. do tibi cap[ut]
Ploti Auon[iae. Pr]oserpina S[aluia],
do tibi fron[tem Plo]ti. Proserpina Saluia,   20
do [ti]b[i] su[percilia Ploti. Proserpin[a]
Saluia, do [tibi palpebra]s Plo[ti].
Proserpina Sa[luia, do tibi pupillas]
Ploti. Proser[pina Saluia, do tibi nare]s,
labra, or[iculas, nasu]m, lin[g]uam,   25
dentes P[loti], ni dicere possit
Plotius quid [sibi dole]at: collum, umeros,
bracchia, d[i]git[os, ni po]ssit aliquit
se adiutare: [pe]c[tus, io]cinera, cor,
pulmones, n[i possit] senti(re; text *qu*: see Kropp) quit   30
sibi doleat: [intes]tina, uenter, um[b]licu[s],
latera, [n]i p[oss]it dormire: scapulas,
ni poss[it] s[a]nus dormire: uiscum
sacrum, nei possit urinam facere:
natis, anum, [fem]ina, genua,   35
[crura], tibias, pe[des, talos, plantas,
digito]s, ungis, ni po[ssit s]tare [sua
ui]rt[u]te. seiue [plu]s, seiue paruum

scrip[tum fuerit], quomodo quicqu[id]
legitim[e scripsit], mandauit, seic   40
ego Ploti(um) ti[bi tr]ado, mando,
ut tradas, [mandes me]nse Februari[o
e]cillunc. mal[e perdat, mal]e exset,
[mal]e disperd[at. mandes, tra]das, ni possit
[ampliu]s ullum [mensem aspic]ere,   45
[uidere, contempla]re.

Translation

Proserpina good and beautiful, wife of Pluto (or if I should call you Salvia), snatch away the health of Plotius, his body and complexion, his strength and manly qualities. Hand him over to Pluto your husband. Let him not be able to avoid this by his designs. Hand him over to a quartan fever, a tertian fever, a daily fever, which may wrestle, wrestle utterly with him and utterly overwhelm, overwhelm him until they snatch away his life. Therefore I consign this victim to you, Proserpina, unless, Proserpina, unless I should call you Acherusian. Send me to summon the three-headed dog, so that he may snatch away the heart of Plotius. Promise that you will give him three offerings, dates, dried figs and a black pig, if he has carried this out before the month of March. These, Proserpina Salvia, I will give you when you have made me possessor of my wish. I give you the head of Plotius, slave of Avonia. Proserpina Salvia, I give you the forehead of Plotius. Proserpina Salvia, I give you the eyebrows of Plotius. Proserpina Salvia, I give you the eyelids of Plotius. Proserpina Salvia, I give you the pupils of the eyes of Plotius. Proserpina Salvia, I give you the nostrils, lips, ears, nose, tongue and teeth of Plotius, so that Plotius cannot say what gives him pain; his neck, shoulders, arms, fingers, so that he cannot help himself at all; his chest, liver, heart, lungs, so that he cannot feel what gives him pain; his intestines, belly, navel, sides, so that he cannot sleep; his shoulder blades, so that he cannot sleep soundly; his sacred vital part, so that he cannot urinate; his buttocks, anus, thighs, knees, legs, shins, feet, ankles, soles, toes, nails, so that he cannot stand by his own effort. Whether more has been written or but little (by him as a curse) – whatever he has written (and however he has done it) and committed to writing as prescribed by the laws (of magic), in such a way I hand over and offer up Plotius to you, so that you may hand over and offer that very person in the month of February. Let him be properly ruined, let him properly depart this life, let him be properly and utterly ruined. Offer him up and hand him over, so that he cannot observe, see or contemplate any month further.

Commentary

1 bona pulchra: for asyndeton bimembre in religious formulae and the like (curse tablets are both quasi-religious and quasi-legal) cf. e.g. *Iuppiter optimus maximus*, and see Skutsch (1985: 233) on the augural expression *pulc(h)er praepes* at e.g. Enn. *Ann.* 86, and also above, 4.14–15 for *uolens propitius* in prayers in Cato. For *pulcher* associated with *bonus* (or *melior, optimus*) see *TLL* X.2.2565.15f. and particularly 2569.1f., citing also *CIL* VI.32328.8 *bone pulch<er> Apo<llo>*. For a similar asyndeton in the same type of context note the second *defixio* from the sanctuary of Isis at Mainz (Blänsdorf 2010a: 166) *bone sancte Atthis Tyranne, adsi(s), aduenias*; also *CIL* XIII.11340.1 *bona santa nomen pia nomen* (Kropp 2008a, 4.1.3/15). For asyndeton bimembre as a marked feature of curse tablets see below, 19.6–7.

2 seiue, deicere: *ei* is often written in this text where it is etymologically justified, but not with complete consistency. Cf. 5 *sueis*, 16 *sei*, 34 *nei*, 38 *seiue* twice, 40 *seic*, but on the other hand 11 *dicere*, 14 *illi*, 26, 33, 37 *ni*. This attempt to preserve *ei* seems to have persisted until the Augustan period. It shows up, for example, in the Gallus papyrus (see Somerville 2007, and, for the text, Anderson, Parsons and Nisbet 1979) and in the letter from Oxyrhynchus (below, 14.5, 14.6, though in the latter case as a false archaism), with some hypercorrection and inconsistency (for example, in the Gallus papyrus alongside correct forms such as *spolieis, tueis* and *deicere* there is also *mihi* for *mihei*), and then it tended to fade. There is a gradual change from the first century BC through to the end of the first century AD visible in various official and formal inscriptions (see on 14.6 for the distinction between etymologically correct and incorrect uses of the digraph, and the rule of Lucilius).

For example, in four late republican documents, the *Lex Cornelia de XX quaestoribus*, the *Lex Tarentina*, the *Lex Antonia de Termessibus* and the *Tabula Heracleensis* (all of these texts may be found in Crawford 1996), *ei* is written constantly, if not consistently. In the Augustan period or thereabouts, however, while there are some documents with frequent or less common use of *ei*, others do not have it at all. The former group includes the two texts mentioned in the previous paragraph, the *Laudatio Murdiae* (*CIL* VI.10230, *ILS* 8394), the second of the so-called *Decreta Pisana* (*CIL* XI.1421, *ILS* 140; for these two inscriptions from Pisa see also Marotta D'Agata 1980) and the *Res gestae* (Scheid 2007), though in this last there are only three examples of *ei*, in dative/ablative plural endings, against numerous instances of *i*. The latter group (without *ei*) includes the *Laudatio Turiae* (*ILS* 8393), the first of the

Decreta Pisana (*CIL* XI.1429, *ILS* 139) and the *Lex Libitina Puteolana* (see for the text Hinand and Dumont 2003; the date is disputed but may be Augustan). If we move to the early post-Augustan period it is not hard to find documents without (or virtually without) *ei*: e.g. the *S. C. de Cn. Pisone patre* (see Eck, Caballos and Fernández 1996), the *Tabula Siarensis* (see Crawford 1996: I.509, 515–18) and the archive of the Sulpicii (*TPSulp.*: see Camodeca 1999). In the last *ei* has been dropped completely, but I longa is constant (see below, 15 Commentary, 'preliminaries'). From various later imperial texts *ei* is also absent: e.g. Claudius' speech of AD 48 recorded in the Lyons inscription (*CIL* XIII.1668), the *Lex coloniae Genetiuae* (of Caesarian date but engraved in the Flavian period: Crawford 1996: I.395), the *Lex de imperio Vespasiani* (Crawford 1996: I.549–53) and the *Lex Irnitana* (copy edited by González 1986), a text of the time of Domitian.

3 salutem, c[orpus, co]lorem, uires, uirtutes: in a long list of terms without connectives there may be asyndetic pairs (e.g. Cic. *Ac.* 2.92 *diues pauper, clarus obscurus sit, multa pauca, magna parua, longa breuia, lata angusta*, with six pairs of opposites, *Orat.* 131 *sed est faciendum etiam ut irascatur iudex mitigetur, inuideat faueat, contemnat admiretur, oderit diligat, cupiat fastidiat, speret metuat, laetetur doleat*, with opposites again, *Phil.* 11.2 *inuisitatum inauditum, ferum barbarum*, this time with pairs of synonyms, Ulp. *Dig.* 2.4.4.1 *liberos parentes, patroni patronae*, here with pairs of complementary terms, from the praetor's edict; cf. Sall. *Cat.* 52.5 *domos uillas, signa tabulas uostras*), and that appears to be the case here. After the initial general term *salutem* there are two pairs that share alliteration. *Vis* and *uirtus* are often combined, though usually with a connective (see Wölfflin 1933: 280, citing e.g. Plaut. *Amph.* 191 and passages from Cicero, Livy and Tacitus). Cf. *defixio* 11 from the sanctuary of Isis at Mainz (Blänsdorf 2010a: 177–8), containing a list with two pairs of alliterative asyndeta: *mentem memoriam cor cogitatum*. Alliterative pairs also occur in Oscan curse tablets (note Rix 2002: 117, Cm 13 **fakinss.fangvam biass.biítam**). See also index, 'asyndeton bimembre', with the entries for alliteration.

4 Ploti: the name has the *o*-form rather than the diphthong *au* throughout this text, which is suggestive of popular or informal speech. In personal names *o*-forms are particularly common: cf. e.g. *Olus, Clodius, Pol(l)a, Plotia* (see Leumann 1977: 72). Names (and titles) belong loosely in the category of address terms, and such terms may be susceptible to popular phonetic developments. Campanile ([1971] 2008: I.357–8) draws attention to an oscillation in the form of a related name as possessed by a single person. At *CIL* I^2.2055 on the lid of an urn there is the naming formula *L. Pomponius L. f. Arsniae gnatus*

Plautus, whereas the side of the urn has *L. Pomponius L. f. Plotus*. Both forms of a name could be used of the same person, with the monophthongal form probably suited to casual speech (see Campanile 2008: I.358, Adams 2013: 86). On the other hand there were writers who made an effort to use the 'correct' form of a personal name (see Adams 1994: 103; see also below, 21.14).

ni possit: this is not the conditional use of *ni* (< *nei*) familiar from classical Latin but an early use equivalent to *nē* 'lest'. It is a usage that occurs throughout this text (26, 33, 37, 44), and once has the earlier form *nei* (34). See Ernout and Meillet (1959: 433) s.v. *ni*, citing e.g. *S. C. Bac.* (*CIL* I².581 *neiquis eorum Bacanal habuise uelet*), and particularly *OLD* s.v. *ni* 1–3, with examples from early Latin, including Plautus, Cato and laws.

5 illunc: the reinforced form of *ille* (with the deictic particle -*c(e)*) had a distinctive history in Latin (we saw the word above, 2.21–2, and for full details of the material in this note, Adams 2013: 454–9). In Plautus *illic* (*illaec* etc.) occurs about 200 times and in Terence about fifteen. Then there are a few attestations in literary texts before the late republican period (see *TLL* VII.1.370.29ff.: writers listed with an example or two include Livius Andronicus, Ennius, Naevius, Pacuvius, Turpilius, Lutatius Catulus, Catullus, Lucretius and the archaiser Gellius). Lutatius Catulus committed suicide in 87 BC, and Lucretius died in 55 and Catullus in about 54. *Illic* does not turn up in any form in Cicero. There are five occurrences in Varro, which are restricted to formulae of sale (*TLL* 370.31), in all of which the original final -*e* is preserved (e.g. *Rust.* 2.2.5 *illasce oues, qua de re agitur, sanas recte esse ...*). This expression is described by Varro as a *prisca formula*. The reinforced pronoun thus disappeared from the literary language by about the middle of the first century BC. It must however have maintained a currency in informal spoken varieties, as it turns up in the letters of Terentianus (Adams 1977a: 45) and in a Vindolanda tablet (*Tab. Vindol.* 343.19). The example here is consistent with a first-century date, but not decisive proof of such.

In both the 'Avonia' (Kropp 2008a, 1.4.4/10) and 'Vesonia' (Kropp 2008a, 1.4.4/10) the feminine form *illanc* occurs.

The reinforced form *istic* also has an interesting distribution (see above, 3.420, and below, 8.1, 17.3).

7 quas: nominative. For comparable -*as* nominative plurals in pronouns/demonstratives in early Latin see Pomponius 150 Frassinetti *ego quaero quod comedim; has quaerunt quod cacent* (see below, 10.3.3), Cato *Agr.* 134.1 *prius quam hasce fruges condantur*, *CIL* I².2685 *hasc(e) mag(istr-) V(eneri) d(onum) d(ant)* (possibly first half of the first century BC, from Minturnae: see Petersmann 1973: 78). For a collection of the epigraphic and literary evidence for such forms see Bakkum (1994: 35–6); also Adams (2003a: 118–19). The origin of these forms remains uncertain. Vendryes (1912: 206, 208) found in the example in this text a provincial or even 'Marsian' feature, in keeping with a tradition of interpreting the language of the text as dialectal (see also Lazzeroni 1962: 116, 117, opting for Campanian, and Petersmann 1973: 88, referring to southern Italian).

In nouns -*as* nominatives are attested from Pomponius onwards (140 Frassinetti *quot laetitias insperatas modo mi inrepsere in sinum*; this example is however open to another interpretation: see below) throughout the Empire in inscriptions from many areas (see Adams 2007: 674–5, with bibliography, and particularly now Galdi 2012; note too *CIL* I^2.1342 (Tibur) *L. l. Naepori Nicephor fullo [liber]ti et libertas [D]iomedei [liber]ti et libertas*, on which see Petersmann 1973: 79; thought to be republican on the evidence of the name *Naepor*, a type regarded as obsolete by the Empire: see Quint. 1.4.26). The -*as* form may be reflected in some Romance varieties (see e.g. Elcock 1960: 62–4, Väänänen 1981a: 108), but there is not agreement on this point (see e.g. Herman 1997, Penny 2002: 118, Maiden 2011: 164, Sornicola 2011: 27–8).

Since the nominal nominative plural in the feminine declension in Oscan and Umbrian was the inherited -*as* (Buck 1904: 113), early nominative examples in -*as* in nouns (such as that above in Pomponius, a writer of Atellan farce, a genre with an Oscan origin) have tended to be seen as Italic-influenced and dialectal. The ending might possibly have been imported into regional varieties of Latin from another Italic language. If so, what those varieties might have been does not emerge from the patchy evidence. Moreover these *s*-plurals are better attested in the Republic in pronouns than nouns, and it is from that fact that any explanation proposed should have its starting point (see Bakkum 1994: 37 for this point). Another uncertainty hanging over nominal examples is that they tend to be open to special explanations. The passage of Pomponius (140) may have a conflated construction, with the accusatives exclamatory. See also Adams (2007: 444), explaining otherwise (as attractio inversa) a supposed case at *TPSulp.* 83 (*purpuras laconicas reliquas quas* ...), which is taken by Calboli (2006: 167) as a sure manifestation of 'l'influence des dialectes italiques'. The -*as* nominatives, pronominal and nominal, seem to have had a non-standard profile, but their precise character, social and regional, in the Republic remains obscure. Galdi's paper (2012) discusses the various theories, and in a review of the imperial evidence stresses the low level of correctness of many of the documents containing the form. On the other hand in the very late period in some texts from Gaul written correctly the ending -*as* is the standard form, or at least notably common (see Vielliard 1927: 109, Pei 1932: 137–8; see also below, 44 Conclusions, 49.12, 50.24).

l]uct[ent, deluctent: both *luctent* and the compound *deluctent* are confirmed by other tablets in the corpus (Kropp 2008a, 1.4.4/10, 11). In curse tablets in asyndeton bimembre a simplex may be followed by an intensifying compound of the same (or different) root (note on the one hand Audollent 1904, no. 250 *obliges perobliges* and on the other hand Audollent no. 140 *uince peroccide*). Cf. e.g. Plaut. *Amph.* 551 *sequor subsequor*, Ter. *Eun.* 962 *dico edico*, Cic. *Verr.* 3.155 *caede concide*, Kropp (2008a) 11.1.1/5 *ligo o<b>ligo*, 11.1.1/13 *uratur … aduratur*.

Luctor is usually a deponent verb, but for republican instances in the active see e.g. Enn. *Ann.* 298 Skutsch (with Skutsch 1985: 476 ad loc.), Ter. *Hec.* 829, Varro *Ling.* 5.61 (with *TLL* VII.2.1730.25ff.). Whereas later such active variants may be of low register (see e.g. 26.5 *obliscere*), in early Latin they are relatively numerous and found in genres of differing stylistic levels (see 3.424). See further below, 6.46 on *contemplare*.

8 eu[in]cant, [uincant]: again this juxtaposition of compound and simplex can be confirmed from elsewhere in the corpus (see Kropp 2008a, 1.4.4/9). Here the order of the two (with the compound preceding) is different, and we might seem to have the old pattern showing iteration of a compound by its simplex (see above, 5.1), a pattern that reflects the operation of the preverb on more than one verb following. For this pairing cf. Manil. 3.63 *euincunt stellas nec non uincuntur et ipsa* (cited by Wills 1996: 442). The motivation of the repetition in a curse tablet can only be intensification, which was occasionally achieved with the compound preceding rather than following. Note Plaut. *Merc.* 681 *disperii, perii misera* = Ter. *Haut.* 404, Pacuvius frg. 199.8 Schierl *retinete, tenete*, Ter. *Eun.* 377 *abduc, duc* (see Lindholm 1931: 85, Renehan 1977: 244, Wills 1996: 443, Schierl 2006: 414; Lindholm and Schierl also cite parallels from Greek).

12 m[e mittas a]rcessitum canem | tricepitem: *arcessitum* is a supine of purpose. There are at least nine constructions expressing purpose used as complements of verbs of motion or of *mitto* in Latin (for a classification see Cabrillana 2011: 23–8): (1) the supine of purpose, (2) *ad* + gerund(ive), (3) *ut* + subjunctive, (4) the future participle (sometimes accompanied by *ut, quasi* or *tamquam*), (5) the present participle, (6) *qui* + subjunctive, (7) the dative of the gerundive, (8) the infinitive, and (9) *ad* + verbal noun. A number of these will come up in the Commentaries that follow (see index, 'verbs of motion', with cross-references), and they have a good deal of interest, because usage changed over time. See Adams and Vincent (forthcoming b).

In early Latin (Plautus and Terence) the supine is the most common construction expressing purpose with verbs of motion. For example, with the two verbs *uenio* and *eo* the supine is found seventy-five times in Plautus and ten times in Terence (for Plautus see Lodge 1924–33: I.504, II.838, and for Terence McGlynn 1963–7: I.165–6, II.264; both works conveniently classify purpose complements with these verbs). Plautus has *ut* thirty-eight times, and Terence eleven times (with these verbs). In the two writers there is only one instance (in Plautus) of *ad* + gerund(ive). Plautus has the infinitive seven times, Terence not all. As for other verbs of motion and the like complemented by the supine, Bennett (1910–14: 453–6) lists three and a half pages of examples from early Latin. For *mitto* with the supine see *TLL* VIII.1189.51ff. (with the cross-reference at 51). The combination here is found in early Latin: cf. Plaut. *Stich.* 196 *hic illest parasitus quem arcessitum missa sum*, Ter. *Andr.* 514–15 *missast ancilla ilico | obstetricem accersitum*. Bennett (1910–14: I.455) lists nine instances of *mitto* + supine in Plautus and Terence, and a few others from other early writers.

Later the supine receded (*ad* + gerund(ive), for example, became common by the classical period), but was kept in archaising genres such as historiography. Various banal phrases (*ire cubitum, cacatum* etc.) maintained a currency, and there are still some examples of the construction in classical prose (see Hofmann and Szantyr 1965: 381–2). Some idea of the fading of the supine later is conveyed by the following figures from Tertullian, *Aduersus Marcionem* 4 (a book of about 120 pages). Here there are fourteen instances of the infinitive (but almost all in biblical quotations), twelve of *ad* + gerund(ive), three of *ut* + subjunctive, two of the future participle and three of *ad* + verbal noun. The supine does not occur.

Tricepitem is for *tricipitem*, under the influence of the nominative *triceps*.

m[e mittas: the restoration of the pronoun in this form is based on other tablets in the corpus (Kropp 2008a, 1.4.4/9, 1.4.4/10). The form is interpreted by Warmington (1940: 283 n. 4) as dative (i.e. 'for me send someone to . . .'), an interpretation inspired by Festus p. 152 Lindsay *me pro mihi dicebant antiqui, ut Ennius, cum ait lib. II* [119 Skutsch, but Skutsch 1985: 271 takes it as an ablative] '*si quid me fuerit humanitus, ut teneatis*'; *et Lucilius* [1227]: '*nunc ad te redeo, ut quae res me impendet, agatur*'. See also Varro *Rust.* 3.16.2 *hereditate me cessa* (cited by *OLD* s.v. *ego*; see also below, 39 Introduction). The dative form *me* would be from *mei* (an alternative form for *mi*), with the *e* representing the long close *e* [ẹ] of early Latin (on which see e.g. Adams 2007: 52–64) (see further below, 39.21). Kroll (1915: 364) and Ernout (1957a: 103), however, take *me* to be accusative. Note the latter: it 'désigne la tablette d'exsécration, glissée dans un tombeau, et qui dans la compagnie du mort, descend jusqu'aux enfers'.

13 qui [Ploti] cor eripiat: there is similar phraseology in a curse tablet from Este (Kropp 2008a, 1.7.2/1), which also addresses Proserpina, and in which the victim is handed over *canibus tricipiti[bus] et bicipitibus ut ere[piant] capita capita cogit(ata) cor.*

polliciarus: for *pollice-*, and thus an early example of closing of *e* in hiatus, but unfortunately not precisely datable (see Petersmann 1973: 86, claiming that this is the oldest example of the phenomenon extant). Another early example is at *Lex Latina tabulae Bantinae* 10 *pariat = pareat,* a text dating from the late second century BC (see also Leumann 1977: 46).

The form of the verb is present subjunctive, with the non-classical ending *-rus* for *-re/-ris.* The ending derives from the inherited second person middle (secondary) ending *-so,* with the addition of *-s* from the active and rhotacism. *-so* usually produced *-re* in Latin, which itself acquired the *-s* of the active and became *-ris* by normal vowel weakening (see Sommer 1914: 494, Leumann 1977: 517, Sihler 1995: 475–6). *-rus* has tended to be taken as a dialectal form, non-Roman and southern (see Petersmann 1973: 86–8, with Adams 2007: 445 for some further bibliography), but the evidence for this view is not decisive. Adams (2007: 445–51) collects and discusses thirteen examples (the conjectural fourteenth example may be disregarded). Of the ten inscriptional examples, two are from Egypt, two from Rome, three from Pompeii, and one from one each of Beneventum, Venusia and Dalmatia (Adams 2007: 449–50). It is impossible from such a corpus to generalise about a specific regional character. Almost all examples are relatively early (republican or first century AD) (see Adams 2007: 450), and the presence of the form in this text is another indication of early date. Whatever its possible geographical restriction, it does turn up particularly in informal documents, such as Pompeian graffiti, private letters and texts associated with Latin-speaking Greeks (see Adams 2007: 450). Two of the examples are in letters printed in this anthology (see 13.5, 14.4).

14 te daturum: the addressee (Proserpina) is feminine, and *daturam* would have been the norm in classical Latin. The presence of this non-inflecting future infinitive (regularly used without *esse*) in the text is a guarantee that it is republican, and probably not late republican. This is a usage, the origins of which are disputed (see the bibliography below), that belongs to early Latin, with hardly any traces lingering beyond the middle of the first century BC. It is discussed by Gellius 1.7 in relation to a possible instance of *futurum* for *futuram* at Cic. *Verr.* 5.167 (70 BC), where editors usually print *futuram.*

There is a slightly later example at Varro *Rust.* 1.68 (*descensurum se mini-tantur*), where the neuter plural subject would usually have generated *descen-sura*, but Varro was prone to hold on to earlier usages (see below, 6 Conclusions, and index, 'Varro, Latin of'). Gellius quotes instances from C. Gracchus, Claudius Quadrigarius, Valerius Antias, Plautus and Laberius. See also Lucil. 538, 1045. See further Postgate (1891, 1894), E. Löfstedt (1956: II.11–14), Hofmann and Szantyr (1965: 343), Leumann (1977: 619), Fortson (2007).

15 ca]rica[s]: dried figs, derived from the place name *Caria*: see *TLL Onom.* 188.49ff.

18 compote: accusative, with omission of *-m*.

19 Ploti Auon[iae: 'of Plotius slave of Avonia'. In Plautus there is alternation between the plain genitive and genitive + *seruos* in identifications of slaves. Note on the one hand *Amph.* 378 *Amphitruonis, inquam, Sosia*, 411 *equidem Sosia Amphitruonis sum*, and on the other hand 148 *sed Amphitruonis illi[c] est seruos Sosia*, 394 *Amphitruonis ego sum seruos Sosia*, 403 *non sum ego seruos Amphitruonis Sosia?* Note too *Curc.* 230 *estne hic Palinurus Phaedromi?*, Ter. *Andr.* 357 *forte ibi huius uideo Byrriam.* Nevertheless *seruus* with the genitive is very frequent in Plautus and Terence (see Bennett 1910–14: II.47), and the norm in classical Latin. See the brief remarks of Kühner and Stegmann (1955: I.414), Hofmann and Szantyr (1965: 59–60). Omissions of *seruus* (or *libertus* or comparable words) continue to occur in inscriptions (e.g. *CIL* VI.3985 *Isochrysus Liuiae ad uestem*, 3972 *Syneros Ti. Caesaris ad imagines*). One context in which omission tends to take place is in naming constructions that state more than one relationship; one of the nouns of relationship may be left unexpressed: e.g. Cic. *Att.* 12.20.2 *Cn. Caepio Seruiliae Claudi pater* 'Cn. Caepio, father of Servilia wife of Claudius', *P. Oxy.* II.244 *Ceri[nthus] Antoniae Drusi ser(uus)* 'Cerinthus, slave of Antonia daughter of Drusus'. See further below, 14.11, on *Chio Caesaris* 'to Chius slave of Caesar') in a letter of probable Augustan date, and 21.15–16 on the genitive without *uxor*.

Here the genitive form of the woman's name is restored with the classical *-ae* ending. In other tablets the feminine genitive ending is sometimes *-aes*. The latter is certainly read four times in the same name in the tablet 'Avonia' (Kropp 2008a, 1.4.4/9), and there is another place where the *-s* is read but the rest of the name is missing. In several other places in this tablet the ending is restored as *-ae*, presumably for reasons of space. In the tablet 'Vesonia' (Kropp 2008a, 1.4.4/10) *Vesoniae* occurs six times and *Vesoniaes* once. *Maximae* occurs six times but *Maximaes* never. The alternations suggest that, if the -*aes* form belonged particularly to a certain regional or social dialect, it was not an invariable component of that dialect. There must have been some oscillation between the non-standard and prestige forms. On the distribution and origin of the -*aes* ending (it must have a Grecising -*s* imposed on the Latinate *ae* digraph; sometimes it has the more overtly Greek form -*es*) see Adams (2003a: 479–86, 2007: 673–4), with further bibliography; also Galdi (2004: 19–22), and below, 14.3. It seems to have started in Latin *nomina* possessed by Greeks, who often had a Greek cognomen, but it spread to some extent to areas that were not particularly Greek (there is an example in one of the Vindonissa tablets (3) from Switzerland: see Adams 2007: 674), and also occasionally to common nouns (*TPSulp.* 82 *libertaes*).

25 labra: the neutral term for 'lips' in educated Latin; the various alternatives (*labeae, labia, labella*) are semantically or stylistically special in different ways (see the table at *TLL* VII.2.775 for distributions). However, in another tablet ('Vesonia', Kropp 2008a, 1.4.4/10) the word is feminine plural (*labras*) instead of neuter. No other early examples of the gender change in this word are noted at *TLL* VII.2.809.49ff., but the general phenomenon (feminine plural for neuter plural) is common in early Latin, and also in curse tablets. Such feminine plurals in early Latin are *armentae* (Perrot 1961: 301), *caementae* (Perrot 1961: 302), *lamentae* (Perrot 1961: 302), *aruae* (Perrot 1961: 304), *fulmentae* (Perrot 1961: 302) and *neruiae* (Varro *Men.* 366; see Perrot 1961: 307); on these terms see also Adams (2013: 406–7). There are also *labeae* = *labia*, which is Plautine (*Stich.* 723: see Adams 2013: 398–9 on this form and its use), and *horreae*, quoted by Nonius p. 307 Lindsay from a speech of Calidius *in Quintum Gallium*. For curse tablets see Jeanneret (1918: 83), citing (apart from *labras*) *bracias, labias, neruias* and *itestinas*. The alternation of form from one tablet to another illustrates the fact that lower social dialects do not have rigidly fixed components; non-standard forms are not necessarily used all the time.

or[iculas: if the reading is right the diminutive is without diminutive force and is used as a standard term for the ears. See below, 7.13, and index, s.v. *auricula*.

28 aliquit, 30 quit: in both cases the voiceless final stop precedes a voiceless consonant at the start of the next word. See further below, 14.6, 22.16.

29 adiutare: the distribution of this frequentative of *adiuuare* shows that it belonged mainly to informal style and lower sociolects after the early period (Adams 1977a: 80). In early Latin it is found in Plautus and Terence but also in tragedy (Accius *trag.* 103), and then later in Lucretius (1.812). It is however only once in Cicero, in a letter (*Ep.* frg. 11(10).3). In Petronius it occurs only in a freedman's speech (62.11) whereas *adiuuo* occurs five times elsewhere in the work. The letters of Terentianus have *a(d)iuto* twice (*P. Mich.* VIII.468.41, 471.28: see below, 22.28) but *adiuuo* once (470.11). *Adiuto* survives in Romance languages (*REW* 172) whereas *adiuuo* does not. Both examples in Terentianus and that in Petronius are construed with the dative, reflecting either Greek influence (cf. βοηθέω + dat.) or the analogy of other verbs of helping in Latin (*opitulor, auxilior* etc.) that take the dative (see Adams 2007: 438). Here *adiuto* is construed with an internal neuter accusative of the pronoun (28 *aliquit*), a construction found with *adiuuo*: cf. Cic. *Att.* 12.14.3 *solitudo aliquid adiuuat*, Theod. Prisc. p. 90.4–5 *ut etiam in tempore aliquid de fysicis adiuuentur* (see Müller 1908: 75).

io]**cinera**: singular for plural, otherwise attested just a few times in medical texts (see *TLL* VII.1.244.68ff.) and now in another curse tablet (see below, 19.8). Jeanneret (1918: 110) cites as a parallel popular French *les foies*. Many body parts come in pairs, and such plurals may influence the naming of single body parts (see E. Löfstedt 1956: I.30–1). The naming of internal organs that are not often seen, except in groups as used in sacrifice or cooking, is perhaps more readily influenced by such analogies than is the naming of single external body parts (note e.g. Eng. 'brains', once a culinary term but also used colloquially of an individual, as in 'he has got no brains'). For the plural *iecinera* in cookery see Apicius 5.3.8, 6.2.5, 7.10.1, 8.8.5. In such contexts the plural denotes a plurality of livers, but they are not readily differentiated and the term for such a collectivity might have come to be applied by some loosely to an individual's liver. See also above, 5.27 on *lienes* in Cato, and index, 'plural for singular, of anatomical terms'.

31 uenter, um[b]licu[s]: the anatomical terms listed in the curse are largely in the accusative dependent on *do tibi*. This leads Warmington (1940: 285 n. 1) to state: '*venter* is here apparently accusative of a colloquial neuter form' (an explanation he then applies to *umbilicus*) (so Ernout 1957a: 104). This explanation is implausible, and not only because *uenter* is not attested in the neuter in the period covered by the *OLD*. Irrational alternations between accusative and nominative are not uncommon in lists. Both cases may be motivated in lists of different types (depending e.g. on whether the terms may be construed as object of a verb, expressed or understood, or as subject of the copula *sunt*, expressed or understood), and alternations are explicable as lapses from one list-case to the other. For switches into the nominative from accusative see the discussion of *P. Mich.* VII.434, *P. Ryl.* IV.612, *ChLA* 4.249 (line 13) at Adams (2003a: 627), and of the Myconos *defixio* (*ILLRP* 1150) at Adams (2003a: 680–1). This last text provides a particularly good parallel for the structure here. It is a long list of names in the accusative (of the persons cursed), with several unmotivated lapses into the nominative. See also Adams (2013: 912, s.v. 'lists, syntax of').

33–4: uiscum | sacrum: the singular of *uiscera*, a term usually found in the plural, was *uiscus, -eris* n. *Viscum* must be an alternative form of the neuter singular, second declension rather than third. Occasionally neuters have two different forms, of the second and third declension (e.g. *penum, -i, penus, -oris*; this noun also had masculine and feminine forms). The following clause *nei possit urinam facere* suggests that the reference is to the urinary tract or bladder (see *OLD* s.vv. *sacer* 4e, *uiscus* 3d), but no parallel for this phrase seems to be found. The plural *uiscera* denotes the undifferentiated internal organs (heart, lungs, liver, intestines), and just occasionally the singular is used in reference to a specific organ, such as the liver (Cels. 4.15.1 *alterius quoque uisceris morbus, iocineris* 'a disease of a second internal organ too, the liver') and heart (Plin. *Nat.* 11.186 *sine illo uiscere* 'without that internal organ', referring back to *cor*) (see André 1991: 203). Here 'the sacred internal organ' is only deducible as referring to some part of the urinary system from the following clause. The point of *sacrum* is not clear. In Greek τὰ ἱερά may indicate the entrails of a victim because these are sacrificed to a god, and it is possible that the epithet and phrase derive from sacrificial language.

34 urinam facere: no doubt a polite expression, which is found in medical language: e.g. Scrib. Larg. 90 *non sine cruciatu urinam faciunt*.

38 paruum: undoubtedly a 'correct' spelling for *parum* (see Kroll 1915: 364).

40 mandauit: following *scripsit* (an asyndeton bimembre of a type discussed in the next note) *mando* does not have the sense that it has elsewhere in the text, of handing over the victim of the curse to face his punishment (see the next note), but must mean 'entrust to writing' (see *OLD* s.v. 2).

41 ti[bi tr]ado, mando: this pair of synonyms is used in asyndeton bimembre three times in lines 41–4. For the combination (but with a connective) see Cic. *carm. frg., Marius* IV Soubiran *tunc se fluctigero tradit mandatque paroni.* Asyndeton bimembre is a pronounced feature of curse tablets, including this one, as we have seen (lines 1, 3, 7, 8). For a few examples of pairs of synonymous or near-synonymous verbs in asyndeton see Preuss (1881: 93–9), citing at 99 instances from this semantic field, such as *dare adsignare, dare legare, dare donare, dare deuouere, reddere restituere.* In high literature see Enn. *scen.* 9 Jocelyn *mortales inter se pugnant proeliant*, and in curse tablets Kropp (2008a), e.g. 2.2.3/1 *rogo oro* three times, 2.3.2/1 *do dono*. On pairs of verbs in asyndeton (and the problem of deciding whether they are genuinely asyndetic) see above, 3.420, 4.3–4. Synonymous pairs such as those in this note pose no such problems: they are real asyndeta.

43 e]cillunc: a doubly reinforced demonstrative, with the deictic particle *-c(e)* as suffix and *ecce* as prefix (if the restoration is correct). According to Lindsay (1900: 164), commenting on Plaut. *Capt.* 169, when a pronoun was prefixed by *ecce* (so e.g. *eccum < ecce + *hom*) the *-ce* particle (as seen e.g. in *hunc*) 'was regarded as superfluous, just as *eccillum, eccistum* are the invariable forms, never *eccillunc, eccistunc*'. Our example suggests that this rule cannot stand as an absolute.

Ecce not infrequently coalesces with demonstratives in Plautus, in such forms as *eccistam* (*Curc.* 615), *eccillum* (*Per.* 392) (see Hofmann and Ricottilli 2003: 144, Perdicoyianni-Paléologou 2006, Fruyt 2011b: 750–1, Adams 2013: 466–8). These compounds are always in the accusative and can invariably be interpreted as exclamatory (and hence detached from the syntax of the clause in which they stand), as distinct from direct object of a verb. Their detachment is sometimes shown by a syntactic hiatus following (see Woytek 1982 on Plaut. *Per.* 392 and also 226, and particularly Lindsay 1922: 244; note too Weiss 2009: 135). In the present passage, however, *ecillunc* would have to be direct object of *tradas, mandes*. This would represent a development beyond Plautine usage, and might be interpreted as a step closer to the Romance demonstratives that are compounds comprising *ecce* (or the like) and *ille, iste* (cf. It. *quello, questo < eccu(m) illu(m), eccu(m) istu(m)*; also Fr. *celui, celle*; on the Italian forms see e.g. Maiden 1995: 116, and see in general Cuzzolin 1997, Adams 2013: 465–6). However, in later Latin there are no signs of usages such as this one.

43–4 mal[e perdat, mal]e exset, | [mal]e disperd[at: whereas *bene* may intensify a verb of favourable meaning (*bene amo* etc.), *male* may be used to intensify words 'possessing an unpleasant, depreciatory etc. sense' (*OLD* s.v. *male* 10; cf. *TLL* VIII.244.13ff.), with a particular frequency in Plautus and informal republican and early imperial Latin. For the phraseology here cf. Plaut. *Epid.* 50 *male perdidit me*, Catull. 14.5 *cur me tot male perderes poetis?*, Hor. *Sat.* 2.1.6 *peream male si non optimum erat* (see further *TLL* 244.31ff. on verbs of this type with *male*). See also Landgraf (1914: 132), Hofmann and Ricottilli (2003: 201).

perdat/disperdat: these seem to be intransitive (see *TLL* X.1.1273.43ff. on *perdo*), meaning 'let him destroy (himself)/be destroyed', perhaps with ellipse of the reflexive (see Feltenius 1977: 41 with 22). Jeanneret (1918: 144) quotes this passage along with various parallels from curse tablets, most notably a group of tablets from Hadrumetum in Africa (found at Audollent 1904, nos. 272–84) containing *frangant* (in curses on racehorses) alongside *cadant* and *disfrangantur* or *disiungantur*, where the meaning must be 'let them be broken' (cf. the compound *disfrangantur*). Intransitivisations are dealt with at length by Feltenius (1977) but have often been discussed (see e.g. Lundström 1943: 73–83). An alternative possibility in the present passage is that Cerberus is loosely envisaged as the subject/agent (see *TLL* X.1.1273.45f., citing Kroll 1915: 364). See index, 'intransitivisation of transitive verbs'.

exset: this looks like a mistake for *exeat*, a verb sometimes used of dying (occasionally with complements such as *e uita*) (see *OLD* s.v. *exeo* 7). Kroll (1915: 364) suspected that it might be for *uexet*, but *uexo* would be weak in this sequence, between verbs of destruction.

disperd[at: intensive compounds in *dis-* were characteristic of colloquial or informal Latin during the Republic and also later, as we will see (see 9.11, and index, 'compound verbs, intensives in *dis-*). This one is found in Plautus and a few times elsewhere in early Latin, then in an early speech of Cicero (*Leg. agr.* 1.2) and in a letter by one of Cicero's correspondents (Vatinius, *Fam.* 5.10a.1; a passage containing also *apage te cum nostro Sex. Seruilio* and the identification *simius non semissis homo*, expressions suggestive of comedy), and occasionally in less formal poetic genres, such as Virgil's *Eclogues* and Ovid's *Amores*. It is common in late Latin.

46 contempla]re: this verb, with its active form, is fully preserved in some other tablets. Here is another active variant of a deponent (see also above, 6.7 on *lucto*) that in early Latin occurs in higher genres as well as lower (see Nonius 753 Lindsay, citing examples from Accius, Naevius, Titinius, Ennius and Plautus). Indeed before Terence the active form seems to have been normal for this verb in dramatic texts of whatever genre (*TLL* IV.650.23ff.).

Conclusions

The text (along with the other members of the group) has numerous features suggestive of or consistent with a republican date prior to the classical period, with about 100 BC as good a guess as any: the etymologically based *ei* spellings, *ni* = *ne*, the reinforced form *illunc*, the pronominal compound with a prefix derived from *ecce*, the nominative plural pronoun form *quas*, the feminine *labrae*, and the non-inflecting future infinitive form *daturum*. Parallels with Plautus were constantly pointed out (see on *ni*, *illunc*, *arcessitum* with *mitto*, *daturum*, *Ploti Auoniae*, *adiutare*, *disperdat*, *male*, *contemplare*), as were several correspondences with Varro (see on *me mittas*, *daturum*; also *oricula* in the meaning it has, for which see *Rust.* 2.9.4, and below, 7.13). Though contemporary with Cicero, Varro held on to older usages that seem to have been eliminated from the educated language by the late Republic. The text has traditional elements with religious associations that were suited to a curse uttered to a deity. Asyndeton bimembre is noticeable (*bona pulchra, corpus colorem + uires uirtutem, luctent deluctent, euincant uincant, trado mando*). Such pairs have stereotyped features. There are pairs of synonyms, pairs comprising simplex and compound and alliterative pairs. The writing is on the whole correct (the nominatives *uenter* and *umblicus* are simple slips of a type not unusual in lists; there is occasional omission of *-m*), but there is a non-standard element to the Latin, ranging from banal low-register or colloquial usages (e.g. the forms *Ploti* and *oriculas*, the compound *disperdat*) to the more distinctive oddities *quas* (nominative), *polliciarus* and (in other texts of the same corpus) the genitive singular *-aes*. These were certainly non-standard, but the evidence for placing them more precisely, whether in social or regional dialects, is lacking. We also saw some oscillation between standard and non-standard forms, as in *labra* versus *labras* and *-ae* versus *-aes*, which is a reminder that high and low social dialects are not rigidly distinct.

7

RHETORICA AD HERENNIVM 4.14: A SPECIMEN OF THE 'SIMPLE STYLE'

Introduction

The *Ad Herennium* is a rhetorical treatise sometimes attributed to Cicero but generally treated as of unknown authorship (see Achard 1989: xiv–xx; also Calboli 1993: 8–10 on the etymologist Cornificius as a possible candidate). It was probably written some time in the 80s BC (between 86 and 82, according to Achard 1989: vii, xi–xiii; cf. Calboli 1993: 17). It has similarities to the *De inuentione* of Cicero (see Achard 1989: xv, Calboli 1993: 25–9), which was of similar date.

In the fourth book, from which our passages 7 and 8 come, the author illustrates the three styles of oratory, and then the faulty variants of each. The first passage here is the sample of the simple style, and the second that of its 'debased' variant, described as 'dry and bloodless'. See Marouzeau (1921: 156–7) (on this and the next text), Caplan (1954), Calboli (1993, and particularly 293 n. 44), Hofmann (1951: 206), Leeman (1963: I.31), Hofmann and Ricottilli (2003: 391–2), Ferri and Probert (2010: 18–21). The text printed here is a composite of those of Caplan, Achard and Calboli.

Text

in adtenuato figurae genere, id quod (1) ad infimum et cottidianum sermonem demissum est, hoc erit exemplum:

nam ut forte hic in balneas (2) uenit, coepit, postquam perfusus est, defricari (3); deinde, ubi uisum est ut in alueum descenderet, ecce tibi iste de trauerso (4). 'heus,' inquit 'adolescens (5), pueri tui modo me pulsarunt (6); satis facias oportet (7).' hic, qui id aetatis ab ignoto praeter consuetudinem appellatus esset, erubuit. iste clarius eadem et alia dicere coepit. hic uix: 'tamen' inquit 'sine me considerare.' tum uero iste clamare uoce ista quae perfacile cuiuis rubores eicere (8) potest, ita petulans est atque acerba (9) – ne ad solarium quidem, ut mihi uidetur, sed pone scaenam (10) et in eiusmodi locis exercitata. conturbatus est adolescens; nec mirum, cui etiam nunc pedagogi (11) lites (12) ad oriculas (13) uersarentur inperito huiusmodi conuiciorum. ubi enim iste uidissset scurram exhausto rubore, qui se putaret nihil habere quod de existimatione perderet, ut omnia sine famae detrimento facere posset?

Translation

Of the simple style, that which has been brought down to the level of humble everyday speech, this will serve as an example:

'It happened that this chap came to the baths. After washing he began to be rubbed down. Then, when he had decided to go down into the pool, unexpectedly this (other) fellow presents himself. "Look here, young man," he said, "your slaves have just assaulted me; you should make amends." The other blushed, since it was contrary to custom that one of his age should have been addressed by a stranger. This other fellow started to say the same things, and more besides, in a louder voice. The first struggled to get words out: "Just let me look into it." Then the fellow proceeds to shout in such a tone that can very readily bring out blushes in anyone – so aggressive and harsh is it, a tone not even employed at the sundial, it seems to me, but backstage, and in places of that kind. The youth was thrown into confusion, and no wonder, since his ears were still ringing with the reprimands of his tutor, and he had no experience of vulgar abuse of this kind. For where would he have seen a buffoon who had exhausted all his blushes, since he thought he had nothing left to lose of his good name, such that he could do anything he liked without damage to his reputation?'

Commentary

1 id quod: a variant reading (adopted by Achard) has *est* between *id* and *quod*.

2 balneas: a variant reading (adopted by Calboli) is *balineas*. The form with *-i-* has been taken to be substandard (see Ferri and Probert 2010: 21), but manuscript evidence is not to be relied on in such a matter.

3 coepit . . . defricari: there are two examples of *coepi* + infinitive in this short narrative, a fact which is suggestive of the reputation that the construction had in some eyes at the time, 'counting as one of the tokens of the slim, plain style' (Rosén 2012a: 123). *Coepi* tends to occur in clusters like this in graphic informal narrative (see e.g. Quadrigarius, *FRH* II.24.F6, two examples, *B. Hisp.* 31.4, 4, 5, 7, Petron. 74.8, 9, 12 (see further below), *Per. Aeth.* 15.2 twice, 30.1, 30.2, Greg. M. *Dial.* 4.40.3, 4 twice, 5, 7, 8).

The frequency of the construction in different types of narrative varies. In some higher-style historical works it is less obtrusive. In the whole of

Tacitus' *Histories* and *Annals* there are just eleven instances of *coepi* + infinitive (see Gerber and Greef 1877–90: I.180 col. 2), six of them in the *Annals*, a work that is almost 400 pages long in a Teubner edition. Ammianus too uses it sparingly (about eighteen times where *coepi* is active). On the other hand in the far less stylised and much shorter *Bellum Hispaniense* (twenty-nine pages in the OCT) there are about forty-four examples (Preuss 1884: 248) (again examples where *coepi* is passive have not been counted), and in the similar *Bellum Africum*, thirty-two (Preuss 1884: 248). In the meagre fragments of the annalist Quadrigarius there are six instances (see *FRH* III.703, index), as many as in the whole of the *Annals* of Tacitus. Even more strikingly, the story of the werewolf told by a freedman in Petronius, of just over one chapter in length (61.6–62), has the construction five times. In the *Peregrinatio Aetheriae*, another short text, there are twenty-three instances, some of them in clusters (see above). This is not to say that the construction itself was substandard or colloquial or vulgar (*coepi* + infinitive could be quoted from all the higher genres; Livy, for example, uses the form *coepit* with an infinitive about sixty-five times, and he has further examples with other forms of the verb), but its constant use, and particularly its occurrence in clusters, seem to have been especially characteristic of what might be called popular/informal/ naive narrative. This view we will see confirmed later (27.7) by the narrative of the persecutions in the *Passio sanctarum Perpetuae et Felicitatis*.

Another issue that has vexed scholars is whether *coepi* + infinitive some-times loses its lexical force and is a mere periphrasis for a perfective tense of the dependent verb. However, if the history of the construction is looked at over a long period it becomes clear that the verb was not weakened into a genuine auxiliary (see e.g. Rosén 2012b: 373). The attempt to find a semantic weakening may be based on an obsession with imposing a single literal meaning on the verb 'begin'. In the passage of Quadrigarius referred to above (*FRH* II.24.F6), one of the examples (*deinde Gallus inridere coepit atque linguam exertare*), if rendered literally into English ('then the Gaul began to jeer and to poke out his tongue'), would most naturally (in English) be taken to mean, not that he started to jeer and poke his tongue out but failed to complete the jeering or extrusion of the tongue, but rather that he started to do so and then repeated the acts. That surely is the force of the Latin too. As Courtney (1999: 147) puts it, '*coepit* ... usefully marks actions spread over some time'; see too Briscoe (*FRH* III.24.8, p. 302 '*coepit* ... indicates the beginning of a repeated action which will eventually have a result'). For a discussion of the actionality of the construction see Rosén (2012a: 128–33), stating that it is indifferent 'to the contrast durative: punctual' (128), and may e.g. be revealed by adverbials 'as either durative or instantaneous, as ongoing or terminative-resultative' (128).

The second example in our passage (*iste clarius eadem et alia dicere coepit*) has the same durative function. So Cicero sometimes combines *coepi* with *dicere* (e.g. *Verr.* 1.20, 4.32, *Mil.* 25) or e.g. *clamare* (see Adams 2013: 827, in another connection).

Coepi + infinitive may also occur at the start of the description of sequences of events marked by adverbs such as *primo, deinde*, where it may be pleonastic with *primo* (see Cic. *S. Rosc.* 26 with Landgraf 1914: 69). In the present passage there is such a sequence, but *deinde* is not preceded by *primo*. Since the rubbing down is completed the verb is not straightforwardly inceptive, but the force may be close to 'he began by being rubbed down and then decided to go down into the pool'.

Coepi does sometimes lack point, as at *B. Hisp.* 39.2 *in speluncam Pompeius se occultare coepit . . . ita ibi interficitur*, where a single act is referred to (see also E. Löfstedt 1956: II.451), but automatic use of the term 'periphrastic' is to be avoided until objective criteria are established for identifying weakened uses. In the meantime we can only say that it is not the construction itself, but rather its incessant use, especially in clusters, that is typical of a type of narrative.

See particularly below, 27.7, where attention is drawn to an old observation about a function of *coepi*.

4 ecce tibi iste de trauerso: *ecce* is a sentence modifier ('look/listen, this fellow . . .', and *tibi* is an ethic dative (see below). *Ecce* and *tibi* are often juxtaposed in this way in classical Latin (see below). Despite the fact that *iste* is independent of the preceding two words, the collocation of the three is a foreshadowing of Italian (Tuscan) *codesto* (*cotesto*) < *eccu(m)* + *tibi* + *istum*. For the derivation see Staib (1996: 362). Note Proudfoot and Cardo (2005: 78): 'There is a third demonstrative in Italian: *codesto*, used to refer to something far away from the speaker, but near to the person addressed.' They cite *dammi codesto libro* ('give me that book [the one you have]'), and add: 'This use of *codesto* is relatively uncommon today, except in Tuscany, being restricted to bureaucratic language, when we want to refer to an office, company or firm (as in English "your company").' See further Maiden (1995: 116).

Calboli (1993: 293 n. 44) refers to It. *eccoti* = *ecce tibi*.

ecce tibi: an ethic dative (*tibi*) is detached and not part of the syntax of the sentence. It is a way of evoking the interest of the reader/listener or (in the first person) of keeping the writer/speaker present as an observer (see Dyck 2008: 140). Such datives are frequently associated with *ecce* and used in the description of sudden arrivals. A verb of motion may have to be understood, as here. For some or most of these features together see Cic. *Att.* 1.14.5 *hic tibi rostra*

Cato aduolat, Att. 2.15.3 *cum haec maxime scriberem, ecce tibi Sebosus!, Att.*
15.4a *ecce autem de trauerso L. Caesar ut ueniam ad se rogat, Cluent.* 75 *ecce tibi*
eius modi sortitio . . .!, De orat. 2.94 *ecce tibi est exortus Isocrates, Luc.* 121 *ecce*
tibi e transuerso Lampsacenus Strato, Off. 3.83 *ecce tibi qui rex populi Romani*
dominusque omnium gentium esse concupiuerit, Phil. 11.2 *ecce tibi geminum in*
scelere par, inuisitatum, inauditum, ferum, barbarum!, Pis. 48 *ecce tibi alter*
effusa iam maxima praeda, S. Rosc. 133 *alter tibi descendit de Palatio et aedibus*
suis, Varro *Men.* 411 *cum dixisset Vitulus, ecce tibi caldis pedibus quidam*
nauicularius semustilatus irrumpit se in curiam (see also Adams 2013: 477).
On the ethic dative (in some of these and other passages) see Hofmann and
Ricottilli (2003: 292–4), Adams (2013: 347–8) and especially now Rosén
(2015).

5 heus, . . . adolescens: *heus* is common in comedy but rare later in prose (for
the later examples see *TLL* VI.2–3.2675.71ff.; these include a number from the
letters of Cicero, who has the word in total fifteen times; see also Hofmann and
Ricottilli 2003: 116–18). The only example in the speeches of Cicero is at *Mil.*
60 *heus tu, Rufio, . . . caue sis mentiare,* in imagined interrogation of a slave.
The language of this last passage must represent that appropriately used to
a slave (*sermo cotidianus*: see Quint. 12.10.40). *Sis,* for example, was not normal
in formal contexts. In speeches of Cicero *sis* is elsewhere only in the early
S. Rosc., at 48 *age nunc, refer animum sis ad ueritatem et considera* (see
Landgraf 1914: 109, and for further details of the use and distribution of the
term, Hofmann and Ricottilli 2003: 288–9, Dickey 2006). Similarly the
combination *heus tu,* which is common in comedy, is ten times used in
Cicero's letters, but otherwise only in a reported exchange at *De orat.* 1.240:
deinde ipsum Crassum manu prehendit et 'heus tu,' inquit 'quid tibi in mentem
uenit ita respondere?'
    The tone of *heus* is well captured by Austin's note (1971: 121) on Virg. *Aen.*
1.321: 'the stranger-girl is no demure miss, waiting to be spoken to. The word
sets the tone for her speech: it belongs to Comedy and to familiar, intimate talk,
and is often followed by a jussive or interrogative sentence.' He points out that
heus is normally used by men in comedy. In our passage the addressee is
likewise a stranger, and similarly an instruction follows.
    Heus, adolescens is a comic address (Plaut. *Epid.* 1, *Men.* 135, *Pseud.*
1137). In specimen passages the author *Ad Herennium* elsewhere sometimes takes words or expressions from comedy (see Adams 2007: 378–9),
and it is a moot point whether his inspiration here is everyday conversational language or comedy itself (on comic language in the *Rhet.* see
below, 8.1).

6 pulsarunt: must derive from the perfect ending *-erunt* with *ĕ* (for which see Sommer 1914: 579 and particularly Leumann 1977: 607–8). This short-vowel form was the only one to continue into the Romance languages (Leumann 1977: 608).

7 facias oportet: *oportet* with a subjunctive complement (which often precedes it, as here) is well established from an early period alongside the more common infinitival construction (see *TLL* IX.2.741.64ff.). The addition of *ut* belongs to late Latin (*TLL* 742.14ff.).

8–9 uoce ista quae perfacile cuiuis rubores eicere potest, ita petulans est atque acerba: high-style prose might have used a subordinate (consecutive) construction, of the type *uoce ista ita petulanti atque acerba ut perfacile cuiuis rubores eicere possit.* For this type of parataxis, which is common, cf. Plaut. *Mil.* 177 *nescio, ita abripuit repente sese subito* (cf. *Mil.* 159, 167, 397, 1261, *Stich.* 338, Pomponius 95–6 Frassinetti *nescio quis molam quasi asinus urget uxorem tuam, | ita opertis oculis simitu manducatur ac molit,* Sall. *Jug.* 84.3 *sed ea res frustra sperata: tanta lubido . . . inuaserat,* Cic. *Att.* 9.19.1 *etsi omnis et illos et qua iter feci maestos adflictosque uidi; tam tristis et tam atrox est* ἀναθεώρησις *huius ingentis mali,* Hor. *Sat.* 1.1.13 *cetera de genere hoc, adeo sunt multa, loquacem | delassare ualent Fabium,* Petron. 70.11 *paene de lectis deiecti sumus, adeo totum triclinium familia occupauerat,* Plin. *Nat.* 11.193 *hinc et in mores crimen bilis nomine: adeo magnum est in hac parte uirus, cum se fundit in animum, Colloquium Celtis* 68b (Dickey 2015) *nescio quid dicam, ita enim perturbatus sum.* On such parataxis see Hofmann and Ricottilli (2003: 252–3). See also below, 18.10.

Achard (1989) prints a variant text, turning the *ita*-construction into direct speech containing a classical consecutive construction: '*ita petulans es atque acer ut ne ad solarium quidem, ut mihi uidetur, sed pone scaenam et in eiusmodi locis exercitatus sis.*' This looks very much like a classicisation of the syntax, and the speech thereby created is too long-winded alongside the snappy utterances that this specimen and the next otherwise have.

perfacile: on compounds in *per-* see Laurand (1936–8: III.271–7), André (1951), Landgraf (1914: 54) on *perfacile* at *S. Rosc.* 20 (also Dyck 2010: 87), Powell (1988: 103), the last remarking that they are 'characteristic of the polite, urbane language of Cicero's dialogues and letters'. In the speeches of Cicero such words are found mainly in the early works, most notably the *Verrines* (see Laurand 1936–8: III.276), and in letters and philosophical works. On the decline of *permagnus*, for example, in the course of Cicero's oratory see Laurand (1936–8) III.272–3. André (1951: 122–35, 146–7) provides a full list of *per*-compounds in Cicero, but not full details of their distribution.

Here are some figures for the distribution across the speeches of a small selection of these words (*perfacile*, adverbial, as here, *perfamiliaris, permagnus, permultus, perpaucus*). The speeches may be divided (arbitrarily) into three chronological groups, those from 81 to 69 (about thirteen speeches), those from 66 to 62 (thirteen), and those from 59 to 44–43 (thirty-two) (see *OCD*² p. 236 for a convenient list of the speeches in chronological order). In the first period above the five words listed occur sixty-one times; in the second period, twenty-two times; and in the third period, only seven times. The decline is striking, particularly given the volume of later works from 59 BC onwards. There are large numbers of such intensives in the speeches against Verres of 70 BC (e.g. *permagnus* 10, *permultus* 20, *perpaucus* 7). Various other words not included in the above list occur only in the *Verrines* (*perlucidus, pernobilis, peropportune, perparuolus, perridicule*).

Achard (1989) prints the variant reading *uel facile*, but the compound gives a better meaning and is suited to the type of narrative.

eicere: in English we would say 'bring out (blushes)' rather than 'throw (them) out', i.e. we would refer to the manifestation of the blushes from our perspective as observers, rather than from the perspective of the person emitting them. Latin sometimes adopts a different perspective from that normal in English, not least in the use of the verb 'go' (see below 27.6 on *exiuit* in the *Passio Perpetuae*). Examples of *eicio* interchangeable with *produco/educo* are cited below, 45.10, with bibliography.

Calboli (1993) prints *elicere* (which seems to have no manuscript support), but in his note on the passage (1993: 293 n. 44) comments on *eicere*.

10 pone scaenam: *pone* + acc. = 'behind' is mainly in early Latin (six times in Plautus; Cato *Agr.* 18.3 *ad parietem, qui pone arbores est*) and later in archaisers such as Apuleius and Tacitus (see *TLL* X.1.2628–9). It cannot be used as an archaism here but must have been current in this phrase: cf. *CIL* I².1492.5 *porticum pone scaenam* (perhaps of the period of Cicero), cited at *TLL* 2629.11f.

11 pedagogi: in koine Greek the αι diphthong had long since turned into a monophthong represented by epsilon (in anticipation of Modern Greek), and the interchange of the two is common in the papyri (Gignac 1976: 192–3, Biville 1995: 40–2). Popular Latin had borrowed the koine form, and the spelling thus has nothing to tell us about the monophthongisation of *ae* in

Latin itself (contrast Ferri and Probert 2010: 20). For parallels see Biville (1995: 40) (e.g. *Clytemestra* in Livius Andronicus).

12 lites: *lis* normally denotes a dispute in law, or a dispute in a more general sense (see *OLD* s.v. 1, 2), but of this and a few other examples the *TLL* (VII.2.1499.71f.) observes that 'vergit hic illic in vim q. e. obiurgatio, convicium sim.'

13 ad oriculas: *oricula* has no diminutive force here: cf. Varro *Rust.* 2.9.4 *auriculis magnis ac flaccis* (of large ears, of dogs). *Auris* did not survive in the Romance languages and was replaced by the diminutive. Early instances already lacking any diminutive idea anticipate that development (on the term see André 1991: 42). Note for example the Johns Hopkins *defixiones*, 'Avonia' 24 *oricula[s]*, 'Vesonia' 25 *oriclas* (Sherwood Fox 1912) (also above, 6.25, where it is not fully preserved), where the word occurs in a list of anatomical terms and is clearly the vox propria for the part in the social dialect reflected by the curses. For the form *oricula* (with *o*), which probably had a popular character (see Adams 2013: 83–4), see the proverb *oricula infima ... molliorem* at Cic. *Q. fr.* 2.14(13).4 and Catull. 25.2 (form *oricilla*). In the last two passages the reference is to the lobe of the ear, and the form thus has a diminutive function, since diminutives could express part of a whole (cf. *pellicula* 'piece of skin', alongside *pellis*, which could be used of the hide as a whole: Adams 1995a: 543). On the semantics and distribution of *auricula* see Adams (1995a: 550–1). See also below, 29.3, and index, s.v. *auricula*.

Conclusions

The 'simple style' of oratory was intended as something that might even be employed on formal occasions, as for example in a speech in which the orator wanted to present facts rather than make a dramatic impression. It is in the nature of classifications of style that they are bound to be vague and unscientific, and any individual's attempt to illustrate a style would inevitably be personal. One certainty is that a distinction would have been perceived between outrightly uneducated speech, and an orator's efforts to present something in a simple way. This passage is syntactically correct throughout. The last sentence is complex, with three subordinate clauses. There are about ten subordinate clauses in a short space. Two of the relative clauses have subjunctive verbs. There is no shortage of passives (about five), whereas in the (admittedly shorter) specimen of the debased simple style (below, 8) none is found.

The author does not overdo informal devices. Amid the subordination there is just one paratactic construction, of a type well represented in less formal literary genres. One clause (beginning *ecce tibi*) has ellipse of a verb of going, in a phrase that was hackneyed and used by the educated. Compounds in *per-* might turn up anywhere. Cicero went off them as his oratorical career progressed, but he continued to use them in dialogues and letters. There was nothing substandard about *coepi* + infinitive, but the two instances in proximity must have been deliberate, to evoke an informal narrative style. The peremptory tone of the newcomer is conveyed by a phrase (*heus, adolescens*) perhaps taken from comedy. There is some evidence that the diminutive *auricula* = *auris* was in use among the educated by the late Republic, though it would not have been admitted by purists in learned discourse. The spelling with *o* (or should we say the pronunciation with a monophthong?) seems to have been acceptable to Cicero in proverbial expressions. The passage is in educated Latin, with some deliberate markers of informality.

8

RHETORICA AD HERENNIVM 4.16: A 'DEBASED' VARIANT OF THE 'SIMPLE STYLE'

Text

Qui non possunt in illa facetissima uerborum adtenuatione commode uersari ueniunt ad aridum et exsangue genus orationis, quod non alienum est exile nominari, cuiusmodi est hoc:

'nam istic (1) in balineis (2) accessit ad hunc. postea (3) dicit: "hic tuus seruus me pulsauit." postea dicit hic illi: "considerabo." post ille conuicium fecit (4) et magis magisque (5) praesente multis (6) clamauit.'

friuolus hic quidem iam et inliberalis est sermo; non enim est adeptus id quod habet adtenuata figura, puris et electis uerbis conpositam orationem.

Translation

Those who cannot properly employ that clever simplicity of diction arrive at a dry and bloodless style, which it is not inappropriate to call 'thin'. The following is of this type:

'This fellow came up to him in the baths. Next he says: "This slave of yours has assaulted me." Next the other says to him: "I'll think about it." Next that fellow used abuse and shouted more and more in the presence of many people.'

This language is silly and mean. It has not attained the character of the simple style, which is speech composed of pure and well-chosen words.

Commentary

1 istic: it was seen earlier (3.420) that the neuter form of this reinforced pronoun (*istuc*) was standard in Plautus (for *istud*), and then survived to a limited extent into the classical period. The history of the masculine nominative form seen here is somewhat different. Apart from this passage it is totally absent from classical Latin (see *TLL* VII.2.495.24ff., citing as well an instance from a tragedy of Seneca, and from Tertullian), though it had been common in comedy. On the history of *istic* see Adams (2007: 379–80, 2013:

457). The author of the *Rhet.* may deliberately have drawn on comic diction to create this specimen of colloquial style. On comic language in the specimen passages in the *Ad Herennium* see Adams (2007: 378–9). Comedy was exploited by various writers to create a pseudo- or literary colloquial style (for Gellius see Holford-Strevens 2010, for Jerome, *Vita Malchi* see Gray 2015: 34–6 and for Augustine see Burton 2007, chapter 2, and particularly the general remarks at 56 n. 41). However, in a letter of Seneca (12.3) (see text 17.3 below), in a piece of quoted dialogue in which a slave is addressed angrily (*unde istunc nanctus es?*), we find the only example of the accusative *istunc* outside comedy (see *TLL* VII.2.496.46). In that context the form *istunc*, used with obvious contempt, looks like a genuine colloquialism uttered in the heat of the moment. If we accept it as such, we ought also to accept the possibility that the nominative *istic* had retained some currency in speech.

On another reinforced demonstrative (*ille* + *ce*), see 2.21–2, 6.5. On the adverbs *istic* and *istoc* see 3.421, 9.10.

2 balineis: the manuscripts do not agree about the form of this noun, with *balneis* attested as well (see Ferri and Probert 2010: 21 n. 17). Caper condemns the longer form (*GL* VII.108.7), but one must agree with Ferri and Probert (21) that 'the distribution of the two forms does not make for a straightforward assessment of their sociolinguistic status' (see above, 7.2).

3–4 postea . . . postea . . . post: for strings of temporal adverbs at the start of clauses as a mark of popular/naive narrative/storytelling style see above, 1.1 (with bibliography), 1 Appendix 3, index, 'temporal adverbs, repetitious'. The author *Ad Herennium* recognises this style as *breuitas* 'brachyology' (4.68), and cites two examples, one with the sequence *inde . . . post . . . inde*, the other with *modo . . . deinde . . . tum . . . deinde . . . post . . . postremo*.

4 conuicium fecit: on *facio* as a support verb see above, 4.8. This expression came up earlier (3 Appendix, passage (3)), where it was cited from Festus commenting on its currency. It occurs for example three times in Plautus, once coordinated with another noun also attested elsewhere in this construction: *Bacch.* 874 *ut ne clamorem hic facias neu conuicium.* It is also at *Merc.* 235 and *Most.* 617, in the latter case with a personal dative (*sic et praesenti tibi facit conuicium*). The single example in Terence is in the type of context commented on by Festus: *Ad.* 180 *ante aedis non fecisse erit melius hic conuicium* ('You'd be wiser not to make a scene in front of my house', Barsby, Loeb). See also *TLL* IV.874.22ff., and note *Att.* 16.8.2 *et ei conuicium graue fecerunt*, Cic. *Cluent.* 74 *conuicium C. Iunio iudici quaestionis maximum fecit.* These two examples share the characteristic that *conuicium* is accompanied by a strong adjective, and thus we see one motivation of the periphrastic verb phrase: it permits the use of a focal adjective. The single-verb equivalent *conuicior* is also used in classical Latin both absolutely, as *conuicium fecit* in the present passage (Livy 42.41.3 *ut accusare potius uere quam conuiciari uideantur*; for other absolute uses see *TLL* IV.872.53ff.) and with a dative of the person abused, as *facit conuicium* at *Most.* 617 above (see *TLL* 872.68ff.).

Support-verb constructions are widespread, not least in classical Latin, including Cicero (for *clamorem facio*, for instance, cited above from Plautus, see *TLL* III.1259.11ff.; see also the last paragraph for Cicero). Occasionally, however, one detects a purist disapproval of such usages, and that may be the case here, in a starkly expressed sentence with several other distinctive terms and expressions. Note Cicero's ridicule of Antony (*Phil.* 3.22), who had said *nulla contumelia est quam facit dignus*. Cicero says *quid est porro facere contumeliam? quis sic loquitur?* ('moreover, what is "making an insult"? Who speaks like this?'). The implied answer is that no educated person does. Cf. Quint. 9.3.13 *et 'contumeliam fecit', quod a Cicerone reprehendi notum est*, commenting on this remark. See also below, 48.2.5. Purist disapproval, however, does not mean that the purist will himself succeed in avoiding a usage.

5 magis magisque: *TLL* VIII.69.9ff., Wills (1996: 112), and also below, 18.4 on such gemination.

6 praesente multis: for the lack of concord see *TLL* X.2.838.55ff. (mainly in early Latin, notably fragments of farce, and occasionally elsewhere; for an inscriptional parallel see *CIL* V.895 (Aquileia) = Diehl 1910, 1464a *posuit titulum de suo astante ciuibus suis*). Such constructions may derive partly from a plural predicate comprising coordinated singulars, such as *Caesare et Cicerone*, with the adjective agreeing in a normal manner only with the first. Also, an example in Terence (*Eun.* 649 *absente nobis*) refers to a single person, with *nobis* a 'pluralis maiestatis' (*TLL* I.213.54f.), and thus the singular may be a constructio ad sensum; cf. also Afranius 6 (*adeste, si hic absente nobis uenierit puer*), which looks the same, though there is no context. In our passage there is a genuine plurality, as is also the case in Atellan farce: Pomponius 43 Frassinetti *praesente amicis*, 167 *praesente testibus*, Novius 57 *praesente omnibus*. The usage is not securely attested in Plautus (see *TLL* lines 56–8), and it would not do on the basis of the single case in Terence to argue that our author here was deliberately imitating comic language. An example in a fragment of Varro quoted by Donatus on the above passage of Terence (*id praesente legatis omnibus exercitu pronuntiat*) also refers to a plurality, and it is possible that such expressions had a limited currency (for the stylistic peculiarities of Varro see index, 'Varro, Latin of'). See in general Hofmann and Szantyr (1965: 445), Bonfante (1967: xiv).

Conclusions

The passage has only four sentences, none with any subordination. Three of these begin with *post(e)a*, whereas in the longer passage of simple style there are only two sentences beginning with temporal adverbs, and these different (*deinde, tum uero*). Here the author has taken a recognised feature of naive narrative style, and caricatured it. The construction *praesente multis* has a parallel in Varro, a writer who retains many old usages that had by the late Republic been rejected in urbane forms of literature. It seems likely that such expressions were lingering on in some quarters. The nominative masculine *istic* has no parallel in the late Republic, and this the author might possibly have taken from comic dialogue, but we also saw a reason for accepting it as genuinely current.

9

LETTER OF MARCUS CAELIUS RUFUS TO CICERO (CIC. *FAM.* 8.15.1–2)

Introduction

This passage is from a letter of Caelius to Cicero dated 9 March 49. In January 49 Scipio had proposed that Caesar be made a public enemy if he refused to dismiss his army. Caelius voted against the motion and joined Caesar. He was then sent by Caesar to put down a revolt at Intimilium in Liguria, a command, as Austin (1960: xiii) puts it, 'which did not seem to him to be of sufficient importance'. The first two sentences of the second paragraph below convey his attitude to this expedition. It is not clear where Caelius was when he wrote the letter (see Shackleton Bailey 1977: I.488). The letters of Caelius preserved in Cicero's *Ad familiares* have some distinctive, non-standard features (on Caelius' Latin see in general Pinkster 2010), and that is true of the present extract. On the life of Caelius and his relations with Cicero see Austin (1960: v–xvi), Dyck (2013: 4–6).

Text

8.15.1 Ecquando (1) tu hominem ineptiorem quam tuum Cn. Pompeium uidisti, qui tantas turbas, qui tam nugas (2) esset, commorit? ecquem autem Caesare nostro acriorem in rebus gerendis, eodem (3) in uictoria temperatiorem aut legisti aut audisti? nunc tibi nostri milites, qui durissimis et frigidissimis locis, taeterrima hieme, bellum ambulando (4) confecerunt, malis orbiculatis (5) esse pasti uidentur? 'quid tam' inquis 'gloriose omnia?' (6) si scias quam sollicitus sim, tum hanc meam gloriam, quae ad me nihil pertinet, derideas. quae tibi exponere nisi coram non possum, idque celeriter (7) fore spero. nam me, cum expulisset ex Italia Pompeium, constituit ad urbem uocare, id quod iam existimo confectum, nisi si (8) maluit Pompeius Brundisi circumsederi. **2** peream si (9) minima causa est properandi isto (10) mihi quod te uidere et omnia intima conferre discupio (11); habeo autem quam multa (12). hui (13), uereor, quod solet fieri, ne cum te uidero omnia obliuiscar.

Sed tamen, qu<odn>am ob scelus iter mihi necessarium retro ad Alpis uersus (14) incidit? ideo quod Intimilii in armis sunt, neque de magna causa (15). Bellieni uerna Demetrius, qui ibi cum praesidio erat, Domitium quendam, nobilem illi (16), Caesaris hospitem, a contraria factione nummis acceptis comprehendit et strangulauit.

Translation

8.15.1 Did you ever see a more foolish fellow than your Cn. Pompeius, who stirred up such trouble, joke that he was? But did you ever read or hear about anyone more vigorous in action or more moderate in victory than our Caesar? Do you now think those soldiers of ours, who in the harshest and coldest of places and in the foulest winter have put an end to the war by walking, are fed on rounded fruit? 'Why', you say, 'all this boasting?' If you only knew how anxious I am, then you would be making fun of this boasting of mine, which has nothing to do with me. I cannot explain these matters to you except face to face, and I hope that this will be soon. As for me, he has decided to call me to Rome when he has driven Pompey out of Italy. That I suppose has already been done, unless Pompey has preferred to be besieged at Brundisium. **2** My desire to see you and to share all intimacies is by no means my least important reason for hurrying there. How many such intimacies I have! But I am very afraid that when I see you I may forget them all, as usually happens.

Nevertheless for what crime has this compulsory trip back to the Alps fallen upon me? It is because the Intimilii are up in arms, and for no good reason. Demetrius, the indulged 'slave' of Bellienus, who was there with a garrison, received bribes from the opposite party and arrested and strangled a certain Domitius, a noble of the area and host of Caesar's.

Commentary

1 ecquando: this term, like *ecquis*, is an indefinite interrogative implying the answer 'no'. *Ecquando* (here 'did you ever see …') tends, according to *TLL* V.2.51.44, to occur in emotional speech and is often in anaphora. So here it is picked up by *ecquis*, and cf. the letter of Cornelia, Nepos frg. 15 (Peter 1906: 39) = frg. 59 (Marshall 1985: 112) *ecquando desinet familia nostra insanire? ecquando modus ei rei haberi poterit? ecquando desinemus et habentes et praebentes molestiis desistere? ecquando perpudescet miscenda atque perturbanda re publica? Ecquando* was not a favourite term of Cicero's. It occurs just a few times in speeches (*Verr.* 2.43, 5.66, *Vat.* 18, *Leg. agr.* 2.17), and at *Fin.* 5.63. This is the only instance in the whole corpus of letters.

2–3 nugas esset: a difficult expression, open to several explanations (see Landgraf 1898 for a general discussion, with early bibliography).

First, *nugas* might be a misspelling of *nugax*, showing assimilation of the consonant cluster *ks*. That is clearly how it was taken by the *OLD*, where the passage is quoted without comment under *nugax*. If it is a misspelling, the assimilated spelling might in theory be due either to the writer, Caelius (reflecting a current pronunciation), or to a late scribe. But the assimilation *ks* > *s(s)* is one of four structurally related assimilations which, though they became influential eventually, are all but unknown (except in a few controversial cases) in classical Latin (see Adams 2013: 145–74). The two early assimilations cited as parallels for *nugax* > *nugas* by Landgraf (1898: 225), *sescenti* < *sexcenti* and *Sestius* < *Sextius*, are both false, because in these it is a threefold consonant cluster that has been reduced. Given the absence of convincing republican examples of the assimilation of *ks* alone, it is unlikely that Caelius himself wrote *nugas*, intending it as *nugax*. A late scribe on the other hand might well have written *nugas* for *nugax*, but any editor who thinks that that is the case has no alternative but to emend to *nugax*. Shackleton Bailey (1977: I.488) says: 'More probably *nugas* was only a colloquial variant of *nugax*.' He therefore has made the implausible assumption that Caelius wrote *nugas* = *nugax*.

An alternative possibility is that *nugas* is the exclamatory accusative *nugas!* ('nonsense, rubbish': see Plaut. *Most.* 1087), fossilised into an indeclinable noun. Indeclinables arising from oblique case forms discussed by Wackernagel (1926–8: I.295–6) = Langslow (2009: 371–2) are *frugi, pondo* and *nequam*. To these can be added town names fossilised in the locative or accusative (note Consentius, *GL* V.349.4–5 *interdum efferuntur nouo modo et quasi monoptota, ut Curibus Trallibus Turribus Sulcis Seruitti Gadir Viniolis Bilbilis*), a process which sometimes produced the form of the name of the town in the Romance languages (e.g. *Aix* < *Aquis* 'at the waters') (see further Adams 2013: 336). None of these derives from an accusative of exclamation, but the feature that most have in common is that it is a case form used particularly often that was fossilised. Therefore behind the use of *nugas* here might well lie the exclamation *nugas!* I cannot cite an exact parallel for the fossilisation of an exclamatory accusative, but at Plaut. *Per.* 264 (*tuxtax tergo erit meo*) *tuxtax* is an onomatopoeic exclamation expressing the sound of the cudgel on the back, which is used in the context as a noun (see Woytek 1982: 257) and as subject of the verb to be, like *nugas* on this second interpretation. This example was drawn to my attention by Wolfgang de Melo. Another of similar type is at Petron. 58.7 *et <ei> qui te primus 'deuro de' fecit* (< δεῦρο δή 'come here', i.e. 'he has made you his "come here"', sc. for sexual purposes, thus = *deliciae*) (see e.g. Cavalca 2001: 80).

There are several comparable instances of *nugas* both in late republican literature and inscriptions. Note Varro *Men.* 513 = 515 Cèbe (1998) *crede mihi, plures dominos serui comederunt quam canes. quod si Actaeon occupasset et ipse prius suos canes comedisset, non nugas saltatoribus in theatro fieret*, 'Believe me, more masters have been eaten by their slaves than by their dogs. But if Actaeon had anticipated and himself had eaten his dogs first, he would not turn up as a source of nonsense for dancers in the theatre'). See Cèbe (1998: 1966): 'Ce substantif indéclinable ... était sans doute à l'origine un accusatif exclamatif mais fut employé de bonne heure comme un nominatif dans la langue parlée d'où il passa dans la langue littéraire' (and reporting in n. 66 a different but implausible explanation). In Pompeian graffiti there are two instances of the expression *tu nugas es* (*CIL* IV.5279, 5282), which are taken by Väänänen (1966: 116) as indeclinables deriving from the accusative of exclamation. Väänänen cites also Cic. *Att.* 6.3.5 *amicos (Appius) habet meras nugas, Ma<ti>nium, Scaptium* ('He has friends who are utter good-for-nothings – Matinius, Scaptius', Shackleton Bailey 1965–70: III.117), which displays the identification of persons abused with *nugae*, an identification that would also be seen in the expression *nugas es(t)* on this second interpretation of the form.

Finally, note *CIL* XV.7059 *nugas uiuas* (on a drinking glass) (drawn to my attention by Giuseppe Pezzini). Here *nugas* appears to be not so much a fossilised form as an internal accusative (lit. 'live a nonsense', 'live lightheartedly').

Twice in speeches in the *Cena Trimalchionis* of Petronius *nugax* is transmitted with parts of the verb 'to be' in the second person: 52.4 *'cito' inquit 'te ipsum caede, quia nugax es'*, 52.6 *suadeo, a te impetres, ne sis nugax.* One wonders whether the original reading might have been *nugas* (see Landgraf 1898: 226), with the Pompeian graffiti providing, as often, an exact parallel to a usage in freedmen's speeches.

3 eodem: referring to Caesar (ablative of comparison), and redundant, in that *Caesare* could be taken with *temperatiorem* as well. For the weakened use of *idem* as a mere anaphoric (= *is, ille*), which occurs from time to time in classical Latin, see *OLD* s.v. 7.

4 ambulando: this is not a use of the ablative of the gerund that is equivalent to a present participle, as it seems to be taken by Hofmann and Szantyr (1965: 379), but is fully instrumental: they finished the war by means of a hard march (see Adams 2013: 727).

5 orbiculatis: a variety of apples and pears mentioned by Varro and Columella, literally 'rounded', which would have been eaten at dessert (Shackleton Bailey (Loeb) 'sugar plums'). See Shackleton Bailey (1977: I.488).

6 'quid tam' inquis 'gloriose omnia?': Shackleton Bailey (1977: I.250) follows C. F. Hermann in printing *quid? tam* instead of the transmitted *quid iam*, citing Plin. *Epist.* 7.4.10 *sed quid ego tam gloriose?* There is no reason, however, to place a question mark after *quid* (contrast the punctuation of the passage of Pliny). Shackleton Bailey's translation (Loeb, letter 149) does not match his punctuation ("'What's all this brag?" you may say'). On issues of punctuation after interrogative *quid* see below, 10.3.2.

6–7 celeriter fore: *celeriter* means 'soon' here, a classical meaning (*OLD* s.v. 3).

8 nisi si: on this 'volkstümliche Abundanz' (= *nisi*) see Hofmann and Szantyr (1965: 668), describing it as common in early Latin, and then found in the *Rhet. Her.*, Varro, Nepos, and in Cicero in early speeches, philosophical works and letters. It is absent from Caesar and Sallust, but occurs in Vitruvius and Livy.

9 peream si: this phrase along with the variant *peream nisi* is rendered by the *OLD* s.v. *pereo* 3b 'may I die if (if not)'. It marks a strong assertion. At *TLL* X.1.1332.14ff. it is cited not from Cicero himself but three times from letters by his correspondents (here and at Brut. *Fam.* 11.23.2 and Cass. *Fam.* 15.19.4). It is also in a letter of the emperor Augustus quoted by Suetonius (*Claud.* 4.6 *peream nisi, mea Liuia, admiror*) (see further below, 12 Conclusions). The few other examples given by the *TLL* are in texts admitting colloquialisms (one is cited above, 6.43–4 from Horace). Cf. below, 13.10 on *dispeream (ni)si.*

10 isto: 'to that place'. This adverb brings up again the subject of non-standard demonstrative pronouns/adverbs in the republican period (see above, 3.421).

For a list of attestations of this adverbial form see *TLL* VII.2.517.55ff., where it is remarked (54f.) that the form, like *istoc*, is used 'nonnisi in sermone cotidiano vel familiari'. Its distribution is indeed strongly indicative of a colloquial character, with most examples found in letters. Caelius himself has it also at *Fam.* 8.9.3. Another of Cicero's correspondents, Plancus, uses it at *Fam.* 10.17.2. Two examples are cited from Cicero's own letters (*Att.* 12.23.1, *Fam.* 9.16.9), and there are also instances in the letters of Seneca and Pliny. Plautus, finally, has it at *Mil.* 455 and *Most.* 837.

The reinforced form *istoc* (not to be confused with *istuc*, which is more widespread) has a very similar distribution (see *TLL* 517.60ff.). It does not occur in Cicero's own letters, but is several times attested in letters by his correspondents, most notably Caelius himself, from whom it is quoted three times (*Fam.* 8.4.1 (with manuscript variation; Shackleton Bailey 1977 prints *istoc*), 8.8.10, 8.9.4: see below). Plancus, again, has it (*Fam.* 10.21). There is also an instance in an epistle of the emperor Caligula quoted by Suetonius (*Cal.* 55.1). An interesting case is in a speech by Hermeros in Petronius' *Cena Trimalchionis*: 57.11 *nam [in] ingenuum nasci tam facile est quam 'accede istoc'*, on which Schmeling (2011: 239) notes: 'Instead of comparing *ingenuum nasci facile est* with another passive happening, Hermeros substitutes a short phrase: "being born a free man is as easy as saying 'come hither'".' Smith (1975: 158) says that *accede istoc* 'is probably chosen as a familiar order by a master to a slave' (cf. above, 9.2–3 on δεῦρο δή). Finally, *istoc* too is found a number of times in Plautus.

The attestations of both forms suggest that they continued in colloquial use over a long period, with a more marked presence in the very insubstantial corpus of letters by some of Cicero's correspondents than in the much bigger corpus of Cicero's own letters. That same feature was also seen above in the distribution of *peream si*. Caelius is the correspondent who stands out in his taste for these terms.

Isto as used here by Caelius can be given a second-person nuance, = 'to that place (where you are)', and that is not infrequently the case with both *isto* and *istoc*. For *istoc* in this sense note Caelius *Fam.* 8.4.1 *tam multa cottidie quae mirer<is> istoc perferuntur* ('so many surprises landing on your doorstep every day', Shackleton Bailey, Loeb), 8.8.10 *libertum Philonem istoc misi* ('there', in the sense of 'to your part of the world'; the adverb follows *istinc* in the previous sentence (on the low tone of which see Austin 1977: 145), translated by Shackleton Bailey as 'from your part of the world'), 8.9.4 *M. Feridium, equitem Romanum, amici mei filium, . . . qui ad suum negotium istoc uenit* (= to Cilicia, where Cicero is; again with second-person reference), Plancus *Fam.* 10.21a *cum primum poterit, istoc recurrere non dubitabit* (to Rome, where Cicero is).

In the Petronian phrase *accede istoc*, however, *istoc* has lost that nuance.

11 discupio: intensive compounds in *dis-* also have an eminently colloquial distribution, and Caelius has two of them in the short correspondence extant (on such forms see above, 6.43–4, and below, 13.10, 38.52). This one sentence has three distinctive usages (*peream si, isto, discupio*).

12 habeo autem quam multa: with *multa* understand *intima*. Shackleton Bailey (1977: I.489) has this note: '*quam* probably = *perquam*'. The *OLD* does not register a usage *quam* = *perquam* (was Shackleton Bailey merely offering a paraphrase?). With both adjectives (as here *multa*) and adverbs exclamatory *quam* may be placed either before the verb of its clause, or after, as here. For the former placement see e.g. Ter. *Haut.* 213 *quam iniqui sunt patres in omnis adulescentis iudices!*, and for the latter *Haut.* 1023 *sed ipse egreditur quam seuerus!* (for such variation with *quam* + adverb see *Haut.* 375 alongside *Andr.* 136).

13 hui: on the exclamation *hui* see Hofmann and Ricottilli (2003: 120–1). It is found only in Plautus and Terence and in the correspondence of Cicero but must have continued in spoken use because it is reflected in Romance languages. From the *TLL* article (VI.2.3074) it can be seen that it is used a number of times by Cicero in his letters to Atticus (particularly before exclamations with *quam* or *quanto*), and also by Cassius (*Fam.* 15.19.4) as well as Caelius.

14 iter mihi necessarium retro ad Alpis uersus: *iter* here has a double adnominal complement, *retro* and *ad Alpis uersus*. On the difference between adnominal expressions used with verbal nouns like *iter* and those with non-verbal nouns, see below, 11.3 (on adnominals see also 9.16 below).

15 neque de magna causa: *de causa* is a common classical expression (*TLL* III.672.27ff.). With *magna* it is cited by the *TLL* (672.73) only from here, Cic. *Fam.* 13.17.1 and from a letter of Quintus Cicero (*Fam.* 16.16.2 (superlative)).

16 Domitium quondam, nobilem illi: 'a notable of the district' (Shackleton Bailey, Loeb). Worthy of note here is the adverb *illi* = 'there, in that place' (from the locative *illei*; the usual adverb of this root is *illic*, with the same base but also with the deictic particle *c(e)*). This is another unusual pronominal form in Caelius. The evidence for *illi* is presented at *TLL* VII.1.367.82ff. It was in use in early Latin, where it occurs about thirty-three times in Plautus and thirteen in Terence. A notable early example is that at Turpilius 9 (*uenire illi*), where it is not static in meaning but complements a verb of motion (*TLL* 368.42f.). Thereafter in the whole of Latin it is attested about fifty times but is accepted by editors in only about twenty places (*TLL* 368.1ff.). The instance in Caelius is perhaps the only attestation in the classical period, where it is defensible particularly because the next word begins with *c* (*TLL* 368.10f.). Here is a form that must have fallen out of use among the educated during the Republic, though presumably maintaining a lingering currency to the end of the Republic in informal speech. The general point is worth stressing again that quite a few pronominal forms, some reinforced by *-c(e)*, some not, that had fallen out of educated use by the late Republic or early Empire continued to be used in informal varieties: cf. *isto* and *istoc* above, 9.10, *illim*, below, 22.24, *illic*,

6.5, and Adams (2013, chapter XX). Caelius had a particular taste for these non-standard forms.

Illi attached to *nobilem* is another adnominal use of an adverb (see above, 9.14). An exact parallel is provided by the occasional adnominal use of *ibi* in Livy, Tacitus and others (*TLL* VII.1.154.5ff., where the usage is inappropriately (but conventionally) described thus, 'ibi ponitur pro adiectivo'). Cf. e.g. Tac. *Hist.* 2.16.2 *Claudium Pyrrichum trierarchum Liburnicarum ibi nauium*. For other adverbs used thus by Tacitus see Heraeus (1929: 147) on Tac. *Hist.* 2.16.2; among his examples there is a case of *illic*, *Hist.* 5.14.1 *memoria prosperarum illic rerum*. The frequency of adnominal expressions is variable from author to author, with a marked increase observable in very late Latin: see index, 'adnominal prepositional expressions', 'adverbs, adnominal', and particularly 11.3, 11.30, 46.5–6.

Conclusions

It is no surprise to find in this letter of Caelius some usages that occur in the corpus of Cicero only in his own letters and those of correspondents, such as *isto* and *hui*. Letters reflect an informal level of the language that does not show up much in higher literary genres. More striking, however, are usages that do not turn up at all in Cicero even in his letters, but are attested in Caelius and usually other Ciceronian correspondents as well, and sometimes too in other letters, for example by Augustus and Caligula. Into this category fall the expression *peream si*, the adverbs *istoc* and *illi* and the intensifying compound *discupio*, which has also surfaced in a soldier's letter of much the same period from Egypt (see 13.10). What are we to conclude from this discrepancy between Cicero and his correspondents? Several of the latter write things that Cicero himself does not allow even in letters (for Caelius categorised as 'slangy', see 13.10), and that is an indication that Cicero's Latin was not entirely representative of the Latin of the educated class of his own period. We should be reluctant to throw around the term 'classical Latin' if it is to imply that there were standardised formal and informal varieties of the language current in the late Republic as represented, merely by chance, mainly by Cicero (because the works of Cicero are the most extensive survivals of the period). The extant letters of Cicero are considerable in extent and those by his correspondents minute by comparison, and yet some of the above usages are far better represented in the correspondents than in Cicero himself. It would seem that Cicero was more restrictive in his linguistic tastes than some others of his class. We have also seen differences between Varro and

Cicero (see index, 'Varro, Latin of'). It would be unsatisfactory to conclude that Cicero was the typical one and the others untypical.

Particularly striking at this informal level are the pronominal forms (including adverbs based on pronouns) that are avoided in more formal Latin of the period. The point was made too that there are several other pronominal forms, not as it happens occurring here, that are also attested at this period only in low-register sources, and in these various cases we have an indication that the pronominal inventories of formal versus informal language were not entirely uniform in the late Republic.

The most interesting usage in Caelius' letter is perhaps the fossilised form *nugas*, which occurs in a number of other informal texts, including Pompeian graffiti, but is never in Cicero. That it is in Varro is another sign of the dissimilarity of the Latin of Cicero and Varro, both of them regarded as highly learned.

10

SOME JOKES RECORDED BY CICERO, QUINTILIAN AND MACROBIUS, MAINLY OF REPUBLICAN DATE

Introduction

Many jokes are collected by (among others) Cicero in the second book of the *De oratore*, Quintilian 6 and Macrobius, *Saturnalia* 2, and most of these are of republican or Augustan date. They are usually attributed to named individuals. Since jokes tend to be made off-the-cuff and are mainly spoken, they fall nicely into the category of Latin talk. Several specimens are selected here from the three writers above. In the Conclusions some general comments will be offered about their linguistic features.

(1) Cicero, *De oratore* 2.256

Text

Alterum genus est, quod habet paruam uerbi immutationem . . ., ut . . . eiusdem responsio illa: 'si tu et aduersus (1) et auersus (2) impudicus (3) es.'

Translation

There is a second type, which is based on a slight modification to a word, . . . as this reply of the same fellow: 'If you are shameless both in front and behind.'

Commentary

preliminaries

This remark is attributed by Cicero to Cato, who is alluded to in *eiusdem*. The joke is classified by Cicero according to the difference by a single letter between *aduersus* and *auersus*. Slight though the remark is, it is an illustration of a type of sexual allusion that is so oblique as to be usable in public. The two key words, *aduersus* and *auersus*, one of them (*aduersus*) an adverb, might in both cases be called locational or positional. Sexual parts or acts may be alluded to, not least by means of adverbs, by oblique reference to the position of the part or site of the act or pose adopted by the performer (cf. e.g. English 'down there'). Similar is the euphemistic use of *ibi* of the vulva at *Mul. Chir.* 853 *et in pesso, cum pepererunt mulieres, suppones ibi, ut melius purgentur*; cf. Ovid *Met.* 4.359 *subiectatque manus* 'she applies her hands below'.

See Corbeill (1996: 152), translating Cato's remarks as '[i]f both from the front and from behind you are shamelessly effeminate'.

1.1 aduersus: if the referent is pathic 'in front', the reference in *aduersus* must be to 'the use of the mouth in fellatio' (Corbeill 1996: 153). For the contrast 'in front/behind' Corbeill (1996: 152) cites a remark attributed to the philosopher Arcesilaus quoted by Gellius 3.5.2, drawing on Plutarch: *'nihil interest' inquit 'quibus membris cinaedi sitis, posterioribus an prioribus.'* On *cinaedi* as assumed to practise oral sex see Juv. 6.O5 with L. C. and P. Watson (2014: 186) ad loc.

1.2 auersus: For the suggestiveness of *auersus* 'turned away' compare Plaut. *Aul.* 637 :: *quid uis tibi?* | :: *pone. Pone* is intended as the imperative of *pono*, but the slave interprets it as the adverb 'behind' and as a request for anal sex. He replies (637) *id quidem pol te datare credo consuetum, senex*, 'that service I am sure you are used to granting, old man' (see Stockert 1983: 171 and the note of de Melo 2011a: 326 n. 42 ad loc.). There is a more protracted joke of the same kind at Plaut. *Poen.* 611–12 (see Stockert 1983: 171): :: *pone nos recede.* :: *fiat.* :: *nos priores ibimus.* | :: *faciunt scurrae quod consuerunt: pone sese homines locant* (see the translation of de Melo 2012a 'Step behind us. :: Yes. :: We'll go in front. :: They do what men about town usually do: they place people behind themselves'; also his note on the last clause, 83 n. 37 'A euphemism for wishing to be the passive partner in anal intercourse').

In both of these Plautine passages note *consuesco*, used vaguely of what a certain type of person 'is accustomed to do' and alluding particularly to a homosexual act. Cf. Plaut. *Pseud.* 780 *neque ego illud possum quod illi qui possunt solent*, Scipio Aemilianus, *ORF* 21.17 (Gell. 6.12.5) *eumne quisquam dubitet, quin idem fecerit, quod cinaedi facere solent*. Note too Plaut. *Asin.* 703, a passage in which the slave Libanus rides on the back of the *adulescens* Argyrippus: *asta igitur, ut consuetus es puer olim. scin ut dicam?* ('stand to then, just as you used to do when you were a boy – know what I mean?').

1.3 impudicus: as Corbeill (1996: 152 n. 61) says, *impudicus* is often applied to a passive homosexual (see too Jocelyn 1999: 102). Note e.g. Sen. *Epist.* 52.12 *inpudicum et incessus ostendit et manus mota et unum interdum responsum et* *relatus ad caput digitus et flexus oculorum* (also Vitr. 2.8.12, juxtaposed with *molles*).

(2) Cicero, *De oratore* 2.275

Text

Ex quo genere est etiam non uideri intellegere quod intellegas: ut Pontidius, 'qualem existimas qui in adulterio deprehenditur?' 'tardum'.

Translation

Of this type also is pretending not to understand what you do understand, as in the case of Pontidius: 'What do you think of a man who is caught in adultery?' – 'Slow'.

Commentary

tardum: commentators point out that the expected response would be a moralising term such as *scelestum*. Instead Pontidius (unknown: see Leeman, Pinkster and Rabbie 1989: 311–12) upset expectations by referring to the slowness of the adulterer in reaching a climax. Verbs of hurrying and the like are not infrequently attested of rushing to a climax (see Adams 1982a: 144–5), and here we have the opposite characteristic.

Much the same joke is at Quint. 6.3.87.

(3) Cicero, *De oratore* 2.277

Text

Est bellum illud quoque ex quo is qui dixit irridetur in eo ipso genere quo dixit: ut, cum Q. Opimius consularis, qui adolescentulus (1) male audisset, festiuo homini Decio, qui uideretur mollior nec esset, dixisset, 'quid tu (2), Decilla (3) mea (4)? quando ad me uenis cum tua colu et lana (5)?' 'non pol (6)' inquit 'audeo, nam me ad famosas uetuit mater accedere (7).'

Translation

That type too is neat, in accordance with which the one who has made a joke is mocked in the very same mode as that of his own joke, as when the consular Q. Opimius, even though he had had a bad reputation as a foppish youth, ventured to say to a jolly fellow Decius, on the grounds that he seemed rather effeminate, but was not, 'Well then, my dear little Decia, when are you coming to me with your distaff and wool?', and the other replied 'I really really don't dare – for my mother told me not to go up to women of ill repute.'

Commentary

preliminaries

See Lucilius 421 (and also 418–20), from which the joke seems to derive. There (419) a certain Quintus Opimius is described as *formosus fuit homo et famosus*, a description that appears to be echoed in the use of *famosas*, directed at Opimius, in the present joke. Chahoud (2010: 93) observes that, while the Ciceronian anecdote is 'constructed in Cicero's typical fashion', it was 'most probably drawn from Lucilius'.

3.1 adolescentulus: diminutives are often used of males to imply or underline effeminacy. In this chapter (10) we will see instances of *muliercula* (Cic. *Verr.* 2.192), *filiola* (*Att.* 1.14.5), *pulchellus* (Apul. *Met.* 8.26), and *adulescentulus* itself, reinforced by *molliculus* (fragment of Titinius cited at Charisius p. 258.4 Barwick). Chahoud (2010: 93) cites Scipio Aemilianus' description of Publius Sulpicius Galus as *adulescentulus ... non modo uinosus sed uirosus quoque*, 'not only fond of wine but also fond of men' (*ORF* 21.17, Gell. 6.12.5) (see further Chahoud 2010: 92–3 on such diminutives, and also below, this section, on names (*Decilla*) given diminutive form).

3.2 quid tu, ...?: *quid tu* (or, in a more general sense, interrogative *quid* followed by a pronoun or name, or sometimes a noun) is a typical conversational phrase, which is common in comedy and Petronius and also found in interactive contexts in Cicero, in speeches and letters (for discussions see Hofmann and Szantyr 1965: 424–5, Stockert 1978, Ricottilli 1978, Hofmann and Ricottilli 2003: 244–5). The combination has however not infrequently been punctuated with the question mark placed after *quid* (for discussion of this issue see especially Ricottilli 1978). A case in point is at Cic. *S. Rosc.* 104, where A. C. Clark (OCT) punctuates *quid? tu, uir optime, ecquid habes quod dicas?* By contrast Leeman, Pinkster and Rabbie (1989: 315) in a citation of the passage punctuate *quid tu, uir optime? ecquid habes quod dicas?*, which I take to be correct (on the problem of punctuation see the following paragraphs). Punctuation of the type adopted by Clark here has been particularly noted in editions of Petronius (on which see Ricottilli 1978). Nor are editors who sometimes punctuate *quid? tu* etc. necessarily consistent. Clark for example punctuates *Cluent.* 71 as follows: *'quid tu?' inquit 'ecquid me adiuuas, Bulbe?').* These last two Ciceronian passages are similar, in that *quid tu* is followed in both by the same question word *ecquid*, and yet different punctuations are adopted.

Typically the *quid tu* construction is followed by another question, introduced by -*ne, an, num* or another question word, such as *ecquid* above. Note e.g. Plaut. *Aul.* 183 *quid tu? recten atque ut uis uales?* ('Well then? Are you in good health, just as you wish?') (see further e.g. *Capt.* 270 with Lindsay 1990: 190 ad loc., *Curc.* 181, *Pseud.* 610). In typical cases such as this the punctuation *quid? tu . . .* would entail taking *tu* as part of the second interrogative clause, but fronted out of that clause and placed before the question word. Fronting might occasionally look possible (see above, 3.416), but there are cases where such punctuation would not be tolerable. Note for example Plaut. *Men.* 1109 *esne tu Syracusanus? :: certo. :: quid tu? :: quippini?* ('Are you from Syracuse? :: Certainly. :: What about you? :: Naturally'). Here there is no following interrogative clause of which *tu* could be a fronted component. *Quid tu?* is a freestanding unit = 'what about you?', and the punctuation *quid? tu* would make *tu* difficult to understand.

There are other passages which show that it would be unsatisfactory mechanically to put a question mark after *quid* in such collocations. At Plaut. *Epid.* 561 (*filiam quam ex te suscepi . . . :: quid eam? :: eductam perdidi*) the meaning can only be 'what about her?', and a division after *quid* would be meaningless. The change of speakers locates *eam* with *quid* rather than *eductam* (see Stockert 1978: 84 on this passage). Even more graphic is the following, discussed by Stockert in the same place: Plaut. *Merc.* 180–1 *eloquar, quandoquidem me oras. tuos pater . . .* | *:: quid meus pater? :: tuam amicam? :: quid eam?* Here the second speaker twice interrupts the first impatient to hear what is to be said about the referents, and again to place the question mark after *quid* would be unsatisfactory: the sense is 'what about . . .?'

Finally note Cic. *Att.* 3.15.3 *sed quid Curio? an illam orationem non legit?* (cited at Hofmann and Szantyr 1965: 425). *An* regularly comes first in a direct interrogative clause, and a question *sed quid?* would be hard to defend.

It should not of course be implied that *quid?* cannot be used as a single-word interrogative (see e.g. for Terence McGlynn 1963–7: II.107 s.v. *qui*). Note for example Cic. *Fam.* 11.21.1 *quid? tu illum tecum solum aut cum Caesare?* (so Shackleton Bailey 1977 no. 411, who translates in the Loeb 'Do you really suppose that he talks only to you or to Caesar?'). Here there is no second question-word following *quid?*, as in examples that have been quoted above.

Tu is appropriately at the head of the acc. + inf. construction, as subject of the understood verb of thinking or the like. For this construction with the verb of thinking expressed note Quint. 6.3.90 *alienam finxit Iuba, qui querenti quod ab equo luto esset aspersus 'quid? tu' inquit 'me Hippocentaurum putas?'* All possible cases of the *quid tu* construction need to be assessed in context.

In our passage *quid tu?* is not a real question, but merely a way of engaging the addressee ('well then, . . .'). Compare Cic. *Att.* 5.21.12 *uoco illos ad me remoto Scaptio. 'quid uos? quantum' inquam 'debetis?'.* Shackleton Bailey (1965–70: III.75) translates: '"Well gentlemen," I said, "how much do you owe?"'.

3.3 Decilla: there is uncertainty about the names here (see Leeman, Pinkster and Rabbie 1989: 314–15 for the variants and discussion), but there is no doubt that the speaker switched from the real name of the male addressee to a feminine variant, implying effeminacy. We leave aside here the possible use of a diminutive form as well (for which see below, 10.4.3), and deal only with the feminine.

The use of the feminine form of the male referent's name belongs to a rich category of abusive terminology in Latin implying someone's effeminacy. This terminology can be put into various groups. First, as here, there are feminine names applied to males. These do not comprise a single type. The type here, where the person's actual name is converted to the feminine, is not common in extant Latin. Among the Perusine sling bullets from the siege of Perusia in 41/40 BC, which contain abusive slogans about Octavian, there is one which reads *pet[o] Octauia culum*, where *Octauia* may be for *Octauiai* or *Octauiae* (see Hallett 1977: 152 on no. 2). Elsewhere in the corpus he is referred to by his earlier name *Octauius*, and the feminine seems to express a charge of effeminacy (on which see Hallett 1977: 157–60). For a collective name see Virg. *Aen.* 9.617 *o uere Phrygiae, neque enim Phryges* (cf. Hom. *Il.* 2.235 Ἀχαιίδες, οὐκέτ' Ἀχαιοί). So too for Greek, Cicero (*Nat.* 1.93) says of Zeno, *Chrysippum numquam nisi Chrysippam uocabat* (see Richlin 1992: 293, and also the extensive note ad loc. of Pease 1955: 456, with material relevant here and also later in this note).

In other cases the victim is assigned a feminine name that is not a modification of his own. Thus Gellius 1.5.3 reports that L. Torquatus in a court case said of the orator Hortensius, who was known for his theatrical delivery: *non iam histrionem eum esse diceret, sed gesticulariam Dionysiamque eum notissimae saltatriculae nomine appellaret.* Hortensius is given a female name (and a feminine adjective), but the name is that of a female dancer of the day. Hortensius replies *'Dionysia,' inquit 'Dionysia malo equidem esse quam quod tu, Torquate,* ἄμουσος, ἀναφρόδιτος, ἀπροσδιόνυσος.'

At Cic. *Prov.* 9 *Semiramis illa* is used of the effeminate Gabinius (see Richlin 1992: 97).

Again, at Cic. *Att.* 4.11.2 there is an allusion to Clodius via the feminine form of another male's name: *quid illa populi Appuleia* ('(tell me in detail about) the People's Appuleia', Shackleton Bailey 1965–70: II.103). Appuleius was the 'nomen of Saturninus, a famous tribune of the people' (Corbeill 1996: 97). There is a double reference in *populi* here, first to Saturninus the tribune and second to the idea that prostitutes were the possession of the 'people' (for which idea see Adams 1983b: 343–4).

There is an uncertainty about *Pediata* at Hor. *Sat.* 1.8.39: *in me ueniat mictum atque cacatum | Iulius et fragilis Pediata furque Voranus.* Gowers (2012: 277 ad loc.) remarks: 'Three types of unmanly sexuality: possibly a *cinaedus* (or a *puer*?), a pathic and an *irrumator*'; Pediata is a 'male pathic effeminate enough . . . to have a woman's name'. Whether this is a modification of the pathic's own name or a nickname is unclear. Given that verbal puns in Latin are often made in indifference to distinctions of vowel length, the name here may indeed be suggestive of *pedicata* (so Gowers).

Second, feminine common nouns that are designations of females are often used of effeminate males, such as the words for 'woman' themselves. Thus, according to Suetonius (*Iul.* 22.2) Caesar declared in the senate that he would *insultaturum omnium capitibus* (with a suggestion of *irrumatio*), which inspired an abusive quip by an unnamed person, that this would not be easy for any woman: *ac negante quodam per contumeliam facile hoc ulli feminae fore.* For *femina* see also *SHA, Tyr. Trig.* 12.11 *Gallienus, sordidissimus feminarum omnium* (see Opelt 1965: 174). Note too *mulier* at Suet. *Iul.* 52.3 *Curio pater quadam eum oratione omnium mulierum uirum et omnium uirorum mulierem appellat,* and also Cic. *Verr.* 2.192 *at homo inertior, ignauior, magis uir inter mulieres, impura inter uiros muliercula proferri non potest* (see Corbeill 1996: 150), *Mur.* 31 *bellum illud omne Mithridaticum cum mulierculis esse gestum* (see Richlin 1992: 97). For a few other examples of *mulier* see Opelt (1965: 155).

Another such designation is *filiola* at Cic. *Att.* 1.14.5: *totus ille grex Catilinae duce filiola Curionis* ('the whole Catilinarian gang with little Miss Curio at their head', Shackleton Bailey 1965–70: I.143). The reference is to C. Scribonius Curio, tr. 50 and son of C. Scribonius Curio, the consul of 76 (for the younger Curio and his sexual reputation see Shackleton Bailey 1965–70: I.310).

Note too Sall. *Hist.* 1.55.22 *Fufidius, ancilla turpis.*

Femina above was not the only such term applied to Caesar. Note Suet. *Iul.* 49.1 *praetereo actiones Dolabellae et Curionis patris, in quibus eum Dolabella paelicem reginae, spondam interiorem regiae lecticae, at Curio stabulum Nicomedis et Bithynicum fornicem dicunt* (a *paelex* was a female rival of a wife), 49.2 *missa etiam facio edicta Bibuli, quibus proscripsit collegam suum Bithynicam reginam.* Here Caesar is called the 'Bithynian queen' for his relations with Nicomedes (see Corbeill 1996: 149). For *paelex* above see also ps.-Cic. *In Sall. inv.* 8.21 *omnium cubiculorum in aetate paelex.*

Of the same type is the use of *noua nupta* in a passage of Juvenal: 2.120 *gremio iacuit noua nupta mariti.* Here the *noua nupta* is a male trumpeter who is married to a certain Gracchus: note 129 *traditur ecce uiro clarus genere atque opibus uir,* 'a man illustrious in family and fortune is handed over in marriage to another man', Braund, Loeb. Note too 137 *interea tormentum ingens nubentibus haeret,* | *quod nequeant parere* ('meanwhile a huge torment clings to these brides, that they cannot give birth').

Suggestive use of marital terminology in reference to an effeminate male is not uncommon. So, we are told, Antony was removed by Curio from the prostitute's profession (Cic. *Phil.* 2.44 *qui te a meretricio quaestu abduxit*), and metaphorically given the matron's *stola* (*tamquam stolam dedisset*) and placed *in matrimonio stabili.* Earlier Antony, on taking the *toga uirilis,* had converted it (metaphorically) into a *toga muliebris,* the mark of a female prostitute (*sumpsisti uirilem, quam statim muliebrem togam reddidisti*).

Finally, for a designation of a female animal (*catula* 'young bitch') applied to a male see ps.-Aur. Vict. *Epit. de Caes.* 23.5–6 *huius corpus per urbis uias more canini cadaueris a militibus tractum est militari cauillo appellantium indomitae rabidaeque libidinis catulam* (see Opelt 1965: 175).

Feminines used of males need not be exclusively abusive. *Pathici* are sometimes presented as applying feminine designations to themselves. There is an interesting case at Apul. *Met.* 8.26: *'puellae, seruum uobis pulchellum en ecce mercata perduxi.' sed illae puellae chorus erat cinaedorum.* Here the speaker is an old effeminate (8.24 *cinaedum et senem cinaedum*), who addresses his band of *cinaedi* as *puellae.*

This last passage may serve to introduce a third, miscellaneous, class of terms suggestive of effeminacy. The *senex cinaedus* not only uses *puellae* of the *cinaedi* but also has a feminine participle (*mercata*) in reference to himself. This latter usage is of particular interest. It is not only feminine names or nominal designations applied to males that may imply effeminacy. A variety of usages appropriate to females could be brought into service. Note Pomponius 150 Frassinetti *ego quaero quod edim; has quaerunt quod cacent.* Here *has* is a feminine nominative, and it may refer to pathics (see Buchheit 1962: 253), though the context does not allow certainty. For the form see above, 6.7 and Adams (2003a: 118 with n. 32). Also worth noting is the occasional application of a term denoting the female sexual organ to the anus of a male pathic (*CIL* IV.1261 *cunnus*: see Adams 1981: 263, Solin 2008: 64).

3.4 mea: the use of *mea* with *Decilla* is significant. Women in comedy use the *mi*-form of address frequently, more so than men (see Adams 1984b: 68–73, Dickey 2002: 221). Men for their part 'virtually never use *mea* to an unrelated woman unless they have a romantic interest in her' (Dickey 2002: 221). The point here is that Opimius not only converts the name of the effeminate Decius into a feminine, but also issues an invitation to 'her' to come to him for sexual purposes. Dickey (2002: 223) suggests as an explanation of *mea* that 'perhaps the speaker is feigning romantic interest in [Decius] as part of the taunt', and that suggestion is confirmed by the phrase *quando ad me uenis*. *Venio ad* (along with a few roughly equivalent verbs) is regularly used euphemistically of the woman (e.g. a prostitute) 'coming/going to' the man for sex (see Adams 1982a: 176 for a few literary examples). For further instances see Plaut. *Asin.* 195 *illa alio ibit tamen* ('she will go off elsewhere (for sexual purposes)'), Hor. *Sat.* 1.2.122 *neque cunctetur cum est iussa uenire*, Audollent (1904), no. 230A.7 (Carthage) *[c]oge illam uenire ad me amante aestuante*, 265A *neque somnu uideat donec at me ueniat puellạ[r]ụ d[eli]cias* (also 265B), ps.-Hippocr. *De conceptu* 198 Mazzini and Flammini *sic ad uirum suum accedat*, 233 *non uadat ad uirum suum*. These last two cases are shading into the meaning 'have intercourse with'; note Soranus Lat. p. 32.16–17 *et si fieri potest ad uirum suum in totum non accedat*, which might mean 'and if possible she should not go to her husband at all'; or could it mean 'she should not go all the way with her husband'? The man for his part may 'await' the arrival of the woman, as at Hor. *Sat.* 1.5.82–3 *usque puellam | ad mediam noctem exspecto*.

3.5 cum tua colu et lana: these references to women's work are difficult to interpret. Such symbols of femininity are almost the antithesis of sex, and may seem to strike an odd note here. Thus at Ovid *Ars* 2.685–6 a woman forced to have sex dreams of her wool as she submits without being aroused: *odi, quae praebet, quia sit praebere necesse, | siccaque de lana cogitat ipsa sua*. Perhaps the attribution of the *colus* and *lana* to a male in our passage is simply meant to portray him as womanly in a general sense. On the other hand there are many Greek vases from the fifth century onwards depicting women spinning or winding wool, who are approached by young men with gifts or money-bags (see Davidson 1997: 87). Davidson remarks that the money-bags 'seem to make the men's intentions quite clear', adding that no one 'really disputes what the men in these scenes are after'. There seems however to be no firm agreement whether these women are prostitutes, and if so what the functions of the spindles are (see Davidson loc. cit., with bibliography). See however *The Times* May 11 2015 (p. 3), quoting Virginia Postrel: 'For the Ancient Greeks, spinning had [an] association with sex. Greek vases depict prostitutes spinning. It was a productive occupation while waiting for clients.' So here women's work may be envisaged as an interlude between sexual acts. Cf. Hom. *Il.* 1.31 'she walks to and fro before the loom and tends my bed'.

3.6 pol: the speaker, having been characterised as effeminate, at first plays along with this notion by using *pol* in his reply, a term which in comedy, and particularly that of Terence, is strongly associated with the speech of women, though not exclusive to them (see for details Adams 1984b: 50–4, and above, 3.433). Titinius, cited by Charisius p. 258.6 Barwick, has a *magister* ascribe both *pol* and *edepol* to an effeminate youth, according to Charisius: p. 258.3–6 *denique Titinius in Setina, molliculum adulescentulum effeminate loquentem cum reprehendere magis<ter> uellet, 'an' inquit 'quia "pol edepol" fabulare? edimedi'* (see Adams 1984b: 52, *TLL* X.1.2525.74ff.). Charisius' comment reveals a notion that effeminates might speak in an 'effeminate' way, an idea that is met with elsewhere in Latin (see Adams 1984b: 53 with the bibliography at n. 43, and L. C. and P. Watson 2014: 195 on Juv. 6.O23; see also Phaedr. *App.* 10.2–3 *fracte loquendo et ambulando molliter* | *famam cinaedi traxerat certissimi*), and not least in our present joke.

It is not only *pol* that is significant here, but the whole phrase *non pol audeo*, which must be meant to catch the diffident tone that has traditionally been associated with women ('I really really would not dare!'). Compare the use of *licet* ('may I') by the effeminate soldier at Phaedr. *App.* 10.20 asking (*uoce molli*: on his manner of speech see the last paragraph) to fight the enemy, a remark suggestive of feminine deference (see Adams 1984b: 53–4).

From this point Decius suddenly goes on to the attack, reversing the roles both of himself and of his addressee. He now adopts a male role, and represents Decius as the woman (of ill fame) (see the next note).

3.7 nam me ad famosas uetuit mater accedere: the expression 'go/come to' someone for the purpose of sex was, as we saw above, 10.3.4, often used of the woman coming to the man, but was also reversible and is here applied to the man going to prostitutes (see the material at Adams 1982a: 175–6, which includes examples of *uenio* of the man going to a brothel; also perhaps Novius 8 Frasinetti *cum ad lupam nostram tam multi crebro conmetant lupi*). For *accedo* itself note Sen. *Contr.* 2.7.4 *tantum non ultro blandientes ut quisquis uiderit non metuat accedere*, 'all but making eyes invitingly to ensure that no-one who sees you is afraid to approach' (Winterbottom, Loeb, of 'approaching' women in the street), Petron. 140.11 *accessi temptaturus an pateretur iniuriam* (of approaching a male with an indecent proposal). Both of these examples are similar, of going up to someone and making a suggestion. In our passage the meanings 'my mother forbade me to proposition women of ill repute' and 'my mother forbade me to visit women of ill repute' would both be possible, with the latter preferable. For *famosas* see Livy 39.43.2 *famosam mulierem*, Suet. *Tib.* 35.2 *feminae famosae*, and Adams (1983b: 342), Chahoud (2010: 93 with n. 24).

(4) Cicero, *De oratore* 2.286

Text

Saepe etiam sententiose ridicula dicuntur, ut M. Cincius, quo die legem (1) de donis et muneribus tulit, cum C. Cento prodisset et satis contumeliose 'quid fers (2), Cinciole (3)?' quaesisset, 'ut emas,' inquit 'Gai, si uti uelis (4).'

Translation

Often also jokes are uttered sententiously, as for example in the case of M. Cincius. On the day when he carried a bill concerning gifts and presents, when C. Cento had come forth and asked rather insultingly, 'What are you bringing, my good Cincius?', he said 'That you pay, dear Gaius, for anything you use.'

Commentary

4.1 legem: Cincius' law was brought forward in 204 BC (Wilkins 1890: 152 ad loc.).

4.2 quid fers: *fers* here has several, perhaps three, meanings (*TLL* VI.1.540.84 refers only to an ambiguity; for greater detail see Leeman, Pinkster and Rabbie 1989: 329), which I will number (a–c) as I propose them. The primary meaning (a) given to the verb in the reply of Cincius is obvious: it picks up *legem tulit* earlier, hence '(I am proposing a law) that you ...' That is not the sense that had been intended by Cento. But what did Cento mean?

   Wilkins (1890: 152) says that this is an 'expression used to those who were offering goods for sale', without quoting any evidence. There seems little point in such an unsupported suggestion, and I will henceforth leave it aside.

Quid fers is a question found several times in Plautus addressed to someone who has just come on the scene: *Stich.* 319–20 *unde is? quid fers? quid festinas?*, *Merc.* 161 *tibi equidem a portu apporto hoc – :: quid fers? dic mihi.* The meaning (b), particularly in the second passage, could be (asked of someone just encountered), 'what news do you bring?'; in this second passage *apporto* does not have a concrete object: the line is translated by de Melo in the Loeb as 'you . . . are the one I'm bringing this news for from the harbor'. If *quid fers* was a formula of greeting, it is likely that that is one reason why it was adopted by Cento.

But *donis et muneribus* earlier in the passage suggests another possibility (c), that Cento was hinting secondarily at the idea 'what gifts are you offering?' For *fero* of the bringing of gifts see *TLL* V.1.2022.82ff. s.v. *donum. Fero* is also used with *munus* (e.g. Virg. *Aen.* 4.218). On this view he would deliberately have been misunderstanding the aim of a bill *de donis et muneribus*, as bestowing not restricting *dona* (see Leeman, Pinkster and Rabbie 1989: 329).

A variant on this view would be that Cento merely used the formula (b), but was mischievously taken by Cincius to mean (c), who consequently as a put-down chose to adopt meaning (a). There are reasons for adopting this interpretation: see the final note of this section.

4.3 Cinciole: Cento adopts the diminutive form of Cincius' name in a chance meeting in the street, and this is described by Cicero as insulting. Names in Latin (and Greek, particularly in Old Comedy) were readily given a diminutive form, almost invariably for affectionate purposes, but to accost someone who was not an intimate out of the blue in this way might well have been offensive. Here is a collection of diminutives of names in Latin (I have not restricted myself to vocatives) (see further Hofmann and Ricottilli 2003: 297–300), along with some material from Greek.

Plaut. *Cas.* 739 Olympisce mi, mi pater, mi patrone (the character's name is Olympio; the address is meant to be affectionate).
Plaut. *Poen.* 421 mi Milphidisce, mea commoditas, mea salus.
Plaut. *Stich.* 739–40 te expetimus, Stephaniscidium, mel meum (cf. 736 *Stephanium*).
Ter. *Ad.* 763 edepol, Syrisce, te curasti molliter (here the slave Syrus addresses himself in an aside; according to Martin 1976: 209, this reflects his tipsiness).
Ter. *Hec.* 81 sed uideon ego Philotium unde haec aduenit? | Philotis, salue multum (note the following *Philotis*).
Cic. *Att.* 1.8.3 Tulliola, deliciolae nostrae, tuum munusculum flagitat ('My darling Tullia is demanding your little present', Shackleton Bailey 1965–70: I.115).

Cic. *Att.* 6.5.4 et puellae salutem Atticulae tuae dices nostraeque Piliae.

Cic. *Att.* 14.20.2 Tertullae nollem abortum ('I am sorry to hear of Tertulla's miscarriage', Shackleton Bailey (1965–70: VI.61), who says (1965–70: VI.239) that since Cicero uses the diminutive again at 15.11.1, this 'was probably her usual name in the family circle'; she was Junia Tertia, 'one of M. Brutus' three half-sisters' (Shackleton Bailey 1965–70: VI.238); the instance at 15.11.1 is in a list of names, not in an emotive context – *deinde multis audientibus, Seruilia, Tertulla, Porcia, quaerere quid placeret* –, and that supports Shackleton Bailey's suggestion).

Catull. 12.17 haec amem necessest | ut Veraniolum meum (*Veranius* is in the preceding line).

Catull. 45.13 mea uita Septimille (in a poem about Septimius).

Juv. 6.105 nam Sergiolus iam radere guttur | coeperat (the affectionate diminutive used by a woman Eppia of a gladiator Sergius, her lover).

Tac. *Ann.* 6.5.1 illos quidem senatus, me autem Tiberiolus meus ('They will be protected by the senate, but I by my pet Tiberius', Woodman 2004).

Evidence for the use of diminutive forms of names also comes from a few names that have taken on a fixed diminutive form, such as *Paterculus* (see Hansen 1951: 32), *Fenestella* (Leumann 1977: 306), *Felicla* (Leumann 1977: 284), *Hispallus* (< *Hispanus*: Leumann 1977: 306). See also *CIL* VIII.7614 <u>*Quintulus*</u> *Numisius Arator* (see Schulze 1904: 460 n. 5) and above on *Tertulla* in Cicero. On female cognomina with the ending *-illa* see Leumann (1959: 80–3): these look like diminutives and may have been interpreted as such, but they probably in origin have a Greek suffix.

For Greek (Old Comedy) see e.g. Dover (1968: 104) on Aristoph. *Nub.* 80 Φειδιππίδη, Φειδιππίδιον ('wheedling diminutive'). Also Dover on *Nub.* 222–3 ὦ Σώκρατες, | ὦ Σωκρατίδιον, Olson (1998: 151) on Aristoph. *Pax* 382 ‘(E)ρμίδιον, using the phrase 'wheedling diminutive' taken from Dover. See also *Ach.* 404 Εὐριπίδη, Εὐριπίδιον with Olson (2002: 179) ad loc., adopting again the same phrase. Another possible case is at Eubulus 105.1 Hunter, Αἰγίδιον for Αἴξ. See further Schmidt (1902: 208–9), Petersen (1910: 174–6), López Eire (1996: 138–9).

Dickey (1996: 50–1) mentions various diminutives addressed to prostitutes in Lucian's *Dialogi meretricii*, but in all cases but one the prostitute's name is always in the diminutive (Dickey 1996: 50), and that may have been the standard form. In the case of just one woman the non-diminutive address also occurs in the same dialogue (1.8: see Dickey 1996: 51). Dickey says (51) that diminutives addressed to persons other than prostitutes are very rare, but she does give some examples, including four from Aristophanes that have only slight overlap with those above. See further Headlam and Knox (1922: 14) on Herodas 1.6.

4,4 'ut emas,' inquit 'Gai, si uti uelis': *emo* is not infrequently used absolutely (*TLL* V.2.511.69ff.), but this is a special use derived from a proverb (see *TLL* 512.12ff., and particularly Otto 1890: 124). There was a proverb 'buy rather than ask', with variants, such as 'nothing is more expensive that that which is bought by prayers' (see e.g. Cic. *Verr.* 4.12 *profecto hinc natum est: 'malo emere quam rogare'*. Cincius it seems has contrived to suggest that Cento has asked (for gifts) (meaning c above, 10.4.2), when he probably used a formula meaning 'what news?' (meaning b). The response of Cincius is by implication 'don't ask for what you want but buy it'.

Gai: the use of the praenomen by Cincius in his response is also significant. The normal use of the praenomen was for reference to or address of close relatives (see Dickey 2002: 63–4). It could also be used to non-relatives as a mark of contempt (see Adams: 1978: 162, Dickey 2002: 64, with the references at n. 48). Cincius matches the over-familiarity in Cento's use of the diminutive by himself adopting the praenomen, to convey a false and offensive bonhomie.

(5) Quintilian 6.3.83

Text

Illud uero, etiam si ridiculum est, indignum tamen est homine liberali, quod aut turpiter aut impotenter dicitur: quod fecisse quendam scio qui humiliori libere aduersus se loquenti 'colaphum (1)' inquit 'tibi ducam, et formulam scribam quod caput durum (2) habeas.'

Translation

On the other hand, foul or brutal language, however funny, is unworthy of a decent citizen. I know a case of this, when a man said to an inferior who had spoken freely against him, 'I will give you a clout on the head, and then bring an action against you for having such a hard head' (Russell, Loeb)

Commentary

5.1 colaphum: a significant example of *colaphus* (see above, 2.24), a word for 'blow' that was to survive in Romance languages (e.g. It. *colpo*, Fr. *coup*). Literary equivalents were *ictus, plaga* and *uerbera*. The word goes back to

Sicilian Greek and must have entered Latin from the south via the slave trade. Early on it is associated particularly with blows delivered to lower-class characters (on the word see Adams 2003a: 351 n. 100, 2007: 439, 2013: 17, Clackson 2011b: 252–3). The low tone of the word is clear from this context. The remark is described by Quintilian as unworthy of a decent citizen, and the blow itself is delivered to a social inferior. There are still then hints of its original associations. For the sense of *duco* here, of delivering a blow, see *OLD* s.v. 11a, citing Phaedr. 5.3.2.

5.2 caput durum: on the one hand this is meant literally (the person's 'hard head' damages the one who strikes him), but there was almost certainly a metaphorical meaning as well, referring to stupidity, shamelessness or the like (it is hard to be more precise, since examples are so few; for metaphorical uses of *durus* applied to body parts see *TLL* V.1.2308.235ff., but not citing this passage). Note Petron. 39.5 *itaque quisquis nascitur illo signo, multa pecora habet, multum lanae, caput praeterea durum, frontem expudoratam*. Schmeling (2011: 152) observes that 'with a sense of humour T[rimalchio] puts the *scholastici* here [the passage goes on to say that these were born under this sign of the Zodiac] . . . so that he can make fun of their thick heads'.

(6) Macrobius, *Saturnalia* 2.2.9

Text

Faustus Sullae filius cum soror eius eodem tempore duo moechos haberet, Fuluium Fullonis (1) filium et Pompeium cognomine Maculam, 'miror' inquit 'sororem meam habere maculam (2) cum fullonem habeat (3).'

Translation

When his sister had two lovers at the same time, Fulvius, the son of Fullo, and Pompeius, who had the cognomen Macula, Faustus, son of Sulla, said, 'I am surprised that my sister has a stain when she has a launderer.'

Commentary

6.1 Fullonis: I have not followed Kaster in his recent *OCT* and Loeb editions in printing this with an initial lower-case letter, since a completely balanced double entendre is achieved if it is taken instead as a cognomen (for *Fullo* as a name see *OLD* s.v. 2b), of the father of the referent but by implication of the son as well: it is a surprise that the sister has two lovers, Fullo and Macula, at the same time, and even more so that she has a *macula* despite having a *fullo* 'launderer'.

6.2 maculam: *macula* can be used of a stain on garments caused by semen, usually the garments of the male himself but here those of the woman. See Suet. *Nero* 28.2 *olim etiam quotiens lectica cum matre ueheretur, libidinatum inceste ac maculis uestis proditum affirmant*, Plin. *Nat.* 36.21 *ferunt amore captum quendam, cum delituisset noctu, simulacro cohaesisse, eiusque cupiditatis esse indicem maculam* (on *cohaereo* in this passage see Adams 1982a: 181). Note also the verb at Hor. *Sat.* 1.5.85 *immundo somnia uisu | nocturnam uestem maculant*, and see further Adams (1982a: 199).

6.2–3 habere, ... habeat: for the commonplace sexual use of *habeo* that underlies both instances of the verb here see Adams (1982a: 187).

(7) Macrobius, *Saturnalia* 2.4.6

Text

Vrbanitas eiusdem innotuit circa Herennium deditum uitiis iuuenem. quem cum castris excedere iussisset et ille supplex hac deprecatione uteretur, 'quo modo ad patrias sedes reuertar? quid patri meo dicam?', respondit, 'dic me tibi displicuisse.'

Translation

A witticism of his gained notoriety in connection with Herennius, a young man sunk in vice: when Augustus ordered him out of his camp, the young man threw himself on Augustus' mercy, saying, 'How can I return home? What will I tell my father?' Augustus replied, 'Tell him I did not please you' (Kaster, Loeb).

Commentary

preliminaries

This is a joke of Augustus. A version of the anecdote is also at Quint. 6.3.64, but it is less precise there and does not have the name of the youth, though the punch line is the same. The youth is sunk in vice here (in Quintilian he is merely discharged with ignominy by Augustus), which is likely to be a reference to pathic tendencies.

displicuisse: the negative correspondent of *placeo*, tending to a sexual sense. *Placeo* is commonly used of pleasing a lover, by attributes, often unspecified, of any type (*TLL* X.1.2259.59ff.: e.g. Publil. *Sent.* M32 *mulier quae multis nubit multis non placet*; note here the negation), but it can be used explicitly of giving sexual pleasure: e.g. Mart. 7.30.8 *qua ratione facis, cum sis Romana puella, | quod Romana tibi mentula nulla placet?*, 'how is it, since you are a Roman girl, that no Roman *mentula* pleases you?'. Here there is a failure to give pleasure. Quintilian (9.2.69) cites as an example of ambiguity *duxi uxorem quae patri placuit*, 'I married the woman who pleased my father' (the father approves the woman as wife for his son, with the secondary meaning that she was the father's lover). At Sen. *Contr.* 1.6.10 *displiceo* itself is used non-specifically of displeasing a lover, in an opposition with *placeo*: *non aliam sibi magis placere sed illam displicere dixit*. At *TLL* V.1.1416.41ff. several examples of *displiceo* 'sensu amatorio' are cited. In our joke there is a vagueness, but the idea seems to be either that Augustus displeased the youth as a potential lover, or that Augustus the *pedicator* failed to please him.

Conclusions

This is not the place to analyse jokes as jokes, nor would it do to imply that jokes have specific linguistic features that set them apart from other forms of discourse. We may however highlight some of the phenomena that appear in the highly selective corpus above.

Names in Latin offered potential for offensive remarks and double entendres, and it is play with names that is the most prominent feature seen here. Cognomina were meaningful, and the literal meaning might be drawn on to make a joke, as in the cases of *Macula* and *Fullo*. The gender system of Latin was exploited when a masculine name was converted into a feminine form, or a marked feminine designation applied to a male. The possession by individuals in the Latin system of several names opened the way for a type of name inappropriate to the context to be adopted on occasion, such as the use of a praenomen to a stranger. The *mi*-form of vocatival address was also used out of context in one of the jokes above.

A cursory look at the jokes assembled by Cicero and the others would show that diminutives constantly occur in humorous remarks. Diminutives may be not only affectionate but also contemptuous and disparaging. Names in Latin could be readily converted into diminutive form, for a variety of purposes. Another category of diminutives that turned up were those used to imply effeminacy.

A majority of the jokes above have a sexual point, which is always merely implied. It is a common attitude that the punch line of a joke if it is to be witty must not be too explicit. An implication of effeminacy lies behind most of the sexual jokes here, conveyed by such allusive terms as 'turned away', 'to be behind', 'failure to please', or the use of feminine forms or diminutives. Adultery and prostitution are also the subject of jests.

Those collecting jokes openly disapproved of the coarse or the over-direct, and partly for that reason the corpus provided by the three writers cited here is in remarkably polite language. The one term with low social associations commented on above was *colaphus*, and Quintilian disapproved of the joke containing that. There are of course sexual jokes, for example in epigram and in graffiti, that make use of blatant obscenities, but our jokes were mostly spoken not written, with an addressee and sometimes perhaps an audience. Speakers, particularly when dealing with sex, may show some reserve in public gatherings.

11
VITRUVIUS ON THE LARCH
(2.9.14–16), OF THE AUGUSTAN
PERIOD

Introduction

Vitruvius here describes a property of the larch as discovered by Caesar during a campaign. The military section of the passage appears to mimic stylistic features of Caesar's *commentarii*. Vitruvius' treatise on architecture cannot be dated precisely but it seems reasonable to place it between 35 and 25 BC (see Fleury 1990: xxiii and the whole discussion from xv to xxiv). The Latin is that of a practical man, not a man of letters with a full training in rhetoric, and Vitruvius himself (1.1.18) expresses an unease that he might sometimes have violated the rules of grammarians. The language is less standardised than that of Cicero and Caesar. At least some of its features are related to the genre. We should not expect scientific prose to match in every respect political oratory or military reports. The text printed here is close to that of Fensterbusch (1964), but with changes to the punctuation, and with one other change mentioned in the Commentary. There are a few other textual notes in the Commentary.[1]

Text

2.9.14 Larix uero, qui (1) non est notus nisi is municipalibus qui sunt circa ripam fluminis Padi (2) et litora maris Hadriani, non solum ab suco (3) uehementi amaritate (4) ab carie aut tinea non nocetur (5) sed etiam flammam ex igni non recipit, nec ipse per se potest ardere, nisi, uti (6) saxum in fornace ad calcem coquendam (7), aliis lignis uratur (8); nec tamen tunc (9) flammam recipit nec carbonem remittit, sed longo spatio (10) tarde comburitur. quod est (11) minima ignis et aeris e principiis temperatura (12), umore autem et terreno (13) est spisse solidata, non habet spatia foraminum, qua possit ignis penetrare, reicitque eius uim nec patitur ab eo sibi cito noceri, propterque pondus ab aqua non sustinetur, sed cum portatur (14) aut in

[1] I am grateful to Jan Felix Gaertner and David Langslow for their comments on a version of this chapter.

nauibus aut supra abiegnas rates conlocatur. **15** Ea autem materies (15) quemadmodum sit inuenta, est causam cognoscere (16). Diuus Caesar cum exercitum habuisset (17) circa Alpes imperauissetque municipiis praestare commeatus (18), ibique esset castellum munitum, quod uocaretur Larignum (19), tunc qui in eo fuerunt naturali munitione confisi noluerunt imperio parere. itaque imperator copias iussit admoueri. erat autem ante eius castelli portam turris ex hac materia (20) alternis trabibus transuersis uti pyra inter se composita alte, uti possent de summo sudibus et lapidibus accedentes repellere. tunc uero cum animaduersum est alia eos tela praeter sudes non habere neque posse longius a muro (21) propter pondus iaculari, imperatum est fasciculos ex uirgis alligatos et faces ardentes ad eam munitionem accedentes mittere. **16** Itaque celeriter milites congesserunt. posteaquam (22) flamma circa illam materiam uirgas comprehendisset (23), ad caelum sublata efficit opinionem (24), uti uideretur iam tota moles concidisse. cum autem ea per se extincta esset et re quieta turris intacta apparuisset, admirans Caesar iussit extra telorum missionem eos circumuallari. itaque timore coacti oppidani cum se dedidissent, quaesitum unde essent ea ligna quae ab igni non laederentur. tunc ei demonstrauerunt (25) eas arbores, quarum in his locis maximae sunt copiae. et ideo id castellum Larignum, item materies larigna est appellata. haec autem per Padum Rauennam deportatur; in colonia Fanestri, Pisauri, Anconae reliquisque quae sunt in ea regione municipiis praebetur. cuius materies (26) si esset facultas adportationibus ad urbem (27), maximae haberentur in aedificiis utilitates (28), et si non in omne, certe tabulae in subgrundiis circum insulas (29) si essent ex ea conlocatae, ab traiectionibus incendiorum aedificia periculo (30) liberarentur, quod eae (31) neque flammam nec carbonem possunt recipere nec facere per se (32).

Translation

2.9.14 The larch, which is only known to those provincials who are around the riverbank of the river Po and the shores of the Adriatic Sea, is not only not harmed by rot or worm because of the intense bitterness of its sap, but it does not even admit flame from a fire nor can it burn alone itself, except that, like stone in a kiln for producing lime, it may be burnt with the help of other firewood; but not even then does it receive flame or produce charcoal, but is slowly consumed over a long period. Because the mixture derived from the elements of fire and air is slight but it (the mixture) is tightly packed with moisture and the earthy element, (the larch) does not have wide pores where the fire can penetrate, and it repels its force and does not suffer itself to be quickly harmed by it; and because of its weight it is not supported by water, but when it is transported it is either placed on boats or on top of pine rafts. **15** The story behind how that timber was discovered is a matter of knowledge. When Divus Caesar had his army in the region of the Alps and had ordered the municipalities to furnish provisions, and there was a fortified stronghold there, which was called Larignum, then those who were in it, trusting to the natural fortification, refused to obey the order, and so the commander ordered troops to be moved up. There was before the gate of the stronghold a tower of this timber raised aloft with alternate cross-beams like a funeral pyre, so that from the top they could repel anyone approaching with stakes and stones. But then, when it was noticed that they had no other weapons but stakes and that they could not throw them far from the wall because of their weight, the order was given to approach and throw bundles of twigs bound together and burning torches against the fortification. **16** And so the soldiers quickly piled them up. After the flames had seized the twigs around the timber, they rose skyward and created an impression that the whole mass had now collapsed. But when the flames had burnt themselves out and things were quiet and the tower had emerged intact, Caesar in wonder ordered them to be walled in by a rampart beyond the range of their weapons. And so when the townsmen, compelled by fear, had surrendered, it was asked where those timbers came from that were not harmed by the fire. Then they showed him those trees, of which there is a great abundance in these parts. And for that reason the fort is called Larignum, and likewise the timber is called *larigna*. This is transported down the Po to Ravenna. It is supplied at the colony of Fanum, at Pisaurum, Ancona and the other municipalities that are in that region. If there were a facility for the transportation of this timber to the city, there would be very great benefits in buildings; if not in general, certainly if planks in the eaves around apartment blocks were put in place consisting of this timber, the buildings would be freed from the danger arising from the crossing over of fires, because these (planks) can neither catch fire nor take in charcoal nor produce it themselves.

Commentary

1 larix ... qui: this is the only instance of *larix* in the masculine cited by *TLL* VII.2.977.26. Cetius Faventinus in his epitome of Vitruvius gives the word feminine gender (12, p. 271.8 Krohn *larix uero a castello Laricino est dicta*). The feminine is also in Pliny (*Nat.* 16.219) and Palladius (12.15.1). Various tree names changed gender from feminine to masculine in the history of Latin (*alnus, fagus, fraxinus, populus, pinus*: see e.g. Väänänen 1981a: 226, Stotz

1998: 150; but note that these end in -*us*, and the analogy of the usual masculines of the second declension must have been the determinant: cf. Adams 2013: 385–6), as did *arbor* itself. The Gallo-Romance reflexes of *larix* vary between masculine and feminine (see *FEW* V.193). On the other hand in Italian dialects reflexes are masculine (so It. *larice*) in the north and the south. Tree names in Italian are almost universally assigned masculine gender (I am grateful to John Trumper for detailed information about Italian dialects).

Whatever the motivation of the masculine here, there are some anomalies of gender in Vitruvius (see Adams 2013: 396, 404, 409, 432), a phenomenon also found in Varro (see Adams 2013: 395, with cross-references) and indicative of a lack of standardisation in the classical period.

The diminutive of *genu* 'knee' is used by Vitruvius alone of extant writers in the masculine (8.6.6 *geniculus: TLL* VI.2–3.1810.2; incidentally, the alleged feminine *genicula* at Anon. *Val.* 50 is certainly neuter plural, despite *TLL* 1810.3: see Adams 1976a: 54). *Geniculus* is metaphorical in Vitruvius (of the knee or elbow-joint in a water-pipe: see *OLD*). Semantic differentiation is one determinant (see Adams 2013: 386) of gender variation (e.g. *cubitus* 'elbow' alongside *cubitum*, a term of measurement: see the next paragraph but one), though it has to be said that metaphorical uses of *geniculum* are well attested (*TLL* 1810.36ff.) and the masculine is not otherwise cited for any of these.

At 3.1.2 Vitruvius uses the word for 'nose' as a neuter (*nasum*). This is the gender of the term in early Latin (see Plaut. *Amph.* 444, *Men.* 168, *Mil.* 1256, Lucil. 267, 582, 942). The masculine nominative *nasus* is first at Cic. *Nat.* 2.143.

In the same passage (3.1.2) Vitruvius uses the anatomical term *cubitus/-um* 'elbow, forearm' as a neuter (*cubitum*). On the other hand twice (10.13.6) he uses the neuter plural *cubita* as a term of measurement ('cubits'). Where the gender of the term can be determined in other writers, usually the masculine *cubitus* is used of part of the arm, and the neuter of the measurement (*TLL* IV.1274.39ff.), but that is not a distinction that Vitruvius has observed.

Lactem for *lac* or *lacte* turns up for the first time in extant Latin at Vitr. 7.14.2 (see *TLL* VII.2.815.68ff.); the next example is in a freedman's speech in Petronius (71.1: see below, 18.21). The gender is indeterminate in the context in Vitruvius but has to be masculine or feminine.

Rudens 'rope' is usually masculine in Latin, but at Vitr. 10.15.7 is feminine (*rudentibus maioribus extentis, per quarum asperitates* . . .), a gender that it also has in Plaut. *Rud.* 938. Again Vitruvius has preserved the gender of early Latin.

Similarly *frons*, which in classical Latin is usually feminine, is in Vitruvius both masculine (10.11.7) and feminine (2.8.4), as it had been in Plautus (m. *Mil.* 201, f. *Rud.* 318).

The term for 'harbour', which is usually masculine (*portus*), is neuter at 2.8.11 (*portum utile* GH; so at 2.8.13 G and H have *portum*, which is corrected to *portus* by S). Note *TLL* X.2.59.58 'genus neutr. vix recte suspicatur Fensterbusch ad VITR. 2, 8, 11'. There is in this case a change of declension as well, from fourth to second. There is no other neuter form of the second declension cited at *TLL* 59.51ff. The variation in this term is paralleled in *angiportus* versus *angiportum*.

Vitruvius' use of *pelagus* is also anomalous, though gender change is not necessarily at issue. The word is for the most part in Latin a neuter of the second declension in *-us* (cf. *uulgus*) (*TLL* X.1.989.42ff. with cross-references), with occasional variants in *-um*, as at 2.8.14 *in pelagum eduxit classem*. This form (without an adjective in agreement) might be either masculine or a remodelled neuter.

There is other morphological variability in Vitruvius that is not gender-related. For example, he uses both *uas* and *uasum* and *uase* and *uaso*.

2 circa ripam fluminis Padi: *ripam* is translated by Granger (Loeb) as if it were plural, probably rightly: Vitruvius surely does not mean that the larch grew on only one side of the Po. This must be a collective use of the term, embracing both banks of the river (cf. Eng. 'riverbank', as in the title of the children's television programme 'Tales of the Riverbank') (David Langslow provided this parallel, and I am grateful to Brian Campbell for other information used in this note). Note Hyginus *Agr.* p. 87.14 Thulin = p. 90.24 Campbell *circa Padum autem cum ageretur, quod flumen torrens et aliquando tam uiolentum decurrit, ut alueum mutet et multorum late agros trans ripam, ut ita dicam, transferat* ('Now, when there was a dispute in the area of the Po because the river surges down sometimes in such a raging torrent that it changes its course and carries across its bank, so to speak, the land of many people over a wide area', Campbell 2000: 91). Here the Po in flood is described as bursting its banks, obviously on both sides, but the singular is used (it 'carries the fields across its bank' in the sense that as it widens it moves the fields into the river, across the new banks, as it were). For *ripas* in such a context see Livy 4.49.2, Sic. Flacc. *Agr.* p. 122.10 Thulin. For the singular note also *Grom.* I.365.27 Lachmann *plurisque super ripam paludis sacra paganorum inueniuntur*.

For the use of a collective singular to embrace a set of two members the obvious parallel lies in the singular use of anatomical terms denoting body parts that come in pairs: e.g. Hor. *Sat.* 1.2.102–3 *Cois tibi paene uidere est | ut nudam, ne crure malo, ne sit pede turpi; | metiri possis oculo latus, Odes* 2.2.23 *quisquis ingentes oculo inretorto | spectat aceruos.* Various idiomatic phrases containing *manus* have indifferently a plural or collective singular, such as *manibus/manu* 'by force' (*OLD* 8b; cf. also 9f), *committere et sim.* + *manus/manum* of joining battle (*OLD* 9c), *aequis manibus/aequa manu* 'on equal terms' (*OLD* 9e). To 'go on foot' is usually expressed by *pedibus* (*OLD* 6a), but for the singular see Ovid *Pont.* 3.1.28 *nec pede quo quisquam nec rate tutus eat.* The ears as the organ of hearing are usually expressed in the plural (*OLD* s.v. *auris* 2), but for the singular see Hor. *Epist.* 2.1.187 *uerum equitis quoque iam migrauit ab aure uoluptas* | *omnis ad incertos oculos,* Quint. 1.5.19 *illa (uitia) uero non nisi aure exiguntur quae fiunt per sonos.* Good examples of collective/generic singular anatomical terms in Vitruvius himself are at 1.2.4: *uti in hominis corpore e cubito, pede, palmo, digito ceterisque particulis symmetros est eurythmiae qualitas.*

3 ab suco: some editors (Rose and Müller-Strübing 1867, Krohn 1912) prefer the variant reading *suci,* but this has the consequence that the passive verb *nocetur* is complemented by two separate expressions with *ab* (*ab suci ... amaritate* and *ab carie aut tinea*), apparently with different functions. Marini (1836) attempted to get round this problem by printing *ob succi uehementem amaritatem,* but *ob* is out of the question: Vitruvius admits this preposition only in the formula *quas ob res,* four times. Far better (with Fensterbusch 1964 and Callebat, Gros and Jacquemard 1999) is the adnominal expression *ab suco* linked to *amaritate* and expressing the source of the *amaritas,* with *amaritate* a causal ablative ('because of the bitterness coming from the sap').

The adnominal is entirely in keeping with Vitruvius' style. Vitruvius was not examined by Wharton (2009) in his account of the distribution of adnominal prepositional expressions (which have sometimes wrongly been claimed not to have been allowed in Latin at all: see Wharton 2009: 184; see too in general on such expressions Kühner and Stegmann 1955: I.213–18, Hofmann and Szantyr 1965: 428; also *TLL* I.16.59ff.), but they are particularly common in the work (for further details see below, 11.30, and also 7, 12, 20, 23, 27, 28, 29). Wharton (2009: 198) found no clear diachronic trends in the distribution of such usages, but a 'high degree of variability from author to author'. He also suggested (199) that adnominal prepositional phrases (APPs) with non-verbal nouns were a 'normal feature of everyday, spoken Latin, whereas APPs attached to verbal nouns [were] more typical of higher or more literary registers of Latin' (notably Tacitus) (see above, 9.14 for an example with a verbal noun). So in the speeches of the freedmen in Petronius APPs attached to non-verbal nouns are the norm, and that is the case with most of the examples that will be noted below in this passage of Vitruvius.

For comparable examples to that here see Vitr. 5.10.3 *non enim a uapore umor corrumpere poterit materiem* 'moisture from the heat' (cited by Wistrand

1933: 73),[2] 6.1.3 *sanguine multo ab umoris plenitate . . . sunt conformati*; also
6.1.3 *ex caelo roscidus aer* (with *ex*). Note too e.g. Ovid *Met.* 8.410, *Ars* 2.179 *ab
arbore ramus*, Tac. *Ann.* 11.31.3 *interrogantibus quid aspiceret, respondisse
tempestatem ab Ostia atrocem.*

Sometimes, as in the expression in the present context and in the passages
from Ovid just cited, this use of *ab* would be replaceable with a genitive.
A particularly clear case of this 'genitival' use derivable from the separative is
at 7.3.6: *cum ab harena . . . non minus tribus coriis fuerit deformatum*, 'when it
has been laid out with not less than three coats of/from sand'. A few sentences
later there is (7.3.6) *cum tribus coriis harenae . . . solidati parietes fuerint* (cf.
also 7.3.8 for the genitive). The equivalent separative > genitival use of *de* was
eventually to lead to the Romance genitive.

Adnominal expressions come up often in our texts, in one or two with
striking frequency: see index, 'adnominal prepositional expressions',
'adverbs'.

4 amaritate: this is the only literary example of the noun *amaritas* cited by the
TLL (otherwise there is just one case in a gloss). *Amaritudo*, the usual formation, is not used by Vitruvius. The suffix *-tudo* was particularly productive in
early Latin (Rosén 1981: 61), but its productivity declined during the Republic,
as part of a tendency for the number of functionally overlapping nominal
suffixes attached to the same root to diminish (Rosén 1999: 62–6; see however
Langslow 2000: 309–13 on the continuing use of *-tudo* in forming medical
terms; also below). That does not explain Vitruvius' usage here, given the
continuing currency of *amaritudo*. He did, however, have something of a taste
for formations in *-tas*. He is the only writer extant (apart from his summariser
Cetius Faventinus) to have *macritas* (2.4.3). *Macritudo* had been used by
Plautus (*Capt.* 135). The commonplace *macies* is not used by Vitruvius.
More striking is his use, five times, of *plenitas* (1.4.6, 5.9.5, 6.1.3, 7.8.2, 8.2.2),
a term found in no other writer apart from a few grammarians commenting on
it. The usual term *plenitudo* is not used by him. He was also the first writer to
use *spissitas* (2.9.8), a word cited otherwise only from Pliny (*Nat.* 18.304) by the
OLD. *Spissitudo* is in Seneca and Scribonius Largus. Another oddity is *similitas*
(2.9.5). This is cited by the *OLD* from only one other writer, Caecilius (216).
Similitudo was common, and is used six times by Vitruvius himself. If he felt
that the *-tas* formation was particularly suited to his technical treatise, that
does not mean that he set out to avoid terms in *-tudo*. Particularly striking is
grauitudo at 1.6.3, a medical term, of a '[h]eavy or oppressed condition (of the

---

[2] This same section has two other APPs: *tergulae sine marginibus, camarae in caldariis.*

body or its parts)' (*OLD* s.v.). Vitruvius alone has this word in the period covered by the *OLD*. It occurs in late Latin (*TLL* VI.2.2309.72ff.), perhaps most notably in the medical writer Caelius Aurelianus. Langslow (2000: 313) has observed an unmistakable 'clustering of derivatives in *-tudo* in the vocabulary related to disease', and *grauitudo* falls into that category. One other term worth mentioning is *salsitudo* (1.4.11), cited by the *OLD* only from here.

5 ab carie aut tinea non nocetur: here Vitruvius uses *tinea* ('the larva of a moth, beetle, etc.', *OLD* s.v., but possibly referring to woodworm) in the singular, but cf. 2.9.13 *a tineis et carie non laeduntur*. This is a familiar type of collective or generic singular, in reference to types of animals (E. Löfstedt 1956: I.14, 18–19).

Noceo governs a dative rather than an accusative, and thus according to the school rule (see e.g. Gildersleeve and Lodge 1895: 220, §346 R. 1) when expressed in the passive it ought to be impersonal and retain its dative object (*larix, cui ab carie aut tinea non nocetur*). Vitruvius, however, gives the verb the personal passive construction of ordinary transitive verbs, not only here but also at 2.7.3. On the other hand he has the expected impersonal passive construction in this same section, *nec patitur ab eo sibi cito noceri*, an illustration of the variability of his syntax. An ambiguous construction occurs at 1.1.15: *si <u>uulnus mederi</u> aut aegrum eripere de periculo oportuerit*, 'if it is necessary for a wound to be healed or to snatch a sick person from danger' (alternatively one might understand an indefinite personal subject of *mederi*, 'if it is necessary for one to heal ...', with *mederi* taking an accusative object rather than a dative; Vitruvius uses both the accusative (8.3.4) and dative (e.g. 6.8.6) with this verb, another sign of the lack of standardisation to his Latin).

In fact the rule is not as absolute as it is made out to be. Kühner and Stegmann (1955: I.103) cite for the passive use of *noceo* Sen. *Dial.* 5.5.5 *non noceri uult*, as well as examples of other verbs that govern a dative used in the personal passive. *Imperor* for example occurs at Hor. *Epist.* 1.5.21. *Persuadeo* is so used at *Rhet. Her.* 1.10 (*si persuasus auditor*), by a correspondent of Cicero (Caecina, *Fam.* 6.7.2), at *B. Afr.* 55.1, and sometimes in Augustan poetry (see Gibson 2003: 356 on Ovid *Ars* 3.679). Wölfflin and Miodoński (1889: 90) point out that, though the personal passive construction with *persuadeo* is permitted by the author of the *B. Afr.*, it was not permitted by Caesar, and it might be added that whereas Cicero's correspondent Caecina allows it Cicero himself does not. There are many such differences between Cicero's practice and that of his correspondents (see the Commentary on Caelius, text 9, and also below, 11.16 on *est* + infinitive). If Cicero's usage reflects some sort of grammarians' idealised standard, standardisation was far from absolute among the educated in the late Republic and Augustan period. Gender variations in Vitruvius (see above, 11.1) have the same story to tell.

Vitruvius twice elsewhere as here uses the prepositional expression *ab carie* (usually with *tinea* as well) with a passive verb (cf. 2.9.13 *non laeduntur*, 7.3.1 *uitiantur*). He does not have the ablative *carie* on its own with a passive verb. Here is a notable feature of his syntax: inanimate or abstract agents are often expressed in the passive by means of the preposition *ab*, just as in all types of Latin animate, particularly human, agents are expressed in this way. The *ab*-expression with inanimates is unusual, in that normally classical Latin prefers the plain ablative of inanimate agents. However, the Vitruvian construction is logical, in that (e.g.) *caries* is an agent (it is coordinated with an animate, *tinea*), and not an instrument. Its role is brought out by the fact that *caries* is also employed by Vitruvius in the nominative as the perpetrator/cause of an event (7.3.1 *cui nec caries nec uetustas nec umor possit nocere*; cf. 1.5.3). There is a worldview inherent in the use of *ab* in the passive with such inanimates: natural processes, forces of nature, natural phenomena such as heavenly bodies and rivers are seen as doers in their own right, whether or not any personification was felt. The same attitude is also to be seen in the common use of terms denoting forces of nature and the like as the subject of reflexive verbs (rivers hurl themselves along, the moon moves itself, and so on: see Adams 2013: 693–4, 695–6, 709–11 (the last on Vitruvius)). Similarly Langslow (2000: 193–201) has shown that in medical writers there is a 'considerable element of corporeality, animacy, and even anthropomorphism implied in the vocabulary used of physiological processes, and of the actions and effects of disease on the body and of medical remedies on both body and disease' (194).

There are numerous comparable expressions in Vitruvius (details below). Many of them, however, are not unambiguously agentive. There is also a well-established use of *ab* to convey cause/source, as for example at Livy 30.6.1 *ab eodem errore credere et ipsi sua sponte incendium ortum* ('because of/as a result of/from the same error they too believed that the fire had broken out of its own accord') (see Kühner and Stegmann 1955: I.495–6). How, for instance, are we to take 9.1.16 *feruens ab ardore solis efficitur*? Does *ab ardore solis* mean 'by the heat of the sun' (agentive) or 'because of/from . . .'? Nevertheless there are places where it would be implausible to give an *ab*-expression with a passive verb in Vitruvius anything other than an agentive meaning, as at 4.1.4 *ab aqua est deuorata*, where a town is 'swallowed up by water'. Even when a causal interpretation is possible, the *ab*-expression is usually ambiguous and may be taken as agentive as well.

Here are some details of Vitruvian usage. In the following nineteen alphabetically numbered subdivisions (arranged alphabetically by agent noun) there is quoted first a prepositional phrase or two from Vitruvius, followed usually by passages in other writers containing the same term used in the ablative without a preposition. Comparative material is taken particularly from Cicero's philosophica, where the same forces of nature often come up. Cicero rarely uses the preposition with such terms.

(a) 5.9.6 *ab aere umores ex corporibus exsugantur molestiores* (cf. 3.3.11); cf. Stat. *Silv.* 3.2.70 *fugimus exigua clausi trabe et aere nudo. Aere* is used once by Vitruvius with a passive verb.

(b) 6.3.11 *sin autem inpedientur ab angustiis.* There is one instance of the ablative with a passive (8.3.3).

(c) 2.9.14 *ab aqua non sustinetur,* 4.1.4 *ab aqua est deuorata,* 8.3.8 *ab ipsa aqua unguntur,* 9.8.8 *ab aqua subleuatur;* cf. Cic. *Cato* 57 *ubi enim potest illa aetas . . . umbris aquisue refrigerari salubrius?, Nat.* 2.27 *qui aquis continetur,* 2.129 *facile enim illa (oua) aqua et sustinentur et fetum fundunt,* Virg. *Aen.* 8.549 *pars cetera prona | fertur aqua,* Ovid *Ars* 1.476 *dura tamen molli saxa cauantur aqua,* Livy 21.28.7 *ne secunda aqua deferretur.* The ablative is used by Vitruvius once with a passive verb (apart from clear instrumental uses, where someone does something with water).

(d) 9.1.16 *feruens ab ardore solis efficitur;* cf. Cic. *Rep.* 6.21 *medium autem illum et maximum solis ardore torreri, Div.* 1.114 *ardore aliquo inflammati atque incitati, Nat.* 2.31 *acerrimo et mobilissimo ardore teneatur. Ardore* is not used without the preposition by Vitruvius.

(e) 6.1.2 *premuntur a calore,* 6.1.3 *non exhauritur a caloribus umor* (also 6.6.2, 8.3.10); cf. Cic. *Nat.* 2.25 *omnes igitur partes mundi . . . calore fultae sustinentur,* 2.31 *homines bestiaeque hoc calore teneantur,* 2.136 *ut facile et calore . . . et terendo cibo et praeterea spiritu omnia cocta atque confecta in reliquum corpus diuidantur, Tusc.* 1.69 *urantur calore, Mul. Chir.* 143 *caloribus soluuntur. Calore/caloribus* do not occur in Vitruvius with a passive verb.

(f) 2.9.16 *ab igni non laederentur* (so at 8.3.19; note too 8.2.4 *ab ignis uapore percalefactum*); cf. Cic. *Div.* 1.17 *aetherio flammatus Iuppiter igni | uertitur* (from his own poetry). Most examples of *ab igni* cited at *TLL* VII.1.298.20ff., apart from those in Vitruvius himself, are not with passive verbs (e.g. *ab igni . . . tutus* at Caes. *Civ.* 2.10.5 is quite different), but cf. Ovid *Met.* 8.514 *inuitis correptus ab ignibus,* where there is an obvious personification. *Igni* is found once with a passive verb in Vitruvius.

(g) 2.3.1 *cum ab imbribus in parietibus sparguntur*; cf. Hor. *Epist.* 1.11.11 *imbre lutoque* | *aspersus*, Livy 21.31.12 *imbribus auctus ingentem transgredientibus tumultum fecit*, Amm. 17.7.13 *aureo quonam imbri perfusa*. *Imbre/imbribus* are never with a passive verb in Vitruvius.

(h) 10.5.1 *percutiuntur ab impetu fluminis*; cf. Cic. *Off.* 1.49 *quasi uento impetu animi incitati, Tusc.* 2.30 *profiteri se neque fortunae impetu nec multitudinis opinione . . . terreri* (but both examples metaphorical), Livy 24.10.8 *prouoluta uelut impetu torrentis*, 35.21.5 *Tiberis infestiore . . . impetu illatus urbi*, Sen. *Nat.* 1.1.6 *maiore impetu impulsae* (of clouds) (cf. *Nat.* 2.22.2), 3.27.14 *eodem impetu omne pecus . . . mersum est*, Curt. 8.13.16 *impetu amnis ablati sunt. Impetu* is twice in Vitruvius with passive verbs.

(i) 2.7.5 *ab natura rerum probata durare poterunt. A natura* is found with a passive verb in Vitruvius fourteen times. *Natura* (ablative) occurs five times. The prepositional expression is common, at least in genres in which a personified Nature might have been felt to be at work. In Cicero *a natura* is found with passive verbs (particularly *dari*) more than fifty times, almost exclusively in the philosophical works (e.g. *Div.* 2.96 *corrigerentur ab natura* (see Pease 1963 ad loc.), *Fin.* 2.45 *rationem habent a natura datam*, 5.24 *appetitus a natura datur, Off.* 1.13 *animus bene informatus a natura*). Cicero was not, however, consistent: there are also in the philosophica many examples of the plain ablative *natura* with passive verbs (e.g. with *dari* at *Fin.* 2.33, 3.66, 5.2; see further Merguet 1892: 646–7). Livy has the plain ablative at 6.18.10 and 29.21.11 but *a natura* never.

(j) 2.9.6 *flectitur ab onere*, 6.8.4 *cunei ab oneribus parietum pressi*; cf. Sall. *Hist.* frg. 1.98 *onere . . . deprimebantur*, Cic. *Verr.* 5.63 *nauem onere suo . . . depressam*, Livy 26.45.3 *onere ipso frangebantur*, 38.40.12 *impeditos oneribus*, Apul. *Met.* 1.9 *octo annorum onere . . . distenditur*. Vitruvius has *onere/oneribus* once with a passive verb.

(k) 10.16.11 *et ab aquae multitudine et ab ruina specus omnes sunt oppressi.* Cf. 2.8.3 for *ab ruina*. Vitruvius does not have the plain ablatives *ruina* or *multitudine* with passive verbs. Contrast Cic. *Div.* 2.20 *ruina igitur oppressus esset*, Livy 44.5.7 *simili ruina inferioris pontis deferebantur*.

(l) 2.4.3 *ab sole et luna et pruina concoctae resoluuntur* (see also 6.1.10, 8.2.3 for *ab sole* with passive verbs). For the prepositional construction in Cicero see *Nat.* 2.118 *iis qui a sole ex agris tepefactis et ex aquis excitantur* (with Pease 1958 ad loc: 'the sun seems here personified'). Livy has *sole* at 26.17.14 but *a sole* never. *Sole* without preposition is not so used by Vitruvius.

(m) 2.3.4 *a tempestatibus non dissoluuntur* (so 2.7.3, 2.7.5); cf. Cic. *Att.* 11.16.4 *tempestatibus retentus est, Acad.* 2.8 *quasi tempestate delati, Tusc.* 5.5. *magna iactati tempestate confugimus* (cf. for the ablative Caes. *Gall.* 3.12.3, Livy 23.40.6, 29.18.5, 29.27.14, 37.13.2). *Tempestatibus* occurs twice in Vitruvius with passive verbs.

(n) 1.4.3 *ab ignis uapore percalefactum* (so 7.8.2, 8.2.4); cf. Cic. *Cato* 51 *tepefactum uapore, Nat.* 2.118 *terrae, maris, aquarum uaporibus aluntur. Vapore* is never used without a preposition with a passive verb by Vitruvius.

(o) 2.8.18 *in tecto tegulae fuerint fractae aut a uentis deiectae*; cf. Plaut. *Per.* 773–4 *nos uentisque fluctibusque | iactatae,* Cic. *Fam.* 16.9.1 *ibi retenti uentis sumus, Nat.* 2.26 *maria agitata uentis, Tusc.* 1.119 *sin reflantibus uentis reiiciemur,* Livy 21.58.8 *et mox aqua leuata uento* (cf. 24.8.13, 29.27.10, 37.24.9). Vitruvius has *a uentis* three times with passives, *uentis* never.

(p) 7.3.1 *abiegnei ab carie et ab uetustate celeriter uitiantur* (also 10.2.13); cf. Cic. *Nat.* 1.28 *quae uel morbo uel somno uel obliuione uel uetustate delentur, Tusc.* 3.32 *nam neque uetustate minui mala nec fieri praemeditata leuiora,* 3.74 *cum constet aegritudinem uetustate tolli,* Apul. *Met.* 4.18 *capulos carie et uetustate semitectos.* At 7.3.1, as remarked above early in this note (p. 172), Vitruvius also writes *cui nec caries nec uetustas nec umor posit nocere,* with *uetustas* (and *caries*) overtly expressed as agents in the nominative. He has *uetustate/-ibus* three times with passive verbs.

(q) 8.6.13 *sin autem eripietur lumen a ui uaporis,* 10.6.3 *ut ab aquae ui ne dissoluantur*; cf. Cic. *Cluent.* 138 *mare uentorum ui agitari atque turbari,* Suet. *Dom.* 15.2 *titulus excussus ui procellae … decidit. Vi* + genitive occurs twice in Vitruvius with passive verbs.

(r) 9.1.4 *cetera sub terram subeuntia ab eius umbra obscurantur*; cf. Cic. *Cato* 57 *ubi enim potest illa aetas … umbris aquisue refrigerari salubrius?, Tusc.* 2.36 *parietum umbris occuluntur. Vmbra* (ablative) is not used thus by Vitruvius.

(s) 7.4.1 *ab umore ne uitientur* (so 8.1.5); cf. Cic. *Nat.* 2.40 *cum sol igneus sit Oceanique alatur umoribus,* 2.43 *marinis terrenis umoribus longo interuallo extenuatis alantur,* Curt. 8.10.25 *terra umore diluta. Vmore* occurs five times with passive verbs.

Also worth noting is 8.3.2 *ex his autem qui non sunt aperti, sed a saxis continentur,* though *a* is an emendation for *aut.* The preposition would be in line with Vitruvian usage, because a rock formation is a natural phenomenon.

With the nouns listed above (apart from the last) there are fifty-five instances of *ab* complementing passive verbs in Vitruvius, compared with just twenty-four instances of the plain ablative. These figures are at variance with what one finds in classical and literary texts in general. An examination of Cicero's philosophical works shows that he almost invariably uses only the plain ablative with the same terms (except *ab natura*). This material gives a clear impression of a mannerism of Vitruvius' syntax, though it would be possible (as pointed out at the start of this note) to be more specific about semantic distinctions. There seems to have been a feeling among literary stylists writing in prose against referring to an abstract entity or phenomenon of nature as if it were agent of an action, a feeling based perhaps on an unwillingness to be seen as personifying abstractions. To call the prepositional usages 'vulgar', the usual explanation resorted to for any non-Ciceronian usage, would be unreasonable, not least because of the ambiguities between an agentive and causal interpretation: the causal use of *ab* was widespread and literary. It seems preferable to set up a generic distinction between literary prose in general and technical writing (including verse: note Lucr. 3.429 *a tenui causa magis icta mouetur*), with the practitioner of a technical *ars* not afraid to give surface expression in passive constructions to the agency of forces of nature (see also the discussion of Langslow 2000: 193–201).

Some parallels to Vitruvius' usage are found in another technical text, Celsus' medical work. Note the following instances of *ab* with terms expressing body parts, bodily functions or abstractions construed with the passive:

2.1.9 ab aestate tantum proxima pressos interemit.

2.8.41 a menstruis defecta est.

3.21.4 si a stomacho retentum est.

3.27.2A deinde retento spiritu ab ipsa exercitatione potius superiores partes mouendae.

4.1.11 supraque elapsa ab ipsa uulua sustinetur.

7.12.3A si (uua) . . . nihilo minus autem ultra iustum modum a pituita deducta sit (perhaps causal rather than agentive).

But Celsus sometimes goes beyond Vitruvius, by using *ab* and the passive with a concrete noun designating not a natural force but an inanimate object:

7.4.4B id sanescit, quod a lino relictum est et id, quod ab eo mordetur, inciditur ('that which has been released from the thread undergoes healing, and that which is still "bitten" by it, is being cut into'; the thread by which the patient is bitten is tied by the medical practitioner and is logically an instrument, but here it seems to be personified).

7.5.1C quae maior fit, si ab illo telo, dum redit, corpus laniatur ('this becomes more severe if the body is lacerated by the missile itself while the missile is coming out').

7.5.4C ne quis neruus aut uena aut arteria a telo laedatur ('lest any sinew or vein or artery is harmed by the weapon'; strictly the weapon is an instrument by means of which the doctor might harm the patient as he withdraws it from the body, or should we talk of 'source' in these last two cases?; alternatively some prefer to speak of ab + ablative as 'causal': see e.g. Fedeli 1980: 382 on Prop. 1.16.14).

Practical men probably had a habit of personifying the tools or objects with which they worked, but there tends to be an ambiguity about such examples. At Ovid Ars 1.763, for instance (hic iaculo pisces, illic capiuntur ab hamis), ab hamis in alternation with an instrumental ablative certainly looks instrumental, but one might give some local force to the preposition: fish are caught (by men) 'from hooks', i.e. by being detached from hooks carrying bait.

For the agentive/causal use of ab in Pelagonius see 204.1 id accidit cum praeclusi sunt a cruditate nimia meatus, 252 si forte ab axe fuerit percussus, 287 ad eos qui a feno malo laeduntur (the same construction with the active verb laedo at 181 favours the interpretation that ab indicates source/cause: si . . . aut a nimio tractu aut a pondere dorsum laeserit), 448.2 optandum est ut potius priora equi ab istis tuberculis et ab ipsa passione teneantur (here the agentive interpretation seems better).

6 nisi, uti: at first sight this looks like the use of nisi ut(i) + subjunctive = 'except that', as at 6.2.1 nulla architecto maior cura esse debet, nisi uti proportionibus ratae partes habeant aedificia rationum excactiones (see OLD s.v. nisi 6 c). There follows immediately a comparison: larch may burn with other timbers, just as stone in a lime-kiln. Marini (1836) ad loc. catches the force of the comparison as follows: 'Nempe, uti saxum in fornace ad calcem efficiendam coquitur.' The presence of modal uti in Marini's paraphrase ('as stone . . .') highlights a lack of clarity in Vitruvius' text. There is no modal uti present on the above interpretation of nisi uti, and it would have to be deduced by the reader that the subject of uratur is the larch rather than saxum, which would be appositional to the subject. The meaning would be clearer if Vitruvius had written ut(i) twice: nisi ut, uti saxum in fornace ad calcem coquendam, aliis lignis uratur. A haplography might have caused the loss of one ut(i). It is indeed a moot point whether the required comparison could possibly be extracted from the clause if nisi uti did mean 'except that'. If the text is to be retained it seems preferable to separate nisi and uti, punctuating with Marini nisi, uti . . . coquendam, aliis. On this view we would have nisi = 'except that', = nisi quod, for which see above, 2.24.

The form *uti*, which is common in early Latin (see above, 1.2 on Ennius and Cato), was used mainly by archaisers (e.g. Sallust) from the late Republic onwards, or at least by those who did not move with the times. Vitruvius uses *uti* more often than *ut*, if the manuscripts are to be trusted; even though there is bound to have been some scribal inaccuracy, the considerable frequency of *uti* makes it likely that Vitruvius admitted the form freely. *Vti* outnumbers *ut* by 421:234 (1.8:1) (details from Callebat *et al.* 1984, with good classification of the uses). These figures conceal some variations of usage. First, modal *uti* (= 'as', as suggested for the present passage, with a noun rather than a verbal construction) is proportionately more common than *uti* as a subordinating conjunction: it is preferred to *ut* by 184:51 (3.6:1), whereas as a subordinating conjunction *uti* outnumbers *ut* by 229:183 (1.2:1). Second, within the work Vitruvius' taste shows some fluctuations. It is in books 3–6 that *uti* is at its most frequent: *uti* (modal) is preferred to *ut* by 76:13 (5.8:1), and *uti* (conjunction) is preferred by 122:56 (2.1:1). In books 1–2 *ut* is at its most frequent. As a conjunction *ut* outnumbers *uti* here, by 45:41, and modal *ut* is outnumbered only by 35:18 (1.9:1). For books 3–6 as forming a stylistic unit see below, 11.9 on *tunc/tum*.

7 saxum in fornace ad calcem coquendam: a double adnominal construction (for another see below, 11.29), which shows the freedom with which Vitruvius was prepared to attach prepositional expressions to nouns. *In fornace* is attached to *saxum* and *ad calcem coquendam* to *fornace*. *Fornax ad calcem coquendam* is a composite expression for 'lime-kiln'. Here as often the head nouns are concrete not verbal.

8 aliis lignis uratur: *aliis lignis* is an instrumental ablative, = 'by means of/with the help of other pieces of wood', which comes close to expressing accompaniment ('along with').

9 tunc: in Vitruvius *tunc* outnumbers *tum* by 89:37. This is a reversal of earlier classical practice: in the *Rhet. Her.*, Cicero and Caesar it is *tum* that is overwhelmingly preferred (details may be found in Hofmann and Szantyr 1965: 520, and particularly in the long discussion of Svennung 1935: 407–18, with the comparative table at 409; see also above, 1.11 on early Latin). Vitruvius' preference is an anticipation of things to come, as *tum* was gradually eliminated and is absent from many late writers. Other early imperial writers, such as Seneca, also already prefer *tunc*. Celsus, however, a notable classiciser, still greatly prefers *tum* (see the index of Richardson 1982). In Vitruvius there are fluctuations of preference in different books. In books 1–2 *tunc* is preferred by only 21:13, whereas in books 3–6 it outnumbers *tum* far more markedly, by

30:3. There are also places, not taken into account in these figures, where manuscripts are split.

For a comprehensive treatment of *tum* and *tunc* in Augustan poetry, see Gaertner (2007).

10–11 longo spatio tarde: Vitruvius presumably preferred to use the nominal phrase *longo spatio* rather than *diu* alongside a second adverb, and *diu* might not have given precisely the required sense (the substance does not merely burn for a long time but is reduced to ashes over a long time). He did however have something of a taste for temporal circumlocutions comprising noun + adjective standing as equivalents or near equivalents of either adverbs or single nouns (for such circumlocutions in late Latin see Adams 1976a: 84 with bibliography, and on the classical period see below). *Diu*, for example, is not favoured in some late texts (though its comparative *diutius* is more common), and may be replaced by circumlocutions such as *tempus + longum, multum, diuturnum* (see Adams 1976a: 84). For circumlocutions in Vitruvius note 8.2.9 *ideo diutius non potest permanere, sed breui spatio fit frigida* (*breui spatio* is interchangeable with *mox*, as also at 9.praef.15 and 9.8.13; Vitruvius never uses *mox*; for this phrase and its equivalence to *mox* see *TLL* II.2173.67ff., citing examples not only from Vitruvius but also *Rhet. Her.* 4.31, *B. Alex.* 47.5, Sall. *Cat.* 56.2, *Jug.* 87.3, Livy 29.36.3: Cicero is not listed, but he is cited numerous times at 2173.28ff. for *breui tempore = mox*), 2.3.2 *per uernum tempus*, 4.1.9 *circum uernum tempus*, 2.9.10 *paulum tempus*, 1.4.2, 6.praef.3 *nullo tempore* (Vitruvius does not use *numquam*), 2.9.2 *autumnali tempore*, 6.4.1 *uespertino tempore* (cf. 1.4.1 *uespere*), 9.3.1 *sostitiale tempus*, 9.7.1 *aequinoctiali tempore*, 5.11.4, 6.1.9, 6.7.5 *per hiberna tempora*, 6.8.5 *hibernis temporibus*. For *uernum* with and without *tempus* in Cato and Varro see above, 5.6; and for another such circumlocution in Cicero (*omni tempore*) see Adams (2003b: 570–1). Expressions of these types are also in Lucretius (e.g. 1.26 *tempore in omni = semper*, 3.553 *in paruo ... tempore = mox*).

11 quod est . . .: this long sentence (to *conlocatur*) lacks coherence because of a change of subject (not specified in the text) halfway through. The subject of *est* and *est . . . solidata* must be *temperatura* (on which see below), but then the subject changes at *non habet* to the tree itself, which continues as subject to the end of the sentence. Krohn (1912), however, introduces the words <*namque ea materies*> before *quod est* as the beginning of a new sentence. With this change *materies* becomes subject of *est* and remains subject for the rest of the sentence, and *minima ... temperatura* has to be reinterpreted as a descriptive ablative. Much earlier Marini (1836) had achieved a consistent subject throughout by changing *larix ... qui* to *larix ... quae*. Thus the larch is subject throughout, and *minima temperatura* is again taken as an ablative. However, this emend-ation entails changing *ipse* to *ipsa* too. Abrupt changes of subject are not unusual in technical prose (see below, 11.31), and I see no reason to suspect the text printed here.

12 ignis et aeris e principiis temperatura: *e principiis* is another adnominal prepositional expression, replaceable in this context with a genitive, and the genitives *ignis* and *aeris* are dependent on it. *Principia* is Vitruvius' term for the four Empedoclean elements fire, air, earth, water (Gk. στοιχεῖα), an equiva-lence he states explicitly at 1.4.5. *Principia* had been used in this way by Cicero (e.g. *Tusc.* 1.22) and Varro (*Rust.* 1.4.1) (*TLL* X.2.1311.69ff.). Lucretius for metrical reasons had used *primordia* (*TLL* X.2.1271.61ff.), with *principia* substituted for it in the genitive plural (see Munro 1886: II.34 on Lucr. 1.55, with a good note on terms for atoms and elements; also 1886: II.189 on Lucr. 3.262; for a few remarks about *elementum* in Latin and alternatives see Lumpe 1959: 1075–6; also Diels 1899: 68–91 on *elementum*, and 7 on synonyms in Latin). *Temperatura* is a distinctively Vitruvian term for the mixture of elements in the proper proportion (see Zellmer 1976: 280); most of the examples cited at *OLD* are from Vitruvius. Other writers use other suffixal derivatives on the same root, namely *temperamentum* (*OLD* s.v. 1a) and *temperatio* (*OLD* s.v. 1), an indication of the variety of abstract nominal suffixes available in Latin and the element of personal preference. Vitruvius makes a distinction at 1.4.5 between *mixtio*, of the mixing of the elements (Gk. μεῖξις), and *temperatura*, of the natural proportion of the mixture: *e principiis, quae Graeci στοιχεῖα appellant, ut omnia corpora sunt composita, id est e calore et umore, terreno et aere, et ita mixtionibus naturali temperatura figurantur omnium animalium in mundo generatim qualitates.* *Mixtio* itself has an emi-nently Vitruvian flavour: he uses the word twenty-four times but never has *mixtura* (for which in such a context see Lucr. 2.978). Indeed for the period down to the end of the second century AD covered by the *OLD* no other writer is cited for *mixtio*, whereas *mixtura* is quite widespread (on the latter see the *TLL* and also Zellmer 1976: 227–9). There are about 276 different nouns in *-tio* in Vitruvius, an extraordinary number, which would be worth studying in detail.

It would be wrong to talk of an established and fixed scientific or philoso-phical vocabulary in Latin; these various suffixal formations in Vitruvius might reflect either his own choices or the influence of his teachers.

13 terreno: *terrenus* is used adjectivally by Cicero and others in philosophical language in reference to the element consisting of earth, as at *Tusc.* 1.42 *terreno principiorum genere* (see *OLD* s.v. 4). Vitruvius is the first to use it substantivally (about eighteen times) in the neuter of this element (so later Columella at 8.14.2). He also has the adjectival use sometimes, as at 8.praef.2 *terreni principii*. For substantival neuter adjectives in technical prose see above, 5.2.

14 portatur: larch cannot be floated down-river because it is too heavy to be supported by the water: it has to be transported by boats or rafts. *Porto* may be used of carrying by hand (*TLL* X.2.46.12ff.), but equally it may be used of transportation by other means, such as by vehicle: see e.g. *B. Afr.* 75.3 *plaustris merces portabant* and *TLL* 45.60ff.

15 materies: *materies* occurs seventeen times in Vitruvius whereas *materia* occurs fifty-seven, but the bare statistics conceal an interesting distinction. Thirteen or fourteen instances of *materies* are in the nominative singular, whereas *materia* occurs in the nominative singular just four times. It follows that in the nominative singular *materies* outnumbers *materia* by 13/14:4, whereas in the oblique cases *materia* outnumbers *materies* by 53:3/4 (at 2.9.13 *materies* may be either nominative or genitive). In the accusative singular *materiam* outnumbers *materiem* by 6:2, and in the genitive singular *materiae* outnumbers *materies* by 15:1/2 (Vitruvius does not use the genitive form *materiei*: see further below, 11.26). In the ablative singular only *materia* is used. Here we have revealed the major factor determining the passage of fifth declension nouns into the first declension (on which see e.g. Väänänen 1981a: 106): the uncertainties in the inflection of the fifth declension first must have caused it to be avoided in oblique cases, though for a time the nominative singular was still regularly used. It is commonly the case in inflecting languages that the nominative (and accusative) are more resistant to change than other case forms, perhaps because they are more frequently used (so it was only Latin nominative and accusative forms of nouns that survived in Romance languages, if some special cases are left aside). Lucretius uses *materies* as the nominative, twenty-two times (and also *materiem* as the accusative, nine times versus one instance of *materiam*), but *materia* furnishes the genitive (*materiai* forty-two times, *materiae* three times). Various other terms of this type, such as *notities* and *amicities*, behave in similar ways in Lucretius, though tokens are not so numerous, and metrical factors come into it (*materies*, for example, is very convenient in the nominative). Full details may be found in Bailey (1947: I.74). Lucretius' preference for *materiem* in the accusative is not metrically determined.

16 est causam cognoscere: this is the Grecising construction *est* + infinitive 'it is possible'. The manuscripts have *est causa* + inf., but that construction does not ring true (see Fensterbusch 1964: 542 n. 138). The example of *est* + inf. here is typical of the way in which the construction is used at this period. There is one example in the Ciceronian corpus, in a letter of Balbus and Oppius to Cicero: *Att.* 9.7A.2 *sed cum etiam nunc quid facturus sit magis <sit> opinari quam scire*. Here, as in Vitruvius, one dependent infinitive is a verb of knowing (*scire*) and, again as in Vitruvius, dependent on the infinitives is an indirect question that precedes the *est*-construction. Similarly in a fragment of Varro *ap.* Gell. 18.12.9 there is again a preposed indirect question dependent on the infinitive, and the verb is one of perception, a type which does not differ fundamentally from a verb of mental acquisition: *inter duas filias regum quid mutet, inter Antigonam et Tulliam, est animaduertere*. A second example of the construction in Vitruvius, in this same chapter, also has a verb of perception: 2.9.11 *est autem maximum id considerare Rauennae* ('one can observe that in greatest abundance at Ravenna'). Gratwick (2002: 49) notes that in the majority of cases the verb dependent on this construction is one of perception. It is of interest that all four of the instances just cited from prose are in late republican/Augustan writers other than Cicero (see Adams 2005a: 94), and Livy 42.41.2 (a speech) can also be added. Cicero rejected the construction but his restrictiveness was not shared by educated contemporaries. Grammars of 'classical Latin' are based very much on Cicero (and Caesar), but the educated language of the time was less standardised than Ciceronian practice might suggest. For a collection (not entirely complete) of examples down to Gellius see Gratwick (2002: 49–50 n. 17). The construction is represented for example in Augustan poetry (Virg. *Aen.* 6.596, 8.676, Ovid *Met.* 3.478).

17 cum exercitum habuisset: the imperfect *haberet* might have been expected here. The use of the pluperfect for imperfect is particularly common in the verbs 'be' and 'have' both in the indicative and the subjunctive (*fuerat, fuisset, habuerat, habuisset*). It is cited from this period from writers other than Caesar and Cicero, namely the ps.-Caesarian works, Sallust, Nepos, Livy, and particularly Vitruvius (Kühner and Stegmann 1955: I. 140–1; see also Adams 1976a: 68, 159 n. 137). Where *habeo* is concerned one may sometimes suspect a conflation of thought with the corresponding dynamic verb (here e.g. *duxisset*; note too the coordinated *imperauisset*). The encroachment of pluperfect subjunctive forms on imperfect has some significance for the Romance languages, in that the pluperfect subjunctive survives in the west with imperfect meaning (see Adams 2007: 520 with bibliography). On late Latin see below, 45 Conclusions, 'Literary and late Latin', 48.1.2.

18 imperauissetque municipiis praestare commeatus: *impero* + infinitive occurs twice in this section, and Vitruvius provides no examples of the construction *impero ut* + subjunctive. Here is another departure by Vitruvius from the 'norms' based on the practice of Cicero and Caesar. The infinitive goes back to early Latin in verse and is common in poetry, but it is hardly cited from this period in prose (see however Sall. *Jug.* 47.2, Sen. *Contr.* 10.2.13) (details at *TLL* VII.1.585.35ff.). The one possible Ciceronian instance (*Verr.* 2.43 *quid interest utrum praetor imperet uique cogat aliquem de suis bonis omnibus decedere*) is a special case, as the infinitive is determined by the coordinated *cogo*, to which it is nearer. In the encroachment of infinitive complements of verbs on the *ut*-construction, poetry anticipates later developments in the language.

Impero with the acc. + inf. is a different matter: this construction is established in classical prose (*TLL* 585.54ff.).

19 quod uocaretur Larignum: the subjunctive seems unmotivated (there is an early emendation *uocabatur*, which is printed by Rose and Müller-Strübing), and the tense is slightly odd too, as the place was still called Larignum (see §16), and the present or perfect might have been expected (though this is a pedantic point, as narrators of past events may express timeless facts in the past too). The subjunctive might be explained by resorting to the notion that there has been 'attraction of mood' after *habuisset, imperauisset* and *esset*. An alternative possibility is that Vitruvius was attributing the information to some informant ('which, they said, was called …'). An unmotivated subjunctive, in a causal *quod*-clause, is found in this chapter at 2.9.11 *est autem maximum id considerare Rauennae, quod ibi omnia opera et publica et priuata sub fundamentis eius generis* habeant *palos*. According to Hofmann and Szantyr (1965: 575), whereas in classical and much post-classical Latin the subjunctive is used with causal *quod* only as a Modus obliquus, in late Latin unmotivated subjunctives (possibly reflecting the influence of *cum*) become common, as too with *quia*; they cite examples from Hyginus *Fab.* and inscriptions. If the text here is accepted the development can be pushed back into the first century BC. Later in the chapter (§16) *posteaquam* is construed with a subjunctive (see below, 11.22–3; also 27.5).

In this and the following sentences down to about *circumuallari* (§16) there is a good deal of phraseology that can be paralleled in Caesar and the ps.-Caesarian works:

(a) *naturali munitione confisi noluerunt imperio parere*: cf. Caes. *Civ.* 1.42.2
      confisus *praesidio legionum trium et* munitione *fossae*; cf. also *Gall.* 3.9.3

natura loci confidebant, Civ. 3.80.3 se *confidere munitionibus* oppidi. With the second part of the clause cf. *Gall.* 5.2.4 *neque imperio parebant*, Civ. 3.95.2 *imperio paruerunt*.

(b) *itaque imperator copias iussit admoueri*: cf. *B. Afr.* 25.2 *propius eius regnum copias suas admouere*, 51.3 *cum propius oppidum copias admouisset*. With the opening expression *itaque imperator* cf. *B. Hisp.* 29.3 *itaque Caesar*.

(c) *uti possent de summo sudibus et lapidibus accedentes repellere*: cf. *B. Alex.* 20.2 *hi primum nauigia hostium lapidibus ac fundis a mole repellebant*, *B. Afr.* 87.5 *lapidibus fustibusque equites reppulerunt*.

(d) *tunc uero cum animaduersum est*: cf. *Gall.* 6.27.4 *cum est animaduersum* (cf. *Civ.* 3.68.3). *Tum uero* (usually with the preferred *tum* for *tunc* here) is a common sentence opening in Caesar (e.g. *Gall.* 2.2.4, 3.23.2, 3.26.4, 5.37.3, 7.47.4, *Civ.* 1.81.1).

(e) *itaque celeriter*: for this sentence opening see *B. Afr.* 95.2.

(f) *flamma ... comprehendisset*: cf. Caes. *Gall.* 8.43.3 *opera flamma comprehensa*. *Flamma* is used either in the plural or as a collective singular (see *OLD* s.v. 1), as here. All twelve instances in Vitruvius are singular.

(g) *admirans Caesar iussit*: cf. *Gall.* 7.44.2 *admiratus quaerit ex perfugis causam*.

It is not clear what is to be made of these correspondences. Were they determined merely by the nature of the subject matter? None of the phrases is particularly distinctive. Or did Vitruvius have some familiarity with the style of military reports, into which he fell when dealing with an incident during one of Caesar's campaigns? Or might he have had a written source, perhaps by Caesar himself? It is suggested that Vitruvius could have been present himself in Caesar's army (see Callebat, Gros and Jacquemard 1999: 172 n. 15.2), in which case he might have seen a written report.

20 turris ex hac materia: *ex hac materia* should probably be construed as adnominal, though it might go with *composita*. The primary complement of this latter, however, is *alternis trabibus transuersis*, and *ex hac materia* looks detached from the participle.

21 longius a muro: the meaning is 'far from the wall', not 'further from the wall': the comparative is indistinguishable from a positive in function. On such comparatives (e.g. *celerius, citius, diutius*), which become particularly common in later Latin and low-register texts, see Hofmann and Szantyr (1965: 168–9), and below, 23.8–9, 26.9–10. Vitruvius himself uses *diutius* sometimes without clear comparative force: 8.2.9 *ideo diutius non potest permanere, sed breui* *spatio fit frigida,* 8.3.18 *ouum in aceto si diutius positum fuerit, cortex eius mollescet et dissoluetur.* Note too *celerius* at 8.6.12 *ita qui non celerius inde effugiunt, ibi interimuntur.*

22–3 posteaquam . . . comprehendisset: the subjunctive (*comprehendisset*) in a *posteaquam*-clause is scarcely attested (see now *TLL* X.2.196.58ff.; also Hofmann and Szantyr 1965: 598–9), and then usually in later Latin. The tiny number of possible cases in Cicero tend to be emended to *postea, cum/quom* (details at *TLL* loc. cit.). The analogy of *cum* was presumably the determinant (see above, 11.19 on causal *quod* with the subjunctive at 2.9.11). *Postquam* likewise is used with the subjunctive only very rarely in the earlier period, as at *B. Afr.* 40.5, 50.3, 91.3, Val. Max. 5.7.ext.2, though it occurs in later Latin (see *TLL* X.2.251.44ff.); again a few examples in classical writers are either variant readings or considered doubtful (details at *TLL* loc. cit.).

23 circa illam materiam uirgas: another adnominal prepositional expression.

24–5 efficit opinionem, uti uideretur iam tota moles concidisse: two features of this construction are typical of the educated language of the period. First, *opinionem* is elaborated by an explanatory *ut*-clause. For abundant examples from the classical period see *TLL* IX.2.718.55ff.: e.g. Caes. *Civ.* 1.47.1 *sed haec eius diei praefertur opinio, ut se utrique superiores discessisse existimarent.* Second, *uideretur* might seem redundant, in that it carries on the idea already expressed by *opinionem.* In explanatory *ut*-clauses following *opinio* there is often a redundant verb of the semantic field 'think', as is noted at *TLL* 718.55f. 'epexegeticum q. d. (saepe per abundantiam cum verbis sentiendi . . .)'. For *uideor,* as here, in the dependent clause the *TLL* cites (718.61f.) Q. Cic. *Pet.* 21 *in hanc opinionem adducendi, ut . . . iis uicissim nos obligari posse uideamur.*

25 tunc ei demonstrauerunt: *tunc* is used three times in this passage, and three sentences are introduced by *itaque.* Another four sentences are introduced by *autem.* The format of Vitruvius' narrative is somewhat repetitive. For the constant use of temporal adverbs (and anaphorics, on which see further below, 11.31) as a mark of popular narrative style see above, 1.1, 1 Appendix 3, and index, 'temporal adverbs, repetitious'.

26 cuius materies: *materies* is genitive; so possibly at 2.9.13 *materies uena directa,* though there it may be nominative with a descriptive ablative following. *TLL* VIII.448.43 quotes this old form of the genitive in this word only from Vitruvius; in the fifth declension the *-ēs* form, under the influence of the second declension, had the *s* replaced by *ī* (cf. *-ās* > *-āī*). For relics of the old genitive form in words of the fifth declension see Neue and Wagener (1892–1905: I.569–72). There is slight evidence for the occasional use of such forms by Cicero. According to Gellius (9.14.6–7) Cicero said *dies* for *diei* at *Sest.* 28, and according to Charisius p. 87.11–19 Barwick Cicero used *pernicies (causa)* (*S. Rosc.* 131; but see Dyck 2010: 14 with n. 48, preferring *pernicii*). Mostly however these forms are attested in earlier Latin or archaisers (*rabies* is at Lucr. 1083; see also Skutsch 1985: 569 on Enn. *Ann.* 406 *dies*, and the discussion of Garcea 2012: 230–4).

27 adportationibus ad urbem: *ad urbem* is adnominal.

28 in aedificiis utilitates: *in aedificiis* can be taken as adnominal.

29 tabulae in subgrundiis circum insulas: a double adnominal construction, with the first prepositional expression qualifying *tabulae* and the second *subgrundiis*. This is the second such double adnominal in the passage (cf. above, 11.7).

30 ab traiectionibus incendiorum … periculo: the *ab*-expression qualifies *periculo* and is adnominal.

It is appropriate to review the frequency of these adnominal prepositional expressions in the passage. We have noted eleven such expressions (two of them double) in a passage of just 374 words, an incidence (very roughly) of about 30 examples per 1,000 words. Wharton (2009: 201) has calculated the frequency of adnominal prepositional phrases per 1,000 words of text in thirteen writers from Cato through to Gregory of Tours. There is variation from 1.3 in Augustine to 3.0 in Tacitus, with an average of 2.2 (see Wharton 2009: 192). Vitruvius was not included in his survey, but it is obvious, even allowing for the shortness of this passage and the unreliability of statistics based on a small sample, that adnominal expressions are an extraordinary feature of his style. The incidence of 30 is close to that of a sample from a modern Romance language (French, 26) noted by Wharton (2009: 191), and also similar to that (as we will see) from a late Visigothic text with proto-Spanish features (below, 46.5–6). It would be rash to conclude that Vitruvius already shows in this respect a proto-Romance feature. His usage alongside that of literary prose brings out the diversity of the language and is another indication of the difference between high literature and technical writing.

31 eae: the apparatus of Rose and Müller-Strübing (1867) reports *eae* from Joc. (Fra Giocondo, edition of 1511) and *ea* from GH; Callebat, Gros and Jacquemard (1999) also list three fifteenth-century manuscripts as having *eae*. The two modern editions just referred to print *eae*, but some other editors, including Fensterbusch (1964), prefer *ea*. There is a lack of clarity about the use of the pronoun here, whichever form is adopted.

If *ea* is accepted, it might be either neuter plural (subject of *possunt*) or feminine ablative. If it is neuter plural, what does it refer to? Vitruvius has been talking about the timber (*materies*) larch, and the feminine prepositional expression two clauses before, *ex ea* (*conlocatae*), refers back to *materies* at the start of the same sentence. Four or five sentences earlier we have the neuter plural expression *ea ligna*, again of larch timbers, and it is possible that Vitruvius has slipped into thinking of *ligna* as an alternative to *materies* (a possibility we might call a). There is a neuter plural noun just before, *aedificia*, but Vitruvius could hardly be referring to that in *ea* (possibility b), because he has just made it clear that the buildings as a whole would not be made of larch, but only the planks around the eaves: it would not make sense to maintain that he meant that 'the buildings (as a whole) cannot catch fire'. If *ea* were ablative singular (possibility c), the reference might indeed be to *materies* ('because of that (timber) they cannot catch fire'). However, such a use of the ablative looks too inexplicit, and its presence would raise the question what the subject of *possunt* is. The best solution (possibility d) is to accept *eae*, which would refer back two clauses to the planks of larch (*tabulae*), which indeed cannot catch fire, and their presence would prevent the crossing over of fire from one building to another. The imprecision of the writing consists in having two instances of *is* in close proximity, with different referents. Allusive use of demonstratives or anaphorics (where the reader has to deduce the referent and changes of number may occur) is a feature too of late technical prose (see Adams 1995a: 589–91 on *is* in medical and veterinary Latin).

One other feature of the adjectival use of the anaphoric *is* in the passage is its redundancy: so §§15 *eius castelli, eam munitionem*, 16 *eas arbores, id castellum, ea regione*. So at 16 pronominal *ea* (*ea per se extincta esset*) could be omitted. Such redundancy, whether in the use of *is, idem, ipse* or terms such as *supradictus*, is a mark of technical, including legal, prose (see above, 5.2–4). Note for example Cato *Agr.* 157.10 *lotium conseruato eius qui brassicam essitarit: id calfacito . . . item pueros pusillos si laues eo lotio, numquam debiles fient. et quibus oculi parum clari sunt, eo lotio inunguito . . . si caput aut ceruices dolent, eo lotio caldo lauito . . . et si mulier eo lotio locos fouebit.* See further Langslow (2005: 298 with n. 42), Adams (2013: 491–2).

32 neque flammam nec carbonem possunt recipere nec facere per se: the position of infinitives that are the primary complement of auxiliary verbs is

distinctive in Vitruvius. As here, infinitives frequently come after the governing verb, a feature that has been noted by others (see Morgan 1906: 500–1).
In the passage discussed here note §§14 *nec ipse per se potest ardere, qua possit
ignis penetrare, nec patitur ab eo sibi cito noceri*, 15 *est causam cognoscere,
noluerunt imperio parere, uti possent . . . repellere, neque posse . . . iaculari,
imperatum est . . . mittere*, 16 *uti uideretur . . . concidisse* (ten examples, in both
positive and negative clauses, with no instances of the reverse order). Various
factors seem to have influenced the order. When *possum* is negated the
infinitive almost always comes after it (126:24), but when it is not negated
the two orders are equally common (74:76) (see Morgan 1906: 501). With this
auxiliary, negation therefore is a determinant of postposition of the infinitive,
though that said the incidence of postponement when there is no negation is
rather high compared with that in some other classical writers. With *uideor*
anteposition and postposition seem to be equally frequent; *uidentur esse* is
preferred to *esse uidentur*, no doubt because the latter produces a hexameter
ending. With *uolo* on the other hand postposition is strongly preferred, by
22:6. With *debeo* as with *uideor* the two orders are equally common (anteposition 31, postposition 28), though there is at least one collocational peculiarity:
debet esse is preferred to *esse debet* by 7:2, but *fieri debet* to *debet fieri* by 10:1.
Thus (on a superficial review of limited data) rhythmical, lexical and collocational determinants were at work, but it remains true that the incidence of
postposition compared with that in some other texts (e.g. Caesar) is high.

Conclusions

Vitruvius was not far removed from Cicero in time but his Latin is different in
important respects. It would not do to dismiss it as 'plebeian' or the like, an
implication that can readily be found in the literature. Despite his apology at
1.1.18 for a lack of grammatical training he was highly educated. He quotes
literary Greek often, is familiar with philosophy and at 9.praef.16–17 lists
Ennius, Accius, Lucretius, Cicero (on rhetoric) and Varro (on the Latin
language) as Latin authors with whom he is familiar.

Technical discourse

To some extent Vitruvius' differences from 'classical Latin' can be put down to
the fact that he was writing in a genre that was technical and of which we have
no specimens in this period. The most prominent usage in the above passage
that may be genre-related is the preposition *ab* with what we would see as
inanimate nouns, in association with passive verbs, to mark agency (though

with some ambiguities). Ciceronian prose and that of Livy far prefer the ablative. Vitruvian usage is, however, the more logical, in that forces of nature and the like are not instruments employed by man to effect actions but agents in their own right, whether or not they are consciously viewed as personified. It is possible that practitioners of or writers on technical *artes* were more attuned to see natural forces at work and to allow them their true character as agents (see also Langslow 2000: 193–201, cited several times above). We saw some parallels in the medical writer Celsus, and there is an indirect parallel of a different kind in Vitruvius himself and writers such as Celsus and Pliny the Elder, namely the use of terms designating the same or similar natural forces and phenomena as subject of reflexive verbs (see Adams 2013: 695–711). An alternative form of expression, more favoured in non-technical prose, was to have the natural phenomenon as subject of a passive verb: 'the disease eases itself' thus becomes 'the disease is eased'.

Another feature of Vitruvius' prose is the quantity of abstract verbal nouns (in some cases probably coined by Vitruvius himself) formed by a variety of suffixes. For example, we noted that alone of writers covered by the *OLD* Vitruvius uses *mixtio* (twenty-four times), and that he has as many as 276 different abstracts in *-tio*, which have never been analysed in their entirety for their currency in other writers. He also exploited the suffix *-tas*, and several such formations that are confined to his work were noted. We observed the particularly Vitruvian abstract *temperatura*, and also his adoption of the suffix *-tudo* in a medical context (*grauitudo*). It does not matter how many such terms might have been coined by Vitruvius himself. The point is that suffixal derivatives, though spread throughout Latin, were a characteristic of technical texts at all periods, and Vitruvius might either have been using a technical vocabulary he had picked up from his teachers, or exploiting suffixes that he himself felt appropriate to technical writing.

We pointed out a number of adnominal prepositional expressions, attached mainly to non-verbal nouns. The sample is only small, but it is obvious from a cursory look at the rest of the work that the sample does not give a false impression. The frequency of these adnominals in Vitruvius far exceeds that in the numerous literary texts surveyed by Wharton (2009). There are two ways of accounting for it. First, it is possible that such expressions were common in ordinary speech, and that Vitruvius was influenced by that. Wharton drew attention to adnominals attached to non-verbal nouns in the speeches of the freedmen in Petronius. Alternatively, adnominals might have been normal in technical discourse. An examination of (e.g.) Celsus, Scribonius and Pliny the Elder from the early period might be worthwhile.

Vitruvius and early Latin

The standardisation of syntax and morphology apparently displayed by Cicero and Caesar gives a false picture of the diversity of the written language of the time, and it may be false even for Cicero himself, reflecting the normative influence of either ancient grammarians or more modern editors on his textual transmission. For example, the manuscripts of Cicero preserve examples of the indicative in indirect questions, but these are systematically emended away by editors, even from contexts in which they may be defended. No editor, however, would emend away the indicative from the text of Vitruvius. The indicative in Cicero seems intolerable to those brought up on the idealised classical Latin of modern grammar books, whereas Vitruvius can be put aside as not capable of holding on to the standard. The reality might rather be that there was some variation in educated usage. We also saw evidence in the ancient grammatical tradition for the occasional use by Cicero of the -es genitive in the fifth declension, though most editors would be reluctant to print such forms.

In some respects Vitruvius is closer to old Latin than classical Latin. For example, there are gender variations or anomalies in his work that associate him particularly with the earlier period. In *nasum* he preserves the old Latin gender of the word, his use of *rudens* as feminine is paralleled in Plautus, and his use of *frons* as both a masculine and feminine again has a parallel in Plautus. Another near-contemporary, Varro, also shows some variability of gender and connections with earlier Latin. We should not see these usages as deliberate archaisms. Some writers simply lagged behind current trends. If we had more of the works of Varro and the writings of other contemporaries of Cicero we would probably be confronted by a more diverse picture of republican educated Latin. Another of Vitruvius' preferred old forms is *uti* for *ut*, though in this manuscripts are not reliable. The genitive in -es seen in *materies* is also an old type, admitted by Lucretius (in a different word), but he was a poet, and even he preferred the first-declension forms -ae/-ai. Another preference of Vitruvius' redolent of an earlier period is his use of *memoro*, twelve times, against no instances of the compound *commemoro* (see also Morgan 1906: 476). In Plautus the simplex is common, outnumbering *commemoro* by 90:15. In Cicero on the other hand the compound is very frequent, but *memoro* occurs just four times, usually in special contexts (once only in the speeches, at *Verr.* 4.107 in a mythologising context) (see Adams 1974a: 55 for details).

Other divergences from classical practice

Not all divergences in Vitruvius from classical practice (i.e. that of Ciceronian and Caesarian prose) represent the lingering on of old usages that were fading from educated language.

There are usages that are attested in Latin of the period and perhaps earlier but are rigidly excluded by Cicero. A case in point is the Greek-inspired (?) construction *est* + infinitive. This goes well back (at least as far as Cato), and has good literary credentials (not least in poetry, including Virgil), even if it is not widespread. It cannot be dismissed as vulgar. It is found in other prose of the period, namely in Varro, correspondents of Cicero and Livy. Cicero's motives in rejecting the construction cannot be determined, but this rejection is not representative of educated practice.

The personal passive (as distinct from impersonal) use of verbs governing the dative (such as *noceo*) has a similar distribution. It is avoided by Cicero but admitted by one of his correspondents and by the author *Ad Herennium*, avoided by Caesar but admitted in the ps.-Caesarian works, and admitted in Augustan poetry.

The pluperfect of *habeo*, used where an imperfect is expected, shows much the same pattern. It is not quoted from Cicero and Caesar, but again is found in the ps.-Caesarian works, but not only there: it is in Sallust, Nepos and Livy.

The use of the subjunctive with *post(ea)quam* in direct (as distinct from indirect, or quoted) clauses seems to have been an innovation of the late Republic, on the analogy of *cum*. It is sometimes emended away, but is retained in the ps.-Caesarian works and Vitruvius.

If we were merely finding a contrast between Cicero and Caesar on the one hand, and the ps.-Caesarian works (with Vitruvius) on the other, the conventional narrative might be upheld, according to which the ps.-Caesarian works and Vitruvius were substandard. But there is more to it than that, because other writers too sometimes side with Vitruvius against Cicero and Caesar, namely the author *Ad Herennium*, Sallust, some of Cicero's correspondents, Varro, Livy, Nepos, Virgil and other poets. There was a split of sorts in late first-century literary language, with Cicero and Caesar more restrictive than numerous contemporaries. Not all of the latter were simply substandard writers. Their differences from Cicero and Caesar reveal that the literary language was not entirely standardised. Standardisation is never absolute.

Sensible remarks about Vitruvius and his relation to 'classical Latin' can be found in the old discussion by Morgan (1906, e.g. at 468–9). He refutes the contention of J. L. Ussing that phenomena in Vitruvius 'point to the decadence of the Latin language and to its transition to the Romance tongues' (Morgan 1906: 468), a contention that led Ussing to believe that Vitruvius wrote in the third century AD (1906: 469). Morgan observes (469) that the 'gist of the linguistic part of Ussing's argument seems to consist in his belief that if a writer lived in the "classical period" his style must therefore be "classic"', and he goes on to stress that Vitruvius was educated but a technical writer.

12

FROM A LETTER OF AUGUSTUS
(SUET. *AVG*. 76.2)

Introduction

According to Suetonius, Augustus' autograph letters revealed his use of every-day language: *Aug.* 87.1 *cotidiano sermone quaedam frequentius et notabiliter usurpasse eum, litterae ipsius autographae ostentant.* The fragment quoted here, which has several notable lexical items, bears this out. The fragments of the private letters of Augustus are quoted mainly by Suetonius, and have been collected by Malcovati (1948: 6–28), in which collection this fragment is numbered XI. In the conclusion below some remarks are included about features of other fragments.

Text

ne Iudaeus quidem, mi Tiberi (1), tam diligenter sabbatis ieiunium seruat quam ego hodie seruaui, qui in balineo (2) demum post horam primam noctis duas buccas (3) manducaui (4) prius quam ungui inciperem.

Translation

Not even a Jew, Tiberius, so carefully observes fasting on the Sabbath as I have observed it today. At the baths eventually after the first hour of the night I had two mouthfuls to eat before I began to be anointed.

Commentary

1 mi Tiberi: the *mi*-address (on which see Dickey 2002: 214–24; also above, 10.3.4) is regular in the fragments of Augustus' private letters. *Mi Tiberi* occurs five times (cf. also Suet. *Aug.* 51.3, 71.2, 71.3, *Tib.* 21.5), and the single exception with this name (*Tib.* 21.4 *iucundissime Tiberi*) has an emotive adjective instead. *Mea Liuia* occurs three times (*Claud.* 4.1, 4.4, 4.6) (see Dickey 2002: 217–18, noting that in a speech of Augustus, as distinct from letters, she is *Liuia*). There is also a case of *mi Gai* (Gell. 15.7.3).

2 balineo: see above, 8.2.

3 buccas: *bucca* = 'cheek' was standard Latin (see André 1991: 38), but by a metonymy the term shifted meaning to 'mouth' and the distribution of that secondary usage is suggestive of a colloquial character (see André 1991: 57, noting that it occurs in farce, as Pomponius 158 Frassinetti, Menippean satire and epigram). Note too Cic. *Att.* 1.12.4 *si rem nullam habebis, quod in buccam uenerit scribito*, a slangy variant for *in mentem uenire* (*quod dicerem* etc.): *OLD* s.v. *mens* 1b. *Bucca* in this secondary meaning is widespread in Romance languages (e.g. It. *bocca*, Fr. *bouche*, Sp., Pg. *boca*: see *REW* 1357). It is however a moot point whether *duas buccas* here means 'two mouthfuls' or 'two cheeks full'. If the latter, the meaning is the classical one, and the point would be that he had only one mouthful.

4 manducaui: this seems to be the first instance of the verb in its Romance meaning 'eat' (as distinct from the earlier sense 'chew'): see *TLL* VIII.273.36ff. at 74f. It turns up in a speech of Trimalchio in Petronius (see Stefenelli 1962: 64–5), and was no doubt non-standard (see further Adams 2013: 21). There is also a literary example in the first-century (?) translator of Homer, Attius Labeo, who is twice disparaged by the scholia to Persius (at 1.4, where his translation technique is described as *ridicule satis*, and at 1.50, where he is described as a *poeta indoctus* and as having composed *foedissime*). The line quoted at 1.4 is: *crudum manduces Priamum Priamique pisinnos*, = *Il.* 4.35 ὠμὸν βεβρώθοις Πρίαμον Πριάμοιό τε παῖδας. *Manduco* renders βεβρώθοις (< βιβρώσκω) and *pisinnos* παῖδας. See also Courtney (1993: 350), Burton (2000: 162–3).

Conclusions

Suetonius above in referring to the everyday language he said he had seen in Augustus' letters lists a few examples, and in the extant fragments of private letters there are some usages worth noting here.

Peream (ni)si (Suet. *Claud.* 4.6) is a phrase found in Caelius and other correspondents of Cicero but not in Cicero himself (see 9.9), and in various colloquial sources (see 6.43–4 for Hor. *Sat.* 2.1.6, and on the intensive *dispeream si* see on the soldier's letter below, 13.10). *Misellus* in the same letter (*Claud.* 4.5) was an emotive diminutive used by Cicero only in letters (*Att.* 3.23.5, *Fam.* 14.4.3). Also in the same letter there are two instances of the instrumental *qui* meaning 'how': *Claud.* 4.5 *qui uellem*, 4.6 *qui possit ... non uideo*. This term (see *OLD* s.v. 1–2) is found for example in Plautus and Terence, in Horace's *Satires* (1.1.1, 1.1.108, 1.3.128, 2.3.108) and *Epistles* (1.16.63), in certain contexts in Cicero (see above, 4.5), and in Catullus (24.7). It is described by Gowers (2012: 62) as unpoetic.

A fragment of a letter to Virgil quoted by Priscian *GL* II.533.13 has the preposition *ab* with the name of a town: *excucurristi a Neapoli*. On this usage, which tended to be avoided by purists but is notable for its frequency in Livy, see Adams (2013: 329–30), and below, 18.22. Suetonius tells us (*Aug.* 86.1) that Augustus used prepositions with the names of towns for clarity (see Adams 2013: 328). He was no pedant, as is also clear from the anecdotes cited in the last paragraph below.

At *Aug.* 76 Suetonius discusses Augustus' eating habits, and he quotes three extracts from letters. One has the verb *manduco*, in our passage. Another (*Aug.* 76.2) has *comedo*, which had some currency at this period (see 5.19), though the simplex *edo* long persisted in literary texts (see the table at *TLL* V.2.100, and also below, 38.53). The third (76.1) has *gusto*: *nos in essedo panem et palmulas gustauimus*. The verb does not mean so much 'taste' here as 'consume a little (of some food)'. Cf. Lucil. 1183 *gustaui crustula solus* (again with a diminutive object), Petron. 62.13 *nec postea cum illo panem gustare potui*. See *TLL* VII.2.2367.45ff. There was not necessarily anything slangy about the usage, but the three passages reveal a certain colour and variety to Augustus' informal prose.

The greeting to Tiberius at Suet. *Tib.* 21.4 (*uale, iucundissime Tiberi, et feliciter rem gere*) has conventional components (see 21.6 on *iucundus*, and 23.11–13 on expressions of *felicitas* in letters), but is put in an unusual way. Augustus liked the all-purpose phrase *rem gero*: cf. Suet. *Aug.* 71.3 *frater tuus magnis clamoribus rem gessit*.

The (long) letter just cited (*ap.* Suet. *Aug.* 71) has a remarkable section about gaming (with dice), which illuminates the force of various verbs of throwing at this time. It is worth quoting not because it is revealing of Augustus' style but because it highlights changes that were to occur in the language in general and will come up in this anthology: 71.2 *talis enim iactatis, ut quisque canem aut senionem miserat, in singulos talos singulos denarios in medium conferebat, quos tollebat uniuersos, qui Venerem iecerat*. Here *iacto* is first used of the throwing of the dice. It refers to repeated action, and the frequentative preserves its original force. Later *iacto* was to lose this frequentative meaning and become a synonym of *iacio*, which it ousted, and even to undergo a weakening, > 'put' (see 40.5). There follow two more verbs of throwing, *miserat* and *iecerat*, both used synonymously of a single throw. *Iacio* was eventually to fall out of use, to be replaced not only by the frequentative but also by *mitto*, which itself tended to acquire the meaning 'put' (on the semantic field see 27.10, 40.5, 44.36.3, 44.37.9, 50.29).

In a letter to Livia Augustus at one point switches within a single sentence from *eum* to *illum*, in reference to the same person (Tiberius), who repeatedly in the letter is referred to by *is*: Suet. *Claud.* 4.2 *sin autem* ἠλαττῶσθαι *sentimus* eum ... *praebenda materia deridendi et* illum *et nos non est hominibus* τὰ τοιαῦτα σκώπτειν καὶ μυκτηρίζειν εἰωθόσιν. Is this switch unmotivated? It might look like some unmotivated switches in late texts (see 27.9, 27.11; also 2.21–2), but it could be argued that here *ille* has been chosen as more suited to the strong contrast with *nos*.

Twice Augustus uses the exclamation *medius fidius* in the same phrase: *Tib.* 21.6 *ualde medius fidius Tiberium meum desidero*, Gell. 15.7.3 *quem semper medius fidius desidero*. The exclamation is several times put into the mouths of speakers by Petronius: 17.4 *misereor medius fidius uestri* (spoken by a woman; there is little substance to any claim that it was used mainly by men: see Charisius p. 258.1 Barwick *edio fidio, per Iouem uel fidem filiumque Iouis Herculem. quae iuratio propria uirorum est*; cf. Hofmann and Ricottilli 2003: 139), 104.5 *pessimo medius fidius exemplo*. An instance at 129.6 (*medius fidius peristi*), also spoken by a woman, has tended to be eliminated by editors treating *fidius* as an interpolation (see Schmeling 2011: 494). For earlier examples see *OLD* s.v. *Fidius* (from Cato onwards, and a few times in Cicero's speeches and a dialogue), but the *OLD* treatment is sketchy, without the examples from Augustus or Petronius; the *TLL* has bypassed the oath. The instance in Cato (*ap.* Gell. 10.14.3) is in the same phrase as one of those in Petronius (*rei quoque publicae medius fidius miserear*).

On the expression *ad summam* at Suet. *Aug.* 71.3 see Leiwo (2010a: 283–4), and below, 18.9.

Finally, Augustus' hostility to linguistic pomposity is revealed by various anecdotes about him. He rebuked Tiberius for writing (probably in a letter) *peruiam* rather than *obiter* (Charisius p. 271.16–18 Barwick), the popular word (for details of its distribution see Adams 2003b: 568–9). He also corrected Gaius Caesar in a letter for using *calidam* rather than *caldam* (Quint. 1.6.19: see Adams 2013: 93–4).

13

SOLDIER'S LETTER OF THE LATE FIRST CENTURY BC (AUGUSTAN PERIOD) FROM QASR IBRÎM, EGYPT (*P. RAINER CENT.* 164, *CEL* 9)

Introduction

The letter comes from the hilltop fortress town of Qasr Ibrîm in Egyptian Nubia, about 150 miles south of Assam. The place 'came within the Roman sphere of influence, but not into Roman occupation, after the expedition of Cornelius Gallus (29 B.C.)' (Anderson, Parsons and Nisbet 1979: 127). It was occupied in 25 or 24 by the expedition of Gaius Petronius, who fortified it and installed a garrison of 400 men. It is likely that Ibrîm was abandoned by the Romans in 20 BC, but the evidence is not decisive (see the discussion of Anderson, Parsons and Nisbet 1979: 127–8). The text belongs roughly to the last quarter of the first century BC. It is too fragmentary to translate, but has a number of interesting elements that allow some observations on the level of the Latin. In particular it has some parallels with the colloquial style of Catullus in the shorter poems and with the letters of Caelius and of others. For a commentary see the notes of the editor, P. J. Parsons, and also Cugusi (1992: II.18–21).

Text

Valerius · de · te · et · centuria scripsi[
uos · disperise · hoc · esst · te · non · esse ... [
.] . [ ] ... on.tam · bonum · et · . en . [
disperire · non · inim · fa[ ]nus[
petr[. .]misererus · eius · . . m . [5
reuerti · et · sucesorem · t[
literas · respectat · ut · tibi · su[
]e me · si · mentior · n . [
] · minus · auxilio^{mi} sint · . [
discupio · satis·facere · set · [10

non · sufragatur · test . [
. u . ium · Valutium · [
quae · soliam · de · te[ ] . . [
    ] . os · renumer . [
]ạ salua sana · ual [15
]luom · cupimu[s
]mei · omṇ[
] . . ṇị · milites · option[
]mịum · ten . [

Commentary

2 disperise: for this compound see two lines further on, and the note below (13.10) on *discupio*. The meaning is probably metaphorical ('you are done for' or the like: see Parsons, *P. Rainer Cent.* 164, pp. 486–7).

esst: a number of non-literary texts display an obsession with the writing of geminated *s* even where the gemination had no historical justification (see below, 15.7), an obsession that may spring from an awareness that in some environments *ss* was undergoing simplification and from a desire to counter that development (with inevitable hyper-correction). The spelling *esst* need have had no phonetic basis. Baehrens (1922: 76–7) cites from inscriptions a number of instances of *ss* written unhistorically before *t* (as e.g. in *magisster*), but in these the *t* is not in final position in the word as it is in *esst* and the *ss* may reflect an adjustment in the syllabification (*magis-ter* > *magis-ster*) caused by the common juxtaposition of *s* and *t* in the same syllable (e.g. in *stare*). For *esst* itself Parsons cites *CIL* IV.1097a add. p. 202. The writer of our text also shows a complementary tendency to simplify geminates, including *s* (*disperise, sucesorem, sufragatur*). In the document of C. Novius Eunus of AD 37 (below, 15) *s* is constantly geminated but other geminates are simplified (see 15.7). In both cases we see a tendency to fall into phonetic spellings in competition with a desire to be correct.

4 inim: this must be for *enim*. There has occurred a regressive vocalic assimilation of a type attested early in the history of Latin (Leumann 1977: 101). Accented *e* in an open initial syllable with *l, m* or *n* following is assimilated to an *i* or *o* in the next syllable (e.g. *cinis* < *cenis*).

5 misererus: here is another informal text with a second person middle form in -*rus*: see above, 6.13, and below, 14.4 (also Adams 2007: 445–51).

8 si mentior: on this expression see Parsons, *P. Rainer Cent.* 164, p. 487, citing Ovid *Met.* 9.373, Petron. 62.14.

10 discupio: remarkably, this short and fragmentary text has three intensive compounds in *dis-* (so *dispereo* in lines 2 and 4), a type also found in the Johns Hopkins *defixiones* (see 6.43–4) and Caelius (see 9.11, on the same verb *discupio*, and also below). The *OLD* s.v. *dis-* notes: 'An intensifying force as in *disamo, discupio* is app. colloquial.' Parsons (*P. Rainer Cent.* ad loc. on *discupio*) observes: 'The word's credentials are all colloquial: Plaut., *Trin.* 932; Cat. 106.2 (ribald joke); Cic. *Fam.* 8.15.2 (not Cicero, but the brash and slangy Caelius)' (this last is our text 9 above). Caelius also shares with Catullus a use of another such intensive, *discrucior* with acc. + inf.: Cael. *Fam.* 8.3.1 *nunc cottidie non esse te ad quem cursitem discrucior*; cf. Catull. 66.76 *afore me a dominae uertice discrucior*. This usage occurs elsewhere only in Plautus (*Bacch.* 435 *propter me haec nunc meo sodali dici discrucior miser*) and in a letter of Cicero (*Att.* 14.6.1 *discrucior Sextili fundum a uerberone Curtilio possideri*) (see *TLL* V.1.1364.51f.). In these passages both Caelius and Catullus use the verb in expressions of regret at separation from someone, and Caelius' use of *discupio* (above, 9.11) is similarly in an expression of desire that a separation should be ended: *peream si minima causa est properandi isto mihi quod te uidere et omnia intima conferre discupio*. It is possible that in our present letter the verb was also accompanied by an infinitive construction. Here is evidence for a colloquial manner of speaking current in fashionable circles in the late Republic. *Discrucio* had a literal use (of severe torture) that is not confined to colloquial texts (*TLL* 1363.82ff.). But in (medio-)passive forms, of mental 'torture', it has a restricted distribution consistent with an educated colloquial character down to the late Republic, followed by obsolescence (*TLL* 1364.32ff.). In addition to those cases cited above taking an acc. + inf. construction, *discrucior* is found (in other constructions) in Plautus and Terence, but just once in the speeches of Cicero (*Q. Rosc.* 31). There are examples in the correspondence of Fronto and scattered cases in later Latin.

Dispereo earlier in the letter is another intensive in *dis-* used by Catullus and a few other writers prone to colloquialisms of roughly the same period. There is possibly a difference of status between the literal uses (of utter destruction) and hyperbolical uses. There is not obviously anything colloquial about the former, but two hyperbolical uses (*TLL* V.1.1405.46ff.), in expressions of despair (e.g. *disperii miser*) and in the formula *dispeream si, nisi*, have typically restricted distributions. The latter occurs twice at Catull. 92 (2, 4), and also at Hor. *Sat.*

1.9.47 (cf. in the same satire *interream si* at 38) and Prop. 2.21.9 (see Fedeli 2005: 617); see further *TLL* 1405.50ff.

satis·facere: for the splitting of a compound by interpunction see below, 14.5, 20.4 and *CEL* 3.3, 9.10 and 10.5, with the notes of Cugusi ad locc. Note in the Ankara version of the *Res gestae* at 20 (Scheid 2007) *per·fecissem.*

13 soliam: whether this is a noun (*solea*) or verb (*soleo*) (probably the latter), it has an early instance of the closing of *i* in hiatus. See 6.13 on *polliciarus.*

15 salua sana: this looks like an alliterative asyndeton bimembre comprising two near-synonyms ('safe and sound'), though the fragmentary word pre-ceding might also have been an adjective (Parsons however takes it to be *familia*, and Cugusi as *omnia*). Cf. *ChLA* 3.204 = *CEL* 156, a receipt from an unidentified place (Puluinos) in Egypt dated AD 167: *miserat mi[hi] Cornelius Germanus procurator meus quas has res [i]ntra scriptas meas, salbas, sanas recepisse scripsi nonarum Octobrium ad Puluinos.* The pairing was old but was not always with asyndeton: note Plaut. *Amph.* 730 *sana et salua sum*, Cic. *Fam.* 12.23.3 *sanae et saluae rei publicae* (see also Wölfflin 1933: 273, 274, Cugusi 1992: II.20). An asyndeton bimembre often com-prises two terms that are virtual synonyms, and such pairs may be alliterative too (see above, 4.14–15 'special pairs of adjectives', 6.41, 18.12 (*sicca sobria*), and index, 'asyndeton bimembre'). Many examples can be found in Preuss (1881): e.g. *oro obsecro* (95), *certus clarus* (112), *purus putus* (112–13), *laetus lubens* (113).

16]luom · cupimu[s]: Parsons (see *P. Rainer Cent.* 164, pp. 483, 488) argues that this formula (reconstructed as *ual[ere te hilarem et sa]luom cupimu[s]*) is the earliest infinitival valediction in either Greek or Latin, antedating ἐρρῶσθαί σε εὔχομαι, and thus it seems that a Latin formulation has influenced Greek in this case. On Greek-derived formulae in Latin letters see below, 20.3. See Cugusi's note on *CEL* 9.16 and Adams (2003a: 79–80) for the relevant for-mulae in the two languages.

The accusative ending *-om* after *u* was still the norm in the letters of Terentianus (Adams 1977a: 10).

Conclusions

The interest of this non-literary text of the Augustan period from a remote part of the Empire is that it displays usages quotable particularly from literary texts of informal type of much the same period. Parallels were cited above from letters of Caelius and Cicero, and from Catullus' shorter poems and Horace's

Satires. The form *misererus* can be paralleled in another non-literary letter of the Augustan period, below, 14.4. The texts in our collection numbered 9 (letter of Caelius), 12 (letter of Augustus) and 13 all hang together both in date and aspects of phraseology, and together they illuminate the language variety drawn on by Catullus and Horace.

14

LETTER FROM OXYRHYNCHUS, POSSIBLY OF AUGUSTAN DATE (BROWN 1970, *P. OXY.* XLIV.3208)

Introduction

In this personal letter, the circumstances of which are not fully explained by the writer, the names are all Greek, and the characters seem to be slaves (see Cugusi 1972–3: 675). The editio princeps was by Brown (1970), who attributed the letter to the Augustan period, and it is also published as *P. Oxy.* XLIV.3208 and *CEL* 10. The text printed here is that of *P. Oxy.*, but the various editions do not differ in any significant way. There is a discussion of the linguistic features by Cugusi (1972–3: 675–87); also id. (1992: II.21–4).

In the original text most interpuncta are placed on the line (see the note at *P. Oxy.* ad loc.), but here I have followed convention in putting them in the medial position.

Text

Suneros · Chio suo · plur(imam) · sal(utem). · s(i) u(ales) b(ene). · Theo
    adduxsit · ad · me · Ohapim
regiuṃ · mensularium · Oxsyrychitem, · qui quidem · mecum · est · locutus
de · inprobitate · Epaphraes. · itaque · nihil · ultra · loquor · quam · [[no]]
ne patiarus · te · propter · illos · perire. · crede · mihi, · nimia · bonitas
pernicies · homiṇ[i]ḅus est uel maxsuma. · deinde · ipse · tibei · de·mostrabit   5
qu[i]t · rei · sit · qum · illum ad te · uocareis. · set · perseruera [*sic*]:
qui · de · tam pusilla · summa · tam · magnum · lucrum · facit
dominum · occidere · uolt. · deinde · ego · clamare · debeo · siquod · uideo
'deuom · atque · hominum' · [[fidem · si · tu · [.] · ista · non · cuibis]].
tuum · erit · uindicare · ne · alio · libeat · facere. *vac.*   10

Back: Chio · Caesaris

Translation

Suneros to his friend Chius very many greetings. If you are well, good. Theo brought to me Ohapim, the royal banker of Oxyrhynchus, who spoke with me about the wickedness of Epaphras. Therefore I say nothing more than that you should not let yourself perish on their account. Believe me, excessive goodness is a disaster to men, perhaps the greatest there is. He himself will reveal to you what the matter is when you have summoned him to you. But persist: he who makes such a big profit from such a tiny sum is willing to kill his master. Then I ought to cry out, if I have any insight, 'by gods and men'. It will be yours to exact vengeance so that no one else conceives the will to do it.

To Chius, slave of Caesar.

Commentary

2 mensularium: this term for 'banker', like *mensarius*, looks like a calque on τραπεζίτης < τράπεζα 'table'. For a discussion of the semantic field see Cugusi (1972–3: 683), pointing out that in the Ciceronian and Augustan periods *argentarius* and *mensarius* were more usual (see also Brown 1970: 141, and on earlier aspects of the semantic field, Shipp 1955: 139–41). *TLL* VIII.758.31ff. cites few examples of *mensularius*, but one of them (Sen. *Contr.* 9.1.12) is from about this period. The diminutive *mensula* that provides the base is attested from early Latin (Plaut. *Most.* 308, Lucil. 1062), and it seems to be used of a banker's table by Fronto p. 66.25 van den Hout (so *TLL* VIII.758.17ff.). Editors (so *OLD*) usually take the preceding *argentariis* with *mensulis* (*scis ut in omnibus argentariis mensulis, perguleis, taberneis . . .*), but van den Hout (1988) puts a comma after *argentariis* (which becomes substantival), and says unconvincingly (1999: 184) that *mensulae* are booths of any kind. The *OLD* citing the passage of Fronto gives the noun the meaning 'money changer's counter'.

  Oxsyrychitem: omission of the nasal (in this position a velar nasal) before a stop (see Cugusi 1972–3: 676, and below, 15.14 and also index, 'spellings, omission of nasal before stop').

3 Epaphraes: a hybrid in more senses than one. The genitive ending *-aes*, which is common in the first declension in inscriptions (see above, 6.19, with bibliography), represents a Latinisation (of spelling) of the Greek ending *-es* (see Adams 2003a: 479–86). Ἔπαφρᾶς in Greek would be expected to have a genitive in -ᾶ (see Adams 2007: 674). Greek names in *-as* (such as *Aeneas*) regularly lost the final *-s* in Latin (Adams 2003a: 372 with n. 138; for *Epaphra* in Latin inscriptions see Fraser and Matthews 1997: 144), and the genitive of such a name in Latin would usually be *-ae* (so *Aeneae*, which in early Latin appears in the nominative without the final *-s*). *Epaphrae* has been Grecised, but in the wrong way (for Greek).

4 patiarus: for forms of this type see above, 6.13 and 13.5. It is of note that the form occurs in the same text as a genitive in -*aes*, and that the same combination is found in the Johns Hopkins *defixiones* (see 6.13, 6.19). The milieu of the present text is Greek, with all the personal names of Greek origin, as we noted, but it is not possible to characterise precisely the varieties of Latin to which these forms might have belonged.

crede mihi: a phrase typical of epistolography, which occurs in two forms, *mihi crede* and *crede mihi*. There is a classic discussion of the distribution of the two by Landgraf (1914: 187), and refinements are made by Cugusi (1972–3: 681). In Cicero's correspondents *crede mihi* is the norm, whereas in Cicero himself *mihi crede* is constant. It does not, however, seem convincing to argue from this with Cugusi and Landgraf that *crede mihi* was more colloquial and *mihi crede* somehow more refined. Imperatives are often placed in first position and unemphatic pronouns for their part do not as a rule come in first position. The order *mihi crede* is thus abnormal on two counts, and cannot but have given special emphasis to the personal pronoun. *Crede mihi* was more self-effacing than the reverse order, and it would only have been a person of marked self-esteem who would regularly have written *mihi crede*. Cf. *ausculta mihi/mihi ausculta*, below, 16.2.

5 maxsuma: for the artificial *xs* spelling for *x*, which occurs in inscriptions and not infrequently in Vindolanda tablets, see Adams (1995b: 90–1).

The vowel 'intermediate' (see Quint. 1.4.8) between *ī* and *ŭ* in unstressed syllables before a labial was early represented by *u* but came increasingly to be written with *i*. A grammatical fragment of Varro (269: Funaioli 1907: 291) attributes the change to Caesar (cf. Quint. 1.7.21; for a full collection and discussion of the grammatical *testimonia* see Garcea 2012: 148–52), but there was not a sudden switch in orthography, and the old spelling lingered on. On the one hand already in the Gallus fragment (Anderson, Parsons and Nisbet 1979), which antedates Gallus' death in 26 BC, and comes from the same Egyptian site as the present letter, there is the spelling *maxima*. Similarly in the *Res gestae* of Augustus (soon after AD 14?) mainly *i*-spellings occur (including several cases of *maximus* and *manibium*; also 2 *legitimus*, 14 and elsewhere *decimus*; *clupeus* however is at 34 of the Ankara version: see Scheid 2007: clxiv). On the other hand from much the same period we have the *S. C. de Cn. Pisone patre* (AD 20), and in this *u* is still preferred to *i*, by 20:2 (for the text see Eck, Caballos and Fernández 1996). In the archive of the Sulpicii (*TPSulp.*) from Pompeii (see Camodeca 1999, and text 15 below), consisting of precisely dated legal documents spanning roughly the period AD 30–60, there are five instances of *u* before labials, but these are outnumbered by *i*-forms (by 15:5).

In the Vindolanda tablets there are still cases of the *u*-spelling, notably in the term *contubernalis*, which alternates in the corpus with *contibernalis* (see Adams 2003a: 536). In the *Lex Irnitana* of Flavian date the *i*-spelling predominates (thirty-eight examples), but the *u*-form also occurs seventeen times (figures taken from the text of González 1986).

Spelling reform does not take place overnight, and personal preference was a factor.

tibei: the old form of the dative (see Leumann 1977: 62, 64), which coexists with the form *tibe*, showing the long close *e* that was transitional between the original diphthong *ei* and CL *ī* (see below on 14.9). For early inscriptional examples of the two forms (and of *sibei/sibe*) see Neue and Wagener 1892–1905: II.349). Suneros writes *ei* several times (see below, 14.6 on *uocareis*), and also has the *e*-spelling in *deuom* (below, 14.9). See further above, 6.2, and also below, 26.12.

de·mostrabit: for *demonstrabit*, with assimilation to *s* of the consonant cluster *ns* (cf. *cosul* for *consul*, and see Leumann 1977: 146, Väänänen 1981a: 64).

Here again is a point separating the parts of a compound (see above, 13.10), in this case after the preverb *de*. This is also a text in which prepositions are usually divided from the dependent noun or pronoun by a point, whereas in some texts with interpuncta the two elements are left undivided (see e.g. Adams 1995b: 96, 2003b: 532). See also below, 20.4 (*de·est*), where the point might possibly be an attempt to counter a contraction.

6 qu[i]t: such *t*-spellings were first determined by assimilation to a following voiceless consonant (as here). These assimilations, and the coexistence of pairs of terms such as *at* and *ad, quot* and *quod, reliquit* and *quid*, caused uncertainty about the correct written forms, and sometimes *-t* was written even before a voiced consonant or *-d* before a voiceless (see Adams 1977a: 27–9, id. 1990a: 237, id. 1995a: 91, id. 2013: 157–62; also Cugusi 1972–3: 676, above, 6.28, 30, and below, 22.16; also index, 'spellings, *t/d* in final position'). Later in this line *set* is written before a voiceless stop.

uocareis: future perfect (CL *uocaueris*). In classical Latin the *i* of the future perfect is short (usually: see further below), and historically too it was short. There was a distinction between the original length of the *i* in the perfect subjunctive (long, from an *ī*-optative) and that in the future perfect (short, from a short-vowel subjunctive) (see Leumann 1977: 609–10: e.g. Plaut. *Mil.* 156 *diffregeritis*), but the short vowel became the norm in both by the classical period. However, there are some early relics of the long form in the perfect subjunctive (see Leumann 1977: 610; also Neue and Wagener 1892–1905: III.

428-9, Meiser 1998: 215). The spelling in the present letter shows that the writer, who had a taste for old-fashioned orthography, thought that the vowel in the future perfect too was originally long. Such analogical confusions are understandable, given that the two categories eventually ended up with an *i* of the same quantity, and also that in some contexts either a perfect subjunctive or future perfect may be possible. Note *ambulareis* at *CIL* I².2138 (with the same *ei*-spelling as that here), which may either be future perfect or perfect subjunctive: *heus tu, uiator lasse, qu[i] me praetereis, | cum diu ambulareis, tamen hoc ueniundum est tibi* (taken by both Ernout 1914: 311 and Neue and Wagener 1892–1905: III.428 as future perfect). Future perfect forms with *ī* start to turn up occasionally in classical poetry from Catullus onwards, as in *fecerimus* at Catull. 5.10 (see further Neue and Wagener 1892–1905: III.430; the other examples cited, Ovid *Met.* 6.357, *Pont.* 4.5.6, 4.5.16, *Priap.* 73.4, are all second person plural). Cicero's clausulae suggest that he too admitted *ī* in the future perfect (see Fordyce 1961: 107 on Catull. 5.10). Presumably, while both future perfect and perfect subjunctive usually had a short vowel by CL, there was a lingering memory of the old *ī*-form of the perfect subjunctive (for examples in classical poetry see Neue and Wagener 1892–1905: III.428-9), which was occasionally allowed to influence the future perfect by analogy, and a historically incorrect long vowel future perfect gained some currency for a while (perhaps mainly in the plural for some reason). Grammarians were not clear about the original distinction of vowel quantity between future perfect and perfect subjunctive: note Agroecius, *GL* VII.116.1-2 *fuerimus coniunctiuo modo tempore praeterito perfecto, i breuis est; et fuerimus eodem modo tempore futuro, i longa est.*

  Those at this period who had an archaising taste for the old digraph *ei* (the diphthong itself had given way to *ī*) attempted to use it where it was etymologically justified, i.e. in positions where there had originally (or at least transitionally) been a diphthong rather than *ī* (this is so for example in the Gallus papyrus: see Somerville 2007, and also above, 6.2). So it was that earlier Lucilius (364-6) had advocated the spelling *ei* for the nominative plural *puerei*, in which it was an old form, but *i* in the genitive singular *pueri*, in which the *ī* was original. In *uocareis*, however, *ei* has been adopted as a marker merely of what the writer thought was *ī*. This 'false' use of *ei* as a means of indicating a long vowel is sometimes found. For example, in the *Tabula Heracleensis*, which was possibly Caesarian in date (Crawford 1996: I.360), the *ei* in the genitive singular at 58 (*operisue faciumdei causa*) is not etymological or of the type recommended by Lucilius: this is a false archaism.

7 pusilla … magnum: for the opposition *pusillus/magnus* see Vitr. 5.6.7 *in pusillo et in magno theatro*. In poetry *pusillus* occurs mainly in lower genres, such as comedy, Menippean satire, Catullus and Horace's *Satires* (see *TLL* X.2.2736.45f.). In Cicero it is found only twelve times, and ten of these cases are in the correspondence (*TLL* 47f.) and only one in a speech, and that early (*Verr.* 2.185). In the late Republic the word must have been informal/ colloquial.

   lucrum facit: a standard phrase for making a profit (e.g. Plaut. *Merc.* 95 *lucrum ingens facio, Capt.* 327, Brut. *ap.* Cic. *Fam.* 11.20.2: *TLL* VII.2.1723.61ff., Cugusi 1972–3: 682).

8 siquod: an interesting expression, for which on the face of it *si quid* would have been expected in classical Latin. In the masculine *si qui* is a not infrequent non-standard variant for *si quis*. The lexicon to Vitruvius of Callebat *et al.* (1984) shows, for example, that Vitruvius eighteen times uses *si qui* (singular, and pronominal not adjectival; in the plural and as an adjective *qui* is normal) for *si quis*, and has *si quis* only twice (see also E. Löfstedt 1956: II.92–3). The neuter use of *quod* for *quid* in such an environment, however, is a different matter (cf. above, 5.11). Vitruvius has only *si quid* (five times), and examples of *si quod* (where *quod* is pronominal) are very difficult to find. Apparent cases are usually explicable in other ways (see E. Löfstedt 1956: II.81–2 n. 2). A possible instance at *Tab. Vindol.* 250.6 (*s̩i̩ quod a te petierit*) may be taken as containing a parenthetical *quod*-clause (relative) (see Bowman and Thomas 1994: 222; also Adams 1983a: 73). In our letter *siquod* certainly looks equivalent to *si quid*, but it is just possible that *quod* is a relative ('if I see which thing', 'that sort of thing', i.e. a slave intending to kill his master, = *quod si uideo*). It is of note that *siquod* is written as a single word, which would be surprising if *quod* were intended as a relative.

9 deuom: the term *diuus* (for the more banal *deus*) belonged to high and poetic style and to various old formulae, including this one: cf. Plaut. *Aul.* 300 *diuom atque hominum clamat continuo fidem.* The archaic genitive plural form in *-om* outnumbers *diuorum* (*TLL* V.1.1652.31ff., 1653.67ff.), and is found particularly in formulae.

   Diuus originally had an *ei* diphthong in the first syllable (for *ei*-spellings see *TLL* V.1.1649.22ff.), and the *e*-spelling here represents the intermediate stage between the early and classical forms, viz. the long close *e* that was eventually to become *ī*. In this letter the spelling is probably not a reflection of speech but rather archaising (see Adams 2007: 138 n. 69, 442 and also 150, along with

52–62 on the history of the *e*-spelling in general; see too above, 14.5 on *tibei*, and 6.12, 15.13, 25.9 and particularly 26.12).

The scribe first wrote *fidem* and then crossed it out along with the following words, thereby leaving the genitives unattached. Cugusi (1972–3: 680) points out that, though *fidem* is normal in an expression such as *pro deum (atque hominum) fidem*, ellipse of *fidem* occasionally occurs, as at Ter. *Ph.* 351 *pro deum immortalium* (see *TLL* VI.1.666.43ff., and also X.2.1439.30 f., adding Cic. *Orat.* 156 'pro deum' dico uel 'pro deorum').

cuibis: Cugusi (1972–3: 678–9) was probably right to see this as representing *cuiuis*, in which case it would be an early spelling *b* for *u* (on early examples see Adams 2013: 183–4).

10 alio: the usual dative is in *ī* (masculine and feminine), but there are occasional analogical forms derived from the masculine and feminine declensions, such as the feminine *aliae* at Plaut. *Mil.* 802 and *alio* at *Rhet. Her.* 2.19 (*ut aliud alio iudici aut praetori aut consuli aut tribuno plebis placitum sit*). For a collection of examples of both *alio* and *aliae* see Neue and Wagener (1892–1905: II.536–7); also *OLD* s.v.

11 Chio Caesaris: Chius is presumably the slave of Caesar (see Brown 1970: 140, Cugusi 1972–3: 676), and if so here is the use of the genitive without *seruus* that was also seen in the Johns Hopkins *defixio* (6.19; see also below, 21.15–16, and for the full expression gen. + *seruus*, see 15(a).11). The whole text is suggestive of the world of slavery, and not least in the expression *dominum occidere uolt* (see the remarks of Cugusi 1972–3: 675).

Conclusions

The language and orthography are consistent with an Augustan or certainly a relatively early date. The use of the *ei*-spelling faded after the Augustan period (see 6.2). *e*-spellings (as in *deuom*) reflecting the long close *e* were mainly early (see Adams 2007: 52–62 cited at 14.9 above), but there are signs that they might have had a literary vogue as an archaism in the Augustan period (see Adams 2007: 149–50, and below, 26.12). Second person forms such as *patiarus* are mainly early (republican and early imperial). The *ī* of the future perfect implied by the *ei*-spelling in *uocareis* turns up in late republican and Augustan verse. The *u* of *maxsuma* is by no means proof of an early date, but is not inconsistent with one.

The writer's aspiration to write correctly is seen in his orthography. He uses the old spelling *tibei*, and *deuom* is archaising on two counts. *Vocareis* is a false orthographic archaism. He does not write *x* on its own but always *xs* (*adduxsit, Oxsyrychitem, maxsuma*).

However, he lapses a number of times into non-standard usages, most notably in *Epaphraes* and *patiarus*, two morphological forms also found in the Johns Hopkins *defixio* (text 6). Both of these, whatever their regional distribution might have been, were undoubtedly current in mundane social circles, and the former was almost by definition associated with the servile world. Neither is admitted by the highly educated as a concession to informality or casual style. Also non-standard are the dative form *alio* and *si quod* for *si quid* (if it is indeed such).

15

LEGAL DOCUMENT FROM THE ARCHIVE OF THE SULPICII, DATED 18 JUNE AD 37 AT PUTEOLI (*TPSVLP.* 51)

Introduction

The document is a receipt for a loan, in two versions. The exterior version (b) is written by a scribe and is spelt correctly for the most part. The interior version (a) is written by a freedman (of Greek origin), C. Novius Eunus, and contains phonetic and other types of misspellings and errors. To refer to this version as a specimen of 'Vulgar Latin' would miss the point, given that the language is formulaic and legal. Nor do the phonetic spellings necessarily betray features of uneducated speech: the underlying pronunciations might in some, if not all, cases have been general across all spoken varieties (e.g. the omission of final -*m*). The spelling errors are worth classifying, but we cannot always say whether they reflect standard or stigmatised pronunciations. There are however also errors of other types. What the two versions definitely do display are differing levels of literacy, with the Greek freedman emerging as a real-life equivalent of the uncultured freedmen of Greek origin, probably of much the same date and from the same part of Italy, portrayed in the novel of Petronius. See Landi (1983), Wolf and Crook (1989), Adams (1990a), Flobert (1995a), Seidl (1996), Calboli (1999, 2006).

Text

(a) *scriptura interior*
Cn(aeo) Acceronio Proculo C(aio) Petronio Pọntio co(n)s(ulibus),
X̣IV k(alendas) Ìulias.
C(aius) Nouius Eunus scripsi me accepisse {ạḅ}
mutua ab Eueno Tì(berii) Cessaris Augustì
liberto Primiano apssente per   5
Hessucus ser(uum) eìus et debere eì sesterta
decem milia nummu, que eì redam
cum petiaerit, et ea sesterta decem mi-

lia, <q(uae)> s(upra) s(cripta) s(unt), p(roba) r(ecte) d(ari) stipulatus [[ets]] est
    Hessucus
Eueni Tì(berii) Cessaris Augustì l(iberti) Primiani   10
ser(uus), spepodi ego C(aius) Nouius Eunus;
pro quem iìs sestertis decem milibus
num<<m>>u dede ei pignoris ar<<ab>>onis
ue nomine tridici Alxadrini modium
septe milia plus minus et ciceris faris   15
monocpi lentis in sacis ducentis modium
quator milia plus minus, que ominia
possịta habeo penus me in horeis Bassianis
puplicis Putolanorum, que ab omini
ui periculo meo est, [[dico]] fateor.   20
        vac.
actum Putolis.

(b) *scriptura exterior*
Cn(aeo) Acerronio Proculo C(aio) Petronio Pontìo Nigrìno cọ(n)ṣ(ulibus),
quartum [*sic*] kalendas Ìulias.
C(aius) Nouius Eunús scrìpsi me acçepisse mútua ab Eueno
Tì(berii) Caesaris Augustì libertọ Ṗrimiano apsente per
Hesychum seruum eìus et deḅere eì sestertium   5
decem mìllia nummum, quae eì reddam cum
petìerit, et ea HS X m(illia) n(ummum), q(uae) s(upra) s(cripta) s(unt), p(roba)
    r(ecte) d(ari) stipulátus est
Hesychus Eueni Tì(berii) Caesaris Augustì l(iberti) Prìmianì
seruus, spopondì ego C(aius) Nouius Eunús; proque
iìs séstertiìs decem m[ill]ibus nummum dedì   10
eì pignoris arrabonisue nomine trìtìcì Alexandrìnì
modium septem mịḷḷia [plu]s mịnus et cicerìs farris monocopì
lentis ìn saccìs duc[en]tìs [mod]ium quattuor mìllia p(lus) m(inus),
quae omnia reposita habeo penes me ìn horreìs
Bassìanìs publicìs Pu[teo]lanorum, quae ab omnì uì   15
perìculo meo esse fat[e]or. act(um) Puteolìs.

Translation

(b) In the consulship of C. Acerronius Proculus and C. Petronius Pontius Nigrinus, four[teen] days before the Kalends of July, I, C. Novius Eunus, wrote that I have received a loan from Euenus Primianus freedman of Tiberius

Caesar Augustus in his absence, through the agency of his slave Hesychus, and that I owe him ten thousand sesterces in cash, which I shall give back to him when he asks for it, and those ten thousand sesterces written above, Hesychus, slave of Euenus Primianus freedman of Tiberius Caesar Augustus, stipulated be duly paid in good coin, and I, C. Novius Eunus, promised to do so; and for those ten thousand sesterces in cash I have given him as pledge or security seven thousand *modii*, more or less, of Alexandrian wheat, and four thousand *modii*, more or less, of chickpeas, spelt, (*monoc(o)pi?*) and lentils in two hundred sacks, all of which I have in my possession in store in the public Bassian granaries of the people of Puteoli, which I acknowledge to be safe from all violence [?: see the Commentary], at my risk (if that should turn out not to be the case). Transacted at Puteoli.

Commentary

preliminaries

Certain orthographic features are worth noting at the start. I have used in the texts an acute accent to indicate an apex, and a grave to indicate I longa.

In the scribal version (b) there is a subtle use of the apex. There are just five cases, all of them correctly placed over long vowels (3 twice, 7, 9, 10). The two apices on the second syllable of *Eunus* (3, 9) are noteworthy, and imply a Greek pronunciation of the name (Εὔνους), which may reflect Eunus' continuing Greekness; the name was easily Latinised. Cf. *TPSulp.* 16.6. The apex on the first vowel of *séstertiis* is correct (see Leumann 1977: 488) (*sestertius* = *sēmis* + *tertius*), as are those on the first vowel of *mútua* and on *stipulátus*. Quintilian (1.7.2) remarked that it would be silly to place apices over all long vowels, and the scribe here was clearly sparing and using his judgment. The apex is used quite differently, and in a very consistent way (almost always over *a* and *o*), by the military scribes at Vindolanda, a fact which suggests that they had received a specific type of instruction (see Adams 1995b: 97–8, 2003c, 531–2). There are many apices in the archive of the Sulpicii, and also cases of I longa (see below), which are listed in appendices in Camodeca (1999). Eunus himself in the interior version makes no use of the apex, though he does use I longa sometimes.

The scribe in the exterior version writes I longa thirty-six times, for the most part but not always to represent *ī* (note Plaut. *Aul.* 77–8, using *litteram longam* in an image which shows that the audience at that time must already have been familiar with the letter form). There are five errors, where I longa is used for *ĭ*, in the second syllable of *tritìci* (11) (in this word the first *i* should be long and the second short, and this looks like a mechanical error with I longa used in the wrong syllable), in *ciceris* (12) and *in* twice (13, 14) and in *petierit* (7) (but here the *i* would have been long in the full form *petiuerit*, and the scribe might have been influenced by that). There are two, and probably three, places where I longa is used for yod, in *Iulias* (2) and *eius* (5) (for the phonetics of this word see Sturtevant 1940: 146, Leumann 1977: 13, and see also on the orthography *TLL* VII.2.456.58ff.), and in *Pontio* (1), in which it is likely that there was already yodisation of the vowel in hiatus after a stop. On the use of I longa to represent yod see in particular Marichal (1988: 60–5), noting (64) that at La Graufesenque the I longa does not usually mark a vowel but yod; see also Adams (2013: 104–8). There remain twenty-eight cases above where I longa represents *ī*. The scribe achieved almost total consistency, as there is only a small number of cases in which *ī* is not so rendered (in the final syllable of *scripsi*, and in *liberto Primiano*). Marichal's discussion shows that different corpora had different ways of employing I longa (see too the preceding paragraph on the variable use of the apex). For this scribe it was a marker of *ī*.

In Eunus' own version things are different. He offers only nine instances of I longa (two for yod, in *Iulias* and *eius*, and the rest for *ī*). The ability to use I longa consistently was a mark of literate culture (see the discussion of Marichal 1988).

The notes that follow apply to the interior version of Eunus (a).

1 Acceronio: the wrong consonant has been doubled here, a mechanical error. Cf. *[T]urranium* at Terentianus, *P. Mich.* VIII.468.54 (see Adams 1977a: 35). For a comparable example at Bu Njem see Adams (1994: 107).

5–6 per Hessucus: it is possible that the nominative for accusative is a slip. However, in Greek documents (inscriptions, ostraca) of the early imperial period personal names dependent on prepositions (including διά, the equivalent of *per*) are often left in the nominative case, and they are also sometimes uninflected (i.e. used in the nominative form) when they are direct object of a verb or have some other oblique-case role. For instances dependent on prepositions see e.g. Bernand (1988), 35 διὰ Δίδυμος [ἱερέως θρησκ]εύοντος, [π]ροσεδρεύοντος, *O. Claud.* II.233.6–7 ἐκομισάμ(ην) . . . [. . . παρ]ὰ Πανίσκος, Baillet (1920–6), 1862 Ποτάμων ἱστόρησα σὺν Ποτάμων πατρί (for further examples see Adams 2013: 207).

This practice must reflect the special character of personal names: it was the nominative form that expressed the essence of a person's identity, and for that reason there was a tendency for the nominative or base form to be adopted when strict syntax required an oblique case (see Adams 2013: 210–13). In two of the above examples, while the name is in the nominative, nouns or participles in agreement with it are inflected. Eunus was a Greek and he might have been influenced by a contemporary Greek practice. There are also cases of *per* with the nominative in later Latin (see Adams 1994: 99–102, particularly on *per kamellarius Iassucthan* in *O. Bu Njem* 77, of the mid-third century; also Galdi 2004: 396–8 on some inscriptional examples, and Bastardas Parera 1953: 24 and Westerburgh 1956: 250 on early medieval Latin). See further below, 41 Commentary, 'preliminaries', 46.4–5.

7 redam: for *reddam*. This text (along with the rest of the oeuvre of Eunus) provides marked and early evidence for degemination of consonants other than *s* (see Adams 1990a: 238–40): cf. here *arabonis, faris, sacis, quator, horeis* (in every case between vowels). If *ss* is left aside, the document has a false geminate in *Acceronio* above, and geminates only in *accepisse* and *nummu*. There is similar evidence from Pompeian graffiti (see Väänänen 1966: 62 for intervocalic degemination). For an account of degemination (and lenition, which will come up below) in the Romance languages see now Loporcaro (2011: 150–4). Degemination 'co-occurred with lenition throughout western Romance . . . Central and southern Italo-Romance, south of the Apennines, is the only Romance area that remained unaffected either by lenition or degemination' (Loporcaro 2011: 151). Loporcaro (151) believes that in western Romance 'degemination probably spread from Gaul'. The early evidence from around Pompeii complicates the chronology within Italy. See further on the Latin evidence Kiss (1972: 74–82), Väänänen (1981a: 58–9).

Eunus' treatment of *s* is in contrast to his treatment of other geminates. He constantly writes *ss*, after long vowels (e.g *Hessucus*), *p* (*scripssi, apssente*) and after short vowels (*possita*). There are twenty-eight cases in the corpus (Adams 1990a: 239), most of them false geminates, though in *promissi* (*TPSulp.* 68, Eunus) the geminate is etymologically justified. By contrast the scribes in the exterior versions do not double *s* in these ways. There is a similar, but not identical, use of *ss* in Vindolanda tablets (see Adams 1995b: 89, 2003c: 539). There *ss* is frequently written in environments where the geminate was historically correct though not usually written, i.e. after long vowels or diphthongs and deriving usually from assimilation/assibilation within the consonant clusters *tt, ts, dt*. Most notable is the spelling *missi* of the perfectum of *mitto* and its compounds (eleven such examples are listed by Adams 1995b: 89), as in Eunus' *promissi*. Quintilian (1.7.20) implies that a simplification of the geminate in such environments (he cites *caussae, cassus* and *diuissiones*; with the second compare *occassionem* at Vindolanda, *Tab. Vindol.* 225) had taken place after the time of Cicero and Virgil. The constant writing of the geminate in these environments suggests that scribes had received orthographic instruction which attempted to counter the simplification that had occurred or was occurring in speech. This would represent a taste for the old-fashioned in spelling (cf. the attempt to restore *ei* where it was etymologically justified: see above, 14.6 with references). Just occasionally writers at Vindolanda got things wrong, by doubling an *s* where the geminate was not justified, as in *nissi* (*Tab. Vindol.* 343.20) and *resscribere* (*Tab. Vindol.* 645), and herein lies what seems the most plausible explanation of the geminations in Eunus (but cf. Seidl 1996: 107–9). Writers who had had inculcated in them a sense that *ss* was often right and should be written wherever it was etymologically justified were bound occasionally to write it by hypercorrection where it did not belong. That happened only rarely among the competent scribes at Vindolanda, but an uncultivated writer such as Eunus might have had to resort to writing the geminate almost everywhere except at the end of words.

See also above, 13.2.

8 petiaerit: the monophthongisation of *ae* occurred early in non-city Latin (see Adams 2007: 78–88 for republican evidence, all but exclusively from outside Rome; cf. Adams 2013: 71–2). Eunus always writes *e* and not *ae* (Adams 1990a: 230), except in this one place, where the digraph is hypercorrect, for original *ĕ* (rather than for *ē*).

In the Romance languages the reflex of *ae* merged with that of CL *ĕ*, and that development is anticipated in such hypercorrect spellings as the one here. For the same hypercorrection (*ae* for *ĕ*) in Pompeian inscriptions see Väänänen (1966: 24). There is an example in Terentianus (*P. Mich.* VIII.469.11 *resçreibae*), and another elsewhere in the archive of the Sulpicii, in a document of a certain Diognetus, slave of C. Novius Cypaerus (*TPSulp.* 45 *aeodem = eodem*). The same, short monophthongal, outcome of *ae* is also attested to by Greek transliterations of Latin employing epsilon to represent the sound of the original *ae*. There is a case in the second century in a document of Aeschines Flavianus of Miletus (*SB* III.1.6304 = *CPL* 193), who writes βετρανε for the genitive of *ueteranae* (see the discussion of the text at Adams 2003a: 53–62). The witness to this last document, Domitius Theophilus, writing Latin in Latin script, has *aeadem* for *eadem*; see above for this form, and also e.g. *aeorum* for *eorum* in a letter of Rustius Barbarus at *O. Faw.* 1.12 (see below, 26.2). The earliest inverse spelling (*ae* for *ĕ*) in the Spanish inscriptions, according to Carnoy (1906: 77), is *Naerua* in an inscription from the end of the first century AD. Coleman (1971: 186) gives examples of *ae* for *ĕ* from the inscriptions of various regions.

In the documents of Eunus, with their relatively early date, it is possible that the constant spelling with *e* reflects a long-standing feature of the speech of this

Campanian region, distinguishing Campanian Latin still at this period from the speech of the city. The evidence of the archive is supported by a literary testimonium. According to Varro (*Ling.* 7.96) rustics (in Atellan farce) called the character Pappus/pappus *Mesius* not *Maesius* (see Adams 2007: 154–5 with n. 100 on the passage and its difficulties), and these rustic characters can only have been Campanians. Since Oscan, unlike Umbrian, seems to have preserved the diphthong *ai*, such a monophthong in Campania cannot with any confidence be put down to the influence of the substrate (Adams 2007: 154–5). The Pompeian graffiti, also of the first century, show up the same characteristic as the archive of Eunus. In these the *e*-spelling abounds (see Väänänen 1966: 23–4 for the evidence).

11 spepodi: it is a curiosity that the scribe uses the later assimilated form *spopondi*, whereas Eunus uses the archaic form *spe-* (for which see Adams 1990a: 244, citing Gellius' discussion at 6.9.12, 15). It seems unlikely that Eunus, a phonetic speller, adopted the form from his own usage (the term is legal and would not have been in common use). It is more likely that he had a slightly different version of the document from that used by the scribe, or that the scribe modernised the spelling if he were reproducing Eunus' version. The nasal has also been omitted before a stop.

12 pro quem: hypercorrect for *proque*. Eunus omits final *-m* nine times (Adams 1990a: 236).

iìs sestertìs: the scribe writes *iìs séstertiìs*, distinguishing the two vowels in the ending of the demonstrative and noun. Eunus does so in the demonstrative, but in the noun the spelling reflects the contraction that occurred in speech (and not only that of the uneducated) when two vowels of similar quality were in hiatus (see e.g. Väänänen 1966: 39–40, 1981a: 44–5, Leumann 1977: 120, Coleman 1999: 33; for examples of this contraction in Augustan poetry see e.g. Platnauer 1951: 68).

More problematic is the omission of the vowel in hiatus in *sesterta* (twice in this document), where the following vowel is of different quality, and in *Putolanorum* (likewise). Such omissions are a feature of the writing of Eunus (see Adams 1990a: 233–5). In *sesterta* the omission is after the accent. In *Putolis* (several times in the corpus: Adams 1990a: 233) it may look to have occurred under the accent (*Putéolis*), but there is evidence in such words for a shift of accent (> *Puteólis*; cf. *mulíere* > *muliére*: see e.g. Kramer 1976: 36, 37 with footnotes). Omission of the vowel grapheme in these various environments is common in inscriptions and other documents (see e.g. Svennung 1936: 9–29, Kiss 1972: 53–4, Adams 1977a: 19–20, id. 1994: 105, id. 2013: 108–10). The original vowel would not have been lost but converted to yod, effecting various palatalisations later. The omission in writing reflects the reduction in the number of syllables, if not the new sound. An alternative was to use I longa to mark the yod, as seems to have been done by the scribe in *Pontio* (see above, 'preliminaries').

13 dede: the scribe writes instead *dedi*, with the *ī* marked by I longa. Eunus' *e* must represent the long close *e* that was an intermediate stage between the original *ei* diphthong and CL *ī* (see above, 14.5, 14.9, and index, 'spellings, *e* (long close) for *ei/ī*'). In Pompeian graffiti of much the same date and provenance as this text a parallel use of the *e*-spelling in the first person singular of a perfect verb form occurs twice in *futue = futui* (*CIL* IV.1517, 2200 add. p. 215) (see Väänänen 1966: 23, Adams 2007: 442–3). The period in which such *e*-spellings derived from *ei* genuinely represented a feature of speech was probably restricted to the Republic and not much beyond; there is evidence from about the Augustan period that *e*-spellings had acquired an old-fashioned flavour and were written by those with stylistic aspirations (see 14.9, 26.12). It seems unlikely, however, that someone scribbling an obscenity on a wall would have adopted archaic orthography, and it 'becomes likely that in the area of Pompeii in the mid-first century AD there was a variety of speech in which the expected long final *i* (stemming from an earlier *ei* diphthong) of the first-person singular perfect ending had an open articulation that caused it to be heard as an *e*' (Adams 2007: 443).

13–14 pignoris ar<<ab>>onisue nomine: on this use of *nomine*, which possibly replaces the old unsupported genitive of the 'rubric', see Adams (1990a: 244–5), Flobert (1995a: 148). In document 52 in this corpus Eunus uses instead the unaccompanied genitive. See however Calboli (1999: 342).

14 tridici: the spelling with intervocalic *d* occurs in Eunus' next tablet too, where the other intervocalic stop is also voiced (*tridigi*). Reflexes in Romance show voicing of one or the other consonant (*REW* 8924, citing Borm. *tridik*, Obw. *trédi*, Log. *trigu* (note too OSard. *tridigu*, cited at *FEW* XIII.308), Sp., Pg. *trigo*; see also Seidl 1996: 106). Intervocalic voicing of voiceless stops, generally referred to as lenition (see e.g. Loporcaro 2011: 150–4, and also below, 37.2–3), left its mark on western Romance, with Romania and a good deal of Italy unaffected (see the table of correspondences at Väänänen 1981a: 56–7). Whether there was a general tendency to voicing in this environment at the early period to which this text belongs is unclear (for what evidence there is, apart from *tridicum*, see Adams 1977a: 30–1). Certainly in the term *triticum* voicing is quite well attested in non-standard documents of the early Empire (see also Flobert 1995a: 149), including the Pompeian graffiti. For a Pompeian example see *CIL* IV.8830 (Väänänen 1966: 54 with n. 2). In the ostraca of Bu Njem *tridicum* is the only form (five times) (Adams 1994: 108). It seems best to treat *tridicum* as a special case, with lenition starting in particular lexical items (lexical diffusion) rather than working more generally all at once (see also Siedl 1996: 105–6). The first stop is between two near-identical vowels, the first of them under the accent, a position in which voicing might have been particularly favoured (see Väänänen 1966: 54 n. 2). Whatever the distribution of the pronunciation, it must certainly have been current at Pompeii in the first century. For another such correspondence between Eunus and Pompeian graffiti see above on *dede*.

Alxadrini: this spelling for *Alexandrini* may look like a slip but it is repeated by Eunus in *TPSulp.* 52, and it may be treated as reflecting a syncope (of the *e*), and as also showing omission of the nasal before a stop. A pewter tablet from London (Hassall and Tomlin 1999: 375) with an (accusative) list of valuables has the form *Alxadri* (*pastellos auri VIII sabanum Alxaḍri | mappam …*). The text has many uncertainties, but the form seems to share the same characteristics as that in Eunus. There are quite a few syncopated spellings in the documents of Eunus (Adams 1990a: 231–2). Nasals are often omitted in substandard writing, including Pompeian inscriptions (see Väänänen 1966: 67–8, 1981a: 63, Adams 1990a: 241; also above, 14.2, and index, 'spellings, omission of nasal before stop'). Cf. with this instance *CIL* VI.4428 *Alexadrus* (see Gordon *et al.* 2006: 280 (5) for further such examples from Roman inscriptions). There are ten such omissions in the corpus of Eunus (Adams 1990a: 241), including *spepodi* for *spepondi* in this text and three times elsewhere. Whether Eunus' Greekness was a factor here it is impossible to tell. However, the omission of nasals before stops is 'very frequent' in Greek papyri of the period (Gignac 1976: 116–17).

16 monocpi: obscure, but see Flobert (1995a: 148), suggesting 'une légumineuse'.

lentis: like various other terms for plants used as foodstuffs (e.g. *faba*), *lens* is typically used in the collective singular (see *OLD* s.v.); so too its diminutive *lenticula*. Note too *cicer* here (chick peas). On this type of collective see E. Löfstedt (1956: I.14), and above, 4.10 and below, 17.2.

18 penus me: for *penus* = *penes* cf. *CIL* III.6441 *(Maximina) defuncta penus colonia(m) Sirmi(um)*; *TLL* X.1.1053.39ff. Has the term been given another adverbial ending (cf. e.g. *tenus* and particularly *penitus*: see Flobert 1995a: 148), or has there been some sort of mechanical conflation with the noun *penus*, with a genuine adverbial form with this ending not really existing at all? See also Calboli (2006: 164–5).

19–20 que ab omini ui periculo meo est, [[dico]] fateor: the correct formula (in the scribal version) has *esse*, in an acc. + inf. dependent on *fateor. Ab . . . esse* as it has been translated above would be a tmesis, = *omni ui abesse*. For *abesse* = 'be safe from' see *OLD* s.v. 9b. For tmesis of preverbs in Latin see Wackernagel (1926–8: II.171–2, 175) = Langslow (2009: 613, 617–18), Marouzeau (1949b: 150–4). However, another possibility is to take *ab* in sense 25 of the *OLD* s.v. ('in respect of'), and *uis* in sense 19 ('value, amount'), hence 'in respect of the full value': 'which I acknowledge are my liability/are held at my personal risk in respect of their full value'.

With the finite verb *est, fateor* becomes parenthetical and the construction paratactic. The same construction occurs also in this corpus in 52, again in the hand of Eunus. Such parataxis with a variety of verbs is common, particularly in colloquial texts, from Plautus onwards (see Hofmann and Ricottilli 2003: 250–1, Adams 2003c: 554–5; also above, 3.417, and index, 'parataxis, parenthetical use of verbs of saying and the like'). Cf. Plaut. *Aul.* 88 *pauper sum, fateor, patior* (with Stockert 1983 ad loc.), Ter. *Ad.* 188 *leno sum, fateor, TLL* VI.1.337.9ff., and see further Calboli (1999: 337–8).

Que (= *quae*, plural), subject of *est*, is possibly a Grecism (see Calboli 1999: 341). The construction is repeated by Eunus in document 52. Alternatively one might suggest a sort of dictation error, with Eunus hearing *esse* as *es(s)'* and interpreting it as *est* (on the assumption that there was a tendency for the final *-t* in this verb to be lost in pronunciation: for this phenomenon in the verb 'to be' see Adams 2013: 155; cf. below, 25.27). Twice elsewhere (*TPSulp.* 52, 67) Eunus writes *ets* for *est*, and this mistake could be due to his insertion in the wrong place of the *t* that he knew to be correct in the written form. Another possibility is that *est* represents a constructio ad sensum, with the collectivity that precedes inspiring a singular verb. The neuter plural *omnia*, which occurs in the preceding clause with *quae*, is sometimes treated as a collective singular, and not only in late Latin (see Norberg 1944: 55–6).

The error *[[dico]]*, according to Flobert (1995a: 150), reflects the fact that **fatíum** means 'say' in Oscan. Eunus might simply have written the most banal verb possible in such a sentence and then have had it corrected.

The spelling *omini*, preceded two lines earlier by *ominia*, is of a type that occurs no fewer than six times in Eunus' small corpus in this word (see Adams 1990a: 232). Cf. too *recete* (52), *Septeberes* (67) and *Octoberes* (68). However these forms are to be explained, they cannot but represent his pronunciation. The anaptyxis particularly in *ominis* is of a type that can be paralleled in Oscan, and it is possible that Eunus' pronunciation was Oscan influenced (see Flobert 1995a: 148–9). However, this is no more than a possibility (for reservations see Adams 2003a: 120 n. 42). Anaptyxis in this environment in Latin goes back to an early period (*mina* < μνᾶ), and in *omnis* can be cited from a variety of Latin inscriptions, papyri and documents (see Adams 1990a: 232 with nn. 15, 17). To this material can be added the Visigothic slate tablet (Velázquez Soriano 2004) 123.I.4 (*omenibus*). Anaptyxis is also quite common in Greek papyri (Gignac 1976: 311–12).

Conclusions

It is not clear whether Eunus copied the text from a written exemplar, or had it dictated to him. Certainly there are phonetic spellings that suggest he might have been listening to speech, up to a point. Perhaps he was overseen by someone as he copied out the text.

Various influences on the writing can be discerned. Some misspellings are banal (e.g. omission of *-m*, contraction of *ii*), with the pronunciations behind them particular to no single social dialect. On the other hand *dede* for *dedi* may reflect a local pronunciation. The spelling *omini* is unusual, adopted repeatedly, and open to several explanations, all of which have been allowed above. The uninflected name *Hessucus* dependent on the preposition *per* is a usage more readily associated at this period with Greek. Eunus' Greekness is also implied by the punctuating of his own name. One or two other possible Grecisms were seen (the use of *que* with a singular verb, and also various spellings, such as *Alxad-*, of a type frequent in contemporary Greek), but usually there is an alternative explanation. That goes too for the various Oscanisms that have been proposed by scholars.

Eunus does seem to have had some sort of training in Latin literacy. He displays an obsession with writing *ss*, sometimes writes I longa, and has a hypercorrect digraph *ae*. He comes across as a Greek living in a specific part of Italy, whose literacy in Latin was imperfect.

16

SEXUAL VERSES FROM POMPEII
(*CIL* IV.2360, 4008, 8229)

Introduction

These verses are in iambic senarii (see *CLE* 45). For an interpretation of the context see the Commentary, 'preliminaries'.

Text

amat qui scribet, pedicatur qui leget,
qui opscultat prurit, paticus est qui praeterit.
'ursi me comedant, et ego uerpa qui lego.'

Translation

The writer of this is performing an amatory act: the reader is being buggered. The listener is aroused: the passer-by is his pathic. 'May bears eat me, for I, the reader, am a stupid prick.'

Commentary

preliminaries

It is arguable that there is not a random series of clauses with sexual content in these verses but that the two parts of each line complement each other. In the first line the first impression that one has it that *amat* must mean 'is in love', but the second part of the line suggests otherwise. *Amo* may refer not only to love in the emotional sense, but also euphemistically to sexual acts (Adams 1982a: 188). Indeed at Cic. *Cat.* 2.8 both *amo* and *amor* allude to *pedicatio*: *alios ipse amabat turpissime, aliorum amori flagitiosissime seruiebat.* The meaning of the line seems to be 'the writer is committing a sexual act: the reader is being buggered' (with the second part explaining the first). Could the placement of the inscription have been such that the reader had to stoop to read it? The obvious meaning of the first part of the second line is 'he who listens (to this act taking place) is aroused'; and then 'the passer-by is his pathic/victim'. The second part implies a consequence of the first. In the final line the second part seems to explain the first, as was suggested above for the first line (see below on the last line). The reader speaks at the end, having realised that he has been made a fool of. First he curses himself, and then declares that he is a *uerpa*, which in the context has a weakened meaning, 'fool' or the like.

See Courtney (1995), no. 79 (with commentary p. 301).

1 scribet, leget: these are both present tenses, with *e* written for the expected *ī*. There are numerous such misspellings at Pompeii in the final syllable of both nominal and verbal endings (see Väänänen 1966: 21–2, Adams 2013: 58–9). The verbal instances are found mainly in the perfect and present tenses of third conjugation verbs, but there are also two instances of *pugnabet*. There are no grounds for seeing them as regional, as comparable forms are found in other non-literary documents of the early Empire, such as the letters of Terentianus (*P. Mich.* VIII.468.38 *uolueret, aiutaueret,* 470.24, 471.33 *dicet*), the ostraca of Wâdi Fawâkhir (*O. Faw.* 2.3, 3.2, 4.10 *scribes,* 3.11 *mittes:* see below, text 26), the Vindolanda tablets (*dabes* three times, *dabet* and *signabet* once each are all in *Tab. Vindol.* 643) and the Vindonissa tablets (*dabes* is at *Tab. Vindon.* 15, 31 and 53). In final syllables *i* must have tended to lose its tension and to undergo opening, a forerunner of its ultimate merger with CL *ē* (a merger only possible once distinctions of vowel length had been undermined). For the evidence and discussion see Adams (2007: 141–2), id. (2013: 51–61; also 43–51 on the loss of phonemic distinctions of vowel length). See also below, 22.33, 26.3, 42.3, and index, 'endings, verbal, *e* for *i* …'; also 'spellings, *e* for short *i*, in verb endings'.

By contrast the two presents in the next line, *prurit* and *praeterit,* have *i*-spellings. The vowel of the third person singular, present tense, of fourth conjugation verbs and of *eo* (and compounds) was originally long (in the latter case deriving from a diphthong) (see Questa 2007: 17 on Plautus, but without citing evidence for the length of the vowel, perhaps because there would usually be a consonant at the start of the next word and evidence for length is hard to find; also *TLL* V.2.626.57 for *īt* in early Latin; in Terence *redit* unambiguously has *ī* at *Hec.* 347, whereas in *uenit* at *Ad.* 60 the vowel is short, probably because of iambic shortening; at *Haut.* 276 *prodit* may be scanned with either a long or short vowel in the second syllable), but long vowels were later subject to shortening before *-t.* None of the numerous *e*-spellings for *i* collected from Pompeian inscriptions by Väänänen (1966: 22) is in a fourth conjugation verb, and it seems likely that the old long pronunciation still lingered on in speech.

2 opscultat: *ausculto* was potentially subject to two different phonetic developments, each leading to types of recomposition.

First, from dissimilation caused by the *u* in the second syllable *ausculto* was sometimes modified to *asculto* (note Caper, *GL* VII.108.6 *ausculta non asculta*; for the dissimilation cf. *Augustus* > *Agustus* and Adams 2013: 86–7). The initial vowel was then subject to reinterpretation as the prepositional prefix *a/ab* (see *TLL* II.1534.43ff. for the form *absculto*), and that reinterpretation opened the way for the replacement of *a* with the synonymous *e(x)* (**e/ex-sculto*). For substitutions of this kind cf. *Tib. Vindol.* 182.16 *exungia* = *axungia* (Adams 1995b: 102); at *Mul. Chir.* 599 the form *absungia* betrays the reinterpretation of the first vowel of *axungia* as representing the prefix *a(b)*; also *O. Bu Njem* 84, 85 *propositus* = *praepositus* (Adams 1994: 109–10, *TLL* X.2.2070.35ff.). It. *ascoltare* derives from the initial dissimilated form, whereas Fr. *écouter* and Sp. *escuchar* derive from the secondary form with its prefixal substitution (see Bloch and von Wartburg 1968: 211).

Second, the *au* diphthong was not infrequently converted to a form of *o*, particularly in slangy or popular terms (see e.g. Adams 2013: 81–7). A monophthongised form *osculto* (not registered by the *TLL*) might have been falsely interpreted as an assimilated form of *obsculto*. Such an interpretation would be based on the assumption that 'original' *obsculto* had developed to *opsculto* by means of devoicing of *b* before voiceless *s*, and that that in turn had been assimilated to *osculto* (for the assimilation *ps* > *s(s)*, attested particularly at Pompeii, see Adams 2013:172–3). False recomposition to *obsculto/opsculto* then became possible (for false recomposition of such assimilated forms see Adams 2013: 169–70).

The various deformations undergone by *ausculto* show that it was in popular use, and that is also suggested for the classical period onwards by its distribution. It survives widely in the Romance languages (see above). In the early period it is common in Plautus and Terence (and occurs as well in Afranius, Caecilius and Pomponius; for citation of some early examples see Nonius p. 370 Lindsay), but is also found in tragedy (at Enn. *scen.* 247 Jocelyn, in a phrase (*ausculta mihi*) also used a number of times by Plautus (Jocelyn 1967: 384–5), and at Pacuvius 85 = 77 Schierl *magis audiendum quam auscultandum censeo*). At least one of the attestations in tragedy (that in Pacuvius), along with the presence of the word in a fragment of a speech by Cato (*ap.* Gell. 1.15.9 *itaque auditis, non auscultatis*), suggests that it would be wrong to assume that in the early Republic it was exclusively a low-register term. The phrase *ausculta mihi* may look colloquial, but the other two examples, in formal contexts, seem rather to be semantically determined. *Ausculto* meant 'listen (to)' (whence 'obey') rather than 'hear', whereas *audio* shared both meanings. It is obvious from two of the instances just cited that *ausculto* allowed a distinction to be made between an act of listening and one of hearing.

In the classical period *ausculto* is far less frequent. There is just a single instance in Cicero (*S. Rosc.* 104), in an early speech in which he admitted a few non-standard usages later avoided, and there it is in the old colloquial (?) phrase *mihi ausculta* (for the word order of which see above, 14.4) and in juxtaposition with another imperative, as sometimes in old Latin (see Landgraf 1914: 203 on this use and for some details of distribution). This is the only instance in classical prose, if one disregards Varro's discussion of the word (*Ling.* 6.83). It is admitted however by Horace in the *Satires* (2.7.1) and by Catullus (67.39), in a colloquial context (note the phraseology at line 37, *qui tu istaec, ianua, nosti*, on which see Adams 2013: 458). It would seem that *ausculto* had declined in respectability. Its survival in Romance shows that it was not a mere archaism (though it was of course open to archaisers later to use it suggestively, in allusion to old Latin), but had descended into varieties of the language that were largely submerged. It occurs quite often in the Vulgate and *Vet. Lat.* (see the *TLL* s.v.), and just occasionally in later literary writers.

paticus: used of a passive homosexual (or sometimes a woman), *pathicus* is well attested in Latin, in inscriptions and lower literary genres (Catullus, the *Priapea*, Juvenal and Martial: see now *TLL* X.1.704.39ff.), yet until recently it had not turned up in Greek itself (though reflected in παθικεύεται at Nicarchus, *AP* 11.73.7) (Adams 1982a: 190, Bain 1997: 81). It has now appeared in Greek in a graffito from Aphrodisias (Rouché 1989: 245), as noted by Bain (1997: 81–2). Various terms in Latin to do with effeminacy or passive homosexuality are of Greek origin, namely *catamitus* (on which see *TLL Onom.* 255.51ff., Adams 2003a: 163), *cinaedus* (see Jocelyn 1999: 109–12 on the semantic development of this term, with bibliography) and *malacus* (Plaut. *Mil.* 668), though there were numerous others of Latin origin (for a list see Jocelyn 1999: 102).

Greek words attested in Latin but not or hardly at all in Greek itself include e.g., in Laberius, *eugium* (24, 139; see Panayotakis 2010: 183–4), *balanistria* (?) (ap. Nonius p. 149 Lindsay but not in this form: see the discussion of Panayotakis 2010: 143–4), *cacomnemon* (ap. Gell. 16.7.8: see Panayotakis 2010: 147–8), in Petronius, *babaecalus* (37.10: Cavalca 2001: 38), *spataloci-naedus* (23.3: Cavalca 2001: 158), and, in Lucilius, *moechocinaedus* (1058). There are various reasons why a Greek word may appear in Latin but not Greek. First, it might have been a vulgar term submerged in Greek but picked up by Latin and admitted into lower genres. That seems to be the case with *pathicus* and also *eugium*. The recent appearance of παθικός at Aphrodisias shows that the term was indeed in use in Greek. Second, it might have been a dialect term from Magna Graecia unknown in Attic/Ionic. *Colaphus* for example is common and was long-lived in Latin but in Greek literature is found only in the Sicilian Epicharmus (see Adams 2003a: 351 n. 100; also 10.5.1). Third, it might have been a (humorous) coinage made by a Latin speaker or writer (so perhaps *spatalocinaedus*; see also Panayotakis 2010: 148 on *cacomnemon*). There are also of course many terms of Greek origin in Latin that were deformed in the process of borrowing and therefore do not exactly replicate the Greek term, such as nouns borrowed from the Greek accusative (e.g. *cratera, crepida*) or genitive forms (e.g. *abacus, elephantus, trygonus*) (see above, 2.24, 2.25), verbs borrowed from the aorist form (*campsare*), and numerous hybrids of different types (see e.g. Cavalca 2001: 261 s.v. 'ibridismi', Adams 2003a: 815 s.v. 'hybrid words, inflections', id. 2013: 563–4). See also above, 2.5 (for a term, like this one, that had apparently entered Latin from contemporary Greek, *machaera*), and below, 18.10.

3 et ego uerpa qui lego: there are two ways of taking this expression. First, *uerpa* may be nominative with *sum* understood, with the expression forming one of those contemptuous or abusive identifications of a person with a *mentula/uerpa*, which are not uncommon in Latin. Cf. *CIL* IV.1655 *Hysocryse puer, Natalis uerpa te salutat* (cf. 1375 *Natalis uerpe*), 8617 *uerpes* [= *uerpa es*] *qui istuc leges*, 8931 *mentules*, Catull. 115.8 *non homo, sed uero mentula magna minax* (see further Adams 1982b: 37–9). Second, with Housman (1931: 406 = Diggle and Goodyear 1972: 1179) one may take *uerpa(m)* as accusative, and object of *comedam*, derivable from *comedant* earlier in the line, in which case the reader is made to wish *irrumatio* on himself. The first interpretation now seems preferable to me, first because of *CIL* IV.8617 quoted above, where the reader is unambiguously identified with a *uerpa* in a very similar line (see further Courtney 1995: 301, citing a further inscriptional example with the same implication), and second because *comedo* is not the usual verb applied in this way to an act of *fellatio/irrumatio* (see Adams 1982a: 139 for a collection of examples, none with *comedo*; *uoro* 'swallow' is the most usual; for a few others see the Conclusions below).

Verpa was a gross word for an erect penis, recorded in literature only in Catullus (28.12), Martial (11.46.2) and the *Corpus Priapeorum* (34.5), but it is common in graffiti (for details see Adams 1982a: 12–14). Notable is its not infrequent use, as here, *pars pro toto* of the person to whom it belongs. The semantic weakening (here from 'prick' to 'fool') is of a type that is not unusual in Latin sexual terminology (see Adams 1982a: 272 s.v. 'weakening of obscenities').

Et with *ego* here seems to be an explicative use wherein (see Hofmann, *TLL* V.2.895.78) 'parataxis copulativa explicationi inservit', such that it has the role of *enim* (Virg. *Aen.* 11.272 is cited). The wish to be consumed by bears (a general curse upon oneself) is explained by this expression (= 'for I am a fool').

Conclusions

The linguistic interest of the Pompeian graffiti lies in the fact that they have a *terminus ante quem* that is quite early (AD 79), and that they present the earliest substantial body of genuinely popular Latin, which throws light on the tone of some of the Latin admitted by Catullus in particular (in his shorter poems) (we also saw Catullus illuminated by text 13 above). He makes use of *pathicus*, like the writer of these verses, of *uerpa* (in a context in which it occurs in another Pompeian graffito, based on the metaphor of eating: 28.12–13 *nam nihilo minore uerpa | farti estis*; cf. *CIL* IV.1884 *qui uerpam uissit, quid cenasse illum putes?*, with Courtney 1995: 301 on the latter, his text no. 80), and he also employs another such basic term, *mentula*, *pars pro toto*, as *uerpa* is employed in our present text. Another basic obscenity (found in our inscription) that is common to Pompeian graffiti and lower literary genres (including Catullus) is *pedico* (thirteen times at Pompeii, three times in Catullus, in hendecasyllables, and in mime and epigram: see Adams 1982a: 123). A notable instance is in the epigram of Augustus quoted by Martial (11.20: on the question of authenticity see Kay 1985: 111), which also contains *futuo* and *mentula*. The use of obscenities is not class-related but may be determined by the circumstances of an utterance (which in Latin include literary genre and intent, with basic words particularly capable of expressing aggression), though individual attitudes to such terminology may vary. Augustus is also recorded as using *penis* of Horace, *pars pro toto* (Suet. *Vita Hor.*; see Adams 1982b: 39).

Another connection between our passage and Catullus, from a different lexical sphere, lies in the use of *ausculto*.

The Pompeian graffiti are the first corpus providing extensive evidence for the writing of *i* for *ĕ*. Many such spellings are in final syllables, particularly in verb endings. It is not convincing to appeal to Oscan influence (see Adams 2013: 59). At a slightly later period, when we start to get non-literary documents from scattered areas (Britain, Egypt, Switzerland) not exposed to Oscan, the same types of misspellings again turn up. They are best seen as representing an early stage in the developments that were to lead to a front-vowel merger. In our text 16 the different endings in the present tense, third person singular, of third and fourth conjugation verbs are of historical significance.

17
PASSAGE FROM A LETTER
OF SENECA (*EPIST*. 12.1–3)

Introduction

This letter is about old age, and notably that of Seneca himself. At the start, part of which is quoted here, he recounts a visit, real or imaginary, to one of his estates near Rome, and an exchange he had there with two slaves, one the *uilicus* of the estate, the other a decrepit slave whom he had known in the distant past but no longer recognises. The letter has been much discussed. A recent and comprehensive account of its aims, structure and subtleties, with extensive biography, may be found in P. and L. C. Watson (2009). The interest of the passage for the present book is that it reports, both directly and indirectly, talk between master and slaves. Seneca portrays himself as angry and aggressive, and as callously speaking of the second slave as it he were not there. The encounter may be fictitious (see Griffin 1976: 277, referring to several passages: 'These slaves must have existed, but did the scenes described really take place?'), with Seneca perhaps presenting his aggression tongue-in-cheek, but the description is interesting nevertheless as a specimen of address between social unequals. There are some noteworthy linguistic touches, the most interesting of which (*istunc*) seems to have gone all but unnoticed. One question that suggests itself is whether the Latin may reflect in places not that of real life but of comedy. Comic language was often imitated in later literature (see above, 8.1, with bibliography). This question is taken up in the Commentary.

For the date of the *Epistulae morales* see Griffin (1976: 396). The dramatic date is probably between winter 63 and autumn 64, and the date of publication between autumn 64 and spring 65. Seneca was born between 4 BC and AD 1, and would thus have been into his sixties when this incident supposedly took place.

Text

12.1 Veneram in suburbanum meum et querebar de inpensis aedificii dilabentis. ait uilicus mihi non esse neglegentiae suae uitium, omnia se facere, sed uillam ueterem esse. haec uilla inter manus meas creuit: quid mihi futurum est, si tam putria sunt aetatis meae saxa? **2** iratus illi proximam occasionem stomachandi arripio. 'apparet' inquam 'has platanos neglegi: nullas habent frondes. quam nodosi sunt et retorridi rami, quam tristes et squalidi trunci! hoc non accideret si quis has circumfoderet, si inrigaret.' iurat per genium meum se omnia facere, in nulla re cessare curam suam, sed illas uetulas esse. quod intra nos sit, ego illas posueram, ego illarum primum uideram folium. **3** conuersus ad ianuam 'quis est iste,' inquam 'iste decrepitus et merito ad ostium admotus? foras enim spectat. unde istunc nanctus es? quid te delectauit alienum mortuum tollere?' at ille 'non cognoscis me?' inquit: 'ego sum Felicio, cui solebas sigillaria adferre; ego sum Philositi uilici filius, deliciolum tuum.' 'perfecte' inquam 'iste delirat: pupulus, etiam delicium meum factus est? prorsus potest fieri: dentes illi cum maxime cadunt.'

Translation

12.1 I had come to my country estate and was complaining about the expenses generated by a building that was falling apart. The bailiff said to me that it was not the fault of his negligence, and that he was doing everything he could but that the villa was old. This villa grew in my hands. If stones of the same age as me are so rotten, what is about to become of me? **2** Angry with him, I seized the next opportunity of venting my spleen. 'It is obvious,' I said, 'that these plane trees are being neglected: they have no foliage. How knotty and dried up are the branches, how grim and rough the trunks! This would not happen if someone dug around them and watered them.' He swore by my guardian spirit that he was doing all he could, and that in no respect was his attention flagging, but they were old. Entre nous, I was the one who had planted them, I was the one who had seen their first leaves. **3** Turning to the door, I said: 'Who is this, this creature worn out and deservedly moved forward to the door? His prospects are after all outside. Where did you acquire this one? What delight did you get in carrying off someone else's dead?' But the other said: 'Don't you recognise me? I am Felicio, to whom you used to bring little figures. I am the son of the bailiff Philositus and your little pet.' I said: 'He is completely off his head. He has become a little boy again, even my pet. It *is* certainly possible: his teeth are falling as I look.'

Commentary

1 non esse neglegentiae suae uitium: the bailiff replies to Seneca's complaints about the dilapidated state of the building, that 'it is not my fault'. This is not the sort of remark made by slaves in comedy.

omnia se facere: the *uilicus* twice within a few sentences responds defensively to Seneca's aggressive complaints by saying that 'he is doing everything' (exactly the same phrase below). The phrase, which recurs in Seneca, can mean 'to do everything in one's power': e.g. *Ben.* 7.14.1 *quaeritur an, qui omnia fecit, ut beneficium redderet, reddiderit* (The question is, whether anyone who has done everything in his power to return a benefit has returned it', Basore, Loeb). Cf. *Ben.* 7.14.3, 7.14.4. Such a phrase might degenerate into a defence resorted to by someone under suspicion of falling short in some duty. Note *Ben.* 7.16.2 *in omni quaestione propositum sit nobis bonum publicum; praecludendae sunt excusationes ingratis, ad quas refugere non possint et sub quibus infitiationem suam tegere. 'omnia feci.' fac etiamnunc* ('In the case of every question, let us keep before us the public good; the door must be closed to all excuses, to keep the ungrateful from taking refuge in them and using them to cover their repudiation of the debt. "I have done all in my power," says he. Well, keep on doing so', Basore, Loeb). *Omnia feci* is presented here as the assertion of a person keen to establish that he has done his duty, but it is not good enough: he must keep on doing so. The tense used by the bailiff is not the same: he 'is (still) doing all in his power'.

sed uillam ueterem esse . . . 2 sed illas uetulas esse: note that the *uilicus* uses *uetus* of the house, but then the diminutive of the plants. See below, §2 on *uetulus*.

quid mihi futurum est: Summers (1910: 168) ad loc. cites for this phrase Cic. *Att.* 10.12.1 *quidnam mihi futurum est* ('what is to become of me?', an expression there of despair; the passage continues *quis me non solum infelicior sed iam etiam turpior?*). A word search turned up just two further examples accompanied by the dative as here, both in Plautus. Seneca's example is not however overtly 'comic', and it is more likely that this was a hackneyed phrase:

Plaut. *Men.* 663 quid mihi futurum est, qui tibi hanc operam dedi? ('What reward am I going to get, who did you this service?', de Melo, Loeb).

Plaut. *Truc.* 633 quid mihi futurum est, quoi duae ancillae dolent | quibus te donaui? ('What will happen to me? The two slave girls I presented you with are paining me').

There are also expressions (sometimes of hopelessness) containing *quid futurum est* but without the dative, three of them together in a letter of Cicero (*Fam.* 9.17.1):

ex me quaeras quid de istis municipiis et agris futurum putem ('you ask me what I think is going to happen about those towns and lands').

immo uero, si me amas, tu fac ut sciam quid de nobis futurum sit ('on the contrary, you please be the one to let me know what is going to become of us').

deinde quod scire quoque mihi uideor quid futurum sit ('second, because I think I know too what is going to happen').

The first Plautine example is quite unlike that in Seneca.

2 iratus illi: in this letter *ille* not *is* is the usual third person pronoun: cf. *2 illas uetulas esse, ego illas posueram, ego illarum primum uideram folium,* 3 *at ille, dentes illi cum maxime cadunt,* 4 *complectamur illam, si illa scias uti, illa quae mergit,* 5 *et illam quoque in extrema tegula stantem,* 9 *quod ille . . . faciebat, ille beatissimus est,* 10 *quam illi trado.* There are twelve instances of *ille* (pronominal) in the letter, and none of *is.* Evidence comes up in this anthology in non-literary texts for the spread of *ille* vis-à-vis *is* (see below, 18.6, and index s.v. *ille* 'in relation to *is*'), an extension that is anticipatory of the eventual disappearance of *is* by the time of the Romance languages, but by the early Empire even in literary texts there are some signs of the encroachment of *ille* on *is* (on this feature of the Latin of Seneca the Elder see Pinkster 2005).

retorridi rami: *retorridus* 'parched, dried up' is used often in agricultural contexts, of plants etc. (e.g. Varro *Rust.* 1.9.5 *prata retorrida,* Col. 11.2.87 *retorridae frondis*; several times elsewhere in Seneca himself, as e.g. *Epist.* 86.18: see *OLD* s.v. a).

On Seneca's knowledge of agriculture see Griffin (1976: 290 with n. 3).

quam tristes et squalidi trunci: with this use of *tristis* cf. e.g. Ovid *Met.* 8.789 *triste solum, sterilis sine fruge, sine arbore tellus,* Plin. *Nat.* 17.240 *odit et corylum, ni procul absint, tristis atque aegra* (with a personification) (see *OLD* s.v. 8a).

iurat per genium meum: the oath ascribed to the *uilicus* is servile, and used as a form of characterisation by Petronius too (see below, 18.5). Every man had his *genius* or guardian spirit, but swearing by the *genius* of one's master or patron was a habit of slaves and freedmen. For a collection of such passages (including inscriptional) see *TLL* VI.2.1831.43ff. Conversely for cursing the *genius* of a master see Petron. 53.3 *Mithridates seruus in crucem actus est, quia Gai nostri genio male dixerat.* The freeborn might refer to their own *genius,* but note Sen. *Epist.* 95.41 *quid tam dignum censoria nota, si quis, ut isti ganeones loquuntur, sibi hoc et genio suo praestet?* ('Or what [is] so worthy of the censor's condemnation as to be always indulging oneself and one's "inner man," if I may speak as the gluttons do?', Gummere, Loeb). There is disapproval here, and Seneca refrains from speaking in his own voice, attributing the remark to *ganeones.* The censor's mark was used when someone was struck off the list of senators or knights.

in nulla re cessare curam suam, sed illas uetulas esse: for *nulla res* see above, 5.34–5.

uetulas: the diminutive had a recognised use of old plants or animals. See Cic. *Fin.* 5.39 *itaque et uiuere uitem et mori dicimus, arboremque et nouellam et uetulam et uigere et senescere.* The predominating use of the other diminutive here, *nouellus* ('young'), is in reference to animals or plants (see *OLD* s.v. 1a, b), which suggests that it, and perhaps *uetulus* too, originated as rural usages. On *uetulus* in this connection see Hanssen (1951: 22–3, 110). Unlike *nouellus, uetulus* was more common of humans: *OLD* s.v. a; for the 'rural' use see b. It had a disparaging tone of people, and occurs only once thus in a speech of Cicero, the early *Pro Quinctio* (29 *cum isto gladiatore uetulo*). Cicero uses it several times in the letters (see Ruckdeschel 1910: 17–18).

ego illarum primum uideram folium: here in reference to a plurality of trees Seneca uses the collective singular *folium.* This is a typical collective applied to plants (see 15.16, with references). *Folium* is very common in the plural (see the *TLL* article *passim*), but the singular is used sometimes by e.g. Pliny the Elder when describing the characteristics of a type of tree: note *Nat.* 15.127 *Cypriam esse folio breui, nigro, per margines imbricato crispam* (cf. the singular *baca* in the next section, of a different tree: *est enim caerula baca*), 16.38 *pinus atque pinaster folium habent capillamenti modo praetenue longumque,* 17.91 *uitis sibi sufficit, mobili folio iactatuque crebro solem umbra temperans* (contrast Hor. *Odes* 1.23.5–6 *mobilibus . . . foliis*); further examples may be found at *TLL* VI.1.1012.

3 iste decrepitus: the adjective, of disputed etymology (see de Vaan 2008: 164), is applied particularly to old men (and sometimes women): see *TLL* V.1.218.14ff. It is found in both Plautus and Terence, and occasionally in literature over a long period, but does not survive in the Romance languages. It looks like an emotive, sometimes (as here) disparaging, term of the literary language.

Decrepitus is used five times of old men in Plautus, three times in asyndeton bimembre with *uetus* or *uetulus,* combinations that look stylised or 'proverbial' (see Preuss 1881: 9): *Epid.* 666 *nos uetulos, decrepitos duos, Merc.* 291 *senex uetus, decrepitus, Merc.* 314 *uetulus, decrepitus senex.* There are also two instances of *decrepitus* in Terence. The word occurs just once in the whole of Cicero (*Tusc.* 1.94), where he has it in reference to certain creatures (*bestiolas quasdam*) which according to Aristotle live for just one day. A creature which has lived to the eighth hour, *prouecta aetate mortua est*. One which lives until sunset, is *decrepita*. It is a stronger term than *prouecta aetate* here, and presumably than *uetus/uetulus*, expressing extreme decrepitude: in the three asyndeta above it follows *uetus/uetulus*, and the asyndeta are of that type in which the second term intensifies the first. Timpanaro (1978: 172) refers to the type as 'asindeto accrescitivo', as at Lucr. 1.557–8 *longa diei | infinita aetas*, 'lunga, (anzi) infinita', 'the long, nay infinite, age of days'. The second term means much the same as the first but is stronger, almost a correction. Cf. Plaut. *Bacch.* 732 *quid si potius morbum mortem scribat?*, 'What if he's writing a greeting of illness and death to him instead?' (de Melo, Loeb). *Mortem* caps *morbum*, though alternatively here there may be a sequential relationship, with death following disease (for this pair see Wölfflin 1933: 267).

Though *decrepitus* faded from literature, it was always available as a means of stressing extreme old age and/or unfitness for some task. It is even used (with the latter function) by Echion in Petronius in a notoriously substandard speech (45.11 *dedit gladiatores sestertiarios iam decrepitos, quos si sufflasses cecidissent*), which undermines any idea that the word was 'archaic' or the like.

At Aug. *Conf.* 9.8.17 there is the phrase *famulae cuiusdam decrepitae*, of an old slave of Augustine's mother Monica. Burton (2007: 53) comments: 'The old woman is broken down, *decrepitus*, an adjective in classical Latin rare outside comedy; there is some evidence of its revival in post-classical Latin, but it is likely to have remained in part at least a conscious archaism' (cf. Summers 1910: 169 'a colloquial, probably old-fashioned word'). In a footnote (53 n. 33) Burton adds: 'Plautus and Terence together provide seven of the eight Perseus instances. Most of the later examples in *TLL* 5.1.217–8 are from Christian authors, but Apuleius and Symmachus also feature.'

The phraseology in Seneca is not at all suggestive of the language of comedy, or of deliberate archaising. Seneca himself has a few other instances of *decrepitus*. Note first *Dial.* 10.11.1 *decrepiti senes paucorum annorum accessionem uotis mendicant: minores natu se ipsos esse fingunt.* At *Epist.* 26.1 he explains the point of the word. He fears that he has now left old age behind. *Senectus* is the name of a weary age, not a broken one, and a different word is needed for his own state, *decrepitus*, 'in reach of the end': *modo dicebam tibi in conspectu esse me senectutis: iam uereor ne senectutem post me reliquerim. aliud iam his annis, certe huic corpori, uocabulum conuenit, quoniam quidem senectus lassae aetatis, non fractae nomen est: inter decrepitos me numera et extrema tangentis.* For Seneca *decrepitus* is a word adopted for its semantics ('on his last legs'), not for its earlier stylistic associations. See also frg. 36.10 *Archimimus, senex iam decrepitus.* Seneca's explanation above matches the use of the word at

Jerome, *Vita Malchi* 2.2 (of a woman): *ualde decrepita et iam morti proxima.* The example in our letter has exactly that meaning.

ad ostium admotus? foras enim spectat: he has been moved to the door and is looking out, because he is ready to be carried out for burial. Summers (1910: 169) says of *foras spectat* that it 'must refer to the ancient custom of setting corpses with their feet turned towards the door, symbolically of their coming departure'. He cites among other passages Pers. 3.105, on which Kißel (1990: 481) has a collection of references. Summers (1910: 169) adds that 'the phrase was probably a colloquial one'. But the phraseology is related to the specific situation. Seneca turns to the door (*conuersus ad ianuam*), and sees the slave stationed there (*merito ad ostium admotus*), presumably as doorman. He is gazing outside. The implication is indeed that he is ready to be carried out to the grave, but there is no necessary reference to the laying out of a corpse feet first (in which position it could hardly 'look outside').

unde istunc nanctus es?: the seemingly unobtrusive pronoun *istunc* is the most noteworthy term in the passage. This reinforced accusative (i.e. *istum* + *c(e)*, nominative *istic*) is the single occurrence of that form attested outside early comedy, a point made at *TLL* VII.2.496.46. So we saw at 8.1 that its nominative correspondent, *istic,* which had been common in comedy, is found just once in classical Latin, in a special context in the *Rhet. Her.* (in a specimen of a debased simple, i.e. vulgar, style). Thereafter there are two isolated examples, in a tragedy of Seneca and in Tertullian.

The pronoun *iste* + *c(e)* was a significant term stylistically (see Adams 2013: 456–8). It was widely current in the earlier Republic, but then faded from the educated language, with different forms having different histories. The neuter singular *istuc* had a survival into classical Latin and beyond (see below on Seneca himself), whereas the neuter plural *istaec* was confined to markedly colloquial contexts by the classical period (see above, 3.420, and Adams loc. cit.). *Istic* and *istunc* for their part are so rare after early Latin that the question arises whether those using them might have been deliberately drawing on comic language for artificial effect.

That is a hard question to answer. The author *Ad Herennium* (above, 8.1) certainly made a habit of dipping into comedy in his specimen passages. But the present example, in a contemptuous and dismissive reference to an old slave spoken in his presence, is more suggestive of a continued currency in speech of this sort. The base form *iste* itself, with its second person reference, readily assumed a tone of disparagement or contempt, and the reinforced form might well have had this implication even more strongly, and that might account for its rarity in literature. It has to be conceded that 'scribes have doubtless in many cases emended to the commoner form' (Summers 1910: 169), but even so the distribution of the reinforced forms as a group is consistent with a decline in currency among the educated (with the possibility, we are suggesting, of an ongoing survival in speech). Seneca does sometimes use the neuter form *istuc* (e.g. *Epist.* 16.7, 27.8, 28.4, 29.9, 35.2, 85.24, 88.19).

In comedy *istunc* is occasionally used of a slave in his presence, without a name:

Plaut. *Amph.* 699 et istunc et te uidi.
Cas. 406 quid tibi istunc tactio est? (referring to a slave who has just been punched).

But *istunc* is not only used of slaves. It is e.g. used adjectivally in a neutral way, for example, at *Curc.* 601 *rogita unde istunc habeat anulum*, *Epid.* 440 *si istunc hominem quem tu quaeritas | tibi commonstrasso* (of someone not present). In the two references to slaves cited above it does not have a tone of contempt.

Different views will be taken of Seneca's source here. My own is that the language and presentation of the encounter are not reminiscent of comedy, and that Seneca might have been drawing on a colloquial register.

alienum mortuum tollere: *tollo* here obviously means to pick up and remove for burial (someone else's dead). The usage is not given a separate lemma by the *OLD*.

ego sum Felicio: for an inscription dedicated to a freedman Felicio, described as a *delicium*, see Setaioli (1998) (notably 150 on *Felicio* as a slave or freedman's name).

deliciolum: see below, next note but one.

perfecte: not a banal and widely used intensifier, like e.g. *omnino*. In the Republic it occurs only in the *Rhet. Her.* (three times) and in Cicero's rhetorica and philosophica (eight times), and it thus seems to have been at home in technical or academic prose. It is used six times by Seneca in the letters. For details see *TLL* X.1.1382.35ff.

pupulus, etiam delicium meum factus est?: the correction of *pupulus* by *delicium* implies that *delicium* was the more emotive word, referring to a close relationship with another (note *meum*). In a letter of Jerome (14.1) there is a collocation *paruulus delicatus* (*tu quasi paruulus delicatus contemptum rogantis per blandimenta fouisti*), in which *paruulus* merely denotes a child but *delicatus* is associated with a form of behaviour.

There is a good discussion of the diminutive *pupulus* and its base form *pupus* by Heraeus (1937: 167–8). On the question of etymology see André (1978: 63), de Vaan (2008: 500). The reduplication is typical of nursery language (cf. *mamma, tata, dida, titta, pappa*; also the whole section of Heraeus, and particularly André 1978, chapter V, entitled 'nursery-words'). For *pupus* see e.g. Varro *Men.* 546 *ac mammam lactis sugentem pascere pupum* (on the interpretation of which see Cèbe 1999: 20–41) (cf. Suet. *Cal.* 13). For the feminine *pupa* see *CLE* 92.11, cited below at 21.12–14. The attestations of *pupus, pupa, pupillus* and *pupula* can all now be seen in *TLL* X.2 s.vv. (cf. too *pusus, pusio* and *pusa*, which may be of the same root). These are not literary words at all, rarely surfacing. *Pupulus* must have been a term of talk within households, with only one other literary attestation in this sense (see *TLL* X.2.2672.23ff.: cf. Catull. 56.5 *deprendi modo pupulum puellae | trusantem*).

It has usually been assumed by commentators and others (see e.g. Laes 2003: 303) that Seneca and Felicio were playmates as children, and thus contemporaries, but P. and L. C. Watson (2009: 219; cf. 213 n. 6) find reasons for suggesting that Felicio would have been in his mid-fifties or even younger at the dramatic date of the letter (AD 63–4), whereas Seneca himself was in his sixties (214 with n. 14). On this view the relationship between Seneca and the slave would be uncertain. The roles of *delicia* were diverse: note Laes (2003: 324): '*Delicia* can be natural children, substitute children, foster children, pampered pets, entertaining little jesters, objects for erotic pleasure' (cf. Slater 1974). The words of Felicio himself (*ego sum Philositi uilici filius, deliciolum tuum*), and particularly the diminutive, imply that he was some sort of favourite or plaything (and indeed younger), though the relationship would hardly have been sexual (cf. Laes 2003: 318: 'Seneca (*Epistles* 47.7; 95.24) deplores the use of young persons who serve their masters not only at table, but also in bed').

Delicium and also *delicatus -a* are commonly used, not least in epigraphy, of child favourites in their diversity (see Laes 2003: 307 for inscriptional examples), but the diminutive *deliciolum* is quoted by the *TLL* only from this passage.

cum maxime: Summers (1910: 161) notes that this combination is very common in Seneca, stating: 'It lays stress on the fact that the action of the verb takes (or took) place when it does (did), representing such English phrases as "just now", "even as I write (speak)", and occasionally "at this of all times".' The reference is to the loss of the milk teeth but also to Felicio's present state.

Conclusions

Seneca presents himself as (among other things) well versed in the language of agriculture. The bailiff is characterised in status by his oath *per genium meum*, and he also speaks defensively towards his social superior by twice adopting the formula *omnia facere*, of 'doing everything in his power', which probably sounded like a lame excuse. The main interest lies in the exchange at the end between Seneca and Felicio, which, even if it is fabricated and intended as tongue-in-cheek with its references to the moribund state of the slave, still must have had an element of reality if it were to have any point as a specimen of talk between social unequals. Seneca uses only third person verbs of Felicio in his presence, in addressing the bailiff. The normal third person pronoun in this letter is *ille*, but three times in a short space *iste* is used of Felicio, along with the instance of the reinforced *istunc*. Only once is *ille* used of Felicio when the addressee is the bailiff rather than the reader; there is also one instance when the reader is addressed. I have ruled out the possibility that there may be deliberate reminiscence of comedy in the language here, and have taken *istunc* to be a colloquialism of uncontrived speech, here (like *iste* itself) with an obvious note of contempt. Felicio refers to himself in his single utterance with the extremely rare (no doubt affective) diminutive *deliciolum*, which Seneca in his response converts into *delicium*. It is of interest that in the context in which it is used, *pupulus* could only have been relatively unemotive compared with *delicium*.

18
FREEDMAN'S SPEECH FROM THE
SATYRICA OF PETRONIUS (37.1–38.2)

Introduction

This passage is from a speech by a character who is intended to be of Greek origin. He is taken to be Hermeros (see Boyce 1991: 90, and also Schmeling 2011: 135). Hermeros' Latin is very distinctive, with a marked, and often unusual, Greek element, and a high level of vulgarisms (see Boyce 1991: 90–4, Adams 2003a, index s.v. 'Hermeros'). I have assumed in placing the speech at this point that the conventional Neronian date for the *Satyrica* is about right, but it is only fair to acknowledge that this is controversial, and that arguments have been produced for a later, second-century, date (see the overview by Vannini 2007: 85–95, with the bibliography at 85–7; note particularly Flobert 2003). Later (19.6–7) I will comment on an expression, hitherto attested in a running text only in a freedman's speech (the combination in asyndeton *ago agino*), which has now turned up in curse tablets that can be dated to about AD 80, that is to roughly the time of the conventional date of Petronius' novel.

For further discussion of this passage see the commentaries of Perrochat (1939), Marmorale (1961), Smith (1975), Schmeling (2011).

Text

37.1 '... Longe accersere fabulas coepi sciscitarique, quae esset mulier illa, quae huc atque illuc discurreret. **2** 'uxor' inquit 'Trimalchionis (1), Fortunata appellatur (2), quae nummos modio metitur (3). **3** et modo modo (4) quid fuit? ignoscet mihi genius tuus (5), noluisses de manu illius (6) panem accipere. **4** nunc, nec quid nec quare, in caelum abiit (7) et Trimalchionis topanta est (8). **5** ad summam (9), mero meridie si dixerit illi tenebras esse, credet. **6** ipse nescit quid habeat, adeo saplutus est (10); sed haec lupatria (11) prouidet omnia, est ubi non putes. **7** est sicca, sobria (12), bonorum consiliorum (13) – tantum auri uides – est tamen malae linguae, pica puluinaris (14). quem amat, amat; quem non amat, non amat. **8** ipse [Trimalchio] fundos habet, qua milui uolant (15), nummorum nummos (16). argentum in ostiarii illius cella plus iacet quam quisquam in fortunis habet. **9** familia uero babae babae (17), non mehercules puto decumam partem esse quae dominum suum nouerit. **10** ad summam, quemuis ex istis babaecalis (18) in rutae folium coniciet (19).

38.1 nec est quod putes illum quicquam emere. omnia domi nascuntur: lana, citrea (20), piper; lacte gallinacium (21) si quaesieris, inuenies. **2** ad summam, parum illi bona lana nascebatur: arietes a Tarento emit (22) . . .'

Translation

37.1 '. . . I began to draw the conversation out and to ask who that woman was who was running about here and there. **2** 'It's the wife of Trimalchio,' he said, 'she's called Fortunata, who measures her cash by the *modius*. **3** And what was she just now? If your *genius* will pardon me, you would have been unwilling to take bread from her hand. **4** Now, God knows why, she's on top of the world, she's Trimalchio's one and only. **5** In short, if she says to him at high noon that it is dark he will believe her. **6** He does not know what he has got, he is so filthy rich. But this tart foresees everything, she's where you don't realise. **7** She's dry sober and good at planning – you see all the gold – but she has a bad tongue, she's a magpie on a couch. Whom she loves she loves, whom she doesn't love she doesn't love. **8** His lordship has estates as far as kites fly, cash to end all cash. More silver is lying in his doorkeeper's cubicle than anyone has in his entire fortune. **9** As for the household, well, well, I don't think there's a tenth of them who know their own master. **10** In short, he will toss any of those fine fellows into a leaf of rue.

38.1 And don't think that he buys anything: everything is grown at home, wool, citrus fruit, pepper. If it's hen's milk that you're after, you will find it. **2** In short, not enough good wool was being produced for him: he bought rams from Tarentum . . .'

Commentary

1 uxor … Trimalchionis: for the presence (or absence) of *uxor* in such expressions, see 21.15–16.

2 Fortunata appellatur: without relative, an omission common in naming constructions, which are rendered thereby parenthetical. See Havers (1928: 118); cf. e.g. Curt. 4.2.12 *ferreae manus (harpagonas uocant).*

3 nummos modio metitur: she measures her money by the *modius* instead of counting it. Cf. Hor. *Sat.* 1.1.95–6 *diues | ut metiretur nummos.* A proverbial idea, and the phraseology (with *metior*) presumably established.

4 modo modo: on gemination of adverbs and interjections see Wölfflin (1933: 295–6), Wills (1996: 106–19) (but without *modo modo*). For *modo modo* see *TLL* VIII.1311.74ff. (citing several examples from the freedmen's speeches). Cf. for such intensification *Per. Aeth.* 3.1 *subis lente et lente per girum*; also above, 8.5 *magis magisque*. Alliterative pairs are a feature of this passage: cf. *nec quid nec quare, sicca, sobria.*

5 ignoscet mihi genius tuus: on the servile character of reference to a master's *genius* see Smith (1975: 80) and Schmeling (2011: 136) ad loc., and see above, 17.2 on Seneca's encounter with a (slave) *uilicus*, who (*Epist.* 12.2) *iurat per genium meum.*

Schmeling also draws attention to the polite third person address of a person by means of an abstract noun, in this case denoting the person's guardian spirit. Such abstract terms of address became common in bureaucratic language, particularly in address of the emperor (Svennung 1958: 68–85, Coleman 2012: 194–9). Note in a recent Vindolanda tablet (Bowman, Thomas and Tomlin 2011, 880.A.6) *peto, domine, de bon[itate] tua* ('I ask, master, of your goodness'), with Coleman (2012: 198).

The future *ignoscet* is taken by Smith and Schmeling as a courteous substitute for the imperative (for which see Petersmann 1977: 171–2, Adams 1995a: 460–1, 469), as is certainly the case at Cic. *Att.* 9.6A *festinationi meae breuitatique litterarum ignosces* ('you must forgive my haste and the brevity of this letter', Shackleton Bailey 1965–70: IV.141). An alternative is to take the clause as conditional, without an expressed *si*, particularly as the clause is not free-standing but is followed by a clause to which it is subordinate (which is not the case in the example from Cicero just quoted). On such conditional constructions (found elsewhere in the freedmen's speeches: note 61.8 *fecit assem, semissem habui*) see Hofmann and Ricottilli (2003: 254–6) and also Bertocchi and Maraldi (2011: 94–7). Note e.g. Hor. *Sat.* 1.3.49–53 for a series of such clauses, and Plaut. *Amph.* 995 *amat: sapit.* A comparable paratactic relationship between two juxtaposed clauses without a subordinating conjunction is seen also in the last sentence of this passage, where the clause *parum illi . . .* is implicitly causal or temporal ('because/when') (see below).

6 de manu illius: on *ille* as a weak anaphoric (= *is*) without deictic force in this passage (five times) and elsewhere in the freedmen's speeches see Adams (2003b: 13–17). On this use of *ille* see also Adams (1977a: 44) (it outnumbers *is* markedly in the letters of Terentianus), Flobert (1995b: 484), Pinkster (2005), André (2010) (Augustine preferred *ille* in the *Sermons* but *is* in the *Confessions* and *Civ. Dei*), Dickey (2012: 159–60), and see above, 17.2, and below, 22.10, and index s.v. *ille*, 'in relation to *is*'. In our passage within a short space four examples of *ille* without any variation refer to Trimalchio, and it could not be said that it has any function such as to mark a change of subject (cf. Pinkster 1987a: 377): it is simply anaphoric.

On *de* for *ex* (or *ab*), both of which it ousted in the history of Latin, see e.g. E. Löfstedt (1911: 103), Hofmann and Szantyr (1965: 262–3), Adams (2003a: 567 with bibliography), id. (2011: 259), and also below, 26.8–9. There is nothing substandard or late about this use. *De manu* is already in Cicero (*Verr.* 4.24), and alternates in the classical period with the plain ablative *manu* and *e(x) manu* (*TLL* VIII.346.76ff.).

7 nec quid nec quare, in caelum abiit: cf. Cic. *Att.* 2.19.2 *Bibulus in caelo est nec quare scio.* The passage of Cicero has exactly the same combination of the idiom with *caelum*, and an expression of the type 'I don't know why'. The language must be hackneyed. As the text stands there is a double ellipse in *nec quid nec quare*, first of a subjunctive verb in the *quid/quare* clause, which is paralleled in the passage of Cicero (cf. e.g. Mart. 1.32.1 *nec possum dicere quare*, and on the general type see Hofmann and Szantyr 1965: 424, citing Livy 1.23.8 *neque, recte an perperam* (sc. *fiat*), *interpretor*), and second of a main verb such as *scio*. Given the Ciceronian parallel, David Langslow suggests to me that the first *nec* might be a corruption of *nescio*. For the alliterative synonyms *quid quare* cf. *sicca, sobria* below, 18.12. For the idiom with *caelum* see also Cic. *Att.* 2.9.1 *in caelo sum* (of public standing: Shackleton Bailey 1965: 369–70).

8 Trimalchionis topanta est: the Greek expression here (for which, with τά not τό, see Hdt. 1.122), which is imitated at Livy 40.11.4 *Demetrius iis unus omnia est* (see Briscoe 2008: 441–2), is problematic because of the singular article and (apparent) plural *panta*. For a discussion of the interpretations that have been advanced see Cavalca (2001: 177–8). See also Biville (1995: 221–3), Schmeling (2011: 137), noting that πάντα here with τό may be taken as 'a concept independent of morphology and syntax'. On the tendency for *omnia* to be fossilised in Latin in the singular, see 23.10–11.

9 ad summam: occurs three times in this short passage and six times in all in the speeches of Hermeros, out of fifteen examples in the whole work (see Leiwo 2010a: 283–4, Schmeling 2011: 137; also Stefenelli 1962: 35), and thus seems to be intended by Petronius as idiolectal (so Leiwo), particularly since the speeches of Hermeros do not occupy much space. On its distribution elsewhere see Stefenelli loc. cit. and Leiwo (2010a: 284) (e.g. Cicero's correspondence, including a letter by Caelius at *Fam.* 14.14.2 *uelim . . . ad summam animo forti sitis*; also Hor. *Epist.* 1.1.106). An example in a letter of Augustus quoted by Suet. *Aug.* 71.3 (*ad summam tamen perdidit non multum*) retains its literal sense 'in total', but Hermeros sometimes uses the expression merely to introduce a new thought, as is particularly clear in the last sentence of this extract. In other cases it has much the force of 'to cut a long story short' (note too Cic. *Att.* 14.1.1 *ad summam, non posse istaec sic abire* ('In sum, his opinion is that it cannot all just pass quietly off', Shackleton Bailey 1965–70: VI.5; the language here is colloquial, with the form *istaec* for *ista*, and the idiom *sic abire*; the example in Caelius cited above has much the same force).

10 ipse nescit quid habeat, adeo saplutus est: for this type of colloquial paratactic construction, with the *adeo*-clause tagged on at the end instead of introducing a consecutive *ut*-clause (i.e. *adeo saplutus est, ut nesciat*), see above, 7.8–9.

  saplutus: ζάπλουτος is in classical Greek (Herodotus, Euripides, *al.*), but it also turns up in names in Latin inscriptions in the western Roman Empire, and must have been in use in western Greek of the period (Biville 1990: 107): *CIL* XIII.2851 *Saplutus, CIL* XIII.7072 *Saplutius, CIL* VIII.7219 *Zaplutus* (see further Cavalca 2001: 148–9). The first example of zeta in a Latin inscription is dated 81 BC (Biville 1990: 101). Greek zeta was generally converted into *s* in initial position in Latin before the Greek letter became established (e.g. Ζώσιμος > *Sosumus* in inscriptions: Biville 1990: 108). We have already seen the diversity of the popular Greek words that found their way into Latin (see 2.24, 2.25, 16.2, and also index, 'loan-words, from Greek to Latin'; for a term that had entered Latin from koine Greek, see 2.5).

11 lupatria: probably a hybrid formation, with Latin base and Greek suffix (but on the problems of interpretation see Neumann 1980). On such hybrids, which sometimes have elements from vernacular languages (e.g. Etruscan) and not merely Greek, see Adams (2003a: 420–2), id. (2013: 563–6); they are often of popular character. On *-tria* in Latin see André (1971: 103). In Greek the suffix is attached to a verbal root (cf. πορνεύτρια < πορνεύω, λαικάστρια < λαικάζω), but in this term (on the interpretation adopted here) its range has been extended and it is attached to a nominal base. Borrowed suffixes may take on a life of their own in the borrowing language. For a hybrid of the reverse type, cf. κλιβανίκιος 'cooked in a *clibanos*' at Athenaeus 113B: a Greek–Latin hybrid, with extended use of the Latin suffix, which has participial function here. An emendation to *lupatris* (< *lupatrix*) in our passage (Neumann, and mentioned with approval by Schmeling 2011: 138) would be more convincing if *lupatrix* were attested. See also Hofmann and Ricottilli (2003: 456), with bibliography.

12 est sicca, sobria: an asyndeton with alliteration, with both terms having much the same meaning (see above, 13.15, with references), as is often the case with pairs in asyndeton. The second adjective does however have the effect of specifying the precise sense to be given to the more general first adjective. For *siccus* of sobriety see *OLD* s.v. 7. For this pair see e.g. Mart. 12.30.1 *siccus sobrius est Aper*, and for further examples Wölfflin (1933: 275) (several times e.g. in Seneca). Schmeling (2011: 138), though translating 'thrifty and sound' and stating that *sicca* 'might refer to character rather than physiology', refers to the sexual use of *sicca* (the opposite of *uda*), of a woman who is not aroused, but that cannot be relevant in this phrase. For another asyndeton bimembre containing *siccus*, in the related meaning 'thirsty', see Hor. *Sat.* 2.2.14 *siccus inanis | sperne cibum uilem* 'thirsty and hungry'.

13 bonorum consiliorum: *consili boni* is in an epitaph of a woman at *ILS* 7454 (see Schmeling 2011: 138).

14 pica puluinaris: '(she is) a magpie on a couch'. An identification (as distinct from a simile, i.e. 'she is like a magpie') of a type much favoured in the popular style of Plautus (see e.g. Fraenkel [1922] 2007: 28, 36–7, 51–2, Hofmann and Ricottilli 2003: 219, 324) and also by the freedmen. Cf. e.g. Plaut. *Merc.* 361 *muscast meus pater*, Pomponius 174 Frassinetti *porcus est, quem amare coepi, pinguis, non pulcher puer*, Petron. 38.16 *phantasia non homo*, 44.6 *piper, non homo*, 57.2 *quid rides, inquit, ueruex?*, 58.4 *mus, immo terrae tuber*, Schol. Juv. 4.77 (of a jurist) *ut liber uulgo, non homo diceretur*.

15 qua milui uolant: H has *qua*, but in the scholia to Persius 4.26 the proverb is given with *quantum* ('as far as kites fly', of a great area or distance: see Smith 1975: 81–2), and editors usually change. However, meaning 4b of *qua* in the classification of the *OLD* ('as far as, wherever') would seem to justify retention of the text.

16 nummorum nummos: cf. e.g. Plaut. *Trin.* 309 *uictor uictorum*, *Truc.* 25 *summa summarum*, Petron. 43.8 *olim oliorum*. The construction is sometimes regarded as Semitic (see Hadas 1929, Petersmann 1995: 538), and certainly it has eastern parallels (see the discussion of Johansen and Whittle 1980: II. 408–10 of ἄναξ ἀνάκτων at Aesch. *Suppl.* 524), but the type of genitive can be loosely paralleled within Latin (as too Greek) itself and the source is not necessarily external. Bennett (1910–14: II.34) takes the genitive to be partitive, with 'words denoting preeminence' (cf. the type dependent on a superlative, as *pessumarum pessuma*, with Bennett 1910–14: II.24); on the whole question see Hofmann and Szantyr (1965: 55), and also Schmeling (2011: 139). Johansen and Whittle (1980: II.409) argue that such genitives in Greek and Latin may be either partitive or 'objective'. They take that at e.g. *Trin.* 309 above to be clearly partitive, whereas an example at Ovid *Her.* 8.46 (*dux erat ille ducum*) looks objective, and that at Hor. *Epist.* 1.1.107 (*rex denique regum*) either partitive or objective. A partitive construction is found in Greek tragedy showing a substantival adjective reinforced by the same adjective in the genitive case: e.g. Soph. *OC* 1238 κακὰ κακῶν and see Broadhead (1960: 173) on Aesch. *Pers.* 681 πιστὰ πιστῶν, interpreting the genitive as partitive; also Johansen and Whittle (1980: II.409), with the same interpretation. Since such constructions had been around in Latin since Plautus it should not be argued from this evidence that Hermeros is being characterised as of Semitic origin (on this issue see Adams 2003a: 274, with bibliography).

17 babae babae: Hermeros is much given to Greek exclamations (as well as to other types of Greek words), and this feature is undoubtedly intended as a form of characterisation reflecting his background (see Boyce 1991: 92–3, Cavalca 2001: 37, Adams 2003a: 21). Βαβαί expresses surprise or amazement. It is found as well in Plautus. Exclamatory terms are readily borrowed from one language into another (see e.g. Adams 2003a: 21).

18 quemuis ex istis babaecalis: on the various meanings that have been attributed to the previously unattested *babaecalus* (it is not in Greek, and in Latin an example at Arnob. *Nat.* 4.22.4 must be from Petronius). The etymology remains obscure: see Cavalca (2001: 37): βαβαί + καλός, καλῶς, καλεῖν (?); *-culi* (?). It is highly unlikely that Petronius made the word up. It must have been current among the types he was satirising, like *saplutus*, for which we have a little more evidence suggesting its western currency.

19 in rutae folium coniciet: an obscure expression, on the possible interpretations of which Schmeling (2011: 140) may now be consulted.

20 citrea: if feminine it denotes a citrus tree; if neuter plural (sc. *mala*) the fruit of the citrus tree. The text is corrupt, and *cedria* 'resin from cedar' has been proposed. See further Schmeling (2011: 141).

21 lacte gallinacium: the word for 'milk' (CL *lac*) does not occur in the narrative of the novel. Here the disyllabic neuter form is used, whereas Trimalchio at 71.1 uses the masculine *lactem* (with *unum*). CL monosyllables with an additional syllable in the oblique cases are several times made disyllabic in freedmen's speeches: cf. 47.4 *Iouis*, 62.13 *bouis*, and note too the neuter *excellente* for *excellens* at 45.4 and 66.3, which also gives an imparisyllabic neuter the same number of syllables in the nominative as in the oblique cases (see index, 'nouns, imparisyllabic, remodelled'). See also below, 22.27 on *lites* = *lis*. The neuter *lacte* is old (Ennius, Plautus, Caecilius, Cato and Varro: see Stefenelli 1962: 51) and was not stigmatised: there was discussion of which nominative form, *lac* or *lacte*, was 'correct', and some support for *lacte* (see Garcea 2012: 157–8 for testimonia). The form *lactem* is found first in Vitruvius (see above, 11.1; its gender there is indeterminate), and for the first time as an unambiguous masculine in Petronius cited above. Alternation between the masculine *lactis/lactem* and neuter continued for a long time. In the sixth century, Anthimus, also writing in Italy, has the masculine *lactis* seven times, the neuter *lacte* once. See Adams (2013: 426, 429–30).

'Bird milk' (of various types) is a proverbial expression in many languages for a great rarity. See Otto (1890: 152) for examples from Latin (Plin. *Nat.* praef. 24) and Greek (quite common: γάλα ὀρνίθων). So e.g. in Bulgarian there is an expression *ot pile mljako* 'milk from a bird' (with *pile* used not in its usual meaning, = 'chicken', but = 'bird', as commonly in proverbs) (information from Iveta Adams).

22 ad summam, parum illi bona lana nascebatur: arietes a Tarento emit: there is parataxis here. The first clause might have been introduced by a temporal or causal conjunction (on one occasion when/because he was not getting any good wool, he bought rams from Tarentum), but the clauses are merely juxtaposed and the relationship between the first and the second has to be deduced. See Kühner and Stegmann (1955: II.158), Hofmann and Ricottilli (2003: 259), and particularly now Halla-aho (2009: 69–75); often the asyndetic causal or explicative clause follows the main clause, as later in this same speech: 38.6–7 *reliquos autem collibertos eius caue contemnas: ualde sucos[s]i sunt* (cf. 42.6 *planctus est optime – manu misit aliquot*, 43.7 *plane Fortunae filius, in manu eius plumbum aurum fiebat*, 45.3 *non debemus delicati esse, ubique medius caelus est*, 45.6 *et habet unde: relictum est illi sestertium trecenties*; cf. Plaut. *Aul.* 376 *atque eo fuerunt cariora: aes non erat*). The type above with the causal clause preceding is called by Hofmann and Szantyr (1965: 830) 'asyndeton conclusivum' (of the type (*SHA, Pesc. Nig.* 7.8) *uinum non accepimus, pugnare non possumus*, discussed by Tidner 1922: 77). Another example from the *SHA* is discussed by Hallén (1941: 105–6), with bibliography. See too some of the material from Plautus, Petronius and non-literary letters cited by Halla-aho (2009: 73–4), under the general heading of 'paratactic asyndeton'. For examples in a popular acclamation (cited by Tidner 1922: 77) see *SHA, Comm.* 19.9 *innocentes sepulti non sunt: parricidae cadauer trahatur. parricida sepultos eruit: parricidae cadauer trahatur.* Constructions of this type seem to have been widely current in popular and literary discourse, but were clearly associated by Petronius with popular speech. However, on the difficulty of classifying their stylistic level, see Halla-aho (2009: 75).

arietes a Tarento emit: in the next sentence (38.4, not in our selection) the speaker says *apes ab Athenis iussit afferri*. The preposition with the name of a town may look unclassical, but it was hardly substandard. Livy uses the expression *ab Roma* fifty-four times with verbs of motion, but *Roma* (abl.) never (Adams 2013: 330–1), and there are instances of *ab* with names of towns in other classical writers (see e.g. *TLL* I.14.42ff., 15.31ff., with examples from e.g. Cicero and Virgil, and also above, 12 Conclusions, on Augustus). For the preposition in a context such as that here cf. Cato *Agr.* 135.1 *tegulae (emantur) ex Venafro*. In this context the prepositional expression may as readily be taken as adnominal as adverbal: 'rams from Tarentum' may be bought from a dealer who is not in Tarentum. Their wool was of exceptional quality and no doubt they were traded in different places, with the phrase 'from Tarentum' becoming a defining one suggestive of quality. It is *de* that usually has this characterising use (see Adams 2013: 275–6, and index s.v. *de*, 'defining, characterising').

Conclusions

The most distinctive feature of this passage is the accumulation of unusual Greek loan-words (*topanta, saplutus, babaecalis*; cf. *babai babai*) along with the possible hybrid *lupatria*. These are unusual either in having an abnormality (*topanta*) or in being otherwise unattested (*babaecalis, lupatria*) or in having an association with the western Empire (*saplutus*). We mentioned at the start the marked element of Greek in Hermeros' speeches. Notable usages put into his mouth elsewhere include 41.3 *plane etiam hoc seruus tuus indicare potest* = 'your humble servant', where the noun phrase with a third person verb could be rewritten with the first person pronoun *ego* and a first person verb. This is a usage with Semitic associations (see Adams 2003a: 274, with bibliography): cf. Vulg. Gn 44.18 *oro domine mi loquatur seruus tuus uerbum in auribus tuis* (see Rubio 2009: 198; for such phraseology surviving in Romance – but presumably ultimately reflecting biblical influence – see Wagner 1933: 13, citing parallels from colloquial Italian and Spanish; also Stefenelli 1962: 66). Another curiosity is at Petron. 58.7: *Athana tibi irata sit curabo* (*Athana* is a plausible emendation of *satana*, possibly reflecting southern Italian influence (?): Adams 2003a: 21 n. 65, 149). Whatever we are to make of the details, Hermeros was an exotic character. He is also characterised as servile by his appeal to the *genius* of his addressee.

As is typical of freedmen's speeches, there is the odd unparalleled expression (*in rutae folium coniciet*) underlining our poor knowledge of everyday Latin, but Hermeros is also given some widespread usages associated with informal or low-register style, and indeed found elsewhere in this anthology. I would single out his use of various types of paratactic syntax, and preference for *ille* over *is*. We also find emphatic gemination, ellipse, an identification of a type common to Plautus and Petronius in particular, some hackneyed expressions and one case of non-standard morphology (*lacte*).

19

CURSE TABLET FROM THE SANCTUARY OF ISIS AND MATER MAGNA AT MAINZ (BLÄNSDORF 2010a: 173–5, TEXT no. 8), OF THE SECOND HALF OF THE FIRST CENTURY AD

Introduction

The remains of two temples dedicated to Isis and Mater Magna which were uncovered in the centre of the city of Mainz in 1999 can be dated to 'the early Flavian period, or even late in the reign of Nero' (Blänsdorf 2010a: 141), or more precisely (Blänsdorf loc. cit.) fairly closely to the decade 71–80. The hands of the curse tablets found there 'are comparable to those dated around the middle of the first century', and none is later than the early second century (Blänsdorf 2010a: 146).

Text

Obverse

Tiberius Claudius adiutor:
in megaro eum rogo te, M<a>
t<e>r Magna, megaro tuo recipias. et Attis domine, te
precor, ut huc ostiam accep-   5
tum abiatis, et quit aget aginat, sal et aqua illi fiat. ita tu
facias, domna, it quid cor eoconora
cedat.

Reverse

deuotum defictum   10
illum menbra,
medullas AA (?).

nullum aliud sit,
Attis, Mater Magn<a>.

Translation

Tiberius Claudius *adiutor*:
    In the hall, I ask you, *Magna Mater*, in your hall receive him. And Lord Attis, you I pray that you (both) have him as victim entered in the account, and what he does and conducts, may it turn to salt and water for him. So, Mistress, may you do something which cuts his heart and liver.

Him, cursed, fixed with a spell – namely his limbs, marrow – let there be nothing else, Attis, *Magna Mater*.

Commentary

1 Tiberius Claudius adiutor: the nominative heading (a name + title) is detached from the syntax of the rest of the curse. For the unconstrued nominative of names in curse tablets see below, 37.6–21 (though there the names are not a heading), and Adams (2013: 212–13, 215–16).

2 in megaro: this Greek loan-word (usually rendered 'hall', but see further Blänsdorf 2010a: 174) has hitherto been hardly attested in Latin. There are just two instances cited at *TLL* VIII.604.1ff. (*CIL* XIV.18, 19), and there in the context of Isis worship (note *CIL* XIV.18 <*Isi*>*aci magar(um) de suo restitu(erunt)*, where *Isiaci* denotes worshippers of Isis).

2–3 in megaro eum ... megaro tuo recipias: the repetition of *megaro* (the second time without the preposition) is not crude but artificial and rhetorical, or, as Wills (1996: 68) puts it in reference to examples in Silver epic, 'the syntax has truly become a figure'. Typically the repetition occurs after a verb such as *inquam* (found for example in Cicero: see Wills 1996: 65), or after a digression or intervening clause, as in the present case. Wills (1996: 67–8) collects many examples from epic poetry. Note e.g. Val. Fl. 1.344–5 *nunc ille dies (det Iuppiter oro)* | *ille super quo* ... Here the intervening element is *rogo te, M<a>t<e>r Magna*.

2–4 rogo te ... recipias: for the construction *rogo* + subjunctive see now Halla-aho (2009: 81–5).

5–6 huc ostiam acceptum: *huc* has to be taken (with Blänsdorf) as a misspelling of *hunc*, as the parallel cited from Audollent (1904), no. 138 (*hanc ostiam* *acceptam habeas*) shows. Nasals are so frequently omitted (as in *huc*) before stops in non-literary documents, such as the Vindolanda tablets and archive of the Sulpicii, that the spelling must be phonetic and representative of some varieties of speech. See index, 'spellings, omission of nasal before stop'.

The masculine gender of *hostia* would be anomalous. No examples are registered in the *TLL*, and the word has an overtly feminine form. The gender change in such a word is not of one of the normal types (for which see Adams 2013: 383–452), nor is it of a type occurring in curse tablets (for which see Kropp 2008b: 264–5). One can however get around the apparent error by taking *hostiam* as appositional ('have him, as victim, entered up').

acceptum abiatis: the second word has two phonetic spellings, omission of the initial aspirate and closing of *e* in hiatus. For this phrase in curse tablets see Blänsdorf (2010a: 175). It is common in legal Latin (see Thielmann 1885: 418; also 385–6). Note the switch to second person plural.

6–7 quit aget aginat, sal et aqua illi fiat: 'what he does and undertakes, may it become ...' Here *quit* (for *quid*) is clearly a relative pronoun, replacing CL *quod*. The same is true in the next line (*facias ... it quid*) (= *id quod*). On the use of *quid* for *quod* (relative), a substandard usage, see Hofmann and Szantyr (1965: 554) (contrast the different phenomenon, the possible indefinite use of *quod* for *quid* after *si*: see above, 5.11, 14.8). It is found in freedmen's speeches in Petronius (see Adams 2013: 763–4), and also in Pompeian graffiti (see Väänänen 1966: 122). These examples along with those in the present text all belong to the first century AD, and the non-literary instances again reveal the accuracy of Petronius' presentation of the freedmen's Latin.

Aget and *aginat* are both presents: for the *e*-spelling in *agit* see 16.1. The same combination occurs in another of the Mainz tablets, though not in asyndeton (Blänsdorf 2010a: 172 no. 7.7–8) *quidquid agit, quidquid aginat*. *Agino* is tentatively taken by Leumann (1977: 552) to be from ἀγινέω (though others would derive it rather obscurely from a noun *agina*, which has a technical meaning hard to relate to the sense of the verb).

This attestation of the phrase is of real interest, because the verb occurs elsewhere in literature (leaving aside a few glosses, for which see Blänsdorf 2010a: 173) only in Petronius, in a freedman's speech and in the same asyndetic combination: 61.9 *per scutum per ocream egi aginaui*. Our tablet is probably virtually contemporaneous with Petronius, and provides further evidence that Petronius was drawing on real varieties of speech in his *Cena*. The asyndeton bimembre in Petronius is a typical one, juxtaposed as it is with another asyndetic pair, but the speaker has lost the alliteration by using the phrase in the perfect tense.

Asyndeton bimembre, often with types of assonance, is a pronounced feature of curse tablets (see 6.1, 6.3), and there are other examples in this tablet (see below, 19.10) and elsewhere in the corpus (Blänsdorf 2010a nos. 2.2 *adsi(s)*, *aduenias*, 2.4–5, *Castorem*, *Pollucem*, 2.6–7 *malam mentem*, *malum exitum* (a phrasal pair, with marked alliteration), 11.1–2 *mentem memoriam cor cogitatum* (two alliterative pairs juxtaposed), 16.15 *membra m[ed]ullae*, 16.18 *laetus libens*, 17.10 *uitam ualetudinem*). There are also some longer asyndeta. Note too text no. 7 from the *Fons Annae Perennae*, also from Mainz (Blänsdorf 2010b: 238), with three pairs of different types: *sacras santas . . . tollatis pertolla{e}tis . . . oculus dextru sinesteru*.

8 eoconora: as Blänsdorf notes (2010a: 175), this is a misspelling of *iecinora*, a word that created considerable spelling confusion. It is also plural for singular, of the liver of a single person. On this usage in another curse tablet see above, 6.29.

10 deuotum defictum: another asyndeton bimembre, with repeated verbal prefixes; *aget* and *aginat* also have repeated fore-elements (*ag-*), but they are not prefixes. The same phrase is in a curse tablet from Barchín del Hoyo, Hispania Tarraconensis (Curbera, Sierra Delage and Velázquez 1999, Kropp 2008a, 2.1.2/1 *pro me pro meis deuotos defixos inferis, deuotos defixos inferis*), where it is juxtaposed with an asyndetic pair of prepositional expressions, with the preposition repeated as in Petronius' *per scutum per ocream* above (19.6–7). Asyndeta with repeated fore-element are very common and ancient (for Latin examples see above, 3.420), with parallels in other early Indo-European languages (particularly in the case of compound adjectives, such as those with a privative prefix: see West 2007: 109–10).

Syntactically this phrase is of interest. It is an accusative that appears to be free-standing ('him, cursed, fixed with a spell'), in that there is no expressed verb. An exact parallel, with the same phrase, is in the curse tablet from Barchín del Hoyo, just cited, on which Curbera, Sierra Delage and Velázquez (1999: 282) speak of the syntax as 'confused', with participles 'apparently used instead of finite verbs'. But the victims of a curse may be referred to in a free-standing list either in the nominative, or in the accusative (with a verb of handing over or the like easily understood, e.g. *dono*), or inconsistently, in a mixture of cases. The Myconos *defixio* (see Solin 1982), for example, basically has names in the accusative without any expressed verb, with a few lapses into the nominative (see Adams 2003a: 680–1, id. 2013: 227; also Kropp 2008b: 280 for alternations). Here Tiberius Claudius, after being named in the nominative in the heading, becomes the victim to whom things are to be done, and as such he can be referred to in the accusative as patient of implied acts.

The Spanish tablet just referred to is bilingual, and does indeed have a pair of finite verbs in the Greek version (δίδωμι παραδίδωμι 'give, consign') governing the accusatival names, but it does not have an exact equivalent of the Latin phrase *deuotos defixos*. The writer of the Latin version chooses not to express the implied governing verb of consigning, which can be understood from the Greek version. Bilingual texts are often complementary, with one not having all the elements of the other (see Adams 2003a: 824 s.v. 'texts, bi-/trilingual … with complementary versions'), and this specimen illustrates that phenomenon nicely, in that each version has something that the other does not.

Defictum is described by Blänsdorf (2010a: 175) as a 'Vulgar form of *defixum*', but in fact *fictus* is the original form of the participle of *figo* (with *fixus* a remodelling on the analogy of the perfect *fixi*) (see Leumann 1977: 615). *Fictus* occurs in Varro (*Rust.* 3.7.4) and Lucretius (3.4: see the note of Munro 1886: II.177–8), and is commented on by Diomedes (*GL* I.377.11–12) as existing alongside *fixus* (with citation of Scaurus, *De uita sua* for the form *confictus*).

10–12 deuotum defictum illum menbra, medullas: as the text stands there is an accusative pronoun *illum*, and then two nouns denoting body parts in the same case. *Menbra* and *medullas* can be interpreted as appositional to the pronoun, and standing to it as part to the whole ('him, cursed, fixed with a spell – namely his limbs, marrow'). This is an old type of partitive apposition, attested for example in Plautus and Homer, and found in a curse tablet from the Hamble Estuary (see 33.15–17). *Menbra medullas* is another alliterative asyndeton bimembre, found in another tablet in the corpus (see above, 19.6–7).

Conclusions

Curse tablets are usually linguistically contrived up to a point, because they employ traditional language with roots in legal and religious idiom. This tablet contains alliterative asyndeta bimembria of traditional types, an ancient type of partitive apposition, the legal phrase *acceptum habere* and a rhetorical repetition. Another traditional element is the detached nominative heading. Otherwise the Latin is substandard, and not only in its phonetic spellings such as *abiatis*. *Quit* for *quod* is not educated usage, and neither are the plural use of the word for 'liver' or its bizarre form.

Two usages particularly stand out, both of them with parallels in the freed-men's speeches in Petronius, namely the asyndeton containing the verb *aginare*, and the use of *quit* just mentioned. The tablet is roughly contemporary with Petronius' novel, and Petronius in composing his speeches was drawing on the same level of language as that which came naturally to the drafter of the curse.

20

LETTER FROM THE MYOS HORMOS ROAD (EGYPT), END OF FIRST CENTURY/FIRST QUARTER OF SECOND (CUVIGNY 2003: II.409, M689)

Introduction

Myos Hormos was a Red Sea port from which the Romans constructed a road into the eastern desert of Egypt in the first century AD. Various letters come from desert stations on the road.

Text

Manilius · Felix · dec(urio) Nouelio
curatori · Maximiano · salute.
recte facies · per amaxas · mittas
nobis · aqua ·, quia · de·est · nobis
et · unde potere · non abemus,   5
ẹt · cura tibi · sit · celerius · mittere.

m^2 opto te bene ualere.

Translation

Manilius Felix the decurion to Novellius, *curator* at Maximianon, greetings. Please send us by wagon water, because we have a lack of it and do not have anything to drink, and see that you send it quickly. I hope you are well.

Commentary

2 curatori Maximiano: Halla-aho (2013: 180 n. 52) remarks that 'the name of the fort, Maximianon, is wrongly inflected in the dative *Maximiano* (after *curator* in the dative) although it should be in the genitive (*Maximiani*)'. The form is unexpected, but is unlikely to have been regarded as a dative. It is more likely to be a locatival ablative, a usage that becomes common in second declension words from the Augustan period (see Adams 1983a: 72 with n. 8, with bibliography, id. 2013: 338–9), and adnominal ('curator at Maximianon'). Cf. *Tab. Vindol.* 22.8–9 (*centurioni*) *regionario Luguualio* ('to (so and so), regional centurion at Luguualium').

3 recte facies: construed with a subjunctive following. This is not a normal Latin way of making a request, and is clearly modelled (see Halla-aho 2009: 56–7, ead. 2013: 180–1) on the Greek formula (= 'please'), καλῶς ποιήσεις (with various complements, such as an infinitive or aorist participle), which is very common in contemporary Greek letters. On the Greek construction in papyrus letters see Leiwo (2010b: 99–106). Latin letters from Egypt of this period often adopt Greek-style epistolary formulae (see e.g. Cugusi 1981: 735–6, Adams 1977a: 4–5, and on the transfer of formulae from one language to another see in general Adams 2003a: 76–83, and also 591–2 (on 'convergence')). For the opposite phenomenon (a Latin epistolary formula influencing Greek) see above, 13.16.

amaxas: for this loan-word in Egyptian Latin see *O. Faw.* 5 and Adams (2003a: 444). Cf. *amaxitem* in the same corpus, *O. Faw.* 1.

4 de·est: for the interpunct in this position, which betrays a continuing perception that the verb was a compound (whereas double compounding, as e.g. in *adalligare* < *ad* + *ad-ligare*, reveals that a compound structure was no longer perceived as such) and perhaps also betrays a keenness to resist a contraction, cf. above, 13.10 on *satis·facere*, 14.5 on *de·mostrabit*. On the other hand in the prepositional phrase *per amaxas* the preposition is not divided from the noun. The interpuncta in this text are sometimes placed between words, as in the fourth line, and sometimes between phrases, as in the third and fifth lines. The latter placement represents the first stage in the development of 'grammatical' punctuation, but typically texts are not consistent in following one system or another (see below, 26 Commentary, 'preliminaries', Adams 1996, Dickey 2010: 197–8).

5 unde potere non abemus: for the infinitive (instead of a relative clause with generic subjunctive) dependent on *non habemus* cf. e.g. Schol. Juv. 7.87 *non habebat unde se sustentare*, and Hofmann and Szantyr (1965: 539), Adams (2013: 770–1); also below, 45.10. This form of the infinitive (for *potare*) does not seem to be registered in the *TLL*, and is not open to an obvious explanation, because first conjugation verb forms were stable and productive (see e.g. Väänänen 1981a: 135).

6 cura tibi sit: *cura tibi est* + infinitive is an old literary construction cited by the *TLL* IV.1456.20ff. mainly from poetry (from Virgil onwards). There is an alternative construction showing *curae* (predicative dative) instead of the nominative, which is also old and literary (and found in prose) (*TLL* 1457.44ff.).

celerius: on this comparative use and its Greek equivalent in epistolography see below, 23.8–9.

Conclusions

This text is to some extent phonetically spelt, with for example degemination (*Nouelio*), and omission of final *m* (*salute*; sometimes scribes made a special effort to get this greeting right: see Adams 1994: 107 on the regular correct form at Bu Njem, amid many omissions in other words) and of the initial aspirate (*abemus*). There is also some substandard morphology (*potere*) and syntax (*unde potere*). But what most stands out is the evidence for convergence of formulae in the Greek and Latin letters of Roman military personnel serving in the east at this period.

21
LETTER OF CLAUDIA SEVERA FROM VINDOLANDA (*TAB. VINDOL.* 291), OF THE EARLY SECOND CENTURY

Introduction

This is a letter by Claudia Severa, wife of Aelius Brocchus, to Sulpicia Lepidina, wife of Flavius Cerialis, prefect of the Ninth Cohort of Batavians stationed at Vindolanda in Period 3 (the end of which was 'in or not long after AD 103': Bowman and Thomas 1994: 19). It is one of several letters by women found at Vindolanda. 292 is also from Claudia Severa to Lepidina. 293 is possibly by the same woman. 294 is by an unnamed woman. 635 is a fragmentary letter, again from Severa to Lepidina. 291 and 292 are both in two hands. In each a second hand, that of Claudia herself, writes a 'full and intimate closure' (Bowman and Thomas 1994: 256). As the editors remark (256), the 'evidence for correspondence between literate women of the equestrian officer class is of no less interest than their presence itself at Vindolanda'.

The letter is an invitation to the birthday celebration of Severa.

Text

i

Cl(audia) · Seuerá Lepidinae [suae
                    [sa]ḷ[u]ṭem.
iii Idus Septembṛ[e]ṣ, soror, ad dieṃ
sollemnem nạtalem meum rogó
libenter ḟaciás ut uenias   5
ad nos, iụcundiorem mihi

ii

[diem] interuentú tuo facturá si
[.].[c. 3]ṣ. *uacat*
Cerial[em t]ụum salutá. Aelius meus [
et filioḷụs ṣalutant. *uacat*   10

m² *uacat* sperabo te, soror,

uale, soror, anima
mea – ita ualeam –
karissima et haue.

Back
m¹ Sulpiciae Lepidinae   15
Cerialis
a S[e]uera.

Translation

Claudia Severa to her Lepidina, greetings. On 11 September, sister, for the day
of celebration of my birthday, I ask warmly that you set about coming to us,
sure to make (the day) more delightful to me by your coming, if you (are here).
Greet your Cerialis. My Aelius and our little son send greetings.

I will long for you, sister. Farewell, sister, my dearest – so help me – soul, and hail.

To Sulpicia Lepidina, wife of Cerialis, from Severa.

Commentary

3–4 ad diem sollemnem natalem meum: *ad* is not temporal but expresses
purpose. *Sollemnem* goes with *diem* ('ceremonial day': cf. Suet. *Aug.* 75 *festos et
sollemnes dies profusissime . . . celebrabat*), with *natalem meum* in apposition
('for the ceremonial day, my birthday').

4–5 rogó libenter faciás ut uenias: *facias ut* is virtually redundant here; the
sense would be much the same if Severa had written *rogo ut uenias* or *rogo
uenias*. The subject of *facio* is the same as that of the dependent verb. What
Severa has done here is to convert the formula *fac ut uenias* (see Plaut. *Men.*
437 *facito . . . ut uenias*, Ter. *Andr.* 712 *huc face ad me ut uenias*; see also the
numerous examples of *fac ut* et sim. followed by other second person verbs
collected by Bennett 1910–14: II.224–7) from overtly imperatival into dependence on *rogo*, a conversion that presumably made it more polite.

Usually in the *facio ut*-construction when the subject of the dependent verb
is the same as that of the higher verb (as in our passage), that higher verb is
imperative, as *fac/facito* in Plautus and Terence above (see again Bennett's
examples). For an instance where *facio* is not imperative see Cic. *Att.* 11.23.2
sed tardius iter faciebat. eo feci ut [eo] celeriter eunti darem (cited by Thielmann
1886: 204), which is translated by Shackleton Bailey (1965–70: V.57) as 'but as
he is making a rather leisurely journey I thought it best to give this (i.e. *litteras*)

to a fast traveller'. It would be possible to rewrite here as *eo celeriter eunti dedi*, but *feci* stresses the deliberateness of the act. This quasi-redundant use of *facio ut* (with both verbs having the same subject) in late Latin gave way to *facio* + infinitive: see e.g. Vict. Vit. 3.27, p. 47.12 *nam si haec praesens uita sola fuisset et aliam, quae uere est, non speraremus aeternam, nec ita fecissem ad modicum atque temporaliter gloriari* (= *gloriatus essem*: see *TLL* VI.1.104.58, and the examples immediately before; also Thielmann 1886: 204–5, Norberg 1945: 81, Bastardas Parera 1953: 160–1, Hofmann and Szantyr 1965: 325; for Old French, Gougenheim 1929: 330–8, especially 335–8).

In our passage (where incidentally *libenter* goes with *rogo*, 'I ask you warmly') *facias ut* seems to be of a different order from the Ciceronian and late construction, because it can be directly derived from the imperatival *fac ut uenias*.

6 iucundiorem: *iucundus* was an emotive word, and not in favour in the higher forms of poetry or prose (historiography): see *TLL* VII.2.592.19ff., Axelson (1945: 35 n. 18), Moussy (1964), and below. Though *iucundus* often seems interchangeable with *gratus*, it was potentially stronger in meaning (see Moussy 1964: 391): note Cic. *Att.* 3.24.2 *nam ista ueritas, etiam si iucunda non est, mihi tamen grata est.* For further observations see Fordyce (1961: 218) on Catull. 50.16 ('the *iucundus* is one whose company gives pleasure') and (taking a different line) Krostenko (2001: 11 n. 22, 286 n. 126). Cicero has *iucundus* (and *gratus*) often (and not only in letters), but it is almost totally absent from historians, tragedy and epic (details of distribution are at Moussy 1964: 397–8). It is found in Catullus, Horace's *Satires, Epistles* and *Epodes* (but not *Odes*), Ovid's lesser works but not the *Metamorphoses*, Propertius, Tibullus, Juvenal and Martial. Tacitus has *iucundus* in the minor works and once in the *Histories* (3.56.3), but not in the *Annals*, whereas *gratus* is common in the *Annals* (and other works).

Gratus does not occur in vols. 2 and 3 of the Vindolanda tablets. For *iucundus* see also 225.23, and for the adverb *iucundissime*, 629. Our example is in line with Fordyce's remark above. In letters of Augustus note *uale, iucundissime Tiberi* (Suet. *Tib.* 21.4), *iucundissime et, ita sim felix, uir fortissime* (same letter), *aue, mi Gai, meus asellus iucundissimus* (Gell. 15.7.3). See too Catull. 14.2 *iucundissime Calue*, Mart. 10.47.2 *iucundissime Martialis*.

7 interuentú tuo facturá si: *interuentus* is here used of an arranged, rather than a chance, coming on the scene, and has a parallel in *interuenit* at 343.36 (*constituerat se uentur|um nec interuenit*, 'he had agreed that he would come but did not turn up'), where again the visit had been agreed in advance. In both passages *interuen-* picks up a use of the verb *uenio*. *Interuentus* serves as the abstract verbal noun corresponding to *uenio*; the verbal noun *uentus* was virtually non-existent.

After *si* the text breaks off, but Bowman and Thomas (1994: 258) think that *a[deri]s* is a possible restoration. They translate this part as: '... to make sure that you come to us, to make the day more enjoyable for me by your arrival, if you are present (?)'.

This is an interesting use of the future participle *factura* (with a conditional clause). The participle, accompanying a verb of motion, is akin to the use expressing purpose (see 27.6), but the accomplishment of the act is subject to a condition. The future participle accompanied by a conditional clause appears first in the Augustan period (see Riemann 1885: 305, Kühner and Stegmann 1955: I.761, Hofmann and Szantyr 1965: 390). Note Livy 21.17.6 *Ti. Sempronius missus in Siciliam, ita in Africam transmissurus, si ad arcendum Italia Poenum consul alter satis esset* ('Tiberius Sempronius was sent to Sicily, thus to be in a position to cross to Africa, should the other consul be enough to keep the Carthaginian out of Italy'). Oakley (1998: 591), citing Hor. *Carm.* 2.3. 4–8 *moriture Delli | seu ... seu*, notes that the usage appears in Augustan literature and adds that Livy characteristically 'affected the construction more than other writers'. Horace also has it in the *Satires* in an elliptical conditional (cf. 18.5 above): 2.8.44 *haec grauida ... | capta est, deterior post partum carne futura*' ('this ... was caught while pregnant. (If caught) after spawning, it would have been inferior in flesh'). The nuance of the participle may be variable. In the Vindolanda example *factura* without a following *si*-clause would unambiguously express purpose ('come to us in order to make the day more enjoyable'). The addition of the *si*-clause changes the implication ('come to us, destined to make the day more enjoyable if you do'). According to Hofmann and Szantyr (1965: 390), these uses of the future participle are less well known from late Latin, except in poets such as Prudentius, but it is doubtful whether there has been any systematic investigation.

The presence of the construction in a private letter not intended for publication is intriguing. Nisbet and Hubbard (1978: 56) on the above passage of Horace's *Odes* state that the 'attributive use of the future participle was alien to the spoken language (except for *futurus*), but because of its brevity was cultivated in the Silver Age'. Given that it has now turned up in a private letter from one woman to another, we must either, in agreement with the implication of Nisbet and Hubbard, say that Claudia Severa had literary aspirations, or query Nisbet and Hubbard's statement that it was 'alien to the spoken language'. This latter view is not based on evidence, and indeed at much the same time as Severa's letter Terentianus used a future participle expressing purpose with a verb of motion, in a letter of marked informality: *P. Mich.* VIII.467.8

s[cias] ạutẹṃ [ra]pi me in Syriam exiturum cum uexillo ('know that I am being hurried off to Syria to go forth with an attachment'). Whatever the status of the participle in these uses in the Augustan period, it was clearly at home in lower registers a century later. There is no subtlety to the way in which Severa has expressed herself here. The phrasing is repetitive ('come, to make me happy by your coming, if you come'), and the banality of the condition does not have a literary look.

There are three future participles in the short letters of Severa (291, 292). One (292.b.iii.3–4) is straightforward, in an indirect question (*scies quiḍ sim actura*), but the third, at 292.c.v.2, is intriguing: *eram et Brigạe ṃansụṛạ*. The context is unfortunately fragmentary, but this one may express intention ('intending to remain at Briga'). The future participle is very restricted in early Latin. Laughton (1964: 118) states: 'In early Latin the participial form is found frequently in the periphrastic conjugation *-urus est*, but its independent participial use is very rare indeed; according to some scholars it is non-existent.' Laughton goes on (119–22) to discuss the small number of predicative uses in Cicero (apart from *futurus*, which is common: see above). For its rather more frequent use expressing intention in literature of the Augustan period see Riemann (1885: 304–5) and Kühner and Stegmann (1955: I.761). See also 27.6.

I am grateful to John Briscoe and Trevor Evans for information used in this note.

9 Cerial[em t]ụum salutá Aelius meus: *tuus* refers to 'your (husband)' and *meus* to 'my (husband)'. This is a recurrent usage of the Vindolanda correspondence. *Mea* accompanies a name in the nominative three times in reference to a wife (244, 622 *Seuera mea*, 626 *Claudia mea*). For *Aelius meus* see also 635. *Cerialem tuum* is also in the greeting of the next letter, 292. At *TLL* VIII.917.57ff. there are many instances quoted of *meus* with names in cases other than the vocative, but although these are classified according to the relationship of the referent to the writer, there is no explicit category for husbands or wives (for *meus* in the vocative with names see 916.57ff.). See further the material at Köhm (1905: 174–5).

10 filiolụs: the diminutive (also at 623 and 635 in the same context) of a child (cf. e.g. Cic. *Att.* 1.2.1 *filiolo me auctum scito, salua Terentia*).

11-12 sperabo te, soroṛ, uale, soror: the vocative *soror* occurs three times in this short letter. There are letters between men in which *frater* occurs more than once, but in different parts of the text (248, 301, 310, 311, 345, 670). Here it is possible to speak of gemination, with the instances separated by just one word, undoubtedly an affectionate form of address. For an account of vocative gemination in its different forms (in poetry) see Wills (1996: 50–8, particularly 56–7). Cf. Ovid *Her.* 7.191 *Anna soror, soror Anna, meae male conscia culpae*, 11.61 '*uiue, soror, soror o carissima*' *aisti* (though in our passage *soror* does not have its literal meaning: for *soror* as an address rather than kinship term see Dickey 2002: 125). For separations of the repeated vocatives see Wills (1996: 57).

For *sperabo te* Petersmann (1992: 289) cites Ter. *Eun.* 195 *me speres*. An object of affection may be the one 'hoped for': see Plaut. *Poen.* 1268 *sperate, salue* (spoken by a girl to her father), Ovid *Her.* 11.123 *o frustra miserae sperate sorori* (Dickey 2002: 360). Note too Dickey loc. cit. on the address term *spes*: 'Term of affection and praise for anyone but lovers, always with *mea* or another possessive.'

12–14 anima mea – ita ụạḷeam – karissima: this phrase is interesting for several reasons. What is the point of *ita ualeam*? Noteworthy too is the word order.

Bowman and Thomas (1994: 258) note that they cannot parallel the expression *ita ualeam*, and it may well be unparalleled, but it does belong to a type. It is a parenthetical exclamatory wish introduced by *ita* ('so help me, on my life'), here inserted into another phrase to place emphasis on a word or words of the other phrase. Note Cic. *Fam.* 2.13.3 (Shackleton Bailey 93, Loeb) *qui<s> hoc putaret, praeter me? nam, ita uiuam, putaui*, translated by Shackleton Bailey as 'who would have thought it? – except me! For upon my soul, I *did* think it'. Inserted between *nam* and *putaui* the expression emphasises the following *putaui* (Shackleton Bailey uses italics). Note too *Fam.* 16.20 (Shackleton Bailey 220) *sollicitat, ita uiuam, me tua, mi Tiro, ualetudo* ('I am *anxious*, I can tell you, my dear Tiro, about your health'). Here Cicero stresses his anxiety, and the presence of the exclamation puts emphasis on the word preceding. Again there is a dislocated word order, with *ita uiuam* intruding between *sollicitat* and its object; there is incidentally a second dislocation following, with *mi Tiro* placed between *tua* and *ualetudo* (and emphasising in this case *ualetudo*). For a double dislocation (of a more contrived type) in a more literary genre note Catull. 66.18 *non, ita me diui, uera gemunt, iuerint* (here the emphasis is on the following *uera*: 'not *genuine*, so help me, is their grief'). Emphasis on a following word is also to be seen in the expression used by D. Brutus to delay his execution (Val. Max. 9.13.3; cf. Sen. *Epist.* 82.12). He first withdrew his neck and then when told to present it more steadily uttered the words (to buy a moment of time, according to Valerius), *ita uiuam, dabo*, 'so help me, I *will* give it' (i.e. in a minute or two, with the emphasis on the future tense). A letter of Augustus (Suet. *Tib.* 21.4) has the expression *iucundissime et, ita sim felix, uir fortissime* ('delightful, and, so help me, bravest man'), with the contrast of bravery with mere pleasantness brought home by the intrusive exclamation. Note finally Prop. 1.7.3 *atque, ita sim felix, primo contendis Homero*, where again the exclamation leads into the striking point, that Ponticus rivals Homer himself. For a few other examples see *TLL* VII.2.526.65ff., Hofmann and Szantyr (1965: 529 b, 634 e, in the latter place on the intrusive placement of such wishes), Fedeli (1980: 189), Bowman and Thomas (1994: 258) and Hofmann and Ricottilli (2003: 141). At Petron. 57.6 in a freedman's speech there is a verb of the opposite meaning to *ualeam* in a parenthetical wish that has exactly the same emphasising role: *spero, sic moriar, ut mortuus non erubescam* ('I hope, so help me, that when *dead* I am not embarrassed').

In our passage I take it that the intrusive expression stresses the word following, 'my *dearest* soul'. The combination of *uale*, which immediately precedes, with a vocative phrase containing an intrusive *ita*-expression has a parallel in the letter of Augustus just cited (Suet. *Tib.* 21.4 (where *uale* follows the quoted passage)).

In another letter to Lepidina (294), also by a woman (see Bowman and Thomas 1994: 263), there is a comparable phrase (*ita sim salua*), though it does not seem (in a fragmentary context) to intrude into another phrase.

Anima also occurs as an address term in the second letter by Claudia Severa. It is used a few times in writings by women addressed to women, and by men addressing women, and in emotional contexts where males are addressed (see Adams 1995a: 120, with modifications by Dickey 2002: 158–9). An example, little noticed if at all, is in a Roman epitaph, *CLE* 92.11 *haue, pupa blanda, anima m[ea]* (addressed by the male deceased to a girl: see *TLL* X.2.2674.24ff. for the meaning of *pupa*, and see above, 17.3 on *pupulus*).

14 karissima: the superlative is the normal form of this word in address in the Vindolanda tablets and indeed in other corpora of letters. In *Tab. Vindol.* vol. 2 there are thirteen certain cases of the superlative in the vocative, and in vol. 3 seven (also the non-vocative *fratri karissimo* at 670). So at *O. Faw.* 2.19–20 there is *frater k[a]rissime* and at *O. Claud.* 2.9–10 *frater karissime*; cf. in Terentianus *patri karissimo* at *P. Mich.* VIII.467.1 (cf. Petron. 48.7 *Agamemnon mihi carissime*, 71.5 *amice carissime*, in freedmen's speeches). *Soror karissima*, which is also at 292, 293 and 635, may look markedly affectionate, but the absence of the positive form of the adjective, and the use of the superlative in the masculine not only with *frater* or *domine frater* (247, 255, 306, 331, 611, 622, 632) but also with *domine* alone (285, 288, 613, 623), suggest that the superlative had become totally banal in address (see Dickey 2002: 134–6). In the corpora of letters referred to in this note there is only one example of the adjective in the positive, and that is not a term of address (Terentianus *P. Mich.* VIII.467.18 *karum*). The placement of *ita ualeam* before *karissima* (see above on 12–14) apparently reinvigorates the superlative.

Also illustrated by this word is the persistence of the old-fashioned spelling with *k* before *a* (part of a system, with *q* used before *u* and *c* before other letters: see below, 22.25–6) There are just two possible instances of *carissime* in the Vindolanda corpus, vols. 2 and 3 (255, but the reading is uncertain, 306). Note too the index to *CEL* III, 352 for a long list of forms of this adjective with *k*. It is also of note that Cerialis at Vindolanda receives a letter from a Karus, who spells his name with a *K* (250.1). Personal names may attract formal or 'correct' spellings (see Adams 1994: 103; but see 6.4), and the *K* in this name raises the question how *carus* would have been spelt in literary texts of the period. Petersmann (1992: 286) in referring to *k*-spellings classifies them as 'Vulgar Latin peculiarities in the sphere of orthography', but they should be seen as archaising and 'correct'. See further Adams (1977a: 32).

15–16 Sulpiciae Lepidinae Cerialis: 'to Sulpicia Lepidina (wife) of Cerialis'. The same expression (without *uxori*) is also at the end of the next letter, 292, where it seems to be followed by a second instance of the same genitive use: *a Seuera B[rocchi*. This is a classic use of the genitive of possession, and is originally a reflection of the *patria potestas* of a *paterfamilias*. Such expressions, without a kinship term to which the genitive is attached, express a variety of relationships, wife of, son of, daughter of, slave of (see e.g. Kühner and Stegmann 1955: I.414, Hofmann and Szantyr 1965: 59, and, on the gamonymic, Kajava 1994: 20–4 and Horsfall 2006: 254). At the end of letter 301 there is *Candido Genialis praef(ecti)*, where the meaning is 'to Candidus slave of Genialis the prefect', an expression that is possibly followed by a variant construction (*a Seuero . . . .i seruo*), but the reading is uncertain. The construction with *seruo* however certainly occurs at the end of 347: *a Rh]eno Similis seruo*. See also above, 6.19, 14.11, 18.1.

There is good early inscriptional evidence for gamonymics in the 340 Praenestine cippi, which date from the early/mid-third century BC to the 80s BC and name 130 women (see Kajava 1994: 20). There are three main types there, an early one in which the husband's name is expressed by a possessive adjective (*CIL* I^2.561 *Dindia Macolnia*: see Kajava 1994: 21, 23), and then the types both without and with *uxor* (e.g. I^2.143 *Curtia Rosci*, 184 *Luscia M. uxor*, 300 *Seruia M. f. Cinsi uxor*) (for examples see Kajava 1994: 21, 24 n. 33; the second type sometimes has a patronymic as well, as in the last example cited).

Though the plain genitive from early on was rivalled by gen. + *uxor*, it persisted for centuries in literary language. For an example in the annalist Cn.

Gellius (in a prayer) see *FRH* II.14.F5 *Neria Martis* 'Neria wife of Mars'. For Cicero note e.g. *Att.* 12.20.2 *Cn. Caepio Seruiliae Claudi pater*, 'Cn. Caepio, father of Servilia wife of Claudius', and for later examples see e.g. Virg. *Aen.* 3.319 *Hectoris Andromache*, Val. Max. 1.5.4 *Caecilia Metelli*, Plin. *Epist.* 2.20.2 *Verania Pisonis*, Quint. 6.3.74 *Domitia Passieni*, Suet. *Caes.* 50.1 *Postumiam Ser. Sulpici, Lolliam Auli Gabini, Tertullam Marci Crassi, etiam Cn. Pompei Muciam*, and the further instances cited by Kühner and Stegmann and Horsfall locc. cit. (last paragraph but one).

For the genitive with *uxor* see Cic. *Tim.* 3.75 *Artemisia illa, Mausoli, Cariae regis, uxor*. *Vxor* tends to be expressed for clarity when there is also a filiation present: e.g. Cic. *Rep.* 2.46 *Lucretiae, Tricipitini filiae, Collatini uxori*, 30.12.11 *Sophonbiba, uxor Syphacis, filia Hasdrubalis Poeni, occurrit*.

Conclusions

Vindolanda letters tend to be lumped together and regarded as specimens of 'Vulgar Latin', and Severa's letter has not escaped that treatment. Petersmann's paper (1992) on 'vulgar' elements in Vindolanda tablets notes several such features in this letter, namely the orthography of *karissima* (though Petersmann also oddly points out that the spelling is old: 1992: 286–7) and the expression *sperabo te* (1992: 289), which is regarded as one of those early popular features that resurface in 'vulgar language' at a later period. Severa's letter, and not least the part in her own hand, is certainly intimate and informal in tone, but intimacy of expression is not to be equated necessarily with 'vulgarity'.

The letter is correctly spelt throughout, in Severa's greeting as well as the body of the text. Severa uses the archaising *k* before *a* in *karissima*. There are no deviations from standard morphology. In the syntax the most notable construction is the use of the future participle with a conditional clause, a usage previously associated with high-style literature of the Augustan period. The vocabulary is emotive (*iucundiorem*, the diminutive *filiolus*, the repetitions of *soror*, *sperabo te*, *anima mea*, the exclamatory *ita ualeam*, employed for the purpose of emphasis).

22

LETTER OF CLAUDIUS TERENTIANUS (*P. MICH*. VIII.471, *CEL* 146), OF THE EARLY SECOND CENTURY

Introduction

The letters of Claudius Terentianus, who as a veteran settled at Karanis in Egypt, are dated to the first quarter of the second century. The corpus is bilingual, containing five letters in Latin and five in Greek to the same addressee, Tiberianus, referred to as the father of Terentianus. The Latin letters, including the present one, have been much discussed and indeed reproduced in recent times (see e.g. Adams 1977a, Kramer 2007: 59–74, Strassi 2008: 32–4; further bibliography at Kramer 2007: 59–60; see also the editions mentioned in the heading above), but 471 in particular is such an important specimen of non-literary Latin that I have thought it essential to this anthology. Terentianus clearly used different scribes, and there are spelling variations from letter to letter (see Halla-aho 2003). I print here the text of Kramer (2007), with his subscript dots (see his reproduction of the text at 67).

Text

dico illi, da mi, di[c]o, a[e]s paucum; ibo, dico, ad amicos   10
patris mei. item acu lentiaminaque mi mandauit;
nullum assem mi dedit. ego tamen incebinde collexi paucum aes ed ibi ad [.]uaroclum et [.]g[.]iuan
et emi pauca que espediui. si aequm tempus esset se exiturum Alexandrie silui[t]. item non mi d[e]dit aes quam   15
aureum matr[i] mee in [u]estimenta. hoc est, inquid,
quod pater tus m[i] mandauit. quo tempus autem ueni
omnia praefuerunt et lana; et matrem meam au-
te praegnatam inue[n]i; nil poterat facere. dende pos paucos dies parit, et non poterat mihi succurrere. item litem   20
abuit Ptolemes pater me[us] sopera uestimenta mea, et factum est illi uenire Alexandrie con tirones et me reli-

quid con matrem meam. soḷi nihil poteramus facere,
absentia illim aḅit[u]ri. [m]ạter mea: speç[t]ẹmus illum
dum uenit et uen[i]o teqụm Alexandriẹ ẹt deduco te   25
usque ad naue. Saturninus iam paratus erat exire
illa die quạndo tam magna lites factam est. dico illi: ueni interpone te si potes aiutare Ptolemaeo patri
meo. non magis qurauit me pro xylesphongium
sed sum negotium et circa res suas. attonitus   30
exiendo dico illi: dạ m[i] pạuqum aes, ut possim uenire
con rebus meis Alexandria, im inpendia. negabit se
abiturum. ueni, dicet, Ạlexandrie ed dabo t[i]bi. ego
non abiui. mater ma nos assem uendedi lentiamina
            [ut] ueniam Alexandrie.   35
        verso
Claudio Tiberiano [pat]ṛ[i   a Cla]ụḍ[io] Teren[tiano

Translation

I say to him, 'Give me', I say, 'a little money. I will go', I say, 'to the friends of
my father.' Likewise he handed over to me a needle and linens, but didn't
give me a single *as*. Nevertheless I got together a little bit of money from here
and there and I went to . . . and bought a few things for which I settled up. He
did not say that if the time were right he would go to Alexandria. Likewise
not so much did he give *me* money, but rather an *aureus* to my mother for
clothes. 'This', he said, 'is the instruction your father gave me.' But when
I came everything was present, even the wool, but I found my mother
pregnant. She could do nothing. Then after a few days she gives birth, and
she could not help me. Likewise my father Ptolemes had a dispute over my
clothes, and it turned out that he went to Alexandria with the recruits and he
left me with my mother. We could do nothing on our own, intending to
depart from there because of his absence. My mother said: 'Let us wait for
him until he comes and I will come with you to Alexandria and I will escort
you right up to the ship.' Saturninus was already prepared to go on the day
when such a dispute occurred. I say to him: 'Come, intervene, if you can help
my father Ptolemaeus.' He paid no more attention to me than to a sponge
stick, but (occupied himself) with his own business and over his own affairs.
Astonished I say to him as I take my leave: 'Give me a little money, so that
I can come with my things to Alexandria – for expenses.' He said he would
not have any. 'Come', he says, 'to Alexandria and I will give it to you.' I did

not go off.[1] My mother did not have an *as*. I sold linens so that I could come to Alexandria.

To Claudius Tiberianus, father, from Claudius Terentianus.

Commentary

10 di̱co̱ illi, da mi, di[c]o̱, a̱[e]s paucum; ibo, di̱co̱, ad amicos: notable here is the heated repetition of the verb of saying in quoting speech, of the sort that could be paralleled from colloquial English. Similar types of pleonasm are found sometimes in Latin. Note that here *dico illi* introduces the quoted speech, and then immediately after a verb of saying is inserted within a phrase of the speech. Cf. e.g. Greg. Tur. *HF* 5.44, p. 253.4–5 *cumque haec mihi recitare iussisset, ait 'sic' inquit 'uolo'*, where *ait* is at once followed by *inquit* within a phrase of the speech (for further such examples see E. Löfstedt 1911: 229–30). These last cases are not, however, identical to ours. They reflect a mechanical tendency to insert *inquit* within a speech near the start, with occasional indifference to whether a verb of saying has already preceded. The repetition of *dico* in the letter looks like a graphic colloquial manner of reporting a spoken exchange.

This letter is replete with quoted direct speech (cf. lines 17, 24, 27, 31, 33). There is just one certain acc. + inf. (32–3 *negabit se abiturum*), of very simple type, with one clause and the accusative pronoun attached to the higher verb. *Se exiturum Alexandr̲ie s̲i̲lui[t]* (14–15) is presumably another, but the final verb is problematic (see below). These statistics bring out the fact that in conversational style speakers will often prefer the vividness of quoted speech to a more formal indirect construction, a point that is sometimes neglected in discussions of the acc. + inf. versus the *dico quod-/quia*-construction. See further below, 47.12, and also Adams (2005b).

Illi occurs (as a pronoun) in this letter at 22, 24, 27–8 and 31. *Is*, which does not occur at all, has been replaced in this corpus by *ille* (Adams 1977a: 44), which does not convey its usual deixis (see further above, 18.6 on Petronius, and index s.v. *ille*, 'in relation to *is*').

There is some variability in the letters between the dative forms *mihi* and *mi*. In this letter *mi* is preferred by 6:1, whereas in 467 *mihi* alone is used (ten times) (see Adams 1977a: 20). The variation probably reflects the practices of different scribes.

The prepositional complement *ad amicos* follows its verb *ibo*, and that is the regular place of prepositional expressions in this text (ten times). Only the

---

[1] On the text translated from this point see the Commentary.

temporal expression *pos paucos dies* precedes the verb (19–20). See further below, 22.19 on the comparable placement of infinitives after the governing verb.

11, 34 lentiamina: the expected spelling is *linteamina*. The form here is also attested in Greek letters in a bilingual glossary (see Kramer 2001: 72–3). One might explain it in two ways. If it is phonetically inspired, there is represented closing of the second vowel in hiatus, along with a vocalic misspelling, *e* for ï, in the first syllable. Alternatively in a long word there might have been a mechanical reversal of two vowel graphemes.

For this word in Latin Bible translations see Burton (2000: 100) (though he does not cite these documentary examples). The term does not differ in meaning from *linteum*, with which it alternates in different codices of the Old Latin Gospels. Burton observes that its 'use by the OLG translators is a further example of their preference for derived over simple forms'. Terentianus has the term twice (in this letter), but does not use *linteum* (which, however, survives in Romance (*REW* 5072), unlike the derivative).

11 mandauit: the verb occurs several times in the Johns Hopkins *defixiones*, where it is juxtaposed with *trado* and means roughly 'hand over' (6.41), but there may be a special nuance here. Terentianus particularly wants money (that is the theme of the whole letter), but what he gets instead are a needle and linen. The two clauses *acu ... mandauit* and *nullum ... dedit* stand in asyndeton (so Cugusi, *CEL* II. 170), with the first perhaps expressing a concession. The force is possibly 'he did, it is true, let me have/allow me a needle and linen' (something less desirable), but did not give me any money'. For *mando = permitto* see *TLL* VIII.262.41ff.

12 incebinde: the editors read and print *inc ebinde*, which is also accepted by Cugusi (*CEL*). Despite this agreement I do not believe that *ebinde* can be right and would emend to *ed inde*. How can *ebinde* be explained as a mistake for *abinde*? *Hinc et inde* is an idiomatic phrase, and *hinc abinde* has not as far as I am aware been paralleled. The confusion of *d* and *b* is easy. See Adams (1977a: 7 n. 5), Kramer (2007: 68).

12–13 collexi: the classical form of the perfect was *collēgi*, a long-vowel type that was undermined by developments in the vowel system: the present stem *collĭg-* and the perfect stem *collēg-* would eventually have been pronounced with the same vowel. The sigmatic perfect (as in *collexi*) was the one type of perfect that continued to be well represented in the Romance languages (see Väänänen 1981a: 143), and in Latin itself it encroached on other types. Note Caper, *GL* VII.94.14–16 *non est sorbo sed sorbeo, nec sorbsi sed sorbui. sic et* *absorbui non <u>absorbsi</u>, ut Lucanus* (4.100). *coactus non coctus dicendum. abscondi non <u>absconsi</u>.* Caper's example from Lucan shows that such encroachment was not confined to lower social dialects. The variability of the perfect forms of this root is brought out by the fact that the usual perfect of *intellego* is *intellexi* (see *TLL* VII.1.2096.68ff.) whereas *intellegi* is also attested in classical Latin, as at Lucr. 6.17 (see Munro 1886: II.352 ad loc., noting that the best manuscripts of Sallust have *intellegit* at Sall. *Jug.* 6.2). Again, the usual perfect of *neglego* was *neglexi*, but *neglegerit* is found in the fragmentary republican historian Licinius Macer, *FRH* II.27.F8a–b (see also Oakley's note, *FRH* III.425, citing Lebek 1970: 288). The form *lexerit* is quoted from *CIL* III.12484 by *TLL* VII.2.1123.33f. The form *collexi* is quite well attested in later Latin (*TLL* III.1606.17ff.), for example in the *Vetus Latina*. It is obvious that a consistent perfect form of *lego* and its compounds had not been achieved even in classical Latin, and occasional aberrant forms such as that here may simply reflect the variability from verb to verb and need not be connected with a general development in the language.

13 paucum aẹṣ (see also 10, 31): *paucus* is not used here in the usual classical manner as a count adjective in the plural ('few, a few'), but as a mass adjective in the singular ('a little', = *paruus*), a use surviving in Romance languages (e.g. It. *poco*, Fr. (*un*) *peu*). This usage is attested quite early (*OLD* s.v. 3, *TLL* X.1.804.45ff.), and there are hints that it was substandard. At *Rhet. Her.* 4.45 the phrase *pauco sermone* is described as exhibiting *abusio*. There are examples in two texts that show other departures from educated norms: *B. Afr.* 67.2 *magno inuento hordei . . . numero, pauco tritici*, Vitr. 1.1.6 *pauca manu infinitum numerum exercitus Persarum cum superauissent* (see also Adams 2005a: 87). By the second century *paucus* with singular terms indicating money seems to have been idiomatic (see *TLL* 804.65ff.), and Gellius twice has the same expression *aere pauco* (9.4.5, 20.1.31). See also below, 50.44.

On the spelling *aes*, see below, 26.2.

ed ibi aḍ: *ibi* seems to be the full form of the perfect tense of the verb 'go', *iui* for the classical *ii*, which was subject to contraction. In late non-literary texts there is a handful of such forms of the verb and its compounds (see Adams 2013: 117 for a collection, and see further below, 26.8–9, 27.2), but with *u* inserted rather than the *b* here (cf. Terent. *P. Mich.* VIII. 467.16 *et iui*, 471.34 *abiui*, 472.3 (Tiberianus) *exiuerim*, *O. Bu Njem* 67 *exiuimus*, *P. Amh.* II.26.5 *rediuit*); the insertion of the glide countered the contraction. On glide insertion see below, 33.7–8.

B for V is common in this corpus (Adams 1977a: 31); on the distribution of such spellings see Adams (2007: 626–66), id. (2013: 187–90).

14 et emi pauca que ẹspẹdiui: there are uncertainties about the last word here. I now believe (in contrast to what I said earlier, 1977a: 31) that the verb is probably *expedio* in the sense 'sort out' (financially) (see Cugusi 1992: II. 170 ad loc.; also Pighi 1964: 68–9, Lehmann 1988: 14 n. 3; contrast Kramer 2007: 69). The tense does not favour the interpretation of the verb as being *expeto* 'want' (an imperfect would have been expected), on which view we would have to assume voicing of the intervocalic *t*. The implication seems to be that he bought a few things and settled the bill (in full). The verb is attested in this financial sense (*TLL* V.1608.44ff., *OLD* s.v. *expedio* 3b). There are other, looser, parallels. In the Vindolanda tablets the near-equivalent verb *explico* (compare the primary meanings of *expedio* and *explico*, *OLD* s.vv. 1) is several times used of 'sorting out' financial matters (see 301.5, 343.4, and Bowman and Thomas 1994: 324 on the second passage). Note too the Greek letter of Terentianus, *P. Mich.* VIII.479.16, where there is a comparable verb (ἐκπλέκω) of unravelling one's affairs: ἀλ[[αλ]]λὰ [ο]ὔπω τὰ μετέωρά μου ἐξέπλεξα ἕως σή[με]ρον ('but until today I have not yet disposed of my affairs, which remain unsettled'). See too *P. Mich.* VIII.477.16, 37.

On the assimilation *ks > s(s)* see Adams (2013: 170–1).

14–15 se exiturum Alexandṛie: the verb of motion is accompanied by a locative rather than the accusative *Alexandriam*. The usage occurs with the same verb in a freedman's speech at Petron. 62.1 (*forte dominus Capuae exierat*). It is castigated by several grammarians: see Diomedes, *GL* I.455.27 *si interrogati quo pergamus respondeamus 'Romae' (fieri soloecismum)*, Pompeius, *GL* V.289.31 *quando … dicitur 'quo uadis?', et tu dicis 'Romae' soloecismus est*. There are parallels for the use of a static complement with verbs of motion from quite early (e.g. *intus* for *intro*; see also above, 9.16 on a use of *illi* in Turpilius), but the locative of the name of a town for the accusative is striking and must have been substandard. On this topic see Adams (2013: 332–7).

15 ṣịluị[t]: the restoration *siluit* inspires no confidence and the meaning of this sentence is therefore uncertain.

15–16 item nọn mi d[e]dit aes quam aureum matr[i] mee in [u]estimenta: here the first editors emended *quam* to *quamquam* and added *dedit* after *uestimenta*, a case of rewriting a slightly abnormal text. The construction can be paralleled (not least in Livy), and the text can stand. Strictly, after the negative *non* we might have expected *tam*, which would then be picked up by the correlative *quam*. For this (full) construction see e.g. Ter. *Eun.* 393 *non tam ipso quidem dono quam abs te datum esse* ('Not so much with the gift itself but with the fact that it comes from you', Barsby, Loeb). For the elliptical construction without *tam* see Livy 26.31.2 *sed non quid ego fecerim in disquisitionem uenit, quam quid isti pati debuerint* (also 5.15.9, 26.18.3; 35.49.7 is almost certainly corrupt); see too Kühner and Stegmann (1955: II.458), citing numerous examples and observing that these are often unnecessarily changed by editors. There is a case at Tac. *Ann.* 3.8.1 (*quem haud fratris interitu trucem quam remoto aemulo aequiorem sibi sperabat*), about which Woodman and Martin (1996: 122–3) express reservations, but without compelling reason. Ogilvie (1965: 377) on Livy 2.56.9 notes that the ellipse of *tam* after a negative in this construction in Livy is usually in direct speeches, and suggests that it might have been a colloquialism. Weissenborn (1856: 296) on the same passage remarks that *quam* comes close to the meaning of *sed*, as we have translated here.

16 inquid: cf. 22–3 *reliquid*. These spellings have nothing to do with the pronunciation of third person verb forms in general. Various monosyllables and other 'weak' grammatical words, including clitics (such as prepositions) and connectives, that ended in *-t/-d* were prone to have the final consonant assimilated in voice to the following vowel or consonant (see above, 14.6). *Ed dabo* at 33 in this letter has an assimilation of the final consonant to the following *d*. Once assimilated spellings came into being they were sometimes used in phonetic contexts in which they did not belong (contrast e.g. *P. Mich.* VIII.468.30 *ed praeterea*), and a spelling confusion set in between the original form and that which had arisen by assimilation. Terms affected include *apud/aput*, *sed/set* and *ad/at* (a confusion enhanced by the fact that there were two separate words distinguished thus) as well as *et/ed*. Another such pair was *quid/quit*, and that alternation has here influenced two verb forms ending in *-quit*. For bibliography see above, 14.6. For further examples from late Latin see Lundström (1948: 17). See also 6.28, 30, 14.6, and index, 'spellings, *t/d* in final position'.

17 pater tus: with the form *tus* = *tuus* cf. *sum* = *suum* at line 30. By contrast at 30 there is the usual form *suas*. Such contraction occurs when the vowel *u* would have been juxtaposed with a *ŭ* in the ending. The same phenomenon is to be seen also in the *Tablettes Albertini* (see below, 41.3 on *in perpetum* and also Adams 2013: 110–13).

mandauit: the meaning cannot be the same here as at line 11. The referent did not give Terentianus money as he gave an *aureus* to his mother. The only possible antecedent of *hoc* (16) in the context, if it is to be given a concrete sense, would be *aureum*, but that is masculine. *Hoc* must therefore refer to the content of the preceding sentence: this (i.e. not giving money) is what your father enjoined on me. It follows that here *mando* means 'instruct, give as a commission'. Cf. Plaut. *Epid.* 130–1 *quod mandasti <tu> mihi | impetratum est*, and particularly the contemporary text from Egypt, *O. Claud.* 135.4 *tu cura id quod tibi mandaui.*

    quo tempus: in late and medieval Latin there are cases of neuters of the third declension (e.g. *crimen, pignus, caput, nomen, lumen, latus, medicamen, mel*) used in the nominative/accusative form when an ablative is expected (usually with prepositions governing the ablative: see below). A possible instance of *tempus* so fossilised is at *Actus Petri cum Simone* 1 *Pauli tempus demorantis Romae et multos confirmantis in fide, contigit etiam quendam ... audire* ('at the time (= *tempore*) when Paul was living in Rome and strengthening many in the faith, it happened that a certain man heard'), though here *tempus* might just be taken as standing in an independent sentence with the copula omitted ('It was the time when ...'). Other examples of *tempus* for *tempore* in late texts may be found at Norberg (1943: 36). Similarly *nomen* is quite commonly used for *nomine* 'by name' in late Latin (for examples see Norberg 1944: 15–16, and also B. Löfstedt 1961: 242). For an example in this anthology see below, 47.11.

    Texts with third declension neuters used in the nominative/accusative form instead of the ablative include the *Compositiones Lucenses* (see Svennung 1941: 121) and the Oribasius translations (Mørland 1932: 107–8); see also in general B. Löfstedt (1961: 233–5) (with further bibliography), Havers (1928: 121). The use of a neuter form, open to the interpretation that it was accusative, with ablative-governing prepositions one might be tempted to put down to the tendency for the accusative to become the prepositional case (a phenomenon exemplified in this letter: see line 22), but there is more to it than that, not only because this syntactic development will not explain the present instance of *tempus* and those cited by Norberg above (or examples of *nomen* = *nomine*), but also because in some texts (e.g. the Oribasius translations: see Mørland 1932: 108) it is largely third declension neuters as distinct from nouns of other types that appear in the accusative instead of the ablative with prepositions. Sometimes too, as in the present case, where the noun has the nominative/accusative form, an adjective in agreement has the correct ablative form (for a few examples see some of the material cited by B. Löfstedt 1961: 234). Neuter nouns of the third declension were tending to become indeclinable, with the nominative/accusative used as a base form (see Mørland 1932: 108, and also Adams 2013: 429). See index, 'nouns, third declension neuters, fossilised ...'.

18 praefuerunt: 'were present', a meaning derived from the adjective *praesens* (Youtie and Winter 1951: 39, Adams 1977a: 82). The *OLD* s.v. *praesum* 3 cites along with our passage Titinius 146, but there is little context there and the meaning is not certain. See now *TLL* X.2.956.30ff., which does not include the passage of Titinius; the examples are imperial, from Tertullian onwards after Terentianus.

18–19 et lana; et matrem meam aute: this (minus the punctuation) is the text of the papyrus, but the second *et* has raised doubts. Youtie and Winter (1951: 40) translate thus, 'wool as well as linen (?)', thereby making the assumption that a word such as *linum* has been omitted after the second *et*. If on the other hand the text is accepted (see Cugusi, *CEL* II.171), we have a combination of connective (*et*) and (mild) adversative (*aute*), with *autem* the third element in the clause (counting *matrem meam* as a unit). As Cugusi points out, both *et autem* and *et . . . autem* are well attested from the earliest period, not infrequently following an earlier *et* (*TLL* II.1593.68ff.), and the text can therefore stand: cf. e.g. Tert. *Scorp.* 9.10 *qui se negauit Christianum, in Christo negauit, negando se esse in Christo, dum negat se Christianum; et Christum autem in se negando . . .* I have punctuated with a semi-colon after *lana*, with the *et* before it having the function defined at *TLL* V.2.873.81 as 'notio ante memorata accuratius definitur', and given there the equivalence 'et quidem' ('everything was to hand, and indeed the wool').

Autem is a conspicuous component of the style of Terentianus (eleven examples, four of them in a cluster within six lines at the opening of letter *P. Mich.* VIII.467 (4–9): 4, 6, 8, 9, 22, 468.12, 25, 34, 38, 472.17, 18; see also Adams 1977a: 59). Some of these are loosely adversative, but in other cases the particle does no more than tack on an afterthought. For example, at 467.2–3 (*an[te omn]ia op[to te] fortem et h[i]larem [e]t saluom mihi esse cum nostris omn[ibus], quoti[en]sque aute[m a t]ẹ habe[o no]uom mihi bene est*) Terentianus first says that he hopes Tiberianus is well, and then adds (with *autem*) 'whenever I get news from you, I am well'. Here *autem* is connective or explanatory. At 468.10–12 (*habes amicla par unu amictoriạ [pa]r unu sabana par unu saccos par unu ẹ[t] sṭṛ[a]glum lini[u]. emeram aute illuc con culcitam et pulbin[o]*) Terentianus tells the addressee that he will receive numerous items, including a pair of sacks and a linen bedspread. He then adds in a new sentence that he had bought that (the bedspread) along with a cushion and pillow. The addition is introduced by *autem*, but there is no adversative sense; the remark is an afterthought, attaching as it were the pillow and cushions to the associated bedspread.

There is another place in Terentianus (apart from that in our letter) where *autem* is in third place, at 468.34, *sollicitus sum autem*; here the enclitic verb *sum* has precedence, just as at 467.18 the auxiliary *habeo* forces *enim* into third place (*neminem habeo enim*). Terentianus seems to have been happy to place colourless auxiliary verbs before sentence-connecting particles.

The frequency of *autem* contrasts with the absence of *quidem* from the letters. The contrast probably reflects the state of the non-literary language at this time. Similarly in the contemporary Vindolanda tablets Bowman and Thomas list five examples of *autem* in the index to the second volume (1994), but none of *quidem*, and nine examples (three of them uncertain) of *autem* in the index to the third volume (2003), compared with one of *quidem*, in a fragmentary text the stylistic level of which is unclear. In Vitruvius there are 714 instances of *autem* but only nine of *quidem*. Contrast however Langslow (2006: 184 n. 12) on the frequency of *quidem* in the Latin version of Alexander Trallianus. See also below, 27.10.

The only other particle used with any frequency by Terentianus is *enim* (five times: 467.18, 470.11, 12, 18, 20). *Nam* never occurs. Similarly no examples of *nam* are listed by Bowman and Thomas (1994, 2003) at Vindolanda, whereas *enim* occurs fourteen times in the second volume and four times in the third. In Vitruvius *enim* outnumbers *nam* by 210:20. The particles cannot be treated as a single category at this period. Some were still current but others had been lost.

In the third-century Bu Njem ostraca there are no examples of *quidem*, *autem* or *enim*. None of the particles *quidem*, *autem*, *enim* or *nam* is reflected in the Romance languages, but they must have disappeared from use in stages.

19 praegnataṃ: there are several terms for 'pregnant' of this root in Latin, with variations of suffix. The earliest form seems to be *praegnas* (*TLL* X.2.659.78ff.), which is attested in the earliest manuscripts of writers from Plautus onwards. *Praegnans* is a later remodelling, facilitated by the loss of *n* before *s* and consequent availability of *ns* as more 'correct', and by the currency of the present participle ending *-ans*. This form according to *TLL* X.2.660.12ff. is found particularly in the earliest manuscripts of the *Vetus Latina*. *Praegnax* is a remodelling of *praegnas* with a familiar suffix (for the evidence see *TLL* 660.16ff.). *Praegnax* occurs at *CLE* 498.4 = *CIL* IX.3968 and is transmitted several times in the manuscripts of Varro *Rust.* (e.g. 2.4.7), but not accepted by editors. There are several late examples, as at *Mul. Chir.* 129 *equa praegnax*. Finally there is *praegnata*, which as well as here is also at *Mul. Chir.* 769 (see *TLL* 663.26ff.). Kramer (2007: 70) points out that *praegnata* is reflected in

Ibero-Romance. This form in turn generated a verb *praegno*, = 'make pregnant' (*TLL* 663.16f., 25f.).

nil poterat facere: an expression of hopelessness or helplessness used twice by Terentianus, with slightly different implications. Here the meaning is 'she could do nothing (to help)'. At 23 on the other hand (*soli nihil poteramus facere*) the sense is 'we could achieve nothing on our own'. A similar phrase is *omnia facere*, used twice by a bailiff at Sen. *Epist.* 12.1, 2 in response to Seneca's charge that he had been neglecting his country estate (see above, 17.1). The reply *omnia se facere* is also an expression of hopelessness: he was doing all in his power, but it was of no use.

The dependent infinitive here follows the governing verb, as is always the case in this letter (seven times; the problematic and textually uncertain construction in 14–15 is left aside).

dende: for Romance forms (e.g. Sp., OPg. *dende*) with this or a similar graphic form see *REW* 2525. Etymologically the word contains $\bar{e}$ + $\breve{\imath}$, but *dein-* is regularly scanned as a single syllable in classical Latin (see *OLD* s.v. *deinde*), as is *dein-* in *deinceps*. This scansion is traditionally put down to 'synizesis' (see *OLD*), the phonetics of which tend not to be addressed. The Spanish and Portuguese reflexes above (now obsolete) must derive from a form with the ordinary CL $\bar{e}$ in the first syllable; had the base of the Romance terms had CL $\breve{e}$ in the first syllable, that vowel would have undergone spontaneous diphthongisation (even in a closed syllable in Spanish), producing the non-attested form **diende* (information from Adam Ledgeway). Similarly the late Latin compound *deintro* is reflected as *dentro* in Spanish, where the first *e* can only continue $\bar{e}$; otherwise there would have been diphthongisation (**dientro*). Presumably Terentianus' spelling represents a form with CL $\bar{e}$ in the first syllable, the proto-Romance form. For the coalescence of a long vowel (of a prefix) + short vowel (of the root) into a long vowel with the quality of the first cf. *cogo* < **cō-ăgo*. It remains unclear in what way (or ways) the term was pronounced in the early period; for the scansion *dĕīnde* in Terence see Questa (2007: 439).

19–20 pos paucos dies: the spelling *pos* represents not a general loss of final *-t* but a reduction of the threefold consonant cluster across the word boundary, and the pronunciation that it reflects must have been standard, to judge from Cicero's remark that he would prefer to say *posmeridianas* rather than *postmeridianas* (*Orat.* 157 *et posmeridianas quadrigas quam postmeridianas <quadriiugas> lubentius dixerim*). For a full account of the form *pos* see now *TLL* X.2.156.60ff. The majority of attestations are before a word beginning with a consonant, particularly *t* (156.70ff.); for the rare instances before a vowel see 157.38ff. See also Adams (2013: 153, 156).

20 parit: it is simplest to take this as a historic present rather than some sort of remodelling of the CL reduplicated perfect *peperit* (despite Adams 1977a: 52). Historic presents throughout Latin constantly alternate with past tense verbs. There does seem to be a remodelled form at Audollent (1904), no. 268.2 *peri(t)* = *peperit* (Jeanneret 1918: 55–6).

21 Ptolemes: represents the Greek form Πτολεμές = Πτολεμαῖς rather than Πτολεμαῖος: see Gignac (1981: 26), Kramer (2007: 71).
   sopera: on this form, with a late anaptyxis, see Kramer (2007: 71).

21–2 et factum est illi uenire Alexandrie: for *factum est* + (dative) and infinitive see *TLL* VI.1.101.79ff., Adams (1977a: 63). It is quoted first from the *Vetus Latina* and may reflect Greek influence. An example in the Vulgate at Act 16.16 corresponds to *contigit* in an Old Latin version (cod. *d*) and to ἐγένετο in the Greek (see *TLL* loc. cit.), and that reveals the meaning of the construction ('it happened to him to' = 'he happened to'). In a Greek letter on papyrus there is an example of ἐγένετο with the same construction: *P. Mich.* VIII.503.2–3 καταπλέοντί μοι ε[ἰ]ς Ἀλεξανδρίαν διὰ σπουδῆς ἐγέ[ν]ετο γενέσθαι εἰς τὸ καταγώγιον. There are no grounds for attempting to impose on an established use of *factum est* a causative interpretation ('it was made to him to' > 'he was made to'), given that the attested use fits the context well. On *factum est* + infinitive see also Kramer (2007: 71).

22 con tirones: an unambiguous instance of *cum* + accusative; possible examples such as *con culcitam* (468.12) and *con fratrem* (470.10) are open to the alternative explanation that the *-m* has been mechanically added where it does not belong, as in *factam* at 27 (see Adams 1977a: 36–7 for the evidence from the letters). There was a tendency for the accusative to oust the ablative with prepositions in non-standard usage, a tendency which by many was resisted. Unambiguous cases of the accusative with prepositions normally governing the ablative are also found in Pompeian graffiti (Väänänen 1966: 120–1). On the (late) spelling of *con* see Kramer (2007: 71).

24 absentia illim aḅit[u]ri. [m]ạter mea: this is how the line is printed by Cugusi and Kramer. Youtie and Winter add *illius* after *absentia*, and also a verb of saying (*dicit*) after *mea*.
   Illim has the same ending as *istim, utrim-que, in-de, illin-c, hin-c, interim* (see Walde and Hofmann 1938–54: I.692, Leumann 1977: 482). The reinforced

form *illinc* (with *c(e)*) was better established and longer-lived than *illim*, which had a shadowy existence: from the literary attestations we would conclude that it did not last beyond Cicero. It is found in Plautus and Terence, Pomponius, once in Lucretius (3.881), and occasionally in Cicero, in letters but not only there: there are a few instances in speeches and the philosophica. An instance at *Phil.* 2.77 (an emendation generally accepted) is in a love letter attributed to Antony and quoted indirectly. The example in Terentianus shows that the form had lived on far beyond the classical period in ordinary usage. Here is another pronominal/adverbial form that was fading from the educated language by the late Republic but maintained an existence in speech after that (see above, 9.10, 9.16 with cross references, and also Adams 2013: 454–9 on forms of *ille* reinforced by *-c(e)*).

Absentia can be used absolutely (see Kramer 2007: 72), and there is no need for the addition of *illius*. We might translate 'without (him)', and thus semantically *absentia* is a precursor of It. *senza* 'without' (see Kramer 2007: 72).

[m]ater mea: 'spẹc[t]ẹmus illum': ellipse of a verb of saying with quoted speech is common in all varieties of the language: cf. e.g. Virg. *Aen.* 1.37 *cum Iuno aeternum seruans sub pectore uulnus | haec secum* (sc. *locuta est*), Hor. *Sat.* 1.5.56–8 *prior Sarmentus: 'equi te | esse feri similem duco.' ridemus, et ipse | Messius 'accipio', caput et mouet.* See e.g. Heidemann (1893: 73–8), E. Löfstedt (1956: II.244–6), Hofmann and Szantyr (1965: 424).

Spectemus has the meaning of *exspectemus*. It is not a simplex pro composito but reflects an assimilation of the initial consonant cluster (*eksp* > *esp*) and then aphaeresis of the *e* before *s* + consonant (Adams 1977a: 21, Kramer 2007: 72).

25–6 et uen[i]o tequm Alexandriẹ ẹt deduco te usque ad naue: present tenses where a future might have been possible, on which usage see Adams (2013: 666–72, with bibliography). It is usually a first person singular, as here, that is used thus (but see Adams 2013: 670 for some different examples). In the letters of Terentianus there are about a dozen future tense finite verbs (one or two periphrastic, comprising *-urus* + *est*), only two of which are in the first person singular (both in this letter: 10 *ibo*, 33 *dabo*; on the context of the latter see Adams 2013: 669). See further Adams (1977a: 49).

Tequm has *q* written before *u*, which is old orthography. As part of the same spelling system the scribes sometimes too write *k* before *a* (see above, 21.14 and Adams 1977a: 32–3). Consistency was not achieved. In this letter we have *pạuqum* at 31 but *paucum* at 13 (see further Halla-aho 2003). Note too *qurauit* at 29.

27 illa die: on the gender of *dies* in late low-register texts (predominantly feminine), see E. Löfstedt (1911: 192–5). In early Latin there had been a semantic distinction between the masculine and feminine, but that did not last (see Adams 2013: 393, with bibliography). In this same letter Terentianus also has the masculine (20 *pos paucos dies*), possibly because this was an old and formulaic phrase (see *TLL* V.1.1042.64ff.).

quạndo tam magna lites factam est: on temporal *quando*, which (unlike *cum*) survived widely in the Romance languages (*REW* 6932) but in the classical period is restricted in use, with substandard, archaic and also regional associations, see Adams (2007: 158–60).

On *tam magnus* as a replacement of *tantus* see Adams (2007: 344–7), with details of its distribution in literary texts. It survives in Ibero-Romance but cannot convincingly in the Latin period be treated as a regionalism. Many of the literary examples are contextually determined (e.g. when *tam magnus* is coordinated with another adjective modified by *tam*), but that is not always the case; Tacitus, for example, has four instances, three in the minor works and the other in a speech in the *Annals*, which cannot be so explained. The phrase was an occasional variant for *tantus*.

Lites (for *lis*) is nominative singular; on monosyllabic nominatives of imparisyllabic nouns modified (for the most part in non-standard texts) to bring them into line with the syllabic structure of the oblique cases see on *lacte* (18.21), and also below, 33.10 on various modifications to *sanguis*; also Adams (1977a: 42–3). *Litis* is possibly nominative singular at *CLE* 543.3 (see *TLL* VII.2.1496.41ff.). Here the *e* may represent a vocalic misspelling (for *ĭ*), or the term might have been given the nominative form of terms such as *gurges*, *poples*, *fomes* (for which type see Leumann 1977: 372–3). *Factam* has a hypercorrect final *-m*.

28 ueni interpone te: for the reflexive use of *interpono* = 'take a hand, intervene' see *OLD* s.v. 9a (classical), but taking the infinitive *aiutare* as going with *interpone te*; it is dependent on *(si) potes*. For the asyndeton of two imperative verbs see index, 'asyndeton bimembre, of imperative verbs'.

aiutare Ptolemaeo: for the frequentative and its construction with the dative see 6.29. On the various misspellings of the term, including that here, and their significance, see Adams (2013: 121–2).

29 non magis qurauit me pro xylesphongium: two constructions have been conflated here, *non magis curauit me quam xylesphongium* and *habuit me pro xylesphongio* (Adams 1977a: 60). ξυλοσπόγγιον was a sponge on a stick for cleaning the private parts. Transferred into Latin the term can be called a popular borrowing. The *OLD* cites just one other (epigraphic) example. On the form here, with *e* for *o* as the linking vowel, see Adams (1977a: 8). The aspiration of the stop (*ph* for *p*) is a type of spelling found in Greek papyri

(Gignac 1976: 87–8). Gignac (1976: 86) interprets such evidence as indicating that aspirated stops tended to lose their aspiration in various positions in spoken Greek.

30 sed sum negotium et circa res suas: *sum negotium* is object of *qurauit* in the previous line. Terentianus then changes construction and complements the same verb (understood) with the prepositional phrase *circa res suas*. The change of construction is understandable because *curo* could vary its construction according to meaning. It usually has an accusative, with meanings such as 'watch over, look after, care for' (*OLD* s.v. 1), but with the meaning 'regard with anxiety, worry or care about' (*OLD* 8) it may in classical Latin have a dative, or, significantly for the present passage, be complemented by *de* (*OLD* 8b). *Circa* is a variant for *de* (for *circa = de* see *TLL* III.1092.79ff.). Hence 'he looked after his own business and worried about his own affairs'.

For *sum = suum* cf. *tus = tuus* earlier in the letter (17).

31 exiendo dico illi: I have elsewhere (1977a: 54, 2003a: 745) suggested that, since earlier in the letter Saturninus was the one 'going out' (*exire*), so here *exiendo* must allude to him. Since the *illi* that comes two words later certainly refers to Saturninus, therefore *exiendo* would on this argument be some sort of dative form in agreement with *illi*. But it is inexplicable as a dative form, and I now accept Cugusi's argument (*CEL* II.175) that the word order is also against taking *exiendo* as agreeing with *illi*, from which it is separated. *Exiendo* must be a non-standard alternative form to the ablative of the gerund *exeundo*, used as an equivalent of the present participle and referring to Terentianus himself, meaning 'astonished, taking my leave I say to him . . .' B. Löfstedt (1983: 460) also takes the form in this way. For the ablative of the gerund used thus (the forerunner of the Romance present participle) see Adams (2013: 734 and the whole of the chapter). *Exeo* is often used of going forth on long distance travel (see lines 14–15), but it could also be used of merely leaving a place such as a house or taking one's leave from someone (e.g. Plaut. *Epid.* 650).

32–3 negabit se abiturum: has the phonetic spelling error here (*negabit* for *negauit*) triggered a mechanical lapse into a future infinitive where a present infinitive (*habere*) might have been expected (see Adams 1977a: 48–9, following Youtie and Winter 1951: 40)? B. Löfstedt (1983: 460) on the other hand cites Svennung (1935: 430) on the occasional use of the future participle for the present, i.e. *amaturus = amans*. This explanation is not convincing, because *nego* needs an infinitive complement, not a participial. *Abiturum* represents *habiturum esse* and could hardly in this text be replaced by *habentem esse = habere*.

An alternative is to take *se* as a mistake for *me* ('he said that I would not have it'). Finally, we might take the future infinitive at face value ('he said that he would not have any', i.e. while he was here). The point, on this last interpretation, given that there is a promise of money in the next few words if Terentianus comes to Alexandria, might be that he would not have money to give until he was in Alexandria. This final interpretation seems now the simplest to me.

33 dicet: present not future, with the misspelling *e* for *ĭ*, which, we have seen, is common in non-literary documents of the early imperial period in the final syllable of verb forms (see 16.1 with bibliography, and index, 'spellings, *e* for short *i* in verb endings'). There are four such verb forms in this corpus (see Adams 2013: 51–2).

34 mater ma nos assem uendedi lentiamina: I print here (like Cugusi and Kramer) the transmitted text, which is not however meaningful.

The editors proposed *no<n haben>s assem uendedi<t>*, which at least has the merit of making some sense. From *ueni* in the previous line we might translate: 'come, he says, to Alexandria, and I will give it to you (i.e. the money you are asking for). I didn't go off. My mother, not having an *as*, sold some linens so that I can come to Alexandria.' The difficulty with this interpretation is that *habens* is not convincing, and the insertion requires a further change, to *uendedi<t>*. Present participles are very rare in the corpus (see Adams 1977a: 53–4), and there is no certain case in agreement with the subject of a verb (*pergentes* at *P. Mich.* VIII. 470.21 has no clear context). It is awkward to introduce such a participle by emendation.

Pighi (1964: 72) takes the preceding *abiui* in line 34 to stand for *habui*. But the verb-form in *-iui* (of an *eo*-verb) is typical of this corpus and of other non-literary texts (see on *ibi* at line 13 above), and a verb of this meaning suits the context. The other person is reported as having said 'come to Alexandria', but Terentianus reveals that he 'did not go'. Pighi then suggests that *abiui* = *habui* has a double subject in asyndeton, *mater ma* + *nos*. The asyndeton is implausible, and the violations of agreement serious. An initial verb may sometimes not match in number a following subject, but here as well there would be a mismatch of person, in that the first person singular verb is followed immediately by a noun that would require a third person singular verb. Moreover, even if one took *nos* implausibly to be the 'primary' subject (despite its position after *mater ma*), it would not agree in number with the verb. This is a far-fetched interpretation that can be rejected.

Another suggestion (see Cugusi, *CEL* II, 175, who lists possibilities) is that *mater ma* introduces (as earlier in the letter) direct speech, with ellipse of the verb of saying. *Nos* thus becomes subject of *uendedi* (implausible), *assem* has to be taken as an accusative of price or the like, and the 'mother', as distinct from Terentianus, becomes the one who is to go off to Alexandria (cf. 25, where she raises the possibility of going with Terentianus). The sense would thus supposedly be 'we [sic] have sold the linen garments for an *as* so that I can come to Alexandria'.

There is an additional difficulty with this interpretation, which concerns the use of *as*. The letter turns on Terentianus' failure to secure money from someone, and throws some light on monetary terminology. The letter as extant opens (10) with Terentianus demanding a 'little bit of money' from someone. The phrase *aes paucum* recurs in an identical demand at 31 (*da m[i] pauqum aes*), and also earlier in the letter where Terentianus reveals that he has collected a little money (12–13 *collexi paucum aes*). There is yet another instance of *aes*, without *paucum*, at 15: *item non mi d[e]dit aes quam aureum matr[i] mee*. There is no doubt that *aes* in these contexts (particularly in conjunction with *paucum* 'a little') is a collective term for 'money, cash', as distinct from denoting a specific type of bronze or copper coinage. Though *aes* originally meant 'copper or bronze money', and thence a 'copper or bronze coin' (see *OLD* s.v. 2), this general meaning is very well attested (*OLD* s.v. 3), and, as Ulpian remarks, *aes* could even be used to embrace gold coins (*Dig.* 50.16.159 *etiam aureos nummos 'aes' dicimus*). Indeed at 15, quoted above, *aes* 'money' might be taken to include gold coin (= 'he gave my mother gold coin, but he did not give me any money').

In addition to these four instances of *aes* there are two cases of *as*, and one of these suggests a distinction between the two words. The first is at 11: *acu lentiaminaque mi mandauit; nullum assem mi dedit*. Terentianus complains that he has been given a needle and linen cloth, but not a single *as*. A common use of *as* is to indicate a 'penny, regarded as a coin of small value, a copper' (*OLD* s.v. 2). In this sense *as* may be accompanied by *unus* (note *OLD* s.v. 2b, '*unius assis aestimare*, to care as little as a halfpenny for, regard as worthless', and see Catull. 5.3 *rumores ... senum ... omnes unius aestimemus assis*). The example in Terentianus is suggestive of *unus as*, negated, = 'he gave me not a single penny'. This sense of *as* suits the context perfectly, and sets up a distinction of meaning in the letter between *as* and *aes*: it would be implausible to suggest that in a single letter Terentianus used one word four times and the other twice without making a distinction between them.

I return to line 35. It would hardly have helped Terentianus or his 'mother' to get to Alexandria if one or both of them sold some material for a mere *as*. The presence of *nullum* with *assem* in the earlier passage suggests to me that *nos* conceals the negative *non*, but for the reasons given above we need a solution which does not entail the insertion of a present participle such as *habens*. I propose the following text and punctuation: *ego non abiui. mater ma no<n> assem. uendedi lentiamina [ut] ueniam Alexandrie* ('I did not go. My 'mother' (had) not an *as*. I sold linen garments to be able to come to Alexandria'). I am suggesting an ellipse of a verb such as *habuit*. For ellipse of *habeo* in the letters of Cicero, see the material assembled by Heidemann (1893: 86–7): e.g. *Fam.* 16.18.3 *sed tu nullosne tecum libellos?* ('But have you no books with you?', Shackleton Bailey, Loeb). Verbal ellipse is very common (as Heidemann's dissertation brings out; see also Kühner and Stegmann 1955: II.551–4, Hofmann and Szantyr 1965: 423–4), and there is indeed another example in this same letter, as we saw, where again *mater mea* is subject (24: verb of saying implied). Note in the passage of Cicero just cited the negative *nullos*. Verbal ellipse is often facilitated by the presence of an adverb, as it would be here by a negative (see Kühner and Stegmann 1955: II.551).

The advantage of this interpretation is that it does not require the change of *uendedi* to *uendedit*. It also makes sense in the context that it should have been Terentianus who sold the *linteamina*, as we have already been told that he was given them (11). One must assume an error by a scribe in writing *nos* for *non*. It is possible that Terentianus said *no* for *non*, and that the scribe falsely interpreted his intention. *No* is not uncommon in inscriptions (see the examples collected by Diehl 1910: 159; also Jeanneret 1918: 63), and is reflected in some Romance languages (see Väänänen 1981a: 67).

I mention an interpretation favoured by Cugusi (1992: II. 175): *mater ma nos [= nobis] assem uendedi(t) lentiamina* ('my mother sold for us linen cloths for an *as*'). Quite apart from the unsatisfactory sense of *assem* in a positive sentence of this type, *nos* for *nobis* fails to convince. Cugusi cites *Appendix Probi* 220–1 (on *noscum* and *uoscum* for *nobiscum* and *uobiscum*), but these are not true parallels because the accusative rather than the ablative has been used as the case selected by the preposition *cum*, a common phenomenon. It would be a different matter entirely to propose that the passage contained an unmotivated use of the accusative for the dative of a pronoun. Pronominal indirect objects are used correctly in the letters, as in subliterary Latin in general.

Kramer (2007: 74) offers an interpretation along the same lines, in that *nos* is taken to be equivalent to *nobis* and *assem* to be used instead of an expected ablative: *mater m<e>a <dixit>: 'no<bi>s asse{m} uend<i>di l<i>nt<e>amina'*, translating 'Meine Mutter sagte: Uns habe ich für einen Pfennig die Leinentücher verkauft.'

Lehmann (1988) follows the editors Youtie and Winter, but he does remark pertinently (15 n. 7) that Pighi 'tries to save *nos*, but with severe harm to the syntax'.

See also Strassi (2008: 34 n. 62) for a brief note listing these various possibilities.

Conclusions

The letters of Terentianus are quite early for non-literary documents. Terentianus is of much the same date as Tacitus. Although his Latin is a world apart from that of the historian, it is interesting to note the odd correspondence.

This letter is dramatically written and quotes conversations verbatim, and is by definition colloquial in tone. Various features of the Latin and the evidence that the letter presents about the state of the language are worth listing.

We have a limited ability to date spoken developments, and virtually any new non-literary text will suggest the redating of some phenomena. The fossilised use of *tempus* and the form *praegnata* occur here centuries before other attestations. On the other hand the adverb *illim* clearly lived on longer in speech than might have been deduced from the literary evidence.

The letter contains usages inadmissible in educated writing at this time and indeed for centuries beyond, namely the directional use of the locative *Alexandrie*, the form *exiendo* and the accusative expression *con tirones*. This use of the locative, and also *adiuto* + dative, can be paralleled in freedmen's speeches in the *Cena Trimalchionis*, and it becomes certain that in such cases Terentianus was drawing on real language of a type stigmatised by the educated classes.

On the other hand not all non-standard variables are excluded from educated usage, and there are some cases in point here. The elliptical expression *non ... quam* for *non tam ... quam* may be unusual in the literary language, but it does occur, and indeed in Tacitus. The sigmatic perfect form *collexi* is not the educated norm, but there was some variability between long-vowel and sigmatic perfect forms of *lego* and its compounds even in the literary language. The 'mass' use of *paucus* (= *paruus*) was castigated in the late Republic but by the second century must have risen in status, because it is admitted by Gellius in the same expression as that used by Terentianus.

Terentianus' use of particles is of interest. The fact that he uses *autem* freely but not others suggests that it was still widely current, and that we should not speak of a disappearance en bloc of particles from lower-class speech at this period.

Finally, there is a possible Grecism in the letter, the use of *factum est* with dative and infinitive.

23

LETTER FROM MONS CLAUDIANUS (EGYPT), OF THE SECOND CENTURY (*O. CLAVD.* 367)

Introduction

For the text see Van Rengen (1997: 209). Mons Claudianus was the site of Roman quarries in the desert about 140 km NE of Qena in the Nile valley (see Bingen *et al.* 1992: 8 for a map). Large numbers of ostraca mainly in Greek have been found there. 366, in Greek, is apparently by the same person to the same addressee as the Latin text printed below (see Van Rengen 1997: 207). The writer is Teres, *curator* of Raima, and the recipient Anius Rogatus, *duplicarius.* The Latin is better written than the Greek, and Van Rengen suggests (209) that, if the writers of the two letters are the same person, 'le latin est sa langue maternelle'. There are parallels between the Latin and the Greek. Corresponding to the comparative *celerius* (with a verb of sending) the Greek has ταχύτερον, also with a verb of sending (see below). The Greek has two ἵνα constructions and the Latin two *ut* (on the extension of ἵνα clauses in later Greek possibly under the influence of Latin *ut* see Horrocks 2010: 129). Corresponding to *rogo te* is ἐρωτῶ σε. For a discussion of mundane practical bilingualism at Mons Claudianus, and of the language choice in this pair of letters, see Adams (2003a: 590–2). The letter is fragmentary but is still of some interest, not least because communication between Teres and Anius was in both languages on similar subjects.

Text

Anio Rogat[o] Ter[es]
curator *vac.* salu[tem].
rogo te, dominc,
misi tibi per tabe-
llarium st[. . .]   5
ut clauem . . l[. . .]
.eas in co[. . .]r[.]
ut celerius mihi

remittas · Ani, o-
mnia clauem b-   10
onam. opto te be-
ne ualere et
felicem esse.

Translation

Teres the *curator* to Anius Rogatus, greetings. I ask you, Lord – I sent you by
a *tabellarius* . . . so that a key – that you quickly send me back, Anius, a key
good in every respect. I hope that you are well and happy.

Commentary

3 rogo te: the clause dependent on this formula does not come until line 8
(*ut celerius mihi* . . .). Teres has inserted an explanatory afterthought before the
ut-clause. Halla-aho (2009: 56) points out that *rogo* is by far the most frequent
verb in Latin non-literary letters, which, as she says, is natural, given that such
letters were written to take care of practical matters, though from the point of
view of lexical history it is significant that the typical verb is *rogo* and not one of
its synonyms, *oro* and *peto*. The three constructions found with *rogo* in letters,
ut + subjunctive, plain subjunctive, and imperative, vary in their relative
frequency from corpus to corpus (for some details see Adams 1995a: 117,
Halla-aho 2009: 82–3). In his Greek letter Teres uses the equivalent verb with
the aorist imperative of the verb of sending (366.11 ἐρωτῶ σε πέμσον).
The greater the distance between *rogo* and the dependent clause, the greater
the likelihood that *ut* rather than the plain subjunctive would be used (Halla-
aho 2010: 246). For a particularly long separation (with a parenthetical clause
one of the separating elements, as here) see Plin. *Epist.* 6.12.5.

4–6 misi tibi per tabellarium . . . ut clauem: there are gaps in the text but the
initial verb of sending is clearly picked up by a purpose clause introduced by *ut*.
The phraseology in the Greek at one point is very similar, with an equivalent
initial verb phrase and a correspondent to the *ut*-clause (and also the same
Latin noun *tabellarius*, though as direct object of the verb): 366.7–8 ἔπεμσά σοι
τὸν ταβελάρειν εἶνα πέμσεις ὄνον.

8–9 ut celerius mihi remittas: this clause is dependent on *rogo te* at 3 (see
above). Of note is the comparative adverb *celerius* where the positive *celeriter*
would have been possible. Again the Greek has the same construction, with
a verb of much the same meaning: 366.9 ταχύτερον ο<ὖ>ν αὐτὸν πέμσον.

Celerius seems to have been widely current for *celeriter*, particularly in informal Latin (on the type of comparative see Hofmann and Szantyr 1965: 168–9; also *TLL* III.753.39ff. for examples 'sensu positivo pro celeriter'; see too Adams 1977a: 58, above, 11.21 for a comparable comparative, and below, 26.9–10 on *sepius*). *Celerius* is well represented in non-literary Latin letters. In the archive of Terentianus it is found three times in the letter of Tiberianus (*P. Mich.* VIII.472.4, 10, 3); *celeriter* does not occur in the archive. Terentianus does however have ταχύτερον in one of his Greek letters (479.13). Rustius Barbarus from Wâdi Fawâkhir uses *celerius* in an almost identical context to that in the present letter: *O. Faw.* 2.15–17 *rogo te ut . . . [mi]ttas mi celerius* (for this letter see below, 26). We also saw *celerius* earlier with the verb 'send' in a letter from the Myos Hormos road (20.6). There had been convergence of popular Greek and Latin in the preference for the comparative form of adverbs with this meaning. There is an instance in speech at Sen. *Apoc.* 13.2 (*'celerius' inquit Mercurius 'et uenire nos nuntia'*), the idiomatic character of which is seen in the ellipse of the verb of going. Also, in the bilingual school exercise *Colloquium Celtis* (see Dickey 2015) note 55a *explica te celerius*/ἔκπλεξόν σε ταχύτερον and 70e *surge celerius*/ἀνίστασον ταχ<ύ>τερον. Note too line 17 of the poem of Iasucthan from Bu Njem (Adams 1999: 112).

For a comparable comparative use see e.g. Plaut. *Curc.* 276 *exi exi exi, inquam, ocius.*

10–11 omnia clauem bonam: this adverbial use of *omnia* may look like a Grecism but is not necessarily so by this date. The same use of *omnia* occurs in Virgil, where it is indeed modelled on πάντα: *Aen.* 4.558 *omnia Mercurio similis* (cf. Hom. *Il.* 23.66 πάντ᾽ αὐτῷ μέγεθός τε καὶ ὄμματα κάλ᾽ εἰκυῖα). It was largely avoided by imperial poets, but picked up by late prose, where Greek need not still have been the model. There is an example in one of the bronze tablets of Vipasca (Portugal), which can hardly be explained as a Grecism: I.3.1 (Domergue 1983: 51) *conductor balinei sociusue omnia sua impensa balineum . . . calfacere . . . debeto* ('the contractor in charge of the bath or his associate must warm the bath entirely at his own expense'). See too text no. 5 (*defixio* from Mainz) in Blänsdorf (2010a: 170) *quidquid conabitur, quidquid aget, omnia illi inuersum sit*; later, *omnia interuersum surgat*. The subject of *sit* is an understood neuter singular such as *id*, resuming *quidquid*, with *omnia* adverbial, 'let it go completely wrong', though this is the sort of context that might have contributed to the fossilisation of *omnia* as a singular (cf. *Comp. Luc.* S 21 *quod uos legitis, nos omnia probatum habemus*, and also Norberg 1944: 55–6). Incidentally the passages cited from Plautus and Petronius by Blänsdorf (2010a: 171) are not parallels for the wording of the *defixio*. A few apparent examples of *omnia* in the earlier period are better explained as internal accusatives (*TLL* IX.2.623.57ff.). See further Wölfflin (1885: 95–8), citing numerous late instances.

11–13 opto te bene ualere et felicem esse: for the wish of *felicitas* cf. *Tab. Vindol.* 645.ii.19 *opto sis felicissimus* (cf. 641.ii.8), *P. Oxy.* I.32.28 *estote felicissi[mi]*, and note the letter of Augustus *ap.* Suet. *Tib.* 21.4 *uale, iucundissime Tiberi, et feliciter rem gere.* See also Cugusi (1983: 63 with n. 94), and above, 12 Conclusions.

Conclusions

The Latin writing of Teres appears to be competent and correct. The interest of the letter lies in the evidence it provides for language use in a remote part of the Roman Empire in the army. It is unclear what determined the choice of language on a particular occasion (see Adams 2003a: 591–2 for various possible factors), but on the face of it Teres has used both languages indifferently to the same addressee. He falls into the same formulae and phraseology in the two languages, and we referred above to an element of 'convergence'. For this term see above on 20.3 (*recte facies*). In such communities formulae were readily taken over from one language to the other (see also above, 13.16 for a Latin formulation transferred into Greek). There was a mundane practical bilingualism in operation.

24

ANOTHER LETTER FROM THE MYOS HORMOS ROAD (EGYPT), OF THE PERIOD OF HADRIAN (CUVIGNY 2003: II.405, M1107)

Introduction

On Myos Hormos and the Roman road into the desert see the Introduction to text 20.

Text

Aelius Caluentius *vac.* Festo *vac.* suo

                              salutem

cámellos quattuor misi at te. tu cura ut

quam primum aquae onerentur et one-

ratos expelle eos ut hora frugda per   5

noctem reuertantur. eosdem camel-

los iube adaquentur et r[eue-?]

niant. bene ualere

te opto

uale.

Translation

Aelius Calventius to his friend Festus, greetings. I have sent you four camels. See that as soon as possible they are loaded with water and when they are loaded dispatch them so that they return during the night at the cold time. Give orders that those same camels are watered and let them come back. I hope that you are well. Farewell.

Commentary

3 at te: the familiar assimilation of final -*d* in a monosyllable to the following consonant (see Quintilian 1.7.5, who shows himself indifferent to the distinction between *ad* and *at*, which suggests that he probably saw such assimilations as inevitable in speech (of the educated): see Colson 1924: 93, Adams 2013: 158–9, 192). See above, 14.6, 22.16, and index, 'spellings, *t/d* in final position'.

4 quam primum: classical = 'as soon as possible' (*OLD* s.v. *primum* 4b).

aquae onerentur: camels (rather than *aquae*, plural) are the subject of this verb, as is shown by *oneratos* ('let them be loaded, and when they are loaded . . .'). This means that *onerentur* is complemented by a genitive singular, *aquae*. Verbs of filling and the like (cf. *plenus*) may be complemented by an ablative ('fill with') or partitive genitive; for a pot 'loaded with' (genitive) gold see Plaut. *Aul.* 611 *aulam onustam auri*. However, with *onerare* the ablative is overwhelmingly preferred. At *TLL* IX.2.635.32 just one example of a genitive construction is cited, from early tragedy (Pacuv. 291 *postquam est oneratus frugum et floris Liberi*) (see Schierl 2006: 463 on fr. 227 in her numeration). It is easy to appeal to the analogy of *plenus* in explaining the Pacuvian usage, since in early Latin *plenus* is construed mainly with the genitive (see Schierl), but centuries later in an informal letter written in the Egyptian desert the genitive complement looks remarkably artificial and stylised, particularly since the form of the verb belongs to the infectum and is not participial. The writer seems to have been a stylist with old-fashioned tastes.

4–5 onerentur et oneratos expelle eos: the 'participial resumption' seen here has good literary credentials both in prose (from early Latin onwards) and verse: see the detailed account of Wills (1996: 311–25). For such resumption in an extreme form see Scipio Aemilianus Africanus minor, *ORF* 21.33: *ui atque ingratis coactus cum illo sponsionem feci, facta sponsione ad iudicem adduxi, adductum primo coetu damnaui, damnatum ex uoluntate dimisi.*

5 expelle: in this context it would seem difficult at first sight to give the verb the meaning 'expel', with an implication of banishing, rejecting. One possibility is that the verb has the sort of weakened sense (e.g. 'send forth') that E. Löfstedt (1911: 267) attempted to find for it (without success) (cf. *TLL* V.2.1638.58ff.; again the few examples are not striking). Alternatively the idea might be 'drive them off/forth' (see *OLD* s.v. 4, of driving cattle out, for example to graze), with the implication that they will use their homing instinct and return to base.

hora frugda: *hora* cannot have its precise meaning 'hour' here, but is used loosely of time, *tempus*. For this loose use see *TLL* VI.2.2962.55ff. (occasional examples from the classical period onwards), Adams (1995a: 578–9).

The misspelling in *frugda* (with *u* for *ī*) is abnormal and seems inexplicable in accordance with any linguistic development.

6–7 eosdem camellos iube adaquentur: *eosdem camellos* is a striking proleptic accusative. The camels are not the ones receiving the orders, and *camellos* cannot be construed as closely dependent on *iube*. So in this construction in early Latin the 'governing verb is frequently one which cannot alone take the accusative in the sense demanded by the context' (Bennett 1910–14: II.222–3). Thus at Plaut. *Bacch.* 555 (*dic modo hominem qui sit*, 'tell me who he is') *hominem* cannot be construed as object of *dic*; logically one might have expected it to be in the nominative, as predicate with *qui sit*. At Cato *Agr.* 31.1 (*uectes iligneos, acrufolios, laureos, ulmeos facito uti sient parati*) the addressee is not instructed to 'make levers', but to see that they are prepared, and logically a nominative *uectes ilignei* as subject of *sient parati* would have been correct. The proleptic accusative is syntactically independent in these cases both of the higher verb, and of the verb in the dependent construction. So it is in the example from the present letter. It is not clear why Halla-aho (2009: 113–14) finds this example abnormal or incorrect, suggesting a syntactic contamination.

On the history of the proleptic accusative see now Halla-aho (2012). She observes, for example, that in early Latin an imperative governing verb, as here, is a standard type. It is demonstrated that the construction changes its shape in late Latin, where it is not to be seen as a mere continuation of earlier types. In classical and early imperial Latin it may be archaising, as in Varro and the *Bellum Africum*. Structurally the present example is so similar to that at Cato *Agr.* 31.1 above that Calventius seems to have adopted an old type.

The presence of *eosdem* raises a question of interpretation. There are two ways of explaining it. First, it might be given its strong meaning 'the same', and interpreted as reflecting the writer's wish to stress that the same animals, and not replacements, should be sent back with the water. That, however, was made clear enough in the previous sentence. A second possibility is that *eosdem* is virtually redundant, or equivalent to an anaphoric such as *eos* or *illos*. The weakened or redundant use of *idem* as an anaphoric can be paralleled at all periods (and in the literary language) (see the discussion of Svennung 1935: 300–6), and is particularly common in technical writers who make a show of precision in referring to an object under discussion. Here is an example from Celsus: 2.7.11–13 *at si sanguis aut pus in urina est, uel uesica uel renes exulcerati sunt. si haec crassa carunculas … habet, … utique in renibus uitium est. at si paulatim destillat …, in eadem uesica uitium est* (cited by Svennung 1935: 302). In a general discussion of conditions of the bladder the writer could not have moved on to a different bladder, and *eadem* could be deleted. There follow a few examples from Pelagonius: 24.2 *de his omnibus facis modium et pridie in aqua munda eundem modium infundes*, 57 *linteola ... uulneribus inponito ... et cum ad sanitatem eadem uulnera peruenerint*, 181 *si ... equus ... clauum fecerit, utilissimum est farinam hordeaciam imponere ... tamdui, quamdiu idem clauus cadat*, 190 *sanguis de brachiolis mittendus est eodemque sanguine ... omne corpus perungendum est*. In most of these sentences the whole phrase containing *idem* might have been omitted, and the same is true (on the second interpretation) of *eosdem camellos*. See further above, 5.2–4 and Adams (2013: 494–8).

7 iube adaquentur: for *iubeo* construed with a plain subjunctive without *ut* (a construction that must have its origin in parataxis) see the examples at *TLL* VII.2.579.73ff. The construction goes back to early Latin, is not usual in classical Latin prose but was certainly acceptable in literary prose by the time of Tacitus, who has it several times. On the history of this type of construction (with various other verbs) see the remarks of Penney (1999: 257–9), who illustrates it not only from early comedy and classical poetry but also Vindolanda tablets (257 n. 24).

Conclusions

This is a remarkable letter. It is correct throughout, apart from the spelling *frugda*, but what is most striking is the stylised and old-fashioned character of the Latin. The letter has participial resumption of a literary kind, an old and very abnormal genitive use with *onerentur*, a proleptic accusative of old type, and a use of *iubeo* with the subjunctive. There are four passive or deponent forms in what is a very short text. The writer also used two different verbs of returning.

25
SURVEYOR'S INSCRIPTION FROM ALGERIA (*CIL* VIII.2728 = 18122 = *ILS* 5795), COMMEMORATING THE CONSTRUCTION OF AN AQUEDUCT, *c.* 153

Introduction

The inscription was found at Lambaesis, but relates to the construction of the aqueduct for Saldae (modern Bejaia), on the north coast of Algeria. The text is inscribed on a hexagonal base, of which only three sides survive. Recent translations into English may be found in Lewis (2001: 345–6) and Cuomo (2011: 144–5), though both contain inaccuracies and in one or two places that of Lewis is excessively free. Parts are translated into French by Laporte (1994), but with errors.

Text

. . . Etrusco (1): 'et Salditani, ciuitas splendissima (2), et ego cum Salditanis rogamus te, domine, uti Nonium Datum, ueteranum leg(ionis) III Aug(ustae), libratorem (3), horteris ueniat (4) Saldas, ut quod relicum (5) est ex opere eius perficiat.' profectus sum et inter uias (6) latrones sum passus (7); nudus saucius (8) euasi cum meis; Saldas ueni; Clementem procuratorem conueni. ad montem me perduxit, ube (9) cuniculum dubii operis (10) flebant (11), quasi reliquendus habebatur, ideo quot (12) perforatio operis cuniculi (13) longior erat effect(a) quam montis spatium. apparuit fossuras (14) a rigorem (15) errasse, adeo ut (16) superior fossura dextram petit (17) ad meridiem uersus (18), inferior similiter dextram suam petit at septentrionem: duae ergo partes relicto rigore errabant. rigor autem depalatus erat (19) supra montem ab orientem in occidentem. ne quis tamen legenti (20) error fiat (21) de fossuris, quot est scriptum 'superior' et 'inferior' sic intellegamus (22): superior est pars qua cuniculus aquam recipit, inferior qua emittit. cum opus adsignar(em), ut scirent quis quem modum suum perforationis haber(et) (23), certamen operis inter classicos milites et gaesates (24) dedi (25) et sic ad compertusionem (26) montis conuenerun (27). ergo ego (28), qui primus libram feceram (29), ductum atsignaueram (30), fieri institueram secundum formam, qu(a)m Petronio Celeri pro(curatori) dederam, opus effectum aqua missa dedicauit Varius Clemens pro(curator).

modios V.

ut lucidius labor meus circa duc(tum) (31) hoc Saldense (32) pareret (33), aliquas epistulas subieci.

Porci Vetustini ad Crispinum: 'Benignissime, domine, fecisti (34) et pro cetera humanitate ac beniuolentia tua, quod misisti ad me Nonium Datum euocatum, uti tractare (35) cum eo de operibus, quae curanda suscepit. et ideo, quamquam tempore urguerer et Caesarea festinarem (36), tamen Saldas excucurri (37) et aquae ductum bene inchoatum sed magni operis inspexi et quod absolui sine curam Noni Dati non potest, qui it simul diligenter et fideliter tractauit. et ideo rogaturus eram, concedere nobis (38), uti mensibus aliquis (39) rei agendae immoraretur, nisi incidisset infirmitatem contractam (40) . . .'

Translation

. . . to Etruscus: 'Both the people of Saldae, a most splendid city, and I along with the people of Saldae, ask you, lord, to encourage Nonius Datus, veteran of the Third Legion Augusta, surveyor, to come to Saldae, so that he may complete what remains to be done of his work.' I set out and en route endured brigands. I escaped naked and wounded with my men. I came to Saldae and met Clemens the procurator. He took me to the mountain, where they were bewailing their tunnel of dubious workmanship, on the grounds that they thought it would have to be abandoned, because the excavation of the work of the tunnel had been made longer than the width of the mountain. It became clear that the passages had departed from a straight line, to the extent that the upper passage made for the right towards the south, and the lower passage similarly made for its right towards the north. Therefore the two parts, having left the straight line, were missing (each other). But the straight line had been marked out with stakes on top of the mountain from east to west. So that no mistake may be inflicted on the reader concerning the passages, let us understand as follows that which is designated 'upper' and that which is designated 'lower'. The upper is the part where the tunnel receives the water, while the lower is that where it releases it. When I was assigning the work so that they would know who had what portion of the excavation as his lot, I set up a work contest between the naval men and the mercenaries and in this way they came together at the meeting point of the reciprocal excavations of the mountain. Therefore I, who had first made the levelling and assigned the aqueduct and set in progress the job according to the plan which I had given to Petronius Celer the procurator – the completed work was dedicated by Varius Clemens the procurator with the release of the water.

Five modii.

So that my toil over this aqueduct at Saldae might be more clearly apparent, I have attached some letters.

Letter of Porcius Vetustinus dispatched to Crispinus: 'You acted most kindly, lord, and in line with your usual humanity and benevolence, in sending to me the reservist Nonius Datus, so that I might deal with him concerning the works which he undertook to take care of. And for that reason, though I was pressed for time and was hurrying to Caesarea, nevertheless I made a quick detour to Saldae and inspected the aqueduct, which had begun well but is a big job which cannot be completed without the supervision of Nonius Datus, who has dealt with it both carefully and reliably. And for that reason I was about to ask you to grant us that he dwell on the project for some months, had he not fallen into an illness contracted . . .'

Commentary

1 Etrusco: the recipient of the epistle was M. Valerius Etruscus, *legatus* of the army in Africa in 151. The sender seems to have been Varius Clemens, the procurator.

2 Salditani, ciuitas splendissima: strictly Saldae, not the *Salditani*, was the city, but this is a constructio ad sensum, made easier by the fact that a *ciuitas* might be seen as a collection of *ciues*. For comparable constructions where collectives are associated with a plural see e.g. E. Löfstedt (1956: II.147–8), Hofmann and Szantyr (1965: 438–9), though usually the collective (such as *ciuitas* here) is picked up by a following plural (Hofmann and Szantyr 1965: 436–7) (note e.g. Vitr. 1.3.1 *aedificatio autem diuisa est bipertito, e quibus* . . ., where *partes* has to be understood from *bipertito*). Note however Eutrop. 7.13.2 (cited by E. Löfstedt 1956: II.147) *Britannis intulit bellum, quam nullus Romanorum post C. Caesarem attigerat* (where *terram* or *insulam* must be understood with *quam*).

On *ciuitas* in this sense see Adams (2011: 259–60).

3 ueteranum leg(ionis) III Aug(ustae), libratorem: a *librator* (< *librare*) is one who does 'levelling' (see below, 29 on *libram feceram*), and hence more generally a surveyor. The term is also found in letters of Pliny to Trajan (*Epist.* 10.41.3, 10.61.5). The phrase here does not mean (with Lewis 2001: 345) 'retired surveyor'.

4 horteris ueniat: *hortor* + subjunctive is classical: see *TLL* VI.2.3012.21ff. (e.g. Cic. *Att.* 4.15.10 *ut te hortetur quam primum uenias*).

5 relicum: banal phonetic spelling of *reliquum*, with *u* or [w] lost before a back vowel.

6 inter uias: cf. Turp. *com.* 196 *inter uias epistula excidit mihi*. The usual expression for 'on the way, en route' is *in uia* (see *OLD* s.v. *uia* 1 c), but for *inter* = *in* see Svennung (1935: 360–1).

7 latrones sum passus: it is usually inanimates or abstracts which one endures or is subjected to, but cf. e.g. Tac. *Hist.* 2.95.3 *magna et misera ciuitas eodem anno Othonem, Vitellium passa*.

8–9 nudus saucius euasi: for the expression 'escape wounded' cf. Tac. *Ann.* 14.7.1 *euasisse ictu leui sauciam. Euado* is often used absolutely with a predicative adjective, particularly of escaping 'unharmed' (with *incolumis, intactus, illaesus*: examples in the *TLL* s.v.); 'escaping wounded' is far less common. There are no grounds for converting in translation the verb phrase into the plural, with Lewis (2001: 345) ('my staff and I were stripped and injured, but escaped').

Datus shows an awareness of stylistic effects in his use of the asyndeton bimembre *nudus saucius*. This is the type of which the second member caps the first (see above, 17.3). Asyndeton bimembre, as we have seen, is common in formulaic language (see index, 'asyndeton bimembre'), but in the later period in particular it is also associated with high or graphic style, and is not unusual, for example, in Sallust and Tacitus (see Goodyear 1972: 252–3). Here it is obvious that Datus is striving for a narrative rapidity: he uses three short main clauses (or sentences) in succession without any connection (sentence asyndeton), and the phrasal asyndeton within the third sentence enhances the staccato style. Goodyear notes (1972: 253 with n. 3) that Tacitus used such asyndeta particularly in battle descriptions, and the context here is of much the same type. The asyndeton *nudus saucius* (or *saucius nudus*) is not otherwise attested and was clearly not formulaic. Nor is it usual for these two adjectives (or variants of them) to be linked in other ways (cf. Livy 38.27.8 *Galli . . . saucii aut inermes, nudati omnibus rebus*).

9 ube: for this spelling see e.g. *TPSulp.* 45 (AD 37), *Tab. Vindol.* 642, and Adams (2007: 151 n. 95). The spelling is old-fashioned. The early form of the word had a diphthong spelling (*ubei*), and the long close *e* (represented by *e*) was an intermediate stage between the diphthong and the later *i*-spelling (representing first a long vowel, and then a short by iambic shortening). The intermediate form lingered on as old orthography (cf. e.g. the Augustan letter, above at 14.9; also index, 'spellings, *e* (long close) for *ei/ī*').

10 cuniculum dubii operis: the syntax here is ambiguous. *Dubii operis* may be a descriptive genitive dependent on *cuniculum*, with *opus* having the sense 'workmanship' (*OLD* s.v. 6). It is taken thus in the translation. Cuomo (2011: 145), however, translates 'they were crying over a tunnel, uncertain about the work', in which case *dubii* would be masculine nominative plural and *operis* a dependent genitive of respect (cf. e.g. Livy 33.25.5 *dubios sententiae patres*). For *dubius* with a genitive see the index grammaticus of the *TLL* article, V.1.2125.76ff. This construction seems to have been literary and found mainly in historians and poets. That would not rule it out in this writer with his stylistic affectations, but the first interpretation seems better, as it is natural to bewail a tunnel of poor workmanship.

10–11 cuniculum . . . flebant: *fleo* was a literary word which did not survive in the Romance languages, where it was replaced by reflexes of *plango* and *ploro*. For details see Rohlfs (1954: 33 with map 16), Väänänen (1981a: 76–7). The transitive use of *fleo* = 'bewail' had a marked literary flavour: most of the examples cited at *TLL* VI.1.900.69ff. are from poetry.

12 ideo quot: for the misspelling of *quot* cf. *at septentrionem* (line 19), *quot est* (22), *it simul* (= *id*) (38). Such errors are banal. See index, 'spellings, *t/d* in final position'.

13 perforatio operis cuniculi: *operis* looks redundant here, as *perforatio cuniculi* would give the same meaning. *Opus* of building works sometimes has a defining genitive (such that the phrase might have been rewritten with *opus* omitted), as in Trajan *ap.* Plin. *Epist.* 10.91 *explora diligenter, an locus ille quem suspectum habes sustinere opus aquae ductus possit* (see *TLL* IX.2.846.54ff.), and one may suspect official or technical pleonastic pomposity. For this type of pretentious circumlocution in veterinary and medical works see Adams (1995a: 357), Langslow (2000: 223). Cf. the constructions discussed below, 45.8.

14 fossuras: this term, with its suffix *-ura*, is also used a number of times in a concrete sense by the architect Vitruvius (*TLL* VI.1.1215.51ff.). Suffixal derivatives in *-ura* had a special place in the language of the *gromatici* (Josephson 1940: 283–8).

15 a rigorem: here and in *ab orientem* below, and also in *sine curam* in the following epistle, the accusative appears to be used for the ablative, but these are probably a stonecutter's spelling errors. In the plural expression *de fossuris*, where *-m* could not be mechanically added, the ablative is used.

Rigor was a surveyors' technical term for a straight line, which is well represented in the *gromatici* and also found in a few official inscriptions (Josephson 1940: 282–3, *OLD* s.v. 3b, Cuomo 2011: 148 with n. 26).

16 adeo ut: this is a consecutive construction (though for a different interpretation of it, described as 'falsch', see Kübler 1893: 176) with two indicatives in the *ut*-clause, and is one of the earliest manifestations of the phenomenon if anacolutha are left aside (see Hofmann and Szantyr 1965: 639, citing this example as the first case; also Kiss 1982: 72). The indicative use anticipates Romance practice (on which see e.g. Salvi 2011: 377)), and is found often in low-register texts of the late period (details with bibliography in Hofmann and Szantyr loc. cit.). Instances in the learned jurist Gaius are taken by E. Löfstedt (1956: II.431) to be Grecisms, a view that is not entirely convincing (see Hofmann and Szantyr loc. cit.). The fact is that technical writers, however correct (on the whole) and complex their Latin, were more prone to departures from standard syntax than were littérateurs and pedants (see the Final Conclusions below, 5.1). Vitruvius shows an awareness of this in his remark at 1.1.18.

17 dextram petit: the form *petit* (twice) is a banal phonetic spelling, reflecting contraction of the identical vowels.

Peto with *dextram* (twice) is that use which 'indicat ... directionem, quo quis (quid) tendit' (*TLL* X.1.1956.35). Among examples cited are Virg. *Aen.* 3.563 *laeuam cuncta cohors ... petiuit*, Ovid *Met.* 3.642 *laeuam pete*, *Trist.* 3.1.31 *petens dextram*.

18 ad meridiem uersus: not 'was turned towards the south' (Cuomo 2011: 145). This is the postposition *uersus* (with *ad*) 'towards'.

19 depalatus erat: *depalo* 'mark out with stakes' is hardly attested but does occur in another inscription (*CIL* XI.3932) of marking out land, and it must have had a quasi-technical status (see Cuomo 2011: 148 n. 25). The simplex *palo*, as well as being used of staking in a vineyard, is attested in an architectural context (*TLL* X.1.157.17).

20 legenti: for the substantival use of this present participle (in the dative) see Adams (1973: 129). The usage is imperial, and attested in literary writers such as Livy (in his preface: 1.praef.4), Seneca (*Epist.* 45.13, 86.15) and Quintilian (3.1.2, 10.1.16). Cicero preferred *lector*. Vitruvius has *legens* (in the plural) four times in the preface to book 5, where he also has *lector* (also plural) once, the only instance in his work.

21 error fiat: *errorem facere*, here in the passive, does not mean 'make a mistake' oneself but 'cause a mistake' in someone, with the dative (here *legenti*) or *in* + ablative used to express the person on whom the error is inflicted. See Livy 10.9.13 *id credo cognomen errorem in aedilibus fecisse* ('caused a mistake'), 25.10.4 *errorem et tuba audita ex theatro faciebat* (here without a complement), Sen. *Epist.* 67.6 *nihil erit quod tibi faciat errorem*, Tac. *Ann.* 4.63.1 *sed par forma aut aetas errorem adgnoscentibus fecerat* (also *TLL* V.2.819.2ff.). The expression was imperial (it is quoted first from Livy) and literary. The literary flavour here is enhanced by the use of the passive (the examples cited by the *TLL* are active), the hyperbaton (with *quis* and *error* separated) and the equally literary *legenti*.

22 de fossuris, quot est scriptum 'superior' et 'inferior' sic intellegamus: *quot est* . . . is not a relative clause referring back to *fossuris* (as it is translated by Lewis 2001: 346 and Cuomo 2011: 145). The antecedent of *quot* has to be understood (*id* or the like) as object of *intellegamus* ('what has been designated X, (that) let us understand in the following way'). It is thus a relative-correlative construction with the resumptive element in the main clause omitted (for parallels see e.g. 1 Appendix 2, and index, 'relative clauses, resumptive pronoun . . . omitted'). A comma should not be placed after *inferior*.

23 ut scirent quis quem modum suum perforationis haber(et): this is the type of double indirect question which has two question-words (cf. Eng. 'he knew who was doing what'), though there has been a (mistaken) tendency to see in such constructions a use of *quis* = *quisque*. The type is known in classical Latin: e.g. Cic. *Q. Rosc.* 21 *considera . . . quis quem fraudasse dicatur.* For later Latin see e.g. Victor Vitensis 3.19 *notariis scribentibus, quis quid diceret.* For further details and bibliography see Adams (1976a: 33–4). The *ut*-clause here obviously explains the purpose of the 'assignment of the work' just mentioned, the aim being to make it clear who had to do what. Lewis (2001: 346) implausibly takes the *ut*-clause as explaining the following clause *certamen . . . dedi*, 'I organised a competition between the marines and *gaesates* (Alpine troops) so that they could learn each other's method of tunnelling'. The logic of such an aim would be unclear, but more seriously the words *quis quem modum suum . . . haberet* cannot bear this meaning. Laporte (1994: 748) prints *quis* and *quem* as a single word (*quisquem*). *Quisquem* for *quisque* would be possible if there were only one verb (*scirent*, with *modum suum* as its object*)*, but *haber(et)* demands the presence of at least one term introducing the indirect question, which *quisque* would not provide.

24 gaesates: this derivative of *gaesum* ('Gallic javelin': see Delamarre 2003: 174 on the Celtic origin of the word) usually has the suffix *-atus/-ati* (pl.), and this is the only third declension variant cited at *TLL* VI.2.1667.65. It was possibly influenced by the associated *milites*. The reference here has usually been taken to be to mercenaries (see Cuomo 2011: 144 n. 11), though the evidence is not clear-cut; see *TLL* 1667.38, 53 for the variable military implications of the term at different periods. Laporte (1994: 750–1) states that the Gaesates were an auxiliary troupe raised in origin in Raetia and armed with the *gaesum*, but the question deserves a systematic discussion.

24–5 certamen operis . . . dedi: Datus has here imitated the language used in reference to the putting on of games, spectacles and the like. *Do* is regularly used of 'presenting' a show (*TLL* V.1.1677.65ff.). *Certamen* referring to such competitions often, as here, has a defining genitive (e.g. *cursus TLL* III.881.14f., *armorum* 881.50, 84, *saliendi* 882.2, *luctandi* 882.3, *comoediarum* 882.27). A 'contest of work' is an unusual concept (cf. Ovid *Met.* 13.159).

26 compertusionem: this word is attested only here, and it is not clear whether it is a technical term or a coinage by Datus. The base is *pertundo*, which means 'bore a hole through', usually with the object penetrated standing as object, though at Vitr. 10.16.6 it is the holes themselves (*foramina*) that are object (see *TLL* X.1.1825.124ff.). This passage of Vitruvius is itself about tunnelling, overseen by an architect: holes are bored (*pertudit*, with the *architectus* as subject) into a tunnel occupied by the enemy, following the construction of a *fossura* used to locate the tunnel of the enemy. The non-compounded derivative noun *pertusio* is also attested several times in a late medical text (*TLL* X.1.1833.65ff.) (of boring through), though it does not turn up in architectural contexts.

The compound *compertusio* conveys the reciprocity of tunnelling from both directions. There are two possible ways of taking the term and the verb phrase in which it occurs, one of them straightforward, the other not so obvious but almost certainly the right one.

First, *ad* might have a final meaning, giving the sense 'and so they gathered for the joint tunnelling operation'. This is the meaning of the noun given by the *OLD* (so *TLL* III.2058.75 f. 'i. q. actio communis pertundendi, perforandi'). On this interpretation the reference in the verb is to the gathering of the two groups of tunnellers before the excavation began.

But it is not convincing to have Datus at this point merely describing an initial gathering of the tunnellers. He is, on the contrary, boasting about the climax of the operation, because he states a conclusion (introduced by *ergo*) in the very next sentence, 'therefore I completed the work': *ergo . . . opus effectum*, resuming *compertusionem*. *Compertusio* must have passed from an abstract to a concrete meaning (a common semantic development of abstract verbal nouns), expressing the meeting point of the joint tunnelling within the mountain (so in effect Cuomo 2011: 145). Literally we might render 'and in this way (i.e. consequent on the competition that Datus had set up) they met at the point of reciprocal boring through of the mountain'. *Conuenerun* is the climactic verb, denoting the meeting in the middle of the mountain. It is possible that Datus coined the compound (and the concrete meaning) for the occasion, but the base noun certainly existed, and it is likely that it was used technically of tunnelling.

Lewis's translation 'and so they began driving through the mountain' is exceedingly vague (where is the inceptive verb?), and disregards the semantic issues.

27 conuenerun: there are various abbreviated verb forms in the inscription, and this might be another. It does not come at the end of a line, where omissions by abbreviation are most common. It is alternatively possible that the form is a phonetic spelling. Such omissions go back to early Latin: e.g. *CIL* I².30 *dedron* (Rome). In most Romance languages final *-t* was lost. It was mainly in the Romance of France (also Sardinia) that *-t* was preserved, into the medieval period (see e.g. Rohlfs 1966: 434–5 (on Italy), Vincent 1988: 37, Harris 1988: 213 (on Old French), Jones 1988: 326 (on Sardinian), Väänänen 1981a: 69). Thus *cantat* > OFr. *chantet*, but It., Sp., Pg., *canta; cantant* > OFr. *chantent*, but Cat., Sp. *cantan*, Pg. *cantam* (see Väänänen 1981a: 69). In later non-literary Latin documents there are sporadic omissions. For example, in the curse tablets considered by Jeanneret (1918: 63–4) omission is especially noticeable in third person plural verb forms. Jeanneret lists eleven instances in the plural, including three in a single sentence (Audollent 1904, no. 272.a. 11–12 *cadan frangan disiungantur male guren palma*). The same curse tablet also has *possin* (13, at the end of a sentence), but on the other hand *cadant, Blandus* (9). Almost all omissions in this text are before a consonant (indeed in the first word of *cadan frangan* before a double consonant), but at Audollent no. 111.3 a compound of *esse* shows an omission before a vowel (*adsin ad Plutonem*). It is virtually impossible in inscriptions to distinguish between abbreviations, omissions that reflect simplification of a consonant cluster, and unconditioned omissions. For a survey of such omissions in non-literary documents of the Empire see Adams (2013: 150–7).

28 ergo ego . . .: there is a breakdown in the syntax here. *Ego* is left hanging without a finite verb in the main clause of which it would be subject. Regular syntax would have been achieved if Datus has written *opus effeci* instead of *opus effectum* (see below), a phrase which is not even unambiguously in the same sentence as *ego* as things stand: it is most obviously object of *dedicauit*.

Initial hanging nominatives are not unusual even in literary language (see e.g. Adams 2005a: 92–3), where they may focus the subject (for example when someone or something new is introduced to the context), but here there is not a main clause of any type if we take *opus effectum* as object of *dedicauit*, and it is likely that a mistake has been made rather than that the nominative has been left hanging deliberately. Datus might have lost the thread in his draft, or did the stonecutter leave out a word? If Datus had intended a participial resumption (*ego . . . opus effeci, effectum . . . dedicauit Varius . . .*) a stonecutter might have omitted one of the two similar verb forms. On participial resumption see Wills (1996: 311–17) and above, 24.4–5.

29 libram feceram: *libra* was an 'instrument for determining horizontal direction, a level' (*OLD* s.v. 4; see Lewis 2001: 109–19), but that cannot be the precise meaning here, standing as it does as object of *feceram*. The reference must be rather to the act carried out by the level, 'I had made/done a levelling'. Brian Campbell notes *per litt.* that Datus presumably 'laid down a series of markers to establish the gradient from the water source, and to mark the correct alignment of the tunnel' (on levelling see Vitr. 8.5). This 'verbal' use of *libra* is not noted by the *OLD* or *TLL* but is registered by Lewis (2001: 321), 'procedure of levelling', or 'survey in general'. The abstract verbal noun *libratio* has the meaning 'levelling' (*OLD* s.v. 1a), and indeed it is used with *facio* (in the passive) at Vitr. 8.5.3 *dicet non posse fieri ueram ex aqua librationem*. The substitution of the concrete noun for the abstract verbal looks like surveyor's jargon ('to do a level'). *Facio* here is a support verb, though without an explicit verbal noun as object (see index, '"support" verbs').

30 ductum atsignaueram: this is the second occurrence of the verb in the inscription. The first (which is spelt differently, with *ad-*; a typical case of indifference to spelling regularity) makes clear the meaning in this context. The reference is to the formal assigning of the task by the surveyor to the workers, with explicit instructions about how the job was to be done. This sense is not obviously to be picked up from the *OLD* article. Datus has expressed himself slightly elliptically here, in speaking of 'assigning the aqueduct', as distinct from assigning the building of the aqueduct (= *opus ductus*), whereas earlier he had used *opus* redundantly.

   Here and below Datus uses *ductus* on its own without the genitive *aquae*, whereas in the epistle of Porcius Vetustinus at the end of this text there is an accusative *aquae ductum*. For the elliptical usage *TLL* V.1.2172.12ff. cites this inscription and *CIL* II.4509, as well as various examples from Frontinus, *De aquaeductu*, e.g. 124.1 *illud nulli dubium esse crediderim, proximos ductus, id est qui a sexto miliario lapide quadrato consistunt, maxime custodiendos, quoniam et amplissimi operis sunt et plures aquas singuli sustinent*, where it is obvious that substantial structures are referred to, as distinct from mere channels (see also Rodgers 2004: 132–3). *Ductus* on its own displays the professional's brevity when referring to his own subject. Pliny when writing as governor of Bithynia to the emperor Trajan about an aqueduct first uses the full form with genitive (*Epist.* 10.37.1 *in aquae ductum*) and then switches to the shorter form (*in alium ductum*).

31–3 lucidius . . . pareret: Datus had earlier used *apparuit*, but the simplex is not uncommon in later Latin (see E. Löfstedt 1911: 58, Väänänen 1987: 151). There are several instances in British curse tablets (34.6, 35.14–17).

The adverb *lucide*, a synonym of *clare*, was an imperial term, attested from Valerius Maximus and Seneca onwards. Similar combinations to that here, such as *lucide claret, patet, apparet*, are quoted from later Latin (*TLL* VII.2.1708.51ff.).

31 labor meus circa duc(tum): for *circa* expressing that over which *labor* is expended see Quint. 2.16.14 *circa quae omnia multus hominibus labor est*. Imperial phraseology again (*TLL* III.1090.66f.).

31–2 duc(tum) hoc Saldense: the words *hoc Saldense* show that *duc(tum)* here is neuter. Both *ductus* and *aquaeductus* have a neuter variant (see *TLL* II.364.47ff., V.1.2170.31ff.; also Adams 1976a: 90).

34 Benignissime, domine, fecisti: both Laporte (1994: 741) and Cuomo (2011: 145) translate as if *benignissime* were a vocative adjective agreeing with *domine*, which is impossible.

35 uti tractare: presumably *tractarem* with omission of -*m*, though a tendency in later Latin for final *ut* + subjunctive to be conflated with the final infinitive, producing a mixed construction *ut* + infinitive, is accepted by the handbooks (E. Löfstedt 1911: 250–1, Norberg 1943: 256–8, Hofmann and Szantyr 1965: 643). Examples which can be accounted for by a simple phonetic explanation should not be explained thus. The form *uti* for *ut* is old-fashioned, and used twice in this letter. See above, 1.2, 11.6.

36 Caesarea festinarem: omission of -*m* in the accusative place name.

37 excucurri: in the context the sense of this compound is clear: it means to make a temporary diversion/detour from one's intended course. The meaning is not registered by the *OLD* or, it seems, the *TLL*, but the *OLD* does note (s.v. 2b) a related metaphorical use, 'to go off into a digression' (in speaking), and we have here, apparently for the first time, the literal correspondent to that meaning.

38 rogaturus eram, concedere nobis: in classical Latin an *ut*-construction, not an infinitive, would have complemented *rogo*, but the (acc. +) inf. with many verbs encroaches on *ut* in the imperial period, particularly in poetry where infinitives are metrically useful (some details in Hofmann and Szantyr 1965: 356). The first example of the infinitive cited with *rogo* is at Catull. 35.10 *manusque collo | ambas iniciens roget morari*, and there are others in Ovid (Hofmann and Szantyr loc. cit.).

39 mensibus aliquis: the ablative plural form *aliquis* is quite well attested in some literary writers, such as Livy (e.g. 45.32.6) and particularly Pliny the Elder (see Neue and Wagener 1892–1905: II.481, *TLL* I.1608.51ff.), but it was scarcely standard (for *aliquibus* see *TLL* 1608.48ff.; this is not a form that often turns up but it is found in Cicero and is common in the purist Celsus). The ablative expressing duration of time becomes widespread in the imperial period, such as in funerary inscriptions stating the lifespan of the deceased, in which *mensibus* itself is commonplace (see e.g. E. Löfstedt 1911: 51–6, Hofmann and Szantyr 1965: 148). Educated purists, however, such as Tacitus, stuck to the accusative of duration, and it was 'bei mehr oder weniger vulgärsprachlichen Schriftstellern' such as the author of the *Peregrinatio Aetheriae* that the ablative was frequent (E. Löfstedt 1911: 54). Note Servius on Virg. *Aen.* 1.47: *licenter in istis elocutionibus et accusatiuo et ablatiuo utimur. dicimus enim et 'tota nocte legi' et 'totam noctem legi'. honestior tamen elocutio est per accusatiuum.* See index, 'ablative, expressing duration of time'.

40 incidisset infirmitatem: *incido* would normally be accompanied by *in* + accusative, and it is possible that the stonecutter omitted *in* in error. However, *incido* + accusative (with the accusative dependent on the preverb, an old construction of the type seen at Cato *Agr.* 141.2 *agrum terram fundumque meum suouitaurilia circumagi iussi*, where the first three nouns are governed by *circum*-) is well attested, not least in later Latin, though editors often emend (for a full treatment see *TLL* VII.1.905.67ff.; also Müller 1908: 136–7). For an instance metrically guaranteed see Lucr. 4.568 *quae pars uocum non auris incidit ipsas*.

Conclusions

The interest of this inscription lies in the fact that most of it is the work of a professional in one of the practical disciplines, surveying. There was a time when the Latin of practical texts (such as medical and veterinary works, works on agriculture, the architectural treatise of Vitruvius) was dismissed as 'plebeian', 'rustic', 'vulgar' or the like (on this subject see the remarks of Langslow

2000: 1–3; a particularly influential book in generating this idea was that of Cooper 1895). Occasionally technical practitioners themselves made disparaging remarks about their own Latin (so Vitruvius at 1.1.18) which gave encouragement to Cooper and others in their classifications, but it was one thing not to have received a full rhetorical education and to be unfamiliar with the latest grammatical doctrines (a failing of which Vitruvius seems to have been conscious), and quite another to be uneducated. Vitruvius and no doubt others like him had been educated in a range of learned disciplines, such as mathematics, music and philosophy, and at one point too (9.praef.16–17) Vitruvius parades his acquaintance with Ennius, Accius, Lucretius, Cicero and Varro. Cuomo (2011: 165) correctly remarks that '[r]ecent scholarship has been anxious to demonstrate that technical writers were fully conversant with the literary traditions of their time, and that they consciously presented themselves as participating in the same culture as their, usually élite, addressees'.

Datus was manifestly proud of his achievement in completing the tunnel, and the monument he set up is a grand one. There are three elements of his Latin that need to be stressed. First, he sets out to express the grandeur of his achievement in suitably literary Latin. Second, he presents himself as a technical expert, and that presentation is enhanced by the use of jargon, technical terms and pompous forms of expression. Third, he sometimes lapses from the grammatical standard. That is not surprising. There is no absolute distinction between an educated standard on the one hand and substandard language on the other. Users of the standard language will sometimes switch into disparaged forms of expression either deliberately to achieve a casual style, or inadvertently. Technical writers in particular were not obsessive followers of the rules of grammarians. In the following three paragraphs some summarising remarks will be made about each of the above three components of Datus' Latin.

The opening sentences of Datus' narrative describing his arrival to save the day are especially marked by literary phraseology and are reminiscent of staccato narrative passages in historians. The artificial asyndeton bimembre *nudus saucius* was no mere formula but possibly his own invention, and *saucius* is used predicatively with *euado* as it was once used by Tacitus. He opts for the literary verb *fleo* over its more mundane synonyms, and construes it with the accusative in the manner of poets. *Patior* with a personal object looks stylised. Later there is imperial literary phraseology scattered about, as in the clause beginning *ne quis*, where there are two lexical items and a hyperbaton of the type that can be paralleled in literary texts, and in the sentence introducing the epistle of Porcius Vetustinus. *Dextram petit* is a phrase that can only be paralleled in Virgil and Ovid, but it was probably banal.

When Datus comes to the details of the tunnelling his Latin is replete with technical terminology (*rigor, fossura* with its distinctive suffix, *perforatio*, the use of *adsignare, depalare*), not all of it, one assumes, readily comprehensible to the layman, such as *libram feceram*, with its 'verbal' use of *libra* for *libratio*, and particularly *compertusionem*. Also notable is the redundant use of *opus* with the genitive *cuniculi*, a type of verbosity that can be paralleled in other technical texts, such as medical works. The use of *ductus* without *aquae* reflects the professional's occasional elliptical style, as does the expression *ductum atsignaueram*.

Datus' most striking departure from standard language is in his use of the indicative (twice) in a consecutive construction. The verbless main clause introduced by *ego* looks crude but may reflect a stonecutter's error, and the same may be true of ablatival prepositions construed with the accusative (with *-m* falsely added) and of the form *conuenerun*. Also significant, both in morphology and syntax, is the ablative expression *mensibus aliquis*, but that is in the letter of Vetustinus.

26

SOLDIER'S LETTER FROM WÂDI FAWÂKHIR (EGYPT), POSSIBLY OF THE SECOND CENTURY (*O. FAW.* 2, *CPL* 304, *CEL* 74)

Introduction

This is part of a small corpus of Egyptian military letters in the name of Rustius Barbarus. For discussion of the Latin of the whole corpus see Cugusi (1981); also id. (1992: II.62–7). On the date of the corpus see the remarks of Cugusi (1981: 752–3) (uncertain, but possibly early second century AD or a bit before that). For the punctuation of this text, see below, Commentary, 'preliminaries'.

Text

Rustius Barbarus Pompeio fratri suo salutem
opto deos · ut bene ualeas · que mea uota sunt ·
quid · mi tan · inuidiose scribes aut · tan leuem
me iudicas · si tan cito uirdia mi non · mittes
stati amicitiam tuam · obliscere debio ·   5
non sum talis · aut · tan leuis · ego te · non
tanquam · amicum · habio set · tamqua[m]
fratrem · gemellum · qui de unum ·
uentrem · exiut · huṇ[c uer]bum sepi-
us tibi ṣc̣ṛibo · set tu · [. . .]as · me · [[.]]   10
iudicas accepi · fasco c̣ọḷịc̣los et
unum casium · misi tibe · per Ạṛṛi-
ạnum · equitem · chiloma ẹntro ha-
[b]et · collyram · I · et · in lintiolo ·
[ ] · alligatum · quod · rogo te ut ·   15
em[as] mi matium · salem et
[mi]ttas mi · celerius · qui-
a pane uolo facere
uale frater ·
k[a]rissime   20

Translation

Rustius Barbarus to his brother Pompeius, greetings. I pray the gods that you are well, which is my wish. Why do you write to me with such ill will and judge me so fickle? If you do not send me the greens very quickly, I ought immediately to forget your friendship. I am not such a person or so fickle. I do not regard you as a friend but as a twin brother who came from the same womb. This (word?) I keep on writing to you, but you . . . judge. I have received . . . (?) cabbages and a single cheese. I sent you by the *eques* Arrianus a box. Inside it has one pasta dish (?) and, bound in a linen cloth, . . . which . . . I ask that you buy me a *matium* of salt and send it to me quickly, because I want to make bread. Farewell, dearest brother.

Commentary

preliminaries

Cugusi's interpretation (1981: 734) is as follows: *Rustius Barbarus Pompeio fratri suo salutem. opto deos ut bene ualeas, quae mea uota sunt. quid mihi tam inuidiose scribis aut tam leuem me iudicas? si tam cito uiridia (?) mihi non mittis, statim amicitiam tuam obliuisci debeo? non sum talis aut tam leuis. ego te non tamquam amicum habeo, sed tamquam fratrem gemellum qui de uno uentre exiuit. hunc uerbum (?) saepius tibi scribo, sed tu alias (?) me iudicas. accepi fascem (?) cauliculorum et unum caseum. misi tibi per Arrianum equitem chiloma: intro habet collyram I et in linteolo (denarium?) I (?) alligatum, quod rogo te ut emas mihi matium salis et mittas mihi celerius, quia panem uolo facere. uale, frater karissime.*

Interpuncts are not placed regularly between words in this text but are sporadic. Sometimes they seem to mark off groups of words that belong together, as is particularly clear in the second line, but often they are more haphazardly placed. We perhaps see the start here of grammatical punctuation, but consistency has not been achieved. See above, 20.4.

2 opto deos ut bene ualeas que mea uota sunt: the opening formula is of Greek type. Cf. Terentianus *P. Mich.* VIII.468.3–4 *ante omniạ ọpto te bene [ual] ere, que m[ihi ma]xime uoṭ[a su]nt,* alongside his Greek letter 476.2 πρὸ μὲν πάντων εὔχομαί σε ὑγιαίνειν καὶ εὐτυχεῖν μοι, ὅ μοι εὐκταῖόν ἐστιν. See Adams (1977a: 4–5), Cugusi (1981: 735), and on formulae transferred in both directions between the two languages, above, 13.16 and 20.3.

que: later in the letter there is *sepius* for *saepius*, and the digraph *ae* does not occur in the text. In the first letter of the corpus there is a hypercorrect digraph (*aeorum*), for original *ĕ*, and also a correct use in the monosyllable *aes*. Terentianus, in whose corpus the original diphthong is often represented by *e*, three times has *aes* in text 22 above, and it is likely that the digraph was more tenacious in this monosyllable: the form *es* would have lacked distinctiveness (see Adams 2013: 74). The hypercorrect example above further suggests that the open *e* derived from *ae* early showed shortening. We have seen that already in the archive of the Sulpicii from Pompeii in a text dated 18 June AD 37 there is an instance of *petiaerit* for *perierit* (above, 15.8).

3 tan inuidiose: in this text *tan* occurs four times and *tam* not at all. Both *tanquam* and *tamquam* occur once. In monosyllables and grammatical words final *-m* was assimilated in place of articulation to the following phoneme, as is shown by Cicero's remark (*Fam.* 9.22.2) that *illam dicam* might constitute a *cacemphaton* (*landicam* 'clitoris'). Such assimilation is the origin of the spelling *tan*, which, once established in particular environments, sometimes spread to other contexts where it could not have represented the pronunciation (see in general Adams 2013: 129–30). With *leuis* (twice in this letter) it was, however, phonetic (before the alveolar/dental consonant), and in *tan cito* it must have represented the velar nasal.

   scribes: in this context the tense can only be present, not future: *e* has been written for original *ĭ*. On the other hand in the next line *mittes* looks like a future (despite Cugusi's interpretation). In writing tablets of the early imperial period the misspelling *e* for *ĭ* is not uncommon in the final syllable of verb forms (see above, 16.1 with bibliography). It is possible that the readjustment in the vowel system that was to lead in most areas of the Romance world to the merger of *ĭ* and *ē* as a close *e* got under way in final (unstressed) syllables, with a loss of tension of *ĭ* causing its opening in the direction of the place of articulation of CL *ē*. The indeterminacy of the tense of *mittes* here points to the potential for confusion in the tense system that lay ahead.

4–5 si tan cito uirdia mi non mittes stati amicitiam tuam obliscere debio: taken out of context, and following as it does a future conditional clause, *obliscere debio* might seem translatable as a future periphrasis ('I will immediately forget your friendship'), in which case *debeo* might seem to anticipate a use of its reflex in Sardinian (see Adams 2013: 653 with bibliography). However, the next clause (*non sum talis aut tan leuis*) rules out such an interpretation. The sense is 'I should forget your friendship but am not so fickle as to do so'. Alternatively with Cugusi the speaker may be taken as asking a question ('should I?') and replying to himself in the negative. On the interpretation and punctuation adopted here (without question mark) the clause *non sum talis aut tan leuis* has an adversative relationship to the previous clause but is asyndetic (without *sed*). For this type of asyndeton see Hofmann and Ricottilli (2003: 258), citing e.g. Plaut. *Pers.* 44 *quaesiui, nusquam repperi.* See also above, 18.22.

tan cito: = 'very quickly': for *tam* + adjective/adverb as an intensive combination or superlative equivalent see the numerous examples from classical Latin collected by Krebs and Schmalz (1905: II.640); also Adams (1977a: 56), and the index to Eusebius of Vercelli, *CC* 9, p. 475. The usage is common in Livy: e.g. 34.50.4 *quod admoniti essent ut tam pio tam necessario officio fungerentur*, 42.5.5 *tam pio erga propinquos, tam iusto in ciuis, tam munifico erga omnis homines regi.* See also Kay (2010: 320) on an epigram of Martial castigating one Sextilianus for his constant use of *tantus* = 'very big'.

uirdia: a nominal use now attested several times in the eastern desert of Egypt (see the text published by Bülow-Jacobsen *et al.* 1994: 35), whereas previously it was known from glosses, where it is equated with CL *olera*, 'vegetables, greens' (for discussion see Bülow-Jacobsen *et al.* loc. cit.). *Virdia* is represented in Romance (*REW* 9367), but *olera* is not. The question arises whether it means 'vegetables' in general here, or 'cabbages'. The reflexes in Romance mean either 'Savoy cabbage' or 'cabbage' in general (e.g. Sp. *berza*). The presence of *coliclos* in our present text (line 11) tells against the specialised meaning. *Brassica* was on the way out of use in classical Latin, and has only a limited survival in Romance. *Caulis* and its diminutive *cauliculus* acquired the sense 'cabbage', and that is likely to be the meaning of *coliclos* here. One would not expect syncope under the accent (< *uirídia*), but the syncope must have started in the form *uíridis* > *uirdis* and spread to the rest of the paradigm.

5 obliscere: for *obliuiscere* or, in its classical deponent form, *obliuisci.* For the loss of [w] between vowels of similar quality, cf. *diuitis* > *ditis, lauatrina* > *latrina, audiui* > *audi (audii), diuinus* > *dinus* (see e.g. Väänänen 1981a: 51, 142). The active forms cited at *TLL* IX.2.110.34ff. are mainly late, starting with an instance in the *Vetus Latina*. This may be the earliest active example attested (see Cugusi 1981: 745). Deponent verbs were already showing a tendency to switch into the active at the time of Plautus, but there was no steady or unbroken decline in the category (see on the whole question Flobert 1975, and see above, 3.424). The freedmen in Petronius both convert deponents into actives (see e.g. Schmeling 2011: 181–2 on e.g. *loquere* at 46.1) and by hypercorrection actives into deponents (see Schmeling 2011: 186 on 45.7

delectaretur). On Terentianus see Adams (1977a: 52). There was probably a purist reaction against the loss of deponents. The literary language never lost them entirely and even substandard texts display an effort to retain them (see 47.15).

debio: there is no more common misspelling in this corpus than *i* for *e* in hiatus, which points to closing in this environment and possible yodisation. In this text note also *habio, casium* and *lintiolo*, and for the rest of the corpus see Cugusi (1981: 743) (seven examples). For the early evidence for this phenomenon see Adams (2013: 102–4).

8 gemellum: the diminutive *gemellus*, whether with the literal meaning 'twin', as here, or with a derived sense, is not common in classical Latin, though it is well represented in the Romance languages (*REW* 3721: e.g. It. *gemello*, Fr. *jumeau* (with modification of the first syllable)). Cicero, for example, does not have *gemellus* but uses *geminus* freely. Ovid had something of a taste for *gemellus*, and there are instances in the shorter poems of Catullus, in Horace's *Satires* and *Epistles*, and in Virgil's *Eclogues*, a distribution suggesting an informal character. *Geminus* also has some Romance survivals (*REW* 3723), and there cannot have been a clear-cut stylistic distinction between *gemellus* and *geminus*.

8–9 de unum uentrem exiut: André (1991: 189) states that *uenter* of the womb was 'surtout poétique', and then cites this passage to show that it was 'aussi dans le langage familier'.

De is presumably used with the accusative here, though when the dependent terms are singular and end in *-m* the possibility has to be allowed that there has been a mechanical addition of *-m* (with a vocalic misspelling in *unum*). For an unambiguous instance of the accusative with a preposition normally taking the ablative see above, 22.22, with the note.

The use of the preposition *de* in conjunction with a compound in *ex-* represents an early sign of the encroachment of *de* on *ex*, which was eventually ousted by the other (see above, 18.6 with bibliography). The pattern seen here has early literary parallels, such as *Rhet. Her.* 4.51 *eicite eum de ciuitate*, Cic. *S. Rosc.* 34 *de manibus uestris effugit* (cf. 149 *de manibus erepta*), *Vat.* 31 *de balineis exeunti, B. Afr.* 11.2 *de manibus . . . egredi.* In Caesar *exeo* is construed with *ex* at e.g. *Gall.* 1.5.1, 2.33.1, 7.20.10, but with *de* at 1.2.1.

In *exiut* there has been syncope in the final syllable of the verb form, a syncope that was usually resisted because the full ending constituted a morpheme. Examples occur only in low-register inscriptions. For *exsiut* (sic) see *ILCV* 3053A, and cf. *CIL* XI.3541. In first conjugation verbs note *CIL* III.12700 *curaut*, IV.2047 *pedicaud*, VI.24481 *donaut* (Väänänen 1966: 45, id. 1981a: 44, Cugusi 1981: 744). The syncopated form eventually caught on in an extensive part of the Romance world. See Väänänen (1981a: 143) on *cantau(i)t* > OIt. *cantao* (mod. *canto*), Sp. *cantó*, Pg. *cantou* (see further Adams 2013: 117).

The form *exiut* must derive from *exiuit*, where the *u* is not normal in classical Latin (in which one would expect *exiit*, with a tendency to contraction into *exit*). The *u*-form, which has late parallels in substandard texts, implies the insertion of a glide to counter contraction (see above, 22.13 for parallels).

9–10 sepius: the comparative use for the positive is paralleled by that of *celerius* at line 17 below (on which see above, 23.8–9). *Saepe* faded from use in non-literary imperial Latin (see below, 29.2), but the comparative was more tenacious (see Stefenelli 1962: 24). Pelagonius for example uses *saepius* but not *saepe*. For such comparatives earlier (*longius, diutius*) see above, 11.21.

10 set tu: for the spelling *set* in this environment see line 7.

11 fasco coliclos: the first word is obscure: is it perhaps a second declension variant for *fascem*? See B. Löfstedt (1983: 460), taking the phrase as equivalent to *fascem cauliculorum*. On this interpretation the construction might be partitive apposition (= *coliclos fascem*, 'cabbages, a bundle'), but with an unusual word order, paralleled however later in the letter (see below, 26.16 on *matium salem*). Or *fasco* might be ablative ('cabbages in a bundle'). The form *fasco*, however, remains obscure.

Coliclos (probably 'cabbages': see above, 26.4–5) has syncope and the 'rustic' monophthong for *au* (on which see Adams 2013: 81–7). In *caulis* 'stem, stalk of a plant such as a cabbage', then 'cabbage', and its diminutive *cauliculus* the *o*-spellings were established already in early republican literature, if manuscripts are to be trusted (for *colis* see *TLL* III.652.20ff., and for *coliculus*, 651.27ff.; cf. Adams 2013: 84–5, and above, 4.16). They occur particularly in agricultural writers. Both Cato (*Agr.*) and Varro (*Rust.*) prefer *coliculus* to *cauliculus* (by 2:0 in each case). Cato has *caulis* four times and *colis* once, whereas Varro has only *colis* (four times). Columella also has only *coliculus* as the diminutive form (ten times), but prefers *caulis* to *colis* by 25:7. If the figures may be taken at face value there is a distinction in the three agricultural writers between the base form and its diminutive. All three have only the *o*-form of the diminutive, but *caulis* outnumbers *colis* in two of the three.

12 tibe: there are four instances of this form in the corpus of Rustius Barbarus. There are two ways of explaining the spelling.

Originally the second syllable had a diphthong *ei* (see 14.5). That proceeded to *ī* in the usual way, which was subject to iambic shortening (> *ĭ*). An intermediate stage in the development *ei* > *ī* was a long close *e*. For the inscriptional evidence for such *e*-spellings see Adams (2007: 52–62). The spelling *tibi* could have two phonetic realisations, with the second vowel grapheme representing either the original long vowel, or the short consequent on iambic shortening.

As for *tibe*, the first possibility is that the *e* is parallel in type to that seen above in *scribes* (see above, 26.3). The shortened second *i* in a final syllable might have undergone opening to a type of close *e* prior to merging (once phonemic distinctions of vowel length had been lost) with CL *ē* and producing the close *e* of most Romance languages. Thus *tibe* could be a 'modern' form reflecting developments in progress during the Empire.

The second possibility is that *tibe* is old-fashioned, a spelling reflecting in origin the long close *e* that existed for a time in the Republic. On this view the *e*-spelling that once had a basis in speech might have been maintained to some extent in the written language as an archaism. There is some evidence for archaisms of this type. The letter of Suneros (above, 14), which has the archaic *tibei*, also has *deuom* for original *deiuom*, where there is not only the old *e*-spelling but also the archaic genitive plural form (see 14.9). The surveyor writes *ube* for *ubi* (see above, 25.9).

There is also anecdotal evidence of a vogue for such *e*-forms in written imperial Latin (see Adams 2007: 149–50). According to Quintilian (1.7.24), Asconius Pedianus said that Livy wrote *sibe* and *quase* rather than *sibi* and *quasi*: *'sibe' et 'quase' scriptum in multorum libris est, sed an hoc uoluerint auctores nescio: T. Liuium ita his usum ex Pediano comperi, qui et ipse eum sequebatur. haec nos i littera finimus* ('*[s]ibe* and *quase* are found in texts of many writers, but whether the authors intended them, or not, I do not know; I learn the fact that Livy used these forms from Pedianus, who himself followed the example. We spell these words with a final *i*', Russell, Loeb). Quintilian is not talking about speech but about spellings in manuscripts. Livy and many others wrote *sibe* and *quase*, and Asconius Pedianus, having seen such forms in Livy, followed the *auctoritas* of the respected author. It is inconceivable that Livy and other literary figures used such spellings as a reflection of a proto-Romance vowel merger that was taking place in speech. They must have been using orthography with an old-fashioned flavour to it.

On the other hand the present letter is full of phonetic spellings (see the Conclusions below), but otherwise devoid of archaisms. The question is best left open.

13 chiloma: χείλωμα 'box, coffer': see *P. Oxy.* X.1294.5. Here is a Greek word that may be otherwise unattested in Latin (see also Cugusi 1981: 740–1). It does not appear in the *TLL*, and this is the only example cited by the *OLD*. In military communities in the Eastern Desert where Greek was the dominant language loan-words readily passed ad hoc from Greek into Latin even when there might have been a Latin equivalent available. In this same corpus note *O. Faw.* 5b.5 *amaxe* (= *amaxae*), Gk. ἅμαξα (see Cugusi 1981: 740; in Latin now also in a text from the Myos Hormos road: see above, 20.3). For further such terms see Adams (2003a: 443–7).

13–14 ẹntro ha[b]et: *habet* is not impersonal (= Fr. *il y a*) but has *chiloma* as subject (see too Cugusi 1981: 749–50). The *e* of *entro* if it is correctly read would probably reflect Greek influence (ἐν-). *Intro* is usually directional ('to within'), and the static correspondent *intus* would have been expected here. Quintilian (1.5.50) notes the confusion of the pair as a solecism (*hoc amplius 'intro' et 'intus' loci aduerbia, 'eo' tamen 'intus' et 'intro sum' soloecismi sunt*). But the failure to distinguish them goes well back (see above, 5.24 on Cato; also Lucil. 1215), and was not entirely avoided in the literary language. Russell (2001: I.148 n. 58) notes that Quintilian himself comes close to breaking the rule at 11.3.99 *pollice intus inclinato*. *Intus* (which originally meant 'from within', a sense found in Plautus: *TLL* VII.2.102.39ff.) in particular is often interchangeable with *intro* in literary Latin (e.g. Lucretius, Ovid, Celsus, Pliny, Tacitus: see *TLL* VII.2.106.42ff., Adams 2013: 334, 589). *Intro* for *intus* is more restricted in distribution (see *TLL* VII.2.55.54ff., citing, apart from Cato, Vitr. 5.10.2, *Mul. Chir.* 21 and a few late examples).

14 collyram: this is κολλύρα, tentatively defined by *OLD* as a 'kind of pasta', and by the *TLL* III.1667.42 as 'genus quoddam panis'. It is found in Plautus (*Per.* 92), then is virtually unattested in literary texts (apart from the *Vetus Latina* and a metaphorical example in Tertullian), but is reflected in Romance (of coarse bread) (Italian dialects, Portuguese: *REW* 2055). See also Cugusi (1981: 738–9).

15–16 quod rogo te ut em[as] mi: with Cugusi's suggested supplement before *alligatum* (*denarium*), *quod* might seem to be a substitute for *quo* (see Cugusi 1981: 750). *Quod* became something of a universal subordinator in late Latin (see E. Löfstedt 1907: 15–19, id. 1936: 14–21, Hofmann and

Szantyr 1965: 579–82), and *quod* for *quo* is cited from the very late period (see Bonnet 1890: 394 on Gregory of Tours, Stotz 1998: 134). However, there are other possibilities here. There may be an anacoluthon caused by a mechanical use of the expression *quod rogo* followed by a construction that did not fit it. Alternatively *quod* might be causal.

16 matium salem: the construction here is partitive apposition ('a *matium* of salt'), but the word order is abnormal for Latin, in which in this construction in expressions of quantity the term for the whole regularly precedes that for the part ('salt, a *matium*'), as e.g. at Terentianus *P. Mich.* VIII.468.10–11 *habes amicla par unu amictoriạ [pa]r unu sabana par unu saccos par unu.* The reverse order is, however, common in koine Greek texts from the same region and period (for details see Adams 2006): cf. *O. Florida* 1 ἔχεις δέκα ἡμέρας κομμιᾶτεν, *O. Claud.* II. 227 κομείσατε μ[αρ]σίππιν σείναπιν ('receive a bag of mustard'), 228 κομίσατε . . . σεύτλια δέσμην γ' καὶ ἄλλη(ν) δέσμη(ν) σέρις ('receive beets three bunch (sic) and another bunch chicory'), I.139 εἵνα . . . τὸ πρόσλοιπον δώσομεν τὴν τειμήν ('so that we . . . can give the rest the price'), I.141 καταγρα[φ]ὶν γράψις τοὺς ἐργάτας ('write a list the workmen') (examples from Adams 2006: 2–3). The construction with this order survives in modern Greek: δυο κιλά πατάτες 'two kilos of potatoes', δέκα τόνοι τσιμέντο 'ten tons of cement', πλῆθος κυναίκες 'a crowd of women' (see Adams 2006: 3, with bibliography).

Such reversals do occur in very late Latin (Norberg 1944: 6 n. 1, Hofmann and Szantyr 1965: 57). At this date, however, the departure from the normal Latin order probably reflects interference from Greek, in a text from a Greek milieu with other Greek elements. It is possible, as we saw above (26.11), that *fasco coliclos* is of the same type (cf. above, in this paragraph, *O. Claud.* II.228).

There are one or two other types of apposition in which there may be a movement from the part to the whole. This order can occur in expressions with *genus* (cf. Ausonius, *Mosella* 310 *omne genus uolucres*). Also, we saw at 3.421 that in double locatival expressions the term for the whole may come second. Note for example Cic. *Verr.* 2.50 *in curia Syracusis* (part > whole) alongside *Verr.* 5.160 *Syracusis in lautumiis* (whole > part) (for this example and other variations of the same type see Müller 1895: 547 and *passim*). A distinctive feature here, however, is that the terms are locatival, and in the first example *Syracusis* is a locatival adnominal rather than a pure apposition.

17 [mi]ttas mi celerius: for this expression see above, 20.6 (letter from the Myos Hormos road) *cura tibi sit celerius mittere*, and for the use of the comparative see 23.8–9 (and above in this text, 26.9–10).

Conclusions

This text is notable for its phonetic spellings, which fall into at least nine or ten types and comprise at least twenty tokens. The types are: *e* for *ī* in final syllables, syncope, assimilation of final *-m*, assimilation of final *-d*, vocalic contraction (in *mi*), closing of *e* in hiatus, omission of final *-m*, loss of [w] between two vowels of similar quality, *e* for *ae*, *o* for *au*, *e* for original *ei* (?). By contrast a letter of similar date from the Myos Hormos road (text 24) has just a single spelling error (24.5 *frugda*; the *u* looks more like a slip than a phonetic spelling). We should not however conclude that the speech of the two writers differed, as most of these misspellings represented features of speech in general at this period. The difference between the writers is in the level of their literacy. The other letter, as we saw, has some literary usages as well as correctness of spelling, and is a reminder that we should not lump all non-literary documents together as specimens of 'Vulgar Latin'. There were differences of educational level among those stationed in Egypt.

The present letter starts with a Greek-style epistolary formula, and has Greek syntactic interference in *matium salem*. It also has some extremely rare Greek loan-words (*chiloma, collyram*). Its bilingual background is obvious.

Non-standard features include *obliscere, exiut, sepius* and *celerius*.

27

PASSIO SANCTARVM PERPETVAE ET FELICITATIS 10, OF THE EARLY THIRD CENTURY

Introduction

The *Passio* concerns the execution of a small group of Christians which is thought to have taken place in the amphitheatre at Carthage on 7 March 203 (see Bremmer and Formisano 2012b: 2). The account of the execution seems to have been written within a decade or so of this date (see Heffernan 2012: 60–7 for the evidence, dating the composition to 206–7 or possibly 208; see also Bremmer and Formisano 2012b: 2). Linguistically the text contains little or nothing to suggest that it might have been written later than this period. We will see several features (the use of verbs of the semantic field 'go', the absence of *quod-/quia-* clauses for the acc. + inf.) in the following extract that associate the work with the early centuries AD rather than with, say, the fourth or fifth century. The distinctive word order of the narrative parts, which in a number of respects is markedly non-classical, does have parallels in late Latin, but it also has similarities to that of Old Latin versions of the Bible and indeed the letters of Claudius Terentianus, corpora which belong to a much earlier date.

The text, as Bremmer and Formisano (2012b: 5) put it, 'combines three different authorial voices' (see also Heffernan 2012: 61). A compiler provided the introduction, conclusion and narrative portions towards the end (14–21). Second, Vibia Perpetua narrates her dream about her own ordeal (3–10). According to the compiler (2.2), Perpetua had left an account written in her own hand, and this he took over. Third, there is a narrative by Saturus (11–13) of his dream, *quam ipse conscripsit* (11.1).

The narrative of Perpetua has attracted considerable attention, as may be seen from the recent volume edited by Bremmer and Formisano (2012a). It is widely regarded as a moving autographical account written by a woman, of a type that has not survived from antiquity. Whether the compiler is to be trusted about his sources is, however, a question that must be considered. Men often wrote in the voice of women, and it is not impossible that the compiler made the narratives up himself and gave them an air of authenticity by asserting that he had had access to written stories (for bibliography on the question of authorship see Ameling 2012: 80 with n. 12). I will produce a good deal of evidence showing that the narrative of the compiler is very different linguistically from that of Perpetua (and also Saturus). This evidence will come up mainly in the Commentary, but in the Conclusions the question of the genuineness of Perpetua's narrative will be reviewed.

Heffernan (2012: 74) argues that, although 'the redactor is singly responsible for sections XIV through XXI, he did not hesitate in his construction of the *Passio* to make changes in the *hypomnemata* of Perpetua and Saturus'. He advances arguments in the following pages (down to 78) for finding at least editorial insertions into the narratives.

There is also a Greek version of the *Passio*, which is cited sometimes below. Opinions have differed whether the Latin is a translation of the Greek, or vice versa, but the consensus now seems to be that the Latin version is the original one (see the discussion of Heffernan 2012: 79–99, which provides a lot of evidence for the primacy of the Latin; cf. Barnes 2010: 69–71 and Bremmer and Formisano 2012b: 3–4). A difficult sentence of the following extract discussed in the Commentary below (8) supports the idea that the Greek is a translation of the Latin.

Perpetua is described by the compiler (2.1) as *honeste nata, liberaliter instituta*. She is regarded therefore as of upper-class birth, and educated (on the interpretation of these phrases see Ameling 2012). In the conclusion we will make an assessment of the character of the Latin attributed to an educated woman of the early third century.

Text

10.1 Pridie quam pugnaremus, uideo in horomate hoc: uenisse Pomponium diaconum ad ostium carceris et pulsare uehementer. **2** et exiui ad eum et aperui ei; qui erat uestitus discincta candida, habens multiplices galliculas. **3** et dixit mihi: 'Perpetua, te expectamus; ueni.' et tenuit mihi manum et coepimus ire per aspera loca et flexuosa. **4** uix tandem peruenimus anhelantes ad amphitheatrum et induxit me in media arena et dixit mihi: 'noli pauere. hic sum tecum et conlaboro tecum.' et abiit. **5** et aspicio populum ingentem adtonitum; et quia sciebam me ad bestias damnatam esse, mirabar quod non mitterentur mihi bestiae. **6** et exiuit quidam contra me Aegyptius foedus specie cum adiutoribus pugnaturus mecum. ueniunt et ad me adolescentes decori, adiutores et fautores mei. **7** et expoliata sum et facta sum masculus; et coeperunt me fauisores mei oleo defricare, quomodo solent in agone. et illum contra Aegyptium uideo in afa uolutantem. **8** et exiuit uir quidam mirae magnitudinis ut etiam excederet fastigium amphitheatri, discinctatus, purpuram inter duos clauos per medium pectus habens, et galliculas multiformes ex auro et argento factas, et ferens uirgam quasi lanista, et ramum uiridem in quo erant mala aurea. **9** et petiit silentium et dixit: 'hic Aegyptius, si hanc uicerit, occidet illam gladio; haec, si hunc uicerit, accipiet ramum istum.' **10** et recessit. et accessimus adinuicem et coepimus mittere pugnos. ille mihi pedes adprehendere uolebat; ego autem illi calcibus faciem caedebam. **11** et sublata sum in aere et coepi eum sic caedere quasi terram [non]^1 calcans. at ubi uidi moram fieri, iunxi manus ut digitos in digitos mitterem et apprehendi illi caput; et cecidit in faciem et calcaui illi caput. **12** et coepit populus clamare et fauisores mei psallere. et accessi ad lanistam et accepi ramum. **13** et osculatus est me et dixit mihi: 'filia, pax tecum.' et coepi ire cum gloria ad portam Sanauiuariam. et experrecta sum. **14** et intellexi me non ad bestias, sed contra diabolum esse pugnaturam; sed sciebam mihi esse uictoriam. **15** hoc usque in pridie muneris egi; ipsius autem muneris actum, si quis uoluerit, scribat.

Translation

10.1 On the day before we were to fight, I saw this in a vision: Pomponius the deacon came to the door of the prison and was hammering on it violently. **2** And I went out to him and opened it for him. He was dressed in an unbelted tunic, white, and had on intricate sandals. **3** And he said to me: 'Perpetua, we are waiting for you, come.' And he held my hand and we began to go along a rough and winding route. **4** After much effort we reached the amphitheatre out of breath, and he took me into the middle of the arena and said to me: 'Do not be afraid. I am here with you and toiling with you.' And he departed. **5** And I caught sight of a huge crowd, who were spellbound; and because I knew that I had been condemned to the beasts, I was surprised that beasts were not being let loose on me. **6** And there came forth against me an Egyptian of foul appearance with his assistants, to fight with me. There came to me too handsome youths, my assistants and supporters. **7** And I was stripped and became male; and my supporters began to rub me down with oil, as they are accustomed to do in a contest. And I saw that Egyptian opposite rolling in the sand. **8** And there came forth a man of amazing size, such that he even reached beyond the highest point of the amphitheatre. He was beltless, sporting purple down the middle of his chest between two purple [?]^2 stripes, and ornate

---

^{1} On the text here see the Commentary.
^{2} See the Commentary on the meaning of this passage.

sandals made of gold and silver, and carrying a rod like a trainer of gladiators, and a green branch on which there were golden apples. **9** And he called
for silence and said: 'This Egyptian, if he defeats her, will kill her with
a sword. If she defeats him, she will receive this branch.' **10** And he withdrew. And we approached each other and began to throw our fists. He
wanted to get hold of my feet, but I kept hitting his face with my heels. **11**
And I was raised into the air and I began to strike him as if I were treading
the ground. But when I saw that a pause was occurring, I joined my hands
together so as to force the fingers of one hand into those of the other,
and I caught hold of his head; and he fell on his face and I trod on his
head. **12** And the people began to shout and my assistants to sing psalms.
And I went up to the trainer and received the branch. **13** And he kissed me
and said to me: 'Daughter, peace be with you.' And I began to go in triumph
to the Gate of Life. And I woke up. **14** And I realised that I would not fight
with beasts but against the Devil; but I knew that victory was mine. **15** This is
what I did up until the eve of the show; as for what transpired at the show
itself, let him write of it who will.

Commentary

1 uideo in horomate hoc: *horoma* (*horama*) is a very rare Greek loan-word
(for Lat. *uisio*), attested here for the first time (see *TLL* VI.2.2964.56ff.,
Heffernan 2012: 254–5).

A striking feature of this chapter and indeed of the whole of the two martyrs'
narratives is in the word order, which has a definite 'rightward orientation'.
Various elements that might be described loosely as satellites of the
verb (nominal direct objects, object pronouns, whether accusative or dative,
prepositional expressions, infinitives dependent on a verb, the acc. + inf.
construction) tend to be placed to the right of the verb, whereas in a classical
text these would often be to its left. Similarly genitives are regularly to the right
of the word on which they depend. This rightward orientation, which is also
a characteristic of the Romance languages that sets them apart from classical
Latin, is related to a tendency for finite verbs, particularly in main clauses, to
move leftwards towards the beginning of the clause (on this point see particularly below, 2 on *aperui ei*). In a number of respects the word order of
Perpetua and Saturus may be described as proto-Romance in type, though
'popular' developments in the language need not have been its main determinant; the influence of the Latin Bible has to be taken into account (see the
Conclusions below). The compiler's narrative does not share this orientation,
at least to the same extent.

In the present passage the direct object *hoc* comes after the verb (VO order). The verb itself is at the start of the clause, which is the main clause of the sentence. Here are some figures to do with V and O.

In the narrative of Perpetua (chapters 3–10) in main clauses VO (whether the object is nominal or pronominal) outnumbers OV when the verb is finite by 37:11. In subordinate clauses on the other hand it is OV that is preferred, by 16:7. This last point must be stressed, as it is relevant to the source of Perpetua's Latin. This old and persistent feature of subordinate clauses in Latin (see e.g. Linde 1923, Adams 1976a: 123, 131–2 with n. 46, 136, id. 1977a: 69, with bibliography) is not characteristic of the Latin translations of the New Testament, in which VO is the predominating order in both types of clauses, under the influence of the Greek version, the word order of which is generally kept by translators (see below, 38.57). The narrative word order in this respect in the present text seems unlikely to have been determined by imitation of an Old Latin version; it looks genuinely Latinate.

Finite verbs are rarely at the end of their clause, whether or not it is the object that comes after, and this is particularly the case in main clauses. In main clauses in the present chapter there are 37 finite verbs that are not at the end of the clause. By contrast just 5 finite verbs are placed at the end of a main clause. Two of these (at 10.10) are in juxtaposed clauses in which there are pairs of antithetical terms that go forward in their clauses, leaving the verbs at the end. Two other examples (at 10.15: *hoc … egi* and *ipsius autem muneris actum, si quis uoluerit, scribat*) are not part of the narrative proper but form Perpetua's statement that her narrative is over, and she was possibly using a different style. There are incidentally several clauses containing a verb alone, such that it is not meaningful to speak of final or non-final position, and these have been left out.

In subordinate clauses in this chapter there are six finite verbs in non-final position, compared with four in final position. Final position is thus statistically more apparent in subordinate clauses than in main, but even in subordinate clauses verbs that are in final position are slightly outnumbered by those that are not.

We may now compare object–verb position in the other narratives (of Saturus, chapters 11–13, and of the compiler, 14–21) with that of Perpetua. Saturus' placement of the object of finite verbs is much the same as Perpetua's. In main clauses VO predominates by 12:2. In subordinate clauses VO again predominates, but only by 4:3.

There is a sharp distinction between these two narratives of the martyrs and the compiler's chapters. Overall in the latter OV (where the verb is finite) outnumbers VO by 35:7. This is a reversal of the preference shown in the other two narratives. The overall figures for the narratives of Perpetua and Saturus have VO predominating by 60:32. We may break down the figures for the compiler's narrative. In main clauses OV predominates by 19:6, and in subordinate clauses by 16:1. The difference in this case between main and subordinate clauses is minimal: OV is the compiler's preferred order.

2 et exiui ad eum: on the glide *u* inserted in *exii* and such forms see above, 22.13, 26.8–9.

The prefix of the verb here is not semantically empty, but the simplex would nevertheless have been possible in this context (see further below). Verbs of 'going' are of some interest in the narratives.

Eo was disappearing from use from the late Republic in monosyllabic and weak forms (*i, is, it*; the perfect forms *ii, iit* also would have been contracted in speech) (see Adams 2013: 794–5). There are just four instances of *eo* in the three narratives, all of them in disyllabic or polysyllabic forms (10.2, 13 *ire*, 10.3 *ibamus*, 12.6 *ite*). *Vado* does not occur. This verb becomes by far the most common suppletive of *eo* in the later Empire, whereas in the early centuries AD in low-register texts, such as the letters of Terentianus in the early second century and the Bu Njem ostraca of the third century, it is lacking (see Adams 2013: 811–17). Compounds of *eo* are preferred in this earlier period to *eo* in its weak forms. Among these is *exeo*, which, despite its prefix, could often have been replaced by *eo* without loss of meaning (e.g. *exire in exsilium* and *ire in exsilium* would express the same idea): see the observations of Burton 2000: 160 about compounds of *eo* as substitutes for the simplex in the Old Latin Gospels; also Adams 2013: 818–19. There are too various other phonetically heavier verbs of motion, such as *pergo*.

The first two narratives in this text are full of verbs of this semantic field. *Exire* occurs eight times (in the present passage and at 3.8, 7.4, 10.6, 10.8, 11.2, 13.1, 13.2; *exierat* at 11.9 means 'had passed away'). *Accedo* occurs four times (8.3, 8.4, 10.10, 10.12; it is obvious that the last example, in the expression *accessi ad lanistam*, could have been replaced by *ii*). *Transeo* is used twice (7.9, 11.8) and *abeo* once (10.4). *Introeo* is in Saturus' narrative at 11.10, 12.1, 12.2, 12.5, and at 9.2 Perpetua has *intrat ad me*. At 3.3 *profectus est* might have been replaced by *(ab)iit*. In the compiler's narrative there are five verbs of 'going' (loosely interpreted), two of them not found outside his chapters (16.4 *introeundi*, 18.1 *processerunt*, 20.6 *accessit*, 21.1 *prodeo*, 21.7 *se . . . transtulerunt*). *Prodeo*, complemented by the adverb *illo*, is another compound of *eo*, which in the context might have been replaced by the simplex; *se transtulerunt* is translated by Musurillo (1972) as 'they went'. The complete absence of *uado* is very striking; the terms for 'going' in the text seem to associate it with the earlier centuries AD.

The prepositional expression *ad eum* comes after the verb. Statistics for the placement of prepositional expressions by Perpetua are given here only from the present chapter, which has an abundance of examples. Such expressions come after the verb (by which in this context is meant not only finite verbs but also infinitives and participles) eighteen times. In fifteen of these cases the verb is finite, and only once (10.7) is the prepositional expression in a subordinate clause. On the other hand there are eight instances of prepositional expressions before the verb. However, of these only one (10.11 *ut digitos in digitos mitterem*) precedes a finite verb, and then in a subordinate clause. Overall then prepositional expressions following finite verbs outnumber those preceding by 15:1. If we restrict ourselves to main clauses, postposition of the prepositional expression predominates by 14:0. Different forms of verbs (participles, infinitives) and their prepositional complements might be treated separately, but it is enough for our purposes to observe the tendency with finite verbs and in main clauses.

Saturus' usage is much the same as that of Perpetua. With finite verbs he prefers postposition of the prepositional expression by 18:8. Again there is a distinction between main and subordinate clauses. In main clauses postposition predominates by 15:4. In subordinate clauses it is anteposition that outnumbers postposition slightly, by 4:3.

By contrast, in the narrative of the compiler prepositional expressions that are satellites of finite verbs precede the verb forty-two times and follow it only thirteen times. The figures for main clauses are: anteposition twenty-six times, postposition nine; and for subordinate clauses: anteposition sixteen times, postposition four. Again, as in the case of OV versus VO above, we see that in the compiler's narrative leftward placement of the modifying element predominates in main as well as subordinate clauses.

et exiui ... (3) et dixit ... et tenuit: another distinctive feature of the narratives of both Perpetua and Saturus is the frequency with which *et* begins a sentence (see Amat 1995: 450, Ameling 2012: 92, the latter noting that *et* occurs 152 times in Perpetua's narrative). In this chapter, for example, there are twenty-one sentence-initial instances on the punctuation used here (that of Musurillo 1972). Editors may of course adopt different punctuations, but it remains true that the narrative advances by means of coordinated main clauses or sentences, with subordinate clauses kept to a minimum. Overall in Perpetua's narrative there are sixty-three cases of sentence-initial *et*. Moreover it is used in stereotyped ways: most notably, it is constantly followed by a finite verb. In the present chapter twenty of the twenty-one instances have the verb immediately after, and in chapter 7, six of the nine.

In the short narrative of Saturus initial *et* occurs twenty-six times, and in fifteen of these cases it is a finite verb that follows. There is however one difference from the other narratives: twice Saturus writes *et dum* (11.5, 13.5), a combination that it is not adopted by Perpetua or the compiler (see below).

In the narrative of the compiler sentence-initial *et* (on Musurillo's punctuation) occurs just thirteen times, and not once is it followed directly by the verb. In ten of the thirteen cases it is followed either by a subordinator or by a particle/adverb. *Et cum* occurs in these chapters five times (15.5, 18.4, 19.6, 20.9, 21.7), and *et ita* (16.4), *et utique* (18.9), *et ubi* (20.4), *et nunc* (21.1) and *et statim* (21.2) once each; the remaining examples are at 15.6, 20.6 and 20.7. Perpetua hardly ever uses initial *et* in these ways: there are just five comparable cases in her sixty-three instances (*et cum* is at 6.5, *et ubi* at 8.1, *et statim* at 3.9, *et quomodo* at 6.8, and *et quia* at 10.5).

Initial *et* is a characteristic of biblical style: see e.g. Vulgate Mc 15 (about twenty-eight examples, depending on the punctuation adopted), Act 12.7–11 (seven examples), 13.4–6 (four examples). Moreover in the Vulgate *et* is often followed by a verb (at least a dozen times e.g. in Mc 15). Here are a few sentences of the Vulgate alongside sentences of Perpetua. At Mc 10.35 (*et accedunt ad eum Iacobus et Iohannes*) *et* + verb are followed by a prepositional expression, and then comes the subject. Cf. e.g. *Perp.* 4.4 *et erat sub ipsa scala draco*. At Mc 10.32 (*et praecedebat illos Iesus*) *et* + verb are followed by a pronominal object and then the subject. Cf. *Perp.* 7.7 *et extendebat se Dinocrates*. This is not the place to compile detailed statistics from the Latin Bible, but it seems plausible to suggest that it has influenced the style adopted by or given to Perpetua.

The consequence of such frequent use of *et* in our text is that subordination is unusual in the martyrs' narratives. It is also worth noting that the literary connective *-que* never occurs in these two narratives, though it occurs in sections overtly written by the compiler (1.5, 20.1, 21.5).

et aperui ei: the dative pronoun *ei* comes after the verb. In the discussion of pronoun position that follows statistics will first be given from the whole of the accounts of the two martyrs. There is no great difference in pronoun position between the narrative of Perpetua and that of Saturus (a breakdown of the figures will be given further below), but we will see reasons for thinking that the narrative of the compiler belongs to a different tradition.

There is a particular interest to the placement of what may be called 'object pronouns', a term used here to embrace personal pronouns in the accusative and those in the dative. The latter are for the most part datives of the indirect object, but I will not distinguish in any statistics given between these and the 'sympathetic' (or possessive) dative, though examples of the latter type will receive brief mention again later. It will become clear that placement varies strikingly depending on the nature of the clause, and that it is the behaviour of object pronouns in main clauses that represents an innovation compared with classical Latin. Another matter that will come up concerns the relative frequency of juxtaposition of the pronoun with the verb, compared with separation from the verb. Some comparisons will be made between the word order of these narratives and that of the letters of Terentianus.

In classical Latin the influence of 'Wackernagel's law' constantly causes unemphatic pronouns to be placed fairly early in the sentence, in a position approximating to second, and with the pronoun often behind an emphatic or focused host word. The consequence is that such pronouns, in main clauses as well as subordinate, are usually before the verb (and often separated from it). By contrast in the letters of Terentianus I noted (1977a: 69–70) that object pronouns were almost obligatorily juxtaposed with the verb (with juxtaposition outnumbering separation by 73:8). A juxtaposed pronoun may precede or follow the verb, and it was pointed out (Adams 1977a: 70) that these placements are related in Terentianus to the nature of the clause. In main clauses postposition of the pronoun predominates over anteposition by 36:8, whereas in subordinate clauses it is anteposition that predominates, by 14:6.

The *Passio Perpetuae* may be about 100 years later than the letters of Terentianus, but object pronoun placement is very similar. Overall in chapters 3–13 juxtaposition occurs seventy-four times and separation only fourteen times (for the examples see below, Appendix).

In main clauses object pronouns are placed after the verb forty-nine times, and before it eighteen times. This latter figure would be reduced further if emphatic pronouns, which always had a tendency to move leftwards to the initial position in the clause, were excluded. At 6.8 *mihi* is in a contrast, as probably is *me* at 5.2. The two anteposed examples at 10.10 are in contrast with each other. The figure for anteposition of weak object pronouns thus goes down to fourteen, and might possibly be reduced further if one analysed all contexts to identify possible emphatic uses (*nos* and *te* at 9.1 and 10.3 look to be candidates).

In subordinate clauses by contrast anteposition of the pronoun occurs seventeen times, and postposition only four times. The difference between pronoun placement in main and in subordinate clauses is if anything sharper than it had been in Terentianus.

If the figures for the narratives of Perpetua and Saturus are separated, the preferences of the two turn out to be much the same. In main clauses in Perpetua postposition of the pronoun predominates by 34:14, and in Saturus by 15:4. In subordinate clauses in Perpetua anteposition of the pronoun predominates by 13:2, and in Saturus by 4:2.

Object pronouns are not particularly common in the narrative of the compiler, but they are common enough to suggest some differences between his practice and that of the other two. Overall in these chapters anteposition of the pronoun outnumbers postposition by 12:5. In subordinate clauses there is the expected predominance of anteposition, by 6:1. One thing that is distinctive about this section, however, is that anteposition of the pronoun is just as frequent in main clauses as postposition (anteposition six times, postposition four times). Another is that separation of the pronoun from the verb outnumbers juxtaposition by 10:8. Separation is particularly apparent when the pronoun precedes the verb (separation nine times, juxtaposition three times).

There are only traces in chapters 3–13 of what might be regarded as distinctive Wackernagel placements. At 11.4 (*quod nobis dominus promittebat*) *nobis* is in second position in the clause and separated from the verb. At 10.10 (*ego autem illi calcibus faciem caedebam*) the sympathetic/possessive dative *illi* belongs semantically with *faciem*, but it has moved away from it to an early position in the clause (note too the preceding sentence, *ille mihi pedes adprehendere uolebat*). On the other hand at 11.2 (*quorum manus nos non tangebant*) *nos* is not in the Wackernagel position. In the compiler's narrative Wackernagel placements are found at 15.7, 16.2, 19.5, 21.7.

A glance at the list of main clauses in which the pronoun follows the verb in the martyrs' narratives (see the Appendix) might lead one to suggest that there is still a type of Wackernagel placement in evidence here, in that the verb is often in first position in the clause, followed by the pronoun in second position, and then by any other elements (e.g. 4.7 *calcaui illi caput*). On this view the only change in the language would have consisted in a leftward movement of the verb towards the beginning of the clause. However, it is by no means always the case that the pronoun, placed after the verb, is in second position in its clause: note 4.1 *tunc dixit mihi frater meus*, 4.2 *fidenter repromisi ei dicens*, 4.7 *quasi timens me*, 9.2 *coepit . . . prosternere se in faciem*, 12.5 *quattuor angeli subleuauerunt nos*. In an example such as the first a genuine Wackernagel placement would have produced either *tunc mihi dixit frater meus* or *tunc mihi frater meus dixit*, and it follows that several tendencies were at work: (1) the pronoun is felt to be closely associated with the verb and juxtaposition is the norm; (2) in main clauses the favoured position for the pronoun is immediately after the verb; and (3) the verb is showing signs of leftward movement, away from clause-final position (though not in subordinate clauses) towards the head of the sentence, or, one might alternatively say, to a position before its object and miscellaneous satellites. Note the words put into the mouth of the unnamed man in the arena at 10.9: *hic Aegyptius, si hanc uicerit, occidet illam gladio; haec, si hunc uicerit, accipiet ramum istum*. This speech brings out the different orders of subordinate versus main clauses. There are two conditional clauses, each with the verb at the end and the object pronoun placed before it. There are two main clauses (with unexpressed subject), each with the order VO, one with a pronominal and the other with a nominal object. In the first the instrumental *gladio* is also to the right of the verb.

uestitus discincta candida: in theory *candida* might be nominal here, of a *candida uestis*: so *TLL* III.245.27. However, it is more likely that *discincta* is a nominalised participle, with *candida* its epithet (see below, 27.8).

4 uix tandem: 'with difficulty after much time and effort' (see *OLD* s.v. *uix* 1b). The combination was a favourite of Virgil's (see Horsfall 2003: 132 on *Aen.* 11.151).

peruenimus anhelantes: *anhelo* is often used in literary Latin in the present participial form, and not least in the nominative in agreement with the subject of a verb (e.g. Catull. 63.31, Virg. *Aen.* 10.837, Apul. *Met.* 2.32). Present participles, particularly following a main verb, are characteristic of all the narratives, and there are some recurrent patterns (see the Conclusions).

induxit me in media arena: *in* + accusative might have been expected here, but (leaving aside the possibility of scribal error) the distinction between *in* with the ablative and with the accusative is somewhat arbitrary, and even in early literary Latin the type of usage here can be paralleled (see e.g. Halla-aho and Kruschwitz 2010: 148–9 on early tragedy). Note too 10.11 *sublata sum in aere*. Heffernan (2012: 259) oddly comments on the present passage that this 'may be a very early instance of the breakdown between the ablative and the accusative'. The real confusion is between static and directional expressions, i.e. those expressing 'place at' versus 'motion towards', and that is a confusion which is early and often manifested outside the inflectional case system (e.g. in the failure to distinguish between *intus* and *intro* or *ubi* and *quo*, and in the possession by *ad* of a static as well as directional meaning) (see above, 5.24, 26. 13–14). There is no evidence here for any breakdown of the case system. For a different type of indeterminacy between accusative and ablative see above, 25.39.

noli pauere: *paueo* does not survive in the Romance languages. It is common in poetry and in the historians Livy and Tacitus (see *TLL* X.1.806.74ff. for details). It is however also frequent in the Latin Bible (particularly OT: *TLL* 807.4), and the combination here (with *nolite*) is cited from the *Vetus Latina* at *TLL* 807.30ff. The writer took the expression from biblical Latin.

conlaboro: a verb used exclusively in Christian Latin, from the *Vetus Latina* onwards (see *TLL* III.1574.56ff.; also Ameling 2012: 100 n. 120, Heffernan 2012: 260). There is no need to translate here as if *conlaboro* were a present with future meaning.

5 aspicio populum ingentem: *populus* of a crowd of spectators goes back to Plautus (e.g. *Asin.* 4) and recurs throughout Latin (*TLL* X.1.2728.42ff.).

quia sciebam me ad bestias damnatam esse: Perpetua uses the acc. + inf. fifteen times. She has no substitute *quod-* or *quia*-clauses (which do not occur anywhere in the text). Speech is constantly quoted in direct form, by Perpetua and also by Saturus and the compiler. Of her fifteen acc. + inf. clauses, only one (3.8) precedes the higher verb. Another (4.2) is split around the higher verb. All the rest come immediately after the higher verb.

Perpetua's placement of the acc. + inf. is in contrast to that of the compiler. In his sections there are ten cases of the acc. + inf., six of which precede the verb (18.3, 18.9, 19.2, 19.4, 20.6, 21.11). The construction follows the higher verb at 15.2, 16.1, 16.4 and 21.5. Placement before the verb is the more literary order; in mundane prose (such as that of non-literary texts) of the Empire the acc. + inf. when it does occur is simple in structure and almost invariably placed after the higher verb (see Adams 2005b). There are no examples of the acc. + inf. in the narrative of Saturus. Perpetua's placement is again of the VO type.

The absence of *quod-*/*quia*- clauses associates the text with the early Empire (see Adams 2005b on the absence of the construction from non-literary texts of the first few centuries of the Empire) rather than with, say, the fourth or fifth century (on which period see e.g. 31.7, 39.18 below).

mirabar quod non mitterentur mihi bestiae: a familiar type of *quod*-clause, used to express the ground of the emotion with verbs of emotion such as 'surprise', 'joy', 'anger', 'pain', 'praise', 'blame' (see e.g. Gildersleeve and Lodge 1895, §542). However, the subjunctive here seems unmotivated. The content of the *quod*-clause seems factual and the oblique mood is not required (for the distinction see Gildersleeve and Lodge 1895, §539). Unmotivated uses of the subjunctive with causal *quod* are quoted usually from later Latin (see Hofmann and Szantyr 1965: 575); we also saw an unmotivated subjunctive with relative *quod* in Vitruvius (11.19). There is another such subjunctive in Perpetua's narrative: 7.1 *obstipui quod numquam mihi in mentem uenisset nisi tunc.* More difficult to interpret is 7.8 *ego dolebam quod et piscina illa aquam habebat et tamen propter altitudinem marginis bibiturus non esset.* The first part of the *quod*-clause is factual and has a classical indicative. In *bibiturus non esset* there is a switch into the subjunctive, which may be potential ('he would not be able to drink it'). There are two other *quod*-clauses with the subjunctive following verbs of this type in the text, one in the narrative of Perpetua and the other in that of the compiler (5.6 *ego dolebam casum patris mei quod solus de passione mea gauisurus non esset*, 18.9 *gratulati sunt quod aliquid et de dominicis passionibus essent consecuti*), in both of which the content of the *quod*-clause might be taken as subjective.

Also worth mentioning is 3.4 *tunc paucis diebus quod caruissem patre domino gratias egi et refrigeraui absentia illius.* The question here is whether *quod caruissem patre* complements *gratias egi* ('I thanked the Lord because I was/had been without my father for a few days'), in which case it would be the same type of *quod*-clause as that with *mirabar* above (and again with a possibly unmotivated subjunctive), or whether alternatively *quod* is temporal and goes rather with *paucis diebus* ('during the few days when I was/had been without my father'). Musurillo (1972) takes it in the first way, as do Farrell and Williams (2012). Heffernan's translation (2012) ('Then for a few days, freed from my father, I gave thanks to the Lord and was refreshed by my father's absence') does not make his interpretation clear, but his note (2012: 158 '*Quod* could *also* be read in a temporal sense') shows that he has, like the other translators, connected the *quod*-clause with *gratias egi* (the italics are mine). The word order suggests strongly that *quod* is temporal (for temporal *quod* see Hofmann and Szantyr 1965: 580–1). In this text a *quod*-clause complementing *gratias egi* would be expected to follow the higher verb (cf. the examples above). If for once the clause were taken as preceding the higher verb, a further difficulty would lie in the placement of *paucis diebus*, outside the *quod*-clause in which it belonged. On the other hand *paucis diebus* is just the sort of phrase that may be followed by temporal *quod* (cf. *Per. Aeth.* 2.2. *his diebus quod sanctus Moyses ascendit*). Usually temporal *quod* is followed by an indicative verb, but contrast *B. Hisp.* 37.3 *quarto die nauigationis, quod ... profecti sine aqua fuissent* (on which note Hofmann and Szantyr 1965: 580 'Konj. nach *cum*'). The pluperfect tense of the subjunctive I take to be one of those mainly late uses equivalent to an imperfect subjunctive: see above, 11.17, and index, 'pluperfect subjunctive, for imperfect'.

6 et exiuit quidam contra me Aegyptius foedus specie cum adiutoribus suis pugnaturus mecum. ueniunt et ad me adolescentes: the advance of the

Egyptian and of the youths is seen from Perpetua's perspective, and English would say not 'went forth' (*exiuit*) but 'came forth', just as in the next sentence Perpetua uses *ueniunt* of the same sort of motion towards her. In Latin however from early on *ire* is sometimes used with this sort of orientation (i.e. of motion towards an observer describing the event) (see Adams 2013: 796 with cross-references). See also above, 7.8–9 on *eicio*.

   exiuit ... pugnaturus: a future participle expressing purpose/intention with a verb of motion. The Greek version also has a future participle here. The construction occurs twice elsewhere in the work, once in the narrator's preface. Cf. 1.5 *cui missus est idem omnia donatiua administraturus* (here the Greek has a present participle), 7.7 *et extendebat se Dinocrates quasi bibiturus* (different construction in Greek).

   The earliest example of the construction extant in Latin is in a fragment of a speech by C. Gracchus (*ORF* 44, from Gell. 11.10.4) *qui prodeunt dissuasuri, ne hanc legem accipiatis*. Earlier in the same passage there is a use of *ut* with the same verb (Gell. 11.10.2). Wackernagel (1926–8: I.286) = Langslow (2009: 360) suggested that here *dissuasuri* was a correction of an earlier supine of purpose (*dissuasum*), made in accordance with later usage. The participle is defended by Laughton (1964: 119–20) and Courtney (1999: 127). There is also possibly a case in an early speech of Cicero: *Verr.* 1.56 *P. Seruilius, uir clarissimus, maximis rebus gestis, adest de te sententiam laturus*. See Laughton (1964: 120) for a discussion of this passage, where there is a textual uncertainty.

   Most examples of the classical period are from historians and other literary texts: e.g. *B. Afr.* 25.4 *dum alios adiuturus proficisceretur*, Sall. *Hist.* 2.71 *multi ... accurrere falsum filium arguituri*, Livy 10.26.7 *Galli ad Clusium uenerunt legionem Romanam oppugnaturi*, 21.32.10 *subiit tumulos, ut ex aperto ... uim per angustias facturus* (note *ut* here and see below for *tamquam* and ὡς), 21.61.1 *transgressus Hiberum Hasdrubal cum octo milibus peditum, mille equitum, tamquam ad primum aduentum Romanorum occursurus*, Tac. *Ann.* 14.8.4 *si ad uisendum uenisset, refotam nuntiaret, sin facinus patraturus, nihil se de filio credere*. For classical poetry see Virg. *Aen.* 9.400 *an sese medios moriturus in ensis | inferat* (of intention to die: see Horsfall 2008: 394 on various examples of *moriturus* in Virgil, not all of them with verbs of motion; cf. 9.554 *haud aliter iuuenis medios moriturus in hostis | inruit*, 10.881 *nam uenio moriturus*).

   Since in classical Greek (including prose and historians) the future participle with a final sense is found with verbs of motion (see Kühner and Gerth 1898–1904: II.16 and particularly 61; also Goodwin 1898: 335, Jannaris 1897: 503 §2157), sometimes accompanied by ὡς, it is possible that Greek influence played a part in classical Latin (*ut* and *tamquam* too seem to be modelled on ὡς: see Riemann 1885: 304). However, the usage did not remain peculiar to high literature: note in a letter of Terentianus (*P. Mich.* VIII.467.8) *s[cias] autem [ra]pi me in Syriam exiturum cum uexillo,* 'know that I am being hurried off to Syria to go forth with an attachment' (see also above, 21.7 on *factura* in the Vindolanda letter). Such usages are scattered about in later Latin: e.g. Hyg. *Fab.*14.27 *nataturus ad eas in mare se praecipitauit,* Tert. *Marc.* 4.9.11 *in uanum ergo descendit quasi legem destructurus* (cf. 4.11.2 *descendit ad legem destruendam*). In later Greek the future participle as a purpose complement of verbs was recessive, though occasionally found (see Blass, Debrunner and Rehkopf 1976: 284 with n. 2, 316 with n. 1; also Bauer, Arndt and Gingrich 1957: 310 ε).

On Latin see further Riemann (1885: 304), Kühner and Stegmann (1955: I.761), Hofmann and Szantyr (1965: 390), Oakley (1997: 585).

7 coeperunt me fauisores mei oleo defricare: editors print *fauisores* here but *fautores* in the same sense in the previous sentence (6). *Fautores* is a variant reading in some manuscripts at this point (see the apparatus of van Beek 1936 and Heffernan 2012). *Fauisor* is an anomalous formation, on which Hofmann at *TLL* VI.1.382.14f. writes: '*favisor* et *favisio* a *favere* ducta esse videntur, ita ut terminationem a *provisor, provisio* acceperint'. It is attested from the second century onwards, in Gellius (14.3.9) and Apuleius (*Apol.* 93). Given its use by Gellius, it would not do to suggest on the basis of the Apuleian example that it was an 'Africanism' (cf. Amat 1995: 450). In earlier Latin the form *fauitor* occurs.

Coepi + infinitive is constant in this chapter (six times) and recurs throughout the text (eleven times in Perpetua: 4.10, 7.2, 8.3, 9.1, 9.2, 10.3, 10.7, 10.10, 10.11, 10.12, 10.13; three times in Saturus: 11.2, 13.4, 13.8; twice in the compiler's narrative: 18.8, 20.8). The order of the elements is significant: thirteen times *coepi* precedes the infinitive, with anteposition of the infinitive only at 8.3, 9.1 and 20.8). There are no apparent differences in this respect between the three narrative sections of the text. It was suggested earlier (7.3) that the construction itself was not substandard, but that repetitive clusters were a feature of popular narrative style. The usage of this text seems to confirm that view. In this chapter *coepi* is used to mark new stages in the action and the fight. I would draw attention to a little-noticed observation of Wölfflin and Miodoński (1889: 69) on *B. Afr.* 41.1, that *coepi* (in such clusters) may have the function of a temporal particle ('quasi munus particulae temporalis sustinet'), and that certainly captures its role here (= *tum, deinde*). So in a much later work, the *Vita sanctae Euphrosynae*, from which there is a passage in this selection (below, 47), *coepit* + infinitive regularly comes in a sequence in which it may be rendered 'and then he did such and such' (see chapters 4, 5, 12, 13), usually after another verb or (three times) after a *dum*-clause (4, 12, 13: *dum* = *cum* in this work).

In earlier Latin anteposition of the infinitive is far more common with this verb (see Adams 2013: 826), and the preferred order seen in this text is consistent with the rightward movement of the word order noted above in these narratives. The word order of the Greek version does not always correspond to that of the Latin. At 8.3 the Latin has *de ea bibere coepit* and the Greek ἤρξατο ἐξ αὐτῆς πίνειν; cf. too 9.1 *nos magnificare coepit* with ἤρξατο ἡμᾶς τιμᾶν. At 10.3, 18.8 and 20.8 the Greek does not have an auxiliary verb. In every other case the Greek has ἄρχομαι, and it precedes the infinitive.

Placement of the infinitive with other auxiliary verbs in the text is less regular than that with *coepi*.

quomodo solent in agone: for *agon* in Latin see *OLD* s.v. (Pliny the Younger, Trajan, Suetonius).

in afa uolutantem: *afa* is for *haphe* < ἀφή, a technical term used of the sand that was sprinkled on wrestlers. It is already in Martial (7.67.5) in this sense.

8 uir quidam mirae magnitudinis: for the literary phrase *mira magnitudo* see *TLL* VIII.121.39. It tends to be applied to animals of exceptional or ominous size, as at Livy 21.22.8 (of a snake), 27.4.13 (of snakes again), Jer. *Vita Malchi* 8.2 (*hirci mirae magnitudinis*). Perpetua uses it thus at 4.4 (*draco cubans mirae magnitudinis*). Note too 4.3 *uideo scalam aeream mirae magnitudinis pertingentem usque ad caelum* (of something miraculous).

discinctatus: a word quoted by *TLL* V.1.1314.63f. only from this passage. The expected form is *discinctus* (*TLL* V.1.1316.38ff.), which is well attested from the classical period onwards (e.g. Virg. *Aen.* 8.724) in the sense 'sine cingulo' (see *TLL* 1316.39). *Discinctus* is the past participle of *discingo*. *Discinctatus* is thus a participial/adjectival form that has been augmented by the redundant suffix *-atus*. Parallels are *bonatus* in a speech by Trimalchio in Petronius (74.16) and *belliatus* in Plautus (*Rud.* 463), in which term *-atus* has been further augmented (by *-i-*). On these last words see Stefenelli (1962: 138–9) and Adams (2013: 563), and on augmented adjectives in general see Adams (1995a: 537–9), id. (2013: 545–59). See also below, 41.4 on *pullatus*.

Earlier in this same chapter of the *Passio* (10.2) *discinctus* itself occurs (*uestitus discincta candida*). *Discincta* there is taken as nominal (deriving from ellipse of *uestis*) by *TLL* V.1.1316.72ff. See also Heffernan (2012: 256).

purpuram inter duos clauos per medium pectus habens: a difficult clause. *Clauus* may indicate a purple stripe (*OLD* s.v. 4), traditionally a mark of status (of equestrians and senators). This garment has two *claui*. *Purpura* may mean (among other things) either 'purple textile' (hence 'garment') or 'purple strip' (see *OLD* s.v. 3, *TLL* X.2.2702.53ff.). If it is given the first meaning (of a garment such as a tunic), the clause is very hard to understand ('wearing a purple garment between two purple stripes down the middle of the chest'?). In what sense could the garment itself be between the stripes, since the stripes run down the middle of the chest? It makes more sense to take *purpura* as referring to a purple stripe, this one running down the middle of the chest, between the other two, which would run from the shoulders. That is what the Greek has, referring to a 'garment which had purple not only running from the two shoulders, but also at the middle on the chest': ἐσθῆτα, ἥτις εἶχεν οὐ μόνον ἐκ τῶν δύο ὤμων τὴν πορφύραν, ἀλλὰ καὶ ἀνὰ μέσον ἐπὶ τοῦ στήθους. The point would seem to be that this was a very special tunic. A normal type, sometimes illustrated in art (see the note of Heffernan 2012: 265), had two stripes running down from the shoulders, but this one had an additional one at the centre of the chest.

Musurillo (1972: 119) translates 'He was clad in a beltless purple tunic with two stripes (one on either side) running down the middle of the chest.' Heffernan (2012: 130) similarly has 'He was wearing an unbelted robe, a purple garment with two stripes running down the middle of his chest.' Neither has paid attention to the meaning of *inter*: the Latin clearly says 'between two stripes', and *purpuram inter duos clauos* cannot be given the sense 'purple garment WITH two stripes'. That is not a use of *inter* that I have been able to find anywhere. I have considered the possibility that the meaning might be 'purple garment within, bounded by, bordered by two stripes' (so Farrell and Williams 2012: 19, 'a purple tunic framed by two stripes in the middle of the chest'), but against that stands the phrase *per medium pectus*: two stripes down the middle of the chest could not form the edges or border of the garment. What the Latin unquestionably says is that the *purpura* is between the two stripes, and that suggests that the Greek above accurately presents the meaning of the Latin. One possible (and indeed desirable) modification of the interpretation adopted here is that the *claui* in this case were not purple, but of a different colour, despite what the Greek says. That is how *claui* is tacitly taken by Musurillo, Heffernan and Farrell and Williams.

The Greek above reads like an attempt to interpret the difficult Latin, and might be used to support the view that the Greek version is a translation of the Latin.

ferens uirgam quasi lanista: the Greek here has ὡς βραβευτὴς ἢ προστάτης μονομάχων. Later (12), where the Latin has *accessi ad lanistam*, the Greek again uses βραβευτής: προσῆλθον τῷ βραβευτῇ. A βραβευτής was a judge (at the games), and it might seem to be better suited to the context. However, there is no evidence here to suggest that the Greek version has primacy and has been mistranslated in the Latin; quite the contrary. There can be no doubt that the reference in *lanista* is to the *summa rudis*, a 'title given to the head instructor in a gladiatorial school' (*OLD* s.v. *rudis* 3b; his deputy was the *secunda rudis*). The *summa rudis* is often depicted bearing a rod (here *uirga*), and acting as umpire or referee in a gladiatorial bout. That is so for example in two fourth-century mosaics from the Via Appia, now in the Museo Arqueológico Nacional in Madrid, which are reproduced by Junkelmann (2008: 136–7 figs. 215, 216). The Greek here looks like a banalisation of the Latin, making explicit in βραβευτής a role that is merely implied in the Latin; that the translator had *lanista* before him may be deduced from the juxtaposed προστάτης μονομάχων in the first passage. The giant incidentally is not stated to be a *lanista/summa rudis*: the Latin says that he was acting like one. I am grateful to Kathleen Coleman for the material used in this note.

9 si hanc uicerit, occident illam gladio: although *illam* follows *hanc*, there is not a deictic contrast of the type often expressed by *hic/ille*. Both *hanc* and *illam* have the same referent, and *illam* is no more than a weak anaphoric equivalent to *eam*, referring back to the person just mentioned. This same alternation is at 7.6: *pro hoc ergo orationem feceram; et inter me et illum grande erat diastema.* For a very similar alternation in Plautus, see above, 2.21–2. For other such switches in this text and elsewhere, see below, 27.11.

On *ille* for *is*, used without any emphasis or deictic force but as a weak anaphoric, see below, 27.11.

haec, si hunc uicerit, accipiet ramum istum: the speaker is presumably displaying the branch to the crowd, and *istum* cannot have its old second person reference but must express proximal deixis ('this branch that I am holding'). *Iste* survives in a number of Romance languages as a replacement for *hic* (see e.g. Väänänen 1981a: 120–1), but its nuances in Latin texts are notoriously difficult to sort out, and second person reference may often be weakly discerned even when there is a temptation to take the word as equivalent to *hic* or *ille*. Here, however, *iste* is unambiguously used with the meaning of *hic* (see also below, 38.58). It has possibly been chosen for variation, following a string of four instances of *hic* and *haec* referring to the male and female participants in the fight, who must be imagined as standing alongside the speaker, and as being indicated by a gesture as he switches attention from one to the other. This use of *iste* is abnormal for the text.

10 et accessimus adinuicem: *adinuicem* is a typical later compound adverb, here expressing reciprocity, 'we came together, i.e. one to the other'. There is a collection of examples of the compound at *TLL* I.689.30ff., from the *Vetus Latina* (and then Vulgate) onwards. The term also occurs in literary texts, including Jerome's letters and Vegetius (*Mul.*). In this text cf. 7.6 *ita ut uterque adinuicem accedere non possemus*. For a full account of reciprocal expressions in Latin see Thielmann (1892), dealing with *adinuicem* at 367.

  mittere pugnos: 'to throw our fists' (of boxing; the Greek has παγκρατιάζειν). At *TLL* X.2.2559.60 this is the only example of the phrase cited. *Mitto* is the usual term for 'throw' in the narratives of chapters 3–14. Here are the examples: 3.3 *mittit se in me*, 9.2 *coepit barbam suam euellere et in terram mittere*, 13.2 *et miserunt se ad pedes nobis*, 13.3 *ut uos ad pedes nobis mittatis*. For the reflexive use of *mitto* (above) see *TLL* VIII.1166.24ff., a usage that goes right back in the literary language (see e.g. Virg. *Aen.* 4.253–4), as does *mitto* 'throw' in general (see above, 12 Conclusions). In later texts *mitto* seems to be the favoured verb of throwing for a while (as compared with *iacio* and *conicio*: see Adams 1974b: 158), though in the longer term it was the frequentative *iacto* (in the form *iecto*) that prevailed in Romance (see *REW* 4568), with *mitto* acquiring the weakened sense 'put' (see Adams 1974b on the whole semantic field, with 159–60 on *iacto*). There is no example of *iacio* or *conicio* of throwing in the martyrs' narratives. *Proicio* is used of throwing to the ground at 6.5 (*iussus est ab Hilariano proici*), but both *eicio* and *deicio* have weakened or metaphorical meanings. At 4.7 (*lente eiecit caput*) a snake is described by means of *eicio* as slowly poking its head out, and the presence of *lente* would suggest that the verb had undergone semantic weakening of a type often shown by verbs of throwing (see e.g. *OLD* s.v. 2c, of poking out the tongue, admitted by Cicero). At 3.1, 5.1 and 6.5 *deicio* is used in the sense 'dissuade' someone (from a course). The examples of *deicio* at *TLL* V.1.40.27ff. (also *OLD* s.v. 10) in the sense of diverting someone from an opinion are not quite the same, as there is usually a local complement (e.g. Cic. *Att.* 15.11.2 *de illo inani sermone*), whereas in this text the verb is used absolutely thus. Note 5.1 *pater meus . . . ascendit ad me, ut me deiceret, dicens*, where it is translated by Musurillo (1972) as 'persuade' ('with the idea of persuading me'), when in fact the meaning must be 'dissuade' (from facing martyrdom). At 6.5 Musurillo does translate as 'dissuade'. These three examples make an addition to the material in the *TLL*, which is brief at this point and does not clearly bring out the existence of an absolute use.

There is one example of *iacto* in the first two narratives, at 5.5 (*se ad pedes meos iactans*), where it is in the same context as *se mittere* in this text at 13.2 and 13.3 (quoted above). See *TLL* VII.1.49.22ff. for this reflexive construction, which is quoted first from the *Vetus Latina*; there are additional late examples cited by Adams (1974b: 149) from veterinary and medical texts, some of them showing weakening to the idea of placing. *Mitto* 'throw' does not occur in the compiler's narrative, but note 20.3 *prior Perpetua iactata est*. See index, s.vv. *iacto, mitto*.

ego autem: *autem* is adversative. For *autem* in the martyrs' narratives see also 4.5, 5.1, 10.15, 11.3, 11.7. *Autem* is also well represented in the compiler's narrative (15.6, 18.8, 19.4, 20.1, 21.9). All examples in the compiler's sections are adversative or contrastive, but several times in the other two sections the particle seems to be a sentence connective empty of contrastive force (4.5, 5.1, 11.7). On the continued vitality of *autem* in mundane or low-register texts of the Empire (and the rarity of *quidem*), see above, 22.18–19, and below, 29.1. *Quidem* is not in the narratives of Perpetua or Saturus (see below).

There is a far richer assortment of particles in the compiler's sections than in the other two narratives combined. The following nine particles, providing twenty-nine tokens, are used by the compiler alone (in 14–21): *certe* (21.1), *ita* (15.7, 16.4, 17.3, 20.3, 20.6), *itaque* (15.4, 19.3, 19.5, 19.6, 20.2; cf., in the introduction, 1.5, 1.6), *nam* (15.2, 19.2, 21.8; *enim* is common to all three narratives: 5.4, 5.6, 7.9, 11.4, 18.5, 20.5), *quidem* (18.4, 19.2, 21.8), *scilicet* (16.3, 19.2), *tamen* (14.3, 16.1, 17.2), *uero* (14.2, 15.1, 18.4), *utique* (16.3, 18.9, 21.3, 21.11). Also, the connective *-que* occurs only in the compiler's sections (20.1, 21.5; cf. 1.5).

For further remarks about sentence connectives in the different narratives see the Conclusions.

11 eum sic caedere quasi terram [non] calcans: this is another difficult passage. The idea does not seem to be that she was raised aloft by the Egyptian, but rather that she rose by supernatural forces (see Heffernan 2012: 269); the Greek has ἰδοὺ ἐπῆρα ἐπ᾽ ἀέρος. She then struck him, presumably with the feet (on this point see below). But what does the *quasi*-clause mean? I have considered the possibility that it is generalising, = 'as one (a flying creature) who does not walk on the ground'. However, giving *quasi terram non calcans* such a quasi-substantival meaning in the absence of a noun in agreement is not convincing. Farrell and Williams (2012: 19) have: 'Then I was floating in mid-air and started hitting him without really touching the ground.' This is excessively free (*sublata sum*, for example, cannot have a continuous meaning), and 'without really touching the ground' cannot be related precisely to *sic ... quasi terram non calcans.* 'As if not touching the ground' would be expected to imply 'but actually doing so', which is not the case here as Perpetua is aloft. This difficulty is merely passed over by a rendering such as this. Musurillo (1972) translates: 'Then I was raised up into the air and I began to pummel him without as it were touching the ground.' If *quasi* were given a temporal meaning 'while not touching the ground' (see the next paragraph for an alleged example of this type) such a translation might be justified, but it is ruled out by the preceding *sic*, which is an anticipation of *quasi* ('in such a way as if').

I would suggest a minor change to the text (deletion of *non*). The meaning becomes 'I began to strike him as if I were treading the ground'. While hovering aloft she walks on him as if he were the ground. Heffernan (2012) retains the negative but translates very freely in such a way as to show that he wishes to understand the passage much as I have just taken it: 'I began to strike him stepping on his face, as though I were unable to step on the ground.' The Latin does not say this, but, retaining the negative, one might make this translation more literal as follows: 'I began to strike him, as if I were not treading on the ground (but on him)'. Perfect sense is achieved by deletion of the negative, without any need to understand a missing clause as I have had to do in the above variation of Heffernan's translation. Since Perpetua was manifestly flying, it is easy to see how a scribe, missing the point of the comparison, should have added *non*. Note the similar idea at 4.7 *quasi primum gradum calcarem, calcaui illi caput et ascendi*. Perpetua treads on the head of the snake as if it were the first step of a ladder (note Musurillo's translation: 'Then, using it as my first step, I trod on his head'; E. Löfstedt 1911: 128 implausibly takes *quasi* here as temporal); so in the present passage she treads on the Egyptian as if he were the ground.

The Greek version of our passage also has a negative, but it is very close to the Latin and does not help with the difficulty (οὕτως ... ὡς μὴ πατοῦσα τὴν γῆν).

iunxi manus ut digitos in digitos mitterem: here *mitto* does not mean 'throw', but 'put into', a forceful act of putting and not the same as that described by *pono*, which refers to a careful act, as at 11.7 *quattuor illi angeli qui gestabant nos, deposuerunt nos*. For this distinction see Adams (1974b).

et apprehendi illi caput: *is* and *ille* both recur in the narratives. Some examples of *ille* are motivated, either by the needs of deixis or by some other special factor, but in other cases the term is a weak anaphoric replaceable by *is*. In most classical Latin *is* is the anaphoric pure and simple, with *ille* conveying marked deixis and often contrastive, but, as we have seen, from the early Empire (and not least in low-register texts such as the letters of Terentianus) a weakened use of *ille*, interchangeable with *is*, is identifiable (see above, 22.10, and index s.v. *ille*, 'in relation to *is*').

Illi here can be interpreted as adnominal: it is a 'sympathetic', or some might say possessive, dative, which cannot but be taken as closely associated with *caput*; it is not purely a satellite of the verb. The Greek has αὐτοῦ; αὐτός is used throughout the Greek version, with hardly any variation, whether the Latin has *is* or *ille*.

In this sentence *illi* follows *eum* (*coepi eum sic caedere*) without any change of referent or, it seems, emphasis, and it could have been replaced by *ei*. The same is true in the next sentence, where *illi* is used a second time with the same referent (*calcaui illi caput*).

There is a mannerism to be seen here, namely the unmotivated switch within a short space from *is* to the weak anaphoric use of *ille*. Exactly the same mannerism turns up in the narratives of both Saturus and the compiler. In Saturus note 13.5 *et dum loquimur cum eis, dixerunt illis angeli.* For the compiler's narrative see 20.6 *manum ei tradidit et suscitauit illam*, 21.5 *reddidit ei hereditatem, pignus relinquens illi.* It is also the case that in our passage (see 27.9 above) *illam* follows *hanc* without change of referent in a context in which *eam* would have been possible (see the note), and, as we saw, there is an identical alternation in this text at 7.6, where *illum* follows *hoc*, with the same referent. Such switches may be found in other informal sources: e.g. Codex Palatinus (*e*) of the Gospel of John 19.3 *ueniebant ad eum . . . et dabant illi* (the Vulgate has *is* in both places), Vulg. Io 6.66 *multi discipulorum eius abierunt retro, et iam non cum illo ambulabant* (the Greek has αὐτός in both places in these two passages), Patr. *Conf.* 33 *inquisiui eum et ibi inueni illum*, sermon *ap. ALL* 14 (1906) 259 §111 v *introiui in eum et statui illum publicanum.*

It is worthwhile to identify weak versus emphatic examples of *ille* in the three narratives, and to compare their distribution with that of *is*.

In Perpetua's narrative *ille* is often marked or emphatic. Here are the examples. First, at 10.10 *ille* is twice in a contrast (with *mihi/ego*): *ille mihi pedes adprehendere uolebat; ego autem illi calcibus faciem caedebam.* Second, note 3.4 *tunc paucis diebus quod caruissem patre domino gratias egi et refrigeraui absentia illius.* Here *illius* refers to *patre*, but after *patre* a second participant is introduced (*domino*), and *illius* thus refers back to the more distant of the two (distant deixis). Third, at 7.9–10 (*et orabam pro eo omnibus diebus . . . natale tunc Getae Caesaris. et feci pro illo orationem die et nocte*) it may seem that the two pronouns are interchangeable. The referent (Perpetua's brother) is the same in both sentences, and the verb phrases virtually identical. However, *illo* comes immediately after a reference to another person (the emperor Geta). If *pro eo* had followed this the reference would most naturally have been to Geta; *illo* expresses distant deixis again. Fourth, at 6.8 (*neque ille ... neque mihi*) *ille* is contrastive. Fifth, at 3.8 (*tabescebam ideo quod illos tabescere uideram mei beneficio*) the subject accusative *illos* is contrastive ('I was wasting away because I saw that they were wasting away because of me').

Once these emphatic uses are eliminated, we are left with the following distribution. In chapters 3–10 *is* outnumbers *ille* by 15:4 (these figures embrace object accusatives, datives of the indirect object, adnominal datives, genitives and instances dependent on prepositions).[3]

In chapters 11–13 (narrative of Saturus) *ille* outnumbers *is* by 8:3.[4] In this section some instances of *ille* may be taken as strong anaphorics (12.4, 12.5), but in about six cases *ille* seems to be replaceable with *is*. This is particularly clear at 13.3–5, where there is a succession of four instances of *ille* all with the same referents, interspersed among which are two instances of *is* also referring to the same persons. These uses are more striking than but no different in type from those at 10.11 in Perpetua, where *ille* occurs twice in succession with the same referent.

In the narrative of the compiler (14–21) there are twelve instances of pronominal *is* compared with ten of *ille*.[5] I would take five of the ten cases of *ille* to be interchangeable with *is* (15.5, 19.5, 20.6, 21.2, 21.5).

The occurrences of the two pronouns in the three narratives are not numerous enough for meaningful statistical comparisons to be made. What is most striking is that all three have weak uses of *ille*, and all three turn up the same mannerism, whereby there is an apparently unmotivated switch from *is* to *ille*.

13 coepi ire cum gloria: for *cum gloria*, an old expression, see *TLL* VI.2.2075.44ff. ('fere i. q. gloriose'). Such uses of *cum* (with abstract nouns and without an accompanying adjective) are found in all three narratives (cf. 11.7, 12.5 *cum admiratione*, 21.8 *cum silentio*).

---

[3] For *is* see 3.2 *dixi ei*, 4.2 *repromisi ei*, 4.3 *carnes eius*, 5.6 *confortaui eum*, 6.5 *pro senecta eius*, 7.2 *pro eo*, 7.4 *in facie eius*, 7.5 *mors eius*, 7.9 *labori eius*, 7.9 *pro eo*, 8.2 *de ea*, 8.3 *de ea*, 10.2 *ad eum*, 10.2 *aperui ei*, 10.11 *coepi eum sic caedere*. The four instances of *ille* have been commented on above (7.6, 10.9 (on these two examples see also above, 27.9), 10.11 twice).

[4] 11.9 *quaerebamus de illis*, 12.4 *post illos ceteri seniores stabant*, 12.5 *osculati sumus illum*, 13.3 *diximus illis*, 13.3 *complexi illos sumus*, 13.4 *coepit ... cum illis loqui*, 13.5 *dixerunt illis angeli*, 13.5 *sine illos refrigerent*; 13.4 *segregauimus eos*, 13.5 *dum loquimur cum eis*, 13.6 *conturbauerunt eos*.

[5] *Is*: 16.1, 16.2 twice, 16.4 twice, 18.9, 20.6, 20.8, 21.5 twice, 21.7, 21.11; *ille*: 15.1, 15.5, 15.6 twice, 16.4, 19.5, 20.6, 21.2, 21.5, 21.7.

14 mihi esse uictoriam: Musurillo (1972) translates 'I would win the victory', and Heffernan (2012) 'victory was to be mine'. Both see a future reference in *esse*, and certainly victory does lie in the future. This is the use of present for future implying immediacy, which also occurs in this anthology in a veterinary text (29.2): the victory is as good as won already. Farrell and Williams (2012) translate as I do. A graphic instance of the present where an English speaker might have expected a future is seen in Perpetua's firm refusal to do something requested of her by her persecutors: 6.3–4 '*fac sacrum pro salute imperatorum.*' *et ego respondi: 'non facio.'* For this usage cf. Plaut. *Mil.* 444–5 *mitte.* :: *manufestaria's. non omitto.* On the remarkable present for future *consumor* in one of the compiler's chapters (21.2) see below, 29.2.

15 usque in pridie muneris egi; ipsius autem muneris actum, si quis uoluerit, scribat: see *TLL* X.2.1230.23ff. for *in pridie usque* at Tert. *Scap.* 2.5, and also 1231.55ff. for *pridie* following *ad, usque ad, in* and *intra*. Most examples are late and non-literary, but *ad pridie* is cited from Cic. *Att.* 2.8.2. Such examples may fall into the category of compound adverbials, for which see above on *adinuicem*, and Adams (2013: 582–611), though *in pridie* may be taken as a prepositional expression (for the ambiguity of interpretation see *TLL* 1230.22f.).

In the expression *ipsius muneris actum*, the genitive, which seems to be emphatic, is placed before the noun. This is an unusual placement for the genitive in the narratives of Perpetua and Saturus. There are just three other such cases, all in Perpetua. One is in the expression *uerbi gratia* (3.1), where *gratia* has its conventional position after the genitive, and the other two are both with *beneficio* meaning 'thanks to, because of' (3.6 *turbarum beneficio*, 3.8 *mei beneficio*), a late 'prepositional' usage. Perpetua has the genitive after its noun forty-eight times, and Saturus five times. In these two narratives therefore postposition of the genitive outnumbers anteposition by 53:4 (in the ratio 13.25:1). This preference is typical of many late texts (see e.g. Adams 1976b: 73), and is another aspect of the emergent VO character of the language. In the *Peregrinatio Aetheriae*, for example, postposition of the genitive predominates in the ratio of about 15.5:1, and in the *Anonymus Valesianus II* by about 10:1 (see Adams loc. cit.). In classical Latin genitive position is very variable and determined by many factors, but the bare figures for Caesar, Cicero, Sallust and Varro show postposition of the genitive occurring roughly 55 per cent of the time (see McLachlan 2012: chapter 3, table 1, chapter 4, table 2.8). In informal texts of a few centuries later a move had occurred towards mechanical placement of the genitive after its noun most of the time.

Postposition of the genitive is also preferred in the compiler's narrative, but by no means as markedly as in the other two. Postposition outnumbers anteposition by 42:13 (in the ratio of 3.2:1). There are signs here of old literary patterns. At 18.2 there are two instances of genitival chiasmus in the same sentence (juxtaposed phrases having on the one hand the order NG and on the other GN): *ut matrona Christi, ut Dei delicata, uigore oculorum deiciens omnium conspectum*. Again, there are several cases of enclosing order (where a genitive is enclosed between a preposition and its dependent noun): 16.1 *de ipsius constantia*, 19.2 *de martyrii sui uoto*, 21.7 *in eorum corpore*. For a different type of enclosing order see 15.2 *instante spectaculi die*. And at 20.4 two genitives are split around the governing term: *pudoris potius memor quam doloris*. Perpetua does not use the enclosing order: contrast e.g. 3.3 *cum argumentis diaboli*, 3.5 *in ipso spatio paucorum dierum*, 3.7 *in meliorem locum carceris*, 4.3 *in lateribus scalae*, 4.6 *in caput scalae*, 4.6 *in nomine Iesu Christi*, 4.8 *in habitu pastoris*, 4.10 *ad sonum uocis*, 5.2 *ad hunc florem aetatis*, 5.2 *in dedecus hominum*, etc. It is obvious that old types of literary variation persisted in the literary language, but that in informal Latin placement had become far more stereotyped, and of VO character.

Appendix: object pronouns, direct and indirect, in chapters 3–13

1 Main clauses

1.1 Pronoun comes before the verb

3.8 uniuersi sibi uacabant, 4.2 crastina die tibi renuntiabo, 4.6 non me nocebit, 5.2 ne me dederis in dedecus hominum, 5.4 ne uniuersos nos extermines, 5.5 et se ad pedes meos iactans, 6.6 tunc nos uniuersos pronuntiat, 6.8 neque mihi feruorem fecerunt, 9.1 nos magnificare coepit, 10.3 Perpetua, te expectamus, 10.7 coeperunt me fauisores mei oleo defricare, 10.10 ille mihi pedes adprendere uolebat, 10.10 ego autem illi calcibus faciem caedebam, 10.11 coepi eum sic caedere, 11.7 honorem nobis dederunt, 13.2 et sic nos reliquistis, 13.3 et complexi illos sumus, 13.7 et sic nobis uisum est.

1.2 Pronoun comes after the verb

3.2 et ego dixi ei, 3.3 mittit se in me, 3.9 factus est mihi carcer, 4.1 tunc dixit mihi frater, 4.2 fidenter repromisi ei dicens, 4.2 et ostensum est mihi hoc, 4.6 et conuertit se, 4.6 et dixit mihi, 4.6 Perpetua, sustineo te, 4.7 quasi timens me, 4.7

calcaui illi caput, 4.9 et aspexit me, 4.9 et dixit mihi, 4.9 et clamauit me, 4.9 dedit mihi quasi buccellam, 5.5 basians mihi manus, 5.6 et confortaui eum dicens, 6.2 et extraxit me, 6.5 et doluit mihi casus patris mei, 7.1 profecta est mihi uox, 7.3 ostensum est mihi hoc, 7.7 et extendebat se Dinocrates, 8.1 ostensum est mihi hoc, 9.2 coepit . . . prosternere se in faciem, 10.2 aperui ei, 10.3 et dixit mihi, 10.3 tenuit mihi manum, 10.4 et induxit me, 10.4 et dixit mihi, 10.9 occidet illam gladio, 10.11 apprehendi illi caput, 10.11 et calcaui illi caput, 10.13 et osculatus est me, 10.13 et dixit mihi, 11.5 factum est nobis spatium, 11.7 deposuerunt nos, 12.5 angeli subleuauerunt nos, 12.5 et osculati sumus illum, 12.5 traiecit nobis in faciem, 12.6 dixerunt nobis, 12.6 dixerunt nobis seniores, 12.7 et dixit mihi, 13.2 et miserunt se ad pedes nobis, 13.3 et diximus illis, 13.4 et segregauimus eos, 13.5 dixerunt illis, 13.5 sinite illos, 13.5 dimittite uobis inuicem, 13.6 et conturbauerunt eos.

2 Relative and subordinate clauses

2.1 Pronoun comes before the verb

3.1 cum . . . me pater uerbis euertere cupiret, 3.3 ut oculos mihi erueret, 3.7 qui nobis ministrabant, 4.5 qui postea se propter nos ultro tradiderat, 4.5 quia ipse nos aedificauerat, 4.6 sed uide ne te mordeat draco ille, 5.1 ut me deiceret, 5.2 si his te manibus ad hunc florem aetatis prouexi, 5.2 si te praeposui, 7.1 quod numquam mihi in mentem uenisset, 7.10 ut mihi donaretur, 10.9 si hanc uicerit, 10.9 si hunc uicerit, 11.2 quorum manus nos non tangebant, 11.4 quod nobis Dominus promittebat, 13.3 ut uos ad pedes nobis mittatis, 13.8 qui nos satiabat.

2.2 Pronoun comes after the verb

4.1 ut . . . ostendatur tibi, 10.5 mirabar quod non mitterentur mihi bestiae, 11.7 ubi uiderunt nos, 11.7 qui gestabant nos.

Conclusions

The authorship of the three narratives

Word order

It is clear that the Latin of the compiler's narrative is subtly different from that of the other two narratives. I have deliberately here taken no account of the first two chapters of the work, which form the compiler's introduction. These belong to a different genre. The first chapter in particular is composed in a high style, with long sentences and a lot of subordination, and it would be pointless to compare such a passage with the informal narrative of Perpetua. Chapters 14–21 are a different matter. Here there is a narrative that completes the story of the martyrdoms. Like the other narratives, it combines description, written in short sentences, with quoted direct speech. There is only a very short peroration in a more rhetorical style at the end of chapter 21 (11). If there are linguistic differences between these three narratives, belonging as they do to the same genre and having the same components, these must have a significance, though it remains to be discussed what that might be.

There are systematic distinctions between the word order of 14–21 (i.e. by the narrator), and that of 3–13 (with the narratives of Perpetua and Saturus indistinguishable in this respect). The martyrs' narratives have VO characteristics (I use OV and VO here to embrace a variety of features and not only the position of the object in relation to the verb), particularly in main clauses. Subordinate clauses retain OV characteristics, and that is no surprise, because final position of the verb was much more tenacious over a long period in subordinate than main clauses. On the other hand the narrative of the compiler has OV characteristics, found not only in subordinate clauses but also in main clauses.

There is a general importance to the word order of this text. It has become conventional to stress the part played by pragmatic factors in determining variability of word order (e.g. between OV and VO) in Latin texts. It is true that in most texts there is a good deal of variation, and that at least some of this can be put down to the needs of emphasis. But there are two other truths about Latin word order that need to be stressed.

First, between the early period and Romance there was a shift from a language in which OV features were common and in some texts (e.g. the works of Caesar) predominant, to languages in which VO features had become widespread. In the intervening centuries variability is commonplace, determined to some extent by the sorts of pragmatic factors that have often been discussed. There is no clear-cut chronological progression from OV to VO.

Second, in post-classical Latin there are certain texts that have marked VO characteristics (particularly in main clauses), with little of the variability just referred to. Such texts include the letters of Claudius Terentianus, the *Peregrinatio Aetheriae*, the *Itinerarium Antonini Placentini*, the grammatical work of the African Pompeius, the bilingual *colloquia* edited by Dickey (2012), the *Anonymus Valesianus II*, the Vulgate of the NT (see below, 38.57), and now two of the narratives in the *Pass. Perp.* It would be perverse to argue that the VO features of this substantial corpus were due entirely to pragmatic determinants, which just happened to produce a different result in these texts from that which they produced in many other texts of the same periods. I would prefer to suggest that in the higher literary language conservatism and imitation of earlier models caused the preservation of a variability that included many OV features, whereas a different, VO, style was emerging in less literary texts, determined possibly by popular developments, and certainly in some texts by the influence of the Latin Bible (itself subject to the influence of biblical Greek).

And so we come to the significance of the *Pass. Perp.* Here we have three narratives of exactly the same date and dealing with exactly the same subject in much the same way. It would be stretching credibility to suggest that the conflicting patterns in 3–13 compared with 14–21 were due to the chance effects of pragmatic influences. It is far more likely that the compiler has composed his narrative within a literary tradition using old OV patterns, whereas the other narratives have been given patterns of a different type. The question that must be addressed later is whether the word order distinctions between 3–13 and 14–21 reflect the work of different authors. First it will clarify things to summarise the features of word order that have been identified in the Commentary.

Verb and object
When the verb is finite, in main clauses in Perpetua VO outnumbers OV by 37:11 and in Saturus by 12:2. In the compiler's narrative OV predominates by 19:6.

In subordinate clauses in Perpetua OV predominates by 16:7 and in Saturus by 4:3. In the compiler's narrative OV predominates by 16:1.

Prepositional expressions
When the verb is finite, in main clauses in Perpetua (chapter 10) postposition of prepositional expressions predominates by 14:0, and in Saturus by 15:4. In the compiler's narrative anteposition predominates by 26:9.

In subordinate clauses in Perpetua (chapter 10) anteposition and postposition both occur once. In Saturus anteposition outnumbers postposition by 4:3. In the compiler's narrative anteposition predominates by 16:4.

Object pronouns (accusative and dative)
In main clauses in Perpetua postposition of the pronoun predominates by 34:14 and in Saturus by 15:4. In the compiler's narrative anteposition occurs 6 times and postposition 4 times.

In subordinate clauses in Perpetua anteposition predominates by 13:2 and in Saturus by 4:2. In the compiler's narrative anteposition predominates by 6:1.

Separation versus juxtaposition of object pronouns and the verb
In Perpetua and Saturus juxtaposition of object pronoun and verb outnumbers separation by 74:14. In the compiler's narrative separation predominates by 10:8.

Placement of the acc. + inf. construction
In Perpetua the acc. + inf. follows the higher verb 13 times and precedes it only once. The construction does not occur in Saturus. In the compiler's narrative the acc. + inf. precedes the higher verb 6 times and follows it 4 times.

There is no point in distinguishing between higher verbs that are in main clauses and those in subordinate.

coepi + *infinitive*
In Perpetua postposition of the infinitive predominates by 9:2 and in Saturus by 3:0. In the compiler's narrative it predominates by 2:1.

Position of dependent genitives
In Perpetua and Saturus postposition of the genitive predominates by 53:4 (= 13.25:1). In the compiler's narrative it predominates by 42:13 (= 3.2:1).

It is worth setting out these figures in a table. In the case of three of the elements above (object, 'object pronouns', prepositional expressions) separate figures were given for each showing their placement in main versus subordinate clauses. In the tables below, one for main clauses and the other for subordinate, the figures for these three elements have been combined. The tables present the distributions in the narratives of Perpetua and Saturus on the one hand and of the compiler on the other.

	Main clauses	
	Element follows V	Element precedes V
3–13	127	35
14–21	19	51

In Perpetua and Saturus these elements come after the verb four times as often as before. In the compiler's narrative they come before the verb almost three times as often as after.

		Subordinate clauses
	Element follows V	Element precedes V
3–13	18	42
14–21	6	38

In both sections anteposition predominates in subordinate clauses (overall by 80:24, or roughly 3:1), but this predominance is more marked in the compiler's narrative (by about 6:1, as against 2.3:1 in the other sections).

The two tables considered together nicely illustrate the long-standing conservatism of word order in subordinate clauses, where the persistent tendency for the verb to be placed at or near the end of the clause has the consequence that associated elements must often precede the verb. By contrast in main clauses there is a sharp difference between the compiler's practice and that in the other two narratives. VO orders are strongly preferred in 3–13 and OV orders almost as strongly in 14–21. In neither 3–13 nor 14–21 is the one order or the other absolute. There was a good deal of freedom still, with individual preference, emphasis, rhythmical and pragmatic factors probably having an influence, but it is obvious that the narratives of Perpetua and Saturus belong to a different style.

The other three placements for which figures were set out above (of the acc. + inf. in relation to the higher verb, of the infinitive with *coepi* and of the genitive in relation to the governing word) reveal again the VO characteristics of the narratives of Perpetua and Saturus, and in the case of the acc. + inf. there is the same distinction between 3–13 on the one hand and 14–21 on the other (the latter with more marked OV character).

> Some other differences between 3–13 (particularly 3–10)
> and 14–21

There are some further stylistic differences between 3–13 (particularly Perpetua's narrative) and the compiler's sections.

A feature of Perpetua's account is the frequent use of *tunc* (she never has *tum*, which does not occur in the text: on the significance of this see above on texts 1.11, 11.9). The repetitive use of *tunc* and other temporal adverbs has been observed in popular narrative (see index, 'temporal adverbs, repetitious'). Perpetua uses *tunc* ten times, sometimes more than once within a short space (note 3.3, 3.4, 3.8 and 6.3, 6.6, 6.7). Saturus on the other hand has *tunc* only once, though his section is short. So the compiler admits *tunc* only once (21.4) as a temporal connective in his rather longer narrative (at 20.8 *a quodam tunc catechumeno* it is adnominal and does not introduce a sentence). The compiler for his part uses other particles (not shared by Perpetua) for advancing the narrative. It was remarked earlier (27.10) that he has numerous tokens of nine literary particles not found at all in the other narratives.

That observation may now be extended. First, the compiler has two equivalents of *tunc*, namely *dehinc* (18.8, 20.5) and *exinde* (20.10, 21.6), which do not appear in the other narratives. Second, he had a taste for *ita* or *itaque* at the start of a sentence (*ita* five times, *itaque* five times in the narrative and also at 1.5, 1.6: see 27.10). These have little or no semantic weight and could either be omitted or replaced in many cases by *tunc*. It was seen earlier (11.25) that in Vitruvius' story about the larch *tunc* and *itaque* alternate. There are fourteen occurrences of the four terms just noted in the compiler's narrative, but none of these is used in the narratives of Perpetua and Saturus. Comparing the distribution of these various terms with that of *tunc* in the different parts of the text we find that *tunc* predominates by 11:0 in the narratives of Perpetua and Saturus, but the other terms predominate over *tunc* by 14:1(2 if we include 20.8: see last paragraph) in the compiler's narrative. Perpetua does once have *deinde* (9.1), but this is not used by the compiler.

Another difference, as was noted above (27.2), between 3–13 and 14–21 lies in the use of sentence-initial *et*. In Perpetua and Saturus it is constant, and followed often by a verb, whereas in the compiler's section it is less frequent and mostly followed by subordinators or adverbs. It was pointed out that whereas the compiler has *et cum* six times, Saturus alone has *et dum*.

It is established that Perpetua's narrative is repetitive in phraseology (see Ameling 2012: 92 with bibliography). This characteristic is particularly noticeable when she uses a distinctive phrase more than once. Her father is described as *consumptus taedio* at 5.1 and 9.2. *Rumor cucurrit* is used at 5.1 and 6.1. *Mirae magnitudinis* occurs twice within a few lines at 4.3 and 4.4, as well as at 10.8. The clauses *quem retro uideram* and *quam retro uideram* occur in consecutive sentences at 8.1–2. At 10.10–11 *caedo, apprehendo, calco, facies* and *coepi* are all repeated. *Pauci dies* (in various case forms) is several times used in chapter 3 (3.4, 3.5 twice; cf. 5.1, 7.1); at 3.5 it is twice in one sentence. There are clusters of examples of *tunc* (see above). *Ascendo* occurs six times in 4.3–7. *Circumstantes* (nominative) is at both 4.8 and 4.9. The formula *ostensum est mihi hoc* is at 4.2, 7.3, 8.1.

There is the same repetitiveness in Saturus' narrative. *Introeo* is used four times within a short space (11.10, 12.1, 12.2, 12.5). *Sine cessatione* occurs at 11.6 and 12.2, and *cum admiratione* at 11.7 and 12.5. *Vidimus* occurs twice in the same sentence at 12.3. *Locus* is used three times in the opening section of 12. *Gestamur ab ipsis quattuor angelis* (11.5) is soon followed by *quattuor illi angelis qui gestabant nos* (11.7).

Such repetitiveness is not a feature of the compiler's narrative.

A curious quirk of the narrative of Perpetua is the taste shown there for *uniuersi*, which outnumbers *omnes* (*uniuersi*: 3.8, 4.9, 5.4, 6.6, 7.1, 9.2; *omnes*: 4.3 (*omne genus*, a set phrase), 5.2, 7.5, 7.9). *Vniuersi* is also used in Saturus' narrative (13.8), but the compiler has only *omnes* (17.3, 18.2, 19.2, 20.8, 20.10). However, this variation may be semantically determined rather than related to changes of authorship. *Vniuersi* is usually applied to the group of martyrs, by the martyrs themselves, and it seems likely that it expresses an idea of solidarity, with *omnes* a more detached term suited to a mere observer. *Omnes* is not used by Perpetua of the martyrs (note 7.5 *omnibus hominibus*, 7.9 *omnibus diebus*).

Similarities between the narratives

One should not overemphasise the differences between the various narratives. There are also similarities, which some might take as suggestive of single authorship. One of these, common to all three narratives, has already been commented on, namely an unmotivated use of *ille* following *is* with the same referent (27.11). Another is the shared VO word order of the narratives of Perpetua and Saturus, and the contrast that both present in this respect with the narrative of the compiler: did a single redactor simply switch into a different word order for the narratives he was attributing to the others?

Particularly striking are the similarities between two visions seen by Perpetua and Saturus, and the language used to describe them: 4.8 *et uidi ... in medio sedentem hominem canum in habitu pastoris, grandem, oues mulgentem*, 12.3 *et uidimus in eodem loco sedentem quasi hominem canum, niueos habentem capillos*. In both cases the sentence begins with *et uidi(mus)*. The present participle *sedentem* precedes in both the noun in agreement, and is itself immediately preceded by a locatival expression with *in*. The object noun phrase is the same (*hominem canum*) in both passages, and has the same word order. Finally, descriptive phraseology follows the noun, containing an accusatival present participle in both cases. It is hard to believe that two different writers could have come up with such matching phraseology:

particularly distinctive is the placement of *sedentem* and of its locatival satellite, which in both respects represents a departure from VO order. There are similar phrases in biblical Latin, which may be the general source, as e.g. at Vulg. Is 6.1 (*uidi dominum sedentem super solium excelsum et eleuatum*) and Io 20.12 (*et uidit duos angelos in albis sedentes unum ad caput et unum ad pedes*), but the locative phrase usually follows *sedentem*; it is the position of the locative in the *Passio* that is at least suggestive of an idiolect.

There is a systematic distinction between the causal uses of *quod* and *quia* throughout the narratives. *Quod* is regularly used only to complement verbs of emotion (*miror, doleo* etc.) (five times, in two of the narratives, those of Perpetua and of the compiler, or six times if we accept the example at 3.4; see above, 27.5), almost always with a subjunctive verb. *Quia* is otherwise the regular causal conjunction (3.5, 10.5, 13.2, 13.6, 15.2, 15.6, 16.2). The only departure from this distinction is at 3.8, where *ideo quod* is used and does not complement the usual type of verb found with *quod*.

Sine cessatione is used in the narratives of both Perpetua (8.2) and Saturus (11.6, 12.2). This is an uncommon expression that goes back to the *Vetus Latina* and is used mainly by ecclesiastical writers (see *TLL* III.956.61ff.). It is a surprise to find three examples within a short space.

Present participial constructions have a prominent place in all the narratives. Participles come after the main verb particularly often, in the nominative in apposition to the subject. I draw attention to some recurrent patterns.

Several times there are three coordinated present participles: 5.5 *haec dicebat … basians mihi manus et se ad pedes meos iactans et lacrimans*, 17.1 *uerba iactabant, comminantes iudicium dei, contestantes passionis suae felicitatem, inridentes concurrentium curiositatem*. In both passages the main verb is one of saying. Sometimes again pairs of following participles are coordinated: 7.10 *et feci pro illo orationem die et nocte gemens et lacrimans* (for *lacrimans* see also the first of the passages above), 13.6 *sic ad te conueniunt quasi de circo redeuntes et de factionibus certantes* (see also 10.8). We saw *habentem* (12.3) in an earlier paragraph in this section conveying descriptive information. For the nominative *habens* see 7.7 *erat piscina plena aqua, altiorem marginem habens*, 10.2 *erat uestitus discincta candida, habens multiplices galliculas*, 10.8 *exiuit uir quidam … purpuram inter duos clauos per medium pectus habens*, 11.5 *quod tale fuit quasi uiridiarium arbores habens rosae*. *Gaudens* is in all three narratives (8.4, 13.8, 18.3), and *dicens* is in those of Perpetua and the narrator (4.2, 5.1, 5.6, 6.2, 20.10, 21.1). The latter (introducing direct speech) is also biblical.

Who wrote Perpetua's narrative?

There are two possibilities. First, the compiler might genuinely have had Perpetua's written account of her experiences, and have incorporated it (along with that of Saturus) in the text. On this view it would have to be assumed that he not only made editorial insertions (on which see Heffernan 2012: 74–8) to give the narratives coherence, but also influenced the style of the originals in subtle ways (unless it is to be assumed e.g. that the compiler, Perpetua and Saturus all happened to share a mannerism in the use of weakened anaphoric *ille*).

Second, the compiler might have written the whole text himself, adopting a different style in the other two narratives in an effort to characterise the martyrs as inspired in their accounts by biblical language. His model (in some respects) might have been an Old Latin version of the Bible. We have seen a good deal of biblical language in the martyrs' narratives (see the next section for a summary). Their word order is relevant too: on the VO characteristics of the *Vetus Latina* (taken from the Greek), see 38.57, and also below, this section, on the Vulgate. The distinctions of word order between the compiler's sections and those of Perpetua and Saturus are certainly marked, but would be more suggestive of differences of authorship if Perpetua and Saturus differed in this respect from each other. As it is, it is not implausible to suggest that the compiler deliberately used more VO patterns in the other two narratives, perhaps with the Bible mainly in mind. Variations of word order may turn up in a single work or single author. It has recently been pointed out by Dickey (2012: 136) that in the *Colloquia Monacensia-Einsidlensia* (a bilingual school exercise with a preface and scenes from everyday life) '[m]any sections of the colloquia are written entirely in Latin of the VO type, but the entire preface (1a–q) is emphatically in the literary OV tradition'. Presumably the OV patterns were perceived as being more literary and formal; Dickey herself refers to the use of OV order as a 'display of erudition'. Imperial writers were capable of varying word order patterns to suit the genre. In the present work the word order of the preface is far more complicated than that of any of the narratives. Or again, Jerome's word order in the treatises and epistles is complex and variable, but in his Vulgate (NT) we find a profusion of VO patterns. Note, for example, the following five sections from the Gospel of Mark (15.16–20), where the word order is relentlessly VO:

Milites autem duxerunt eum in atrium praetorii, et conuocabant totam cohortem, et induunt eum purpura, et inponunt ei plectentes spineam coronam.

et coeperunt salutare eum: haue rex Iudaeorum. et percutiebant caput eius harundine: et conspuebant eum: et ponentes genua, adorabant eum. et post-quam inluserunt ei, exuerunt illum purpura, et induerunt eum uestimentis suis: et educunt eum et crucifigerent eum.

By contrast (e.g.) the opening two sections of the *Vita Malchi* (below) show mainly OV features, with just a little artistic variation, such as a chiasmus in the first main clause, and the postponement of two antithetical prepositional expressions in the last sentence:

Qui nauali proelio dimicaturi sunt, ante in portu et in tranquillo mari flectunt gubernacula, remos trahunt, ferreas manus et uncos praeparant, dispositumque per tabulata militem pendenti gradu et labente uestigio stare firmiter assuescunt, ut quod in simulacro pugnae didicerint, in uero certa-mine non pertimescant. ita et ego qui diu tacui – silere quippe me fecit, cui meus sermo supplicium est –, prius exerceri cupio in paruo opere, et ueluti quamdam rubiginem linguae abstergere, ut uenire possim ad historiam latiorem.

The Greek original was the major influence in the first passage, but even so the VO character of the Latin NT (Vulgate, but the *Vetus Latina* is no different) is so obvious that any Christian writer would be familiar with it and able to exploit the same patterns in a simple Christian narrative.

There would be an interesting consequence of accepting that a single author was responsible for the whole work. We would have another writer who, like Petronius in the *Cena Trimalchionis*, adopted a different style to characterise persons less cultivated than himself. The features of style given to Perpetua and Saturus (on this assumption) would have required no great literary expertise. The repeated use of temporal adverbs, for example, had long been associated with popular style, and is a stylistic tic exploited by the author *Ad Herennium* to characterise the simple and over-simple styles of oratory. The constant use of *et* at the start of a sentence followed by a verb might have been taken from the *Vetus Latina* (see 27.2).

It has to be conceded finally that the authorship of Perpetua's narrative cannot be established with certainty. There are arguments in favour of both possibilities, but a decisive argument is lacking. The Latin has a superficial simplicity but is subtly complex. My own inclination is to say that, despite the substantial evidence set out above for the distinctive-ness of the martyrs' style, there is significant biblical pastiche in Perpetua's Latin, which could easily have been put there by a single author of the whole text.

Perpetua's Latin

The Latin used by or attributed to Perpetua is informal but correct. The use of *in* with the ablative where an accusative might have been expected is far from abnormal and could be paralleled in the literary language. *Cupiret* for *cuperet* at 3.1 (if the text is to be trusted) is not a straightforward vulgarism. It also occurs at Lucr. 1.71, and occasional fourth conjugation forms of *-io* verbs of the third conjugation turn up from early on in literary Latin (e.g. Ennius: see Munro 1886: II.37 on Lucr. 1.71; also *TLL* IV.1429.32ff.). There is a scattering of low-register terms in her narrative, some of them admitted by the educated in appropriate contexts. She has the popular verb for 'kiss', *basiare* (5.5 *basians mihi manus*). It is found in colloquial and low-register texts, such as the shorter poems of Catullus and Petronius, and survives in the Romance languages (see Stefenelli 1962: 34–5 for details). She also has *osculor* (10.13), which is the only verb of this meaning in the sections by the compiler (21.7). So too Saturus has *osculor* (12.5). Other informal elements are *manduco* (4.9) and the compound *commanduco* (4.10), and *impropero* 'curse, blame' (9.2), a usage that Perpetua again shares with a freedman in Petronius (38.11: see Stefenelli 1962: 57) and also with the *Vetus Latina* (see *TLL* VII.1.696.53ff.). The repetitive use of *tunc* as a feature of popular narrative style has been mentioned in these Conclusions, and the partitive use of *de* with verbs of eating and drinking (8.3 *de ea bibere coepit*) comes up elsewhere (see 31.12, and index s.v. *de*, 'expressing partitive object'). This too can be paralleled in biblical Latin. *Coepi* + infinitive used in profusion had long been characteristic of more informal narrative. The augmented suffixal derivative *discinctatus* is of a type that is mainly low-register.

We have stressed the influence of biblical narrative, as for example the use of *et* at the start of sentences. *Noli pauere* and *sine cessatione* were probably recalled from the Bible. The first is followed immediately by another Christian (and biblical) usage, *conlaboro*. At 7.1 Perpetua writes: *et dolui commemorata casus eius*. The participle is from the middle *commemoror* 'recall, remember'. It is apparent from *TLL* III.1835.17ff. that this usage is attested overwhelmingly in biblical Latin, particularly the *Vetus Latina* (see too Rönsch 1875: 353–4, Burton 2000: 182–3). Perpetua's use of postponed *habens* (see the last section but one of these Conclusions) also has a biblical look about it: cf. e.g. Vulg. Mt 26.7 *accessit ad eum mulier habens alabastrum unguenti pretiosi* (so Mc 14.3), Mc 3.1 *et erat ibi homo habens manum aridam*.

Another influence on the Latin of Perpetua was inevitably the time at which she wrote. Her narrative is full of elements typical of later Latin. We have seen, for example, two compound adverbs, *adinuicem* (note too 7.6; but at 9.1 *inuicem*) and *in pridie*. Another is *desub* at 4.7 (where the prefix has full force). Such compounds are not alien to earlier Latin, but they occur in profusion from about the time of the *Vetus Latina*, amid some resistance from grammarians (see Adams 2013, chapter 23). The unmotivated use of the subjunctive in causal *quod*-clauses is mainly late.

28

THE MAGERIUS MOSAIC (THIRD CENTURY)

Introduction

The Magerius mosaic is from the village of Smirat in Tunisia, near Thysdrus, modern El Djem. It was first published by Beschaouch (1966). It is thought to date from the mid-third century AD (see Beschaouch 1966: 147–50), and probably decorated a villa (that of Magerius: see below). The mosaic represents a *uenatio*, or beast hunt, and four named hunters are depicted killing four leopards, also named. In two places the vocative *Mageri* occurs, on each side of the mosaic. Magerius was the presenter of the show, or *editor* (twice the verb *edes* occurs in the acclamations to be discussed here), and *Mageri* must express a repeated chant of the crowd. There are two extended pieces of Latin, first the words of the *curio* or herald addressed to the people and asking that the *uenatores*, who belong to a group called the Telegenii, be given 500 denarii (per leopard), and second acclamations of the crowd.

The texts and image contain scenes from different points in the day. The leopards are shown as either still resisting or in their death throes, yet night has fallen according to one part of the Latin. I believe that there are more acclamations than one, spoken at different times.

The Telegenii were an African sodality (*sodalitas/familia uenatorum*) with a recurrent emblem and a tutelary deity (Dionysus), and they were available for hire for the mounting of *uenationes* (see Beschaouch (1966: 150–6).

The acclamations belong to a formulaic popular genre attested in both Greek and Latin of the Empire (though traceable well back before then) from the circus, the arena, the senate and gatherings of other sorts, including religious. There has been a good deal of interest in acclamations in recent decades (see e.g. the general book of Aldrete 1999), but no comprehensive collection of the texts in either Greek or Latin, a lack which makes it difficult to identify all the formulae in such a text.

A fuller account of the interpretations offered here may be found in Adams (2016).

The acclamations (10–26) following the speech of the herald are printed below with the line divisions that appear on the mosaic. The translation of this second part is split into paragraphs representing one possible division of the acclamations.

Text

Speech of the herald
per curionem
dictum: domini mei, ut
Telegeni
pro leopardo
meritum ha-   5
beant uestri
fauoris, dona-
te eis denarios
quingentos.

Acclamations
adclamatum est: 10
exemplo tuo mu-
nus sic discanp [*sic*]
futuri, audiant
praeteriti. unde
tale, quando tale?   15
exemplo quaesto-
rum munus edes,
de re tua mu-
nus edes.
sta dies.   20
Magerius do-
nat. hoc est habe-
re, hoc est posse,
hoc est ia. nox est:
ia munere tuo   25
saccis missos.

Translation

Through a herald it was said: 'My lords, so that the Telegenii may have the reward of your favour for (each) leopard, give them 500 denarii.'

It was shouted forth: 'By your example let future generations/benefactors (?) learn that a show is like this, and let past generations/benefactors (?) hear (that it is like this). By whom (has a show) such as this (ever been presented), when (has a show) such as this (ever been presented)? On the example of the quaestors (of Rome) you will present a show, from your pocket you will present a show. This is the day! It is Magerius who is presenting it!'

'This is to have the wherewithal, this is to have power, this is the moment!'

'It is night: now discharge (the Telegenii) from your show by (award of) the bags of money!'

Alternatively divisions might be placed at the end of 15, of 19 and after *donat* at 22. It seems certain that a new acclamation begins at 24 (*nox est*), because at this point the show is over.

Commentary

The speech of the herald

The herald asks for 500 denarii per leopard, but the boy is bearing twice that amount. The request for 500 denarii and the appearance of the boy with a much greater sum cannot be simultaneous.

1–2 per curionem dictum: the herald was merely the mouthpiece of the Telegenii, who spoke 'through' him. *Curio* originally meant 'priest of the *curia*' (*TLL* IV.1489.29ff.), but developed the sense 'herald' (1489.43ff.).

2 domini: the crowd here are addressed as *domini* 'lords' (cf. Suet. *Claud.* 21.5 for this crowd address). See Dickey (2002: 88–9), citing Seneca's comment (*Epist.* 3.1) that 'when we run into people whose names we don't remember, we address them as "master"'.

4 pro leopardo: this phrase is unambiguously in the *ut*-clause, and not in the second clause attached to *denarios quingentos*, as it is always taken in translations (i.e. as '500 denarii per leopard'). It must however imply that.

The acclamations of the crowd

There are at least two ways of taking the lines from *exemplo tuo* to *Magerius donat*.

First, they might have been uttered late in the day, in response to the herald's request for payment. It is a (remote) possibility that the phrase *munus edes* means not 'you will present a show' (i.e. soon, with the utterance coming early in the day), but something like 'you will become presenter of the show in the full sense' (sc. 'if you agree to pay the *uenatores*)', which might put the remark towards the end of the day. This interpretation is open to objections.

Second, this part might have been spoken early in the day. On this view it cannot be a response to the request of the herald, as this must have been near the end of the show. It would follow there must have been a time lapse between the first acclamation(s) and the last, which is uttered as night falls.

I have argued elsewhere (Adams 2016) that the second possibility is the right one, and will not go through all the arguments again here, though a few points must be made.

The general opinion has been that the whole right-hand text (and not only the opening part) is a direct response to the herald's request and is thus a demand by the crowd that Magerius pay the *uenatores* (first possibility above: see e.g. Dunbabin 1978: 68, Rouèché 1984: 183). Thus the acclamation (singular) could only have taken place at the end of the day, once the fights were over and the leopards slaughtered. Problems are raised for this inter- pretation by the repeated future tense *edes*, and the standard meaning of the phrase *munus edere*, here with its future verb. This phrase cannot refer to the mere award of prize money. It is a far more comprehensive expression, referring to the mounting by a benefactor of a whole show, the total cost of which would far exceed the prize money. A glance at the thirteen meanings of *edo* distinguished by the *OLD* shows that the verb cannot mean anything like 'pay'. It means rather 'display, exhibit, hold' (see meanings 11, 12), and thus while it is suited to *munus* meaning 'show' in general, it is not suited to some such meaning as 'payment'. The conclusion cannot be avoided that *munus edes* has to mean what the verb phrase elsewhere means (see below, 28.17), namely 'you will present a show'.

If we accept the future tenses and the semantics of the phrase at face value, it is clear that the initial acclamation must have been uttered before the show has got under way. The crowd are in place and Magerius takes his seat. As he does so he is acclaimed by the crowd, who chant that he is about to mount a spectacle that will outdo all others. He is first addressed anonymously, and later is triumphantly named, 'this is the day, it is Magerius who is presenting it!'

It is not only the meaning of *munus* and *edo* that favours this interpretation. A second argument lies in the words *exemplo quaestorum* preceding the first instance of *munus edes*, 'you will present a show on the example of the quaestors'. Evidence for the history during the imperial period of quaestors at their own expense presenting shows to the people, that is whole events, is collected by Beschaouch (1966: 145–6). If Magerius is to act on the model of the quaestors, he is about to mount a show. The second *munus edes* is immediately followed by the phrase *sta dies*, i.e. in the context 'this is the day when you will present a show'. This phrase would not be appropriate if *munus edes* referred in a limited way to the mere granting of prizes.

The right-hand text thus would not express a single acclamation uttered at one moment of time, but several acclamations spread over the day, the last when night has already fallen.

We might alternatively contemplate the possibility that *munus edes* has its proper meaning 'you will present a show', but nevertheless alludes (at the end of the whole performance) in a restricted way to the granting of rewards (see above). Could the sense be 'you will become the presenter of the show (when you have paid the prizes demanded by the herald)'? But there is no such condition expressed in the Latin.

The second acclamation on my first division above (that of the translation) consists of the triumphant three-line celebration of the wealth and power of Magerius, with each clause introduced by *hoc est*. The show is no longer simply foreseen, but a demonstration of wealth must be before the spectators, possibly as the performers enter the arena (note particularly the phrase *hoc est ia*).

The third acclamation runs from *nox est* to the end of the text. The show is now over, and payment is made to the *uenatores*. The syntax here is particularly problematic (see below).

10 adclamatum est: a standard way of introducing an acclamation in the *Historia Augusta* (e.g. *Alex. Sev.* 7.1, 8.2 (without *est*), 9.4, 10.3, *Gord.* 5.7, *Tac.* 7.4); see also the Conclusions below on the same usage in *acta ecclesiastica* reported in Augustine *Epist.* 213.

12 sic discanp: Bomgardner (2009: 168) translates 'may future benefactors (*munerarii*) understand the spectacle'. But that is to disregard *sic*, which is predicative, with *esse* understood (for predicative *sic* with *esse* see *OLD* s.v. *sic* 5a). *Sic* with *est/esse* 'is so' is potentially ambiguous, as it may look back (= 'is as previously indicated, seen') or forward (= 'as is about to be indicated/seen': see *OLD* s.v. 2, 3). Since on the interpretation adopted here the show is yet to begin, *sic* is taken to be prospective ('let them learn that this is what a show is like').

Beschaouch (1966: 139, 140) takes *futuri* and *praeteriti* as referring to benefactors (understanding *munerarii*). Such adjectives/participles are used in the nominative plural without an understood noun in a general sense, usually in oppositions resembling this, of those of the past, present or future (see *TLL* X.2.1017.56ff., citing this example among others). However, generations of the past could hardly learn of anything from the grave, whereas some past benefactors might still be around to learn that they had been surpassed by Magerius. Ellipse of *munerarii/editores* looks an attractive possibility.

Discanp is not a normal type of misspelling, and is probably a slip (or due to damage?).

The expression *exemplo tuo ... discant* 'by your example let them learn' recalls a remark by Ammianus at 28.4.33 that at every show (*in omni spectaculo*) every performer (in a long list *uenator* itself occurs) is constantly hailed with the cry *per te illi discant* 'through you let them learn' (drawn to my attention by William Slater). I take it that *illi* refers not to the spectators but to other performers or to opponents, = 'you show them'. Magerius is to show other *editores* what a show should be like.

14–15 unde tale, quando tale?: it is natural here to take *unde* in the sense *a quo* (i.e. with personal reference, 'by whom'), with Magerius implicitly compared to other benefactors. This personal use is as old as Plautus and Cato, with various nuances (*OLD* s.v. 2, Hofmann and Szantyr 1965: 208–9, Väänänen 1981a: 126; cf. also above, 4.5). Cf. e.g. Plaut. *Men.* 782–3 *ludibrio, pater, | habeor. :: unde? :: ab illo quoi me mandauisti, meo uiro*, Cic. *Att.* 15.13a.2 *sed perscribe, quaeso, quae causa sit Myrtilo ... et satisne pateat unde corruptus* ('But pray tell me all about Myrtilus' case ... and whether it is sufficiently clear who suborned him', Shackleton Bailey 1965–70: VI.185, changing the passive to active). I take it that these clauses on the mosaic are free-standing direct questions, with ellipse of *munus* and also of a verb. A verb of doing, offering, presenting (*facio, do, dono, edo* or the like) has to be supplied, almost certainly in the past tense, probably *edo* (i.e. *editum est*), given the phraseology of the acclamation elsewhere (see further next note on *edes*). The two clauses taken as direct questions are a suitable follow-up to the words *audiant praeteriti* (= 'let past *editores* hear of it as so – after all, who in the past ever put on a show such as this is to be?'). *Tale* is prospective on the interpretation adopted here (= 'of such a kind as we are about to see before us') (see *OLD* s.v. 2b).

Verbal ellipse is a feature of acclamations, and may occur later in this text itself (see below, 25–6 on *saccis missos*). A classic example is *Christianos ad leonem* (see e.g. Tert. *Apol.* 40.2; cf. *SHA, Comm.* 18.10 *exaudi Caesar: delatores ad leonem. exaudi Caesar: Speratum ad leonem*).

17 munus edes: this is a regular expression of the mounting of a spectacle, particularly gladiatorial (*OLD* s.v. *munus* 4, *TLL* V.2.94.27ff.): e.g. Livy 28.21.1 *Scipio Carthaginem ad ... munus ... gladiatorium ... edendum rediit*, CIL VIII.7969 *munus gladiat(orium) et uenat(ionem) ... M. Cosinius ... Celerinus ... edidit. Munus* was not a neutral term simply denoting a show in the manner of *spectaculum*. It implies that that show has been organised at someone's expense as a civic duty or public benefaction. It focuses on the role of the *editor*, whereas the focus of *spectaculum* is on the spectators. As for *edere*, this is the 'verbe le plus commun, et de loin, pour exprimer l'organisa-tion d'un spectacle' (Chamberland 2012: 275). Chamberland (276) notes that he has found about 125 to 130 attestations, from the first century onwards but mainly in the second and third centuries. The implication is that the subject has paid for the show himself, rather than from public funds (see Chamberland 2012: 276 and particularly 277, making a distinction in this respect between *edere* and *curare*).

The repetition of the phrase is a refrain, and such refrains are typical of acclamations, usually in the imperial period with invariant word order. There are some strikingly repetitive acclamations in the *Historia Augusta*, with verb phrases recurring with the same word order. At *Comm.* 18–19 a long senatorial acclamation is reported. Among other repetitive elements it has at 5–6 a sequence of four instances of *unco trahatur*, and then at 19.2–6 a further sixteen instances of the same phrase with the same order. Three times in successive sentences at 18.10 there is the expression *parricida trahatur*, and then at 19.9 two instances of *parricidae cadauer trahatur*. Another repeated refrain with the same word order is at *Pass. Perp.* 21.2 *populus . . . reclamauerit: 'saluum lotum! saluum lotum!'* (on this passage see further below, 28.25–6). Aldrete (1999: 138) notes that repetitions in senatorial acclamations in the *Historia Augusta* range from a few to 'an astounding eighty iterations' (see further the Conclusions below on a text recording the numbers of such repetitions on a particular occasion).

The phrases accompanying the repeated *munus edes* are varied in the two clauses (*exemplo quaestorum, de re tua*). Such variation in the complements of refrains is elsewhere attested in acclamations (see the Greek inscription (*SEG* 34.1306) from Perge in Pamphylia of the late third century AD quoted and discussed by Kuhn 2012: 306–8, in which a single refrain (αὔξε Πέργη) is accompanied by more than a dozen different phrases).

20 sta dies: *sta* is for *ista*. Aphaeresis of the *i* (the inverse or hypercorrect variant of the prothetic vowel that often developed before *s* + stop, as in *estercus* for *stercus* or *iscola* for *schola*) in this pronoun is well attested in late Latin (for examples see Adams 2013: 464; for aphaeresis in general, Sampson 2010: 56–8). *Iste* is not infrequently used in a temporal meaning of the present time (*TLL* VII.2.509.79 'spectat ad ipsum tempus praesens'), with *dies* itself (masculine or feminine) or a synonym (*lux*) or with *nox* (see the examples of these and comparable phrases at *TLL* 510.1ff.). *Iste dies* at Lucan 6.158 (*non paruo sanguine Magni iste dies ierit*) means 'today', and *nox ista* at Val. Flacc. 1.670 means 'tonight'. Note particularly *Per. Aeth.* 35.1 *maximus labor nobis instat hodie nocte ista*, where the underlined words form a sort of compound meaning 'tonight'. Moreover the reduced form survives in Italian in various compound temporal expressions, *stamattina, stasera, stanotte* (*REW* 4553). In the dialect of Bagno di Romagna (Northern Italy) the expression *ste di*, 'this day, today', is in use in opposition to *l'altre di*, 'the other day' (information from Francesco Camagni), and in Bolognese (spoken not far away), *sto de* (information from Anna Chahoud). See also Parry (1991: 627).

21–2 Magerius donat: Beschaouch (1966: 139) shows that he takes this phrase to be an editorial insertion by excluding it from the inverted commas that enclose the rest of the text apart from the initial *adclamatum est*. If it were an editorial comment one would expect the verb to be in the perfect tense, like *dictum* at the start of the herald's speech, and *adclamatum est*. I take it to be a dramatic naming of the benefactor by the crowd.

23 hoc est posse: for the substantival use of *posse* see *TLL* X.2.153.62ff. (sometimes in classical Latin and common in late Latin). For the substantival infinitive see below, 29.2, 29.3.

24 hoc est ia. nox est: this punctuation is necessary, rather than *hoc est. ia nox est*. The mosaic itself shows this, as there appears to be strong punctuation after *ia*. Also, after the two instances of *hoc est* + predicate another such predicative construction seems required.

Adverbs are not infrequently used as predicates of the verb 'to be' in Latin, where an English speaker might expect an adjective or noun. Adverbs used thus include *palam, frustra, recte, bene* and *procul* (e.g. Cic. *Pis.* 11 *quae sunt palam*) (see e.g. Salonius 1920: 208, Adams 1976a: 92, Hofmann and Ricottilli 2003: 337). However, in the present context *iam* would have to be substantivised to provide a predicate parallel to the preceding substantivised infinitives, = 'this is the precise moment' (?), and that would be very odd. Salonius (1920: 209–11) cites examples of the adverbs *mane, tarde* and *sero* from later Latin that are close to substantival, but these are not good parallels for the present case. Such words refer or may refer to periods in the day, and a term meaning e.g. 'late (in the day)' might be reinterpreted to mean 'in the evening'. It is indeed the adverb *sero* that lies behind the masculine nominal reflex = 'evening' in French (*soir*: see Bloch and von Wartburg 1968: 595, and below, 44.36.1).

An alternative might be to understand a noun such as *munus* as predicate, = 'this is the show now', i.e. 'this is it now', but the problem with that is that the third *hoc est* would not have an expressed predicate, which in this rhetorical tricolon it surely needs.

The expression remains a difficulty, but it is possible that here we have an extremely rare instance of a near-substantival use of an adverb. Could it be that there was heard at shows a single-word acclamation *iam!*, uttered right at the start as the performers appeared? If so the meaning here might be 'this is the "now"'. For the adverbial use of *iam* in the sort of meaning required, = 'de tempore praesente et instante', see *TLL* VII.1.102.74ff.

Beschaouch (2006: 1404) also takes *hoc est ia* together, but then punctuates the next bit as *nox est ia. 'munere tuo ...'* rather than as *nox est: ia munere tuo. . .* His punctuation shows that *nox est ia* is taken, like *Magerius donat*, as an editorial insertion. In his earlier paper Beschaouch (1966: 139) also treated *nox est ia* as a unit, but included these words in the acclamation. I would prefer to see this second phonetic spelling *ia* standing in an exclamatory acclamation rather than in an aside (see the Conclusions below). The present tense in such a phrase as *nox est (iam)* does not look at all like an editorial comment, which would only be explicitly such with a past tense (*erat*).

25–6 munere tuo saccis missos: this is the most difficult phrase in the acclamations.

The ablative *saccis* cannot be rendered '(sent off) <u>with</u> the bags of money', as it has constantly been taken, because such a meaning would require the presence of *cum*. Accompaniment is not expressed by the plain ablative without *cum* except in phrases, mainly military, of a certain type, viz. when the noun is accompanied by an adjective, as e.g. *omnibus copiis* and similar (e.g. Caes. *Gall.* 3.11.5 *ipse eo pedestribus copiis contendit*; see further Ernout and Thomas 1953: 87, Hofmann and Szantyr 1965: 114–15). *Cum* is obligatory with *mitto* even when the noun is accompanied by an adjective (see Hofmann and Szantyr 1965: 114, citing Caes. *Civ.* 2.38.1 *cum mediocribus copiis missum*).

This is not the place to collect renderings of *saccis* that disregard the absence of *cum*. These go back to Beschaouch (1966: 139), who renders 'que les Telegenii soient renvoyés de ton munus avec des sacs'. He did however, unlike others, address the syntax, describing *saccis* (143) as 'ablatif d'accompagnement', and he also paid attention to the problem of *missos*.

If *saccis* does not express accompaniment, what could it express? The simplest explanation is that it is instrumental, with *missos* referring to the Telegenii, who are 'released', i.e. 'discharged' from the show by means of the grant of the money-bags (the syntax of *missos* I deal with below). *Mitto* is regularly used of the discharge of someone from some duty or office (see *OLD* s.v. 3a–b, *TLL* VIII.1173.51ff., especially 1174.1ff.). *Mitto* (and the noun *missio*) had a technical meaning in reference to gladiators. Coleman (2006: 221) on Mart. *Spect.* 31.3 puts it thus: '*missio* represents discharge from the authority of the *editor* who has sponsored the spectacle, so that a gladiator who is *missus* will return to his barracks to train for future engagements; it does not mean discharge from service as a gladiator.' Coleman goes on to state the two circumstances under which such a *missio* or reprieve might be granted (a gladiator who had surrendered might sometimes be granted a reprieve, or if two gladiators had fought to a draw both might be deemed worthy of a reprieve), and adds (232) that this sort of *missio* is not to be confused with the unconditional release from service of a victorious gladiator. It is important to note that *mitto* in the sense of 'discharge' from some sort of service, including the gladiatorial use of a reprieve, is attested in the idiom *missum facere* (= *mittere*) (for this expression see *OLD* s.v. 3a–b, both lemmata, and the end of this note, below).

The Telegenii were clearly not (at least in their entirety) gladiators in the conventional sense of slaves, condemned criminals or prisoners of war (for the various types see the rich discussion of Ville 1981: 228–46). They were a professional guild characterised by Beschaouch in a series of papers (1966, 1985, 2006) as a *sodalitas uenatorum*. Bomgardner (2009: 169) calls them 'the best known troupe of itinerant *venatores* of antiquity', and remarks that a 'spectacle given by a professional troupe in the hopes of attracting payment at the end is something new in our repertoire of spectacles'. Whatever the status of the *uenatores* themselves, slaves or free, they must have been chosen and esteemed for their expertise in killing dangerous animals, as payment is demanded precisely for that. Pride was taken in demonstrating that expertise under handicap, as we see from the behaviour of one of the hunters, Spittara, who is on stilts, and the best performers would not readily have been let go by the managers of the sodality. Conventional gladiatorial terminology of reprieve or release from service would therefore not be appropriate of the members of such a guild, but it may well be that old terminology had been given a new twist in reference to such a professional troupe; they were 'discharged' from the show at the end by means of the formal award of payment.

The expression on this mosaic (*missus* along with the ablative of *saccus*) occurs elsewhere, and looks like an African formula applied to professional troupes on such occasions. On a stone preserved in the Museum of Tebessa in Algeria there is a three-line inscription *Sadunti | ob merita | missos sacco* (*CIL* VIII.1884, *ILAlg.* I.3079, *AE* 1986.726), which has been discussed by Beschaouch (1985: 454–8). Beschaouch takes *Sadunti* to be the vocative of a name *Saduntius*, which, like the vocative *Mageri* on the Smirat mosaic, must belong to the *editor*. *Missos* is regarded (457) as an accusative of exclamation, as he also takes it in the Magerius mosaic (see immediately below), and *sacco* like *saccis* is interpreted as an ablative of accompaniment (457; note the translation on the next page, 'Qu'en récompense de leur vaillante prestation ils (= les bestiaires) quittent l'arène <u>avec un sac d'argent chacun</u>' (my emphasis)). Again this rendering of the ablative will not do, but again the ablative may refer to the discharge of the combatants by means of the award of a bag of money.

On this view of the verb phrase in the two African documents, the *saccus* or *sacci* might have come to symbolise the discharge from the show of the professional *uenatores*, at least at this time in North Africa, just as the *rudis* or wooden rod symbolised the release of gladiators (on which see Coleman 2006: 232). An instrumental ablative is well suited to this idea: the bag of money discharges them, or they are discharged by it. Crucial to this interpretation is the meaning of *missos* in this context. I am not taking it merely in the sense 'sent away', which might indeed require a complement expressing accompaniment, but rather in a technical sense, of discharging. They are discharged 'by the sack' (cf. English 'get the sack'). The elliptical character of the expression *saccis missos* makes it certain that it must have been commonplace (or it would not have been understood), and it was probably regional and expressive of a local custom in the signing off of such professional guilds at the end of a performance. Representations of money-bags on the prize table appear in Roman works of art depicting contests (see Dunbabin 2010, especially 343–4 with n. 77, and figures 11, 12, 19, 33, 36, 37; also, for literary evidence, Coleman 2006: 230), and the handing over of these presumably marked the discharge.

There are two ways of explaining the syntax of *missos*.

First, it may be an accusative of exclamation (so Beschaouch 1966: 143; and see above on the other African formula). The use of exclamatory accusatives is a marked stylistic feature of acclamations. A vivid example is recorded in the *Pass. Perp.* (21.2), at the point at which the martyr Saturus becomes the victim of a leopard (see above, 28.17). He is covered with blood by a single bite, and the crowd call out in irony *saluum lotum! saluum lotum!* This is an accusative of exclamation, and it might be rendered 'look at him healthy and washed, healthy and washed!' Moreover *saluum lotum*, like *missos*, is elliptical, in that no name, noun or pronoun is expressed with it, such as *Saturum*.

The second possibility is to understand *fac* with *missos*. *Facio aliquem/ aliquid missum* is an idiom equivalent to *mitto* on its own (= e.g. *mitto aliquem*) in various of its senses (see OLD s.v. *mitto* 3a–b, 4a 5; also the brief comment at *TLL* VI.1.119.59–60). For e.g. *facio missum* = *mitto* 'release' see OLD s.v. *mitto* 3b. Moreover sometimes in the *facio missum* construction *facio* is omitted, and indeed when it would be imperatival (see Heidemann 1893: 60): note Cic. *Att.* 15.20.3 *sed acta missa* (where Shackleton Bailey 1965–70:

VI.269 allows omission of either *sint* or *faciamus*, but *fac* would be just as likely), *Fam.* 9.7.2 *sed ridicula missa* ('but joking aside': sc. *fac*). On this view *missos (fac)* would be an instruction shouted to Magerius, 'discharge (them) from your show'. The expression *missum fecit* is indeed used in a gladiatorial context at *CIL* VI.10194 = *ILS* 5088 (quoted and discussed by Coleman 2006: 221–2: see above), of the granting of a reprieve (*Rom(ae) mun(eris) eiusd(em) die VIIII Fimbriam lib(erum), (pugnarum) VIIII, miss(um) fe(cit)*), and it would not be out of place in the present context, of discharging performers.

I incline to this second explanation, partly because the Ciceronian examples just quoted show that ellipse of *fac* (or another jussive form) was idiomatic with such uses of *missum*, and partly because at the very end of the perform-ance a directive by the crowd to Magerius to pay the *uenatores* seems particularly appropriate. In the Algerian text discussed above the phrase *missos sacco* is preceded by vocative address of the *editor* (*Sadunti*), and that vocative would be better suited to an implied imperative intended for him than to an exclamation.

Conclusions

The Latin of the acclamations is distinctive but not substandard.

There are three definite phonetic spellings, *iam* without the final *-m* twice and *sta* for *ista*. Otherwise in the two texts final *-m* is correctly written five times. All the misspellings are in exclamatory phrases, and it is possible that they were intended to convey the sounds of the crowd's shouts.

Stylistic features of the acclamations worth emphasising here are the use of refrains, and ellipse.

I use the term 'refrain' to refer to a whole phrase repeated. There are two refrains in this text. The first acclamation has *munus edes* at the ends of juxtaposed clauses. Later *hoc est* occurs three times. The format of the mosaic and the small space allowed to the Latin almost certainly mean that the repetitions uttered on the day itself have been reduced in the record. We saw above (28.17) the extent of the repetitions in the late imperial senate as emerges from the *Historia Augusta*. Another text that illustrates the place of repetitions in acclamations is at Augustine *Epist.* 213 (*CSEL* 57). This text records *acta ecclesiastica* and describes the election of a bishop, Eraclius. Augustine delivered a speech that was constantly inter-rupted by acclamations of the *populus*, and the *acta* state the number of repetitions. I quote just one group of these acclamations and the numerical insertions (*Epist.* 213.6, pp. 378.15–379.3):

'de hac accessione aliquid adclamate.' a populo adclamatum est: 'fiat, fiat' (dictum est uicies quinquies); 'dignum et iustum est' (dictum est uicies octies); 'fiat, fiat' (dictum est quater decies); 'olim dignus, olim meritus' (dictum est uicies quinquies); 'iudicio tuo gratias agimus' (dictum tredecies); 'exaudi, Christe, Eraclium conserua' (dictum est octies decies).

Fiat, fiat alone was repeated thirty-nine times at this point. A few other features are worth noting: the phrase *adclamatum est* at the start, the address of Augustine in the second person by the crowd (note *tuo*), and the naming of Eraclius, the key figure, only at the end, as the second-last word (cf. *Magerius donat*), though he is alluded to earlier. This last feature is also to be seen in another of the groups of acclamations, that at *Epist.* 213.3, p. 376.8–10.

Acclamations tend to be elliptical partly because events are unfolding before the spectators and sometimes only key words need to be expressed, and partly because they are formulaic. In this text the clauses *unde tale, quando tale* have both nominal and verbal ellipse, and *saccis missos* may have an imperative omitted, and is also without a noun. The same is true of the other attestation of this formula, *missos sacco*.

29

PELAGONIUS, *ARS VETERINARIA* 34 (FOURTH CENTURY)

Introduction

Pelagonius was the author of an *Ars ueterinaria* which survives mainly in the manuscript Florence, Bibl. Riccardiana 1179 (R), but also partly in Einsiedeln, Stiftsbibl. 304 (514) (E) (for further details see the Introduction to text 30). The interest of E is that it preserves some parts that are not in R. If the two manuscripts are compared it becomes clear in places that there must have been more versions of Pelagonius than one circulating in antiquity. In text 30 below I give a short passage in which the two manuscripts differ, and note a linguistic feature of the treatise that emerges from the version in E.

Pelagonius is mentioned in extant literature only by Vegetius (in the *Mulomedicina*), whose other work, the *Epitoma rei militaris*, is known to have been written at some time between 383 and 450, possibly in the later part of the 4th century (see now Reeve 2004: v, viii–x). Pelagonius dedicated the treatise to a certain Arzygius, and he presented his veterinary instructions in the form of epistles to named addressees, presumably wealthy horse owners (for details of this and the other subjects mentioned in this Introduction see Adams 1995a: 3–12). This convention was taken over from Apsyrtus, a Greek veterinary writer, parts of whose work survive in the Greek hippiatric corpus (*CHG*). Apsyrtus (whose dates are unknown) was used extensively by Pelagonius. Each chapter of Pelagonius' treatise seems to have begun with an epistle, including the present one (the third), where R has the heading *Pelagonius Arzygio suo* (33), though usually any personal elements in these epistles have been dropped in transmission (note however e.g. the start of 24). The present section (34) is probably part of the epistle that began chapter 3. The content is taken from an extant portion of Apsyrtus, and it is of interest to examine Pelagonius' translation technique. Pelagonius used a number of sources (details in Adams 1995a: 4–8), including Columella, as we will see below. He also shared a lost source with the *Mulomedicina Chironis*, and was himself used by Vegetius, who sometimes changed the Latin in various ways.

Text

34.1 Febres autem curantur sic. sanguis sic de temporibus mittitur et de facie et ab omni cibo abstinetur. tantum potum praebendum esse iubeo moderate et alia die deambulet sensim et stabuletur calido loco. si temporis opportunitas patitur, herbis uiridibus recreandum est aegrum pecus; si tempus in hieme est, faenum et hordeum et tisanam praeberi utilissimum est. **2** plerumque autem etiam cum non febricitat, signa in ipso eadem inuenies, id est grauatam ceruicem, caput ad terram demissum, recumbere in latere. hordeum praebeto: si adpetierit, sine febre est. de labore uel de ostocopo talia eueniunt. si autem febriat et hordeum recusat et anorectus plerumque est et tristis, solum tamen potum requirit; febris autem triduo si perseuerauerit, moritur. **3** qui autem aut tactu auriculae aut uenae, quae in latere est sub armum, putant se posse febrientem intelligere, uerae rationis ignari sunt, quia nec ostendit se de uenis intellegere febrientem. ei tamen, qui de labore uel de ostocopo supradicta signa habuerit, sanguinem detrahere contrarium est, quia et labore fatigatus et sanguinis emissione exhaustus sine uiribus fit. febrientem utilissimum est sanguinare, quia et leuiora sentit suspiria et uenae ferro relaxatae recipiunt citius sanitatem.

Translation

34.1 Fevers are treated as follows. Blood is let thus – from the temples and face, and the animal is kept off all food. I instruct that only drink must be offered, in moderation, and that on the next day he should go for a walk, cautiously, and be stabled in a warm place. If the season is appropriate and allows it, the sick beast should be restored with green grass; if the season is winter, it is most useful for hay and barley and pearl barley to be offered. **2** Often, even when he does not have a fever, you will find in him the same symptoms, that is the neck weighed down, the head lowered to the ground, and his lying on his side. Offer barley: if he shows an appetite for it, he is without fever. Such conditions originate from toil or fatigue. But if he has a fever and refuses barley and is generally without appetite and depressed, he nevertheless needs drink on its own. But if the fever lasts for three days, he dies. **3** But those who, by touching either the ear or the vein which is on the flank under the shoulder think they can diagnose a fevered animal, are ignorant of true reason, because the diagnosis of a fevered animal is not revealed from the veins.[1] Nevertheless in the case of one who has the aforementioned symptoms from toil or fatigue it is

---

[1] On the text translated in this clause see the Commentary.

counter-indicated to draw blood, because wearied by the toil and exhausted by the letting of blood he is rendered without strength. It is most useful to let blood from a fevered animal, because he experiences lighter breathing, and the veins, eased by the iron, recover their health more quickly.

Commentary

1 febres autem: in this short passage there are four instances of *autem*, which are usually adversative, though it is hard to see much point to the present case. *Autem* is very frequent in the text (some sixty times). *Quidem* by contrast is rare (six times), and in most cases (four) is in epistles, a significant distribution (see below, 29.3 on *nec* for this point). Here we see a continuation of the pattern already observed (22.18–19, 27.10): *autem* had greater vitality than *quidem* for a period during the Empire.

sanguis sic de temporibus mittitur: *sic* looks redundant and is deleted by Ihm (1892) and Fischer (1980) on the grounds that it has been introduced by confusion from the previous sentence. But *sic* is not infrequently used in this way in technical texts, to lead into a key word that comes straight after (see Svennung 1935: 401, Adams 1995a: 627). There is another instance at 11.1: *intelligitur autem morbus regius sic ex oculis uel maxime* (cf. *Mul. Chir.* 269).

The Greek at this point (*Hipp. Ber.* 1.5, *CHG* I, p. 2.12) has θεραπεύεται δὲ οὗτος αἵματος ἀφαιρέσει ἐκ τῶν κροτάφων ἢ τοῦ προσώπου, but there is a variant reading in the Paris manuscript (see the app. crit.), which begins θεραπεύονται δὲ οὕτως, and it is almost certain that Pelagonius had a Greek text with οὕτως rather than οὗτος.

mittitur: directives are expressed in variable ways in the text of Pelagonius, and the variability may to some extent be due to scribal changes. Here we have a 'descriptive passive indicative' standing for a directive. A practice is described (such and such is done) in such a way as to imply that the reader should follow this practice. The construction continues in *abstinetur*, but in the next sentence another passive is a jussive subjunctive (*stabuletur*). But since the ending is the same as that of the indicative *abstinetur* in the previous sentence it is not impossible that the scribe fell mechanically into that ending without noticing that the mood was different. Or was Pelagonius himself responsible for the variation? There are many other variations in the forms of directives in this single chapter, which could not be emended away. At 1 a gerundive is used (*recreandum est aegrum pecus*), and there is a similar construction earlier, but dependent on *iubeo* (*potum praebendum esse iubeo*: see further below). Twice (1, 3) *utilissimum est* is used with the infinitive: instruction in the form of persuasion. A prohibition is also expressed as persuasion at 3 (*sanguinem detrahere contrarium est*). Once (2) there is a -*to* imperative (*hordeum praebeto*). Finally, there are two jussive subjunctives (*deambulet* at 1 as well as *stabuletur*). Pelagonius seems to have thought it appropriate, particularly in an epistle, to express instructions in a varied way, but the possibility of scribal tampering makes it hard in many places to be certain about the text. On directives in Pelagonius see Adams (1995a: 204–8, 460–8), and on similar variation in another late instructional text (the cookery book of Apicius) see Grocock and Grainger (2006: 98–102); on variations in earlier (agricultural) prose see Hine (2011).

tantum potum praebendum esse iubeo: noteworthy here is the use of *iubeo* with the gerundive in an infinitive construction (instead of a gerundive on its own, or *iubeo* with an infinitive), a conflation, or, perhaps better, a sort of 'harmonic redundancy' (for the term see Pinkster 1989: 315; also Adams 1995b: 198 n. 107 for bibliography on the general phenomenon). There are other examples in Pelagonius, as at 31.2 *cui succurrendum hoc modo Cornelius Celsus iubet* (see Adams 1995b: 218 with 198 n. 107; also Hofmann and Szantyr 1965: 374, 378). For comparable redundancy see 140.2 *huic sanguinem de temporibus aut de facie detrahendum esse necessarium*. The construction of the present passage is unlike the Greek (*Hipp. Ber.* 1.5, *CHG* I, p. 2.14 μόνου τοῦ πόματος κατὰ μικρὸν διδομένου), and we must have a favoured Pelagonian idiom. It is a usage of late Latin: for an extensive collection of material (but not including examples from Pelagonius) see *TLL* VII.2.583.39ff.

Here Pelagonius uses *tantum* 'only' (translating μόνου: see above). At 2, however, he writes *solum autem potum*, with *solum* (adjective or adverb?) this time rendering μόνον in the same expression (*Hipp. Ber.* 1.6, *CHG* I, p. 3.3). This is an interesting lexical variation, and perhaps a sign of Pelagonius' stylistic aspirations. It is not clear whether there is a stylistic distinction between *tantum* and *solum* (adverb) in late Latin, as the evidence for their distribution does not seem to have been collected. In the *Peregrinatio Aetheriae tantum* is the usual word (eleven times). *Solum* occurs there nine times, but six of these examples are in the expression *non solum . . . sed et*, in which *tantum* does not occur.

alia die: in some late, particularly low-register, texts this phrase is used to mean 'on the next day' (so in the *Peregrinatio Aetheriae*: see E. Löfstedt 1911: 145, and for bibliography, Hofmann and Szantyr 1965: 208). It was *alter* that replaced *alius* in the Romance languages, but this usage represents an (originally hypercorrect?) encroachment of *alius* on *alter*. Hofmann and Szantyr loc. cit. find *alius dies* of 'the following day' already at Plaut. *Aul.* 531 *spes prorogatur militi in alium diem* (so Löfstedt says that the usage is in Plautus), but that interpretation is needless (note de Melo 2011a, 'The soldier's hope is put off until another day').

herbis uiridibus recreandum est aegrum pecus: Pelagonius made extensive use of Columella, in the form both of verbatim quotations and stylistic imitation (see Adams 1991b with bibliography). Here he has recalled Col. 6.31.1 *ac uiridibus herbis, cacuminibusque arborum recreatur aegrotum pecus* (see Adams 1991b: 77–8, id. 1995a: 200). Pelagonius uses the adjective *aeger* only four times, always in this phrase, which he clearly took from Columella. The main manuscripts of Columella at this point have *aegrotum*, but Palladius 14.5.3, quoting Col. 6.5.2 (on which see below), also has *aegrum pecus* where the manuscripts of Columella have *aegrotum* (see Adams 1991b: 77), and it is likely that both Pelagonius and Palladius had a version of Columella with *aegrum*.

A significant example of *aegrum pecus* in Pelagonius is at 21.1, in a verbatim quotation of the passage of Columella just referred to (6.5.2–3): *eoque medicamine saliuandum est aegrum pecus* (Col. *aegrotum*). Noteworthy here is the association of *aegrum pecus* with a gerundive (as a form of directive) and its placement after the verb. There can be no doubt that in our present passage Pelagonius had recalled the Columellan construction. The Greek source here is not equivalent in phraseology: *Hipp. Ber.* 1.5, *CHG* I, p. 2.16–17 προάγειν αὐτὸν δεῖ ἐπὶ τὴν νομήν, ἐὰν ᾖ ὁ καιρός. The sick animal is referred to merely by a pronoun, νομή 'pasturage' is more general than the expression *herbis uiridibus*, and δεῖ + infinitive is a more banal usage than the stylistically marked gerundive (on which see below). Pelagonius' equivalent (*si temporis opportunitas patitur*) to the final clause of the Greek here also appears more pompous than the straightforward use of καιρός. *Opportunitas* with *temporis* is, however, classical phraseology, cited at *TLL* IX.2.773.76ff. from Cicero, Caesar and Livy. We see Pelagonius putting effort into his composition, drawing on a Greek source but using phraseology from an admired Latin writer.

It is natural here to take *pecus* (*-oris*), which is often a collective, as referring to a single beast (= *pecus, -udis*). This usage, where the term denotes a single member of a particular species, is to be distinguished from the collective use denoting the species itself (see *TLL* X.1.950.30ff., where the distinction is carefully made across a variety of species). The particularising use of *pecus, -oris*, of a single animal, is attested from the late Republic and particularly Augustan period in literary Latin including poets (details may be found in the *TLL*). For the word used of single equine animals (Columella onwards) see *TLL* X.1.952.29ff.

The gerundive as a directive is a stylistically marked construction, and Columella was Pelagonius' model. While there are many hundreds of imperatives and imperatival substitutes in the text, there are hardly more than forty gerundives replaceable with an imperative, a substantial number of them in epistles (see Adams 1995a: 197–200).

si tempus in hieme est: 'if the season is in winter', an unusual phrase: one would expect *hiems* (nominative) in agreement with *tempus* (cf. 316 *si hiems fuerit*). The Greek has χειμῶνος (*Hipp. Ber.* 1.5, *CHG* I, p. 2.15), though not in an identical context. However, for such predicative prepositional expressions see Bulhart (1955: e.g. 47, 55) (e.g. Ovid. *Met.* 9.454 *Byblis in exemplo est*) and *TLL* VII.1.788.46ff.

praeberi utilissimum est: *utilissimum est* + infinitive is a type of 'persuasive directive' (see above, 29.1 on *mittitur*) favoured by Pelagonius. There is another example in this passage at 3, and six others in the text. The Greek (*Hipp. Ber.* 1.5, *CHG* I, p. 2.16) has δεῖ + infinitive. The second example (at 3) corresponds to ἀναγκαῖον + infinitive (*Hipp. Ber.* 1.8, *CHG* I, p. 3.15). On the other hand at 141.1 Pelagonius has *oportet* where the Greek of Apsyrtus has δεῖ (*Hipp. Ber.* 33.5, *CHG* I, p. 166.20). He varied his rendering of simple Greek forms of expression.

2 plerumque autem etiam cum non febricitat: here *plerumque* translates πολλάκις (*Hipp. Ber.* 1.6, *CHG* I, p. 2.21 πολλάκις δὲ μὴ πυρέσσων ἔστιν). *Plerumque* was an eminently 'Pelagonian' word, which occurs nine times in the text, seven times in epistles (Adams 1995a: 158). A term of the same meaning that is even more favoured is *frequenter*, which occurs twenty times in epistles and ten times in other parts of the text (details in Adams 1995a: 159–60). *Saepe* by contrast is all but excluded (two examples, both of them comparatives). *Saepe* leaves no trace in Romance and was in decline in ordinary (as distinct from high-style) usage from at least the time of Petronius (see E. Löfstedt 1911: 276–8, Lundström 1948: 119, Stefenelli 1962: 23–6, Adams 1976a: 120), though its comparative form seems to have retained a wider currency (see Stefenelli 1962: 24, and above, 26.9–10). *Frequenter* itself does not survive in Romance (though the influence of its comparative *frequentius* may be seen in the late regional term *suuentium*, a conflation of *subinde* and -*entius*/-*m*: see Adams 2007: 466), but it seems to have been current in later Latin (see Stefenelli 1962: 25).

Plerumque occurs a second time in this passage (not corresponding to anything in the Greek).

id est grauatam ceruicem, caput ad terram demissam, recumbere in latere: *recumbere* is a striking nominal use of the infinitive, standing as object of the verb and coordinated with two accusatives. For a similar structure see Cato, *FRH* II.5.F33 *pleraque Gallia duas res industriosissime persequitur, rem* *militarem et argute loqui* (see further Adams 1995a: 479–80, above, 28.23, below, 29.3 on *intellegere*, and 35.8–9, for a slightly different construction in a British curse tablet).

de labore uel de ostocopo talia eueniunt: *ostocopus* occurs twice in this short passage (cf. 3). It ought to refer to 'bone-fatigue' (ὀστοκόπος), but the Greek source does not have this term at all, but twice has the less specific κόπος 'fatigue' (*Hipp. Ber.* 1.6, *CHG* I, p. 2.24, 1.8, p. 3.13), and it is possible that in Latin the compound had been generalised in meaning (for details see Adams 1995a: 304–5). The compound seems to have had some currency in Latin veterinary language: it occurs in the form *stocopus* (with aphaeresis) at *Mul. Chir.* 240.

anorectus plerumque est et tristis: cf. Apsyrtus *Hipp. Ber.* 1.6, *CHG* I, p. 3.2 ἔστιν ἀνόρεκτος καὶ σκυθρωπός. *Anorectus* also occurs in a passage taken from Apsyrtus at 140.2, though there the extant Greek does not have the term. The *TLL* (so too Souter 1949) cites *anorectus* only from Pelagonius, and it seems that it was a term without real currency in Latin and merely transferred from the source.

si autem febriat et hordeum recusat: *febriat* is subjunctive, but then there is a switch into the indicative in the same conditional clause. It looks as if the writer or a scribe has mechanically given the same -*at* ending to the second verb without noticing that it conveys a different mood. For this sort of error see above, 29.1 (note on *mittitur*), and index, 'indicative, mechanically used'.

febris autem triduo si perseuerauerit, moritur: *moritur* strictly refers to future time. When the present tense has future reference the verb is usually in the first person singular from early Latin onwards, but examples in other forms turn up particularly in later Latin (see Adams 2013: 669–70; also index, 'present tense, for future'). Twice, at 30.2 and 30.4, when drawing on Columella Pelagonius converts (it seems) first person plural futures of the source into presents (see Adams 1995a: 470: *custodimus* and *uitamus* for *custodiemus* and *euitabimus*). At 140.2 the second person *laedis* has future reference. With the example in the present passage may be compared 141.3 *sane rhododafnen si burdo comederit, uesica ipsius rumpitur et inde moritur.* A motivation for the present tense *moritur* may be suggested. In early Latin there are places where the present is used to indicate the immediate, as distinct from more remote, future (Adams 2013: 667), and here similarly the present implies instant death (cf. on 27.14). Note particularly Diosc. II, p. 227.15–16 *perhibent Afri, quod die, qua quisquis a scorpione fuerit hic percussus et comederit ocimum, statim moritur.* For a present indicative used in reference to sudden death see also *Pass. Perp.* 21.1 *ecce prodeo illo, et ab uno morsu leopardi consumor* ('I go in there and am done for with one bite of the leopard'). The speaker does not say this as he is being consumed, as the leopard has not yet been released: it is an event that follows immediately, as described in the next sentence.

Triduo occurs fifteen times in the text of Pelagonius and *per triduum* forty times, whereas the unaccompanied accusative is attested only once (in *R*) (374) (see Adams 1995a: 169, 446). The plain accusative conveying duration was in decline in later Latin.

3 auriculae: here the diminutive translates a non-diminutive in Apsyrtus (ὠτός at *Hipp. Ber.* 1.8, *CHG* I, p. 3.10). *Auris* was displaced by *auricula* in the Romance languages, and an example such as *auricula* here, apparently without any diminutive force (there are no grounds for seeing the sense 'inner ear', on which see Adams 1995a: 550–1), loosely foreshadows that displacement (see above, 7.13). Pelagonius prefers the classical *auris* (by 19:11), but in the lower-register *Mulomedicina Chironis* the diminutive is preferred (by 44:5) (see Adams 1995a: 551 for details).

quia nec ostendit se de uenis: the transmitted text has the plural *ostendunt*, but this can hardly be correct and I would now change to *ostendit*, which is translated here. If the plural is kept the translation would have to be something like 'because they do not show that they diagnose a fevered animal from the veins', or 'because they show that they do not diagnose a fevered animal from the veins', neither of which seems meaningful. I believe that a scribe has misunderstood the nature of the infinitive *intellegere*, which I take to be the subject of the verb (*ostendit*), and not dependent on it in an acc. and inf. construction, and has accordingly changed to *ostendunt* believing that *mulomedici* described as lacking true reason must be the subject. The Greek of the source Apsyrtus at this point (*Hipp. Ber.* 1.8, *CHG* I, p. 3.12–13) has οὐδεμία γὰρ ἀπόδειξίς ἐστι διὰ τούτων πυρετοῦ, 'for there is no diagnosis/exhibiting of fever through these means'. It is obvious that *intellegere febrientem* renders ἀπόδειξις πυρετοῦ, which means that *intellegere* is another infinitive used as a noun (see above, 29.2 on *recumbere*). *Ostendit se* 'shows itself' corresponds to ἔστι in the Greek, with *intellegere febrientem* as its subject: the diagnosis of the fevered animal is not revealed from the veins.

Earlier (1995a: 480) I tried to resolve the textual problem by suggesting the change *febrientem* to *febrientes*, 'those suffering from fever do not reveal themselves from the veins', but this leaves a 'final' use of the infinitive *intellegere*, = 'for diagnosis', which is hard to believe.

Nec as a negative replaceable by *non* occurs four times in Pelagonius (Adams 1995a: 160), three times in epistles (here and at 267.2, 363; cf. 60.2). It is associated particularly with old Latin and juristic language, but there are also scattered examples in late low-register texts such as the *Peregrinatio Aetheriae* and *Mulomedicina Chironis* (see E. Löfstedt 1911: 88–9, id. 1956: I.340–1, Hofmann and Szantyr 1965: 448–9). It is hard to know what to make of these. Was the usage really still current at a submerged level (Löfstedt in both places observes that an instance at *Mul. Chir.* 380 is eliminated by Vegetius *Mul.* 2.113.1), or could it have been taken up occasionally as pretentious? The distribution in Pelagonius would favour the second possibility, as there is evidence that he wrote up epistles in a higher style (see Adams 1995a: 160–2).

sanguinare: Pelagonius has three different verbal expressions for 'let blood' in this passage, *sanguis . . . mittitur, sanguinem detrahere* and *sanguinare*; note too 3 *sanguinis emissione*. On the formation and use of *sanguinare* see Adams (1995a: 221–2, 506–8). The verb had earlier been intransitive, meaning 'bleed' or 'thirst after blood', but the use seen here survives in Romance and is attested in a curse tablet. All three examples in Pelagonius are in passages based on Apsyrtus.

Conclusions

See the Conclusions of text 30.

30
PARTS OF PELAGONIUS, *ARS VETERINARIA* 404, FROM TWO DIFFERENT MANUSCRIPTS

Introduction

Until 1989 the veterinary work of Pelagonius was known from a single manuscript, R (see above, 29), but in that year Corsetti published a paper demonstrating that the manuscript Einsiedeln, Stiftsbibl. 304 (514) (E), of the 8th or 9th century, also has substantial sections of Pelagonius (see further Adams 1992b, 1995a: 3, 171–9, 202–4, 205–7, 461–2). Some of these sections in E have a better text than that of R and reveal that R has been tampered with in transmission. Here I present a very short passage in which E manifests a feature of Pelagonius' lexical style (or perhaps that of his source at this point: see Adams 1992b: 506 with n. 64) that has been suppressed in this passage in R. I also quote below the corresponding passage of Vegetius, which clearly comes from a version of Pelagonius similar to that of R (which means that the R-version goes back to antiquity), and a passage from the Greek veterinary writer Eumelus, which is close to the version of E (which means that the fuller version also goes back to antiquity). Little is known about Eumelus. He has traditionally been regarded as a source of Pelagonius, but I have argued (1984a; cf. 1995a: 5–6) that there is good evidence that Pelagonius did not draw on Eumelus, nor Eumelus on Pelagonius; rather, that both drew on a lost Latin veterinary writer.

Texts And Translations

R

eum cum diligentia constringito et sanguinem de ceruice et cruribus detrahito, clausumque in tenebris contineto, donec cibum modice appetat.

Tie him up with care and let blood from the neck and legs, and keep him shut up in darkness until he shows a moderate appetite for food.

E

... detrahito uentremque et crura pluribus punctis uirito [= urito]. si coleatus est, testis adimidio [= adimito] clausumque ...

Let (blood) and burn the belly and legs with numerous points. If he has testicles, remove the testes and (keep him) shut up ...

Eumelus (*Hipp. Ber.* 101.6, *CHG* I, p. 349.8–13)

τοῦτον ἐπιμελῶς δέσμει καὶ αἷμα ἐκ τῶν σκελῶν καὶ τοῦ σπονδύλου λάμβανε, καὶ τῷ αὐτῷ αἵματι σὺν οἴνῳ τὸ σῶμα ἀπότριβε, καὶ τὴν κοιλίαν καὶ τοὺς κροτάφους κεντήμασι πολλοῖς καυτῆρος ἔγκαιε. καὶ ἐὰν ἐνόρχης ἐστί, τοῦτον εὐνούχιζε. καὶ ἐν τόπῳ σκοτεινοτέρῳ κατάκλειστον ἔχε, μέχρις οὗ τροφῆς ὀρεχθῇ.

Tie him up carefully and let blood from the legs and the neck(?), and with the same blood along with wine rub the body, and burn the belly and temples by means of many points made by a cauterising instrument. And if he has testicles, castrate him, and keep him shut up in a rather dark place until he has an appetite for food.

Vegetius, *Mulomedicina* 2.107.1

quem caute, ne medentem laedat, diligenterque constringito. sanguinem de ceruice et de cruribus ei detrahito rursumque in tenebris contineto, donec appetat cibum.

Cautiously, in case he hurts the one treating him, and carefully tie him up. Let blood from his neck and and legs, and keep him again in darkness until he has an appetite for food.

Commentary

detrahito, clausumque (R): after *detrahito* E has several clauses not in R but which are very close to the section καὶ τὴν ... εὐνούχιζε in Eumelus, and must have been in the original version of Pelagonius. By contrast in Vegetius there is no sign of these clauses, which shows that already by his time there was available a version of Pelagonius depleted at this point. *Rursumque* in Vegetius has no point in the context, and it is obviously a corruption of *clausumque*, which should be restored to the text. *Rursumque* is retained by Lommatzsch in the Teubner, though he notes the reading of Pelagonius in his apparatus. E now alongside the Greek of Eumelus makes the emendation obligatory. In most respects the Greek is very similar to E, though κροτάφους 'temples' occurs where the Latin has *crura* 'legs', an inexplicable variation.

It is the additional section in *E* that has the linguistic interest in this passage, and I turn now to that.

coleatus: this adjective is based on the basic (probably offensive) term for 'testicle', *coleus* (on which see Adams 1982a: 66). The noun occurs in epigram (in both Martial and the *Corpus Priapeorum*) but not satire, in a Pompeian graffito (*CIL* IV.4488), and twice in freedmen's speeches in Petronius (39.7, 44.14). It survives in Romance languages (*REW* 2038). The adjective was previously attested only in the Atellan farce of Pomponius (34 Frassinetti *insilui in coleatum eculeum*, 64 *conspicio coleatam cuspidem*). The first of these examples is similar to that in Pelagonius (*eculeus* means 'small or young horse'). Previously the term in Pomponius had looked like a humorous coinage by the poet himself, but it now seems possible that he was drawing on the slang of horsemen.

It is not only the adjective *coleatus* that has turned up in E. The noun itself is at 3.5 (481bis) in the phrase *coleos foueto*. *Colei* is nowhere found in R, in which *testes* occurs five times, twice indeed (65, 153) with *foueto* (see Adams 1992b: 506). The presence of *coleatus* and *colei* in E (and presumably in Pelagonius' work itself) is of a general interest. Before the discovery of some Pelagonius in E I noted (1982a: 232–3) that veterinary writers were less fastidious than medical in their acceptance of basic excretory terminology (*merda, caco* and *meio* in its remodelled first conjugation form, based on the analogy of *cacare*, are all in Pelagonius), and we can now add these terms to the inventory of basic terminology that would not be expected in medical texts (see further Adams 1992b: 506–7, id. 1995a: 420).

Conclusions

Again we see that technical writing, including that on mundane subjects, is not to be confused with substandard writing. Practical texts may be full of literary artifice. That Pelagonius was a conscious stylist is obvious in text 29. He departs from a literal rendering of Apsyrtus to incorporate phraseology and a construction from Columella (*herbis uiridibus recreandum est aegrum pecus*), an admired predecessor. The passage has a lot of variation, for example in the way in which directives are expressed. There is not a single imperative apart from one in *-to*, but the passive indicative (a 'descriptive' directive), the jussive subjunctive, both active and passive, the gerundive, *iubeo* + infinitival gerundive, and 'persuasive' forms of expression (*utilissimum/contrarium est* + infinitive) all occur. There is also lexical variation, as in the expressions for letting blood, and the pair *tantum/solum potum* where the Greek has a single adjective.

Departures from classical norms are not necessarily to be dismissed as vulgar: they may be typical late Latin, or motivated, or have some other explanation. *Sub armum* looks like an accusative with a preposition where an ablative is expected, but the phrase may be a scribal deviation. *Moritur* with future reference implies immediacy. *Triduo* expressing duration of time, if it is not again merely a scribal aberration, typifies a late development. *Nec* for *non* may be deliberately old-fashioned rather than substandard.

Alia die looks substandard. *Si ... febriat* (subjunctive) is odd, in a clause which has the coordinated indicatives *recusat* and *est*, and it is possible that the ending is an anticipation of the ending of the next verb; but if so, was the anticipation Pelagonius' or that of a scribe? *Auricula*, to judge from the *Mulomedicina Chironis*, was now the current term for 'ear' in ordinary speech. It ousted *auris* by the time of Romance. Pelagonius for the most part used the old term *auris* (an indication of his conservative style), but was prepared to admit the diminutive. *Sanguinare* in the sense which it has here was possibly low-register.

Colei and *coleatus*, finally, alongside various coarse excretory terms found elsewhere in the text (see above), suggest that those dealing with animals were more down to earth when referring to bodily functions and sexual parts than was the norm in high literature.

31

LETTER OF PUBLICOLA
TO AUGUSTINE (AUG. *EPIST.* 46,
CSEL 34)

Introduction

This letter was written by a certain Publicola to Augustine some time after 395, posing more than twenty questions on religious problems. Publicola seems to have been a landowner on the African *limes* in the territory of the Arzuges, who was worried by the possible pollution caused by the local Berbers employed to transport and look after foodstuffs by tenant farmers. The Berbers swore loyalty 'by their own demons', and Publicola was concerned particularly whether such oaths might pollute either the persons who received them or the goods themselves. It is of considerable interest that we also have Augustine's reply (*Epist.* 47). Only very rarely do we find pieces of Latin on the same subject and of the same place and date of composition, but reflecting different educational or social levels of the language. Publicola's letter is not only naive in its presentation but has a number of marked proto-Romance features. Augustine's avoidance in his reply of these same features is so stark that he seems to have been distancing himself socially from the language of his addressee, and the impression created is one of condescension. It is well known that Augustine advocated the accommodation of one's usage to that of more humble Christian addressees (see Adams 2013: 14–15 and index s.v. 'Augustine'; also below, 31.6), but there is no sign of linguistic accommodation in his letter. There is a comprehensive discussion (with translation) of the religious significance of the letter by Shanzer (2011), and also of such matters as its date and the identity of the writer, the identification of the Arzuges and features of the Latinity. Particularly significant in view of the remarks above about Augustine's avoidance of linguistic accommodation is Shanzer's observation (section 13) that Augustine appears not to have liked or even to have known Publicola, who seems to have approached him without any prior acquaintance. Augustine's letter ends very abruptly.

The following selection omits only the preface and conclusion of the letter.

In the Commentary to this text the many cross-references to Publicola's letter employ the section numbers found in the edition of the text (and printed in our text and translation in bold).

Text

46.1 In Arzugibus, ut audiui, decurioni, qui limiti praeest, uel tribuno solent iurare (1) barbari iurantes (2) per daemones suos. qui (3) ad deducendas bastagas (4) pacti fuerint (5) uel aliqui ad seruandas fruges ipsas, singuli possessores uel conductores solent ad custodiendas fruges suscipere quasi iam fideles epistulam decurione mittente uel singuli transeuntes, quibus necesse est per ipsos transire. mihi disceptatio in corde nata est, si ille possessor, qui susceperit barbarum, cuius fides per daemonum iurationem firma uisa est, non coinquinatur (6) uel ipse uel illa, quae custodit, uel ille, qui deducitur a deductore barbaro. sed hoc debes scire, quia (7), qui iurat barbarus, a possessore pro seruandis frugibus accipiat aurum uel a uiatore deductor; sed tamen cum hac ueluti mercede, quae solet dari a possessore uel a uiatore, iuramentum etiam illud (8) in medio est mortale datum decurioni uel tribuno, quod perturbat me, ne polluat illum, qui suscepit barbari iuramentum (9), uel illa, quae custodit barbarus. quacumque enim condicione etiam auro dato et obsidibus datis, ut audiui, tamen iuramentum iniquum medium intercessit. dignare mihi autem definitiue rescribere et non suspense, quod, si ipse scribas dubitanter, ego in maiores dubitationes incidere possum, quam antequam interrogassem.

2 hoc etiam audiui, quia ipsi homines conductores (10), qui praesunt rei meae, iuramentum per daemones suos iurantibus barbaris accipiunt pro reseruandis frugibus. si, cum illi ergo iurant per daemones suos, ut custodiant fruges, non polluunt ipsas fruges, ut, si inde manducauerint Christianus sciens uel de pretio ipsarum rerum <usus> fuerit, coinquinetur, significare dignare.

3 item ab alio audiui quod conductori non iuratur a barbaro, et alter dixit quia iuratur conductori. si etiam falsum mihi dixit ille, qui dixit iurari conductori, si iam pro hoc quod solum audiui, non debeo uti de (11) ipsis frugibus uel de pretio ipsarum propter auditum solum, quia dictum est: 'si quis autem dixerit: "hoc immolaticium est idolis", nolite manducare propter illum'? si tamen etiam haec causa similis est causae de immolaticio? quod si ita est, quid debeo de ipsis frugibus uel de pretio ipsarum facere?

4 si debeo requirere de utroque, qui mihi dixit quia non iuratur conductori, aut qui dixit quia iuratur conductori, et dictum uniuscuiusque probare per testes, qui uerum dixit de illis duobus, et tam diu non contingere de ipsis frugibus uel de pretio (12), quam diu mihi probatum fuerit, si uerum dixit ille qui dixit quia non iuratur conductori?

5 si barbarus, qui per iuramentum suum iurat malum, fecerit illum Christianum conductorem uel tribunum, qui limiti praeest, iurare (13) sibi pro fide illi seruanda pro custodiendis frugibus per ipsum iuramentum mortale, per quod ipse iurat, si solus ille Christianus coinquinatur? si non et illa, quorum causa iurat? aut si paganus, qui limiti praeest, iurauerit barbaro pro fide illi seruanda per mortale iuramentum, si non inquinat, pro quibus iurat? si quem misero ad Arzuges, si licet ei iuramentum accipere a barbaro illud mortale et si non coinquinatur, si susceperit tale iuramentum Christianus?

6 si de area trituratoria tritici uel cuiuscumque leguminis aut torculari, de qua daemoni oblatum est, si licet inde manducare Christianum scientem (14)?

7 de luco si licet ad aliquem usum suum Christianum scientem ligna tollere?

8 si quis uadens ad macellum emat carnem (15), quae non sit immolaticia, et cogitationes duas habuerit in corde, quod immolata sit et non sit immolata, et illam tenuerit cogitationem, qua non immolatam cogitabit, si manducauerit, si peccat?

9 si qui (16) bonam rem, de qua dubitat, an bona aut mala sit, faciat, cum putat bonam, cum tamen putasset et malam, si peccatum adscribatur ei?

10 si quis dixerit, quod immolaticium est, mentiens et postea dixerit iterum (17), quia mentitus est, et ad fidem uere mentitus est, si licet Christianum inde manducare aut uendere et de pretio uti ex eo, quod audiuit?

11 si Christianus aliquis ambulans passus necessitatem uictus fame unius diei uel bidui uel multorum dierum, ut iam durare non possit, ita occurrerit, ut in ipsa necessitate famis, in qua sibi uidet iam mortem proximare, inuenerit cibum in idolio positum, ubi nullus sit hominum, et non possit inuenire alium cibum, debet mori aut exinde cibari?

12 si Christianus uideat se a barbaro uel a Romano uelle interfici (18), debet eos ipse Christianus interficere, ne ab illis interficiatur? uel si licet sine interfectione eos inpugnare uel repellere, quia dictum est, 'non resistere malo'?

13 si murum possessioni debet Christianus facere propter hostem et si ille Christianus, qui fecerit murum, causa non existit homicidii (19), cum inde aliqui coeperint pugnare et interficere hostes?

14 si licet de fonte bibere uel de puteo, ubi de sacrificio aliquid missum est? si de puteo, quod in templo est et desertum factum est, debet inde Christianus bibere? si in templo, quod colitur, idoli puteus ibi (20) sit uel fons et nihil ibi factum sit in eodem puteo uel fonte (21), si debet haurire aquam inde Christianus et bibere?

15 si Christianus debet in balneis lauare uel in thermis, in quibus sacrificatur simulacris? si Christianus debet in balneis, quibus in die festo suo pagani loti sunt, lauare siue cum ipsis siue sine ipsis?

16 si in solio, ubi descenderunt pagani ab idolis uenientes in die festo suo et aliquid illic in solio (22) sacrilegii sui fecerint et scierit Christianus, si debet in eodem solio descendere?

17 si Christianus inuitatus ab aliquo adpositam habuerit carnem in escam, de qua dictum fuerit illi, quia immolaticia est, et non manducauerit eam;

postea autem ad aliquem (23) translatam ipsam carnem aliquo casu inuenerit uenalem et emerit eam aut adpositam habuerit ab aliquo alio inuitatus et non cognouerit eam et manducauerit, si peccat?

18 si de horto uel de possessione idolorum uel sacerdotum eorum debet Christianus sciens holus emere uel aliquem fructum et inde edere?

46.1 Among the Arzugi, I have heard, the barbarians are accustomed to swear to the decurion who is in charge of the *limes*, or the tribune, swearing by their own demons. Those barbarians who have agreed to conduct transport or in some cases to protect the crops themselves (*in situ*), these are accustomed to be taken on to look after their crops by individual landowners or tenant farmers, or individual travellers who must pass through their territory, if the decurion merely sends a letter, as if they are already trustworthy. For me the question has arisen in my head whether the landowner, who has taken on a barbarian whose loyalty has seemed to be guaranteed by his swearing by demons, is being defiled – either himself, or alternatively the goods which (the barbarian) is looking after, or the person who is escorted by the barbarian transporter. You ought to know that the barbarian who swears the oath receives gold from the landowner for looking after the crops, or, in his role as a transporter, from the traveller; yet along with this type of payment, which is accustomed to be given by the landowner or by the traveller, that mortal oath has been openly offered up to the decurion or tribune, a thing which worries me, in case it pollutes the one who has received the barbarian's oath, or the goods which the barbarian is guarding. For whatever the terms, even if gold or hostages are given, as I have heard, nevertheless an improper oath has inserted itself openly into the proceedings. Please write back to me precisely and not ambiguously, because if you for your part write with hesitation, I can end up in greater doubt than I was before I had asked.

2 This I have also heard, that the tenant farmers themselves, who are in charge of my property, accept an oath for the keeping safe of the crops sworn by the barbarians in the name of their own demons. Please indicate whether, when they therefore swear by their demons to guard the crops, they are not polluting the crops themselves, with the consequence that, if a Christian knowingly eats some of them or <makes use of> some of the price achieved by the same things, he is defiled.

3 I have also heard from another that an oath is not sworn by the barbarian to the tenant farmer, and yet my other source said that an oath IS sworn to the tenant. Even if the one who said that an oath was sworn to the tenant told me a lie, should I now, because of this thing that I have only heard, refrain from making use of the crops themselves or the price accruing from them on account of hearsay alone, given that it is stated: 'If anyone shall say, "This is an offering to idols", do not eat it on account of him'? Is the present case similar to that of the offering? Because if that is so, what should I do about the crops themselves or the price therefrom?

4 Should I ask both of them, that is the one who said to me that an oath is not sworn to the tenant, and the one who said that an oath IS sworn to the tenant, and should I test through witnesses the assertion of each one of them, to see who out of the two of them told the truth, and should I refrain from touching any of those crops or any of the money therefrom until it has been established for me if the one who said that an oath is not sworn to the tenant told the truth?

5 If the barbarian, who swears by means of his own evil oath, makes the Christian tenant or the tribune in charge of the *limes* swear to him by the same mortal oath by which he himself swears, that he will maintain loyalty to him for guarding the crops, is that Christian alone defiled? Are not also those goods (defiled), on behalf of which he swears the oath? Or if the pagan who is in charge of the *limes* swears to the barbarian by a mortal oath that he will maintain loyalty to him, does he not defile the goods on behalf of which he swears the oath? If I send someone to the Arzuges, is it permissible for him to receive that mortal oath from the barbarian, and is he not defiled if, being Christian, he accepts such an oath?

6 Is it permissible for a Christian knowingly to eat (produce) from a threshing floor for wheat or any legume or from a press from which offerings have been made to a demon?

7 Is it permissible for a Christian knowingly to take logs from a (sacred) grove for some purpose of his own?

8 If someone were to go to the market and buy meat which was not sacrificial, and if he has two notions in his head, that it may be sacrificial or may not, and if he fastens onto the notion that it is not sacrificial, does he sin if he eats it?

9 If anyone were to do something good, but about which he has doubts whether it is good or bad, and does it at the time when he thinks it is good, though previously he had also thought it was bad, should a sin be ascribed to him?

10 If someone has said that (something) is sacrificial, but telling a lie, and if later on the other hand he has said that he told a lie, and if truly on good authority he did lie, is it permissible for a Christian to eat some of that or to sell it and to use the profit from that which he has heard the truth about?

11 If some Christian out of necessity is on a walk and is overcome by hunger of one or two or many days' duration, so that he can no longer last – if it comes about that in the very extremity of the hunger, in which he sees that death is now approaching him, he finds food placed in a temple devoted to idols, where there is no one about, and he can find no other food, should he die or eat some of it?

12 If a Christian sees that he will be killed by a barbarian or Roman, should the Christian himself kill them to avoid being killed by them? Or is it even permissible without killing anyone to fight against or repel them, given that it is stated, 'I prefer not to resist'?

13 Ought a Christian to make a wall for a property to cope with an enemy? And the Christian, who has made the wall – is there not a case of homicide (against him) when some people have begun to fight from there and to kill enemies?

14 Is it permissible to drink from a spring or well where something from a sacrifice has been thrown? From a well which is in a temple and has become deserted – ought the Christian to drink from there? If in a temple which is devoted to worship there is there a well of an idol or spring, and nothing has been done there in the same well or spring, should a Christian draw water from there and drink it?

15 Should a Christian wash in baths or hot baths in which sacrifice is made to images? Should a Christian wash in baths in which pagans are washed on their festival day, whether with them or without them?

16 In a pool where pagans have descended when they come from the idols on their festival day, and have done something of their sacrilege there in the pool and the Christian knows this – should he descend into the same pool?

17 If a Christian, having been invited by someone, has meat served up to him for dinner, of which he has been told that it is sacrificial, and has not eaten it – but afterwards has by some chance found the same meat, which had been transferred to someone else, on sale and has bought it, or has had it served up to him by someone else by whom he has been invited and has not recognised it and has eaten it – does he sin?

18 From a garden or property belonging to idols or their priests should a Christian knowingly buy vegetables or some fruit and eat some of it?

Commentary

1 solent iurare: in this text dependent infinitives almost invariably follow the higher verb (23:3). In the reply by Augustine, however, infinitive position is more variable.

1–2 iurare . . . iurantes: the expansion of a finite verb by a (present) participle of the same meaning has different motivations. In literary Latin it is e.g. an occasional stylistic tic to have the verb accompanied by a synonymous participle from a different verb: see Hofmann and Szantyr (1965: 797), citing Sil. 9.586 *ferens ... portat*, and Kroll (1929) on Catull. 64.179 *at gurgite lato |* *discernens ponti truculentum diuidit aequor* (with some poetic parallels; also Fordyce 1961: 300, with further examples from Catullus). This is an extended type of repetition that hardly seems to be treated by Wills (1996); his 'participial resumption' (311–25) is of different type, with the participle, usually perfect but sometimes present (318), in a different clause, as at Ovid *Met.* 3.390 *ille fugit fugiensque* (see too Hofmann and Szantyr 1965: 812).

On the other hand sometimes inept repetitions are found: note Vitr. 6.8.4 *cum cunei ab oneribus parietum pressi per coagmenta ad centrum se prementes extruderent incumbas* (of buildings resting on piers, with arches constructed with wedges: 'since the wedges, being pressed down by the weight of the walling though the vertical joints, might press themselves towards the centre and push out the upper course of the pillars'). Here the reflexive *se prementes* seems to have the same function as the passive of the same verb that precedes, and could probably have been omitted (though this case differs from the others here in that *pressi* is not a finite verb).

In the present passage *iurantes* could certainly have been omitted without altering the meaning, but here we have a mannerism of biblical and thence of Christian Latin in general, considered ultimately to be of Hebrew origin. For *faciens facio* as a Hebraism in biblical Latin see *TLL* VI.1.124.22ff. See also Väänänen (1987: 87), Velázquez Soriano (2004: 551), with bibliography, Burton (2011: 488), and below, 46.7. At *Per. Aeth.* 12.11 *reuertentes ... regressi sumus* the Christian idiom has been subjected to lexical variation.

3 qui: a preposed relative which would often be picked up in the following main clause by a resumptive pronoun (e.g. *eos*), but there is none here. See above, 1 Appendix 2, 4.11.

4 bastagas: a term ('transport') of doubtful origin that is attested in late Greek (βασταγή) as well as late Latin (see *TLL* s.v.). But did one language take it from the other, or did both draw on a common source?

5 pacti fuerint: this must be an absolute use of *paciscor* ('make an arrangement, come to an agreement': *OLD* s.v. 4), with the gerundive a loose complement rather than directly dependent on the verb, 'for the purpose of conducting transport they came to an agreement'. Nothing comparable is quoted by the *TLL*, and this example does not appear either.

6 mihi disceptatio in corde nata est, si ille possessor, qui susceperit barbarum, cuius fides per daemonum iurationem firma uisa est, non coinquinatur: *disceptatio ... nata est* is followed by an indirect question (*si ... non* *coinquinatur*) that has two features worthy of note: it is introduced by *si* (not *utrum, num, an, -ne*), and the dependent verb is indicative not subjunctive. The same construction is found at 2 *si, cum illi ergo iurant per daemones suos, ut custodiant fruges, non polluunt ipsas fruges, . . . significare dignare*. In the letter in its entirety there are two indirect questions with a subjunctive verb, 1 *quae qualis sit per litteras expono*, 9 *de qua dubitat, an bona aut mala sit*. Of these the first consists of the hackneyed phrase *qualis sit*. The indicative type introduced by *si* is arguably far more numerous in the letter than the two examples quoted here might suggest; we return to this point below, 31.11.

Augustine's use of the indirect question in his reply (*Epist.* 47) is in contrast to that of Publicola. There are seven indirect questions in the letter (pp. 130.3, 130.5, 130.22, 131.15, 131.17, 134.17, 136.11), all of which have a subjunctive verb, and all of which are introduced by *utrum* not *si*. Sometimes these classicising indirect questions take up in part the wording of Publicola himself, who had not used the classical construction. Note for example p. 130.4–6 *ubi te uolo prius considerare* <u>utrum</u>, *si quispiam per deos falsos iurauerit se fidem seruaturum et eam non seruauerit, non tibi* <u>uideatur</u> *bis peccasse*, alongside the construction quoted in the lemma at the start of the previous paragraph.

The use of *si* to introduce an indirect question (and indeed sometimes with an indicative verb in the dependent clause, for which see some of the examples in this paragraph, and those at the end of the next paragraph) goes back to early Latin (see Kühner and Stegmann 1955: II.426), though there may be difficulties of interpretation, with the *si*-clause sometimes arguably conditional (see Bräunlich 1920: 75–84, Bodelot 1987: 82), as at Ter. *Ph.* 674–5 '*quantum potest me certiorem' inquit 'face,* | *si illam dant'*, 'if they are giving me the girl, let me know as soon as possible'; contrast e.g. Ter. *Ph.* 553 *uide si quid opis potes afferre huic*. *Si* is not the normal subordinator in higher-style classical Latin, but there are examples scattered about, particularly in informal genres or special contexts (see e.g. Kühner and Stegmann loc. cit.). For example, in a letter of Caesar at Cic. *Att.* 9.7 C.1 there is *temptemus hoc modo si possumus omnium uoluntates recuperare* (with *possumus* usually emended to *possimus*). This same construction *temptemus si* (and + indicative) is found in a speech by a freedman in Petronius: 33.5 *temptemus tamen si adhuc sorbilia sunt*. For *uide si* (as above in Terence) see e.g. Petron. 71.12 *inscriptio quoque uide diligenter si haec satis idonea tibi uidetur*, Terentianus *P. Mich.* VIII.469.6–7 *uide si potes imbenire*; cf. Hor. *Epist.* 1.7.39 *inspice si possum donata reponere laetus*. At Livy 34.3.5 (in a speech) note *id modo quaeritur, si maiori parti et in summam prodest*. Here the indicative verb is defended against emendation to *prosit* by Briscoe (1981), who makes the point (1981: 49) that *si* is found with the indicative in such contexts in early Latin. For *quaero si* (but this time with a subjunctive) see Vitr. 7.1.1 *et si plano pede erit eruderandum, quaeratur solum si sit perpetuo solidum* ('. . . it must be enquired whether the soil is solid throughout'), where the initial *si*-clause is conditional and of different type from that after *quaeratur*. Such *si*-clauses are well represented in Vitruvius (note e.g. the double construction at 7.5.4, *neque animaduertunt si quid eorum fieri potest necne* 'nor do they consider whether any of them can occur or not'), though Morgan (1906: 488) plays down their significance by arguing that most are conditional (contrast Kühner and Stegmann loc. cit.). On *si* in later Latin see below, and also Adams (2013: 750, 757, 758, 763, 767, surveying early to late Latin).

We turn specifically to the significance of Publicola's use of the indicative (on which construction see Adams 2013: 747–73). In early Latin and also later many clauses containing the indicative are not really indirect at all, but if these are left aside the indicative maintained a life, particularly in informal registers or contexts (notably in speeches in the *Aeneid* and speeches by the freedmen in Petronius: see Adams 2013: 756, 762–5; some of the examples quoted in the previous paragraph are from low-register texts or contexts). By the period of this letter there were still purists insisting on the subjunctive, but reading between the lines we can see that things had changed. Note Diomedes, *GL* I.395.15–24 (who is dated to the second half of the fourth century or the fifth century): *hanc speciem in consuetudine parum multi obseruant inperitia lapsi, cum dicunt 'nescio quid facis', 'nescio quid fecisti'. eruditius enim dicetur 'nescio quid facias', 'nescio quid feceris'. . . . praeposito sermone interiecta parte orationis, 'quid quare cur' et similibus, subiunctiua sequitur species.* Not many, he says (*parum multi*), observe the rule (that the subjunctive should be used), lapsing 'because of ignorance'. The implication is that, try as the grammarian might, preserving the subjunctive construction was a hopeless task. Grammarians themselves often used the indicative. For example, for *si* with the indicative see Pompeius, *GL* V.215.27 *uideamus si potest aliquis hoc intellegere*, 217.17 *uideamus si non erit secunda coniugatio*. By contrast *utrum* in Pompeius seems almost always to generate a subjunctive (see Adams 2013: 767).

In his dealings with Publicola, however, Augustine seems almost self-consciously to have presented himself as a purist, with his avoidance of various non-classical constructions seeming to set up a difference of status between the naive seeker of advice and his condescending instructor. Elsewhere Augustine ridicules grammarians and their out-of-date rules (e.g. *De musica* 2.1.1, *Doctr. Christ.* 4.10.24, *Serm.* 1.18.29, 37.14; cf. the Introduction to this text), advising accommodation to the usage of humble Christians (note *In Psalm.* 138.20 *melius est reprehendant nos grammatici, quam non intellegant populi*), but in this letter he shows no linguistic accommodation at all. This point is illustrated further in the next note, and beyond.

7 sed hoc debes scire, quia: another feature of the text is the frequency of *quod-/quia*-clauses compared with the acc. + inf. The former construction occurs also at 2 *audiui quia*, 3 *audiui quod* (note that *quod* and *quia* interchangeably complement the same verb), *dixit quia*, 4 *dixit quia* three times, 8 *cogitationes habuerit quod*, 10 *dixerit quod, dixerit quia*, 17 *dictum fuerit quia*. The acc. + inf. occurs at 3 *dixit iurari* (immediately following *dixit quia iuratur*), 9 *putat bonam, putasset et malam*, 11 *uidet iam mortem proximare*, 12 *uideat se a barbaro uel a Romano uelle interfici*. The *quod-/quia*-construction predominates by 11:4. There are perhaps lexical determinants at work here. *Dico* almost invariably has *quia* (or *quod*), whereas two of the four cases of the acc. + inf. follow *uideo*, which is not in this text construed with *quod/quia*. The incidence of *quod-/quia*-clauses in this text is high even for late Latin. Herman (1989: 134–5) stated that for five or six centuries the frequency of such clauses (whether with *quod, quia* or *quoniam*) remained constant (at only about 10 per cent of the cases where one might expect an acc. + inf.). Herman added that exceptionally in a few writers the figure of 10 per cent is exceeded, citing the *Peregrinatio* (20 per cent) and Lucifer of Cagliari (15 per cent). Publicola by contrast uses the *quod-/quia*-construction two-thirds of the time. For refinements of Herman's presentation of the incidence of *quod/quia* see Calboli (2012: 440). See also above, 22.10 on Terentianus, and below, 39.18 on Patrick (in whom the acc. + inf. is conspicuously rare, its incidence well out of line with Herman's figures), 47.12 (on another text in which it is very rare), and index, 'accusative + infinitive and substitutes'.

Again Augustine's reply contrasts with Publicola's letter. He uses the acc.+ inf. twenty-seven times, but a *quod*-construction only once, at p. 134.18–19 *si eam cogitationem tenuerit, quod immolaticia non sit*, where it is taken over from Publicola: 8 *et cogitationes duas habuerit in corde, quod immolata sit et non sit immolata*. This is not a striking example, because it is not obvious from the lexica that *cogitatio* with an acc. + inf. was a normal or classical construction. Augustine's usage in the letter is the more interesting in that in other works he does make use of *quod/quia* and even *quoniam* (see Haverling 2012: 92). For example, he admits it in his correspondence with the learned Jerome (see *Epist.* 73.3, p. 265.21, 81, p. 351.4, 82.7, p. 357.4, 82.7, p. 357.8, 82.11, p. 361.13, 82.15, pp. 365.20, 366.1, 82.17, p. 368.1, 82.22, p. 374.17, 82.24, p. 377.4; this list is not exhaustive). Compare on the one hand *Epist.* 82.22, p. 374.17 *uerum scripsit se uidisse Petrum non recte ingredientem ad ueritatem euangelii* and 82.24, p. 377.4 *scripsit ad Galatas uidisse se Petrum non recte ingredientem ad ueritatem euangelii* with on the other 82.15, p. 365.20 *inciderat ut de illo Paulus uerissime scriberet quod eum uidisset non recte ingredientem ad ueritatem euangelii.*

On the use of the acc. + inf. in Augustine as compared with clauses of the *quod*-type, see Dokkum (1900: 67–8). In two early works, written before Augustine's conversion to Christianity (*Contra Academicos, De beata uita*), there are just five and four examples respectively of *quod*-clauses, compared with 400 and 100 respectively of the acc. + inf. The ratio of the acc. + inf. to *quod*-clauses in these two works is 80:1 and 25:1. On the other hand in three works written after his conversion, the *City of God, Confessions* and *Epistles*, there are in total 347 *quod*-, *quia*- and *quoniam*-clauses, compared with 3,961 of the acc. + inf. In the *Confessions* the ratio of the acc. + inf. to the other construction is only 5:1 (416:87), and in the *Epistles* 9:1 and *City of God* 18:1. As Dokkum (1900: 68) puts it: 'Procul dubio hujus incrementi nulla alia causa fuit nisi auctoritas Sanctae Scripturae.' Augustine's early works by contrast are very Ciceronian. In the letter to Publicola his practice is indistinguishable from that of classical Latin.

8 iuramentum etiam illud: *iuramentum* is used for 'oath' by Publicola throughout the letter (eleven times, nine times in the quoted part). In just one place he has *iuratio* instead (1 *cuius fides per daemonum iurationem firma uisa est*). Augustine in his reply uses only *iuratio* (p. 131.14 *ne ab alio iurationem accipiamus,* p. 131.22 *quam illa iuratio confirmat*). With the first of Augustine's examples cf. Publ. 1 *suscepit . . . iuramentum,* 2 *iuramentum . . . accipiunt,* 5 *iuramentum accipere, susceperit . . . iuramentum. Iuramentum* is described by Donatus as used *uulgo* (Ter. *Andr.* 728, 2 '*iurandum' pro 'ius iurandum' aut, ut uulgo dicitur, 'iuramentum'*), and it is found often in the Old Latin Bible translations and the Vulgate. In the latter it occurs about fifty-one times in the OT and six times in the NT, whereas there is only one instance of *iuratio* in the whole work (Sir 23.9). The classical term *ius iurandum* has receded but is still in use (twelve times OT, nine times NT). Unlike *iuratio, iuramentum* is well represented in Romance languages (for details with bibliography see *TLL* VII.2.663.48ff.), but possibly as a late learned borrowing. See also Perrot (1961: 131, 285).

9 qui suscepit barbari iuramentum: it can be seen from the previous note that, while Publicola here and at 5 uses the expression *suscipere iuramentum*, in two other places he has *accipere iuramentum*. At 5 the two expressions alternate in the same sentence. In later Latin in particular (but not exclusively there) *suscipio* encroached on *accipio* (and *excipio*) (see Adams 1976a: 112–13). In this text *suscipio* (= *accipio*) is used four times, and *accipio* twice. Again there is a contrast with Augustine, who has only *accipio* (pp. 131.15, 132.11, 135.4).

10 ipsi homines conductores: *homines* seems redundant. For the most part in the letter *conductor* is used on its own (= 'one who rents something, lessee', here it means 'tenant'), either in the plural (1) or, usually, in the generalising or collective singular (seven times in sections 3–5). Only once elsewhere is it accompanied by a demonstrative (5 *illum Christianum conductorem*). For *homo* accompanied by an appositional noun see *TLL* VI.2.2885.60ff. Such expressions can be found sometimes in early and classical Latin (e.g. Plaut. *Cas.* 564 *hominem amatorem illum*, Cic. *S. Rosc.* 8 *homines sicarios atque gladiatiores*): note Dyck (2010: 72) '*homo* used with a defining term indicates the class or group to which one belongs', citing *OLD* s.v. 4b, and see also Landgraf (1914: 30), citing some interesting cases from Cicero. There is however another possible influence here: according to *TLL* 2885.60 the usage is often in Holy Scripture with a Hebrew model ('saepe in script. sacra sec. hebr.') (see e.g. Vulgate Dt 2.14 *hominum bellatorum*). For the equivalent use of ἄνθρωπος in NT Greek see Bauer, Arndt and Gingrich (1957: 68) s.v. 3ε: note e.g. Lc 7.34 *ecce homo deuorator* (ἄνθρωπος φάγος). The Septuagint has examples of ἀνήρ and ἄνθρωπος translating Hebrew expressions with *ish* ('man') before an occupation noun, as e.g. at Gn 46.32 = Vulg. *et sunt uiri pastores* (see Schleusner 1820–1: I.273, 280). In the Septuagint the usage is replicating the Hebrew, but Greek itself had long had such a usage (see LSJ s.vv. ἀνήρ VI.1, ἄνθρωπος 4), just as appositional *homo* goes well back in Latin. I am grateful to John Lee for information used in this note.

11 si iam pro hoc quod solum audiui, non debeo uti de . . .: this sentence introduces what is the most distinctive syntactic feature of the whole letter, that is the use of *si* at the head of what at least look like direct questions. This is a usage that is potentially bewildering in the text, because it tends to occur in the same sentence as a straightforward conditional clause. That is the case here, as we have at the start of the sentence the conditional clause *si etiam falsum mihi dixit ille*. In the next section (4) by contrast the initial *si*-clause (*si debeo requirere*) is interrogative, whereas later in the sentence *si uerum dixit ille* is conditional. On the other hand in section 5, where there are again two *si*-clauses of the same two types, their order is reversed: *si barbarus . . .* is conditional, whereas *si solus* is interrogative. Sometimes the two types of *si*-clauses are juxtaposed, as at 8 *si manducauerit, si peccat*, where the first is conditional but the second interrogative. The interrogative use occurs at least once in every section of the text from 3 to 18, with the single exception of 11.

The question arises whether we have a genuine use of *si* functioning as an interrogative marker at the head of direct questions. Before addressing this question we ought at least to consider whether it might be a Grecism. It is true that εἰ is attested at the start of direct questions in biblical Greek, both the NT and LXX, but it does not seem to have been a genuinely current Greek usage. See Blass, Debrunner and Rehkopf (1976: 365–6 (citing e.g. Mt 12.10)). The usage is described as unclassical, in the LXX, and possibly a Hebraism. On this view we might find the 'Grecism' particularly in a biblical Latin text, imitating a Greek original. Jannaris (1897: 478) even goes so far as to say that the assumption that εἰ occurs as a direct interrogative particle in biblical Greek 'is based on a misconception, since εἰ here is nothing but an itacistic mis-spelling of the colloquial ἦ'. Whatever the truth of this, an African sending earnest theological questions to a bishop who never mastered Greek is unlikely to have used a string of conscious Grecisms, though it is not impossible that he had picked up a mannerism from biblical texts.

However, I would not take *si* throughout this passage as a direct interrogative particle at all, but as the use of *si*, already illustrated from the letter, introducing *indirect* questions. A clue to the interpretation of the syntax is to be found in Cicero's *Topica* (84). In this passage there is first a verb of questioning, *aut simpliciter quaeritur aut comparate*, 'the question is posed either in the simple form or by way of comparison', Reinhardt 2003). There then follows a series of indirect questions, superficially free-standing but all of them dependent on this initial *quaeritur*. The first and second are: *expetendane sit gloria . . . praeponendane sit diuitiis gloria*. The last two are *aequumne sit ulcisci . . . honestumne sit pro patria mori*. Immediately preceding these there is *si expetendae diuitiae, si fugienda paupertas*. What Cicero has done here is to vary the form of the indirect question by switching to the *si*-type, but the dependence on *quaeritur* is still obvious and it would be unconvincing to suggest that he has used *si* as a direct interrogative particle in the middle of his other indirect questions. For the correct interpretation see Reinhardt's note (2003: 353), calling the construction an indirect question and observing that the construction with *si* is rare in Cicero. Its admission here is motivated by a desire for variation.

The structure of Publicola's letter is similar to that of the passage of Cicero. Publicola gets his questions under way (2) with an indirect question intro-duced by *si* but dependent on the verb phrase *significare dignare*, 'kindly see fit to indicate if . . .' Then follows the long sequence of questions introduced by *si*, which look free-standing but can be attached to *significare dignare*, just as Cicero's *si*-clauses can be attached to *quaeritur*. When Publicola gets to the end of his specific questions he has a concluding paragraph (not quoted here), and at this point he puts a general summarising question with which the verb phrase is repeated (18, p. 128.15–16 *si quid autem aliud apertius aut melius in scripturis inueneris, dignare mihi significare*). The two instances of the verb phrase frame the questions with *si*.

On this interpretation the letter is replete with indirect questions introduced by *si* and containing an indicative verb.

There are extensive discussions and illustrations in the literature of the use of *si* supposedly introducing direct questions: see Rönsch (1875: 404), E. Löfstedt (1911: 327), Svennung (1935: 514 n. 3), Hofmann and Szantyr (1965: 464), Väänänen (1987: 96), Herman (1996), Pinkster (2015: 334). The most convincing examples are in biblical translation texts corresponding to εἰ or in writers who might have picked up a mannerism from the Bible. The examples at *Per. Aeth.* 45.3 (*et sic singulariter interrogat episcopus uicinos eius, qui intrauit, dicens: 'si bonae uitae est hic, si parentibus deferet, si ebriacus non est aut uanus?'*) illustrate the ambiguities inherent in this construction. *Si* was probably generated by the preceding *interrogat*, even though the author has then inserted a redundant *dicens*.

12 tam diu non contingere de ipsis frugibus uel de pretio: here the partitive phrase *de (ipsis) frugibus* has the role of object of *contingere* (on *ipsis* here see the last paragraph of this note). It is striking that in this letter verbs of eating and drinking (and bland replacements such as 'use') regularly have a partitive complement, either a *de*-expression or *(ex)inde* (rather than a pronoun in the accusative). The only accusative is at 17: *et non manducauerit eam* (*carnem*). Contrast the following partitive expressions, most in the context of eating: 2 *si inde manducauerit*, 2 *de pretio ipsarum rerum <usus> fuerit*, 3 *non debeo uti de ipsis frugibus uel de pretio ipsarum*, 10 *si licet Christianum inde manducare aut uendere et de pretio uti*, 11 *debet mori aut exinde cibari*, 18 *holus emere uel aliquem fructum et inde edere*.

Augustine does not use partitive expressions in his reply. Note the following: p. 132.4 *utitur mundis reliquis fructibus*, p. 132.17 *non debemus inde aliquid usurpare* (*inde* is used here but the verb is given an accusative object), p. 133. 17–18 *non autem peccat, qui cibum postea nesciens manducauerit*, p. 134.2 *si putauerimus non uescendum holere*, p. 134.4 *apud Athenas cibum sumere*, p. 136.12 *illud in alimentum sumere*.

Manducare de (also *ab, ex*) is illustrated at *TLL* VIII.274.67ff. from biblical translations and treated as a Grecism based on the use of ἀπό or ἐκ, and it is possible that Publicola was recalling a biblical idiom (see below, 38.51 on the *Vetus Latina*). However, this partitive use of *de* cannot be dismissed as purely a Grecism in Latin, as it goes back to an early period and can be found in texts over many centuries. Note e.g. *CIL* I^2.48, XIV.2577 (= *ILLRP* 100) *de praidad Fortune dedet*, *CIL* I^2.49, XIV.2578 (= *ILLRP* 221) *de praidad Maurte dedet*, Plaut. *Stich.* 400 *ibo intro ad libros et discam de dictis melioribus*, and for a collection of examples spread chronologically see Adams (2013: 273–5); see also earlier, 4.3 on a comparable use of *ex* but also on an example with *de* in Cato. When grammaticalised this use of *de* produced the partitive article of Romance (see below, 50.29–30), and *inde* too in this sense has an outcome in e.g. Fr. *en* (*j'en ai mangé*) and It. *ne* (*ne ho mangiato*). Moreover Publicola does not merely use *de/inde* with *manduco*, but also e.g. with *contingo* and *utor*. What is striking about his usage of *de* and *inde* is its regularity. The *de*-expressions referred to above from early Latin onwards are thinly scattered and adopted ad hoc rather than grammaticalised, whereas in one or two semantic fields they have become the norm for Publicola, and there is a hint of grammaticalisation. Similarly in Anthimus *de*-expressions standing as either subject or object of a verb (e.g. *manducare*) are quite common (Liechtenhan 1963: 54–5).

Liechtenhan (1963: 69) also glosses *inde* at Anthimus 7.10 (*et inde intingendo in oximelli simplici ad hora facto*) with *i. q. partem eius (?)*, and the same gloss would be applicable to the cases of *(ex)inde* above in Publicola. This usage is native to Latin. It has its origin in the partitive use of *inde* attached to a noun, as at Plaut. *Mil.* 711 *dant inde partem* (*TLL* VII.1.1119.47ff.). From an early period *inde* is sometimes used with a verb but without a supporting accusative noun, as at Sall. *Cat.* 22.2 *inde quom . . . omnes degustauissent* (*TLL* 1120.6ff.).

Augustine seems to have made a show of rejecting these usages.

In the expression *de ipsis frugibus*, *ipsis* is contrastive, in that the reference is to use of the crops themselves as distinct from the profit accruing from them. The adjectival use of *ipse* is quite common in the text, but usually the term can be given a strong meaning of classical type and is not relevant to uses possibly anticipating the direct article (contrast 50.29–30 below).

13 fecerit . . . **iurare:** for *facio* + infinitive see below, 50.42.

14 de area trituratoria tritici uel cuiuscumque leguminis aut torculari, de qua daemoni oblatum est, si licet inde manducare Christianum scientem?: the initial phrase *de area* . . . is left hanging, and then picked up by the resumptive *inde*. Pronominal resumption of a hanging term, whether that is in the nominative or an oblique case as here, can be paralleled from the early period onwards (see above, 2.25, 3.416, below, 31.19).

Augustine did not like the form of expression, of 'eating from the threshing floor'. Cf. p. 132.1 *item si de area uel torculari tollatur aliquid*, where a subject (*aliquid*) is supplied along with the verb *tollatur*.

Souter (1949: 431) quotes only one other (late) instance of the adjective *trituratorius* 'for threshing', but the term is of regular formation. From *tero, tritus* there was formed in late Latin an abstract verbal noun *tritura* (cf. *mixtus* > *mixtura*, along with e.g. *coniectura, natura, scriptura, uectura*: Leumann 1977: 315; see Souter 1949: 431 for examples of *tritura*). The next step was the forming of a denominative verb *trituro* from *tritura* (Souter cites two late examples; see also below on Isidore). In late Latin there are various such denominatives, e.g. *lituro, mensuro, mixturo*, and also (in a gloss) *culturo* (see *CGL* VI.525 s.v. *holerare*). From *trituro* was formed *triturator* (one example cited by Souter, from Augustine), and from that, by the usual process, *trituratorius* (see Leumann 1977: 33: e.g. *saltatorius*). In relation to the present passage Isid. *Etym.* 15.13.16 is of interest: *alii aream uocatam dicunt quod pro triturandis frugibus eradatur, uel quod non triturentur in ea nisi arida*. *Trituro* itself is not commented on here, but it is treated as the normal verb for threshing on a threshing floor.

15 si quis uadens ad macellum emat carnem: *uadens* is perfective ('if anyone, having gone to the market, should buy . . .'). The perfective use of the present participle became commonplace (see index, 'present participle, perfective'), but it can be found sometimes even in classical Latin. *Vadens* is a typical late replacement of one of the phonetically weaker forms of *ire*, a verb which occurs twice in stronger compounded forms at 1 (*transeuntes, transire*). A little later at 11 *ambulans* has nothing to do with suppletion of *ire* but refers to a forced act of walking (but cf. below, 47.7). For *uado* see index, s.v., and also Adams (2013: 811–17).

16 si qui: a non-standard variant for *si quis* (well attested, for example, in Vitruvius: see E. Löfstedt 1956: II.92–3), but here it is surrounded by two instances of *si quis*, and an editor ought to contemplate emendation.

17 et postea dixerit iterum: for the adversative use of *iterum* (= 'on the other hand') see *TLL* VII.1.562.59ff. (imperial and mainly late), *OLD* s.v. 3.

18 si Christianus uideat se a barbaro uel a Romano uelle interfici: a curious use of *uelle*, which if translated literally would give an absurd meaning, 'if a Christian sees that he wants to be killed by a barbarian or Roman'. It can be translated as a future tense auxiliary ('if he sees that he will be killed'). Uses of *uolo* that come close to expressing futurity turn up throughout Latin (see e.g. Hofmann and Szantyr 1965: 314), though scholars have tended to be uncritical in interpreting them as such (on which point see Pinkster 1987b, id. 1989). Such a future periphrasis has a Romance survival. In Romanian the standard form of the future is periphrastic, consisting of the auxiliary verb *voi* followed by the infinitive (Mallinson 1988: 407), and deriving it seems from *uolo* (*cantare* etc.). Apart from this literary form there are various other more popular exponents of futurity in Romanian, one of them with reduced forms of the above auxiliary. In the present passage, however, it would not do to identify a grammaticalised future periphrasis. Publicola has probably contaminated ad hoc his passive construction with the required active ('if he sees that a barbarian or Roman wants to kill him'). Contaminations of passive constructions with active are common (see e.g. Norberg 1944: 24–31).

19 et si ille Christianus, qui fecerit murum, causa non existit homicidii: the nominative *ille Christianus* is left hanging (cf. above, 31.14).

20 ibi: redundant, after *in templo*.

21 ibi ... in eodem puteo uel fonte: see index, 'locative/temporal expressions, double'.

22 illic in solio: see the previous note.

23 aliquem: 'someone else' (cf. the fuller expression *aliquo alio* later in the sentence): see *OLD* s.v. 6, E. Löfstedt (1911: 174), Adams (1995a: 170 with n. 63).

Conclusions

The most interesting feature of the present text is the contrast it shows syntactically with Augustine's reply. Various usages, most of which can be described as proto-Romance, are eliminated by Augustine or used with much lower frequency: the *dico quia-/quod*-construction, the indicative in indirect questions, indirect questions introduced by *si*, partitive complements of verbs of eating and the like, and the unvarying placement of dependent infinitives after the governing verb. Was Augustine consciously distancing himself linguistically from his addressee or even making a display of condescension? It would probably be possible to parallel the contrast between the two letters in English letters between, say, an educated official and an unlettered correspondent: the correspondent, unpractised in writing, sends a letter full of misspellings and other non-standard features to an official unknown to him personally, and the official in his reply falls over backwards to admit only standard usages. The effect, whether deliberate or not, is to set up a difference of status between the two. It was pointed out above (31.7) that in his (acrimonious) correspondence with Jerome, his equal or even cultural superior, Augustine was prepared to use the *dico quod*-construction. It was not unacceptable among the educated at this period (though used less often than the acc. + inf.), but a show of extreme purism could be made, if appropriate, by means of an unwavering adherence to the older construction. Note the following recommendation of Marcus Aurelius on how to react to solecisms in another (*Meditations* 1.10): (from Alexander the grammarian), 'not to be captious; nor in a carping spirit find fault with those who import into their conversation any expression which is barbarous or ungrammatical or mispronounced, but tactfully to bring in the very expression, that ought to have been used (ἀλλ᾿ ἐπιδεξίως αὐτὸ μόνον ἐκεῖνο, ὃ ἔδει εἰρῆσθαι, προφέρεσθαι), by way of answer, or as it were in joint support of the assertion, or as a joint consideration of the thing itself and not of the language' (Haines, Loeb) (drawn to my attention by Danuta Shanzer).

Publicola's Latin has other features that have emerged above. There are signs of ineptitude, as in constructions that are left hanging, and in the probable conflation of a passive construction with the corresponding active. He had also picked up mannerisms from biblical texts, such as the expansion of a finite verb by its own present participle, and the use of *homo* with an appositional occupation noun. It is possible that the constant use of *si* to introduce questions comes from this source, but we suggested another explanation. Otherwise there are numerous late, and not necessarily substandard, usages.

32

CURSE TABLET FROM LONDON BRIDGE (HASSALL AND TOMLIN 1987: 360–1 no. 1)

Introduction

This text is on an '[i]rregular piece of sheet lead . . . found in 1984 on the north foreshore of the Thames' (Hassall and Tomlin 1987: 360). The addressee is probably Neptune (see below), but the motive for the curse is not stated.

Text

tibi rogo, Metu-
nus, u(t) m(e) uendic-
as de iste nu-
mene, me uendicas ante qo̧-
d uen(iant) die(s) no-   5
uem, rogo t̥e,
Metunus, ut (t)u
mi uend̥[i]cas
ante qo̧[d]
uen(iant) di(es) n[o]ue-   10
m.

Translation

I ask you, Metunus, that you avenge me on this name, (that) you avenge me before nine days come. I ask you, Metunus, that you avenge me before nine days come.

Commentary

1 tibi rogo: for the hypercorrect construction of *rogo* with the dative see the Spanish curse tablet discussed by Sánchez Natalías (2014), and also the late British Christian inscription from Caldey Island, Pembrokeshire in

Nash-Williams (1950: 180 no. 301) (*rogo omnibus ammulantibus*). In the early medieval *Vita sanctae Euphrosynae* (see below, text 47) there is an expression (7) *interrogauit monacho* (but possibly a misspelling of the accusative). Later in the present tablet the classical construction *rogo te* is written instead.

1–2 Metunus: a god of this name is not known, and Hassall and Tomlin (1987: 360) must be right to suggest that Neptunus, who is invoked in the British curse tablet dealt with next (33), is intended. An assimilation of *pt* > *t(t)* (cf. e.g. *CIL* VIII.466 *otimi* and *otimo, ILCV* 4580 *set(em), CIL* IX.2827.26 (AD 19) *scritus*) and a confusion of the initial nasal would lie behind the misspelling. For this non-standard (but proto-Romance) assimilation see Adams (2013: 171–2).

In Romance, apart from a few fossilised forms, the Latin vocative as a separate inflectional entity has disappeared (see Wackernagel 1926–8: I.306 = Langslow 2009: 384–5), and that is unsurprising, given that in Latin itself the only distinctive vocative form is in names of the second declension singular. Stray late examples of the nominative for vocative (in the second declension), such as that here (which is repeated six lines later), are to be expected in non-standard texts, but signs of the loss of the vocative are not abundant, and there is even a competing tendency for the vocative to encroach on the nominative in some areas (see Adams 2007: 570–1). But note *Tab. Vindoniss.* 30.4–5 *tum, faustus Ṭullus, [qui de] amoribus ig<n>oraṣ,* Wright and Hassall (1973: 325 no. 3) *dono tibi, Mercurius.* There are various inscriptions from Pompeii with the following form (nominative of name with *uale*): e.g. *CIL* IV.4844 *Latimius, ua(le)* (see Svennung 1958: 271–2, Väänänen 1966: 115). Certain examples from Plautus onwards are of a special type: e.g. *Asin.* 691–2 *mi Libane, ocellus aureus,* Augustus *ap.* Gellius 15.7.2 *aue, mi Gai, meus asellus iucundissimus.* Here the nominative element is not a name, and it stands in apposition to a name in the vocative. Further examples of this last type may be found in Svennung (1958: 246–7). Note e.g. Virg. *Aen.* 6.834–5 (with Austin 1977: 257). See also E. Löfstedt (1956: I.99–100), Hofmann and Szantyr (1965: 25).

3–4 de iste numene: *numene* is for *nomine,* the *u* determined by a confusion with *numen,* a term which also has a place in curse tablets (Hassall and Tomlin 1992: 311, no. 5 (Uley) *deo sacto Mercurio Honoratus conqueror numini tuo*). For the same confusion see Hassall and Tomlin (1993: 312, no. 2) (Ratcliffe-on-Soar, Notts.: text 36 below) *ç̣uicumquẹ ṇụm[e]n inuolasit mola illam,* where *numen* can only refer to the thief (see also *Tab. Sulis* 102, cited by Hassall and Tomlin 1987: 363). For confusions of *nomen* and *numen* in epigraphy see Prinz (1932: 60–1, 93).

In a curse tablet the *nomen* of the victim of the curse is of importance, and where possible is specified. The person cannot be offered to the gods but in some cases his name can be (see Jeanneret 1918: 106). Note the curse tablet edited by Corell (1993), where the name, placed in apposition to *nomen*, is offered up to the gods: *dis · imferis · uos · rogo · utei recipiates · nomen Luxsia · A(uli) · Antesti · filia*; cf. *Tab. Sulis* 8 *a nomin[i]bus infrascrip[tis] deae exactura est: Senicia(n)us et Saturninus <sed> et Ann[i]ola*. Where the name is not known *nomen* may still be used, without specification (see further text 33), a practice facilitated by the currency in later Latin of *nomen* in the sense 'person', a usage paralleled by that of ὄνομα in Greek and probably determined by Greek influence, particularly in Christian Latin (see E. Löfstedt 1950: 43–5 and especially Mohrmann 1965: 346–8). On 'cursing the *nomen*' see further Németh and Bounegru (2013), in connection with a curse tablet from Dacia.

In the second syllable *e* is written for original *ī*, a spelling also found in this text three times in *uendicas*. For *uendicas* = *uindicas* in medieval Latin see B. Löfstedt (2000: 267); cf. now the curse tablet from Uley published by Tomlin 2015: 398, no. 21 last line. The misspelling is consistent with the occurrence in late British Latin of the merger of *ī* and *ē* as close *e* that shows up in many Romance languages, but has been questioned for Britain for no good reason (see Adams 2007: 652–3 for British evidence). *Numene* may have the same phenomenon, but the spelling was perhaps generated by the nominative form.

Iste is not inflected, and the form is wrong both in case and gender. Pronouns in later Latin (perhaps most notably *idem*) have a tendency to be fossilised (see particularly B. Löfstedt 1961: 247–51, with bibliography; also e.g. Svennung 1935: 324–5), but *iste* used thus does not seem to be paralleled (see however Stotz 1998: 119 n. 34 for an example of the expression *iste medicamentum*).

4–5 ante qọd: *q(u)od* is used twice (cf. 9) for the usual *antequam*. This anticipates OFr. *ainz que* and is attested in the *Pactus legis Salicae* (24.6 *si <quis> uero infantem in uentre matris suae occiderit aut ante quod nomen habeat*), a text from Gaul; cf. too *Leg. Alamann.* 50.1, p. 109.8, 50.2, p. 109.13 *antea quod* (with *ante quod* a var. lect. in both places). See Norberg (1943: 240–1), Herman (1963: 94), Hofmann and Szantyr (1965: 580), Adams (1976a: 73–4). The parallel subordinator *postquod* is more common (for which see now *TLL* X.2.164.59ff.).

This is not the only correspondence between British curse tablets and the Salic Law (see below, 35.10–11 on *baro*).

5 uen(iant) die(s): *dies uenit* is an old phrase (*TLL* V.1.1046.33ff.); *dies* is also often subject of compounds of *uenio*, such as *aduenio*.

The text is so badly spelt, with abbreviation of the verb *ueniant* twice, omission of several final letters, and omission of the two final letters of *dies* in a later line, that it would be rash to attribute any linguistic significance to the form *die* for *dies*. In early Latin there is a tendency for *-s* to be lost after a short vowel and before a consonant, but this tendency is strongly resisted in non-literary texts of the Empire (for a survey of which see Adams 2013: 135–43). Occasional omissions after a long vowel, as here, are hard to interpret (for a few examples from elsewhere and some discussion, see Adams 2013: 136, 237). In British tablets note *sua* alongside *mentes* at *Tab. Sulis* 5.5, and *habea* at *Tab. Vindol.* 643 (ii) (Adams 2003b: 538).

7–8 ut . . . uend[i]cas: there are two instances of *uendicas* in *ut*-clauses (cf. line 2). On the indicative in final *ut*-clauses (both independent wishes and dependent constructions) see Hofmann and Szantyr (1965: 642–3). Examples are late and not particularly common, though in some medieval texts the indicative with *ut* is not unusual (Bastardas Parera 1953: 157, Stotz 1998: 412 with n. 73). Though the subjunctive is in general recessive in subordinate clauses in the transition from classical Latin to the Romance languages (for example in indirect questions and consecutive clauses), it is retained in final clauses (see Salvi 2011: 375–6, and the whole section 375–9). In Latin the writer sometimes merely loses the thread of the utterance and an indicative construction is not a genuine rival of that with the subjunctive. Cf. the threefold wish at *Tab. Vindoniss.* 40, each part introduced by *ut = utinam: ut a{c} cohorte mi rescribas, u[t] semper in mentem abes, ut mi rescribas.* Notable here is the lapse into the indicative in the second clause. The error is reminiscent of a defective acc. + inf. in Terentianus: *P. Mich.* VIII.468.43 *scias Carpum hic errasse, ed ịnụ[e]ṇtus est Dios in legione, et a[cce]pisse me . . .* The writer forgot momentarily that he was using a subordinate construction and switched into the indicative. He then recovered the construction. It is just possible that in the Vindonissa tablet *ut* is explanatory ('as you always have me in mind'), but that does not seem as convincing as the other explanation. Stotz (1998: 413) also draws attention to instances of the type *ut uenias et . . . ambulas*, where the ending of the first verb has been mechanically imposed on the second (for which phenomenon see above, 29.2, and index, 'indicative, mechanically used'). The examples in the present text cannot be accounted for in these ways.

Conclusions

I draw attention here merely to the features of this text that associate it with continental non-literary Latin of the late imperial period, and also with the

Romance languages, namely the nominative for vocative, which is also in a Swiss tablet, *tibi* with *rogo*, also attested in Spain, the *e*-spelling for *i* (supposedly of a 'non-British' type but attested there), *antequod*, with attestations in other areas and connections with Romance, the proto-Romance consonantal assimilation that is part of the explanation of *Metunus*, and the use of final *ut* + indicative, which can be paralleled for example in Switzerland. This is not a specimen of the 'archaic British vulgar Latin' that is asserted by some to exist, but a mundane specimen of late non-standard Latin. This theme is pursued further in the Commentaries on the following British tablets.

33

CURSE TABLET FROM THE HAMBLE ESTUARY, HAMPSHIRE (TOMLIN 1997: 455 no. 1)

This is another tablet on sheet lead, which was found in 1982 'rolled up on the foreshore. It is inscribed with nineteen lines of fourth-century cursive writing' (Tomlin 1997: 455). The god addressed is again Neptune, but in this case the nature of the theft is specified.

Text

domine Neptune,
t(i)b(i) d(o)no ominẹm quị
(solidum) inuọlạu[it] Mụ-
coni et argenṭi[olo]ṣ
sex. ide(o) dono nomi(n)a   5
qui decepit, si mascel si
femina, si puuer si puue-
lla. ideo dono tibi, Niske,
eṭ Neptuno uitam, uali-
tudinem, sanguem eiụṣ   10
qui conscius fueris eiụṣ
deceptionis. animus
qui hoc inuolauit et
qui conscius fueriṭ ut
eum decipias. furem   15
qui hoc inuolauit sanguem
eiius consumas et de-
cipias, doṃiṇ[e] Ṇẹ[p]-
tune.

Translation

Lord Neptune, I give you the man who has stolen the *solidus* of Muconius and the six *argentioli*. Therefore I give the names (of him) who snatched them away, whether male or female, whether boy or girl. Therefore I give you, Niskus, and Neptune the life, health, blood of him who has been privy to that theft. The mind which stole this (?) and which has been privy to it, may you destroy it. The thief who stole this, may you consume his blood and swallow it up, Lord Neptune.

Commentary

2, 5–6 d(o)no ominẹm ... dono nomi(n)a qui decepit: the alternation between *(h)ominem* and *nomi(n)a* seems slightly odd, and in particular the plural *nomina* is not expected.

A pronominal antecedent for *qui* in line 6 has to be understood here, and it would have been in an oblique case (*eius*). A pronominal antecedent in the nominative is readily omitted (of the type *gloriam reportauit qui hostes uicit*, for *is ... qui*), but omission is less usual when the pronoun would have to be in another case. Later in the text (*animus qui hoc inuolauit*) there seems to be an identical omission (= *animus eius*), unless the 'mind' is personified as the thief (see further below, 33.12–15). Note too lines 16–17 from the poem of Q. Avidius Quintianus found at Bu Njem (see e.g. Courtney 1995, no. 40, Adams 1999: 110–11), *noli pigere laudem uoce reddere | ueram qui uoluit esse te sanum tibi* (for *laudem ei/eius*: see Adams 1999: 125). For an account of the phenomenon (I have in mind here specifically the type where it is an antecedent, and not a resumptive pronoun which would follow the relative clause, that is omitted), with bibliography, see Hofmann and Szantyr (1965: 555–6, dealing with both types just distinguished); also Kühner and Stegmann (1955: II.281–2). Such omissions are difficult to characterise stylistically in the absence of a comprehensive collection. They occur in early Latin, including Plautus (Lindsay 1907: 7; e.g. *Mil.* 156 *ni hercle diffregeritis talos posthac quemque in tegulis | uideritis alienum*: understand *ei* or *eius* with *talos*; the speaker here explicitly affects an edict style (see line 159)) and laws (see Degrassi, *ILLRP* 511 n. 4 on the *S.C. de Bacch.*), but are merely scattered about, it seems, in the classical period, though found sometimes in Cicero, particularly in the philosophica, and Caesar. Later they occur in archaising (or legal) style (note *S.C. de Cn. Pisone patre* 50 *crudelitate unica, qui* (= *eius qui*)), and in late Latin are found particularly in technical texts such as the *Mulomedicina Chironis*. On the legal use and its origin, see Dyck (2004: 292), Powell (2005: 130) (see also below, 42.17 for examples and bibliography on technical texts).

3 inuọḷ̣au[it]: this verb for 'steal' is found three times in this text. The idea behind the usage must be that of the thief 'swooping on' the object to be stolen (cf. the use of *inuado* at Mart. 8.59.13). *Inuolo* is constant in British curse tablets. Tomlin's index (1988: 263) lists about thirty examples from the Bath curse tablets, against just one case of *furo(r)*. See too Hassall and Tomlin (1996: 440, no. 1 (Uley)) *inualauiit*, with a vocalic assimilation, and id. (1993: 312, no. 2 (Ratcliffe-on-Soar): below, text 36), four times in the archaising form *inuolasit*. For an African example in a curse see Audollent (1904), no. 122 *Proserpina, per tuam maiestatem te rogo oro obsecro uti uindices quot mihi furti factum est quisquis mihi imudauit inuolauit . . . tunicas VI . . . Inuolo* 'steal' has a conspicuously colloquial distribution (note *TLL* VII.2.259.41 f. 'praecipue in sermone vulgari pro verbo furandi'), a character which is confirmed by its abundant presence in recently published curse tablets. It is found in one of the shorter poems of Catullus (25.6), and three times in speeches by freedmen in the *Cena Trimalchionis* of Petronius (43.4, 58.10, 63.8) (see Stefenelli 1962: 80). It is only in the meaning 'steal' that the verb lives on in Romance (see Stefenelli 1962: 80 for details).

6 decepit: *decipio* occurs three times in this text and its derivative noun *deceptio* once. Tomlin (1997: 457) was right to point out that more than mere 'deception' is at issue here. In fact the various uses in the text, which differ slightly but are relatable to a basic idea, illustrate certain nuances identified in the verb in late Latin by E. Löfstedt (1936: 102, 157–61). Numerous words in the later period changed meaning because of popular etymologising or etymological analysis (see e.g. E. Löfstedt 1936: 93–104), and that is true of *decipio*, in which the transparent presence of *de* + *capio* led to a meaning 'snatch away' (E. Löfstedt 1936: 159; Tomlin 1997: 457 also notes this analysis). This sense may be observed in the inscriptional use of the participle *deceptus* applied to children who have died prematurely, 'snatched away': e.g. *CIL* V.7962 *immatura morte decepta* (E. Löfstedt 1936: 159), a usage that was to be generalised such that the word acquired the meaning 'kill, destroy, crush' (see E. Löfstedt 1936: 158, Svennung 1935: 336 n. 3). The meaning 'snatch away' is clear in this first example in this text, where it picks up *inuolauit* 'stole'. The verbal noun *deceptionis* refers to the theft and continues the meaning 'snatch away' of the verb. The *TLL* s.v. does not give the meaning 'theft' for the noun.

It is relevant to this text to note that E. Löfstedt (1936: 102) drew attention to a quite early use of *decipio* (in Apuleius), which is also derivable from the meaning 'snatch away': *Met.* 10.34 *iamque tota suaue fraglante cauea montem illum ligneum terrae uorago decepit* ('and now when the whole theatre was full of a sweet fragrance a chasm in the earth swallowed up that wooden mountain'). The chasm snatched away or, in the context, swallowed up the object.

The last example of *decipio* in the present curse is coordinated with *consumas*, with the culprit's blood as its object, and it comes close to expressing the same combination of ideas, 'snatch away > swallow up'.

Finally, in the free-standing wish/request *ut eum decipias*, where *eum* refers to the *animus* of the the thief, we have the general meaning of destruction alluded to above, 'may you destroy it'.

This single text illustrates the late semantic ramifications of *decipio* perhaps better than any of the material collected by Löfstedt.

mascel: *masculus, figulus* and *uernaculus* all have in the imperial period, besides the syncopated forms *masclus, figlus* and *uernaclus*, variants in -*el* (*mascel, figel, uernacel*). *Mascel* is (e.g.) at *CIL* II.1110, *figel* at *CIL* X.423 and *uernacel* at *CIL* VIII.10891. Various explanations of the -*el* form may be found in the literature, none of them decisive (see Sommer 1914: 337, Leumann 1977: 142, Meiser 1998: 133.). The form *mascel* was criticised by grammarians (*GL* IV.211.12, *TLL* s.v. *masculus*), and must have been considered substandard.

7–8 puuer, puuella: glides between two vowels of dissimilar quality in hiatus (for the phenomenon see Adams 2013: 113–18, and also below, index, 'hiatus, insertion of glide'). Cf. e.g. *O. Bu Njem* 86 *duua, tuuos, Tab. Vindol.* 186 *Februuar-* (three examples), *CIL* IV.3730 *poueri = pueri, CIL* XI.6289 = *ILCV* 531 *puuer* (= *puer*), *Tab. Sulis* 31.5 *suua*, Hassall and Tomlin (1992: 311, no. 5; also below, 35.7) *tuui*, Tomlin and Hassall (2007: 351, no. 8) *futuue. Clouaca* for *cloaca* was admitted by Varro in the *Menippea* (290), and it turns up in inscriptions (see *TLL* III.1358.37ff.). For *plouebat = pluebat*, see Petron. 44.18. See also above, 22.13 on *ibi*.

9–10 uitam, ualetudinem: for this alliterative combination see the curse tablet from Carmona (Seville) edited by Corell (1993): *ualetudine(m) uita(m)*. The verbal pairing *uiuere ualere* is old (from Plautus) and common (see Wölfflin 1933: 280; also 277). For such alliterations in curse tablets see 6.3, 19. 6–7, 19.10, 19.10–12.

10 sanguem: this accusative form for the expected *sanguinem* reflects a popular tendency to standardise the number of syllables in the nominative and oblique cases of third declension nouns (contrast the different solution seen at *Physica Plinii Bambergensis* 13.32 *et si cui se sanguinis suffudit*; see also above, 22.27, and index, 'nouns, imparisyllabic, remodelled'). Similarly B. Löfstedt (2000: 247) illustrates a genitive form *sanguis for sanguinis* from late texts. *Sanguem* occurs twice in this text and in other British curses, from Bath (*Tab. Sulis* 44.6) and Uley (Hassall and Tomlin 1996: 440, no. 1). There is also an instance in Greek letters in an unpublished tablet from Uley (cited by

Hassall and Tomlin 1996: 441). For examples in manuscripts of late texts (including versions of the *Vetus Latina*) see Bulhart (1967: xvi); for the *Vet. Lat.* see below, 38.53). This cluster of examples (many of them new, and British) supports the argument of Stefenelli (1962: 117–18) that Romance terms such as It. *sangue*, Fr. *sang*, Cat. *sanc*, Pg. *sangue* reflect this remodelled accusative rather than the old neuter term *sanguen* (see Adams 2007: 586).

11 qui conscius fueris: a mistake for *fuerit*.

12–15 animus qui hoc inuolauit . . . ut eum decipias: there are two ways of construing *animus* here. First, it may be used loosely (pars pro toto or by personification) of the thief, 'the mind which stole this, may you destroy it'. In this case the initial placement of *animus* would represent attractio inversa, i.e. fronting out of the relative clause, = *qui animus hoc inuolauit*, 'which mind stole this'. For attractio inversa in a comparable text, not a curse proper but a shaming on stone of a wrongdoer, from the tomb of Vesonius Phileros at Pompeii, see *AE* 1964, no. 160 lines 3–5 *amicum hunc quem speraueram mi esse, ab eo mihi accusatores subiecti et iudicia instaurata.* Alternatively in our text, as suggested above (2, 5–6), the antecedent of the relative clause may be understood as a pronoun in the genitive (*eius*), 'the mind of him who stole this, may you destroy it' (an omission of a type definitely occurring at lines 5–6). On this interpretation the detached or hanging nominative forms a construction of well-established type. A nominative not infrequently stands outside the syntax of the clause in initial position, usually picked up later by a resumptive pronoun (here *eum*) in the case required by the syntax. Cf. e.g. Cato, *FRH* II.5.F76.19 (Gell. 3.7.19) *Leonides Laco, qui simile apud Thermopylas fecit, propter eius uirtutes omnis Graecia gloriam atque gratiam praecipuam claritudinis inclitissimae decorauere monumentis.* This was sometimes a focusing device (see index, 'nominativus/accusativus pendens', and 5.7–8).

14–15 ut eum decipias: this is the old free-standing use of *ut* to express a wish/request/instruction. It is common in curse tablets from Britain (see Adams 1992a: 6–7), is found in wishes addressed to the gods (see Adams 1992a: 6), and also had a lingering survival in late low-register texts such the *Mulomedicina Chironis* (e.g. 691 *ut eum ossum fractum eximas*; here an instruction). See further Hofmann and Szantyr (1965: 331), Svennung (1935: 511–12) (for late examples). Cf. below, 34.4–5.

15–17 furem qui hoc inuolauit sanguem eiius consumas: here if the construction were attractio inversa the term for 'thief' would derive its case from the relative clause (nominative, *fur*). The accusative *furem* is not unconstrued but can be taken as object of *consumas*. The verb, however, has an additional object in *sanguem*, and the construction may be interpreted as a partitive apposition, with the term for the whole preceding that for the part. For a comparable example cf. Plaut. *Men.* 858–9 <u>hunc senem</u> | *osse fini dedolabo assulatim* <u>uiscera</u>, where again a personal noun is primary object of the verb and in apposition to it later stands an anatomical term denoting part of the person. Note too *Mil.* 204 *dextera digitis rationem computat*, where, unusually, the two nouns are in the ablative. The construction is old, and can be paralleled, for example, in Homer (see Chantraine 1963: 42), from whom Virgil might have taken it at *Aen.* 10.698–9 *Latagum . . .* | *occupat os faciemque*, though alternatively it might have been picked up from Ennius. For Latin see further Hofmann (1924: 83, 85), Hofmann and Szantyr (1965: 44), and for Latin and some other Indo-European languages, Hahn (1953: 101–3); also Adams, Lapidge and Reinhardt (2005: 128). For a similar partitive apposition see above, 19.10–12 (curse tablet); also index, apposition, 'partitive/specifying/ defining'.

Eiius also has a glide in hiatus.

Conclusions

The question that always arises when one considers a late British curse tablet written in badly misspelt Latin is whether it reflects genuine currency of the Latin language in Britain in about the fourth or fifth century, or consists merely of little-understood formulae put together from some phrase book. We can say without hesitation that the present text was written by a speaker of a real variety of late Latin. Decisive evidence for this view lies in the uses of the verb *decipio*. These are not, as the editor points out, formulaic in curses. They are genuine later meanings that had been illustrated by Löfstedt from texts of about the second to the fourth centuries. Also of note (and not only in this text) are the accusative *sanguem*, which there is reason to regard as a proto-Romance form, and *inuolo* 'steal'. The language of the text is not detached from that of the Continent or from developments in progress that were to lead to the Romance languages, and we may underline again how far-fetched it is to categorise British Latin as special and archaic.

34
CURSE TABLET FROM ULEY, GLOUCESTERSHIRE (HASSALL AND TOMLIN 1996: 440 no. 1)

Introduction

This tablet was 'found in 1978 at the temple of Mercury on West Hill. It is shallowly inscribed on both sides in an idiosyncratic Old Roman Cursive of third-century date' (Hassall and Tomlin 1996: 439).

Text

carta que Merçurio dọna-
tur ut maneçilis qui per[i]erunt
ụltiọnem requirat; qui iḷlọṣ
inualauiit ụṭ iḷli saṇguem [e]t sanita-
tem ṭọlla[t]; qui ipsos manicili[o]ṣ tulit   5
[u]ṭ quantociçịus iḷli pareat quod
ḍeum Mercurium r[o]gamus [. .]. .ura
q[.]oṣ.nç.u[2–3]lat.

Translation

The sheet (of lead) which is given to Mercury, so that he exact vengeance for the gloves which have been lost. Who stole them, from him may he remove the blood and health; who took the same gloves, to him may it become obvious as soon as possible what we are asking of the god Mercury . . .

Commentary

2 maneçilis: a term virtually non-existent in Latin until British curse tablets started to turn up. *Manicillium* is cited just once by the *TLL*, from a gloss (*CGL* II.476.24) where it appears alongside χειριδίον, 'glove'. Apart from the two examples here (which have both passed into the masculine) there is an instance in a Bath curse tablet (*Tab. Sulis* 5 *manicilia dua*), where the numeral suits the meaning 'glove'. The relative 'frequency' of the term in Britain may be a cultural phenomenon reflecting the northern climate (see Adams 2007: 613). Distinctive forms of clothing might well have been in use in Britain. Another such term is *capitulare* (originally a neuter but also attested as a masculine), indicating some sort of headgear, a word not reflected in Romance. Given the paucity of subliterary Latin surviving even in Britain the word is now remarkably well attested there (see Adams 2007: 613 for details). It is found at Vindolanda, Bath, Caistor-by-Norwich, Uley and the City of London. Whatever the headgear referred to, the object was clearly much used in Britain, and with it its designation, and the same must have been true of *manicilia*.

For the misspelling of the type in the second syllable in British tablets, see above, 32.3–4 on *uendicas*.

qui per[i]erunt: 'which have been lost', in the sense 'have been removed, taken away': see *TLL* X.1.1337.7ff.

3–4 qui illos inualauiit: the construction is of the relative-correlative type, with a resumptive pronoun (*illi*) in the main clause. *Ille* is the only pronoun in the text. The *o* of *inuolauit* has been assimilated to the stressed vowel (for this type of vocalic assimilation see Adams 1977a: 14–17). This is not an isolated form in British tablets but had some currency. There is now an instance of *inualauerit* on a lead tablet from Silchester, Hampshire (Tomlin 2009: 324 no. 16), and *alauerint* (with letters missing at the beginning) in a tablet from Pagans Hill (Hassall and Tomlin 1984: 339) must be from *inualauerint* (see Tomlin 2009: 324). The spelling with double *i* in our text is hypercorrect against the contraction of *ii*.

4–5 ut ... tolla[t]: for the *ut*-construction see 33.14–15.

sanguem [e]t sanitatem: for this alliterative combination see *Tab. Sulis* 41.3. For alliterative pairs in curse tablets see above, 6.3, and index, 'asyndeton bimembre, in curse tablets'.

5 ipsos manicili[o]s: since the gloves have remained the subject throughout (note *manecilis, illos* earlier), either the noun or the demonstrative might seem otiose: the meaning would have been transparent if *manicilios* had been used on its own, or alternatively a demonstrative (*illos* or even *ipsos*). This is one of those seemingly redundant uses of *ipsos* in which scholars have tended to see the origin of one of the Romance definite articles (that derived from *ipse*). However, repetitious specification of an object under discussion by means of terms meaning 'the very, the same, the aforementioned' is a feature of technical, including legal, Latin, and the redundancy suits the style of curses, which have features both of religious and legal language. *Ipsos* might be translated here as 'the same': for this use see Adams (2013: 492–500). See also below, 45.1, and index, 'technical writing, (specifying style)'.

tulit: often in late Latin treated as the perfect of *tollo* (with which it is juxtaposed here), and given the meaning 'remove, steal' (see Adams 1992a, 2–3, id. 2003a: 736 n. 22, Hassall and Tomlin 1996: 441). For *tollo* 'steal' in classical Latin see *OLD* s.v. 11. The meaning 'steal' is not however registered for *fero* by the *OLD* (cf. s.v. 35a, 'carry away').

6 quantocicius: Hassall and Tomlin (1996: 441), bracketing the second *ci*, compare *Tab. Sulis* 54.9 *quantocius* (see Tomlin's note on the word, 1988: 184). That term might be intended here, in which case there would indeed have been a dittography. Hassall and Tomlin state that it is 'just possible that the scribe coined a new form, *quanto citius*'. But the combination *quanto citius* occurs at Varro *Rust.* 1.67 and sometimes later (Tert. *Idol.* 8.3, Aug. *Civ.* 15.1: *TLL* III.1211.29f.). It is a correlative expression meaning literally 'by how much the more quickly', but the semantic change to the meaning here ('as quickly as possible') is easy, and replicated in *quantocius* itself, for which the meaning given by Souter (1949: 338) is 'the quicker the better'. On the misspelling *ci* for *ti* see B. Löfstedt (1961: 169), citing an example of *cicius* for *citius*.

illi: this is again a resumptive pronoun in a relative-correlative construction. It is unusual by early standards because postponed: the pronoun usually comes at the start of the main clause. On the order seen here see below, 39.10.

pareat: Hassall and Tomlin (1996: 439) translate: 'that he provide what we ask the god Mercury [. . .] as quickly as possible for the person who has taken these gloves'. In a note (1996: 441) they suggest that *pareat* is a misspelling of CL *pariat* 'accomplish'. This interpretation is not convincing. Mercurius would thus be the (unexpressed) subject of *pareat* and the expressed object of the verb in the next clause. The same usage is said to occur in another Uley tablet (Hassall and Tomlin 1992: 311, no. 5) (see the next text, 35), but there the context raises doubts about this view (see the discussion at 35.14–17). *Pareat* is CL *pareo* (see *OLD* s.v. 6, E. Löfstedt 1911: 58–9, Väänänen 1987: 151) = *appareo*, and the prayer is that it should soon become obvious, to the one who has committed the theft, what punishment has been requested of the god Mercury.

Conclusions

This is another British text manifesting typical developments of the period rather than any alleged British conservatism. For the neuter under threat in late Latin (*manicilios*) see Adams (2013: 425–31). The meaning of *tulit* is late and widespread. One possible regional feature here is the form of *inuolo* with *a* in the second syllable, but that is a substandard innovation, not an archaism.

35

ANOTHER CURSE TABLET FROM ULEY, GLOUCESTERSHIRE (HASSALL AND TOMLIN 1992: 311 no. 5)

Introduction

This is another tablet found in 1978 at the temple of Mercury on West Hill. Hassall and Tomlin (1992: 310) note that the tablet, which is complete, 'has been inscribed in Old Roman Cursive (*c.* AD 150 – *c.* AD 275) by a practised hand using a stilus'.

Text

deo sacto Mercurio Honoratus
conqueror numini tuo me perdidisse rotas duas et uaccas quattuor et resculas plurimas de
hospitiolo meo.   5
        rogauerim genium nu-
minis tuui ut ei qui mihi fraudem
fecerit sanitatem ei non permittas nec iacere nec sedere nec
bibere nec manducare si baro   10
si mulier si puer si puella si seruus
si liber nissi meam rem ad me
pertulerit et meam concordiam
habuerit. iteratis praecibus rogo numen tuum ut petitio mea   15
statim pareat me uindica-
tum esse a maiestate tua.

Translation

Honoratus to the holy god Mercury. I complain to your divinity that I have lost two wheels and four cows and very many small things from my dwelling.

I would ask the genius of your divinity that to him who cheated me, to him you do not allow health, nor the ability to lie, sit, drink or eat, be he man or woman, boy or girl, slave or free, unless he shall bring my property to me and make peace with me. With my prayers repeated I ask your divinity that my petition should be immediately fulfilled (and that it become obvious) that I have been avenged by your majesty.

Commentary

1 sacto: for the loss of the nasal (in this case a velar nasal) before a stop, see index, 'spellings, omission of nasal before stop' (e.g. below, 36.3, for another British example). The spelling *sactus* occurs several times in British inscriptions and has a parallel at Vindolanda (*Tab. Vindol.* 609 *Sactius = Sanctius*) but does not represent a regional pronunciation (as it has been taken), as there are parallels from various other parts of the Empire (see Adams 2007: 593–4).

4 resculas: a rare diminutive, but found at Apul. *Met.* 4.12.

5 hospitiolo: the possessive *meo* favours the meaning '(humble) house, cottage, abode' rather than 'inn, lodging place'. The meaning is well attested from Jerome onwards (*TLL* VI.2–3.3037.1ff.). The diminutive is presumably suited to the affecting description of a theft: cf. Greg. Tur. *HF* 6.45, p. 319.5–6 *hospitiola pauperum spoliabant, uineas deuastabant.* The same word (and prepositional phrase) is conjectured by Tomlin (1991: 308) in another Uley tablet (*anulus aureus de hos[pitiolo . . .*), and read by him (1991: 309 (d)) in line 6 of the Pagans Hill curse tablet (*de hospitiolo m[eo]*) originally published by Hassall and Tomlin (1984: 339, no. 7) with *hospitio*. Tomlin (1991: 309 (c)) also conjectures *quas pe[rdidi de hospi]tiolo meo* for *Tab. Sulis* 12 lines 2–3. He points out (loc. cit.) that the sense 'lodging house' is not likely for the countryside around Uley and Pagans Hill, well away from towns. The term seems to have been favoured locally (*casa* was a far more familiar word, surviving widely in Romance languages; *hospitiolum* does not survive anywhere). *Hospitium* occurs in a Bath tablet (*Tab. Sulis* 99.1–2), where it could mean either 'lodging' or 'house'. For *hospitium* meaning 'house' see *ILS* 5920 (cited by Tomlin), and also the school exercise *Colloquium Celtis* (Dickey 2015), 47c *scopa hospitium*, where the Greek has σάρισον τὴν οἰκίαν.

For *hospitium* of a stable at Vindolanda see Adams (2003b: 564), a usage for which see now the Visigothic slate tablet no. 54 (Velázquez Soriano 2004), and also below, 36.7. Could that even be the meaning of the diminutive here?

A comparable word to *hospitiolum* now attested at Vindolanda is *casula* (*Tab. Vind.* 643.ii.3).

7 tuui: with glide: see 33.7–8.

7–8 ut ei qui … ei non: the resumptive pronoun *ei*, following the earlier *ei*, antecedent of the relative, is redundant. Resumptive pronouns are not infrequently superfluous (though often used for clarity or some other purpose), but usually pick up a noun or name rather than a pronoun, as here: see 2.25, 3.416, 5.7–8 (the last on the functions of pronominal resumption). For a pronoun repeating the same pronoun see Plaut. *Aul.* 144–5 *id quod in rem tuam optumum esse arbitror,* | *ted id monitum aduento, Men.* 162 *id enim quod tu uis, id aio atque id nego, Pseud.* 430–2 *nam istaec quae tibi renuntiantur, …* | *…* | *fors fuat an istaec dicta sint mendacia.* These examples all have the same structure as that in the curse (*is qui … is*).

8–9 sanitatem ei non permittas nec iacere nec sedere. . .: here a noun in the accusative appears to be coordinated with a series of infinitives. This is not however quite the same construction as that seen above in Pelagonius (29.2), where a substantival infinitive is coordinated with and has the same role as some nominal accusatives. *Permitto* with the dative and infinitive is an old construction (*OLD* s.v. 6a). What is slightly unusual here is the mixing of the accusative construction (*sanitatem*) with the infinitival, a mixing which in effect converts the infinitives into substantives.

10 manducare: in British curse tablets at Bath (*Tab. Sulis* 41.5) and Pagans Hill (Hassall and Tomlin 1984: 339 no. 7).

10–11 si baro si mulier: *baro* is a Germanic word which obviously means in the context 'man' (for discussion of the term see Adams 1992a: 15–17, id. 2007: 600). It is a feature of British curse tablets. For further examples see Hassall and Tomlin (1989: 328, no. 2) (Uley), Tomlin (1991: 295 no. 1) (no provenance), Hassall and Tomlin (1994: 294 no. 1) (Brandon). There are also four examples in the Bath curse tablets. There seems now to be a case at Vindolanda (713 *bar. nes*). The term is also found on the Continent in Gaul in barbarian law codes in much the same 'man/woman' opposition. Cf. e.g. *Pactus legis Salicae* 31.1 *si quis baronem <ingenuum> de uia sua ostauerit* ('if anyone pushes from his path a (freeborn) man'), with which is juxtaposed (in the next section) 31.2 *si quis mulierem ingenuam … de uia sua ostauerit.* At *Leg. Alamann.* 69, p. 136.11 *baro* is opposed to *femina.* The meaning of *baro* given by *FEW* XV.68 is 'freier mann' (cf. section 1a. 'Tapferer mann, mann'). OFr., MFr. *baron,* for example, is cited, and given such senses as 'homme brave, valeureux;

homme' (*Chanson de Roland*), 'homme distingué par ses hautes qualités'. Sp. *varón* has the sense 'man of worth', but also, more generally, 'man, male, boy'. The weakened meaning (cf. the semantic development of *uir*) is foreshadowed in the curse tablet, whereas in the Salic law the word still retains (to judge by the epithet used at least with its feminine correspondent) something of the earlier sense (see also Gaeng 1969: 3–4 on the sense 'chief, noble' in the Fredegar chronicles). *Baro* 'free/distinguished man, man' seems very much a north-western word, but it remains unclear by what route it found its way into British curse tablets; possibly it had been introduced to Britain by soldiers of German origin. The much earlier literary Latin word *baro*, defined by the *OLD* as 'blockhead, lout', was almost certainly not of the same origin (it is claimed as Etruscan: see Adams 2007: 391 with n. 110; the word is not in de Vaan 2008). *Baro* in the sense(s) discussed above was clearly a late borrowing into Latin.

12 nissi: for the hypercorrect gemination of *s* see *Tab. Vindol.* 343.20, with Adams (1995b: 89 with n. 29).

14 praecibus: *pr-* often is followed by a hypercorrect digraph *ae* for *ĕ*, as e.g. in *praetium* (see Adams 1976a: 44). That is because phonetic spellers might be aware that a preverb *prae-* existed, and prone to see it where it did not belong.

14–17 rogo numen tuum ut petitio mea statim pareat me uindicatum esse a maiestate tua: Hassall and Tomlin (1992: 311) translate the last lines thus: 'I ask your divinity that my petition may immediately make me vindicated by your majesty', taking (310) *pareat* to stand for *pariat* 'accomplish'. What would be odd on this interpretation is the acc. + inf. apparently standing as object of *pariat* = 'produce, accomplish'. The *TLL* article does not seem to recognise such a construction.

It is likely that the spelling (with *e*) is correct, and that the verb *pareo* is used in these passages (cf. 34.6) as a quasi-legalism appropriate to curse tablets, in a sense that may be a slight extension of that normally found. *Paret* = 'is clear, evident' is particularly common in legal formulae and language (see *OLD* s.v. 6, *TLL* X.1.373.38ff.). It may be used impersonally or with a subject, and a dependent clause such as an acc. + infin. may complement it (see *TLL* 373.66ff.). The author of the *TLL* article (Breimeier) points out that the usage tends to take on a variety of semantic nuances, and that (e.g.) it sometimes comes close to being equivalent to *fieri, adesse, exsistere* (*TLL* 373.11).

In the present passage there seems to have been a conflation of constructions, *petitio mea pareat* + *pareat me uindicatum esse a maiestate tua.*
The meaning of the second construction would be '(I ask your divinity that)
it may become evident that I have been avenged by your majesty'. The meaning
of the first would be '(I ask ... that) my petition may be immediately carried
out' (= *fiat*) (alternatively 'may become immediately obvious').

At 34.6 *pareat* could either be given its traditional sense, as it was
translated ad loc., or the slightly extended sense, = *fiat* ('may what we are
asking of the god Mercurius befall him as quickly as possible').

Conclusions

In this text we see illustrated (in *baro*) the fact that Latin in Britain was not cut
off but subject to foreign influences. *Hospitiolum* belongs to late Latin. It had
obviously caught on in Britain, but was not confined to there. The writing of
this text is on the whole correct, even hypercorrect, though the legalistic final
clauses caused the writer trouble, on the interpretation adopted here.

36

CURSE TABLET FROM RATCLIFFE-ON-SOAR, NOTTINGHAMSHIRE (HASSALL AND TOMLIN 1993: 312 no. 2)

Introduction

This text, on an irregular piece of sheet lead, was found in 1990. It is 'written from right to left in mirror-image capital letters' (Hassall and Tomlin 1993: 310). The document is discussed by Mullen (2013), with a plausible solution to one of its problems (at line 5, where the editors print *paulatoriam* with capital letters).

Text

nomine Camụlorigi et Titocune molam quam perdederunt
in fanum dei dẹụọụị. cuicumquẹ ṇụm[e]n inuolasit
mola illam ut saguin suum mịṭtat usque diem quọ
moriatur. q[ui]cumque iṇuọ[l]a[sit] hụrta moriatur,
et paụlaṭọṛiam quicumque [illam] inuolạsit   5
et ipse <moriato> mo[ri]atur. quicumqui illam
inuolasit et VẸRTOGṆ ḍe ospitio uel uissacio,
quicumque illam inuolasit, a deuo moriotur.

Translation

In the name of Camulorix and Titocuna I have dedicated in the temple of the god the mule which they have lost. Whichever person stole that mule, may he lose his own blood until the day he die. Whoever stole the hurdle (?), may he die; and the fodder basket, whoever stole it, may he die also. Whoever stole it and the (VẸRTOGṆ) from the stable, or the double bag, whoever stole it, may he die by the god.

Commentary

1 Camụlorigi et Titocune: both are Celtic names (see Hassall and Tomlin 1993: 312). The genitive of the first should have final *s*, which is restored by the editors, but the form with the ending *-i* could be kept, because confusion with the endings either of the second declension genitive or the third declension dative is not impossible. There is a semantic overlap between the genitive and dative (expressing possession), and confusions do occur. For the *-i* ending in a third declension name with genitive function, see *Froilani* in the Visigothic slate tablet (below, 46.4). Note too the slate tablet 63.2–3 *[in] nomine [pa]tri et filii*, with Velázquez Soriano (2004: 523), on syncretism of genitive and dative. For the reverse phenomenon, genitive for dative, see Adams (2013: 463).

molam: this may be either the term for 'millstone', or a misspelling for *mulam* (female mules were particularly desirable because of their temperament and working abilities, and the feminine was even used sometimes as the generic term for 'mule': see Adams 1993). A mule is a more likely object of theft than a millstone (note the theft of cows in text 35). For this misspelling of *mula* see Hassall and Tomlin (1993: 313) ad loc., citing a few examples and also a false etymology of *mula*, from *molendo* and *molas* (Isid. *Etym.* 12.1.57 *molendo ducat in gyro molas*). Misspellings showing *o* for an original *ū* are not infrequently motivated by false analogies or etymologies (see Prinz 1932: 93–4).

perdederunt: recomposition, a banal phenomenon (see Adams 1977a: 8 with n. 8).

2 c̨uicumqu̧e: the 'dative' form is used where a nominative is required (*quicumque*). Four times later in the text the formula *quicumque inuolasit* occurs, and that surely must be intended here too. The mistake, if it is one, is superficial, because the dative and nominative forms had the same pronunciation (for the same sort of error, see below, 49.22). On this view the masculine by classical standards is wrong here, as *numen/nomen* is neuter. Various third declension neuters retained their neuter form in later Latin while being used as with masculine agreement. Note *nomen et numen deae | uotis perennem quem dicare* in the poem of Q. Avidius Quintianus from Bu Njem (see Courtney 1995, no. 40, Adams 1999: 110), where *nomen et numen* appears to be followed by masculine agreement both in the adjective *perennem* and the relative *quem* (on the interpretation see Adams 1999: 125). For mixed-gender phrases in late Latin (often showing a third declension neuter noun with a masculine adjective) see Adams (2013: 428–31).

An alternative possibility is to accept *cuicumque* with the editors (313) as a dative, and to take it as equivalent in function to the genitive *cuiuscumque*. They translate literally as 'whoever's name stole it'. This seems forced, given the repetitive nature of the curse, with the *quicumque*-clause used four times hereafter.

Numen has been confused with *nomen* and used with a meaning close to 'person' (with the masculine agreement arguably a sort of constructio ad sensum); on *nomen* with this meaning see e.g. Salonius (1920: 416). On the confusion *nomen/numen*, which is widespread, see above, 32.3–4. The potential for confusion was increased by the fact that *numen* as well as *nomen* had a place in curses (see above, 35, and for this point, 32.3–4).

inuolasit: a false archaism. Strictly the form is a sigmatic future or subjunctive, but it is here used as if it were a simple past tense, equivalent to *inuolauit*. See Adams, Lapidge and Reinhardt (2005: 15), de Melo (2007: 238 n. 26, 343). De Melo (2007: 343) notes that this example 'shows how certain ritualistic structures were preserved even when their meaning was no longer clear, at least at this educational level'. Such forms usually have *ss*, but a simplification would be banal.

3 ut saguin suum mittat: the (velar) nasal of *sangu-* was, it seems, not heard, as in *sacto* (35.1). This is unlikely to be the old literary neuter *sanguen* (see Adams 2007: 586). It is either an abbreviation for *sanguinem*, or a misspelling for the remodelled accusative *sanguem* that is found in these texts (33.10).

The *ut*-clause is free-standing again, expressing a wish/request (see above, 33.14–15). The subject of the verb must be the culprit, who is either to let his own blood, or to lose it. For *mitto = amitto* see *TLL* VIII.1177.1ff. The latter interpretation is the more likely. Compare the wording of a curse tablet from Leicester (Tomlin 2009: 329 no. 22), *peto ut uitam suam perdant ante dies septem*.

usque diem quo: *usque* for *usque ad* (Hofmann and Szantyr 1965: 254). It is found with names of towns from Terence onwards, and with other nouns from Celsus onwards and particularly in later Latin.

4 hurta: an obscure word; the *h* is certain. Hassall and Tomlin (1993: 314) suggest that it might be a mistake for *furta*, a word which would have to have a concrete meaning, 'objects of theft'. *Furta* can have this meaning (*TLL* VI.1.1648.26ff.), but so far only one object has been mentioned, the *mola*: a second object in the list of objects stolen would be appropriate here. There is a Germanic word *hurda* 'hurdle, fence', which is reflected in Old French (*REW* 4243, *FEW* XVI.269–70; found especially in the north of France) and might be possible here; these tablets have a Germanic element (see 35.10–11 on *baro*), which must have been introduced by Latin speakers coming from the Continent, where *hurda* was certainly in use among Latin speakers. One might speculate that a piece of hurdle fencing had been removed when the mule was taken.

Far less likely is *horda* 'pregnant (cow)'. The first vowel might in theory have been closed to *u* under the influence of the following *r* + consonant (see B. Löfstedt 1961: 82), but the word seems to have been rare, dialectal and early.

paulatoriam: Mullen (2013: 268) makes a good case that this is a substantivised feminine adjective *pabulatoria*, with ellipse of the feminine variant of *corbis* (a noun attested in both masculine and feminine), = 'fodder-basket'. Columella (6.3.5) has the masculine phrase *corbis pabulatorius*. The phonetics are slightly obscure, but there would have to be an underlying B/V confusion on this interpretation. *TLL* X.1.5.41f. reports as manuscript misspellings of *pabulum* both *pauulum* and *paulum*. On B/V see further on *uissacio* below.

5–6 quicumque [illam] inuolasit et ipse <moriato> mo[ri]atur: a relative-correlative construction.

6 quicumqui illam: in *-qui* for *-que* there has probably been a mechanical spelling error, determined by the preceding *qui-*.

This is a text in which *ille* occurs three times, *is* not at all. In 35 on the other hand *is* is used twice, *ille* not at all. The language was moving towards the elimination of *is*, but those with stylistic aspirations might keep it.

7 VERTOGN: obscure, but the beginning is certainly suggestive of the Celtic term for a fast dog used in hunting (see Delamarre 2003: 317 s.v. *uertragos*), a word that entered Latin particularly in Celtic provinces (as in *Tab. Vindol.* 594), and survives mainly in Gallo-Romance (for details see Adams 2007: 322).

ospitio: given the context this word may well refer to stables or housing for animals. For this meaning attested at Vindolanda and elsewhere, see above, 35.5.

uissacio: this looks like a misspelling of *bisaccium*, denoting a double bag, a term found only at Petron. 31.9 (*asellus Corinthius cum bisaccio*) but widely reflected in Romance languages (see Adams 2003b:18). Gemination of the wrong consonant is a common mechanical error. This would be another rare case of B/V confusion in a British text (see Adams 2007: 651–5, and also Mullen 2013: 268–9).

It is unlikely that *uel uissacio* is part of the *de*-expression that precedes, as the objects of theft that seem to be referred to here could hardly have been kept in a bag, double or otherwise. *Vissacio* must be an accusative, with a banal omission of *-m* and vocalic misspelling, the word referring to another stolen object (punctuate with a comma after *ospitio*). The meaning 'saddle-bags' (see Mullen 2013: 268) would be appropriate to the context.

8 a deuo moriotur: *moriotur* is a misspelling for *moriatur*. *Morior ab* (with an animate agent expressed as inflicting the death) is not usual in classical Latin (but see *TLL* VIII.1493.33ff.: note Sen. *Contr.* 5.3 *moriuntur non alter ab altero sed uterque a patre*, 'they die, not at each other's hands, but both at their father's', Winterbottom, Loeb) (cf. ἀποθνῄσκω ὑπό).

There are various ways of explaining *deuo*. First, *deuos* is the Celtic equivalent of Lat. *deus* (Delamarre 2003: 142–3). The same form occurs at *RIB* 306 (*deuo Nodenti*) also in a Celtic context (Nodens was a Celtic deity). Perhaps the writer of the curse has lapsed into the Celtic word (note the Celtic names of the victims). Second, the word might be the Latin *deus*, with the insertion of a glide (see Adams 2007: 602). The glide [w] after a front vowel is odd for Latin (where [j] would be expected in such a position), but there are British parallels suggestive of a local pronunciation. Cf. Welsh *pydew* < Lat. **puteuus* (Adams 2007: 589–90 with bibliography), and also *euum* = *eum* in the curse tablet (with Celtic names) from Leicester, below, 37.1. A third possibility is that the form is a misspelling of Lat. *diuus*, but used as a noun that term belonged to high and poetic style, and to a few formulae (on the word and type of misspelling see above, 14.9).

Conclusions

This text displays (in *inuolasit*) the aspiration to archaism typical of curse tablets, which sometimes preserve legal or religious terminology. On the other hand it is a product of its time, containing hints of Germanic (*hurta?*) and Celtic influence (*deuo?*). Again there is in evidence a development (B/V confusion) sometimes thought not to be 'British'.

37

CURSE TABLET FROM LEICESTER (TOMLIN 2008, 2009: 327 no. 21)

Introduction

This is one of two inscribed lead tablets 'found in 2005 during excavation of a large courtyard-house in the north-east quarter of Roman Leicester (*Ratae Corieltauvorum*)' (Tomlin 2008: 207).

Text

daeo Maglo od euum qui frudum	
fecit de padoio, od elaeum qui	
furtum de padaoium saum,	
qui saum Seruandi inuola-	
uit.	5
S[il]uester Riomandus	
Ṣ[e]nilis Venustinus	
Voruena	
Calaṃịnus	
Felicianus	10
Rufaedo	
Vendicina	
Ingenuinus	
Iuuentius	
Alocus	15
Cennosus	
Ġermanus	
Senedo	
Cunouendus	
Regalis	20
Niella	
[[sẹ2–3iạṇus]].	
od antae nonum diem	
illum tollat	
qui saum inuolauit	25
Seruandi.	

Translation

To the god Maglus I give him who did a theft (?) from the slave quarters, I give him (?) who (did) a theft (of) the cloak from the slave quarters, who stole the cloak of Servandus. Silvester, Riomandus, Senilis, Venustinus, Vorvena, Calaminus, Felicianus, Rufaedo, Vendicina, Ingenuinus, Iuventius, Alocus, Cennosus, Germanus, Senedo, Cunovendus, Regalis, Ni(g)ella, Se... (deleted). May he destroy him before the ninth day who stole the cloak of Servandus.

Commentary

1 daeo: for this form in inscriptions, with hypercorrect *ae* for *ĕ* (see above, 15.8), see *TLL* V.1.886.74f. The digraphs of the classical written language were beyond this writer. The three instances of *ae* are all hypercorrect, and twice (in renderings of *paedagogium*) *a* is used instead of either *ae* or the phonetic spelling *e*. Similarly in *frudum*, if it represents *fraudem* (see below), *u* is written, though the usual phonetic spelling was with *o*.

euum: this form has the abnormal [w] glide after a front vowel that may be 'British': see Adams (2007: 590), and above, 36.8 on *deuo*.

1-2 od ... od: Tomlin (2008: 208–9) reviews the possible explanations of these forms and opts for a reversal of *do*, which is the best solution in this early part of the document. *Do* for *od* does not work so well, however, in line 23 (where it is followed by the third person verb *tollat*). *Do ... tollas* would be one thing ('I hand him over: may you destroy him ...'), with an introductory *do* and then a jussive subjunctive addressed to the god. Tomlin quotes as parallels (209 n. 9) two passages in which the verb of giving is indeed followed by a <u>second</u> person jussive subjunctive. In his third parallel, quoted to illustrate a third person jussive subjunctive in such a context (*RIB* 323 *do tibi ... non redimat*), the god is still addressed, and is not the subject of the third person subjunctive verb, as would have to be the case in the present tablet: the subject at *RIB* 323 is the victim of the curse ('I give him to you ... may he not redeem'). This example is not then a parallel to the construction suggested by Tomlin in the present curse. Tomlin's translation (208) brings out the awkwardness of taking *od* as standing for *do*: 'I give (that the god Maglus) before the ninth day take him away'. This interpretation might just stand, but the construction that would be simplest here would be a free-standing wish/request introduced by *ut* (*ut ... illum tollat qui*, 'may he destroy him who'). The structure of the clause *od antae nonum* *diem illum tollat* is very similar to that at the end of text 32, where 'Neptune' is also asked to punish a thief before nine days are up, with a *rogo ut-*construction leading to the verb of avenging (*rogo ṭe Metunus ut (t)u mi uenḍ[i]cas ante qọ[d] uen(iant) di(es) n[o]uem*). The only difference is that the god is referred to in the third person in one text and the second in the other. *Vt* is definitely to be expected at this point in the present curse, and *od* could well here be for *ut*. The spelling *o* for *ŭ* is common in late Latin, and *ut* not infrequently has the form *ud* (see e.g. the examples from Terentianus at Adams 1977a: 27–8). It does not matter that the form *od* for *ut* is not yet established in the Latin of Roman Britain, as many of the phenomena in these curse tablets are unique. On this view *od* in this tablet would be variously for *do* and for *ut*, which some would find unacceptable, but such texts are riddled with inconsistencies. I can see nothing problematic either (cf. Tomlin 2008: 209) about the combination of a dative construction in line 1 ('I give to the god Maglus') with the third person wish at the end ('may he destroy him'). In text 34 above the tablet is 'given to' Mercury, and then there is a curse also of the form *ut tollat*.

qui frudum fecit de padoio: in this context (with a *de*-expression following) *frudum* could contain a metathesis and derive from *furdum = furtum*. There is evidence in the tablet for developments affecting voiceless stops (see 37.2–3). Alternatively *fraudem* may be intended. For the *u* Tomlin (2008, 2009 with n. 14) cites *frudem* from *Tab. Sulis* 32, adding that the second declension ending may be due to confusion with *furtum*. The *de*-expression is better suited to theft 'from' than to wrongdoing/fraud, and the expression seems to be repeated immediately, with the spelling *furtum* (but omission of the verb: see below). Repetition of the verb phrase denoting theft is a feature of the last tablet above, 36.

2 elaeum: Tomlin (2008: 214) notes that the clause in which this term occurs is equivalent to that with *euum* just before and that with *illum* later, and accordingly takes the form as a pronoun, which it must be. The *e*-spelling in the first syllable can be paralleled in curse tablets (see Jeanneret 1918: 19; but see Tomlin 2008: 214 n. 19 for reservations about one of Jeanneret's examples) and occasionally elsewhere (see Mihăescu 1978: 175, citing *CIL* XIII.7645 *con elo*, from Gondorf on the Mosel). The *ae* in the second syllable must be hypercorrect for *ĕ*, in which case there would have been a conflation of *illum* with *eum*.

2–3 qui furtum de padaoium saum: if this clause is to be made meaningful *fecit* must be understood from the previous clause (ellipse of *facio* is commonplace: see e.g. Heidemann 1893: 57–63, and above, 28.25–6), and *saum = sagum* must be construed as object of the verb phrase *furtum (fecit)*, with this periphrasis taking on the construction of the single verb (*furor*) to which it is equivalent, and thus governing an accusative (a type of 'incorporation': see above, 4.8, and below 47.3). However, since the next *qui*-clause repeats in a grammatical form the content of that here, with the transitive verb *inuolauit*, it is possible that the present clause represents a false start, with the writer realising that *saum* was not appropriate as object of *furtum fecit* and switching to *inuolauit*.

Tomlin (2008: 209) must be right to take *padaoium* as representing *paedagogium*. He tentatively takes the meaning to be 'slave quarters', while acknowledging the unclarity. The *TLL* article, which was written before the Leicester tablet was published, defines one of the uses thus (X.1.31.4): 'de loco, aedificio ubi paedagogiani instituuntur'. It is unlikely that slaves were being taught in the conventional sense in Leicester, in which case the term might have been generalised to refer to a building in which slaves were merely quartered (see further Tomlin 2008: 209).

The most remarkable feature of this text is exemplified in the last two words of the lemma, namely the omission of intervocalic *g*, twice in *paedagogium* and once in *sagum*. There are two other cases of *saum* in the text, a sixth and seventh omission in *padoio* and an eighth and ninth in *Ri(g)omandus* (line 6: see Tomlin 2008: 214 n. 26) and *Niella* for *Nigella* (21). The letter is retained between vowels just once, in *Regalis*. The omissions occur indifferently both before and after the accent. This is the phenomenon of lenition, a term that may be used to cover on the one hand voicing of voiceless intervocalic stops (e.g. Sp. *fuego* < *focus*) and on the other frication (> [j]) or loss of voiced intervocalic stops (on the terminology see Loporcaro 2011: 150). Omission of the *g* in writing could reflect either loss or frication. Some details of the treatment of intervocalic *g* in different areas of Romance are given by Bourciez (1946: 166–8). In the east it was largely retained. Thus Rom. *lega* < *ligare*. So it was persistent in central Italy (e.g. It. *legare*), though sometimes lost before the accent. In the Iberian peninsula and southern Gaul it was maintained after the accent (Sp. *llaga*, Pg. *praga*, Occ. *plaga* < *plaga*) but was often lost before an accented vowel (Sp., Pg. *liar* < *ligare*). Northern Gaul (French) pushed lenition furthest. Intervocalic *g*, whether original or derived from voicing of an earlier intervocalic *k*, underwent frication (Fr. *plaie* < *plaga*, *payer* < **pagare* < *pacare*) or in some environments total loss. The Leicester tablet suggests that British Latin was aligned in this respect with the Latin of the northern part of Gaul (though the text might of course have been written by a native of Gaul). The various distinctions above are not absolute, and individual lexical items may have their own histories. The reflexes of *sagum* do not show a *g* in any of the Romance areas (Gallo-Romance, Italo-Romance,

Ibero-Romance: *REW* 7515). For the (usually specialised) reflexes of *nigellus* see *REW* 5916, citing Rom. *negel* on the one hand and OFr. *neel* and Occ. *niel* on the other. In It. *niello* the *g* is lost before the accent.

6–21 S[il]uester ... **Niella:** the names in the list are partly Latin and partly Celtic. On the latter (*Seneda, Cunouendus, Ri(g)omandus, Voruena, Cennosus*) see Tomlin (2008: 215). The names are in the nominative without any obvious syntax, a feature of curse tablets (see above, 19.1, and Adams 2013: 227–8).

Conclusions

This is a tablet that comes from a distinctly Celtic milieu, with possessors of Celtic names apparently mixing with possessors of Latin names in a *paedagogium*. The tablet has a particularly striking feature, namely the evidence throughout that in the writer's speech intervocalic *g* had undergone lenition. A second feature is the glide in *euum*, which is abnormal for Latin and may show a local development (cf. *deuo* in 36).

I conclude with a few remarks about this small group of British curse tablets together. They reflect a living Latin of the time, say of the third to fifth centuries. The etymological use of *decipio* and its derivative noun (text 33) is a late innovation that fits the period nicely. The accusative form *sanguem*, which is almost certainly the forerunner of Romance terms for 'blood', we will see (38 below) in the *Vetus Latina*, in a version of this period. Uses of *hospitium* and *hospitiolum* (35, 36) can be paralleled in later Latin, and not least that from Britain. Glides in hiatus are a feature of 33, and those in 36 and 37, as was remarked above, may be regional. The language in Britain was subject to external influences. In 35 and 36 we saw a definite and a possible Germanic loan-word (*baro, hurta*). Celtic names are found in both 36 and 37.

This corpus shows the hazards of making negative assertions of the type 'such and such did not occur in British Latin, which was archaic' (on this notion see further below, 39 Introduction). Confusions of the vowels *e* and *i* are found in texts 32 and 34; contrast Jackson (1953: 86–7). The B/V confusion is attested in several items in 36; contrast Jackson (1953: 89) 'Latin *v* and *b* remained rigidly distinct in British', adding that this was because they were pronounced in Britain as [w] and [b] respectively. *Quantocicius* in 34 has *ci* for *ti*, another phenomenon supposedly not British (Jackson 1953: 91). The fact that there are Latin loan-words in British Celtic that preserve such distinctions might simply mean one of two things: that the loans entered the language before the mergers had taken place in Latin, or that the borrowings were learned rather than popular. This old distinction between a learned and a popular ('acoustic') borrowing must always be kept in mind: learned borrowings preserve learned features of the source language, which might have undergone change at a more popular level. Are there studies of Latin loan-words in Celtic that make a systematic attempt to distinguish these two types of borrowings, or to determine dating criteria? *Fides*, for example, which went into Welsh from the original *ī*-form (see Jackson 1953: 87), was not a popular term but religious. *Vendicas* for *uindicas* on the other hand is in a non-standard text (32 above) also containing *ut* + indicative, a usage revealing a distinct lack of education. Whatever loan-words might appear to be telling us, the Latin curse tablets from Britain throw up misspellings that are typical of non-literary tablets of whatever region, and any characterisation of 'British Vulgar Latin' must be based on the growing corpus of primary texts.

38
GOSPEL OF JOHN (6.51–69) FROM THE *VETVS LATINA* (CODEX PALATINVS, *e*), AND THE CORRESPONDING PASSAGE FROM THE VULGATE

Introduction

Both the Old Latin versions of the Bible and the Vulgate were of considerable influence in later Latin. Much extant Latin from about the third century onwards was written by Christians familiar with at least one version of the Latin Bible, which they quoted and also imitated, consciously or otherwise. Many Christian writers knew little of classical literature, and the Latin Bible became a stylistic model (see for example below, 39 on Patrick). The Latin Bible is a translated text, based partly on Greek and partly on Hebrew (on the latter either directly or indirectly). Constructions alien to ordinary Latin are commonplace, and these were sometimes picked up by Christians and used even in non-biblical contexts. Verbs of saying, for example, under Greek and ultimately Hebrew influence are often complemented in the Vulgate and old translations by *ad* rather than the dative, and *dicere ad* et sim. spread from there to theological writers and even to authors who, though they knew the Bible, were not writing on Christian themes (such as the anonymous author of the *Historia Apollonii*: see text 43). Since the Romance languages have lost the dative and replaced it with reflexes of *ad* (with nouns; pronouns are a separate case), it is possible that the *Vetus Latina* and Vulgate had a part in promoting a general development of the language.

The Vulgate version of the Gospels, the work of Jerome, was a minimal revision of Old Latin versions (see Burton 2000: 6). Of the nature of Jerome's revisions Burton (2000: 192–9) offers a clear account in an appendix. The earliest extant Old Latin versions of the Gospels are not before the fourth century, and thus were in circulation alongside the Vulgate. There is not in every case a clear-cut distinction between the Old Latin and the Vulgate, because some Old Latin versions show the influence of the Vulgate, and Old Latin readings found their way into the Vulgate. Burton (2000: 7) states that of 'the thirteen main manuscripts traditionally classed as Old Latin . . ., no fewer than six are mixed texts'.

The Old Latin Gospels (OLG) are traditionally classified into several groups, representing the 'African' tradition, the 'European', the 'North Italian' and 'mixed texts' (see Burton 2000: 14). The major representative of the African tradition is the Codex Bobbiensis (*k*), which is a fourth-century lacunate African codex containing just part of Mark and Matthew (Burton 2000: 16). The Codex Palatinus (*e*), which is attributed to the fifth century, is described by Burton (2000: 17) as follows:

Its text is closest to *k* in the portions where both are extant, and shows many African features characteristic of *k* in portions for which *k* is not extant; however, it is overlaid throughout with a European element.

For refinements related in particular to John see Burton's fourth chapter (2000: 62–74).

For the *e* version of the Old Latin I have used the online *Vetus Latina Iohannes*, ed. P. H. Burton, J. Balserak, H. A. G. Houghton and D. C. Parker (available at: www.Iohannes.org).

Where one version or another appears to differ from the Greek, that may be because the translator had before him a Greek reading different from those extant. That is a possibility that must be kept in mind, but in the interests of brevity it will not be repeatedly laboured in the following Commentary.

One reason for comparing a passage from the Vulgate with the corresponding one from an OLG version is that differences may throw light on Jerome's attitude to constructions and terms used in the other version. We will return to this subject in the conclusion, but it needs to be said here that the determinants of differences are far more complex than a mere tendency on Jerome's part to favour an educated variant over a substandard.

The Greek text is also printed below.

Texts

Codex Palatinus (*e*)

6.51 'Ego sum panis uibus, qui de caelo discendi. si quis manducauerit de meo pane, uiuet in aeternum. panis autem quem ego dedero, caro mea est pro saeculi uita.'

52 discertabantur itaque Iudaei ad inuicem, dicentes: 'quomodo potest hic nobis carnem suam dare manducare?'

53 dixit illis Iesus: 'amen, amen dico uobis: nisi ederitis carnem fili hominis et biberitis sanguem eius, non habebitis uitam in uobis.

54 qui edet carnem eius et bibet sanguem eius, habet uitam aeternam: et ego suscitabo illum nouissima die.

55 caro mea uere est esca, et sanguis meus uere est potum.

56 qui edet carnem meam et bibet sanguem meum, in me manet et ego in ipsum.

57 et sicut me misit pater uibus, et ego uibo propter patrem: et qui ediderit, et ipse uibet propter me.

58 hic est panis qui de caelo discendit. non quomodo manducauerunt patres uestri, et mortui sunt: qui edediderit panem istum uiuet in aeternum.'

59 haec dixit in synagoga, docens Capharnaum.

60 multi ergo ex discentibus eius dixerunt: 'durus est sermo iste: et quis potest audire eum?'

61 cognouit ergo Iesus apud semetipsum quoniam murabant discipuli eius. dixit illis: 'hoc uos scandalizat?

62 quid si uideritis filium hominis ascendentem in illo ubi fuit prius?

63 spiritus est qui uiuificat: caro nihil prode est. uerba ista quae ego locutus sum, uobis spiritus et uita est.

64 sed ex uobis sunt quidam, qui non credunt.' sciebat enim ab initio Iesus quis esset qui eum traditurus erat.

65 et dicebat: 'propterea quia nemo potest uenire ad me nisi fuerit illi datum a patre meo.'

66 exinde multi ex discentibus eius abierunt retrorsum et iam non ambulabant cum eo.

67 dixit ergo Iesus ad XII discipulos suos: 'numquid et uos uultis ire?'

68 respondit Simon Petrus: 'domine, ad quem imus? uerba uitae aeternae habes:

69 et non credimus, et cognouimus quia tu es Christus filius dei?'

Vulgate

6.51 'Ego sum panis uiuus, qui de caelo descendi. si quis manducauerit ex hoc pane, uiuet in aeternum: et panis quem ego dabo, caro mea est pro mundi uita.'

52 litigabant ergo Iudaei ad inuicem, dicentes: 'quomodo potest hic carnem suam nobis dare ad manducandum?'

53 dixit ergo eis Iesus: 'amen, amen dico uobis: nisi manducaueritis carnem filii hominis et biberitis eius sanguinem, non habetis uitam in uobis.

54 qui manducat meam carnem et bibit meum sanguinem, habet uitam aeternam: et ego resuscitabo eum in nouissimo die.

55 caro enim mea uere est cibus, et sanguis meus uere est potus.

56 qui manducat meam carnem et bibit meum sanguinem, in me manet, et ego in illo.

57 sicut misit me uiuens pater, et ego uiuo propter patrem: et qui manducat me, et ipse uiuet propter me.

58 hic est panis qui de caelo descendit. non sicut manducauerunt patres uestri manna, et mortui sunt: qui manducat hunc panem, uiuet in aeternum.'

59 haec dixit in synagoga, docens in Capharnaum.

60 multi ergo audientes ex discipulis eius dixerunt: 'durus est hic sermo: quis potest eum audire?'

61 sciens autem Iesus apud semetipsum quia murmurarent de hoc discipuli eius, dixit eis: 'hoc uos scandalizat?'

62 si ergo uideritis filium hominis ascendentem ubi erat prius?

63 spiritus est qui uiuificat: caro non prodest quicquam. uerba quae ego locutus sum, uobis spiritus et uita sunt.

64 sed sunt quidam ex uobis, qui non credunt.' sciebat enim ab initio Iesus qui essent credentes, et quis traditurus esset eum.

65 et dicebat: 'propterea dixi uobis, quia nemo potest uenire ad me, nisi fuerit ei datum a patre meo.'

66 ex hoc multi discipulorum eius abierunt retro, et iam non cum illo ambulabant.

67 dixit ergo Iesus ad duodecim: 'numquid et uos uultis abire?'

68 respondit ergo ei Simon Petrus: 'domine, ad quem ibimus? uerba uitae aeternae habes:

69 et nos credidimus, et cognouimus quia tu es Christus filius dei.'

Greek

6.51 ἐγώ εἰμι ὁ ἄρτος ὁ ζῶν ὁ ἐκ τοῦ οὐρανοῦ καταβάς· ἐάν τις φάγῃ ἐκ τούτου τοῦ ἄρτου ζήσει εἰς τὸν αἰῶνα, καὶ ὁ ἄρτος δὲ ὃν ἐγὼ δώσω ἡ σάρξ μού ἐστιν ὑπὲρ τῆς τοῦ κόσμου ζωῆς.

52 ἐμάχοντο οὖν πρὸς ἀλλήλους οἱ Ἰουδαῖοι λέγοντες· πῶς δύναται οὗτος ἡμῖν δοῦναι τὴν σάρκα [αὐτοῦ] φαγεῖν;

53 εἶπεν οὖν αὐτοῖς ὁ Ἰησοῦς· ἀμὴν ἀμὴν λέγω ὑμῖν, ἐὰν μὴ φάγητε τὴν σάρκα τοῦ υἱοῦ τοῦ ἀνθρώπου καὶ πίητε αὐτοῦ τὸ αἷμα, οὐκ ἔχετε ζωὴν ἐν ἑαυτοῖς.

54 ὁ τρώγων μου τὴν σάρκα καὶ πίνων μου τὸ αἷμα ἔχει ζωὴν αἰώνιον, κἀγὼ ἀναστήσω αὐτὸν τῇ ἐσχάτῃ ἡμέρᾳ.

55 ἡ γὰρ σάρξ μου ἀληθής ἐστιν βρῶσις, καὶ τὸ αἷμά μου ἀληθής ἐστιν πόσις.

56 ὁ τρώγων μου τὴν σάρκα καὶ πίνων μου τὸ αἷμα ἐν ἐμοὶ μένει κἀγὼ ἐν αὐτῷ.

57 καθὼς ἀπέστειλέν με ὁ ζῶν πατὴρ κἀγὼ ζῶ διὰ τὸν πατέρα, καὶ ὁ τρώγων με κἀκεῖνος ζήσει δι' ἐμέ.

58 οὗτός ἐστιν ὁ ἄρτος ὁ ἐξ οὐρανοῦ καταβάς, οὐ καθὼς ἔφαγον οἱ πατέρες καὶ ἀπέθανον· ὁ τρώγων τοῦτον τὸν ἄρτον ζήσει εἰς τὸν αἰῶνα.

59 ταῦτα εἶπεν ἐν συναγωγῇ διδάσκων ἐν Καφαρναούμ.

60 πολλοὶ οὖν ἀκούσαντες ἐκ τῶν μαθητῶν αὐτοῦ εἶπαν· σκληρός ἐστιν ὁ λόγος οὗτος· τίς δύναται αὐτοῦ ἀκούειν;

61 εἰδὼς δὲ ὁ Ἰησοῦς ἐν ἑαυτῷ ὅτι γογγύζουσιν περὶ τούτου οἱ μαθηταὶ αὐτοῦ εἶπεν αὐτοῖς· τοῦτο ὑμᾶς σκανδαλίζει;

62 ἐὰν οὖν θεωρῆτε τὸν υἱὸν τοῦ ἀνθρώπου ἀναβαίνοντα ὅπου ἦν τὸ πρότερον;

63 τὸ πνεῦμά ἐστιν τὸ ζῳοποιοῦν, ἡ σὰρξ οὐκ ὠφελεῖ οὐδέν· τὰ ῥήματα ἃ ἐγὼ λελάληκα ὑμῖν πνεῦμά ἐστιν καὶ ζωή ἐστιν.

64 ἀλλ' εἰσὶν ἐξ ὑμῶν τινες οἳ οὐ πιστεύουσιν. ᾔδει γὰρ ἐξ ἀρχῆς ὁ Ἰησοῦς τίνες εἰσὶν οἱ μὴ πιστεύοντες καὶ τίς ἐστιν ὁ παραδώσων αὐτόν.

65 καὶ ἔλεγεν· διὰ τοῦτο εἴρηκα ὑμῖν ὅτι οὐδεὶς δύναται ἐλθεῖν πρός με ἐὰν μὴ ᾖ δεδομένον αὐτῷ ἐκ τοῦ πατρός.

66 ἐκ τούτου πολλοὶ [ἐκ] τῶν μαθητῶν αὐτοῦ ἀπῆλθον εἰς τὰ ὀπίσω καὶ οὐκέτι μετ' αὐτοῦ περιεπάτουν.

67 εἶπεν οὖν ὁ Ἰησοῦς τοῖς δώδεκα· μὴ καὶ ὑμεῖς θέλετε ὑπάγειν;

68 ἀπεκρίθη αὐτῷ Σίμων Πέτρος· κύριε, πρὸς τίνα ἀπελευσόμεθα; ῥήματα ζωῆς αἰωνίου ἔχεις,

69 καὶ ἡμεῖς πεπιστεύκαμεν καὶ ἐγνώκαμεν ὅτι σὺ εἶ ὁ ἅγιος τοῦ θεοῦ.

Translation (of Codex Palatinus)

6.51 'I am the living bread who came down from heaven. If anyone shall eat some of my bread, he will live forever. The bread that I shall give is my flesh, for the life of the world.'

52 So the Jews disputed in turn, saying, 'How can this fellow give us his flesh to eat?'

53 Jesus said to them, 'Amen, amen I say to you: unless you shall eat the flesh of the Son of Man and shall drink his blood, you will not have life in you.

54 He who shall eat his flesh and shall drink his blood has eternal life, and I will revive him on the last day.

55 My flesh truly is food, and my blood truly is drink.

56 Who shall eat my flesh and shall drink my blood, he remains in me and I in him.

57 And just as the living Father sent me, I too live because of the Father; and he who shall eat, he himself too will live because of me.

58 This is the bread that came down from heaven, not in the way that your ancestors ate and died: he who shall eat this bread will live forever.'

59 This he said in the synagogue, teaching at Capharnaum.

60 Many then of his disciples said, 'Hard is this message, and who can listen to him?'

61 So Jesus knew within himself that his disciples were murmuring with disapproval. He said to them, 'This shocks you?

62 What if you shall see the Son of Man ascending to that place where he was before?

63 It is the spirit that gives life. The flesh is of no benefit. These words that I spoke, are for you the spirit and life.

64 But there are some of you who do not believe.' For Jesus knew from the beginning who it was who would betray him.

65 And he said, 'For this reason, because no one can come to me unless it shall have been given to him by my Father.'

66 Then many of his disciples went off back, and no longer walked with him.

67 So Jesus said to his twelve disciples, 'Do you too not want to go?'

68 Simon Peter replied, 'Lord, to whom do we go? You have the words of eternal life:

69 and we do not believe, and we knew that you are Christ Son of God?'

Commentary (lemmata from Codex Palatinus)

51 discendi: this spelling for *descendi* (cf. line 58) is found sometimes in literary manuscripts (see *TLL* V.1.641.59f.) and inscriptions (*ILCV* 3762 *discindentib.* : see the index to *ILCV*, vol. III, p. 512 s.v.). For examples in the *Itin. Ant. Plac.* see Milani (1974a: 342). It is partly due to a tendency for similar prefixes to be mixed up (cf. most notably *pro, prae, per*), and is partly under the influence of verbs of similar structure (*discedo, discindo*), which might affect scribes writing mechanically. Note Caper, *GL* 7.92.1–2 *descendit dicimus, non discendit. Discenderunt* is at 6.16 in *e*.

si quis manducauerit de meo pane: this is the familiar partitive prepositional expression standing as object of the verb. The instance here comes directly from the Greek (ἐκ τούτου τοῦ ἄρτου), but the construction also has Latin antecedents going back to the earliest literature (see Adams 2013: 273–5, and 31.12). For a collection of examples from translation literature see *TLL* VIII.274.67ff. Here the Vulgate has *ex*, whereas *e* has the current (and proto-Romance) preposition *de*. There is the same variation between the two versions in this chapter at 11 and 26. At 50 *e* has *ex eo*, the Vulgate *ex ipso*. In the Vulgate version of the Gospels the only partitive construction with *manduco* is that showing *ex* (Lc 22.16, Io 6.26, 6.50, 6.51). Note too Vulg. Io 6.39 *non perdam ex eo* (ἐξ αὐτοῦ; omitted by *e*). See further below, 40.5.

The Vulgate has *ex hoc pane*, which is equivalent to the Greek (above), but *e* has *meo* for *hoc*, which corresponds to a variant reading in the Greek (τοῦ ἐμοῦ ἄρτου).

For this use specifically of *ex* see above, 4.3, and index s.v. *ex*, 'expressing partitive object'.

quem ego dedero: in relative clauses (including longer ones) in Bible translations *ego* often follows the relative pronoun (as in the Greek): cf. 38.63 below, and Vulg. Io 4.14. This is a mannerism also found in Patrick (see below, 40.4).

52 discertabantur itaque Iudaei: the compound *discertor* (for ἐμάχοντο; the Vulgate has *litigabant*) should be noted. *Certo* is a commonplace classical verb, and it can mean 'dispute' (*OLD* s.v. 4), the meaning here of the compound. In late Latin it has a deponent by-form *certor*, which is common in the *Vetus Latina* (*TLL* III.899.19ff.). *Discertor*, however, is attested in this place only (*TLL* V.1.1309.76ff.). It is one of those intensives in *dis-* that go back to much earlier Latin and have a distinctively colloquial profile (see above, 6.43–4, 9.11, 13.10).

nobis carnem suam dare manducare: the Greek has ἡμῖν δοῦναι τὴν σάρκα [αὐτοῦ] φαγεῖν, the Vulgate (with MSS variations to the word order) *carnem suam nobis dare ad manducandum*. Both constructions complementing *dare* are noteworthy.

First, the infinitive. There is an old construction in Latin, *do bibere* (see e.g. Kühner and Stegmann 1955: 1.681). *Do edere/manducare* might be seen on the one hand as an extension of this, though it does not turn up until late Latin (see *TLL* V.1.1688.72, Norberg 1943: 216; few examples cited). On the other hand an influence was biblical Greek (see the example above, and Bauer, Arndt and Gingrich 1957: 313d). *Do manducare* is itself found in the Vulgate (about nine times in the Gospels: see e.g. Io 6.31; compare *da mihi bibere* at Io 4.7, 4.10), and there is no significance to the fact that in our passage the Vulgate and *e* have different constructions.

Second, the *ad*-construction. According to Hofmann and Szantyr (1965: 378), *do* (along with similar verbs) with *ad* + gerundive/gerund was already current in the early period, but they cite no examples, and neither Kühner and Stegmann nor the *TLL* s.v. *do* have a separate entry for this complement. See however Enn. *Euh.* X.131 Vahlen *exemplum ceteris ad imitandum dedit* (but this fragment is not necessarily in the words of Ennius himself: see the Introduction to text 1), Cic. *Cluent.* 84 *pecuniam Staieno dedit Oppianicus non ad corrumpendum iudicium sed ad ...* More common, it seems, in the classical period is *do* (et sim.) + plain gerundive (Kühner and Stegmann 1955: I.731, *TLL* V.1.1692.68ff.: e.g. Ovid *Fast.* 4.547–8 *papauera . . . | dat tibi . . . bibenda*, Scrib. Larg. 9 *uuam passam . . . dabimus commanducandam*). *Do ad manducandum* appears in later Latin (e.g. Veg. *Mul.* 2.148.1 *iecur eius coctum ad manducandum dabis*; see too below, 50.72), and is historically significant, because, conflated with *do manducare*, it led to the proto-Romance construction *do ad manducare* (see 50.72). *Dare ad manducandum* in our passage is the only instance of the phrase in the Gospels of the Vulgate, but note Vulg. 2 Cor 9.10 *qui autem administrat semen seminanti, et panem ad manducandum* (Greek εἰς βρῶσιν).

53 dixit illis Iesus: here the Vulgate has *eis* (*dixit ergo eis Iesus*). *e* uses both *is* and *ille* to render the single Greek word αὐτός. In chapter 6 of John I have counted in *e* twenty-four instances of *is* and twenty-three of *ille*. To some extent choice is determined by the case of the pronoun. Only *is* is used in the genitive singular (*eius* ten times). There is evidence from other texts for the persistence of this form until very late (see index, s.v. *is*, 'persistence of genitive *eius*', and also Pinkster 2005: 60–1 on the strong position of *eius* already in classical Latin). On the other hand only *ille* is used in the dative singular and plural (thirteen times). The accusative *eum* is used freely (nine times; *illum* seven).

The practice of the Vulgate is very different. In chapter 6 I have counted forty-four instances of *is* (including many datives, singular and plural), but just six instances of *ille*. Three of these are contrastive (with *is*: 20, 29, 39). One isolated oddity is an alternation at 66: *ex hoc multi discipulorum eius abierunt retro, et iam non cum illo ambulabant* (translating αὐτός in both cases; see above, 27.11 and 39.8 on such alternations; *e* here has *is* in both clauses). *Is*, as we have remarked elsewhere, was not to survive in the Romance languages, and it had long been under threat from *ille* (see index, s.v. *ille*, 'in relation to *is*'). Jerome was holding firmly to the old literary word.

After *dixit* the Vulgate has *ergo*, rendering οὖν, whereas the Codex Palatinus has nothing corresponding. At 68, however, where the Vulgate has *respondit ergo ei Simon Petrus* but *e* has *respondit Simon Petrus*, the extant Greek has no particle (but here *ei* of the Vulgate, omitted in *e*, does render αὐτῷ). On the other hand at 60 and 67 both have *ergo* corresponding to οὖν.

In the use of particles and connectives there is variability among translators. Note 51, where *e* has *panis autem quem*, with *autem* translating δέ, but the Vulgate *et panis quem*; 52, where οὖν is rendered by *itaque* in *e* but *ergo* in the Vulgate; 57, where *e* has *et sicut me misit* but the Vulgate *sicut misit me*, where both the absence of *et* and the placement of the object pronoun *me* (see below, 38.57) after the verb match the Greek; 61, where δέ is rendered by *ergo* in *e* but *autem* in the Vulgate (see Burton 2000: 91, noting that in the OLG this empty Greek particle is translated variously by *et, autem* or *uero*: add *ergo*); 62, where ἐὰν οὖν is translated by *si ergo* in the Vulgate but *quid si* in *e*; 66, where ἐκ τούτου becomes *exinde* in *e* but is translated literally in the Vulgate (*ex hoc*).

Burton's conclusion (2000: 91) on similar phenomena is worth quoting: 'This is not high literary art, but it points to two important facts: first, that the OLG are not *wholly* literal translations, and secondly, that their translators are apparently at home in Latin.'

ederitis: twice earlier (in this passage) *e* has *manduco* (51, 52), but now there is a switch to *edo*, the early literary verb. The variation persists throughout the passage, in which *manduco* is used three times and *edo* five. In the Vulgate version there is no such variation: *manduco* occurs throughout, eight times. The variation of *e* is closer to the Greek, which alternates between the old literary word ἐσθίω (φαγεῖν) and the later koine word τρώγω, which originally meant 'chew' (see Shipp 1967: 129, and above, 2.9). The Greek has forms of φαγεῖν at 51, 52, 53 and 58, but ὁ τρώγων at 54, 56, 57 and 58. The Palatine translator has in each case rendered this substantival use of τρώγω by a *qui*-clause containing a form of *edo* (*edet* at 54 and 56, *ediderit* at 57 and 58 (*edediderit*)). There is only one place in the passage where *edo* is used to render ἐσθίω (φαγεῖν), at 53, where ἐὰν μὴ φάγητε is translated by *nisi ederitis*. The choice of the old Latin word in the other places to translate the koine word is something of a curiosity. All three instances of *manduco* (see above) render ἐσθίω (φαγεῖν).

On renderings of ἐσθίω in the Old Latin versions see Burton (2000: 41–3). Burton takes a passage of Matthew and tabulates the readings in fifteen manuscripts (whether *manduco, edo, comedo, cibum capio/accipio* or *ceno*). He concludes (41–2): 'It is clear that the usual European translation is *manduco*, while the African traditions use *manduco* and *edo* roughly half and half.' On the African tradition as sometimes preferring a rendering that was of higher register, and was not to survive in Romance, see Burton (2000) at e.g. 19 and 163.

sanguem: this form of the accusative occurs in our extract also at 54 and 56, where the Vulgate has the classical *sanguinem*. Some examples of *sanguem* (almost certainly the proto-Romance form) in manuscripts are collected by Bulhart (1967: xvi), but we have seen that British curse tablets are now turning up examples of the form (see above, 33.10).

non habebitis: the Vulgate and the Greek both have a present tense here.

54 nouissima die: the Vulgate has the masculine of *dies* (*in nouissimo die*). There had long been gender variation in this word, in the early period with semantic significance (see Adams 2013: 393). In low-register texts of the late period it is usually the feminine that is favoured (see E. Löfstedt 1911: 192–5; also above, 22.27). I have not noted any patterns in Bible translations, despite the distinction above between the Vulgate and *e*. The distribution of masculine versus feminine in the Vulgate, for example, is variable. In Genesis the masculine predominates by about 41:10 (the figures are approximate because there are textual variations in particular passages) and in the Gospel of Matthew by 13:7, yet in Luke the feminine is preferred by 23:13. It is possible that one gender or the other was favoured in certain types of phrases (*die qua*, for example, seems particularly frequent), but this is a possibility that remains to be investigated.

The Vulgate has the preposition *in*, of which there is no equivalent in the Greek (τῇ ἐσχάτῃ ἡμέρᾳ). *In die* for *die* goes back to early Latin (see above, 5.6), and turns up from time to time, e.g. in Pelagonius (see Adams 1995a: 166). There is exactly the same variation between the two versions at Io 6.39.

55 caro mea uere est esca: the Vulgate here has *cibus* not *esca* (Gk βρῶσις). *Esca* is however not absent from the Vulgate: in the Vulgate Gospels *cibus* and *esca* both occur eight times.

On the distribution of *esca* across *Vet. Lat.* manuscripts of John see Burton (2000: 62, 67, 70, 73). It is found particularly in a group which, though from the European tradition, are 'closely based on the African tradition, represented in John by *e* alone'.

Esca is quite widespread from early Latin onwards, but it does seem to have been recherché or stylised by the classical period, except in the specialised meaning 'bait' (see *OLD* s.v. 2, Powell 1988: 191, and the transitional example Cic. *Nat.* 2.125 *ad quas (ranas) quasi ad escam pisces cum accesserint confici a ranis atque consumi*; cf. *inesco* 'entice animals with bait'), a sense which lives on in Romance languages (see *FEW* III.244–5); note also Varro *Rust.* 3.17.3, where the word denotes food for fish, but not specifically bait (see further below). In Cicero *esca* is confined to the philosophica (with eight instances of *esca* and forty-seven of *cibus*), where it is three times combined with *potio* (*Div.* 1.115, *Fin.* 2.90, *Nat.* 2.59; see also *Nat.* 2.125, quoted above, 2.134, 2.160, *Sen.* 44, frg. V.81); cf. *potum* in the present passage. It is found there particularly in theoretical contexts, of food as an abstract entity. *Cibus* is used by Cicero nine times in the speeches (*esca* not at all). Livy has *cibus* forty-three times but *esca* only twice, in special contexts. It is in one of the prophecies of Marcius (25.12.6), which have old-fashioned features, of food for fish, birds and animals (see above). The other example is at 41.20.3, in a passage from Polybius where Polybius talks specifically of dates and Livy generalises (see Briscoe 2012: 104 ad loc.). Livy's motive for choosing *esca* there is not clear, but the passage, about Antiochus IV, is odd. In Celsus *esca* occurs just twice (at 1.2.8 possibly for variation near several instances of *cibus*; it is also there linked to *potio*), *cibus* dozens of times.

In late Latin *esca* does not however disappear. Biblical influence is probably to be seen in (e.g.) the *Peregrinatio Aetheriae*, which has *esca* three times but *cibus* not at all. Personal whim comes into lexical choice. In the notoriously low-register *Mulomedicina Chironis esca* is ubiquitous, whereas in the more correct Pelagonius, writing on the same subject, only *cibus* is used.

potum: neuter by-form of *potus*: see TLL X.2.366.38ff., citing this example and a few others from late Latin.

56 et ego in ipsum: the Greek has ἐν αὐτῷ, the Vulgate *in illo*. The accusative form typifies the indifference to case distinctions with *in* in some late Latin (see index s.v. *in*, '+ ablative for accusative and vice versa'). *Ipse* is used here as an anaphoric demonstrative pronoun = *is* (it is not adjectival), a usage barely touched on by Abel (1971: 140–54) in his discussion of *ipse*; he concentrates on adjectival uses. For *ipse* = *is* in the *Peregrinatio Aetheriae* see van Oorde (1929: 108–9), s.v. I.

57 et sicut me misit pater uibus: the Vulgate here has a different word order, with the object pronoun after the verb: *sicut misit me uiuens pater*. The word order of the Vulgate is that of the Greek (ἀπέστειλέν με ὁ ζῶν πατήρ). There are other such variations between versions. At 6.39 *e* has *qui me misit*, whereas the Vulgate has *qui misit me* (at the end of a sentence). The Greek has a participial construction, with the pronoun after the participle: τοῦ πέμψαντός με. The order in *e* is more Latinate in this last example than that of the Vulgate. In relative clauses verb-final position continues over many centuries to be the norm, and it is highly unexpected to have a pronoun object at the end of such a clause; far more often it comes immediately after the relative (cf. above, 27.2). The same variation is found at 44: in *e, qui me misit*, in the Vulgate *qui misit me* (much the same participial construction in the Greek). At 36 the Vulgate has *quia et uidistis me*, whereas *e* omits the object (*quia uidistis*). At 57, where the Vulgate has *qui manducat me*, *e* likewise gives the verb no object (*qui ediderit*). The Greek has a participial verb with the object pronoun after it. And at 64 there is again a difference of order: *qui eum traditurus erat* in *e*, but *quis traditurus esset eum* in the Vulgate. In the Greek the object pronoun comes after another participle. There does seem to have been a systematic

Latinisation of pronoun position in relative clauses in *e*, though ideally a larger sample should be investigated.

On the whole however the various versions follow the word order of the Greek closely. I offer some statistics from chapter 6 of the Vulgate version for object position (of nouns and pronouns) with finite verbs (OV versus VO). In this chapter VO predominates by 50:11. What is particularly significant is that there is no tendency at all for a lingering of the order OV in subordinate clauses. In subordinate clauses VO predominates by 33:3, and in main clauses by 17:8. The predominance of VO in subordinate clauses is a non-Latinate feature determined by the Greek. *e* has the same general preference, despite its habit of moving pronouns in relative clauses to the pre-verbal position. Nouns are not moved in this way in *e*.

58 non quomodo manducauerunt patres uestri, et mortui sunt: the Vulgate here has *non sicut*. *Quomodo* becomes widespread in late Latin and has an extensive Romance survival, whereas *sicut* does not live on. Grevander (1926: 91) lists a number of places where the more literary writer Vegetius replaces *quomodo* in his source the *Mulomedicina Chironis* with *sicut* (and other expressions): e.g. Veg. *Mul.* 2.48.11 *sicut superius declaratum est* = *Mul. Chir.* 111 *quomodo in flemina superius demonstraui.* On *quomodo* in late Latin see Grevander (1926: 92), Svennung (1935: 509–10).

The *Holy Bible: New Revised Standard Version* (London, 2007) renders the Greek of this passage (οὐ καθὼς ἔφαγον οἱ πατέρες καὶ ἀπέθανον) as '(This is the bread that came down from heaven), not like that which your ancestors ate, and they died. (But the one who eats this bread will live for ever).' 'Not like that which' is an interpretation of the original. Literally the Latin and Greek mean: 'not in the way in which your ancestors ate, and died: (he who shall eat this bread will live forever).' This becomes understandable in English if the clauses are transposed: 'he who shall eat this bread will live forever – not in the way in which your ancestors ate, and died'.

qui edediderit panem istum: *istum* translates τοῦτον, whereas the Vulgate has the classical *hunc. Iste* was to replace *hic* in the Romance languages. *Iste* is used by Latin Bible translators to render no other Greek demonstrative (see Abel 1971: 71; see however below, 38.63), and in such renderings *iste* is equivalent to *hic* (see Abel 1971: 72–4 on factors influencing the choice of *iste*). *e* (like *k*, another African version) shows a particular taste for *iste* = *hic*: see Abel (1971: 45–6). Note also 60 (*e*) *durus est sermo iste*, where the Vulgate has *durus est hic sermo* (= οὗτος). See also above, 27.9.

Edediderit is a dittography, not committed elsewhere in the extract.

59 docens Capharnaum: the Greek has a preposition, ἐν Καφαρναούμ, which is also in the Vulgate (*in Capharnaum*). The Vulgate place name appears to have the wrong case, accusative for ablative, but it is likely that, being exotic, it is merely uninflected. Place names, particularly but not exclusively names that were exotic, were sometimes fossilised and treated as indeclinable in both Greek and Latin. They might be given a preposition, as in the Vulgate here, or even used without any case marker. On exotic names used in these ways see Adams (2013: 207, 343–4), and for Latin names Adams (2013: 336, 341–2). Note too the examples of the 'accusatiuus fixus' listed by Bulhart (1967: xvi). See also, for related treatments of place names, below, 39.15, 41.4.

60 ex discentibus: in *e* there is alternation in this passage between the substantival present participle *discentes* (so at 66) and *discipuli* (61, 67). The Vulgate has *discipuli* in three of these places: at 67 (*dixit ergo Iesus ad duodecim*) it has no noun, in line with the Greek (τοῖς δώδεκα). Note that in this last passage *ad* with the verb of saying corresponds to the dative of the Greek. The motivation of the preposition in this context is obvious. Greek can use the dative of the definite article with the non-inflecting numeral, but Latin must resort to a different case marker. The rendering at least shows a sense that *ad* could play a dative role. *e* by contrast adds the noun *discipulos*, but keeps *ad* instead of using the dative inflection. The Greek word in each case is μαθητής, which is commonplace in the NT of the disciples of Jesus (Bauer, Arndt and Gingrich 1957: 486–7). The substantival present participle οἱ μανθάνοντες is attested in classical Greek (Xen. *Mem.* 1.2.17: see LSJ s.v. μανθάνω I, 'learners, pupils'), but there is no sign of it in the NT, and it is to be assumed that different translators used different renderings of the same Greek noun. E. Löfstedt (1959: 122) (cf. Väänänen 1966: 124) notes that *discentes* is used substantivally in Pompeian graffiti (*CIL* IV.275 *Saturninus cum discentes*, 698) (the accusative shows the level of the Latin), and points out that it is avoided for *discipuli* in the Vulgate but is used in the *Vet. Lat.* Theological writers influenced by the *Vet. Lat.* sometimes use it (see Tert. *Marc.* 4.22.7 *tres de discentibus*). For the survival of *discens* in some Romance dialects see *REW* 2654. See further on this word Adams (1973: 126–7).

quis potest audire: infinitives regularly come after the governing verb, in both *e* and the Vulgate, following the practice of the Greek. See in this chapter 10, 21, 31, 44, 52, 65, 67.

61 cognouit … quoniam murabant: *murabant* is a haplography for *murmurabant*. The Vulgate here has a subjunctive (*murmurarent*) in the *quia*-clause:

on such variations of mood, the motivations for which are difficult to pin down, see Adams (1976a: 94–6, with bibliography). In the Vulgate *quod, quia* and *quoniam* are used indifferently to introduce such clauses, translating ὅτι (Plater and White 1926: 119). In *e quoniam* is sometimes found as here where the Vulgate has *quia* (e.g. Io 1.32, 2.17, 2.18, 2.22, 5.24), but more often than not *e* shares *quia* with the Vulgate (e.g. Io 3.2, 3.33, 4.19, 4.20, 4.21, 4.25, 4.27, 4.42, 4.44, 4.47, 4.51, 4.52, 5.28, 5.32, 5.42, 5.45), and there seems to be no significance to the variations. Later in the extract (69) the same verb is used with *quia* in both *e* and the Vulgate. *Quoniam* itself is also found in such contexts in the Vulgate version of the Gospels (e.g. Mt 2.16, 3.9, 9.6, 24.44, Mc 12.12, 12.14, Lc 21.31, Io 11.40).

62 quid si: interpreting ἐὰν οὖν of the Greek (Vulg. *si ergo*, a more literal rendering).

   ascendentem in illo ubi: the Vulgate has simply *ascendentem ubi*. There are two ways of taking *in illo*. First, *illo* is frequently used as an adverb (*TLL* VII.1.385), with directional or static meaning, 'to where, where', and this phrase may be a compound form (cf. compound adverbs such as *inante, incontra*: see particularly *TLL* VII.1.799.39ff.). Second, there may be ellipse of *loco* (with *in* + abl. directional rather than static). Prepositional expressions with *locus*, some of them redundant, are not uncommon (see below, 44.37.5 on *ad locum ad speluncam*).

63 caro nihil prode est: *prode* is a late adverb extracted by popular etymology from *prodest*, the genuineness of which usage is clearer from instances such as *Per. Aeth.* 8.3 *prode illis est*. See E. Löfstedt (1911: 184–6), id. (1959: 175), the latter discussion with further bibliography. The word occurs in the *Vet. Lat.* and a variety of late texts, and survives in Romance (see E. Löfstedt 1911: 175 and particularly *TLL* X.2.1594.7ff.). Here the Vulgate has *non prodest quicquam* (Gk οὐκ ὠφελεῖ οὐδέν).

   uerba ista quae ego locutus sum: the Vulgate has *uerba quae ego locutus sum. Ista* here translates the definite article of the Greek (τὰ ῥήματα). There is a good discussion of *iste* corresponding to the Greek article by Abel (1971: 80–1). First, the usage is not found in the Vulgate. Second, in the Old Latin translations it is rare. Third, it is not concentrated in any particular *Vet. Lat.* manuscript: the few examples are scattered about. An example such as the present one is best seen, not as evidence that *iste* was being weakened into a definite article, but merely as reflecting the translator's sense that a deictic demonstrative was appropriate to the context.

   spiritus et uita est: the nouns here are predicates of the verb 'to be'. The subject of *est* is the neuter plural *ista uerba*. In the Greek the neuter plural τὰ ῥήματα is subject, and the verb is singular as here in *e*: πνεῦμά ἐστιν καὶ ζωή ἐστιν. In the NT singular verbs with neuter plural subjects are recessive, but still occur (Blass, Debrunner and Rehkopf 1976: 110–11). The Vulgate has eliminated the error (by Latin standards) of concord: *spiritus et uita sunt*.

65 propterea quia nemo potest uenire: between *propterea* and *quia* there has been an omission in *e* (Vulgate *dixi uobis*, corresponding to the Greek διὰ τοῦτο εἴρηκα ὑμῖν).

66 abierunt retrorsum: here *retrorsum* (εἰς τὰ ὀπίσω) is not pleonastic with the prefixed verb (on such pleonasm see index, 'pleonasm, of adverb and verbal prefix'), but adds the information that they went away, back to where they came from. The Vulgate has *retro*. Both are classical words, with Romance outcomes.

68 domine, ad quem imus?: the Vulgate has the future here (*ibimus*), which corresponds to the future of the Greek (ἀπελευσόμεθα). On present for future see index, 'present tense, for future'.

Conclusions

The translators of the Gospels did not operate on mechanical principles such that a Greek word was always rendered by a single Latin term. In *e*, *ille* and *is* are both used to render αὐτός, and μαθητής is translated indifferently by *discens* and *discipulus*. Various semantically empty Greek particles receive variable renderings. On the other hand a particular translator (or tradition) might try to give two Greek synonyms different Latin equivalents. The translator of *e* tended to make a distinction between ἐσθίω/φαγεῖν (*manduco*) and τρώγω (*edo*), whereas the Vulgate has *manduco* for both.

There is one very distinctive feature of *e*. The translator has Latinised the word order of relative clauses containing an object pronoun by placing the pronoun before the verb, whereas in the extant Greek and in the Vulgate the pronoun is oddly placed, by Latin standards, at the end of the clause. It is possible that he was using a divergent Greek text, but it is at least as likely that he made a subtle change.

On the other hand the translator of *e* retained a Grecism in using *uerba* with a singular verb, a discord avoided by the Vulgate.

The Latin of *e* is in many respects more 'popular' than that of the Vulgate. We noted the (unique) intensive *discertor*, a category of compound that has come up before, the accusative (proto-Romance) form *sanguem*, the encroachment of *ille* on *is* as the third person pronoun (an encroachment resisted in the

Vulgate), the use of *discens* and *prode*, the fossilised place name *Capharnaum* without case marker, the use of *de* rather than *ex* in partitive expressions, the neuter gender of *potum*, the use of *iste* for *hic* (a particular feature of *e*), the occasional use of present for future, and the indifference to the old case distinctions with the preposition *in*.

But it would be inappropriate simply to characterise *e* as substandard or the like. *Edo* for *manduco* was an old literary word, which by this period had been replaced not only by *manduco* itself but also by its compound *comedo* (see above, 5.19). Similarly *esca* for *cibus* was literary or stylised. There is a quirky mixture in the version of the popular and the old-fashioned, reflecting the fact that translating in writing is an artificial act for which the translator does a certain amount of groping about for the vox propria, which may take him beyond everyday usage.

Nor is the Vulgate itself consistently classicising. In this extract *dies* is on the one hand given its more literary gender, but is used with the preposition *in*, which was not the norm in classical Latin. There is also an alternation between *is* and *ille* with the same referent in a single sentence, rendering αὐτός in both cases, where it is *e* that is classical. The Vulgate uses *manduco* freely as well.

39
PATRICK, *CONFESSIO* 42–3 (FIFTH CENTURY)

Introduction

Patrick, the 'apostle of Ireland', was born somewhere in Britain but as a youth was captured by Irish raiders and taken as a slave to Ireland. After six years he escaped and returned to his family in Britain. Exact details of his dates and life are unknown and controversial, but it is certain enough that much of his career fell in the fifth century (see e.g. Hanson 1968: 171–88, Dumville *et al.* 1993: 13–18). It is of no consequence to the student of the Latin language whether his writings belong to the early or later part of that century, since it is impossible to distinguish periods of Latin with that precision. He went back to Ireland later as a cleric and missionary. The two works bearing his name that are regarded as genuine are the *Confessio* and the *Epistola ad milites Corotici*. The extracts in this section and the next are from the *Confessio*.

The Latin of Patrick has intrigued scholars because it was written in late antiquity well away from those areas of the Continent where the language always remained current and gave rise to the Romance languages. Specimens of Patrick's Latin have been included in this book, partly because of its seemingly marginal character, and partly because of some of the claims that have been made about its sources. Hanson (1968: 158), for example, states that '[c]learly Patrick's Latin is Vulgar Latin', and then becomes more specific (163): 'No doubt the Latin he learnt before he was kidnapped was the archaic Vulgar Latin of the British rural aristocracy.' Implicit here is the idea that there was a better class of Latin speakers in Britain, distinguishable from the hoi polloi of the Continent and speaking an old-fashioned variety of the language (for a demolition of this romantic notion, which goes back to Jackson 1953, see Gratwick 1982; also Greene 1968: 77, Thompson 1985: 41 n. 5, Adams 2007: 583–93, and above, 37 Conclusions).

Even Bieler (on whose writings see below) cannot refrain from making similar claims. He states (1952: 66), on the basis of no evidence, that 'British Latinity was comparatively less advanced than the language of the earlier provinces', and, worse (1952: 74), attributes certain 'remarkable parallels' between Patrick and Varro to the common influence on them of the '"rustic" language of the countryside' (cf. his reference at 1993: II.131 to the 'conservative language of the countryside'). Two such parallels are cited (1952: 74 n. 47). One (*Conf.* 10 *quis me credit*) has a banal late use of an accusative with a verb normally taking the dative (see below, 39.21). The supposed parallel in Varro, if the reading is right (*Rust.* 3.16.2 *a quo hereditate me cessa*), would show a different, old Latin, phenomenon, of a type not unexpected in Varro, who retains many features of the earlier period. In Varro *me* would be an early spelling for the contracted dative *mi* (spelt with the diphthong *ei* at Novius 50 Frassinetti). The *e* would represent early Latin long close *e*, an intermediate form between the diphthong *ei* and CL *ī* (for further discussion see 39.21; also index, 'spellings, *e* (long close) for *ei/ī*'). The long close *e* and its representation by *e* in writing did not continue much beyond the Augustan period, and it is far-fetched to find it in the fifth century, particularly since Patrick elsewhere has *credo* unambiguously with the accusative (see 39.21). Bieler's other parallel, *Conf.* 10 *denudare imperitiam meam*, is not the sort of expression uttered in the countryside, and indeed the alleged Varronian parallel, which is not exact, is found in Varro's *De lingua Latina* (9.112 *suam inscientiam denudat*), not in the *Res rusticae*. Varro, the most learned Roman of his day, was no country bumpkin. We merely have here similar metaphorical uses of *denudo*, a verb often metaphorical not only in classical Latin but also in the Latin Bible and theological works, from which Patrick probably picked it up.

In the last few decades, as we have glimpsed in texts 32–7, a good deal of new Latin has come to light in Britain (for a brief summary of sources, now out of date, see Adams 2007: 579–80), and in its uneducated forms (e.g. in curse tablets) it bears little resemblance to the Latin of Patrick, nor is it more 'archaic' or 'less advanced' than Latin from Continental sources (see 37 Conclusions). Whether Patrick's Latin has any identifiable traces of real spoken language, whether it contains any usages that there might be reason to think were current in Britain, or whether on the contrary it is entirely bookish, are questions that will have to be addressed here. In the Commentary below and that on text 40, and in the Conclusions to 40, attention will be devoted to its sources.

The best work on Patrick's language is that of Bieler, whose philological commentary on the two texts (1993; a reprint, cited here, of the first version of 1950–1) bears comparison with that of E. Löfstedt (1911) on the *Peregrinatio Aetheriae*. Hanson's comment (1968: 162), that the 'work of Bieler upon Patrick's Latin is confined very largely to comments upon individual words', is unfair, as Bieler provided an extensive 'index grammaticus' (1993: I.123–50) listing the many features that emerge from the commentary, and also wrote a general article on Patrick's language (1952) using his own commentary. Even less satisfactory is Hanson's next assertion, that Bieler did 'not on the whole make judgements about the quality or provenance of Patrick's Latin'. The commentary is replete with information about the sources of the Latin. I will refer whenever appropriate to Bieler below, but will also in places go beyond or question some of his detail. Important too is Bieler (1947), on Patrick's text of the Bible. Patrick's text of much of the OT and in the NT of Revelation was a version of the *Vetus Latina*, and that of Acts was the Vulgate. That of the rest of the NT and in the OT of the Psalter was pre-Vulgate, but with some corrections from the Vulgate (see further Hanson 1968: 180–1, Dumville *et al.* 1993: 15–16). Also worth noting is Bieler (1948), on a late Latin term (*exagellia*) used by Patrick, which was not necessarily of biblical origin (see also Bieler 1993: II.129).

Some mention will be made of the four lectures by Mohrmann (1961a) on the Latin of Patrick.

The term 'vulgar Latin' was not only applied to Patrick's Latin by Hanson. It occurs sometimes in Bieler's commentary (1993: II.117 'As often in late vulgar Latin'; II.136–7 'the construction is too frequent in vulgar Latin to be ignored'; II.172 '[r]edundant demonstratives in relative clauses are a feature of late Vulgar Latin' (on which idea see below, 39.7); similarly at II.179 he refers to 'vulgar texts' and at II.186 to a 'vulgar vocalism'; see too Bieler 1952: 68 on the 'vulgarisms' in Patrick's Latin, and 1952: 81 on a usage 'typical of Vulgar Latin'), but far more often he identifies usages as belonging to 'late Latin'. Mohrmann on the other hand prefers such phrases as 'normal colloquial Latin', 'colloquial elements of the living language' (1961a: 16), the 'stream of living Latin' (1961a: 21), asserting that such 'can go back only to a personal contact with living – and that means continental – Latin' (1961a: 21). She explicitly distinguishes this living or colloquial entity from Vulgar Latin (1961a: 16): 'there are, in Patrick's Latin, many syntactical elements which belong to very normal colloquial Latin of the beginning of the fifth century. These elements do not belong to vulgar Latin.' We will return to such claims in the Conclusions to text 40, addressing the question whether there is any real evidence for 'living Latin' in Patrick.

Text

42 Et etiam una benedicta Scotta (1) genetiua (2) nobilis pulcherrima adulta (3) erat, quam ego baptizaui; et post paucos dies una causa uenit ad nos (4), insinuauit nobis responsum accepisse a nuntio dei et monuit eam (5) ut esset uirgo Christi et ipsa deo proximaret (6): deo gratias, sexta ab hac die optime et auidissime arripuit illud quod etiam omnes uirgines dei ita hoc faciunt (7) – non sponte patrum earum (8), sed et persecutiones patiuntur et improperia (9) falsa a parentibus suis et nihilominus plus augetur numerus (et de genere nostro qui ibi nati sunt nescimus numerum eorum (10)) praeter uiduas et continentes.

Sed ex illis maxime laborant quae seruitio detinentur (11): usque ad terrores et minas assidue perferunt (12): sed dominus gratiam dedit multis ex ancillis suis, nam etsi uetantur tamen fortiter imitantur (13).

43 Vnde autem etsi uoluero amittere illas (14) et ut pergens in Brittanniis (15) – et libentissime 'paratus eram' quasi ad patriam et parentes (16); non id solum sed etiam usque ad Gallias uisitare fratres et ut uiderem faciem (17) sanctorum domini mei: scit deus quod ego ualde optabam, sed 'alligatus spiritu', qui mihi 'protestatur' si hoc fecero, ut futurum reum me esse designat (18) et timeo perdere laborem (19) quem inchoaui, et non ego sed Christus dominus (20), qui me imperauit ut (21) uenirem esse cum illis (22) residuum aetatis meae, 'si dominus uoluerit' et custodierit me ab omni uia mala, ut non 'peccem coram illo' (23).

Translation

42 Also there was a blessed Irishwoman, a native, noble, beautiful, and grown up, whom I baptised, and after a few days she came to us for a reason, and made it known to us that she had received a response from an angel of God, and he advised her to be a virgin of Christ and to draw near to God herself. Thanks be to God, on the sixth day from this she seized truly and eagerly on that course which all virgins of God also adopt, not with the approval of their fathers, but rather they suffer persecutions and false reproaches from their parents, and nonetheless their number goes on increasing (but of our (Christian) family, those who are reborn there, of them we do not know the number), quite apart from widows and those practising continence.

But of these, those women who are kept in slavery suffer most of all. They constantly endure, to the extreme of terror and threats. But the Lord has given his grace to many of his maidservants, for although they are forbidden they bravely emulate him.

43 Therefore even if I want to let go of them and, proceeding to Britain – and 'I was ready' and willing (to go) to my native land and parents – and not only that but also to (go) all the way to Gaul, to visit the brethren, and to see the face of the saints of my Lord. God knows that I wanted it very much, but I am 'bound by the Spirit', who 'testifies' against me if I do that, inasmuch as he indicates that I will be guilty (if I do), and

I am afraid of wasting the labour which I began – not I myself, but Christ the Lord, who ordered me to come to be with them for the rest of my life, 'if the Lord shall will' and shall keep me from every wicked way, so that I do not 'sin before him'.

Commentary

1 una benedicta Scotta: here is a context in which *una* cannot be given any numerical force but is close to an indefinite article (= *quaedam*). Alleged early examples of this usage tend to be open to alternative explanations, despite Wackernagel (1926–9: II.151) = Langslow (2009: 587), quoted here from Langslow: 'Towards the end of antiquity, the use of *unus* as the indefinite article is common and regular, although it is difficult to determine how far back in time it goes in the colloquial language' (one must query here 'regular'; see particularly Fruyt 2011b: 731–2 on the absence of full grammaticalisation of *unus* as an article in late texts). It is further observed there that there are equivalent usages in the Greek NT, and it might be added that this indefinite use of *unus* is attested in late Christian texts, including Bible translations (see Rönsch 1875: 425, id. 1887–9: II.56, Bonnet 1890: 259, Salonius 1920: 237–8). This case introduces at once an important aspect of Patrick's Latin. The articloid use of *unus* might be described as anticipatory of 'proto-Romance' and as belonging to 'living Latin' (Mohrmann's term: see above), but that does not establish that Patrick knew it from varieties of speech: he might have seen it in written texts. Identifying Latin in Patrick that was living to him and not merely bookish will turn out to be an almost impossible task, though some suggestions will be offered below.

2 genetiua: the adjective *genetiuus* goes back to the classical period (Ovid), where it can mean 'of or connected with birth' (*OLD* s.v. 1a; cf. *TLL* VI.2.1805.20, glossing with 'nativus, naturalis, originarius'). Here however it means 'a native of a place', and is equivalent to CL *indigena*. In this sense it is quoted by the *TLL* VI.2.1805.30ff. from the *Vetus Latina* (Lv 16.29 Lugd., where the Vulgate has *indigena*, and from the same book at 17.15, where the Vulgate also has *indigena*); the only other possible examples (inscriptional) cited there have only the abbreviation *gen*, which is open to other interpretations. The passage of Patrick is not quoted at this point by the *TLL*. Here we see a precise source of Patrick's Latin, the *Vet. Lat.*, which will be illustrated further below and comes up often in Bieler's commentary. *Genetiuus* does not, however, seem to have been common in Old Latin versions: Patrick was capable of picking up and noting rare usages in a biblical source. *Genetiuus* is not found in the Vulgate at all. It has no reflexes in the Romance languages, and cannot have been widely current in spoken Latin.

2-3 genetiua nobilis pulcherrima adulta: for the asyndeton cf. *Conf.* 12 *rusticus profuga indoctus.* Patrick was not without stylistic affectations, a point that will be taken up in the Conclusions to 40.

4 una causa uenit ad nos: I have taken this as another weakened use of *una*, 'for a (certain) reason' rather than 'for a single reason'. Bieler (1993: I.133–4) suggests this ('idem fere quod articulus linguarum modernarum'), translating 'for some reason', but in his translation (1953: 34) he renders 'for a particular reason'.

5 insinuauit nobis responsum accepisse a nuntio dei et monuit eam: *insinuo* here means 'inform, tell'. Cf. *Conf.* 27 *propter anxietatem maesto animo insinuaui amicissimo meo quae in pueritia mea una die gesseram.* At *Conf.* 22 *insinuaui* is indistinguishable from *dixi: sicut superius insinuaui, uiginti et octo dies per desertum iter fecimus,* referring back to 19.

This is a late usage, with the verb becoming equivalent to one of saying (see *TLL* VII.1.1916.84ff., drawing attention to specific examples in the article elsewhere; Souter 1949: 210 gives the meaning 'make known' from the mid-third century). Note e.g. Heges. 5.19, p. 338.27 *insinuauit Caesari, mirari se, quod cunctarentur Romani murum succedere,* an example glossed in the 'index grammaticus' of V. Ussani (*CSEL* 66, p. 563) with 'notum fecit'. The usage is not overwhelmingly biblical, but is found in Christian writers. There are just three examples in the Vulgate (e.g. Act 17.3 *adaperiens et insinuans quia Christum oportuit pati, et resurgere a mortuis*; the Greek here has παρατιθέμενος, a verb rendered 'demonstrate, point out' by Bauer, Arndt and Gingrich 1957: 628 2c). It is another word that does not survive in Romance.

Here there is first an acc. + inf. *responsum accepisse* without an expressed subject accusative pronoun (*se*). For such an omission, of a type that goes back to the earliest period (see Hofmann and Szantyr 1965: 362, with bibliography too on late texts, de Melo 2006; cf. also below, 43.4), see also *Conf.* 23 *putabam ipso momento audire uocem ipsorum.* There is then slippage into an indicative verb (*monuit*), which is part of the information reported by the woman and ought logically to be part of the acc. + inf. (i.e. = *et eum monuisse se*).

There are various ways of interpreting such slippage. First, a non-native speaker may fail consistently to apply a rule that he has to remember because it is alien to him. Modern composers of Latin make such mistakes, and it is possible that Patrick has done so here. Second, there is evidence that outside high literature the acc. + inf. was used in a very rudimentary way, without subordinate clauses or strings of coordinated infinitives (see Adams 2005b), and it was certainly not a normal construction for Patrick (see the next paragraph). A non-literary writer who was himself a native speaker might sometimes lapse when faced with the need to report something complex. Note Terentianus, *P. Mich.* VIII.468.43–5 *[sci]as Carpum hic errasse ed i̯ṇu̯[e]ṇtus est Dios in legione et a[cce]pisse me* (see Adams 2005b: 201). Here there is first an acc. + inf., then a switch into the indicative, after which Terentianus gathered his thoughts and returned to the infinitive. Third, in some cases an apparent lapse might be explained otherwise. We might here for example put strong punctuation after *dei* and assume that thereafter Patrick as narrator takes over the reporting of the woman's revelation.

The acc. + inf. is an unusual construction for Patrick (see below, 39.18), and therefore he might have been prone to slips. In the following there may be a run of infinitives with accusative subjects interrupted by a clause with a finite verb: *Conf.* 4 *ut didicimus; . . . Iesum Christum, quem cum patre scilicet semper fuisse testamur, ante originem saeculi spiritaliter apud patrem <et> inenarrabiliter genitum ante omne principium, et per ipsum facta sunt uisibilia et inuisibilia, hominem factum, morte deuicta in caelis ad patrem receptum.* But it is more likely that the participles depend on *praeter* earlier.

There is a switch of construction of a different type, but which is worth noting, at *Conf.* 23: *rogamus te, . . . ut uenias et adhuc ambulas inter nos* (from the subjunctive with *ut* into the indicative, though an influence here was the fact that the indicative ending of *ambulas* was the same as that of the subjunctive of *uenias*: see index, 'indicative, apparent indicatives in *ut*-clauses'; also 'indicative, mechanically used'). See also Bieler (1993: II.151), rejecting the idea that *ambulas* is under the influence of the Old Irish *a*-subjunctive.

Nuntius is here used in the meaning 'angel'. Note Bieler (1993: II.171: '*Nuntius* "angel" belongs to an early stage of ecclesiastical Latin, when Greek terms were literally translated . . . This practice was soon abandoned, and Greek terms were borrowed freely.' Bieler added that the survival of the archaic term in an Insular text of the fifth century was noteworthy, but it would not do to imply that the term was in some sense current: Patrick had access to early Christian texts, and it is uncertain where he would have picked this up.

On the accusative pronoun *eam* (*monuit eam*) see below, 39.8.

6 deo proximaret: a distinctive verb, which is again relevant to the sources of Patrick's Latin. *Proximo* occurs first in Apuleius, as an intransitive verb meaning 'approach, be near' and the like (*TLL* X.2.2368.38ff.: e.g. *Met.* 2.16 *ecce*

Photis mea ... proximat, 3.26 *me praesepio ... proximantem*). It is common in Old Latin versions, employed both intransitively and also in various transitive uses (see *TLL* X.2.2369.55ff.). Multiple examples from the *Vet. Lat.* may be found in the *TLL* article (as well as others in Christian writers influenced by Old Latin versions). A slightly specialised intransitive use is glossed by the *TLL* (2369.29ff.) as follows: 'in religione Iud. vel Christ. respicitur relatio inter deum propitium, opitulantem et homines ei obsequium, venerationem sim. praestantes'. The present passage is cited, along with two from the *Vet. Lat.* and a few others from Christian texts: we might say, 'draw near to God' (note Vulg. Hbr 7.19 *per quam proximamus ad deum*). Here is a verb that is not common in the Vulgate (eight examples, mainly from the OT and none from Acts; see too Lundström 1948: 104 for statistics from a few works). Bieler (1993: II.171) notes that in the Vulgate the verb is often eliminated where the early translations had it. Patrick must have known it from early Bible versions (or theological writers). According to *REW* 6794 it does however survive in Gallo-Romance (see also Greimas 1968: 515, citing *proismer* 'approach' from the thirteenth century). The lexicon of the Latin Bible does not consist only of artificial terminology (see e.g. the whole of Part III of Burton 2000), but this may not be a genuine Latin survival into Romance but a re-coinage, in Gallo-Romance itself, from the adjective (see *FEW* IX.489, 490 n. 3).

7 auidissime arripuit illud quod etiam omnes uirgines dei ita hoc faciunt: here there is a redundant pronoun (*hoc*) in the relative clause, repeating what is expressed by the relative pronoun *quod*. Bieler (1993: II.172) says that '[r]edundant demonstratives in relative clauses are a feature of late Vulgar Latin', but that is to give a false impression of the source of Patrick's Latin here; nor is there any point in offering classical Greek examples. The construction is a Hebrew one, and as such it found its way into the Septuagint, the Greek NT and the Vulgate (see E. Löfstedt 1959: 91, Adams 2003a: 469); Löfstedt indeed describes it as 'hopelessly un-Latin'. For Latin biblical examples see Vulg. Lc 3.16 *cuius non sum dignus soluere corrigiam calciamentorum eius* (same construction in the Greek), and Nm 14.31 as quoted and discussed by Augustine (*Loc. Hept.* p. 588.1–4 *CSEL* 28) (same construction in the LXX, from the Hebrew). Augustine's comment on the construction *quam ... ab ea* is revealing: '*et hereditate possidebunt terram, quam uos abscessistis ab ea': usitatum esset: 'a qua uos abscessistis'; nunc uero et 'quam abscessisis' dictum est nouo more, et additum est 'ab ea'* ('... regular would be "from which you departed", but these days also "which you departed" is said in a new way, and there has been added "from that"*). Augustine goes on to remark on this last phrase, *sicut Scripturae loqui solent* (see E. Löfstedt 1959: 91). There is no suggestion here that the redundant *ab ea* is 'Vulgar Latin'. For Augustine it is not normal but a scriptural usage, and the accusative *quam* he sees as a modernism. The source of the construction in Patrick is likely to have been biblical.

That said, there are examples also of such constructions in late substandard Latin texts (and even a few earlier literary texts) uninfluenced by the Bible, 'springing probably from *ad hoc* conflations rather than from established usage' (Adams 2003a: 612). See further E. Löfstedt (1907: 94–8), Ahlquist (1909: 114–15), Hofmann and Szantyr (1965: 556–7), *TLL* VI.2.2743.21ff. One might leave open the possibility that Patrick too merely stumbled into a crudity of expression (the whole clause is over-complicated: see below), but that should not be attributed to the influence of Vulgar Latin.

Bieler (1993: II.172) notes that *auidissime arripui* is at Aug. *Conf.* 7.21.27, and suggests that Patrick's phrase may be modelled on this. However, *auidissime* was one of Patrick's adverbs (52 *auidissime cupiebant*), and the correspondence may be a chance one.

illud quod . . . ita hoc: the type of construction seen in *quod . . . ita* (where a pronoun, demonstrative or relative, in this case *quod*, has *ita* after it, either attached or postponed) has been discussed by E. Löfstedt (1950: 7–9). Usually there is no pleonasm at all and the adverb has a clear function, as for example at Cic. *Att.* 16.9 *quod quidem ita credo*, cited by Löfstedt (9) and translated by Shackleton Bailey (1965–70: VI.189) 'which I believe is the case', but such combinations had a stereotyped character and could sometimes develop into a type of pleonasm (Löfstedt loc. cit.). Here ('that which also all virgins of God do, so') the force of *ita* is weak to non-existent. Bieler (1993: II.172) sees *ita* and the immediately following *hoc* as constituting the pleonasm, but in this pleonastic use of *ita* it is regularly the pronoun that precedes (see the material collected by Löfstedt), and we must take *ita* with the preceding *quod* (as in several other cases cited by Löfstedt at 9), and *hoc* as an independent resumption of *quod* (and a different construction, as seen above). Bieler cites as a parallel for his interpretation Greg. Tur. *HF* 2.27, p. 72.13 *cum haec ita dixissent*, but this is not a parallel at all, as *haec* precedes: it therefore supports the interpretation given here. The whole clause is garbled, with a construction of Hebrew origin mixed up with a pleonastic Latin form of expression. *Quod ita* (with redundant *ita*) is a feature of the *Vita sanctae Euphrosynae* (see 47.23).

8 non sponte patrum earum: *sponte* + genitive 'by the will of' is first quoted from the imperial period (*OLD* s.v. 3a). Note Tac. *Ann.* 2.59.2 *non sponte principis* 'without the emperor's consent'.

Earum here is reflexive, for *suorum* (see Bieler 1993: I.132): cf. *Conf.* 9 *qui . . . sermones illorum ex infantia numquam mutarunt.* There are two complementary developments in the history of Latin affecting reflexives (both of which are in Patrick), and this exemplifies one of them (for recent discussions of such phenomena see e.g. Fruyt 1987, Bertocchi 1989, de Melo 2010: 93–9). I start with the other.

First, *suus* itself was not always strictly reflexive in classical Latin, and as a result 'in registers of Latin lacking in Classical purity *suus* gradually acquired the anaphoric function of the genitive forms of *is*' (Wackernagel 1926–8: II.93 = Langslow 2009: 516). There are late texts in which *suus* is often used for *eius* or *eorum* (so Gregory of Tours: see Bonnet 1890: 696–7; see too below, 47.15 on the *Vita sanctae Euphrosynae*, and also Boucherie 1871: 52). As Wackernagel notes, the 'end point of this evolution has been reached in Romance, where the modern reflexes of Lat. *suus* denote simply belonging to any given constituent' (Wackernagel 1926–8: II.93 = Langslow 2009: 516). This use of *suus* is also represented in Patrick (see Bieler 1993: I.132 'pronomen reflexiuum indirectum uel perperam usurpatum').

Second, there is the reverse usage seen above in our passage, whereby *eius* etc. (or *illius* etc.) is used for *suus* (see again for Gregory of Tours Bonnet 1890: 696, and in general the account of Hofmann and Szantyr 1965: 175).

The outcome of such usages in the Romance languages varies. The genitive forms of *is* were dropped everywhere, in keeping with the loss of *is* in general (see further below, this note) in favour of *ille* (and hence it follows that Patrick's *earum*, reflexive or not, is partly Latinate rather than purely proto-Romance). Spanish dropped all derivatives of *illius/illorum*, 'generalizing descendants of SUUS in both reflexive and non-reflexive roles' (Harris 1978: 88). In Italy on the other hand *suus* tended to be restricted to the singular, both reflexive and non-reflexive, with *illorum* providing the corresponding plural form (*loro*; cf. Fr. *leur* too, of the same origin): see Harris (1978: 89 and the whole section 87–95); also Wackernagel (1926–8: II.79) = Langslow (2009: 498), and Hofmann and Szantyr (1965: 175).

Bieler, in attempting to discover 'pre-Romance' elements in Patrick's Latin, refers (1952: 67: n. 12) to his 'tendency to use the reflexive pronoun in the singular, the non-reflexive in the plural' (see also 75, and Bieler 1993: II.106). For the possible Romance significance of such a distinction see the previous paragraph; it is to be assumed that Bieler was not referring merely to *suus* used in singular forms, which would not be relevant here, but to its use in reference to a single possessor.

If a proto-Romance distinction were already to be found in Patrick it might comprise *illorum* (*illarum, eorum, earum*) serving as the plural (i.e. referring to a plurality of possessors), reflexive and non-reflexive, complemented by *suus*, used as both a reflexive and non-reflexive of a single possessor. But the figures given later in this note for occurrences of *is* and *ille* show that the genitive singulars *eius* and *illius*, though outnumbered by the plural genitives *eorum*, *earum* and *illorum*, are nevertheless well represented. It should also be noted that, apart from *is* and *ille*, Patrick also uses *ipse* as a demonstrative (usually of God), and the singular possessive genitive *ipsius* occurs four times (*Conf.* 39, 44, 48, 60). As for *suus*, it occurs nine times in the *Confessio* (18, 26, 32, 34, 42 twice, 49, 58, 59). Seven of these examples refer to a single possessor (usually God), but one of those at 42 (*parentibus suis*) and that at 49 (*ex ornamentis suis*) refer to a plurality.

Thus there is not a clear-cut distinction here between *suus* with singular reference and *eorum*/*illorum* with plural, because Patrick admits on the one hand the singulars *eius* and *illius*, as well as *ipsius*, and on the other *suus* with plural reference. Bieler (1993: II.106) cites, and was no doubt influenced by, the demonstration of Pei (1932: 202–6) that 'the scribes of Merovingian charters, so far from distinguishing between reflexive and non-reflexive meaning, are consistent in using *suus* of a single proprietor, *eorum illorum ipsorum* of several persons'. Pei (1932: 202) summarises thus for his corpus: 'The syntactic state of affairs with regard to the possessive pronoun is already fully Romance.' It is not the case that there is the same distinction in Patrick, and it would not do to suggest on the basis of our figures that he was already reflecting a spoken proto-Romance form of the language.

What we certainly do find is that Patrick in a more general sense was under the influence of popular, mainly late, developments, in that *suus* and *eius* etc. were not always kept distinct. At *Conf.* 9 (cited at the start of this note) we might indeed be tempted see him using what was to become the proto-Romance *illorum* as a reflexive, but that is not to say that he need himself have been drawing on the spoken language. Confusions of *suus* and *eius* etc. are widespread in texts, including the Vulgate (Plater and White 1926: 71). Bieler's own conclusion on the matter in his commentary is rather more guarded than that in the article of 1952 (1993: II.106 'Patrick's usage, though still within the terms of Latin syntax, might foreshadow the later Romanic development'). Contrast 'It is this "pre-Romance" element in his Latinity that first strikes the linguist' (1952: 67, with n. 12 referring to the possessive). At best Patrick's usage is transitional.

I turn now to some details of the incidence of *is*. Patrick is one of those imperial writers in whom *is* has receded before *ille* (on which phenomenon see above, 18.6, with bibliography, and index, s.v. *ille*, 'in relation to *is*'). Bieler (1993: I.132) gives some global figures for the two works (*is* 44, *ille* 86), but these almost certainly include examples in biblical quotations. In the *Confessio* I have noted 19 examples of *is* (pronominal: I have not included adjectival *is* or *ille* in these figures) in passages not printed in italic (indicating a biblical source) by Bieler. These show restrictions in the case forms admitted. The case is genitive in 10 instances (*eius* 5, *eorum* 4, *earum* 1; for the persistence of *eius* over a long period see 38.53 and the references there). The accusative singulars *eum* and *eam* occur seven times (*eum* 5, *eam* 2). There remain 2 instances of *id*, one in the formula *id est* (*Conf.* 44), the other in a phrase (*non id solum*) that also looks formulaic (43).

On the other hand I have counted 47 examples of *ille*, in a much wider range of cases: *ille* 1, *illum* 1, *illud* 3, *illius* 1, *illi* (dat.) 6, *illos* 3, *illas* 1, *illorum* 5, *illis* (dat.) 13, *illis* (abl., dependent on prepositions) 13. Note the predominance of *eius* over *illius*.

To some extent there is a complementary distribution of the two terms. In the masculine and feminine accusative singular *is* is preferred to *ille*, by 7:1. In the genitive singular and plural *is* is also preferred, by 10:6 (the figures for the singular are 5:1). *Ille* by contrast is the only term used in the masculine nominative singular, the dative singular and plural, the masculine and feminine accusative plural, and the ablative plural. An interesting alternation is found at *Conf.* 33: *inquisiui eum et ibi inueni illum*, which replicates something we saw in the *Passio Perpetuae et Felicitatis* (see 27.11) and the Vulgate (38.53).

As for the possessive uses (see also above), with reference to a single possessor *eius*, *illius* and *ipsius* occur 10 times, *suus* 7. In reference to plural possessors *eorum*, *earum* and *illorum* occur 10 times, *suus* twice.

Do we see in Patrick's use of *is* and *ille* the influence of 'living' Latin? Patrick does, it is true, like other late writers, prefer *ille* to *is*, most notably in the narrative chapters 18–19, where *ille* occurs 13 times and *is* only once. However, he shows a taste for *eum* and *eam* rather than *illum* and *illam*, and that cannot be put down to the influence of spoken Latin. In the seven passages of freedmen's speeches quoted at Adams (2003b: 13–14) there are 30 instances of *ille* indistinguishable from *is*, and of these 13 are in the accusative singular *illum*; *eum* does not occur in these passages. It was the phonetically 'weak' forms of *is* that were early subject to loss (see e.g. Adams 1977a: 44; also Bieler 1952: 84). *Eum* and *eam* were in effect monosyllabic, with the initial vowel in hiatus subject to yodisation.

Patrick's use of *is/ille* bears a resemblance to that in one of the versions of the *Vet. Lat.*, the Codex Palatinus (*e*) of the Gospel of John. Figures for chapter 6 of *e* are given above, 38.53. There *is* is used freely in the genitive singular and accusative singular, but only *ille* is used in the dative singular and plural.

The distribution in Patrick is much the same, and he might well have been influenced by an Old Latin version. The frequency of the various case forms of the two pronouns in late Latin is however a subject that could do with more extensive investigation, and the observations here are only tentative.

Finally, the placement of object pronouns, direct and indirect, is of also some interest in Patrick. Almost invariably those considered here, *is* and *ille*, are placed after the verb. Of the 7 instances of *eum* and *eam*, 5 are after the verb. Of the other 2 instances, 1 is preposed, but the other (37) is in fact a subject accusative in an acc. + inf. The one instance of *illum* is after the verb, as are 2 of the 3 of *illud*, and all 3 instances of the plurals *illos* and *illas* that are dependent on verbs rather than on a preposition. There are thus 11 instances of postposition of accusatives, compared with 2 of anteposition. Such placement is not the norm for classical Latin.

It is much the same for the dative. There are 19 instances of the datives *illi* and *illis*, of which 17 follow the verb.

9 improperia: this is a term that is attested for the first time in the *Vet. Lat.* and is common there. It does occur in the Vulgate, but *opprobrium* is usually used instead (a term which Patrick also has himself, at *Conf.* 37, but in a biblical citation). In Fischer's concordance of the Vulgate (1977) the occurrences of *opprobrium* occupy two columns, those of *improperium* about one third of a column (twenty-two instances). The *TLL* VII.1.695.77ff. says that *improperium* occurs from the *Itala* onwards 'apud Christianos minus eruditos', adding that it is avoided by such as Cyprian, Ambrose, Jerome and Augustine (except in biblical quotations); cf. Bieler 1993: II.172 'a uox Christiana, and typically "low"', 'frequent in the O.L. version, but avoided in Jerome's independent translations'. See also Rönsch (1875: 32). The usual Greek correspondents are ὄνειδος and ὀνειδισμός (details may be found in the *TLL* article, and also Rönsch 1875: 32–3). *TLL* VII.1.696.3 cites the same verb phrase as that here, *improperium passa est*, from Ier 15.9 (Iren. 4.33.2). *Improperium* is a derivative of *impropero* 'blame', a usage that goes back to a freedman's speech in Petronius (see above, 27 Conclusions, 'Perpetua's Latin').

10 qui ibi nati sunt nescimus numerum eorum: for the interpretation of *nati* ('reborn') I follow Bieler (1953: 34; cf. Hanson 1978: 117 n. 2).

Bieler (1993: I.127) (so too Mohrmann 1961a: 17) classifies the construction (*qui ibi nati sunt*) here as a 'nominatiuus pendens', but it can be taken as a relative-correlative construction of old type (see 1.11, 4.11) (= *qui ibi nati sunt, eorum numerum nescimus*); Patrick has departed from the expected word order (by not having *eorum* at the start of the main clause), but that is all; on that feature see above, 34.6, and below, this note. The relative-correlative construction is found in the Vulgate (derived from the Greek NT), for example three times in the Sermon on the Mount as reported by Matthew (Mt 5.19, 5.41, 7.21); cf. e.g. Mt 10.22, 10.33, 12.32. In biblical language it is found particularly in gnomic utterances. It would have been from biblical or theological sources that Patrick picked it up. See also *Conf.* 24 *qui dedit animam suam pro te, ipse est qui loquitur in te.*

In the same place Bieler quotes the following (taken by Patrick from Mt 12.36) as another instance of the 'nominatiuus pendens': *Conf.* 7 *uerbum otiosum quod locuti fuerint homines reddent pro eo rationem.* But *uerbum otiosum* is certainly an accusative (see the next paragraph), fronted out of the relative clause by attractio inversa (= *quod uerbum otiosum locuti fuerint, pro eo rationem reddent*). Attractio inversa also goes back to early Latin (see e.g. 1.11, 1 Appendix 2, 4.11). In the late period it is found in theological writers and thus belonged to the corpus that influenced Patrick. See e.g. *Didasc. Apost.* 9.6 *pastor qui constituitur in uisitatione praesbyterii et in ecclesiis omnibus et parrociis, oportet eum sine quaerella esse* (with Tidner 1938: 97, noting that while such constructions are in Christian texts, they are far from being confined to those). Here there is again a departure in the main clause from the expected position of *eum*, and that is a feature that might be investigated diachronically, both in relative-correlatives and in attractio inversa (cf. above, 34.6). It occurs for example in a relative-correlative in the Vulgate at Mt 12.32: *et quicumque dixerit uerbum contra filium hominis, remittetur ei* (same construction in the Greek).

For an accusatival instance of attractio inversa in the Vulgate see Mt 21.42, Mc 12.10, Lc 20.17 *lapidem quem reprobauerunt aedificantes, hic factus est in caput anguli* (λίθον ὃν ἀπεδοκίμασαν οἱ οἰκοδομοῦντες, οὗτος ἐγενήθη εἰς κεφαλὴν γωνίας), which refers to Ps 117.22 (where *lapis* is another reading). These NT passages show unambiguously that the fronted noun has the case that it would have had in the relative clause. By contrast in one of the examples in the previous paragraph we saw that the noun is nominative, but it still takes its case from the relative clause (not from any 'hanging' character) (cf. also above, 1.11 for the fronted noun in attractio inversa as having the case of the relative pronoun).

Mohrmann (1961a: 17) also quotes the following as a hanging nominative in Patrick: *Conf.* 52 *omnia quaecumque nobiscum inuenerunt, rapuerunt illud,* but this too is a variant on attractio inversa. Even though it would not be possible to put *omnia* (which is redundant with *quaecumque*) into the relative clause, the placement resembles that of the fronting of attractio inversa.

The lack of concord between the singular resumptive pronoun *illud* and the plural *omnia quaecumque* here is of a type that goes back to early Latin: a neuter pronoun can resume a term of whatever number or gender (see above, 5.5).

It is however true that there are some genuine hanging nominatives in Patrick, described by Mohrmann (1961a: 17) as a 'typical feature of living, unbookish language'. One cannot dismiss the construction unequivocally as unbookish, as it has a long history in literature (see further Adams 2013: 215–20, with examples and bibliography). At *Conf.* 18 (*et gubernator displicuit illi*) one might punctuate with a comma after *gubernator* ('and the helmsman – it displeased him') the structure is typical, in that the focal nominative is resumed by a pronoun in the required case (examples from Plautus, Cato and Cicero at Adams 2013: 215–16; also above, 3.416), but this case is indeed striking because the separation of noun from resumptive pronoun is so short: usually there is a longer gap (but cf. Iren. Lat. 2.102.4–5 B *deus, uera opera eius* alongside Vulg. Dt 32.4 *dei perfecta sunt opera*, cited by Lundström 1943: 53 with another similar example). The detached nominative is rather longer at *Epist.* 12 *et filii Scottorum et filiae regulorum monachi et uirgines Christi enumerare nequeo*. Here there is no resumptive pronoun, but that feature too of hanging nominative constructions can be paralleled in the classical period (see *B. Afr.* 25.1, cited by Adams 2013: 216). Again, Mohrmann (1961a: 18) quotes as an appositional detached nominative *Epist.* 19 *Coroticus cum suis sceleratissimis, rebellatores Christi*. This, with its appositional nominative following a *cum*-expression, has an exact parallel in Cicero (*Phil.* 2.58 *sequebatur raeda cum lenonibus, comites nequissimi*; see Adams 2013: 217, Spevak 2014: 329 for discussion).

Such departures from strict concord are probably to be explained variably in different contexts, as for example deliberately arresting to convey focus, as due to loss of the thread of a sentence (anacoluthon), as sometimes showing indifference to strict syntax for the purposes of informality, or as related to ancient writing materials, which did not make corrections easy. The presence of examples in Patrick does not set him apart from the literary tradition.

Indeed the learned Varro is notorious for anacolutha and other signs of carelessness or rapid writing (Laughton 1960: 2, 20–2; see also Norden 1958: I. 194–200 for an assessment of Varro's Latin). Such features should not be taken as indications of poor education, as they tend to be.

Noteworthy in our passage is the switch to masculine (*qui ibi nati sunt*) after Patrick has been talking about women. He has generalised, to all of those reborn.

11 quae seruitio detinentur: *seruitium* here means 'slavery'. At *Conf.* 49 on the other hand *seruitus* means '(Christian) service'. This distinction is not general in the work (note e.g. *seruitus* at chapters 35 and 49).

12 usque ad terrores et minas assidue perferunt: translated by Bieler (1953: 34) as: 'All the time they have to endure terror and threats.' This cannot be right, as *terrores* and *minas* are dependent on *usque ad* and not objects of the verb. *Perfero* is sometimes used absolutely in classical Latin, and goes on being so used in late Latin (*TLL* X.1.1361.64ff.). The sense is thus something like 'they go on constantly enduring, to the point of being subject to terror and threats'. Alternatively an object may be understood from the previous clause (*labores aut sim.*, extracted from *laborant*).

13 imitantur: according to Bieler (1993: II.173) this is equivalent to *conantur*, but the basic meaning of the verb (*OLD* s.v. 1a) is 'copy the conduct, action, practice of', and that fits here. In his note Bieler renders 'they strive bravely' but in his translation (1953: 35) 'they follow Him bravely'.

  etsi uetantur ... fortiter imitantur: Patrick exploits homoeoteleuta and sound effects quite often (see below, 40 Conclusions).

14 unde autem etsi uoluero amittere illas: translated by Bieler (1953: 15) as 'Wherefore, then, even if I wished to leave them' (better, 'shall ever wish').

  Amittere does seem to mean 'leave'. One can derive such a use from various earlier nuances. For the ideas 'give up, abandon' (but with abstract object) see *OLD* s.v. 5; for 'let go one's hold of, release' (but literal, not metaphorical') see *OLD* s.v. 3; and for 'be parted from, lose', see *OLD* s.v. 9. Patrick had a taste for the verb with this meaning: cf. *Conf.* 36 *sed ut patriam et parentes amitterem*, 58 *quapropter non contingat mihi a deo meo ut numquam amittam 'plebem' suam*. For a parallel from Commodian (*Instr.* 2.9.4) see Bieler (1993: II.166).

15 ut pergens in Brittanniis: a banal confusion of the ablative with accusative in a directional meaning (further examples in Patrick are cited by Bieler 1993: I.129). *Hiberione*, for example, a close transliteration of the Old Irish word (Bieler 1993: II.89), is treated as an indeclinable, serving both for accusative and ablative (Bieler 1993: I.127). Se also index, s.v. *in*, '+ ablative for accusative and vice versa'.

  Bieler (1993: II.173) aptly remarks that this chapter (43) 'is an anacoluthon from beginning to end'. The *etsi*-clause is broken off at this point and not strictly completed, though the chapter roughly comes around to expressing the idea that, much as he might like to leave and return to Britain, he is restrained by the Spirit from abandoning his converts. This main clause as I have just expressed it does not follow on from the *etsi*-clause in the Latin, but comes after the *scit deus quod*-construction.

Bieler has no note on *et ut pergens*. He translates the first clause (1953: 35) as: 'Wherefore, then, even if I wished to leave them and go to Britain', which is by no means a rendering of *et ut pergens*. In late Latin there are sometimes found present participles where a finite verb is expected (see Eklund 1970: 119–205, Adams 1976a: 60–5, Pitkäranta 1978: 80–4, and below, 48.4.3), and these are open to diverse explanations, as due to anacoluthon, textual corruption, incompetence etc. (see the thorough discussion of Eklund). In the present case, however, it could not be said that *et* coordinates a present participle to a finite verb, a common pattern in substandard texts (see index, 'present participle, coordinated to main verb by *et*'), because it would not be to a finite verb that it was coordinated but to the infinitive *amittere*.

One possibility is that the sentence is simply unfinished: Patrick failed to complete it with a second infinitive.

It is alternatively possible that nothing is missing and that *et* tacks on an explanation (Bieler 1993: I.139 quotes examples of such uses of *et* but does not include this one). Thus 'and indeed as one proceeding to Britain'. The idea then would be 'although I want to leave, and indeed as one proceeding to Britain', a natural thing for a Briton to want to do.

The choice of verb is distinctive. Patrick does not use *uado* as his verb of going (see Bieler 1993: I.134), though it was banal by this period (see Adams 2013: 811–17). *Pergo*, a higher-style term (Adams 2013: 800–4), also occurs at *Conf.* 28 (*Hiberione non sponte pergebam*) and 51 (*pergebam ... etiam usque ad exteras partes*). In the Vulgate there are about 170 examples of *pergo* in the OT, but only two in the NT (Jo 8.1 *perrexit*, Act 22.5 *pergebam*), a distribution that brings out the stylistic level of the verb (Jerome's OT is more literary in its lexicon than the NT, which is based on Old Latin versions). As for *uado* in the Vulgate, it is used freely in the NT (more than a column of examples in Fischer's concordance (1977); there are about four columns of examples in the OT). The verb was also used in the *Vet. Lat.* (see Burton 2000: 159–60).

Nor does Patrick use *eo* in finite forms, and the only instances outside biblical quotations are at *Conf.* 17 (*cito iturus*) and 18 (*ire*). *Iter facio* occurs twice (*Conf.* 19, 22), a commonplace phrase that goes back to Plautus. Bieler (1993: I.134) also lists *ambulo* (*Conf.* 23, 52) among verbs of going, but it is not clear that it does not mean specifically 'walk'. *Venio* and compounds (including *deuenio*) are used freely.

A straightforward explanation of Patrick's avoidance of *uado* in favour of *pergo* might be that, like a historian, he preferred the high-style term. But his word choice in other semantic fields is not consistent. Bieler (1952: 82) points out that, unlike the writer of the *Peregrinatio Aetheriae*, Patrick prefers the high-style *interficio* to the mundane *occido*, but on the other hand sides with the *Peregrinatio* in preferring the mundane *inuenio* to the higher-register *reperio*. There is a quirkiness about his word choice, which makes it difficult to classify him simply as a mundane late Christian writer. This quirkiness could be put down to a variety of reasons: one possibility is that he had not picked up Latin words in context, such that he could evaluate their stylistic level.

16 libentissime 'paratus eram' quasi ad patriam et parentes: Bieler (1953: 35) has 'and how I would have loved to go to my country and my parents', and I have taken *ad patriam et parentes* in this way too (i.e. = 'to go to . . .'). This interpretation assumes an ellipse of an infinitival verb of going (e.g. *ire*) dependent on *paratus eram*. It is true that *paratus* can be construed with *ad* ('ready for'), as e.g. at Cic. *Div. Caec.* 41 *paratior ad usum forensem* and *Mil.* 25 *ad omne facinus paratissimus* (see further *OLD* s.v. *paratus* 3, 4, *TLL* X.1. 426–30, with many examples of different types), but often there is a verbal idea to the prepositional complement (so gerunds of the type *ad dicendum* occur in this construction). There might be some meaning to the phrase 'ready for one's parents', but the implication of travel is strongly present in the context (cf. *pergens in Brittanniis, usque ad Gallias uisitare fratres*). Ellipse of a verb of going is commonplace (see on Cicero Heidemann 1893: 50–7, and for bibliography Hofmann and Szantyr 1965: 424). It occurs typically when there is a local or temporal expression present that implies motion (as here), as for example at Ter. *Andr.* 361 *ego me continuo ad Chremem* (on this point see Heidemann 1893: 50). Not infrequently it is an infinitive that is omitted, after a verb of will or intention, as in the present passage: e.g. Cic. *Att.* 9.1.3 *deinde Arpinum uolebamus*, 16.10.1 *statueram enim recta Appia Romam* (see Heidemann 1893: 53 for more examples).

Also of note here is the presence of *quasi* after *paratus eram*. This might be the late use of *quasi* introducing (or here implying) an infinitive, as in phrases of the type *uidetur quasi, conatur quasi* (see Adams 1995a: 484–5), *coepit quasi* (e.g. Vulg. 2 Sm 13.6 *quasi aegrotare coepit*).

17 sed etiam usque ad Gallias uisitare fratres et ut uiderem faciem: there is an ambiguity about the syntax of *uisitare*. On the punctuation adopted here it might be dependent on *paratus eram*. But it was argued above that *ad patriam et parentes* following *paratus eram* has ellipse of a verb of going. If that is accepted, a comma might be put after *Gallias*, thereby coordinating *usque ad Gallias* with the earlier *ad patriam et parentes*, with both *ad*-expressions thus associated with the understood verb. Then *uisitare* would become a final infinitive, in the idiom 'go to visit', a usage which will be illustrated in another connection below (39.22): 'I was ready (to go) to my native land and parents; not only that, but even (to go) as far as Gaul, to visit . . .' There follows *et ut uiderem*, a final use of *ut*, which would be coordinated with the final infinitive *uisitare* ('to visit . . . and to see . . .'). There is a good deal of syntactic inconcinnity in Patrick (see Bieler 1993: I.146, and below, 40 Conclusions, 'Patrick's Latin is severely limited').

18 qui mihi 'protestatur' si hoc fecero, ut futurum reum me esse designat: the use of *ut* here is not straightforward. Bieler (1993: II.163) quoted the passage as illustrating *ut* = *ut qui* as a 'peculiar feature of his individual language'. He did not explain what he meant by *ut qui*. I would take *ut* as explicative/causal, = 'in that, in as much as' (cf. *OLD* s.v. 21a). For causal *ut* (glossed with *quia*) see the late Christian examples cited by Bulhart (1967: xliii).

Designo used as a verb of saying with the acc. + inf. is pure late Latin (*TLL* V.1.719.57ff., Bieler 1993: II.174). The examples cited by the *TLL* are not biblical but in Christian writers.

According to Mohrmann (1961a: 20), this is one of only two cases of the acc. + inf. in the *Conf.*, and one of only four in the whole of Patrick (cf. Bieler 1993: II. 103). Mohrmann refers to 41 for the second instance of the acc. + inf. in the work, a wrong reference for 42 (*insinuauit nobis responsum accepisse*), where, we saw above (39.5), in a following coordinated dependent clause Patrick switches into the indicative: he did not have control of the construction. The acc. + inf. is certainly rare in Patrick, but Mohrmann's figures are not quite accurate. She does not cite *Conf.* 23, cited above at 39.5 (also without an expressed accusative pronoun, as at 42 just quoted). Note too 48 *deus scit 'neminem' illorum 'circumueniri'*, where the biblical passage alluded to (2 Cor 7.2) has *neminem circumuenimus* and the acc. + inf. is Patrick's own construction.

Object clauses introduced by *quod, quia, ut* and *cur* are said by Mohrmann to occur about twenty times. It might be added that often too the verb of saying is followed directly by reported words, without any connective; the higher verb is thus parenthetical (i.e. there is parataxis): e.g. *Conf.* 19 *tu dicis deus tuus magnus et omnipotens est*, 31 *'audenter dico' non me reprehendit conscientia mea*, 33 *sed scit deus, si mihi homo hoc effatus fuisset, forsitan tacuissem propter* '*caritatem Christi*', 44 *spero autem hoc debueram*, 59 *certissime reor, si mihi hoc incurrisset, lucratus sum animam cum corpore meo, Epist.* 13 *nesciunt miseri uenenum letale cibum porrigunt ad amicos et filios suos.* Bieler (1993: I.142–3) quotes almost twenty such cases from the two works: this construction is as common as that introduced by *quod, quia* etc. The parenthetical construction is old (from Plautus onwards) and widespread, particularly in low-register texts, including Vindolanda tablets (see Adams 2003b: 554–5, with further bibliography).

For similar treatment of a conditional construction in reported speech to that at *Conf.* 33 and 59 just cited, see Terentianus, *P. Mich.* VIII. 467.9–10, with Adams (2005b: 201). Conditional clauses embedded in the acc. + inf. were beyond the competence of some writers, and embedding was not attempted.

Thus in Patrick the *quod-/quia*-construction and the paratactic far outnumber the acc. + inf., which is remarkable, because for the most part late writers admitting *quod*-type clauses still prefer the acc. + inf. An exception we saw was Publicola (see 31.7; see also above, 22.10, and below, 47.12). Two other significant exceptions are the *Vet. Lat.* and Vulgate versions of the NT, in which reported speech is regularly introduced by *quod, quia* or *quoniam*, under the influence of the ὅτι-construction of the Greek NT (see Plater and White 1926: 119–20, Burton 2000: 189–90). The parenthetical construction is of the type with which Patrick might possibly have been familiar from real speech, but the frequency of the *quod*-type could just as well reflect the influence of Latin Bible versions.

19 timeo perdere laborem: 'I am afraid of losing' (Bieler 1953). For classical Latin the *OLD* makes a distinction between *timeo ne* 'to be afraid that something will happen' (*OLD* s.v. 3a), and *timeo* + infinitive, either 'to be afraid to' (*OLD* s.v. 4a: e.g. Tib. 1.4.21 *nec iurare time*), or 'to be afraid of experiencing something' (*OLD* s.v. 4b: e.g. Sen. *Nat.* 6.32.8 *ego autem perire timeam* 'I would be afraid of dying'). Our example might fall into this last category, but equally it might be interpreted as equivalent to *timeo ne perdam*. Cf. *Conf.* 10 *erubesco et uehementer pertimeo denudare imperitiam meam*.

20 et non ego sed Christus dominus: *et* here tacks on an explanatory afterthought. For a list of such passages see Bieler (1993: I.139 (d) 'introducitur parenthesis uel epexegesis').

21 qui me imperauit ut: *impero* in classical Latin takes a dative of the person ordered. For the late use of the accusative of the person see *TLL* VII.1.584.34ff., 585.10ff., with further cross-references. The analogy for the construction is provided by *iubeo*. Bieler (1993: 175) says (obscurely) that *me* here 'is probably *mihi*', with a cross-reference to *quis me credit* at *Conf.* 10, on which (117) he states, 'perhaps foreshadows the unstressed pre-verbal pronoun of Romance (*Qui est-ce qui me croit?*)' (see the Introduction above). What he means by this is not entirely clear. There is a weakly attested early dative alternative to *mi*, namely *mei* (for which see *TLL* V.2.254.41ff., and the Introduction above), which, if it genuinely existed, might have undergone the early development *ei* > *e*, with the *e* representing the phoneme long close *e* (on which see e.g. Adams 2007: 52–64). Indeed a (doubtful) dative form *me* is attested occasionally early (see *TLL* V.2.255.8ff., the Introduction above, and also 6.12). Invoking (without any explanation) this old Latin phoneme (see above, p. 446) and mixing it up with Romance developments is very far-fetched. In fact dative- (or ablative-) governing verbs intermittently switch to an accusative complement throughout Latin. Cf. *Conf.* 4 *quem credimus et expectamus*. Contrast the hypercorrect dative for accusative at 59 *peto illi det mihi* (on *peto* + dat. see Bieler 1993: II.187; also E. Löfstedt 1956: I.205, id. 1959: 129).

22 ut uenirem esse cum illis: *uenio* + final infinitive instead of *uenio ut* (i.e. infinitive complementing a verb of motion, and not necessarily *uenio*, or alternatively a verb instigating motion such as *mitto*) is a construction not found in classical prose (apart from Varro: see below). It has an interesting distribution (early Latin, poetry, archaisers and then late Latin: for early examples, notably in Plautus, see *OLD* s.v. *uenio* 3b, Bennett 1910–14: I. 418–19, Kühner and Stegmann 1955: I.680–1, Hofmann and Szantyr 1965: 344–5, Lebek 1970: 220, Penney 1999: 253–4, Calboli (2009: 131–2), Adams and Vincent, forthcoming b).

There are republican examples in prose in two of the early annalists (Calpurnius Piso, *FRH* II.9.F29.5 *idem Cn. Flauius Anni filius dicitur ad collegam uenisse uisere aegrotum*, a passage written in the contrived 'simple' style of annals (see *FRH* III.209); Coelius, *FRH* II.15F9 *Sempronius Lilybaeo celocem in Africam mittit, uisere locum ubi exercitum exponat*), and in the classical period one in Varro (*Rust.* 2.1.1 *uisere uenissemus*). Note that the infinitive (*uisere*) is the same in Varro as that in the annalists, which suggests a formulaic expression: cf. Plaut. *Cas.* 855–6 *eximus ... uisere*, Ter. *Hec.* 189 *it uisere*, 345 *iit uidere*, Ph. 102 *eamus uisere*, Turp. 154 *progredior ... uisere*. In the second century AD, Apuleius and Gellius, both notorious archaisers, have several examples of the same infinitive (Apul. *Met.* 6.9 *interuisere uenisti*, Gell. 16.3.2 *aegrum isset uisere* (note *aegrum* here and *aegrotum* in Calpurnius above), 16.19.5 *proficiscitur ... uisere*).

There is another instance at *Conf.* 37 *ueneram . . . praedicare*, which Bieler (1993: II.167) ad loc. calls a 'Greek construction', noting that it is frequent in the Bible. There are no grounds for considering the early examples of the construction to represent a Grecism (with the possible exception of those in classical poetry), as it is quite widespread in writers who did not admit Greek syntax, but it is likely that in late Latin it was revived or extended under Greek influence, particularly in Christian writers as reflecting Bible transla-tions. In the Vulgate version of the NT the construction is constant. In the Gospels for example I have noted about nineteen examples of *uenio* + infinitive (e.g. Mt 2.2, 5.17 twice, 8.29, 9.13, 10.34, 10.35, in every case corresponding to the Greek), compared with about four examples of the verb complemented by *ut* and one complemented by *ad* + gerundive. It is a different matter in the Vulgate version of the OT. There *uenio ut* and *uenio ad* + gerundive are the norm (note e.g. 2 Sm 13.5 *cumque uenerit pater tuus ut uisitet te*, 2 Sm 13.6 *et quasi aegrotare coepit cumque uenisset rex ad uisitandum eum*, where the verb of the complement is of the type seen above as generating an infinitive in early Latin; note also *aegrotare* in the second passage), and the infinitival construction is only occasional (e.g. 3 Rg 10.1). The preference shown in the OT for *ut* must reflect its more literary character in the eyes of Jerome.

This use of the infinitive also turns up in bilingual school exercises (see Dickey 2012, 2015), corresponding to the same construction in the Greek versions. Some impulse might have been given in the late period to the construction in Latin through its use in bilingual schoolrooms. Note e.g. (from Dickey 2012):

Coll. Mon.–Eins. 2e processi . . . salutare / προῆλθον . . . ἀσπάσασθαι.
3e prodii . . . salutare / προῆλθον . . . ἀσπάσασθαι.
3 f eo salutare / ἀπέρχομαι ἀσπάσασθαι.

Noteworthy here is the phrase *eo salutare*, given that in this expression *eo* was earlier complemented by the supine of purpose *salutatum* (Plaut. *Bacch.* 347, Cic. *Att.* 2.7.2, Mart. 2.18.3).

Thus the construction was current in early Latin (prose as well as poetry), though perhaps subject to lexical restriction, then it seems to have faded, except among archaisers, but was later revived and extended, at least partly under Greek influence. Patrick's model would have been biblical.

23 custodierit me ab omni uia mala, ut non 'peccem coram illo': *ut non* looks like a final use (for *ne*), a late usage found for example in the *Vet. Lat.* (see Hofmann and Szantyr 1965: 535, 643–4), but, as is not unusual in apparent cases of *ut non* for *ne*, the construction might be interpreted as loosely consecutive ('if he shall keep me from every evil path, <u>in such a way that</u> I do not sin') (see below, text 42.4 for a usage of complementary type). Bieler (1993: II.175) for the phraseology compares 1 Reg (= 1 Sm) 25.39 *seruum suum custodiuit a malo* and Ps 118.101 *ab omni semita mala prohibui pedes meos* (Bieler quotes with *uia* for *semita*).

Conclusions

Conclusions to the discussions of Patrick will be found at the end of text 40.

40
PATRICK, *CONFESSIO* 48–9

Text

48 Vos scitis et deus qualiter inter uos conuersatus sum (1) 'a iuuentute mea' in fide ueritatis 'et in sinceritate cordis'. etiam ad gentes illas inter quas habito, ego fidem illis praestaui et praestabo (2). deus scit 'neminem' illorum 'circumueniri'. nec cogito, propter deum et ecclesiam ipsius, ne 'excitem' illis et nobis omnibus 'persecutionem' et ne per me blasphemaretur nomen domini; quia scriptum est: 'uae homini per quem nomen domini blasphematur.'

49 Nam 'etsi imperitus sum in omnibus', tamen conatus sum quippiam seruare me (3) etiam et fratribus Christianis et uirginibus Christi et mulieribus religiosis, quae mihi ultronea munuscula donabant (4) et super altare iactabant ex ornamentis suis (5) et iterum (6) reddebam illis et aduersus me scandaliza-bantur cur hoc faciebam (7); sed ego propter spem perennitatis (8), ut me in omnibus caute propterea conseruarem, ita ut <non> me in aliquo titulo infideli caperent uel ministerium seruitutis meae nec etiam in minimo incredulis locum darem infamare siue detractare.

Translation

48 You know and God knows how I have lived among you 'from my youth' in loyalty to the truth 'and in sincerity of heart'. Even to those pagans among whom I live – to them I have given and shall give loyalty. God knows that of them 'no one is cheated'. Nor do I contemplate such a thing, on account of God and His church, lest 'I stir up' for them and for all of us 'persecution', and lest the name of the Lord be blasphemed through me, for it is written: 'Woe upon the man through whom the name of the Lord is blasphemed.'

49 For 'although I am ignorant in all things', I have made some effort to preserve myself, and indeed for the sake of Christian brethren and virgins of Christ and religious women, who kept on freely presenting me with little gifts and throwing (putting?) some of their ornaments on the altar; and I gave them back again to them, and they were offended with me because I was doing this. But I, in hope of eternity, (was doing this) so as to preserve myself cautiously in every respect on this account, such that they would not catch me or the ministry of my service out under some pretext of infidelity, nor I provide even in the slightest respect an opportunity to unbelievers to defame or disparage me.

Commentary

1 uos scitis et deus qualiter inter uos conuersatus sum: following *scio*, the *qualiter*-clause might seem to be equivalent to an acc. + inf., but in such collocations *qualiter*, like *quomodo*, can usually be given its modal sense 'how, in what manner' (see Herman 1963: 44–5), and that is the case here. Cf. *Conf.* 35 *breuiter dicam qualiter ... deus saepe de seruitute liberauit.* On *qualiter* virtually indistinguishable from *quod* with verbs of saying in Merovingian Latin see Pei (1932: 292, 294–5).

2 ad gentes illas inter quas habito, ego fidem illis praestaui et praestabo: an interesting construction, containing a resumptive pronoun in the main clause (*illis*) that looks redundant. We have seen this sort of resumption going back to early Latin (see 2.25, 3.416, 5.7–8), but what is noteworthy here is the case usage. The verbs of giving are first, it seems (but see the next paragraph), complemented by *ad* + noun, and then the dative of the pronoun is used with the same function. An inflectional form with dative function lived on in the pronominal system even to some extent in Romance, whereas the dative was lost with nouns. There are late texts in which the dative is used with pronouns but the *ad*-construction sometimes with nouns (see Adams 2013: 286, and below, 50.45).

Also striking here is the fact that *praesto* is a verb of giving. In Romance *ad* survived as the exponent of the nominal indirect object with verbs of whatever semantic field, giving, saying and similar, whereas in most late Latin texts that attest the prepositional construction, it occurs mainly with verbs of saying (see Adams 2013: 278–88, and particularly Adams and de Melo, forthcoming). But this Latin evidence is not entirely satisfactory, because it tends to be in texts subject to the influence of either Greek or the Vulgate. In the Vulgate the *ad*-construction occurs almost exclusively with verbs of saying (see 43 Appendix), whether under Greek or, indirectly, Hebrew influence. Do we then have a hint here of Patrick's exposure to a form of submerged Latin in which *ad* did not merely complement *verba dicendi*? Certainly in some very late and early medieval texts *ad* was not only used with verbs of saying (see Pei 1932: 238, Adams 2013: 288, Adams and de Melo, forthcoming; also below, 50.45). Also of interest are possible conflations of construction, with *ad* governing a dative (see below, 47.8). One such cited by Svennung (1935: 337) shows a mixed construction with the same verb as that here: Diosc. 3 PA p. 421.21–2 *sanitatem prestat a danimalibus* (= *ad animalibus*) *et omnibus* (= *hominibus*), translating ἀνθρώποις καὶ ζῴοις. Could such an example represent an unconscious surfacing of the spoken construction in an author given to using the old literary construction in writing?

It has to be said, however, that there is another way of taking *ad* in our passage of Patrick, namely in the sense 'regarding' (see *OLD* s.v. 29b; also Bieler's translation, 1953: 36, 'Likewise, as regards the heathen'). Bieler is not consistent in his interpretation of this passage. Despite the above translation, in the commentary (1993: II.127) he refers to *Conf.* 48, 'where *ad* with the accusative of a noun corresponds to the dative of the pronoun (*illis*)', adding that such a distinction is normal 'in Merovingian Latin and the Romance languages'.

Another possible case of *ad* for the dative is at *Epist.* 13 (cited by Mohrmann 1961a: 17) *nesciunt miseri uenenum letale cibum porrigunt ad amicos et filios suos. Porrigo* can be complemented by *ad* (examples may be found at *TLL* X.1. 2758–9), usually it seems of stretching something out towards/in the direction of someone or something (e.g. Livy 30.21.7 *uoces manus ad caelum porrigentium auditas*). When an object is held in the hands and offered or given to someone the dative is normal (see the comment at *TLL* X.1.2760.3f. and some of the examples that follow), but it is hard to be sure that an *ad*-expression such as that here did not have a nuance in the mind of the writer that set it apart from the dative. On the other hand this sentence of *Epist.* 13 concludes with the following: *sicut Eua non intellexit quod utique mortem tradidit uiro suo*. Here in a parallel metaphorical context the verb of handing over is complemented by a dative, and it is not obvious that the earlier *ad* differs in function.

Bieler (1993: II.126–7) raises the question whether Patrick uses *ad* for the dative at *Conf.* 13 *genti ad quam caritas Christi transtulit et donauit me*. This is not a convincing example. *Transfero* is regularly in classical Latin used with prepositions, most notably *in* + acc., but also *ad* (e.g. Ulp. *Dig.* 36.1.21(20) *ad heredem suum transtulerat legatum*).

Bieler goes on to liken an example of *ad* at *Conf.* 38 to our present instance: *ut clerici ubique illis ordinarentur ad plebem nuper uenientem ad credulitatem*, 'that clerics were ordained for them everywhere, for a people just coming to the faith', Bieler 1953: 32). It is true that the dative pronoun *illis* is resumed appositionally by *ad*, but there the parallel ends, as neither the dative nor the preposition expresses the indirect object. These are final uses ('for their benefit'), and *ad* is in alternation with the dative in this function even in classical Latin (see Adams 2013: 291–2).

I return to the present passage. *Gentes* here has its familiar late meaning found in Christian writers, 'pagans' (see e.g. E. Löfstedt 1959: 74–5). This is usually a collective plural (see *TLL* VI.2.1862.42ff.), originating from the plural use of 'foreigners' as seen from a Roman perspective (i.e. opposed to the *populus*: see *TLL* VI.1.1850.32ff.). There is however a different and particularly interesting use of *gentes* at *Conf.* 18: *sed uerumtamen ab illis speraui uenire in fidem Iesu Christi, quia gentes erant.* This is not a collective but a particularising plural ('because they were pagans'), of a small group of pagans (the sailors with whom Patrick was hoping to sail to Britain). Behind this usage lies a singular use of *gens*, of an individual pagan. This is quoted first from the *Vetus Latina* (*TLL* VI.2.1864.40ff.): Mt 18.17 (cod. *e*) *si ecclesiam contempserit, sit tibi quasi gens aut publicanus* (the Vulgate has *ethnicus*, from the Greek). A few other examples are cited by the *TLL* from Christian writers. It is of note that in one of the Bath curse tablets the word is used in the singular of a single pagan (*Tab. Sulis* 98.1 *seu gens seu Chistianus ... furauerit* (see Adams 1992a: 10–11). The use had clearly reached Britain in Christian circles. Here for once (but see further the Conclusions below) we can parallel a usage in Patrick in a popular British document of much the same period, but his source is still likely to have been biblical or ecclesiastical Latin.

The classical perfect form is *praestiti*, but *praestaui* is attested sometimes in late texts (e.g. *Mul. Chir.* 458 *praestasse*: see *TLL* X.2.913.46ff., without this example and citing juristic and a few other late texts; note too Lundström 1948: 41). By contrast at *Conf.* 23 Patrick has *praestitit*.

3 conatus sum quippiam seruare me: this adverbial neuter *quippiam* is also found at *Conf.* 34 *ita ut imitarem quippiam illos.* It is an old literary usage going back to Plautus (see *OLD* s.v. *quispiam*[2] 1c).

4 quae mihi ultronea munuscula donabant: the placement of the dative pronoun *mihi* should be noted. Not only is the pronoun preposed (i.e. before the verb), but it comes early in the sentence in the 'Wackernagel' position. Usually in Patrick object pronouns come after the verb (see above, 39.8). But in relative clauses containing an object pronoun, direct or indirect, throughout the *Confessio* the pronoun is regularly placed in second position attached to the relative: cf. 3 *gratiam quam mihi dominus praestare dignatus est*, 34 *qui me fidelem seruauit*, 34 *qui me seruauit*, 34 *qui mihi †tanta diuinitate cooperasti†*, 34 *quicquid mihi euenerit siue bonum siue malum*, 34 *qui mihi ostendit*, 34 *qui me audierit*, 38 *qui mihi tantam gratiam donauit*, 43 *qui mihi protestatur*, 43 *qui me imperauit*, 45 *quae mihi a Domino monstrata sunt*, 46 *quod mihi ostensum fuerat*, 47 *qui mihi crediderunt* (fourteen examples). There are few exceptions: 60 *qui adorant eum*. 31 belongs in a different category: *quos ego retuli uobis*. When there is a first person verb in a relative clause *ego* is often given the second position by Patrick (cf. above, 38.51).

In six of the examples just quoted the relative clause contains words in addition to the object pronoun and the verb, which are inserted before the verb: the pronoun is genuinely in the Wackernagel position.

Wackernagel placement of the object pronoun is not however regular in other types of subordinate clauses. In *Conf*. 34 for example, where there is a series of relative clauses containing the pronoun in second position (see above), note by contrast *ita ut hodie offeram illi sacrificium* and *ita ut imitarem quippiam illos*. See also 19 *ut hodie confidenter cibum mittat uobis*, 38 *ut clerici ubique illis ordinarentur ad plebem*, 43 *si ... custodierit me*, 53 *ut det mihi postmodum*, 55 *ut hoc mihi praestaret*, 57 *ut donaret mihi bibere*, 58 *ut det mihi perseuerantiam*, 58 *ut reddam illi testem*.

There are interesting distinctions at work here. The pronoun placement in relative clauses looks too subtle to represent a taught rule. Patrick had imbibed a sense that *mihi* in particular should be attached to the relative pronoun, but from where had he acquired this sense, from writings or native Latin speech?

Here are some figures from two contrasting texts, Cicero and the Vulgate, for the incidence of *qui mihi* as compared with *qui ... mihi*. In the whole of Cicero there are eighty-one instances of *qui mihi*. By contrast here are some figures for separation of the two elements (I am grateful to Giuseppe Pezzini for information used here):

7 qui X mihi
2 qui X X mihi
3 qui X X X mihi.

Thus juxtaposition outnumbers separations by means of one, two or three words by 81:12. Nor are all cases of separation significant, because sometimes *mihi* is in second position in a colon. There is evidence here for this manifestation of Wackernagel's law in the classical period.

In the whole of the Vulgate there are only seven instances of *qui mihi*. Here are the figures for separation:

31 qui X mihi (normally X is the main verb)
20 qui X X mihi
1 qui X X X mihi.

Separation outnumbers juxtaposition by 52:7. Patrick could hardly have picked up the pattern *qui mihi* from the Vulgate (see also above, 38.57).

The evidence of the Vulgate is not relevant to the question whether Wackernagel's law was still operating by about the fourth century, because it is a work that is variously influenced by both Hebrew and Greek.

Patrick must either have been familiar with the pattern from Latin speech, or have acquired it from written works other than the Bible. As it happens there is some contemporary evidence from Britain itself, in the Bath curse tablets (*Tab. Sulis*), which are written in a variety of Latin well down the educational scale, and are dated roughly to the fourth or fifth century. In these *qui* is regularly followed immediately by an object pronoun, with hardly any separations. *Qui mihi* occurs five times (4.1, 7. ii.4, 32.5, 98.9, 107.1) but *qui ... mihi* never. There are also six other instances of *qui* with an object pronoun attached (4.3, 5.3, 38.5, 44.5, 66.3, 100.2), and only one case of separation (54.4). Further evidence from Britain, but several centuries earlier, is found in the Vindolanda writing tablets (*Tab. Vindol.*). In these I have noted five instances of *qui* + object pronoun, with no cases of separation. *Qui mihi* itself occurs at 311.i.6, *qui me* at 710.3, and *qui tibi* at 311.i.9, 661.4, 707.1.

There does seem to be evidence here that the Wackernagel pattern *qui mihi* persisted in ordinary Latin well into the late Roman period, and indeed in Britain itself. The possibility cannot be ruled out that Patrick had not merely observed the order from reading late texts but that he was familiar with it from Latin speech, whether heard on the Continent or in Britain itself. The phrase *qui mihi* might have had almost formulaic status.

It would however be of interest to have statistics from a wide range of late texts for the incidence of *qui mihi* versus *qui ... mihi*, and the conclusions offered here can only be tentative. It is at least worth noting that in the *Itinerarium Antonini Placentini* and *Anonymus Valesianus II*, both of the sixth century, the pattern *qui mihi* is much in evidence (see Adams 1976a: 131–2, but without statistics).

For discussion of the significance of these relative clauses see the Conclusions below.

ultronea: the adjective is first in Apuleius and in Christian Latin is in Cyprian (see Bieler 1993: II.181).

5 super altare iactabant ex ornamentis suis: *ex ornamentis suis* 'some of their ornaments' is a partitive phrase standing as object (for which see 4.3, 31.12, 38.51). On *iacto* 'throw', the regular term in late Latin with this meaning, see 27.10, and index, s.v. *iacto*. The verb also had a weakened meaning, 'put' (*TLL* VII.1.61.70ff.), which may be intended here.

6–7 iterum reddebam: the adverb reinforces the idea expressed by the pre-verb. This form of pleonasm goes back to early Latin (see index, 'pleonasm, of adverb and verbal prefix').

7 aduersus me scandalizabantur cur hoc faciebam: *scandalizo* 'offend' is a word that is not attested in Latin of the period covered by the *OLD*, and which in Greek turns up in the Bible. It is common in the NT of the Vulgate (twenty-eight times, seven times in the OT): e.g. Mt 5.29 *quod si oculus tuus dexter scandalizat te, erue eum.*

Cur has shifted here from its interrogative meaning 'why?' to a causal meaning, 'for, because'. The semantic change replicates that in *quare*, which in the secondary meaning produces Fr. *car.* An early example of *quare* in this meaning is at Pompeii (*CIL* IV.2421 *Rufa ita uale quare bene felas*) (on *quare* see E. Löfstedt 1911: 323–4, commenting on *Per. Aeth.* 40.2 *arguit Thomam, quare incredulus fuisset,* Herman 1957, Wackernagel 1969: I.783, Väänänen 1966: 126). In an example such as that from the *Peregrinatio* just cited it is easy to see how the usage might have developed from the reporting of a direct question: 'he accused Thomas: why had he been disbelieving?'

For *cur* approaching this sense see Cic. *Att.* 3.13.2 *quod me saepe accusas, cur hunc meum casum tam grauiter feram,* translated by Shackleton Bailey (1965–70: II.29) 'You repeatedly take me to task for bearing what has happened so hard' (see E. Löfstedt 1911: 324). Note too Quint. 1.3.15 *nunc fere neglegentia paedagogorum sic emendari uidetur ut pueri non facere quae recta sunt cogantur, sed cur non fecerint puniantur* ('As it is, we try to make amends for the negligence of the *paedagogi* not by forcing boys to do the right thing but by punishing them for not having done it', Russell, Loeb). Colson (1924: 36) ad loc. expresses some doubt about *cur* here, but does cite several other interesting cases, remarking that in all 'the idea of interrogation may be latent'. See also Tac. *Ann.* 15.60.3 alongside 15.61.1 (*conqueror + cur, quod*). In late Latin *cur* is often used in the sense it has in Patrick, in e.g. Jerome (e.g. *Epist.* 27.1, p. 17 Labourt, 37.4, p. 67, 46.3, p. 102, 52.6, p. 180; cf. *quare* at e.g. 49.15, p. 140) and Lucifer of Cagliari (see the index of Hartel 1886: 358 s.v. *cur* (= *quia*)).

8 sed ego propter spem perennitatis: this sentence as it stands is incomplete, as the *ita ut*-clause following is left hanging and there is no main clause. Bieler (1993: II.182) writes: 'After *perennitas* we have probably to assume ellipse of *hoc faciebam*', and it is true that to add these words would restore sense. But there is a difference between a deliberate ellipse (as e.g. when an epic poet leaves out a verb of saying) and an anacoluthon, and it is likely that Patrick lost the logic of the rather long sentence.

Conclusions

I comment first on some attitudes to the Latin of Patrick.

'Patrick is *sui generis*'

Bieler (1952: 65) states: 'Too long has the Latinity of St. Patrick been treated as something *sui generis*.' This is very apt. If we did not know who wrote the two works attributed to Patrick and knew nothing of their geographical origin we would not be able to assign them to any particular region of the later Roman Empire. There is virtually nothing about the Latin that could be described as specifically British or Irish, though we have been able to parallel two features in the Bath curse tablets (see on *qui mihi, gentes*). It is typical late Christian Latin, heavily influenced by the language of Bible translations, written by someone not completely adept at literary style, but nevertheless not without stylistic pretensions. It has idiolectal features, but every piece of Latin has, and those in Patrick do not point to an Irishness or Britishness (cf. Bieler 1952: 75 n. 51 'Nothing in Patrick's Latin points definitely to one province of the Empire rather than to another').

'Patrick wrote as he spoke'

According to Thompson (1985: 43), 'what Patrick writes is not far removed from the Latin which he spoke'. This assertion is very unconvincing. Occasionally Patrick himself puts simple speech into the mouth of a humble character, as twice at *Conf.* 18, but his own discourse, though containing many late and substandard usages, some of them with outcomes in the Romance languages, has an artificiality (see the next section of these Conclusions), acquired from various sources.

For example, Patrick uses a large number of abstract verbal nouns of the type rarely heard in speech, such as *retributio, correptio, agnitio* (*Conf.* 3), *qualitas* (6), *infantia* (9), *excusatio, praesumptio, captura, imperitia, breuitas* (10), *mensura, reprehensio, consolatio* (14), *captiuitas* (15), *splendor, grauitudo* (20), *conculcatio* (26), *anxietas, incredulitas* (27) etc. (see the list at Bieler 1993: I.126, arranged by suffix).

He also has numerous unusual polysyllabic adverbs (see Bieler 1993: I.124 for a list of 'aduerbia minus usitata'), such as *fiducialiter* (*Conf.* 14), a term whose use in late Latin derives from Bible versions, both those of the *Vetus Latina* and of the Vulgate. See *TLL* VI.1.702.8ff. 'totus usus fluxisse videtur ex sacra scriptura, in cuius vetere versione Latina nec non in Hieronymiana hoc adverbium saepius invenitur'. *Inenarrabiliter* (4) is rare, and confined to late Christian writers (*TLL* VII.1.1294.10ff.). *Incunctanter* (37) is more common, but again late and mainly Christian. *Inlicitate* (44) by contrast (on which see Bieler 1993: II.176) is a word that is not even registered by the *TLL*. Fifteen of the adverbs listed by Bieler loc. cit. have the suffix -*iter*.

'Patrick's Latin is severely limited'

Hanson (1968: 163) stresses the limitations of Patrick's Latin. He 'had no literary devices, no store of syntactical variations, no reserves of vocabulary, no art at all, in using Latin'. Every aspect of this assertion must be corrected.

As far as absence of 'reserves of vocabulary' is concerned, within numerous semantic fields Patrick displays considerable lexical diversity. Both *taceo* (*Conf.* 3) and *sileo* (11) are used (I give examples not full lists in this paragraph). As verbs of fearing there are *timeo* (9), *metuo* (17) and *pertimeo* (10). As well as the mundane *laetus* (32) we find *gaudibundus* at 24, a word hardly attested in Latin (examples in Apuleius, Cyprian and Virgilius Maro Grammaticus). Many verbs of the semantic field 'say' occur, not all of them mundane: *inquit* (7), *dico* (18), *exclamo* (18), *respondeo* (18), *testor* (11), *loquor* (18), *memoratus* 'mentioned' (29), *narro* (46), *insinuo* and *designo*, both in our selection, *effor* (33), an archaism, *praefor* (10), *expono* (61), *refero* (31). Twice (24, 25) *effitior* is used in the form *effitiatus est*, translated by Bieler (1953) as 'he spoke'. Bieler (1993: II.152) takes *effitior* to be a coinage based on *infitior*; the *TLL* has an entry for *effiteor* (< *fateor*) with one example from *Not. Tir.*, but has no entry for *effitior*. Patrick uses a range of abstract nouns interchangeably in reference to his own inadequacy: *imperitia* (10), *inscientia* (11), *insipientia* (46), *modicitas* (50), *ignobilitas* (56), *ignorantia* (62). Both verbs meaning 'promise' (*promitto, polliceor*) are used, at 38 and 39. There is a variety of verbs for bestowing, granting: *praesto* (in one of our extracts), *dono* (38), *largior* (33), *offero* (37), *distribuo* (50), *do* (52), *erogo* (53). Both *seruitium* (42) and *seruitus* (49) are found, and not with any consistent distinction of meaning. *Ministerium* at 49 (with *seruitutis* dependent on it) is of much the same meaning. So there are *scio* and *sapio* (both e.g. at 2), and *cuncti* (32) as well as *omnes* (for the distinctiveness of the use of *cuncti* at this period see Lundström 1948: 109). *Litterae* ('epistle') is used (*Epist.* 21 *gerulus litterarum*: on the expression see Bieler 1993: II.209), as well as the more common *epistola* (the usual word in imperial Latin). Patrick has *nequeo*, a literary word, three times, and *non possum* six or seven (Bieler 1952: 82, 1993: I.134). *Desidero*, *cupio* and *opto* all occur several times (Bieler 1952: 81).

Patrick also often pairs synonyms or near-synonyms, a very old manner-ism, as at *Conf.* 4 *credentes et oboedientes,* 8 *se . . . subtrahere uel abscondere,* 9 *instructus atque eruditus,* 10 *spiritus . . . et animus,* 12 *sustulit me et . . . adleuauit,* 13 *audite et scrutamini,* 15 *post aerumnas et tantas moles (aerum-na,* an old literary word (Quint. 8.3.26), is listed just six times from the Vulgate by Fischer 1977), 15 *numquam speraui neque cogitaui,* 37 *cum fletu et lacrimis,* 37 *nullo modo consensi neque adquieui,* 40 *bene et diligenter,* 40 *praemonet et docet,* 40 *ammonet et docet,* 45 *rideat . . . et insultet,* 46 *narrabant et dicebant,* 47 *ad roborandam et confirmandam fidem,* 55 *miser et infelix.* At *Epist.* 18 two synonyms are found in asyndeton bimembre, an artificial structure (*mendacibus periuris;* the biblical source does not have the phrase; could however *mendacibus* be intended here nominally and *periuris* adjectivally?).

Of interest above is the phrase *instructus atque eruditus,* for which there seems to be no exact parallel in Bible translations. The literary connective *atque* is noteworthy, as it is not normal for Patrick (only one other example in the *Confessio,* 4 *iudex uiuorum atque mortuorum,* in a 'credal formula': Bieler 1952: 83). The Brepols database turns up just two other examples of the collocation in this form. One is in Columella (11.3.65 *instructum atque eruditum omni opere rustico*), which Patrick would not have known. The other is in Orosius (7.13.2 *libris de Christiana religione conpositis instructus atque eruditus*), a fifth-century writer who was a pupil of Augustine. Otherwise the two adjectives sometimes occur together in late Latin, but without an expressed connective, as in the sermon of Augustine edited by Étaix (1976), p. 48 line 245 *sic imbutus, sic instructus, sic eruditus ex lege dei,* ps.-Aur. Vict. *Epit. de Caes.* 20.8 *Latinis litteris sufficienter instructus, Graecis sermonibus eruditus.* Bieler (1993: II.115) compares 2 Tim 3.16–17 *ad erudiendum in iustitia . . . ad omne opus bonum instructus,* but this bears little resemblance to Patrick's expression. Had Patrick picked up the phrase from an ecclesiastical writer, or did he form it himself, in keeping with a taste for combinations of synonyms? Bieler (1952: 83) says without explanation that it is a 'parody of literary style', but it seems most likely to me that Patrick saw it in an ecclesiastical text. The phrase makes it clear that Patrick was not merely writing biblical pastiche, and that he had a literary sense.

Also of note above is *post aerumnas et tantas moles.* The combination is not biblical. *Moles* in the metaphorical sense 'labor, negotium, difficultas' is an old literary usage, sometimes occurring in late, including Christian, writers (*TLL* VIII.1340.12ff.), but the only example that I have found (*TLL* VIII.1340.55) even remotely resembling that here is at Ruricius *Epist.* 2.8 (*CSEL* 21, p. 382.

15–16) *aerumnarum mole depressi*. Patrick was not entirely derivative in his use of artificial Latin.

There are as many as fifty-one words used by Patrick that are not biblical, i.e. not found it seems in either the Vulgate or versions of the *Vetus Latina* (see Bieler 1952: 78).

Bieler (1952: 77) gives some statistics in an attempt to assess Patrick's 'word power'. His vocabulary numbers about 1,341 words, but more than half the text 'is made up of only 74 vocables'. The vocabulary of the Vulgate, we are told for comparison, totals about 7,000 words. These figures are meaningless. Patrick's texts are very short, and the Vulgate is very long. Moreover the subject matter of the texts is limited. Patrick's command of the Latin lexicon is best assessed from his use of individual lexemes, not from pointless word counts.

There is also a good deal of syntactic variation. For example, as we have seen, for reported speech et sim. Patrick uses clauses introduced by *quod, quia* or *ut* (for the last see *Conf.* 18 and the examples at Bieler 1993: I.141), the acc. + inf. (sometimes), parenthetical verbs of saying and the like, and direct quoted speech. He uses the infinitive of purpose under some circumstances, but also purpose clauses introduced by *ut*. The syntactic inconcinnity at 13 (*cum humilitate et ueraciter*) is of a type that would be noted as typically stylised if it were in Tacitus.

Patrick exploits sound effects, in a way that would be considered artistic in another writer (and is artistic in Patrick). Note for example *Conf.* 16 *fides augebatur et spiritus agebatur*, where the coordinated verbs show homoeoteleuton, alliteration, identity of length and just a single letter distinguishing them. At 55 (*mihi melius conuenit paupertas et calamitas quam diuitiae et diliciae*) there are two pairs of coordinated nouns in a contrast. Each pair has homoeoteleuton. The second pair is alliterative (for which pair in late Christian Latin see Wölfflin 1884: 383), and the two words have identity of syllabic structure. At 16 (*ante lucem excitabar ad orationem per niuem per gelu per pluuiam*) there is an old type of asyndeton, with each noun preceded by the same preposition (cf. e.g. Plaut. *Cas.* 664 *sub arcis, sub tectis latentes*, *Most.* 392 *cum hac cum istac*). The tricolon is also of ascending length. Patrick had something of a taste for asyndeta, sometimes with just two members, and not infrequently these display other artistic touches as well (for a list of examples see Bieler 1993: I.146). At 46 (*qui saepe indulsit insipientiae meae, neglegentiae meae*) there is a three-syllable homoeoteleuton in the two nouns (which are in the category of 'near-synonyms'), a five-syllable homoeoteleuton in the two phrases, and epiphora as well (*meae* repeated at the ends of the phrases). At *Epist.* 5 there is an asyndetic pair with a three-syllable homoeoteleuton (*patricida fratricida*), at *Epist.* 18 a pair of virtual synonyms (*mendacibus periuris*: see above) and at *Epist.* 17 a type with a privative adjective (*horrendum ineffabile*). All of these are old literary types.

There is no need to labour the literary pretensions of Patrick further. In Bieler's lists may be found cases of hyperbaton, chiasmus, ascending cola, inconcinnity and variation, etymological figures, alliteration, litotes, anaphora etc. (1993: I.145–50).

'Living Latin'

The main question to consider here is whether there is any sign of a spoken 'living Latin' (to use Mohrmann's phrase) or 'vulgar Latin' (so Bieler and others) in Patrick's writings. Those such as Bieler who refer to 'pre-/proto-Romance' features are implying the same, that Patrick was influenced by real Latin speech.

We know little about the Latin spoken by native Britons at this time,[1] despite the claims, so easy to find in the literature, that they 'spoke an old-fashioned variety', that 'all educated Britons spoke Latin', that 'Patrick's Latin was or was not basically "Continental"', and so on. There is (see texts 21, 32–7) more Latin from Britain available to us now than there was at the time of Jackson's book (1953), in the form of curse tablets and writing tablets, but a good deal of it was definitely written by outsiders to Britain (the Vindolanda tablets), and there is no certainty either that all the curse tablets, from Bath, Uley and elsewhere, were the work of native Britons. The Germanic term for 'man', *baro*, in Bath tablets and elsewhere is suggestive of outsiders (on the word see 35.10–11). Nor does the evidence of curse tablets support the notion of a local 'archaising' Vulgar Latin (see below, 37 Conclusions).

The Roman inscriptions of Britain are even less satisfactory. They are limited in extent and not rich linguistically. Moreover inscriptions from all over the Empire were often set up by mobile groups such as traders and soldiers rather than by local populations.

Those making claims of the type referred to above are usually basing themselves on speculation rather than evidence. As a speculation without

---

[1] According to Greene (1968: 76) the 'common word *planta* [i.e. *OLD planta*[2] "young shoot detached from the parent-plant"] . . . has been borrowed into both Welsh and Irish in the meaning "children"', and he goes on to assert: 'the important thing to note is that this colloquial extension is not attested from any Latin document; British Latin *planta* must have been a word like modern English *kids*'. This assertion is false: see now *TLL* X.1.2326.52, noting from late texts a metaphorical use '(de) iuuenibus uel aliquid incipientibus'.

foundation I would single out Bieler's listing (1952: 75) of the spelling *pos tergum* (*Conf.* 46) among features that 'might reflect colloquial habits which Patrick acquired among those "brethren in Gaul"'. We know that even Cicero would not have pronounced the *t* of *post* before *tergum*, as he tells us himself that he would say *posmeridianas* rather than *postmeridianas* (*Orat.* 157), and the consonantal simplification there generated by the following *m* would be even more likely to occur before a word beginning with *t* (see *TLL* X.2.156.70ff.). Here was a general speech habit, tied neither to a region nor to a social class nor to a period (see further Adams 2013: 153, 156). Cicero would not himself have written *pos tergum*, but the spelling became widespread (see *TLL* X.2.156.80ff.) under the influence of a pronunciation that was normal. We do not know whether Patrick spelt the phrase in this way himself, but whether or not he did so is irrelevant to the sources of his spoken Latin. Those in late antiquity writing *pos tergum* were probably not analysing the sounds of their or anyone else's speech but recalling a written example.

Expressions such as 'living Latin', 'vulgar Latin', 'pre-Romance' are not technical terms with an agreed meaning, though they are thrown around as if they were. Some distinctions must be made.

I start with another strong claim made by Bieler (1993: I.39): 'The language of Confessio and Epistola, as we read them to-day, is so typically "pre-Romance" as would be unthinkable in Ireland after the fifth century.' We have already seen (39.8) that one of the 'pre-Romance' features advanced by Bieler (the use of possessives) is no such thing. There are linguistic phenomena in Patrick that were to survive in Romance languages, but how did he acquire them, from written texts or from Latin speech? Consider the following example.

It was noted above (39.6) that *proximo* 'approach' might survive in Old French, if one follows *REW* 6794. It could then be a pre-Romance usage admitted by Patrick. But to describe it as that and to imply that he knew it from speech would be far-fetched, because the verb is found in the *Vetus Latina* in this sense and also scattered about in Christian texts. It is from Bible translations and possibly theological works that Patrick would have known it.

The Latin Bible is full of phenomena that lived on into Romance, and as Patrick was an attentive student of various versions he could not help but reproduce some features of living Latin. In this class belong *unus* anticipatory of an indefinite article, *uenio* + infinitive of purpose, conflation of *eius* etc. and *suus* with reflexive and non-reflexive meanings, *quod-/quia*-clauses for the acc. + inf., hanging nominatives, the partitive use of *ex*-expressions standing as object of a verb, *cur* with causal meaning. Another, which does not come up in our selection, is the use of the infinitive in relative clauses. Note *Conf.* 18 *locutus sum ut haberem unde nauigare cum illis.* For this construction in late Latin see Adams (2013: 770–1). It is found in non-Christian texts such as the *Historia Augusta* (*Maximin.* 29.5), but is also well represented in the *Vetus Latina* and some Christian writers (Augustine, Gregory the Great). Bieler (1952: 67 n. 12) refers to it as a 'typically Romance construction' (and it does survive), but that is to disregard the likelihood that Patrick took it from written texts. Incidentally, the infinitive here in a relative clause following a main verb that is not negated (*haberem*) is unusual, but not without parallel (see Hofmann and Szantyr 1965: 539, and Adams 2013: 771 for instances in an African poem of the third century).

Clearly what we must consider is whether Patrick has any usages that (a) cannot be explained away as deriving from biblical and Christian texts, and (b) are candidates, because of some special feature, for the designation 'living Latin'. The issues that have to be faced may be illustrated by two contrasting cases.

First, the use of *is* versus *ille*. Like other late writers and a few earlier ones Patrick loosely foreshadows the later history of Latin into Romance, in that he prefers *ille* to *is* as the third person pronoun (without contrastive deixis). However, the predominance of *ille* in his work is not as marked as it is even in some much earlier low-register texts, such as the letters of Terentianus and the speeches of freedmen in Petronius. In some case forms, even the phonetically weak accusative singular, he prefers *is*. The incidence of the pronouns in his work does not accord with that of the book of the Vulgate which we considered (38.53), nor could it derive from living speech. It either comes from the *Vetus Latina* (see 38.53), or is quirky (see 39.8), a term we have used of one or two other of his linguistic choices, as of *pergo* in preference to *uado*.

The second case is that of pronoun placement in relative clauses, which is a different matter. We saw that Patrick's taste for juxtaposition of the object pronoun with the relative (*qui mihi ...*) meets criterion (a) above, in that juxtaposition is rare in the Vulgate, and he cannot have acquired it from there. Some additional figures supporting such a conclusion happen to be provided by Ramsden (1964: 43) from sample passages of the *Vetus Latina*. Ramsden was not specifically concerned with juxtaposition of pronoun and relative, but with anteposition versus postposition of the object pronoun in relation to the verb in relative clauses. In three of his Latin specimen texts (*Cena Trimalchionis*, the letters of Terentianus, *Peregrinatio Aetheriae*) the pronoun mainly precedes the verb, whereas in *Vetus Latina* versions of Matthew and Mark (for those used see Ramsden 1964: 28 n. 2) the pronoun more often follows (cf. above, 38.57). Here is further evidence for the distinctiveness of relative clauses containing an object pronoun in Latin Bible translations, and their separateness from those in Patrick.

As for criterion (b), some different findings of Ramsden are also suggestive. In his selection of early Romance texts anteposition of the pronoun (before the verb) in relative clauses is regular, with no exceptions (Ramsden 1964: 55–6). The pronoun is still in the old Wackernagel second-position in clauses in which it immediately precedes the verb and follows the relative (pattern *qui mihi* V: see the examples quoted by Ramsden at 56, such as *La chanson de Sainte Foy* (11th c.) 197 *Deus, qu'm guardestz de tot mal vez*).

In this Old French example the clause contains some other words (a prepositional expression), which are placed after the verb. We have moved on a little here from the common Latin pattern, whereby the verb in a relative clause is in final position, the object pronoun in the Wackernagel position, and other words are between the pronoun and the verb. This early order is seen e.g. in Patrick himself (*Conf.* 45 *quae mihi a domino monstrata sunt*). In Romance by contrast the object pronoun is constantly juxtaposed with the verb, which is the outcome of a tendency that can be seen in late Latin and some low-register texts from quite early on, namely that separation of pronoun and verb declines in frequency (see Adams 1976a: 130, id. 1977a: 69–70). So it is in the Romance example above that the pronoun retains the Wackernagel position, but the verb has moved leftwards to join it, which entails a relocation of other elements to follow the verb. Patrick himself has this Romance pattern three times in *Conf.* 34: *qui me fidelem seruauit 'in die temptationis' meae* (here *me fidelem* is a unit, and *fidelem* is not genuinely an intrusive element separating the pronoun from the verb); *qui me seruauit 'ab omnibus angustiis meis'; quicquid mihi euenerit siue bonum siue malum*.

We thus see a mixture of stages in Patrick's relative clauses containing an object pronoun. Almost invariably the pronoun is in second position. Sometimes other words in the clause are placed between the pronoun and verb, which produces a distinctive Wackernagel placement, in that the pronoun is not only in second position but separated from the verb. On the other hand there are cases where other elements in the clause do not separate the pronoun from the verb but are postponed, and this is the above Romance pattern. The mixture of orders is consistent with a transitional stage of the language, with the old pattern coexisting with but giving way to the new. It is hard to see how this subtle blend could be due to imitation by Patrick of tendencies he had observed in written texts. Here he may indeed reflect 'living Latin'.

Are there any other usages of a type that may have come from contact with spoken varieties? One or two suggestive cases are at least worthy of mention.

First, Patrick may have one or two instances of *ad* for the indirect object, as at *Conf.* 48, with a verb from the semantic field 'give' (*praesto*). In biblical Latin *ad* is often used in this function with verbs of saying, but not with verbs of giving, and this example does not look biblical. The sentence at 48 also seems to anticipate Romance in that it has a contrast between *ad* with a noun and the dative with a pronoun. There are however uncertainties about how to take *ad* in this context, and the other examples too are problematic.

Second, Patrick's ways of reporting speech are interesting. That he uses *quod*- and *quia*-constructions is neither here nor there. What is more striking is that, unlike most late authors, whether Christian or not, he hardly ever uses the acc. + inf., and that he often has parataxis, which was undoubtedly a construction of spoken Latin, though it does find its way into literature.

Third, the ellipse of a verb of going can be paralleled in colloquial texts, such as the letters of Cicero, but in Patrick the omission might not be idiomatic but a slip or anacoluthon.

There is nothing else worth mentioning under this heading. To an over-whelming extent the substandard and proto-Romance elements in Patrick's Latin might derive from a close reading of Bible translations and other Christian writings.

Biblical Latin

The most important influence on Patrick's Latin was biblical, both directly and indirectly through Christian writers influenced by the Bible translations. That fact emerges from every page of Bieler's commentary. *Genetiua, improperia* and *proximo* are all associated with the Old Latin versions. Notable is the particularising plural *gentes* of a small group of pagans present in the scene. *Gens* 'pagan' in the singular is not only in the *Vetus Latina* but also in a Bath curse tablet. Biblical influence is to be seen not only in the use of individual lexemes but more generally in syntactic features. The redundant use of a resumptive pronoun in a relative clause is ultimately a Hebraism, which found its way from there into Greek and Latin Bible versions. Relative-correlative constructions are quite widespread at all periods of Latin, but they are a feature of the Greco-Latin Bible in gnomic utterances, and Patrick might have noticed them there. There is no need to dwell further on biblical Latin in Patrick; in the previous section we listed some proto-Romance usages that Patrick probably knew from the Bible.

Bilingualism

One final topic that ought to be mentioned, though it did not come up in our selection, is Patrick's bilingualism and the possible influence on his Latin of Old Irish. As Bieler (1952: 73) puts it, the evidence is meagre. An interesting item is the phrase *sugere mammellas* at *Conf.* 18, for which see Bieler (1993: II. 139–40). This comes from the *Vetus Latina* (Os 14.1 cod. *k*), but alludes to an Irish rite of admission to friendship, = *dide a ciche-som*. Thus the phrase is pure Latin with a Latin source rather than a manifestation of bilingual interference, but is made to bear a cultural allusion. One or two other similar cases have been noted (see also Bieler 1993: II.147–8); for a few other possible items see also Greene (1968: 78).

Mohrmann's discussion of bilingualism (1961a: 9–12) concentrates on alleged infelicities of expression in Patrick that supposedly reveal him to be a second-language user. I find none of these conclusive. Nor is Mohrmann convincing when she suggests (1961a: 12–15) that Patrick was dictating his text. Ellipses and anacolutha can be found in many literary texts, and with a variety of determinants.

41
FROM ONE OF THE ALBERTINI TABLETS (*TABLETTES ALBERTINI* XIV.1–9), OF THE LATE FIFTH CENTURY

Introduction

The Albertini tablets are writing tablets on wood, numbering forty-five. They were discovered in 1928 on the border of Algeria and Tunisia 100 km south of Tebessa and 65 km west of Gafsa (Tripolitana), and are dated to the years 493–6 during the reign of Gunthamund, the third king of the Vandals. They are mainly deeds of sale in formulaic language but contain a number of local words, some of them of African origin. For the text (which I have punctuated) see Courtois *et al.* (1952); on the language see Courtois *et al.* (1952: 63–80), Väänänen (1965), Adams (2007: 549–62, 644–7), id. (2013: 213–14). The date of this tablet is given as 18 February 496.

Text

anno dodecimo domini regis Gunthamundi sub die xii k(a)l(endas) martias
    u̯e̯n̯[dentibu]-
s Messius Victorinus et Fotta uxor eius ex culturis suis Mancianis, sub dominio
Fl(aui) Gemini Catullini fl(am)i(nis) in perpetum, in locis et uocauulis suis:
    locus qui apell[atur]
in pullatis, firustellum unum in quo sunt oliue arb arbores tredeci,
    inter adf̯i̯n̯[es],
a marino et septentrione Victorinus uenditor, ab africo Saturninus, a choro
    h̯h̯(eredes)   5
Venenati; it(em) alio in loco locus qui apellatur in pullatis, sussanu, oliue
    arbores qui̯nque,
inter adfines, a marino hh(eredes) Iaderis, a choro hh(eredes) Processani, ab
    africo hh(eredes) Iaderis, e̯t̯
ex hac die emit Geminius Felix folles pecunie numero trecentos, quos acceper-
unt Victorinus et Fotta uxor eius et secum sustulerunt.

Translation

In the twelfth year of our lord king Gunthamundus twelve days before the kalends of March, with Messius Victorinus and his wife Fotta selling from their cultivated fields acquired by the law of Mancius, under the jurisdiction of Flavius Geminius Catullinus, the permanent flamen, in places (and) bearing their own names: the place which is called 'In the friable fields', one strip in which there are thirteen olive trees, within those bordering on them, to the north-east and north Victorinus the vendor, to the south-west Saturninus, to the north-west the heirs of Venenatus; likewise elsewhere the place which is called 'In the friable fields, upper (?)', five olive trees, within those bordering on them, to the north-east the heirs of Iader, to the north-west the heirs of Processanus, to the south-west the heirs of Iader, and from this day Geminius Felix has bought (this place) for three hundred *folles* of money, which Victorinus and Fotta his wife have received and taken with them.

Commentary

preliminaries

This is a formulaic text, which must have been produced from a model document. The model would not have had the names, and these have been inserted, probably into gaps, often without due attention to the context. As a result there are breakdowns of agreement, with the nominative tending to be used instead of the correct oblique case. This phenomenon reflects mechanical composition, not any developments being undergone by the case system, but the asyntactic use of the nominative of a personal name for an oblique case does at least show that the nominative was felt to be the base form of a name (see Adams 2013: 204–6). Some Latin names survive in Romance in their nominative form (Fr. *Charles* < *Carolus, Sartre* < *Sartor, Georges* < *Georgius*: see Bastardas Parera 1953: 23–4 and Lloyd 1987: 275 for Spanish, Ewert 1943: 130, Buridant 2000: 82–3 and Smith 2011: 283 for French), against the general trend for the accusative of nouns to serve as the Romance etymon, and that is a reflection of the special status of the nominative form of names. Cf. above, 15.5–6 and below, 46.4–5.

1 dodecimo: cf. *ILCV* 1361 *dodecimu*, 2687 *dodeci*, 2917 and *CIL* XIII.7645 *dodece* (with Kramer 2007: 119). On the suppression of a vowel in hiatus when the phonetic environment was of a type to impede its development into a semivowel ([j] or [w]) see Väänänen (1981a: 46–7). Cf. the note below, 41.3.

2 Messius Victorinus et Fotta uxor eius: a string of nominative names (with an appositional nominative *uxor*), which strictly ought to be in the ablative in agreement with *uendentibus* (see below).

ex culturis suis: the concrete use of *cultura* (of cultivated fields) is characteristic particularly of the *gromatici* (*TLL* IV.1322.71ff.).

3 in perpetum: regularly written for *perpetuum* in this corpus (see Väänänen 1965: 27), whereas the *u* is retained in the form *perpetuo* (see XII.12, XV.24) (where the *o* is long). The back vowel was in some way absorbed by the identical back vowel following. Here the development is post-tonic (*u* in hiatus is commonly lost after the accent and before the back vowels *u* and *o*, as in *quattor* < *quattuor*: for details see Väänänen 1981a: 47, and see also the next paragraph), but *suus* shows the same contraction even though the first *u* is under the accent. *Suus* retains its full form when the second vowel is other than *u*, but *suum* and *suus* are regularly contracted. *Sum* occurs seventeen times and *sus* once (X.4); *suum* is found just once (VII.20) and *suus* not at all. By contrast *suis* (forty-six times), *sui* (four times), *suoru(m)* (six times), *suo* (three times), *suam* (eleven times) *sue* (once), *sua* (twice) and *suos* (four times) are never reduced. Compare, for example, XXXI.5 *emtorem sum* with XXXII.4 *emtore suo*, and XXXI.7 *sum esse dixerit* with XXXII.5 *suam esse dixerit*. See also above, 22.17, and Adams (2013: 110–13). The retention of *u* in *perpetuo* may be due to the analogy of parts of the paradigm where loss of *u* would not be normal (e.g. *perpetua(e), perpetui*) (see however the next paragraph)

   The post-tonic loss of *u* in hiatus is not confined to subliterary texts. The form *promiscus* for *promiscuus*, for example, is well attested in literary manuscripts (details at *TLL* X.2.1852.70ff.; the *TLL* does not give the evidence for *perpetus*), not least of Tacitus (see Goodyear 1972: 309–10). *Promiscam* is confirmed by the metre at Plaut. *Rud.* 1182. This last case shows that the loss must have spread beyond environments where the *u* was before a back vowel, a feature that does not show up in the Albertini tablets.

   in locis et uocauulis suis: cf. III.4–5 *particellas agrorum in diuersis locis cum bocabulis suis*, which seems to mean '. . . in different places bearing their own names'. Väänänen (1965: 20 n. 2) raises the question whether the prototype here would have been *in locis et cum uocabulis suis. Et* looks to be explanatory: 'in certain places – and with their own names'.

   locus: strictly the object of *uendentibus*, but the *locus qui* formula in this text (for which see also below, 41.6) is constantly left unchanged (e.g. XVIII.6).

On the other hand for the accusative *locum* see XVI.6. At XIX.6 *locus* (nominative) is followed some words later by the accusative participle *ab[e]nte* (lacking *-m*) in agreement with it. The expression *in locus* also occurs: e.g. VI.4 *in locus qui est in* . . . (see further the index of Courtois *et al.*, 1952: 321). Such errors of syntax are due to careless handling of formulae, but it is the nominative that keeps asserting itself out of syntax. For pure carelessness note for example the omission of *inter adfines* at XVIII.7–8 (on which expression see below). For *locus qui* see also below, 48.2.4.

4 in pullatis: this phrase seems to be a locatival prepositional expression (found four times in the corpus), which has been fossilised as the name of a locality or type of locality. Twice it is preceded (as here) by *locus qui apellatur*, and once the equivalent *pullatis* (without preposition) is preceded by *locus qui dicitur*. Locatival prepositional expressions, particularly with *ad*, were often substantivised as the name of a place. See in particular Väänänen (1977: 40–2), noting (40) that the 'caractère discursive voire populaire des tours "hypostatiques" est indiqué, notamment dans les occurrences anciennes, par la présence d'un *vocatur, dicitur (vulgo)* ou semblable' (as we have in the present passage). Väänänen (40–1) cites e.g. Plin. *Nat.* 3.85 *colonia autem una quae uocatur ad Turrem Libisonis*, Suet. *Galba* 1 *ut hodieque ea uilla ad Gallinas uocetur*, Paul. Fest. p. 57.6 Lindsay *Capralia appellatur ager, qui uulgo ad Caprae Paludes dici solet.* The base of *pullatus* was *pullus* (see *TLL* X.2.2581.49, comparing *atratus* and *candidatus*), a colour term that was used in Campania, according to Columella (2.10.18), of friable soil (see above, 4.10, and Adams 2007: 206). The suffix *-atus* may be semantically empty (see Adams 2007: 560, and for this phenomenon, above, 27.8). It is tentatively suggested at *TLL* X.2.2582.14 that these phrases may derive from ellipse of *oliuis* ('among the black olives' or 'black-olive trees'; so 'the place that is called the black olive grove'?), given that olives are always present in the context.

firustellum: presumably for *frustellum*. For the anaptyxis see Väänänen (1965: 33, and also 17 and 48 on the term). The construction is that of partitive apposition, with *firustellum* in apposition to the preceding *locus*. *Frustellum* (*-illum*) is hardly attested and then late. It occurs in a direct speech in the *Peregrinatio Aetheriae* (14.2) and in a medical recipe in Marcellus (20.26), but it must long have had a subliterary existence, since it forms the base of *frustillatim*, which is at Plaut. *Curc.* 576 and Pomponius 165 Frassinetti. The diminutive *frustellum* must be of similar meaning to *particula*, of a parcel of land, a term which is also in the corpus.

4–5 inter adfin[es] a marino, et septentrione Victorinus uenditor: the location of a piece of land that is subject of a transaction is defined by a list of the owners of the properties that surround it: it lies 'between the neighbours X to the north-east and north, Y to the south-west', etc. It follows that *Victorinus uenditor* should be in the accusative in apposition to *adfines*. On a charitable view we might describe *Victorinus uenditor* as a 'nominative of apposition', a mainly late construction (see Adams 2013: 216–20; see also below, 46.4–5) which can, however, arguably be quoted from Cicero (*Phil.* 2.58 *sequebatur raeda cum lenonibus, comites nequissimi*; see also above, 39.10). But we should probably not use grammatical terms to explain what has happened here. It is likely that blanks in a model document were filled in carelessly, with persons named mechanically in the nominative case. For a mainly correct variant on this formula, which only gradually breaks down, see XVI.8–11 *inter adfines eiusdem loci qui iungitur a meridie Victorrino a corro Vigilliano uenditor ab africo Vigillianus* ('within those bordering on this same place, which is joined to the south to Victorinus ...'). The construction is correct as far as *Vigilliano*, and then the drafter lapses into the nominative (*uenditor, Vigillianus*). A comparable breakdown, with a lapse into the nominative, is at XVIII.17–18 *in nomine Victorini et Donata uxor eius emtores suos* (with as well an accusative at the end).

5 a marino: *marinus* (sc. *uentus*) is a wind that blows from the direction of the sea. In any region it took its meaning from the direction of the sea, and accordingly has various Romance reflexes with different meanings (see Adams 2007: 555–6 for details). From the contexts in which it occurs in this corpus it may de deduced that the sense is 'north-east wind' (see Väänänen 1965: 47, Adams 2007: 555).

6 oliue arbores: *oliue* is genitive ('trees of the olive'), and the phrase goes back at least as far as Columella (5.11.13). *Oliua* also occurs in the genitive plural (for the forms of the expression see *TLL* IX.2.565.3ff.).

sussanu: unclear: see Väänänen (1965: 51).

8 folles ... trecentos: Geminius Felix buys the property at 'three hundred *folles* of money'. *Folles* were a type of coin, the value of which is discussed by Courtois *et al.* (1952: 203–5; see also Väänänen 1965: 48). *Folles trecentos* is a clear case of the accusative of price, a constant construction in the corpus. In its earlier manifestations the construction shows (internal) neuter pronouns such as *quantum* (Petron. 43.4), *tantum, nihil* (for further such instances see Adams 2013: 321). Nominal examples (as distinct from the *quantum*-type) are cited by E. Löfstedt (1936: 172–3). These are very late, in e.g. Gregory of Tours, the *Vita Caesarii Arelatensis* and the *Actus Petri cum Simone*. The construction with nouns is discussed also by Norberg (1943: 103–4), who adds to Löfstedt's examples others from late law codes such as the *Edictus Rothari, Leges Alamannorum, Liutprandi leges* and the *Lex Curiensis*. Norberg (1943: 104) observes that the Romance use of nouns without prepositions in expressions of price and value must go back to this late use of the accusative (rather than to an ablative). Later (1956: 256–7) Norberg added several instances. For a few medieval examples see Bastardas Parera (1953: 52).

Conclusions

Here is a text that has certain substandard features that do not derive from changes taking place in the language, but from the mechanical filling in of gaps in a formulaic document. It is however of interest that it is the nominative which is regularly used out of syntax as the base form, mainly of personal names but sometimes also of common nouns such as *uenditor* and (in particular) *locus*. There have been attempts to establish that the accusative became a sort of default case, but there is plenty of evidence, if 'default' is to be used, that the nominative was in some respects a competitor for that role (see Adams 2013: 254–5, and also 202–3).

The passage has some banal phonetic spellings, such as *dodecimo, perpetum* and *tredeci*, and a few interesting syntactic and morphological phenomena, such as the accusative of price and the prepositional locality name. The meaning given to *marinus* is local.

42
TWO VERSIONS OF A PASSAGE FROM THE *PHYSICA PLINII*

Introduction

The *Physica Plinii* is the title now given to a medical compilation of about the fifth or sixth century (for details about this and the rest of the contents of this Introduction see Adams and Deegan 1992: 89–91, with bibliography). Its origins ultimately lie in the medical material scattered about in the *Natural History* of Pliny the Elder, which was extracted by an unknown compiler, perhaps in the fourth century, and brought together in a work now known as the *Medicina Plinii*. This work in its turn became the basis of the *Physica Plinii*, but the latter used other sources as well.

The manuscripts of the *Physica* survive in two main recensions (a third, which has never been edited and is very corrupt, is disregarded here). The first is now known as the *Bambergensis*, as it is transmitted in a Bamberg manuscript of the late ninth or early tenth century, and in part in another Bamberg manuscript of the late eighth or early ninth century. There are also excerpts in a ninth-century manuscript from St Gall. This so-called Bamberg version has been edited separately by Önnerfors (1975), a passage from whose text is printed below.

The other recension is referred to as the 'Florentine' or *Florentino-Pragensis*. This is transmitted by three later manuscripts, of the fourteenth and fifteenth centuries. This version has been edited separately in three volumes, the second by Wachtmeister (1985). The second passage below is quoted from his edition, and it corresponds to the Bamberg passage.

The Bamberg and Florentine recensions of our two passages (and others) have some substantial differences. A question that must be asked is whether these are due simply to the vagaries of textual transmission, that is to corruption in one or both branches. Or are there signs that a redactor might have been at work, systematically changing the Latin in one or the other version? We will return to these questions in the Conclusions.

There is another, indirect, source of evidence for the Latin text. The Anglo-Saxon medical work known as Bald's *Leechbook* made extensive use of the *Physica*, translating various passages closely. The extant manuscript of the

Leechbook is thought to have been written around the middle of the tenth century, probably at Winchester (for details and bibliography see Adams and Deegan 1992: 87–9). There is also internal evidence suggesting that the part of the manuscript containing the *Leechbook* is a copy of an exemplar compiled at the court of King Alfred in the late ninth century (Adams and Deegan 1992: 88). The passages of the *Physica* embedded in the Old English are thus approximately as early as the earliest manuscripts of the Latin work. It is sometimes possible, when our two Latin versions diverge, to see which reading the translator had, and in one or two places it is obvious that both Latin versions are corrupt, with the Old English pointing to an emendation. Attention will be drawn in the Commentary to relevant passages of the Old English, which are cited here in modern English translation. The Old English text itself, with translation, is cited at Adams and Deegan (1992: 93), and there are also numerous comments on the Old English in the commentary at Adams and Deegan (1992: 94–9).

In the Commentary below the lemmata are taken from *Bamb.*, but comparisons with the other version are constantly made.

Texts and Translations

Physica Plinii 'Bambergensis' 83.42–3

83.42 Conficis ad duri<ti>a (1) splenis: uessicam porcinam recentem aceto acerrimo plenam (2) ponis (3) super duritiam splenis et ita fascias; ne lauetur (4); per triduum sit ligatam (5), postea soluis, et inuenies uessicam uacuam et duriciem emollittam doloresque sedatos; res est fisicam et probatissima. postea dabis potionem talem: herba centauriam quam uolueris (6) in puluerem redigis quasi cocliarium trium (7) seu amplius, addis herbe sauine puluerem cocliaria tria (8), ... omnia cribrata (9). hinc dabis ieiuno in uini potione cocleare plenum (10), febrienti in calda aqua tepida (11); ne pix remaneat (12) cum reliquo puluere. **43** confectio aciti squilliticis (13) ad splenem (14): squille cortices comminute pondo III mittis in dolium uitreum cum aceti acerrimi *ff* VI et ponis in sole calido diebus canicularibus, ut macere diebus (15) XL; ex hoc aceto dabis splenitico cocleareum plenum (16); post horam celerius manducet, quia res est ualde uehemens. qui numquam eos usus est, adde illis quispiam mellis (17). non solum autem spleniticis saluberrimum est, sed etiam stomachi<ci>s (18) et ptisicis plurimum prodest nec non et sanguinem ex ore iactantibus (19); sed et contra omnes morbos interaneos facit. preterea scabiem ac prodiginem (20) statim tollit, si inde cerotum facias ac perungas; fiat autem sic: mittis ex ipso aceto in ollam noua cocliaria V cum olei emina, ut simul coquat (21); super addis (22) sulfuris uiui cocliaria V et cere modicum et simul ferueat (23), donec exquoquatur acetum; tollis et agitans, hinc infundis scabiem (24) et prudiginem perungues (25).

83.42 Prepare (this) for hardness of the spleen. Put a fresh pig's bladder full of the sharpest vinegar over the hardness of the spleen and so tie it. Let it not be washed. For three days let it be bound on. Afterwards remove it, and you will find the bladder empty and the hardness softened and the pains eased; it is a scientific and proven remedy. Afterwards give a potion of the following kind: the plant centaury, any you wish, reduce to powder of roughly three spoonfuls or more, add powder of savin, three spoonfuls, . . . all sieved. From this give to him, fasting, in a drink of wine a spoonful, and if he is fevered in warm water that is tepid; and see that pitch does not remain with the rest of the powder. **43** Preparation of squill vinegar for the spleen: put three pounds of the rind of squill, crushed, in a glass vessel with six sextarii of the sharpest vinegar, and put in a hot sun in the dog days of summer, to soak for forty days. From this vinegar give to the splenetic person a spoonful. After an hour let him eat quickly, as the thing is very strong. Who has never taken it, add for him some honey (*or* (for him) add to it some honey). But it is not only most beneficial for the splenetic, but it also benefits greatly those suffering in the stomach and from consumption, as well as those throwing up blood from the mouth. But it also helps against all internal ailments. In addition it immediately removes scab and itch, if you make with it a wax ointment and smear it on. It should be made as follows. Put into a new pot five spoonfuls from the vinegar with half a sextarius of oil, so that it cooks together. Add five spoonfuls of live sulphur and a little wax, and let it boil together, until the vinegar is cooked away. Take it and shake, and from it drench the scab and smear the itch.

Physica Plinii 'Florentino-Pragensis' 2.18.26, 29

2.18.26 Item ad duritiam uel dolorem splenis: uesicam porcinam recentem aceti acerrimi plenam pones super duritiam splenis et ita fasciabis; et non leuetur per triduum nec soluetur. postea solues et inuenies uesicam uacuam et duritiam emollitam et dolores sedatos; est enim res phisica et probatissima. postea dabis potionem talem: herbam centauream qualem uolueris in puluerem rediges et eius pulueris coclearia tria, herbe sauine pulueris coclearia tria, picis uirginis pulueris coclearia tria; omnia cribrabis et inde dabis ieiuno in uini potione coclear plenum, febricitantibus uero in aqua tepida; nec pix remaneat cum reliquo puluere ... **29** item ad splenem acetum squilliticum facies sic: squille corticis comminute pondo III mittes in dolium uitreum cum aceti acerrimi sextariis V ac pones in sole calido diebus canicularibus, ut macerentur per dies XL, et ex hoc aceto dabis splenetico coclear plenum, et post horam celerius manducet, quia res est ualde uehemens, qui numquam illo usus fuit; addesque illi modicum mellis, et hoc non solum spleneticis saluberrimum est, sed et stomaticis et ptysicis plurimum prodest nec non et sanguinem exscreantibus; sed et contra omnes morbos interaneos facit et scabiem ac pruriginem statim tollit, si inde cerotum facies et perunges. fiet autem sic: mittes ex ipso aceto in ollam nouam coclearia V cum olei hemina atque simul coques, et super addes sulphuris uiui coclearia V et cere modicum, iterumque simul ferueat, dum excoquatur acetum. postea tolles et agitabis et ex eo infundes scabiem et pruriginem perunges.

2.18.26 Likewise for hardness or pain of the spleen. Put a fresh pig's bladder full of the sharpest vinegar over the hardness of the spleen and so tie it. And let it not be raised for three days or removed. Afterwards remove it and you will find the bladder empty and the hardness softened and the pains eased; for it is a scientific and proven remedy. Afterwards give a potion of the following kind: reduce the plant centaury, of whatever type you wish, to powder, and of that powder three spoonfuls, of the powder of savin three spoonfuls, of the powder of virgin pitch three spoonfuls – sieve all and from it give him, fasting, in a drink of wine a spoonful, but if they are fevered in tepid water; and see that pitch does not remain with the rest of the powder ... **29** Likewise for the spleen make squill vinegar as follows: put three pounds of the rind of squill, crushed, in a glass vessel with five sextarii of the sharpest vinegar, and put in a hot sun in the dog days of summer so that it is soaked for forty days, and from this vinegar give to the splenetic person a spoonful, and after an hour let him eat quickly, because the thing is very strong for one who has never taken it. And add to it a little honey, and this is not only most beneficial for the splenetic, but also greatly benefits those suffering in the mouth and from consumption, as well as those who are spitting blood; but it also helps against all internal ailments, and immediately removes scab and itch, if you make with it a wax ointment and smear it on. It will be made as follows. Put into a new pot five spoonfuls from the vinegar with half a sextarius of oil and cook together, and add five spoonfuls of live sulphur and a little wax, and let it again boil together, until the vinegar is cooked away. Afterwards take it and shake, and drench the scab from it and smear the itch.

Commentary

1 ad duri<ti>a: *Flor.-Prag.* adds *uel dolorem*, and that is translated in the Old English.

2 aceto acerrimo plenam: *plenus* seems normally to be construed with the ablative in *Bamb.* (cf. 1.13, 15.4, 39.2, 56.6).[1] *Flor.-Prag.* usually has the same ablative construction (*Flor.-Prag.* 1.1.13 = *Bamb.* 1.13, *Flor.-Prag.* 1.16.4 = *Bamb.* 15.4, *Flor.-Prag.* 1.40.2 = *Bamb.* 39.2, *Flor.-Prag.* 1.57.7 = *Bamb.* 56.6). The presence of the genitive for ablative in *Flor.-Prag.* in the present passage cannot be of any general significance. The genitive is the construction in early Latin through to Cicero, who has it almost 200 times but the ablative only five times. Quintilian (9.3.1) notes the change of construction, remarking that the ablative for genitive *iam dicitur* (for further details see Hofmann and Szantyr 1965: 77, *TLL* X.1.2407.34ff.). Systematic figures for the choices of later writers do not seem to be available, though the ablative alone is used in the Oribasius translations (Hofmann and Szantyr 1965: 77).

3 ponis: imperatival use of the present indicative, a non-standard construction particularly widespread in late technical texts (for some details see Hofmann and Szantyr 1965: 326–7, Väänänen 1981a: 134). *Flor.-Prag.* here has the future *pones*, and that is a recurrent distinction between the two versions. In this passage in *Bamb.* the present indicative occurs twelve times and the future only four times, and three of the latter examples are in the form *dabis*. In the corresponding passage of the *Flor.-Prag.* the future occurs twenty-one times, and there are no instances of the present indicative as imperatival. For this use of the future, which is found in classical Latin, see e.g. Väänänen (1981a: 134).

Two observations may be made about this variability. First, in third conjugation verbs there would now have been no distinction of pronunciation between futures in *-ēs* and presents in *-ĭs* (cf. above, 16.1 with cross-references). Some late scribes might have had no clear idea what tense they were using, and that would have caused an element of haphazard variation. Second, the variations between the two versions can be added to other evidence that late scribes of technical texts did not set out to reproduce exactly the imperatival forms in the texts they were copying (see Adams 1995a: 461–2). The new pieces of Pelagonius, for example, in the manuscript *E* constantly have different imperatival forms from the other manuscript, *R* (Adams loc. cit.). It is an impossible

---

[1] These examples come from the index of Önnerfors (1975: 152), but a full list of examples of *plenus* is not given there.

task for an editor to determine what imperatival form the original author actually used in a passage. The future probably has better literary credentials than the imperatival present: but did the scribes of *Flor.-Prag.* 'improve' the text by introducing it, or did the scribes of *Bamb.* make the Latin more banal by dropping it (inconsistently)?

4 ita fascias; ne lauetur: the other version differs considerably. *Leuetur* must be the subjunctive of *leuare* 'raise'. Bald's *Leechbook* at this point has 'then bind it on so that it will not slip off, but let it be bound there firmly for three days' (see Adams and Deegan 1992: 93 for the Old English and translation). 'Washing' has little point here, and the Old English suggests a simple emendation of *Bamb.: labatur* for *lauetur* '(in such a way that) it does not slip, < *labor, labi* (see Adams and Deegan 1992: 94). *Leuetur*, which is only in some manuscripts of the *Flor.-Prag.* (others also have *lauetur:* see Adams and Deegan 1992: 94 n. 52), must be a rewriting of the text. It is obvious too that the Old English translator had *Bamb.*'s *sit ligata(m)* (with *per triduum*), which has been dropped in the other version.

The construction *ita . . . ne*, which looks like a consecutive construction with *ne* for the expected *ut non*, is of a well-established type in technical prose from Scribonius Largus and Celsus onwards (see Adams 1995a: 480–2 for examples and discussion). The head verb is usually imperatival, and parataxis must originally lie behind the construction ('tie it on thus: let it not slip'): it is only superficially consecutive. For further bibliography on this usage see Adams and Deegan 1992: 94 n. 53). See also above, 39.23 for a complementary usage.

5 per triduum sit ligatam: hypercorrect addition of *-m. Flor.-Prag.* is very different: *non leuetur per triduum nec soluetur.* The second subjunctive form ought to be *soluatur*, but the verb has mechanically been given the same ending as the previous one (see index, 'indicative, mechanically used'). For *non* (rather than *ne*) in a subjunctive prohibition (anticipating the loss of *ne* in Romance) see Hofmann and Szantyr (1965: 337) (common in late Latin, but found even in classical Latin sometimes). See also below, 42.12 on *ne pix remaneat* and variant.

6 herba centauriam quam uolueris: *Flor.-Prag.* has *qualem* ('of whatever type') for *quam*, and that is almost certainly a rewriting of the text. When *centauria* is introduced in this work (see the examples listed in the index by Önnerfors 1975: 129) types of the plant are not explicitly distinguished (though it is true that two types were recognised, *centaureum maius* and *centaureum minus:* see André 1985: 55). *Quam* is readily taken here as the indefinite use that is common when there is no expressed antecedent (*OLD* s.v. *qui* 15b), = 'any centaury plant you wish', a generalising use that allows for the possibility that different types may be available without spelling it out. *Qualem* looks like the effort of a literally minded redactor who wanted nothing to be left unsaid.

7 quasi cocliarium trium: *quasi* here means 'approximately'. Cf. *Mul. Chir.* 306 *huic sanguinem emittere quasi ad sextaria III*, 360 *necato in loteo quasi mensuram Atticam* (see also *OLD* s.v. 8). The Old English translator ('so that there are three spoonfuls or more') seems to have been rendering a text with *quasi* (but giving it a different nuance from that suggested above), which is only in *Bamb.* (see Adams and Deegan 1992: 95).

8 puluerem cocliaria tria: 'powder, three spoonfuls', a partitive apposition typical of recipe language, which in texts regularly alternates with the genitive construction even in the same sentence (see e.g. Svennung 1935: 198–200, Adams 1995b: 115; also below, index, 'apposition, partitive . . .'). So it is that in *Bamb.* later in this same passage we find a genitive instead (*sulfuris uiui cocliaria V*). By contrast in the present context *Flor.-Prag.* has the genitive (*eius pulueris coclearia tria*). In *Flor.-Prag.* the genitive is regular in such recipes; in the long chapter (2.18) from which our passage comes there are dozens of instances of the genitive but not any, it seems, of partitive apposition. Variability of construction looks more authentic for a technical work, and it is likely that a later redactor, regarding the genitive as more literary, decided to standardise. There is similar standardisation, we saw above (42.3), in the regular use of the future to express instructions.

8–9 addis herbe sauine puluerem cocliaria tria, . . . omnia cribrata: there is a lacuna here in *Bamb.* The other version has *herbe sauine pulueris coclearia tria, picis uirginis pulueris coclearia tria; omnia cribrabis.* The Old English translation clearly used the same Latin as that of *Flor.-Prag.* ('three spoonfuls of boiling pitch, powdered. Sift all': see Adams and Deegan 1992: 93, 95). A little later *Bamb.* itself has *ne pix remaneat*, which shows that it too must have been copied from a text containing the earlier reference to pitch. There has thus been a simple scribal error (an omission).

'Sift all' here corresponds to *omnia cribrabis* of *Flor.- Prag.* rather than to the (seemingly unattached: see below) participial construction *omnia cribrata* of *Bamb.* In the extreme variability in which instructions were expressed in recipe language scribes did sometimes replace imperativals with participial constructions (Adams 1995a: 461–2). Here the meaning would be 'add A, B (missing from text), all sieved', with *omnia cribrata* appositional to *cocliaria*.

The use of *omnia* here, particularly in *Flor.-Prag.*, is typical of recipes: a string of ingredients is resumed by *omnia*, which becomes the primary object of the directive that follows (Adams 1995a: 447). Cf. *Flor.-Prag.* 2.18.10, where a sequence of five ingredients is picked up by *omnia tunsa in aceto colliges* (note the participle with *omnia*, as in *omnia cribrata; Bamb.* 83.9 is the same at this point), 2.18.19, where fifteen ingredients are followed by *omnia uero sicca in puluerem redacta cum reliquis permiscebis*, 2.18.25, with four ingredients and then *tundes omnia*. See also above, 5.7–8 on *(haec) omnia* in such contexts in much earlier Latin.

10 hinc dabis . . . cocleare plenum: *Flor.-Prag.* has *inde* for *hinc*. Later both versions have *inde* in a similar context (*si inde cerotum facias/facies*). At the end *Bamb.* has *hinc* again (*hinc infundis scabiem*), where this time *Flor.-Prag.* has *ex eo*. Both *hinc* and *inde* literally express source ('from this/from that'), and from that idea there derive uses overlapping with the partitive genitive (*hinc cocleare plenum* = 'a spoonful of this') or instrumental ablative (*hinc infundis scabiem* = 'drench the scab with this': see below, 42.24). Into the same general semantic category fall uses of *ex* (see index, s.v. *ex*, 'expressing partitive object', and below, 42.16 on *ex hoc aceto*) and *de* (index, s.v. *de*, 'expressing partitive object'). The use of *inde* referred to above is perhaps better known than that of *hinc* because of its widespread Romance survival, for which see above, 31.12 (but see Hofmann and Szantyr 1965: 209 on *hinc*; also TLL VI.2.2799.65ff., 2802.8ff. for examples approaching an instrumental force). On *inde* see below, 50.59–60.

cocleare plenum: this noun has a variety of inflectional forms. The corresponding passage of *Flor.-Prag.* has *coclear*. A little later *Bamb.* has *coclearium plenum* (this a back-formation from the plural *coclearia*), where again *Flor.-Prag.* has *coclear*. For examples of the forms, all common, see TLL III.1398.125ff. *Bamb.* alternates between *cocleare* and *coclearium*, and there is a trace too of a masculine *cocliarius*, in a masculine accusative form (see Önnerfors 1975: 130–1 for details). *Flor.-Prag.* seems to have standardised to *coclear*. Wachtmeister (1985: 274) says of *cochlear* (in this book) 'sescenties', and then cites just one instance of 'Coclearius uel -ium' (22.13). 'Sescenties' cannot be accurate of the singular alone (it must embrace plurals too), but it must be the case that other singular forms are all but non-existent in that version.

11 febrienti in calda aqua tepida: *febrienti* corresponds to *febricitantibus* in *Flor.-Bamb.* The two verbs *febrire* and *febricito* were synonymous, and both were well established in medical texts (see Adams 1995a: 500–1 for figures showing their distribution). Choices from writer to writer are so variable that it is impossible to distinguish between them stylistically (see Adams loc. cit.). What is interesting is that the two versions of this work display a different preference. *Bamb.* prefers *febrire*: Önnerfors (1975: 137) lists fifteen examples, compared with just two of *febricitare*. By contrast Wachtmeister (1985: 288) lists twenty-three examples of *febricitare*, making it clear, by the use of *et al.* three times against different categories of examples, that the list is far from complete. Only two examples of *febrire* are given. It follows that in the scribal tradition there has been indifference to the original author's word choice. Either he preferred one verb to the other, in which case one of the versions has misrepresented his usage, or he used both verbs freely, in which case each version has falsified by opting for one verb rather than the other.

Bamb. has *febrienti* in the singular, following on from *ieiuno*. *Flor.-Prag.* switches from the singular (*ieiuno*) to the plural *febricitantibus*. Such changes of number in referring to the patient in medical texts are common (and found even in Celsus: see Adams 1995a: 589–90), and it cannot be determined what was originally written.

calda aqua tepida: Önnerfors deleted *tepida*, but wrongly. The Old English translator clearly had this text, as the *Leechbook* has a phrase meaning 'hot water made lukewarm' (Adams and Deegan 1992: 95). *Calida* was an imprecise term for hot water that might range in temperature from boiling to lukewarm. Note Pel. 168 *in calidam feruentissimam mittes*, Apic. 1.12.2 *in calidam feruentem merge*. Both Pelagonius (82 *cum aqua calida, sed tepida*) and *Bamb.* itself elsewhere (10.1 *ad cinerem calidum, sed tepidum*) have *calidus* modified by *tepidus* (introduced by *sed*). The fact that we have an idiom here, that *calda aqua tepida* compared with *in aqua tepida* (*Flor.-Prag.*) is clearly lectio difficilior, and that the Old English agrees with *Bamb.*, establishes that *Bamb.* is right and that the other version has made the text more banal (see further Adams and Deegan 1992: 95–6).

12 ne pix remaneat: *Flor.-Prag.* has *nec* for *ne* introducing a prohibition. The Old English translator seems to have had *ne*, as he translates in a final sense ('so that ... not'), which is possible for *ne* but not *nec* (see Adams and Deegan 1992: 96). For *non* (i.e. a variant of *nec*) with the subjunctive in prohibitions see above on *non leuetur* (also in *Flor.-Prag.*).

13 aciti squilliticis: *acetum scilliticum* is squill vinegar, that is vinegar made from the bulbous seaside plant *scilla* (see Cels. 4.16.2 *acetum ... quod a scilla conditum est*; on the plant see André 1985: 229–30). The form *squilla* is attested in Varro (*Rust.* 1.7.7). For the expression *acetum squ/cilliticum* see Önnerfors

(1975: 111 on 75). -s has been added to the adjective by mistake here (mechanical confusion with third declension genitive ending?).

14 ad splenem: the final use of *ad* here is typical of medical language. A distinction exploited by some writers but not universally was between *ad* ('for the treatment of') with disease names and the dative of the patient (see above, 5.1).

15 ut macere diebus: Önnerfors (1975: 115 on 66) interprets *macere* as for *macerent*. On the omission of final *-t* in inscriptions and elsewhere in both early and imperial Latin see Adams (2013: 148–56; conclusions 156–7; 149 for omissions of *-nt* in early Latin). In the imperial period in the plural it is usually only *t* (not *nt*) that is omitted (see above, 25.27), and it is simpler to take the form here as standing for *maceret*. Although the ingredients to be soaked are a plurality, this sort of singular (with the whole mixture collectively treated as subject) is common in recipes, and indeed occurs twice in this extract (see below, 42.21 on *ut simul coquat*). For comparable phenomena in Varro see Laughton (1960: 17–18); see also below, 50.63, and index, 'singular, for plural in reference to ingredients'; cf. also index, 'concord, violations of'.

   Flor.-Prag. here has *ut macerentur per dies. Macero* 'soak' would be expected to be passive in classical Latin, but the intransitivisation (deriving perhaps from deletion of a reflexive) is typical of later Latin (in particular) and not least of technical texts. The phenomenon has been discussed in detail by Feltenius (1977), though the intransitive use of *macero* itself does not seem to be paralleled. *Macere(t)* versus *macerentur* is again a lectio difficilior, and the Old English too has an intransitive (= 'so that it may . . . soak'). It is likely that *macere(t)* has been 'corrected' in *Flor.-Prag.*; indeed *per dies* in the same version alongside the ablative expressing duration in *Bamb.* (*diebus*), a construction widespread in late Latin, also looks classicising. We will see another intransitivisation later in the passage in *Bamb.* (42.21) but not *Flor.-Prag.* See index, 'intransitivisation of transitive verbs'.

16 ex hoc aceto dabis splenitico cocleareum plenum: *ex* here expresses source (of a spoonful 'from this vinegar'), but it is interchangeable with a partitive genitive (on such uses see Adams 2013: 307–8; cf. above, 42.10, and also 4.3, with cross-references on the partitive use). Later in the passage there is the same use of *ex*: *mittis ex ipso aceto in ollam noua cocliaria V*. At the end of the extract from *Flor.-Prag.* we also find this: *ex eo infundes scabiem* ('from this drench the scab'). Here *ex* again indicates source, but in this context it approaches an instrumental function ('with this'). There are even (in Tacitus) uses of *ex* that are equivalent to the subjective or objective genitive (see Adams 2013: 265–6).

17 post horam celerius manducet, quia res est ualde uehemens. qui numquam eos usus est, adde illis quispiam mellis: here, as Önnerfors notes, *eos* must be a mistake for *eo, illis* for *illi* and *quispiam* for *quippiam*.

On the punctuation of Önnerfors printed here (with a full stop after *uehemens*) the relative clause has to go with what follows ('who has never used it, for him add some honey'; *illi* I have taken here in this sample translation to be personal, but it might be neuter, referring to the medicament).

The Old English translator has a different clause division, with the *qui*-clause explaining the previous clause (= 'then immediately give something to drink, because it is very strong for someone who has never taken it previously'; for the Old English itself, and for the manuscript punctuation as supporting this clause division, see Adams and Deegan 1992: 96).

The other Latin version (*Flor.-Prag.*) undoubtedly has the same clause division as the Old English, though Wachtmeister has obscured that fact by his punctuation. Here is how I have punctuated in the text above: *et post horam celerius manducet, quia res est ualde uehemens, qui numquam illo usus fuit; addesque illi modicum mellis, et hoc non solum …* Wachtmeister, however, places a full stop after *uehemens*, no doubt following Önnerfors in the *Bamb.* But a crucial element is the attachment of *-que* to *addes*, which means that *addes* starts a new theme and cannot introduce the main clause following the relative clause. It could only be taken in this latter way if *-que* were treated as redundant (as it is treated by Wachtmeister). This is implausible (see the discussion of Adams and Deegan 1992: 97–9).

-que has a far higher frequency in *Flor.-Prag.* than in *Bamb.* (for details see Adams and Deegan 1992: 97–8). *-que* was a literary connective which disappeared without trace in the transition to the Romance languages (for details of its distribution see further index, s.v. *-que*). Note Adams and Deegan (1992: 98): 'That *-que* was systematically introduced into the Florentine version by a classicising redactor can be deduced from passages common to *Flor.* and *Bamb.* which derive from the *Medicina Plinii*. In the Bamberg version connectives are used much as they are in the *Medicina Plinii*, whereas the corresponding passages of *Flor.* show a higher frequency of *-que* than that in the *Medicina Plinii* or *Bamb.* The close correspondence between *Bamb.* and the *Medicina Plinii* suggests that in this respect *Bamb.* is similar to the original *Physica. Flor.* on the other hand seems to have been revised by a redactor with a taste for the literary enclitic.' This evidence shows that the discrepancies between the two versions are not to be put down merely to accidents and errors in transmission. Some conscious revising took place, in an effort to improve and standardise the Latin.

Relative clauses without an expressed antecedent (which would have been in an oblique case on the second clause division above) are common in late technical texts (see Svennung 1935: 480 n. 2, E. Löfstedt 1936: 142–4, Hofmann and Szantyr 1965: 555–6, Adams and Deegan 1992: 97), though not only there, and there are other examples in both versions of the *Physica*: note e.g. *Bamb.* 57.29 *ad tussim ueterem, qui disperantur* (alongside 57.23 *ad tussim, ei qui iam disperatus est*). See further 33.2, 5–6, and index, 'relative clauses, without expressed antecedent in oblique case'.

18 stomachi<ci>s: the other version has *stomaticis.* Two separate words seem to have been confused in the tradition, < στομαχικός and στοματικός.

19 ex ore iactantibus: *iacto* is commonly used of vomiting forth (OE = 'one who spews blood': Adams and Deegan 1992: 93 n. 48) in imperial medical texts (*TLL* VII.1.50.68ff.). *Exscreo* on the other hand in *Flor.-Prag.* is used rather of spitting, coughing up, expectorating. It is possible that a corruption of *ex ore* lies behind *exscr-.*

20 prodiginem: *Flor.-Prag.* has the correct form *pruriginem.* When the letter *r* occurs in a sequence of syllables in a word, dissimilation (or loss) is prone to occur. The form *plur-* is quite common (*TLL* X.2.2390.3ff.). For dissimilated forms of the same structure as that here (showing *d* for the second *r*) see Schopf (1919: 99–100), citing e.g. *proda* for *prora*, *prudere* for *prurire*, *radum* for *rarum.* Much the same material is at Baehrens (1922: 70).

21 ut simul coquat: this is the intransitive use of *coquo* (see *TLL* IV.928.15ff.; cited first from Pliny *Nat.* 18.32; Hofmann and Szantyr 1965: 296). Here and immediately below (*simul ferueat*) there is a singular verb, though the ingredients being heated are plural. This is a constructio ad sensum: Önnerfors (1975: 115 on 74 and 75) aptly paraphrases 'totum quod coquitur' (cf. above, 42.15 with cross-references), and the singular might well have achieved formulaic status in recipes with the number of ingredients regarded with indifference. Note particularly *Mul. Chir.* 888 haec omnia *contundito, donec bene* coquat (the numerous ingredients are crushed into a unity before cooking; see Oder 1901: 361 on *donec* apparently equivalent to *tunc*, on which see also *TLL* V.1.2003.45ff., Hofmann and Szantyr 1965: 630, glossing with *denique*, 'dann, endlich', but not citing this example).

   Flor.-Prag. personalises *coquat* (*coques*), but keeps the singular *ferueat.*

22 super addis: I have printed *super addis* in the text after Önnerfors, but in reality this is the compound verb *superaddis.* For this and other such compounds with redundant *super-* in late Latin see Adams (1976a: 116).

23 simul ferueat: *Flor.-Prag.* has *iterumque* preceding this phrase, and the Old English also has an equivalent of 'again' (Adams and Deegan 1992: 99). Similarly the final sentence of the extract in *Flor.-Prag.* begins with *postea*, and there is an equivalent to this too in the Old English (see Adams and Deegan 1992: 93 n. 48) but not in *Bamb*.

24 hinc infundis scabiem: originally *infundo* was used of pouring something (a liquid) onto something or someone. Here we have a secondary sense, of drenching something or someone with something by pouring (*TLL* VII.1.1509.20ff.). The meaning goes back e.g. to Ovid and Vitruvius, but early examples often have the verb in the passive. For the type of active, transitive use seen here in late medical texts see *TLL* VII.1.1510.39ff. *Hinc* is instrumental ('drench with this'), but the idea of source is still apparent ('drench from this') (see above, 42.10).

25 prudiginem perungues: Önnerfors has a comma after *prudiginem*, but it is obvious that Wachtmeister has the right punctuation; there are two verbs, one with *scabiem* and the other with *pruriginem*.

Conclusions

The Old English and the two Latin versions

The Old English sometimes agrees with *Bamb.* against *Flor.-Prag.* (see the notes numbered 11 *calda aqua tepida*, 12 *ne pix remaneat*, 15 *ut macere*, 19 *ex ore iactantibus*) and sometimes with *Flor.-Prag.* against *Bamb.* (see 1 *ad dur-i<ti>a*, 8–9 *addis herbe sauine ...*, 17 *post horam celerius manducet ...*, 23 *iterumque*). In one place the translator had a different text from that of both extant Latin versions (see 4 *ita fascias: ne lauetur*), and his text was undoubtedly right. Thus the Latin version available to the translator was independent of our extant Latin versions. The importance of the Old English is obvious. Considered alongside one or the other of the Latin versions it several times helps to establish what the original author must have written (see 4 *ita fascias: ne lauetur*, 11 *calda aqua tepida*, 15 *ut macere*).

The relationship between the two Latin versions

Is it justifiable to speak of 'versions'? What are the reasons for the differences between the two traditions?

In one case a discrepancy between them is due merely to corruption in one branch (see 8–9 *addis herbe sauine ...* on a lacuna in *Bamb.*). Similarly *exscreantibus* in *Flor.-Prag.* for *ex ore iactantibus* (19) seems to derive from a corruption in the source manuscript. On the other hand at 4 *ita fascias: ne lauetur* the difference is more striking, and suggestive of the activities of a redactor in the *Flor.-Prag.* branch. *Lauetur* in *Bamb.* alongside the Old English can be accounted for as a very simple corruption (for *labatur*). *Leuetur* on the other hand looks like an inept emendation by a scribe, with additional rewriting.

There are indications that the Latin of the Florentine version has been improved and standardised. That is nowhere clearer than in its high frequency of the literary connective *-que*, along with the evidence that *Bamb.*, with far fewer instances, is closer to the main source (see 17 *post horam celerius manducet …*). The variation between partitive apposition and genitive in *Bamb.* (see 8 *puluerem cocliaria tria*) looks authentic for a technical text, in which case the marked preference for the (more literary) genitive in *Flor.-Prag.* must reflect standardisation. Other signs of standardising in keeping usually with literary ideals in *Flor.-Prag.* lie in the consistent use of the imperatival future instead of the present (or of alternation between future and present) (see 3 *ponis*), the preference for *febricito* (see 11 *febrienti in calda aqua tepida*), and the single form given to the noun *coclear* (see 10 *cocleare plenum*). *Macerentur* must be an improvement to the text (see 15 *ut macere*; also, in the same note, see on *per dies* for *diebus*).

The Latin of the *Physica*

This is not a straightforward topic, given the existence of two versions, but once allowance is made for surface corruption, scribal errors and standardising, various features emerge. There are lots of misspellings in *Bamb.* which must be attributed to scribes rather than the original author. *Eos* for *eo* with the verb *utor*, for example (see 17 *post horam celerius manducet*), is an obvious scribal mistake and does not fit the context. Gross departures from classical norms of orthography in *Bamb.* (notably *macere* (15) without an ending and *prodiginem/prudiginem* (20, 25)) cannot reliably therefore be blamed on the first author.

The variations between the imperatival uses of the present and future indicatives in *Bamb.* (3) are typical of late technical texts and are likely to be authentic, with the present no doubt substandard in the eyes of purists. Other usages with a place particularly in technical language are the pseudo-consecutive construction *ita ne* (see 4 *ita fascias*), the resumptive use of *omnia* in recipes (see 8–9 *addis herbe sauine …*), intransitivisations of transitive verbs particularly in recipes (see 15 *ut macere*, 21 *ut simul coquat*), the use of the third person singular of verbs in recipes in reference to a plurality of ingredients (see again on *ut macere* and *ut simul coquat*), a usage only partly eliminated by *Flor.-Prag.* and likely to be authentic, *ex* expressing source in contexts in which it approaches a partitive or instrumental meaning (16), a final use of *ad* with disease names (see 14 *ad splenem*), and relative clauses of which the antecedent (in the expected oblique case) is not expressed (see 17 *post horam celerius manducet*), a usage found in both versions. Several of these usages are likely to have been regarded as substandard (certainly the singular for plural, and also the present indicative for imperative), but the point is that they all had a traditional place in a technical genre of writing and are not directly relevant to the educational level of the original writer.

43

TWO VERSIONS OF *HISTORIA APOLLONII REGIS TYRI* 40.1–15

Introduction

The *Hist. Apoll.* is a work of uncertain authorship and date, but it is late and probably later than the fourth century (see below, 43.3 on *quoquam*, and 43.9 on *uado*). The date conventionally ascribed to it is the fifth or sixth century (so the *TLL* index; cf. Kortekaas 1984: 101, Panayotakis 2012: 1), and that must be about right. It is generally believed that the work derives from a now lost original, quite possibly in Greek (on the history of this view see Kortekaas 1984: 11, with further details at 107–14), though Panayotakis (2012: 9–10) has recently expressed reservations about some of the evidence used to argue for a Greek original. Certainly the Latin is not mere translationese, and it has Latin stylistic models, notably, as we will see in the Appendix below, the Vulgate version of the Old Testament. Kortekaas (1984: 114–15) is inclined to attribute the work to Italy, favouring Rome or central Italy; some of the material cited at 114 from earlier studies is dubious. One Italian usage, but northern (though not in the following extract), is *fio* (in this case *facti*) as an auxiliary with a past participle, at 10.4 (*exhilarati facti adclamationibus gratias agebant*) (see Adams 2007: 466–70 for the regional distribution of this usage).

The *Hist. Apoll.* is one of several late Latin texts extracted in this volume that exist in more than one recension (see Kortekaas 1984: 9–12, and on the manuscripts, 14–96). Whereas a copyist might seek to reproduce the text of a revered classic such as Virgil's *Aeneid* exactly, other, more mundane, works were subject to revisions of different types by redactors who thought such a text might be improved. The second recension (B) is less wordy than the first, and it eliminates some non-classical features found in A. Some details will be given in the Conclusions at the end.

I cite here both versions of the passage, with a translation only of the first, the second being mainly a simplification. However, an addition made in B is translated within square brackets in the text. The passage of the first recension is cited from Panayotakis (2012), that of the second from Kortekaas (1984). Two changes of punctuation have been made to the text of A as printed by both Kortekaas and Panayotakis. First, the speech of Athenagoras in 11–12 has been made to end at *reuocem* rather than *Tharsiam*. Second, in 14 the comma after *omnium* has been removed and put after *tenebris*.

Texts

Rec. A

40.1 Athenagora uero ait intra se audito nomine: 'et Tharsia Apollonium <nominat> patrem.' et demonstrantibus pueris peruenit ad eum. **2** quem cum uidisset squalida barba, capite horrido et sordido in tenebris iacentem, submissa uoce salutauit eum: 'aue, Apolloni.' **3** Apollonius uero putabat se a quoquam de <s>uis contemptum esse; turbido uultu respiciens, ut uidit ignotum sibi hominem honestum et decoratum, texit furore<m> silentio. **4** cui Athenagoras, princeps ciuitatis, ait: 'scio enim te mirari, sic quod nomine salutauerim: disce quod princeps huius ciuitatis sum.' **5** et cum Athenagora nullum ab eo audisset sermonem, item ait ad eum: 'descendi de uia in litore ad nauiculas contuendas et inter omnes naues uidi nauem tuam decenter ornatam, amabili aspectu eius. **6** et dum incedo, inuitatus sum ab amicis et nautis tuis. adscendi et libenti animo discubui. inquisiui dominum nauis. qui dixerunt te in luctu esse grandi; quod et uideo. **7** sed pro desiderio, quo ueni ad te, procede de tenebris ad lucem et epulare nobiscum paulisper. **8** spero autem de deo, quia dabit tibi post hunc tam ingentem luctum ampliorem laetitiam. **9** Apollonius autem luctu fatigatus leuauit caput suum et sic ait: 'quicumque es, domine, uade, discumbe et epulare cum <m>eis ac si cum tuis. **10** ego uero ualde afflictus sum meis calamitatibus, ut non solum epulari, sed nec uiuere desiderarem.' **11** confusus Athenagora subiit de subsannio nauis rursus ad nauem et discumbens ait: 'non potui domino uestro persuadere, ut ad lucem uenire procederet. **12** quid faciam, ut eum a proposito mortis reuocem?' itaque bene mihi uenit in mente: 'perge, puer, ad lenonem illum et dic ei ut mittat ad me Tharsiam.' **13** cumque per<r>exisset puer ad lenonem, et leno audiens non potuit eum contemnere: licet autem contra uoluntatem, uolens misit illam. **14** ueniens autem Tharsia ad nauem, uidens eam Athenagora ait ad eam: 'ueni huc ad me, Tharsia domina; hic <est> enim ars studiorum tuorum necessaria, ut consoleris dominum nauis huius et horum omnium sedentem in tenebris, horteris consolationem recipere, et eum prouoces ad lumen exire, lugentem coniugem et filiam.

Rec. B

Athenagoras ait intra se: 'et Tharsia patrem Apollonium nominabat.' et demonstrantibus pueris peruenit ad eum. quem ut uidit barba caput

squalidum in tenebris iacentem submissa uoce ait: <'Apolloni, aue!'>
Apollonius putans se ab aliquo suorum contempni, turbulento uultu respiciens
uidit ignotum sibi hominem honesto cultu decoratum. furorem silentio texit.
Athenagoras ait: 'scio te mirari quod ignotus homo tuo nomine te salutauit.
disce quod princeps sum huius ciuitatis, Athenagoras nomine. descendens in
littore ad nauiculas co<ntu>endas, inter ceteras uidi nauem tuam decenter
ornatam et laudaui. nautis uero tuis inuitantibus libenti animo discubui.
inquisiui dominum nauis. dixerunt in luctu morari; quod uideo. prosit ergo,
quod ueni. procede de tenebris ad lucem, discumbe, epulare paulisper. spero
enim de deo quia dabit tibi deus p<ost ta>m ingentem <luctum> et laetitiam
ampliorem.' Appollonius uero luctu fatigatus leuauit caput et dixit: 'quisquis
es, domine, uade <et discumbe>, epulare [et discumbe] cum meis ac si cum
tuis. ego autem afflictus calamitatibus grauibus non possum epulari, sed nec
uiuere uolo.' Athenagoras confusus ascendit in nauem et di<s>cumbens dixit:
'non potui persuadere domino uestro ut uel ad lucem rediret. quid enim
faciam, ut eum reuocem a propositio mortis?' bene mihi uenit in mentem:
'uade, puer, ad [Leo]Ninum lenonem et dic illi ut mittat ad me Tharsiam.' est
enim scholastica, et sermo eius suauis, ac decore conspicua. potest enim ipsa
exhortari, ne talis uir taliter moriatur.' ['For she is scholarly and her speech is
sweet, and she is conspicuous for her beauty. For she can by herself encourage
such a man not to die in such a way.'] leno cum audisset nolens dimisit eam. et
ueniente Tharsia dixit Athenagoras: 'domina, hic est ars studiorum tuorum
necessaria: consolans nauis huius dominum sedentem in tenebris, coniugem
lugentem et filiam, exhorteris ad lucem exire.

Translation (of A)

1 But on hearing the name Athenagoras said to himself: 'Tharsia too <names>
Apollonius as father.' And with the servants showing the way he went to him. **2**
When he had seen him lying in the dark with a filthy beard and unkempt and
squalid head, in a low voice he greeted him: 'Greetings, Apollonius.' **3**
Apollonius thought he had been mocked by one of his crew; looking round
with wild expression, when he saw a man unknown to him who was noble and
distinguished, he concealed his rage in silence. **4** To him Athenagoras, the
leading man of the state, said: 'I know that you are surprised that I have greeted
you thus by name. You should know that I am the leading man of this state.' **5**
And when Athenagoras had heard not a word from him, he also said to him:
'I came down from the road onto the shore to look at the boats, and among all
the vessels I saw your vessel decked out with good taste, its appearance
delightful. **6** And while I was walking along, I was invited by friends and sailors

of yours. I went aboard and willingly took up a reclining position. I enquired after the master of the ship. They said that you were in deep grief, which I can also see. 7 But as a concession to the desire which brought me to you, come forth from darkness to the light and dine with us for a while. 8 I place my hope in god, that after grief as vast as this he will grant you greater joy.' 9 But Apollonius, wearied by grief, raised his head and spoke as follows: 'Whoever you are, my lord, go, recline and dine with my men as if with your own. 10 But I have been greatly afflicted with my disasters, so that I was longing not only not to dine but not even to live. 11 Confused, Athenagoras went up from the hold again to the vessel, and reclining said: ' I could not persuade your master to proceed to come to the light. 12 What am I to do, to recall him from his resolve to die?' And so it came about that I had a good idea: 'Go, boy, to that pimp and tell him to send Tharsia to me.' 13 And when the boy had gone off to the pimp, the pimp, listening, could not scorn him: although it was against his inclination, he readily sent her. 14 Tharsia, on coming to the ship – Athenagoras, on seeing her, said to her: 'Come here to me, Miss Tharsia, for here the art of your studies <is> required, so that you may console the master of this ship and of all these men as he sits in darkness, and may encourage him to accept consolation, and may rouse him to come forth to the light, as he grieves for his wife and daughter.'

Commentary

1 Athenagora: on this form in Latin of a Greek name in -ας (as *Aenea* in early Latin) see Adams (2003a: 372). Such forms are common in the classical period. For the variability of the spelling of the name in this version (it occurs with the Greek ending immediately after at 4) see Panayotakis (2012: 420).

<nominat>: the verb is added from the second version. *Habet* would fit the context as well, and ellipse of *habeo* is not infrequent in classical Latin (see Heidemann 1893: 86–7). However, an expressed verb rather than an ellipse seems to be needed here, but what it should be is not certain.

2 quem cum uidisset squalida barba . . . in tenebris iacentem: a conventional (postponed) participial construction in A (see below, 43.14). More striking is B *quem ut uidit barba caput squalidum in tenebris iacentem*. Kortekaas (2007: 659) has a note on the passage but does not remark on the oddity of the syntax of *caput squalidum* (neuter), which is followed by the masculine participle *iacentem*. *Quem . . . caput squalidum* could at a pinch be taken as a partitive apposition: cf. Plaut. *Merc.* 859 *hunc senem osse fini dedolabo assulatim uiscera* (where *uiscera*, expressing the part, is in apposition to *hunc senem*; for this type of construction see on 33.15–17). But that possibility is undermined by the postponed masculine accusative participle *iacentem* agreeing with *quem* ('whom when he saw – the head squalid with a beard – lying'?). *Barba caput squalidum* looks like an asyntactic expression within *quem ... iacentem*, and may be an error, though some might accept it as a parenthesis or 'accusative absolute' (on which see Hofmann and Szantyr 1965: 143).

3 putabat se a quoquam de <s>uis contemptum esse: the meaning of *quoquam* can only be 'by one/a certain one' of his crew, = *quodam*. *Quisquam* is used in a positive clause rather than, as usually, in a negative one, and the meaning thus changes from 'anyone' to 'someone'. This is a late usage. Wölfflin (1896: 507) cites an example in a positive clause from the *Regula* of Benedict; see also Linderbauer (1922: 111) on Ben. *Reg.* 54.6 *quod si etiam a parentibus suis ei quidquam directum fuerit.* An example such as this, however, in a *si*-clause (so that of Wölfflin), is not as striking at that in our passage, because in a conditional clause there is an ambiguity to the pronoun ('something/anything'), whereas in the present passage the meaning 'anyone' is not possible. Panayotakis (2012: 478) refers to his note on 39.4 (2012: 469) for this use of *quisquam* (*me autem ueto a quoquam uestrum appellari*), but although this example is a parallel for the substantival use, it is semantically different because it is in the usual negative context (*ueto*). See further Hofmann and Szantyr (1965: 196), referring to Verecundus (sixth century) for the use of the word in positive sentences. Is *quoquam* perhaps corrupt?

B changes to *putans se ab aliquo suorum contemni*, which is a normal usage. Kortekaas (2007: 660) says nothing about the use of *quisquam*, other than that the word was on the wane in late Latin.

turbido uultu: the second recension changes *turbido* to *turbulento*. Of the two adjectives, only *turbidus* survives in Romance, mainly Italian and dialects (see *REW* 8994). I do not have information for the distribution of the pair in late Latin.

respiciens, ut uidit: *ut uidit*, usually postponed as here, is a temporal expression so ubiquitous in the text as to be a striking mannerism (e.g. 12.7, 14.1, 14.9, 16.2, 17.1, 18.7, 27.1 etc.). So *ut audiuit* is also common (24.6, 24.7, 25.1 etc.). Earlier in this chapter (2), where A has *quem cum uidisset*, B has *quem ut uidit*. *Vt uidit* occurs five times in Cicero, and is common in poetry, particularly in first position in the line (six times for example in Virgil: *Aen.* 2.519, 10.365, 10.441, 10.790, 11.40, 11.854). In both this text (e.g. 14.1, 14.9) and in Virgil (2.519, 10.441, 11.40, 11.854) it sometimes ushers in direct speech. It is frequent in Hyginus' *Fabulae*, a work possibly of the second century AD: e.g. 27.2 *Medus Aegei* *et Medeae filius ut uidit*, 36.2 *quod Deianira ut uidit* (cf. *Hist. Apoll.* 27.1 *quod ut uidit*), 95.2 *quem Palamedes ut uidit* (cf. *Hist. Apoll.* 16.2 *quem ut uidit rex flentem*), 105.4 *quod Agamemnon ut uidit. Vt audiuit* is also Ciceronian (for both see *De orat.* 1.240 *ex quo ut audiuit commotumque ut uidit hominem*; in this same passage of lively narrative *ut . . . uidit* occurs a little earlier as well, at 239; on this passage see further below, on 43.12), and it too is found in Hyginus *Fab.* (101.2 *hoc Telephus ut audiuit*). There is a generic similarity between the *Fabulae* and the *Hist. Apoll.*, in that the former consists of mythological narrative in a simple and repetitive style. Many sentences have the format 'when he saw, he . . .', and not only when the temporal conjunction is *ut*: cf. in Hyginus *cum uidit* (36.1, 68.4), *postquam uidit* (67.8), *cum uidisset* (79.2, 84.3, 88.9). In the present chapter of the *Hist. Apoll.* we have just seen at 2 (A) *quem cum uidisset*.

The phrase *ut uidit* is not a normal one in the prose historians (only two examples) (information from Harm Pinkster). Nor is it a mannerism of the Vulgate. There are a few examples in the Gospels, translating the participle ἰδών, singular or plural (Mc 6.49, Lc 8.28, 8.34, 17.14), and two examples in Acts, translating ὡς εἶδεν (-ον). Twice in Luke (8.34, 17.14) *ut* follows a relative pronoun. It is hard then to attribute the usage to a specific stylistic model.

Another shared feature of Hyginus and the *Hist. Apoll.* is the repetitive 'folk tale' use of the pronoun *is* (see e.g. *Fab.* 50.2, 51.2, 54.3, 55, 64.4), for which mannerism see above, 1.8, 1 Appendix 3. Cf. below, 43.6 on a repetitive use of *qui = et is* in our text.

4 sic quod nomine salutauerim: Panayotakis (2012: 479) says that *sic* anticipates the *quod*-clause and cites an example of the combination *sic quia* from early Latin (Plaut. *Most.* 450 *quid uos? insanin estis? :: quidum? :: sic, quod foris ambulatis* ('What about you? Are you all mad? :: Why? :: Well, because, you're strolling about outside', de Melo, Loeb). However, there is a pause there between *sic* and the explanatory *quod*-clause ('for this reason, namely that . . .'), and the examples at *OLD* s.v. *sic* 6 usually indeed have *sic* separated from the explanatory clause. In our passage the key word is *nomine* (it is a surprise that he has been greeted by a stranger thus, BY NAME), and it seems likely that *sic* anticipates that, though displaced slightly from it. The function of *sic*, despite the displacement, seems to be exactly the same as that at 20.2 *quid est, magister, quod sic singularis cubiculum introisti?* (cf. Kortekaas 2007: 273, translating 'alone like this'). Cf. above, 29.1.

Kortekaas (2007: 662–3) and Panayotakis (2012: 479) supply *te* before *salutauerim*, but the supplement is unnecessary. *Saluto* is not infrequently used elliptically like this (see *OLD* s.v.1a, where four examples are cited, three of them from Livy and Tacitus). Note Plaut. *Pseud.* 968 *eho, an non prius salutas?* (translated by de Melo, Loeb, 'Oho! Aren't you greeting me first?'). Cf. in this text 8.5 *aue, inquam, Apolloni, resaluta* ('greetings, I say, Apollonius, greet (me) in return'). Panayotakis himself elsewhere (2012: 123) comments on the absolute use of *saluto*.

There are other instances of pronominal ellipse in the *Hist. Apoll.* Note 28.5 *iurauit fortiter nec barbam nec capillos nec ungues dempturum*, 29.9 *sic uotum faciens neque capillos dempturum neque ungulas*, 31.3 *ut audiuit laudare Tharsiam et suam uituperare filiam*. In these three places the omission of the subject accusative in an acc. + inf. is allowed by Kortekaas and Panayotakis, whereas at 13.8 a pronoun is supplied by both: *uidens autem <se> Apollonius a ciuibus laudari* (see Panayotakis 2012: 211).

disce quod princeps huius ciuitatis sum: Panayotakis (2012: 479) notes (citing the *TLL*) that *disco* complemented by a *quod-* or *quia*-clause is attested elsewhere only in Christian authors and biblical Latin. Whether there is any significance to that is unclear, since so much extant late Latin happens to be Christian. Kortekaas (2007: 663), also referring to *TLL*, and describing the combination here as very rare in Latin, sees Greek influence (to be exact, he states 'partly influenced by Greek'), but such dependent constructions are banal in late Latin, and the head verb is surely of little significance. The three instances that he cites to demonstrate (partial) Greek influence are all from the Vulgate version of the OT, where Greek is not necessarily the determinant.

Dependent clauses with *quod/quia* in this text have an interesting distribution. They are in the minority compared with the classical construction (contrast e.g. Patrick, 39.18). The work is full of cases of the acc. + inf., both in the narrative and speeches. The acc. + inf. clause is not infrequently long or complex. Here is a small selection from the narrative:

3.1 intra domesticos uero parietes maritum se filiae gloriabatur (here the construction, with the infinitive *esse* understood, precedes the higher verb).
6.6 atque ita onerari praecepit naues frumento (here the components of the construction are split around the higher verb).
14.6 statim rex iussit eum dignis uestibus indui et ad cenam ingredi (here there are two coordinated elements in the dependent construction).

There is a literary feel to these examples. In low-register non-literary texts acc. + inf. constructions that do occur are usually short and simple and placed after the higher verb, often with a subject accusative pronoun attached to the verb (Adams 2005b).

The following examples (intended as a complete list) of the alternative construction (showing a clause introduced by *quod* or *quia: quoniam* does not occur in this use in the text) are from A:

6.1 Thaliarche, secretorum meorum fidelissime minister, scias quia Tyrius Apollonius inuenit quaestionis meae solutionem.

8.6 audi, forsitan quod nescis, quia proscriptus es.

21.7 certe dixi uobis quia non apto tempore interpellastis.

22.4 nata dulcis, noli de aliqua re <u>cogitare quia</u> talem concupisti, [ad] quem ego . . . sed ego tibi uere <u>consentio quia</u> et ego amando factus sum pater.

30.1 cara nutrix, testor deum, quod si fortasse aliqui casus mihi euenissent, antequam haec mihi referres, penitus ego nescissem stirpem natiuitatis meae.

31.4 puto quia mortuus est aut in pelago periit.

32.6 tu scis, deus, quod non feci scelus.

32.15 deus, tu scis quia purus sum a sanguine Tharsiae.

33.7 ignoras, misera, quia in domum auari lenonis incurristi?

33.9 tu autem nescis quia apud lenonem et tortorem nec preces nec lacrimae ualent.

38.1 crede nobis, quia si genesis permisisset, sicut haec omnia damus, ita et filiam tibi reddidissemus.

40.4 disce quod princeps huius ciuitatis sum.

40.8 spero autem de deo quia dabit tibi post hunc tam ingentem luctum ampliorem laetitiam.

There are just fourteen examples here. Their most striking feature is that they are all in speeches. The acc. + inf. is also common in speeches, but it seems that the author has excluded the *dico quia*-construction from the narrative. The subordinating construction in every case but three is *quia*. The higher verb is always in the first or second person or is imperative. Five times the higher verb is *scio, nescio* or *ignoro*. The dependent verb is always indicative, except at 38.1, where the subjunctive is determined by the nature of the conditional construction. Most of the dependent clauses are straightforward, without coordination or embedded subordinate clauses (30.1 and 38.1, just referred to, are exceptions), and are of the type expressed regularly elsewhere in the text by the acc. + inf.: thus the choice of the *quia*-construction has not been determined by the complexity of the dependent clause. Throughout the work only the acc. + inf. is used when the higher verb is in the third person. Also of note are the accumulations of examples (of *quia/quod*) in close proximity to each other in passages of dialogue, as in this chapter and at 32 and 33.

The author seems to have regarded the *quia*-construction as more appropriate to conversation than to impersonal narrative (see also the Conclusions below).

5 et cum: for sentences beginning with *et* (see also the start of 6) as a mark of biblical style see 27.2.

cum … nullum ab eo audisset sermonem: *nullum sermonem* here must mean 'not a single word'. *Sermo*, translating λόγος, came to be used in the sense 'word (of God)' in Christian Latin, where it is a synonym of *uerbum* (see Lundström 1943: 36, Souter 1949: 375, Mohrmann 1961b: 671, ead. 1965: 109–11, Stotz 2000: 69, id. 2002: 78 n. 6). Souter (1949 375) (without examples) gives the secular meanings 'expression, phrase, word' as attested from the second century AD onwards. There is a substantial collection of examples in this last meaning (i.e. = 'word' in the singular, 'words' in the plural) in Arnaldi, Turriani and Smiraglia (1939–64: III.139), from e.g. Boethius, Cassiodorus, Paulinus *et al.* (e.g. Cassiod., *GL* VII.144.20 *minutus labor syllabis litterisque tractandis modo factus ex nominum deriuatione, modo ex casibus sermonum* … (23) *m quoque littera in quibusdam sermonibus scribi datur*). Note too *Colloquium Celtis* (Dickey 2015) 34a *sermonis declinationem* = τοῦ ῥήματος κλίσιν ('inflection of the word, verbal inflection'). Panayotakis (2012: 480) quotes the expression *sermonem audire* from the Vulgate (e.g. Io 19.8 *cum ergo audisset Pilatus hunc sermonem magis timuit*), but *sermonem* refers to a whole utterance.

ait ad eum: the use of *ad* in relation to the dative of the indirect object is of considerable interest in this text, and throws light on the author's stylistic models. It is dealt with separately in the Appendix below.

descendi de uia in litore ad …: here in a main clause with numerous components the verb is placed first. Verb-final position, particularly in main clauses, is hardly to be found in this extract (40.1–15). Here are some figures embracing only finite verbs (participles, infinitives and imperatives are excluded; the last in particular regularly come at the start of the clause and their inclusion would skew the figures).

In main clauses non-final position of the verb outnumbers final position by 20:3 in this extract. The three instances of final position are unremarkable, because all are in short clauses (3 *Apollonius uero putabat*, 6 *et libenti animo discubui*, 11 *et discumbens ait*). In subordinate clauses final position is a little more prominent, but even in these non-final position predominates by 10:6. Overall in clauses of both types non-final position predominates by 30:9.

The distributions are similar if we take into account only the orders VO versus OV (i.e. if we include only instances of finite verbs that have a direct object expressed). In main clauses VO is preferred to OV by 6:0. In subordinate clauses too VO is preferred by 5:2. In both types of clauses VO predominates by 11:2. The lack of distinction between main and subordinate clauses seems to replicate that in the Vulgate, which derives from the Greek original (see 38.57).

ad nauiculas contuendas et inter omnes naues: diminutives not infrequently interchange with their base form without distinction of meaning. In this text see 28.5 *nec ungues dempturum* alongside 29.9 *neque capillos dempturum neque ungulas.* Note also e.g. *Mul. Chir.* 923 *medicamentum ad clauos morticinos. herbam urceolariam et absungia et sale contundito et imponito, tertio die soluito, clauolus cadet* (see Adams 1995a: 316), *Vitae patrum* 5.2.9 *uade et sede in cellula tua, et cella tua docebit omnia* (for further alternations see e.g. Adams 1976a: 105, id. 1995a: 303, 544, 552, 553).

In the Vulgate *nauicula* is used only in the Gospels, seventeen times.

aspectu eius: the *Hist. Apoll.* is one of those late texts in which the genitive is mainly placed after its noun. In the present chapter there are ten instances of NG but none of GN. In this chapter, along with chapters 30–5 and 39, there are in total sixty-two instances of NG and thirteen of GN. Those of the latter type not infrequently show an enclosing order, that is the genitive is enclosed between the noun and an associated element, such as a preposition, participle or adjective (32.10, 34.14, 35.4, 35.12).

6 libenti animo discubui: *libenti animo* is an old phrase going back to Plautus and found in Cicero and later Latin, including the *Peregrinatio Aetheriae* (*TLL* VII.2.1327.35ff.). In the *Per. Aeth.* it occurs four times, whereas *libenter* occurs only once in the equivalent sense (van Oorde 1929: 121). The phrase is adverbial in function, and provides a background to the emergence of *mente*, a synonym of *animo*, as an adverbial suffix in the Romance languages. For a discussion of such phrases (including those with *animo*) see Bauer (2010). The combination (with *discubui*) in the present context is of interest, because twice earlier the adverb *libenter* is used with the same verb (39.9 *cum uidisset omnes tam libenter discumbere ... quod omnes libenter discumbitis*), and this brings out the adverbial function of the phrase. *Animo*, unlike *mente*, was never grammaticalised as an adverbial suffix. Cf. 24.10 in this text for *satis animo libenti*; also 3.1 *simulata mente*, 9.2 *turbata mente*, 38.5 *stupenti mente*. There are also phrases with *uultu* that are quasi-adverbial: 4.3 *irato uultu respiciens*, 40.3 *turbido uultu respiciens*.

inquisiui dominum nauis: a use of *inquiro* that is unusual by classical and indeed later standards. Kortekaas (2007: 666) translates 'I asked about the master of the ship', and that seems to be right. In classical Latin there is a construction *inquiro in aliquem*, meaning 'make inquiries about (a person)' (*OLD* s.v. *inquiro* 3b). From later Latin the *TLL* VII.1.1818.33f. cites a construction *inquiro aliquem* = *in aliquem* from legal Latin, but the examples given are passive, and the present example is in a neutral not a legal context. Nevertheless the meaning in the context must be 'I made enquiries about', because the sailors answer that he is in mourning. The classical meaning 'search out' (a person or thing) (*OLD* s.v. 1 and below) would not suit the answer given.

At 6.4 there is a slightly different transitive use of the verb: *inquirit omnes quaestiones auctorum omniumque pene philosophorum disputationes* ('he investigated/looked into all the speculations of historians and the debates of almost all the philosophers': cf. e.g. Lucr. 4.1189, *OLD* s.v. *inquiro* 2). There is a different transitive use again at 6.2: *inquires inimicum eius* ('search out': *OLD* s.v. 1; a meaning referred to above: see Kortekaas 2007: 62 'seek out some enemy of his').

qui dixerunt: a connective relative at the start of the sentence, = *et ii*. This is a mannerism loosely comparable to the use of *et* starting sentences, and to the popular narrative style that makes redundant use of *is* (for which see Panayotakis 2012: 480 on *aspectu eius*). The introductory use of *qui* is a mark of the narrative style of the *Itinerarium Antonini Placentini* (see 44.7). At 37.1 (rec. A) in that text it even occurs in conjunction with a first person verb: *qui perambulantes per heremum octaua decima die uenimus ad locum*. In the present text cf. 1.5 *qui cum luctatur*, 3.1 *qui cum simulata mente ostendebat*, 7.4 *qui ut uidit*, 8.7 *cui Apollonius ait*, 8.13 *cui Hellenicus ait* (cf. 13.5, 14.10, 15.2, 15.3, 16.2, 16.9, 19.3 etc.). For the usage in the NT see Mt 2.9 *qui cum audissent*, 2.13 *qui cum recessissent*, 2.14 *qui consurgens*, 2.21 *qui surgens* (3.12, 4.4). See also Kortekaas (2007: 666).

7 sed pro desiderio, quo ueni ad te: Kortekaas (2007: 667), translating 'in response to the desire which brought me to you', says that *pro* is equivalent to *propter*, and bibliography on that late usage is cited. It is however doubtful whether there is a precise equivalence of this type (similarly contrast Panayotakis's rendering, 2012: 481). I would prefer to take the phrase in the sense 'as a concession to/indulgence of the desire' (that brought me here), a nuance easily derived from conventional uses of the preposition as classified by the *OLD* s.v. 13–16. In fact four times in Anthimus the phrase is used in reference to a food craving, in the sense 'as an indulgence to a craving': e.g. p. 13.8 *nisi forte pro desiderio aliquis interdum sumat* 'unless by chance someone sometimes eats it indulging a craving' (cf. 14.12, 20.7, 21.2). An example in Trajan *ap.* Plin. *Epist.* 10.119 is slightly different: *nec proficere* *pro desiderio athletarum potest*, lit. 'nor can it be of assistance on behalf of the athletes' claim'.

8 spero autem de deo: for the late Latin expression *spero de (deo)* see 14.11 and Panayotakis (2012: 224, 481); also Kortekaas (2007: 668). *Autem* marks as often a transition to a new thought and is a mere sentence connector.

9 leuauit caput suum: an old literary phrase (*TLL* VII.2.1232.7ff.), which continued to occur in later Latin (see e.g. *Pass. Perp.* 4.9).

There is an interest to this semantic field in late Latin. In classical Latin *leuo* and *tollo* overlap to a considerable extent, and both can be used of raising up e.g. a part of the body. Note on the one hand Stat. *Theb.* 11c.556–7 *leuauit | ad caelum palmas* (see *OLD* s.v. *leuo* 1a) and on the other Livy 5.21.15 *manus ad caelum tollens* (*OLD* s.v. *tollo* 3b). In late Latin, however, particularly of an informal kind, the two verbs are not infrequently more sharply differentiated (but see below, final paragraph to this note). *Leuo* is usually used in the sense just noted, often with a personal object (expressing a part of the body, or the whole person in the form of a reflexive expression, the latter also a usage that goes well back: *TLL* VII.2.1231.53ff., citing e.g. Virg. *Aen.* 4.690, Livy 7.26.5). *Tollo* on the other hand has often lost any idea of raising and is used particularly in the imperative in the sense 'take', sometimes in a context where there is an ambiguity and one might translate 'pick up/take', but sometimes where the idea is rather 'take' (something handed over), without any suggestion of picking up, raising (see further below, 50.29). Below are listed, first, all instances in the text of *leuo* (and two of its compounds, which are used identically). There are seven examples, all with the types of personal objects noted above:

17.5 peractoque conuiuio leuauerunt se uniuersi.
29.3 nutrix uero eius eleuans se dixit ei.
32.6 eleuans ad caelum oculos.
32.15 in caelum leuans oculos.
33.9 alleua te, misera.
34.15 alleua te, domina.
41.5 ad haec uerba leuauit caput Apollonius.

Tollo is more frequent. There are, first, a few old uses:

7.2 spectacula tollerentur ('spectacles were abolished': see *OLD* s.v. 14).
25.12 iussit infantem tolli (of accepting a child: *OLD* s.v. 2a; Panayotakis 2012: 326).
31.5, 31.7, 32.9 tollere de medio (implying 'kill': see *OLD* s.v. 13a; Panayotakis 2012: 390).

41 (in verse) line 10 animum ad sidera tolle ('raise', metaphorically, a literary use: *OLD* s.v. 5c).

Here are the remaining examples:

12.8 dedit unam (partem) iuueni dicens: 'tolle hoc, quod habeo, et uade in ciuitatem' ('take this', with no idea of picking up).

17.6 tollite, famuli, haec, quae mihi regina donauit: aurum, argentum et uestem (ambiguous between 'take' and 'pick up').

19.6 rex accepit codicillos ... datque Apollonio dicens: 'tolle, magister ... hos codicillos et perfer ('take', with no idea of picking up).

21.3 tolle, magister Apolloni, hos codicillos et lege.

26.1 tollite hunc loculum cum omni diligentia et ad uillam afferte (here the idea of lifting is possible, but *tollite* can still be translated 'take').

26.9 tolle ampullam unguenti et ... corpori puellae superfunde ('pick up' > 'take').

34.12 tolle libram auri integram (here something is handed over).

38.3 tollite haec omnia et ferte ad nauem.

There are eight instances here, all of them imperative, and all meaning 'take'. Panayotakis (2012: 198) notes that the imperative is often followed by another one (six times above), and he cites parallels from biblical Latin. That is not, however, specifically a biblical usage (Panayotakis also cites Petron. 79.11 *res tuas ocius tolle et alium locum ... quaere*, but on this see now Schmeling 2011: 334, on 'the expanded sense of *res tuas ocius tolle* as a formula used in expelling a mistress or divorcing a wife'), but is the late colloquial norm. Below by way of illustration are cited all examples of the verb from the school exercises edited by Dickey (2012 and 2015):

Coll. Mon.–Eins. (Dickey 2012)
9b tolle, coque diligenter pulmentaria.
Coll. Harl. (Dickey 2015)
3b tolle omnes libros.
25c tolle nobis mutatoria in balneum.
28a cito fac et tolle sabana.
Coll. Mont. (Dickey 2015)
4f tolle quae opus sunt et ueni mecum.
6b tolle coronam ('take the crown': not of picking up but of something handed over).
12c tu, puer, tolle lagunam et imple aquam.
18f parti eum, tollamus partes ('divide it up, let's take the parts').
20f tolle lucernam, dormire uolo ('take/remove the lamp, I want to sleep').

Coll. Celtis (Dickey 2015)
55b tollite soleas . . . pone.
56b tolle res et balnearia.
Cf. 70e leua te, puer.

In this last text (*Coll. Celtis*) there is the same distinction between *tolle* and *leuo* as that in the *Hist. Apoll. Leuo* does not occur in the other texts.

Every example but one of *tollo* in the four texts is an imperative, and the one exception is imperatival (jussive subjunctive). Also four times the imperative is followed by another. On the semantics of *tolle* see also Dickey (2015: 79).

On *tollo* see further e.g. E. Löfstedt (1911: 182–4). *Leuo* itself, despite the distinctions seen above, was not entirely immune from such weakening in late texts: see below, 46.7 for bibliography.

uade, discumbe et epulare: for *uado* elsewhere in this text see 12.8 *uade in ciuitatem*, 14.4 *uade celerius*, 27.5 *uadit ad magistrum suum*, 38.3 *ego enim uado*, 41.9 *uade*, 41.10 *quo uadis*, 41.14 *uadam*, 42.2 *uadam* (nine examples). For *eo* see 12.2 *quo itaque ibo*, 17.6 *eamus*, 31.12 *ibat*, 39.12 *qui eat*. There are four examples only of *eo* in the work, all in forms of two or more syllables. Six of the nine examples of *uado* are in forms of which the corresponding form of *eo* was monosyllabic. *Vado* thus is used mainly (but not entirely) as a replacement of the monosyllabic forms of *eo*. *Vadam* (future) is also used alongside (and more often than) *ibo* (on the history of *uado* see Adams 2013: 811–17).

Again a comparison is worth making with the texts edited by Dickey.

In the *Coll. Harl.* (Dickey 2015) the only form of *uado* used is the imperative *uade* (four times), as a substitute for the monosyllable *i* (1d, 10f, 25a, 27a). There are eight instances of *eo*, all in forms of two or more syllables (*eamus* at 3d, 12e, 18h, 18j, 23g, *ibas* at 14a, *ibo* at 15c, *ire* at 24c). There is an absolute distinction between the two verbs, with *eo* used except in monosyllabic forms and *uado* not intruding except as a substitute for the monosyllable.

The situation is identical in the *Coll. Mont.* (Dickey 2015). *Vado* occurs just once (4d), in the form *uade*. *Eamus* occurs five times (8b, 13c, 16a, 19b, 20c) and *eat* once (14a).

In the *Coll. Celtis uado* is used once, in the imperative (44b). *Eo* occurs thirteen times, always in forms of more than one syllable (*eo* 17a, 18, *eamus* 28b, 46c, 59b, 60a, 60c, 64a, *ire* 28c, *eunt* 37a, *ite* 62a, 65, 69b).

So in the *Coll. Mon.–Eins.* (Dickey 2012) *uado* is used only for the monosyllabic forms of *eo* (*uadis* once, 7a; *uade* four times: 9g twice, 9j, 9n), whereas the longer forms of *eo* are still used (2g *eo*, 3f *eo*, 4k *eamus*, 8c *ire*, 10d *imus*, *eamus*, 11s *eamus*).

There is a distinction to be seen between the four *Colloquia* and the *Hist. Apoll.*, which may reflect the different dates of the respective works. In the *Colloquia uado* is used only to replace monosyllabic forms of *eo*, whereas in the later work *uado* has also encroached to a slight extent on non-monosyllabic forms.

With *Hist. Apoll.* 14.4 *uade celerius et dic illi*, cf. *Coll. Mon.–Eins.* 9g *uade ad Gaium et dic illi*, 9j *uade iterum et dic illi*, 9n *uade, dic illi*, *Coll. Harl.* 27a *uade ad fratrem et dic ei*. For this 'go and say' formula see also below, 43.12 for a passage of *Anon. Val. II*, and 43.14 (Gregory the Great).

On avoidance of monosyllabic forms in the *Hist. Apoll.* see Panayotakis (2012: 49), on the nominative *is*.

Vade is often associated with other imperatives, as in the present passage and in some of those just quoted, either with a connective, as in most cases in the last paragraph but one, or without, as in our passage of the *Hist. Apoll.* and at *Coll. Mon.–Eins.* 9n, above (cf. e.g. Vulg. 4 Rg 4.3 *uade, pete*). Pairs of imperatives without connective go back to the earliest period (see below, 45.14).

On *uade* see also below, 47.7.

10 non solum epulari: = *non solum non* (on the ellipse see Kortekaas 2007: 669, Panayotakis 2012: 482). On the tense of *desiderarem* see Kortekaas loc. cit.

11 subiit de subsannio nauis rursus ad nauem: *subsannium* is a rare hybrid compound denoting the hold of a ship (see Panayotakis 2012: 464). Athenagoras 'went up' (*subiit*: Kortekaas 2007: 670, Panayotakis 2012: 482) 'from' (*de*) the hold to the boat proper, i.e. apparently the deck, but *nauem* is an oddity (of part of the boat; a use not it seems in the *TLL*). B also has (*ascendit*) *in nauem*. The change to *lucem* that has been suggested does not look compelling (see further Kortekaas, Panayotakis locc. cit.).

Of note here is the placement of the two prepositional expressions after the verb in a main clause (see further index, 'word order, position of prepositional expressions'). When the verb is finite (as distinct from a participle, imperative or infinitive, which show their own tendencies of word order), postposition of prepositional expressions is the norm in this text. In this chapter there are thirteen cases of the order V + prep., compared with three of prep. + V in main clauses. In subordinate clauses the frequency of the two orders is much the same: four instances of V + prep., against three of prep. + V.

Here are figures from some other chapters:

	Main clauses		Subordinate clauses	
	V + prep.	prep. + V	V + prep.	prep. + V
Chapter 41	5	3	0	2
Chapter 46	5	3	0	5

Here we see a tendency for postponement to be avoided in subordinate clauses, and that is a reflection of the long-standing persistence of verb-final position in such clauses. By contrast no distinction was noted above (43.5) between subordinate and main clauses in the placement of direct objects in relation to the verb. These conflicting patterns underline the need for a systematic examination of late Latin word order, in which the possible influence of the Vulgate (inter alia) would have to be taken into account.

uenire procederet: for *procedo* + final infinitive see Panayotakis (2012: 483), and on the text Kortekaas (2007: 671).

12 bene mihi uenit in mente: 'perge, puer . . .': the phrase *uenit in mente* introduces direct speech. At *TLL* VIII.724.2–3 just two instances of the phrase with quotations following are referred to: Sen. frg. 119 Haase (vol. III, p. 443) *et tandem illi uenit in mentem: 'ab alio exspectes, alteri quod feceris'*; also Scaev. *Dig.* 33.7.20.pr. The phrase in our passage introduces words to be spoken, and it is not quite the same. For *bene* in this type of context Heraeus (1937: 114 n. 1 on Petron. 66.5 *bene me admonet domina mea*) cites *SHA*, *Tyr. trig.* 20.1, *Claud.* 10.1 *bene uenit in mentem*, as well as our passage. There is a large collection of examples of *(mihi) in mentem uenit* at *TLL* VIII.723.52ff. It goes back to early Latin and is common in Cicero. An example at *De orat.* 2.240 occurs in a piece of direct (and forceful) speech (*'heus tu,' inquit, 'quid tibi in mentem uenit ita respondere?'*) in a vivid narrative passage in which *ut uidit* also occurs, twice (2.239: see above, 43.3).

There is no need to add *-m* to *mente*, as the failure to observe a distinction between *in* + accusative and *in* + ablative is widespread (earlier in this chapter, at 5 *descendi . . . in litore*, the ablative cannot be removed by a single-letter emendation).

Perge is resumed immediately (13) by a different form of the same verb (*cumque per<r>exisset*). There are other resumptions of various types in the text: 13.5 *remisit remissamque*, 13.6–7 *recedite . . . et cum recessissent* (similar to that in our passage), 14.4–5 *dic illi . . . et cum dixisset ei* (so again), 17.2–3 *et permisi et permitto . . . permisso*), 20.4 *legit perlectoque nomen ibidem non legit*,

23.1 *uocantur amici, inuocantur uicinarum urbium potestates ... quibus con-uocatis*, 26.11–12 *supponite ... suppositas*, 34.2–3 *ingreditur ... dum fuisset ingressus*, 38.4–5 *titulum legit ... perlecto titulo*. Resumptions in literary Latin are discussed by Wills (1996, chapter 12). The phrases quoted above exemplify the author's stylistic aspirations.

The writer goes in for other features of assonance, such as the rhyming effects at 1.5 *cum luctatur cum furore, pugna<t> cum dolore, uincitur amore*.

On *pergo* see above, 39.15.

et dic ei ut mittat ad me Tharsiam: for *dico ut* see *TLL* V.1.986.69ff. The usage goes back to early Latin but is mainly in informal sources, such as letters (e.g. of Cicero). Note for example *Rhet. Her.* 4.63, in a racy specimen of character delineation, in which a master addresses a slave: *ei dicit in aurem aut ut domi lectuli sternantur aut ab auuncluo rogetur Aethiops qui ad balneas ueniat*.

For the construction with an imperative verb in conversational style in late Latin see *Coll. Harl.* (Dickey 2015) 15b *dic illi ut maneat me, Coll. Mont.* 11b *coquo dic ut pulmentaria bene condiat, Anon. Val. II* 88 *ambula Constantinopolim ad Iustinum imperatorem, et dic ei inter alia, ut reconciliatos ... restituat* (a notable example, because the usual formula *uade et dic* (see above, 43.9 on *uado*) has been changed by the replace-ment of *uade* with *ambula*, a change that shows that *ambula* means no more than 'go': see Adams (2013: 810, and below, 47.7).

For *dic* with the plain subjunctive see e.g. Petron. 70.10 (Trimalchio) *dic et Menophilae ... discumbat*, and below, 45 Conclusions, 'Linguistic characterisation'.

13 et leno audiens: *et* introducing the main clause after a temporal clause could be defended (see Hofmann and Szantyr 1965: 482 on apodotic *et*, with bibliography; also Kortekaas 2007: 673, Panayotakis 2012: 484, Galdi 2014). Panayotakis' objection (2012: 484) that *audiens* elsewhere always has a complement is not a conclusive one. He accepts the change to *haec* (and discusses various other proposed solutions).

licet autem contra uoluntatem, uolens misit illam: *uolens* immediately after *contra uoluntatem* looks like an absurdity, which is not resolved by changing *uolens* to *nolens* (which would simply repeat the idea of *contra uoluntatem*). Nor is the possibility (discussed by Kortekaas 2007: 673, Panayotakis 2012: 485) that the expression might be seen as a parallel to expressions such as *uolens nolensque* convincing. We could perhaps translate *uoluntas* with either of the meanings listed by the *OLD* s.v., 3, 7 ('approval, inclination'): although it was against his own inclination (we might say 'better judgment'), he did so readily enough in response to the entreaty.

14 ueniens autem Tharsia ad nauem, uidens eam Athenagora ait ad eam: typical late participial constructions. First, both participles are perfective in meaning. Second, the first construction is left hanging, such that it resembles a nominative absolute. There is no need to see Greek influence here (so Kortekaas 2007: 674). See further below, 44.37.2, 44.36.1, on such participial uses. The second version changes *ueniens . . . Tharsia* to *ueniente Tharsia*, and eliminates the participle with *Athenagoras*.

   hic <est> enim ars . . . necessaria: the second version here has *est*, but the ellipse of the copula in the present tense is so banal that there is no need to add it in the first version.

   ut consoleris . . . horteris consolationem recipere: the last three words, coming after *consoleris* a little earlier, add little, and are eliminated in the second version (see Kortekaas 2007: 675, Panayotakis 2012: 486 for examples of *consolationem recipere*; it is a periphrastic or support-verb construction that serves as the passive of the deponent verb *consolor*) (see below, 47.3 for a comparable expression).

   sedentem in tenebris . . . lugentem coniugem et filiam: long participial constructions, often postponed like this, had always been a feature of literary Latin. We have seen them in another late text (27 Conclusions, 'Similarities between the narratives'). Cf. earlier in this passage (2) *squalida barba, capite horrido et sordido in tenebris iacentem.*

Appendix: *ad* and the dative

Rec. A

The following examples from chapter 40 of the dative of the indirect object and of expressions with *ad* encapsulate most of the features of a system of sorts operating in this text in the expression of the indirect object (which in classical Latin is regularly conveyed by the dative but in Romance by prepositions with non-clitics, though there are remnants of the old inflectional system in clitic pronouns: see e.g. Adams 2013: 278, and Adams and de Melo, forthcoming): 40.4 *cui Athenagoras, princeps ciuitatis, ait . . .* (5) *item ait ad eum . . .* (8) *dabit tibi . . .* (12) *dic ei . . .* (14) *ait ad eam . . .* (16) *dabo tibi.* In this text this aspect of case grammar has the following features:

   (1) With verbs other than those of saying the old dative is still the norm. Here is a fairly comprehensive collection of the dative constructions with selected verbs: *do* (9.6, 10.3, 14.6, 15.1, 16.10, 17.2, 17.7, 17.8, 22.5, 25.12,

34.11, 34.12, 40.8, 40.16, 41.11, 41.12 twice, 51.6, 51.9), *dono* (17.6, 39.3, 39.8, 51.10, 51.12), *redono* (46.10), *reddo* (12.10, 38.1), *trado* (18.3, 20.6, 20.7, 22.6, 46.9), *denego* (17.9), *ostendo* (14.9, 16.3, 42.7, 49.2, 50.7), *demonstro* (13.1), *tribuo* (51.8), *assigno* (14.7), *affero* (16.6), *confero* (46.11), *offero* (35.4), *profero* (8.12), *refero* (30.1). This list of verbs could no doubt be extended.

I have noted only two instances of *ad* that might have been replaced by the dative with verbs of this general category. Notable is 34.11 *quantum dedit ad te iuuenis?*, a question which is immediately answered by means of the dative: *quater denos mihi aureos dedit*. The other is at 32.14: *qui iunctus sum ad pessimam uenenosamque serpentem et iniquam coniugem*; for verbs of joining with the dative see 22.4 *quem ego . . . tibi coniungere adoptaui*, 24.2 *iuncta sibi puellula*.

(2) With verbs of saying other than *ait*, the dative is also the norm. For example, with *dico* I have noted twenty instances of the dative, mainly pronominal (6.1, 14.4, 14.5, 21.7, 24.3, 24.4, 24.5, 29.3, 34.7, 35.9, 37.2, 39.8, 39.13, 40.12, 41.12, 47.3, 49.2) but sometimes nominal (10.1, 14.5, 48.2). *Dico* is used with *ad* only twice (24.6 *dixit ad coniugem*, 39.11 *dixit ad gubernum*). *Dic ei* (and pronominal variants), which is constant, was probably current in ordinary speech (see above, 43.12).

With other verbs loosely of this semantic field the dative is regular: e.g. *confiteor* (37.3), *expono* (28.2, 35.13), *indico* (2.5, 7.4, 15.5, 15.6, 34.11), *iuro* (14.1, 18.5, 22.5), *nuntio* (31.6, 48.9), *promitto* (32.4), *respondeo* (20.3, 42.8, 42.14, 42.16). One exception is at 6.5: *ad semetipsum locutus est dicens*.

(3) With *ait* it is a different matter. This is regularly complemented by *ad* in expressions of two types, those with a personal pronoun, and those with a name or noun. On the other hand when the complement is a relative pronoun the plain dative is the norm. All three of these categories do admit of some exceptions. I take the three types in turn.

First, I have counted forty instances of *ad eum/ad eam/ad eos* with *ait*, as e.g. 4.3 *sic ait ad eum*.[1] In chapters 41–3 alone, where conversations are reported, there are eighteen examples. There seem to be only two exceptions in this

---

[1] 4.3, 5.1, 8.11 *et ait ad eum*, 14.6, 16.5 *et ait ad eam*, 25.9, 31.14, 33.6 *et ait ad eam*, 33.10 *et ait ad eum*, 34.5 *et ait ad eam 'erige te'*, 34.15 *et ait iuuenis ad eam 'alleua te'*, 35.5 *et ait ad eam leno*, 35.6 *et ait ad eum puella*, 35.7 *et ait ad eum*, 35.9 *et ait ad eam*, 35.13, 39.3 *ait ad eum 'dona'*, 39.9, 40.5, 40.14, 41.6 *et ait ad eam*, 41.10 *et ait ad eam Athenagora*, 41.11 *et ait ad eum Tharsia*, 41.13, 42.1 *et ait ad eum Tharsia*, 42.5 *et ait ad eam Apollonius*, 42.6, 42.7, 42.10, 42.11, 42.13, 42.15, 43.1, 43.3, 43.5, 43.6 *et ait ad eam Apollonius*, 43.7, 43.8, 50.5, 50.11. The examples quoted here are all of types that will come up below in this Appendix in the discussion of the Vulgate version of the OT and its relationship to the *Hist. Apoll.*

category, at 19.3 (*quos uidens rex subridens ait illis*) and 21.1 (*ait illis*). In both the pronoun is *ille*. When the pronoun is *is, ad* is standard.

Second, I have counted seven instances of *ait* with *ad* and a noun or name: 9.6 *Apollonius autem ad Stranguillionem ait*, 17.2 *sic ait puella ad patrem suum*, 20.2 *quae <ad a>mores suos sic ait*, 24.3 *conuersus ait ad gubernatorem*, 26.6 *ad famulos ait*, 38.3 *ait ad famulos suos*, 51.8 *ait ad coniugem*. There are three exceptions: 7.4 *ait cuidam puero*, 26.1 *ait famulis suis* (contrast this with the two cases of *ad* above with the same noun), 27.6 *ait discipulo suo*.

Third, I have counted sixteen instances of *cui* with *ait* (7.5, 8.7, 8.13, 9.2, 12.11, 14.10, 15.3, 17.8, 18.4, 20.6, 24.9, 31.17, 33.9, 34.11, 40.4, 46.10) and one instance with *quibus* (32.17). For a rare variant see 16.9 *ad quem rex ait*.

Various observations may be made about these facts.

First, there is support here for the view that in the late Latin period there was no general encroachment of *ad* on the dative of the indirect object. That encroachment is only to be seen to any significant extent with verbs of saying. There is other evidence elsewhere suggesting that the development started with verbs of saying (Adams 2013: 278–88; also Adams and de Melo, forthcoming).

Second, there is one noteworthy feature of *ad* with such verbs in our text. *Ad* is used to mark the addressee even when the conversation is private, between equals, or without any suggestion that the voice has to be projected. Earlier, and in some late texts as well, *ad* only complements verbs of saying when the utterance is a public one (as for instance in the address of crowds), or of the type that might be described as 'speaking at' the addressee (Adams 2013: 281–2, 285–6, and Adams and de Melo, forthcoming). We are beyond that stage in this text, in which *ad* is employed whatever the nature of the utterance.

Third, the usage is lexically restricted in a narrow and rather odd way, in that *ad* is the norm with *ait* but not with *dico*. Avoidance of *ad* with *dico* does not show up in other late texts that I have looked at, such as the *Actus Petri cum Simone* (see Adams 2013: 285–6).

It was noted above that when the pronoun is *is* (*eum, eam, eos*) *ad* is regularly used with *ait*, whereas when the pronoun is *ille* the dative is preferred. Could the pronoun be the determinant of the construction? That cannot be the whole story. With *dico* both *illi* and *ei* are used, with the latter predominating (*illi*: 14.4, 24.5, 39.11; *ei*: 14.5, 29.3, 34.7, 37.2, 40.12, 41.12, 47.3 (*eis*), 49.2). It is not the pronoun but the verb that determines the construction. In this writer's idiolect for some reason *ait* was associated with *ad*, *dico* with the dative.

Rec. B

In the second recension of the *Hist. Apoll.* there are only twelve instances of *ad* expressing indirect object, all of them with verbs of saying. In many places an *ad* in Rec. A is eliminated. I list first all the examples, by chapter and line number in the edition of Kortekaas (1984):

4.6 ad iuuenem ait.
13.17 ad suos ait.
14.1 rex ad amicos ... ait.
17.10 ait ad famulos.
26.17–18 ad famulos ait.
35.17 ait ad eam.
38.7 ad famulos ait.
38.17 ait ad suos.
39.30 ait Athenagora ad unum de ser<u>is.
41.16 ait ad eam.
41.24 ait ad eam.
42.5 ait ad eum.

In six cases the addressees are groups of people, and these examples might display the old use in which crowds are addressed. On the other hand there are four cases of *ad* + *eum/eam*, one of *ad iuuenem* and one of *ad unum*.

What stands out here is the reduction in the number of instances of *ad eum/ eam* (forty in the earlier recension). The scribe does seem to have set out to avoid this usage, but without total success.

Here are the places where B has removed *ad* as found in A. I have not quoted all passages in full (again the numeration is that of Kortekaas 1984):

4.10 respiciens iuuenem ait (= A *sic ait ad eum*).
16.11 ait (= *ait ad eam*).
24.6 conuersus ad gubernatorem ait (= *conuersus ait ad gubernatorem*).
24.17 respiciens coniugem suam ait (= *conuersus dixit ad coniugem*).
25.26 ait (= *ait ad eum*).
31.31 ait (= *ait ad eum*).
33.18 ait Tharsiae (= *ait ad eam*).
33.28 ait (= *ait ad eam*).
34.25 quantum tibi dedit iuuenis (= *quantum dedit ad te iuuenis*).
34.34 ait (= *ait ... ad eam*).
35.8 ait (= *ait ad eam*).
35.13 ait (= *ait ad eum*).

35.22 dixit (= *ait ad eam*).
39.8 ait (= *ait ad eum*).
39.26 ait (= *ait ad eos*).
40.31 dixit (= *ait ad eam*).
41.26 ait (= *ait ad eam*).
41.28 ait (= *ait ad eam*).
41.31 ait (= *ad eum ait*).
42.1 ait (= *ait ad eum*).
42.10 ait (= *ait ad eum*).
42.14 ait (= *ait ad eam*).
42.20 ait (= *ait ad eum*).
42.24 ait (= *ait ad eam*).
42.29 ait (= *ait ad eum*).
43.1 ait (= *ait ad eum*).
43.8 ait (= *ait ad eum*).
43.12 ait (= *ait ad eum*).
43.15 ait (= *ait ad eum*).
43.19 ait (= *ait ad eam*).
50.12 ait (= *ait ad eos*).
50.24 cui ait (= *ait ad eum*).
51.19 ait (= *ait ad coniugem*).

There are twenty-nine cases here of *ad eum/eam/eos* eliminated in B, and other places where B has either been rewritten more radically or does not preserve passages with the *ad*-construction (the passages of A, with Panayotakis' numbering, are 8.11, 14.6, 35.6, 40.5, 41.11, 41.13, 42.5, 42.13, 43.5, 43.6). Notable is the replacement at 34.25 of *ad te* by the dative with *dedit*.

There are two other categories to be identified in the first list (of twelve examples) above (at the start of this section).

First, there are those places where B has the same usage as A (though in a few cases with changes of terminology). These are:

4.6 ad iuuenem ait (A has *ait ad eum*).
26.17–18 ad famulos ait.
35.17 ait ad eam.
38.7 ad famulos ait.
39.30 ait Athenagora ad unum de ser<u>is (A has *Antenagora dixit ad guuernum*).
41.16 ait ad eam.
41.24 ait ad eam.

Second, there are a few places where the scribe seems to have introduced the usage himself:

13.17 ad suos ait (A has *intuens famulos suos ait*).
14.1 rex ad amicos . . . ait (A has *rex autem . . . conuersus ad amicos suos ait*).
17.10 ait ad famulos (A has *intuens famulos . . . dixit*).
38.17 ait ad suos (A has *suos allocutus est dicens*).
42.5 ait ad eum (A has much the same speech but without the introductory phrase).

The redactor of B does not come across as a rigorous or consistent classiciser, but he does show a resistance to the *ad*-construction.

The Vulgate version of the OT and the *Hist. Apoll.*

There are similarities between the practice of the *Hist. Apoll.* (i.e. A) as described above and that of the Vulgate of the OT. A characteristic of the OT is the frequency with which *ait ad* (or *aio ad*) is used with accusative forms of *is*. The usage is not a feature of the NT, as we will see. An oddity of the latter, which is not strictly relevant here, is variability in the frequency of the *ad*-construction vis-à-vis the dative from book to book. In Matthew, for example, *ad* is very unusual, whereas in Luke it is common. Even in the latter, however, *ad* + *is* is rare. It is *ille* that is preferred with *ad* in the NT books that allow the construction. Some further details will be given below, and it will be shown that the variation between *ad* and the plain dative is determined largely by the Greek version of the NT. I start with *ait ad eum* et sim. in the OT (some further information about Bible translations will be found in Sznajder 2012).

ait ad eum

In the OT in the expression *ait/aio ad* the dependent pronoun is almost invariably *is* rather than *ille*. Here are just a few examples from a much larger number:

ad eum (Gn 8.21, Nm 22.8, 23.27, 1 Sm 15.28, 28.9, 2 Sm 1.3, 1.14, 1.16, 2.1, 13.24, 4 Rg 10.15).
ad eam (Gn 24.45, 2 Sm 14.5).
ad eos (Gn 39.14, Ex 5.4, 19.14, Lv 10.4, Ios 4.5, 10.25, Za 3.4).

In the NT on the other hand *ait* is used frequently with *ille* as its complement, often in the dative (e.g. Mt 9.15, 11.4, 12.39, 13.11, 13.28, 14.31, 15.3,

15.28, 15.34, 18.32, 19.16), but not infrequently with *ad* (see Lc 2.49, 8.22, 9.3, 9.13, 9.50, 9.62, 11.5, 11.39, 15.3, 19.13, 24.17). *Is* in the dative is also found with *ait*, but perhaps not as frequently as *illi* etc. (see e.g. Mt 16.2, 17.11, 19.4, 19.14). What is striking, however, is the rarity of *ait ad eum* etc. I have noted an instance at Lc 19.9 *ait Iesus ad eum*, but no others on a cursory inspection. Even if I have missed some, *ait ad eum* is an idiom of the OT, not of the NT.

There are also phrasal similarities between the OT and *Hist. Apoll.* in the use of *ait*. For example, the formula *et ait ad eum/eam* is common in the *Hist. Apoll.* (for examples see n. 1 above); cf. e.g. Nm 22.8 *et ait ad eum*, Ios 4.5 *et ait ad eos*. The subject, whether a name or noun, may follow the pronoun, as at *Hist. Apoll.* 35.5 *et ait ad eam leno*, 41.10 *et ait ad eam Athenagora*, 41.11 *et ait ad eum Tharsia* (so 42.1), 42.5 *et ait ad eam Apollonius*; cf. 1 Sm 15.28 *et ait ad eum Samuel* (so 2 Sm 1.14, 1.16), 2 Sm14.5 *et ait ad eam rex*. Or again, in both texts such expressions may be followed by an initial imperative, as at *Hist. Apoll.* 34.5 *et ait ad eam 'erige te'*, 39.3 *ait ad eum 'dona'*; cf. Ex 19.14 *ait ad eos 'estote parati'*, Lv 10.4 *ait ad eos 'ite et colligite'* (also Ios 4.5, 10.25).

Further similarities and differences

There is more to be said about the use of *ait* and its complements in the OT. Some other features of its use may be paralleled in the *Hist. Apoll.*, but not all of them. I list a few features of both types.

First, as in the *Hist. Apoll.*, so in the OT *ait ad* is used with names and nouns: e.g. Gn 17.19 *et ait deus ad Abraham* (cf. 48.21, Nm 34.16), Gn 3.14 *ad serpentem*, 24.65 *ad puerum*, Ex 3.13 *ad deum*.

Second, in the OT also *cui ait* is found: 1 Sm 4.16, 4 Rg 2.2, 4.3, 20.9, 20.14, 2 Par 18.14, Tb 5.13, Idt 12.3. However, in contrast to the *Hist. Apoll.*, *cui* is not invariable in the OT with this verb. For *ad quem/quam* see e.g. Gn 27.13, Ios 17.15, Dn 5.13.

Third, in the OT, unlike the *Hist. Apoll.*, *ait* is not only complemented by *ad* + accusative forms of *is*. *Is* also occurs with the verb in the dative: e.g. Gn 15.5, 42.33 and often.

Fourth, there is a difference between the OT (and the NT) on the one hand and the *Hist. Apoll.* on the other in the use of *dico* and its complements. In neither the OT nor the NT is there any restriction placed on the use of *ad* with *dico*. For *dico ad + eum* etc. in the OT see e.g. Gn 37.6, 37.13, 39.8, 40.8, 43.11, 47.29, 48.8, Ex 2.18, 4.2, 4.11, 5.21, 10.3, 12.21, 16.3, 32.2. In Luke in the NT I have noted twenty-five cases of *dico ad illum*, and eleven examples of *dico ad eum*.

Dico is not restricted in the OT to *ad*-complements: it also occurs with the dative (e.g. Gn 12.7 *dixit ei*, 12.18).

The variations between dative and *ad* with these verbs in the OT probably reflect variations in the Hebrew, between one Hebrew preposition אֶל, matched by *ad*, and another, לְ, matched by the dative (information from John Lee; see also Sznajder 2012: 283).

Explanations

How are we to explain the variability in the *Hist. Apoll.*, between the different types of complements with *aio* and *dico*, and between the relative dative *cui* alongside *ad* + *eum* etc. with *aio*? The variations in the complements in the Vulgate (not only the OT but also the NT: see further below) can be put down largely to the influence of the texts being translated. That is not an explanation that can necessarily be resorted to for the *Hist. Apoll.* (but see the next paragraph). Nor can we explain *ait ad eum* from the spoken language. The evidence is that the dative of pronouns was very persistent in late texts with verbs of saying (see e.g. Adams 2013: 286), in anticipation of the Romance survival of inflected pronominal (clitic) forms expressing indirect object (see also below, 50.45). Moreover the pronoun *is* itself was replaced by *ille*, and *ad eum* thus looks doubly odd when considered in relation to possible spoken usage.

The phrasal similarities noted above between the *Hist. Apoll.* and OT in the use of *ait ad eum* etc. suggest to me that the author, who has a lot of biblical phraseology (see e.g. Panayotakis 2012: 1, 8, and his Index locorum 681–2, where references in the commentary to the Vulgate are collected), had picked up this mannerism from the Vulgate version of the OT and used the phrase as a formula. He may also have taken note of examples of *cui ait*. These phrases apart, he had not studiously examined the biblical uses of verbs of saying and their complements, and thus otherwise fell into contemporary Latin usage when using *dico*. This last remark is made on the assumption that we do not have to posit the existence of a lost Greek original lying behind the Latin text. If the Latin were a mere translation of a lost work, then the reasons for the syntactic variability with verbs of saying would be impossible to determine.

Some remarks about the NT

It is noteworthy that the use of *ait ad eum* etc. in the *Hist. Apoll.* can be related to the Vulgate version of the OT but not that of the NT. For completeness I give some statistics below for indirect object complements of verbs of saying (mainly *aio* and *dico*, but a few other verbs that fall into this category have also been included) in selected passages of two Gospels (Matthew 1–8, Luke 1–6). There is a difference between the two, with the dative preferred in Matthew and *ad* used as often as the dative in Luke. The variation is entirely determined by the Greek version: in almost every case *ad* in the Latin corresponds to πρός in the Greek, and the dative in the Latin to the dative in the Greek. It is possible that the practice of Luke (Greek version) was influenced (as in other respects) by the Septuagint.

In Matthew 1–8 there are no prepositions with verbs of saying. There are forty-three examples of the dative with such verbs. I have noted just one discrepancy between the constructions of the Latin and the Greek (at 3.15).

In Luke 1–6 there are twenty-nine examples of *ad* with verbs of saying. On the other hand there are thirty-four examples of the dative. I noted only about eight places in the two groups of examples where the construction of the Latin does not correspond to that of the Greek. *Ait ad eum* (et sim.) does not occur in the selection, and *ille*, whatever the construction, outnumbers *is* (by just 9:8 in Matthew but 29:7 in Luke).

Conclusions

The *Hist. Apoll.* is a narrative text containing a lot of speech. One difference has been detected here between speeches and narrative, in the distribution of verba dicendi + *quod/quia*. This construction is confined to speeches, and the head verb is always in the first or second person, or imperative. Despite the widespread use of such dependent constructions in late Latin, there are some signs that they continued to be felt by some purists to be less 'literary' than the acc. + inf. We saw this attitude in Augustine's letter to Publicola (31.7).

The work is rich in its stylistic influences. Though it is not overtly Christian, it has exploited the language of the Vulgate (see Kortekaas 1984: 101–6 on Christian influence more generally). The account of *ad* and the dative above suggests not merely imitation of the Vulgate but specifically of the OT. The frequent use of *et* at the start of sentences (see 43.5) is a feature of biblical style, which had been picked up by other late writers of narrative texts (see 27.2). Some idea of the extent of literary phraseology may be gained from Panayotakis's Index locorum. The temporal use of *ut* with *uidit* and *audiuit* (see 43.3) was an old literary usage, found notably in Hyginus' *Fabulae* and adopted incessantly in this work. The author also had a taste for assonance and various types of verbal resumption (see 43.12).

The work reveals itself linguistically in virtually every sentence to be a product of late antiquity (see Kortekaas 1984: 97–101, with examples and further bibliography). See e.g. 43.5 on *sermo*, 43.6 on *inquiro*, 43.9 on the distinction between *leuo* and *tollo*, 43.9 on the use of *uado*, 43.14 on participial usage. The word order has marked VO characteristics (see 43.5, on verb position and the position of the genitive, 43.11, on placement of prepositional expressions). The Latin looks idiomatic, and is not obviously translationese (see e.g. 43.6 on *libenti animo*, 43.10 on *non solum*, with Panayotakis referred to there, 43.12 on *bene mihi uenit in mente*).

This is a work surviving in two recensions, and is another of those late works the wording of which was clearly not treated as sacrosanct by scribes. The second recension eliminates some of the verbosity of the other, and also some non-classical usages. On the elimination of many examples of *ad* for the dative see the Appendix. See also 43.3, on the removal of *quoquam*, and 43.14, on the conversion of the hanging participle *ueniens* to an ablative absolute. Various expressions or usages dropped by B have not been commented on above. They include, for example, the elliptical *non solum* (10).

44
ITINERARIVM ANTONINI PLACENTINI 36-7, WITH DIFFERENT VERSIONS

Introduction

This work, attributed to the second half of the sixth century (Geyer 1898: xxvi, Milani 1977: 36–8: probably after 560), records a journey to Jerusalem. It has attracted less attention than the *Peregrinatio Aetheriae*, which belongs to the same genre, but has its own linguistic interest. The text is printed by both Geyer and Milani in two versions. The first is based on the manuscripts referred to as G (Sangallensis 113, s. VIII–IX) and R (Rheinaugiensis, now Turicensis, 73, s. IX exeuntis–X exeuntis) (Geyer 1898: xxvii). The other in Milani's edition is based on sixteen manuscripts, but in that of Geyer on only three, referred to as Br (Bruxellensis Bibl. R. 2922 (7430)), M (Monacensis, Bayer Staatsbibl. 19149) and B (Bernensis, Burgerbibl. 582). A full account of the manuscripts is given by Milani (1977: 47–57), who regards the second version as a reworking of the text after the Carolingian reforms; she incidentally refers to M above as D. Of the manuscripts of the first version (G and R), R is described by Geyer as showing much greater conformity 'ad praecepta grammaticae' (1898: xxvii). For Geyer, G is full of 'lacunis, mendis orthographicis et grammaticis', but he expresses some uncertainty whether these are to be attributed to the author or to the scribe (1898: xxvii 'quae [lacunae etc.] utrum auctoris an librarii culpae tribuendae sunt, saepe difficillimum est diiudicatu'). Such uncertainties highlight the fact that a late text traditionally considered 'vulgar' might owe its deviations from standard norms as much to scribes as to the original author, or conversely its non-standard deviations, if original, might have been partly corrected by the scribes of some manuscripts. The editing of such texts poses different problems from the editing of literary texts. Two works with a weak textual basis of which the language might well have been vulgarised are the *Peregrinatio Aetheriae* and the *Mulomedicina Chironis*.

I quote below, first, two chapters of Geyer's attempt to produce a critical edition of the first recension (referred to here as Rec. A; section numbers are taken from Milani's edition of 1977), and, second, the two chapters as they are printed in Milani's edition of the second recension (B). Only the first recension is translated here, as the second is much less complicated, and also truncated. The Commentary has lemmata from Geyer's edition of Rec. A, though it does contain some comparisons between the two versions.

Milani does not offer a critical edition of the first recension, but prints G and R alongside each other. I have not followed her in that, which would be wasteful of space here, given that any significant differences between the two manuscripts and any inadequacies in Geyer's edition can be pointed out and discussed in the Commentary. Milani does however provide a critical text of the second recension. She discusses the relationship between the manuscripts of this version at 59–69, with a stemma at 68.

References in the Commentary to other passages of the *Itinerarium* are based on Geyer's text, with Milani's section numbers added.

On aspects of the language of the work see Milani (1974a, 1974b), Burton (2011: 497–9), Galdi (2015).

Texts

Rec. A

36.1 Ambulantibus nobis per heremum dies V uel VI cameli nobis aquam portantes, sextarium mane et sextarium sero per hominem accipiebamus. **2** amarescente aqua illa in utres in felle mittebamus in ea harenam et indulcabatur. **3** familia autem Saracenorum uel uxores eorum uenientes de heremo, ad uiam sedentes in lamentatione, et sareca missa ante se petiebant panem a transeuntibus. **4** et ueniebant uiri ipsarum, adducebant utres cum aqua frigida de interiore parte heremi et dabant, et accipiebant sibi panes et adducebant resticulas cum radices, quorum odor suauitatis super omnia aromata, nihil licentes; quia anathema habebant et dies festos suos celebrabant. **5** populus autem, qui per ipsum maiorem heremum ingrediebatur, numerus duodecim milia sexcenti.

37.1 Qui perambulantes per heremum octaua decima die uenimus ad locum, ubi Moyses de petra eduxit aquas. exinde alia die uenimus ad montem dei Choreb. **2** et inde mouentes ut ascenderemus Sina, et ecce multitudo monachorum et heremitarum innumerabilis cum crucis psallentes obuiauerunt nobis, qui prostrati in terra adorauerunt nos, simili modo et nos facientes flentes. **3** et introduxerunt nos in uallem inter Choreb et Sina, ad cuius pede montis est fons ille, ubi Moyses uidit signum rubi ardentis, in quo et oues adaquabat. **4** qui fons inclusus est intra monasterium, quod monasterium circumdatum muris munitis, in quo sunt tres abbates scientes linguas, hoc est Latinas et Graecas, Syriacas et Aegyptiacas et Bessas, uel multi interpretes singularum linguarum. in quo sunt condita monachorum. **5** et ascendimus in monte continuo milia tria, et uenimus ad locum ad speluncam, ubi absconditus fuit Helias, quando fugit ante Iezabel. **6** ante ipsa spelunca surgit fons, qui inrigat montem. **7** inde ascendimus milia continuo tria in summum cacumen montis, in quo est oratorium modicum, plus minus pedes sex in latitudine et in longitudine. in quo nullus praesumit manere. **8** sed orto iam die ascendent monachi et faciunt opus dei. **9** in quo loco omnes pro deuotione barbas et capillos suos tondent et iactant, ubi etiam et ego tetigi barbas.

Rec. B

36.1 Ambulantes per heremum dies VI, camelis nobis aquam portantibus, sestarium mane et sestarium uespere cotidie dabatur per hominem. **2** amarescente aqua in utres in modum fellis, mittebamus in eam harenam et indulcabatur. **3** familia autem Sarracenorum uel uxores eorum uenientes de heremo, cum lamentatione in uia sedentes, sarcina deposita, petebant panem a transeuntibus. **4** et ueniebant uiri ipsarum de interiore parte heremi adducebantque utres cum aqua frigida et accipiebant sibi panes et adducebant restes cum radicibus, quarum odor suauissimus super aromata et dies suos festos celebrabant. **5** populus autem, qui per ipsum maiorem heremum ingrediebatur ad explorandum, numero XII milia sexcenti.

37.1 Qui perambulantes heremum, octaua die uenimus ad montem dei Choreb. **2** et inde mouentes ut ascenderemus montem Syna, ecce multitudo monachorum et heremitarum cum crucibus psallentes obuiauerunt nobis, prostrati in terram adorauerunt nos, simili modo et nos facientes lacrimauimus. **3** tunc introduxerunt nos in uallem inter Choreb et Syna, ad cuius pedem montis est fons ille, ubi Moyses adaquabat oues, quando uidit ardentem rubum. **4** qui fons inclusus est infra monasterium, in quo monasterio sunt tres abbates scientes linguas, hoc est Latinam, Graecam, Syram et Aegyptiacam et Bessam. **5** inde uenimus ad speluncam, ubi absconditus fuit Helias propheta, quando fugit Iezabel mulierem perfidam. **6** ante ipsam speluncam surgit fons, qui irrigat ipsum montem. **7** inde ascendimus in summum cacumen montis, in quo est oratorium modicum habens in longitudine pedes sex, similiter et in latitudine. in quo nullus manere praesumit. **8** sed orto iam die ascendunt monachi de supradicto monasterio et celebrant ibi officium. **9** in quo loco multi pro deuotione tondent capillos suos et barbas, nam et ego ibi tetigi barbam meam.

Translation (of A)

36.1 While we were walking through the desert for five or six days, camels carrying water for us, we received a sextarius in the morning and a sextarius in the evening per man. **2** If that water became bitter in the bladders, turning into something bile-like, we put sand in it and it became sweet. **3** A family of Saracens or rather their wives had come from the desert and were sitting at the roadside in lamentation, and they had spread cloth before them and were asking passers-by for bread. **4** And their husbands kept coming, bringing bladders with cold water from the inner desert, and handing them over and receiving loaves themselves, and they kept bringing string bags with roots, the sweet smell of which surpassed that of all spices, and they were not entertaining any bidding (for) them because they had a curse (hanging over such behaviour) and because they were celebrating their holy days. **5** The people who arrived through the greater desert numbered 12,600.

37.1 Walking through the desert we came on the eighteenth day to the place where Moses drew water from stone. Then on the next day we came to Choreb the mountain of God. **2** And leaving there to ascend Sinai – and lo a countless multitude of monks and hermits with crosses and singing psalms met us. They threw themselves on the ground and did obeisance to us and we too weeping acted in the same way. **3** And they took us into the valley between Choreb and Sinai, at the foot of which mountain there is that fountain where Moses saw the sign of the burning bush, and in which he also watered the sheep. **4** This fountain is enclosed within a monastery, which is surrounded by fortified walls, in which there are three abbots fluent in languages, that is Latin and Greek, Syriac and Egyptian and the language of the Bessi, and many interpreters of individual languages. Here there are the stores of the monks. **5** And we went up on the mountain for fully three miles, and we came to the place – to the cave – where Elias was in hiding when he fled before Jezabel. **6** In front of the cave there rises a spring which waters the mountain. **7** From there we went up fully three miles to the very summit of the mountain, where there is a little oratory, more or less six feet wide and six feet long. Here no one dares to stay the night. **7** But at daybreak monks ascend and do the work of God. **8** Here they all as an act of devotion cut off their beards and hair and throw them down, and here I also put some touches to (my) beard.

Commentary

36.1 ambulantibus nobis . . . accipiebamus: an incoherent sentence, whatever text is adopted, which illustrates the indifference of some late writers to participial agreement. *Ambulantibus nobis*, which is printed by Geyer, comes from R; G has *ambulauimus nobis*. The latter is an attractive reading, because verbs of motion are sometimes used with the reflexive dative in late Latin, usually with the implication 'on our own, in isolation'. On the text (and for parallels) see E. Löfstedt (1911: 141), Dahlén (1964: 88), and for the sense of such a dative see Dahlén (1964: 89 n. 1): 'we walked on our own through the desert for five or six days'; see also Milani (1974b: 384). Similarly *uagari sibi* is found in an inscription on a brick from London: *RIB* 2491.147 *Austalis dibus XIII uagatur sib<i> cotidim*. Note too *Edict. Roth.* 216 *et uadant sibi ubi uoluerint liberi* ('and let the children go off where they want'; cf. Fr. *ils s'en vont* < *illi sibi inde uadunt*, with an additional marker of separation, *inde/en*), 217, p. 96 *mortuo . . . marito, uadat sibi una cum filiis suis et cum omnis res suas* ('when the husband . . . is dead, let the wife go off/depart along with her sons and all her possessions'). Norberg (1943: 168) cites Aug. *Epist.* 34.3, *CSEL* 34, p. 24.16 *uadam mihi ad eos, qui nouerunt exsufflare gratiam in qua ibi natus sum, destruere formam quam in utero eius accepi*. On such reflexive dative constructions see Adams (2013: 357–8).

If *ambulantibus nobis* is accepted it would either be dative (of advantage) with *portantes*, in which case *nobis* is repeated needlessly later in the clause, or an ablative absolute followed by a breakdown in the syntax. *Cameli . . . portantes* is a hanging participial construction (for which see below, 44.37.2 on *mouentes*), followed by a change of subject in the final verb of the sentence. *Ambulauimus* does not improve the structure of the sentence, as *cameli . . . portantes* remains unattached.

The second recension is different but offers no improvement. Here the camels appear in an ablative absolute (*camelis . . . portantibus*), but *ambulantes* is now left hanging, because there is a switch into the third person singular passive in the main verb (*dabatur*).

ambulantibus nobis per heremum: the word order of this text is typical of that seen in other late texts in this anthology (see index, 'word order', various subdivisions). Modifying elements, such as the prepositional expression here, are mainly to the right of the verb or the governing term. Here are some figures from this passage alone. First, prepositional expressions follow the verb (whether finite or participial) twenty-two times and precede it six times (twice in subordinate clauses). Second, genitives follow their noun eleven times and never precede it. Third, objects follow finite verbs thirteen times and precede five times (three times in subordinate clauses). Finally, there is one dependent infinitive only, and that follows the governing verb (37.7 *praesumit manere*).

sextarium mane et sextarium sero: it is in this sort of context (in opposition to *mane*) that *sero*, originally = 'late in the day', would have acquired the meaning 'in the evening', which it must have here; the second recension has the classical *uespere*. In some Romance languages the nominalised adjective *serus* survives in the feminine with the meaning 'evening' (e.g. It. *sera*), and in others in the masculine (e.g. Fr. *soir*) (see *REW* 7841). The feminine (which is found for example in the *Peregrinatio Aetheriae*) probably derives from an ellipse of the feminine form of *dies* (*sera dies* > *sera*), whereas the masculine must derive from *sero* itself. For the semantic development one might compare Sp. *tarde* (adverb) < Lat. *tarde* 'late, too late' (*REW* 8573), which may be used as a feminine noun meaning 'afternoon, evening' (*buenas tardes* 'good afternoon, good evening'). For further details see E. Löfstedt (1911: 75).

36.2 amarescente aqua illa in utres in felle: *fel* here cannot mean 'bile' literally, but must mean more generally 'bitter liquid', or perhaps 'bitterness', in a more abstract sense; the second recension has *in modum fellis*. At *TLL* VI.1.424.48f. the example from the first recension is cited with the lemma 'evanescente notione primaria i. q. amaritudo', along with just two other weakened instances, both from the Vulgate, which must be the source of the usage. *In utres* must comprise *in* + accusative where the ablative is expected, and *in felle* must show either *in* + ablative where the accusative is expected, or *in* + accusative with omission of *-m*. *Fel* is originally neuter, but the form *fellem* is otherwise attested (*TLL* VI.1.422.28).

indulcabatur: a late denominative (*Vetus Latina*, Vulgate, Christian and medical writers). The simplex *dulco* is also found in later Latin (*TLL* s.vv.).

36.3 familia . . . petiebant: the present participles *uenientes* and *sedentes* (the first perfective: 'having come') are coordinated to the finite verb *petiebant* by *et*. This feature, which is eliminated in the second recension, is common in late texts (for many examples, some from the present work, see Eklund 1970: 172–7). See also below, 47.16, 48.4.3.

uel uxores eorum: *uel* seems to introduce a correction here (*OLD* s.v. 3). In one place later (37.4 *uel multi interpretes*) it is replaceable with *et*, and that might just be so here too. The other recension also has *uel*.

sareca: this is an alternative form of *serica* 'silk cloth', which is used particularly in medieval Latin of fabric or a tunic, originally of silk but not necessarily so: see Niermeyer (1976: 938).

missa: the second version has *deposita*, a difference illustrating the intrusion of *mitto* into the semantic field 'put' (see further below, 44.37.9 on *iactant*, and also above, 27.10, and below, 50.29).

36.4 et dabant, et accipiebant sibi panes: *et dabant* is omitted by R and the second version. Whether or not it is accepted (it fits well before *et accipiebant*), *sibi* refers to the male Saracens, who bring water for the women and receive bread for themselves. *Sibi* is a dative of advantage and contrastive, and is not 'pleonastic'. The passage from *et ueniebant* to *radices* has a pedestrian structure, with five imperfect verbs in short clauses tacked on one after the other mainly by *et* (with the verb following immediately after *et*, a mannerism seen in the *Pass. Perp.* and in biblical style: see above, 27.2), though the first instance of *adducebant*, at the head of its clause, is in a relation of clausal asyndeton with the previous verb *ueniebant*. The second recension has here *adducebantque*. Different punctuations would be possible, but in any case the narrative drifts on without subordination or temporal/logical connectives, with all the finite transitive verbs preceding their objects. The imperfects seem to indicate repeated actions.

resticulas cum radices: the second version has *restes cum radicibus* (with the accusative a variant reading). For *cum* + accusative see e.g. in this text 7.7 *cum luminaria*, 8.3 (G) *cum paleas*, 11.4 (G) *cum rugitos* (further examples in the index of Milani, 1977: 322). See also below, 44.37.2 on *cum crucis*, and also index, s.v. *cum* '+ accusative'.

Resticulas ought to mean 'strings, little cords' (*restis* 'rope'). Either these were attached to the roots, which might then be slung across the shoulder, or the reference is to string bags, nets made of string. Both the base noun (so the second recension) and the diminutive have Romance reflexes (but mainly *restis*) (*REW* 7250–1).

odor suauitatis: so both G and R. The second recension has *odor suauissimus*, alongside which *suauitatis* is manifestly an abstract noun in the genitive with adjectival role. For the expression, which is biblical, see *TLL* IX.2.470.73ff. Structures of this type are not uncommon in Christian Latin under Hebrew/biblical influence (see e.g. Hofmann and Szantyr 1965: 64, Petersmann 1977: 72), though sometimes found elsewhere (note Petron. 93.4 *moderationis uerecundiaeque uerba*, with Habermahl 2006: 250).

aromata: '(that of) all spices', a *comparatio compendiaria* (Kühner and Stegmann 1955: II. 566–7, Hofmann and Szantyr 1965: 826), for 'surpassed (the sweet smell) of all spices'. It is an ancient form of comparison going back in Greek to Homer (see e.g., particularly on later Greek, Rydbeck 1967: 78–80).

nihil licentes: this is the verb *liceor* 'make a bid' (usually at auction), presumably here of haggling informally over the price. See *TLL* VII.2.1357.81ff., quoting this passage at 1358.22f.

36.5 populus autem . . . numerus duodecim milia sexcenti: the second version has a logical construction with *numero* for *numerus*. In the first version there is probably either textual corruption (in *numerus*), or an anacoluthon, with the sentence disrupted by the relative clause and *populus* left hanging: 'the people – their number (was) 12,600'. Alternatively some might be tempted to see a specifying apposition (see Milani 1974b: 414); cf. 18.4 *lapis, unde clausus monumento, ante os monumenti est, color uero de petra* (though here the copula can be understood).

37.1 perambulantes: perfective. G has *perambulantibus*.
alia die: for this phrase see above, 29.1.

37.2 et inde mouentes: here *mouentes* is a hanging initial nominative, as there is a change of subject in the main verb that follows (*obuiauerunt nobis*), with the referents of *mouentes* now expressed in the dative *nobis*. Again the participle is coordinated to the main verb by *et* (see above on 44.36.3). The second version removes the coordination but leaves *mouentes* hanging. A syntactic construction might have been produced by a dative *mouentibus*, but *nobis* could hardly be left separated from it by such a distance.

Mouentes is used intransitively for the reflexive *se mouentes*, in the sense 'departing' (from there), < 'shifting ourselves'. Both the reflexive use and the intransitive are found in the *Per. Aeth.* (and given the meaning *abire* by van Oorde 1929: 133): note 16.5 *qui sanctus monachus uir ascitis necesse habuit post tot annos, quibus sedebat in heremum, mouere se*, alongside 10.7 *et iterato post lectione facta est oratio, et gratias deo agentes mouimus inde* (note the same phrase with *inde* as that in the present text). An early instance of the reflexive in this sense (and looking slangy) is in a Pompeian graffito: *CIL* IV.8400 *moue te, fellator* (see Väänänen 1966: 113; = 'go away'). Note too Cic. *Att.* 4.9.2 *ego me de Cumano moui a. d. V Kal. Mai.* ('I left Cumae on 26 April', Shackleton Bailey 1965–70: II.101). Cic. *Att.* 9.1.1 (*postquam ille Canusio mouerat*) is translated by Shackleton Bailey (1965–70: IV.121) as 'after he marched from Canusium', and in his note (358) he understands *castra* as object of *mouerat* (so it seems *TLL* VIII.1546.32). That is possible, but not certain in this context, where a few lines earlier *profectus erat* had been used of the same event (*nam Canusio VIII<I> Kal. profectus erat Gnaeus*); *mouerat* looks like the intransitive use, = 'departed', and it is just as easy to derive such an intransitive from ellipse of the reflexive, given Cicero's own use of the full phrase in the required sense, as from ellipse of *castra*. A similar example is at Livy 33.26.6 *priusquam <a>ut hi praetores ad bellum prope nouum . . . proficiscerentur aut ipsi consules ab urbe mouerent* (see on the intransitive use *TLL* VIII.1546.15ff., 29ff., but without much semantic classification or citation of late examples).

The classical examples, most notably in Livy, tend to be in military contexts (see *TLL* 1546.30) and open to the interpretation that there has been ellipse of *castra* (note e.g. Livy 10.20.6 *ex quibus inquirendo cognoscit ad Volturnum flumen sedere hostem, inde tertia uigilia moturum*), though it is usually possible to assume ellipse of the reflexive pronoun (see further *OLD* s.v. 6b). The history of intransitive *moueo* has not been fully written.

At Ter. *Eun.* 912–13 (*moue uero ocius | te nutrix. :: moueo*) the meaning is more literally 'move (yourself) more quickly', though the alternation of the explicit reflexive with *moueo* suggests that the intransitive use may indeed sometimes have originated from ellipse of a reflexive pronoun even in the earlier period.

cum crucis: so G, which must be *cum* + acc. pl. (see above, 44.36.4 on *cum radices*). R has *cruce*, which is correct in syntax but does not look right because a plural seems required. It may be a correction of *cruces*. Milani prints *cum crucibus* in the second version, but there is another reading, *cum cruces*, adopted by Geyer.

obuiauerunt nobis: *obuiare* is a late word for *obuiam ire*, which according to *TLL* IX.2.317.33ff. is not definitely attested until the *Vetus Latina*. It has reflexes in the Romance languages (*TLL* 317.35ff.).

adorauerunt nos, simili modo et nos facientes flentes: these participles in G, better punctuated with a comma between, can be taken in agreement with the preceding (second, nominative) *nos*, though the Latin is awkward, with *nos* repeated. The clause beginning *simili*, which must mean 'we too acting in the same way, weeping', lacks a finite verb. R omits *flentes*. In the second recension the construction is more straightforward: *simili modo et nos facientes lacrimauimus*.

37.4 qui fons inclusus est intra monasterium, quod monasterium circum-datum muris munitis: the repetition of the antecedent (*monasterium*) in the relative clause is something of a mannerism in these pilgrimage texts (on the *Per. Aeth.* see E. Löfstedt 1911: 81–3). Cf. in this text 15.1 *est illa arbor, ubi ascendit Zachaeus uidere dominum, qui arbor . . .*, 32.1 *ex qua fons processit, quae fons . . .*, 32.3 *ubi Esaias a serra secatus est uel iacet, quae serra . . .* This stylistic tic seems to reflect the authors' keenness to have everything on their pilgrimage precisely specified.

The masculine *fons* is in R and the second recension. G however has the feminine (*quae fons inclausa est*). *Fons* is one of numerous nouns of variable or changing gender in the history of Latin. It is masculine in classical Latin, but the feminine turns up in later Latin (see *TLL* VI.1.1022.38ff.), and survives in Romance reflexes (e.g. Sp. *fuente*: see Stotz 1998: 140 for details). In earlier

Italian *fonte* varies between masculine and feminine in both literal and metaphorical meanings (so in Petrarch: information from Nigel Vincent). Similar variability can be seen in *arbor* (G) in 15.1, cited in the last paragraph, where masculine and feminine are in the same sentence (note too R *quae arbor, inclausus*). *Arbor* was originally feminine, but it changed to masculine in later Latin and Romance (see Adams 2013: 385–6, and the whole of chapter XIX on gender variation). On gender variation in the present text see the comprehensive account of Milani (1974b: 361–71).

in quo sunt tres abbates scientes linguas, hoc est Latinas et Graecas, Syriacas et Aegyptiacas et Bessas: the main determinant of the illogical plurals *Latinas, Graecas* etc. must be a mechanically written agreement with the preceding *linguas*. See however Wackernagel (1926–28: I.96) = Langslow (2009: 130) on his fifth type of plural for singular: the plural may be used 'when the idea is of something relatively extended in a spatial sense, while the singular is used when the relevant object is regarded as a unitary mass' (quoted from Langslow). Did the writer (or scribes) perhaps allow *Latinas* etc. because of the wide currency of Latin and various of the languages beyond their places of origin? The second recension has *linguas*, followed by the expected singulars *Latinam* etc. On balance the plurals are probably to be explained in the way suggested first above.

condita: for this substantival use see *TLL* IV.149.10ff. (with this passage at 25f.).

37.5 et ascendimus in monte continuo milia tria ... (7) inde ascendimus milia continuo tria: *continuo* in these two places might seem to be translatable with a temporal meaning ('at once'), or alternatively in the sense 'without a break', i.e. we made the ascents in one unbroken advance (so too at 31.1 *continuo milia XX de Hierusolima uenimus in monte Gelbuae*). But the word is common in the text, and any temporal meaning is ruled out in cases where no action or movement is referred to at all: see 2.3 *inter Sidona et Tyrum et Saraptam continuo milia septem*, 25.3 *inter sepulchra habet continuo gressus XX*, 29.3 *continuo medium miliarium a Bethlem in suburbio Dauid ibi iacet* (cf. the second recension *miliario semis de Bethleem in suburbe Dauid iacet Dauid*). In these passages a measurement is given, and indeed every example of *continuo* in the text is accompanied by a measurement (usually *milia* or an equivalent) and a numeral. Behind the usage must lie the meaning 'in a straight/unbroken line' (so it seems *TLL* IV.728.19ff., 'i. q. continenter ... de loco'): so 'we went up the mountain a straight three miles', with the idea presumably being that the distance specified was no more and no less, i.e. 'fully, a good', a meaning that seems to be at 42.4 also: *nam liquor ipsius unguenti tenet continuo per milia duo*.

ad locum ad speluncam: so R; G has *ad locum speluncae*. For pleonasm of
the type in R in local phrases, where *locus* or another vague term such as a local
adverb is immediately specified by a more precise appositional term, see *Mul.
Chir.* 92 *quodcunque iumentum in eo loco inter maxillas fistulam fecerit*, and
Adams (2013: 586), along with E. Löfstedt (1911: 144) and *TLL* VII.2.1583.17ff.
(the latter two citing the passage from the *Itin. Ant. Plac.*). On the phenomenon in general, see above, 3.421 and the bibliography there, and also index,
'locative/temporal expressions, double'. *Locus* in such double expressions need
not be pleonastic, for example if it precedes an exotic place name and thus
makes clear the nature of the name (see below, 46.3), but with a common noun
such as *spelunca* it has no obvious point. The second recension eliminates the
pleonasm (*inde uenimus ad speluncam*). The same usage is found twice at 41: 1
exinde uenimus . . . ad locum ad LXXII palmas et XII fontes . . ., 5 *et inde
uenimus ad locum ad ripam* (and is eliminated in both places again by
the second recension). In this text such pleonasm is probably a consequence
of formulaic composition. The formula *(ex)inde uenimus ad locum* recurs (so
e.g. in 41 again, 4 *exinde uenimus ad locum ubi filii Israhel . . .*), and sometimes
the writer probably committed himself to the full formula before stating the
specific goal, which rendered *ad locum* redundant. On the tendency to fossilisation of *locus* in another formulaic text (*Tablettes Albertini*), see above, 41.3.
See also below, 46.2–3.

For another type of pleonasm in a local expression see this text, 42.1 *intus
autem in pelago ipso*, where *intus* redundantly introduces *in* (on this type, from
Plautus onwards, see above, 5.8 on Cato *Agr.* 157.3 *subtus suppurat sub carne*;
for such expressions in this work see Milani 1974b: 401).

ubi absconditus fuit Helias: *absconditus fuit* (with *fuit* not *est*) is not
a genuine passive with an implied agent that might have been expressed by
ab, because Elias was not hidden by someone else but hid himself. Nor would it
be convincing to suggest that the verb is middle. *Absconditus* is adjectival (see
OLD s.v. *absconditus* 1 for this use) and *fuit* used to indicate a state in the past
('was hidden, in hiding'). Participles with *fui* rather than the usual perfect
passive formant *sum* can often be interpreted as adjectival. A very similar case
can be found in Cicero at *Sest.* 69: *quo patefacto ferroque deprenso, ille inclusus
domi tam diu fuit quam diu inimicus meus in tribunatu*. This is translated by
Kaster (2006: 71) as follows: 'after the plan was uncovered and a weapon seized,
<u>he shut himself up</u> in his house for the balance of my enemy's tribunate' (my
emphasis). He was not shut up by someone else, which would be the implication of a genuine passive periphrasis, but was in hiding of his own volition in
his own house (more literally, 'he was for the balance of my enemy's tribunate
shut up at home') (cf. *OLD* s.v. *inclusus* 1). *Fuit* has to be understood as well in

the *quam diu* clause, where *est* would have given the wrong meaning. Cicero appears largely to have avoided *fui* as a perfect tense auxiliary (see Blase 1903: 174); see however Neue and Wagener (1892–1905: III.139–40) (apparent cases may be due to textual corruption) and the next paragraph.

Similarly Riemann (1885: 215) collects and discusses instances of past participle + *fui* in Livy, and makes a semantic observation. *Fui* marks not a past *action*, but a *state* which existed in the past, sometimes with the idea that this state has ceased, sometimes without this idea. This remark leads Riemann to note as a consequence that in certain passages the participle has taken on the force of an adjective, which is the case in our passage. Note for example Livy 9.11.3, where the semantic field of the periphrasis is the same as that just seen: *restituat legiones intra saltum quo saeptae fuerunt* (Riemann: 'où elles se trouvaient enfermées').

Another occasional function of *fui* in classical Latin was to effect an explicit contrast between a past state/action (*fui*) and a present state (*sum*). See e.g. *Lex agr.* 77 [*quei*] . . . *factei createiue sunt fueruntue* (Neue and Wagener 1892–1905: III.135, Hofmann and Szantyr 1965: 322). There are examples of this type in Cicero (see Neue and Wagener loc. cit., Blase 1903: 173), as at *De orat.* 1.187 *omnia fere, quae sunt conclusa nunc artibus, dispersa et dissipata quondam fuerunt.*

In the present text genuine aoristic perfective passives (as well as stative perfect passives) are still regularly formed with *sum* rather than *fui*: e.g. 22.4 *est columna, ubi flagellatus est dominus*, 22.7 *est . . . et corona de spinis, qua coronatus est dominus*, 22.7 *et lancea, de qua in latere percussus est dominus*, 22.8 *sunt et lapides multae, cum quibus lapidatus est Stephanus*, 22.9 *est et columnella, in qua crux posita est beati Petri, in qua crucifixus est Romae*, 23.2 *in praetorio, ubi auditus est dominus*, 23.4 *petra . . . in qua leuatus est dominus, quando auditus est a Pilato.* This is a tiny selection from many examples. There is just a small number of participles with *fui* that seem to be real perfect passives, though even some of these are open to doubt: 16.3 *cellula, ubi fuit inclausa uel iacet sancta Pelagia in corpore*, 18.2 *ubi corpus domini Iesu Christi positum fuit*, 18.2 *lucerna aerea, quae in tempore ad caput ipsius positum fuit*, 19.3 *locus, ubi crucifixus fuit, paret.* The last two examples should be compared with two of the formations with *est* just cited. See also Milani (1974b: 383) on *fui*.

The interest of the *fu-* formation is that it survives in Romance as a passive referring to a past action: see e.g. Rohlfs (1969: 128) on It. *la porta fu chiusa.* The Latin evidence however suggests that *fui* for *sum* in aoristic perfect passives was very slow to catch on. It has been often noted in studies of late Latin texts that passive periphrases with *fui* are all but non-existent but that those with (in particular) *fueram* rather than *eram* (and also *fuissem* rather than *essem, fuero* rather than *ero* and *fuerim* rather than *sim*) are commonplace. In the *Anonymus Valesianus II* forms with *fui* do not occur (though the perfect passive with *sum* is found thirty-nine times) but the pluperfect with *fueram/fuissem* rather than *essem/eram* is the norm (Adams 1976a: 67). The same is true of the Ravenna Papyri (Adams loc. cit.). In Victor Vitensis past participle + *fui* does not occur but in the formation of the pluperfect passive *fueram* greatly outnumbers *eram* (Pitkäranta 1978: 75). In Gregory of Tours formations with *fui* are extremely rare but those with *fueram/fuissem* are commonplace (Bonnet 1890: 642). For further details see de Melo (2012b: 98–100), Burton (forthcoming), Danckaert (forthcoming); also Leumann (1921).

Similarly in our present text, whereas *sum* predominates heavily over *fui* in the perfect, in the other tenses of the passive (or deponent) perfectum the *fu-* forms are used almost without exception (9:1). Most such forms happen to be future perfect, but there are also two pluperfects, one of them indicative and the other subjunctive. The full list is as follows: 2.2 *factus fuerat*, 3.3 *si suspensa fuerit*, 7.7 *dum impletus fuerit*, 7.7 *dum soporati fuerint*, 10.4 *quicquid ibi iactatum fuerit*, 12.1 *dum aliqua ex ipsis mortua fuerit*, 13.6 *dum collectus fuerit*, 34.1 *dum nupta fuisset*, 42.2 *si impletus fuerit*. The only instance of an *es-* form is 20.3 *titulus, qui ad caput domini positus erat*.

This distinction between the formation of the perfect passive (where *fu-* is very much in a minority) and other tenses of the perfectum passive (where *fu-* forms rival those with *es-*) goes back at least to the early principate. The rich collection of pluperfect forms with participle + *fueram* at Neue and Wagener (1892–1905: III.142–5) contains many from the Augustan period, most notably in Livy (see also Blase 1903: 221; for Livy see the extensive discussion of Riemann 1885: 217–23). Riemann at first attempts to set up some distinctions between *fueram* and *eram* + participle, but then lists (220–2) a large number of examples in which he can find no difference between them. This evidence suggests that the *fueram*-forms had primacy over those with *fui* in the remodelling of the passive periphrases.

Riemann (1885: 223–5) has a final section on formations with *fuero, fuerim* and *fuissem*, in which he again makes some distinctions between the new periphrases and those with *ero, sim* and *essem*, but then (224) once more lists examples of new forms that cannot be distinguished from the old. These periphrases may therefore be bracketed with those containing *fueram* as behaving differently from the cases of *fui* + past participle.

There are relevant remarks in commentators on Augustan texts. Bömer (1969: 510) on Ovid *Met.* 3.228 (*fuerat ... secutus*) provides extensive evidence from Augustan poetry, and not exclusively of pluperfect indicative forms (cf. e.g. 3.521 *fueris dignatus* with Bömer 1969: 573). Bömer says that there are four examples in Virgil (*Aeneid*), one in Propertius (1.15.35) and numerous in Ovid (about ten examples are cited from the *Met.*, *Trist.* and *Pont.*). Cf. also Kenney (1996: 127) on Ovid *Her.* 17.23 *delenita fuissem*, where the usage is described as characteristically Ovidian and as avoided by careful stylists with the exception of Livy. It is put down to metrical convenience in Ovid.

There are also numerous examples from the Augustan period in Hyginus, *De astronomia* and Vitruvius (for details see de Melo 2012: 95–8).

Helias, quando fugit ante Iezabel: for *fugio ante* 'flee before', a Christian usage, see *TLL* VI.1.1478.10ff., though citing few examples. See also e.g. *Itin. Theod.* 5 *ubi habitauit sanctus Dauid septem annis, quando fugiebat ante Saul*, Greg. Tur. *HF* 4.28, p. 161.8 *Lyghnus ... in pauimento conruit et fugientem ante eum duritiam pauimenti tamquam in aliquod molle elimentum discendit.*

An alternative biblical/Christian idiom with *fugio* has prepositional expressions containing words for 'face', such as 'flee before/from the face of': e.g. Vulg. Gn 16.8 *a facie Sarai dominae meae ego fugio* (cf. LXX ἀπὸ προσώπου Σάρας τῆς κυρίας μου ἐγὼ ἀποδιδράσκω), 1 Sm 31.1 *fugerunt uiri Israhel ante faciem Philisthim* (cf. LXX ἔφυγον οἱ ἄνδρες Ἰσραὴλ ἐκ προσώπου τῶν ἀλλοφύλων), Greg. Ilib. *Tractatus Origenis* 5.35 (*CC* 69, p. 42.302) *fugit ante faciem eius*, Per. Aeth. 4.2 *ubi fuit sanctus Helias propheta, qua fugit a facie Achab regis*, Isid. *Quaest. In Vet. Test. In Reg.* 3.1, *PL* 83, col. 412 *fugit ante faciem eius securus de uictoria ... fugisse Dauid a facie bellantis aduersus se filii*. Such expressions are very common in the Vulgate version of the OT, e.g. Ex 2.15 *fugiens de conspectu eius*, Nm 10.35 *fugiant ... a facie tua*, Dt 28.7 *fugient a facie tua* (see further Fischer 1977 s.v. *fugio*; for a few other examples see *TLL* VI.1.1478.3ff.). They derive ultimately from the Hebrew Bible. There are two verbs 'to flee' in biblical Hebrew, **brh** and **nws**, and both can take the preposition 'before' (literally either 'to the face of' (**lifnei**), or 'from the face of' (**mippenei**), or even 'from to the face of' (**millifnei**)), to give the meaning 'to flee from'. For **nws** with such complements see e.g. Koehler and Baumgartner (2001: 681a), and for **brh** Koehler and Baumgartner (2001: 156a) (information from Philip Alexander and John Lee). Jerome's methods of rendering such expressions were variable. We noted places above where he has *a facie* + genitive. In the following passage he has *ante* where the Septuagint has 'from the face of': Vulg. 2 Par 10.2 *fugerat quippe illuc ante Salomonem* = LXX ὡς ἔφυγεν ἀπὸ προσώπου Σαλωμὼν τοῦ βασιλέως. Note too Ex 14.25 *fugiamus Israhelem* = LXX φύγωμεν ἀπὸ προσώπου Ἰσραήλ, Ios 10.11 *cumque fugerent filios Israhel* = LXX ἐν δὲ τῷ φεύγειν αὐτοὺς ἀπὸ προσώπου τῶν υἱῶν Ἰσραήλ.

Given the frequency of *fugio ante* in Christian texts, it is a curiosity that in the whole of the Vulgate there is just a single example of this phrase (cited at the end of the last paragraph; expressions of the *a facie* type are much preferred). How then did *fugio ante* get into Christian literature? Surely not from the single instance in Jerome's Bible. Similarly in the Septuagint there is only a single example of φεύγω ἔμπροσθέν τινος, and that in a different passage from Jerome's example of *fugio ante* (2 Sm/Kgds 24.13). Nor does φεύγω occur with πρό, ἔναντι, ἐναντίον or ἐνώπιον. It therefore seems out of the question that the usage entered the Old Latin versions as a direct translation from the Septuagint. The Latin phrase is thus a puzzle; perhaps it originated as a watering down of phrases of the *ante faciem*-type, but it is unclear when or where for the first time that watering down might have occurred.

Iezabel in our passage of the *Itin. Ant. Plac.* is accusative in function, whether dependent on *ante* or the verb. It is an instance of a foreign name left uninflected (for which see Adams 2013: 207, 343–4, with bibliography). The second version has *mulierem perfidam* following the name, with the appositional expression used to convey the case.

37.7 oratorium modicum: this is a text in which the regular word for 'small' is *modicus* (nine times: cf. 3.3, 5.5, 9.3, 23.5, 41.2, 41.4, 41.6, 42.1). *Paruus* is found only once, at 7.3 (*uocatur Iordanis, paruus omnino*). Terms for 'small' and 'big' tend to be constantly replaced because they become mundane through frequency of use. *Paruus* leaves no trace in the Romance languages (unlike its diminutive *paruulus*: see *REW* 6262), but neither does *modicus*. Another late text in which *paruus* hardly occurs but *modicus* is common in the *Per. Aeth.* (see E. Löfstedt 1911: 71–3).

in quo nullus praesumit manere: on *nullus*, by which *nemo* is eliminated in some late texts particularly of low register, see Hofmann and Szantyr (1965: 205), with bibliography. For *nullus* as subject of *praesumo* + infinitive see Greg. M. *Dial.* 3.26.2 *nullusque ultra praesumeret eius cellulam nisi humilis intrare.*

Sentences are often introduced by connective relatives in this text. In this passage (chapter 37) note *qui perambulantes* (1), *qui fons* (4), *in quo sunt* (4), *in quo loco* (9). This is another feature of the naive specifying style (see also above, 43.6).

37.8 ascendent: not future but present (Rec. B *ascendunt*). There are numerous such presents, including *ascendent*, also in the *Per. Aeth.*: see Väänänen (1987: 58), Adams (2013: 653); also Lundström (1948: 37–8). In this text at 2.2

(*multae uirtutes illic fient*) *fient* must be present; the second recension has (2a.2) *uirtutes multae fiunt*: for this usage see Adams (1977a: 51). Note too 9.5 *descendit ros sicut pluuia et colligent eum medici* (*colligunt* second recension), 11.5 *omnes fundent illos colathos in fluuium et tollent inde aquam* (*fundunt*, *tollunt* second editon), 15.3 *nam quod fallent homines de uxore Loth* (*dicunt* second recension), 18.3 *ingredientes exinde benedictionem tollent* (*tollunt* second recension), 40.8 (*tollent* again), 42.1 (*fundent*; so in this case the second recension); see also Milani (1974b: 381). In imperial low-register writing tablets *-et* often appears for *-it* in verb endings in the singular, and these misspellings must originate in changes in the vowel system (Adams 2013: 51–9): most notably, in the second person of the third declension, forms such as *scribĭs* and *scribēs* became identical in pronunciation (cf. above, 16.1). However, *-ent* for *-unt* must reflect not a phonetic development but a morphological, i.e. a partial falling together of third and second conjugation endings in the present tense. In a part of the Romance world the present ending *-ent* has been generalised to verbs of all conjugations apart from the first (see e.g. Väänänen 1981a: 137), though the development is not neat or straightfor-ward, and there are some instances of the reverse change, notably in *habunt* (rather than *habent*) producing Fr. *ont* (for forms such as *habunt*, *debunt* and *ualunt* in Latin writing tablets see Adams 2003a: 746–7). *-ent* endings are only occasional in this text. The author was clearly familiar with the old *-unt* ending but sometimes (if the manuscripts are to be trusted and the forms not merely scribal) could not help lapsing into *-ent*, a tendency suggestive of a change in progress but not completed.

37.9 capillos suos tondent et iactant: the regular verb for 'throw' in this text is *iacto*: cf. 8.5 *ipsos nummos in aqua iactas*, 10.4 *quicquid ibi iactatum fuerit*, 19.5 *ubi ... iactas melum*, 31.3 *ternas lapides portantes et super ipsum tumulum iactantes*. The classical verbs *iacio* and *conicio* do not seem to occur. *Mitto* for its part, which had a long life as a verb of throwing, is used in a weakened sense of putting, twice in this selection (44.36.2, 44.36.3). In this text the components of the semantic field 'put–throw' are an antici-pation of Romance, where *iacto* is well represented in the meaning 'throw' and *mitto* in the meaning 'put' (for details of the semantic field see Adams 1974b). See also index, s.v. *iacto*.

tetigi barbas: *barba* is sometimes used in the plural of 'a large or unkempt beard' (*OLD* s.v. 1a). The second recension changes to *barbam*. *Tango* is used here in an unclassical meaning, apparently of putting light touches to, touching up lightly, virtually = 'trim'. Souter (1949: 413) cites Cassiodorus for the meaning 'tamper with, alter, change'.

Conclusions

This is a text that it is all but impossible to edit in the conventional way. The nature of the original author's departures from classical norms cannot be determined with certainty because the manuscripts are so variable, and have variants that are non-standard in different ways (see 44.36.1 on *ambulantibus nobis* versus *ambulauimus nobis*, both followed by a hanging participle). At 7.1, for example, in the first edition Geyer prints *in qua sunt termas ex se lauantes salsas*, with an *-as* form standing as subject of the verb 'to be'. Such a usage might be defensible at this period (see Adams 2013: 231, 251–2, 341–2, 374; see also Milani 1974b: 372), but is this text justifiable? Alongside G's *termas . . . salsas*, R has *termis ex se leuantes salsis*. In the second edition Geyer and Milani print *in qua sunt termae salsae*, without indicating any variants. A few pages later in the first edition (10.1) Geyer prints *in quo loco sunt termae ex se lauantes* (*terme* R: see Milani). Though *termas* is possible in the first passage, its textual basis is weak. Would a systematic collection of the manuscript attestations of nominative uses of *-as* versus *-ae* clarify this problem (see Milani 1977: 317 for *-as*)? It is not unlikely that one would find such variability that establishing what the author wrote would be hopeless. On this subject see Galdi (2015: 55–61).

There is also uncertainty in the use of present participles. These may, for example, be coordinated to a main verb or left hanging. At 16.2 (*nam respicientibus* (sc. *nobis*) *in ualles illas et perambulantes monasteria multa . . . . uidimus multitudinem*) an ablative and nominative are coordinated, with both having the same referents. Some nominative participles look like substitutes for the ablative absolute, even in the second recension (e.g. Rec. B 11.4 *diaconi tenentes sacerdotem, descendit sacerdos in fluuium* (= *tenentibus diaconis*), but whether we should speak of such as genuine nominative absolutes is a moot point (contrast Milani 1974b: 389; on the issues, see further below, 48.4.3). The narrative is markedly participial, and that reflects the influence of biblical style, but the writer seems not to have understood classical systems of agreement and subordination. He knew the present participle forms (notably the nominative and dative/ablative plural forms), but writes as if they had no basis in current usage to guide him. But the real problem for an editor is that there is no consistency from manuscript to manuscript.

There are other aspects of Christian and biblical influence, and that is no surprise, since the narrative describes a pilgrimage to biblical sites. A notable Christian usage is the complementing of *fugio* with *ante*, and we also mentioned the frequent use of finite verbs immediately following *et*. *Odor suauitatis* is a biblical phrase.

Such a late text is bound to have late features (see e.g. on *indulcare* and *obuiare*), some of them relevant to Romance developments (see on *sero, mitto/ iacto* and *ascendent*), but even so manuscript variation may make it uncertain what the author himself wrote. The *-ent* third person plural present ending of the third conjugation is not consistently used in the manuscripts G and R. The nominative plural *-as* is not invariable for *-ae*.

The second recension is more correct than the text of G and R, and there must have been some scribal correction of an earlier version. However, that version itself is not consistently classical (see three paragraphs above on 11.4; also 44.36.1 on *ambulantes*).

45

PASSAGE FROM THE *DIALOGUES* OF GREGORY THE GREAT (1.2.2–3)

Introduction

Gregory the Great (*c.* 540–604), of noble Roman family, became Pope in 590. His *Dialogues* can be dated to the years 593–4 (de Vogüé and Antin 1978–80: I.25–7). Gregory presents himself as taking part in the dialogue, his interlocutor being a deacon called Peter (on the identity of whom see de Vogüé and Antin 1978–80: I.44). The purpose of the *Dialogues* is explained in the prologue to book 1, 7–10. Peter states (1.prol.7) that he does not know whether there have been Italians whose lives have been marked by miracles, and the Pope undertakes to narrate what he knows of such people. Numerous Italian saints are then described for the deacon (see de Vogüé and Antin 1978–80: 46). The Latin of Gregory is learned, but the linguistic interest of the *Dialogues* here lies in the speeches that are put into the mouths of humble characters.

The present passage deals with a *uir reuerentissimus* Libertinus, who was *praepositus* of the monastery of Fondi at the time of King Totila (1.2.1). The incident has been attributed to 542, when Totila was travelling from Tuscany to Naples via Samnium (see de Vogüé and Antin 1978–80: II.25 nn. 2–3). Gregory says (1.2.1) that he heard the story from a *religiosus uir* Laurentius, who is still alive and at the time had been *familiarissimus* with Libertinus. The Goth Darida is otherwise unknown.

There is a long discussion (with bibliography) of Gregory by Banniard (1992: 105–79), dealing for example with problems of communication between the Pope and Christians at this period, and his intended addressees.

Text

1.2.2 In eadem prouincia (1) Samniae (2), quam supra memoraui, isdem uir pro utilitate monasterii carpebat iter (3). dumque (4) Darida Gothorum comes cum exercitu in eodem loco uenisset (5), dei seruus ex caballo in quo sedebat (6) ab hominibus eius (7) proiectus est. qui iumenti perditi damnum (8) libenter ferens, etiam flagellum quod tenebat diripientibus obtulit, dicens: 'tollite (9), ut habeatis qualiter hoc iumentum minare (10).' quibus dictis protinus se in orationem dedit. cursu autem rapido praedicti ducis exercitus peruenit ad fluuium nomine Vulturnum. ibi equos suos coeperunt singuli hastis tundere, calcaribus cruentare. sed tamen equi uerberibus caesi, calcaribus cruentati (11), fatigari poterant, moueri non poterant, sicque aquam fluminis tangere quasi mortale praecipitium pertimescebant. **1.2.3** cumque diu caedendo sessores singuli fatigarentur, unus eorum intulit quia (12) ex culpa quam seruo dei in uia fecerant, illa sui itineris dispendia tolerabant. qui statim reuersi post se (13) Libertinum repperiunt in oratione prostratum. cui cum dicerent: 'surge, tolle (14) caballum tuum', ille respondit: 'ite cum bono (15), ego opus caballi non habeo (16).' descendentes uero inuitum eum in caballum de quo deposuerant leuauerunt et protinus abscesserunt. quorum equi tanto cursu illum quem prius transire non poterant fluuium transierunt, ac si ille fluminis alueus aquam minime haberet. sicque factum est ut, dum seruo dei unus suus caballus redditur, omnes a singulis reciperentur.

Translation

1.2.2 In the same province of Samnium, which I mentioned above, the same man was making a journey for the good of the monastery. When Darida, count of the Goths, had come with an army to the same place, the servant of God was thrown from the horse on which he was sitting by the count's men. Bearing the deprivation of his lost horse with equanimity, he also offered the whip that he was holding to those who were pulling him down, saying: 'Take it, so that you may have the means to drive this horse.' So saying he devoted himself forthwith to prayer. By a rapid advance the army of the aforementioned general reached the river called Volturnus. There they each proceeded to beat their horses with spears and to bloody them with their spurs, but the horses, struck by the blows and bloodied by the spurs, could be worn out but could not be moved, and they dreaded to touch the waters of the river as if it was a deadly precipice. **1.2.3** And when by constant beating the riders were each worn out, one of them suggested that they were suffering these inconveniences to their journey because of the wrongdoing that they had inflicted on the servant of God en route. Immediately retracing their steps they found Libertinus prostrate in prayer. When they said to him, 'Get up and take your horse', he replied, 'Off you go, and good luck, I do not need the horse.' But they got down and lifted him against his will onto the horse from which they had dislodged him, and forthwith departed. Their horses crossed the river which previously they could not cross with such speed that it was as if the bed of the river had no water. And so it came about that when the man of God was given back his only horse, they recovered all their horses, one apiece.

Commentary

1 in eadem prouincia: in this passage *idem* occurs three times and *praedictus* once, and these terms are recurrent in Gregory's narrative. There are texts throughout Latin literature in which the thing/person under discussion is often redundantly specified by these and other terms, such as *is*, *ille* and *supradictus*. Such specification is common in legal and technical works, but also in late narrative texts such as the *Peregrinatio Aetheriae* (see above, 34.5, and Adams 2013: 492–500, with bibliography at 496).

2 Samniae: some manuscripts have *Samnii*. Cf. *Dial.* 3.26.1 *in Samnii prouincia*. It is not clear why there should be a feminine form of this place name, and it is certainly not clear that it should be printed in the text.

3 carpebat iter: both *carpo uiam* and *carpo iter* are phrases at home mainly in poetry (see *TLL* III.493.74ff.).

4 dumque: *dum* does not have its classical meaning here but has been conflated with *cum* ('after he had come') (see below, 47.1, and index, s.v. *dum = cum*, and also Hofmann and Szantyr 1965: 614). So in the final sentence of the passage *dum* does not express concomitance but introduces an event that precedes that of the main clause ('when, after'). Cf. e.g. 1.5.4 *cui ipsum esse dum a pluribus fuisset adstructum*, 3.37.14 *dum concessum fuisset*. Also characteristic of late Latin is the reinforcement of the subordinator by *-que*; so *cumque* becomes common in late Latin (see Adams 1976a: 77–8, with bibliography), and is found later in this passage (1.2.3).

5 in eodem loco uenisset: by this period even a writer as learned as Gregory might use a locatival complement (here *in* + abl.) with a verb of motion, if the manuscripts are to be trusted (see index s.v. *in*, '+ ablative for accusative and vice versa'). Cf. the adverbial parallels 1.2.9 *ubi uis ire* (in a speech, and picked up in the reply by *ibi ire disposui*), 2.30.1 *dicens: 'ubi uadis?'* (in another speech). See also below, 48.3.2.

6 dei seruus ex caballo in quo sedebat: the horse of Libertinus is here called a *caballus*. Later the soldiers in speech also refer to it as a *caballus*, and Libertinus in his reply uses the same word. Then *caballus* is twice again used of the animal in the narrative. In the same passage *equi* is used three times, always of the soldiers' horses. There must be a significance to the choice of words. *Caballus* is not the usual word of the *Dialogues*, where *equus* is regular and *iumentum* (on which see below) occurs sometimes (see de Vogüé and Antin 1978–80: II.25 nn. 2–3, who note that there is only one other instance of *caballus* in the work, at 1.9.11; it refers to the horse of a *presbyter*, which is twice in the previous section (10) called an *equus*). In the present tale the use of *caballus* might be pejorative, implying that the horse of Libertinus was of lower quality than that of the cavalrymen (on the pejorative use see Adams 1995b: 124), or alternatively the implication might be that this is the word that would have been used even of a good horse by such a humble character (and indeed by the cavalrymen themselves, as in their short speech: on evidence from Vindolanda that soldiers used *caballus* even of horses of good quality see Adams 2003b: 564), whereas *equus* was the word to be expected in educated narrative. In the later passage the *presbyter* is not presented in a good light, and *caballus* is used of his animal immediately before he delivers an enraged speech revealing an avarice that puts an end to his ecclesiastical ambitions. There is no suggestion that this horse was of low quality, as it is sold for a dozen gold *solidi*. It seems rather that the everyday word is used as the behaviour of the *presbyter* descends to a lowly level: literary language gives way to the mundane.

7 ab hominibus eius: this plural use of *homines* designating soldiers is an old classical usage quoted from Cato onwards (see *TLL* VI.2–3.2889.43ff., and also now *Tab. Vindol.* 155, 157), though none of the examples cited there has a possessive genitive, as here.

8 iumenti perditi damnum: 'the loss of the lost horse'. This pleonastic phrase is obviously related to those cases of the genetivus inhaerentiae in which a noun has dependent on it in the genitive another noun of much the same meaning, such as *mens animi* (Plaut. *Cist.* 210, *Epid.* 530, Lucr. 3.615, 4.758, 5.149, 6.1183, Catull. 65.4) or *symphoniae consonantiam* (Vitr. 5.5.5); in the latter case Greek and Latin synonyms are associated in this way (see in general Hofmann and Szantyr 1965: 63, and for many examples Weijermans 1949). In the present example, however, the pleonasm lies not in the genitival noun but in the participle in agreement. Hofmann and Szantyr (1965: 785, 795) cite Amm. 24.5.4 *inter exordia obsidii coepti*, suggesting (795) that the origin might lie in an expression such as Amm. 22.12.3 *immodica rerum secundarum prosperitate*, where *res secundae* is a unit equivalent to a single noun in the genitive, but the pleonasm lies only in its adjectival part. This type of pleonasm is a feature of Apuleius (see Koziol 1872: 33–5), who may have started a trend among later writers. Note for example *Met.* 4.19 *numerosae familiae frequentia*, 8.23 *annonae copiosae beata celebritas*, 8.29 *fictae uaticinationis mendacio*.

A further example is cited by Sittl (1882: 96) from Arnobius, *Nat.* 2.35, p. 76.25 (*CSEL* 4) *uitae incipientis exordium*. There is also a closely related type of redundancy, where it is the base noun that is accompanied by an adjective that forms a pleonasm with the dependent genitive (see Koziol 1872: 35), as at Apul. *Met.* 10.23 *publicam populi caueam*. Sittl (1882: 96) cites too Arnob. *Nat.* 3.29, p. 131.25 *in continua serie perpetuitatis*.

Our example from Gregory does not seem to have been noted. Such phraseology surely had a literary or artificial flavour. The genetivus inhaerentiae (of the conventional type) becomes particularly common in late literary/ artificial style, as was shown by Sittl (1882: 92–4) (calling the phenomenon 'tumor Africus') and particularly Weijermans (1949: 26–51), the latter citing numerous examples from Gregory at 47–8; see also e.g. Wölfflin (1900: 367) on Jordanes.

iumenti: *iumentum* is twice used in this passage of a saddle horse, and that is a reference which it often has (note e.g. Amm. 23.5.13 *militem celsi nominis cum bellatoriis iumentis exstinxit*, 'it killed a soldier of lofty name along with war horses). It differs however from *equus* in several ways, two of which may be mentioned here (for further details see Adams 1990b: 441–2, id. 1995a: 135–40). First, *iumentum* was capable of embracing all the equids, horses, mules and donkeys, whereas *equus* excluded the latter two categories (Adams 1995a: 135–6). Second, in literary texts *equus* was favoured in reference to racehorses, military horses or noble horses in general (Adams 1995a: 136–7), whereas *iumentum* was general enough to be suitable when the reference was to a horse of low quality. Such a use can be seen at *Dial.* 1.4.10 *et quotiens ad alia tendebat loca, iumentum sedere consueuerat, quod esse despicabilius iumentis omnibus in cella potuisset*, and also perhaps in the present passage.

9 tollite: *tollo* means here 'take (it)', as later in the passage in a speech of the soldiers (*surge, tolle caballum tuum*). In the later case in particular any idea of raising (the typical semantic component of the verb in classical Latin) is out of the question, and the imperative could be replaced by *accipe, sume* or *habe*. On this use of *tollo* (and particularly of its imperative forms) see above, 43.9.

10 ut habeatis qualiter hoc iumentum minare: here Gregory has put into the mouth of Libertinus a substandard use of the infinitive for subjunctive in a relative clause of potential type (here without an expressed antecedent) (for this construction with bibliography see Adams 2013: 770–1). An early example (end of first century, start of second) was seen above (20.5) in a letter from Egypt, Myos Hormos road (*et unde potere non abemus*). The verb of the main clause is often *habeo* (see the examples at Adams 2013: 770). Sometimes the

apparent infinitive can be explained otherwise, as merely showing omission of
-*m*, but that is not so here. It is worth comparing the present passage with
another, where Gregory is speaking in his own voice: 1.5.2 *unde lampades
accenderet omnimodo non haberet*. The contexts are similar. The higher verb
again is *habeo*, and the relative clause, introduced by *unde*, is again without an
antecedent. Here however Gregory uses the classical potential subjunctive (and
preposes the dependent construction). The difference between the two passages suggests that Gregory was deliberately characterising some of his speakers linguistically (see the Conclusions below).

It is also of note here that *minari* has passed from deponent to active, and
the meaning is of interest too. The reference is not to threatening the horse
aimlessly, but to driving it on, a derived sense of the original meaning
'threaten'. A clear instance of this secondary meaning is at Schol. Juv.
6.526 *hanc igitur Io in tantum persecuta est Iuno, ut per omnem mundum
eam minaret*, 'this Io therefore Juno so pursued that she drove her all over
the world'. Fr. *mener* 'lead' derives from this usage: see Bloch and von
Wartburg (1968: 401) 'Lat. pop. *mināre* "pousser des animaux devant soi
en criant"'. There occurred a shift in orientation, from 'drive (in front of
one)', to 'lead (towards one)', i.e. by going in front, a shift that might have
taken place in the context of moving groups of farm animals, because the
position of the shepherd aut sim. in relation to the flock would vary. The new
sense 'drive', as Bloch and von Wartburg imply, is associated exclusively
with the active form *minare* (*TLL* VIII.1031.34ff., citing e.g. Paul. Fest.
p. 21.13 Lindsay *agere modo significat ante se pellere, id est minare*).
The *TLL* (1031.45) glosses the usage with 'agere, pellere, trahere', but it is
not clear that the third gloss (implying the shift of orientation mentioned
above) is appropriate to the Latin examples cited.

Such a shift did however take place in at least one other verb in the Latin
period, *eicio*, which from 'throw out' (away from oneself) occasionally shifted
to the secondary meaning 'take out' (towards oneself): see above, 7.8–9, and
TLL V.2.308.36ff., Rönsch (1875: 361–2), id. (1887–9: III.33–4), E. Löfstedt
(1911: 264–6), id. (1956: II.445), and Svennung (1935: 537), citing Col. 8.11.15
(*educi*) alongside the derivative passage Palladius 1.28.6 (*eici*). Note too *Coll.
Mon.–Eins.* 9 c (Dickey 2012) *aperi loculum et eice clauem cellarii* = ἄνοιξον τὸ
γλωσσοκόμον καὶ ἐξάγαγε κλεῖδα τοῦ ταμιείου ('open the casket and take out
the key of the cellar'), and particularly two instances from Soranus Lat.
(Mustio) (pp. 86.8, 87.4) of *eicere* used of the midwife at the moment of
delivery 'drawing out' (towards herself) the newborn (e.g. 87.4 *foras eiciat*).
The subject is not the mother, 'casting it out'.

11 hastis tundere, calcaribus cruentare … uerberibus caesi, calcaribus cruentati: double 'participial resumption' (for the term see Wills 1996: 311–13 and the whole of chapter 12), but with the two resumptions differing in type. The participle *cruentati* picks up the infinitive of the same verb, but *caesi* picks up the infinitive of a different (but synonymous) verb (*tundere*). For the latter type see Wills (1996: 318–19; also 312 on Cicero's preference for such variation), calling it 'substitution'. Similarly *calcaribus* is repeated with *cruentare/cruentati*, but with *tundere/caesi* there is variation (*hastis/uerberibus*). Also of note is the marked alliteration of *c*. Participial resumption is found particularly in Ovid (Wills 1996: 311), and is also noticeable in Livy's opening chapters (Wills 1996: 312). Gregory's phrasing here is contrived. See also index, 'resumption, participial'.

12 intulit quia: for *infero* with the meaning 'propose, suggest' see *TLL* VII.1.1381.82, with the examples at 1382.15f., 60 (with acc. + inf.) and 1382.52 (with *quia*, and citing this example).

Quia for the acc. + inf. is common in this text, and not only in speeches by humble characters (cf. e.g. 43.4 on the different practice of the *Hist. Apoll.*). This example is in Gregory's narrative. Peter for example has *fateor quia* at 3.37.18, and Gregory *scimus quia* at 3.37.19. For some details about the distribution of *quod* and *quia* in late Latin see e.g. Herman (1963: 40–2), suggesting that in the sixth century *quod* predominates in Gaul but *quia* in Italy. Statistics are not given from Gregory. It is not the case, however, that Gregory uses only *quia*. For the *quod*-construction see 1.2.4, 1.4.1, 1.4.2, 1.4.3, 1.4.5 (twice), 1.4.15, 1.4.19, 1.4.20, 1.5.6, 1.7.2. For the *quia*-construction in this same section see 1.3.3, 1.4.14 (twice), 1.4.16, 1.4.17, 1.5.2, 1.7.2.

The acc. + inf. is also frequent in the text. One difference between this and the *quod-/quia*-construction lies in their placement in relation to the higher verb. In e.g. the preface to book 1 note on the one hand *quia* at 10 *cum mihi luce clarius constet quia Marcus et Lucas … didicerunt*, and also 10 *hoc uero scire te cupio quia …*, but on the other the acc. + inf. at 5 *sed tamen se perdidisse meminerit*, 7 *non ualde in Italia aliquorum uitam uirtutibus fulsisse cognoui*, 7 *et quidem bonos uiros in hac terra fuisse non dubito*, 7 *signa tamen atque uirtutes aut ab eis nequaquam factas existimo*, 9 *si se esse aliquid aestimat*, 10 (the first part of the second passage quoted above in this paragraph) *hoc uero scire te cupio*. The *quia*-construction is used in the preface when the dependent clause follows the higher verb, but the acc. + inf. when it precedes (with a little overlap) (on this tendency in later Latin see Herman 1989, Adams 2013: 745). At 10 *scire te* (acc. + inf.) precedes the higher verb, but the *quia*-construction dependent on *scire* follows it.

This distinction seems to hold up to a point throughout the work, but it is not absolute. For examples of the acc. + inf. placed before the higher verb see 1.2.9 (twice), 1.2.10, 1.3.1, 1.4.1, 1.4.8, 1.5.4 (twice). On the other hand for the acc. + inf. postponed see 1.2.7, 1.4.3, 1.4.6, 1.5.4, 1.6.2. It is the placement of the *quod-/quia*-construction that is the more distinctive, as it rarely comes before the higher verb. In the selection considered for statistical purposes in this paragraph (from 1.2.1 to 1.7.2) it is preposed only at 1.4.14 (twice): e.g. *suo domino quia ipse esset quem quaereret indicauit* (the second example is very similar).

13 reuersi post se: for this local use of *post se*, replaceable with *retro* but redundant with *re-uersi*, see *TLL* X.2.178.8ff. (from the first century AD but mainly late). Note the striking use at 1.3.3, *tremefactus post semetipsum concidit* ('he fell backwards'). For pleonasm of the type where the prefix of the verb is reinforced by an additional element or elements (found at all periods) see Adams (2013: 586–7), and index, 'pleonasm, of adverb and verbal prefix'.

14 surge, tolle: 'get up and take': the double instruction is expressed by two imperatives in an asyndeton bimembre. Pairs of imperatives may from the earliest period either be in asyndeton (but see above, 4.3–4 for problems of interpretation) or explicitly coordinated, with asyndeton probably more peremptory and calling for immediate action, and coordination expressing a more measured instruction that two acts are to be carried out in sequence. For the second type in this text see 3.37.11 *surge et concitus fuge ... surge et uade*, 3.37.14 *surge et flexu genu tende ceruicem*, 4.54.2 *uade et dic episcopo proiciat*. Cf. on the one hand Livius Andronicus *trag.* 22 Ribbeck *porrige, opitula*, Plaut. *Asin.* 925 *surge, amator, i domum*, *Aul.* 192 *tace, bonum habe animum*, 193 *dic, si quid opust, impera*, 767 *i, refer*, Ter. *Ph.* 152 *cape, da hoc*, 994 *abi, tange*, Terentianus, *P. Mich.* VIII.471.28 *ueni, interpone te si potes aiutare Ptolemaeo, Coll. Mon.–Eins.* 9a (Dickey 2012) *tolle, coque*, 9n *uade, dic illi*, 10o *descende, fomenta me*, and on the other hand Plaut. *Aul.* 103 *tace atque abi intro*, 142a–3 *utere atque | impera*, 270 *propera atque elue*, 329 *hunc sume atque abi intro illo*, 350 *prodi atque ostium aperi*, 394 *Apollo, quaeso, subueni mi atque adiuua* (note that here a god is addressed), Ter. *Hec.* 787 *i atque exple animum, Coll. Mon.–Eins.* 9g (Dickey 2012) *uade ad Gaium et dic illi*. See further above, 43.9.

15 ite cum bono: neither this phrase nor the prepositional expression alone appears in the *TLL* or *OLD* s.v. *bonum*, but the meaning is obvious enough, 'go with good fortune', = 'good luck'. For *bonum* 'good fortune' see

OLD s.v. 3 citing e.g. Varro *Men.* 172 *sapiens et bonum ferre potest modice et malum fortiter aut leuiter.* 'Good luck' is often in Latin expressed by the phrase *bona fortuna* (see Adams 2003a: 81). Here we have an expression of farewell (= 'good speed'). There are similar expressions of complementary type (of welcome) in the colloquia edited by Dickey (2012, 2015): *Coll. Mon.–Eins.* 6a *bono die uenisti, Coll. Mont.* 10b *bono pede conuenisti* (see Dickey 2015: 124).

16 ego opus caballi non habeo: *opus habeo* 'I need' is not a classical phrase; the *OLD* s.v. *opus* 12, 13 cites only the verb 'to be' with *opus* in this sense. *Opus habeo* appears from the *Vetus Latina* onwards (see *TLL* IX.2.861.28ff. for details). Diomedes found fault with the usage, by implication perhaps deriving it from the Greek equivalent: *GL* I.316.32–5 *nam ut Graeci dicunt* χρείαν ἔχω, χρείαν εἶχον, *nos non dicimus 'opus habeo', 'opus habebam', sed 'opus est mihi', opus erat mihi'; et quod illi dicunt* χρείαν σου ἔχει ὁ πατήρ, *nos dicimus 'pater uult te', 'praeceptor uolebat te' et similia.* This is a familiar attempt by a grammarian to reinstate a classical usage, with *nos non dicimus* implying as usual 'we should not say (but do)'. *Opus habeo* in a Latin text often renders the Greek phrase, as in the *Vet. Lat.* (cod. *d*) at Mt 26.65 (see *TLL* 861.37), where Jerome in the Vulgate writes instead *quid adhuc egemus testibus.* In the popular Latin of the second century as represented by the Vindolanda tablets *opus* with *esse* is still the norm (*Tab. Vindol.* 218.2, 255.8, 642.ii.5, 667.1; so too in Terentianus: see *P. Mich.* VIII.467.10). However, if the Latin expression started as a Grecism, it must have gained currency, as here in Gregory it is put into the mouth of a humble character (and Gregory reputedly never himself learnt Greek properly). Note too *Coll. Mon.–Eins.* 5a (Dickey 2012) *quid opus habes mutuari*, alongside τί χρείαν ἔχεις δανείσασθαι (also 5c, where the Latin is conjectural, 6a).

Conclusions

Literary and late Latin

Gregory's own Latin is educated and classicising. We noted some contrived patterns of words modelled on earlier literary Latin (the variation on the genetivus inhaerentiae, participial resumption), and the literary phrase *carpebat iter.* The word order also has marked OV characteristics, with objects usually preceding the verb (other than imperative forms) and dependent infinitives preceding the higher verb. Despite this Gregory belonged to his time, and usages that had once been innovations rejected in the literary language are now freely admitted, such as *dum* used indistinguishably from *cum*, locatival expressions complementing verbs of motion, and *quod-/quia*-clauses for the acc. + inf.

Noteworthy in this category is a usage that does not come up in this passage. I refer to his use of the pluperfect subjunctive of two auxiliary verbs, *possum* and *debeo*, in effect for the imperfect subjunctive, though in the case of *debuisset* there is more to it than that. Note e.g. 3.37.10 *aduesperescente autem die, uir dei Sanctulus ab eisdem Langobardis petiit, ut relaxari eique uita concedi debuisset*, 'but when evening was drawing in, the man of God Sanctulus asked of the same Lombards that he (another person) ought/should be released and that life ought/should be granted to him'. The translation 'ought to have been' is impossible, and it may be said that *debuisset* has been used for *deberet*. However, even *deberet* would not have been used in such a context in classical Latin: infinitive + *debuisset* is here equivalent to the imperfect passive subjunctive forms of the two verbs in the infinitive: = *petiit ut relaxaretur eique uita concederetur*, 'he asked that he (should) be released and life granted to him'. There are thus two features of *debuisset* to be distinguished. First, it seems to represent an attempt to make explicit a modal nuance that the imperfect subjunctive of *relaxari* and *concedi* would itself have been capable of expressing in classical Latin. Second, the tense is pluperfect for imperfect.

An illustration of this use of the pluperfect with the other auxiliary is at 1.4.14 *ita ut* <u>*tremeret*</u>, *atque ad insinuandum hoc ipsum quod uenerat uix sufficere lingua* <u>*potuisset*</u>, 'in such a way that he trembled and his tongue could scarcely raise the strength to convey the thing that he had come to convey'. Here the pluperfect subjunctive *potuisset* is coordinated with the imperfect subjunctive of another verb, though the time reference of both is the same. Here too there is the sort of redundancy that was seen above in *debuisset*. The sense would not be altered if *potuisset* were deleted and *sufficere* converted to the subjunctive *sufficeret*.

For examples of the two auxiliaries in the pluperfect subjunctive where, instead of a pluperfect auxiliary + infinitive, the imperfect subjunctive of the verb currently in the infinitive might have been expected see 1.4.10 *et quotiens ad alia tendebat loca, iumentum sedere consueuerat, quod esse despicabilius iumentis omnibus in cella potuisset* (= *quod esset*), 1.4.15 *coepit uehementissime urguere, ut statim exire debuisset* (= *ut statim exiret*), 1.5.4 *atque obnixe peteret ut sibi debuisset ostendi* (= *ut sibi ostenderetur*), 1.7.2 *cogitaret, quod saltem ad condimenta holerum nutrienda locus isdem aptus potuisset existere* (here *posset existere* would be possible, but again the same sense would be given by *existeret*), 3.37.12 *Langobardis placuit, ut eum capite truncare debuissent* ('it was agreed by the Lombards that they ought to cut off his head'; here *deberent* would be tolerable, but *truncarent* would give the required sense).

There is also a use of the present subjunctive of *debeo* expressing a modal nuance that might have been expressed by the plain (present) subjunctive of the dependent verb: 1.4.17 *rogat pater uester ne fatigari debeatis* (= *ne fatige-mini* '(your father asks) that you not tire yourselves'), 3.37.17 *ut habeam unde pro uobis debeam orare* (= *unde pro uobis orem*, 'so that I may have the means of praying for you').

In the western Romance languages the original pluperfect subjunctive replaced the imperfect (see 48.1.2), and here we see an anticipation of that development, but it seems to be restricted in this text to just two verbs, whereas in the later *Annales regni Francorum* a wide range of verbs displays a pluperfect subjunctive functioning as the earlier imperfect (48.1.2). In the present text the imperfect subjunctive is used freely in other verbs with classical functions. Gregory's practice suggests that the encroachment of the pluperfect subjunctive form on the imperfect began in certain modal verbs.

Linguistic characterisation

Gregory modified his Latin to suit the characters, some of them mundane, whom he constantly introduced. This feature was seen in the use of the infinitive for subjunctive in a potential relative clause introduced by *qual-iter*. The use of *caballus* too was intended either to characterise the usage of Libertinus, or to characterise his horse. Here is a selection of short extracts from speeches elsewhere in the work, all of them containing distinctive usages:

1.4.7 moxque hortum isdem pater ingressus est, coepit ex eius ore quasi satisfa-ciens ipse qui hanc arripuerat diabolus clamare, dicens: 'ego quid feci? ego quid feci? sedebam mihi super lactucam. uenit illa et momordit me'.

On this use of *mihi* with *sedeo* see Adams (2013: 357), and also above, 44.36.1.

1.9.18 placet tibi, domine, ut de nutrimento matris meae manducare non possim? ecce enim gallinas, quas nutrit, uulpes comedit.

For *manduco de* in another sixth-century Italian writer (of substandard Latin), Anthimus (e.g. 10.15), see above, 31.12 (with cross-references on the usage); also index s.v. *de*, 'expressing partitive object'.

2.18 ut dei uiro in monasterium uino plena duo lignea uascula, quae uulgo flascones uocantur, deferret . . . 'uide, fili, de illo flascone, quem abscondisti, iam non bibas, sed inclina illum caute, et inuenis quid intus habet.'

Here is the same partititive use (see above) of *de* standing in an object relation to the verb, but of drinking not eating. Also of note here is the Germanic (?) (see Ernout and Meillet 1959: 239) term *flasco* (reflected in Italian and French but hardly attested in Latin: see *TLL* VI.1.876.66ff.; the other literary example cited there, from Ennodius, a late writer of Gallic origin but bishop in Pavia, is a jesting use of a drunk), along with the jussive construction *iam non bibas* where *ne* (after *uide*) is expected, *illum* with *inclina* instead of *eum*, and the present *inuenis* with future reference. On this passage see Banniard (1992: 117–18).

2.30.1 ei antiquus hostis in mulomedici specie obuiam factus est, cornu et tripedicam ferens. quem cum requisisset, dicens: 'ubi uadis?', ille respondit: 'ecce ad fratres uado, potionem eis dare.'

Here note the infinitive of purpose *dare* with a verb of motion, a construction found elsewhere in speeches. Cf. 1.4.14 *qui uehementer iratus coepit clamare, dicens: 'quid est hoc? ego te misi hominem deducere, non faenum portare.* Otherwise Gregory uses conventional purpose complements:

1.2.11 cumque pro utilitate monasterii ad constitutionem causae egressus fuisset.
1.4.4 cum . . . dei famulus pro exhortandis ad desideria superna fidelibus paulo longius a cella digressus est.
1.4.8 egredere ad praedicandum.
1.4.11 mittatur igitur, si placet, qui huc eum exhibeat.
1.4.13 hunc ego misit, ut eum ad se sub celeritate perduceret.
1.4.21 coeperunt eosdem monachos foras trahere, ut eos aut per tormenta discuterent aut . . .
1.5.4 ad uidendum eum quidam rusticus uenit.
1.5.4 is qui ad uidendum eum uenerat.
1.6.1 concurrerunt omnes ut ignem extinguerent.
1.7.5 ad exhibenda extraneis opera pergerent.
1.9.8 ad benedictionem dandam in sua domo declinaret.
1.9.10 ad exercendum aliquod opus discessit.
1.9.14 ad eum Gothi hospitalitatis gratia uenerunt.
1.10.2 ad dedicandum oratorium processit.

3.14.6 nam die quadam ad uesperum in horto monasterii fecit iactari ferramenta, quae usitato nos nomine uangas uocamus. dixit itaque discipulis suis: 'tot uangas in horto proicite, et citius redite.'

For the meaning of *uanga* (also found at Palladius 1.42.3) see Souter (1949: 435): a spade with a crossbar on which to rest the foot. It is reflected only in

Italian (*vanga* 'spade': *REW* 9137). Ernout and Meillet (1959: 712–13) describe it as '[s]ans doute mot de provenance germanique' and note that the Latin word was *bipalium*. Gregory refrains from using the word in his own person, except in a descriptive relative clause. This word, along with *flasco* above, was clearly local.

Tot with *uangas* is possibly indefinite (for which use see Hofmann and Szantyr 1965: 197), but the meaning is not easy to grasp. Perhaps the speaker is imagined as pointing to a collection of *uangae*, in which case the meaning would be 'all of those you see'. Alternatively he may mean 'quite a few, a number of' (unspecified).

4.54.2 uade et dic episcopo proiciat hinc foetentes carnes quas hic posuit, quia si non fecerit, die trigesimo ipse morietur.

For the construction with *dic* see e.g. *O. Max.* 254 (Bülow-Jacobsen *et al.* 1994: 34, text no. 4) *dic Ama . . . Antonino acc[i]piat ab ho . . . ati epistulam*, and particularly *TLL* V.1.987.20ff. (a usage quite widespread from early Latin onwards in conversational contexts; several times in Cicero's letters and also in speeches in poets and Livy), and Penney (1999: 257–8). See also above, 43.12.

46

VISIGOTHIC SLATE TABLET (VELÁZQUEZ SORIANO 2004, no. 40.II), OF THE FIRST HALF OF THE SEVENTH CENTURY

This Visigothic corpus consists of more than 150 texts incised with a sharp instrument on pieces of slate found in an area to the south of Salamanca between Avila and the Portuguese border. The script falls into the category of Visigothic cursive, and the texts are dated roughly from the sixth to the eighth centuries. The corpus is of variable content, embracing for example legal documents, epistles, curse tablets, phylacteries, various Christian texts, school exercises and inventories (see the list of contents to Velázquez Soriano's edition). The present document is a declaration of a servitude (presumably a rustic or praedial servitude, an easement in common law: see *OLD* s.v. *seruitus* 3, a 'liability resting on a property by which the owner is bound to give certain defined facilities to a neighbour, e.g. right of way'). On the language of the texts there is little written, but see Velázquez Soriano (2004: 473–553, with the commentary *passim*), Herman (1995), García Leal (2008), Adams (2013: 371–5; also 913, index, s.v. 'Visigothic slate tablets').

Text

Profesio de ser[uitute].
ego Vnigild(us) de locum Langa
Tomanca, dum uenisse ad loc[um . . .]
tum lirigiare ad domo Froilani, ego adduxsi teste ipse Froila, fraude ad do-   5
mo Desideri. dum istare in dom(o) Desideri,
fu(i)t ueniens Froila et dix(it) mici: 'leua, leuita,
et uadam(us) ad domo Busani et Fasteni [. . .]'
sucisit fuim(us) ad domo Busani [..] unam ra[. . .]
[. . .] pro Froilane et dixsit nouis: 'uadam(us)   10
ad fragis, ad uinias p[o]stas et pono te ibi in fragis et leuaui de domo Desideri p[. . .]rales duos, dolabra una,
[. . .]o quanto laspare una'.

Translation

Declaration of a servitude. I, Unigildus, from the place Langa Tomanca, when I had come to the place . . . to litigate at the house of Froila, I brought as witness Froila himself, because of the fraud at the house of Desiderius. While I was in the house of Desiderius, there came along Froila and he said to me: 'Up you get, clerk, and let us go to the house of Busanus (?: *or* Busa) and Fastenus.' It transpired we went to the house of Busa . . . on behalf of Froila and he said to us: 'Let us go to the strawberries, where there are vineyards planted, and I will put you among the strawberries; and I have taken from the house of Desiderius two . . . and one hoe . . .'

Commentary

2–3 Vnigild(us) de locum Langa Tomanca: an adnominal *de*-expression marking origin. For adnominal *de* indicating domicile or origin in later Latin see *Per. Aeth.* 10.3 *faciens iter cum sanctis, id est presbytero et diaconibus de Ierusolima*; cf. 49.1 *incipiunt se undique colligere turbae non solum monachorum uel aputactitum de diuersis prouinciis, id est tam de Mesopotamia uel Syria uel de Egypto aut Thebaida* (but ambiguous between adverbal and adnominal). The usage can be paralleled from early Latin with a different preposition: e.g. Plaut. *Capt.* 509 *Philocratem ex Alide* (see further Coleman 2006: 163). Republican Latin also used the adnominal ablative with this function: see e.g. Plaut. *Asin.* 499 *Periphanes Rhodo mercator diues, Merc.* 940 *uideo ibi hospitem Zacyntho*, Caes. *Civ.* 1.24.4 *N. Magius Cremona* (with Coleman loc. cit.). Adnominal prepositional phrases in general are old and classical with a variety of functions: see e.g. above 2.16 (with bibliography), 2.25, 11.3 (on Vitruvius, with cross-references), and index, 'adnominal prepositional expressions'. A typical classical instance is at Cic. *Pis.* 61 *scriba ad aerarium . . . commurmuratus sit* (the scribe did not 'mutter at the treasury', but was a 'treasury scribe').

The adnominal use of *de* itself, marking provenance (loosely speaking), can be quoted from classical and early imperial Latin (see *TLL* V.1.54.79ff., e.g. Cic. *Cluent.* 163 *cauponem de uia Latina*, Mart. 1.41.12 *de Gadibus improbus magister*, with Citroni 1975: 134), but it tends to have a special, characterising, function (see Väänänen [1956] 1981b: 95, Adams 2013: 275–6). At Mart. 5.78.26 (*nec de Gadibus improbis puellae | uibrabunt*) the point is not merely that certain girls happen to be from Cadiz. They are a type, girls from Cadiz, notoriously disreputable dancing girls. Note too Cic. *Phil.* 2.65 *exsultabat gaudio, persona de mimo*, 'he rejoiced like a character from a mime/a mime character', where the expression is descriptive rather than purely a statement of provenance.

3 dum uenisse: for *cum uenissem*. For *dum* = *cum* in late Latin see above, 45.4.

ad loc[um . . .]: for *locus* redundantly specifying a place, see above, 44.37.5. Sometimes, as perhaps here, the motivation for *locus* might have been the insignificance of the place named (cf. 46.2–3 above), and the need felt to define it as a locality: see e.g. *Per. Aeth.* 4.2 *nam hic est locus Choreb, ubi fuit sanctus Helias propheta.*

4 lirigiare: presumably for *litigare*, but the reason for the misspelling is not obvious (see Velázquez Soriano 2004: 228).

This must be an infinitive of purpose complementing the verb of motion *uenisse* (for this construction see above, 39.22; also index, 'infinitive, final, with verbs of motion and the like'). In early Spanish, verbs of motion are regularly used with an infinitive and without an intervening preposition (as was later to be the case): see Menéndez Pidal (1944: 349–50), citing examples from the *Poema de Mio Cid* (e.g. *vayamos los ferir, fuesse los molinos picar*), and stating that it was current in all ancient texts.

ad domo Froilani: *domus* occurs six times in this text, always in an oblique case, and always with a preposition. Twice it is used with *ad* in a directional sense ('to'), twice with *ad* in a static sense ('at') (cf. e.g. It. *a*, Fr. *à* for the combination of meanings), once with *in* (static) and once with *de* ('from'). There has been a complete abandonment of the classical prepositionless uses of *domum, domi* and *domo*. The novelty lies in the invariable use of prepositions to convey these ideas, not in the use of the prepositions themselves. Already by the Augustan period (e.g. in Livy) prepositions start to appear with *domus* in contexts in which classical Latin would have used an unaccompanied oblique case form (see Kühner and Stegmann 1955: I.483, Woodcock 1959: 6).

The name *Froila*, here in the genitive, is Gothic. The ablative *Froilane* occurs later in the text, and the genitive ought to have been *Froilanis*, but it has been contaminated with the second declension inflection and given the ending -*i*. This name survived in Old Spanish in the form *Fruela*, reflecting the nominative *Froila*, and also in a different form, *Froilán*, reflecting the oblique case form, *Froilane* (see Penny 2002: 14). The declension-type -*a*, -*anis* was acquired by late Latin from Gothic/Germanic. It forms a parallel to the native Latin type -*o*, -*onis*, and occurs particularly in names, as in *Attila, Attilanis* ('little father', from *atta* 'father') (see in general Piel 1960: 430). On relics of this formation in Spanish from the time of the Visigothic rule in Spain see Penny (2002: 14–15) (mostly in Germanic personal names, such as *Froilán*, but also in one or two common nouns of Germanic origin, such as *guardián* 'guardian' <

*wardjane). For Germanic names of this formation in Gregory of Tours see Bonnet (1890: 380). Some parallels are *scriba, scribanis* (*scribanem* > Fr. *écrivain*; see Bloch and von Wartburg 1968: 212 s.v.), where the inflection has spread to a term of Latin root, and *barba, barbanis* 'uncle' (for which in Latin see Adams 2007: 511–12). See Adams (2013: 372, 375 n. 1).

4–5 adduxsi teste ipse Froila: here *ipse Froila*, a nominative form, is object of the verb. *Teste* is accusative. On one interpretation *teste* might be the primary object with *ipse Froila* an appositional nominative ('I brought a witness, Froila himself'). But personal names particularly in late and early medieval Latin may be left in the nominative when dependent on a preposition or object of a verb (see above, 15.5–6, with bibliography, and in this Visigothic corpus 11 *p(er) Sigerius*). It is perhaps a surprising revelation that the witness should be Froila, who has just been mentioned in an oblique case as the one at whose house the hearing is to be held. Hence 'I brought as witness – the said Froila', with the nominative inspired by its identifying powers, of the type seen in curse tablets (see above, 15.5–6, and index, 'nominative, detached, in headings'). Some, it is true, might see such a use as not really different from a nominative of apposition. See also Velázquez Soriano (2004: 229).

5–6 fraude ad domo Desideri: the prepositional expression is adnominal, and striking by the norms of classical Latin, where a participle such as *facta* would have been expected with *fraude*. In this text of just eleven lines (omitting the defective last two lines) and seventy-four words there are three adnominal prepositional expressions (cf. *Vnigild(us) de locum Langa Tomanca, ad fragis ad uinias p[o]stas*; in this last example the first *ad* is part of a verb phrase and the second is adnominal: see below on line 11). This is a remarkably high incidence. For the frequency of such constructions per 1,000 words of text in a variety of classical writers (with an average of 2.2), see Wharton (2009: 201), and above, 11.30. By contrast the figure for the slate tablet is almost 40. Wharton (2009: 191) notes a substantial increase in the incidence of adnominals in some modern languages, including the Romance language French, the figure for which is given (at 192) as 26. The high figure for the slate tablet is statistically meaningless, given the size of the text, but the writer was clearly uninhibited in his use of the construction, in line with what must have been the state of the language. We saw a much earlier work (not examined by Wharton) with a high incidence of such constructions, that of Vitruvius (for details see above, 11.30).

6 dum istare in dom(o) Desideri: here *istare* (for *istarem*; < *starem* with prothetic vowel) should not be taken in its old sense of standing, as standing rather than sitting is not an issue in the context. The next speaker tells the writer to 'get up' (*leua*), implying that he was sitting. We seem to have here an anticipation of the role of the verb in modern Ibero-Romance varieties as the copula for place/state/condition (e.g. Sp. *estar*; versus *ser* for many non-locative copular functions). Various Latin anticipations of this Romance use are cited without necessarily being decisive (see e.g. Väänänen 1981a: 97), e.g. *Per. Aeth.* 24.6 *item mittet uocem diaconus, ut unusquisque, quomodo stat, cathecuminus inclinet caput*, which is translated by Wilkinson (1971: 124) 'but now the deacon calls every catechumen to stand where he is and bow his head' (in effect giving *stat* its literal sense). See Hofmann and Szantyr (1965: 395), citing *Per. Aeth.* 2.2 *lapis . . . ibi fixus stat* (but again *stat* can be given its full meaning), and now the more comprehensive account of Nuti (2015).

7 fu(i)t ueniens: the first word has been read as *f(u)it* or *fu(i)t* but either way we might seem to have a periphrasis with present participle + verb 'to be'. This construction has been exhaustively treated by Eklund (1970: 11–74). He shows that there are probably no genuine cases before AD 150 (apparent cases can be explained away, as having for example an adjectival use of the participle with the copula). After 150 the great majority of examples are in translation literature and determined by Greek. Examples from this period that are not in translations are dealt with by Eklund (1970) at 68–73 and are limited in number, though they are numerous in one writer, Lucifer of Cagliari (Eklund 1970: 68 and particularly Hartel 1886: 37–8), who, as Eklund puts it, must have picked up a strange construction and made it a feature of his style. Note p. 66.25 *eam dare formam, quae non fuisset de lege ueniens domini* (Hartel lists two further examples with this participle but both references are wrong). Haverling (2010: 491–7) has recently provided some refinements to this narrative of the history of the usage, noting (496): 'Gregory of Tours and the Merovingian texts have a growing number of such constructions . . ., and by then it is safer to assume that the development toward the Romance system of imperfective periphrases had begun.'

However, it is not certain that the instance in the present text is a genuine periphrasis. Certainly an imperfective/progressive meaning of the type mentioned by Haverling could not be given to the combination here.

One alternative translation might be: 'while I was in the house of Desiderius, Froila was (there), having come (with me)'. On this view *ueniens* would have a perfective meaning (a common use), and *fuit* would be an ordinary copula. There is however no local term for 'there' in the Latin, which makes this second interpretation implausible.

If it is felt that the context seems to require the meaning 'while I was in the house of Desiderius, Froila came up and said . . .' (surely the most natural interpretation), a third possibility is that we have here the use of *fuit* as a verb of motion (for which usage see below, line 9 on *fuim(us)*), with in this case a pleonastic specification by means of a present participle of much the same meaning, but here changing the orientation of the verb (from 'go' to 'come'). There are such pleonasms in classical Latin (see Hofmann and Szantyr 1965: 797, and both Kroll 1929 and Fordyce 1961 on Catull. 64.179), but the model is more likely to have been a usage of later Christian Latin, for which see above, 31.1–2, with bibliography.

leua, leuita et uadam(us): *leua* here is the intransitive use of the verb with reflexive meaning, = *leua te*, which is illustrated from very late Latin by *TLL* VII.2.1236.69ff., Norberg (1943: 180), Feltenius (1977: 100–1); for *leuo* in general in late Latin see above, 43.9. The meaning here is 'get up/rouse yourself, and let us go'. Very similar is Agnellus 144, p. 372.18, cited by Norberg: *surge, leua, uade*. The noun *leuita* is well attested in medieval Latin of a deacon or clerk or minor ecclesiastical official: see Stotz (2002: 523); also id. (2000: 279). Usually it denotes a deacon or some such official but may sometimes be used of a clerk who is not a priest; perhaps in any case the referent here was a member of the Church. *Subleuita* is also attested (see Stotz 2004: 987, index).

Later in this text (11–12) *leuo* has a late meaning 'take, remove' (with diminution of the idea of raising). For *leuo* in this sense see *TLL* VII.2.1235.39ff., Svennung (1935: 581) (then > 'steal', e.g. *Tab. Sulis* 44.1).

7–8 sucisit fuim(us) ad domo Busani: if *sucisit* has been correctly read and represents *successit* it would have to be taken as impersonal. For the impersonal use see *OLD* s.v. *succedo* 7b, 'it turned out well, succeeded'; here '(so) it transpired we went to the house of B'. The verb would be close to an adverb in function, = 'and so we went . . .' For a verb phrase becoming an adverb from its parenthetical use cf. Fr. *peut-être*, which is foreshadowed by an adverbial use of *potest fieri* in a Vindolanda tablet: 656 *uidit autem me potest fieri apud aurifices* (see Adams 2003b: 554).

Fuimus must be that use of the verb 'to be' implying motion, which is quite well attested in Latin (see now Petersmann, 2002–3; also Adams 2007: 348 with further bibliography). Cf. e.g. Petron. 42.2 *nec sane lauare potui; fui enim hodie in funus, Per. Aeth.* 9.6 *et licet ea loca . . . iam nosse, id est quando Alexandriam uel ad Thebaidem fueram,* 20.2 *ibi statim fui ad ecclesiam,* 23.1 *ubi cum peruenissem, fui ad episcopum uere sanctum ex monacho.*

In Spanish the verb *ir* 'to go' suppletively uses *ser* 'be' in the preterite (e.g. *fui ayer al mercado* 'I went to the market yesterday'). What is interesting in the present text is that *fuim(us) ad domo Busani* follows immediately on *uadam(us) ad domo Busani*, with *fuimus* in the same expression providing the past tense of *uado*. The phrase mirrors modern Spanish *fuimos a casa*, and our text provides evidence of a proto-Spanish suppletion.

For this use of *fui* in medieval Latin texts from Spain see Bastardas Parera (1953: 141–2), but these are somewhat later than the present text.

11 ad uinias: this is surely not coordinated (i.e. in asyndeton) with *ad fragis*, but must be an adnominal specification of the location of the strawberry patch, 'where the vineyards are planted', 'at the vineyards that have been planted'. *Fraga* 'wild strawberries' is originally neuter plural. The ablative form *fragis* with *ad*, if indeed it is ablative, looks hypercorrect; cf. texts 13, 14, 40a in the same corpus for *inter nobis*. On this last expression see Isid. *Etym.* 1.33.1 with Velázquez Soriano (2004: 523, 524).

pono te: the old first person use of the present tense with future reference: see index, 'present tense for future'.

ibi in fragis: pleonasm in an expression of place, of a type that goes back to early Latin, with *ibi* specified by a more precise phrase. See index, 'locative/temporal expressions, double', and for *ibi* in such expressions, from both early and late Latin, see *TLL* VII.1.152.8ff.

11–12 leuaui: here of taking: see above on line 7.

13 laspare: obscure: see Velázquez Soriano (2004: 232).

Conclusions

The word order of this text has marked VO characteristics. Direct objects are not numerous (there are just three), but all are placed after the verb. More numerous are local complements of verbs. There are eight, and all come after the verb. Both datives of the indirect object follow the verb, in juxtaposition with it. Finite verbs are always early in their clause, either in first or second position (following *ego* or the subordinating conjunction *dum*). The result is that satellites (the accusatives, datives and local expressions mentioned above) are positioned later in the sentence. All six genitives come after their noun, and adnominal prepositional phrases follow the noun to which they are attached. Dependent terms of whatever type are always to the right of the determining term, whereas in any classical text placement to the left is commonplace.

There is in evidence a movement towards a case system in which oblique case functions are expressed by prepositions. This we saw in the regular use of *domus* with prepositions marking location, direction and separation, roles in classical Latin usually expressed by the locative, accusative and ablative. On the other hand the possessive genitive (of personal names) is still standard (cf. below, 50.40–1), with no trace of the *de*-construction.

Finally, the text has some proto-Spanish features. *Fui* is in a complementary relationship with *uado*, with the one serving as the verb 'go' in the past and the other in the present. Also, *stare* is used with the function of copula. One of the names exemplifies the *-a, -anis* nominal formation, which left a mark in Spanish.

47

PASSAGE FROM THE *VITA SANCTAE EVPHROSYNAE* (17)

Introduction

The Life of Euphrosyne tells of a young woman from Alexandria who disguised herself as a eunuch and spent thirty-eight years in a male monastery, in solitary confinement. She did this to escape a betrothal arranged by her father. He for his part searched in grief for his daughter. At last he found her, but soon afterwards she died. The father entered the monastery himself, and spent his remaining years in the cell that had been occupied by his daughter. On the history of this tale see Reisdoerfer (2011: 227 with nn. 1–2, and also some of the rest of his introduction). The date of the death of the saint is traditionally 470 (Reisdoerfer 2011: 227 with n. 3).

The text was edited by Boucherie (1871), an edition that has been drawn on by several anthologies in the past (Muller and Taylor 1932: 236–42, Iliescu and Slusanski 1991: 269–75). Boucherie used a ninth-century manuscript now in the Bibliothèque interuniversitaire de Montpellier, section de médecine (ms H55, fol. 139r–142v) (BuM). This manuscript was revised by a corrector of the twelfth century, but only a selection of these corrections was reported by Boucherie (see Reisdoerfer 2002: 712). BuM is a Merovingian version, a Gallic text perhaps of the seventh or eighth century with some regional characteristics. There is too a version preserved in the Bibliothèque municipale de Valenciennes (ms 168 fol. 211r–212v, s. 13) (BmV), edited for the first time by Reisdoerfer (2011). Also, a fragment is contained in a manuscript of the eleventh century in the Bibliothèque municipale de Rouen (ms U3) (BmR), it too edited for the first time by Reisdoerfer (2002). A few other known manuscripts are also listed by Reisdoerfer (2011: 229). There is a Greek version of the Life (see Boucherie 1883), but its relationship to the Latin versions is difficult to establish (see Reisdoerfer 2011: 228 with n. 8).

The text I have used here is from an online edition of Reisdoerfer, which reports the witnesses named above with textual variants, which are not listed here: http://w3.restena.lu/cul/VSE/VSE/000VSE.html.

Numerals in the Commentary refer to chapters of the text not printed here.

Text

17 Et dum fecit (1) beata puella in ipsa cella (2) retrusione (3) trigenta et octo annus (4), facta est egruta, in qua egrotudine (5) recessit. dum enim iacebat (6), uenit pater (7) suus in monasterio, et post orationem dixit ad abbati (8): 'si iubes, domini, uideam (9) dumnum (10) Ismaracdum istum eunuchum, quia satis diligit illum anima mea.' iussitque abbas magistro suo nomen Agapio (11) ducere patrem puelle dicens quia forsitam in hoc corpore non uidebit illum (12). dum autem apertus est ustius (13) et uisitaretur in aegritudinem (14), intrauit pater suus et iactauit se in collo suo et osculauit os suum (15) dicensque ei (16): 'ora pro me, uir dei, ut donet mihi deus consolationem pro filia mea, quia adhuc incertus sum pro illa ubi consistit (17).' dixitque ei ancilla dei: 'non sis tristis, domni pater (18), quia deus satis facere tibi habet (19) quideuinit filia tua (20). hoc te rogo solo, ut obseruis (21) hic in isto monasterio (22) tres dies et semper dignes uisitare me.' quod ita et fecit pater suos (23).

Translation

And after the blessed girl was confined in that very cell for thirty-eight years, she fell ill, in which illness she departed the world. And while she lay ill, her father came to the monastery and after prayer said to the abbot: 'If you bid it, lord, may I see lord Smaracdus the eunuch, because my soul delights in him greatly.' And the abbot ordered his master called Agapius to take the father of the girl, saying that perhaps he will not see him in this mortal body. And when the door was opened so that attendance might be made on the illness, her father entered and threw himself on her neck and kissed her mouth, and said to her: 'Pray for me, man of God, so that God may give me consolation for my daughter, because I am still uncertain on her behalf where she is.' And the maidservant of God said to him: 'Do not be sad, lord father, because God will give you satisfaction as to what has become of your daughter. This only I ask you, that you keep watch here in this monastery for three days, and always see fit to visit me.' And this her father did.

Commentary

1 et dum fecit: this is a text in which *dum* has assumed the functions of *cum*. It can sometimes still be translated 'while', as a few lines later (*dum enim* *iacebat*), but it also has the temporal meaning of *cum* ('when, after'), as here and in *dum autem apertus est ustius* below. It is also frequently causal, as in the opening chapter (1), *dum diuitia erat illi* (cf. e.g. 8, 9, 11 twice etc.). In the temporal sense it has in the present passage it may be followed by a perfect indicative, as e.g. at 4 *et dum uinit*, 12 *dum autem pater suos reuersus est*, 18 *dum autem uidit*, or indeed by a pluperfect subjunctive, as at 4 *dum ... cummorassent*, 19 *dum ... uidisset*. I have noted well over twenty instances of *dum* in the work, but none of *cum*. See index s.v. *dum = cum*.

2 beata puella in ipsa cella: unlike some very late works (see texts 49 and 50), this is not a text in which there is anything approaching a regular 'articloid' use of a demonstrative, whether *ille* or *ipse*. There is some specification of the revered characters of the story, particularly by *ipse*, but such specification has not become mechanical as a marker of definiteness. For example, at the start of chapter 4 the abbot is referred to as *ipsi sanctissimus abbas*, but then the demonstrative is dropped throughout much of the rest of the chapter, where we find *ad abbatem, abbas, ad abatti, ad abbatem*. There is however one example of the phrase *ipse uir sanctissimus*. Both uses of *ipse* in reference to the abbot in the chapter are accompanied by the superlative adjective *sanctissimus*. Again, in chapters 9–10 the abbot is first referred to as *ipse beatus abbas* (9), and then eleven times becomes *abbas* (in various cases) without a demonstrative.

The girl too, who is often merely *puella*, is *ipsa castissima* in 7 and twice in 9. By contrast in three other places in 7 *puella*, without an epithet, is also without *ipsa*. A superlative adjective however is not always accompanied by *ipse* (note 18 *sancta castissima ancilla dei*).

The 'father of the girl' (*pater puelle*), a constant phrase throughout the work, is almost invariably without specification (with a few exceptions, as at 12 *ipse pater*).

Another term that is sometimes (but by no means always) given a demonstrative is *monasterium* (2, 13, 14, 22 *ipsum monasterium*).

All of the nouns referred to in this note are repeatedly used without a specifier, and it is in traditional functions of *ipse*, not in Romance practice, that one should seek its motivations. It stresses the importance of someone ('the very'), particularly with an epithet.

3 retrusione: for *retrusionem*. *Retrudo* often means in the early medieval period 'confine (in a monastery)' (see Niermeyer 1976: 918). Here *fecit* is used as a support verb with the verbal noun *retrusio* 'confinement' (for which see Niermeyer 1976: 918). 'To make a confinement' is the equivalent of 'to be confined', here = *erat/fuerat/fuit retrusa*. Elsewhere the author does indeed use *retrudo* itself: 11 *uolo ut una cella retrudas te*, 14 *bonum hominem eunuchus de palatium Thodosio imperatori retrusum*, 22 *in cellam ubi filia sua fuit retrusa*. This last example is in much the same context as *fecit . . . retrusione*. We will see constructions with support verbs in another early medieval text from this area (see below, 48.2.5), which however are removed from an 'improved' version of the work, presumably because they had a reputation for being 'popular'. See above, 4.8, 8.4, and also index, 'support verbs'.

Such constructions are quite common in the text. Later in this chapter *donet . . . consolationem* is equivalent to *consoletur*. See also 1 *curam habens pauperum*, 2 *qualem tribulationem haberet in corde* (contrast 13 *dum omnes serui dei tribulati essent pro hac causa*), 4 *ubi peregrini recepcionem habebant*, 4 *coepit in cor suum zelum habere conuersationis eorum*, 8 *inimicus impedimenta et recogitacionis facit*, 11 *multos fecit inimicos scandalum in anima* (contrast, immediately after, *unde animas scandalizentur*), 15 *conloquium habentes*. At 18 similarly *habeas . . . tristiciam* is a 'nominalisation' (for the term see Langslow 2000: chapter 6) of *sis . . . tristis*. At 11 just quoted *inimicos* is a misspelling of *inimicus*, of the devil, and *multos* looks like an accusative plural object of the support-verb construction *fecit scandalum*, = 'scandalised many'. This would be a type of the phenomenon sometimes referred to as 'incorporation', whereby in this case *facio* + object behaves like a transitive verb and takes an object (see above, 4.8, 37.2–3(?)).

4 trigenta et octo annus: 'for thirty-eight years', with *annus* for *annos*. This is a common spelling at this period, particularly with *annus* or *solidus* (see Pei 1932: 55, 143, B. Löfstedt 1961: 86–8, Adams 1976a: 42, with further bibliography). The spelling is not significant historically, and is hard to explain decisively. Speculations may be found in the works above.

On the form *trigenta* see B. Löfstedt (1961: 60–3). He points out (60) that in his Lombard corpus *uiginti* more often than not retains an *i* in the second syllable, whereas *triginta* (along with other words for tens) often has an *e*. He concludes (62) that the penultimate vowel of *uiginti* must have been closer than that of *triginta*, and puts that down to the palatalising influence of the final *ī* of *uiginti*. In French *uiginti* gives *vingt* but *triginta* gives *trente*. The phonetics however are disputed (see the whole discussion of Löfstedt).

5 egrotudine: the easiest explanation of this form is that *aegritudo* has been conflated with *aegrotatio*.

6 dum enim iacebat: for *iaceo* 'lie ill' see Adams (1977a: 79–80). *Enim* is merely transitional or perhaps adversative (Hofmann and Szantyr 1965: 508).

7 uenit pater: the semantic field 'come'/'go' is of interest in this text. *Venio*, which survives in Romance, occurs throughout (about sixteen times). On the other hand *eo* 'go' has disappeared completely, except in the compounds *introeo* (4) and *exeo* (4, 9, 16); on the persistence of the latter, often interchangeable with *eo*, see above, 27.2, with bibliography. *Vado* occurs once, in the imperative form *uade* (7; on the imperative use see above, 43.9). Its past tense equivalent is *ambulo*, which does not retain the old sense 'walk' but means 'went'; this verb is also used once in the future perfect. The meaning can be seen clearly at 21, where it is construed with a final infinitive (*ambolabat osculare*, 'he went to kiss', i.e. 'he went and kissed'). Cf. 1 *ambolabat in monasterio*, 4 *ambulauerunt in monasterio*, 8 *ambolauit in monasterio*, 9 *si ambulauero in monasterio*, 13 *ambolabat ad ipso monasterio*. Complemented by *in monasterio* the verb means 'went (into a monastery),' i.e. 'entered'. There is a general similarity to French, in which *eo* has disappeared except in the future (*j'irai* etc.). In the present tense the paradigm is split between *uado* (so e.g. the imperative *va*, with which compare *uade* above) and *ambulo* (if it is indeed *ambulare* that lies behind *aller*: see e.g. Bloch and von Wartburg 1968: 19), and in the imperfect, past historic and perfect the basis is *aller/ambulare*. It is hard to find even in very late Latin instances of *ambulo* that have a more general meaning than 'walk' (see above, 43.12, and Adams 2013: 809–10), and a text with *ambulo* regularly used for *eo* is a real rarity.

There are a few other verbs that may be mentioned. *Accedo* occurs at 4 and 5, where it means 'go/went'. *Intro* is scattered throughout (6, 9, 11, 17, 19, 22). *Redeo* is not used; for *reuertor* see below, 47.15.

8 dixit ad abbati: in this context (complementing a verb of saying) we find both *ad abbatem* and *ad abbati*. For the former see 4 *dixit pater puelle ad abbatem*, 10 *dixitque illi ad abbatem*; for the latter, 4 *dixit pater puelle ad abbati*. For the *ad*-construction with another noun see 10 *dixitque abas ad monachum, sapientissimo seruo dei*; for the classical dative in such contexts see e.g. 9 *nuncia domno abbati quia*, 9 *dixit abbati*, 13 *coepit abbas dicere patri puellae*.

Here are some figures for the use of *ad* versus the dative in this text, with verbs of saying and with verbs of giving.

For (clitic) pronouns with verbs of saying the dative is preferred, by about 29:1. The only instance of *ad* is at 12: *dixerunt ad illum*. Here is evidence for the persistence of inflected forms in clitic pronouns, a persistence that lasts into Romance. With verbs of giving similarly there are no instances of *ad* + pronoun, but eight of the inflected dative.

With nouns the *ad*-construction with verbs of saying (as illustrated at the start of this note) is better represented, but it is nevertheless slightly outnumbered by the dative construction (by 8:5). So with verbs of the semantic field 'give' the dative is preferred to the *ad*-construction, by 7:2 (for the latter see 1 *pecuniam ad pauperes erogans*, 10 *offerens quingentos solidos ad abbatem*; cf. Tac. *Ann.* 16.17.5 *pecuniam in Tigellinum . . . erogabat*).

There are two ways of explaining the form of *ad abbati*. First, in this text *ĕ* in final position often appears as *i*, as e.g. in *ipsi* for *ipse* and in *domini* in the next note (see also below, 47.18). The accusative *abbate* (with the loss of final *m*) might have been spelt *abbati*. Pei (1932: 42) cites *abbati* for *abbate* in Merovingian Latin. The second possibility is that the old dative construction might have been conflated with the new equivalent *ad*-construction. For such conflations in late Latin see 40.2, and Adams and de Melo (forthcoming, 8.1). There may be a similar mixing of constructions at 10, quoted in the first paragraph of this note, where an *ad*-phrase appears to be followed by an appositional dative (*seruo*), though the latter could also be interpreted as accusative with loss of *m*.

There is no significant difference between the constructions with verbs of saying and those with verbs of giving in this text. This too represents a development towards Romance usage, because for a long time in later Latin the *ad*-construction was all but confined to verbs of saying (see below, 50.45, and also Adams and de Melo, forthcoming).

9 si iubes, domini, uideam . . .: *iubeo* does not mean 'order' here: rather, 'if you permit/see fit, may I see the . . . ' This is a late use of the verb, dealt with at *TLL* VII.2.584.3ff. (with bibliography). For the phrase *si iubes* see *TLL* 584.45ff.

10 dumnum: for the spelling with *u* see B. Löfstedt (1961: 70), who cites it (69) from Lombard laws, and attributes it to the assimilatory (closing) influence of the following *m*.

11 iussitque abbas magistro suo nomen Agapio: the words *magistro suo Agapio* are either accusative (as would be usual with *iussit*) or dative (perhaps on the analogy of *impero* + dative). There are many accusatives of this form in the text. *Nomen* 'by name' would be expected to be ablative (*nomine*). Cf. 10 *dixitque abas ad monachum, sapientissimo seruo dei nomen Agapio*. For the correct use see 1 *uir magnificus, nomine Pafnutius*, 14 *adduxitque magistrum puellae Agapio nomine ipsi abbas* (*Agapio* must be accusative). Third declension neuters not infrequently display a fossilised nominative/accusative use where an oblique case is expected. See

above, 22.17 on the phenomenon in general and for bibliography on fossilised *nomen* itself.

A different naming construction at 10 (*Ismaracdus habeo nomen*), where the
name is given its base (nominative) form though seemingly in apposition to an
accusative, goes back to classical Latin (see Adams 2013: 222).

12 dicens quia forsitam in hoc corpore non uidebit illum: in this text the acc.
+ inf. is very rare. Speech is reported to an overwhelming extent by direct
quotation (for this phenomenon much earlier, see above, 22.10), usually
introduced by *dico*, as three times in this chapter. For example, in the first
ten chapters alone there are thirty-four cases of such direct quotation, and just
two of the acc. + inf. (or attempts at the acc. + inf.): 3 *contegit genetricem suam
de hac lucem migrauit* (the attempted construction *contigit genetricem suam
migrasse* has broken down and the infinitive is replaced with a finite verb), 5
apertum est omnibus uolentibus esse saluos (is *se* to be understood here?). Verbs
such as *iubeo, rogo, inuito* superficially with an acc. + inf. have a different
construction: the accusative is direct object of the verb, and the infinitive is
final. Verbs of saying (mainly *dico*) are sometimes complemented by *quia*, as
here (8, 18, 19), but never by *quod*. There are also mixed constructions, such
that *dicit quia* (or the like) is followed by quoted direct speech: e.g. 9 *cogitauit
in se ipsam dicens quia, si ambulauero in monasterio puellarum,* 9 *nuncia
domno abbati quia eunuchus de palatio occurrere tibi uolit.* For a comparable
mixed construction of a different sort (indirect question) see 12 *interrogabat
familiam suam quideuenisset filia mea.*

I stress two general points: the virtual loss of the acc. + inf., such that
attempted uses are likely to go astray, and the eclipse of *quod*, with verbs of
saying, by *quia*. See above, 31.7, 43.4, 45.12.

13 apertus est ustius: the noun is *ostium*, with a change of gender. For the
form cf. in this text 5, 11 *ustium*; also 9 *ustiarius*. B. Löfstedt (1961: 99) sees in
this the palatalising effect (with closing) of the following yod, comparing *bistia*
for *bestia*. Romance outcomes go back to a form with $\bar{u}$ (It. *uscio*, Fr. *huis*, OSp.
uzo), on which see *FEW* VII.439. The masculine in the present text contrasts
with the feminine (deriving from the neuter plural) in another Gallic text
(below, 49.7).

14 et uisitaretur in aegritudinem: *et* should probably be changed to *ut*: 'so
that it might be attended upon the illness'.

15 intrauit pater suus et iactauit se in collo suo et osculauit os suum: here
are three phrases in which *suus* is not reflexive but equivalent to *eius* ('kissing
his own mouth' would be a particular absurdity). Earlier in the chapter there is

another such case (*uenit pater suus*), but also a genuine reflexive use (*iussitque abbas magistro suo*). *Suus* thus marks a single possessor in the Romance manner, whether in a reflexive function or not. This non-reflexive use of *suus* is common in the text, but there is not consistency: note for example 20 *ambolabat osculare pedis eius*, where *eius* is used in the classical way with the object of the same verb of kissing. Similarly, in contrast to *pater suus* here, at 3 we find the classicising *paterque eius docebat*. Of plural possessors *eorum* is usually used, for example non-reflexively, in the classical manner, at 1 *post exitum eorum*, 4 *conuersationis eorum*. On the other hand at 13 (*ut omnes fratres de cellola eorum congregarentur*) it might have been replaced in classical Latin by *sua*. There is the beginning of a Romance-type distinction, between *suus* of a single possessor, reflexive or not, and *eorum* of plural possessors (see above, 39.8). It is not however absolute yet, partly because, as we saw, *eius* is sometimes used of a single possessor in the classical manner, and also because *suus* rather than *eorum* is at least once used of plural possessors (reflexively) (3 *pro filios suos*).

iactauit se: cf. 13 *iactauit se ante pedes beati abbatis*. An intransitive equivalent (with deletion of the reflexive) to this use of the verb is at 4: *iactauit ad pedes eius*. For *se iactare* see above, 27.10.

osculauit: there are still some deponents in this text, but they are slightly outnumbered by conversions into the active. Deponents are *commoror* (6, 7, 9), *dignor* (7), *loquor* (15, 16), *nascor* (4), *reuertor* (12, 13, 14, 16 three times), *sequor* (7) (fourteen examples). The activisations are *amplexo* (16), *commoro* (4, 19), *consolo* (14, 22), *conuerso* (6), *digno* (17, 18), *furo* (12), *lamento* (12), *miro* (3, 11), *moro* (19), *obliuisco* (13, 20), *osculo* (16, 17, 21) (eighteen examples).

16 dicensque ei: here is a case, so typical of late narrative texts, where a present participle is coordinated to a finite verb. Cf. 20 *et ueniens abba uelociter et ipsi inruens super sancto corpusculo uirginis et dicens* (no finite verb). See index, 'present participle, coordinated to main verb'.

17 ubi consistit: 'where she dwells', or better 'is'. Both meanings, 'dwell' and 'be', are common for this verb in medieval Latin: see Niermeyer (1976: 255, meanings 1 and 2). Cf. 4 *ambulauerunt in monasterio ubi ipsi sanctissimus abbas consistebat*, 4 *beati sunt hominis isti qui in hoc habitaculo consistunt*, 9 *ueni consistere uobiscum* ('I have come to live with you'), 10 *dum iuuenis es solus non potes consistere*, 22 *in ipsa retricione decim annus consistens*.

Consistit is indicative in an indirect question, as is *quideuinit* in the next sentence. There is no consistency of mood in indirect questions in the text.

For the indicative see as well 5 twice (both times in clauses introduced by *si*, a recurrent construction from early on), 12, 13 three times (eight examples), and for the subjunctive, 2, 7 four times, 12 (six examples). See index, 'indirect question' (with reference too to the type with *si*).

18 domni pater: *domni* is for *domine*. Original *ĕ* in final syllable often appears in this text and other early medieval texts as *i*, a spelling that has different explanations in different environments (see the comprehensive treatment of B. Löfstedt 1961: 39–56; for examples in Merovingian texts see Vielliard 1927: 18–19, Pei 1932: 40–2; see too, on Gregory of Tours, Bonnet 1890: 13–17). For instance, the spelling is common in this text and elsewhere in nominative pronouns, such as *ipsi* for *ipse* (e.g. 4; see also B. Löfstedt 1961: 53–4, with bibliography). Romance forms such as OFr. *li*, Fr. *il*, It. *il, egli*, have a close *i*, and it is suggested that *ille* etc. were influenced by *qui* (B. Löfstedt 1961: 54). In the case of a vocative form such as *domni* it is possible that there was influence from the commonplace vocative *fili*, or alternatively one might fall back on the indeterminacy of short front vowels in final open syllables (see Bonnet 1890: 114).

19 deus satis facere tibi habet: here infinitive + *habeo* has a future meaning (for this proto-Romance construction see e.g. Adams 2013: chapter XXV, with bibliography). There is another future periphrasis at 13: *age domino gracias, quia quando iusserit dominus, sic cognuscere habis quideuinit filia tua*, 'give thanks to the Lord, because when the Lord shall have ordered it, then you will know what has become of your daughter'. In both passages the infinitive precedes *habeo* in the Romance manner, with juxtaposition of the two elements in one case, and separation by a pronoun in the other; in some areas of Romance pronominal insertion did continue (see Adams 2013: 652–3 with bibliography).

On the other hand at 8 (*habeo cum suo adiutorio saluare animam meam*) there is an ambiguity about the periphrasis ('with His help I will save my soul', or 'must'), and here the order is different and the elements are separated. Earlier in the chapter (*quid tibi habeo dicere*) the construction is classical, 'what can I say to you?'

For inflected futures of the classical type in the text (including one in this chapter) see 3 *erit*, 6 *eris*, 6 *commorabitur*, 8 *inuenient*, 9 *erit*, 12 *captiuabit*, 17 *uidebit*, 18 *preparabis*. Note the three examples from the verb 'to be'; for the survival of the future of this verb into Old French see Buridant (2000: 267).

Well represented are presents with future reference. Note particularly the self-address by the girl at 9: *si ambulauero in monasterio puellarum, pater meus querit me et si inuenerit, me habet pro meo sponsum, dum potens est, trahit me* *de monasterio. uerumtamen <u>muto</u> me sicut eunuchus, nimine cognuscenti, et <u>intro</u> in monasterio uirorum ubi nulla erit suspectio.* There are five such presents here, two of them in the apodosis of conditional sentences following a future perfect in the *si*-clause. For this pattern see too 9 *se saluaueris animam meam, in isto loco offero omnia*; cf. 10 *quomodo iusseris, sic facio.* At 8 (*et ubi uolet pater tuus dimittit suam*) *dimittit* has future reference (*uolet* is possibly a present form).

20 quideuinit filia tua: this phrase recurs: 12 *quideuenisset filia mea*, 12 *quidiuinit filia tua*, 13 *quideuinit filia tua*. Muller and Taylor (1932: 240 n. 11) compare with *quideuenisset* Fr. *qu'était devenue*, 'what has become of'.

Deuenio 'become' = *fio* (Fr. *devenir*) is typical of late Latin: see *TLL* V.1.850.77ff.; cf. the special usage illustrated by Adams (2013: 723).

There has been simplification of the geminated *d* across a word boundary (*quid deuenit*). The spelling with *i* (*uin-*) is of some interest. It is common in very late texts in the perfect of *uenio* and compounds. For examples from Lombard laws see B. Löfstedt (1961: 22), and for Merovingian texts see Pei (1932: 20); see also the bibliography at B. Löfstedt (1961: 26). B. Löfstedt (1961: 26–7) sees such forms as originally assimilatory, that is as under the influence of the following *ī* in the first person singular perfect of verbs such as *feci* (another in which the spelling is common) and *ueni*. These forms were more than merely orthographic: cf. Fr. *je vins, il vint, je fis* etc. (B. Löfstedt 1961: 27 with further evidence and literature).

21 ut obseruis: *obseruis* for the subjunctive *obserues*. The spelling *i* for *e* in verb forms, not least of the present subjunctive of the first conjugation, is particularly common in late Italian texts (see B. Löfstedt 1961: 50–2), and survives in the Italian present subjunctive (e.g. *compr-i*, first, second and third person singular subjunctive of a verb of the first conjugation). It is also well attested in early medieval Gallic texts (B. Löfstedt 1961: 50). For some evidence see Vielliard (1927: 20), who states: 'cela s'explique par ce fait que, aux raisons d'homophonie entre *i* et *e* atones, se joignent les raisons de confusion entre les différentes conjugaisons'. See also Pei (1932: 41). See in this text 7 *ut uisitis*, 10 *ut ... superit*, 13 *ut manifestit*.

22 hic in isto monasterio: see index, 'locative/temporal expressions, double'. In this context *isto* is synonymous with *hoc*.

23 quod ita et fecit pater suos: *ita* following the relative is superfluous. Cf. 11 *quod ita et fecit*, 13 *quod ita et fecerunt*. For this redundant use of *ita* see above, 39.7, with bibliography.

Conclusions

Here is an early medieval text from the area of Gaul that in a few respects presents the language a stage further on towards Romance than is usual in late texts. I know of no other text (though there are probably others) in which *ire* has been ousted in the past tenses by *ambulo*, a verb that was tenacious in holding on to its old meaning 'walk'. *Vado* is used in the present imperative, and there is thus a distinction of the sort found in Gallo-Romance.

Ad for the dative of the indirect object with nouns is used with verbs of giving as well as saying, whereas in many late texts it occurs only with verbs of the latter type. Nevertheless the dative (of nouns) has not been dropped; by contrast in the Italian text 50 there is already a Romance distinction between clitic pronouns (used always in the dative with this function) and nouns (used only with *ad*). The present text does however display the preservation of the dative of pronouns, which was to have Romance consequences.

The acc. + inf. has all but disappeared, and attempts to use it show ineptitudes. It was now a literary construction, little understood.

Suus is the usual possessive in non-reflexive functions of a single possessor. It has encroached on *eius*, but not ousted it completely. Of plural possessors *eorum* is usually used. *Eorum* was not to survive in Romance, where it was replaced by *illorum*, but the complementary relationship between *suus* (of single possessors, in a reflexive and non-reflexive sense) and *eorum* (of a plurality) is a step along the way to some varieties of Romance.

There are examples of demonstratives (notably *ipse*) that in isolation might look 'articloid', but regular specification of definite nouns is not a feature of this text, which in this respect is well behind texts 49 and 50.

There are two instances of infinitive + *habeo* expressing futurity, one with juxtaposition of the two elements, the other with separation by a pronoun, both Romance patterns. However, the classical future (along with the future perfect) is still well represented (as is the present with future reference). Both cases of the *habeo*-construction are in *quia*-clauses, whereas the future is several times in simple main clauses. It is hard, even impossible, to find late texts in which the *habeo*-construction has genuinely ousted the old future. Texts that have examples tend to have them in complicated structures, which possibly indicates that the periphrasis developed first in educated varieties of the language.

48

SELECTED PASSAGES FROM THE *ANNALES REGNI FRANCORVM*, IN TWO VERSIONS

Introduction

The *Annales regni Francorum* have been called the 'most important single narrative source for Carolingian history' (McKitterick 1983: 4–5). There are two redactions of much of the *Annales* (a text that has not been edited since 1895). The first version (printed on the left-hand pages of the text of Kurze 1895) may have been written at the court of Charlemagne (Scholz and Rogers 1970: 2). It is a composite work, which was probably put together by several authors. A conventional view is that the first part of this first version, which is the only part that will concern us here, covers the years 741–95 (Scholz and Rogers 1970: 4), though Collins (1998) has more recently reopened the question of the stages of composition. It was composed by a writer or writers little touched by the Carolingian revival of learning, and is full of regionalisms and non-standard features (see Adams 1977b). Part of this first version was revised in a second edition, which is printed by Kurze on the facing pages. This is written in a classicising style with reminiscences of several classical authors. Local and non-standard usages found in the first version are constantly removed. This revised version is thought to have been used by Einhard for his life of Charlemagne (but for reservations see Collins 1998: 197, 207; verbal parallels may be found in the notes of Halphen 1967 to his edition of the Life). In the following four extracts (**1–4**) there is first a passage from the first edition, and then the corresponding section from the revised version. The Commentary is mainly about the first version, but some comparisons are made between the two, and a few observations are offered about details of the second.

The *Annales* are arranged by year. Cross-references in the Commentary of the form a. 769 are to a year of the narrative, i.e. in this case anno 769.

(1) a. 745

Text

(first version)

Tunc Carlomannus confessus est Pippino germano suo (1), quod uoluisset (2) seculum relinquere; et in eodem anno (3) nullum fecerunt exercitum (4), sed praeparauerunt se uterque, Carlomannus ad iter suum et Pippinus, quomodo germanum suum honorifice direxisset cum muneribus.

(second version)

Hoc anno Carlomannus, quod diu ante praemeditatus est, patefecit fratri suo Pippino, saecularem conuersationem se uelle dimittere et habitu monachico deo seruire. propter hoc dimissa expeditione anni praesentis ad uota Carlomanni perficienda et iter illius dispondendum (nam Romam proficisci statuerat) et Pippinus uacabat, dans operam ut frater honorifice ac decenter illo, quo desiderabat, perueniret.

Translation

(first version)

Then Carloman confessed to his brother Pippin that he wanted to leave the secular world; and in the same year they formed no army but both prepared themselves, Carloman for his journey and Pippin for sending his brother off honourably with gifts.

(second version)

In this year Carloman revealed to his brother Pippin that he wished to abandon the secular life and in a monk's garb to serve God (a thing that he had long previously contemplated). For this reason the expedition of the present year having been abandoned, in order to carry out the wishes of Carloman and to arrange his journey (for he had decided to set out to Rome), and Pippin was free, devoting himself to seeing that his brother should with the appropriate honours reach the place that he desired.

Commentary

1.1 germano suo: twice in this passage *germanus* is used for 'brother', and both times it is replaced in the second edition by *frater*. *Germanus* 'brother' (along with the feminine *germana* 'sister') goes back to early Latin (*TLL* VI.2.1916.48ff.), but its use in the first edition is a little surprising, as it is *frater* and *soror* that survive in Gallo-Romance; *germanus* is associated particularly with the Romance languages of the Iberian peninsula (*REW* 3742). For *germanus* see also a. 753 (twice), a. 769. All three of these latter examples are replaced in the second edition by *frater*.

1.2 uoluisset: the pluperfect subjunctive here has an imperfect meaning, as does *direxisset* towards the end of the passage, where the literal sense is 'he prepared how he might send off . . .' Here we have a proto-Romance usage, as the pluperfect subjunctive was 'preserved in the west with imperfect meaning' (Elcock 1960: 142). There are many such pluperfect subjunctives in the first edition (for a list, by no means complete, see Adams 1977b: 281), which are eliminated from the second. Note e.g. a. 787 *misit Romaldum filium suum cum magnis muneribus, postolare de aduentu iamdicti domni regis, ut in Beneuento non introisset* ('. . . to demand . . . that he should not enter Beneventum'); also (same year) *eo quod sub iureiurando promissum habebat, ut in omnibus oboediens et fidelis fuisset domno rege Carolo* (here incidentally *promissum habebat* seems to be a genuine perfect equivalent). Parallel uses of the pluperfect subjunctive can be found in late texts from various areas (see e.g. Bonnet 1890: 640, Haag 1899: 920, Vielliard 1927: 224, Bastardas Parera 1953: 155–6, Adams 1976a: 68, id. 2007: 520). It was pointed out earlier (45 Conclusions, 'Literary and late Latin') that Gregory the Great restricted this usage to certain auxiliaries. On earlier Latin see above, 11.17.

The second edition (with *patefecit*) has the classical acc. + inf., whereas the first edition (with *confessus est*) has a *quod*-clause. It would be wrong to suggest that at this period (or indeed much earlier, say in the fourth century) the *quod*-construction was in any way substandard, but the acc. + inf. was always available for someone who wanted to make a demonstration of his command of the old literary language (see above, 31.7, 43.4).

1.3 in eodem anno: the second edition has *hoc anno* (without the preposition). See below, 48.3.1.

1.4 nullum fecerunt exercitum: for this phrase, of putting an army together, see a. 787, p. 78 *et iussit alium exercitum fieri, id est Franci Austrasiorum, Toringi, Saxones . . . et tertium exercitum iussit fieri partibus Italiae.* It is an expression with outcomes in the Romance languages: see Stefenelli (1962: 58). See also below, 48.3.1 for *exercitum reficio* in classical Latin.

There is an ineptitude at this point in the second edition. The clause containing the ablative absolute *dimissa expeditione* has no finite verb but is left hanging, and is coordinated to the next clause by *et* (*et Pippinus uacabat*). This is an anacoluthon that is more typical of the first edition (see below, 48.4.3). Its presence in a text that is usually correct by classical norms illustrates how readily the run of a sentence might be lost when there are participial and other verbal elements (here gerundives) present.

(2) a. 758

Text

(first version)

Pippinus rex in Saxoniam ibat (1), et firmitates (2) Saxonum per uirtutem (3) introiuit in loco qui (4) dicitur Sitnia, et multae strages factae sunt (5) in populo Saxonum; et tunc polliciti sunt contra Pippinum omnes uoluntates eius faciendum (6) et honores in placito suo (7) praesentandum usque in equos CCC per singulos annos.

(second version)

Pippinus rex cum exercitu Saxoniam adgressus est; et quamuis Saxonibus ualidissime resistentibus et munitiones suas tuentibus, pulsis proelio propugnatoribus per ipsum, quo patriam defendere conabantur, uallum intrauit. commissisque passim proeliis plurimam ex ipsis multitudinem cecidit coegitque, ut promitterent se omnem uoluntatem illius esse facturos et annis singulis honoris causa ad generalem conuentum equos CCC pro munere daturos.

Translation

(first version)

King Pippin went into Saxony, and he entered the fortresses of the Saxons by force at the place called Sythen, and many massacres were done among the people of the Saxons; and then they promised Pippin to do all his wishes, and to present honours at his assembly, to the extent of 300 horses each year.

(second version)

King Pippin attacked Saxony with his army; and although the Saxons resisted most strongly and defended their fortifications, the defenders were repulsed in battle and he entered through the very rampart by which they were attempting to defend their land. Battle was joined everywhere and he cut down a great multitude of them and forced them to promise that they would do his every wish and each year as a mark of respect at a general assembly would give him as a tribute 300 horses.

Commentary

2.1 Pippinus rex in Saxoniam ibat: *ibat* here seems interchangeable with
a perfect tense ('he went'); cf. the revised version, *Saxoniam adgressus est.*
For the imperfect with what looks like perfect meaning in medieval Latin
see Stotz (2000: 320), and for texts of this region Vielliard (1927: 222–3),
Pei (1932: 278). The 'aoristic' or narrative uses of the imperfect in
classical Latin discussed by Hofmann and Szantyr (1965: 317) may have
subtle motivations in particular contexts; see also Pinkster (1998: 232–4)
for such motivated uses in Merovingian hagiographic texts. By contrast
note particularly a. 769 (first edition), where *ibat* is located within
a sequence of perfect verbs, which also contains *iuit*: *Carolus benignissi-
mus rex iuit ad Aequolesinam ciuitatem, et inde sumpsit plures Francos
cum omni utensilia et praeparamenta eorum et ibat super flumen
Dornoniam et aedificauit ibi castrum.* Each of the events would have
occupied a limited time, and the perfect was considered appropriate to
the description of all but one of them. It would be unconvincing to
suggest that here the imperfect was used to mark a particularly durative
event, because the crossing of the river would have taken no more time
than travel to the city or the building of a *castrum.* The writer has slipped
into an imperfect serving the same function as *iuit* earlier in the sentence.
For this use of the imperfect in Old French (particularly Anglo-Norman)
see Buridant (2000: 368–9). See also, on Latin of different periods,
Haverling (2010: 476–87).

In the *Vita sanctae Euphrosynae* at 1 (*ambolabat in monasterio*) the
imperfect is used in a phrase which elsewhere in the text also has the
perfect (see 47.7 for the examples), and there is also a textual variant
(BmV *ambulauit*). Note too 13 *dum autem non potebat portare dolores
pater puelle, ambolabat ad ipso monasterio et iactauit se ante pedes beati
abbatis.* The act of going is complete before the father throws himself at
the feet of the abbot. There does not seem in the context to be any
significant semantic motivation to the imperfect (but see below), but
there may have been something special about the verb itself, *ambulo,* in
the original meaning of which the imperfect often had point (of going for
a walk, durative), and indeed about verbs for 'go' in general (see above,
previous paragraph), which in many contexts in the imperfect are markedly durative. There was perhaps a mechanical extension of such imperfects to different contexts. Or did the writer at *Vita Euphrosynae* 13 above
perceive a contrast between the instantaneous throwing of the father at
the abbot's feet, and his more protracted journey to the monastery?

2.2 firmitates: *firmitas* here has a concrete meaning, 'fortress', a sense in which it survives only in Gallo-Romance (OFr. *ferté*, Occ. *fermetat*: see *REW* 3319, *FEW* III.575–6). It is used in the first edition of the *Annales* (apparently its earliest attestations) but not in the second edition, and was no doubt a regionalism of the type avoided by the later edition, which here has *munitiones*. For further details about this usage (which occurs in other annals from the region) see Adams (1977b: 262–3).

2.3 per uirtutem: the meaning is 'by force', = CL *ui, per uim*, a late and medieval usage. See Önnerfors (1975: 108 n. on *Phys. Plin. Bamb.* 82.77), B. Löfstedt (1976: 157 = id. 2000: 209), Adams (1977b: 271–2), Stotz (2000: 112–13). This is another usage typical of the first edition (cf. e.g. a. 776 *ad debellandum per uirtutem ipsum castellum*). In the second edition at this point the narrative is rewritten and there is no exactly equivalent phrase: note the threefold alliteration *pulsis proelio pugnatoribus.*

2.4 in loco qui: on this formulaic expression see above, 41.3. The accusative (directional) would be expected (see index, s.v. *in*, '+ ablative for accusative and vice versa').

2.5 multae strages factae sunt: cf. a. 775 (first edition) *stragem . . . fecit*, ibid. *stragia . . . facta*, a. 788 (first edition) *stragia . . . facta est*. An old expression (cf. Livy 8.39.9, 26.4.8, 35.21.6), and one of numerous support-verb constructions in the first edition comprising *facio* + object and usually interchangeable with a single verb (see Adams 1977b: 278 for further examples, such as *aliquod tempus moram faciens* at a. 746, with which compare a. 787 *aliquod dies ibi moratus est*). The second edition of the present passage has *caedo: plurimam ex ipsis multitudinem cecidit*. It usually eliminates such constructions (see Adams loc. cit.), which suggests continuing disapproval among purists (cf. above, 8.4, and also 4.8).

2.6 polliciti sunt contra Pippinum omnes uoluntates eius faciendum: the second edition has a classical future infinitive in the active with the verb of promising (*promitterent se omnem uoluntatem illius esse facturos*). In the first edition *omnes uoluntates* is clearly direct object of *faciendum*. The construction is repeated in the next clause (*honores . . . praesentandum*), and again the second edition classicises (*daturos*).

Various ways of explaining the construction of the first edition suggest themselves. First, we might consider starting with a usage that goes back to early Latin and had some currency in much later Latin. The gerundive is sometimes used as an impersonal passive and construed with an accusative object. This construction (but expressing obligation/necessity) turns up in Plautus (e.g. *Trin.* 869 *agitandumst uigilias*), and thereafter it retained some life as an archaism (Hofmann and Szantyr 1965: 372). It then re-emerged in later Latin (usually in non-standard texts), again with the idea of obligation/necessity (e.g. Philagrius p. 78 *et si tibi manifesta signa plenitudinis apparuerint, euacuandum patientes*: see Svennung 1935: 476–7, Hofmann and Szantyr loc. cit.).

It is a problem that our examples cannot be taken as expressing obligation/necessity but would have to be given a future meaning (literally 'would be done all his wishes'); they therefore cannot be related directly to the early Latin construction. It is true that the gerundive came to be used sometimes in later Latin with future meaning (Hofmann and Szantyr 1965: 312–13), as for example at Julius Valerius 1.50, p. 61.20 *praenuntio tibi fore actus tuos humanorum omnium fortiores nomenque per saecula porrigendum* and Victor Vitensis 1.47, p. 12.3 *promittens multis eum diuitiis cumulandum* (cited by Pitkäranta 1978: 73, who takes *cumulandum* to be a substitute for the future passive infinitive, = *cumulatum iri*). However, in these last examples and the others cited in the literature the gerundive is not impersonal, and it seems excessively convoluted to invoke an early construction that would have to have been conflated with a later use. These two examples, it should be stressed, are not the same as that in our passage because they are gerundives with subjects in agreement, whereas in our example *faciendum* governs an accusative object.

It is preferable to take *faciendum* (and *praesentandum*) as equivalent to an active verbal noun or infinitive. Hofmann and Szantyr (1965: 378) draw attention to the late accusative of the gerund with e.g. *iubeo*, citing Cael. Aurel. *Chron.* 1.4.78 *iubentes eam a lauacro abstinendum* 'ordering the keeping her away from bathing'. Thus the present example may be translated 'they promised the doing of all his wishes'. This usage is common in Fredegar (another Frankish work of this period). For details (including examples with verbs of promising, both *promitto* and synonyms) see Haag (1899: 924), Odelstierna (1926: 45–54): e.g. 3, p. 160.24 *cumta, que sui . . . perpetrauerant, emendandum spondedit.*

In *contra Pippinum* the preposition virtually has the role of the dative of the indirect object. Stotz (2002: 86) cites this usage from Irish texts; contrast the examples at *TLL* IV.751.38ff.

2.7 in placito suo: *placitum* here means 'assembly' (cf. e.g. a. 757 (first edition) *rex Pippinus tenuit placitum suum in Compendio*, where the second edition has *ubi tunc populi sui generalem conuentum habuit*). In this sense the term occurs eleven times in the first edition down to a. 795 but is absent from the second edition; so in the present passage it is replaced by *generalem conuentum* (for further details see Adams 1977b: 263–4). This usage is cited first from the Gallic writer Gregory of Tours, who has it a number of times (*TLL* X.1.2273.74ff.), and it also occurs in one of the versions of the Salic Law (*TLL* loc. cit.). Later it is common in other annals of Francia (see Adams 1977b: 264 for examples). Its Gallo-Romance reflexes show a similar but more specialised meaning, 'judicial hearing, assise, court of the king or a magnate' (*FEW* IX.6, Adams 1977b: 264). Here is another usage that was clearly widespread locally but was rejected by the classicising second edition.

(3) a. 767

Text

(first version)

Et in eodem anno in mense Augusto (1) iterum perrexit partibus Aquitaniae (2); Bituricam usque uenit. ibi synodum fecit (3) cum omnibus Francis solito more in campo (4). et inde iter peragens usque ad Garonnam peruenit. multas roccas et speluncas conquisiuit (5), castrum Scoraliam, Torinnam, Petrociam, et reuersus est Bituricam.

(second version)

Iam prope aestate confecta mense Augusto ad reliquias belli profectus est, et Bituricam ueniens conuentum more Francico in campo egit. indeque ad Garonnam fluuium accedens castella multa et petras atque speluncas, in quibus se hostium manus plurima defendebat, cepit. inter quae praecipua fuere Scoralia, Torinna et Petrocia. reuersusque Bituricam exercitum in hiberna dimisit.

Translation

(first version)

And in the same year in the month of August he again went to the area of Aquitaine; he came as far as Bourges. There he held an assembly with all the Franks in the usual way in a field. And from there undertaking a journey he reached the Garonne. He captured many castles on cliffs and caves, namely Ally, Turenne and Peyrusse, and returned to Bourges.

(second version)

And now with summer almost done in the month of August he set out for the remnants of the war, and coming to Bourges he conducted an assembly in the Frankish manner in a field. And from there proceeding to the river

Garonne he captured many castles and rocks and caves, in which many a band of the enemy were defending themselves. Among these the main ones were Ally, Turenne and Peyrusse. Returning to Bourges he dismissed his army to winter quarters.

Commentary

3.1 in eodem anno in mense Augusto: in juxtaposed temporal expressions the first edition has *in* with the ablative where CL would have used the plain ablative; the second edition has the classical *mense Augusto*, and also *iam prope aestate confecta*, a phrase that is modelled on Caes. *Gall.* 7.32.2 *iam prope hieme confecta* (see Kurze 1895: 25 n. 3). At the end of the previous sentence Caesar (§1) had written *exercitum ex labore atque inopia reficit*, and the second edition for its part at the end of the previous sentence has *exercitum a labore refecit*. For this commonplace use of *in*, see Hofmann and Szantyr (1965: 148), Adams (1976a: 50, with bibliography), index, s.v. *dies*, '*in die*', and above, 48.1.3.

3.2 perrexit partibus Aquitaniae: the phrase *partibus Aquitaniae* requires comment both for the meaning of *partes* and for its syntax. *Partibus* I take to be redundant: the phrase does not refer here to '(certain) parts of Aquitaine' but 'the region of Aquitaine (in general)', though there is no reason why in a particular context it should not refer to part of a whole (place) (see the extensive collection of material at *TLL* X.1.489ff.). *Partes* (= *regio*) is particularly well established in late Latin (see Svennung 1922: 122–4, E. Löfstedt 1956: II.440–1, id. 1959: 113, Pitkäranta 1978: 124–5, the latter two commenting on this general meaning), and not least in the first edition of the *Annales* (but not the second) (Adams 1977b: 274–5). Note that it does not appear in the second edition of the present passage, where the semantically unrelated *ad reliquias belli* occurs instead. *Reliquias belli* is a literary expression, which also occurs at a. 769 (second edition): *remanentibus in ea transacti belli reliquiis*. With the latter Kurze (1895: 29 n. 2) compares Velleius 2.114.4 *reliquiis totius belli in Dalmatia manentibus*, from where the redactor took his wording.

   In the first edition *partibus* has two meanings: first, 'in the region of', as at a. 778 *cum audissent Saxones quod ... Carolus rex et Franci tam longe fuissent partibus Hispaniae*, and second (as here), 'to the region of' (cf. e.g. a. 748 *Grifonem uero partibus Niustriae misit*) (see further Adams 1977b: 274). In the first meaning *partibus* is a locatival ablative, and in the second sense too I would now interpret it as ablative. Static (i.e. locative, in this case in the ablative) adverbials frequently (particularly but not exclusively in late Latin) were used with a directional meaning (as e.g. *Romae* for *Romam* with verbs of motion) (see index, 'directional/static expressions/terms confused', and also Adams 2013: 332–7). *Ibi* for example regularly complements *uenio* in the first edition (e.g. a. 773, a. 774) (see above, 45.5 on *ibi*).

This use of *partes* has a parallel in Greek in τὰ μέρη (see Svennung and Löfstedt locc. cit. in the last paragraph but one).

3.3 synodum fecit: *synodus* is commonly used in the first edition of an assembly, either ecclesiastical or political. In the second edition it is usually avoided, and here for example is replaced by *conuentus*. The word survives only in Old French (*REW* 8500, *FEW* XII.497: in Old French it usually but not exclusively indicates an ecclesiastical assembly; OFr. *senne* is given the meaning 'assemblée quelconque' by *FEW*). For details of its use in this text see Adams (1977b: 263). Note that *fecit*, a multi-purpose verb in the first edition, is replaced here by *egit* in the second.

3.4 in campo: *campus* at a. 794 (first edition) is used in reference to the *-feld* part of a Germanic compound (*in campo qui dicitur Sinistfelt*), and here too it is probably equivalent to CL *ager*, though the meanings 'plain' (usually given to CL *campus*) and 'field' (usually given to CL *ager*) are not clearly distinguishable.

3.5 multas roccas et speluncas conquisiuit: the second edition gets rid of *roccas*, and replaces *conquisiuit* with the classical *cepit*: *castella multa et petras atque speluncas . . . cepit.*

Rocca, a non-Latin word but of uncertain origin, must mean here 'fortification built on a high rock or cliff', a meaning that it has in numerous Gallo-Romance place names (*FEW* X.440, quoting this passage and stating 'hier hat das wort bereits die vielen ortsnamen zugrundeliegende bed. "auf einen felsen gebaute burg"'). It is replaced in the second edition by *petra*. *Rocca* survives in a number of Romance areas, including Gallo-Romance (see *REW* 7357).

Conquiro is used often in the first edition in various closely related meanings that it did not have in classical Latin, namely 'capture, conquer, subdue, acquire by force'. Note for example a. 775 *praedam multam conquisiuit* ('acquire by force'), a. 786 *multos Brittones conquesierunt una cum castellis et firmitates eorum* ('capture'). It is avoided completely in the second edition, the classicising redactors of which must have been aware that the usage was not classical. The reflexes of the word in Old French and Occitan (which derive from the recomposed form *conquaero*) have all of the meanings listed above. The term is not restricted to Gallo-Romance but was obviously current there. For details see Adams (1977b: 275–6).

(4) a. 774

Text

(first version)

Et dum peruenisset (1) in loco qui (2) dicitur Ingilinhaim, mittens quatuor scaras in Saxoniam (3): tres pugnam cum Saxonibus inierunt et auxiliante domino uictores extiterunt (4); quarta uero scara non habuit pugnam (5), sed cum praeda magna inlesi iterum reuersi sunt ad propria.

(second version)

Rex autem domum regressus, priusquam eum Saxones uenisse sentirent, tripertitum in eorum regiones misit exercitum, qui incendiis ac direptionibus cuncta deuastans, compluribus etiam Saxonum, qui resistere conati sunt, interfectis cum ingenti praeda regressus est.

Translation

(first version)

And when he had reached the place called Ingelheim, sending four divisions into Saxony. Three entered battle with the Saxons and with the help of the Lord emerged as victors. The fourth division did not have a battle, but they returned again to their own places with great booty, unharmed.

(second version)

But the king, having returned home, sent an army divided into three divisions into the territory of the Saxons before they noticed that it had come. This laid everything waste with arson and plunderings, and also many of the Saxons who attempted to resist were killed. The army returned with huge booty.

Commentary

4.1 dum peruenisset: on *dum* for *cum* see index s.v. The redactor of the second edition eliminates it.

4.2 in loco: a static expression with a verb of motion (for the expected *in/ad locum*): see above, 48.3.2 for *partibus* (locatival for directional) in such a context. Contrast e.g. a. 795 (first edition) *rex uenit ad locum qui dicitur Cuffinstang.*

4.3 mittens quatuor scaras in Saxoniam: *mittens* is a hanging participle in a context in which a finite verb is expected (cf. *misit* in the second edition). It is clear, particularly from the second edition, that the sending of the troops into Saxony followed the king's return to Ingelheim ('having returned home, he then sent'), and that would seem to rule out the possibility of taking *mittens* to be a perfective present participle describing an action that preceded the return home (i.e. 'when he had reached Ingelheim, having previously sent troops into Saxony'). In the second edition the expression 'before they noticed that *eum* had come' presumably refers to his army.

Participial hanging constructions are particularly common in late narrative texts, as we have seen elsewhere (see above, 44 Conclusions, and index, 'present participle', for all the types referred to in this note). In this text note e.g. a. 755 (first edition) *Pippinus rex ... in Italiam iter peragens, ... Haistolfus Langobardorum rex ... clusas Langobardorum petiit*, where the initial participial construction is left unattached. Another type shows a participle coordinated with a finite verb, as at a. 746 (first edition) *ibique aliquod tempus moram faciens et inde ad sanctum benedictum in Casinum usque peruenit* (cf. e.g. a. 761, a. 762, first edition). For the coordinated participle coming after the finite verb see a. 763 (first edition) *Pippinus rex habuit placitum suum in Niuernis et quartum iter faciens in Aquitaniam.*

It is hard to know whether we should speak of a genuine and productive finite/absolute use of the present participle that had caught on in late narrative texts, or of anacolutha (on the problem of interpretation see too above, 44 Conclusions; also e.g. Eklund 1970: 119–71, Adams 1976a: 60–5, Pitkäranta 1978: 78–85). Some examples do look to be exact equivalents of the ablative absolute (e.g. a. 773 (first edition) *et tunc ambo exercitus ad clusas se coniungentes, Desiderius ipse obuiam domni Caroli regis uenit*). However, the fact that an ablative absolute too may be coordinated with a main verb (see above, 48.1.4, and also e.g. a. 774 (first edition) *et reuertente domno Carolo rege a Roma, et iterum ad Papiam peruenit*) is suggestive of a lack of control over (or indifference to) the logic of participial syntax; nor is there any attempt at consistency (note alongside the previous example a. 775 (first edition) *et inde reuertente praefato rege, inuenit . . .*). A striking confusion is to be seen at a. 775 (first edition), in a sentence in which there is first an ablative absolute, then a present participle in the nominative with the same subject, followed by coordination of these two constructions to the main verb by *et: hoc audiente domno Carolo rege, iterum super Saxones cum exercitu irruens et non minorem stragem ex eis fecit.* The narrative seems to advance by means of a series of discrete verbal elements, whether finite verbs, absolute constructions or participles, with little attempt to form them into a logical whole, and that is a procedure that is due not so much to the state of a living language but to mechanical and formulaic composition.

Scara is a Frankish word (cf. Germ. *Schar*) which is used constantly of a troop of (Frankish) soldiers in the first edition (down to the year 784) but is always replaced in the second edition (here by *tripertitum ... exercitum*). On its status see Hincmar *Epist. Ad dioec. Rem. episc. 3 bellatorum acies, quas uulgari sermone scaras uocamus, dispositas.* It survived in Old French (*FEW* XVII.95–6, giving the forms *esciere* and *eschele* the meaning 'corps de troupes rangées en bataille'). For further details see Adams (1977b: 259–60). *Scara* is one of several Frankish words admitted in the first edition but eliminated from the second. Others are *wadius* (a. 667) and *alodem* (a. 777). Both of these have reflexes in Gallo-Romance (see Adams 1977b: 260–1). There seems to have been a purist reaction against the use of Germanic words in Latin texts after the Carolingian revival, and that accounts for their avoidance in the second edition (details in Adams 1977b: 261).

4.4 auxiliante domino uictores extiterunt: two formulae of the first edition: cf. e.g. a. 755 *et domino auxiliante beatoque Petro apostolo intercedente Pippinus rex cum Francis uictor extitit.*

4.5 non habuit pugnam: *habeo* with an object (for a precise verb) is, like *facio* (see above, 48.2.5), also used as a support verb (see index s.v. *habeo*, 'as support verb'. In the first edition there is also (a. 775) *uictoriam habuerunt* (see Adams 1977b: 279). E. Löfstedt (1911: 147) cites e.g. *Per. Aeth.* 5.7 *habuerunt concupiscentiam*, and notes that such expressions are frequent in Vitruvius. For examples from this period and region, see above, 47.3.

Conclusions

The two versions of the *Annales* if compared illustrate the diversity of early medieval Latin. Some texts are so classicising that they scarcely betray their late date or place of origin. Others may to some extent show Latinising of the vernacular, that is the use in Latinate form of terms and constructions that there is reason to believe were current in the proto-Romance of the area in which they were written. We have seen this feature in one of the Spanish slate tablets, and it is obvious in the first edition of the *Annales*. This version contains a number of words (some of them Frankish) or meanings of words that are non-classical but have reflexes in Gallo-Romance (*firmitas*, a use of *uirtus, placitum, synodus, rocca, conquiro* and *scara*; we also referred to *wadius* and *alodem*). All of these are avoided in the second version, whose compilers were so well versed in classical Latin that they were able to steer clear of many late and regional usages. The first edition may be treated as a specimen of late regional Latin, though it has other elements as well. Another of its proto-Romance features is the use of the pluperfect subjunctive with imperfect meaning, which lived on in the west.

Other usages in the first edition are merely typical of late or informal Latin in general, such as the use of the preposition *in* in temporal expressions where classical Latin would have used the ablative, and the use of locatival phrases with directional meaning. The gerund with *polliceor* is anomalous but can be paralleled in late Latin, including that of Francia.

On a different subject, Kurze pointed out various verbatim quotations of classical writers in the second version. We saw above wording taken not only from Caesar but also from Velleius. There must have been a text of Velleius available in Carolingian France, and a systematic computerised investigation of the whole second edition might reveal more classical reminiscences, some of which could have light to throw on the textual transmission of classical writers. The archetype of the few surviving manuscripts of Velleius is lost, and it is an interesting question whether the *Annales* might have something to contribute to the history of the text.

49
A DESCRIPTION OF THE BASILICA
OF SAINT-DENIS OF 799

Introduction

For the text see Stoclet (1980a, 1980b), Bischoff (1981, 1984c). It occupies fols. 159v and 160r of the manuscript Karlsruhe, Augiensis CCXXXVIII of the ninth century, which once belonged to the Abbey of Reichenau (details in the works above). The description is dated precisely at the end of the text. The most notable feature of the Latin is that it contains a definite article, *ille*.

Text

Basilica sancti Dyonisii (1), ubi beatissimus corpus (2) suus (3) requiescet (4), habet de longo pedes CCXLV. de latus habet pedes CIII (5). de alto usque ad camerato (6) habet pedes LXXV. excepto habet ille fundamentum (7) pedes XIII et ille tictus habet de alto pedes XXX et illa casubula (8) habet pedes de alto XXXIII. in summo sunt inter totum (9) de alto pedes CXL. habet ipsa ecclesia fenestras CI, columnas infra ecclesia (10) capitales L, alias columnas XXXV. excepto habet columnas de licio V (11). in summo sunt intus illa ecclesia columnas inter totum XC (12). excepto habet foras (13) per illos porticos de illa ecclesia (14) columnas capitales LVIIII, alias columnas minores XXXVII. excepto habet columnas de licio VII. in summo sunt columnas deforas per ipsos porticos CXXX [*sic*: *i.e.* CIII] et in summo sunt inter totum infra illa ecclesia et deforas columnas CXCIII.

Habet ipsa ecclesia luminaria mille CCL et mittunt in illa luminaria de oleo modios VIII (15) et ad uno quemque festa (16) in anno semper per tres uices (17). et habet in illa ecclesia portas paratas de auro et argento II (18). alias portas habet paratas de iborio et argento II. excepto habet hostia parata I de iborio (19) et de argento et excepto habet alia hostia II paratas (20) de argento Dagoberto regis bone memoriae (21), qui tale monasterio construxit, et Pippino regi Francorum, qui tale ecclesia per sua iussione post mortem suam fecerunt filii sui (22) domnus rex Carolus et Carlemannus.

Habet illa ecclesia arcus maiores XLV, alios arcus minores. excepto habet per illas alias ecclesias infra monasterio LXX columnas et sunt in totum illo monasterio (23) sancti Dyonisii columnas marmoreas CCXLV. anno XXXI Carolo rege.

Translation

The Basilica of Saint-Denis, where his blessed body rests, is 245 ft in length and 103 ft wide. As far as the vaulted ceiling it is 75 ft high. In addition the foundation is 13 ft deep and the roof is 30 ft high, and the crossing tower is 33 ft high. In total it is in all 140 ft high. The church has 101 windows, and within the church there are 50 large columns, and another 35 columns. In addition it has 5 columns of decorative stone. In total there are in the church 90 columns in all. In addition there are outside along the colonnades of the church 59 large columns and another 37 smaller columns. In addition there are 7 columns of decorative stone. In total there are outside along the colonnades 130 [i.e. 103] columns, and in total there are in all 193 columns inside and outside the church.

The church has 1,250 lamps, and they put in the lamps 8 modii of oil, and on each festival of the year they always (do so) three times. And there are in the church 2 doors decorated with gold and silver. There are another 2 doors decorated with ivory and silver. In addition there is 1 entrance decorated with ivory and silver, and in addition 2 other entrances decorated with silver for King Dagobert of good memory, who constructed such a monastery, and for Pippin King of the Franks; who ... on his orders after his death his sons the lord King Charles and Carloman made such a church.

The church has 45 larger arches, and other smaller ones. In addition there are throughout the other churches in the monastery 70 columns, and there are in the whole of the monastery of Saint-Denis 245 marble columns. In the 31st year of King Charles.

Commentary

1 sancti Dyonisii: the other genitives in this text are in the formula *bone memoriae*, in *regi Francorum*, and in *monasterio sancti Dyonisii* in the last paragraph. Thus the genitive is found mainly in names and their epithets. *Regis* in the phrase *Dagoberto regis* probably functions as a dative, a late usage (see below, 49.21). *De* is unambiguously genitival (possessive/partitive) in a common noun in the phrase *per illos porticos de illa ecclesia*. Similarly the Spanish slate tablet retains the old genitive in names (see above, 46 Conclusions, and also Adams 2013: 374–5). There are other *de*-expressions in this text that are genitival but also indicate source/material (*columnas de licio, de oleo modios* (but see below).

2 beatissimus corpus: for the masculine use of *corpus* (or should we say the neuter form with masculine agreement?) see e.g. *Anon. Val. II* 93 *deductus est corpus eius foris ciuitatem* (sometimes emended by editors) and *TLL* IV.999.18ff.

3 suus: this is non-reflexive, and equivalent to CL *eius* (or *illius*). There are four instances of *suus* in the text (the other three at the end of the second paragraph: *qui tale ecclesia per sua iussione post mortem suam fecerunt filii sui*). All four denote single possessors, and none is definitely reflexive (the clause just quoted is incoherent because of a change of construction or textual corruption; at least one instance there, in *per sua iussione*, would have been reflexive if the clause had continued as expected, but if there is a change of subject, as possibly occurs in *fecerunt* (but see below, 49.22), the remaining instances cease to be reflexive). *Eius/illius* does not occur. We have here a Romance-type usage, with *suus*, whether reflexive or not, denoting a single possessor (see above, 39.8, 47.15).

4 requiescet: this is a third conjugation present tense with the commonplace *e*-spelling (see above, 44.37.8).

5 de latus habet pedes CIII: *de latus* is a common phrase of late Latin, meaning 'on the side' and used as either an adverb or preposition (see E. Löfstedt 1911: 67, Wackernagel 1926–8: II.164 = Langslow 2009: 603, Josephson 1940: 193: 200, Hofmann and Szantyr 1965: 236 with further bibliography). That cannot be the meaning here. The phrase obviously refers to the measurement of the building across its width/breadth (= 'crosswise, in width' or the like). The two other measurements, of length (*de longo* ...) and height (*de alto* ...), are also expressed by phrases containing *de*, and the opposition *longus/altus/de latus* strongly suggests that *de latus* (containing in origin a noun with ă, = 'side') has been conflated with the adjective *latus* 'broad, wide', which has ā. It seems possible that the writer has misunderstood *de latus* as if it contained *latus* 'broad', giving it the meaning 'in width'. The other two phrases are not so hard to understand. *Longus* for example is often used substantivally in the neuter in prepositional expressions such as *in longum, in longo, ex longo* (*TLL* VII.2.1642.22ff.). *De longo* I have not found quoted, but note e.g. *Per. Aeth.* 2.1 *uallis ... quae habet ... in longo milia passos forsitan sedecim, in lato autem quattuor milia esse appellabant* ('in length ... in width'). The preposition *de* in our text does not change the meaning materially, and is easy to interpret: *habet de longo pedes CCXLV,* literally 'it has 245 ft of length'. Noteworthy in the passage of the *Peregrinatio* is the contrasting expression *in lato*, which has exactly the same function as *de latus* in our text and suggests that the conflation proposed above has indeed taken place. We might speak of a malapropism, where two different words of similar meaning are confused (see index, 'malapropisms').

6 usque ad camerato: *camerato*, which used as a participle can mean 'vaulted' (see Niermeyer 1976 s.v.), is here used as a noun, designating the vaulted ceiling or roof (see Bischoff 1984c: 216). The equivalent term in classical Latin is *concameratio* (used by Vitruvius).

7 excepto habet ille fundamentum: *excepto* originally was participial in an ablative absolute construction (of the type *excepto hoc*). It then became fossilised and reinterpreted as a preposition, either with the ablative (of the type *excepto filiabus*) or even the accusative. Then, like the synonymous preposition *praeter*, it came to be used as an adverb, with roughly the same meaning as *praeterea*, which is the sense that it has throughout this document. See also Svennung (1935: 645), B. Löfstedt (1961: 215 n. 2), Niermeyer (1976: 388). The examples in this text are particularly clear-cut.

Ille fundamentum is a phrase of mixed gender of familiar type in late Latin (see Adams 2013: 428–31): the neuter form of the noun is remembered, but it is given masculine agreement. This is not the only manifestation of the loss of the neuter in this text. *Hostia* is used twice in the second paragraph as a feminine singular, deriving from the neuter plural *ostia*. Reflexes in Romance (e.g. It. *uscio*, Fr. *huis*, OSp. *uzo*) are usually masculine (see *FEW* VII.439 s.v. *ostium*; these all go back to a form with *ū*: see above, 47.13). On the mixed phrase *hostia II paratas* see below. The only unambiguous neuter in the text is the plural *luminaria*, which occurs twice.

In *ille* we have what is sometimes called an 'associative' use of the definite article (see Adams 2013: 487–8, with bibliography). It is not anaphoric, because there has been no earlier mention of foundations, but a basilica must have foundations and a reader would be aware that these were the definite foundations of the basilica. In the text there are twelve article-like instances of *ille*, some of them associative (*ille tictus, illa casubula, per illos porticos, per illas alias ecclesias*), some anaphoric (*in illa luminaria*, immediately after the first example of this noun, and also various examples of *illa ecclesia*).

Ille does not have the field only to itself. We also find *ipsa ecclesia* (with *illa ecclesia* several times soon after), *per ipsos porticos* (coming soon after *per illos porticos*), and *ipsa ecclesia* a second time at the start of the second paragraph.

There are hardly any nouns that might be described as definite, in either the associative or anaphoric senses, that are without *ille: basilica, ad camerato, infra monasterio.*

Two things stand out here. First, definite nouns that are so specified outnumber those unspecified by 15:3. Second, *ille* is the preferred article element, in anticipation of Gallo-Romance, but it has not ousted *ipse* entirely.

8 casubula: this is taken by Bischoff (1984c: 216) to indicate the *Vierungsturm* or crossing tower, that is the tower above the crossing of the nave and transept, and this is plausible (see below).

The word, the form of which is problematic, is thought to be based on *casula* (see Niermeyer 1976: 155). The semantics of *casula* are clearer than those of *casubula*, and I start with it. *Casula*, diminutive of *casa*, refers to a small dwelling, cell, sanctuary or the like (Niermeyer 1976: 156). It then acquired a metaphorical meaning 'chasuble, cloak' (Niermeyer loc. cit.). The chasuble is a long sleeveless vestment falling straight down to reach the ankles, and sloping at the shoulders. The idea behind the metaphor is presumably that the garment encloses the priest like a small dwelling or hut.

Casubula for its part means 'chasuble, cloak', except in this one passage (see Niermeyer 1976: 155-6). There must be a metaphor behind the present usage too. The squat tower, with a domed top and possibly a pinnacle, resembles a chasuble, with its sloping shoulders and 'pinnacle' represented by the head of the wearer. Alternatively it might have been thought to resemble a hut.

It is not clear what caused the deformation of *casula* to *casubula* (see Bloch and von Wartburg 1968: 124). If we posited an intermediate form *casucula*, showing the augmented diminutive suffix *-cula* (see Leumann 1977: 306-7), attached to the (false) base *casu-* that may be extracted from *casula*, it would remain hard to see the reason for the deformation.

Casubla and *casula* are not separated at *REW* 1752 or by *FEW* II.480. The meaning 'little hut' survives in It. *casipola*, the meaning 'chasuble, vestment' in e.g. Fr. *chasuble*.

9 in summo sunt inter totum: *inter totum* 'in all, all in all' occurs four times, always when the total number of instances of a specific architectural feature is added up. It is not a classical or even late Latin usage. In classical and later Latin of earlier periods two equivalent phrases are *ex toto* and *in totum* (Wölfflin 1887a); for *inter* used as an equivalent to *in* see above, 25.6. In the *Peregrinatio Aetheriae*, *totum* without preposition is often used adverbially (see E. Löfstedt 1911: 49), sometimes with numerals as here: e.g. 1.2 *habet . . . forsitan quattuor milia totum per ualle illa.*

Inter totum is attested in Frankish (Merovingian and Carolingian) Latin in this sense, with numerals: e.g. *MGH, Diplomata regum Francorum e stirpe Merovingica* I (ed. P. Kölzer, Hanover 2001), no. 108, p. 455 *uillam scilicet, quae nuncupatur Monasteriola, cum ecclesia et omnibus suis aiacentibus, hoc est Curtecella, Villena, Balneolis, Suprema, Vuillertiagas,* inter totum *mansos XXX cum terris, domis, edificiis, mancipiis, uineis, pratis, siluis, aquis aquarumue decursibus, cultis et incultis absque ulla uicariorum potestate cungrue teneant atque possideant, MGH, Diplomata regum Germaniae ex stirpe Karolinorum* I (ed. P. Kehr, Berlin 1956), no. 183, p. 156 *dedimus itaque ei quasdam res proprietatis nostrae consistentes in Alamannia in pago qui uocatur Brisahgawe, id est Berga, Andloa et Baldinga et Secchosouua, id est* inter totum *hobas LXXVI cum omnibus mobilibus et immobilibus, quae ad ipsas pertinent.* There are several other such examples (source eMGH).

Italian has an expression *tra tutto*, which is equivalent. *Tra* is from *intra*, which took on the functions of *inter* (*REW* 4508).

10 infra ecclesia: three times *infra* is used as a preposition with the ablative (cf. later *infra illa ecclesia, infra monasterio*). This is a late non-standard usage (see *TLL* VII.1.1485.37ff. for examples), found e.g. in the *Mulomedicina Chironis* (see Ahlquist 1909: 4) and the *Itin. Ant. Plac.*

11 de licio: the phrase occurs twice. The word is *lithium*, which is attested in Greek (Pausanias), but not in Latin of the period covered by the *TLL* (though there is an entry for *lithus*). It indicates a special form of stone, perhaps coloured (see Bischoff 1984c: 217). On the misspelling *ci* for *ti* see e.g. B. Löfstedt (1961: 171), Adams (2013: 123) and index, 'spellings, *ci*/*ti*'.

De here indicates the material from which the object is made: see *OLD* s.v. 8, citing e.g. Virg. *Georg.* 3.13 *templum de marmore ponam.* It may also be translated as a genitive.

12 sunt intus illa ecclesia columnas inter totum XC: *columnas* is subject of *sunt*, with the *-as* ending serving as the nominative plural. There are three other places where *columnas* is subject of *sunt; columnae* does not occur. Various other instances of *columnas* in the text are object of *habet*. This is one of those (mainly Gallic) texts in which the *-ae* nominative plural ending has been ousted (see above, 44 Conclusions, Pei 1932: 137–8, Adams 2013: 252, with further bibliography, 374; also index 'endings, nominal, *-as* nominative plural').

Intus (*illa ecclesia*) is here used with the ablative, as a preposition, a rare late usage: *TLL* VII.2.107.64 cites Caes. Arel. *Serm.* 67.1, *CC* 103, p. 286 *intus anima mea.* It is not unusual for adverbs to be reinterpreted as prepositions. *Foris* is a parallel in late Latin: see *TLL* VI.1.1046.45ff. At *Edictus Rothari* 1 (*si quis foris prouincia fugire temptauerit*) there is the sort of context in which a reinterpretation might have occurred: *foris* might once have been adverbial, with *prouincia* a free-standing separative ablative ('outside, from the province').

13 excepto habet foras: not infrequently in this text *habet* has an expressed subject, as *basilica sancti Dyonisii … habet, habet ille fundamentum, illa casubula habet, habet ipsa ecclesia.* Here however there is no subject, and impersonal *habet* is used as *il y a* in French. Cf. *et habet in illa ecclesia portas paratas, alias portas habet paratas, habet ostia parata I, excepto habet per illas alias ecclesias infra monasterio LXX columnas.* This constant mixing up in a single text of *habet* with a subject and *habet* without is very striking: could the impersonal use have developed from the mechanical extension of this verb form, formulaic in measurements, to non-specific contexts in which the hearer/reader was expected to supply or understand the subject?

14 per illos porticos de illa ecclesia: *porticus* is feminine in classical Latin but changed to masculine on the analogy of other *-us* nouns (see e.g. Petron. 77.4 and Adams 2013: 385, 419).

The genitival phrase *de illa ecclesia* has the prepositional genitive marker *de* combined with the article *illa*, a direct anticipation of Fr. *de la*. For this type of combination see below, 50.29–30.

15 mittunt … de oleo modios VIII: *de oleo* is either a partitive genitive dependent on *modios* ('eight modii of oil') (see Adams 2013: 270–2), or it can be taken independently as the partitive object of *mittunt* ('they put in some oil, eight modii') (see Adams 2013: 273–5), in which case *modios VIII* would be in apposition to *de oleo* and we would have a late variant on the old partitive apposition construction. The latter interpretation seems preferable, since all other genitives and genitive equivalents follow the head word (see above, 49.1, and below, 49.21).

For the verb in this meaning see index, s.v. *mitto* 'put'.

16 ad uno quemque festa: the feminine *festa* 'festival' survives widely in Romance (*REW* 3267: e.g. It. *festa*, Sp. *fiesta*, Fr. *fête*). It derives from the neuter plural *festa* (Stotz 1998: 18, 38). For the neuter singular *festum* (and the plural) earlier see *TLL* VI.1.631.65ff. The writer has given the feminine noun masculine agreement here, for obscure reasons.

17 per tres uices: see below, 50.26.

18 portas paratas de auro et argento: the use of *de* here recurs throughout the paragraph (*paratas de iborio et argento, parata … de iborio et de argento, paratas de argento*). It is not clear whether the reference is to doors made entirely of (e.g.) gold, in which case the use would be that indicating the material from which something is made (see above, 49.11), or with (some) gold, a quasi-instrumental use retaining an idea of source and with a partitive idea as well (Adams 2013: 300).

19 iborio: the origin of this term ('ivory') lies in the old adjective *eboreus* 'of ivory' (< *ebur*), which has been substantivised. Romance terms such as Fr. *ivoire* are generally regarded as 'borrowings' of this (substantivised) adjective (see e.g. Bloch and von Wartburg 1968: 347; also *REW* 2817), but clearly the nominal use was at least as old as the eighth century. Perhaps the misspelling in the first syllable represents the old phenomenon of pretonic closing of ĕ in an initial syllable (for which see B. Löfstedt 1961: 38; also below, 50.51).

20 hostia II paratas: another mixed-gender phrase (cf. *ille fundamentum* above, 49.7, 49.16), with the neuter plural form of the noun retained but given feminine plural agreement. This expression resembles the ambigenerics, particularly of Italy, that is nouns treated as feminine plural in adjectival and participial agreements, but themselves retaining the neuter plural form of classical Latin (see Adams 2013: 431–7). Most of the evidence for phrases of this type in late Latin comes from Italian texts.

21 Dagoberto regis bone memoriae: there are two ways of taking this expression. First, *bone memoriae* may be dative, with the other phrase a mixed possessive comprising a possessive dative and genitive juxtaposed ('to the good memory of King Dagobert'). Alternatively *Dagoberto regis* may be a 'dative' phrase ('for King Dagobert of good memory'), with *regis* one of those stray uses of 'genitive for dative' found particularly in Merovingian Latin (see Adams 2013: 463, with bibliography). This latter possibility is the more likely, given that the coordinated phrase *Pippino regi* is unambiguously dative. Moreover *bonae memoriae* is a formulaic genitive phrase attached to the name of the dead (*TLL* VIII.673.75ff.), and the word order virtually demands that *bone memoriae* be dependent on *Dagoberto regis*, rather than that *Dogoberto* be dependent on *memoriae*: such leftward dependence cannot be introduced in a text of this date without very good reason (see above, 49.15). The addition of the -*s* to *regi* could also be a simple slip.

Dagoberto and *Pippino regi* are the only datives or dative equivalents in the text: there are no instances of *ad* used with dative function. Again (see on *sancti*

Dyonisii above, 49.1) we have the maintenance of the old oblique case inflections in names and associated epithets.

22 Pippino . . . qui tale ecclesia per sua iussione post mortem suam fecerunt filii sui: on the face of it a conflated construction. *Pippino* appears to be the antecedent of *qui*, but after *ecclesia* the construction changes and his sons become subject of the plural verb *fecerunt*. However, the change of a single letter (*qui* to *cui*) would restore correct syntax ('for whom his sons made such a church on his orders'), and one wonders if there is a dictation error here (cf. above, 36.2).

23 in totum illo monasterio: *in totum* should not be associated with *inter totum*: *totum* is for *toto*, reflecting confusions between nominative and accusative common in many later texts.

Conclusions

This text was written, presumably in Paris, at the end of the eighth century. It contains a regular definite article, *ille*, which foreshadows the definite article of Gallo-Romance. But usage in this respect is not completely fixed, in that there are a few identical cases of *ipse*. Similarly in a northern Italian text not much later than this there is a constant article use of *ipse*, but with *ille* as an occasional variant (below, 50). Could it be that even as late as this the articles had not yet become fixed and invariant in some regions?

Case morphology and syntax show differences from earlier Latin. *-as* is the regular nominative plural ending of the first declension. On the other hand in the first declension the old nominative plural is still in use (*filii sui*). This distinction is found in other texts of the late (Merovingian) period from this area; by contrast in the Visigothic slate tablets, whereas *-as* is the normal feminine nominative plural, there is some alternation between *-os* and *-i* in the nominative plural (Adams 2013: 231). Old genitive and dative forms occur in the text, largely in names and their epithets. There are no cases of *ad* for the dative, but *de* displays some genitival uses, once indeed in conjunction with the definite article. There is clearly some conservatism in case usage, particularly in the names of the saint and of kings. The text ends with a conventional ablative absolute (*regnante Carolo rege*) containing the name of a king. On the other hand in some instrumental phrases with common nouns (of the type *de iborio*) the preposition *de* is used.

The text has only one clear-cut neuter (plural), *luminaria*. Other neuter forms have masculine (*ille fundamentum*) or feminine (plural) agreement (*hostia . . . paratas*). The latter is reminiscent of feminine plural uses of original neuters (with feminine agreement) in Italian texts. Several other words have changed gender because of morphological analogies (*corpus, porticus*).

There is a variety of other late usages, some of them of Romance significance (impersonal *habet, casubula*, non-reflexive *suus*). We have proposed at 49.13 a possible origin of the impersonal use of *habet*, which is suggested by the ways in which the term is used in this text.

50

A TENTH-CENTURY TREATISE ON FALCON MEDICINE FROM NORTHERN ITALY

Introduction

This (incomplete) text on falcon medicine survives in a manuscript in the Biblioteca Capitolare in Vercelli, the hand of which establishes that the manuscript was written not later than the middle of the tenth century (Bischoff 1984b: 172–3), possibly at the time of Bishop Atto of Vercelli (924–60) (Bischoff 1984b: 172). The composition of the work itself might in theory have been (much) earlier, but there are good reasons for dating it very late, possibly not much before the manuscript itself. The interest of the Latin lies in its many proto-Romance features, and in its regional usages, which suggest an origin in northern Italy. Here we see a different case system from that of earlier periods, and an almost obligatory definite article. The lexicon of the work is overwhelmingly of Romance type. The characteristics of the Latin will be summarised in the Conclusions. The text in Bischoff's edition occupies three substantial pages (176–8), with fragmentary part-pages at the beginning (175) and end (179). The extract here contains the first half of the three complete pages.

Because of the importance of cross-referencing in the Commentary, I have used Bischoff's line numbers, which are continuous throughout his whole text. The start of each line is indicated here within the text by numbers in bold.

Text

XVI **23** ... in modum unguenti dum ueniat, et tunc accipe alium acetum et **24** laua diligenter pertusa illa, unde ipsas pennas exire debent, et per modum ma ... ip**25**sum unguentum intromittas in ipsum foramen, unde ipsae pennae exierunt. hoc fac **26** per tres uices. et si plus illi necessarium ad sanandum, apprehende tuas tegulas et cale**27**facies in focum, quousque rubeae sint. tunc apprehende sanguissugam et pone eam **28** super ipsas callidas tabulas et incende eam et fac inde puluerem subtilissimam. tunc **29** tolle pennas de paone de cauda et mitte eas super fumarium et ibi sint, usque dum sugia super ipsas pennas crescat. tunc accipe de ipsa su**30**gia de ipsis pennis et puluerem **31** de sanguissuca tantum de una quantum de alia et fac puluerem subtilissimam. tunc **32** adprehende acetum forte et ipsas pulueres et confice eum insimul non minus liquidum. **33** de aceto laua ipsa foramina fortiter, unde ipsae pennae exire debent. et tunc accipe **34** lardum ueterum et fac inde subtilissimas petiolas et <i>ntinge in ipsa confectione tan**35**tum, ut ipsa confectio ad ipsum lardum teneat firmiter et mitte in ipsis foraminibus, **36** unde ipsae pennae exierunt, per duas uices in epdomada tamdiu, quousque ipsas pen**37**nas exire uideas. nam si antea quam istum totum illi facias, ipsas pennas exire uide**38**ris, nihil illi postea facias, quousque uideas, si ipsae pennae bonae sunt aut adulterae.

XVII **40** Tolle glutonem, quae inter grana nascitur, et testum de osso, qui de capite **41** <hom>inis fuisset, quantum plus uetus potes, qui de longo tempore mortuus fuisset et **42** limatura de aciario mundo simil . . . ipsum testum de ipso capite calimare fac cum lima **43** et glutonem pistare facias, et de unoquoque tantum sit puluis quantum de alio. de **44** ipsa testa hominis paucum plus sit quam in illis aliis duabus pulueribus et mixta insi**45**mul dona ad falconem manducare, sola ipsa carne non nimis, de ipsum totum insimul **46** per nouem dies. certissime, si ipsi pertusi, unde ipsae pennae exierunt, clausi non **47** sunt, absque dubio ipsae pennae ueniunt. nam si ipsae per dies XV non exeunt aut **48** per XX, tunc accipe ipsum falconem et diligenter require ipsos pertusos, unde ipsae **49** pennae exierunt, et ipsos si aliter aperire non poteris, tolle fleotomum, unde homines **50** sanguinem laxare solent, et incide in ipsos pertusos, usque dum illos ueraciter inue**51**nies. tunc tolle cera mundissima et fac inde sicut fistucum et intinge in oleo mundis**52**simo et mitte in ipsos pertusos, unde ipsae pennae exierunt. scias certissime, quia de **53** ipsa infirmitate sanat.

XVIII **54** Tamen super totas istas medicinas nullam sic ueracem inuenimus sicut **55** istam. tolle acetum fortissimum et sucum de agrumen, quae dicitur allio, et mitte in**56**simul et laua ipsos pertusos et cura illos bene et imple illos, quantum plus ibi inde mit**57**tere potes, et usque ad dies XV illum mittas ad aquam, usque dum uideris, si ipsae **58** pennae ueniunt, et si non ueniunt in die XVI., iterum similiter illi fac. scias quod nul**59**lam medicinam de ista infirmitate sic ueracem inuenimus sicut istam, quia inde iam **60** falcones ad sanitatem reduximus.

XIX **61** Ad falcones qui desiccant, aut si fastidium habent. tolle lac caprinum et **62** mitte in frixoria munda et accipe oua II et mitte in lacte et tamdiu simul in ipsa frixo**63**ria bulliat, quousque ipsa oua cum ipso lacte tales sunt sicut patellata, quae homo **64** manducat. uide ut fumus nec flamma nullo modo ueniet ibi et da illi ad manducan**65**dum duas uel tres uices tantum, ut plenam gorgam inde habeat. si enim smaltierit, **66** sanabitur. ista patellata ad falconem ad omnem infirmitatem, quae infra corpus ha**67**bet, adiuuat.

XX **68** Si falco se demonstrat bulsum esse, istam patellatam illi per duas uices primum **69** dones. tolle lardum et fac inde tres petias, quales glutire potest, et mitte illas iacere in **70** melle super noctem. deinde accipe limaturam de ferro subtilissimam et sala inde ipsas **71** petias de lardo non nimis et da illi manducare. et si manducare noluerit, hoc mitte illi **72** in gorgam sicut alia prime. hoc fac per tres dies et nihil aliud illi dones ad manducare.

XXI **74** In quarto uero die tolle pullicinum tenerem et sic illum inebria de uino, quan**75**tum plus potueris, et scalda pectus eius ad focum et batte cum manico de cultello tan**76**tum, ut illius sanguis cum ipso uino in ipsum pectus descendat.

Translation

XVI ... until it reaches the state of ointment, and then take another lot of vinegar and carefully wash the holes from which the feathers should grow, and by means ... put the ointment in the hole from which the feathers grew. Do this three times. And if he needs more to heal him, take your tiles/slates and heat them in the fire until they are red-hot. Then take a leech and put it over the hot tablets and burn it and make from there a fine dust. Then take peacock feathers from the tail and put them over a smoking flue and let them stay there until soot forms on the feathers. Then take some of the soot from the feathers and dust arising from the leech, as much of one as of the other, and make a very fine dust. Then take strong vinegar and the grains of powder and mix it together with them so that it is not too liquid. With vinegar wash the holes vigorously from which the feathers should grow, and then take old bacon and make of it tiny little pieces and dip in the mixture just so that the mixture holds firmly to the bacon, and put it in the holes from which the feathers grew, twice a week until you see the feathers grow. But if, before you do all this to him, you see the feathers growing, do nothing after that to him, until you see if the feathers are good or imperfect.

XVII Take corncockle, which grows amid the wheat, and a splinter of bone which had belonged to the head of a man, the older the better, a man who had been dead for a long time, and filings of clean steel ... File the splinter from the head with a file and crush corncockle, and let there be from each thing as much powder as from the other. From the skull of the man let there be a little more than in the other two powders, and when they have been mixed together give them to the falcon to eat, as the only meat, not too much – from the whole mixture together, for nine days. Certainly if the holes from which the feathers grew have not closed, the feathers are undoubtedly on their way. But if they do not grow in fifteen or twenty days, then take the falcon and carefully look for the holes from which the feathers grew, and if you cannot open them otherwise, take a phlebotomy knife, with which people are accustomed to let blood, and cut into the holes until you genuinely find them. Then take very clean wax and make with it a straw-like shape and dip it in very clean oil and put it in the holes from which the feathers grew. Rest assured that it cures him of the condition.

XVIII Nevertheless over and above all these remedies we have found none as reliable as this. Take very strong vinegar and juice of the sharp plant that is called 'garlic', and put them together and wash the holes and tend them well and fill them with as much as you can put there of it (i.e. of the mixture), and for a full fifteen days put him in water, until you see if the feathers are coming, and if they do not come on the sixteenth day, do the same to him again. Rest assured that we have found no treatment of this condition as reliable as this, because by means of it we have already brought falcons back to health.

XIX For falcons which are desiccated or if they have anorexia. Take goat's milk and put in a clean frying pan and take two eggs and put them in the milk, and let it boil together in the pan, until the eggs with the milk are like an omelette that one eats. Make sure that neither smoke nor flame in any way comes there, and give it to him to eat two or three times only, so that he has his mouth full of it. If he excretes, he will be cured. The omelette helps the falcon for any illness he has which is internal.

XX If the falcon shows that he is breathless, first give him the omelette twice. Take bacon and make it into three pieces of the type he can swallow, and put them to lie in honey overnight. Then take very fine shavings of iron and salt the pieces of bacon with that (but not too much) and give to him to eat. And if he is unwilling to eat, put it into his mouth like the other things (that were tried) first. Do this for three days and give him nothing else to eat.

XXI But on the fourth day take a young chick and inebriate it as much as you can with wine, and burn its breast on a fire and beat it with the handle of a knife so much that its blood descends to the breast with the wine.

Commentary

23 accipe: on verbs of this semantic field in the text see below, 50.29 on *tolle*.

alium acetum: for *alius* in the singular applied to a term for an unspecified quantity of liquid or other substance and indicating a second portion, see *Comp. Luc.* R 22 *teres iarim mundum et mittes in alia urina* ('in another quantity/batch of urine'; the first lot of urine came up at 13–14), δ 3 *et post hec tolle inde et mitte aliut alumen*, Anthim. p. 25.4 *ut illa prima calda fundatur et alia calda missa cum ratione.* Note the parallels here from the *Compositiones Lucenses*, another late text from northern Italy (see further below, next two notes).

24 pertusa illa: the past participle of *pertundo* is not cited as a noun by the *TLL*, but for *pertusus* 'hole' see Niermeyer (1976: 794) and for *pertusum* see Arnaldi, Turriani and Smiraglia (1939–64: II.513). The usage occurs in the *Compositiones Lucenses*: e.g. P 9 *exprimis in uaso uitreo, abentem pertuso modicissi<mum> cera <clausum>. aperies ipsum pertusum* (see Svennung 1941: 57, 68–9). See also *REW* 6436, *FEW* VIII.2.290-1. The gender of the word is variable in this text. In the next chapter it occurs several times as a masculine plural (46 *ipsi pertusi*, 48 *ipsos pertusos*, 50, 52 *in ipsos pertusos*; there are also instances of *ipsos* (49) and *illos* (50) referring to the *pertusi*; in chapter XVIII there is a further instance of *pertusos* (56) with two masculine pronouns in the same line referring to the holes).

This variability underlines an uncertainty in the use of the neuter in this text. There are many apparent neuter forms, but most do not display their gender from the context (note however e.g. 77 *dum ipsum lac callidum est*, 105 *aequale pectus*, 135 *lardum uetus*). At 23 above *alium* (*acetum*) might have been expected to be *aliud*, but that does not establish that the writer has treated *acetum* as masculine: *alium* might have been intended as a neuter form (cf. 32 *acetum forte*). Similarly at 37 *istum* (*totum*) ought to have been *istud*, but *istum* might have been meant as a neuter. At 40 *testum de osso* is picked up by *qui*, and at 55 *agrumen* by *quae* (but see the note ad loc.). At 63 *patellata* (neuter plural) is followed soon after by two feminine forms of the same word. At 140 there is a correct neuter accusative expression *stercus caprinum*, but at 88 (*adprehende stercum passeris et stercum suricis*) and 90 (*de sterco passeris*) it looks as if the word has been treated as masculine.

There are also other abnormalities of gender (28 *puluis*, 51 *fistucum*, 75 *manico*, on which see the notes ad locc.).

For *illa* here (as distinct from *ipsa*) see the next note.

ipsas pennas: nominative, despite the form. For the *-as* nominative plural ending and its possible outcomes in Romance, including Italian, see e.g.

Adams (2013: 251–2), with bibliography (also above, 6.7 on early Latin). In some early medieval texts it is the standard nominative plural ending (see above, 49.12), but in this text it is exceptional. *Pennae* (nom. pl.) occurs nine times in chapters XVI–XVIII, and there are other such forms, including *rubeae* in this chapter and a number of instances of *ipsae*. There is no other *-as* nominative in the text. It is possible that the form here is not a real morphological variant but that the writer conflated this construction with another: note 36–7 *quousque ipsas pennas exire uideas*, 37 *ipsas pennas exire uideris*.

Penna (pl., whether nominative or accusative) occurs fifteen times in XVI–XVIII, and in fourteen of these cases it is accompanied by *ipsae/ipsas*. The one instance without *ipse* is different from the others: 29 *tolle pennas de paone de cauda*. Here the reader is instructed to take feathers from the tail of a peacock, whereas in every other case the feathers are those of the bird under treatment, the falcon. In the passage just cited the reference is indefinite ('feathers/some feathers', not all 'the feathers of the peacock'), whereas in all other cases the reference is specific. *Ipse* is almost (but not quite) an obligatory definite article in this text, and not only with *pennae*. When a new item is introduced to the discourse, it is without *ipse* when first named but thereafter tends to receive *ipse*: English too in such circumstances would pass from indefinite article (or absence of article) to definite article. For example, at 61–2 *lac caprinum, frixoria* and *oua* are introduced without *ipse*, and then in lines 62–3 we have *in ipsa frixoria, ipsa oua* and *cum ipso lacte* (but also *in lacte* at 63). Just as the feathers of the treated bird are regularly named along with *ipse*, so the holes from which they grow are specified thus in chapters XVI–XVIII: 24 *pertusa illa*, 25 *in ipsum foramen*, 33 *ipsa foramina*, 35 *in ipsis foraminibus*, 46 *ipsi pertusi*, 48 *ipsos pertusos*, 50 *in ipsos pertusos*, 52 *in ipsos pertusos*, 56 *ipsos pertusos*: nine examples and no exceptions). There are however exceptions with some other nouns. *Falco* itself, for example, is not always accompanied by *ipse* when the reference is definite (for *ipse falco* see 48, 98, 104, 124; for *falco* alone: 45, 78, 144, 156; *falco* alone is usually, however, indefinite, as at the start of sections about 'a falcon suffering from this or that', as e.g. at 61, 68, 112, 116, 122, 127).

There are seventy-three instances of the specifier *ipse* (adjectival) in the text, against just four of *ille* (3, 24, 44, 96). The density of the occurrences of *ipse* is in places remarkable, as for example in the six lines at 33–8, where there are ten examples of *ipse*, or at 124, where all three nouns are so specified. I know of no other text in which there is such constant marking of definiteness by this means (but see the next paragraph), even if *ipse* is not quite obligatory. However, historically there is a problem to be faced. It was *ille*, not *ipse*, that produced the definite article in this area (see e.g. Maiden 1995: 117, Ledgeway

2011: 411). Are we to assume that there was a sudden change from *ipse* to *ille* in northern Italy after the tenth century, or is the preference for *ipse* to be explained in some other way? Was the grammaticalisation in different areas of a particular demonstrative, whether *ille* or *ipse*, as the definite article something that was only firmly established late, after a period of variability (see above, 49 Conclusions)? The question will be raised again in the Conclusions. As for what motivates the choice of *ille* in this text (see above), there is no apparent unity to the four examples. At 96, for example, *in ipsa confectione* is immediately followed by *illa confectio*. For *ille* with *alius* at 44 (*in illis aliis duobus pulueribus*), cf. *Comp. Luc.* A 32 (with Adams 2013: 509).

The *Compositiones Lucenses*, of similar provenance and period, also have sequences of *ipse*, but without the same consistency in the use of the term. But note e.g. D 5–8 *donec non remaneat in linteolo aliquid de ipso bermiculo, et tolle ex ipsa confectionem; et conficis ipsas pelles ut utrem et mittis ex ipsa per unamquamque pellem lib. dim.*, 22–6 *dimittis refricdare et cuse ipsas pelles sicut utres, quomodo diximus de alithina, et coctionem mittis in ipsos utres et confrica bene et insufflas modicum, ut habeant uentum; et confice bene, donec conbibat ipsum medicamen, et post hec refundis ex ipsis et tolles ipsas pelles.* Here the use of *ipsae* with *pelles* is similar to that with *pennae* in our present text.

For further remarks about the article, see below on 30, 32, 33, 44–5, 62.

exire debent: this must be *exire* in the sense 'grow forth' (*TLL* V.2.1358.51ff.: note e.g. Ovid *Met.* 5.671 *pennas exire per ungues | aspexere suos*). The bird has lost feathers and the attempt to make them grow again is described.

25 in ipsum foramen: the writer has here inadvertently used the singular of the holes. *Foramen* survives in Italian, Spanish and Portuguese (*REW* 3427).

unde ipsae pennae exierunt: i.e. from which the feathers grew in the past.

hoc fac: this is a locution in the text. It occurs at 72, 79 (*hoc . . . facies*), 120 (*fac hoc*), 125, 131 (*hoc illi fac*). There are only four other instances of *hic* in the text, all neuter accusative, and all but one singular (contrast 108 *si hec feceris*). The use of the pronoun was very restricted, and it was perhaps fossilised as a neuter, usually associated with the verb *facio*.

Iste is used adjectivally in the text (and in several forms) with the sense of CL *hic*, an anticipation of its Romance function (see further index, s.v. *iste* = *hic*). Note particularly 54 *nullam (medicinam) sic ueracem inuenimus sicut istam.* A description of the remedy follows, and *istam* is replaceable with *hanc*. See too 37 *antea quam istum totum illi facias* 'before you do all of this to him', 59 *nullam medicinam de ista infirmitate sic ueracem inuenimus sicut istam*, 66 *ista patellata*, 68 *istam patellatam*.

26 per tres uices: *uice(s)* in this new sense ('(three) times') turns up in late Latin (e.g. Palladius 1.28.3 *excusatae matres ab incubatione tribus uicibus per annum fetus edunt*) (see Souter 1949: 442) and is common in the early medieval period in e.g. the *Annales regni Francorum* and other Frankish texts (Adams 1977b: 267). It survives in Gallo-Romance (e.g. *una uice* > Fr. *une fois*) and the Iberian peninsula, but not in Italian, which has *volta* (see *REW* 9445.2, *FEW* XIV.412). In late Italian texts *uice(s)* is nevertheless quite common (see Adams 1977b: 267 for examples), notably in the *Compositiones Lucenses* (see Svennung 1941: 151). See also above, 49.17.

illi: *ille* is the usual third person pronoun in this text, occurring forty times. *Is* has not been dropped entirely (fifteen times). There are some differences between them. First, *is* is preferred in the genitive (*eius* 75, 119, 137; *illius* is only at 76; on the persistence of *eius* see above, 38.53, 39.8). Second, *ille* is favoured in the dative (*illi* twenty-four times; *ei* occurs only four times; on the latter see further below, and for the vitality of *illi* in other late texts see above, 38.53, 39.8). Third, *is* tends to occur in clusters, as four times in this section between lines 27 and 32, and five times near the end of the extant text (XXVII–XXX, between lines 133 and 145). These clusters may reflect a different source or sources, particularly the second cluster towards the end. There *dabis ei manducare* occurs three times (133, 139, 141–2), a phrase that is out of keeping with the usual phraseology of the text: cf. 2 *da illi manducare*, 4 *da illi manducare*, 6 *dona illi ad manducare*, 64–5 *da illi ad manducandum*, 71 *da illi manducare*, 72 *nihil aliud illi dones ad manducare*, 81 *illi manducare dones*. Also anomalous in this final section is *non liceat ei commedere* (145). Here the usual verb of eating (*manduco*) is replaced by *comedo* (for which however see also 103), and *non liceat* is a refined form of prohibition; *comedo* also occurs a second time in the same line. All four instances of the dative *ei* (see above) are in this final section.

Ille was to replace *is* in Romance, and we have already seen some early signs of its inroads (see index s.v. *ille*, 'in relation to *is*').

tuas tegulas: on this phrase see below, 50.28.

26–7 apprehende ... calefacies: here an imperative is coordinated with an imperatival future. This text has the variability of imperativals that is typical of later technical treatises (see e.g. Adams 1995a: 164–5, 204–8, 460–7, and above, 29.1, 42.3). On *apprehende* here see below, 50.29 (on *tolle*).

27 in focum: *in* + accusative, but locatival. *Focus* is probably used here in its Romance sense 'fire' (*REW* 3400) rather than 'hearth' (see e.g. Svennung 1935: 568, id. 1941: 174, Liechtenhan 1963: 68 index s.v., Stotz 2000: 53), though there is an ambiguity ('on the fire/on the hearth').

rubeae: originally spelt with an *o* (long) in the first syllable, and earlier found with the ending *-ius* as well as *-eus*; a form *rubeus* with *ū* is said to occur sometimes in classical Latin alongside *robeus*: see Blümner 1889: 401, *OLD* s.v. *robeus*. In the early period *robeus* existed alongside the adjective *robus*, a dialect colour term said to have been used by *rustici* (Paul. Fest. p. 325 Lindsay) (see Ernout 1928: 220–1, André 1949: 84–5, Ernout and Meillet 1959: 575). Later *robeus/rubeus* was conflated with *ruber* and acquired the short vowel of the latter (André 1949: 85), and *rubeus* (with short first vowel) is reflected in the Romance languages (*REW* 7408, *FEW* X.536). It. *rosso* is from *russus* (*REW* 7466; see André 1949: 83–4), but OIt. *robbio* derives from *rubeus*. *Rubeus* is quite common in the *Compositiones Lucenses* (e.g. A 12, 15, N 19), and no doubt here and in that text we have the form with *ū*.

sanguissugam: the old word for 'leech', *hirudo* (e.g. Plautus, Cicero, Horace), survives only in Occitan (*REW* 4144, *FEW* IV.434), whereas the later term *sanguisuga* (Celsus, Scribonius Largus, Pliny the Elder: note *Nat.* 8.29 *hausta hirudine, quam sanguisugam uulgo coepisse appellari aduerto*) is widespread (*REW* 7575, *FEW* XI.182: e.g. It. *sanguisuga*; the word also survived in the northern parts of France: see Adams 2007: 277 n. 2).

28 super ipsas callidas tabulas: *tabulas* 'tablets' picks up *tuas tegulas* 'your tiles/slates'. It is possible that the reference here is to slate tiles used as writing tablets, given the specificity of *tuas*: in the context these are things that one has around the house as a possession, and stray roofing tiles would hardly fit the bill. For slate tiles as writing tablets see the corpus edited by Velázquez Soriano (2004), and text 46 above.

puluerem subtilissimam: *puluis* is regularly used in the feminine in this text, though in classical Latin it is mainly masculine (but see Adams 2013: 388). For Romance reflexes of *puluere* (generally masculine, but It. *polvere* is feminine), see *TLL* X.2.2626.18ff.; for those of the form *puluera*, which is feminine, see 20ff.

Twice (32, 92) the word is used in the (feminine) plural (*ipsas puluere*). The plural hardly occurs in classical Latin (but see Hor. *Epod.* 17.48, Plin. *Nat.* 11.82), but is sometimes found later (*TLL* X.2.2626.7ff.; note e.g. Amm. 23.6.83, Caes. Arel. *Serm.* 31.2, *CC* 103, 135, Isid. *Etym.* 13.2.1; in the northern Italian work of Anthimus *pulueris* is accusative plural at p. 25.7, and some manuscripts have it in the feminine). In Italian *polveri* in the plural is a standard use. Both instances of *puluere* in this text immediately follow a use of the singular, in the phrase *fac inde puluerem*. The reader is then instructed to do something with or to the (grains of) dust, *ipsas puluere*. The singular seems to be collective (of the substance, generically), the plural particularising (of grains of dust). This particularising use of the plural is very clear at Isid. *Etym.* 13.2.1, where it refers to motes of dust visible in the rays of the sun: *sicut tenuissimi pulueres qui infusi per fenestras radiis solis uidentur.* Svennung (1935: 160) translates *pulueres* as 'pulverised ingredients'.

29 tolle pennas de paone de cauda: *tolle* is used here in the typical late sense 'take' (cf. It. *togliere*) (see above, 43.9). It is the most common verb with this meaning in the text, nineteen times (3, 5, 14, 19, 29, 40, 49, 51, 55, 61, 69, 74, 77, 113, 116, 127, 137, 138, 147). Two other imperatives are used with the same meaning throughout, *accipe* (a verb with limited and specialised Romance survival), twelve times (11, 23, 30, 33, 48, 62, 70, 91, 93, 132, 135, 140), and *adprehende* (for which in Italian and other Romance languages see *LEI* III.1.317, 330; cf. the uncompounded form: e.g. It. *prendere*, Fr. *prendre*), eight times (26, 27, 32, 88, 95, 98, 102, 122). The three verbs are completely interchangeable: note e.g. 23 *accipe alium acetum* / 32 *adprehende acetum forte* / 55 *tolle acetum fortissimum*; 11 *accipe glutonem* / 40 *tolle glutonem*; 48 *accipe ipsum falconem* / 98 *adprehende ipsum falconem*; 88 *adprehende stercum passeris* / 140 *accipe stercus caprinum*; 69 *tolle lardum* / 135 *accipe lardum*.

Tollo is also constant in the *Compositiones Lucenses*, but it does not seem to alternate there with the other two verbs.

de ... de: it is unlikely that the writer means that users of his manual should seek out a peacock and then remove feathers from its tail. *De paone* contains the defining or characterising use of *de*, which goes back to classical Latin and continues through late Latin into Romance (see index, s.v. *de*, 'defining, characterising'). The meaning is 'take peacock feathers'. *De cauda* is a second defining use of a *de*-phrase, specifying *pennas* further: 'peacock feathers, tail ones', > 'peacock tail-feathers'.

mitte eas: the usual word for 'put' in this text is *mitto* (cf. e.g. It. *mettere*, Fr. *mettre*) (twenty-one times: 1, 15, 19, 29, 35, 52, 55, 56–7, 57, 62 twice, 69, 71, 92, 96, 98, 100, 101, 106, 118, 119 (note too 25 *intromittas*). *Pono* (cf. It. *porre*) occurs three times (27, 128, 148). For *mitto* + infinitive see below, 50.69–70. See index, s.v. *mitto*, 'put'.

fumarium: given the meaning 'smoke-room' (where wine was stored) by the *OLD*, but that meaning would not fit with *super*. The Romance reflexes of the word are glossed at *REW* 3568 (cf. *FEW* III.857) with *Rauchfang* 'chimney flue', and some sort of smoking flue/smoke vent must be meant here.

29–30 accipe de ipsa sugia: a noteworthy proto-Romance use of the preposition + article (associative here: for the type see above, 49.7). The *de*-expression stands in an object relation to the verb. There is nothing unusual about a partitive use of *de* in this role, a usage that goes back to early Latin and recurs from time to time (see index s.v. *de*, 'expressing partitive object'). It is common in this text when the noun is indefinite, as at 80–1 (*de passeribus ... de aliis ocellis minutis ... de columbis ... de porco*, 89 *de aloe*, 95 *de lanam*). What is unusual is the presence with it of the article use of *ipsa*. The partitive article of Romance languages (= 'some') shows the coalescence of *de* with the definite article. The same combination is at 101 *si de ipsa aqua biberit* (where water has been previously mentioned and the reference is thus definite). These phrases are direct anticipations of a Romance type, except that in most areas it is *ille* and not *ipse* that generates the definite article (see above, 50.24). Several identical uses of *de ipso/ipsa* are cited from medieval documents of Spain by Bastardas Parera (1953: 34–5), though most of the partitive uses of *de* he quotes are without *ipse*. He also has (34) a single example of *de* + *ille* (in the phrase *de illis sanctis*, subject of a verb). For the combination *de* + *ille* in the description of the Basilica of Saint-Denis, see above, 49.14.

sugia: a Gaulish word, reconstructed for that language in the form *sudia* (Delamarre 2003: 285), with the form here either a misspelling or representing some sort of palatalisation (Delamarre loc. cit.). In Romance the word survives in Gallo-Romance, including that of Provençe (from which it is said to have been borrowed in Lombardy) and in Catalan (*REW* 8425, *FEW* XII.397).

30 de ipsis pennis: the soot is to be collected from the surface of the feathers and *de* is thus local (separative).

30–1 puluerem de sanguissuca: this use of *de* is different. The powder is not taken from the surface of the leech but in effect comprises the leech itself once it has been burnt and crushed. Here *de* can be taken as characterising ('leech powder'), though perhaps with an idea of source ('originating from'). Ambiguities are constant in later uses of *de* (see further below, 50.33).

31 de una ... de alia: a different use of *de* again. Dependent on *tantum* and *quantum*, these phrases are equivalent to partitive genitives, though still with a hint of local (separative) force.

32 acetum forte et ipsas pulueres: the presence of *ipse* with *pulueres* alongside its absence with *acetum* is notable. The *pulueres* are specific, having just been mentioned, whereas *acetum* refers to any vinegar of the right type that happens to be available, and is indefinite.

insimul: a compound adverb widely reflected (from the form *insemul*) in Romance, including Italian (*REW* 4465). The *TLL* has postponed treatment of the compound until *simul*. See Adams (2013: 588), with bibliography.

33 de aceto: the reference presumably is not to the vinegar that has just been mentioned as part of a mixture (which is now 'not very liquid'), but to another lot to be used for washing. Only then is the previously mentioned mixture to be used. *Acetum* on this view is indefinite, and thus without *ipse*.

De is here instrumental, but there is a typical ambiguity, in that the preposition can still just be taken as referring to source ('wash from a quantity of vinegar'). On instrumental *de* (including its ambiguities) see Adams (2013: 299–307). It was to survive in Romance languages (Adams 2013: 299).

It is a striking feature of this text that the old instrumental ablative does not occur. Its functions have been assumed mainly by *de* and *cum*.

For the former see 74 *illum inebria de uino*, 77 *mulge de ipso lacte*, 94 *rade ibi de s<alis> gema* (*gemma* 'crystal'), 124 *de ipsa puluere sala ipsam carnem*, 129 *de ipso ... unge ipsum pedem*, 130 *unge illum de optimo sapone*, 137 *ineb<ria> de uino*.

For *cum* see 42 *calimare fac cum lima*, 75 *batte cum manico de cultello* (*de* here is genitival (partitive)), 98 *mitte illi cum digito in gorgam*, 114 *cum mel ipsam carnem unges*. Three of the nouns here with *cum* denote solids, whereas it is *de* that is used with liquids (a reflection of its original separative sense).

There are also a few cases of *in* and *ad* which are local but approaching instrumental in meaning: 27 *calefacies in focum*, 75 *scalda pectus eius ad focum*, 98 *tene illum in manu*.

34 lardum ueterum: *ueterum* is a neuter singular (for CL *uetus*) constructed by back-formation from the neuter plural *uetera* (see B. Löfstedt 1976: 123 = 2000: 175–6, Stotz 1998: 34 with n. 393). The old form occurs at 135 (*lardum uetus*). There is a good deal of morphological (and gender) variation in the text (see Bischoff 1984b: 174).

petiolas: the base of this diminutive is *pecia/pet(t)ia* (for which see *TLL* X.1.901.26ff.), probably a Gaulish word (see Delamarre 2003: 249–50), which means 'piece' and occurs in some manuscripts of the *Pact. leg. Sal.* at 60.1 (others have *fustes* or *partes*) and also later in this work (69, 71) (for the spelling variation *ti/ci* see above, 34.6 with bibliography). It is also found in the *Compositiones Lucenses* (I 22, 23, 28). It lives on in e.g. Italian (*pezza*), French (*pièce*) and Spanish (*pieza*) (*REW* 6450). *Petiola* is not attested in the period covered by the *TLL* but is common in medieval Latin, not least that of Italy (Arnaldi, Turriani and Smiraglia 1939–64: II.516–17). It is not in *REW*. It may however have survived (as *pezzuola*) in earlier (northern) Italian, attested in Pietro de Crescenzi (Bologna, 13th c.), *Trattato dell'Agricoltura* 2.3.11 (information from Anna Chahoud).

35 ut ipsa confectio ad ipsum lardum teneat firmiter: *teneat* here is intransitive, and complemented by *ad*. It is obvious what the meaning must be: the mixture must adhere, stick to the *laridum*. It is not so easy, however, to parallel this usage (without the resources yet of the *TLL* for the word). Intransitivisations of this kind can often be derived from deletion of a reflexive pronoun (see above, 44.37.2 on *moueo*), and there is indeed a reflexive example of *teneo* that comes close to the required meaning. Arnaldi, Turriani and Smiraglia (1939–64: III.261) cite Cassiodorus *In Psalmos* 32D (*PL* 70) for the construction *ad aliquid se tenere* (glossed by *eo fulciri* 'to be supported by it'): (*homo*) *quia sua leuitate ad firmamentum mandatorum se tenere non potuit, merito puluis dicitur, qui tamquam substantia tenuis uitiorum flatibus uentilatur*, 'man, because in his fickleness he could not hold on/adhere to the support of instructions (received), is deservedly called dust; like an insubstantial substance he is blown by the winds of vice'. Here there is a complement with *ad*, but the act of holding on/adhering to something is metaphorical. There is a closer example to our own at Anthimus p. 2.12, in a similar context: *quomodo in fabrica domus parietis si calcem et aquam quis tantum temperauerit, quantum ratio poscit, ut spissa sit ipsa mixtio, proficit in fabrica et tenit*, 'just as, in the construction of a house wall, if someone mixes lime and water in the correct proportion, so that the mixture is thick, it works in the construction and holds firm'. Anthimus goes on to say that if there is too much water, the mixture does not work. Liechtenhan (1963: 77) classifies *tenit* here as intransitive and glosses with *stabilem esse*. As in the passage on falcons, so here there is a mixture that has to be of the right composition to hold on to something; if too liquid it will not. The only difference between the two examples is that that in Anthimus is absolute, whereas the other has *ad*.

A similar intransitive use from a different semantic field has the meaning (in reference to plants) 'take root' (e.g. Palladius 3.9.8, 3.25.20, 4.9.13, 12.7.6, with Svennung 1935: 449). If plants are planted correctly, they 'hold firm' (in the soil).

In French there is an intransitive use of *tenir à*, but it is metaphorical and not really parallel, meaning 'to be fond of'. However, in an expression such as *il tient à son argent*, 'he can't bear to be parted from his money', it is possible to see a remnant of the literal meaning ('he holds on to his money'). Italian has the same usage. *Tenere a qualcosa* means 'to care very much about something'. Normally it has either a modifier (*molto/poco*) or a locative particle (*tenerci*). Note e.g. *tengo molto al mio denaro* ('I hold on to my money') (information from Anna Chahoud and Giuseppe Pezzini).

The non-metaphorical meaning 'hold to, adhere to' is also attested in thirteenth-century Italian (*Dizionario dell'Accademia della Crusca*, 4th edn (1729–38), s.v. VII 'tenersi per attenersi, stare attaccato'), for example reflexive in Pietro de Crescenzi, *Trattato dell'Agricoltura* 5.4.10 *Quando seguiterà quasi a far filo (lo zucchero) se lo toccherai col dito, o che pendente si tenga alla mestola, sarà cotto* (information from Anna Chahoud).

37 nam si: adversative, 'but if' (see Hofmann and Szantyr 1965: 505–6).

istum totum: *istum* here is equivalent to *hoc*.

illi facias: an old phrase: see Ter. *Andr.* 143 *quid facias illi qui . . .*

40 Tolle glutonem, quae inter grana nascitur: Bischoff (1984b: 180) glosses *glutonem* (which is also at 11 and 43) with *Kornrade* 'corncockle' (Fr. *la nielle rose des blés*), and cites Penzig (1927: 14) for the northern Italian dialect forms *clossòn, glotù*. The corncockle (Agrostemma githago) is a pink flower of European wheat fields. Further dialect forms may be found in Rolland (1899), who deals with the Agrostemma githago at 220–31. The following forms with Rolland's provenance (given in French) are listed by him at 226–7; all are northern Italian:

git, gittone, gittajone, gitterone, gettone, gettajone (italien).
closson (Canelli, Piémont).
gittone, giottone, juttone (Bologne).
gitoun, gioutoun (piémontais).
giotton (lombard, vénitien).
gitton (lombard).
gitun, giutun (Monferrat).
giultun (Monferrat).
gioton (Trévise).
giotton (Plaisance).
giotton (milanais).
glotu (Brescia).

The second and last are the same as those cited from Penzig. The origin of these terms is unclear (CL *glut(t)o* means 'glutton'). However, all, and most obviously those beginning *gi-*, could be based on the Semitic term *git*, attested in Latin from Varro onwards (*TLL* VI.2.1997.4ff.), which is also found in the forms *gitti, gitter* and *gittus* (details in *TLL*). *Git* is defined (*TLL* 1997.4) as 'semen herbae, quae vocatur "nigella sativa"' (see further André 1985: 110–11). These seeds of the Nigella sativa are known variously in English as fennel flower, nutmeg flower, Roman coriander and black cumin, but a late semantic change might lie behind the above northern Italian forms. *REW* 3768a does indeed have some of the dialect forms above under the heading *gittus*. It remains uncertain what the phonetic relationship might be between the *gi-* and *gl-* forms.

The suffix must be *-o, -onis*, here attached unusually for Latin to a non-personal base (*git*?) (but for this type see Leumann 1977: 363). In Italian the suffix *-one* (along with its feminine correspondent *-ona*) denotes bigness (see Rohlfs 1969: 414–18), and some such motivation might conceivably lie behind **gitto* (denoting a whole flowering plant rather than a part, the seeds). For the suffix in Italian attached to a botanical term note Lombard *tejón* 'fir tree' < Lat. *taeda* 'pine tree' (Rohlfs 1969: 416) (reference from Adam Ledgeway).

From a British medieval text the *DMLBS* cites a form *glutho*, suggesting tentatively the meaning 'sweet wine', but it is in a list of plants and must be the same term as that in the present text.

The (apparent) feminine gender in our text is anomalous, but might be explained as a constructio ad sensum (*glutonem, quae herba …*) (see the material at E. Löfstedt 1956: II.146: e.g. Eutrop. 9.9.1 *Moguntiacum, quae (urbs/ciuitas) aduersus eum rebellauerat*). See also below on 55 (*agrumen quae*).

grana: must refer here not to cereal seeds, but to the wheat plants/crops. Cf. It. *grano* 'wheat'. For *granum* of plants/crops see Arnaldi, Turriani and Smiraglia (1939–64: I.241).

testum de osso: CL *testu/testum* means 'earthenware pot' (cf. It. *testo*, a flat earthenware board for cooking bread etc. on). A derived meaning therefrom was 'shard, fragment' (see Bloch and von Wartburg 1968: 632 s.v. *têt*; cf. Fr. *tesson*; also *FEW* XIII.287), hence here 'fragment of bone'. *De* here seems to be the characterising/defining use, 'bone-fragment'.

40–1 de capite <hom>inis: there are twenty-two inflected (classical) genitives in the text. In eleven cases, as here, the genitival term denotes an animate (cf. 44 *testa hominis*, 75 *pectus eius*, 76 *illius sanguis*, 78 *de pectore pullicini*, 88 *stercum passeris*, 88–9 *stercum suricis*, 90–1 *de sterco passeris et suricis*, 93 *lac feminae*, 107–8 *columbi pastum unum*, 137 *pectus eius*). Seven of the other genitives are of the partitive type found for example in recipes where quantities of a substance are recommended (89 *piperis grana*, 89–90 *grana piperis*, 113 *cum piperis granis*, 116 *granum piperis*, 119 *sucum eius*, 122 *geniperis coriam medianam*, 135 *grana apii*). There remain 23 *in modum unguenti*, 93 *in modum auellanae*, 94 same phrase, 99 *horam diei*.

There are many *de*-expressions in the text with a genitival appearance (well over twenty; they are however difficult to classify semantically, as is made clear above in the notes on 30, 30–1, 31), but not a single one is with a noun denoting an animate. Nor is there a prepositional equivalent to a pronominal genitive (contrast the four examples of *eius/illius* above). Similarly in the Visigothic slate tablet (text 46 above) the genitive of animates is well represented, though other inflectional cases are in decline (see above, 46 Conclusions).

These differences aside, in this text there is some overlap between uses of *de* and the genitive. See 59 for an equivalent to an objective genitive (*medicinam de ista infirmitate*). An expression at 83 (*qui medicinam sciunt de falcone*) looks the same, but here *de* may be characterising. For *sucus de*, matching *sucum eius* above, see 55 *sucum de agrumen*, 141 *sucus de mentastro*. *Granum* is several times used with the genitive (see above); contrast 138 *grana de aneto*. Noteworthy is 116–17 *tolle granum piperis I et de aloe mundissimo simile modum*, where *de aloe ... modum* is coordinated with *granum piperis I*. *De*-expressions in three places are dependent on *tantum/quantum*, a partitive use which was conveyed by the genitive in classical Latin: 31 *tantum de una quantum de alia*, 43 *de unoquoque tantum sit puluis quantum de alio* (is *puluis* here nominative in apposition to *tantum*?), 91 *tantum sit de uno quantum de alio*. Not infrequently *de*-expressions still imply separation, or may be interpreted as characterising (the two ideas are not mutually exclusive). Note for example 3 *tolle seta<s> de porco* ('take the bristles of/from a pig'; or 'take pig bristles'). However, there is not always an idea of separation: note 75 *cum manico de cultello* 'with the handle of a knife'. This partitive/possessive idea would have been expressed in classical Latin by a genitive, but again the expression is close to characterising, i.e. equivalent to an adjective.

It does seem that the inflected genitive maintained some vitality, though *de* had intruded into its territory. The types of ambiguities noted in some *de*-expressions go well back in Latin (see e.g. Adams 2013: 270–2).

41 quantum plus uetus potes: this parenthesis seems to refer back to *testum*. The construction is odd by Latin standards. In CL the required meaning ('as old as possible') would be given by the construction *quam* + superlative (*testum ... quam ueterrimum*). Alternatively a parenthetical correlative construction of the *quanto/tanto* type might have had much the same meaning (e.g. *quanto ueterius (inuenire potes), tanto melius erit*). The substitution of *quantum* for *quanto* raises no problem, because this is an equivalence that goes back to the classical period itself (see Oakley 2005: 363 on Livy 10.35.2, citing e.g. Kühner and Stegmann 1955: I.402). It is possible that the second part of these correlations had come to be suppressed such that the first part on its own could be used to convey the same idea as CL *quam* + superlative. The new construction recurs throughout the text: 4 *quantum plus potue<ri>s*, 56–7 *imple illos, quantum plus ibi inde mittere potes*, 74–5 *illum inebria de uino, quantum plus potueris* (clearly equivalent to *quam plurimo*), 128–9 *freca ipsum, quantum melius potueris* (= *quam optime*). *Quantum plus* survives in Italian in constructions of this type: thus *quanto più vecchio puoi*, or more commonly *quanto più vecchio possibile* or *quanto più vecchio si puo* (information from Adam Ledgeway and Giuseppe Pezzini).

plus uetus: comparative. In the formation of the analytic comparative the Romance languages are split between those using *magis* (Romanian, Spanish, Portuguese, Catalan) and those using *plus* (Italian, French, Occitan, etc.) (see e.g. Väänänen 1981a: 118). This use of *plus* only appears to any extent from quite late on (Hofmann and Szantyr 1965: 166 with bibliography). It also seems to occur at 7 (*plus . . . tenerum*) in a fragmentary passage.

qui de longo tempore mortuus fuisset: 'who had been dead/had died long since'. Cf. It. *da lungo/molto tempo* (*da* < *deab*), Fr. *depuis longtemps* (*depuis* < *depost*). On adverbial expressions with *tempus* see above, 11.10–11.

42 limatura de aciario: 'steel shavings'. *Aciarium*, which survives in Romance languages, is the form used in this text (cf. 2 *limatura de aciario minutissimo*), though an alternative form *aciale* was in use (and survives in) the north of Italy (Adams 2007: 475–6). For *limatura* see e.g. *Comp. Luc.* A 27 (also in the Oribasius translations, Gregory the Great and various late medical texts).

ipsum testum . . . calimare fac: *calimare* clearly means 'file', containing as it does *limare*, but the first part is obscure, and the verb may not be otherwise attested.

Facio with the active infinitive where a passive might have been expected (= 'have it filed, make it to be filed') occurs twice in the same clause (cf. *glutonem pistare facias*). This active infinitive lies behind Romance constructions of the type *faire faire quelque chose à quelqu'un*, though here there is no dative/*ad*-complement. The Latin present passive infinitive did not survive into the Romance languages, a loss that can be put down to its lack of phonetic distinctiveness (Norberg 1945: 75). This loss is one of the factors lying behind the disappearance of *facio* + passive infinitive. For late examples of the active construction see Norberg loc. cit.: e.g. Fredegar 3.19, p. 100.29 (*MGH, SS rer. Merov.* II) *duos eiusdem germanos capite truncato in puteum fecisti proi[e]cere*, 4.8, p. 125.26 *omnes Gothos ad Christianum legem baptizare fecit*.

Norberg (1945: 77–80) finds the roots of this construction a long way back. From an early period the analogous verb *iubeo* is sometimes construed not only with an acc. + pass. inf. (e.g. Plaut. *Asin.* 890 *iube dari uinum*) but also with an active infinitive and dependent accusative, without an expressed subject accusative (e.g. Plaut. *Rud.* 659 *iube oculos elidere*), where the subject can be supplied from the context or is an implied generality such as *milites, homines, seruos* (see Norberg 1945: 78 for numerous examples of these types). This usage seems still to be found in the *Vita sanctae Euphrosynae*, at 9 *si iubis me suscipere* 'if you give orders that I be accepted'; cf. also 5 *castissima puella rogauit introducere ipso monacho*, lit. 'asked to introduce the monk', = 'asked the monk to be introduced' (see Muller and Taylor 1932: 237 n. 2). The type of structure *glutonem pistare facio* alongside the expected *facio glutonem pistari* (for which type see e.g. Gell. 2.17.6, Lact. *Mort. Pers.* 24.7, Vulg. Tb 8.22, Macrob. 6.6.2; also some of the examples at Thielmann 1886: 197, 198, 199 etc., *TLL* VI.1.115.37ff.) has been seen as a continuation of the old elliptical active construction. Note Norberg (1945: 80): 'Le type *facio domum aedificare* est donc ... la continuation tardive d'une construction qui était, en effet, très ancienne, et qui s'était maintenue dans la langue populaire à travers toutes les époques, à côté de la construction passive *iubeo oculos elidi*.' Not everyone will find this idea of continuity plausible. It is possible that there has been a change in the nature of the infinitive such that it is united with the 'do'-verb, with the unit governing an accusative (see Vincent, forthcoming).

43 pistare: the classical verb with this meaning was *pinsere*. This developed two first conjugation variants, *pi(n)sare* and **pi(n)siare*, the latter of which is now attested in a manuscript of Pelagonius. Both of these (particularly the first) have Romance reflexes. There was also a late verb *pistare* (attested from about the fourth century: see *Mul. Chir.* 289 and *TLL* s.v.), which survives widely (*REW* 6536: e.g. It. *pestare*) (for details of the semantic field see Adams 1995a: 516–17). Our text has only *pistare* (see too 119, 123). This is either a frequentative or is based on the participle/supine *pistum* (for the latter type cf. *tritare* = *terere*, found in this text).

44 paucum plus sit: 'let there be a little more'. *Paucum* is adverbial, and has the sense of *paucus* commented on above, 22.13. Here it is equivalent to CL *paulum, paulo*.

in illis aliis duabus pulueribus: there are three types of powder in this recipe, from the corncockle, the splinter of bone from the head, and the clean steel.

44–5 mixta insimul dona ad falconem manducare, sola ipsa carne non nimis, de ipsum totum: this is the punctuation of Bischoff. I take *sola ipsa carne* to be accusative, and in apposition to *mixta*, 'give these things mixed together as the only meat'. *Non nimis* for its part seems to be a partitive apposition with *mixta* or *sola ipsa carne*, 'as the only meat, not too much'. For *non nimis* see 70–1 *sala inde ipsas petias de lardo non nimis*, 'salt the pieces of bacon, not too much'. On this punctuation *de ipsum totum* is left hanging awkwardly, and alternatively we might punctuate *sola ipsa carne, non nimis de ipsum totum* ('as the only food, (but) not too much of the whole thing').

There has been no mention of meat in the present passage (in the previous chapter the *lardum* (34) is used only to put in the holes where the feathers are to grow), and therefore the article *ipsa* would be out of place if a new food were being introduced. *Ipsa carne* must refer to the aforementioned ingredients of the mixture, and cannot be taken literally. The meaning seems to be 'as the only "meat"', i.e. 'food', with *carne* generalised.

45 dona ad falconem manducare: *dono* and *dare* are used all but interchangeably in this text. *Dono* occurs nine times (6, 45, 69, 72, 78, 81, 86, 87, 104), five times in the imperative. *Do* is used thirteen times (2, 4, 64, 71, 107 twice, 108, 124, 133, 135, 139, 141, 144 (?)), eight times in the imperative. With the phrase here (which recurs at 78 and 104) cf. the similar example of *do* at 124 *quam ad ipsum falconem dabis manducare*. *Da illi manducare* occurs at 2, 4, 71, and the almost identical *dona illi ad manducare* at 6. There are other uses of both *da illi* (64, 107 twice, 108) and *dona illi* (87).

Another text in which the two verbs are used freely in alternation is the *Vitae patrum* (Salonius 1920: 373). There has not, however, as far as I am aware, been a systematic account of their distribution in later Latin (see however Rönsch 1875: 385, id. 1887–9: III.32). In northern France *dare* was replaced by *donare* and *baiulare* (see *FEW* III.14), but *dare* lived on e.g. in Italy (along with *donare*: see *FEW* III.137).

There are some differences. Only *dono* is used in the subjunctive (*dones*) as a directive (69, 72, 81, 86). *Do* regularly has its complements (accusatives, datives, verbal) following (ten times). The only (partial) exception is at 124 (quoted above), where in a relative clause the complements are split around the verb. At 135 (*insimul da*) *da* is used absolutely. *Dono* by contrast has its complements preceding (or partly preceding) at 68–9 (*istam patellatam illi per duas uices primum dones*), 72 (*nihil aliud illi dones ad manducare*), 81 (*illi manducare dones*) and 86 (. . . *illi dones* (gap in text)). In all four of these instances the verb form is *dones*. Thus in two respects (word order, jussive subjunctive) the passages have a more literary feel to them, and suggest that for this writer *dono* was of higher register than *do*.

In later sections there is a sudden change in the use of *do*. From 124 to the end *da* occurs only once (135), and instead *dabis* makes an appearance, four times (124, 133, 139, 141). Moreover in three of these cases (all but the first), as we saw above on 26, the dative pronoun is the old-fashioned *ei* instead of the ubiquitous *illi* (124 has no pronoun). Another feature of this late part is the appearance twice (145) of *comedo* 'eat', whereas to that point *manduco* had been the almost invariable verb of eating (see above, 50.26). It is likely that a new source came into play.

ad falconem: this phrase, with *ad* expressing the indirect object with a verb of giving, raises the question of the currency of the old dative at this time. There is not a single nominal dative in the work: the dative inflection is confined to pronouns (*illi, ei, cui*), of which there are thirty examples (1, 2, 4, 6, 16, 26, 37, 38, 58, 64, 68, 71 twice, 72, 81 twice, 82, 86, 87, 98, 106, 107 twice, 108, 125, 131, 133, 139, 141, 145). These are mainly datives of the indirect object, but there are also datives of advantage (e.g. 26) and sympathetic/possessive datives (16 *cui tiniolae deuorant pennas*, 71 *mitte illi in gorgam*, 98 *mitte illi cum digito in gorgam*). On the other hand the construction for nouns is exclusively *ad*. The only noun so used in the text is *falco*, understandably, given the subject matter. *Ad falconem* is used with verbs of giving, as here (cf. 78 *dona ad falconem manducare*, 104 *sic dona ad ipsum falconem manducare*, 124 *quam ad ipsum falconem dabis manducare*, 144 <*da*> *de mane ad falconem bibere*), but it is also used instead of the sympathetic/possessive dative (112, 116, 127; see below, 66–7), and instead of the dative with a verb taking a dative rather than accusative object (66–7; see the note ad loc.).

Three points may be made. First, the dative as a nominal inflection seems to have disappeared (unlike the genitive). Second, the distinction between the behaviour of pronouns and nouns is anticipatory of the Romance languages, in which *ad* replaced the dative with nouns but a case system survived to some extent in clitic pronouns, with indirect-object forms partly distinguished from direct-object forms (see Adams 2013: 278, and 286–7 for traces of this distinction in other late texts, a distinction which in our text is now absolute; see also below, index, 'dative, retained in pronouns when lost in nouns'). Third, it is only very late indeed that one starts to find the *ad*-construction to any extent with verbs of giving and the like (see index, 'dative, and *ad*, with verbs of giving versus saying'). The main earlier signs of encroachment by *ad* on the dative are with verbs of saying, where usually *ad* is motivated: it occurs particularly when a crowd is addressed or the voice projected across space, especially in authoritative utterances, and is also found mainly in Christian texts, where Greek was an influence (see Adams 2013: 278–88 for some details, and particularly Adams and de Melo, forthcoming; see also above, '43 Conclusions).

46 unde ipsae pennae exierunt: this clause, qualifying *pertusi*, occurs three times in six lines in this section (cf. 48–9, 52), and is typical of the redundant specifications found in technical texts (see e.g. Adams 2013: 491–2, 496). *Vnde* here has a conventional local meaning ('from which, whence'), but it was tending also to be used as an invariable relative pronoun with a different function: see below, next note.

49 tolle fleotomum, unde homines sanguinem laxare solent: here *unde* is not a local adverb but functions as a relative pronoun equivalent to an instrumental ablative ('a phlebotomy knife, by means of which men are accustomed to let blood'). This is one of the uses that reflexes of *unde* have in early Romance languages. See e.g. Buridant (2000: 590), citing *Aucassin et Nicolette* XIV.7–8 *or ne quidiés mie que j'atendisse tant que je trovasse coutel dont je me peusce ferir el cuer et ocirre* (translated 'n'allez pas vous imaginer que j'attendrais de trouver un couteau pour me poignarder et me tuer', literally 'a knife with which'; *dont* is from *de unde*, but the uncompounded *ont* is also in Old French: *REW* 9062, *FEW* XIV.33). The only instrumental examples cited by the *OLD* (s.v. *unde* 12) are from Hyginus *Fab.* 112.2 *Aiax Hectori donauit balteum, unde est tractus, Hector Aiaci gladium, unde se interfecit.* See also Hofmann and Szantyr (1965: 209), Reichenau Glosses (Klein 1968) 2734 *calamus: penna unde litteras scribuntur.*

Noteworthy in the relative clause is the final position of the verb. In relative and subordinate clauses in this text the verb almost invariably comes at the end of the clause, which represents a preservation of the ancient word order of subordinate clauses. In main clauses the vast majority of verbs are imperatives, and the object and other complements are usually placed after. Here are the subordinate clauses in chapters XVI–XVIII, first (a) those with verb-final placement (twenty-eight), and then (b) those (three) with another term in final position:

(a) 23 in modum unguenti dum ueniat, 24 unde ipsas pennas exire debent, 25 unde ipsae pennae exierunt, 27 quousque rubeae sint, 29–30 usque dum sugia super ipsas pennas crescat, 33 unde ipsae pennae exire debent, 36 unde ipsae pennae exierunt, 36–7 quousque ipsas pennas exire uideas, 37 antea, quam istum totum illi facias, 37 nam si … ipsas pennas exire uideris, 38 si ipsae pennae bonae sunt aut adulterae, 40 quae inter grana nascitur, 40–1 qui de capite <hom>inis fuisset, 41 quantum plus uetus potes, 41 qui de longo tempore mortuus fuisset, 46 unde ipsae pennae exierunt, 46–7 si ipsi pertusi … clausi non sunt, 47 nam si ipsae per dies XV non exeunt, 48–9 unde ipsae pennae exierunt, 49 et ipsos si aliter aperire non poteris, 49–50 unde homines sanguinem laxare solent, 50 usque dum illos ueraciter inuenies, 52 unde ipsae pennae exierunt, 52–3 quia de ipsa infirmitate sanat, 56 quantum plus ibi inde mittere potes, 57–8 si ipsae pennae ueniunt, 58 scias quod nullam medicinam de ista infirmitate sic ueracem inuenimus, 59–60 quia inde iam falcones ad sanitatem reduximus.

(b)   35 ut ipsa confectio ad ipsum lardum teneat firmiter, 55 quae dicitur allio, 58 si non ueniunt in die XVI.

50 sanguinem laxare: the *TLL* s.v. *laxo* cites nothing like this expression of letting blood (see VII.2.1073.19ff., where 'partes corporis' are object), but the usage undoubtedly developed in medical language. The veins were 'relaxed' by blood-letting, as indeed was tension in the whole body. Note Pel. 34.3 *uenae ferro relaxatae recipiunt citius sanitatem, Mul. Chir.* 4 *quae strictura et tensio corporis aliter laxari non potest, nisi per sanguinis detractionem.* As a result we find blood-letting and *laxatio* equated: *Mul. Chir.* 31 *sanguinis detractio, per quam laxationem* . . . So the verb *laxare* must have come to be used of releasing blood.

51 fac . . . fistucum: this is a variant form for CL *festuca* 'stalk, straw' (*OLD* s.v. 1; the *e* is short). The change to *i* in the first syllable is of a familiar type: in initial pretonic syllables closing is well attested, particularly in Italian texts and from early on (e.g. *sinatus* for *senatus:* see Battisti 1949: 113, B. Löfstedt 1961: 38, Sommer and Pfister 1977: 92). *Festuca non fistuca* has traditionally been cited from *App. Probi* 87 (see Baehrens 1922: 51), but Powell (2007: 697 n. 87) reports that the text is entirely illegible. See however Albinus, *GL* VII.302.10 *festucam non fistucam dicito*, and for further evidence for the *i*-form, Heraeus (1900: 314), *TLL* VI.1.625.73f., 77f., Baehrens (1922: 51). The *i*-form does not survive in Romance (see Baehrens 1922: 51 with *REW* 3268).

There is also a change of gender here. *Fistucum* could be either masculine or neuter in this accusative form. The neuter is attested (see *TLL* VI.1.625.75ff., *FEW* III.485–6: e.g. at *CGL* III.428.21; see also Sittl 1885: 578–9 for this and a few parallel forms, where the gender is not always determinable between masculine and neuter; and Bischoff 1984b: 180). Once *festuca* was subject to a switch into the neuter (as a result of some analogy?), it would have been prone to a further switch into the masculine, and masculine as well as feminine forms survive in Romance languages. *Fétu* 'wisp of straw' is masculine in French (OFr. *festu*) (*FEW* III.486), and Italian has *festuca* (see also Bloch and von Wartburg 1968: 260 s.v. *fétu*, citing also OPr. *festuga/festuc* (i.e. in both genders)). The masculine lived on in Raetia and northern Italy (see *FEW* III.486, citing e.g. OLomb. *festugo;* so too *REW* 3268).

52-3 quia de ipsa infirmitate sanat: an intransitive use of *sanare* = *sanari* (possibly derivable from ellipse of the reflexive *se*) is reported for late Latin (Önnerfors 1963: 53-4, Feltenius 1977: 122-3), but that interpretation would not fit *sanat* here because of the tense: a future would be appropriate to the context ('know that he will be cured of the infirmity': cf. *sanabitur* at 134, 136, 139, 142) but not a present ('know that he is cured'?). *Sanat* here must be transitive, with the treatment previously described as subject, and the falcon understood as object ('know that it cures him of the infirmity'). For this elliptical use of *sanare* cf. 115 *scias quia certissime sanabit*.

The preposition *de* in this context, of curing someone 'from' something, replicates the more familiar use of *ex* (for which see *TLL* V.2.1089.57ff.): e.g. Cato *Agr.* 157.8 *sanus fiet ex eo morbo*, Priscill. *Tract.* 2.46, p. 38.16 *quem ex infirmitate sanauerat*. For *ab* see Tert. *Scap.* 4.5 *et quanti honesti uiri … aut a daemoniis aut ualetudinibus remediati sunt!* (Hoppe 1903: 36). *De* replaced *ex* and *ab*.

scias … quia: the construction (*scias*) *quia* here is one of two replacements for the acc. + inf. in the text (so also *quod*): cf. 58 *scias quod nullam medicinam de ista infirmitate sic ueracem inuenimus*, 115 *scias quia certissime sanabit*. The acc. + inf. occurs three times, always in subordinate clauses, and with at least part of the dependent construction preceding the main verb: 36-7 *quousque ipsas pennas exire uideas*, 37 *si … ipsas pennas exire uideris*, 68 *si falco se demonstrat bulsum esse*. The word order and construction are conservative in a subordinate clause (see above 50.49).

55 sucum de agrumen, quae dicitur allio: *agrumen* is for *acrumen* (< *acer*). The word is not classical but is cited by Blaise (1975: 12) from medieval Latin (no examples quoted) and given the meaning *aigreur, amertume* 'sourness, bitterness'. Here it cannot have that abstract sense, but the phrase must mean 'juice of the sharp plant/herb/vegetable, which is called "garlic"'. *Alium* 'garlic' is often spelt with *ll* (see *TLL* I.1619.33, 61). It survives in Romance (*REW* 115). Nowadays It. *agrume* usually means 'citrus (fruit)', but that meaning is not the earliest one. Previously it referred mainly to garlic, leek, onion and such plants with a sharp flavour or odour (source 3rd edn of the *Dizionario dell'Accademia della Crusca* (1691), which mentions the new reference to citrus fruit for the first time: information from Anna Chahoud). Cf. *LEI* I.355, giving various meanings from Italo-Romance, 'ortaggio dal gusto acre', 'cibi di sapore acre, forte'; also the abstract meaning 'sour/sharp taste, acidity'.

The word is masculine in e.g. Italian (*agrume*), and the *-men* form here is presumably neuter. Here we see again (cf. 40 *glutonem, quae inter grana nascitur*) the use of a feminine relative in reference to a (neuter) botanical term, perhaps under the influence of *herba*.

59 medicinam de ista infirmitate: here the *de*-expression is equivalent to an objective genitive, a late usage (see Adams 2013: 272–3).

59–60 quia inde iam falcones ad sanitatem reduximus: 'because by that (medicine) we have already brought falcons back to health'. *Inde* is an invariable pronominal here with instrumental force, and equivalent in implication to *ea medicina* (abl.); *medicinam* is in the previous clause. The instrumental uses cited by *TLL* VII.1118.74ff. are mainly late; the example at Virg. *Aen.* 3.663 is not convincing as a pure instrumental (it expresses source more than anything else, but is nevertheless transitional).

Here are some uses of *inde* in the text:

(a) Instrumental/source
70 *deinde accipe limaturam de ferro subtilissimam et sala inde ipsas petias de lardo*, 'then take very fine shavings of iron and salt the pieces of bacon with them'. Here *inde* may be translated as instrumental, but, like *de* at 124, *de ipsa puluere sala ipsam carnem* 'from the powder salt the meat', it still retains an idea of source, a common ambiguity: see Adams 2013: 299–307, and above on Virg. *Aen.* 3.663; *sala inde* is at 4 too but without surviving context.

(b) Partitive/source
56 *imple illos, quantum plus ibi inde mittere potes*, 'fill them (the holes) with as much as you can put there of it (i.e. of the medicament described previously)'. Here *inde* is partitive (a partitive genitive might have been dependent on *quantum*), but again there is an ambiguity, in that *inde* can still be interpreted as expressing source.

Similar are: 65 *ut plenam gorgam inde habeat* 'so that he has his gullet full of it' (*plenus* regularly takes a genitive), 106 *illi inde plenum* (but there is then a lacuna), 119 *collige sucum eius et m<itte> inde guttas III in ipso oculo* 'collect its juice and put three drops of it in the eye' (here *inde* seems equivalent to the preceding *eius*).

The partitive use is old and classical (*TLL* VII.1.1119.47ff.).

(c) With *facio*
In classical Latin something can be made 'from, out of' something else (*ex: OLD* s.v. 16; *de: OLD* s.v. 8). The most frequent use of *inde* in the text has the word accompanied by *fac*, as e.g. at 28 *incende eam et fac inde puluerem*

subtilissimam 'burn it and make from it a fine powder', 34 *accipe lardum ueterum et fac inde subtilissimas petiolas* 'take old bacon and make from it fine little pieces' (cf. 51, 69, 90, 97, 117, 123, 133). Again the meaning is close to instrumental. This use goes back to early Latin (Plautus, Cato): see *TLL* VII.1.1117.48ff. ('de materia').

61 qui desiccant: the verb is intransitive, with medio-passive meaning, = *desiccantur* or (in accordance with later usage) = *se desiccant,* and is one of those intransitive usages that can be derived from ellipse of the reflexive. For a few parallels from late texts see Feltenius (1977: 125; also 124 for *sicco* used thus).

62 in lacte: in the previous line *lac* is used as the accusative form. *Lacte* should be taken here as ablative, not as the alternative accusative form *lacte* for *lac.* The milk here must be the same as the *lac caprinum* just mentioned, and thus an item already mentioned is not given the usual artcicloid *ipse.* In the next line the writer reverts to the norm in *cum ipso lacte.*

62–3 frixoria ... frixoria: this is a late word for 'frying pan' attested in Latin only in texts or writers with a northern Italian connection (Oribasius translations, translation of Rufus of Ephesus, *Pod., Venantius, Phys. Plin. Bamb.*), and reflected mainly in Italian dialects, including those of the north (see Adams 2007: 479–80 for details).

63 bulliat: two ingredients have been mentioned, milk and eggs, and the singular might seem to imply that only milk is subject of the verb. However, *simul* shows that the author was thinking of both items as boiling together, and the singular must be a constructio ad sensum, with the implied mixture the subject. There are often illogical switches of number in recipes (see above, 42.15).

   patellata: translated by Bischoff (1984b: 181) as 'omelette' (*Omelett*), with some bibliography. The word does not occur in the *TLL* and appears not to be reflected in Romance. The base is *patella* 'pan', and *patellata* must be the participle of a denominative **patellare,* meaning 'pan-cooked (thing(s))'. *Oua* is the subject of *sunt,* and is surely to be understood with *patellata,* given that the *quae* which follows immediately must be neuter plural, as it is object of *manducat.* The original phrase would therefore be *oua patellata,* of eggs pan-cooked (with milk), i.e. 'omelette' (or should we say some sort of pancake?). Then *oua* was dropped by ellipse, leaving a substantival use of *patellata,* which changed gender to feminine. The two other instances of the word that follow are indeed feminine singular (66 *ista patellata,* 68 *istam patellatam*).

63–4 quae homo manducat: not only is *homo* indefinite here (cf. e.g. Fr. *on*), but the verb phrase in which it occurs, like verb phrases in French with *on*, is equivalent to a passive, = *quae manducantur* 'which are eaten/can be eaten'. On indefinite *homo* see Hofmann and Szantyr (1965: 198), noting that the usage is very rare even in late Latin. For Italian see Rohlfs (1968: 231–2). See in general now Bauer (2015).

64 ut fumus nec flamma nullo modo ueniet: the writer conflates here alternative negative constructions, *ut fumus et flamma nullo modo* and *ut nec fumus nec flamma ullo modo*. *Veniet* is indicative in a purpose clause, a late substandard construction (see Hofmann and Szantyr 1965: 642–3; also above, 32. 7–8, and index, 'indicative, apparent indicatives in *ut*-clauses'). In Romance in general, however, the subjunctive is retained in final clauses (Salvi 2011: 375–6). Could there be a morphological confusion here, with the ending used as a subjunctive marker? The construction recurs at 79–80 with a correct subjunctive: *uide ut ipsos cibos nullatenus uomat* (also 99).

65 ut plenam gorgam inde habeat: *gorga* here means 'mouth', or 'mouth and gullet/gorge'. *Gorga* is a late form, showing a typical vowel merger, of *gurga* (for which see *TLL* VI.2.2359.69ff.), which itself is an alternative (feminine) form of CL *gurges*, in its late extended sense 'jaws, gullet' (*TLL* VI.2.2361.10ff.). The change of form is analogous to but not the same as the switch of fifth declension feminines such as *materies* and *luxuries* into the first declension (*materia*, *luxuria*: see e.g. Väänänen 1981a: 106). The difference is that the *e* of *gurges* is not long, and the word is masculine not feminine, and of the third not fifth declension. *Gorga* survives mainly in varieties of Gallo- and Italo-Romance (*REW* 3921), with slight variations of meaning. Fr. *gorge*, for example, means 'throat', but for the sense 'mouth' see Bloch and von Wartburg (1968: 299): 'Usuel au sens de "bouche" dans la région de la Franche-Comté et de la Suisse romande, avec la voyelle *o*.' That seems to be the meaning here. *Gorga* does not appear in the *TLL*, and the only example cited of *gurga* (see above) is not an anatomical term. Some further details may be found at *FEW* IV.337 (*gurga* itself came to be rivalled by a masculine *gurgus*).

Inde goes with *plenam*, 'full of it' (above, 50.59–60 b).

smaltierit: a Germanic word, given at *FEW* XVII.157 the forms **smeltjan* (Frankish), which produces Old French *esmeltir*, and **smaltjan* (Gothic), from which It. *smaltire* comes. The Old French is given the meaning 'fienter (en parlant des oiseaux)', i.e. 'leave droppings, excrete', and that must be the meaning here. In current Italian *smaltire* means 'eliminate', and it can be applied to the elimination of digested food. This last meaning seems to be the original one in Italian, attested from about the twelfth century (see the 1st edn of the *Dizionario dell'Accademia della Crusca* (1612), s.v.). A little later see Pietro de Crescenzi, *Trattato dell'Agricoltura* 3.19.3 *il panìco è duro da smaltire, ma non è del ventre costipativo* (information from Anna Chahoud).

Of particular interest is an example later in the text at 105 (*sedeat quousque smaltitum habeat*), which must mean 'let him sit until he has excreted'. For *sedeo* in such contexts see Adams (1982a: 241). This is an example of past participle + *habeo* as a perfect tense equivalent. Elsewhere in the text there are a few traditional inflected perfects (54 *inuenimus*, so 59, 78 *uoluerit* (future perfect), 100 *uomuerit* (perfect subjunctive), so 101 (or future perfect), 102 *biberit* (future perfect), 103 *commederit* (future perfect or perfect subjunctive), 108 *feceris* (future perfect)). Genuine perfect periphrases with *habeo* that are not open to other interpretations are extremely hard to find, even in very late Latin (see Adams 2013: 642–5 and the whole of chapter XXIV, and particularly now the extensive study of Tara 2014, chapter II), though an unambiguous instance such as this does suggest that the type must have existed beneath the surface.

Smaltierit is an inflected future perfect.

66–7 ad falconem ... adiuuat: *adiuuo* takes an accusative in classical Latin, but in late Latin it sometimes has a dative complement (Hofmann and Szantyr 1965: 89), either on the analogy of other verbs of this semantic field construed with the dative, or under Greek influence (βοηθεῖν), direct or indirect. The same is true of both the simplex *iuuo* (Hofmann and Szantyr loc. cit.) and the frequentative *adiuto* (Adams 1977a: 42 with bibliography, and above, 6.29, 22.28). In late Latin a manifestation of the encroachment of *ad* on the dative is to be seen in the occasional use of dative-governing verbs with *ad* (e.g. *noceo ad*: see further Adams 2013: 292), and that is the phenomenon here.

It is worth mentioning here another striking prepositional expression in the text used for a different type of dative (see also above, 50.45 on *ad falconem*). At 112 note *si autem ad falconem carnes in pedem aut in alio loco foris corpus adcrescerit*. Here *ad falconem* has replaced the old sympathetic/possessive use of the dative (in association with an anatomical term), a replacement, with an outcome in Romance, that it is difficult to parallel even in late Latin (see Adams 2013: 288–90). The construction recurs in this later part of the treatise: 116 *si ad falconem aliqua macula in oculo euenerit*, 127 *si pedes ad falconem inflauerint*. For the old dative use see 98 *mitte illi cum digito in gorgam*, and above, 50.45 on *ad falconem*.

68 bulsum: *uulsus* is the past participle of *uello*, 'pluck, pull (sprain)', a term long since established in veterinary Latin, where it was used of a horse that was 'broken-winded'. It derives from a notion that the lungs could be sprained (see Adams 1990c, id. 1995a: 40–1, 305–8 for details, and mentioning the Hippocratic origin of the idea). The term here must refer to breathing difficulties of some type. For Romance reflexes see Adams (1995a: 306: e.g. It. *bolso*, OPr. *bols*).

69 petias: for this word see above, 50.34 on its diminutive *petiola*.

glutire: this verb meaning 'swallow' goes back to Plautus, and is quite common in late medical texts (Adams 1995a: 610). *REW* 3807 cites reflexes from Neapolitan and Friulian, and also Catalan.

69–70 mitte illas iacere in melle: cf. 100 *mitte eum sedere*. For *mitto* (but in the sense 'send' not 'put') + infinitive see *TLL* VIII.1189.71ff. In Italian *mettere* in the sense 'put, leave' is used with an infinitive, but introduced by *a* (*ad*: for *ad* + infinitive in this text see below, 50.72): *mettile a giacere nel miele, mettilo a sedere*. The construction here is quite common in the *Compositiones Lucenses*, but with the compound *demitto/dimitto*: e.g. D 18 *demitte desiccare* 'leave to dry' (cf. D 21–2, E 8, Q 1–2, T 3–4). With the present example cf. R 17 *demitte illum requiescere*. Contrast *Per. Aeth.* 37.3 *manum autem nemo mittit ad tangendum*.

70 super noctem: 'overnight', a curious phrase for Latin. *Super* is quoted from classical Latin with a temporal meaning, 'during' (Hofmann and Szantyr 1965: 281, Kühner and Stegmann 1955: I.573, *OLD* s.v. 1d), but in phrases of the type *super cenam* 'over dinner', *super mensam*. For medieval examples of *super noctem* see Hincmar, *Annales Bertiniani* a. 864, p. 72 (*MGH, SS rer. Germ.* V. III) *super noctem . . . regreditur*, *Vita Eligii* 2.16, p. 705.12 (*MGH, SS rer. Merov.* IV.II) *neque mensas super noctem conponat neque strenas aut bibitiones superfluas exerceat*.

sala: *salare* survives widely in Romance, including Italian (*REW* 7521).

72 illi dones ad manducare: this construction (*ad* + inf.) is also found at 6 (*dona illi ad manducare*) and 128 (*quae est ad cultellos uel ad rasoria acutiare* 'which is for sharpening knives or razors'), and it alternates in the text with the plain infinitive (cf. just two sentences earlier *da illi manducare*) and with *ad manducandum* (64 *da illi ad manducandum*). The *ad* + inf. construction, which survives in Romance, is discussed in detail by Norberg (1943: 206–31) (see also Hofmann and Szantyr 1965: 378–9, with some further bibliography). The influence of the overlapping gerund construction (with *ad*) must have been one factor in the extension of *ad* to the infinitival construction (see Norberg 1943: 216, and above, 38.52). Norberg loc. cit. cites what would be an early example from the *Vetus Latina*, at Io 6.52 (cod. Verc., s. IV–V), *dare ad manducare*, where the Vulgate has *ad manducandum* and the Greek δοῦναι . . . φαγεῖν. However, the reading of the Vercelli manuscript cannot be verified (information from Philip Burton). The construction seems to be mainly medieval (see Hofmann and Szantyr 1965: 378, along with Norberg's examples). For a few earlier examples see Adams and Vincent (forthcoming b: §12), but in each case either Greek or Hebrew influence has to be allowed; see also Panayotakis (2012: 306). It occurs in the *Compositiones Lucenses* (I 23 *semper eum ibi scalda; et aliud eramen pone ad battere, unam petiam desuper et unam desubtus*; note also in this last passage *scalda, battere* for *battuere* and *petiam*, all of which occur in our text; for the first two see below, 50.75) (see Svennung 1941: 157).

74 tolle pullicinum tenerum: *pullicinus*, originally an adjective (for the extended suffix *-cīnus* see Leumann 1977: 327; cf. *morticinus*), is used here and at 78 in the singular as a noun with the meaning of its Romance reflexes ('chick(en)': e.g. It. *pulcino*, Fr. *poussin*: see *TLL* X.2.2582.33ff. for a full list of reflexes, including those deriving from the alternative form *pullicenus* attested in the manuscripts of the *SHA*). In the period covered by the *TLL* the word occurs just once, at *SHA, Alex.* 41.7, substantivally but in the plural and embracing the young of various birds (see *TLL* 2582.38f.). The Romance specialisation of meaning had taken place by the time of the present text.

75 scalda: this is the verb *excaldare*, with aphaeresis (the complementary tendency to or hypercorrect reaction against the addition of a prothetic vowel before *s* + stop). For the form in another northern Italian text see Anthimus p. 28.7 *bene scaldetur*; see also *Comp. Luc.* I 23, quoted above, 72 (also *Comp. Luc.* I 14). The form with aphaeresis survives in Italian (*scaldare*) and also Romanian, Engadine and Friulian, whereas the initial vowel is retained in French (*échauder*), Occitan and Ibero-Romance (*REW* 2946, *FEW* III.265). A comparable example in the text is *scortica* (5), from *excorticare* (> It. *scorticare*; contrast Fr. *écorcher*: *REW* 2988). On aphaeresis in Latin see now Sampson (2010: 56–9).

batte cum manico de cultello: the form *battunt* for *battuunt* is already attested in Marcus Aurelius *ap.* Fronto p. 50.6–7 van den Hout (Adams 2013: 111). *Battes* occurs also at *Mul. Chir.* 25, accompanied as here by a prepositional instrumental expression for the ablative (*battes de tabella aliqua belle ponderosa*: see Adams 2013: 304). Forms without *u* are also found in the *Compositiones Lucenses* (see Svennung 1941: 104, and above, 50.72); cf. It. *battere* (*REW* 996). Notable in the present passage is the sequence of two prepositional expressions (instrumental + partitive), each with a function that might have been expressed in classical Latin by cases (ablative

+ genitive). On instrumental *cum* see above, 50.33, and also Adams (2013: 296–9); in late Latin this usage is prominent in texts of Italian provenance (Adams 2013: 298), and not least in the *Compositiones Lucenses* (e.g. F 23–4, G 15, I 14–15, K 13, L 20, M 17, N 29, T 15, Z 17, α 16).

Manicus (at least in the Latin lexicographical tradition) is thought to be the same word as *manica*, with a change of gender. *Manica* (usually plural) is used in classical Latin of handcuffs, or various coverings of the hands (see *TLL* VIII.301–2). However, a meaning much the same as that here (though more specialised) is already reported for its (feminine) diminutive by Varro *Ling.* 5.135, listing the parts of the *aratrum* 'plough'. The *manicula* is a cross-piece forming the hand-grip of the plough: *super id regula quae stat, stiua ab stando, et in ea transuersa regula manicula, quod manu bubulci tenetur* ('the straight piece of wood which stands above this is called the *stiua* "handle," from *stare* "to stand," and the wooden cross-piece on it is the *manicula* "hand-grip," because it is held by the *manus* "hand" of the ploughman', Kent, Loeb). The non-diminutive form for its part turns up in glosses with the meaning 'handle' (= *manubrium*), either specifically or by implication of the plough (*TLL* VIII.302.26ff.), and in both the masculine and feminine: *CGL* V.515.51 *steba* [i.e. *stiua*] *manica aratri*, V.115.17 *manubrium quod rustici manicum dicunt*. Another gloss (V.507.16) reads *manubrius manicus*, with *manubrium* as well in the masculine. One possible determinant of the masculine *manicus* might have been the analogy of *manubrium*: a neuter *manicum* (influenced by *manubrium*) might have shifted to masculine, or *manicus* might have been based on the masculine by-form *manubrius*.

In our passage *manicus* is no longer associated specifically with the plough. So it is that in another late Italian corpus, the Ravenna papyri, the original feminine non-diminutive form is attested in the general meaning 'handle' (see *TLL* VIII.302.30ff.): 8.II.11 *cocumella cum manica ferrea*.

Manicus (with the meaning given as *Griff*) has a lemma separate from that of *manica* at *REW* 5303a, and also at *FEW* VI.1.217, though the latter (at 226) refers to *manicus* as concurrent with *manica* in late Latin. There are numerous reflexes, e.g. It. *manico*, Fr. *manche*.

Conclusions

Date

There are no grounds for placing the composition of the work much before the time of the manuscript itself. There is an abundance of usages that are loosely to be described as 'medieval' (see 24 *pertusa*, 29–30 *sugia*, 34 *petiola, petia*, 41 *quantum plus uetus*, 42 *fac* + active infinitive, 45 *ad* for the dative of the indirect object with verbs of giving, 55 *agrumen*, 63 *patellata*, 65 *gorga*).

Origin

Many terms, forms or usages in the text have reflexes in Italy, if not exclusively there (e.g. 27 *sanguisuga*, 28 *puluis* feminine and plural, 34 *petia*, 42 *facio* + infinitive, 43 *pistare*, 55 *agrumen*, 65 *gorga*, 69 *mitto* + infinitive, 70 *salare*, 74 *pullicinus*, 75 *scaldare, manicus*). These are merely consistent with (northern) Italian composition. On the other hand *glutonem* (40) and *frixoria* (62–3) have connections specifically with northern Italy. It is also worth stressing the frequency with which we have been able to quote parallels from the *Compositiones Lucenses* (see on 23, 24, 26, 27, 29, 34, 42, 69, 72, 75). This work survives in a manuscript copied at Lucca in about 800 (see Adams 2007: 465–72), and it was possibly not very different from our text in its time of composition.

Case system

At first glance the text seems to contain a wide range of classical noun inflections in both singular and plural. But in reality not all endings occur, and those that do are not all fully functional. There has been a shift towards prepositions for expressing case roles. Three features of the case system are worth stressing. First, there are no dative inflections in the text except in pronouns. With nouns *ad* is used for various functions earlier expressed by the dative: indirect object, 'sympathetic', with dative-governing verbs (see on 45, 66–7). The preservation of the dative in pronouns is itself of Romance significance, as a partial inflectional case system continued in clitic pronouns. Second, the instrumental ablative is not found in the text (see on 33), though ablative forms are common enough. Prepositions (*cum, de*) are used (with the ablative or accusative) to convey the instrumental idea. Prepositions had long been encroaching on the instrumental ablative, but here the replacement is absolute. Third, *de* was overlapping with various uses of the genitive (see on 40–1), but inflected genitive forms are still always used with animate nouns and pronouns. It is possible that the genitive was the last of the oblique cases to be ousted. Genitival uses of *de* are however difficult to analyse; there is often an idea of source present.

Definite article

Here is a text in which definiteness is marked almost invariably by *ipse*, to the extent that there may be a long sequence of nouns all accompanied by the demonstrative (see on 24). Twice *de* and *ipse* are used together as a partitive article (29–30). Is there another Latin text of any period in which this articloid use is so ubiquitous? However, it was not *ipse* but *ille* that produced the article in northern Italy. Here we have, in an extreme form, the old problem raised by the frequency of article-like uses of *ipse* in areas in which it was *ille* that became the article in the local Romance (for this problem see Adams 2013: 482 with bibliography). The work was probably written as late as 900, at a time when early forms of Romance vernaculars were already starting to appear. Is it possible that soon afterwards a linguistic revolution occurred in northern Italy, with an established article use of *ipse* suddenly replaced by one of *ille*? That does not seem plausible. Might the writer have spotted in earlier texts the frequent use of *ipse* (often equivalent to *idem*) that is just one manifestation of the redundancy of specification that had long been a feature of technical genres (see Adams 2013: 488–50, 513–19), but have increased its frequency as a reflection of an article use of *ille* already current in speech? *Ipse* would on this view have come from the tradition of technical writing going back for centuries, but its new frequency would be based on the existence already of a definite article (*ille*) in speech. Another possibility is that the specification of definiteness by articloid uses was now regular in this area, but that there was still optional variation between *ipse* and *ille* (and *ille* itself is also occasionally used as an article in this text, but not as often as *ipse*). Similarly in the French text discussed earlier (49) there is some alternation between *ille* and *ipse*, with *ille* predominating.

Lexicon

The lexicon of the text has a Romance feel, with many terms unknown or of restricted use in classical Latin now the norm (26 *manducare, uices*, 27 *focus*, 29 *tollo, mitto*, 34 *petiola, petia*, 43 *pistare*, 62–3 *frixoria*, 65 *gorga, smaltire*, 74 *pullicinus*).

FINAL CONCLUSIONS

The phenomena that come up in this anthology are far too diverse to be summarised, but there are some recurrent themes, which I will attempt to bring out here, not discursively but referring to discussions in the commentaries.

1 Periodisation

The texts in this work span more than 1,000 years, and one cannot but say something about 'periodisation', that is the question whether the language can be divided into clear chronological stages. This volume is however an anthology, and any selection of texts is bound to be a weak basis on which to build narratives of chronological change. Indeed the whole of extant Latin literature is an anthology, selected by scribes for copying in line with obsessions of the medieval period. That is why we have so much Cicero and so little Varro, so much Livy and Tacitus but almost nothing of their sources, such a huge amount of Christian writing from later antiquity but relatively little pagan, and so much high-style writing in both prose and verse and so little practical or personal writing on mundane subjects. There is no point in trying to define neat periods in the history of the language from such data. I will say something here about some different periods (loosely defined) in which Latin is extant, but not with the aim of identifying stages in an even progression. That is not to say that the language did not change, but rather that false conclusions can be drawn from imperfect evidence treated as offering the whole truth.

There are quite a few early texts (from about 200 to 160 BC) in our selection. 'Archaic' is sometimes used of the Latin of this period, but it can be an unsatisfactory term, implying for some readers that there was a 'primitive' stage in the history of the language. There is nothing primitive about early Latin. It is diverse in style and register, with subtle variations in individual writers. The fragments of Ennius' *Euhemerus* at first sight look crude, with verbal repetitions, constant use of temporal adverbs and redundant use of *is*, but there are also signs of stylistic artificiality (see 1 Conclusions). Ennius did not have to write like this, as other forms of his output show. Terence (see 1 Appendix 3) and others, including annalists (see e.g. 1.8), sometimes used the same simple narrative style (for Plautus see Courtney 1999: 153–5), but Plautus when he wanted wrote elaborate narrative, abounding in artificial usages, as in a long passage of the *Amphitruo* (see 1 Appendix 4). The 'crude' style is not a sign of the (archaic) times, but a traditional method of narrating events simply. It was associated with folk tales (see 1 Appendix 3 and the first passage of Terence cited there), and may have had input from Greek. Nor did it die out after the early period, but was always available (see e.g. 8.3–4 and index, 'popular/simple narrative style').

There are also generic differences in early Latin texts, which tell against any notion that the language was naive. Notable phenomena that have come up are the use of *atque* before consonants (see 1.6 and 1 Appendix 1), which is all but non-existent in Cato's *De agricultura* but constant in the fragments of his Origines, the use of the archaic form *-ere* of the third person plural perfect (1.11), and the use of present participles governing an accusative object (1.15). For 'register variation' in Plautus see 3 Conclusions.

Texts of the early period do of course have features that largely disappear from use later, such as the uninflected future infinitive form (see 6.14 on *daturum*); this and various such usages have been used to give a rough date to the Johns Hopkins *defixio* (see 6 Conclusions). Others in other texts include *clam* + accusative (1.16), *gestio* in its etymological sense (2.7–8), *facinus* in a neutral meaning (3.418), *enim* in initial position (3.429), *lien* 'spleen' (5.27), early subjunctive forms of *edo* 'eat' (5.19), and *ualidus* with an early meaning (4.13). Such phenomena in Plautus are listed at 3 Conclusions, 'Old Latin features'.

But the Latin of texts of the early period was not a discrete entity. We have seen anticipations of later, including Romance, phenomena, as in Cato's use of *unde* (4.5), of prepositions in various types of temporal expressions (5.6), of *subtus* (5.8) and *pullus* (4.10), and of *sanum* (*facere*) with the adjective showing a lack of concord with the primary (nominal) object of the verb (5.15). In Plautus analytic intensive superlatives are as common as the synthetic type (see 2.24), and although the intensifying element is variable and there is no sign yet of grammaticalisation, his taste for the combination intensifier + positive adjective provides the background to later developments. The verb *fabulor*, which he has often, is mainly submerged later but it continued into Romance languages (3.424). The reflexive dative of advantage, which is sometimes pleonastic, was to have a long history (2.5). Partitive expressions comprising *de* or *ex* standing as object of a verb are already found in Plautus and Cato and anticipate the Romance partitive article. The (apparent) accusative pronoun form *ecillunc* (in the Johns Hopkins tablet) is closer in its syntax to Romance compounds with *ecce* than are comparable forms in Plautus (see 6.43). Some (fading) usages lasted well beyond the early period, particularly but not exclusively in colloquial varieties of the language, such as the adverb *istic* (3.421), the reinforced pronoun *istic*, notably in the nominative and accusative singular forms *istic* and *istunc* (see 3.420, 8.1, 17.3), and the adverb *illi* (9.16). In the Conclusions to the section on Vitruvius (11) we have included a section entitled 'Vitruvius and early Latin', the point being, not that Vitruvius was an archaiser but rather that there is not the sharp division between the early and late Republic/Augustan period that there might appear to be if one uses only Cicero for defining 'classical Latin'.

The classical period (which is taken to mean here the late Republic and early Empire, down to about the mid-first century AD) suffers from its persuasive adjective 'classical', and from at least one other term applied to it ('Golden' Age, as distinct from 'Silver'). I would stress the limitations that have emerged to the standardisation that was supposedly effected during this period; a 'standard language' is readily given adjectives such as 'classical', since it is regarded as controlled. Here is some relevant evidence.

Cicero has not been included in this anthology except in the section on jokes, but he does come up indirectly. In a number of places it has been pointed out that usages found in his (educated) correspondents (or other contemporaries, notably Varro and Vitruvius) are used by Cicero himself either not at all or hardly ever. I would conclude from this that Cicero's Latin cannot be taken as wholly representative of the late republican educated language. It is, inevitably, an idiolect. Because the works of Cicero survive in such abundance, they have traditionally been used to construct a classical Latin that obscures the diversity of the period. Late republican or Augustan deviations from what appear to be Ciceronian norms are traditionally classified as 'vulgar', but that is a tendentious classification when they might just as well in at least some cases be treated as evidence for diversity. See 9.9 (*peream si*), 9.10 (the adverb *istoc*), 9.11, 13.10 (*discupio*), 9.16 (the adverb *illi*), 11.5 (passive use of *persuadeo*), 11.5 (*ab* expressing agency with some abstracts), 11.16 (*est* + infinitive: here Cicero is at variance with a correspondent, and with Varro and Vitruvius), 11.17 (pluperfect of *habeo* for imperfect), 11.18 (*impero* + infinitive), 14.4 (*mihi crede*); see too 22.12–13, on the lack of standardisation in the forms of the perfect of compounds of *lego*. It is also possible that some 'abnormalities' in Cicero have been emended from his text (see 11.26 on the fifth declension genitive singular; another case is the indicative in indirect questions: see Adams 2013: 752–3). It is unfortunate that so little is extant of Cicero's contemporary Varro, who was famous for his learning. What does survive is very different in some ways from the language of Cicero (see Laughton 1960, and the index to the present work, s.v. 'Varro, Latin of').

Cicero's Latin in the speeches changes over time. Usages found in the early speeches are sometimes dropped or reduced in frequency later (see e.g. 1.3 *ibi tum*, 3.421 *istic*, 3.425 *homo* with indefinites, 6.43-4 *disperdo*, 7.5 *sis* 'please', 7.8-9 compounds in *per-*, 9.8 *nisi si*, 14.7 *pusillus*, 16.2 *ausculto*). Such modifications suggest that there was at the period some debate about or at least consideration given to the acceptability of various usages, but any such debate implies stylistic awareness and not necessarily anything so dramatic as a deliberate movement that might be labelled 'standardisation'.

Genre and register, and not merely personal taste, are of course major determinants of diversity in the classical period. So it is for example that usages peculiar to or at least mainly found in epistolography (including the letters of Cicero himself) have often come up. See e.g. 2.24 *ualde*, 3.417 *opinor*, 3.420 *istaec*, 3.421 *istic*, 3.428 *timeo/timor*, 6.29 *adiuto*, 7.5 *heus* (*tu*), 7.13 *oricula*, 9.10 *isto*, 9.13 *hui*, 12.3 *bucca*, 22.24 *illim*.

Another writer not dealt with explicitly but who is sometimes mentioned here, usually as exemplifying abnormalities, is Livy. The question arises why these should appear in his text.

In the Conclusions to 12 it is noted that Augustus in a fragment used *ab* with the name of a town, an exemplification of a practice of his commented on by Suetonius. This is a usage that Livy has constantly (Adams 2013: 329-30), invariably writing *ab Roma*. Nor is it absent from other writers of the classical period (e.g. Sallust), though not frequent. The rule that prepositions are not used with names of towns has hardened into something immutable in the school tradition, but the reality is that practice was more varied, with Augustus and Livy consciously, it seems, taking a decision to use prepositions (Augustus for clarity, we are told). It was also noted that in Livy prepositions start to appear with *domus*, in contexts in which most Latin of the classical period would have a plain case (46.4).

Nisi si for *nisi* is shared by Livy with e.g. Cicero's early works, Varro and Vitruvius (see 9.8). *Fabulor* occurs just once in Augustan literature (it is avoided by Cicero), in a speech in Livy (3.424). The adverb *istic* occurs twice in Livy, both times in speeches (3.421). The redundant use of *homo* with indefinites is found in speeches in Livy (3.425). *Est* + infinitive is in a speech in Livy (11.16). The ellipse of *tam* after a negative in the *tam ... quam* construction is usually in direct speeches (22.15-16).

Livy famously was accused by Asinius Pollio of some sort of provincialism (*Patauinitas*: see Adams 2007: 147-53 for details), and the presence of some of the above usages in his work does make one wonder whether they might be the sorts of things that Pollio had in mind (see 3 Conclusions).

However, a number occur in speeches, and historians did admit informal usages in speeches. By contrast Livy's examples of *ab Roma* are common in the narrative, and are suggestive of a lesser degree of standardisation than is allowed by the grammatical tradition. A more systematic search for such abnormalities both in speeches and narrative might turn up a firmer basis for Pollio's remark, or, alternatively, further evidence for the limits of standardisation.

Thus, the common narrative of Latin periodisation that would have the language moving towards standardisation or even a state of 'perfection' in the classical period (cf. the adjective 'Golden' above) ought to be re-examined.

But it is in the late period (say, from 300 to 600) that easy narratives run into real trouble. The main objection to splitting our extant texts into neat chronological units and implying that these units represent stages in the history of the language as it was spoken lies in the inadequacy of much late Latin as linguistic evidence. It is true that informal writing tablets have been turning up, quite a few of which are in this selection (19–24, 32–7, 46), and that these do bring out some changes that were in progress, but they are minute in extent compared with the amount of Christian Latin. This was heavily influenced by versions of the Latin Bible, and the Bible was a translation text, full of artificiality and translationese. For example, in much late Latin the infinitive of purpose with verbs of motion is confined to biblical Latin or texts inspired by the Bible (see 39.22, and Adams and Vincent forthcoming b). One can learn little or nothing from evidence of this kind about the state of the ordinary language. Even more striking is the use of *ad* with verbs of saying (with unemphatic pronouns as well as names and nouns) in the *Hist. Apoll.* (see the detailed discussion, 43 Appendix). This use can be related to the Vulgate version of the Old Testament, but in most respects not to the Romance languages: it looks artificial (and might indeed derive from a lost Greek original). One might it is true argue that in Christian texts a period of Latin is indeed reflected, the 'Christian period', but the problem is that translationese and its derivatives may be quite unlike ordinary speech. In the Conclusions to Patrick (40) I have attempted to find a distinction between 'living Latin' in Patrick, and biblical Latin. The biblical element is overwhelming, and not much sign of a living language was discovered. There is little point in compiling crude statistics from Christian texts en masse showing the frequency of particular constructions, as if such statistics would point us to patterns of change. Unless biblical quotations and imitations are excluded from the figures (an impossible undertaking), then we would be documenting to a considerable extent the biblical influence on late Latin writing, not developments in speech. Nor is it convincing to assert that Christian writers were addressing the ordinary people and therefore made a habit of using ordinary Latin. The one text, the Latin Bible (in its various versions), that was certainly intended for the ordinary people is replete with translationese, as was remarked above. Many other Christian texts are theoretical and argumentative, and intended for other theorists.

When we move on to a very late period things become different. We find for example a clear awareness of a distinction between that which was 'correct' (i.e. classicising), and that which was deviant or modern, and that awareness leads to the appearance of various texts in more than one version (see 42, 43, 44, 48). Those who were in control of what might be deemed classicising Latin can tell us little about the state of the language, but on the other hand 'deviant' versions may be very revealing.

As a chronological unit the most coherent and distinctive group of texts in this anthology are the last five (46–50), from the early medieval period. These have a profusion of proto-Romance features, which I summarise here.

Two texts have a regular definite article (49.7, 50.24), and in both the article may combine with *de* to form a partitive article (49.14, 50.29–30). In two *suus* is used non-reflexively of a single possessor, equivalent to CL *eius*, which however has not been completely displaced in one of the two texts (47.15, 49.3). There are some distinctive lexical items, anticipatory of areas of Romance (see e.g. 46.7–8 on *fuimus/uado* in a Spanish text and 47.7 on *ambulo/uado* in a Gallic text, 48.2.2 on *firmitas* in a Gallic text, 50.35, 50.40, 50.55, 50.62–3, 50.65 on *teneo, gluto, agrumen, frixoria* and *smaltire* in an Italian text). A Spanish text has a name with a Gothic suffix that was influential in Spain (46.4). There are also signs in these texts of proto-Romance developments in the use of case and prepositions. These are summarised below, 4.4.

I conclude that continuities, real or imagined, between early Latin and later periods need further investigation, that the possible standardisation movement in the classical period is a topic ripe for a detailed study, that statistical studies of linguistic phenomena in texts from the Christian period should distinguish between biblical quotation and imitation on the one hand and free composition on the other, and that early medieval texts offer a huge field for further linguistic study. Any student of the history of a language must have a cut-off point, but a date of AD 600 or thereabouts, a terminus that I (in the past) and others have adopted, has the consequence that some texts in which there is a surfacing of Romance phenomena are excluded.

2 Latin and Greek

For much of the period covered by this volume Latin speakers were in contact with Greeks, and a recurrent theme has been the impact of that contact on Latin.

In the earliest period we find loan-words that had undergone modifications to their Greek base forms, which show that they were acoustic borrowings derived from spoken contacts and not from the reading of high Greek literature (see 2.25 on *elephantus*, a borrowing of the Greek genitive form, and also the examples collected at 16.2). Sometimes the (non-literary) source may be identified, as for example the Greek of Magna Graecia (see 2.24 on *epityra*, 10.5.1 on *colaphus*) or contemporary koine (see 2.5 on *machaera*). Somewhat later, in Petronius, *saplutus* seems to have been current in the west, certainly in Gaul (18.10), and in the same work *lupatria*, if it is a hybrid, is obviously another popular borrowing. Some Greek terms in Latin are all but unattested in extant Greek, a possible sign of their popular character (see 16.2 on *pathicus* and various other terms, along with remarks about alternative reasons why such terms might have been unattested in Greek). The Latin of Hermeros in Petronius is full of Greek, not all of it paralleled or possible to explain (see also 18.8, 18.17, 18.18, 18 Conclusions). Here is exemplified another source of Greek in the Latin of the early Empire: Greeks in Italy imported Greek into their adoptive language.

But not all of the Greek influence on Latin was exerted at a popular level. See, for the early period, 1.15 on the present participle with accusative object, and 11.16 on the construction *est* + infinitive. In later Latin Greek was influential via the Bible: see 39.22 on the revival of the infinitive of purpose with verbs of motion, and 43 Appendix, 'Some remarks about the NT', on *ad* for the dative of the indirect object with verbs of saying.

In the Empire in the east Greek and Latin were in particularly close contact in military circles. That is reflected in the passing of epistolary formulae in letters between soldiers from one language to the other. On a Latin formula apparently transferred to Greek see 13.16. For Greek formulae translated into Latin see 20.3, 26.2. In a pair of letters by the same person, one in Greek and one in Latin, we saw the same phraseology in both (23.8–9); on 'convergence' of formulae see 20 Conclusions. In Latin letters written in the east Greek loan-words were adopted freely (see 20.3, 22.29, 26.13, 26.14).

The translating of a formula of one language into the other might be classified as 'imitation'. On the other hand when in such a letter a Greek construction turns up in Latin form, the term 'interference' is more appropriate (see 22.21–2).

In other parts of the Empire informal writing tablets have elements from vernacular languages, notably Germanic (see 35.10–11, 36.4) and Celtic (36.8, 37.6–21).

3 Regional Latin

It was noted in the section on periodisation above that in the early medieval texts included here there are proto-Romance features, including regionalisms, mainly of a lexical kind. The regular articloid use of *ille* in the description of the Basilica of Saint-Denis (49) is not confined in its Romance survival to France, but it is in that text an anticipation of a Romance usage of the area in which the text was written.

In earlier texts we have noted a few usages that were probably typical of the regions from which the texts originate. There are several probable or possible 'Pompeian' usages in the document of Eunus (see 15.8, 15.13, 15.14, 15.19–20). The curse tablet from Leicester in its constant omission of intervocalic *g* provides overwhelming evidence for lenition in the area from which its writer came, whether Britain or Gaul (see 37.2–3). The same text (37.1), and another British curse tablet, also have an odd *u*-glide in hiatus that can be associated with Britain.

4 Some distributional patterns

Some usages have come up quite often in texts covering a long period, and it may be useful here to select a few of these and to describe any patterns that might have emerged.

4.1 Accusative + infinitive and substitute constructions

In the early second century, in Terentianus, direct quotation is favoured for the reporting of speech (22.10), and centuries later in the *Vita sanctae Euphrosynae* direct quotation is overwhelmingly preferred (see 47.12). There are late texts in this selection in which the acc. + inf. hardly occurs (see 39.18, 47.12; see also 31.7), and in which, if it does, its use may be marked by ineptitudes suggesting that it was no longer genuinely current (see 47.12). A statistical survey of the late period would no doubt show a decline compared with *quod-/quia*-clauses (note, however, that in the *Passio Perpetuae* of the early third century the acc. + inf. is still the norm (see 27.5), even though by that period in early Bible translations the *quod-/quia*-construction would have been in use on the Greek model). What is interesting, however, in some of our texts is that the acc. + inf. could be treated as stylistically marked and exploited for special effects. This is a phenomenon that is apparent in three extracts. Augustine, who after his conversion made quite frequent use of clauses of the *quod*-type, in his reply to Publicola sticks rigidly to the acc. + inf., whereas Publicola had used mainly the *quod*-construction in his own letter (see 31.7). Augustine was distancing himself from his correspondent, who had almost certainly irritated him, and that distancing takes the form of adopting a 'superior', classical style. The author of the *Hist. Apoll.* also seems to have given the acc. + inf. higher status, in that he restricts the *quod*-construction to direct speeches (43.4). There is also some complexity to his use of the acc. + inf. Finally, at a much later period the more 'correct' second version of the *Annales regni Francorum* sometimes replaces a *quod*-construction of the first version with the acc. + inf. (48.1.2).

The conclusion to be drawn is that linguistic change does not always progress evenly over time. The old does not die out overnight but may remain available for use by revivalists or purists who wish to make a point.

4.2 Asyndeton bimembre

Asyndeton bimembre, whereby two words of the same syntactic status are placed together without a connective, is an interesting phenomenon. It is necessary to exclude from this category pairs of words that could not alternatively have been coordinated by the addition of, say, *et*. 'The big bad wolf' could be rewritten with a connective ('the wolf which was big and bad'), whereas 'the disastrous First World War' could not (*'the World War that was disastrous and First'). 'First World War' forms a unit, which is qualified by a single adjective, 'disastrous'. I use old terminology in saying of an example such as this that 'disastrous' and 'First' differ in rank. The distinction is not always made by commentators, who have sometimes classified pairs of differing rank as asyndetic. Asyndeta can have more members than two, but examples with three (especially) or more members are mundane forms of rhetoric, whereas asyndeta bimembria tend to be stylised or formulaic. Asyndeton bimembre occurs in other Indo-European languages, with some specific types, such as pairs of adjectives of which at least one is privative, widespread (see 3.420; also 6.3 and below). I have made a point of commenting on cases of asyndeton bimembre that occur in the anthology, and the distribution of these comments is revealing of the history of the phenomenon in Latin. It declines over time, and tends to be restricted to certain genres or to formulae. I will say something first about its distribution in this volume, and then about types that have been noted here.

Asyndeton bimembre is common in Plautus (though not so in this selection: but see 3.420, and 17.3 for particular types) and also in Cato (see 4.14–15 for a classified collection of examples from the *De agricultura*). It was however stressed that some types in Cato are stylistically marked. In the genre of agricultural writing there is a clear decline from Cato to the *Res rusticae* of Varro (see 4 Appendix). Varro regularly, however, uses three terms together without connectives. Another quite early text in which asyndeton bimembre is frequent is the Johns Hopkins *defixio* (see 6.1, 6.3, 6.7, 6.8, 6.41). Here genre comes into it. *Defixiones* share features with the languages of law and religion, in both of which asyndeton bimembre had a place (for asyndeton in prayers see 4.14–15 on Cato, and for legal language in curses, 19.5–6, 19 Conclusions), and the usage occurs in a later corpus of curses represented in this selection (from Mainz: 19.6–7, 19.10, 19.10–12).

In the imperial and later Latin included here (apart from the above curses) the phenomenon is rare. There is an alliterative formula (*salua sana*) in a private letter of the early Empire (13.15), and another in a freedman's speech in Petronius (*sicca sobria*: see 18.12). It was also noted that another alliterative asyndetic expression (*agere* combined with *aginare*) used by a freedman in Petronius (in a passage not included in this selection) has now turned up in Mainz curse tablets (see 18 Introduction, 19.6–7), which shows that it was a ready-made formula adopted by Petronius for his speaker. In all three of these examples the linked terms are synonymous. A crowd acclamation of the imperial period (*saluum lotum*) came up in passing (28.17, 28.25–6). In the whole of the rest of the anthology we have had little call to comment on the phenomenon. The African surveyor uses a non-formulaic expression, *nudus saucius*, in a context in which it was suggested he was trying to write impressively (25.8–9). We were able to cite a possible case (*mendacibus periuris*; classified as asyndeton by Bieler 1993: 146) from Patrick (40 Conclusions), in a section ('Patrick's Latin is severely limited') in which we argued against the idea that Patrick wrote as he spoke: he had stylistic pretensions. Finally, pairs of imperatives could be used either with a connective or in asyndeton, and this type of asyndeton seems to have lived on until late (see 45.14; also 22.28, 43.9).

In the types of Latin considered here asyndeton bimembre was recessive, occurring in the late period occasionally only in formulae or in contexts in which it was generically determined or in pretentious pieces of writing. It would no doubt be possible to find many more examples in higher-style writings of the period, but this book is about mundane texts, from which it was mainly absent.

I turn now to some of the categories into which examples can be put. An old type (found in other languages too) is that of which the two members have a repeated fore-element, such as a prefix (3.420, 19.6–7, 19.10). The adjectival privative prefix *in-* (or ἀ- in Greek) is one such element. Pairs of adjectives also sometimes show just one such privative term (4.6). Alliterative terms, which are common, also in a sense have a repeated fore-element (4.14–15, 13.15, 18.12, 19.6–7, 19.10–12). It is not only alliteration that is prominent in asyndeta bimembria; there are other forms of assonance too (4.14–15). Sometimes the second element is an intensive compound of the first (6.7), or alternatively a compound may precede its simplex (6.8). There are pairs of synonyms and opposites (4.6, 4.14–15, 6.41, 18.12). Semantically the second term may be an intensification of the first (17.3; also possibly 25.8 *nudus saucius*, where the second is stronger than the first). The second, intensive element may correct the first (= 'A, nay rather B': see 17.3). The combination may be disjunctive (= 'A or B': see 5.35) or adversative (4 Appendix). Finally, the problem of classification raised by some pairs of verbs has been referred to (3.420, 4.3–4), as when the verbs refer to sequential events. More straightforward are pairs of synonymous verbs referring to a single event (see 6.41): these are definitely asyndeta, and stylistically marked.

4.3 Word order

Variations of word order have been noted in this work, determined by such factors as the source of a text, its stylistic level and genre. The last word has not been written on word order, and there is need for a rigorous compilation of statistics from texts over a long period, and also for an attempt to identify the multiplicity of factors that may determine variation.

I start with the orders OV/VO in relative and subordinate clauses. There was a persistent tendency in Latin for the verb in subordinate clauses to gravitate towards the end (see Adams 1977a: 69, with bibliography), with the consequence that the order OV predominates, even in texts in which in main clauses VO is more usual. In the *Anonymus Valesianus II*, for example, a work of the sixth century, VO predominates by 37:26 in main clauses, but in subordinate clauses OV is preferred by 21:6 (see Adams 1976a: 136, id. 1977a: 69).

But there are some conflicting patterns in our texts. At one extreme stands the last text, that on falcon medicine. In this in subordinate clauses verb-final position is almost absolute, predominating over non-final position by 28:3 (see 50.49). A proper comparison with main clauses cannot be made for this text, because in main clauses verbs are almost all imperatives, usually with the object following, a normal pattern throughout Latin. It would seem possible nevertheless that placement of the verb late in subordinate clauses persisted until this time in northern Italy. Further investigation of other early medieval Latin texts might be useful. In Old French, for example, there is some preservation of the order SOV in subordinate clauses, but that order is not invariable but alternates with SVO in response to a variety of factors (see Buridant 2000: 747–8).

At the other extreme there is a passage from the Vulgate version of one of the Gospels, for which statistics are given at 38.57. In that VO is strongly preferred in subordinate clauses as well as main, and indeed even more markedly in subordinate. The obvious reason for this is that the Vulgate has retained the order of the Greek. The order OV was not especially common in subordinate clauses in Greek (see Adams 1977a: 69 n. 7). We did however detect some unease among Bible translators about copying this VO pattern of subordinate clauses from the Greek NT. The translator responsible for the *Vetus Latina* version *e* tended to convert the non-Latin pattern *qui misit me* (found often in the Vulgate, following the Greek) into *qui me misit* (38.57).

Another text in which there seems not to be a sharp distinction between subordinate and main clauses in this respect is the *Hist. Apoll.* In this we saw the order VO preferred in both types of clauses (see 43.5), though the sample was not large and the whole text ought to be examined. The *Hist. Apoll.* is an odd work, showing biblical influence in other respects too (notably in the use of *ad* in expressions of the type *ait ad eum*). It is worth noting that in the Latin letters of Terentianus too VO is preferred in subordinate as well as main clauses. Terentianus was bilingual, and he shows exactly the same preference for VO in the two types of clauses in his Greek as in his Latin letters (for details see Adams 1977a: 68–9). The pattern seen in his Latin subordinate clauses may well reflect Greek influence.

A text that adds another dimension to the picture is the *Passio sanctarum Perpetuae et Felicitatis*. There are variations between different sections of this text. In the narrative of Perpetua there is a predictable distinction between object position in main clauses compared with subordinate. In main clauses VO predominates by 37:11, whereas in subordinate clauses OV is preferred by 16:7 (see 27.1). On the other hand in the compiler's narrative the word order contrasts sharply with that of Perpetua. He prefers OV markedly, but in main clauses as well as subordinate. There seems to have been a choice available. The compiler's sections are more formal, and one aspect of that formality seems to have been a preference for OV even in main clauses. It is true that no attention has been given here to other possible determinants of object place-ment, but on the face of it there are two different traditions at work, a classicising one and another showing a rightward orientation within the Latin sentence (except in subordinate clauses).

There are indeed other signs of this orientation in some parts of the work, with the compiler's sections contrasting with those of the other narratives.

Thus Perpetua herself regularly places the acc. + inf. after the higher verb, whereas the redactor more often than not places it before (see 27.5). In the two narratives of the martyrs, Perpetua and Saturus, postposition of the genitive outnumbers anteposition to an overwhelming extent (see 27.15). In classical Latin its placement is more variable, with the two orders roughly equal in incidence (statistics are given), and no doubt determined by many factors. On the other hand the compiler shows a greater readiness to place genitives before their noun. By contrast the order NG is far preferred to GN in a number of the later texts in this anthology, and was tending to be adopted mechanically (see Index, 'word order, position of genitive'). For further details of the differences between the word order of Perpetua and Saturus on the one hand, and the compiler on the other, see 27 Conclusions.

The Conclusions to 27 also have a comparison between a passage of the Gospel of Mark in Jerome's Vulgate version, and the opening sections of Jerome's own *Vita Malchi*. The former is overwhelmingly VO (i.e. rightward-looking) in its characteristics, the latter mainly OV, with some artistic vari-ation. Jerome was drawing on two different traditions, one from the Greek source, the other with classical connections.

The word order of two of the very late texts in this selection, Gregory the Great (45) and the Spanish slate tablet (46), is commented on in the Conclusions to the two texts. Again we see contrasting patterns. Gregory's Latin has OV characteristics, whereas that of the slate tablet is uniformly VO in type (I am referring not only to objects in relation to the verb, but to local complements of verbs, datives of the indirect object in relation to the verb, genitives in relation to their noun and adnominal prepositional phrases in relation to their noun). There are no exceptions to this general pattern in the tablet. Gregory on the other hand was a learned classiciser, and he was hanging on to literary patterns of the past.

I give finally one further example of the old in competition with the new. In relative clauses in Patrick clitic pronouns (notably *mihi*, used as the basis of a note at 40.4) are regularly placed next to the relative pronoun, even when there are other words present in the clause. This is the old Wackernagel pattern. It is shown that Patrick could not have picked the pattern up from the Vulgate, where it is rare. It is however an order that is still represented in

Bath curse tablets and Vindolanda tablets, and it has to be assumed that it lingered on for centuries. Occasionally however Patrick puts the pronoun before the verb in a relative clause, as usual, but other words of the clause after the verb (see 40 Conclusions, 'Living Latin'). This represents a shift from a Wackernagel placement to a Romance. This coexistence of the old and the new is suggestive of the language in a state of change. In the narratives of the *Passio sanctarum Perpetuae et Felicitatis* too we saw traces of Wackernagel placement lingering (see 27.2), but the main feature of clitic pronouns there is that they are usually juxtaposed with the verb. In Perpetua's narrative such pronouns are usually before the verb in subordinate clauses, but after it in main clauses.

Word order was complex in the later period, and no one approach, statistical, pragmatic or generic, could get to the bottom of it. Individual texts vary. The topic is complicated by the competing stylistic traditions in evidence.

4.4 Case

The relationship between case and preposition comes up in our texts, with innovations mainly to be seen in the very late period.

In earlier Latin we noted a few interesting phenomena, in a general sense anticipatory of things to come. For example, Cato had a taste for prepositions in certain temporal expressions, in which an unaccompanied ablative of time would have been usual (see 5.6). There are partitive expressions with *ex/de* standing as object of a verb already in early Latin (4.3), a usage that was to lead to the Romance partitive article, which, we saw above, appears in two of our very late texts in the form of *de* in combination with an articloid demonstrative (49.14, 50.29–30). A genre-related prepositional usage found in Vitruvius and other technical writers is that of *ab* expressing agency with nouns that are either abstract or denote natural forces or the like (11.5). With these in classical Latin the instrumental ablative was preferred. In Cato there is a common use of *unde* equivalent to *ex quo/qua/quibus*, which was later to survive in Romance (4.5). On instrumental *unde* in a very late text see 50.49.

It is in the texts from 46 onwards that change becomes apparent. In the slate tablet (46), for instance, the various oblique case uses of *domus* (*domum, domo, domi*) have been replaced by prepositions (*ad, de, in*) (see 46.4, 46.5–6, 46.6). *Ad* has encroached on the dative of the indirect object in the *Vita sanctae Euphrosyne* (47.8), but most notably in the text on falcon medicine, in which there is a proto-Romance distinction between the inflected dative with clitic pronouns and *ad* with nouns (50.45). This text also has *ad* where classical Latin uses the sympathetic dative (50.45), and *ad* with verbs normally governing the dative (50.66–7). There are too examples of *de* with a genitival appearance (note e.g. 50.59, where such a phrase is equivalent to an objective genitive), but interestingly none of these is with nouns denoting animates; the genitive inflection is maintained with animates (50.40–1). Similarly in the description of the Basilica of Saint-Denis the genitive remains in use in names (49.1), and in the Visigothic slate tablet (46) there are six or seven genitives, all of them in personal names. Finally, the text on falcons has not a single instance of the instrumental ablative: its functions have been taken over by *de* and *cum* (see 50.33); for notes on uses of *de* in late texts see also 49.15, 49.18, 50.29, 50.29–30, 50.30–1, 50.31.

4.5 Relative clauses

Attention has been drawn in the commentaries to two types of relatives clauses in particular, the relative-correlative type, and attractio inversa (for examples see e.g. above, 1.11). In the first the relative clause is preposed, and picked up in the main clause by a resumptive element (e.g. Cic. *De orat.* 2.248 *quoscunque locos attingam, … ex eisdem locis fere etiam grauis sententias posse duci*). In the second the relative clause again precedes the main clause, but is itself preceded by an antecedent, which however takes its case from the relative clause not the main clause (e.g. Ennius, *Euhemerus* III *tum Saturno filius qui primus natus est, eum necauerunt*; *filium* might have been expected). The second type often seems closely related to the first, in that the antecedent looks to have been fronted out of the relative clause of a relative-correlative construction.

The distribution of these constructions is discussed by Probert and Dickey (forthcoming), and Halla-aho (forthcoming). I comment here on their distribution in the texts collected in this volume.

Both constructions are common in early texts (for relative-correlative see 1.11, 1 Appendix 2, 4.6–7, 4.10, 4.11; for attractio inversa 1.11, 1 Appendix 2, 4.10, 4.11; these examples are in Ennius and Cato, but in the notes other republican attestations are cited as well). Thereafter both all but disappear (in our material, it must be stressed), except in some texts of distinctive type. In the surveyor's inscription and the letter of Publicola there are unremarkable relative-correlatives of imperfect type, in that a resumptive element is lacking (25.22, 31.3). Apart from that there are examples of both types, first, in curse tablets (relative-correlative 34.3–4, 34.6, 36.5–6; attractio inversa 33.12–15), and, second, in the theological writer Patrick and other Christian texts, including the Vulgate (see 39.10). Curse tablets are traditional in language. Christian examples are derived from the Greek Bible. The relative-correlative type seems to have been suited there to gnomic generalisations, as found for example in the Sermon on the Mount.

5 Some remarks on genre

5.1 Technical writing

Technical texts from the early Republic (5 Cato) through the classical period to late antiquity are included in this anthology (11 Vitruvius, 25 surveyor's inscription, 29–30 Pelagonius, 42 *Physica Plinii*, 50 text on falcon medicine). Such works have traditionally been regarded as manifestations of *sermo plebeius* (a term favoured by Cooper 1895). It is impossible to characterise them in a simple formula, and *sermo plebeius* will not do.

There are to be sure departures from expected norms in some of these texts. The surveyor for example has the indicative in consecutive clauses (25.16), and Vitruvius has some nouns in unusual genders (11.1). Pelagonius uses coarse excretory and anatomical terminology that would not have been admitted in high literature (30). The *Physica Plinii* survives in more than one redaction, with an earlier version being 'improved' later, and that suggests that the Latinity of the earlier one had not entirely met with approval.

But technical Latin cannot simply be equated with non-standard. Writers on technical subjects had varying control of educated norms, ranging at one extreme from that of the elegant classicising writer Celsus to that of some of the crude medical texts of late antiquity. The manifest stylistic aspirations of some of the above writers, for example the surveyor and Pelagonius, have been pointed out (e.g. 25.8–9, 25.10–11, 29.1; see too the Conclusions to 25 and 30). Technical Latin should be treated as what it is, technical, and its particular features described. Technical terminology in all the above texts has been discussed in the commentaries. Categories of word formation have been noted, such as the substantivising of adjectives and participles in the neuter (see 5.2, 5.11, 11.13) (see also 11.4, 11.12 on suffixal derivatives in Vitruvius). There are also features of syntax, which, though not unique to technical writing, may be distinctive of such genres. For example, in Cato's medical chapter paratactic conditional sentences are an obtrusive element (see 5.6), and these we paralleled in a parody of doctors' talk found in Plautus (see 5.6, 5.15). Various turns of phrase found in this passage of Cato continued in medical writing for centuries (see 5.1, 5.2, 5.2–4, 5.5, 5.12). The most striking feature of syntax in technical texts noted here is the constant use of *ab* with passive verbs expressing the agency of some natural force in determining an event (see 11.5 on Vitruvius compared with Cicero, and on a few other technical writers).

On the apparent 'non-standard' elements in Vitruvius, see particularly 11 Conclusions, 'Other divergences from classical practice', where it is pointed out that various departures in Vitruvius from the usage of Cicero and Caesar were shared by him with a wide range of educated writers, such as some of Cicero's correspondents, Varro, Livy, Nepos and Virgil. What this shows is not that these writers were using *sermo plebeius*, but that the educated norms of the period should not be constructed from a pair of writers.

5.2 Non-literary documents and some genres of Latin literature

Writing tablets have been exemplifying usages in certain genres of Latin, particularly the shorter poems of Catullus and Horace's *Satires*, and making it clear that lower genres drew on genuine colloquial varieties. See 13.10 (Catullus and Horace and intensive compounds with *dis-*), 21.6 (Catullus, Horace and *iucundus*), 33.3 (Catullus and a use of *inuolo*). The Pompeian graffito also has three usages found in Catullus, *ausculto, pathicus* and *uerpa* (see 16.2, 16.3 and also 16 Conclusions). The combining of *ago* with the obscure verb *agino* is now attested in Mainz curse tablets of the first century AD, a pairing previously only found in a freedman's speech in Petronius (19.6–7), of much the same date. Petronius was (at least up to a point) drawing on real speech in creating the speech of his characters. The future participle *factura* accompanied by a conditional in the Vindolanda letter adds a dimension to the history of this construction (21.7). See also 14.7 (on *pusillus* in a non-literary Augustan letter, and Catullus and Horace). Finally, I mention in passing that the fragmentary letters of Augustus (which however are literary in attestation, not documentary) also have parallels with e.g. Horace (see 12 Conclusions).

6 'Informal' texts and Latin

I take up finally a term that is used in the title of the anthology. 'Informal', like all stylistic designations, is a vague term, and it might be useful here to define some of the categories of texts in the anthology for which it seems particularly appropriate.

Private letters on mundane subjects that were not intended for publication are usually devoid of literary pretension. Various private letters on writing tablets are included here (12–14, 20–4, 26; I include 12, by Augustus, which was not published but is quoted by Suetonius), just one of which (24) is exceptional in its use of studied language. Caelius' letter (9), along with others by him that are extant, survives in literary manuscripts and does have a more serious content, but his extant corpus has striking departures from literary norms. In another letter of a literary kind (17), Seneca quotes his own irritable speech directed at two slaves, as well as their replies, and there are several usages in these spoken parts that are virtually excluded from literary texts.

The Magerius mosaic (28) records verbatim shouts of the crowd at a show in the arena.

Educated writers even working within a formal literary genre may, as Seneca did (see above), deliberately present mundane speech or conversation. Plautus (2, 3), as a playwright, had to do so by definition, though his Latin has a huge stylistic range. The classic depiction of trivial speech is that by Petronius (18). The passages from the *Rhet. Her.* (7, 8) are meant to illustrate run-of-the-mill style, and they also contain speech. The jokes collected here (10) were delivered informally, in spoken form. The *Hist. Apoll.* (43) has speeches as well as narrative, and there is at least one syntactic distinction between the narrative and spoken parts (43.4). Gregory the Great (45) puts spoken Latin into the mouths of humble characters, admitting usages not usual in his normal discourse. The Visigothic slate tablet (46), though it is strictly a legal document, records conversation, which even has a regional Spanish feature.

Finally, the *Vita sanctae Euphrosynae* (47) has spoken parts.

A distinction of a specific type may be made between (e.g.) the letter of Seneca referred to above, and most of the writing tablets in this volume, not only the letters just listed, but also the curse tablets (6, 19, 32–7) and legal tablets (15, 41, 46). Seneca was a prominent literary figure, who just happened to reveal in the letter how he might speak to (or at) slaves in anger. His outburst was certainly not 'formal'. On the other hand those composing (e.g.) curses were working within a genre that might be described as formal, in that gods were addressed and formulaic language was to some extent used. But writers of curses were usually poorly educated, and their efforts are full, for example, of spelling errors. *Defixiones* might be 'formal' texts in a sense, but in another sense they have Latin that would not be thought by the educated suited to formal contexts. Amid their formulae, curses have usages redolent of speech (such as the combining of *ago* with *agino*: see above). We thus have the educated sometimes writing down, and the uneducated writing up.

A number of the texts in this volume, as we just saw, fall into the category 'technical'. Technical Latin is difficult to characterise, and it has been given its own section above. There are again informal features in such texts.

The remaining texts include a narrative deliberately written (up to a point) in a mundane style (1), an obscene graffito (16), the (formal) letter of Publicola that was indirectly portrayed by Augustine as inappropriate in style (31), and the various texts with more than one version (42, 43, 44, 48). In this last group one of the versions is in effect treated by a later redactor as stylistically defective.

The features of all the extracts mentioned in this section have been summarised in the Conclusions to each commentary. Recurrent usages include types of parataxis (3 Conclusions; henceforth in this paragraph 'Conclusions' should be added to all single-digit numbers given; 7.8–9, 15. 19–20, 18.5, 18.10, 18.22, 18), certain reinforced demonstratives and adverbs (3, 6, 8, 9), hanging nouns (2.25, 3.416, 4), low-register lexical items (5, 6, 10, 12.3, 12.4, 18.8, 22.13, 27 Conclusions, 'Perpetua's Latin'), incoherence or carelessness of expression (5, 11.31, 22.29, 25.28), intensive compounds in *dis-* (6, 9, 13.10), popular Greek borrowings and Greek words unattested in Greek (2.5, 2.25, 16.2, 18), deviant morphology and syntax (as *-rus* and *-aes*, 6, 13, 14, *per* + nominative 15.5–6, locative with verb of motion 22.14–15, fossilised *tempus* 22.17, ablative gerund *exiendo* 22.31, *cum* + accusative 22.22, *adiuto* + dative 6.29, 22.28, consecutive *ut* followed by indicative 25.16).

BIBLIOGRAPHY

ABEL, F. (1971), *L'adjectif démonstratif dans la langue de la Bible latine* (Tübingen).

ACHARD, G. (1989), *Rhétorique à Herennius* (Paris).

ADAMS, J. N. (1973), 'The substantival present participle in Latin', *Glotta* 51, 116–36.

(1974a), 'The vocabulary of the later decades of Livy', *Antichthon* 8, 54–62.

(1974b), 'On the semantic field "put-throw" in Latin', *CQ* 24, 142–60.

(1976a), *The Text and Language of a Vulgar Latin Chronicle (Anonymus Valesianus II)* (London).

(1976b), 'A typological approach to Latin word order', *IF* 81, 70–99.

(1977a), *The Vulgar Latin of the Letters of Claudius Terentianus* (Manchester).

(1977b), 'The vocabulary of the *Annales regni Francorum*', *Glotta* 55, 257–82.

(1978), 'Conventions of naming in Cicero', *CQ* 28, 145–66.

(1981), '*Culus, clunes* and their synonyms in Latin', *Glotta* 59, 231–64.

(1982a), *The Latin Sexual Vocabulary* (London).

(1982b), 'Anatomical terms used *pars pro toto* in Latin', *Proceedings of the African Classical Associations* 16, 37–45.

(1983a), 'Language', in Bowman and Thomas (1983), 72–4.

(1983b), 'Words for "prostitute" in Latin', *RhM* 126, 321–58.

(1984a), 'Pelagonius, Eumelus and a lost Latin veterinary writer', *Centre Jean Palerne, Mémoires* 5, 7–32.

(1984b), 'Female speech in Latin comedy', *Antichthon* 18, 43–77.

(1990a), 'The Latinity of C. Novius Eunus', *ZPE* 82, 227–47.

(1990b), 'The meaning and use of *subiugale* in veterinary Latin', *RFIC* 118, 441–53.

(1990c), 'The meaning of *uulsus* in veterinary Latin', *BICS* 37, 153–62.

(1990d), 'The uses of *neco* I', *Glotta* 68, 230–55.

(1991a), 'The uses of *neco* II', *Glotta* 69, 94–123.

(1991b), 'Pelagonius and Columella', *Antichthon* 25, 72–95.

(1992a), 'British Latin: notes on the language, text and interpretation of the Bath curse tablets', *Britannia* 23, 1–26.

(1992b), 'Notes on the text, language and content of some new fragments of Pelagonius', *CQ* 42, 489–509.

(1993), 'The generic use of *mula* and the status and employment of female mules in the Roman world', *RhM* 136, 35–61.

(1994), 'Latin and Punic in contact? The case of the Bu Njem ostraca', *JRS* 84, 87–112.

(1995a), *Pelagonius and Latin Veterinary Terminology in the Roman Empire* (Leiden).

(1995b), 'The language of the Vindolanda writing tablets: an interim report', *JRS* 85, 86–134.

(1996), 'Interpuncts and the enclitic character of personal pronouns in Latin', *ZPE* 111, 208–210.

(1999), 'The poets of Bu Njem: language, culture and the centurionate', *JRS* 89, 109–34.

(2003a), *Bilingualism and the Latin Language* (Cambridge).

(2003b), 'Petronius and new non-literary Latin', in Herman and Rosén (2003), 1–23.

(2003c), 'The new Vindolanda writing-tablets', *CQ* 53, 530–75.

(2005a), 'The Bellum Africum', in Reinhardt, Lapidge and Adams (2005), 73–96.

(2005b), 'The accusative + infinitive and dependent *quod-/quia-* clauses: the evidence of non-literary Latin and Petronius', in Kiss, Mondin and Salvi (2005), 195–206.

(2006), 'Greek interference in Egyptian Latin: an unusual partitive apposition construction', *Oxford University Working Papers in Linguistics, Philology & Phonetics* 11, 1–4.

(2007), *The Regional Diversification of Latin 200 BC – AD 600* (Cambridge).

(2011), 'Late Latin', in Clackson (2011a), 257–83.

(2013), *Social Variation and the Latin Language* (Cambridge).

(2016), 'The Latin of the Magerius (Smirat) mosaic', *HSCP* 108, 509–44.

ADAMS, J. N. and DEEGAN, M. (1992), 'Bald's *Leechbook* and the *Physica Plinii*', *Anglo-Saxon England* 21, 87–114.

ADAMS, J. N. and DE MELO, W. D. C. (forthcoming), '*Ad* versus the dative: from early to late Latin', in Adams and Vincent (forthcoming a).

ADAMS, J. N., LAPIDGE, M. and REINHARDT, T. (2005), 'Introduction', in Reinhardt, Lapidge and Adams (2005), 1–36.

ADAMS, J. N. and MAYER, R. G. eds. (1999), *Aspects of the Language of Latin Poetry* (Proceedings of the British Academy 93) (Oxford).

ADAMS, J. N. and VINCENT, N. eds. (forthcoming a), *Early and Late Latin: Continuity or Change?* (Cambridge).

(forthcoming b), 'The infinitive of purpose with verbs of motion: from early Latin to Romance', in Adams and Vincent (forthcoming a).

AHLQUIST, H. (1909), *Studien zur spätlateinischen Mulomedicina Chironis* (Uppsala).

ALBRECHT, M. VON (1989), *Masters of Roman Prose from Cato to Apuleius: Interpretative Studies*, translated by N. Adkin (Arca, Classical and Medieval Texts, Papers and Monographs 23) (Trowbridge).

ALDRETE, G. S. (1999), *Gestures and Acclamations in Ancient Rome* (Baltimore and London).

AMAT, J. (1995), 'Le latin de La Passion de Perpétue et de Félicité', in Callebat (1995), 445–54.

AMELING, W. (2012), 'Femina liberaliter instituta – some thoughts on a martyr's liberal education', in Bremmer and Formisano (2012a), 78–102.

ANDERSON, R. D., PARSONS, P. J. and NISBET, R. G. M. (1979), 'Elegiacs by Gallus from Qaṣr Ibrîm', *JRS* 69, 125–55.

ANDRÉ, A. (2010), 'La concurrence entre *is* et *ille* dans l'évolution de la langue latine: étude comparative, de Cicéron à Augustine', *Latomus* 69, 313–29.

ANDRÉ, J. (1949), *Étude sur les termes de couleur dans la langue latine* (Paris).

(1951), 'Les adjectifs et adverbes à valeur intensive en *per-* et *prae-*', *REL* 29, 121–54.

(1956), 'Nominatifs latins en -*us* formés sur un génitif grec en -ος', *BSL* 52, 254–64.

(1968), 'Les changements de genre dans les emprunts du latin au grec', *Word* 24, 1–7.

(1971), *Emprunts et suffixes nominaux en latin* (Geneva and Paris).

(1978), *Les mots à redoublement en latin* (Paris).

(1985), *Les noms de plantes dans la Rome antique* (Paris).

(1991), *Le vocabulaire latin de l'anatomie* (Paris).

ARIAS ABELLÁN, C. ed. (2006), *Latin vulgaire – latin tardif VII: Actes du VIIème colloque international sur le latin vulgaire et tardif, Séville, 2-6 septembre 2003* (Seville).

ARNALDI, F., TURRIANI, M. and SMIRAGLIA, P. (1939–64), *Latinitatis Italicae medii aevi inde ab a. CDLXXVI usque ad a. MXXII lexicon imperfectum*, 3 vols. (Turin).

AUDOLLENT, A. (1904), *Defixionum tabellae* (Paris).

AUSTIN, R. G. (1960), *M. Tulli Ciceronis Pro M. Caelio*, 3rd edn (Oxford).

(1971), *P. Vergili Maronis Aeneidos liber primus* (Oxford).

(1977), *P. Vergili Maronis Aeneidos liber sextus* (Oxford).

AXELSON, B. (1945), *Unpoetische Wörter: Ein Beitrag zur Kenntnis der lateinischen Dichtersprache* (Lund).

BAEHRENS, W. A. (1922), *Sprachlicher Kommentar zur vulgärlateinischen Appendix Probi* (Halle an der Saale).

BAILEY, C. (1947), *Titi Lucreti Cari De rerum natura libri sex*, 3 vols. (Oxford).

BAILLET, J. (1920–6), *Inscriptions grecques et latines des tombeaux des rois ou syringes à Thèbes* (Cairo).

BAIN, D. M. (1997), 'Two submerged items of Greek sexual vocabulary from Aphrodisias', *ZPE* 117, 81–4.

BAKKUM, G. C. L. M. (1994), 'The second-declension nominative plural in -*eis*, -*es*, -*is*, and the first-declension nominative plural in -*as*', in Herman (1994), 19–39.

BALDI, P. and CUZZOLIN, P. eds. (2009), *New Perspectives on Historical Latin Syntax I: Syntax of the Sentence* (Berlin and New York).

eds. (2010), *New Perspectives on Historical Latin Syntax II: Constituent Syntax: Adverbial Phrase, Adverbs, Mood, Tense* (Berlin and New York).

eds. (2011), *New Perspectives on Historical Latin Syntax IV: Complex Sentences, Grammaticalization, Typology* (Berlin and Boston).

BAMMESBERGER, A. and HEBERLEIN, F. eds. (1996), *Akten des VIII. Internationalen Kolloquiums zur lateinischen Linguistik* (Heidelberg).

BANNIARD, M. (1992), *Viva voce: communication écrite et communication orale du IVe au IXe siècle en Occident latin* (Paris).

BAÑOS, J. M. (2012), 'Verbos suporte e incorporación sintáctica en latín: el ejemplo de *ludos facere*', *Revista de Estudios Latinos* 12, 37–57.

BARNES, T. D. (2010), *Early Christian Hagiography and Roman History* (Tübingen).

BASTARDAS PARERA, J. (1953), *Particularidades sintácticas del latín medieval* (Barcelona and Madrid).

BATTISTI, C. (1949), *Avviamento allo studio del latino volgare* (Bari).

BAUER, B. L. M. (2010), 'Forerunners of Romance -*mente* adverbs in Latin prose and poetry', in Dickey and Chahoud (2010), 339–53.

(2015), 'Origins of indefinite homo constructions', in Haverling (2015), 542–53.

BAUER, C. F. (1933), *The Latin Perfect Endings -ERE and -ERUNT* (Language Dissertations published by The Linguistic Society of America 13) (Philadelphia).

BAUER, W., ARNDT, W. F. and GINGRICH, F. W. (1957), *A Greek–English Lexicon of the New Testament and Other Early Christian Literature*, 4th edn (Chicago).

BEHAGHEL, O. (1909), 'Beziehungen zwischen Umfang und Reihenfolge von Satzgliedern', *IF* 25, 110–42.

BENNETT, C. E. (1910–14), *Syntax of Early Latin*, 2 vols. (Boston).

BERNAND, É. (1988), *Inscriptions grecques et latines d'Akôris* (Cairo).

BERTOCCHI, A. (1989), 'The role of antecedents of Latin anaphors', in Calboli (1989), 441–61.

BERTOCCHI, A. and MARALDI, M. (2011), 'Conditionals and concessives', in Baldi and Cuzzolin (2011), 93–193.

BESCHAOUCH, A. (1966), 'La mosaïque de chasse à l'amphithéâtre découverte à Smirat en Tunisie', *CRAI* 110, 134–57.

(1985), 'Nouvelles observations sur les sodalités africaines', *CRAI* 129, 453–75.

(2006), 'Que savons-nous des sodalités africo-romaines?', *CRAI* 150, 1401–17.

BIELER, L. (1947), 'Der Bibeltext des heiligen Patrick', *Biblica* 28, 31–58, 239–63.

(1948), 'Exagellia', *AJP* 69, 309–12.

(1952), 'The place of Saint Patrick in Latin language and literature', *Vigiliae Christianae* 6, 65–98.

(1953), *The Works of St. Patrick; St. Secundinus, Hymn on St. Patrick* (Westminster, MD and London).

(1993), *Libri epistolarum sancti Patricii episcopi: Introduction, Text and Commentary*, repr. of edn of 1950–1 (Dublin).

BINGEN, J. *et al.*, eds. (1992), *Mons Claudianus: ostraca Graeca et Latina* I: *O.Claud. 1 à 190* (Cairo).

eds. (1997), *Mons Claudianus: ostraca Graeca et Latina* II: *O.Claud. 191 à 416* (Cairo).

BISCHOFF, B. (1981), 'Eine Beschreibung der Basilika von Saint-Denis aus dem Jahre 799', *Kunstchronik* 34, 97–103.

(1984a), *Anecdota novissima: Texte des vierten bis sechzehnten Jahrhunderts* (Stuttgart).

(1984b), 'Die älteste europäische Falkenmedizin (Mitte des zehnten Jahrhunderts)', in Bischoff (1984a), 171–82.

(1984c), 'Eine Beschreibung der Basilika von Saint-Denis aus dem Jahre 799', in Bischoff (1984a), 212–18.

BIVILLE, F. (1990), *Les emprunts du latin au grec: approche phonétique* I: *Introduction et consonantisme* (Louvain and Paris).

(1995), *Les emprunts du latin au grec: approche phonétique* II: *Vocalisme et conclusions* (Louvain and Paris).

BIVILLE, F., LHOMMÉ, M.-K. and VALLAT D. eds. (2012), *Latin vulgaire - latin tardif IX: Actes du IXᵉ colloque international sur le latin vulgaire et tardif, Lyon, 2-6 septembre 2009* (Lyons).

BLAISE, A. (1975), *Lexicon Latinitatis medii aevi* (Turnhout).

BLÄNSDORF, J. (2010a), 'The defixiones from the sanctuary of Isis and Mater Magna in Mainz', in Gordon and Simón (2010), 141–89.

(2010b), 'The texts from the Fons Annae Perennae', in Gordon and Simón (2010), 215–44.

BLASE, H. (1903), 'Tempora und modi', in G. Landgraf ed., *Historische Grammatik der lateinischen Sprache* I: *Syntax des einfachen Satzes* (Leipzig), 99–288.

BLASS, F., DEBRUNNER, A. and REHKOPF, F. (1976), *Grammatik des neutestamentlichen Griechisch*, 14th edn (Göttingen).

BLOCH, O. and VON WARTBURG, W. (1968), *Dictionnaire étymologique de la langue française*, 5th edn (Paris).

BLÜMNER, H. (1889), 'Die rote Farbe im Lateinischen', *ALL* 6, 399–417.

BODELOT, C. (1987), *L'interrogation indirecte en latin: syntaxe - valeur illocutoire - formes* (Louvain-la-Neuve).

BÖMER, F. (1969), *P. Ovidius Naso: Metamorphosen Buch I–III* (Heidelberg).

BOMGARDNER, D. (2009), 'The Magerius mosaic revisited', in T. Wilmott ed., *Roman Amphitheatres and Spectacula: A 21st Century Perspective* (BAR International Series 1946) (Oxford), 165–77.

BONFANTE, G. (1967), 'La lingua delle atellane e dei mimi', in P. Frassinetti, *Atellanae fabulae* (Rome), v–xxiv.

BONNET, M. (1890), *Le latin de Grégoire de Tours* (Paris).

BOTHE, F. H. (1811), *M. Atti Plauti Comoediarum tomus quartus; in usum elegantiorum hominum* (Berlin).

BOUCHERIE, A. (1871), 'La vie de sainte Euphrosyne', *Revue des langues romanes* 2, 23–62, 109–17.

(1883), 'Vita sanctae Euphrosynae secundum textum Graecum primaevum', *Analecta Bollandiana* 2, 195–205.

BOURCIEZ, E. (1946), *Éléments de linguistique romane*, 4th edn (Paris).

BOWMAN, A. K. and THOMAS, J. D. (1983), *Vindolanda: The Latin Writing-Tablets* (Britannia Monograph Series 4) (London).

(1994), *The Vindolanda Writing-Tablets (Tabulae Vindolandenses II)* (London).

(2003), *The Vindolanda Writing-Tablets (Tabulae Vindolandenses III)* (London).

BOWMAN, A. K., THOMAS, J. D. and TOMLIN, R. S. O. (2011), 'The Vindolanda writing-tablets (*Tabulae Vindolandenses* IV, part 2)', *Britannia* 42, 113–44.

BOYCE, B. (1991), *The Language of the Freedmen in Petronius' Cena Trimalchionis* (Leiden).

BRÄUNLICH, A. F. (1920), *The Indicative Indirect Question in Latin* (Chicago).

BREMMER, J. N. and FORMISANO, M. eds. (2012a), *Perpetua's Passions: Multidisciplinary Approaches to the Passio Perpetuae et Felicitatis* (Oxford).

(2012b), 'Perpetua's passions: a brief introduction', in Bremmer and Formisano (2012a), 1–13.

BRIGGS, W. W. (1983), *Concordantia in Varronis libros De re rustica* (Hildesheim, Zurich and New York).

BRISCOE, J. (1981), *A Commentary on Livy Books XXXIV–XXXVII* (Oxford).

(2008), *A Commentary on Livy Books 38–40* (Oxford).

(2012), *A Commentary on Livy Books 41–45* (Oxford).

BRIX, J. and NIEMEYER, M. (1901a), *Ausgewählte Komödien des T. Maccius Plautus I: Trinummus*, 5th edn (Leipzig and Berlin).

(1901b), *Ausgewählte Komödien des T. Maccius Plautus IV: Miles Gloriosus*, 3rd edn (Leipzig).

(1907), *Ausgewählte Komödien des T. Maccius Plautus III: Menaechmi*, 4th edn (Leipzig).

BROADHEAD, H. D. (1960), *The Persae of Aeschylus* (Cambridge).

BROWN, V. (1970), 'A Latin letter from Oxyrhynchus', *BICS* 17, 136–43.

BUCHHEIT, V. (1962), 'Ludicra Latina', *Hermes* 90, 252–6.

BUCK, C. D. (1904), *A Grammar of Oscan and Umbrian* (Boston).

BULHART, V. (1955), 'Ausdruckweisen für das prädikative Verhältnis im Lateinischen', *WS* 68, 47–64.

(1967), *Gregorii Iliberritani episcopi quae supersunt* (Corpus Christianorum, Series Latina 69) (Turnhout).

BÜLOW-JACOBSEN, A., CUVIGNY, H. and FOURNET, J.-L. (1994), 'The identification of Myos Hormos: new papyrological evidence', *BIFAO* 94, 27–42.

BURIDANT, C. (2000), *Grammaire nouvelle de l'ancien français* (Paris).

BURTON, P. (2000), *The Old Latin Gospels: A Study of their Texts and Language* (Oxford).

(2007), *Language in the Confessions of Augustine* (Oxford).

(2011), 'Christian Latin', in Clackson (2011a), 485–501.

(forthcoming), 'Analytic passives and deponents in classical and late Latin', in Adams and Vincent (forthcoming a).

CABRILLANA, C. (2011), 'Purpose and result clauses', in Baldi and Cuzzolin (2011), 19–92.

CALBOLI, G. (1962), *Studi grammaticali* (Bologna).

ed. (1989), *Subordination and Other Topics in Latin: Proceedings of the Third International Colloquium on Latin Linguistics* (Amsterdam and Philadelphia).

(1993), *Cornifici Rhetorica ad Herennium: introduzione, testo critico, commento*, 2nd edn (Bologna).

(1999), 'Zur Syntax der neuen vulgärlateinischen Urkunden aus Murécine', in Petersmann and Kettemann (1999), 331–44.

(2006), 'Encore une fois sur les tablettes de Murécine', in Arias Abellán (2006), 155–68.

(2009), 'Latin syntax and Greek', in Baldi and Cuzzolin (2009), 65–193.

(2012), 'Syntaxe nominale et subordination en latin tardif', in Biville, Lhommé and Vallat (2012), 439–51.

CALLEBAT, L. ed. (1995), *Latin vulgaire, latin tardif IV: Actes du 4ᵉ colloque international sur le latin vulgaire et tardif, Caen, 2–5 septembre 1994* (Hildesheim, Zurich and New York).

CALLEBAT, L., BOUET, P., FLEURY, P. and ZUINGHEDAU, M. (1984), *Vitruve: De architectura concordance*, 2 vols. (Hildesheim, Zurich and New York).

CALLEBAT, L., GROS, P. and JACQUEMARD, C. (1999), *Vitruve: De l'architecture livre II* (Paris).

CAMODECA, G. (1999), *Tabulae pompeianae Sulpiciorum (TPSulp.): edizione critica dell'archivio puteolano dei Sulpicii*, 2 vols. (Rome).

CAMPANILE, E. (1971), 'Due studi sul latino volgare', *L'Italia dialettale* 34, 1–64 = Campanile (2008), I.337–83.

(2008), *Latina & Italica: scritti minori sulle lingue dell'Italia antica*, 2 vols., edited by P. Poccetti (Pisa and Rome).

CAMPBELL, B. (2000), *The Writings of the Roman Land Surveyors: Introduction, Text, Translation and Commentary* (Journal of Roman Studies Monograph 9) (London).

CAPLAN, H. (1954), *[Cicero]: Ad C. Herennium (Rhetorica ad Herennium)* (Cambridge, MA and London).

CARNOY, C. (1906), *Le latin d'Espagne d'après les inscriptions: étude linguistique*, 2nd edn (Brussels).

CAVALCA, M. G. (2001), *I grecismi nel Satyricon di Petronio* (Bologna).

CÈBE, J.-P. (1998), *Varron: Satires Ménippées XII* (Rome).

(1999), *Varron: Satires Ménippées XIII* (Rome).

CHAHOUD, A. (2010), '*Romani ueteres atque urbani sales*: a note on Cicero *De Oratore* 2.272 and Lucilius 173M', in C. Kraus, J. Marincola and C. Pelling eds., *Ancient Historiography and its Contexts: Studies in Honour of A. J. Woodman* (Oxford), 86–97.

CHAHOUD, A. (forthcoming), 'Verbal mosaics: speech patterns and generic stylisation in Lucilius', in B. W. Breed, R. Wallace, and E. Keitel eds., *Our Lucilius: Satire in Second Century Rome* (in preparation).

CHAMBERLAND, G. (2012), 'La mémoire des spectacles: l'autoreprésentation des donateurs', in *L'organisation des spectacles dans le monde romain* (Fondation Hardt: Entretiens sur l'antiquité classique 58), 261–303.

CHANTRAINE, P. (1963), *Grammaire homérique II: Syntaxe* (Paris).

CHRISTENSON, D. M. (2000), *Plautus: Amphitruo* (Cambridge).

CIGNOLO, C. (2002), *Terentiani Mauri De litteris, De syllabis, De metris*, 2 vols. (Hildesheim, Zurich and New York).

CITRONI, M. (1975), *M. Valerii Martialis Epigrammaton liber primus: introduzione, testo, apparato critico e commento* (Florence).

CLACKSON, J. ed. (2011a), *A Companion to the Latin Language* (Malden, MA, Oxford and Chichester).

(2011b), 'Classical Latin', in Clackson (2011a), 236–56.

CLACKSON J. and HORROCKS, G. (2007), *The Blackwell History of the Latin Language* (Malden, MA, Oxford and Carlton, Vic.).

COLEMAN, K. M. (2006), *M. Valerii Martialis Liber spectaculorum* (Oxford).

(2012), 'Bureaucratic language in the correspondence between Pliny and Trajan', *TAPA* 142, 189–238.

COLEMAN, R. G. G. (1971), 'The monophthongization of /ae/ and the Vulgar Latin vowel system', *TPhS* [no vol. no.] 1971, 175–91.

(1999), 'Poetic diction, poetic discourse and the poetic register', in Adams and Mayer (1999), 21–93.

COLLINGE, N. E. (1985), *The Laws of Indo-European* (Amsterdam and Philadelphia).

COLLINS, R. (1998), 'The "reviser" revisited: another look at the alternative version of the *Annales regni Francorum*', in A. C. Murray ed., *After Rome's Fall: Narrators and Sources of Early Medieval History (Essays Presented to Walter Goffart)* (Toronto), 191–213.

COLSON, F. H. (1924), *M. Fabii Quintiliani Institutionis oratoriae liber I* (Cambridge).

COOPER, F. T. (1895), *Word Formation in the Roman sermo plebeius* (New York).

CORBEILL, A. (1996), *Controlling Laughter: Political Humor in the Late Roman Republic* (Princeton).

CORELL, J. (1993), 'Defixionis tabella aus Carmona (Sevilla)', *ZPE* 95, 261–8.

CORSETTI, P.-P. (1989), 'Un nouveau témoin de l'*Ars ueterinaria* de Pelagonius', *Revue d'histoire des textes* 19, 31–56.

COURTNEY, E. (1993), *The Fragmentary Latin Poets* (Oxford).

(1995), *Musa lapidaria: A Selection of Latin Verse Inscriptions* (Atlanta, GA).

(1999), *Archaic Latin Prose* (Atlanta, GA).

COURTOIS, C., LESCHI, L., PERRAT, C. and SAUMAGNE, C. (1952), *Tablettes Albertini: actes privés de l'époque vandale (fin du Ve siècle)* (Paris).

CRAWFORD, M. H. ed. (1996), *Roman Statutes*, 2 vols. (Bulletin of the Institute of Classical Studies Supplement 64) (London).

CUGUSI, P. (1972–3), 'Le più antiche lettere papiracee latine', *Atti della Accademia delle scienze di Torino: II, Classe di scienze morali, storiche et filologiche* 107, 641–87.

(1981), 'Gli ostraca latini dello Wâdi Fawâkhir: per la storia del latino', in *Letterature comparate, problemi e metodo: studi in onore di Ettore Paratore* (Bologna), 719–53.

(1983), *Evoluzione e forme dell'epistolografia latina nella tarda repubblica e nei primi due secoli dell'impero con cenni sull'epistolografia preciceroniana* (Rome).

(1992), *Corpus epistularum Latinarum papyris tabulis ostracis servatarum*, 2 vols. (Florence).

(2002), *Corpus epistularum Latinarum papyris tabulis ostracis servatarum* III (Florence).

CUOMO, S. (2011), 'A Roman engineer's tales', *JRS* 101, 143–65.

CURBERA, J. B., SIERRA DELAGE, M. and VELÁZQUEZ, I. (1999), 'A bilingual curse tablet from Barchín del Hoyo (Cuenca, Spain)', *ZPE* 125, 279–83.

CUVIGNY, H. (2003), *La route de Myos Hormos: l'armée romaine dans le désert oriental d'Égypte* (Institut français d'archéologie orientale, Fouilles 48/1–2), 2 vols.

CUZZOLIN, P. (1997), 'Quelques remarques syntaxiques à propos de ecce', in García-Hernández (1997), I.261–71.

DAHLÉN, E. (1964), *Études syntaxiques sur les pronoms réfléchis pléonastiques en latin* (Stockholm, Göteborg and Uppsala).

DALBY, A. (1998), *Cato on Farming: De agricultura* (Exeter).

DANCKAERT, L. (forthcoming), 'Variation and change in Latin BE-periphrases: empirical and methodological considerations', in Adams and Vincent (forthcoming a).

DAVIDSON, J. (1997), *Courtesans and Fishcakes: The Consuming Passions of Classical Athens* (London).

DELAMARRE, X. (2003), *Dictionnaire de la langue gauloise*, 2nd edn (Paris).

DE MELO, W. D. C. (2006), 'If in doubt, leave it in', *Oxford University Working Papers in Linguistics, Philology & Phonetics* 11, 1–4.

—— (2007), *The Early Latin Verb System: Archaic Forms in Plautus, Terence, and Beyond* (Oxford).

—— (2010), 'Possessive pronouns in Plautus', in Dickey and Chahoud (2010), 71–99.

—— (2011a), *Plautus* I (Cambridge, MA and London).

—— (2011b), *Plautus* III (Cambridge, MA and London).

—— (2012a), *Plautus* IV (Cambridge, MA and London).

—— (2012b), 'Kuryłowicz's first "law of analogy" and the development of passive periphrases in Latin', in Probert and Willi (2012), 83–101.

DE MEO, C. (1983), *Lingue tecniche del latino* (Bologna).

DE VAAN, M. (2008), *Etymological Dictionary of Latin and the Other Italic Languages* (Leiden and Boston).

DE VOGÜÉ, A. and ANTIN, P. (1978–80), *Grégoire le Grand: Dialogues*, 3 vols. (Paris).

DICKEY, E. (1996), *Greek Forms of Address from Herodotus to Lucian* (Oxford).

—— (2002), *Latin Forms of Address from Plautus to Apuleius* (Oxford).

—— (2006), 'The use of Latin *sis* as a focus-marking clitic particle', *Oxford University Working Papers in Linguistics, Philology & Phonetics* 11, 21–5.

—— (2010), 'The creation of Latin teaching materials in antiquity: a re-interpretation of P. Sorb. inv. 2069', *ZPE* 175, 188–208.

—— (2012), *The Colloquia of the Hermeneumata Pseudodositheana* I: *Colloquia Monacensia-Einsidlensia, Leidense–Stephani, and Stephani* (Cambridge).

—— (2015), *The Colloquia of the Hermeneumata Pseudodositheana* II: *Colloquium Harleianum, Colloquium Montepessulanum, Colloquium Celtis, and Fragments* (Cambridge).

DICKEY, E. and CHAHOUD, A. eds. (2010), *Colloquial and Literary Latin* (Cambridge).

DIEHL, E. (1910), *Vulgärlateinische Inschriften* (Bonn).

DIELS, H. (1899), *Elementum: Eine Vorarbeit zum griechischen und lateinischen Thesaurus* (Leipzig).

DIGGLE, J. and GOODYEAR, F. R. D. eds. (1972), *The Classical Papers of A. E. Housman*, 3 vols. (Cambridge).

DOKKUM, T. (1900), *De constructionis analyticae vice accusativi cum infinitivo fungentis usu apud Augustinum* (Groningen).

DOMERGUE, C. (1983), *La mine antique d'Aljustrel (Portugal) et les tables de bronze de Vipasca* (Paris) (extract from *Conimbriga* 22 [1983], 5–193).

DOVER, K. J. (1968), *Aristophanes: Clouds* (Oxford).

DUMVILLE, D. N. *et al.* (1993), *Saint Patrick, AD 493–1993* (Woodbridge, Suffolk and Rochester, NY).

DUNBABIN, K. M. D. (1978), *The Mosaics of Roman North Africa: Studies in Iconography and Patronage* (Oxford).

(2010), 'The prize table: crowns, wreaths and moneybags in Roman art', in B. Le Guen ed., *L'argent dans les concours du monde grec: Actes du colloque international, Saint-Denis et Paris, 5–6 décembre 2008* (Saint-Denis), 301–45.

DYCK, A. R. (2004), *A Commentary on Cicero, De legibus* (Ann Arbor).

(2008), *Cicero: Catilinarians* (Cambridge).

(2010), *Cicero: Pro Sexto Roscio* (Cambridge).

(2013), *Cicero: Pro Marco Caelio* (Cambridge).

EBELING, H. (1885), *Lexicon Homericum* I (Leipzig).

ECK, W., CABALLOS, A. and FERNÁNDEZ, F. eds. (1996), *Das senatus consultum de Cn. Pisone patre* (Munich).

EKLUND, S. (1970), *The Periphrastic, Completive and Finite Use of the Present Participle in Latin* (Uppsala).

ELCOCK, W. D. (1960), *The Romance Languages* (London).

ERNOUT, A. (1914), *Morphologie historique du latin* (Paris).

(1928), *Les éléments dialectaux du vocabulaire latin*, 2nd edn (Paris).

(1949), *Les adjectifs latins en -ōsus et en -ulentus* (Paris).

(1957a), *Recueil de textes latins archaïques*, 2nd edn (Paris).

(1957b), *Philologica* II (Paris).

ERNOUT, A. and MEILLET, A. (1959), *Dictionnaire étymologique de la langue latine*, 4th edn (Paris).

ERNOUT, A. and THOMAS, F. (1953), *Syntaxe latine*, 2nd edn (Paris).

ÉTAIX, R. (1976), 'Sermon inédit de Saint Augustin sur l'amour des parents', *Revue Bénédictine* 86, 38–48.

EVANS, T. V. and OBBINK, D. D. eds. (2010), *The Language of the Papyri* (Oxford).

EWERT, A. (1943), *The French Language*, 2nd edn (London).

FARRELL, J. and WILLIAMS, C. (2012), 'The Passion of Saints Perpetua and Felicity', in Bremmer and Formisano (2012a), 14–23.

FEDELI, P. (1980), *Sesto Properzio: il primo libro delle Elegie* (Florence).

(2005), *Properzio: Elegie libro II* (ARCA, Classical and Medieval Texts, Papers and Monographs 45).

FELTENIUS, L. (1977), *Intransitivizations in Latin* (Uppsala).

FENSTERBUSCH, C. (1964), *Vitruv: Zehn Bücher über Architektur*, 3rd edn (Darmstadt).

FERRI, R. and PROBERT, P. (2010), 'Roman authors on colloquial language', in Dickey and Chahoud (2010), 12–41.

FISCHER, B. (1977), *Novae concordantiae Bibliorum sacrorum iuxta Vulgatam versionem critice editam*, 5 vols. (Stuttgart).

FISCHER, K.-D. (1980), *Pelagonii Ars veterinaria* (Leipzig).

FLEURY, P. (1990), *Vitruve: De l'architecture livre I* (Paris).

FLOBERT, P. (1975), *Les verbes déponents latins des origines à Charlemagne* (Paris).

(1995a), 'Le latin des tablettes de Murécine (Pompéi)', *REL* 73 (1995), 138–50.

(1995b), 'Traits du latin parlé dans l'épopée: Lucain', in Callebat (1995), 483–9.

(1996), 'Les verbes supports en latin', in A. Bammesberger and F. Heberlein eds., *Akten des VIII. Internationalen Kolloquiums zur lateinischen Linguistik* (Heidelberg), 193–9.

(2003), 'Considérations intempestives sur l'auteur et la date du Satyricon sous Hadrien', in Herman and Rosén (2003), 109–22.

(2011), 'La coriander: du mycénien au latin', *Revue de Philologie* 85, 245–50.

FORDYCE, C. J. (1961), *Catullus: A Commentary* (Oxford).

FORTSON, B. W. (2007), 'The origin of the Latin future active participle', in A. Nussbaum ed., *Verba docenti: Studies in Historical and Indo-European Linguistics Presented to Jay H. Jasanoff by Students, Colleagues, and Friends* (Ann Arbor), 83–95.

FRAENKEL, E. (1951), 'Additional note on the prose of Ennius', *Eranos* 49, 50–6 = Fraenkel (1964), II.53–8.

(1961), 'Two poems of Catullus', *JRS* 51, 46–53 = Fraenkel (1964), II.115–29.

(1964), *Kleine Beiträge zur klassischen Philologie*, 2 vols. (Rome).

(1968), *Leseproben aus Reden Ciceros und Catos* (Rome).

([1922] 2007), *Plautine Elements in Plautus (Plautinisches im Plautus)*, translated by T. Drevikovsky and F. Muecke (Oxford).

FRASER, P. M. and MATTHEWS, E. (1997), *A Lexicon of Greek Personal Names* IIIA (Oxford).

FRUYT, M. (1987), 'Interprétation sémantico-référentielle du réfléchi latin', *Glotta* 65, 204–21.

(2011a), 'Latin vocabulary', in Clackson (2011a), 144–56.

(2011b), 'Grammaticalization in Latin', in Baldi and Cuzzolin (2011), 661–864.

FUNAIOLI, G. (1907), *Grammaticae Romanae fragmenta* (Leipzig).

GAENG, P. A. (1969), 'The extent of Germanic influences on the vocabulary of the so-called *Fredegarius Chronicles*', *Romance Notes* 11, 1–6.

GAERTNER, J. F. (2007), '*Tum* und *tunc* in der augusteischen Dichtersprache', *RhM* 150, 211–24.

GALDI, G. (2004), *Grammatica delle iscrizioni latine dell'impero (province orientali): morfosintassi nominale* (Rome).

(2012), 'Again on *as*-nominatives: a new approach to the problem', in M. Leiwo, H. Halla-aho and M. Vierros eds., *Variation and Change in Greek and Latin* (Helsinki), 139–52.

(2014), 'Some considerations on the apodotic use of *atque* and *et* (2nd c BC–2nd c AD)', *Journal of Latin Linguistics* 1, 63–91.

(2015), 'Some remarks on the language of the *Itinerarium Antonini Placentini*', *Listy filologické* 138, 41–63.

GARCEA, A. (2012), *Caesar's De analogia* (Oxford).

GARCÍA-HERNÁNDEZ, B. ed. (1997), *Estudios de lingüística latina: Actas del IX coloquio internacional de lingüística latina, Universidad Autónoma de Madrid, 14–18 de abril 1997*, 2 vols. (Madrid).

GARCÍA LEAL, A. (2008), 'El orden de palabras en las pizarras visigóticas', in Wright (2008), 453–62.

GERBER, A. and GREEF, A. (1877–90), *Lexicon Taciteum*, 2 vols. (Leipzig).

GEYER, P. (1898), *Itineraria Hierosolymitana saeculi IIII–VIII* (CSEL 39) (Prague, Vienna and Leipzig).

GIBSON, R. K. (2003), *Ovid: Ars amatoria Book 3* (Cambridge).

GIGNAC, F. T. (1976), *A Grammar of the Greek Papyri of the Roman and Byzantine Periods* I: *Phonology* (Milan).

(1981), *A Grammar of the Greek Papyri of the Roman and Byzantine Periods* II: *Morphology* (Milan).

GILDERSLEEVE, B. L. and LODGE, G. (1895), *Gildersleeve's Latin Grammar*, 3rd edn (London).

GONZÁLEZ, J. (1986), 'The *Lex Irnitana*: a new Flavian municipal law', *JRS* 76, 147–243.

GOODWIN, W. W. (1898), *Syntax of the Moods and Tenses of the Greek Verb*, 8th edn (London, Melbourne and Toronto).

GOODYEAR, F. R. D. (1972), *The Annals of Tacitus* I: *Annals 1.1–54* (Cambridge).

GORDON, A. E., GORDON, J. S., JANSEN, U. and KRUMMREY, H. (2006), *Corpus Inscriptionum Latinarum* VI.6: *Fasciculus tertius, grammatica quaedam errores-que quadratarii et alias rationes scribendi notabiliores* (Berlin and New York).

GORDON, R. L. and SIMÓN, F. M. eds. (2010), *Magical Practice in the Latin West: Papers from the International Conference held at the University of Zaragoza 30 Sept.–1 Oct. 2005* (Leiden and Boston).

GOUGENHEIM, G. (1929), *Étude sur les périphrases verbales de la langue française* (Paris).

GOUJARD, R. (1975), *Caton: De l'agriculture* (Paris).

GOWERS, E. (2012), *Horace: Satires Book I* (Cambridge).

GRATWICK, A. S. (1982), 'Latinitas Britannica: was British Latin archaic?', in N. Brooks ed., *Latin and the Vernacular Languages in Early Medieval Britain* (Leicester), 1–79.

(1993), *Plautus: Menaechmi* (Cambridge).

(2002), 'A matter of substance: Cato's preface to the *De agri cultura*', *Mnem.* 55, 41–72.

GRAY, C. (2015), *Jerome, Vita Malchi: Introduction, Text, Translation, and Commentary* (Oxford).

GREENE, D. (1968), 'Some linguistic evidence relating to the British Church', in M. W. Barley and R. P. C. Hanson eds., *Christianity in Britain, 300–700* (Leicester), 75–86.

GREIMAS, A. J. (1968), *Dictionnaire de l'ancien français jusqu'au milieu du XIVe siècle*, 2nd edn (Paris).

GREVANDER, S. (1926), *Untersuchungen zur Sprache der Mulomedicina Chironis* (Lund and Leipzig).

GRIFFIN, M. (1976), *Seneca: A Philosopher in Politics* (Oxford).

GROCOCK, C. and GRAINGER, S. (2006), *Apicius: A Critical Edition with an Introduction and an English Translation of the Latin Recipe Text 'Apicius'* (Blackawton, Totnes).

HAAG, O. (1899), 'Die Latinität Fredegars', *RF* 10, 835–932.

HABERMAHL, P. (2006), *Petronius, Satyrica 79–141: Ein philologisch-literarischer Kommentar* I: *Sat. 79–110* (Berlin and New York).

HADAS, M. (1929), 'Oriental elements in Petronius', *AJP* 50, 378–85.

HAFFTER, H. (1934), *Untersuchungen zur altlateinischen Dichtersprache* (Berlin).

HAHN, E. A. (1953), 'Vestiges of partitive apposition in Latin syntax', *TAPA* 84, 92–123.

HALL, F. W. (1923), 'On Plautus, *Miles Gloriosus* 18', *CQ* 17, 100–2.

HALLA-AHO, H. (2003), 'Scribes and the letters of Claudius Terentianus', in H. Solin, M. Leiwo and H. Halla-aho eds., *Latin vulgaire – latin tardif VI: Actes du VIe colloque international sur le latin vulgaire et tardif, Helsinki, 29 août – 2 septembre 2000* (Hildesheim, Zurich and New York), 245–52.

(2009), *The Non-Literary Latin Letters: A Study of their Syntax and Pragmatics* (Helsinki).

(2010), 'Requesting in a letter: context, syntax and the choice between complements in the letters of Cicero and Pliny the Younger', *TPhS* 108, 232–47.

(2012), 'A historical perspective on Latin proleptic accusatives', *De lingua Latina* 7 (Revue de linguistique latine du Centre Alfred Ernout, Université Paris-Sorbonne) (available at: www.paris-sorbonne.fr/rubrique2315).

(2013), 'Bilingualism in action: observations on document type, language choice and Greek interference in Latin documents and letters on papyri', in M.-H. Marganne and B. Rochette eds., *Bilinguisme et digraphisme gréco-romain: l'apport des papyrus latins* (Actes de la Table Ronde internationale, Liège, 12–13 mai 2011), 169–81.

(forthcoming), 'Left-detached constructions from early to late Latin (nominatiuus pendens and attractio inuersa)', in Adams and Vincent (forthcoming a).

HALLA-AHO, H. and KRUSCHWITZ, P. (2010), 'Colloquial and literary language in early Roman tragedy', in Dickey and Chahoud (2010), 127–53.

HALLÉN, M. (1941), *In Scriptores historiae Augustae studia: commentatio academica* (Uppsala).

HALLETT, J. P. (1977), 'Perusinae glandes and the changing image of Augustus', AJAH 2, 151–71.

HALPHEN, L. (1967), Éginhard: Vie de Charlemagne, 4th edn (Paris).

HANSON, R. P. C. (1968), Saint Patrick: His Origins and Career (Oxford).

(1978), Saint Patrick: Confession et Lettre à Coroticus, with the collaboration of C. Blanc (Paris).

HANSSEN, J. S. T. (1951), Latin Diminutives: A Semantic Study (Bergen).

HARRIS, M. (1978), The Evolution of French Syntax: A Comparative Approach (London and New York).

(1988), 'French', in Harris and Vincent (1988), 209–45.

HARRIS, M. and VINCENT, N. eds. (1988), The Romance Languages (London).

HARTEL, W. (1886), 'Lucifer von Cagliari und sein Latein', ALL 3, 1–58.

HASSALL, M. W. C. and TOMLIN, R. S. O. (1984), 'Inscriptions', Britannia 15, 333–56.

(1987), 'Inscriptions', Britannia 18, 360–77.

(1989), 'Inscriptions', Britannia 20, 327–45.

(1992), 'Inscriptions', Britannia 23, 309–23.

(1993), 'Inscriptions', Britannia 24, 310–22.

(1994), 'Inscriptions', Britannia 25, 293–14.

(1996), 'Inscriptions', Britannia 27, 439–57.

(1999), 'Inscriptions', Britannia 30, 375–86.

HAVERLING, G. V. M. (2010), 'Actionality, tense, and viewpoint', in Baldi and Cuzzolin (2010), 277–523.

(2012), 'Latin tardif littéraire et latin tardif parlé', in Biville, Lhommé and Vallat (2012), 91–102.

ed. (2015), Latin Linguistics in the Early 21st Century: Acts of the 16th International Colloquium on Latin Linguistics, Uppsala, June 6th–11th, 2011 (Uppsala).

HAVERS, W. (1928), 'Zur Syntax des Nominativs', Glotta 16, 94–127.

HEADLAM, W. and KNOX, A. D. (1922), Herodas: The Mimes and Fragments (Cambridge).

HEFFERNAN, T. J. (2012), The Passion of Perpetua and Felicity (New York).

HEIDEMANN, A. (1893), De Ciceronis in epistulis verborum ellipsis usu (Berlin).

HERAEUS, K. (1929), Cornelii Taciti Historiarum libri qui supersunt I: Buch I und II, 6th edn revised by W. Heraeus (Leipzig and Berlin).

HERAEUS, W. (1900), 'Die Appendix Probi', ALL 11, 301–31.

(1937), Kleine Schriften, edited by J. B. Hofmann (Heidelberg).

HERMAN, J. (1957), 'Cur, quare, quomodo: remarques sur l'évolution des particules d'interrogation en latin vulgaire', Acta Antiqua Academiae Scientiarum Hungaricae 5, 369–77 = Herman (1990), 289–97.

(1963), La formation du système roman des conjonctions de subordination (Berlin).

(1989), 'Accusativus cum infinitivo et subordonée à quod, quia en latin tardif: nouvelles remarques sur un vieux problème', in Calboli (1989), 133–52 = Herman (2006), 43–54.

(1990), Du latin aux langues romanes: études de linguistique historique (Tübingen).

ed. (1994), *Linguistic Studies on Latin: Selected Papers from the 6th International Colloquium on Latin Linguistics, Budapest, 23–27 March 1991* (Amsterdam and Philadelphia).

(1995), 'Les ardoises wisigothiques et le problème de la différenciation territoriale du latin', in Callebat (1995), 63–76.

(1996), 'À propos du si interrogatif: évolutions achevées et évolutions bloquées', in Bammesberger and Heberlein (1996), 296–307 = Herman (2006), 65–75.

(1997), 'À propos du débat sur le pluriel des noms italiens (et roumains): à la recherche d'une conclusion', in G. Holtus, J. Kramer and W. Schweickard eds., *Italica et Romanica: Festschrift für Max Pfister zum 65. Geburtstag* (Tübingen), 19–30.

(2006), *Du latin aux langues romanes II: nouvelles études de linguistique historique* (Tübingen).

HERMAN, J. and ROSÉN, H. eds. (2003), *Petroniana: Gedenkschrift für Hubert Petersmann* (Heidelberg).

HINAND, F. and DUMONT, J. C. (2003), *Libitina: pompes funèbres et supplices en Campanie à l'époque d'Auguste* (Paris).

HINE, H. M. (2011), '"Discite . . . agricolae": modes of instruction in Latin prose agricultural writing from Cato to Pliny the Elder', *CQ* 61, 624–54.

HOFMANN, J. B. (1924), 'Syntaktische Gliederungsverschiebungen im Lateinischen infolge Erstarrung ursprünglich appositioneller Verhältnisse', *IF* 42, 75–87.

(1951), *Lateinische Umgangssprache*, 3rd edn (Heidelberg).

HOFMANN, J. B. and RICOTTILLI, L. (2003), *La lingua d'uso latina*, 3rd edn (translation with supplements of Hofmann 1951 by L. Ricottilli) (Bologna).

HOFMANN, J. B. and SZANTYR, A. (1965), *Lateinische Syntax und Stilistik* (Munich).

HOLFORD-STREVENS, L. (2010), 'Current and ancient colloquial in Gellius', in Dickey and Chahoud (2010), 331–8.

HOPPE, H. (1903), *Syntax und Stil des Tertullian* (Leipzig).

HORROCKS, G. C. (2010), *Greek: A History of the Language and its Speakers*, 2nd edn (Malden, MA, Oxford and Chichester).

HORSFALL, N. (2000), *Virgil, Aeneid 7: A Commentary* (Leiden, Boston and Cologne).

(2003), *Virgil, Aeneid 11: A Commentary* (Leiden and Boston).

(2006), *Virgil, Aeneid 3: A Commentary* (Leiden and Boston).

(2008), *Virgil, Aeneid 2: A Commentary* (Leiden and Boston).

HOUSMAN, A. E. (1931), 'Praefanda', *Hermes* 66, 402–12.

IHM, M. (1892), *Pelagonii Artis veterinariae quae extant* (Leipzig).

ILIESCU, M. and MARXGUT, W. eds. (1992), *Latin vulgaire – latin tardif III: Actes du IIIème colloque international sur le latin vulgaire et tardif, Innsbruck, 2–5 septembre 1991* (Tübingen).

ILIESCU, M. and SLUSANSKI, D. eds. (1991), *Du latin aux langues romanes: choix de textes traduits et commentés (du IIe siècle avant J.C. jusqu'au Xe siècle après J.C.)* (Wilhelmsfeld).

JACKSON, K. H. (1953), *Language and History in Early Britain: A Chronological Survey of the Brittonic Languages, 1st to 12th c. AD* (Dublin).

JANNARIS, A. N. (1897), *An Historical Greek Grammar Chiefly of the Attic Dialect* (London).

JEANNERET, M. (1918), *La langue des tablettes d'exécration latines* (Paris and Neuchâtel).

JOCELYN, H. D. (1967), *The Tragedies of Ennius* (Cambridge).

(1999), 'Catullus, Mamurra and Romulus cinaedus', *Sileno* 25, 97–113.

JOHANSEN, H. F. and WHITTLE, E. W. (1980), *Aeschylus: The Suppliants*, 3 vols. (Copenhagen).

JONES, M. A. (1988), 'Sardinian', in Harris and Vincent (1988), 314–50.

JOSEPHSON, Å. (1940), *Casae litterarum: Studien zum Corpus agrimensorum Romanorum* (Uppsala).

JUNKELMANN, M. (2008), *Gladiatoren: Das Spiel mit dem Tod* (Mainz am Rhein).

KAHLE, W. (1918), *De vocabulis Graecis Plauti aetate in sermonem Latinum receptis* (Münster).

KAJAVA, M. (1994), *Roman Female Praenomina: Studies in the Nomenclature of Roman Women* (Rome).

KASTER, R. A. (2006), *Marcus Tullius Cicero: Speech on Behalf of Publius Sestius* (Oxford).

KAY, N. M. (1985), *Martial Book XI: A Commentary* (London).

(2010), 'Colloquial Latin in Martial's epigrams', in Dickey and Chahoud (2010), 318–30.

KENNEY, E. J. (1996), *Ovid: Heroides XVI–XXI* (Cambridge).

KISS, S. (1972), *Les transformations de la structure syllabique en latin tardif* (Debrecen).

(1982), *Tendances évolutives de la syntaxe verbale en latin tardif* (Debrecen).

KISS, S., MONDIN, L. and SALVI, G. eds. (2005), *Latin et langues romanes: études de linguistique offertes à József Herman à l'occasion de son 80ème anniversaire* (Tübingen).

KIßEL, W. (1990), *Aules Persius Flaccus: Satiren* (Heidelberg).

KLEIN, H.-W. (1968), *Die Reichenauer Glossen I: Einleitung, Text, vollständiger Index und Konkordanzen* (Munich).

KOEHLER, L. and BAUMGARTNER, W. W. (2001), *The Hebrew and Aramaic Lexicon of the Old Testament*, revised by W. W. Baumgartner and J. J. Stamm, translated and edited by M. E. J. Richardson (Leiden).

KÖHM, J. (1905), *Altlateinische Forschungen* (Leipzig).

KORTEKAAS, G. A. A. (1984), *Historia Apollonii regis Tyri: Prolegomena, Text Edition of the Two Principal Latin Recensions, Bibliography, Indices and Appendices* (Groningen).

(2007), *Commentary on the Historia Apollonii regis Tyri* (Leiden and Boston).

KOZIOL, H. (1872), *Der Stil des L. Apuleius: Ein Beitrag* (Vienna).

KRAMER, J. (1976), *Literarische Quellen zur Aussprache des Vulgärlateins* (Meisenheim am Glan).

(2001), *Glossaria bilinguia altera (C. Gloss. Biling. II)* (Munich and Leipzig).

(2007), *Vulgärlateinische Alltagsdokumente auf Papyri, Ostraka, Täfelchen und Inschriften* (Berlin and New York).

KREBS, J. P. and SCHMALZ, J. H. (1905), *Antibarbarus der lateinischen Sprache*, 2 vols. (Basel).

KROHN, F. (1912), *Vitruvii De architectura libri decem* (Leipzig).

KROLL, W. (1915), 'Literaturbericht für das Jahr 1912', *Glotta* 6, 348–80.

(1929), *C. Valerius Catullus*, 2nd edn, 1st edn 1922, reprinted with addenda 1968 (Stuttgart).

KROON, C. (1995), *Discourse Particles in Latin: A Study of nam, enim, autem, vero and at* (Amsterdam).

KROPP, A. (2008a), *Defixiones: Ein aktuelles Corpus lateinischer Fluchtafeln* (Speyer).

(2008b), *Magische Sprachverwendung in vulgärlateinischen Fluchtafeln (defixiones)* (Tübingen).

KROSTENKO, B. A. (2001), *Cicero, Catullus, and the Language of Social Performance* (Chicago and London).

KÜBLER, B. (1893), 'Die lateinische Sprache auf afrikanischen Inschriften', *ALL* 8, 161–202.

KUHN, C. T. (2012), 'Emotionality in the political culture of the Graeco-Roman East: the role of acclamations', in A. Chaniotis ed., *Unveiling Emotions: Methods for the Study of Emotions in the Greek World* (Stuttgart), 295–312.

KÜHNER, R. and GERTH, B. (1898–1904), *Ausführliche Grammatik der griechischen Sprache* II: *Satzlehre*, 3rd edn, 2 vols. (Hanover and Leipzig).

KÜHNER, R. and STEGMANN, C. (1955), *Ausführliche Grammatik der lateinischen Sprache: Satzlehre*, 3rd edn revised by A. Thierfelder, 2 vols. (Leverkusen).

KURZE, F. (1895), *Annales regni Francorum inde ab a. 741. usque ad a. 829* (Scriptores rerum Germanicarum in usum scholarum ex Monumentis Germaniae Historicis separatim editi) (Hanover).

LAES, C. (2003), 'Desperately different? *Delicia* children in the Roman household', in D. L. Balch and C. Osiek, *Early Christian Families in Context: An Interdisciplinary Dialogue* (Grand Rapids, MI and Cambridge, UK), 298–324.

LANDGRAF, G. (1898), 'Nugas = nugax', *ALL* 10, 225–8.

(1914), *Kommentar zu Ciceros Rede Pro Sex. Roscio Amerino*, 2nd edn (Leipzig and Berlin).

LANDI, A. (1983), *Il contributo dell'archivio puteolano dei Sulpicii alla conoscenza del 'latino volgare'* (Naples).

LANGSLOW, D. R. (2000), *Medical Latin in the Roman Empire* (Oxford).

(2005), '"Langues réduites au lexique"? The languages of Latin technical prose', in Reinhardt, Lapidge and Adams (2005), 287–302.

(2006), *The Latin Alexander Trallianus: The Text and Transmission of a Late Latin Medical Book* (Journal of Roman Studies Monograph 10) (London).

ed. (2009), *Jacob Wackernagel: Lectures on Syntax, with Special Reference to Greek, Latin, and Germanic*, edited with notes and bibliography by D. R. Langslow (Oxford).

LAPORTE, J.-P. (1994), 'Notes sur l'aqueduc de Saldae (Boujie)', *L'Africa Romana* 11, 711–62.

LAUGHTON, E. (1951), 'The prose of Ennius', *Eranos* 49, 35–49.

(1960), 'Observations on the style of Varro', *CQ* 10, 1–28.

(1964), *The Participle in Cicero* (Oxford).

LAURAND, L. (1936–8), *Études sur le style des discours de Cicéron*, 3 vols. (Paris).

LAZZERONI, R. (1962), 'Le più antiche attestazioni del nom. pl. -ās in latino e la provenienza dei Coloni pesaresi', *SSL* 2, 106–22.

LEBEK, W. D. (1970), *Verba prisca: Die Anfänge des Archaisierens in der lateinischen Beredsamkeit und Geschichtsschreibung* (Göttingen).

LEDGEWAY, A. (2011), 'Syntactic and morphosyntactic typology and change', in Maiden, Smith and Ledgeway (2011), 382–471.

LEEMAN, A. D. (1963), *Orationis ratio: The Stylistic Theories and Practice of the Roman Orators, Historians and Philosophers*, 2 vols. (Amsterdam).

LEEMAN, A. D., PINKSTER, H. and RABBIE, E. (1989), *M. Tullius Cicero, De oratore libri III III: Buch II, 99–290* (Heidelberg).

LEHMANN, C. (1988), 'On the Latin of Claudius Terentianus (P. Mich. VIII, 467–472)', *Cuadernos de Filología Clásica* 21, 11–23.

LEIWO, M. (2010a), 'Petronius' linguistic resources', in Dickey and Chahoud (2010), 281–91.

(2010b), 'Imperatives and other directives in the Greek letters from Mons Claudianus', in Evans and Obbink (2010), 97–119.

LEUMANN, M. (1921), 'Part. perf. pass. mit *fui* im späteren Latein', *Glotta* 11, 192–4.

(1959), *Kleine Schriften* (Zurich).

(1977), *Lateinische Laut- und Formenlehre*, 6th edn (Munich).

LEWIS, M. J. T. (2001), *Surveying Instruments of Greece and Rome* (Cambridge).

LIECHTENHAN, E. (1963), *Anthimi De obseruatione ciborum ad Theodoricum regem Francorum epistula* (Berlin).

LINDE, P. (1923), 'Die Stellung des Verbs in der lateinischen Prosa', *Glotta* 12, 153–78.

LINDERBAUER, B. (1922), *S. Benedicti Regula monachorum* (Metten).

LINDHOLM, E. (1931), *Stilistische Studien: Zur Erweiterung der Satzglieder im Lateinischen* (Lund).

LINDSAY, W. M. (1900), *The Captivi of Plautus* (London).

(1907), *Syntax of Plautus* (Oxford).

(1922), *Early Latin Verse* (Oxford).

LINTOTT, A. W. (1968), *Violence in Republican Rome* (Oxford).

LLOYD, P. M. (1987), *From Latin to Spanish* I: *Historical Phonology and Morphology of the Spanish Language* (Memoirs of the American Philosophical Society 173) (Philadelphia).

LODGE, G. (1924–33), *Lexicon Plautinum*, 2 vols. (Leipzig).

LÖFSTEDT, B. (1961), *Studien über die Sprache der langobardischen Gesetze: Beiträge zur frühmittelalterlichen Latinität* (Uppsala).

(1976), 'Zum spanischen Mittellatein', *Glotta* 54, 117–57 = B. Löfstedt (2000), 169–211.

(1983), 'Rückschau und Ausblick auf die vulgärlateinische Forschung: Quellen und Methoden', *ANRW* 29.1 (1983), 453–79.

(2000), *Ausgewählte Aufsätze zur lateinischen Sprachgeschichte und Philologie*, edited by W. Berschin (Stuttgart).

LÖFSTEDT, E. (1907), *Beiträge zur Kenntnis der späteren Latinität* (Stockholm).

(1911), *Philologischer Kommentar zur Peregrinatio Aetheriae* (Uppsala).

(1936), *Vermischte Studien zur lateinischen Sprachkunde und Syntax* (Lund).

(1950), *Coniectanea: Untersuchungen auf dem Gebiete der antiken und mittelalterlichen Latinität* (Uppsala and Stockholm).

(1956), *Syntactica: Studien und Beiträge zur historischen Syntax des Lateins* I, 2nd edn, II (Lund).

(1959), *Late Latin* (Oslo).

LÖFSTEDT, L. (1966), *Les expressions du commandement et de la défense en latin et leur survie dans les langues romanes* (Helsinki).

LÓPEZ EIRE, A. (1996), *La lengua coloquial de la comedia aristofánica* (Mercia).

LOPORCARO, M. (2011), 'Phonological processes', in Maiden, Smith and Ledgeway (2011), 109–54.

LORENZ, A. O. F. (1869), *Ausgewählte Komödien des T. Maccius Plautus III: Miles Gloriosus* (Berlin).

LUMPE, A. (1959), 'Elementum', *RAC* IV, 1073–1100.

LUNDSTRÖM, S. (1943), *Neue Studien zur lateinischen Irenäusübersetzung* (Lund).

(1948), *Studien zur lateinischen Irenäusübersetzung* (Lund).

MacCARY, W. T. and WILLCOCK, M. M. (1976), *Plautus: Casina* (Cambridge).

McGINN, T. A. J. (1998), *Prostitution, Sexuality and the Law in Ancient Rome* (Oxford).

McGLYNN, P. (1963–7), *Lexicon Terentianum*, 2 vols. (London and Glasgow).

McKITTERICK, R. (1983), *The Frankish Kingdoms under the Carolingians, 751–987* (London and New York).

McLACHLAN, K. (2012), *Verborum ordo – ordo verborum: The Placement of the Dependent Genitive in Classical Latin* (DPhil thesis, University of Oxford).

MAIDEN, M. (1995), *A Linguistic History of Italian* (London and New York).

(2011), 'Morphological persistence', in Maiden, Smith and Ledgeway (2011), 155–215.

MAIDEN, M., SMITH, J. C. and LEDGEWAY, A. eds. (2011), *The Cambridge History of the Romance Languages* I: *Structures* (Cambridge).

MALCOVATI, H. (1948), *Imperatoris Caesaris Augusti operum fragmenta* (Turin).

MALLINSON, G. (1988), 'Rumanian', in Harris and Vincent (1988), 391–419.

MALTBY, R. (forthcoming), 'Analytic and synthetic forms of the comparative and superlative from early to late Latin', in Adams and Vincent (forthcoming a).

MANESSY-GUITTON, J. (1964), '*Facinus* et les substantifs neutres latins en *-nus*', *RPh* 38, 48–58.

MARICHAL, R. (1988), *Les graffites de La Graufesenque* (Paris).

MARINI, A. (1836), *Vitruvii De architectura libri decem* (Rome).

MARINI, E. (2015), 'Les verbes à incorporation de l'objet en latin: essai d'aperçu typologique', in Haverling (2015), 117–32.

MARMORALE, E. V. (1961), *Petronii Arbitri Cena Trimalchionis: testo critico et commento*, 2nd edn (Florence).

MAROTTA D'AGATA, A. R. (1980), *Decreta Pisana (CIL XI, 1420–21)* (Pisa).

MAROUZEAU, J. (1910), *L'emploi du participe présent à l'époque républicaine* (Paris).

(1921), 'Pour mieux comprendre les textes latins: essai sur la distinction des styles', *REL* 45, 149–93.

(1949a), *Quelques aspects de la formation du latin littéraire* (Paris).

(1949b), *L'ordre des mots dans la phrase latine* III: *Les articulations de l'énoncé* (Paris).

(1962), *Traité de stylistique latine*, 4th edn (Paris).

MARSHALL, P. K. (1985), *Cornelii Nepotis Vitae cum fragmentis* (Leipzig).

MARTIN, R. H. (1976), *Terence: Adelphoe* (Cambridge).

MAUERSBERGER, A. (1975), *Polybios-Lexikon* I.4 (Berlin).

MAZZARINO, A. (1982), *M. Porci Catonis De agri cultura ad fidem Florentini codicis deperditi*, 2nd edn (Leipzig).

MEADER, C. L. and WÖLFFLIN, E. (1902), 'Zur Geschichte der Pronomina demonstrativa II', *ALL* 12, 239–54.

MEISER, G. (1998), *Historische Laut- und Formenlehre der lateinischen Sprache* (Darmstadt).

MENÉNDEZ PIDAL, R. (1944), *Cantar de Mio Cid: texto, gramática y vocabulario. Primera parte: crítica de texto – grámatica* (Madrid).

MERGUET, H. (1892), *Lexikon zu den Schriften Ciceros*, second part: *Lexikon zu den philosophischen Schriften* II (Jena).

MIHĂESCU, H. (1978), *La langue latine dans le sud-est de l'Europe* (Bucarest and Paris).

MILANI, C. (1974a), 'Aspetti fonetici del ms. Sang. 133 (*Itinerarium Antonini Placentini*)', *Rendiconti dell'Istituto Lombardo* 108, 335–59.

(1974b), 'Problemi di morfologia e sintassi nell'*Itinerarium Antonini Placentini* (ms. Sang. 133 e ms. Rhen. 73)', *Rendiconti dell'Istituto Lombardo* 108, 360–416.

(1977), *Itinerarium Antonini Placentini: un viaggio in Terra Santa del 560–570 d.C.* (Milan).

MOHRMANN, C. (1961a), *The Latin of Saint Patrick: Four Lectures* (Dublin).

(1961b), *Études sur le latin des Chrétiens* II: *Latin chrétien et médiéval* (Rome).

(1965), *Études sur le latin des Chrétiens* III: *Latin chrétien et liturgique* (Rome).

MOREDA, S. L. (1987), *Los grupos lexemíticos de 'facio' y 'ago' en el latín arcaico y clásico: estudio estructural* (León).

MORGAN, M. H. (1906), 'On the language of Vitruvius', *Proceedings of the American Academy of Arts and Sciences* 41, 467–502.

MORITZ, L. A. (1958), *Grain-Mills and Flour in Classical Antiquity* (Oxford).

MØRLAND, H. (1932), *Die lateinischen Oribasiusübersetzungen* (Oslo).

MOUSSY, C. (1964), '*Grātus* et *iūcundus*', *REL* 42, 389–400.

MULLEN, A. (2013), 'New thoughts on British Latin: a curse tablet from Red Hill, Ratcliffe-on-Soar (Nottinghamshire)', *ZPE* 187, 266–72.

MÜLLER, C. F. W. (1895), 'Zu Caesars Bellum civile', in *Festschrift zum fünfzigjährigen Doctorjubiläum Ludwig Friedlaender* (Leipzig), 543–54.

(1908), *Syntax des Nominativus und Akkusativus im Lateinischen* (Leipzig and Berlin).

MULLER, H. F. and TAYLOR, P. eds. (1932), *A Chrestomathy of Vulgar Latin* (Boston).

MUNRO, H. A. J. (1886), *T. Lucreti Cari De rerum natura libri sex*, 4th edn, 3 vols. (London).

MUSURILLO, H. (1972), *The Acts of the Christian Martyrs* (Oxford).

MYNORS, R. A. B. (1990), *Virgil: Georgics* (Oxford).

NASH-WILLIAMS, V. E. (1950), *The Early Christian Monuments of Wales* (Cardiff).

NÉMETH, G. and BOUNEGRU, G. V. (2013), 'Cursing the nomen', *ZPE* 184, 238–42.

NEUE, F. and WAGENER, C. (1892–1905), *Formenlehre der lateinischen Sprache*, 4 vols. (Berlin and Leipzig).

NEUMANN, G. (1980), '*Lupatria* in Petron c. 37, 6 und das Problem der hybriden Bildungen', *WJA* 6a: 173–80.

NIERMEYER, J. F. (1976), *Mediae Latinitatis lexicon minus* (Leiden).

NISBET, R. G. M. and HUBBARD, M. (1978), *A Commentary on Horace Odes Book II* (Oxford).

NORBERG, D. (1943), *Syntaktische Forschungen auf dem Gebiete des Spätlateins und des frühen Mittellateins* (Uppsala).

(1944), *Beiträge zur spätlateinischen Syntax* (Uppsala).

(1945), '"Faire faire quelque chose à quelqu'un": recherches sur l'origine latine de la construction romane', *Uppsala Universitets Årsskrift* 12, 65–106.

(1956), 'Contributions à l'étude du latin vulgaire', in *Hommages à Max Niedermann* (Collection Latomus 23) (Brussels), 251–7.

NORDEN, E. (1956), *Agnostos Theos: Untersuchungen zur Formengeschichte religiöser Rede* (Stuttgart).

(1958), *Die antike Kunstprosa vom VI. Jahrhundert v. Chr. bis in die Zeit der Renaissance*, 5th edn, 2 vols. (Stuttgart).

NUTI, A. (2015), 'The syntax-semantics interplay of *stare* in late Latin and phenomena of functional differentiation of stative verbs in Romance', in Haverling (2015), 530–41.

OAKLEY, S. P. (1997), *A Commentary on Livy Books VI–X I: Introduction and Book VI* (Oxford).

(1998), *A Commentary on Livy Books VI–X II: Books VII–VIII* (Oxford).

(2005), *A Commentary on Livy Books VI–X IV: Book X* (Oxford).

ODELSTIERNA, I. (1926), *De vi futurali ac finali gerundii et gerundivi Latini observationes* (Uppsala).

ODER, E. (1901), *Claudii Hermeri Mulomedicina Chironis* (Leipzig).

OGILVIE, R. M. (1965), *A Commentary on Livy Books 1–5* (Oxford).

OLSON, S. D. (1998), *Aristophanes: Peace* (Oxford).

(2002), *Aristophanes: Acharnians* (Oxford).

ONIGA, R. (1985), 'Il canticum di Sosia: forme stilistiche e modelli culturali', *MD* 14, 113–208.

ÖNNERFORS, A. (1956), *In Plinii maioris Naturalem historiam studia grammatica semantica critica* (Uppsala).

(1963), *In Medicinam Plinii studia philologica* (Lund).

(1975), *Physica Plinii Bambergensis (Cod. Bamb. Med. 2, fol. 93ᵛ - 232ʳ)* (Hildesheim and New York).

OPELT, I. (1965), *Die lateinischen Schimpfwörter und verwandte Erscheinungen: Eine Typologie* (Heidelberg).

OTTO, A. (1890), *Die Sprichwörter und sprichwörtlichen Redensarten der Römer* (Leipzig).

PANAYOTAKIS, C. (2010), *Decimus Laberius: The Fragments* (Cambridge).

PANAYOTAKIS, S. (2012), *The Story of Apollonius King of Tyre: A Commentary* (Berlin and Boston).

PARRY, M. M. (1991), 'Le système démonstratif du cairese', in D. Kremer ed., *Actes du XVIIIᵉ congrès international de linguistique et de philologie romanes, Université de Trèves (Trier) 1986* (Tübingen), 625–31.

PEASE, A. S. (1955), *M. Tulli Ciceronis De natura deorum libri III: Liber primus* (Cambridge, MA).

(1958), *M. Tulli Ciceronis De natura deorum libri III: Libri secundus et tertius* (Cambridge, MA).

(1963), *M. Tulli Ciceronis De divinatione libri duo* (Darmstadt) (reprint: originally published in two volumes with different pagination in *University of Illinois Studies in Language and Literature* [6], 1920 and [8], 1923).

PEI, M. A. (1932), *The Language of the Eight[sic]-Century Texts in Northern France: A Study of the Original Documents in the Collection of Tardif and Other Sources* (New York).

PENNEY, J. H. W. (1999), 'Archaism and innovation in Latin poetic syntax', in Adams and Mayer (1999), 249–68.

(2005), 'Connections in archaic Latin prose', in Reinhardt, Lapidge and Adams (2005), 37–51.

PENNY, R. (2002), *A History of the Spanish Language*, 2nd edn (Cambridge).

PENZIG, O. (1927), *Flora popolare italiana: raccolta dei nomi dialettali delle principali piante indigene e coltivate in Italia* I (Genoa).

PERDICOYIANNI-PALÉOLOGOU, H. (2006), 'Les emplois de *ecce, eccum, eccistum, eccillum* chez Plaute', *Faventia* 28, 41–52.

PEROCHAT, P. (1939), *Pétrone, Le festin de Trimalcion: commentaire exégétique et critique* (Paris).

PERROT, J. (1961), *Les dérivés latins en -men et -mentum* (Paris).

PETER, H. (1906), *Historicorum Romanorum reliquiae* II (Stuttgart).

PETERSEN, W. (1910), *Greek Diminutives in -ION* (Weimar).

PETERSMANN, H. (1973), 'Zu Cato de agr. 134, 1 und den frühesten Zeugnissen für den Ersatz des Nominativus pluralis von Substantiven der 1. Deklination durch Formen auf -as', WS 86, 75–90.

(1977), Petrons urbane Prosa: Untersuchungen zu Sprache und Text (Syntax) (Vienna).

(1992), 'Zu den neuen vulgärlateinischen Sprachdenkmälern aus dem römischen Britannien: Die Täfelchen von Vindolanda', in Iliescu and Marxgut (1992), 283–91.

(1995), 'Soziale und lokale Aspekte in der Vulgärsprache Petrons', in Callebat (1995), 533–47.

(2002–3), 'Bedeutung und Gebrauch von lateinisch fui: eine soziolinguistische Analyse', Die Sprache 43, 94–103.

PETERSMANN, H. and KETTEMANN, R. eds. (1999), Latin vulgaire – latin tardif V: Actes du Vᵉ colloque international sur le latin vulgaire et tardif, Heidelberg, 5–8 septembre 1997 (Heidelberg).

PIEL, J. M. (1960), 'Antroponimia germanica', Enciclopedia lingüística hispánica I: Antecedentes: onomastica (Madrid), 421–44.

PIGHI, G. B. (1964), Lettere latine d'un soldato di Traiano (P. Mich. 467–472) (Bologna).

PINKSTER, H. (1985), 'The development of future tense auxiliaries in Latin', Glotta 63, 186–208.

(1987a), 'The pragmatic motivation for the use of subject pronouns in Latin: the case of Petronius', in Études de linguistique générale et de linguistique latine offertes en hommage à Guy Serbat (Paris), 369–79.

(1987b), 'The strategy and chronology of the development of future and perfect tense auxiliaries in Latin', in M. Harris and P. Ramat eds., Historical Development of Auxiliaries (Berlin, Amsterdam and New York), 193–223.

(1989), 'Some methodological remarks on research on future tense auxiliaries in Latin', in Calboli (1989), 311–26.

(1998), 'Narrative tenses in Merovingian hagiographic texts', in J. Herman ed., La transizione del latino alle lingue romanze (Tübingen), 299–335.

(2005), 'The use of is and ille in Seneca rhetor', in Kiss, Mondin and Salvi (2005), 57–64.

(2010), 'Notes on the language of Marcus Caelius Rufus', in Dickey and Chahoud (2010), 186–202.

(2012), 'Relative clauses in Latin: some problems of description', in P. da Cunha Corrêa et al. eds., Hyperboreans: Essays in Greek and Latin Poetry, Philosophy, Rhetoric and Linguistics (São Paulo), 377–93.

(2015), The Oxford Latin Syntax I: The Simple Clause (Oxford).

PITKÄRANTA, R. (1978), Studien zum Latein des Victor Vitensis (Helsinki).

PLATER, W. E. and WHITE, H. J. (1926), A Grammar of the Vulgate (Oxford).

PLATNAUER, M. (1951), Latin Elegiac Verse (Cambridge).

POMPEI, A. (2011), 'Relative clauses', in Baldi and Cuzzolin (2011), 427–547.

POSTGATE, J. P. (1891), 'The Latin future infinitive in -turum', CR 5, 301.

(1894), 'The future infinitive active in Latin', IF 4, 252–8.

POWELL, J. G. F. (1988), Cicero: Cato Maior de senectute (Cambridge).

(2005), 'Cicero's adaptation of legal Latin in the De legibus', in Reinhardt, Lapidge and Adams (2005), 117–50.

(2007), 'A new text of the Appendix Probi', CQ 57, 687–700.

PREUSS, S. (1881), De bimembris dissoluti apud scriptores Romanos usu sollemni (Edenkoben).

(1884), Vollständiges Lexikon zu den pseudo-cäsarianischen Schriftwerken (Erlangen).

PRINZ, O. (1932), De o et u vocalibus inter se permutatis in lingua Latina: quaestiones epigraphicae (Halle an der Saale).

PROBERT, P. (2015), Early Greek Relative Clauses (Oxford).

PROBERT, P. and DICKEY, E. (forthcoming), 'Six notes on Latin correlatives', in Adams and Vincent (forthcoming a).

PROBERT, P. and WILLI, A. eds. (2012), Laws and Rules in Indo-European (Oxford).

PROUDFOOT, A. and CARDO, F. (2005), Modern Italian Grammar: A Practical Guide, 2nd edn (London and New York).

QUESTA, C. (2007), La metrica di Plauto e di Terenzio (Urbino).

RAMSDEN, H. (1964), Weak-Pronoun Position in the Early Romance Languages (Manchester).

REEVE, M. D. (2004), Vegetius: Epitoma rei militaris (Oxford).

REINHARDT, T. (2003), Marcus Tullius Cicero: Topica (Oxford).

REINHARDT, T., LAPIDGE, M. and ADAMS, J. N. eds. (2005), Aspects of the Language of Latin Prose (Oxford).

REISDOERFER, J. (2002), 'Incipit Vita sancte Eufrosine qui interpretatur in latino castissima: prolégomènes à une édition critique de la Vita Sanctae Euphrosynae', in D. Walz ed., Scripturus vitam: Lateinische Biographie von der Antike bis in die Gegenwart (Festgabe für Walter Berschin zum 65. Geburtstag) (Heidelberg), 711–30.

(2011), 'C'est l'habit qui fait le moine: édition de la version valenciennoise de la Vita Sanctae Euphrosynae (BHL 2722)', Zeitschrift für antikes Christentum 15, 227–48.

RENEHAN, R. (1977), 'Compound-simplex verbal iteration in Plautus', CP 72, 243–8.

REYNOLDS, L. D. ed. (1983), Texts and Transmission: A Survey of the Latin Classics (Oxford).

RICHARDSON, W. F. (1982), A Word Index to Celsus De medicina (Auckland).

RICHLIN, A. (1992), The Garden of Priapus: Sexuality and Aggression in Roman Humor, rev. edn (New York and Oxford).

RICOTTILLI, L. (1978), 'Quid tu? quid vos? (per il recupero di una locuzione oscurata nel Satyricon)', MD 1, 215–21.

RIEMANN, O. (1885), Études sur la langue et la grammaire de Tite-Live, 2nd edn (Paris).

RIX, H. (2002), *Sabellische Texte: Die Texte des Oskischen, Umbrischen and Südpikenischen* (Heidelberg).

RODGER, A. (2006), 'What did *damnum iniuria* actually mean?', in A. Burrows and A. Rodger eds., *Mapping the Law: Essays in Memory of Peter Birks* (Oxford), 421–38.

RODGERS, R. H. (2004), *Frontinus: De aquaeductu urbis Romae* (Cambridge).

ROHLFS, G. (1954), *Die lexikalische Differenzierung der romanischen Sprachen* (Munich).

(1966), *Grammatica storica della lingua italiana e dei suoi dialetti* I: *Fonetica* (Turin).

(1968), *Grammatica storica della lingua italiana e dei suoi dialetti* II: *Morfologia* (Turin).

(1969), *Grammatica storica della lingua italiana e dei suoi dialetti* III: *Sintassi e formazione delle parole* (Turin).

ROLLAND, E. (1899), *Flore populaire, ou Histoire naturelle des plantes dans leurs rapports avec la linguistique et le folklore* II (Paris).

RÖNSCH, H. (1875), *Itala und Vulgata: Das Sprachidiom der urchristlichen Itala und der katholischen Vulgata*, 2nd edn (Marburg).

(1887–9), *Semasiologische Beiträge zum lateinischen Wörterbuch*, 3 vols. (Leipzig).

ROSE, V. and MÜLLER-STRÜBING, H. (1867), *Vitruvii De architectura libri decem* (Leipzig).

ROSÉN, H. (1981), *Studies in the Syntax of the Verbal Noun in Early Latin* (Munich).

(1999), *Latine loqui: Trends and Directions in the Crystallization of Classical Latin* (Munich).

(2012a), 'Two phrasal verbs: Lat. *coepi* and Gk. ἔβαλον/ἔβαλα, βάλλω/βάζω/βάνω', *IF* 117, 119–72.

(2012b), '*Coepi* + infinitif dans une sélection de traductions en latin tardif', in Biville, Lhommé and Vallat (2012), 365–75.

(2015), 'The Latin "ethical" dative: a distinct category', in Haverling (2015), 240–63.

ROUECHÉ, C. (1984), 'Acclamations in the later Roman Empire: new evidence from Aphrodisias', *JRS* 74, 181–99.

(1989), *Aphrodisias in Late Antiquity: The Late Roman and Byzantine Inscriptions Including Texts from the Excavations of Aphrodisias* (Journal of Roman Studies Monograph 5) (London).

RUBIO, G. (2009), 'Semitic influence in the history of Latin syntax', in Baldi and Cuzzolin (2009), 195–239.

RUCKDESCHEL, F. (1910), *Archaismen und Vulgarismen in der Sprache des Horaz* (Munich).

RUSSELL, D. A. F. M. (2001), *Quintilian: The Orator's Education*, 5 vols. (Cambridge, MA and London).

RYDBECK, L. (1967), *Fachprosa, vermeintliche Volkssprache und Neues Testament: Zur Beurteilung der sprachlichen Niveauunterschiede im nachklassischen Griechisch* (Uppsala).

SALONIUS, A. H. (1920), *Vitae patrum: Kritische Untersuchungen über Text, Syntax und Wortschatz der spätlateinischen Vitae partum (B. III, V, VI, VII)* (Lund).

SALVATORE, M. (1995), *Concordantia Varroniana pars I: Concordantia in M. Terenti Varronis libros De lingua Latina et in fragmenta ceterorum librorum*, 2 vols. (Hildesheim, Zurich and New York).

SALVI, G. (2011), 'Morphosyntactic persistence', in Maiden, Smith and Ledgeway (2011), 318–81.

SAMPSON, R. (2010), *Vowel Prosthesis in Romance: A Diachronic Study* (Oxford).

SÁNCHEZ NATALÍAS, C. (2014), 'Una nueva interpretación de la defixio contra Salpina', *ZPE* 191, 278–81.

SCHEID, J. (2007), *Res gestae Diui Augusti* (Paris).

SCHIERL, P. (2006), *Die Tragödien des Pacuvius: Ein Kommentar zu den Fragmenten mit Einleitung, Text und Übersetzung* (Berlin and New York).

SCHLEUSNER, J. F. (1820–1), *Novus thesaurus philologico-criticus sive Lexicon in LXX et reliquos interpretes Graecos ac scriptores apocryphos Veteris Testamenti*, 3 vols. (Leipzig).

SCHMELING, G. (2011), *A Commentary on the Satyrica of Petronius*, with the collaboration of A. Setaioli (Oxford).

SCHMIDT, K. (1902), 'Die griechischen Personennamen bei Plautus', *Hermes* 37, 173–211.

SCHOLZ, B. W. and ROGERS, B. (1970), *Carolingian Chronicles: Royal Frankish Annals and Nithard's Histories* (Ann Arbor).

SCHOPF, E. (1919), *Die konsonantischen Fernwirkungen: Fern-Dissimilation, Fern-Assimilation und Metathesis* (Göttingen).

SCHULZE, W. (1904), *Zur Geschichte lateinischer Eigennamen* (Berlin).

SEIDL, C. (1996), 'Die finanziellen Schwierigkeiten eines Getreidehändlers und der Profit, den die Linguistik daraus ziehen kann', in H. Rosén ed., *Aspects of Latin: Papers from the Seventh International Colloquium on Latin Linguistics, Jerusalem, April 1993* (1996), 99–115.

SETAIOLI, A. (1998), 'Seneca, lo schiavo Felicione e un'iscrizione di Velia', *Prometheus* 24, 149–51.

SHACKLETON BAILEY, D. R. (1965–70), *Cicero's Letters to Atticus*, 7 vols. (Cambridge).

——— (1977), *Cicero: Epistulae ad Familiares*, 2 vols. (Cambridge).

SHANZER, D. (2011), 'Who was Augustine's Publicola?', *Revue des Études Juives* 170, 429–62.

SHERWOOD FOX, W. (1912), *The Johns Hopkins Tabellae defixionum*, supplementary section to *AJP* 31.

SHIPP, G. P. (1955), 'Plautine terms for Greek and Roman things', *Glotta* 34, 139–52.

——— (1967), 'Some observations on the distribution of words in the New Testament', in E. C. B. MacLaurin ed., *Essays in Honour of Griffithes Wheeler Thatcher 1863–1950* (Sydney), 127–38.

——— (1979), *Modern Greek Evidence for the Ancient Greek Vocabulary* (Sydney).

SIHLER, A. L. (1995), *New Comparative Grammar of Greek and Latin* (New York).

SITTL, K. (1882), *Die lokalen Verschiedenheiten der lateinischen Sprache mit besonderer Berücksichtigung des afrikanischen Lateins* (Erlangen).

(1885), 'Zur Beurteilung des sogenannten Mittellateins', *ALL* 2, 550–80.

SJÖGREN, H. (1900), *De particulis copulatiuis apud Plautum et Terentium quaestiones selectae* (Uppsala).

SKUTSCH, O. (1985), *The Annals of Q. Ennius* (Oxford).

SLATER, W. J. (1974), '*Pueri, turba minuta*', *BICS* 21 (1974), 133–40.

SMITH, J. C. (2011), 'Change and continuity in form-function relationships', in Maiden, Smith and Ledgeway (2011), 268–317.

SMITH, M. S. (1975), *Petronii Arbitri Cena Trimalchionis* (Oxford).

SOLIN, H. (1982), 'Appunti sull'onomastica romana a Delo', in F. Coarelli, D. Musti and H. Solin eds., *Delo e l'Italia* (Opuscula Instituti Romani Finlandiae 2) (Rome).

(2008), 'Vulgar Latin and Pompeii', in Wright (2008), 60–8.

SOMERVILLE, T. (2007), 'The orthography of the new Gallus and the spelling rules of Lucilius', *ZPE* 160, 59–64.

SOMMER, F. (1914), *Handbuch der lateinischen Laut- und Formenlehre*, 2nd and 3rd edn (Heidelberg).

SOMMER, F. and PFISTER, R. (1977), *Handbuch der lateinischen Laut- und Formenlehre* I: *Einleitung und Lautlehre*, 4th edn (Heidelberg).

SORNICOLA, R. (2011), 'Romance linguistics and historical linguistics: reflections on synchrony and diachrony', in Maiden, Smith and Ledgeway (2011), 1–49.

SOUTER, A. (1949), *A Glossary of Later Latin to 600 AD* (Oxford).

SPEVAK, O. (2014), *The Noun Phrase in Classical Latin Prose* (Leiden and Boston).

STAIB, B. (1996), 'Gemeinromanische Tendenzen VII: Wortklassenbildung', *LRL* II.1, 355–67.

STEFENELLI, A. (1962), *Die Volkssprache im Werk des Petron im Hinblick auf die romanischen Sprachen* (Vienna).

STOCKERT, W. (1978), 'Zu den elliptischen *quid*-Fragen in der römischen Komödie', *QUCC* 29, 83–7.

(1983), *T. Maccius Plautus: Aulularia* (Stuttgart).

STOCLET, A. (1980a), 'Une description contemporaine de la basilique carolingienne de S. Denis, près de Paris', *Latomus* 39, 191–2.

(1980b), 'La Descriptio Basilicae Sancti Dionisii: premières commentaires', *Journal des Savants* [no vol. no.] (1980), 103–17.

STOTZ, P. (1998), *Handbuch zur lateinischen Sprache des Mittelalters* IV: *Formenlehre, Syntax und Stilistik* (Munich).

(2000), *Handbuch zur lateinischen Sprache des Mittelalters* II: *Bedeutungswandel und Wortbildung* (Munich).

(2002), *Handbuch zur lateinischen Sprache des Mittelalters* I: *Einleitung, Lexikologische Praxis, Wörter und Sachen, Lehnwortgut* (Munich).

(2004), *Handbuch zur lateinischen Sprache des Mittelalters* V: *Bibliographie, Quellenübersicht und Register* (Munich).

STRASSI, S. (2008), *L'archivio di Claudius Tiberianus da Karanis* (Berlin and New York).

STURTEVANT, E. H. (1940), *The Pronunciation of Greek and Latin* (Philadelphia).

SUMMERS, W. C. (1910), *Select Letters of Seneca* (London).

SVENNUNG, J. (1922), *Orosiana: Syntaktische semasiologische und kritische Studien zu Orosius* (Uppsala).

(1929), 'Om Palladius' *De medicina pecorum*', *Eranos* 27, 46–113.

(1934), 'Annotationes criticae in Catonem', *Eranos* 32, 1–29.

(1935), *Untersuchungen zu Palladius und zur lateinischen Fach- und Volkssprache* (Lund).

(1936), *Kleine Beiträge zur lateinischen Lautlehre* (Uppsala).

(1941), *Compositiones Lucenses: Studien zum Inhalt, zur Textkritik und Sprache* (Uppsala and Leipzig).

(1958), *Anredeformen: Vergleichende Forschungen zur indirekten Anrede in der dritten Person und zum Nominativ für den Vokativ* (Lund).

SZNAJDER, L. (2012), '*Dixit autem serpens* ad mulierem/mulieri *quoque dixit*: la double expression de l'allocutaire dans les propositions introductrices de discours directs dans la Vulgate', in Biville, Lhommé and Vallat (2012), 271–88.

TARA, G. B. (2014), *Les périphrases verbales avec habeo en latin tardif* (Paris).

THIELMANN, P. (1885), 'Habere mit dem Part. Perf. Pass.', *ALL* 2, 372–423, 509–49.

(1886), 'Facere mit dem Infinitiv', *ALL* 3, 177–206.

(1892), 'Der Ersatz des Reciprocums im Lateinischen', *ALL* 7, 343–88.

THOMPSON, E. A. (1985), *Who was Saint Patrick?* (Woodbridge).

THOMSEN, H. (1930), *Pleonasmus bei Plautus und Terentius* I: *Ausgewählte zeitliche (und verwandte) Begriffe* (Uppsala).

TIDNER, E. (1922), *De particulis copulatiuis apud Scriptores historiae Augustae quaestiones selectae* (Uppsala).

(1938), *Sprachlicher Kommentar zur lateinischen Didascalia apostolorum* (Stockholm).

TIMPANARO, S. (1978), *Contributi di filologia e di storia della lingua latina* (Rome).

TOMLIN, R. S. O. (1988), 'The curse tablets', in B. Cunliffe ed., *The Temple of Sulis Minerva at Bath* II: *The Finds from the Sacred Spring* (Oxford University Committee for Archaeology Monograph 16) (Oxford), 59–277.

(1991), 'Inscriptions', *Britannia* 22, 293–311.

(1997), 'Inscriptions', *Britannia* 28, 455–72.

(2008), '*Paedagogium* and *septizonium*: two Roman lead tablets from Leicester', *ZPE* 167, 207–18.

(2009), 'Inscriptions', *Britannia* 40, 313–63.

(2015), 'Inscriptions', *Britannia* 46, 383–420.

TOMLIN, R. S. O. and HASSALL, M. W. C. (2007), 'Inscriptions', *Britannia* 38, 345–65.

TREGGIARI, S. (1981), '*Concubinae*', *PBSR* n.s. 36, 59–81.

VÄÄNÄNEN, V. (1956), 'La préposition latine DE et le génitif: une mise au point', *RLiR* 20, 1–20 = Väänänen (1981b), 89–116.

(1965), *Étude sur le texte et la langue des Tablettes Albertini* (Helsinki).

(1966), *Le latin vulgaire des inscriptions pompéiennes*, 3rd edn (Berlin).

(1977), *Ab epistulis ... ad Sanctum Petrum: formules prépositionnelles latines étudiées dans leur contexte social* (Helsinki).

(1981a), *Introduction au latin vulgaire*, 3rd edn (Paris).

(1981b), *Recherches et récréations latino-romanes* (Naples).

(1987), *Le journal-épître d'Égérie (Itinerarium Egeriae: étude linguistique)* (Helsinki).

VAHLEN, J. (1928), *Ennianae poesis reliquiae*, 2nd edn (Leipzig).

VAN BEEK, C. I. M. I. (1936), *Passio sanctarum Perpetuae et Felicitatis* (Nijmegen).

VAN DEN HOUT, M. P. J. (1988), *M. Cornelii Frontonis Epistulae* (Leipzig).

(1999), *A Commentary on the Letters of M. Cornelius Fronto* (Leiden, Boston and Cologne).

VAN OORDE, W. (1929), *Lexicon Aetherianum* (Amsterdam).

VAN RENGEN W. (1997), 'Correspondance militaire (357–387)', in Bingen *et al.* (1997), 193–222.

VANNINI, G. (2007), 'Petronius 1975–2005: bilancio critico e nuove proposte', *Lustrum* 49, 7–511.

VELÁZQUEZ SORIANO, I. (2004), *Las pizarras visigodas (Entre el latín y su disgregación: la lengua hablada en Hispania, siglos VI–VIII)* (Real Academia Española, Instituto de la lengua castellano y leonés).

VENDRYES, J. (1912), 'La langue des defixionum tabellae de Johns Hopkins University', *RPh* 36, 203–8.

VETTER, E. (1923), 'Zu lateinischen Fluchtafeln', *Glotta* 12, 63–7.

VIELLIARD, J. (1927), *Le latin des diplômes royaux et chartes privées de l'époque mérovingienne* (Paris).

VILLE, G. (1981), *La gladiature en Occident des origines à la mort de Domitien* (Rome).

VINCENT, N. (1988), 'Latin', in Harris and Vincent (1988), 26–78.

(forthcoming), 'Causative constructions in Latin and Romance', in Adams and Vincent (forthcoming a).

VONLAUFEN, J. (1974), *Studien über Stellung und Gebrauch des lateinischen Relativsatzes unter besonderer Berücksichtigung von Lukrez* (Freiburg).

WACHTMEISTER, W. (1985), *Physicae Plinii quae fertur Florentino-Pragensis liber secundus* (Frankfurt).

WACKERNAGEL, J. (1926–8), *Vorlesungen über Syntax*, 2nd edn, 2 vols. (Basel).

(1969), *Kleine Schriften*, 2nd edn, 2 vols. (Göttingen).

WAGNER, M. L. (1933), 'Über die Unterlagen der romanischen Phraseologie', in *Volkstum und Kultur der Romanen: Sprache, Dichtung, Sitte* (Vierteljahrsschrift, Seminar für romanische Sprachen und Kultur an der Hamburgischen Universität VI).

WALDE, A. and HOFMANN, J. B. (1938–54), *Lateinisches etymologisches Wörterbuch*, 3rd edn, 2 vols. (Heidelberg).

WARMINGTON, E. H. (1940), *Remains of Old Latin IV: Archaic Inscriptions* (Cambridge, MA and London).

(1961), *Remains of Old Latin* I: *Ennius and Caecilius*, 3rd edn (Cambridge, MA and London).

WATKINS, C. (1995), *How to Kill a Dragon: Aspects of Indo-European Poetics* (Oxford).

WATSON, A. (1967), *The Law of Persons in the Later Roman Republic* (Oxford).

WATSON, L. C. (2003), *A Commentary on Horace's Epodes* (Oxford).

WATSON, L. C. and WATSON, P. (2014), *Juvenal: Satire 6* (Cambridge).

WATSON, P. and WATSON, L. C. (2009), 'Seneca and Felicio: imagery and purpose', *CQ* 59, 212–26.

WEIJERMANS, L. H. (1949), *De genitivus inhaerentiae in het Latijn* (Nijmegen).

WEISS, M. (2009), *Outline of the Historical and Comparative Grammar of Latin* (Ann Arbor and New York).

WEISSENBORN, W. (1856), *Titi Livi Ab urbe condita* I: *Buch I und II*, 2nd edn (Berlin).

WEST, M. L. (1988), 'The rise of the Greek epic', *JHS* 108, 151–72.

(2007), *Indo-European Poetry and Myth* (Oxford).

WESTERBURGH, U. (1956), *Chronicon Salernitanum: A Critical Edition with Studies on Literary and Historical Sources and on Language* (Studia Latina Stockholmiensia 3) (Stockholm).

WHARTON, D. (2009), 'On the distribution of adnominal prepositional phrases in Latin prose', *CP* 104, 184–207.

WILKINS, A. S. (1890), *M. Tulli Ciceronis De oratore libri tres* II, 2nd edn (Oxford).

WILKINSON, J. (1971), *Egeria's Travels* (London).

WILLS, J. (1996), *Repetition in Latin Poetry: Figures of Allusion* (Oxford).

WINIARCZYK, M. (1991), *Euhemeri Messenii reliquiae* (Stuttgart and Leipzig).

WISTRAND, E. (1933), *Vitruvius-Studier* (Göteborg).

(1972), *Opera selecta* (Stockholm).

WOLF, J. G. and CROOK, J. A. (1989), *Rechtsurkunden in Vulgärlatein* (Abh. Heidelb. Akad. Wiss., Phil.-hist. Kl.) (Heidelberg).

WÖLFFLIN, E. (1884), 'Der Reim im Lateinischen', *ALL* 1, 350–89.

(1885), 'Das adverbielle cetera, alia, omnia', *ALL* 2, 90–9.

(1887a), 'Ex toto, in totum', *ALL* 4, 144–7.

(1887b), 'Die Verba frequentativa und intensiva', *ALL* 4, 197–222.

(1896), 'Die Latinität des Benedikt von Nursia', *ALL* 9, 493–521.

(1900), 'Zur Latinität des Jordanes', *ALL* 11, 361–8.

(1933), *Ausgewählte Schriften*, edited by G. Meyer (Leipzig).

WÖLFFLIN, E. and MIODOŃSKI, A. (1889), *C. Asini Polionis De bello Africo commentarius* (Leipzig).

WOODCOCK, E. C. (1959), *A New Latin Syntax* (London).

WOODMAN, A. J. (2004), *Tacitus: The Annals, Translated with Introduction and Notes* (Indianapolis and Cambridge).

WOODMAN, A. J. and MARTIN, R. H. (1996), *The Annals of Tacitus Book 3* (Cambridge).

WOYTEK, E. (1970), *Sprachliche Studien zur Satura Menippea Varros* (Vienna, Cologne and Graz).

(1982), *T. Maccius Plautus, Persa: Einleitung, Text und Kommentar* (Vienna).

WRIGHT, R. ed. (2008), *Latin vulgaire - latin tardif VIII: Actes du VIIIᵉ colloque international sur le latin vulgaire et tardif, Oxford, 6-9 septembre 2006* (Hildesheim, Zurich and New York).

WRIGHT, R. P. and HASSALL, M. W. C. (1973), 'Inscriptions', *Britannia* 4, 324–37.

YOUTIE, H. C. and WINTER, J. G. (1951), *Michigan Papyri VIII: Papyri and Ostraca from Karanis* (Ann Arbor).

ZELLMER, E. (1976), *Die lateinischen Wörter auf -ura*, 2nd edn (Frankfurt am Main).

SUBJECT INDEX

Page numbers are not used in these indexes. In most references two numbers are given. The first refers to the number (between 1 and 50) of the text as that appears in the list of contents, the second to the number of the lemma in the Commentary to that text (e.g. 42.2).

In a few cases there are three numbers (e.g. 48.1.4). These fall into two groups. First, there are those cases where a 'text' consists not of a single passage but of several scattered passages from the same work or related works (so nos. 10, 48). Here again the first number refers to the number of the 'text' as it appears in the list of contents; the second number then refers to one of the numbered selections within the 'text', and the third to the number of the lemma in the Commentary to that selection. The second group consists of some continuous passages which occupy more than one chapter of the original work (e.g. no. 44). In such cases a number such as 44.36.1 indicates text no. 44 and within that the first section of chapter 36.

Sometimes reference is made in index entries not to the lemmata in the Commentaries, but to the introduction or conclusion of a numbered text (e.g. under 'ablative' below note '50 Conclusions'). These references are self-explanatory.

ablative
  absolute, left hanging 44.36.1, 48.1.4
  adnominal, expressing provenance 46.2–3
  expressing duration of time 25.39, 29.2,
     42.15 (alternating with *per*)
  in directional expressions for accusative
     27.4, 39.15
  instrumental 28.25–6, replaced by
     prepositions in a late text 50.33, 50
     Conclusions
  locatival 20.2
  locatival, fossilised as place name 9.2–3
  of accompaniment 28.25–6
  of gerund 22.31
  with *plenus*, versus genitive 42.2
abstract nouns
  applied to persons in address 18.5
  as mark of Patrick's style 40 Conclusions,
     'Patrick wrote as he spoke'
  in genitive with adjectival role 44.36.4
  with concrete meaning 25.26
  see also suffixation
acclamations
  ellipse in 28.14–15, 28.25–6, 28
     Conclusions

  formulae in 28.25–6
  refrains in 28.17, 28 Conclusions
  repetitions in 28 Conclusions
  with exclamatory accusatives
     28.25–6
  word order of refrains in 28.17
  see also 28 *passim*
accusative
  'absolute' (?) 43.2
  as prepositional case 22.22, 25.15,
     26.8–9
  exclamatory, fossilised 9.2–3
  exclamatory, in acclamations
     28.25–6
  hanging 4.10 (*see also* nominativus/
     accusativus pendens)
  in curse tablets, of the victim of curse,
     without verb 19.10
  in lists 4.10, 6.31
  of price 41.8
  proleptic 24.6–7
  with *cum* 22.22, 44.36.4, 44.37.2
  with *de* 26.8–9
  with verbs normally taking the dative
     39.21

resumption (cont.)
  of relative by resumptive pronoun or
    adverb in correlative part of
    relative-correlative construction *see*
    pronouns, resumptive
  participial 24.4–5, 29.2 45.12, 46.7
  see also relative clauses

school exercises, bilingual 39.22, 43.9, 43.12,
  45.16
scribes
  and spelling variation 22.10
  and training in spelling 15 Commentary,
    'preliminaries', 15.7
Semitic influence (?) 18.16
Sempronius Asellio, annalist 1.9
sexual/excretory terminology 10 *passim*, 16
  passim, 30
simplex pro composito 23.25
singular
  collective, of plants 4.10, 4 Conclusions,
    15.16, 17.2
  for plural in reference to ingredients in
    recipes forming a collectivity 42.15,
    42.21, 50.63
  for plural, in reference to types of animals
    11.5
  for plural, in *ripa* 11.2
  for plural, of things that come in pairs 11.2
Sisenna, annalist 1.9
slave idioms/address 3.433, 7.5, 9.10, 17.2,
  17.3, 18.5
spellings
  a for *ae* 37.1
  ae for short *e* by hypercorrection 15.8,
    35.14, 37.1, 37.2
  au/o 6.4 (in names), 6.25, 7.13, 16.2, 26.11
  b/u 14.9, 22.13, 22.32–3, 36.4, 36.7
  ci/ti 34.6, 49.11, 50.34
  d for *t* between vowels 15.14
  degemination/simplification of
    consonants 13.2, 15.7, 20
    Conclusions, 36.2, 47.20
  e and Greek αι 7.11
  e for *ae* 15.8, 26.2
  $\bar{e}$ (long close) for *ei/ī* 6.12, 14.9, 15.13,
    25.9, 26.12, 39 Introduction

  e for short *i*
    in verb endings 16.1, 22.33, 26.3
    elsewhere 22.11, 22.27, 26.13–14
      (under Greek influence), 32.3–4,
      34.2, 37.2
  ei for long *i*, etymologically justified 6.2,
    14.5, 14.6, 14.9
  ei for long *i*, not justified 14.6
  errors, mechanical 22.11, 36.2, 36.6
  false gemination of consonants 15.1, 15.7,
    36.7
  final -*m*, omitted or falsely added 6.18,
    15.12, 22.27, 25.35, 25.36, 26.8–9, 26
    Conclusions, 36.7, 42.5
  gemination of *s*, etymologically justified
    or otherwise 13.2, 15.7, 35.12
  i for long *e* in the perfect stem of *facio* and
    uenio 47.20
  i for short *e* in final syllable in early
    medieval texts 47.8, 47.9, 47.18
  i for short *e* in pretonic initial syllables
    49.19, 50.51
  i/u, intermediate vowel before nasal
    14.5
  k before *a* 21.14, 22.25–6
  loss of *u* (i.e. [w]) between vowels of
    similar quality 26.5
  m/n in final position 26.3
  misspellings, inexplicable 24.5
  o for long *u* 36.1
  o for short *u* 37.1–2
  omission of final -*s* 32.5, 43.1 (in Greek
    name)
  omission of final -*t* in *post* 22.19–20
  omission of final -*t* in verb forms 42.15
  omission of *g* between vowels *see* lenition
  omission of nasal before stop 14.2, 15.11,
    15.14, 18.5, 35.1, 36.3
  p for *t* in final position (*discanp*) 28.12
  prothetic vowel 46.6
  q before *u* 22.25–6
  t/d in final position 6.28, 30, 14.6, 22.16,
    22.19–20, 24.3, 25.12, 25.27, 26.10,
    37.1–2
  u for *au* (?) 37.1, 37.1–2
  u for long *o* by palatalisation 47.13
  xs for *s* 14.5

INDEX VERBORUM

facio
  as support verb 4.8
  + *contumeliam* 8.4
  + *conuicium* 3 Appendix, 8.4
  + dative 50.37
  + *errorem* 25.21
  + *exercitum* 48.1.4
  faciens facio 31.1–2
  factum est + dative and infinitive
      22.21–2
  + infinitive 31.13, 50.42
  + *libram* 25.29
  + *lucrum* 14.7
  + *lustrum* 4.8
  + *messem* 4.8
  + *missum* (and with ellipse of *facio*)
      28.25–6
  + *omnia* 17.1
  perfect spelt *fic-* 47.20
  recte facies 20.3
  + *retrusionem* 47.3
  + *sanum* 5.15
  + *sationes* 4.8
  + *scandalum* 47.3
  + *sementim* 4.8
  + *stragem* 48.2.5
  + *uindemiam* 4.8
  + *urinam* 6.34
  + *ut* 21.4–5
famosus 10.3 Commentary, 'preliminaries',
    10.3.7
fateor, parenthetical 15.19–20
fauisor (*fautor*) 27.7
febrio/febricito 42.11
fel 44.36.2
felix (et sim.), in greetings 12 Conclusions,
    23.11–13
femina
  of a man 10.3.3
  specifying *lupus, leo* 1.9
fero 10.4.2 (*quid fers*), 34.5 (*tuli* as perfect of
    tollo)
festa 49.16 (with masculine agreement)
fiducialiter 40 Conclusions, 'Patrick wrote as
    he spoke'
figel 33.6
filiola, of a man 10.3.1, 10.3.3

filiolus 21.10
filius 1.10
firmitas 48.2.2
firustellum = *frustellum* (?) 41.4
fistucum, for *festuca* 50.51
flasco 45 Conclusions
fleo 25.10–11
focus 50.27
folium, collective singular 17.2
folles, monetary use 41.8
fons, gender 44.37.4
foramen, uninflected 4.10
foris, preposition 49.12
fortis/fortunatus 2.10
fossura 25.14
fraga 46.11
frequenter 29.2
frixoria 50.62–3
Froila, Gothic name 46.4
frons, of variable gender 11.1
frudum (?) 37.1–2
fugio ante/ante faciem 44.37.5
fumarium 50.29
fundamentum, with masculine agreement
    49.7
futuri, nominal 28.12

gaesates 25.24
gemellus/geminus 26.8
genetiuus 39.2
geniculus, masculine 11.1
genius, and slave language 17.2,
    18.5
gens 'pagan' 40.2
germanus 48.1.1
gerra 2.24
gestio 1.7–8
gestito 1.7–8
git 50.40
glaucuma 2.24
gluto 50.40
glut(t)io 50.69
(g)natus 1.10
gorga 50.65
granum 50.40
grauitudo 11.4
gusto 12 Conclusions

habeo
    as support verb 4.8, 47.3, 48.4.5
    impersonal *habet* and its possible origin
        49.13
    non habemus, with relative clause
        containing infinitive 20.5; cf. 45.10
    pluperfect subjunctive of for imperfect
        11.17
    sexual use of 10.6.2–3
    with infinitive as future periphrasis 47.19
    with *mihi* 2.23
    with perfect participle as periphrastic
        perfect 48.1.2, 50.65
    with *tristitiam* = *sum tristis* 47.3
haphe 27.7
harenosus 4.6
herbosus 4.6
heus 7.5 (with *tu* or *adulescens*)
Hiberione, not inflecting 39.15
hic, adverb
    in correlation with *hic* 3.418
hic, pronoun
    in alternation with *ille* 2.21–2, 27.9
    resumptive in relative clause 39.7
    retained until late in idiom *hoc fac* 50.25
hinc 3.10
    hinc et inde 22.12
    in correlation/juxtaposition with *huc*
        3.418
    = *inde*, of source, partitive or
        instrumental 42.10, 42.24
hirudo 50.27
homo
    accompanied by appositional personal
        noun 31.10
    indefinite 50.63–4
    plural, of soldiers 45.7
    redundant with indefinites 3.425
hora, of time in general 24.5
hordeaceus/hordearius 5.14
horoma 27.1
hortor, + subjunctive 25.4
hospitiolum 35.5
hospitium 35.5, 36.7
hostia
    form *ostia*, with masculine agreement (?)
        19.5–6

huc, in correlation with *hinc* and *huc* 3.418
hui 9.13
hurta 36.4

iaceo 'lie ill' 47.6
iacio 12 Conclusions, 27.10
iacto 12 Conclusions, 27.10, 40.5 (= 'put'?),
        42.19 ('vomit'), 44.37.9 ('throw'),
        47.15
iam, in acclamation 28.24
ibi
    adnominal 9.16
    ibi tum 1.3
    sexual 10.1 Commentary, 'preliminaries'
    temporal 1.3
iborium < *eboreus* 49.19
idem
    repeated 5.2–4, 45.1
    weakened anaphoric use 9.3, 24.6–7
iecur, plural 6.29, 19.8
    form *eoconora* 19.8
    form *iocinera* 6.29
ille
    as definite article (?) 2.27, 49.7
    combined with *de* as partitive article 49.14
    genitive of with reflexive meaning 39.8
    in illo 38.62
    in relation to *is* 17.2, 18.6, 22.10, 27.9,
        27.11, 36.6, 38.53, 39.8, 40
        Conclusions, 'Living Latin', 50.26
    see also is
illi, locatival adverb 'in that place' 9.16
illic, adverb 9.16
illic, pronoun
    history of 6.5
    interchangeable with *hic* 2.21–2
illim/illinc 22.24
immuto 3.432
impero + infinitive 11.18, 39.21
improperium 39.9
impropero 27 Conclusions, 'Perpetua's
        Latin'
impudicus 10.1.3
in
    + ablative for accusative and vice versa
        27.4, 38.56, 39.15, 43.12, 44.4.2,
        44.36.2, 45.5, 48.2.4, 50.27

Printed in Great Britain
by Amazon

74239782R00417